Alias Soapy Smith
The Life and Death
Of a Scoundrel

The Biography of Jefferson Randolph Smith II

By
Jeff Smith
Great-grandson of "Soapy" Smith

KLONDIKE RESEARCH
Juneau, Alaska

In Loving Memory

JOHN RANDOLPH SMITH
1918-1987

He loved to con, but never cheated a soul.

This book is dedicated to my children in the hope it inspires them to always seek the truth, even when the truth is not very nice.

Ashley Nicolet Smith
And
Jefferson Randolph Smith
The great-great-grandchildren of Soapy Smith

Published by Klondike Research
   Art Petersen, Editor
   15845 Glacier Highway
   Juneau, Alaska 99801   (907) 789-9830
   mailto: editor@klondikeresearch.com (klondikeresearch.com)

ISBNs: 0-9819743-0-9 (pbk)   0-9819743-1-7 (cloth)

Library of Congress Catalog Card Number: TBA
               (Case # 1-167206321 03/05/2009)

This book is available directly from Klondike Research for $26 softbound and $43 hardbound + $5 shipping (media mail) and handling. Copies signed by the author are available *by request* at no additional charge except the additional cost of $5 for shipping via the author to the patron. Requests for special inscriptions are welcome. To order, write to the above address with mailing information and a check for the appropriate amount made payable to Klondike Research. E-mail orders may be placed at the above address, and an itemized PayPal bill (at no additional cost to the patron) will be sent for payment.

Bookseller orders are welcome at standard discounts. Contact Klondike Research for terms.

Contents

Preface

I was raised in a household where the life and times of "Soapy" Smith were regularly discussed, studied, and celebrated. Almost every adult in my family owned at least one biography of him. A collection of hundreds of photographs, artifacts, documents, and letters to and from Soapy was divided among his grandchildren. I fondly remember the first time my father took out his portion of the collection and let me hold and read some of the old letters. As I read, handling each letter with great care, I remember deciding to write a detailed biography of my great-grandfather.

My father taught me many things, but two of them have been of immense help in writing this book: be skeptical and always question authority. His collection of books related to Soapy was vast, and he did not trust most of the information they contained. My father did not seek to protect Soapy's image but rather to doubt unverified information about it. I soon saw that this orientation to the printed word about Soapy Smith was for the best. Scores of stories about him are either faulty or based on faulty information. Fortunately, however, spread throughout our house was a treasure trove of information about Soapy, piled in drawers, stacked on shelves, stuffed into filing cabinets. I knew from the start that I had the opportunity to assemble the most factual account of Soapy's life written thus far. Everything I needed was around me. At that time I thought all I had to do was arrange everything in chronological order. Had I known then that it would take twenty-five years to write this biography, most likely I would never have started.

After becoming personally invested in the research for this book and experiencing the exhilaration of a few discoveries and verifications of fact, I came to love the research process and expect to continue the quest for knowledge until my dying day. I cannot imagine ever saying, "OK, I am finished researching this subject."

In some instances, documents and letters made little sense alone, but when merged with the political and social history of the time, they fit into the picture as meaningful parts. So it became clear that for a comprehensive biography, I would have to research beyond the information I already had. Often the histories and stories of Soapy are not documented and so are open to immediate suspicion of manipulation, embellishment, or outright fiction. Not wanting the same fate for this biography, to the greatest extent possible, I have documented all facts and most statements with primary sources. I have taken nothing I read by other writers for granted, suspected the manipulation of everything presented as fact, and re-opened for examination all the old stories. In a number of instances, a completely different story has emerged. Despite comprehensive efforts, however, I found that holes or gaps in Soapy's history would remain if they were not filled in with logical speculation. This I have undertaken with extreme care.

Serious research for this book began in 1985. I took an extended vacation in Colorado, visiting the places Soapy was known to reside. I quickly found that one trip was not enough and took three. In terms of what geographical locales and research opportunities might reveal, my sense is that a lifetime of exploration remains, but I had to stop at some point and begin the writing process, or this book would never have found its way into your hands.

It is important to me for the reader to understand that although I am related to the subject of this book, I do not pretend to believe Soapy was "a good guy" or someone to be admired. I would be untruthful were I to say it is not fun being a descendant of an Old West bad man. The little moments of celebrity are enjoyed. But my primary interest has been the history of Soapy Smith. I am not proud of what he did but rather of what he left behind, an outsized history of a complex character at the center of often rough frontier times. No attempt has been made to mask his crimes. As my father used to tell me, "Jeff, he's more interesting that way," how he really was—his charities, crimes, all.

The truth, however, is not always clear. In these circumstances, fortunately I am often able to present more than one side of an event because of the extensive collection of personal letters in my possession as well as documents, notebooks, and newspaper and police accounts. Sometimes events in Soapy's life are multisided. As has seemed reasonable and possible, I show all sides and then present my own interpretation. The intent throughout has been to present as much information as possible so that readers may have opportunity to decide for themselves where the truth may lie.

Research shows that when Soapy was feeling good or in a charitable mood, he emptied his pockets to those in need. However, research also shows that when in a competitive, ruthless, or bad frame of mind, he could apply smooth flimflam or escalate to outright robbery, physical force, or manslaughter without hesitation. Most information in this book comes from thousands of original and copied items in the Smith family Soapy Smith collection. Letters and documents are the paramount sources for dates, events, places, and names. I was well aware that Soapy's own written words could be exaggerations or lies, so microfilmed newspapers of his time were extremely important sources. These, too, however, were not always accurate. I found it exhilarating when Soapy's letters and documents coincided with newspaper accounts, making for an apparently accurate history of a particular set of events. With Denver's *Rocky Mountain News*, I began with the year 1879 and read every page of every issue for that year. I then moved on to 1880 and repeated the process. And so the method proceeded through 1896. Reading upwards of 90,000 pages took years. It was a daunting task but proved a goldmine of information not known to have been republished anywhere—until now. I have retained significant amounts of this material for a variety of reasons: to document the high volume of activity undertaken by Jeff and his associates, to share interesting and sometimes entertaining aspects of his sector of criminal activity, to show Jeff interacting with major events of his time, and to make this wealth of material a part of today's historical record.

One problem was the inability to present complete stories of court cases. Many crimes and arrests were reported on court dockets and in newspapers, but few made it all the way through the system. A probable cause of this lack is the notorious corruptness of the Denver legal system in the latter nineteenth century. Witnesses were paid off as well as court officials and policemen; thus, some cases were swept away intentionally while others, apparently, were just plain forgotten. Corruption was recognized by the legal system, the media, and the electorate, but little was done to rectify it. In other instances the records are not to be found.

Books were of great use in my research. Those with sources could be easily checked for accuracy, but even so, many of these sources revealed just the same old misinformation being passed down from other books. The worst and most suspicious were accounts without documentation. Many authors added filler (details impossible to know) and fictionalized sequences, apparently thought necessary to spice up and fill out accounts. The worst case scenarios involved a kernel of truth in a bushel of falsehoods. Sadly, once a single piece of forged information was exposed, little of the remaining story could be trusted. I found the stark, non-fictional facts far more pertinent, interesting, and compelling than the romanticized fiction.

Family research into the life of Soapy began shortly after his death in 1898. Soapy's widow, Mary, already had most of her husband's paperwork from his time in "the states" (Georgia, Texas, Colorado...), and when she came to Skagway after his death, she gathered what was left of her husband's documents and possessions. She also traveled to Skagway to find the truth about his death. For decades, she consulted many of her husband's long-standing friends and associates about her husband, including criminals. The author's father and his siblings resided with Mary, known to them as "Mammy." She often spoke of their grandfather's behavior. Mammy loved her beer and whiskey mix, which she said was for her rheumatism. On Saturdays after a few of these concoctions, she would enlighten the author's father with fascinating stories of Soapy. Then for the gift of her stories, she "let him" clean her wooden floors.[1]

Mary passed down a large collection of documents and personal artifacts to her son, Jefferson Randolph Smith III, the author's grandfather. He carried on the quest for information, also meeting with former affiliates and allies of his father. From about 1919 to the late 1940s, he vigilantly assailed publishers and film companies with law suits for attempting to put his father in a bad light. For this reason the author believes the name of Soapy Smith is generally not more well known. In the 1930s while involved in St. Louis political circles, Jefferson thought such exposure could jeopardize his position in the city. He even went so far as to hide the enormous collection of Soapy Smith documents and memorabilia behind wall panels in the basement of the family home. John Randolph Smith, the author's father, told of the hiding place and how he would sneak down and play with the rifle, faro cards, gaming equipment, and old hat and coat secreted there. Unfortunately, the hat and coat deteriorated so badly over the years that they were discarded long before their value was recognized.

Jefferson had nine children, and before his death, he divided the collection among them. John Randolph, and his siblings carried on the historical exploration of their grandfather. Men who had known Soapy were still living, and the Smith siblings were able to question some of these witnesses. In the 1960s they tape-recorded interviews with a number of old-timers who had known Soapy. As a young boy the author recalls

---

[1] John Randolph Smith interview by the author, 01/1981.

several meetings and interviews in the den of the family home. Too young to be allowed in at such times, I would "hang out" just beyond a set of saloon-style swinging doors and listen. Years later I was fortunate enough to be at my father's side during some interviews, such as with Bobby Sheldon, who claimed to have witnessed to the shootout that ended Soapy's life. Later still, the author conducted interviews with persons who had direct connections to Soapy and with descendants of those who had had dealings with him.

The gambling paraphernalia in the family collection generated in John Randolph a fondness for magic and gambling. He studied and performed standard magic acts for neighborhood shows in the early 1920s. He also learned some methods of deception from his father, Jefferson, who had learned them from his father, Soapy himself. I learned from my father, John, those same methods and in turn developed my own magic and gambling shows. From the 1980s through the publishing date of this book, I could be seen at Old West festivals, dressed authentically as Soapy Smith, reenacting the prize package soap sell racket, the shell game, and three-card monte on the tripod and keister my father had made.

In 1977, John Randolph and his brother Joseph Jefferson Smith brought their life of research to a summit with a family reunion in Skagway. This was believed to have been the first time the Smiths had been there since August 1898. Nineteen at the time, I still remembers the concerns my father had about how the family would be received. Would the Smiths be welcomed or scorned? The arrival was kept secret, but somehow the visit was discovered, and waiting at the dock were several members of the Skagway Days of '98 Show to welcome the visitors. The family was warmly embraced, and friendships were forged that continue to this day.

In quoting letters, documents, and newspapers, I have often kept them as published, including misspellings and grammatical mistakes. Occasionally, though, where variations from common usage are thought might inhibit clarity, small adjustments have been made. Where it could be unclear whether an error is mine or appears in the quotation, I have employed the time-honored "*sic*" to signal that what appears is "thus" in the original. Some spellings have changed over the years, and in quotations I have retained the old forms, such as *Spokan Falls*, Washington, but beyond quotation, I have employed modern spelling, for example, *Spokane*. In the case of Skagway, however, the old form, which took many years to change, I have retained as *Skaguay* throughout. Otherwise, from quotation to narrative would result in a constant shift in spelling.

Looking for a capstone comment to the complete the bridge into this biography, I found one in Thucydides (460-400 B.C.), said to be first among great historians. It is from the prefatory comments to his history of the Peloponnesian War. He wrote, "The absence of romance in my history will, I fear, detract somewhat from its interest...." That absence is also the case with this history of Jeff R. "Soapy" Smith. Probably, though, it will not detract for those who find plain truth far more interesting and compelling than romance. Modesty and reality prompt me to confess that it would be foolish to equate the great history of Thucydides with this book. Still, his "objective, critical method" has also been mine, including this claim by the historian: "My history has been composed to be an everlasting possession, not the showpiece of an hour."[2]

Jeff Smith
Corona, California

Acknowledgements

Thanks and recognition are due a great many people. I will begin with some of particular note.

A huge supply of information came from **John Randolph Smith**, the author's father, and from his brother, **Joseph Jefferson Smith**. Joseph's son, **Jefferson Randolph "Little Randy" Smith**, allowed the author to invade his home for the purpose of cataloging and copying his portion of the collection inherited from his father. Without his assistance this narrative would be incomplete. **Geri Murphy**, great-grandchild of Soapy and daughter of **Jacqueline Alice Smith**, sent wonderful scans and copies of her portion of the collection inherited from her mother. Without her assistance, this narrative would be incomplete as well.

Joy Smith Schaftner, the author's aunt, sent photos and information about the rifle with which Soapy died and about the old Smith Georgia Mansion. **Erik Andersen**, great-great-great-grandson of Ira Ellis Smith and Ellen Stimpson Peniston, was a constant aid in early Smith family genealogical history. **Ellen Rafeedie**, a first cousin twice removed of Soapy, aided in research on the early Smith genealogical history. **Curtis Light** faithfully shared his knowledge of "Cap" William Sydney Light, one of the brothers-in-law who worked for Soapy. **Kyle Rosene**, a great grandnephew of Soapy contributed early photographs of the family and one of the Soap Gang. **Mildred Bunny Godard**, a first cousin three times removed, aided in early family history. **Jim Lynch**, a great-grandson, aided with stories from Soapy's sister, Eva Katherine Smith. **Joanne McNelis**, a great-granddaughter, shared her thoughts and artifacts with the author. **Jim Smith**, a great-grandson, shared his knowledge of the early family and his father, Joseph Jefferson Smith.

Other persons and organizations who patiently rendered help and assistance are as follows: **Darryl Beckmann** of Seattle, author of *Alexander Conlin, the Man Who Knows*, gave me concise information about Conlin, a supposed member of the Soap Gang, as well as educated me on the pitfalls of the publishing world. **Pierre Berton**, famed Canadian author. **Jeff Brady**, publisher of the *Skagway News*, has shared his extensive knowledge of the history of Skagway and the surrounding area and generously offered his home upon visits to the city. Since 1977, this respected historian has been a good friend. Special thanks to artist **John Bruce** for working with me to render two conceptual drawings of the shootout on the Juneau Wharf. These are the most accurate images of what actually occurred. (Examples of John's artistry may be seen at http://www.bruceart.net.) **Howard Clifford** of Seattle, noted author

---

[2] Thucydides. *Peloponnesian War*, book I, section 22.

and scholar on the life of Soapy Smith, held different and controversial views on the events in Soapy's life and forced me to dig deeper. **Leland Feitz**, Colorado historian and author, personally showed me the Cripple Creek area and the ruins of Gillette, Colorado, with its earthen outline of the bull-fighting arena with which in 1895 Soapy was possibly involved. **Karl Gurke** of the Klondike Gold Rush National Historic Park, Skagway, who always found time to answer questions and aided in finding photographs of Soapy in Alaska. **Craig and Scott Johnson**, relatives of Samuel and Louis Blonger, succession heirs to the Denver crime lord throne. Like detectives, the author and the Johnsons worked together to solve linking mysteries between the Blongers and Soapy Smith. These two sleuths continue to be of great help. **Diana Kodiak**, Archivist at the National Archives and Records Administration, Pacific Alaska Region, Anchorage. **Roy Minter**, author of a well-researched, comprehensive book on the history of the White Pass and Yukon Railway. **Judith Munns**, curator of the **Skagway City Museum**. **Newnan Historical Society**. **David Wright**, of the Burro Café in Leadville, Colorado, and local historian, searched his records for a sign of Soapy's time in Leadville.

Whit "Pop" Haydn, the award-winning, close-up magician and sleight-of-hand master, has been an imperative instructor in the street methods of confidence men, their swindles, and human nature. Whit taught the author how street routines of nineteenth-century bunco gangs plied their nefarious games, including the shell game, three-card monte, and the handling of playing cards. While watching Whit manipulate the shells or a deck of cards, one can see how victims could easily be fooled into believing they had a "sure-thing" and could not lose. Whit is the producer of the annual Soapy Smith Wake at the Magic Castle in Hollywood, California.

Alaska State Archives staff and particularly **Tatyna Stepanova** and **Abby Focht** for responsiveness and extending hospitality during research. **Alaska State Historical Library** staff and particularly **Sandy Johnston** for photo requests. **Alaska State Library** staff and particularly **Becky Orford** for her responsive interlibrary loan help. **Alaska State Museum** for its fine collection of artifacts and photographs, and **Sorrel Goodwin**, Registrar, for help in obtaining photographs of collection items. **University of Colorado, Boulder,** for its greatly appreciated interlibrary loan of newspapers on microfilm. **Library and Archives Canada**. **Colorado Historical Society** for its indispensable and greatly appreciated photograph collections, city directories, and interlibrary loan of newspapers on microfilm. **Library of Congress** for its *Rocky Mountain News* on microfilm. **Corona Library** and **Karli Mahoney**, Library Assistant, Interlibrary Loans, for indispensable help in obtaining microfilm from all across the country. **Denver Western Heritage Library** for its photograph collections and city directories. **Joanne A. Frodsham** of the State and Military Records, Government Archives Division, Canada, who in 1987 found the two reports stating Frank Reid did not kill Soapy Smith. **Gale Digital Collections**, which allowed me access to their immense digital newspaper collection. **Elmer E. Rasmuson Library**, University of Alaska, Fairbanks, for service in providing photographs. **Royal British Columbia Museum** and **Kelly-Ann Turkington** for appreciated special photograph service. **University of Washington Library, Special Collections** and its efficient, responsive photograph services staff.

Dan Dietz, Vice-President of the Coweta-Newnan Historical society and a curator at the Male Academy Museum, Newnan, Georgia. Dan taught me early Coweta County history. He is responsible for finding the Smith mansion's new location and owners after it had been saved from the wrecking ball. Dan took me to the Smith house as well as the Oakhill cemetery where some of the family members are buried. He also gave me a private tour of the Historical Society's museum, which contains several early artifacts from Dr. Ira Ellis and Ellen Stimpson Smith, Soapy's grandparents. **Donna Dietz**, wife of Dan Dietz, searched cemetery, city, and family records in Newnan. It is only because of Donna and husband Dan that the Smith family plots were located, as the official location maps in the Oakhill cemetery were incorrectly marked.

Reverend Jan Davis was responsible for relocating the Smith mansion in which Soapy was born, thus saving it from being razed. He allowed me to photograph the mansion and gave me a private tour as well. **Joanne and "Tank" Tankersley** and **Jan Jacobs** of the Creede, Colorado, Historical Society. **Craig Gartrell**, Denver, Colorado. He searched Denver archives and gave the author much encouragement for several years prior to his passing. **Jim Richards**, owner of the Days of '98 Show, whom many in Skagway believe to be the reincarnation of Soapy Smith. For years, Jim has portrayed "Soapy" several times a day during the summer tourist season. His wit, charm, and ego gave this author a living, breathing Soapy Smith with whom to communicate. **Steven C. Levi** of Anchorage sent much information while working on his own book projects.

Martin Itjen, old-time and long-time resident, made Soapy Smith a major tourist draw in Skagway and remains a great source of early information. **Harriet Pullen** was a pioneer resident of Skagway who helped keep the legend of Soapy alive. Thanks to her, many early Skagway artifacts, such as Soapy's roulette table and grave marker, were saved.

Appreciated are the proofreading efforts of **Chizuru Araya** from Japan, a close student of English with an interest in the American frontier West. To long-time teachers of composition and literature Professors **Bill Hotchkiss** (poet and novelist of many volumes) and **Ron Silva** (poet and writer), and Professor **Chad Denton** (historian), I am much indebted for their faithful and invaluable proofreading expertise.

Last, but in no way least, my publisher and friend, **Art Petersen**. Retired English professor and Klondike Gold Rush historian who patiently answered all my publishing needs and questions. Art kept a very patient, positive, and upbeat attitude even when mine was not. He never ceased to amaze me with his knowledge of history and the English language. I learned an enormous amount from this man who has become a valued friend.

To those whom I unintentionally did not mention and to those who supported my endeavors, I offer my most sincere thanks.

Foreword
by Art Petersen

I first heard of Soapy Smith at age five from my mother. In 1933, fourteen years before, she worked for a California bank that closed for two weeks to reorganize, and employees were given paid time off at the end of June. As school would be out, she and two women teacher friends planned an adventure: drive to Seattle, sail north, and visit Southeast Alaska and British Columbia. Disembarking in Skagway, as did gold rush stampeders of old, they began at once for the interior. Returning, the trio spent two nights at Skagway's Pullen House. They took Martin Itjen's famous tour, which included the grave of Soapy Smith and stories about the bad man who ruled the town in '98. On the second night, Ma Pullen dined with her guests, and after dessert, she herded them into the parlor for her Soapy Smith "lecture." From her chair, she told of the generous, dangerous, charming criminal, but not long into her eye-witness account of his violent death, she fell asleep. Guests slipped out, and the three friends roamed the town. When a man began following them, they returned by a direct route to rambling Pullen House. "It was creepy," mother said. "Not a door had a lock."

Throughout my younger years, I heard this story occasionally retold, sometimes accompanied by a brief tale or two about the exploits of Soapy Smith. In the overall telling, there was not much about Canada. Rather, Skagway was the focus with its shadowy Soapy Smith. Perhaps in a similar way (through short histories, stories, visits to Skagway), generations have learned of the legendary bad man. Becoming engrossed in Klondike research for four histories, I often saw Soapy again in the pages of books and newspapers, as shadowy as ever—relentless and ruthless in pursuit of robbing, even of the dead, and of orchestrating roguery and murder. Most stories seemed outrageous. And yet....

Then came opportunity to work with Jeff Smith in publishing his decades of research on his infamous forebear. I was pleased to find that Jeff was committed to using documented sources. This approach kept the other Soapy at a distance, that looming, indistinct, long shadow cast by exaggerated tales told over time. There are many of these, such as launched by Ma Pullen. She had met Soapy and claimed to have seen him die. One of the teacher friends of my mother had a friend, Miss Jeannette Garner, who taught in Skagway's high school in 1926-27. In 1981 she wrote to share remembrances of Ma Pullen at that time, including how

> People in town laughed about her "museum" ... and said that the stories she told in her "lecture" were most of them untrue or at least greatly exaggerated. She would not let townspeople in to hear it but one woman put on a veil and went in unrecognized and reported on the "whoppers" she told.[3]

One of these comes from a little book by Mrs. Pullen about how she and her son Royal were at the scene of Soapy's death. To me it is highly suspect. The story's overstatement aside, not one of the many eye-witness reports of the shootout includes a woman with a child near Soapy's body on the Juneau Wharf.

---

[3] Garner, Jeannette, typed enclosure to letter of October 25, 1987. Jeannette shared no "whoppers."

One of the Pullen "whoppers" told to me by my mother was about a Presbyterian minister who wanted to build a church in Skagway and was given several hundred dollars by Soapy for the cause. But that was not all. Soapy next, in the story, helped the minister gather more money from gamblers. Then that night the minister was relieved of the funds by robbers, one of whom was Soapy Smith! Martin Itjen tells a version of this story, but in his (which appears in his guide book), the minister is not robbed; he just accepts the money.[4] Now it so happens that I know these tales to be untrue. I spent five years editing, researching, and preparing the manuscript of the first "man of the cloth" into Skagway in 1897. He was the *Presbyterian* Rev. Robert M. Dickey. He did not solicit funds for a church; rather, recorded in various places, is that a church committee of women did.[5]

Ma Pullen and the colorful Martin Itjen were just two of the progenitors and conveyers of "whoppers" about Soapy. Another was the Honorable James Wickersham in his *Old Yukon: Tales—Trails—and Trials* (1938). He was US District Judge in Alaska from 1900 to 1908 and for fourteen years represented the Territory of Alaska in Congress. Judge Wickersham traveled Alaska and came to know many of its people, and no doubt they shared their stories with the well-liked, honest judge. In the twelve pages devoted to Soapy Smith, Wickersham mixes probable details with numerous time-worn exaggerations that I see now, after close association with Jeff Smith's research and analysis, are surely not true. Among these stories is one about "A Presbyterian missionary" whose "lay brother ... carried the church fund" and who lost all of it gambling with "a well-dressed and agreeable gentleman," not named but who in context could be none other than Soapy Smith.[6] In actuality, only one Presbyterian minister came to Skagway and Dyea in the fall of 1897, Rev. Dickey. He came alone and remained all winter, its only resident minister and living in the back of the church his parishioners furnished the money to build.

One story about Soapy and a minister in Skagway is not enough. Judge Wickerhsam tells "Another ... related to me [him] by a prominent business man of Skagway who assured me of its truth."[7] In this story, an "evangelist" came to Skagway to build a church. Soapy, titled Colonel Smith in this version, gives the minister $300, helps collect $3,000 more, and then orders "henchmen" to rob the evangelist of it all. This story is also surely not true. Nothing shows Rev. Dickey was ever robbed of church funds. It seems clear that in recounting the "Tales" in the last years of his life, the judge assembled his chapter on Soapy Smith from stories he had heard and those told in newspapers and magazines from 1898 to the late 1930s. He had to rely on these because there was no documented, critical literature on the man. The judge himself had no first-hand knowledge of events as he did not arrive in the Territory until 1900, and then it was to Eagle on the Yukon River and to Nome and Valdez that he first went. Tales told by word of mouth have staying power. Some I heard about Soapy

---

[4] Itjen, p. 24.
[5] Rev. Dickey's novel, his diary, a personal letter, and Skagway newspapers, documented in this biography.
[6] Wickersham, p. 15.
[7] Wickersham, p. 16.

Smith have clung to me for over sixty years. When a person of stature like Judge Wickersham gives them the power of print and the prestige of his reputation, their growth is vigorous, uniform, and lasting. Then, like a second-growth forest, the appearance of the original terrain is altered to a significant degree, often totally.

Enter biographer Jeff Smith with his determination to record apparent realities, no matter what they might be. His method was to line out all available information about the man and interpret it based on documentation of strong or at least reasonable authority. His decades of work draws back a curtain on times and details previously unknown about Soapy Smith: when he was a child in the war-time and then Reconstruction South, when a youth scrambling to claim an identity and make a living in Texas, and when a young man ranging the western states. So far, so good: here was a normal-sized man, not a distorted shadow figure of unwavering criminality. But then along the way, Soapy Smith for me began again to assume larger proportions. They were not, however, the result of implausible tales of evil doing but rather of how the world responded to a highly complex and contrary human being, and he to his world. Soapy Smith could and would do evil in terms of "skinning suckers" who would skin him if they could, but he was much more than a crook.

Congressmen, lawmen, criminals, parsons, writers, and businessmen called him *friend* and asked after him. Ability with a pen revealed he held ideals and empathized with suffering. Also appearing was a desire and ability to influence politics, lead men in claiming human rights, command heavily armed men against a misdirected Colorado National Guard, encourage a political march on Washington *before* Jacob Coxey promoted one, lead a Denver regiment to join Coxey's Army, head a military company in Mexico, to go to Cuba, and in Alaska. The man aspired to greatness. Jeff Smith compares Soapy to "The Man Who Would be King" in Rudyard Kipling's story (1889), and that match seems apt. I find him, though, more akin to the driven mystery man in F. Scott Fitzgerald's *The Great Gatsby* (1925). Gatsby's and Soapy's harsh upbringings are similar, and they share similar dualities in their society and in their human nature. There is also a comparable social irony, which Jeff includes from a publication of the time (*The Road*): that Soapy's crimes pale beside those of robber barons large and small of the Gilded Age.[8] The aspirations of these characters from literature and Jefferson Randolph Smith II (*Alias Soapy Smith*) seem thoroughly mixed with Soapy's passions for family, gambling, social position, "skinning suckers," drink, "pals," and the unshakeable code of honor and fierce pride that got him killed.

A clever rascal in one of Shakespeare's plays claims that "Some are born great..., Some achieve greatness..., And some have greatness thrust upon them."[9] And some, like the imposing, contradictory, aggressive, charming, and unforgettable Soapy Smith—his watermarks all through the pages of the last chapters of the American West—have all three. More than any history to date, Jeff Smith's biography shows us how and why.

July 6, 2009, Juneau, Alaska

---

[8] *Gilded Age*: spans from the end of Reconstruction (circa 1877) to the "beginning of modern America" (circa 1900). (*Gilded Age*)

[9] *Twelfth Night* 3.4.38-42. Malvolio speaking to Olivia.

Introduction

Jefferson Randolph ("Soapy") Smith II was an American, 19th-century confidence man, gambler, and crime boss par excellence—perhaps the most accomplished street hawker and all-round bunco artist of his day. Wherever he set up his "tripe & keister" (tripod and suitcase), which held the implements of his nefarious trade, he was certain to draw a large crowd and succeed in molding it to his will. A colorful and complex character of the Old West, he became a ruler of rogues and vagabonds, a friend of the friendless, a protector of criminals, and a contributor to churches. He devoted his God-given talents and abilities to the pursuit of the fast buck by employing every swindling scheme then known to man. He pretended righteousness as he leveraged to his advantage the greed of his fellow man, who himself awaited the opportunity to cheat him. He accomplished his dominance by eliminating chance from his games. In turn, he emptied the pockets of his victims and bluffed them into silence and submission. A favorite saying of his was, "Do unto others what they'd like to do to you, but do it first."[10] This king of misrule was as many sided as he was incomprehensible.

Jeff was a self-taught reader of human nature, and he used his knowledge and criminal skill to exploit the greed and dishonesty of his victims. He knew as soon as he set eyes on a man whether or not he could be "played." He had an unconquerable aversion to making money by honest means and loved the art of fleecing his prey and then arranging it so his victims earnestly thanked him for his services. In the art of sleight-of-hand mechanics, he could deal himself the winning hand in any game without fail or suspicion. In his talents, few equaled him. He was master of the "short-con," including the shell and pea game, three-card monte, and a wide assortment of others. He developed and maintained larger indoor operations, such as fake lottery shops and stock exchange agencies, and mock auction houses. The most infamous of his unique schemes was the prize package soap sell in which he put large-denomination bills inside the wrappers of some cakes of soap and auctioned off the packages for $1 each, then for more as the number of cakes diminished. Only Jeff's men, who seeded every crowd, ever won the larger bills. From this swindle came the sobriquet "Soapy" by which he came to be known throughout the American West.

Jeff had a disarming smile that invited trust, the firm handshake and warm demeanor of a successful businessman, and the silvery personality of a man impossible to dislike. His manners were those of a Southern gentleman and his persuasive powers those of the devil. Almost no crime was beyond his scope when he was in pursuit of the almighty dollar. In times of physical danger he could draw a pistol or knife as smoothly as he could deal aces from the bottom of the deck. In times of trouble, though, he usually preferred to rely on his wits, smooth speech, and dexterity rather than on physical force. He opposed bloodshed, but as violence came with the people and places he did business with, it frequently could not be avoided. Tough and treacherous men filled out the roster of Soap Gang members for these occasions. No one questioned his bravery. He was fearless. Threatened with violence, he was quick

---

[10] Robertson, p. 12

to anger and as quick with his revolver, which was always at the ready. He feared neither policeman nor any foe. He was in the gravest sense of the words *a bad man to cross*.

He knew how to use to his advantage anything he had ever read, from news stories to literature. He wrote and published essays, stories, and poetry that conveyed not only the sporting man's activities but also heart-felt political feelings of the day. Thankfully, he collected and saved most of his writings and business documents, giving us the unique opportunity to view the world as he saw it, or at least as he sought to portray it.

Jeff made friends among the worst and the best in society, from criminals to congressmen. As the protector of criminals and organizer of rogues, grifters, and scoundrels, he was continually at odds with the law, which endlessly pursued him with endless exasperation, and yet, many times he became the ally of the policeman on the beat, helping to catch common criminals, or the ally of clergy on the street, helping to round up aid for hungry families.

Voting strictly Republican, he had political muscle in various precincts sought by corrupt office holders. In recompense, they offered him the favor of immunity from the law for helping them to win elections, only to regret it later when that favor came due again and again. His foes saw him as a dangerous man with solid political power.

Jeff forged to the front as a leader among professional gamblers and sure-thing men. During his career, he built and ruled three criminal empires, two in Colorado and one in Alaska. He opened and operated saloons, gambling establishments, and swindling operations where men of ill virtue preyed upon the innocent. At the same time, Jeff maintained the personal virtues of a dutiful and loving family man who went to great lengths to keep his family from harm or want. He used his considerable intelligence and personality to devise and manage predatory schemes, yet he persisted in showing sympathy and charity to those in need. He was strikingly generous, giving a good percentage of his ill-gotten riches to those less fortunate, preferring the limelight of notoriety and popularity to the accumulation of wealth. He might have contributed more to charitable causes had it not been for a gambling addiction to the card game of faro. He often played nightly until either he or the bank had been broken. His vices were gambling and alcohol, the latter becoming instrumental in his violent finish.

Never reckoning the cost of his actions, Jeff throughout his life was guided by circumstance. An opportunist who rarely planned, he was swift to grab at life's offerings and make the most of them through shrewdness and cunning. At the height of his power in Denver, he boldly admitted to being a confidence man: "I beg to state that I am no gambler," he told a newspaper reporter. "A gambler takes chances with his money, I don't."[11] He seems earnestly to have believed that his successful life of crime should be considered more of a credit to his social standing than a blemish. He once stated, "I consider bunco steering more honorable than the life led by the average politician."[12] Always a step ahead of his competition and the law, still

---

[11] *RMN* 12/02/1894.
[12] *The Road* 02/29/1896.

repeatedly he would stop, spin, and face his troubles head-on. His daring, fanned by successful escapes or confrontations of trouble, increased rather than diminished with age.

He led and organized other bunco men into an army of unstoppable brothers in fraud. He knew how to command and keep their devotion, loyalty, and friendship. And he did the same at city hall. With local city powers in his pocket, Jeff set up a framework of protection and security for himself and his men. Rather than remain in the shadows and be content with his power, Jeff wanted the public to see him. He was a man of Old West mentality in a swiftly evolving New West. His breed was diminishing, but he refused to retire and continued promotion of himself in the public eye. Finally audacity cost him his influence and control, and in the end, his life. However, he never considered himself a rival of society. Rather, he saw himself as a businessman who had a rightful place in it. At Jeff's funeral in 1898, Reverend John Sinclair said of Soapy, "Poor Smith thought he made this [the following] proverb truer to the facts of life, I am told, by revising it to read, 'The way of the transgressor is hard ... to quit.'"[13]

This is the story of a man who had an insatiable appetite for greater things. A self-styled patriot, Jeff longed to be a military leader. He commissioned himself "Colonel" Smith in Colorado and "Captain" in Alaska. Several times, he labored to amass volunteer armies that he would lead into battle, yet he never served in the military. There is little doubt that towards the end, he sincerely began to think he was the man he wanted everyone to believe he was.

This belief, in part, is among the causes of Jeff's violent death at the hands of vigilante foes. Throughout his adult life, and long after his death, his daring crimes along with his good and charitable works were reported regularly in newspapers across the Western states. His life had been dense with exploits and his death shot full of controversy. His was a spectacular and devious life. For some twenty years, Soapy Smith was the top "sure-thing" man of the West, and no one would prove more slippery.

---

[13] The "proverb" is Proverbs 13:15. From the sermon of Reverend John A. Sinclair delivered in Skagway's morgue, July 11, 1898. Reprinted in *Skaguay News* 07/15/1898, p. 2.

Chapter 1
The Smiths in Early America

"*My god, don't shoot!*" These last words spoken by Jefferson Randolph ("Soapy") Smith II ended a career in crime spanning over twenty years, from 1877 to 1898, and all the Western states from Colorado to California and from Texas to Alaska.

Jefferson, or "Jeff" to his friends, stood about 5' 9" with a slight physical build, dark brown hair, beard, mustache, and gray-blue eyes. A bullet ended his life when he was only 37 years old, though his grave marker indicates that he was 38. No one in Skaguay, Alaska, where he was killed, knew that he was born on Friday November 2, 1860. Jeff regularly sent funds to his wife Mary, ranging from $500 to $1000, yet self-appointed authorities taking charge of his estate reported that he was all but broke.[1] Although perhaps the most infamous confidence man of his era and although owning and controlling several saloons and a ship during one of the greatest gold rushes in history, he was reported to have only $148.60 before subtraction of inquest fees.[2]

Jefferson R. Smith II was born to an affluent aristocratic family whose lineage predates the American Revolution. On a commission from the English Treasury, Joshua Smith, Jefferson's great-great-great-grandfather, came in 1760 to the American Colonies with his son George. By 1763, England and the Colonies showed signs of dissent, and so did father and son. When Joshua decided to return to England, George refused to accompany him. George and his wife were expecting the birth of their first child, and they wanted to settle in the Colonies. Joshua returned alone, and in anger, disinherited his son and banished him from the family.

George and his family settled in the Virginia Colony. Their son John was the first family member born in America. During the American Revolution against his former homeland, George enlisted in the Continental Army, earning the rank of captain. Son John also joined the struggle against the English. In October 1779 he fought as a captain with the French at the "Siege of Savannah" under General Casmir Pulaski. John married Martha Manson Hardaway, who gave him two sons, George and Ira Ellis. In 1782, they settled on 641 acres in Dinwiddie County, Virginia. County tax records show they owned 12 slaves and 7 horses.[3]

In the War of 1812, their son George was a captain and Ira Ellis was a sergeant in a rifle company, First Regiment, Virginia Militia. After the war Ira Ellis Smith studied medicine under Caspar Wistar, who taught biology to Merriwether Lewis of the historic exploring team of Lewis and Clark. Ira married Ellen Stimpson Peniston, who was known as the "Belle of Virginia."[4] They had ten boys and one girl. One of the boys died six months after birth, and another died at age ten. One of the boys was named after

---

[1] Receipt for $500 fr Jeff Smith II to Mary E. Smith, 08/28/1897, item 21, author's col. Receipt for $1000 fr Jefferson R. Smith II to Mary E. Smith, 08/28/1897, item 20, author's col.

[2] Document returning ship ownership to original owner. Skagway, Alaska City Museum.

[3] Land & Tax Lists of Dinwiddie County, Virginia State Library, Archives Division.

[4] b. 03/04/1802 to d. 10/23/1860.

Caspar Wistar. Their only daughter, Lillie Katherine Jane, died at age four.[1] In 1828, Dr. Ira Ellis Smith moved his family to Wilkes County, Georgia, later known as Oglethorpe County, where they lived for six to eight years.

On March 25, 1828, the state of Georgia held a land grant lottery for the sale of land ceded to the state in a treaty with the Creek Indians.[2]

> Sec. 11.... The following ... persons shall be entitled to a draw or draws under this act; every male white person of eighteen years of age and upwards, being a citizen of the United States, and an inhabitant within the organized limits of this State for three years immediately preceding this act, including such as have been absent on lawful business, shall be entitled to one draw; every male person of like description, having a wife or legitimate male child or children, resident as aforesaid, or who were born and have ever since resided in this state, shall have two draws....[3]

Ira Ellis won the right to purchase land in the Sixth district of Coweta County, named for the large Coweta Indian population in the region. The land Ira purchased was thirty-nine miles southwest of the future city of Atlanta and seven miles beyond the settlement of Newnan. The Ellises were one of the first families to reside there.[4] Newnan would become a prosperous town for professionals due to its thriving cotton industry. Ira was well-liked and succeeded as a physician and planter.[5] His popularity gained him a seat in the House of Representatives for the Sixth District in the Georgia Legislature; he served from 1832 to 1837 and again in 1851. He was elected a state senator in 1839, 1841-42, 1849, and 1853.[6] According to Edwin Smith,[7] a grandson of Ira, the Smith "family was equal in standing to any in Georgia, ... claiming descent from long lines of well-known people."[8]

Ira Ellis Smith's wife Ellen, in a letter from her sister to a niece, is described as the "Belle of Virginia" and "the Flower of Georgia."[9] Another family letter boldly states that she was the most educated lady in Georgia.[10] Another letter by Ellen's brother John Gilbert Peniston tells of a duel fought in September 1820 over the sixteen-year-old Ellen. It took place in St. Petersburg, Virginia, between R. C. Adams and James B. Boisseau. She was "Educated in Baltimore," and

> her accomplishments equalled her personal charm, so it was no wonder that she should have many lovers. Admiring friends gave her a party in her honor. During the evening one man showed her such marked attention that her escort became jealous and challenged his rival to fight a duel. The next day the word came to Ellen that both men had been killed. A sad shock to her,

---

[1] Ltr fr Ellen Smith Faver to Jefferson R. Smith III, 11/08/1932. Geri Murphy col.

[2] Anderson, p. 14.

[3] Jones, Mary, p. 42.

[4] The Newnan Male Academy museum, Newnan, Georgia.

[5] Ltr fr Ellen Smith Faver to Jefferson R. Smith III, 11/08/1932. Geri Murphy col.

[6] Anderson, pp. 71-72.

[7] b. 05/10/1859. d. 11/01/1941. First cousin of "Soapy" Smith.

[8] *Trail* 01/1920, p. 6.

[9] Jones, Mary, p. 51.

[10] Ltr fr Ellen Smith Faver to Jefferson R. Smith III, 11/08/1932. Geri Murphy col.

though she loved neither of them. ... In old Blandford churchyard both men, Adams and Boisseau, were buried.[1]

As the account goes, Adams offered Ellen a cold drink, thus offending Boisseau, who then challenged Adams to the pistol duel. Their combat took place in a secluded yard behind the Old Blandford church and cemetery.[2] Both men were apparently adequate shots as each was killed by the other.[3] Some blamed Ellen for the deaths, causing her great distress, and she never escaped feeling responsible.[4] It is said that Dr. Ira Smith was the physician present when the duel took place. On December 6 (or 26), 1821, approximately a year after the duel, Ira married Ellen. Their children were well schooled and successful. Among them were 3 physicians, 3 lawyers, 1 professor and president of the Methodist Emory College at Oxford (Georgia), 1 minister, and 1 farmer.[5] Among the children who took up law was Jefferson Randolph Smith, Sr., the father of Soapy Smith.

Between 1830 and 1835, Ira engaged brothers named Cole to build a plantation mansion that he christened Shoal Creek. It stood seven miles east of Newnan, close to Thomas' crossroads on the Old Wynn's Pond Road.[6] From the outside, the house is imposing, appearing larger than it is on the inside. A large center hall is flanked by two spacious rooms, a small kitchen, and a sitting room. Upstairs are two large bedrooms, each with fireplace.[7] Some of the original furnishings and family heirlooms are on permanent display in Newnan at the Male Academy Museum.[8]

In 1844 Moses P. Kellogg came to Coweta county to be a teacher. With a large family to educate, Ira offered Kellogg a teaching job and a place to live in the Smith home. There he would teach eight of the Smith children.[9] School was held in a small room added to the rear of the house.[10] Arrangements were made to open a school on Fayetteville Road for children from the surrounding area.[11] One of Kellogg's brightest students was Ira's son Luther, who went on to become president of Emory College.[12]

Cotton and corn were grown on the Smith Plantation, supplementing the income from Ira's medical practice. In a 1932 letter, Ellen Elizabeth Faver, a cousin of Jeff's (Soapy's), wrote how cotton produced a large portion of the plantation revenue. She explained that at the end of the Civil War, about one hundred slaves had been freed,

---

[1] Jones, Mary, p. 51.

[2] Adams & Boisseau were from prominent families. The church, cemetery, and one of the dueling pistols used in the fight may be seen at the Old Blandford Church museum on US routes 301-460 Crater Road, St. Petersburg, VA.

[3] Ltr fr John Gilbert Peniston to Ellen S. Faver, 3/26/1903. Ellen Rafeedie col.

[4] Statement by Ellen Rafeedie, 04/25/2007.

[5] Smith family genealogical records.

[6] Coweta, p. 350.

[7] "Grandeur gone from decaying house." Newspaper clipping of unknown origin & date, 1960s interview of Ira Ellis Casper Wistar Smith III.

[8] In 1994 the house was moved some distance away and is in the process of being restored.

[9] Jones, Mary, p. 92.

[10] Statement by John R. Smith, 08/10/1977.

[11] Pamphlet by the Newnan-Coweta Historical Society, written by Georgia Hinely.

[12] President of Emory College, later, Emory University. Luther M. Smith (1826-1879), graduated Emory 1848, President 1867-71. (Emory Presidents)

with a small number staying on at the farm until Ira Smith moved to the home of his son, Ira Ellis Caspar Wistar Smith.[1] Edwin Bobo Smith, another cousin of Jeff's (Soapy's), who also came to live with Jeff and his parents for a time, stated that "Their wealth consisted largely of slaves."[2] The 1860 census shows that Ira accounted for fifty-seven slaves living in sixteen houses on his land.[3] During a fact-finding visit to the house in the 1960s, Joseph Jefferson Smith,[4] a grandson of Jeff's (Soapy's), found a black family living in the house. The head of this family, Joseph Jefferson reports, was a man calling himself Ira Ellis Smith.[5] The connection this family may have had with the Smith family is yet to be determined.

Of Dr. Ira Smith's eleven children, the fifth was Jeff's father, Jefferson Randolph Smith Sr.,[6] a lawyer who married Emily Dawson Edmondson.[7] Her family owned the property adjoining the Smith Plantation.[8] Three of the Edmondson daughters married three of Ira's sons. Jeff's cousin Edwin wrote that "Jeff's mother was a lovely Christian woman" and that "his father was college bred and a lawyer of good standing."[9]

Jefferson Randolph and Emily moved in with Ira at Shoal Creek to help care for Ira's ailing wife, Ellen. Another Ellen, the daughter of Columbus Darwin Smith and the granddaughter of Ira, named Ellen Smith Faver, also moved to Shoal Creek. She came after her mother, Nancy Edmondson, died on October 21, 1860. Two days later Ira's wife Ellen also died. In a letter, Ellen Faver Smith writes that ten days later, on November 2, 1860, Jefferson Randolph Smith II was born.[10]

Jefferson and Emily had five children, of whom four survived. They were Jefferson Randolph, Eva Katherine, Emmie Lou, and Bascomb.[11] Ellen Faver, who lived at the plantation until after the Civil War, came to know the first-born child and had good to say of him as a youngster: "I can truly say that a brighter more manly little boy, I have never known."[12] This good opinion did not last. Jefferson Randolph Smith II was to become infamously known by the moniker of "Soapy." Jeff's future exploits brought so much shame and disgrace to his kin in Coweta County that his name was erased from birth records in the family Bible. The eraser marks can be faintly seen to this day.[13]

Jefferson Smith's youth was overshadowed by the Civil War. It began on the early morning of April 12, 1861, when Confederate forces opened fire on the Federal garrison at Fort Sumter in the Charleston, South Carolina, harbor. Georgia was the fifth state to secede from the Union and join the Confederate States of America. Two of Ira's sons, Ira Ellis Caspar Wistar and Columbus Darwin, joined the Confederate

---

[1] Ltr fr Ellen Smith Faver to Jefferson R. Smith III, 11/08/1932. Geri Murphy col.
[2] *Trail* 01/1920, p. 7.
[3] 1860 census, (July 26) Sched. 2—Slave Inhabitants, p. 52, Coweta county, Georgia. (Ancestry.com)
[4] b. 11/16/1909 d. 11/29/1977.
[5] Ltr fr James Rothmund Smith to author, 01/26/2007.
[6] b. 03/21/1831 to d. 09/28/1902.
[7] b. 01/04/1837 to d. 07/01/1877.
[8] Ltr fr Ellen Smith Faver to Jefferson R. Smith III, 11/08/1932. Geri Murphy col.
[9] *Trail* 01/1920, pp. 6-7.
[10] Ltr fr Ellen Smith Faver to Jefferson R. Smith III, 11/08/1932. Geri Murphy col.
[11] b. 1869. d. believed to have died some time in 1920.
[12] Ltr fr Ellen Smith Faver to Jefferson R. Smith III, 11/08/1932. Geri Murphy col.
[13] The Bible was seen and recorded by Joseph J. Smith, but its location is currently unknown.

cavalry to fight for the Southern cause. Both men survived the war. Young Jeff was able to continue his education at a Sabbath school throughout the war.

The War Between the States is a significant part of the history of Newnan and Coweta County. Newnan was known as the "hospital city of the Confederacy," having six field hospitals located city-wide in churches, homes, and other buildings and serving as many as 10,000 wounded soldiers of both the North and South.[1]

On July 30, 1864, the carnage and violence of the war approached Newnan. During the siege of Atlanta, Union Brigadier General McCook with 3,600 Federal cavalry began a campaign of raids against Southern railroads, the final objective of which would be the attempt to rescue 32,000 Union prisoners at Andersonville. In the path of the army advancing on Andersonville was Newnan. Believed at the time was that General McCook intended to capture wounded Confederates at Newnan. The Union troops were only three miles from the town when Major General Joseph Wheeler with 1,400 Confederate cavalry caught up with the Federals, engaged them in battle, and won a victory. Captured were approximately 2,000 prisoners, several ambulances, and a full battery. Also won was the release of about 500 Confederate prisoners that McCook had in his possession.

The Confederate triumph, known as the "Battle of Brown's Mill," probably saved Newnan from the destruction that many Southern cities suffered.[2] In September 1864, Atlanta was being evacuated, and on November 16, Union General William Sherman burned Atlanta to the ground on his "march to the sea." With little opposition, his army destroyed everything useful to the Confederate Army and everything of value to the residents. Little survived. The war came to an official end on August 9, 1865, and with it, the lifestyle the Smith family had always known. In a few short years of horrific fighting, the Confederacy had crumbled and Ira's family empire with it. Before Jefferson grew out of swaddling clothes, life on the Smith Plantation changed irrevocably. Cousin Edwin Smith wrote, "At the close of that struggle, the family were in less affluent circumstances than they had been before."[3] With the war's destruction of Southern resources and the harsh Federal regulations of the Reconstruction era, living conditions grew ever more severe for the family inhabiting "Shoal Creek."

The Federal Reconstruction Act of 1866 enabled the Northern states to occupy and enact harsh laws meant to punish the Southern states for the next decade. One such law banned Southern-educated lawyers from practicing. This law, along with the emancipation of plantation slaves, forced young Jeff's father to abandon his law practice and join the rest of the family in the cotton and cornfields. Enduring the hardships of the coming decade would require basic, "down to earth" measures.

Jeff continued his schooling after the war's end and on into Reconstruction. A Christmas speech written for the Sabbath school play in 1871 shows clear evidence of a good education and signs of wit.

---

[1] Male Academy Museum, Newnan, Georgia brochure.
[2] Coweta County museum records. A detailed account of the Battle of Brown's Mill can be found in Jones, Mary, pp. 151-180.
[3] *Trail* 01/1920, p. 7.

Newnan, GA. Dec. 24 1871

Friends & Patrons. Ladies & Gentleman, we heartily welcome you on this festive occasion. With buoyant & grateful hearts we commemorate the nativity of Him at whose birth the morning stars sang together & the sons of God shouted for joy. Let the community for its blessings, rejoice, and especially should we as a Sabbath school rejoice, that we have been blessed with such kind patrons & efficient teachers. And how can we express our gratitude (and admiration) for this beautiful tree? A tree is known by its fruits, and this one is one that speaks for itself. It must have sprung from a generous soil in a genial clime. Leaden with such rich and luscious fruit, its bending boughs are more persuasive than speech; and the masich[1] it bears would puzzle Linnaeus[2] to classify or name it. Ladies, in our hearts we thank you for it. Again a hearty welcome and a joyous festive Christmas eve to all.[3]

Edwin Bobo Smith[4] was eighteen months older than his Cousin Jeff. The boys were double first cousins as their fathers were brothers and their mothers were sisters. Cousin Ed's family lived "within a stone's throw"[5] of Cousin Jeff's. Growing up together, the boys called one another "brother" and as youths, planned to stay together for life. Here is how Edwin characterized his boyhood relationship with Jeff:

There was a natural affinity besides the tie of close blood relationship, and the inseparable companionship endured for many years. Our ages were nearly the same but his superior daring and adventurous spirit made me a satellite. Hunting and fishing were mutual passions, and we quickly learned to handle guns expertly, ruthlessly decimating the small game in our area. One winter, after agreeing that we were weary of this petty sport of quail and squirrel slaughter, we got a reluctant assent of our elders to go on an extended trip for the bagging of bigger stuff. We headed for the big pinelands of the coastal region south of Savannah, and we got there partly by rail and partly afoot, helped occasionally by riding in the wagon of a friendly farmer. Our minds were set on bringing down the red deer and maybe a bear in the cane breaks, to say nothing of the waterfowl along the streams. The expedition was a triumph and we wrote home of getting seven good-sized bucks, quite a few wild turkeys and no end of marsh hens, but the score took in no bear. On Saint Simon Island we encountered a novelty, something utterly unexpected from which we were enabled to make money; from a

---

[1] *masich*: may be *mastic*, "1. A gum or resin which exudes from the bark.... 2. An evergreen shrub yielding mastic gum...." It fits with the following named botanist who was challenged to name its origin. (*OED*)

[2] *Linnaeus*: Carolus Linnaeus (1707-1778), famed Swedish naturalist and botanist, established system of nomenclature for taxonomy of plants. His published works number 180. (*Encyclopedia Britannica*, 1892)

[3] Copy of original sent to John R. Smith by Joseph J. Smith, 12/08/1969. The original (location currently unknown) is nicely hand written in cursive and very readable. Someone, in different script, perhaps his mother, wrote at the top, "Jeffies Christmas Welcome, Sabbath School play."

[4] b. 05/10/1859, d. 11/01/1941.

[5] Smith, Edwin.

native who got a living that way we learned to be trappers of mink that abound along the reedy shores of that beautiful domain. The skins brought a dollar apiece in the Savannah market and we were in the fair way to become capitalists when a peremptory message summoned the young trappers home. It was a bitter pill to go back when fortune was smiling and Jeff, surveying the fleet of sailing ships that came from all ports of the world into the harbor at Brunswick for lumber and resin and turpentine, said,

"Let's go away on one of them, Ed, and see the world." He must have read my thoughts for the same notion had been fluttering through my mind. Landlubbers as we were we had been mingling with the captains and crews of full-rigged ships, barques and schooners from distant ports and the master of one seeing our quickness to learn the ways of vessels and celerity in skinning up the rope ladders offered to let us work our passage with him to Buenos Aires. If I had only said the word, away we would have sailed on the next tide, but the vision of a sad mother interposed and so the dreams of a pair of embryo sea rovers were frustrated as one wouldn't embark without the other. I have often speculated whether our whole lives would not have been altered had we made that voyage; if we might not have become wedded to the deep and sailed the seven seas to the end of our days.

As it was, we went home, entirely by rail this time by virtue of our mink-gained coin, and though we didn't know what halos were, they had accrued to us as the home folks turned out to hear the wondrous details of the intrepid explorers' exploits in far off spaces. As a consequence, the explorers felt their importance considerably, and as traveled men deemed themselves much superior to the juveniles who had never crossed the county boundaries. It is true they had been away only six weeks, but it seemed six years so much had happened....[1]

To the end, the pair shared a bond. Years later, Edwin became assistant doorman in the US House of Representatives and then reported for the *Washington Post*. In time, Edwin introduced Jeff to the political and social powers of Washington. Some of Ed's facts are flawed. He was a newspaper reporter, after all, and perhaps guilty of using creative license in telling stories about Jeff as a young man. Further, discrepancies occur between Edwin's accounts published in 1920 and his unpublished manuscript in 1937. However, Ed is the only substantive source of information about Jeff's boyhood in Georgia and Texas. In a 1919 interview, Edwin told how

Jeff as a young boy on the farm had a lot of push, delighted in the outdoor life, energetic, and a good manager as well as a hard worker. By the time he was ten years old he was doing a man's work, and he directed things in a way that would have done credit to one of mature years....[2]

Why young Jefferson chose a path of crime over one of commerce or politics is not known, but it can be reasonably supposed that the Civil War and its aftermath

[1] Smith, Edwin; & Ltr by Jefferson R. Smith III, 06/15/1941. Author's col.
[2] *Trail* 01/1920, p. 7.

played a significant part. Key causes included economic destruction and the downslide of his father when Reconstruction prevented him from practicing law. Then followed endless toil on the always-struggling family farm for many years. Jefferson Sr. tried to maintain standing in the community, but he was failing. In 1871 he was an officer of the Independent Order of Good Templars, which met every Monday night at the Masonic Hall in Newnan.[1] A photograph said to be of Jefferson Sr. shows him wearing a Templar's medal.[2] The Knights Templar, however, was (and is) a strict temperance organization; none of its members were to drink. The father, however, did not adhere to the rules, and after he began drinking heavily, he never regained his vigor.

Cousin Ed was witness to the transformation. "The father fell into inebriety," he wrote, "and by the time the family moved to Texas, Jeff had become its main stay....[3] Ellen Rafeedie, a Smith relative, spoke of the distance wedged between father and son owing to the father's alcohol abuse.

> When Soapy was a small child his father would go into Newnan every Saturday and get drunk, and would take Soapy to drive him home. It would make Soapy so mad he would dump his father (who had passed out) in the back of the wagon and whip the mules to go lickedy-split over the rutted road so his father's head would whack with every bump....[4]

For eight harsh years, the Smith family struggled to survive the grim post-war period. Historians have named this period Reconstruction, but its definition is far from the reality of its connotation, which is that of disorganization, corruption, and general privation among citizens of the South. Generally, Reconstruction covers the years 1867 to 1877, a decade of carpetbaggers from the North, spoilers rushing into the void left by politically disenfranchised and professionally dispossessed Southerners. These times were hard enough to turn otherwise reasonable and moral people toward any way of gaining advantage in an unfair world. Then additionally in 1873, the US plunged into a six-year economic depression. Seeing only worsening penury ahead and hearing of opportunities for a new life in Texas, Jefferson's father concluded it was time to migrate. Sometime between 1876 and 1877, the father picked up the remains of his family and moved them to Round Rock, Texas.[5]

The state was a haven for Southerners after the war. Laws were lax, and growth was everywhere. Round Rock had become a prosperous frontier-trading center for ranchers and farmers since arrival of the railroad in 1876, which turned Round Rock into a railway terminus. Round Rock was home to the Smith family for almost five years, but records of Smith activities there are few. The father attempted to resurrect his law practice but without success. The local historical society has indications that the Smith family may have opened a hotel for a short time. It was located on the 100 block of Bagdad Street, which ran parallel to the train tracks.[6] However, earliest

---

[1] Jones, Mary, p. 205.

[2] The photograph, according to the book, may be that of Columbus D. Smith. (Jones, Mary, p. 582)

[3] *Trail* 01/1920, p. 7.

[4] Ltr fr Ellen P. Rafeedie to author, 05/22/1992. Author's col.

[5] Ltr fr Ethel Smith to Jefferson R. Smith III, 1932. Geri Murphy col.

[6] *Round Rock*, p. 275.

records of the hotel are from 1891, well after the Smiths had left Round Rock. Family records make no mention of any such business venture. The only family testimony of this period comes from Cousin Edwin Smith, who also had moved to Texas with his family and found work as a reporter on the *Fort Worth Gazette*. Edwin later wrote that young Jefferson found work in Round Rock as a store salesman and hotel runner whose job was to meet incoming trains and steer travelers toward a local hotel.[1]

Several months after the Smiths' arrival in Round Rock, on Sunday, July 1, 1877, Emily, Jefferson's mother, died of unknown causes. The death propelled the father deeper into depression, and his consumption of alcohol increased. Although growing increasingly resentful of his father, seventeen-year-old Jefferson stayed with his family as the mainstay of his younger his siblings.

Jefferson came from a successful and well-educated family. He had the potential to succeed at the same professions as the majority of his family. The fields of medicine, law, or politics only awaited his choosing. Abilities demonstrated later in life leave no doubt of his drive to succeed, and probably excel, in numerous legitimate fields. The Civil War, though, had taken from Jefferson's family nearly all it had, including an opportunity for higher education. Instead, Jeff was forced to enroll in the school of survival, and with the move to Texas, his curriculum became that of life experiences on the Western frontier. While working hard for his family's well-being and throughout his penurious, difficult youth in Texas, Jeff was on the lookout for any door of opportunity. He would find one soon enough.

Chapter 2

How are you fixed for soap?
From Cheap John to Prize Package Soap Swindler

*The class of people who want to get something for nothing
are no match for those who give nothing for something.*
— *The Daily Standard*, August 2, 1882

Texas in the mid 1870s might not have seemed the ideal location for life-changing opportunities. Chances were even slimmer in the little trail-town of Round Rock, except for one profession that flourished there, that of the confidence man. Jeff was drawn to the skills of the peddler of cheap goods, called a "cheap John," to the almost magical methods of the playing-card manipulator, the dexterity of the three-card monte tosser, and the nimbleness of the shell and pea man. Appealing to Jeff were the elevated levels of cleverness these grifters displayed and how they supported a high standard of living. After discovering his selling skills, he tried the con man's arts and found he had not only ability in them but also a liking for them. Early on they and the world in which they were practiced got into his blood.

At Round Rock, after the death of Jefferson's mother, a letter came to his father from his brother, Luther Martin Smith. He addressed his brother's drinking problem

---

[1] Smith, Edwin; & Ltr by Jefferson R. Smith III, 06/15/1941.

and pleased with Jefferson Sr. to return to Georgia with the children, or at least to send them to him.[1] The father chose to stay in Texas with the children. Jeff knew not to rely on him as the main provider for his younger sisters and brother. Letters from his sisters in Texas and from cousins in Georgia show that Jeff for the remainder of his days provided money to his family whenever possible.[2] The Smith family collections contain few letters between father and son, an indication that Jeff held little respect for his alcoholic father. If Edwin's writings are accurate, Jeff remained in Round Rock for at least a year before striking out on his own. The following long excerpt from Edwin's manuscript about Jefferson addresses this period.

> Young Jefferson found employment at the leading store in Round Rock, and in no time demonstrated that he could sell more goods than pretty near the whole staff of clerks with the proprietor thrown in; gift of gab and magnetism did it, which is about the essence of what is now entitled "intensive salesmanship." Often before his place opened its doors in the morning he would take to the highway to meet some early bird coming in with a full wagon load of valuable products; stopping him, and without asking leave, the pedestrian would climb into the seat by the driver and glibly explain that he represented the only house where the owner would get the highest prices for his chattels and where he could buy the best clothing, boots and shoes, all sorts of ranch supplies, the best in quality, full weight, a square deal—in short his friend would be unjust to himself to trade anywhere else. It is not believed there was ever a single instance of escape from the blandishments of the young impresario; his genius was recognized and rewarded by rapid increases of salary, and when it reached $100 a month he was the town marvel; no such youth had ever come within the ken of that village.
>
> The boom days kept up and as a railway terminus, pro tem, many drummers from St. Louis, Memphis, Galveston and other cities were constant arrivals which accounted for a cluster of many so-called hotels, sorry shacks at best, but affording Jeff another opportunity. He met every incoming train and loudly proclaimed as he went through the coaches that he represented the only first class hotel in Round Rock. One day a losing competitor at the same game, becoming enraged at his rival's luck hurled him violently from the steps of a car. Bruised and bleeding, Jeff waited for him to emerge and as he did, let fly a chunk of coal that caught the fellow squarely in the temple; it took quite a while to bring him back to consciousness, but the crowd that gathered applauded the winner, a magistrate exonerated him, saying he did the right thing, and the defeated bully quit the business of hotel drumming.
>
> A circus came to town. Jeff watched one of the street hawkers selling cheap jewelry. This bird made his spiel and gave so much away for a small price. He watched daily, when not busy with his hotel work.

---

[1] Ltr fr Luther Martin Smith to Jefferson R. Smith II, 11/19/1877. Geri Murphy col.
[2] Ltr fr Henry Marshall Smith to Jeff R. Smith II, 08/16/1884. Ellen Rafeedie col.

At last came a day when the hawker must rush to the corner store for a headache powder. He had watched young Smith, liked his appearance and his look of honesty and sincerity. Calling to Smith, he said:

"Son, stand here in my place for a few minutes and watch my goods. I will reward you on my return."

Young Smith did so. He mounted the soap box with the spreading case before him and eyed more carefully the supplies of finery—broach pins, watches, diamond rings, stick pins, charms, handkerchiefs, garters, socks, etc.

Smith looked longingly in the direction of the disappearing hawker and then clapping his hands he began the hawker's own spiel. He had heard it now a score of times and knew it by heart. A crowd gathered and Smith swept swiftly through the talk. Then he filled the paper bags with the finery just as he had seen the hawker do. And business was brisk.

In the midst of the rush to purchase the hawker's wares, the hawker returned. He looked at the crowd. He looked at young Smith..., smiled, and waved him to continue. Smith did and that marked the beginning of a new career for the man later to become famous—not for selling cheap jewelry and other merchandise for a mere pittance, but for selling a penny cake of soap for as much as $50.

An occasional letter brought me [Cousin Edwin] news of my kinsman's progress in the Lone Star State and what a field it was for the hustling young man. Always he asked me to come out to join him promising that in no event would I go hungry as long as he had a dollar. With some difficulty, I scraped up sufficient funds to buy an immigrant's railroad ticket, part of the journey by water from Morgan City to Galveston. On board ship, a man who looked reliable told me I was simply inviting death to locate in Texas; that it was a God-forsaken country where the chief recreation of the natives was filling strangers with lead; that many men whose kindred back in the states never heard from, had been ruthlessly slain. I was momentarily impressed, but the sense of impending calamity soon vanished and when I got to my destination broke but happy, Jeff and I had a good laugh at the futile effort of the man on the boat to turn back a tenderfoot.

"I've quit the store and other jobs for a much better thing," he confided, after the affectionate welcome. "I've learned a racket that's new in this part of the world, one of the slickest and surest money-makers; I have become a cheap John, a dealer in odds and ends of merchandise, and I go from town to town selling my stuff on the streets. I mount a box; take up a banjo, which I twang to the accompaniment of a few plantation songs like the *Little Old Log Cabin* or *Old Black Joe*; this never fails to draw a crowd and the rest is easy for then they are primed to buy my stock of socks, hanker chiefs, suspenders, razor belts before the rush of customers and it is a bad day if I don't net $20 or $25. In a few towns the merchants were so sore at losing trade that they had regulations passed to drive me out." The story was enchanting and I thought: "This boy will be a millionaire; there's only one Jeff." Plans were formed to induct me into the same profession. I was to learn the cheap John technique and Jeff was to stake me to my first layout. I could sing a little and twanging a banjo took but a few lessons.[1]

A cheap John operation is the predecessor of the *jam auction*,[2] which Jeff would later operate in Denver. An operator sells, usually under high pressure, practically worthless merchandise at a fraction of its value in order to excite and confuse the audience. Sometimes the items are said to be valuable manufacturers' promotional items. First, small, practically worthless items are given away to everyone, then unexpectedly slightly more valuable items are sold to bidders for almost nothing. The procedure is conducted in a way that confuses buyers about whether they are putting up money "as a good faith gesture" that they will get back or whether they are tendering payment. When buyers are thoroughly confused, the cheap John adds the final wrinkle: the sale of almost worthless (but apparently valuable) merchandise for what seem like outrageous "bargain" prices.

Jeff had begun the phase that would shape his life. It was not an overnight transformation as described in earlier biographies of him. In 1920, Jeff's Cousin Edwin stated that Jeff had been educated by a confidence man but failed to name him, if he knew. Numerous histories of Jeff mention the tutors as "Clubfoot Hall" and later as "Old Man Taylor," but no clear information has been found to relate these men to Jeff. Further, Cousin Ed Smith's remarks are the closest known contemporary descriptions of Jeff, and Ed mentions no mentors by name. However, in 1887, a John Taylor wrote several letters to Jeff. Perhaps this is the "Old Man Taylor" written about, but no known provenance shows them to be the same person. The only reliable description of Jeff's educator comes from Edwin in 1920.

> The peripatetic gentleman persuaded Jeff to learn the business, and soon the latter was allowed to take the place of the regular man on the street corners.... He canvassed the entire region, and as the profits ran from 300 to 400 per cent, he became very prosperous. In fact, he was so successful that small towns organized against him and prevailed upon the Texas legislature to pass a law imposing heavy taxes upon traveling salesmen of Jeff's persuasion.
>
> All this time Jeff was supporting his family and was in all respects a good boy.... The change came after he left Round Rock.[3]

Ed did not join Jeff in the cheap John trade nor accompany him when he left Round Rock. His reason being "the Sam Bass incident." Sam Bass was a much-sought-after Texas bank and train robber. On July 19, 1878, Bass, Frank Jackson, and Seaborn Barnes rode into New Town (Round Rock) to case a bank they were planning to rob the following afternoon. Jeff and Cousin Ed witnessed what came next.

> But in the midst of our rehearsals as "cheap John's" something happened in the way of rough drama that rocked the entire state and even

[1] Smith, Edwin, & Ltr fr Jefferson R. Smith III, 06/15/1941. Author's col.

[2] *jam auction*: an auction usually in a pawn shop. (Partridge, *Underworld*)

[3] *Trail* 01/1920, pp. 7-8.

the nation, something that put Round Rock on the map and filled the newspapers with screaming headlines. Jeff and I saw it—the raid of Sam Bass and his outlaw gang and the killing of Bass by sergeant Dick Ware [Richard Clayton Ware] of the Texas Rangers. As a matter of fact, when the thing started, we had been chatting with the Ranger Chief in a restaurant and he was talking to us in great good humor. He was a Georgian, a friend of the family and born within a mile of the old Smith estate. With a small squad he had been on Bass's trail for days but the wily train and stage coach robber was hard to catch; at any rate he wouldn't be taken alive; there was just one more job to pull off in Texas and then a swift dash to the Mexican border. It looked to him that the spoliation of the bank in this small burg ought to be easy and, of all strange things, the robbers and the Rangers got into town within an hour of each other, neither aware of the other's presence. The outlaws dressed as cowboys were going about leisurely but separately, to avoid attention; they were riding splendid stolen horses which they had hitched close to the bank. One of the gang was stupid and brutal enough to shoot the town marshal dead on being told that it was against the law to carry weapons, and it was the roar of his Colt's 45 that started the drama. Dick Ware jumped from his chair, grabbed his Winchester and rushed to the street to see four men making a desperate dash to gain their mounts. In front was their leader and just as he was seating himself, the pair of us who were running along with Dick Ware saw Dick kneel, lower his gun and with deliberate aim, fire. "I think you hit him," said Jeff, but the distance was long and it wasn't certain; the fellow was putting spurs to his horse and galloping off furiously. By this time the other Rangers were in action and had killed Barnes, Bass's lieutenant, and wounded another; the fourth escaped. As to Bass, Jeff was right. Suffering a mortal wound, they found him dying by the roadside on the outskirts of the town; he hadn't the strength to sit longer in the saddle; it was a magnificent piece of workmanship and that day's good work some years afterward got Dick Ware the post of United States Marshal at the hands of Grover Cleveland.[1]

It is not doubted by this author that Jeff and Ed talked with ranger Dick Ware, known to have been a fellow Georgian, or witnessed the shooting, as both wrote about the event, but one mistake in Ed's story suggests that it could be attributed to creative license or imprecise memory when Ed wrote about the events fifty plus years later. Questioned is whether Jeff and Ed were in fact with Dick Ware when he shot Bass. According to historical accounts, Ware was being shaved when he heard the first gunshots.[2] It is possible that after the meal with Jeff and Ed, Ware received his shave,

---

[1] Smith, Edwin, & Ltr by Jefferson R. Smith III, 06/15/1941. Author's col.

[2] The Ranger credited with shooting Seabourne Barnes and mortally wounding Bass was Dick Ware. His full name was Richard Clayton Ware, and he was born in Rome, Georgia, on November 11, 1851. He came to Texas in 1870 and joined the Rangers on April 1, 1876. On the fateful day in Round Rock, he had been in the barbershop when the shooting started. He still had foam on his face when he rushed out and shot Barnes. For a time, who had shot Barnes was in question, but Bass is supposed to have

and the young men could have followed him to the barber's. But if so, it seems Ed should have remembered such a dramatic transition from barber's chair to the street.

In a small notebook in his own handwriting, Jeff wrote about witnessing the shooting but the contents were only briefly viewed by the author who unfortunately could not make any copies or notes at the time.[1]

Ed gave the Sam Bass incident as the cause for not continuing with Jeff in the "cheap John" business. Did Ed have a sense of the shady road that Jeff was headed down and not want to go with him? Or was it the environment of the open, still pretty much untamed west in which hot lead could suddenly be flying that caused Cousin Edwin to shy off? Jeff, though, had no reservation or presentiment about crime or the business end of gun. It would have been well if he had because eventually he did end up in the pathway of a bullet.

So came the second parting with Jeff and I didn't see him again for more than twenty years, yet I kept track of his movements, of how he prospered financially.[2]

For all the information Ed provides about Jeff, not much is certain about Ed. Known is that he followed a calling in newspapers and politics. An undated newspaper clipping reports that he had graduated from Wofford College, South Carolina, and that his "maternal ancestors were natives" of that state, but no school records are known to exist and no known family ancestors from the Carolinas. Another undated clipping puts Ed in Washington, DC, "since the first administration of Grover Cleveland" (1885-1889).[3] There he called home for the remainder of his life.

Sometime before June 1880,[4] the father again packed up his family, minus son Jeff, and moved to Belton, Bell County, Texas, a business center for the surrounding agricultural area with a population under 4,000. In the early 1880s, the Gulf, Colorado, and Santa Fe Railroad reached Belton, and the Missouri-Kansas-Texas Railroad built through in 1882. In 1881 the Santa Fe established Temple eight miles to the northeast, aggressively promoted the location, and Temple quickly surpassed Belton as the county's largest town. Some Belton businesses moved to Temple.[5]

Jefferson Smith, Sr. felt opportunities were better in Temple, and he moved his family there. Success, however, continued to elude him, and his mental and physical decline persisted. He would outlive his son Jeff by six years, dying in 1904, although possibly within the confines of an insane asylum. Young Jeff continued to write and send money to his siblings, but it is not known if he visited them in Belton and Temple.

Some accounts of Jeff have him a cowboy in Texas for a time. This is not true. A couple of circumstances have led to this misperception. Round Rock was indeed the

---

verified that it was the man with shaving foam on his face who did it. Some say it was Ranger Connors, but Connors himself gave the credit to Ware. He also said that it was Ware who delivered Bass the fatal shot to the kidneys. (Bass)

[1] The notebook was verified first hand by the author but no notes or copies of the contents could be made at the time. Geri Murphy col.

[2] Smith, Edwin, & Ltr by Jefferson R. Smith III, 06/15/1941. Author's col.

[3] Undated newspaper clipping of unknown origin. Item 83, author's col.

[4] US Census, 1880, Schedule 1, p. 10. 06/02/1880.

[5] Belton.

starting point for the Shawnee and Chisholm cattle trails to the cow towns of Dodge City, Abilene, and a host of others. The William Devere poem "Jeff & Joe," published in 1897 gives the impression that Jeff "Knowed him [Joe] thirty years or so.... / Worked together, tooth and nail, / Punchin' cattle up the trail...."[1] The poet, though, romanticized this part of the friendship by adding twenty-five plus years to the friendship and throwing in a stint of cowboying. The truth is that Jeff plied his newfound bunco[2] trade in Texas until at least 1879 and did not meet Joe Simmons until arriving in Denver. Joe's granddaughter, Beth Simmons Jackson, states that her father, Joe's son William E. Simmons, was born February 1, 1876, in Denver. So Joe had a new-born son in Denver when Jeff was still living in Texas. The 1889 Denver Directory lists a "J. Simmons" residing at the Clayton Block on Larimer Street. According to Beth Jackson, Joe never lived outside of Colorado and had never been a cowboy. He was a tall, slender gambler known to many as "Gambler Joe" Simmons.[3]

Some time after July 1878, Jeff is believed to have relocated to Fort Worth. The town was growing but wanted to achieve prosperity. As that goal required wide open gambling, the city fathers began "enticing deposed Dallas gamblers to transfer to that city with offers of free rent and $3,500 in cash."[4] Famous gamblers and gunmen like Jim "Longhair" Courtright, Luke Short, and Ben Thompson came and made their living. From 1876 to 1879, Jim Courtright was marshal of Fort Worth, and it is possible Jeff met the famed marshal under not so friendly circumstances. A "J. Smith" was arrested for drunkenness and fined one dollar, but it is not known if this J. Smith was Jeff.[5]

With a population of 6,663 in 1880, this was probably the busiest city Jeff had yet worked. Jeff and his associates may not have been known by name, but they were definitely noticed by the *Fort Worth Democrat*:

> Thievery is becoming so common in the city now, that too much caution cannot be exercised, especially by strangers coming to town from the country. There are always a lot of sharpers ready to fleece the unwary and unsuspecting.[6]

In Fort Worth Jeff most likely completed his secular education in crime and began to assemble his first bunco gang. Four of the earliest known members were E. S. Panknin, Charlie E. Pratt, Ned "Banjo" Parker, and John H. "Fatty Gray" Morris.

Parker, a patent medicine swindler hailing from Springfield, Missouri, stood about 5' 11" and weighed about 225. His first known arrest was for stealing a horse in 1873.[7] He traveled around the west, "selling tooth-paste, singing songs, and selling one dollar chances for drawing money prizes in a lottery which was of course so arranged that he must win."[8] In 1875 he was known as "Professor" Parker to his victims in Golden, Colorado. His methods were disclosed in the *Daily Rocky Mountain News*.

[1] Devere, pp. 109-15.
[2] bunco: as noun, deceit, deception; as verb, to swindle, to rob. (Partridge, *Underworld*)
[3] Ltr fr Beth Jackson to author, 04/20/1991. Author's col.
[4] DeArment, *Knights*, pp. 136-137.
[5] *Fort Worth Daily Democrat* 02/05/1879.
[6] *Fort Worth Daily Democrat* 11/22/1879.
[7] *Daily Arkansas Gazette* 02/25/1873.
[8] *Daily Rocky Mountain News* 10/08/1873, & *Yankton Press & Union & Dakotaion* 07/09/1874.

GOLDEN, September 8, 1875.—A man calling himself Prof. Ned Parker, and hailing from Chicago, gulled the people here last night.... Claiming to be the agent of a Chicago firm, at a salary of $100 per week, sent out by them to advertise a brand of pens called the Colorado No. 2, ... he takes his position in an open wagon, ... and, after playing [his banjo?] and singing to the boys and making a felicitous speech, in which he ... assures the people he is paid the large salary named "for making an ass of himself," ... he displays a lot of small buff envelopes, in which he asserts [that] notes and fractional currency are contained in amounts varying from 25 cts to $100. These, with a certain number of blank envelopes, he puts into an apparently empty box. Before business commences, he displays the large money, puts it into envelopes, and, to all appearances, drops it into the box. He then offers his pens for sale at $1 per box, and makes every purchaser a present of [one of] these envelopes..., to be drawn by the purchaser. If the matter was as represented, it might be a fair transaction, but it is believed to be a downright swindle, as no large money was drawn at all.... It is believed that he has some means of supplying the blank envelopes as fast as they are drawn out, and that he does not put the large money in the box at all. He said he would be here again to-night, but has gone to Central City and Georgetown to give the boys up there a dose. He carried away from here it is believed, about $100 clean.[1]

Ned's "playing and singing" probably included use of a banjo, hence the name "Banjo" Parker. In 1877 he was known to reside at the Grand Central Hotel in Denver.[2]

The earliest record of Morris is in Deadwood, South Dakota, July 23, 1877, where he was involved in swindling a greenhorn out of $57.[3] In 1878 Morris was a popular, well-liked gambler in Fort Worth.[4] He was on friendly terms with many of the influential residents. Admired by the editor of the *Fort Worth Daily Democrat,* his name was often mentioned in glowing terms within its pages. On February 7, 1880, Morris shot a bartender. The *Galveston Daily News* reported the story.

(Special Telegram of the News)

Ft. Worth, February 7.—Last night about one o'clock W. T. Cotton the bar-keeper at "My Theater," a variety show in this city, was shot by John Morris, a prominent gambler. Morris, who was drinking, became angry over a bill presented for drinks he had ordered, disputing the correctness.... During the dispute, Morris drew his six-shooter, and his hands were seized by friends, but wrenching them loose, he threw the pistol down suddenly on the bar counter, the weapon being discharged, but whether accidentally or intentionally is now the question, and Cotton fell, shot through and through, the ball having entered the right breast just below the nipple, ranged upward

---

[1] *Daily Rocky Mountain News* 09/09/1875.
[2] *Daily Rocky Mountain News* 08/23/1877.
[3] Deadwood.
[4] *Fort Worth Daily Democrat* 01/11/1879.

and came out below the right shoulder. Cotton is not expected to live. Morris was arrested.[1]

Cotton died from his wounds, but at the trial in July 1880, Morris was found not guilty of his murder.[2] John Morris was not mentioned in the Fort Worth newspaper again, and presumably he left town. Fifteen days later Jeff was listed as arriving at the Granite hotel in Central City Colorado.[3] Could the two have left Fort Worth together?

These men, and others, worked with Jeff at Fort Worth between 1877 and 1882. Panknin and Pratt kept in contact with Jeff through the years.[4] Ned Parker and John Morris followed Jeff and became mainstay members of the Soap Gang Jeff built in Denver.[5] Letters addressed to Jeff at Fort Worth indicate he might have been residing there as late as December 1882.[6] The methods of the Fort Worth confidence men to skin their prey mirrored those later used in Denver. The *Fort Worth Daily Democrat* published an example of one of the methods employed by bunco gangs there.

A Mr. Cashion "arrived in the city on the train Sunday morning from Monroe County, Tennessee. Mr. A. P. Mathews," with more the bearing of a business man "than a gambler," met Cashion as he walked from the station and represented himself as a land agent who wanted to sell some real estate in the city. Mathews invited the visitor to come to his office to talk about it, and as they walked on for quite a distance, the need was seen to stop at a saloon for a drink Mathews offered to buy. Then Cashion said that he was steered into a room where cards were being played. "By this time his drink had a wonderful effect upon him, and not" feeling himself, he consented to play but did not comprehend very well what was happening in the game.

> He played and lost, lost his all, forty dollars in money and an ordinary silver watch, and now claims that he was drugged, and unconscious at the time, and that he was robbed by three men. He identifies Mathews as one of the parties. Mr. Mathews was arrested yesterday morning by policemen and turned over to Sheriff Maddox, who placed him in jail....[7]

If Cousin Ed Smith's history of Jeff's time in Texas is factual, then while Jeff practiced his new trades there, laws were passed against street sales and gamblers that were directly the result of the handiwork of such men as Jeff in Fort Worth. The city pushed to drive the con men from its borders, and Jeff moved on to safer regions of the country for his line of work. On July 29, 1880 the *Fort Worth Daily Democrat* announced that the days of unrestrained crime and bunco gangs were over.

> Our city court meets as of yore, and dishes out justice on charges of drunk and down, prostitution, vagrancy, vulgarity and profanity in public places, affrays, etc., but the dark deeds of reckless desperadoes, confidence men, "thugs," and manipulators of drugged drinks, have gone into the past never to

[1] *Galveston Daily News* 02/08/1880.
[2] *Fort Worth Daily Democrat* 07/22/1880.
[3] *Daily Register Call* (Central City, CO) 08/07/1880.
[4] Ltr fr E.S. Panknin to Jeff R. Smith II, 03/19/1898. Jefferson R. "Little Randy" Smith col.
[5] *RMN* (*Rocky Mountain News*) 08/02/1889.
[6] Ltr fr John T. Waller of Tombstone to Jeff R. Smith II at Fort Worth, 12/24/1882, Geri Murphy col.
[7] *Fort Worth Daily Democrat* 12/15/1880.

be revived in Fort Worth. There are very few remnants of a once large disorderly element, and they are disappearing day by day.[1]

Jeff is believed to have been one of those who left prior to this publication.

According to Cousin Edwin Smith, Jeff traveled all around the country and then settled for a time in Leadville. Standing 80 miles southwest of Denver at an elevation of 10,192 feet in the Colorado Rocky Mountains, the camp became a town when the discovery of gold in 1860 caused it to boom. Then in 1877, discovery of large deposits of silver extended the town's prosperity into the early 1890s. Older biographies of Jeff described how he started his career here, but no documentary evidence puts him there for any length of time. The perception of Jeff's having lived and worked in Leadville probably stems from a 1920 interview that Edwin gave to *The Trail*. The following paragraph from that interview addresses Jeff's shift from hawker of "cheap John" goods to sleight-of-hand games.

> The change came after he left Roundrock, and Leadville was the lure that carried him away. The license [requirement] on itinerate merchants killed his business, and the whole country was vibrant with news of the wonderful strikes in Colorado's great Carbonate camp. So, with a thousand dollars in his pocket, Jeff "hit the road" for the enticing Colorado mountains when about 17 years old. He tried hard to persuade his cousin to accompany him on this venture, volunteering to pay his way, but to no avail.[2]

Jeff at this time was not seventeen but nineteen years of age. Apparently the author of the article believed Jeff had been born in 1863.

Jeff was in Leadville on July 21, 1880. A photograph documents his being there. The town was honoring the visit of ex-President General Ulysses S. Grant with a parade, and Grant was its grand marshal.[3] A photographer set up his stereoscopic camera on a tripod along Harrison Street to photograph the event. Nineteen-year-old Jeff and some friends were in the street ahead of the parade and engrained himself into Leadville and US history as the ex-president on horse-back is noted as being in the far background. Jeff obtained at least two copies of the photograph and sent them to his family in Texas, writing on the back,

> This is a crew of freighters we met in Leadville on the 21st of July 1880 in the morning on the day that Gen Grant arrived. You can see my photo by looking between the two wagons next to the man with the apron and his sleeves rolled up. (between the two men) J.R.S.[4]

Between youth and manhood, Edwin did not see his cousin again for twenty years, so learning that Jeff had been in Leadville in 1880 caused Edwin to take Jeff's being there for more than it was. The interviewer for *The Trail* relates Edwin's perception that Jeff "did not prosper in Leadville" and how he

---

[1] *Fort Worth Daily Democrat* 07/29/1880.

[2] *The Trail,* 01/1920, pp. 7-8.

[3] *Leadville Weekly* 07/24/1880, p. 1.

[4] Kyle Rosene col.

soon fell in with some of the many tough characters who infested that city.... Failing to find gold growing on the pine trees Jeff again took to the street, and it was here that he earned the sobriquet of "Soapy."[1] As has been stated he had learned some of the rudiments of sleight-of-hand manipulation while hawking his wares in Texas, and in Leadville soon began to specialize on soap.[2]

A strong point against Jeff's ever having settled in Leadville for any length of time comes from the town's well-established *Leadville Herald Democrat.* Eight years later, in 1888, it announced him as a visitor, not a resident:

One of the slickest and best known rascals in the whole western country is reported ... on his way to Leadville.... The gentleman ... —Soapy Smith—is known to many people in Leadville, as he has been here frequently, and always with ... a small valise filled with small cakes of soap in little boxes, and a very pretty Mrs. Smith, who travels with him.[3]

Jeff's visit to Leadville in 1880 was short. Fifteen days later he was known to be sixty miles away, checking into the Granite Hotel in Central City. In the ledger he wrote that he was a resident of Atlanta.[4] With Denver only thirty miles away, he probably soon ventured there.

The earliest account of Jeff performing the infamous prize package soap sell occurred in Denver in 1879. George T. Buffum was the witness, and he recorded what he saw in a 1906 collection of sketches of his frontier experiences.

I first saw him in the spring of 1879. Standing in front of the old Grand Central Hotel one day, I saw approaching me a man driving a bay horse hitched to a light buggy. He stopped by my side and lifted a box from the bottom of the buggy seat, and I noticed that it contained several cakes of soap. Looking at me squarely in the face, he said, "Will you allow me to present you with fifty dollars?" I declined with thanks, though such benevolence might have received more consideration had I been more familiar with his game.[5]

In 1889 when asked how long he had lived in Denver, Jeff replied, "Since 1879, but not steady...,"[6] which matches the year in Buffum's account.

Business licenses obtained in other cities confirm that Jeff continued to travel. He must have been leading a company of shills, cappers, and boosters as they were essential to the success of any bunco operation. Most of the licensing was not recorded or has been lost in time, but a few examples survive to give a glimpse of his travels. The earliest was sent to "J. R. Smith Esqr.," in Fort Worth in response to his request from the Georgia comptroller general in Atlanta, dated March 3, 1881.

---

[1] Contemporary newspapers show Jeff obtained the sobriquet of "Soapy" in Denver, not Leadville.

[2] *The Trail,* 01/1920, p. 8.

[3] *Leadville Herald Democrat* 05/02/1888. Clipping in author's col. The "very pretty Mrs. Smith" is Jeff's wife. He was married on February 1, 1885, and she is known to have traveled with Jeff for a time. The couple's courtship, marriage, and domestic life appear in another chapter.

[4] *Daily Register Call* 08/07/1880.

[5] Buffum, pp. 26-27.

[6] *RMN* 08/06/1889.

Dear Sir-

Your favor of the 24th to grant lender the lease of this state you will have to pay a sum of twenty-five dollars for each day's exhibition in every city or town of five thousand inhabitants; twenty dollars in city or town of four thousand & under five thousand inhabitants; fifteen dollars in city or town with less than four thousand inhabitants; said tax to be paid to the tax collector in each county where the exhibition takes place.

Yours Respectfully   W. A. Wright, Comp Genl.[1]

Compared with licensing costs secured elsewhere, the Georgia fees were high, making it doubtful Jeff ever worked his trade within the borders of his home state.

Between 1881 and 1882, Jeff's whereabouts are uncertain. Family collections contain no personal letter or news clipping to show his activities. To survive, however, is a letter of reference that may explain his whereabouts. Dated May 12, 1882, from the South Pueblo, Colorado, office of the Denver and Rio Grande Railway, it reads,

To whom it may concern

The barer Mr. Jeff. R. Smith has been in the employ of this company for the last fourteen months in the capacity of train baggage master. During that time he has served us it has been to the satisfaction of all concerned. He leaves our employ in good standing.

W. H. Bancroff[2]

The letter bears the superintendent's personal stamp. Two possibilities are that Jeff actually worked for the Denver and Rio Grande and had been on the job, or that the letter is a forgery, perhaps so that Jeff might move about by train, unmolested by railroad security. Either way, what came to be Jeff's life-long focus makes probable that he was swindling train passengers.

In the summer of 1882, Jeff surfaced in Salt Lake City. He purchased a merchant's license to operate on the sidewalk at South Temple, between East Temple 1st and East streets for the term of three months, starting June 11, 1882. The fee was $2.75.[3] Though the license was good until September, he did not stay the full term. During this period, Jeff seems to have been a "hit and run" nomad, staying in each location long enough to swindle victims, and then leaving before facing prosecution.

Less than two months later he was in Portland, Oregon, where he purchased a vendor license dated August 2, 1882.[4] An edition of Portland's *Daily Standard* of the same date exposes the infamous prize package soap sell for the first time.

A Sleight of Hand Performer in the Role of a Street Hawker
He Soft-Soaps the Unsophisticated and Rakes in Their Coin.

As a contemporary sapiently remarked a few days since, "there are some curious phases in human nature." Perhaps one of the most singular is the extreme gullibility of the average human.... ... All that is needed to attract them and charm the hard coin out of their pockets is for some glib tongued

---

[1] Ltr fr W. A. Wright to Jeff R. Smith II, 03/03/1881. Geri Murphy col.

[2] Ltr of reference fr W.H. Bancroff to Jeff R. Smith II, 05/12/1882. Geri Murphy col.

[3] Merchants License in Salt Lake City, Utah, 06/11/1882. Geri Murphy col.

[4] Vendor license, 08/02/1882. Jefferson R. "Little Randy" Smith col.

fellow to stand on the street corner and keep up an incessant talking, and no matter whether he is pretending to give a dollar's worth of lead pencils for a quarter, to sell some nostrum warranted to cure all the ill [that] flesh is heir to or bits of soap with a ten dollar greenback wrapped around them, for one dollar, he is sure of an audience. A "fakir" whose tongue appears to be hung in the middle and run at both ends, has been working the last racket on our street corners for several days. His stock in trade consist of an old valise and stool to support it, and a number of small pieces of alleged soap, an unlimited amount of cheek, a great gift of gab and a considerable skill in sleight of hand. He wraps a greenback around a piece of the soap and drops [undecipherable] among a number of similar looking packages. Then he takes another for $20 and pretends to go through the same operation, but while mixing up the packages with both hands tucks it up his sleeve. After this has been carried on for some time, he picks out all the packages containing greenbacks and opens them to show that they were in the valise, and then the greenhorns rush in and buy his bits of soap at 50 cents each or 3 for a dollar. During about 10 minutes in which a Standard reporter was watching him, he took in about $20 and only gave a $1 greenback and this he sold for $3. The whole business is one of the most transparent frauds imaginable and should be stopped. [T[here can certainly be no law requiring our city authorities to grant licenses to carry on such a hogging gambling game, and we call upon them to refuse this bilk another license and upon the police to see that he is driven off the streets. The class of people who want to get something for nothing are no match for those who give nothing for something, and the law should protect them. Our laboring classes are robbed of thousands of hard earned dollars by the cursed tribe of frauds which infest our city, and it is high time that at least an effort was made to prevent it.[1]

This is the earliest newspaper account of Jeff's soap sell racket, but probably Jeff was running the scam before this date. The price per chance was $.50, equal to $13.69 today, so in 10 minutes, the *Standard* reporter watched Jeff rake in about $274.[2]

The exposé mentions the use of a valise, which is possibly an apparatus known in magic circles as a "switch outfit." It contained a hidden compartment to hide the money cakes of soap with an equal number containing no money. The swindle involved trained shills (or promoters) who worked for Jeff. Rarely, if ever, did professional bunco men like Jeff work alone, and no doubt by this time he had a small-knit assortment of confidence men traveling with him. The fact that he signed the licenses (at least all those he kept) shows that at age twenty-two, he was the leader.

Forty-five days after the description in the *Daily Standard*, Jeff was a few cities away in Salem, Oregon, where on September 16, 1882, he paid $15.25 for the opportunity to, as the license reads, "Hawk his prize soap" for one week's time.[3]

[1] *Daily Standard* (Portland, OR) 08/02/1882.

[2] Tom's Inflation Calculator.

[3] Vendor license in Salem, Oregon, 09/16/1882. Geri Murphy col.

In December, possibly Jeff was still traveling when a letter arrived from John T. Waller, a successful friend in the confidence profession who had perhaps worked with Jeff along the way. In any event, it is clear Waller had taken a great liking to Jeff.

> Friend Jeff
>
> I received your card. I shall not stop in El Paso. You never said what you had been doing. Can you not take time to write a letter and give me some news. I am afraid that you will get busted before you get home. If so send me word [–] as long as I have a dollar you can have half of it. I am doing a good business here. I sold $82.75[1] yesterday. I took in $43.50 last night and it was so cold that I came near freezing. I shall only stay here 2 or three days longer. I got in here last Wednesday. I saw Taylor & his girl on the stage that day going out. I wish you a Merry Christmas & a happy New Year. Address Colorado City, Texas.
>
> Yours truly,   John T. Waller[2]

Waller would be in touch again on numerous occasions.

On January 25, 1883, Jeff acquired a license to "purchase goods" in Gonzales, Texas.[3] Then on May 26, he paid $2.50 for the privilege of selling soap in Nebraska City, Nebraska.[4] Just 4 days later, he bought a license to sell in Washington City, Iowa, some 300 miles away.[5] At some point in 1883 Jeff made his way to Tombstone, Arizona. A small notebook in his handwriting notes money made while there.[6] On December 26, 1883, he paid $4 for a vendor's license in Phoenix, Arizona.[7] Six days later, on New Year's Day, he was arrested in San Francisco for operating the "soap racket." The *Daily Evening Bulletin* gave a detailed description of his methods.

Jeff Smith's "Soap Racket."

> A sharp young man, Jeff Smith by name, who has been working the "soap racket," as it is called, to large crowds on the street corners in the business part of the city for several weeks, was obligated to suspend operations at the corner of California and Front streets this morning at the request of Detectives Ross, Whittaker and Colby. They compelled him to fold up his camp-stool, strap his valise and go with them to the city prison, where he was charged on the register with conducting a lottery game. He appeared a trifle disturbed at the interruption, for it is not probable that he will gull simple countrymen for some time to come. For some time past complaints have come to the police regarding certain swindling soap vendors, whose plan of operations have been ... about the same as Moses' plaint to the Vicar

---

[1] According to Tom's Inflation Calculator, $82.75 in 1882 would be $2,265.70 today.

[2] Ltr fr John T. Waller to Jeff R. Smith II, 12/24/1882. Geri Murphy col. The name Taylor in the letter may be that of John Taylor.

[3] Occupations tax receipt #2065, 1/25/1883. Jefferson R. "Little Randy" Smith col.

[4] License, Jefferson R. "Little Randy" Smith col.

[5] License, Jefferson R. "Little Randy" Smith col.

[6] The notebook was verified first hand by the author but no notes or copies of the contents could be made at the time. Geri Murphy col.

[7] License, Jefferson R. "Little Randy" Smith col.

of Wakefield[1] after his return from the fair. Smith it seems has been in the habit of setting up his stock by opening his valise containing small packages of soap wherever he thought he could attract a crowd. His soap sold for fifty cents a package or three for one dollar, but the attraction was that he rolled greenbacks, one dollar and five dollars, in the packages before the eyes of the crowd, but by skillful manipulation the purchasers never obtained a lucky package. About a month ago another vendor was arrested, but allowed to go on his promising to leave the city. Smith was arrested at the ocean beach on New Year's day, but as he also promised to leave, was allowed to go.[2]

That was just the day before, so this time Jeff was detained for seven days before release "by Police Judge Lawler, who held that the offense charged did not come under the provisions of the ordinance."[3] According to the newspaper, Jeff had been in San Francisco for several weeks, but seven days prior he was in Arizona. It is possible, then, that the soap peddler from a month previous had also been Jeff, that he had come from Iowa to San Francisco and on to Phoenix and returned.

The police court ordered Jeff to vacate San Francisco. He disobeyed and was again arrested on St. Valentine's Day for once more engaging in the soap sell racket. He was not in jail very long, though, as evidence of violating any city ordinance was lacking. The *San Francisco Call* reported that once again "Judge Lawler sustained the motion to dismiss, on grounds that the facts did not bring the case within the law."[4] Possibly Jeff escaped prosecution through bribery, but more probable is that San Francisco in 1884 had few regulations that pertained to bunco men and their games.

It is a sure bet that Jeff worked many cities in between those listed, and if he operated on the day after Christmas in Phoenix and on New Year's day in San Francisco, then it seems reasonable to assume that he worked most days of the year.

While in San Francisco in February 1884, Jeff received a letter from his fifteen-year-old brother Bascomb.

> Mr. Jefferson R. Smith
>
> As it has been a long time since I have written you, I will now try to write again as you will see that I can't write very good, you will have to excuse bad writing and spelling as I am just learning how to write. I hope you will not become disgusted with my letter. I am going to try to learn to write better. I am still at the depot and will try to stay there as long as I can. I see now that I ought to try to learn something. Papa says he is going to raise a big garden this year. He says he is going to send after 10 lbs., of Irish potatoes. He thinks he will make plenty of money, but I think it is doubtful. Brother I would like to travel with you as soon as I learn how to write and read writing better. I am pretty good on the tongue now.

---

[1] *Vicar of Wakefield.* Allusion to the novel by the same name, 1766, by Oliver Goldsmith. Moses is one of the Vicar's sons.

[2] *Daily Evening Bulletin* (San Francisco) 01/03/1884, p. 3.

[3] *Daily Evening Bulletin* 01/11/1884.

[4] *San Francisco Call* 02/14/1884.

Brother, you told me to send you my measure for a suit of clothes and hat and pr. of boots. I don't hardly [sic] know how to send the measures. But will say that my #No. for shoes or boots are #5. Hat 7 ¼. My pants lenth [sic] 27 ½ inches. Waist 29 inches. I will tell you what I think is best you just send suit for age 15 and I think it will fit. It will suit me anyway. Well I have no news of importance to write you at present so I will close for the time. This leaves us all hoping that this will find you the same. Write soon as you get this. Goodbye,   Your brother Bascomb Smith[1]

Bascomb's letter reflects the continued severity of life for the Smiths. As a child, Jeff received a rather decent education whereas his younger brother by nine years had not had that opportunity. In later years, the brothers did work together but with disastrous results. As much as he tried, Bascomb would never match his older brother in executing the wit, tact, or finesse needed to succeed in the world of the bunco gangs.

Jeff re-appeared in Denver periodically during his migrant years of 1879 to 1883. The earliest known return is based on a letter addressed to Jeff in Denver, July 5, 1883, from C. C. Lamos of Chicago, head of a retail and supply company from which Jeff purchased cheap watches for use in various swindles.

Friend Smith

Yours came to hand. And I must say I had given you up as gone. I had asked several old boys and they think you are an "angel from Colorado." Some one said the other day that the Kid [Jeff] died in Colorado. John Waller is doing big work in Montana. I sent him two lots the 3ʳᵈ. He was in Deer Lodge, Montana, and sent him a big freight order to Portland, Oregon. John has made some big money since he left Chicago.

Well Jeff I sent catalogs ... but you can't tell much about them. Anything you want let me know and I will make the price all o.k. you know that.

Hoping you are doing well and catching on good.

I am yours only   C. C. Lamos

Fair lists are not ready yet.[2]

Lamos also supplied gambling equipment (known as sporting goods) and spurious personal items such as jewelry and watches for use by "cheap John" men. This letter shows that Jeff had become a well-liked, repeat customer. It also shows that confidence man John Waller was also a well-respected member of the bunco fraternity. The last comment about "Fair lists" refers to schedule dates for state and county fairs throughout the country, vital information for an ambitious traveling bunco man. It probably cost a sizable amount. That this list was important to Jeff indicates that he was not blindly traveling the west but rather to targeted locations. Lamos next wrote to Jeff in Denver on December 4, 1883, with an apology.

Friend Jeff

Am dam [sic] sorry the watches did not pan out all ok.... You must always send them back at my expense as I hate like the duce [sic] to have

---

[1] Ltr fr Bascomb Smith to Jeff R. Smith II, 02/1884. Jefferson R. "Little Randy" Smith col.

[2] Ltr fr C. C. Lamos to Jeff R. Smith II, 07/05/1883. Jefferson R. "Little Randy" Smith col.

any of the old boys kick on me. I had rather pay the difference myself. 6 oz white watches nice ones 4.25 each, is the best anyone can do. They are nice ones. Just got in a fine lot today. The Silver watches I have just [illegible] up to the Waltham agency here and will see what they say.

He sends this reply and you can't get any made I don't think this season as they are very busy at the factory for holidays.

[John] Waller is still in Oregon doing well as usual he is making big money this year. Wishing you the best of good luck.

I am yours only   Lamos[1]

With the soap racket working so profitably, probably Jeff was not working the "cheap John" swindle at this time, but later he used the low-value watches as prizes in fraudulent lottery drawings and in his Denver auction houses.

It is doubtful Jeff invented the prize package soap sell, but without doubt, he made it famous. The earliest known newspaper account of the con appears July 22, 1876, in the *New York Times.*

THE PRIZE-SOAP SWINDLE.

On July 22, a young man ... stood on the Bowery, and held forth in glowing terms the advantages of purchasing his fifty-cent boxes of scented soap, each box containing a prize in money—all the way from ten cents up to $10. In proof of his statements, he displayed one of the boxes, which contained a genuine bank note, snugly rolled up beside a cake of soap. Among the soap vender's auditors was Everett Glazier, of No. 61 Ridge street, who foolishly relying on the assertions of the swindler, handed him $2 for four boxes of the precious soap. On receiving and examining the boxes, Glazier found that he had been swindled, the "money" being simply old revenue stamps folded up to resemble currency. Glazier demanded his money back, but the swindler declined ... and ran off. He was subsequently captured and gave his name as Frank Ashton, living at No. 41 Ridge street. On being arraigned in the Court of General Sessions, yesterday, Ashton was identified ... as an accomplished swindler named Frank Astor, who had been convicted of a similar offense in 1874. The prisoner pleaded guilty, and Recorder Hackett sent him to the Penitentiary for six months.[2]

Notice of the swindle appeared in Chicago as early as 1878.[3] "Big Ed" Burns, who became Jeff's long-time confederate, declared himself a peddler of soap in Chicago.

In 1884, Jeff's soap-selling activities in Denver may have caused the *Rocky Mountain News* to republish an article from the *Boston Courier* that details a variation of the soap sell racket utilized by other confidence men.

The Soap Caper.

A very successful swindle, operated by street peddlers, is what is technically known as the "soap caper." For the purposes of the swindle—two

---

[1] Ltr fr C. C. Lamos to Jeff R. Smith II, 12/04/1883. Jefferson R. "Little Randy" Smith col.

[2] *New York Times* 08/10/1876.

[3] *Inter Ocean* 01/26/1878, p. 8.

fellows will buy a lot of cheap soap and cut it up into small pieces, which are dainty perfumed and nicely wrapped in fancy colored paper. This is all the stock in trade needed, except a generous allowance of cheek. One of the fellows dresses himself up like a dude, and generally conducts himself so that everybody to whom he appeals makes fun of him. Perhaps he does sell a few pieces of the soap, for it appears to do what is claimed for it, but he purposely makes such an ass of himself that nobody wants to trade with him. Soon, when he is boasting of how much soap he can sell in a day, a common looking fellow in the crowd calls out, "Well, why don't you sell it then?" and at once they get into a wrangle, which is ended by the plain fellow betting that he can sell more soap in ten minutes than the proprietor of the stand can sell in half an hour. The bet is generally quite a large one, and, as sympathy is entirely with the common looking fellow, the crowd comes to his support, and he rapidly sells out his share of the soap, and finally also disposes of the greater part of the other's packages. It is needless to say that the fellows are confederates, and are playing into each other's hands. Two good operators can make tremendous profits by working this game, and they run no risk of being arrested.[1]

A confidential business neighbor of Jeff's in Denver, whose store was alongside one of Jeff's enterprises, described Jeff's soap racket to the *Milwaukee Sentinel.*

Smith was an inveterate gambler, and before he opened his rooms he used to play his "soap" game on the street corners. You could always tell when he was broke. He would appear on the street with a gripsack that opened out flat on both sides, one of those two-box-on hinges sort of affairs, and in this he would have his soap, little cylinders about an inch long, and hundreds of them in the grip. He would pick up one of the pieces of soap, remove the wrapper, place a five or ten dollar bill next to the soap, replace the wrapper, throw it back in the pile, give it a single stir up by running his hands through the pile, and giving them a turn over. Then he would sing out:

"Who will give me a dollar for a pick?"

The dollars would be thrust at him from every direction, and he would take them in and the people, who had been watching the operation and thought they had a dead sure thing, would make their selections, missing the prize, of course. Then "Soapy" would say:

"Gentlemen, you should have taken this one." And picking up a little cube from the top, he would unroll the wrapper, and there would be the ten dollar bill. As his finances recuperated he would increase the prize to a fifty or a one hundred dollar bill, scatter one dollar bills through the heap and raise his price to ten dollars a draw Some days he would take in thousands of dollars at this game. Old gray haired business men, and young fellows, and all sorts of people, would gather about, watch him closely, think they had a

---

sure thing and take a chance. I tried it myself, but I never caught him nor did any one else. It was the slickest game I ever went up against.[1]

As conveyed from a variety of sources, here is how it is believed Jeff operated his prize package soap sell: With great dignity and in a business-like manner, he would stroll to a busy street corner and open up for business. Atop a folding tripod sat a simple valise. Inside the case were small cakes of soap and wrapping paper. The brand Jeff used most in this swindle may have been Sapolio Soap, which was 3¾ inches long, 2½ inches wide, and 1½ inches thick. Sapolio Soap came wrapped in a paper-like tinfoil. A blue paper band encircled the package, inscribed with gold letters spelling "Sapolio."[2] The blue paper band eliminated the need for wrapping paper, but he probably used both techniques for times when Sapolio brand was not available. Jeff would begin a silver-tongued patter "pitch" to draw a crowd. After extolling the wondrous qualities of his soap, he would offer it to the crowd for from $.10 to $.25 a bar. As an inducement to buy, he would add the element of chance to the sale. With flourishing flamboyance, he would take out an eye-catchingly large roll of bills and draw from it denominations ranging from $1 to an astonishing $100. With speedy dexterity, he would wrap the bills around the cakes of soap and cover them with paper. Jeff used paper money, but John Randolph Smith, a grandson of Soapy's, stated that in the beginning, "Jeff used gold coins before modifying to paper money."[3]

After wrapping the soap with the paper, Jeff would carelessly toss the enriched cakes in among other packages equally covered with paper, but containing only soap. He would continue adorning cakes of soap with larger denomination bills until he was satisfied with the size of his crowd. After mixing up the packages, he began to sell them auction style with a starting bargain bid of $1.00 each. For a mere $1.00, an on-looker had the chance to make a day's, a week's, or even a month's pay, or so he thought. One dollar may seem unworthy of Jeff's effort, but it must be remembered that a dollar in 1885 is worth about $29.97 today.[4] At the onset of each sale, few on-lookers were willing to pay more than the one dollar starting bid. A few boosters in the crowd fixed that. One of Jeff's confederates would step forward, make a purchase, and upon unwrapping his bar of soap, loudly proclaim having picked a winning package and wave the prize money for all to see. This show usually encouraged immediate sales. Periodically when needed, another booster would procure another bar or two and win a small profit. The crowd being made aware that the larger bills still remained among the unsold packages was usually enough to cause onlookers to reach for their wallets. The largest profits came when Jeff began to auction the remaining packages to the highest bidder.

The method of how Jeff wrapped the soap packages is based on the conjecture of eye witness accounts and biographers. This author notes that if Jeff used the Sapolio Soap brand that was wrapped with the trademark blue band, he might have made it

---

[1] *Milwaukee Sentinel* 07/30/1899, p. 5.

[2] Sapolio Soap ad, 1879.

[3] Statement fr John R. Smith, 07/01/1985, author's father.

[4] Tom's Inflation Calculator.

appear that he was slipping currency under that wrapper band, eliminating the need to wrap the soap in paper.

The William Collier and Edwin Westrate book *The Reign of Soapy Smith* (1935) presents a fantastic but plausible example of Jeff's soap sell pitch. Its flamboyant style and flowing cadence tend to suggest the silvery sales patter Jeff was known for and make it seem possible that he could have pitched such a spiel.

"WAKE up! Wake-up, you dreamers, and listen to me!" ...

"Wake up! The hour has come to face the problems of our country!" ...

"One question—the supreme question—before us today is vital to the welfare of the republic!" ...

"Gentlemen, the all-important question which I propound to you and for which I earnestly seek the answer is this: *How are you fixed for soap*?"

A quick smile flashed across the face of the speaker as he paused for the briefest moment, then went on:

"I hear no response. I fear I embarrass you. In all honesty, gentlemen, most of you look as though you need soap, and your silence distresses me.

"But, seriously, though my message is that of soap, it is, likewise, a message of hope. For today, to meet that great need, which is so apparent in you, I bring a new soap—a wonder soap." ... "Here is the finest cleansing product ever brought forth by man's scientific ingenuity, the fruit of many weary months of patient research and experiment in my own laboratories.

"Use this soap upon your skin and it will shine like the moon, and your face will gleam with the radiance of the sun at noonday. Is that bald spot growing? Use this soap and patriarchal locks once more will adorn your brow. Is your hair turning gray? Wash your scalp with this soap and to the silver threads will return the pristine glory of youth. Does your conscience keep you tossing, sleepless, in the silent watches of the night? Use this soap and wash your sins away.

"Perhaps this glorious opportunity to purify body and soul should be enough, but, gentlemen, I offer you far more than this. On this day of all days, to introduce this marvelous product, I am giving—yes, *giving*, my friends— enormous cash prizes to those upon whose shoulders the Goddess of Luck has taken her perch. Cleanliness, gentlemen, is next to godliness, but the feel of good crisp greenbacks in the pocket is paradise itself. Step up, my friends, and watch me closely."

From his wallet he extracted a bundle of greenbacks and dropped them into the sample case, their denominations impressively visible—a hundred, several fifties and twenties, numerous ones and twos.

"Through posterity, my friends, my fame will rest upon this soap—this boon to mankind which I am offering to you."

Swiftly, dexterously, he began wrapping the soap cubes in the blue paper. At intervals, with apparent nonchalance, he enclosed a cube in one of the greenbacks; then he wrapped the blue sheet tightly about money and soap and tossed the package carelessly into the growing pile.

"Now, gentlemen, I am offering this miracle working soap at twenty-five cents—if you wish to buy the soap alone. If there be any such among you,"—this in a very deprecating voice—"I will accept your quarter and you will find it to be the best two-bit investment you have ever made.

"*But*—if you have any sporting blood and wish to take a chance on winning one of these little green papers with the big numbers on them, ranging up to one hundred dollars, I will sell you a bar of soap from those I have already wrapped, for the ridiculous price of five dollars—and you will have the privilege of drawing your own package.

"If you have been watching me as closely as I hope, it should be simple to select a bar of soap wrapped in money—and the first man up has the best chance."[1]

In stating that the price per bar of soap was five dollars, Collier and Westrate probably confused the known starting bid and the progressive nature of the auction. Though Jeff advertised the swindle as a sale, it was in fact an auction.

In one theoretical version of the ruse, Jeff would ask an on-looker for the momentary use of his hat in which to mix the packages. If resistant, the hat owner was assured that no harm would come to his headgear and was offered the first choice of one bar for free as recompense. With this encouragement, the hat owner finally lent his hat, and Jeff tossed in the wrapped bars for a good mixing. Unknown to the crowd was that the lender of the hat was a member of the Soap Gang and that the hat was a prop, modified into a "switch-hat," so called for the concealed compartment that opened and closed by means of a small lever inside the sweatband. The compartment contained wrapped bars of soap previously placed there, some of which might have contained money but of small denomination. Most contained no money at all. The lever was activated by hand as Jeff shook the hat, appearing to mix the contents, and the soap bars wrapped with money were switched with those containing little or no cash. The exchanged bars of soap were then dumped out and sold to the unsuspecting victims, known to confidence men as "dupes."

The hat is returned and its owner given first pick as promised. All attention is on the "hat owner" as he grabs a wrapped package off the keister. In pleading tones, Jeff asks the man to wait until he has sold out his supply before opening his package. Ignoring Jeff, presumably because of his excitement, the "hat owner" exclaims, "I had my eye on this one," rips open the paper, and lets out gleeful yells, waiving his newly acquired ten-dollar bill for everyone to see. However, that bill came from the palm of his hand, not the soap. Men in the crowd rush forward with the purchase price in hand, hoping lady luck will be with them as it had been with the hat owner. But upon opening their packages they find no bills, or if so, none of large denomination.

The crowd was made aware that larger bills were still within one or more of the packages. At this point, Jeff began to auction remaining bars to the highest bidder. As the soap packages dwindled and the largest bank notes still appeared unclaimed, a bidding war, fueled by boosters in the crowd, raised the price on the remaining

[1] Collier & Westrate, pp. 1-4.

packages. As the auction continued, here and there money was found; however, it was mostly of small denomination. Occasionally a shout rung out as a 5-, 10-, or 20-dollar bill was found. These fortunate bidders, however, were just shills, or pretend bidders, with pre-palmed bills. These men then circulated, showing off their "winnings" to the crowd of dupes. Few, if any, of Jeff's victims ever won much more than a five-cent bar of soap.

If a crowd were large enough, the process would commence again until the crowd had been played out. Then Jeff would simply close the valise, fold the tripod, and walk away, looking much like any businessman on the street as he blended into the crowd.

It is interesting to note how successful Jeff was at convincing his "customers" to spend increasingly higher amounts per package during the auction portion of his sale. In 1879 in Denver, George Buffum saw Jeff use auction bidding to grab thirty dollars from a victim. Writing forty-five years later in 1906, he described what happened after Jeff said, "How much am I offered for this cake of soap?" Then Jeff's lively cappers[1] would bid against one another, and Jeff would count "one, two, three" and hand over the soap to the successful bidder. Next

> the successful capper showed his hundred dollars to the crowd and insisted upon proper thanks to the protesting Soapy. Smith then took up a cake which in his seemingly careless handling disclosed the hidden hundred-dollar bill. Bidding began; now was the time to be on one's guard, but an unwary onlooker bid it off finally for thirty dollars and got a good cake of soap.[2]

It is possible that at times other members of the gang worked the swindle for Jeff. Roy Daniel White met Jeff in Denver and again in Skaguay. In a recorded interview with the Smith family in 1968, White recalled how in 1898 Jeff wanted to break him "into the soap sell business." Jeff worked enough with him that his memory of the process seventy years later was detailed and vivid. Asserting that he knew "all about it," White said, "Now that soap sell was a very crooked game. Here's the way it works."

White described how Jeff explained the routine of the spieler, how he kept an open grip hanging from a shoulder strap by his side, how it was always kept open, and how "half a dozen shills or boosters" would mix into the group at the right time. The place of sale is "on the main corner of the town."

The following, edited for clarity but conservatively for veracity, is how White explained the soap sell process. Most of the words and phrasing and all of the ideas are his, beginning with White's dramatization of "the pitch."

> Ladies and gentlemen, I'm out here to do some advertising. I'm working for a company that can give millions of dollars away. I expect to give some of those millions away today. I can give the shirt off my back, the shoes off my feet. I can give everything I've got away, there's no law agin it. The company I work for could plaster these here walls of your city with bill boards, advertising that

---

[1] *cappers*: same as *shills* and *steerers*, an assistant in any cheating or in gambling. In US, circa 1859. (Partridge, *Underworld*)

[2] Buffum, pp. 30-31.

would cost a great deal of money. But no. We're going to do the advertising direct, direct to you. We're going to hand out this beautiful soap—soap that's taken from the best that's produced. This soap brings out the beauty of women, and for men, it makes them more handsome than they are. The idea is to get this soap into your hands. We don't care how much money it costs to get it there. Money ain't nothin'. Now I'm going to start mixing in some prizes with this soap right now.

Here [White explains] you pick up a piece of soap and put it and a fifty-dollar bill into an envelope [or perhaps a pre-folded wrapper that *enveloped* the soap] and put it into the bag. Then you put a hundred-dollar bill into that one, a twenty-dollar bill in this one, and another ten-dollar bill down in that one, all of which are mixed in with the soap bars in the bag, and then these shills would walk in and they'd come up, and they'd buy soap and show the crowd what they got, including the hundred-dollar bill. This would cue the spieler to address the crowd:

Now, just a minute, just a minute. Some of you, yes, are going to have your feelings hurt that you didn't get the hundred-dollar bill. I don't want what people win in prizes to be shown, and I don't want these fellas comin' up here and stickin' their hand in again. I don't want to see them get their hands in there twice. I need to get this soap in the hands of those that will take it home and use it, not just for the financial assistance they'll get. But I'm gonna show you how much is in there.

So you start puttin' hundreds, twenties, and fifties down there into the grip again. You figured it was all money; it was all money when you sees it, but you didn't really see it. The way it works, it would come out the other side of the envelope, but it looked like it had gone right in. Anyhow, they all come alive then and bet that with their soap they'd win. Five dollars each for a bar of soap was the cost. And when they'd all got into the game and were ready to draw, you say,

Now one word for you. I don't want any of you to show what you've won until you get home. The reason I don't want one person to see a hundred dollar bill, another one to see a fifty, and then another, he reaches down and gets only a twenty.

So with that settled, they all start grabbin' and didn't dare open their package until later. Then along comes a hack, and the thing to say before getting into it is this: "Well, good day gentlemen. Ladies and gentlemen, I want you to use that soap. I want you to use it! It's worth every cent you paid for it."

When White was asked if he ever performed the pitch, he replied that he had not. "I didn't go into it and he [Jeff] was mad at me because I didn't."[1]

---

[1] Interview on reel-to-reel tape with Roy Daniel White by Justin and Ester Smith, 125 North Daisy, Long Beach, California. 02/10/1968. Author's col.

In general, the confidence man believes in the old saying, "You can't cheat an honest man." Enough truth is in the statement to ease the conscience of the bunco man and perhaps give him some devious pleasure in his art.

Sometimes Jeff's victims did not accept their losses and tried to take their money back physically or would refuse to pay. Jeff's record clearly shows he was not afraid to scuffle, but in case of violence, Jeff tried to have men of tough caliber around to deal with it, such as boxer "Denver Ed" Smith. Most unhappy victims did not become physical but rather headed toward the nearest police station. For this possibility, too, there was a contingency. Members of the Soap Gang were posted outside the circle of activity, and their job was to follow victims they felt might go to the police. If they did, the gang would "slough the policemen," or "fly cops" as the bunco men termed the action. *Sloughing* means to tip off the spieler and steerers when the police were near by or on their way towards the bunco operation. These lookouts would have prearranged signals to warn Jeff, so he could end the swindle and leave the scene before a policeman could get to him.[1] When Jeff had police officers under his pay, he could be notified in advance that trouble was on the way. Sometimes no advance warning system was available, so Jeff would send a member of the gang into police headquarters to file a fake report in order to spy any complaints being made against Jeff. As reported in the *Denver Evening Post*, one day this practice backfired on Jeff when gang member Henry "Yank Fewclothes" Edwards went to police headquarters "to inquire about his pet dog," which really had been lost. The cause of what happened next was that Yank "was known as a friend of Smith's...."

> The lieutenant in charge of the office at the time immediately concluded that "Yank" was there for the purpose of finding out if someone who had just been buncoed had complained, and that he had not lost the dog at all. So the lieutenant sent for "Soapy," had him arrested on the charge of "suspicion," and held him for two hours, waiting for someone to come in and complain about him. No one came and "Soapy" was released.[2]

If caught in the act and faced with being arrested for running a bunco operation, Jeff would loudly protest that he was not a criminal but a legitimate businessman with a legally obtained business license to sell soap. His argument was based on logic and carefully arranged evidence. He could produce a valid business license, and it was a truth that the only money on Jeff's person was the one-dollar bills and some larger denomination bills freely given him by those purchasing soap. The large bills—the $10s, $20s, $50s, and $100 used as prizes—Jeff argued, had gone to the lucky winners, now conveniently absent. Thus, *prima facie* evidence officers found on the scene lacked any cause to arrest Jeff except on suspicion. In reality, all the large denomination "prize" bills were neatly tucked inside the switch-hats worn by Jeff's shills and boosters, long departed from the scene, or hidden away in Jeff's valise. If a customer's complaint against him should gain sway, Jeff would add to the confusion by accusing his accuser of being a confidence man who was trying to fleece him of his

---

[1] *RMN* 08/25/1885.
[2] *Denver Evening Post* 07/31/1898.

earnings. This approach many times caused the arrest of both Jeff and his victim. Should Jeff be arrested and taken to jail, he never lingered long. His comprehensive plans included having a bondsman at the ready to secure his release.

Perhaps newspaper stories about the soap sale-auctions hindered Jeff most. Occasionally the interview of a victim would expose Jeff's operations in detail. Then should a repetition occur, even corrupt police and city officials were expected to perform their duty and shut down the operation. Jeff's custom was to wine and dine newspaper reporters, police officers, and city officials in an attempt to suppress bad press and actions against his business, but graft could not trump bad exposure.

The Soap Gang's choice of victims was regulated. Jeff's unwritten agreement with authorities was that residents would not be victimized, only "others." If a local were swindled, his funds were returned, with a strong admonishment to avoid street sales or games. Victimizing a non-resident did not disturb the local population as much as a crime against a neighbor. Visitors were not local tax payers and could not affect political or social affairs. Keeping to visitors also increased the chance that a case would be dismissed as these victims often did not appear in court. The constraints of time and money caused most complainants to chalk up their losses to experience and leave for home or continue their journey. Others left because they did not want to expose their gullibility and embarrassment. Those more determined might have a portion of their loss returned as an inducement to leave town. Frustration for the district attorneys and courts sometimes led to the arrest and detainment of victims to force them to appear at legal proceedings. However, detentions only intensified effects of the crime, making it easier for victims to choose to drop charges than pursue them. Thus did many victims leave Denver with an education they had not expected.

> Soapy Smith did me about the greatest favor that ever was done me. I stood watching him one day as he manipulated the soap bars on 17th street.... When I felt sure that I could pick the twenty-dollar bill, which I had seen him twine in with the soap that I put up a fiver on the chance. I lost. Then I watched closer than ever, and again being especially convinced of the infallibility of my position, ventured my second five. Again, I was mistaken. That experience was sufficient. I walked away from the spot determined never to gamble again, and I never have. I say that I owe a great deal to Mr. Soapy Smith.[1]

For at least fourteen years, Jeff outwitted the gullible with his soap sell racket. He enjoyed numerous other swindles, such as the shell game and three-card monte, but he always kept the soap bars handy. That swindle worked so well that bunco men from across the country applied to join forces with the successful Soap Gang.

Jeff had been running his prize package soap racket since 1882, but the sobriquet "Soapy" did not appear in print until the *Rocky Mountain News* applied it in July 1884. The paper also called him "Sapolio Smith," probably a reference to Sapolio name brand soap. Gamblers and enemies christened other gamblers with colorful

---

[1] *Trail, 06*/1920, p. 10.

nicknames, and newspapers inadvertently also bestowed them. But as explained by the *Denver Evening Post* in 1898, the genesis of "Soapy" came from a policeman.

> When he [Jeff] first came to Denver one of the officers had the occasion to walk him to jail for selling soap without a license. It was different then from what it is now. Then an officer making an arrest walked his prisoner to the jail, put him in a cell and then wrote the prisoner's name on the police docket. The particular officer dealing with Smith was John Holland. He could not think of Smith's first name, so he wrote … "Soapy" in parenthesis, after "Smith."[1]

Years later, Jeff's wife, Mary, said that Jeff hated being referred to as "Soapy," that his friends always called him "Jeff" and that business associates addressed him as Mr. Smith. Only his detractors and enemies called him "Soapy." In only one letter in the author's collection does Jeff refer to himself as "Soapy," and this use was to command respect and fear.[2] A man who remained confidential due to his close ties with Jeff, told the *Milwaukee Sentinel*,

> "I should like to see the man who would dare have called him Soapy Smith to his face," continued the west sider, with a merry twinkle in his eyes.
>
> "Did you know him?" inquired a bystander.
>
> "Did I know him! Well I rather guess, yes. I was in the book business in Denver, back in the '80s, and 'Soapy' had his 'fleecing' apartments right alongside of my store, and let me tell you he was one of the best of neighbors. His name was Jefferson Smith, and people had to call him 'Jeff' to avoid trouble."[3]
>
> One young fellow got into the habit of accosting people that stopped to look at the goods on display in my windows, and finally began coming into the store to begin his working-in game. I went to Smith and told him about it. I didn't complain, as he was one of my best customers, buying all the latest periodicals and papers of me, besides the cards that he used in his gambling rooms. He merely said: "If ever one of those fellows visits you again, let me know. I'm glad you spoke of it." That settled the matter. My customers were never troubled after. With all the hard name that "Soapy" bore in the west, he was one of the most generous men I ever knew.[4]

Only once did a friend call Jeff "Soapy," and that was in a poem attributed to Soap Gang associate Henry Edwards, better known as Yank V. Fewclothes, the "Poet Laureate of Seventeenth Street."

[How Are You Fixed for Soap?]

A handsome gent steps out to talk,	"How are you fixed for soap? boys,
His voice can be heard away a block;	How are you fixed for soap?
These words we hear as he hollers his wares	Move on up to the box, boys,
At the crossing of the thoroughfares:	How are you fixed for soap?

---

[1] *Denver Evening Post* 08/06/1898.

[2] Ltr fr Jefferson R. Smith II to Editor of *Denver Times* 07/28/1893, item 108, author's col.

[3] *Milwaukee Sentinel* 07/30/1899, p. 5.

[4] *Milwaukee Sentinel* 07/30/1899, p. 5.

"Take your choice among the lot,   "Be a sport there! Show the bunch
Invest a five for a hundred spot;   You ain't a-scairt to play a hunch!
Fat's a-fryin', come on the lope   Any poor rube with an eye that's quick,
And pick out your cube of lucky soap!   Can grab a winner and turn the trick.

"Don't shy away from soap, boys,
Don't shy away from soap;
Use your brains and snatch the gains;
Don't shy away from soap![1]

Henry Edwards, born 1848,[2] was a dealer in honey and beeswax when Jeff brought him into the Soap Gang as a steerer and a booster. Edwards' business card lists the names of Yank V. Fewclothes and Guy Rich, "Dealers in pure honey and beeswax." The address is the Windsor hotel and gives a telephone number as "Main 182." On the back of the card in pencil is what appears to be a reference from Jeff: "Yank is a great fellow. Jeff."[3] This is believed to have been written by Jeff when he left Denver for the last time in 1895. No account of "Guy Rich" has been found. With the pun-like names on the business card, "Fewclothes and Rich," possibly "Rich" was a fictitious partner. Edwards signed all of his correspondence to Jeff "Yank Fewclothes."

Edwards' job as booster was to give "insider tips" to an intended victim on how to win the game the victim was trying to buck. Edwards' alias aptly described his dress.

He never wore a coat; A homespun vest, nondescript pants, a dark heavy cotton shirt with a cravat tied under the collar, made up his wearing apparel, but he was always genial, soft spoken, and easy to meet.... He could be as coy and secretive as a school girl, when it suited his purpose; but he insisted that he was a straight shooter under all circumstances.[4]

Edwards and his wife, Hi-Ki, were close friends with Jeff and his wife, often staying at the Smith house in Denver when Jeff's wife moved to St. Louis.[5] The *Denver Post* noted that Edwards was so close to the Smiths that he was known as "'Soapy' Smith's shadow."[6]

The most common confidence games Jeff employed were swindles known as "short cons." These sleight-of-hand betting games were quick and needed few confederates. Two of the most common were the shell and pea game and three-card monte. These games were frequently set up on street corners, on sidewalks, and in alleyways. Of the shell and pea game, Detective Sam Howe of the Denver police department, who had numerous dealings with Jeff, said of him, "There was never a better manipulator of the shell game, and Smith could draw a gun as handily as he could deal four aces from the bottom of the deck."[7]

---

[1] Collier & Westrate, pp. 36-37.
[2] *Denver Post* 11/15/1914, p. 10. Item 163, author's col. Henry Edwards states he is 66 at time of interview.
[3] Henry Edwards' business card. Item 47, author's col.
[4] Newspaper clipping of unknown origin, 8/28/1931. Author's col.
[5] Ltr to Mary E. Smith fr Hi-Ki & "Yank Fewclothes," 12/13/1895. Item 6, author's col.
[6] *Denver Post* 11/15/1914, p. 10, item 163, author's col.
[7] *Denver Post* 11/15/1914, p. 10, item 163, author's col.

To the uninitiated, the shell and pea game appears to be a gambling game that is easy to play and win, when in fact, through sleight-of-hand, the operator decides whether and when a player wins or loses. Three walnut shells are placed on a flat surface, and a "pea," usually a small, round, pea-sized ball made of a soft pliable material, is placed under one of the shells. The operator moves the three shells around on the flat surface, and a player is invited to bet on which shell covers the pea. Boosters entice victims to wager and often take part in the game, losing some but mostly winning until the victim is lured into betting. The process of enticement worked this way: The booster and the operator trade insults until, slowly, the insults shift to the victim, raising his ire until at last he seeks revenge against the operator by winning the game and taking the operator's money. Insults might include questioning the courage of the victim or perhaps his ability to concentrate. A booster, who has been a regular winner with his wagers in the game, offers whispered "sure-thing" advice to the victim on how to pick the right shell. When the victim is at a high level of angry competition with the operator, he is encouraged to place a large bet on the shell under which he is 100% certain conceals the pea. When the bet is down, the shell is lifted to reveal no pea, and the victim loses. Even if the victim accidentally picks the shell that the pea is under, the shell game manipulator stealthily and easily removes the pea by sleight of hand as he lifts the shell.[1] Victims never catch a practiced operator's deft manipulation of the pea. The expertise of sleight of hand artists still makes a truism of the old adage that "The hand is quicker than the eye."[2]

Three-card monte, another infamous short con game, is a variation of the shell game except with cards rather than shells. The operator, called the "thrower" or "tosser," uses dexterity to manipulate three cards that he throws face down on a table. The cards, sometimes called "tickets," are slightly bent lengthwise so that they look like little tents when face down on the table. The faces of the cards, one of which is an ace, are shown to the audience, and then placing them face down, the thrower pitches them from side to side on the table. The players are then asked to bet on the location of the ace. The tosser uses a false throw, called "the hype," to obscure the location of the ace. The victim wins only when the tosser wishes him to. In order to boost the amount of a wager, a booster befriends the victim and reveals a false method of picking the right card, just as in the shell game. The operator expresses anger over the shill's helping the victim and begins to insult the two men. Eventually the angered victim wants to punish the tosser for his insults, and at an opportune moment, that wish becomes a seeming reality as the tosser becomes distracted and turns his attention from the table. The shill takes advantage of the opportunity to turn up a corner of the ace card, giving the players the decided advantage of a "sure-thing." The card with the turned-up corner is sure to be the ace. The tosser begins another game, seemingly unaware of the altered ace card. The victim, is encouraged to place all his

---

[1] The author has seen this demonstrated numerous times by award-winning magician Whit Haydn, of the School For Scoundrels educational seminar, and of the Magic Castle in Hollywood, CA. Mr. Haydn has aided greatly in the historical performances of confidence games.

[2] The author performs the shell and pea game as "Soapy" at old west gatherings and finds this adage proves true time and again.

ready cash on the table alongside the bet of the shill. The angered victim is more than willing to cheat the tosser at his own game. The tosser begins to mix the cards and while tossing them, deftly repairs the bent ace and bends the corner of another card. Thus is the victim efficiently, quickly, and completely plucked of his money.

Because the victim was all too willing to cheat the tosser, the cons feel justified in taking everything the victim has wagered. Thieving gamesters are followers of the motto "turn about is fair play." Famed confidence man George Devol wrote,

> When a sucker sees a corner turned up, or a little spot on a card in three-card monte, he does not know that it was done for the purpose of making him think he has the advantage. He thinks, of course, the player does not see it, and he is in such a hurry to get out his money that he often cuts or tears his clothes. He feels like he is going to steal the money from a blind man, but he does not care. He will win it, and say nothing about how he did it. After they have put up their money and turned the card, they see that the mark was put there for a purpose. Then they are mad, because they are beat at their own game. They begin to kick, and want their money back, but they would not have thought of such a thing had they won the money from a blind man, for they did think he must be nearly blind, or he could have seen the mark on the winning card. They expected to rob a blind man, and got left. I never had any sympathy for them, and I would fight before I would give them back one cent. It is a good lesson for a dishonest man to be caught by some trick, and I always did like to teach it.[1]

Like the shell game operator, the three-card monte man is an accomplished artist and can switch the position of the ace with stealthy ease. Even if a victim inadvertently picks the ace card, the bunco artist can switch it without being detected. It was three-card monte that the Soap Gang used against John Douglas Stewart that brought down Jeff's empire in 1898, but not because the thrower was caught (as will be told).

As with the prize package soap sell, the shell game and three-card monte had distinct spiels. The following is an example:

> "Here you are, gentlemen; this ace of hearts is the winning card. Follow it with your eyes as I shuffle. Here it is, and now here, now here, and now— where? You win if you point it out the first time; but if you miss, you lose. Here it is, you see; now watch it again. This ace of hearts, gentlemen, is the winning card. I take no bets from paupers, cripples, or orphan children. The ace of hearts. It is my regular trade, gentlemen, to move my hands quicker than your eyes. I always have two chances to your one. The ace of hearts. If your sight is quick enough, you beat me and I pay; if not, I beat you and take your money. The ace of hearts—who will go me twenty? It is very plain and simple, but you can't always tell. Here you are, gentlemen; the ace, and the ace. Who will go me twenty dollars?"[2]

---

[1] Devol, p. 294.
[2] Parkhill, pp. 76-77.

When Jeff arrived on the Western bunco scene, laws had barely begun to include the misdeeds of the confidence men and their games of no chance. The protection of one's money was considered the responsibility of the owner. The courts were involved with crimes of violence and robbery. Those complaining that they had been swindled had to prove the crime, often no easy task when victims did not fully understand how they were swindled. Unless one was robbed at gunpoint, many city law enforcement officials did little to interfere. If a person foolishly lost his money on games of chance, no one was to blame but the gullible participant. The bunco men were considered the lice of society. Newspaper editors, sensing a cause to promote a reader following, took it upon themselves to prod lawmakers into action against the con men. By writing about their exploits, newspapers educated the public, law enforcement, and those holding political office about the workings of the games. This education did more to damage Jeff's business than any law officer or court, and it did not take long for certain street sales and games of chance to be seen as frauds and to pass ordinances against them. Recognizing fraud was one thing, but proving it remained as illusive as ever. So law enforcement looked for other ways to shut down short cons. Thus were Jeff and members of the Soap Gang often brought before a judge for vagrancy. This charge was abhorred by every gambler and confidence man. It was a slap in the face of their self-respect and a particularly low insult. Jeff thought of himself as a businessman, and a successful, respected one at that.

The vagrancy law in Denver was ordinance number 97, effective October 1, 1884.

SECTION 1. All able bodied persons who not having visible means to maintain themselves, and who live idly without employment, or are found loitering or rambling about, or wandering abroad and lodging in tippling houses, bar lounges, out houses, and houses of bad repute, sheds, stables, or in wagons or boxes, or in the open air; ... or placing themselves in the street or other thoroughfares, or in other public places, to beg and receive aid; and all persons upon whom shall be found any instrument or thing used for the commission of burglary, or for picking locks or pockets, and who cannot give a good account of their possession of the same, shall be deemed vagrants.

SEC. 2. On the trial of any person before the Police court of this city charged with being a vagrant, it shall be lawful for the city to introduce, in support of said charge, testimony of the general character and reputation of the defendant touching the offense or charge set forth in the complaint, and the defendant may likewise resort to testimony of a like nature for the purpose of disapproving said charge; and if the defendant, after all the proofs shall have been heard, be found guilty, he or she shall be adjudged to pay a fine of not less than five dollars nor more than one hundred dollars; and the said magistrate before whom the said cause shall be tried, shall enter judgment for said time and costs.[1]

---

[1] *RMN* 10/03/1884, p. 7.

Even with pretext ordinances meant to impede, if not end, Jeff's line of work, still the business of fraud was good. To his family in Belton, Texas, Jeff continued to send money. Despite regular support, however, sometimes more was needed. In a letter dated April 25, 1884, Jeff received an urgent request for help from his father.

> Dear Jeff.,
>
> Write you a few lines in haste. Am very busy with my garden. Had too [sic] pretty severe frosts in succession on the 22nd and 23rd. Considerable damage done but little vegetation totally killed here. Have now grown peas, and will soon have potatoes in abundance. Send at the earliest moment, you can $300.00 to make payment for property. Do not want to fail to raise at least that sum and the time to do it is now.
>
> The girls send their love.
>
> All's well. Let me hear from you immediately upon the reception of this letter.
>
> Yours as ever truly,   Jefferson R. Smith, Sr.[1]

Jeff continued to despise his father but not his younger siblings, and for their sake, his father's requests for financial help were likely answered.

By 1884, Denver was becoming a big regional center, but Jeff still traveled from town to town. The frequency of his trips may have been in part due to attacks against him in the Denver newspapers and courts. On one such trip, Jeff went to Del Norte, a Colorado gold rush camp that supplied the other mining camps in the surrounding San Juan mountains. Jeff purchased a license for $8.50, paid to the marshal himself, to operate his soap sell operation.[2] It is a safe assumption that both Jeff and the marshal made a profit that day. On the license, Jeff listed his home as Denver.

During Jeff's traveling period, he kept cycling through Denver. The city with its growing influx of visitors was a prime location for this bunco man, but for some reason he hesitated making it his home. Perhaps another bunco gang was already entrenched, making settling down in Denver problematic and possibly dangerous. In 1889 when asked how long he had lived in Denver, Jeff replied, "Since 1879, but not steady.... Very near steady for four or five years: I have been here different times; made it my home since 1880."[3] Jeff could have been exaggerating the year to appear a long-time resident of the city. The Denver City Directory for 1883 shows him as residing at the Taney Boarding House.[4] However, the *Rocky Mountain News* still listed him as a "visitor to the city" as late as August 1883. While the dates of residency may not be precise, what is certain is that Jeff came and went from Denver, eventually settled in the city, and found ways to bend it to his will.

In the summer of 1884 Marian Murray was an 18-year-old arrival to Denver from Central City, Colorado. She was hired as a maid in the boarding house where Jeff was living, the Taney. Although no dive, its clientele was of the rougher sort. Many years

---

[1] Ltr fr Jeff R. Smith Sr. to Jeff R. Smith II, 04/25/1884. Geri Murphy col.

[2] Vendor license to sell soap at Del Norte, Colorado, signed by city marshal J. A. Mummings, 09/13/1884. Jefferson R. "Little Randy" Smith col.

[3] *RMN* 08/06/1889.

[4] *Denver City Directory,* 1883-1884.

later, Marian's son wrote that it was while employed there that his mother was introduced to Jeff, who "appointed himself as protector and guardian of the innocent young Irish girl ... and saw to it that none of the roughnecks in the hotel crowd ever caused her a bit of trouble." When Marian's future husband, Ralph E. Cuthbertson, first began to show romantic interests,

> he must have had to convince Soapy that he had the most honorable of intentions toward the Irish lass. She [Marian] always said that Soapy Smith was the product of a cultured southern family environment with all the polish of an educated gentleman.[1]

Jeff had come a long way in just a few years. Working as a hotel clerk and retail clerk, at which he excelled, he next found he had a gift for working a crowd as a cheap John, marking entrance into the world of crime. He followed traveling bunco men, learning and then operating short swindles like the shell and pea game. He favored and mastered the auction con and made the prize package soap sell his own. Jeff must have tired of traveling, though, or perhaps he discovered the right place to plant himself, for of all the cities he had seen, bustling Denver became his location of choice. The time had come, it seems, for someone of Jeff's animation, energy, and organization to assume leadership of Denver's underworld. It would not take long for him to be feared and admired there.

Chapter 3
Soapy Invades Denver, Queen City of the Plains

My business is Selling prize packages. No one is obliged to buy.

—Jefferson R. Smith II
Weekly Register Call, August 2, 1889

In 1859 when Denver was established as a city, it was little more than a rough, frontier settlement at the westward edge of the Great Plains. Its mainstay was freighting to and from the growing number of mines in the Rocky Mountains, the north-south base of which lay 15 miles west. When Jeff arrived 20 years later, with a population of 35,000, Denver was the nation's 26th largest city, and streetcars and utilities were being introduced. In 1877 Denver boasted 3 train lines while most Western cities had but one. Between 1882 and 1884, the city hosted 3 Expositions of National Mining and Industry and had become known as The Metropolis of the Territories and The Queen City of the Plains. By the mid 1880s, 6 railroad lines conveyed a steady flow of passengers to and from the depot at the northwest end of Seventeenth Street, making the mile-high city the booming business center of Colorado.[2] Yet growth was so rapid and the pace of development so burdened that the city's infrastructure lagged far behind. For example, main streets to and from Denver's

---

[1] Ltr fr Robert E. Cuthbertson, circa 1975. Karen Cuthbertson col.
[2] *Encyclopedia Britannica*, 1910. "Denver."

Union Station remained unpaved until 1891,[1] and civil services were seriously lacking, such as an adequate police force.

For Jeff Smith, the tumult and inability to control it made Denver, over all the other Western cities he visited, perfect ground in which to plant the seeds of a vibrant underworld. Moreover, Denver had modern conveniences, the promise of growth, and an open and permissive atmosphere. Horse-drawn and electric streetcars on rails moved business and pleasure seekers along gas-lit streets. Signaling confidence in the future, the tracks went well beyond the city limits to new construction projects. Telephones connected those who could afford them. Arriving daily were people to swell the city. Also constantly arriving and departing were visitors—miners, farmers, salesmen, travelers on their way further west. This was a booming, modernizing Western city with a future.

Gambling, both straight and crooked, had been a thriving industry in Denver from the start. The first Denver town council in 1860 prohibited gambling.[2] That codified prohibition continued, with short periods of exception, but in such a way as to permit gambling. On February 28, 1861, President Lincoln signed legislation making Colorado a territory, and by September, an appointed legislature gave Denver a charter.[3] Under it, Denver "could regulate and license, or prohibit and suppress" a host of activities, such as "'billiard-tables and bowling alleys,'" including "gambling." This power remained unused except "to prohibit three-card monte." Then in 1864 a general law was passed that suppressed gambling and gambling houses throughout the territory. However, so powerful in Denver were gambling interests by this time that the Territorial Legislature, meeting in that city, was persuaded to pass a special act exempting Denver from the general law against gambling.[4] The next legislature, however, repealed that act and through the compromises that only politics can create, created a legal fog about gambling in Denver that entrenched games of chance in the city and made it a battle ground over gambling, culminating in the ridiculous but almost tragic City Hall War of 1894.

What the legislature did was to give the city the power to prohibit gambling or not prohibit gambling. The law also specifically prohibited Denver the power to license it. The city council did prohibit all gambling, putting Denver in accord with the territorial law against gambling, but the city established fines so low and flexible that the effect was, in essence, to regulate gambling by means of fines instead of license fees. Fines could not be less than $10 nor more than $100. Clyde Lyndon King in his history of Denver government (1911) observed the following:

> This policy made inevitable favoritism in police protection, corruption in the police force, and a vacillating municipal policy with all its temptations and ills. Thus the general law was evaded, as it usually is when local public opinion is at variance with the public opinion of the state....[5]

---

[1] *RMN* 11/01/1891.
[2] King, p. 25.
[3] King, p. 28.
[4] King, p. 52.
[5] King, p. 53.

After Colorado statehood (1876), this double standard, of the state outlawing gambling but allowing Denver to prohibit it if it wished, was revalidated in 1878 and again in 1889.[1] Denver was allowed to appear to be in concert with state law, but the fine structure remained the same. Rather than a penalty or deterrent to gambling, the fine structure and its occasional imposition were seen by gamblers as an acceptable business cost and by corrupt city officials and policemen as a means to extract graft on a regular basis. The fines helped the city coffers, although not by much, and everyone was happy. An attempt to marry the spirit and letter of the anti-gambling laws with actual practice would come, but not until a new Populist governor with a righteous hatred of gambling came to Denver in 1892.

The daily arrival of scores of visitors with money to spend made Denver a mecca for gamblers and confidence men. When out-of-towners asked about the legality of gambling, despite state law and a city ordinance to the contrary, visitors were told the city was "free" and "wide-open." True enough, so long as the delicate balance between gamblers and officials was maintained. This practice that allowed honest gambling held the door open for dishonest gambling and other fraudulent schemes. In making Denver a home base, Jeff could run his bunco operations "wide-open" by paying relatively small constabulary and city official costs for the privilege. The police in particular needed to supplement their income. On average nationally,

> Denver's lawmen were underpaid.... Consequently, they were always consuming free drinks in saloons rather than walking their beats. Furthermore, Denver had too few enforcement agents because the city refused to spend the money for the police. In 1878, for example, the *Rocky Mountain News* urged more money for the police. Denver had only one patrolman for each 4,116 citizens. New York and New Orleans, on the other hand, had one policeman for each 400 citizens, and St. Louis and Cincinnati each had one per thousand.[2]

Denver's population in 1880 was 35,629.[3] By 1887, it had climbed to over 65,000, not counting visitors, yet only 43 policemen were on the payroll. These could not even keep the peace very well let alone fight crime. By 1890, with the population ballooning to 106,713,[4] Denver followed only San Francisco and Omaha as the 3rd largest Western city and the 26th largest in the United States.[5] It likely ranked first, however, in its level of corruption, especially throughout the police force. Clark Secrest in *Hell's Belles: Prostitution, Vice, and Crime in Early Denver* studied the scrapbooks of policeman Sam Howe and has rendered a detailed look at underworld crime, the many police who enjoyed it, and those few who fought it.

> Police misbehavior ranged from minor graft taking to drunken murder and covert alliances with criminals, which generated public mistrust of policemen

---

[1] King, pp. 74, 108.
[2] Dorsett, p. 94.
[3] Leonard, p. 44.
[4] Leonard, p. 66.
[5] Leonard, p. 44, & Noel, *City*, p. 67.

at large. Cops were regarded as ruffians who constantly guzzled free beer, smoked cigars, dressed sloppily, and hung around under street lamps talking.

There must have been brave, conscientious men in the ranks, but the reputation of the force was earned by the great number of police who were inclined toward brutality and always eager for a handout. The policemen returned the scorn [of critics] and often displayed contempt for the public.[1]

Bunco gangs easily opened the doors of the city to their operations with bribes, graft, and the promise of influence in elections. In 1884, as reported by the *Rocky Mountain News*, at least two main bunco gangs worked the city.

Denver seems to be peculiarly the chosen field for bunco men. Scores of credulous travelers are swindled every week out of sums greater or less in amount, who make no sign [of what happened], the sentiment of shame over the result of their verdancy making them pocket their losses with what grace they can. Certainly for every ten cases of impudent fraud ... scarcely one is reported. The operations of these *chevaliers of industrie* are carried on in different portions of the city and in various guises. The business is regularly organized by some accomplished leader with from three to five assistants, who work the traveling community for all it is worth. The manipulators are generally well dressed, very smooth and plausible in their conversation, and after having selected a victim but rarely fail to pluck him. At present there are two gangs working the town, and from all accounts, to considerable profit. Some of the schemes are magnificent in their conception and results, others consist in swindling the unwary with bogus railroad tickets at so-called ticket broker offices..., filching from the poor railroad laborer the last $2 ... on the pretext of obtaining for him employment which never comes. Probably of all the schemes practiced the last is the most rascally as it is the meanest.

It is very rarely that any one of either of the classes of confidence men is brought to justice and as soon as a newspaper dares to hint at their misdeeds, it is called upon by numbers of men calling themselves respectable, to make corrections of statements which are calculated to interfere with their legitimate business. That all of these confidence dens are well known to the police goes without saying. Why they are allowed to exist is a conundrum.... For all the information of the authorities it will be the province of THE NEWS some day to furnish a list of these operators, their methods of working in detail and their "places of business."[2]

The *News* would keep its promise.

Historical accounts identify "Doc" Charles L. Baggs as an early bunco gang leader in Denver and Jeff Smith as the rising leader of another gang. Baggs favored large profits from wealthy dupes. These targets required elaborate, "big-store" swindles that usually took place indoors and involved fake businesses. These operations were often on par with large theatrical productions requiring a set and cast of characters, and

---

[1] Secrest, p. 24.
[2] *RMN* 04/19/1884.

could last for days. Baggs left the short cons to Jeff. Most of the time after a big haul, Baggs had to leave his location in a hurry to avoid the official inquiry of higher ups. Jeff, however, could continue operating in the same location because he had many ways of keeping a lid on his businesses, including the rare complaint.

The two dominant gangs in Denver were said to be competitors, and they may have been in some respects as both were organized under different leaders and competed for overlapping portions of the same resource. But apparently plenty was to be had as no instances of warfare between rival gangs are known. Further, plentiful evidence shows that gangs were in the habit of joining forces during city elections to support officials who secretly promised not to interfere with bunco brotherhood businesses run by the gangs that supported them.

By July 1884, the *Rocky Mountain News* reported an alarming increase in bunco gang activity. According to the paper at this time, now at least twelve gangs operated within the city. It is probable that these were actually clusters of confidence men under the direction of Baggs and Jeff. A prominent hotel operator enlightened a reporter on his experience with the problems he witnessed.

> We have had over a dozen guests of our hotel buncoed in the last fortnight and travel is actually falling off on account of it. People are getting afraid to come to Denver. ... [O]ne old cuss ... got beat out of $400 and hadn't a cent left. We let him have $200 to get out of town and he was so mad that he didn't want to send us the money, but we managed to talk him around all right. I wouldn't blame him much if he hadn't though. There are a dozen bunco sharks hanging around this hotel all the time, and by the time a guest gets in [the door] he is either robbed or talked to death.[1]

Jeff and his men worked the lower part of Seventeenth Street near Union Station. This main artery leading to the city center was a cornucopia of easy pickings. Competition was fierce, but Jeff was highly successful for a number of reasons. He organized his men into a disciplined work force, he and his gang supported local businesses with patronage, he bribed police officers and city politicians, and he helped and supported them come election time and during periods of trouble. For elected officials, another inducement to working with Jeff was that they could count on him to be discreet about their relationship.

Jeff paid graft to Denver police officers. An undated notebook in which Jeff kept records shows the names of three officers with dollar amounts next to each name: Detective George Cook, $50, Tim Connors, $50, and Sam Howe, $45.[2] These are not inconsiderable amounts. With 1889 as a sample year, $50 is equal to $1,498.50 today.[3] Coming as a surprise is the name of Howe, who holds a reputation to this day as having been a dedicated police officer with a highly polished reputation.

Jeff also opened doors of favoritism with city officials. Money and the smooth, bold force of his personality were the keys. He was well aware that these powers could revoke their favoritism and abandon him should a public outcry become

---

[1] *RMN* 07/13/1884.

[2] Undated notebook with notes & records handwritten by Jefferson R. Smith II. Author's col.

[3] Tom's Inflation Calculator.

sustained. So he managed that, too, in a variety of ways, including stalling tactics, trickery, bribes, and threats. During periods when the economy was sound and any outcry from the streets was muted, Jeff was allowed to run his swindles almost free of interference. Jeff honed his management abilities to a fine edge, and try as it might for years, the *Rocky Mountain News* was unsuccessful in attempts to blunt that edge.

Finding victims was often as easy as picking up a newspaper. The *Rocky Mountain News* published a daily column called "Hotels and Personals" that made "marks" easy to find. It listed not only the names of newly arrived visitors and their business in Denver but also where they were staying. Another common method of identifying a mark was through the false introduction. When a likely victim was spotted, one of the bunco men might say, "Oh, hello Mr. Jones. How is business in St. Louis?"—knowing full well it was not the victim's name and ready for extend an apology and make a self-introduction. Even easier, of course, at least for one with a practiced eye, was to spot a victim among the herd of people coming out of Denver's Union Station. Then it was a matter of cutting him out and steering him into a corral.

For the most part, Jeff Smith was predictable in his methods. He ran his organization by procedures used by the majority of bunco organizations across the US, and his strategies for control of Denver's bunco underworld varied little from those used in Creede, Colorado, and Skaguay, Alaska. The key rules of successful engagement included leaving the local population out of the games, keeping to visitors and transients, and maintaining a low profile and well away from the limelight.

Social and political recognition, however, attracted Jeff. He would not give up the life of crime yet desired the public persona of an upstanding businessman and public benefactor. Jeff did his best to split the vastly different versions of himself, but by the late 1800s, the sobriquet "Soapy" Smith the criminal and Jeff Smith the businessman were synonymous with organized crime. The successors to Jeff's empire in Denver, Lou and Sam Blonger, made sure not to make the mistake of failing to keep a low profile and thus kept their criminal power in Denver into the 1920s.

Knowing the general fallibility of human nature, the bunco men sought victims greedy enough to be dishonest. The desire to be a winner and to enlarge one's poke or wallet drew most men to consider playing a game of chance, investment, or scheme. Once that close, all the confidence man need do is show the possibility of "a sure thing" and wait for the fish to bite, and bite hard. Faced with "a sure thing," whether rich or poor, educated or illiterate, experienced or innocent, intelligent or unintelligent, those with an avaricious and less than strictly honest nature could be reeled in without any struggle at all. The only difference among these prospective victims was the degree of their greed and their predisposition to be dishonest. To set the stage, a skilled bunco artist could deftly dupe a man into believing that he, "the mark," could exploit another person rather than be exploited by him. Then the measure of the victim would be played upon by the victim himself. To set the play in motion, the victim need only be exposed to the means of exploiting his opponent. This is called "the opening." If that means were not clearly apparent, boosters would arrive to point out how the victim could win by cheating. Vaudevillian and film actor W. C.

Fields memorialized the dynamic of the "sure thing" con with the expression "You can't cheat an honest man."[1] No one is a victim until he marks the con man as his victim. A perfect example of the bunco man manipulating the greed of his victim comes from an article in the November 8, 1879, *Fort Worth Daily Democrat.*

A new swindle is reported as being perpetrated by "artful dodgers" in Pennsylvania.... They send a letter written in the familiar tone of an old acquaintance, reminding the recipient that when he left their boarding house he owed a little bill of, possibly, $2. He is further informed that they can readily sell the jewelry which, among other things, he left behind in a satchel, for $20 or $30. If he will remit the $2 they will send him the satchel and contents. The gullible one knows well ... he never possessed such property, nor boarded in such a place, but he is willing to quietly obtain some other person's valuable jewelry, and therefore sends the $2. He receives nothing. This swindle is based solely upon the idea that a large percentage of people are by nature dishonest enough to take that to which they have not the slightest just claim, if they have the chance. People ... beaten by the trick are served precisely right. There is not the slightest danger that they will put officers of the law upon the track of the swindlers. Shame will keep them from exposing their own crooked intentions.[2]

Among men of the West at this time, though, was a type who would never know this sort of shame. They came and went with an earnest desire for success and a depth of self-reliance. Usually armed and experienced in defending themselves, they were not gentle or easy prey. Jeff and the Soap Gang learned to recognize this type of Westerner and let him pass unmolested. Successful confidence men must have exercised a great deal of discretion. They, too, knew something of the frontier and long since had learned to avoid hard-eyed individuals who disdained shell games and fingered their weapons if anyone seemed too curious or friendly. Preferred were the gullible, the drunks, and the naïve as victims. Men who looked to their own concerns in a purposeful way were rarely molested. Thieves and con men found prey enough among the weak and stupid. Experienced criminals have never been inclined to look for unnecessary trouble.[3]

There were also the innocent, those neither good nor bad but lacking the experience to know better. Of these, as well as the weak, stupid, and greedy, Jeff liked to say that he was doing them a favor by teaching them a lesson. Examples of lessons might include how there was no sure or easy path to profit and riches, how the gambler must be prepared to lose, and how evil it is to try to cheat another man. And then there was the lesson of how foolish it is to try to beat another man at his own game. Greedy cheats were Jeff's favorite students. He figured these men would be after his money if they had the chance to cheat him out of it, so turn about was fair

---

[1] *You Can't Cheat an Honest Man.* Film, 1939. Larson E. Whipsnade (W. C. Fields), a practiced con man, in his first scene states the film's title and demonstrates how honest men cannot be cheated.

[2] *Fort Worth Daily Democrat* 11/08/1879. Note: $2 seems like little today, but in today's dollars would be about $64.28. (Tom's Inflation Calculator)

[3] Hunt, p. 42.

play. Word of Jeff's educational orientation got out, and Denver's press christened Jeff "the hayseed educator of Seventeenth Street."[1]

Along Seventeenth Street in Denver, Jeff created a spider-web network of entrapment. It ran from the train depot to Larimer Street. So saturated with confidence men were these four blocks that they became known locally as the "streets of doom."[2]

> Out-of-town visitors were fleeced so often that Denver gained an unsavory reputation for thieves and bunco artists. "When the average country merchant does summon sufficient courage to visit this city," one *Rocky Mountain News* editorial complained, "he sews his wad of money in his vest lining, takes an affectionate last farewell of his family and friends, leaves directions as to the color he would prefer to have his tombstone painted every summer, and boards the train, filled with certainty that [anyone] who enters Denver leaves hope behind.[3]

In addition to such editorial overstatement was the friendly warning of train porters to passengers before their arrival in Denver. They were advised to avoid gambling on the street and a variety of investment schemes. As a result, Denver became known as a dangerous place for visitors. Rather than slowing predatory activity, however, con men used Denver's reputation to their advantage. To gain a victim's trust, a bunco man would commonly cultivate the appreciation and confidence of his prey by warning him to stay clear of the confidence men and their games. In fact, the friendly con man would offer to guide the visitor past harm and thus steer him to the fraud of choice.

As many as a hundred trains a day brought passengers to Union Station, and diverse were the ways in which a new arrival could be befriended, all casual and natural. One method involved being flattered into a friendly acquaintanceship that promised benefit. Highly prone to this approach was the member of a fraternal organization, of which there were many. Status-seeking men in the latter 19th century yearned to belong to one of hundreds of such groups. Their themes were various, appealing to the patriot, religious, civic, and they bore extravagant names such as the Masons, Knights of Pythias, and the Ancient Order of Nobles. Many had a secret handshake or signal by which members could identify one another. Most also had a lodge emblem in the form of a ring, pin, or charm that could be proudly worn on the hand, coat lapel, or watch chain.

In a typical scenario a newcomer makes his way from the station depot onto the busy city streets. If it is his first visit to Denver, his gate is tentative as he is unsure of the direction of his destination. A friendly voice is heard from behind him, asking if he would like directions. Turning towards the voice, the visitor is greeted by a smiling face under a fashionable hat. The man's robust, confident presence in his well-made clothes is reassuring, and so is something else. "Why, is that the pin of ____?" asks the man, pointing to the other's lapel. "Are you a member of the ____?" The other extends a hand, takes the visitor's, and executes the secret handshake of their order. "*Bowers* is the name," says the other. "Reverend John Bowers." And so the traveler,

[1] Collier & Westrate, p. 139.
[2] Author's interview with Denver historian Craig Gartrell, 07/1985.
[3] Noel, *City*, p. 90.

happy over meeting a fellow lodge member, and a man-of-God at that, trades information with the man: his name, home location, employment, business in Denver, financial state for his trip…, and accepts the offer of his "brother" to show him the way to his destination.

But the visitor is on his way to becoming a victim. A member of the Soap Gang has succeeded in befriending him and gaining his trust. In this fictitious instance he is "Reverend" John L. Bowers, Jeff's premier "Glad-Hander" and "Pin-Man." Bowers has been waiting for this man, spotted him from afar, and carefully watched his approach. After recognizing the man's lodge pin, Bowers adroitly donned the same pin from among the many he carried and came up quickly behind his prey.

In his fact-finding interview, Bowers discovers he is in the company of "Mr. Walker," a business man from a large company in Salt Lake City, a family man with a wife of 5 years and a child of 2, and that he has $200 to cover his week's stay in Denver, surely enough. Bowers agrees and insists on showing Walker to his destination as he knows the city well and would not want a lodge brother pestered by the many confidence men in this part of the city. As the two make their way up Seventeenth Street, Bowers guides the man into disclosing further personal and business details and shares similar details about himself, including that he is a successful mineral investor. At Seventeenth and Market Street, a man rushes up to Bowers and asks how things are. Bowers tells Walker that he needs to talk with this person about a business investment, that it will only take a moment, and steps aside with the man. Within hearing distance of Walker, Bowers says an excellent profit has been earned and hands over a thick envelope. Bowers adds that more could be had by that afternoon if they reinvest immediately. "It's a sure thing," Bowers declares with a smile. The man opens the envelope, partially withdraws a stack of greenbacks, looks at them, pushes them back into the envelope, and presses it back on Bowers. Thanking him profusely, the man departs.

Bowers rejoins Walker, and after traveling a little further, asks if they might step into a cigar store just ahead because he has some brief business to conduct there. And if Walker likes a fine cigar, Bowers would like to buy him one as a welcome gift to a *brother*. Walker assents, and as they approach the store, Walker says he could not help overhearing the investment discussion and asks if he might be allowed to invest as well. Bowers replies that any investment would have to be made right away in cash. Walker replies that he has cash. Bowers asks how much Walker wants to invest.

The men enter the cigar shop, and Bowers asks for a Mr. Smith. Told he is in the back room, conducting business, and not to be disturbed, Bowers explains that it is about important business that he needs to speak with Mr. Smith and says that part of it involves his new friend there, Mr. Walker. The men are led to a back room where five men sit at a table, playing cards and talking about the business atmosphere of Salt Lake City. Bowers is told that Mr. Smith has just stepped out but will return shortly. The men around the table have been eyeing Walker with noticeable discomfort, but when Bowers introduces him as a businessman from Salt Lake City, the men's discomfort vanishes. As coincidence would have it, their conversation had been of that very city. The men apologize for their prior coolness, explaining that gambling is illegal in Denver and that they did not know who Walker was. The victim finds himself the center of attention as he is asked himself and his affairs in Salt Lake City. Walker says he feels fortunate to have bumped into the Reverend Bowers, who has introduced him to such friendly fellows.

Bowers and Walker step back into the store for a cigar and discussion about "the investment," which is in mining. After allowing Walker to ask several more times to be let into the impending investment, Bowers allows him to add three quarters of his ready cash to the investment. A slip of paper is given Walker, and the money is added to the fat envelope of cash. How glad Bowers says he is that he can let his fellow lodge member in on this opportunity because it seems almost certain to produce a handsome profit in a short time, even within an hour or two. A man enters the establishment and is introduced as Jeff Smith, of Bascomb Smith and Company, a local mineral investments firm. Bowers hands Smith the envelope, which immediately is handed to the clerk behind the counter along with a few terse instructions. The three then wander back to the card game where the three are invited to join. Smith has to leave, but Bowers accepts and encourages Walker to do likewise. They may as well amuse themselves while they wait to collect on their investment, and Walker takes a chair pulled up for him. After Walker is introduced to each of the men at the table— business and professional men, some citizens of Denver, some visitors like Walker— they begin to play a friendly game of cards.

The game is draw poker, and Walker experiences a winning streak. Encouraged to bet heavily, Walker soon has a stack of cash in front of him. Before half an hour has passed, Bowers leaves to check on the investment. As the game continues through a series of small wins but larger, steady losses, Walker loses all his winnings and much of what is left of his ready cash. Then his luck dramatically reverses. He is dealt an incredibly strong hand. At that moment a clerk interrupts the game with news that Bowers is on his way back with a fat bankroll from the investment. Walker is ecstatic at the news, but he is also equally excited about his cards. With few funds to bet with, and wishing to recoup his losses as well as a nice profit, he asks if the players would accept a personal check. The men at first resist, but Walker persuades them that his check is good. He writes it for a tidy sum and adds it and the rest of his cash to the pot. The poker hands are revealed and Walker is shocked to see better cards than his and watches painfully as the sizable pot goes to another man.

The jovial smiles and friendly conversation of the men at the table are suddenly gone. The men now look more like desperadoes than peers. Walker is warned that his check had better be good, told he damn well better have been able to afford what he'd lost, told it don't do no good in a town where gambling's illegal 'cause if word gets out about the game, all of them would be arrested. Walker feels not only remorseful over his loss but also afraid (just as the gang wants him to). He excuses himself, leaves the room, passes through the cigar store and back out onto the busy city street, preferring to wait for Reverend Bowers there than inside. What he wants is to get the investment money from Bowers, go to his hotel, and gather himself so that he can attend to his company's business. What a costly and upsetting turn of events. The sooner put behind him, the better. The police? Let's not have them involved! Where's Bowers? Then he appears, coming quickly his way. Why does he look distressed, out of breath? Standing before Walker, Bowers gives him a rueful look. The mining company in which their money had been invested has gone bankrupt. All their money is gone.

After listening to the events that occurred at the card table, Bowers feigns even greater dismay and expresses a sense of personal responsibility. He tells Walker that he suspects some of the men at the table are dangerous characters and that they may come after him to see he causes no trouble. Bowers insists on giving Walker some money (Walker's money to begin with), which conveniently is just enough for train passage back to Salt Lake City. He tells Walker that it would probably be best if he were to leave immediately, let things calm down. Walker could tell his company he had become suddenly sick and felt it best to return home. Bowers quickly adds that if the police were to become involved, it would surely mean only trouble for Walker as the police are often in league with men who gamble. Slowly, Reverend Bowers escorts Walker to the depot, commiserating with his "brother" over such bad luck. Finally, just before boarding his train, Walker thanks the Reverend for his kindness.

This con is known as a closed swindle. It is a theatrical production designed to extract a victim's ready cash and more if possible. Initial events all lead to seclusion, a secluded stage on which the swindle is played. The cigar store is a cigar store, but it is also a front for the backroom swindle. Grifters each have their parts to play in every event, from the time Walker is met coming from a train until deposited on a train that is leaving. Should a victim go to the police to complain, every "witness" at the poker table will claim that Walker is a criminal who enticed "honest" citizens into an illegal gambling game, which, even worse, was crooked.

John Bowers' task was to select the dupe, prepare him, and steer him to one of Jeff's establishments, depending on which was appropriate to the prey. In the case of Mr. Walker, the man who came to Bowers on the street, wanting to know about "the investment," was a shill responding to a cue from Bowers to retrieve information Bowers had gathered and to pique the victim's interest in making a quick profit. With a code only the con men would understand, Bowers gave the shill the information he had gathered, and the shill delivered it to the bunco men waiting in the cigar store. After the victim had put money into the "sure thing" mining investment, Bowers decided whether the dupe had money enough left to lose, hence the poker game setup. The personal information Bowers gathered was used during the card game introductions to help convince Walker he was among friendly men not unlike himself.

During the card game, Walker's reaction to his cash losses were closely monitored to determine when he was ready to quit the game. At that moment, another shill was sent to inform Walker that Bowers was returning with a lot of money. Shortly thereafter Walker is dealt a "sure-thing" hand. With news that a large amount of cash is coming his way, the victim felt far less cautious than he otherwise might about writing a large check to supplement the remainder of his cash. After losing the hand, Walker may still not have suspected foul play as he was soothed by the belief that he is coming into a large return on his investment. Nevertheless, the bunco men around the table intimidated Walker with their change of attitude to distract him from analyzing the series of events. Once Walker learned his investment had been lost, it became Bowers' job to extend sympathy, offer advice to keep Walker out of trouble, give him a little of his own money back, and ease Walker out of Denver before he figured out he has not just been swindled but skinned of cash and more besides.

Another method of hastening the departure of a victim worked this way. As a crooked card game was coming to a finish and the victim's money had been "won," a few bunco men posing as officers of the law would charge into the room and arrest everyone for illegal gambling, including the victim. The badges the men wore were real. Between 1892 and 1894, Jeff and several members of his gang were periodically commissioned as special policemen or temporary deputy sheriffs of Arapahoe County, and not all of the badges were returned at the end of service. While a bunco officer was taking a distraught victim to jail, he was allowed, or even encouraged, to appeal to the "officer" for leniency. He didn't know gambling was illegal, and now having lost heavily in the game, he's also under arrest? It's so unjust. Couldn't he just slip away, catch the next train out of town? Or the "officer" might offer the victim the choice of a night in jail and court the next day, with a good chance of a fine or jail time or both—or the victim could save the City of Denver and himself a lot of time, trouble, and money, and just leave town. The choice was not hard to make. If the prey had been completely depleted of funds, the officer might "find it in his heart" to front enough money to buy the suffering soul a ticket home. And so most victims were neatly disposed of at Union Station with an admonition to mind the law. To this they readily agreed, thanked the "officer," and rolling away out of the city, considered themselves lucky to escape further trouble.

Jeff became successful enough to begin opening up short con establishments such as a lottery office on Sixteenth Street, between Larimer and Lawrence.[1] Colorado had no state-run lottery, but the sale of out-of-state lottery tickets was permitted. The number of lottery shops selling legitimate tickets was outnumbered by those selling fake ones. Selling these tickets, however, produced only a small profit. The real goal was to coax ticket buyers into a manipulated poker game, three-card monte, or some other nefarious swindle involving larger stakes.[2]

Similar to the lottery shop was the policy shop. *Policy*, as it was called, was similar to the numbers racket of modern times. In the 19th century, this was the poor man's gambling game.[3] Numbers were bet upon, and winning numbers came from out-of-state drawings. A player could win as much as 60 to 1, an enticing prospect, but the odds against winning were very high, and few, if any, of Denver's policy shops were legitimate.

---

[1] *RMN* 06/20/1884.

[2] *RMN* 06/20/1884.

[3] *Policy*: A plausible explanation of the etymology of *policy* as a gambling term appears in the film noir *Force of Evil* (1948). Leo runs a small numbers racket; brother Joe wants Leo to join a combine of numbers rackets. Leo resists, says, "I'm an honest man here, not a gangster.... I do my business honest and respectable." Joe replies, "Honest? Respectable? Don't you take the nickels and dimes and pennies from people who bet just like every other crook...? They call this racket Policy because people bet their nickels on numbers instead of paying their weekly insurance premium. That's why, *Policy!*"

The *Rocky Mountain News* exposed all manner of fraud in its pages throughout July 1884 but with little response from the law, even after printing the letter of a traveler's experiences with the con men and the police.

> I am on my way from London, England to Los Angeles, California. I arrived in Denver this morning by the 8 o'clock train. I had to wait until 1:25. Going down the street, a well-dressed young man came up to me and tried to make my acquaintance. He then led me to an office, 507 ½ Larimer Street, first floor. On the door is written "LAND AND MINERAL ASSOCIATION." He presented a lottery ticket: His accomplice in the office said he had won and paid out to him in my presence $200. He then made him take another ticket, played cards and the man won and received again $50. He took another ticket and I drew for him No. 39. The accomplice said I had won a condition purse of $1000, and we both must lay down $50 cash and would then receive the 1000 cash. I did not lay down any money because I mistrusted them. I applied to two policemen and concluded from their answers that they are in league with these swindlers and confidence bank men, and I would ask you, have you not any means of putting down in publication in your paper this rouguery? [sic]
>
> I remain, sir, yours faithfully   J. Weisendaryer[1]

Mr. Weisendaryer seems to have been cautious enough not to take out his wallet and perceptive enough to see that the policemen were in league with the bunco men. The letter to the *Rocky Mountain News*, perhaps written by Weisendaryer before catching his 1:25 train, added momentum to a growing wave of reform.

After this letter, the *Rocky Mountain News* declared war on the bunco men, which included gamblers and saloon proprietors. The editors made it clear that they were not afraid of the gangs or the corrupt city officials and their police minions. The paper bombarded city hall and the police chief with demands to rid the city of confidence gangs. Jeff's unofficial permit to operate freely was revoked. No one at city hall wished to risk his position to protect him and his associates. The *News* seemed to be winning.

Five days later Sheriff Graham visited the *News* and was quoted as saying, "Within nine weeks I have compelled the bunco men to return $22,000 to their victims."[2] Dubious, the newspaper continued to accuse the police board of conspiring with criminals. An initiative to close swindle shops was undertaken, but it was a token effort, and soon after, the streets were filled with lottery offices and policy shops again.

To safeguard his operations, Jeff set about making quiet allies of gamblers, saloon proprietors, the Republican Party of Denver, and some of the city's newspapers. The *Denver Republican* became a friend, but to Jeff's dismay, the Democratic-Party-aligned *Rocky Mountain News* did not. Jeff went about business as usual, with little interference, but always under the watchful eyes of the *News*. This newspaper would become determined to rid Denver of the man they came to call "Sapolio Smith."[3]

---

[1] *RMN 07/*13/1884.
[2] *RMN 07/*18/1884.
[3] Sapolio: A brand name soap sold in 1884.

With the prize soap racket and other short con street swindles as stand-bys, Jeff focused on a variety of big-store cons. One such operation was the fake stock exchange office, often referred to as "the store" and as a "bucket shop" (derived from the bucket into which stock readings were discarded). Jeff and associates knew it affectionately as "the exchange." Victims were lured into the game with the promise of quick profits on an "inside" bogus stock tip. In the late 19th century, investing in stocks was much the same as betting at the horse track, and the action took place behind many false storefronts scattered about the city. Mike Maher, a young member of the Soap Gang, testified in court about how the swindle worked.

The focus at the "exchange" was a clock that was said to be tied to the country's stock exchanges. Out of the clock in an automated fashion came cards that reported the rise and fall of the market. Behind the scenes, eight or nine hundred cards were shuffled and fed at intervals through two slots in the front of the clock, one marked "advance" and the other "decline." The fractions printed on the cards and which slot they came out of indicated whether the market rose or dropped in value. To players of the exchange, it appeared that telegraph-fed stock market reports were coming in, but behind the scenes, percentages were being played by exchange operators. Generally, the longer players bet on the rise or fall of the market, the more they lost. Mike Maher had been arrested on charges of being a Jeff Smith "steerer," but rather than steering victims from the street to the exchange, Mike said his only job was to post quotations coming out of the clock onto a blackboard. No steering was needed, he stated, because the "Exchange" had so many customers that enticing was not necessary.[1]

The "Up and Down" swindle, a bucket shop that masqueraded as a stock exchange, similar to "the exchange," was defined in the *Denver Catholic Register* by early Denver pioneer, Joseph Emerson Smith. He claimed one such set-up operated in a poolroom near Seventeenth and Larimer streets. On a chalkboard were the names of fictitious mining companies. "To one side of the huge board was the regular bucket shop equipment, including cashier's cage, ticker, and tape. The wire ticked sharply and merrily during the trading hours. Markers with green visor eye shades were busy erasing old quotations and chalking up the new. Everything appeared legitimate." As with all of Jeff's offices, the quotations were fake, arranged for the misfortune of victims foolish enough to push their money to the cashier in exchange for a worthless piece of paper.[2]

There was a cut-rate ticket office where train tickets could be had at a discount. Dupes would order tickets and then be politely told to wait for them to be obtained and delivered by a ticket agent. While the victim waited, some "sure-thing" game was always under way in the corner to pass the time. If the dupe started gambling, no "ticket agent" would return until the swindle was complete, and then it was only to announce that none of those particular tickets were available. If the bunco men could not entice gambling, then the agent returned sooner, again with no tickets. Discount tickets were never intended to be sold, only the con games on the premises were real.

---

[1] *RMN* 03/23/1890.

[2] *Denver Catholic Register* 04/24/1941.

In 1896, a *Denver Republican* reporter asked Jeff about his line of work. With his fifteen years of running a wide variety of swindling operations in Denver, Jeff replied with characteristic directness:

> "There isn't a man in this town, who gives more to the poor than I do. What if I do take a few tributes from the other fellows? Don't these guys come here to the city to lose their dough? Guess the roulette wheels would get it if I didn't."[1]

As a home base, Jeff found Denver much to his liking. Arriving permanently in the mid 1880s as the reign of Denver bunco gang boss Charles Baggs was ending, Jeff quickly ascended to a position of power over a large portion of the city's underworld. Jeff's rise, though, caught the attention of the *Rocky Mountain News*. Its relentless war on the bunco gangs would eventually help bring down the empire that Jeff spent over a decade building and maintaining. First, though, Jeff would win many skirmishes and battles, some in the arena of public opinion with "public relations," some in the offices of city hall with graft, some from the upper stories of city hall with dynamite, and some with brute force.

Chapter 4

The Hayseed Educator of Seventeenth Street

I regard "Soapy" Smith and his crowd as the most interesting set of men with whom the police of Denver have ever dealt. Smith was bright, intelligent, fearless, desperate, and there was nothing he could not do in the way of shell games, dice, cards or sure thing propositions. And, say, he could play havoc with a gun, too!

—Denver Police Captain Sam Howe[2]

One of Jeff's chief assets was the unholy band of men who worked for him. These hand-picked confidence artists, referred to as boosters, cappers, handshake-men, pin-men, imposters, ropers, shills, and steerers,[3] were master readers of human nature. They reacted to prey with understanding and precision. Consummate actors, each with a special talent and role to play, they were part of the complex choreography of separating a sucker from his money. They dressed the part for each situation, from men of business to men of God. If a victim became unruly over his loss, their job was to protect the boss. Without these men, Jeff could not have enjoyed such widespread, sustained success. Knowing their value, Jeff paid them handsomely and before anyone else, including himself. In fact at times some received more than their boss.

Early biographers had access to scant factual information about members of Jeff's Soap Gang. Invented yarns and exaggerations where no known facts were available made their stories more interesting. Some of the men said to have worked

---

[1] *Denver Republican* 01/20/1896.
[2] *The Denver Post* 11/15/1914, p. 10, Item 163, author's col.
[3] *boosters ... steerers*: see Glossary.

for Jeff, such as "Ice Box" Murphy, are possibly complete fabrications as not a single separate accounting of their existence could be found.[1]

In prosperous times, Jeff was said to have had a score of talented, loyal men working with him directly and scores more indirectly. These estimates are not unrealistic given the times. In 1889, Police Chief John Farley said, "there were by actual calculation from 600 to 700 boosters and steerers attached to the gambling houses of the city."[2] In 1898 after Jeff's death, two researchers "in a position to judge fairly well," made an accounting of Soap Gang members in Skaguay and beyond. "There were 192 names on their list, all of them suggestive of the underworld and many of them unprintable."[3]

Most were hired on a temporary, as-needed basis, either from other bunco gangs or from new arrivals to the city. A smart and successful bunco man traveling around the states made his presence known to the chief local gang in power. If allowed to operate, he might be required to pay for the privilege or be hired on to work with a local bunco team. To go directly to work without notifying the local organization was considered a transgression. An arrogant defier of the controlling faction was usually encouraged to make an immediate departure from the city or face arrest or worse, removal by force. Denver was no exception. Newly arrived bunco men came to Jeff for permission to operate. If they wanted to work their racket separate from Jeff's businesses, they would have to pay for the privilege in advance and work where told. Some talented newcomers were encouraged to stay on with the gang.

Not all who worked with Jeff were Soap Gang members. Businessmen, police officers, and politicians had much to gain from indirect participation in Jeff's activities. Jeff could do them favors, from steering customers to paying well and regularly to fixing elections. John P. Kinneavy, a successful early Denver businessman, often aided Jeff's businesses and Jeff himself by posting bonds when he had been incarcerated. Just how Kinneavy benefited from his association is not clear, but the relationship was a long one, from 1888 to 1896. Denver Chief of Police John J. Farley was another "associate." Corrupt, he worked to keep Jeff and Soap Gang members out of jail so long as the media did not have him in their sights.

Total allegiance to their boss bonded the Soap Gang. Jeff's men were known to do anything for him. Joe Palmer shot it out with an adversary of Jeff's in Creede and had his thumbs partially shot off, yet he stayed with Jeff until the latter went to the Northwest and to Alaska in 1896. On another occasion, Jeff had an altercation with a faro dealer in Creede. Guessing that the quarrel was about to turn violent, Soap Gang member Peg Leg Charlie Adams stepped up and offered to use his six-guns if Jeff wanted their assistance.[4] The reputation for skill, audacity, and loyalty among Jeff's bunco gang became legendary in Colorado.

---

[1] *Ice Box Murphy*: Collier and Westrate in the *Reign of Soapy Smith* tell the story of how he got his name (pp. 32-33). Murphy wanted to be a safe cracker and on his first job was sent by a gang into a butcher shop to blow its safe. By mistake he blew the ice box and littered the floor with shattered meat. Evidence that an "Ice Box" Murphy ever existed is yet to be found.

[2] *RMN* 07/31/1889.

[3] Andrews, p. 38. Presumably the names are "unprintable" because they are "off color."

[4] Collier & Westrate, pp. 99-100.

Jeff's men spent their idle time in saloons and gambling halls such as the Chicken Coop at 1214 Seventeenth between Larimer and Lawrence streets and the Missouri Club at 1647 Larimer, where during the day an hourly "policy" wheel drawing was conducted. Other locations included the Morgue, the Arcade, and the White House Club.[1] These particular saloons and gaming halls were the gang's personal recreation grounds for drinking and gambling away their earnings. To conduct a swindle in one of these establishments took planning and the permission of the proprietor, who would receive a generous gratuity. The two most notorious playground resorts were the Arcade Restaurant Company and Murphy's Exchange. Located at 1611-13 and 1615 Larimer Street, the Arcade contained a saloon, restaurant, and private clubrooms for gambling running across the second floor. These attached by stairway to Murphy's Exchange on the floor below. The Arcade in 1890 was reported to be the largest gaming house in Denver. It had

> from six to nine faro tables run[ning] all the time, three roulette wheels and two [poker?] tables. There are about forty faro dealers employed at this place, to say nothing of the men in charge of the roulette and poker tables.[2]

The Arcade was one of Jeff's favorite places to drink and gamble.

In 1887, Jeff's business associate Ed Chase and Chase's partner John Hughes acquired the Arcade. It was considered "the best place to eat in Denver...."[3] Jeff spent so much time at the Arcade that some of his mail was addressed there.[4] It was not uncommon for saloons to maintain letter boxes for regular customers.[5] It is said that Bat Masterson and Wyatt Earp dealt faro for Chase in the Arcade.[6]

Murphy's Exchange, also known as "the Slaughter House" because of numerous shooting scrapes there, was next door to the Arcade at 1617 Larimer Street. The *News* wrote, "Every room in it has its story of murder and assassination and most of the crime committed on Larimer Street have been associated with 'Murphy's Exchange.'"[7] Jeff no doubt met and recruited many of his men in the Arcade and Murphy's Exchange. A number of these were adamant admirers of Jeff's methods and became permanent fixtures of the gang, following Jeff wherever he ventured.

The Soap Gang — A Brotherhood of Rogues, Gunmen, Notorious Sneak Thieves, Scoundrels, & Desperate Characters

What follows is a list of some of the men who worked for Jeff. Early biographies of Soapy Smith include information and stories about these gang members, but much of this information is fabricated to fill in blanks where little or no information was known. A thorough reading of period newspapers, primarily the *Rocky Mountain News* (1879-1896), shows that at one time or another, hundreds of men worked for Jeff, and some details about them have emerged. As their short biographies tell, they were among the

---

[1] *RMN* 07/22/1893, p. 1.
[2] *RMN* 05/08/1890, p. 7.
[3] DeArment, *Knights*, p. 173.
[4] *mail addressed there*: Author's col.
[5] Noel, *City*, p. 14.
[6] DeArment, *Knights*, p. 173.
[7] *RMN* 06/20/1894, p. 8.

worst human beings and the best thieves and bunco artists in the West. To each other they were often good friends who stayed in touch throughout their lives.

Most of the men Jeff hired worked with him but a short time, so only one or two newspaper accounts of their activities were found. Then they seemed to disappear from history. Some interesting arrests of bunco men were made, and personal letters to and from Jeff mention the names of numerous men. However, as no clear affiliation with Jeff could be certain and no specific information could be found about most of these many men, they are not listed. To add them would swell this list by a hundred or more but would add little in the way of specific information. Several gang members among the following worked with Jeff for years, and a handful followed him to Alaska and were close by in 1898 when a bullet ended his life.

Allen, J. W.: A capper used in a prize package auction swindle in 1889.[1] As part of a complaint over swindling, arrested with Jeff and Bascomb Smith, John "Fatty Gray" Morris, and John "Shoot-Your-Eye-Out Jack" Vermillion.[2] Allen may have been with Jeff in Pocatello during the 1889 train depot gun battle. In 1892 Creede, aided Jeff by obtaining titles to land lots by being "elected" to the land commission there.[3]

Anderson, J. "Kid": Arrested 1894 as one of the "Big Five" for vagrancy.[4] Arrested later with Jeff for vagrancy as "Kid" Anderson.[5]

Armstrong, Joe: see George Millsap.

Baggs, Charles L. "Doc": Baggs began his crime career as protégé of the famous three-card monte con man "Canada Bill" Jones.[6] Baggs was on his own in the gold camp of Deadwood, South Dakota, where he operated from spring 1877 through February 1879,[7] amassing a reported $100,000. Usually a long-con man, Baggs

> always had his false safe, an enormous affair made of wood with a silver knob, beautifully painted and labeled 'Hull's Patent.' It looked exactly like a heavy iron safe. One day Doc's office in Deadwood caught fire, and he surprised everybody by running down stairs with the massive safe on his back. ... The thing cost him as much as $100. Of course he wanted to save it. He had it made of wood so he could fold it up and carry it around easily from place to place. You know every time the bunco man catches a big 'sucker' he moves his office. When the 'sucker' next comes around he don't find anything but an empty room.[8]

Baggs moved on to Leadville where it is said he made $75,000 and then relocated in Denver where a bunco gang, probably Baggs', is reported to have raked in nearly $25,000 in two months.[9] Baggs is credited with inventing the "gold brick"

---

[1] *RMN* 08/18/1889.

[2] *RMN* 08/18/1889.

[3] *RMN* 03/03/1892.

[4] *RMN* 10/18/1894, p. 8. (See "Big Five" this section.)

[5] *Denver Post* 01/30/1895.

[6] *Canada Bill Jones*: "Many believed [him] to be the greatest monte sharp to ever 'pitch a broad'" (manipulate a card). (DeArment, *Knights*, p. 325)

[7] Deadwood information accessed 06/02/2006, www.deadwoodpoker.blogspot.com.

[8] *St. Louis Globe-Democrat* 03/08/1882, p. 11.

[9] *RMN* 08/29/1880, p. 4.

confidence scam. He fleeced many wealthy and prominent people by selling them counterfeit gold bars. Baggs became such a notorious fixture in Denver that when away from town on a trip it was rumored he may have been killed. On January 9, 1885, a Denver high school held a pretend trial of his murderer. The event was titled "Baggs' Body."[1] Later that year, Doc Baggs retired from Denver and opened the way for Jeff to move the rest of the way in. Baggs left Denver for the last time in March 1885. Seven days into the month he and a Clay Wilson were jailed in South Carolina for selling a gold brick for $3,000.[2] Not known for certain is what became of Baggs after his release, but one story has it that "As late as 1930..., Baggs was in good health at the age of ninety-three, living quite comfortably under another name on an estate located near New York City."

Big Five, The: A group of the most sought after Soap Gang members, arrested together for vagrancy in 1894, called the "Big Five" by the *News*, including John Bowers, C. W. Casey, W. K. Jackson (aka W. H. Jackson), J. Anderson, and Bascomb Smith, Jeff's younger brother.[3]

Blaine, Jimmy G.: See George McAttee.

Bowers, John L. "Reverend" and "Professor": One of Jeff's premier steerers from the late 1880s to 1898. He was known as a "glad-hander" and "grip-man," a confidence man who knew nearly every closely guarded, secret handshake, grip, and password of nearly every lodge and fraternal order. He was very successful as a bunco man perhaps partly because he so warmly embraced his victims in the sprit of brotherhood and as a God-fearing man of the cloth.[4] Bowers could often be seen with newfound "friends" heading towards one of Jeff's entrapments. However, once the charade was no longer required, he could be cold and mean. He was also known as a "pin-man"; hidden on him were said to be most of the pins of the popular lodges. Once spotting an intended victim's emblem, Bowers would quickly sport the same pin, ring, or watch charm and introduce himself as a member of the same organization.

The earliest accounts of Bowers are from Lowell, Massachusetts, in 1875 where he was arrested for breaking and entering.[5] Some time in the 1880s he joined the Soap Gang. The *Denver City Directory* for 1889 lists his occupation as auctioneer with the firm of R. Oppenstein. He married Belle Banning in 1889.[6] In 1891 he was one of Jeff's auctioneers on the corner of Seventeenth and Market streets.[7] Arrested in 1894 as one of the "Big Five."[8] One of Jeff's most loyal men to the very end in Alaska.

Brown, Frank "Blue-Jay": Arrested in Deadwood 1878 for a fight involving faro.[9] Arrested in Denver 1883 for petty larceny,[10] 1885 for assault and battery and carrying

---

[1] *RMN* 01/08/1885, p. 5.
[2] *RMN* 03/07/1885, p. 4.
[3] *RMN* 10/18/1894, p. 8.
[4] *RMN* 08/24/1894, p. 8. And *Denver Post* 02/27/1895.
[5] *Lowell Daily Citizen & News* 02/15/1875.
[6] *RMN* 11/24/1889, p. 2.
[7] *RMN* 02/19/1891, p. 7.
[8] See "Big Five" this section.
[9] Deadwood.
[10] *RMN* 01/28/1893.

concealed weapons,[1] and 1887 on weapons charges.[2] Opened a saloon in Pueblo, Colorado and on April 21, 1888, attempted to shoot the man his wife had been seeing, but his gun misfired and the man returned one shot striking Brown in the face, entering below the left eye and going under the base of the brain.[3] In Denver 1893, arrested for petty larceny.[4] Went to Skaguay with Jeff and was deported after Jeff was killed.

Burns, Edward "Big Ed": Last name sometimes spelled "Byrnes." Soap Gang member in Denver, Creede (listed in poem "Two Little Busted Shoes"), and Skaguay. The career of this hardened, brutal criminal requires an expanded section. At six feet and weighing over two hundred pounds, "Big Ed" liked to fight and was known as a man not to mess with. Reportedly born in Buffalo, New York, about 1842,[5] he was known as a braggart and a mean bully. In 1861 he began buncoing in Chicago.[6] About 1866 he strangled a man to death and was sentenced to nine years in Illinois' Joliet prison.[7] He returned to Chicago after release in 1875 where he was seriously wounded by a bullet in the back from a man said to be a friend.[8] In April 1877 he was reported as the leader of a bunco gang on Chicago's south side where he used his gang to influence votes for political candidates of his choosing. In a fight, Burns was shot in the thigh.[9] Arrested as ring-leader of buncoing and again for vagrancy, he fled Chicago while on $300 bond. Returning in six months, he was arrested on previous charges and for slugging and robbing a John McGuire of $380. Burns was fined $50 and told to behave. In twenty-six days Burns was again arrested for vagrancy. At trial the charge was dismissed because he could show plenty of money, a profession as a peddler of soap, and a saloon in a building he rented from a city alderman.[10] Reapplication for a saloon license was denied. Not able to sell liquor legally, he sold it from a boat on Lake Michigan. He managed to escape several police raids by jumping overboard, thus gaining the moniker "Elephantine Edward of the Floating Palace."[11]

In October 1878 Burns was extradited to Detroit on pick-pocketing charges.[12] In 1879, he went to Leadville, Colorado, joined bunco operations, and had several gunfights. Many in Leadville had had enough of the bunco gangs, and a vigilance committee stormed the city jail with guns drawn and hanged four inmates. On the body of Edward Frodsham, one of the men, was pinned a placard reading,

NOTICE TO ALL

Lot thieves, bunco steerers, footpads, thieves and chronic bondsmen for the same and sympathizers of the above class of criminals. This is our

---

[1] *RMN* 05/26/1885, p. 8.

[2] *RMN* 02/23/1887, p. 6.

[3] *RMN* 04/24/1888.

[4] *RMN* 01/28/1893.

[5] *Inter Ocean* 09/07/1881, p. 8.

[6] *Inter Ocean* 09/07/1881, p. 8.

[7] *Inter Ocean* 06/14/1875, p. 5

[8] *Inter Ocean* 06/14/1875, p. 5, & 06/22/1875, p. 4.

[9] *Inter Ocean* 04/04/1877, p. 8.

[10] *Inter Ocean* 01/31/1878, p. 8.

[11] *Inter Ocean* 07/10/1878, p. 8; 07/26/1878, p. 8; 07/29/1878; & 10/01/1878, p. 8.

[12] *Inter Ocean* 10/04/1878, p. 8.

commencement, and this will be your fate. We mean business. Let this be your last warning, particularly "Cooney" Adams, Connor, Collins, Hogan, Ed Burns, Ed Champ, P. A. Kelley and a great many others who are well known to this organization. We are seven hundred strong.[1]

When a friend of Burns was shot dead by person or persons unknown, Burns vanished. Not long after, an obituary for Burns was published. It read in part,

Ed Burns called himself a sporting man, but he was not recognized by the fraternity.... He was regarded as a bully and a dead-beat, and it is a notable fact that nobody in the city has a good word to say of him upon learning of his fate.[2]

Burns was not dead. He turned up in Denver where on December 8, 1879, he was arrested with three men for stealing a gold watch and chain.[3] He returned to Leadville where in late March or early April 1880, he shot a man named Curley. When Curley died three weeks later, Burns was gone.[4] He traveled to Deming, New Mexico, where, after being caught cheating at faro, a fight ensued in which Burns hit a man from behind and then beat him badly.[5] Burns began operating in Benson, Arizona, where newspapers referred to him as the leader of "the top and bottom gang," named after the bunco dice game of the same name.[6] Newspapers in Chicago and Leadville learned that Tombstone vigilantes had hanged Burns for killing a deputy sheriff, but the report was wrong. Burns had wounded a deputy McComas with a bullet to the thigh. A mob demanded justice, and Burns was arrested and jailed, not hanged. Police officer Morgan Earp was accused of being in league with Burns.[7] In 1881, during clashes between the "cowboys" in Tombstone, Wyatt Earp said that Burns had warned him about threats made by the Clantons and the McLaurys that ended in the gunfight behind the OK Corral.[8] According to Josephine Earp, Burns had been a member of the Wyatt Earp gang in Tombstone at the time of the OK Corral gunfight.[9]

Burns' first arrest in Denver was in June 1883.[10] During a second arrest two months later, he escaped in handcuffs.[11] In 1887 while in Santa Monica and Los Angeles, he was arrested at least three times and was the defendant in the first recorded court case of the shell game in Los Angeles.[12] In Denver in 1889, Burns received fifteen days for stealing a valise.[13] Within two months he was arrested for waving a pistol around on 32nd and Holladay streets, vowing to shoot someone. His

[1] *Daily Register Call* 11/21/1879.
[2] *Inter Ocean* 09/07/1881, p. 8.
[3] *RMN* 12/09/1879, p. 8.
[4] *RMN* 04/15/1880, p. 5.
[5] *True West Magazine, 04*/1995.
[6] *San Diego Union*, 08/26/1881.
[7] *Tucson Daily Citizen, 08/28/1881.*
[8] *Nugget,* 11/17/1881.
[9] Boyer, p. 171.
[10] *RMN* 06/26/1883, p. 8.
[11] *RMN* 08/14/1883, p. 4.
[12] *Los Angeles Times* 03/27/1887, & 08/10/1887, p. 3, & 12/22/1887, p. 3.
[13] *RMN* 05/02/1889, p. 8.

wife had run off with another man, and he was searching for them.[1] In 1890 Burns was in Denver where he was known as a smooth operator. On July 16, 1890, Chief of Detectives Loar gave him twenty-four hours to leave the city.[2] Burns then vanished until 1892 when he showed up in Creede, probably as a member of the Soap Gang.[3] He dropped in and out of the Gang as he traveled around the state. In February 1896 he was with Jeff and "ten fierce men" when arrested for vagrancy in Cripple Creek and ordered to leave. On March 10, 1896, in Denver, he witnessed the saloon shooting of Aquilla "Dick" Hawkins.[4] The *Denver Evening Post* wrote, "He was never suspected of earning a dollar honestly, and was always regarded as a crook who might be guilty of committing any crime from petite larceny to murder."[5] In 1898 he joined Jeff in Alaska and worked for him until deported. His name appears on the roster of Jeff's Skaguay Military Company.

Though large gaps remain in Burns' record, all of it that shows, which is considerable, is bad. In Denver, Creede, and Skaguay, Jeff found uses for such a one as "Big Ed" Burns, who was larcenous, violent, and deadly. About 1908, he was given a five-year prison term for swindling a railroad promoter out of $2,000 in Danville, Kentucky. Two years into serving his sentence, he died at the age of 86.[6]

Cady, Tom P. "Sure-Shot" and "Troublesome Tom": Sometimes spelled "Kady." Operated shell games for Jeff.[7] Known for his nasty temper and habit of carrying a 12-inch dirk.[8] Followed Jeff to Creede in 1892 and back to Denver. Accompanied Jeff to Mexico in the 1894 in effort to recruit a private army for the President of Mexico.[9] Became a prime suspect with Jeff in the 1892 shooting death of Cliff Sparks.[10] Possibly followed Jeff to Alaska and became Dyea's underworld boss.[11]

Casey, W. H. (or C. W. Casey): May also be known as "Handsome" Casey. Arrested 1893 with Soap Gang members for vagrancy.[12] Arrested 1894 as one of the "Big Five."[13]

Chase, Ed, "Big Ed": Business partner of Jeff in several enterprises. Arriving in Denver in 1860, he became first "czar" of the gamblers. His name appears in Deadwood, South Dakota, in May 1878 as manager of the Morton Club House, a gambling room, and on July 8, 1878, Chase shot a man known only as George.[14] In 1889 he was Jeff's partner in the Denver Tivoli Club. In 1890 he became president of the Colorado Policy Association; operators of the shops paid the "Association" to

---

[1] *RMN* 07/25/1889, p. 2.

[2] *RMN*, 07/17/1890. p. 5.

[3] *Tacoma Daily News*, 04/08/1892, & Devere.

[4] *RMN* 03/18/1896, p. 8.

[5] *Denver Evening Post* 02/15/1896, p. 5.

[6] *The Hazel Green Herald* 01/13/1910, & *The Adair County News* 02/02/1910, p. 1.

[7] *San Francisco Call* 09/04/1898.

[8] *RMN* 10/02/1889.

[9] *RMN* 02/01/1895.

[10] *RMN* 10/12/1892, pp. 1-2.

[11] *Gulf Coast Breeze* 06/10/1898.

[12] *RMN* 04/25/1893, p. 3.

[13] See "Big Five" this section.

[14] Deadwood.

protect them from police. For half a century Chase organized the underworld into a voting block that was traded for protection of his numerous sporting houses. Jeff was also a partner in this enterprise.

Conlin, Claude Alexander: Reported Soap Gang member in Skaguay. First swindled by the Soap Gang with the shell game and then taken into the gang roster. In the 1920s Conlin, billed as "The man who knows," became one of the highest paid magicians and mentalists of his time.[1]

Daniels, Tom: Believed first worked in the Doc Baggs gang and later the Soap Gang. An accomplished bunco artist, he once bilked a man in Illinois for $10,000.[2] Arrested with others in a bunco swindle in 1884.[3]

Deutsch, William, "Henry Dutch": Managed several saloons, such as the Palace Theater and the Alhambra, and properties including the building that housed the Tivoli Club. He is listed between 1889 and 1897 as the manager and proprietor. Listed in 1891 news article about saloons illegally open one Sunday.[4]

Eddy, R. M.: Probable Soap Gang member in Skaguay. Believed by this author to be one of the lesser-known gang members able to escape Skaguay to Juneau after Jeff's death. Sixteen days after Soapy was killed, Eddy was interviewed by the *Washington Post* of Washington, DC, in which he spoke of Jeff as a close friend.[5]

Edwards, Henry, "Yank V. Fewclothes," and "Hank": Born 1848.[6] A dealer in honey and beeswax when Jeff brought him into the Soap Gang as a steerer and a booster. Longtime resident of Denver who had stories to tell of Jeff's Denver in 1914. (He is treated at length elsewhere.)

Foster, John H. "the Kid": Skaguay city counsel member. Member of the Blonger Gang in 1923 when arrested in a monumental raid that netted 20 of the main gang and were shut down.[7]

Foster, W. E. "Slim-Jim": Soap Gang steerer in Skaguay. First name often mistaken as "Jim" due to his handle, "Slim-Jim." Foster was one of the men who led John Stewart down the alley beside Jeff's saloon in Skaguay to a three-card monte game in which Foster grabbed Stewart's gold sack and ran with it. Once arrested after Jeff's death, Foster escaped out a second story window and was almost hanged by vigilantes. At trial, he was fined $1,000 and sentenced to a year in prison with an additional six months for assaulting Stewart. Dr. Fenton Whiting of Skaguay called Foster "a dangerous hop head, ..., a killer..., under the dope of course."[8]

Gallagher, Edward "Red" or "Reddy" "Kid": Probable Soap Gang strong-arm man, Denver and Skaguay. Between 1891 and 1893, Bat Masterson financed Gallagher, a popular Denver boxer.[9] Probably after his boxing career waned,

---

[1] Beckmann, p. 2.

[2] *RMN* 02/03/1886, p. 6.

[3] *RMN* 04/19/1884, p. 8.

[4] *RMN* 02/23/1891, p. 8.

[5] See "Eddy" in Index for quotation.

[6] *Denver Post* 11/15/1914, p. 10. Item 163, author's col. Edwards states he is 66 at time of interview.

[7] *Fort Collins Courier* 08/16/1923, p. 3.

[8] Ltr fr Fenton B. Whiting to "Georgie," 07/27/1929, Alaska Historical Library, MS4, Box 13, #3.

[9] *RMN* 08/19/1891, p. 3, & 01/22/1893, p. 2.

Gallagher turned to crime. In 1898 he was in Skaguay. A photograph of the People's Theater shows a poster with his name displayed. He likely worked for Jeff as muscle until Jeff was killed. On September 13, 1898, Gallagher was arrested in Seattle for burglary. The mug shot lists his occupation as bartender.[1] "Red" had a long career in the demimonde. Later in Denver he joined the Blonger Gang. In 1922 he posted bond for Lou Blonger.[2] Evidence shows there might have been two Gallaghers. This author believes Reddy Gallagher and Edward "Red" Gallagher are the same person. Historian Thomas Noel writes,

> Patrick R. "Reddy" Gallagher ... was called "Reddy" because of his red hair and readiness for fisticuffs. As Denver's prime proponent of ... boxing, he was a pugilist himself, coached others, staged many fights, and, in the 1920s, began a long career as a sports writer for *The Denver Post*. Although he supposedly could neither read nor write, Reddy could dictate and knew more about boxing than anyone else around.[3]

The International Boxing Research Organization lists his name as Stephan Gallagher, born February 4, 1865, and reports that on August 13, 1893, Gallagher fought a "fake" fight with "Denver" Ed Smith. Gallagher won the match and stated that "if Smith did not like the decision, he would fight him again."[4]

Hoffses Albert or Alton E. "Big Al": Real name may have been Hoffesky.[5] In 1884 he was a door-keeper for the Palace Theater and was arrested for fraudulently registering a "large number of names" for an election.[6] First recorded as a member of the Soap Gang in October 1894 when he was bailed out by Jeff who hired an attorney as well.[7] He was arrested in the Tivoli Club during a sting operation a little over a month later.[8] He was arrested with the gang twice in February of 1895.[9] Hoffses shot and killed James "Duke of Halstead" Thornton in Chase's office of the Inter Ocean club on October 11, 1906. He was found guilty of voluntary manslaughter.[10]

Jackson, W. H. (also W. K.) "Professor": Soap Gang affiliate and member in Skaguay. Real name may be Turner Jackson as so written during his last court trial in 1898.[11] Called the "Professor" for ability to exude intelligent qualities to convince victims he was an expert in the field he portrayed. Arrested 1894 as one of the "Big Five."[12] Extremely vile and vicious, he followed Jeff from Denver to Alaska and was one of the men who swindled and robbed John Stewart of his gold sack, the affair that

---

[1] Reedstrom, p. 212.

[2] *RMN* 08/26/1922.

[3] Noel, Colorado Catholicism.

[4] Gallagher.

[5] *RMN* 11/02/1884, p. 4.

[6] *RMN* 11/02/1884, p. 4.

[7] *Denver Evening Post* 10/23/1894, p. 2.

[8] *RMN* 12/07/1894, p. 3.

[9] *Denver Post* 02/19/1895. *Denver Post* 02/27/1895.

[10] Parkhill, p. 67.

[11] Criminal case 1014-US vs. Turner Jackson. Record Group 21 – US District Courts. Box 16 – 01/01/05(2). National Archives and Records Administration, Pacific Alaska Region, Anchorage, Alaska.

[12] See "Big Five" this section.

led to Jeff's death. He was on the wharf with Jeff the night Jeff was shot dead. Jackson was convicted and sent to prison for a total of ten years for the robbery of Stewart and the assault on J. M. Tanner.

King, Silas: Probable Soap Gang member. Arrested for bunco steering in 1893[1] and 1895. The latter incident involved a gang member impersonating a police officer.[2]

Leery, Dan, "Mysterious Dan": Soap Gang member "in good standing":

> "Dan" Leery, commonly known amongst the confidence gang as "Mysterious Dan," came up before Magistrate Barnes yesterday on ... vagrancy. He was arrested Saturday night and bailed out by "Soapy" Smith. His standing with the police is sufficiently accounted for by that fact. The evidence was withdrawn against him yesterday morning, the "sucker" having "slept it over," and even the patrolman had forgotten what he had arrested him for.[3]

Lewis, George W.: Gambler and steerer who worked with Charles "Doc" Baggs in Denver as early as 1875. In San Francisco 1882, killed 17-year-old Ed Patterson. Later worked with Jeff. He may be the man involved with the finding of and later suing for possession of McGinty, the petrified man in Creede. Shot and killed by Eugene Borel in Ogden, Utah, February 26, 1893.[4]

Light, William Sidney "Cap": "Cap," as he was called, is short for *Captain*. This sometimes Soap Gang member and lawman with the reputation of a killer, and brother-in-law of Jeff Smith requires an extended section. Born in Belton, Texas, in 1863 or 1864, he was a barber there when in 1883-84, at age twenty, he was offered and accepted the position of deputy marshal and later assistant city marshal. He tended to use his gun at any provocation and was alluded to as a "good sort of fellow—to get away from."[5] He is believed to have been a member of the posse that tracked down and fatally shot local desperado William Northcott on March 24, 1884. In Temple, Texas, June 1887, Light married Eva Katherine Smith, Jeff's younger sister. In 1890 they had a son, William Jeff Light, and in 1892, a daughter, Emma Ruby Light.

In Belton in the fall of 1889, Light killed his second man. Sam Hasley was a trouble-maker with a deputy sheriff's commission that allowed him to carry a gun. Drunk and disorderly, Hasley was ordered by Light to go home. Instead, Hasley rode his horse onto the sidewalk and dared the young lawman to do something about it. Light tried to arrest Hasley, and Hasley drew his revolver. Light drew and fired.

In August 1889 as deputy marshal of Temple, Light was taking prisoner Ed Cooley to jail when Cooley attempted to escape. Light fired at him, but the outcome of that event is unknown. In March 1890, Felix Moralas was drunk and causing trouble in Temple's Cotton Exchange Saloon. When confronted by Deputy Light, Moralas attempted to pull his gun. Light was faster. Moralas sank to the floor and died with, according to the newspaper, "his pistol in one hand and a beer glass in the other."

---

[1] *Denver Post* 02/27/1893.
[2] *Denver Post* 02/07/1895.
[3] *RMN* 08/20/1889.
[4] *RMN* 03/02/1893, p. 5.
[5] *RMN* 12/27/1893, p. 3.

Next, in Brownwood, Texas, Light killed a man who had trifled with him. From Brownwood, he came to Denver in about 1891 and joined up with his brother-in-law, Jeff. He worked as a steerer in the Soap Gang, and his strong-arm experience made him ideal to have around when violence was called into play.[1] He was with Jeff at the Glasson Detective Agency attack in October 1891.

In March 1892, he was appointed deputy marshal in Creede. Here he shot and killed his last man, "Reddy" McCann.[2] McCann's friends accused Light of murder. He fled to Denver[3] and then returned to Temple. Here in June 1892, he applied for a detective position with the Gulf, Colorado & Santa Fe Railroad. He was turned down. It appears Light believed the railroad's chief detective, T. J. Coggins, was responsible for the denial. One day while drinking, Light approached Coggins and struck him repeatedly with his fists and pistol barrel. Light was arrested for the assault, and when asked why he attacked Coggins, he replied, for "causing good men to lose their jobs." At Light's hearing on the assault charge, Coggins rose from his seat, aimed his .44 revolver at Light's head, and fired several shots. One bullet entered near his right ear and another into his neck. Light's wounds were pronounced fatal, but he eventually fully recovered. Coggins was arrested for attempted murder but never faced trial.

Light again took up barbering. When a Denver district attorney sought his arrest for the McCann shooting, a fake obituary for Light appeared in the *News*. Its false information about his life and family seemed designed to keep authorities from tracking Light.[4] Jeff likely had a hand in, if, indeed, he did not write, his brother-in-law's bogus death notice.

His real obituary hints of deaths attributed to Light that never came to justice.

> It was recalled that all his killings and shooting scrapes occurred when the other man's gun was elsewhere, or in other words, when the victim was powerless to return blow for blow and shot for shot. Then the story was told that Light knew more than he cared to tell of a cold-blooded murder where, on a lonely road on a dark night, a Winchester rifle played an important part in removing one whose antagonism was not relished.[5]

Light died when he accidentally shot himself on Christmas Eve, 1893.

> When he met his death he was on a Missouri, Kansas and Texas train bound north from Belton. At Little River those on the car were expecting that an attempt would be made to hold up the train, and Light was examining his pistol, when it fell to the floor and went off, the ball entering the lower part of the groin and severing the femoral artery. He bled to death in a few minutes.[6]

Londoner, Wolfe: Used Jeff and Ed Chase's vote-stuffing powers to become mayor of Denver (1889-1891).[7] In return, Jeff and Ed's crooked games and street

[1] *RMN* 12/27/1893, p. 3.
[2] *Creede Candle* 04/01/1892.
[3] *Leadville Daily & Evening Chronicle* 04/05/1892, p. 2.
[4] *RMN* 10/21/1892, p. 2.
[5] *RMN* 12/27/1893, p. 3.
[6] *RMN* 12/27/1893, p. 3, & *Wild West Magazine* 04/2006, pp. 18-22.
[7] Leonard, *Denver*, p.70.

swindles were "protected." So long as the media did not link the mayor with Denver's criminal element, Jeff had a highly placed friend in government. During the election fraud trial of 1890, the alliance among Jeff, the mayor, and the police chief became known as the "firm of Londoner, Farley & Smith."[1] In 1891, the Colorado Supreme Court voided the election and ordered Londoner from office.[2]

Maher, Mike: Young Soap Gang member who operated the "exchange," a stock market-like fraud. During the 1889 city election for mayor, he admitted in court that he had fraudulently voted nearly one hundred times more than legally allowed.[3]

Masterson, William Barclay "Bat": Born November 26, 1853, in Iberville County, Quebec, Canada, Masterson led an exciting life. He worked as a buffalo hunter, army scout, professional gambler, business manager, frontier peace officer, sports promoter, and newspaper man. He was a lawman in Dodge City, Kansas (1877-1879), and Trinidad, Colorado (1882-1883), and longtime friend of lawman Wyatt Earp. While in Denver, he met and became good friends with Jeff and some of the Soap Gang. He was involved with Jeff in Denver's 1889 election fraud, and from Jeff's partner Ed Chase, in 1888 he managed and possibly purchased the Palace Theater.[4] Although his name appears in connection with the Palace, no evidence exists to show he actually owned it. According to the *News* Masterson had hopes of turning it into a boxing exhibition theater.[5] The Palace was sold to William Devere, the stage manager in 1891.[6] In 1892 Masterson worked for Martin "Mart" H. Watrous, managing the Denver Exchange saloon and gambling complex in Creede. He later managed the infamous Arcade clubrooms and restaurant for Pete and Charlie Persson.[7] Jeff and Bat corresponded until near the time of Jeff's death.[8]

McAttee, George: Alias "Jimmy Blaine."[9] Worked with Jeff from the early 1880s into the mid 1890s. A Harvard graduate whose big win at a gambling table in Salt Lake City transformed him into a gambler. It is written that "he existed almost entirely through the generosity of Jeff Smith, who fed him, clothed him, and kept him in pocket money, cigars, and liquor ... as a sort of court jester. The fallen alumnus of Harvard university became the regular butt for his benefactor's good-natured pranks."[10] Arrested with John Hamm and others on October 14, 1889. In 1892 became the caretaker or "keeper of the Petrified Man."[11] In December 1895 was arrested in Cripple Creek, Colorado, for vagrancy.[12] Served a 28-day sentence and was released January 25, 1896. Two days later he fell dead in a Cripple Creek restaurant.[13]

---

[1] *RMN* 08/18/1889.

[2] Leonard, *Denver*, p. 71.

[3] *RMN* 03/31/1890.

[4] Secrest, pp. 143-145. Ortiz, p. 45. *RMN* 09/05/1889, p. 3.

[5] *RMN* 09/05/1889, p. 3.

[6] *RMN*, 10/27/1887, p. 5 & 11/15/1887, p. 1.

[7] DeArment, *Bat*, p. 345.

[8] *Jeff and Bat corresponded...*: See Index for location of ltrs.

[9] *RMN* 10/02/1889.

[10] *Denver Republican* 01/28/1896.

[11] *Denver Republican* 01/28/1896.

[12] *RMN* 10/15/1889, p. 7.

[13] *Denver Republican* 01/28/1896.

Millsap, George "Joe Armstrong": Believed originally a member of the "Doc" Baggs gang as arrested with others from it in 1884.[1] Possibly leader of a rival gang after Baggs left, which may have included J. B. Palmer, Billy Kelly, Cornelius Sullivan, and Tom Daniels. Later believed to have joined the Soap Gang. Arrested 1878 for assault.[2] A newspaper reported his having served eleven months in the Colorado penitentiary for theft. Arrested in Cheyenne 1878 for assaulting his wife with intent to kill. Called "one of the hardest customers in Cheyenne."[3] Arrested 1879 in Denver using the alias "Joe Armstrong" and again in 1886,[4] perhaps to be kept from being extradited back to Cheyenne for trial. Once bilked a man in Kansas City of $13,000.[5] Reported as being "known from the Missouri to San Francisco."[6]

Mizner, Wilson: Soap Gang member in Skaguay. Mizner had been a miner, confidence man, ballad singer, medical lecturer, cardsharp, hotel man, Broadway playwright, Hollywood screenwriter, restaurateur, songwriter, and prizefight manager. Alva Johnston, author of *The Legendary Mizners* (1942), writes of Mizner, "He was an idol of low society and a pet of high." In 1897 at age twenty, he arrived in Skaguay from San Francisco with good training from underworld masters. In Skaguay, Johnston writes, he received polishing and finishing from

> the greatest American professor of sharp practice, gentle larceny, and all-around crime—the celebrated Soapy Smith, the American version of *The Man Who Would be King*. ... Of all Mizner's idols and mentors, none had a greater influence on his life than Soapy.[7]

In 1929, Mizner had become a partner in Hollywood's Brown Derby restaurant. He had known Wyatt and Josephine Earp in Alaska, probably Nome. When Earp died on January 13, 1929, in Los Angeles, Mizner was among the pallbearers.[8]

Morris, John H. "Fatty Gray," and "Fatty": A slick and despicable early member of the Soap Gang acquired by Jeff in Fort Worth, Texas. Talents included the "diamond game" in which fakes were sold as real. A steerer posing as an appraiser would examine the stones and pronounce them worth much more than asked for them.[9] Early on, "Fatty" dropped out of sight for a time and then rejoined Jeff in 1887.[10] He had written from New Orleans, February 13, 1887, asking to come

> Friend Jeff,
>
> Doc Watts and Jim Cambell came in town the other day and told me they saw you at St. Louis. Further more said that Denver was about to be opened up again, if so I would like to get [in on] the in side. I can assure you of more

---

[1] *RMN* 04/19/1884, p. 8.

[2] *RMN* 01/11/1878.

[3] *Weekly Register Call* 01/17/1879.

[4] *RMN* 04/04/1879. And 08/14/1886, p. 2.

[5] *RMN* 02/03/1886, p. 8.

[6] *RMN* 05/18/1886.

[7] Johnston, pp. 83-84. The Man Who Would Be King: title of a short story by Rudyard Kipling, 1889.

[8] *Los Angeles Times* 01/17/1929. "Pioneer Folk gather at Rites of Peace Officer."

[9] *RMN* 05/18/1886.

[10] Telegram fr Charles Anderson in Deadwood, SD, to "Fatty Gray" in Denver, 05/06/1887. Geri Murphy col.

money then any one on the account of playing different then before, which is called the Sucker Send or Mr. Parker. It would take to long to explain it in writing but it is stronger then Straight Send. I have made considerable money since coming here at it and at [indecipherable]. You [the person conducting the swindle] can send them to New York for their money and they will bitch it [indecipherable]. I sent a telegram to Emporia, KS for 1000 because with it ... [they] never kicked [at being sent to another city to collect]. Watts told me that if you know my whereabouts you would send for me. If so I will come immediately. This is a confidential letter and I wish you would not show it around town. Do you know where Rebel [indecipherable] is? Let me know the particulars if you have time to write.

Yours Respectfully   "Fatty Gray"   J. H. Morris
        P.O. New Orleans, La[1]

In 1889, after his association with Jeff and his criminal methods and home address were exposed in the *Rocky Mountain News*,[2] he left the Soap Gang and Denver behind. Fatty was killed in a saloon in Murray, Utah, but the date is unknown.[3]

Palmer, Joe: This Soap Gang member, a fighter and intensely loyal to Jeff, was rewarded with Jeff's friendship and trust. Palmer's known criminal record begins ominously in Montgomery County, Georgia, when with nine others, at about age nineteen, he was charged with conspiracy and murder. On the night of May 2, 1881, ten men disguised themselves, went to the home of a black man named Jerry Hamilton, called him out, and beat him with clubs so badly that he died.[4] No trial outcome was found. Seven months later a story in Chicago's *Daily Inter Ocean* told of "two thugs named Joe Kelley and Joe Palmer" who robbed a telegraph operator at gunpoint for "only a few dollars." The men were quickly arrested and identified, but while being photographed, they fiercely resisted, with Palmer trying to stab an officer with a pair of shears. Both were subdued and "locked up in the dungeon...."[5]

Palmer came to Denver and joined the Soap Gang. In 1892 while protecting Jeff in Creede, both his thumbs were shot off. In 1893 as a Denver saloonkeeper, he was arrested for larceny,[6] but in 1894 he was commissioned as a deputy sheriff in Arapahoe County.[7] With partners in 1895, he operated the Missouri House saloon.[8] Also in 1895 when Jeff had gone on a tear and was surrounded, Palmer was with him and said, "If yer goin' to shoot'er up, Jeff, I'm widge."[9] But Palmer did not go with Jeff to Alaska. He remained in Colorado, operating out of Denver and continuing to add to

---

[1] Ltr fr John Morris to Jeff R. Smith II, 02/13/1887. Jefferson R. "Little Randy" Smith col. The many instances of nonstandard diction, spelling, and style are as they appear in the Ltr.

[2] RMN 07/31/1889.

[3] *Denver Post* 11/15/1914, p. 10. Item 163, author's col.

[4] *Georgia Weekly Telegraph & Messenger* 06/17/1881.

[5] *Daily Inter Ocean* 11/29/1881, p. 8, & 11/30/1881, p. 6.

[6] *RMN* 05/03/1893, p. 3.

[7] *RMN* 10/14/1894, p. 14.

[8] *RMN* 11/15/1896, p. 11. And *RMN* 12/27/1896, p. 5.

[9] *Denver Times* 05/16/1895.

his record of trouble. In 1897 he was involved in a severe attack on a gambler.[1] The *Denver Evening Post* reported what happened in court when Palmer appeared before the police magistrate. The assistant city attorney asked Officer Kennedy what he knew of Palmer. "Nothing good," was the reply. "He is no good." Asked whom Palmer associated with, Kennedy said, "Thieves, vagabonds, confidence men." When asked if Palmer was ever known to work, Kennedy said, "He kept a saloon about a year ago," and "He is known as a confidence man. He admits it. He was one of Soapy Smith's right hand men." Palmer, however, had witnesses who spoke on his behalf, claiming he had "worked on a farm all summer raising tomatoes..., and after his return, worked for one of the political leaders, investigating ... the last election."

Finally the magistrate said, "Mr. Palmer has a bad record. But lately it seems, he has earned his money honestly. He is discharged."[2] This finding, based on tomato farming, suggests Joe Palmer had himself a powerful political insider. Others like Jeff apparently found Palmer an asset worth protecting.

In 1898 in Colorado Springs, Palmer was on one side of a battle between factions of the Denver Silver Republican party. A standoff occurred between scores of armed men in a Colorado Springs opera house. In the fight, a rifle bullet scored the cheek of Palmer and took "a piece from the end of his nose." In reporting this fracas, the *Denver Evening Post* listed some of Palmer's story, writing that he was

> familiarly known as "Rubberneck" Palmer, who ... is well known all over the state as a bad man, buncoer, and political thug. During the boom at Creede he gained a reputation as a gun fighter. ... He has been a bunco steerer and for a time he worked with such characters as Tom Quinn, known as the "Ring Con Kid," "Beefsteak" Mike Hennessy, "Third Rim" Casey, "Soapy" Smith, "Rev." Joe Bowers and others of that ilk. ...
>
> Palmer has been arrested many times for bunco games and highway robbery, but he has influential relatives here and was never convicted of anything greater than assault and battery. ... For a long time he lived with a woman on "the row" and compelled her to contribute to his support. The woman finally got tired of this and threw him out.... Since that time he has been "steering" for a "big mit"[3] joint on Seventeenth street and the "Pickwick club," crooked gambling dens known to the police, but immune because they pay rent to a man with a big pull. He usually takes what it pleases him to call an active part in local politics and attempts to control the vote of a certain element of "hop fiends," but he is not a success as a politician.... He has been beaten nearly to death on numerous occasions in houses of ill repute for his actions towards the women of those resorts. ... He is considered lucky to have lived so long.[4]

---

[1] *Denver Evening Post* 12/18/1897, p. 2, & 12/20/1897, p. 9.

[2] *Denver Evening Post* 12/20/1897, p. 9.

[3] *big mit* or *mitt.* "A confidence game involving fraud in a card game." (Partridge, *Underworld*)

[4] *Denver Evening Post* 09/08/1898, p. 10.

In 1907, at age forty-five, Palmer was placed in the county hospital's insane ward. He was reported to have been imagining for some time that "he was being pursued by some of his old-time enemies and [that] they were threatening to shoot him."[1]

Palmer, L. S.: Member of the Doc Baggs Gang (arrested 1884 with other members[2]) and later of the Soap Gang. "L. S. Palmer" appears on a property lease in Creede 1892. Jeff secured access to prize Creede lots, some through the powers of Denver "ladies" who persuaded land owners to lease to him. Palmer's name also appears as a member of the Denver Improved Order of Red Men, Comanche, No. 23, of which Jeff was a member.[3] Joe Palmer and L. S. Palmer may be the same person.

Panknin, E. S.: One of the earliest Soap Gang members. Jeff met Panknin in Fort Worth between 1877 and 1882. An 1898 letter shows they kept in touch.[4]

Parker, Ned "Professor," "Banjo": A mainstay member of the Soap Gang since 1889,[5] in April working with Jeff in election fraud.[6] In July 1889, Parker named an accessory to Jeff in the near deadly assault on *News* editor John Arkins.[7] A traveling bunco man throughout the west from early on. In 1877 listed as staying at the Grand Central Hotel in Denver.[8] He is dealt with prominently in this book.

Pratt, Charlie E.: Among earliest known Soap Gang members. With Jeff in Fort Worth (*circa* 1876-79). In Spokane, Pratt opened a vaudeville theater called The Louvre. As letters to Jeff show, Pratt remained in contact throughout Jeff's life. One is written on 5/20/1895 on stationary from The Louvre.[9] Another dated 10/7/1896 cites conditions in San Salvador, Guatemala. Jeff wrote to him in February 1897. The letter of reply addresses hard times trying to make money in Guatemala and advises Jeff not to come. One line from the letter sums up the bad conditions: "If you have got any enemies you want to fix, send them down here."[10]

Roberts, G. E. "Auctioneer": Soap Gang member. In 1889, an "auctioneer" in Jeff's mock auction house on Seventeenth Street, and in 1889, arrested for swindling along with Jeff and Bascomb Smith, J. W. Allen, John "Fatty Gray" Morris, and John "Shoot-Your-Eye-Out-Jack" Vermillion.[11] Roberts may have been with Jeff in the August 30, 1889, Pocatello depot gun battle.

Saportas, E. W.: Brother of William Saportas. General manager of the Packing Guide & Information Company of Alaska, a probable front for swindling. Killed onboard the *Clara Nevada* when it sunk on February 5, 1898.[12]

---

[1] *Durango Wage Earner* 12/26/1907.

[2] *RMN* 04/19/1884, p. 8.

[3] *RMN* 01/16/1893.

[4] *Alaska–Yukon Magazine,* 12/1907, p. 335.

[5] *RMN* 08/02/1889.

[6] *RMN* 03/20/1890, & 03/15/1890, p. 6.

[7] *RMN* 07/30/1889.

[8] *Daily RMN* 08/23/1877.

[9] Ltr to Jeff R. Smith II fr Charlie Pratt, 05/20/1895. Geri Murphy col.

[10] *Alaska–Yukon Magazine* 12/1907, p. 335.

[11] *RMN* 08/18/1889.

[12] *Skaguay News* 02/18/1898, p. 4.

Saportas, William F. "Billy": Brother of E. W. Saportas. Said to be a New York City newspaper reporter,[1] he joined up with the Soap Gang in 1897 in Skaguay. Proprietor of the Holly House restaurant and lodging house[2] He worked as a reporter for the *Daily Alaskan* where he could control what was reported in the newspaper as well as steer victims to Jeff's establishments.

Simmons, Joe "Gambler Joe": Soap Gang member. Managed Jeff's Tivoli Club in Denver, 1890, and Jeff's Orleans Club in Creede, 1892. According to William Devere's poem "Two Little Busted Shoes," Simmons also dealt faro for Jeff in Creede.[3] Simmons and Jeff had worked together in Denver from Jeff's earliest times there, and they were the best of friends. So when Joe died of pneumonia on March 18, 1892, Jeff took it hard, openly displaying emotion. Both Creede newspapers,[4] a poet, and the *Illustrated Police News*[5] told of Jeff's mourning. The poem "Jeff and Joe," written and published by Devere in 1892, addresses their friendship.[6]

Smith, Bascomb (also **Bascom**): Younger brother of Jeff Smith, born 1869. Joined the Soap Gang around 1887.[7] In 1889 Jeff opened a cigar store and named it Bascomb, Smith & Company. The store was a front for swindles and set-up poker games in a back room. Bascomb was involved with Jeff in fights and the gun fight at the Pocatello train depot on August 30, 1889.[8] In 1892 Bascomb joined his brother in Creede. In 1893 he held a deputy sheriff commission, which he was known to abuse.

> John Cooney was arrested at a late hour last night for an assault to kill at Nineteenth and Larimer. His head was badly beaten. It is claimed by his friends that he is an innocent party, and that he was assaulted by two deputy sheriffs—Bascom[b] Smith and Ingersoll. The stories of the different parties are conflicting. Two shots were fired in the melee.[9]

On June 23, 1893, Bascomb shot and killed "Shotgun Harry" Smith, a rival gambler.[10] Luckily for Bascomb, many friends witnessed the gunfight, and it was ruled self-defense. Then on a drunken spree with Jeff, Bascomb beat Arcade owner John Hughes nearly to death. That excess landed Bascomb a one year prison sentence.[11]

After release, Bascomb did not rejoin his older brother. When Jeff was killed, Bascomb did what he could to see that his brother's widow received his estate, but most of it had already been stolen. According to family genealogy, Bascomb is believed to have died in 1920 at age 51.

Smith, Ed "Denver Ed": Hired brawler for the gang. Born in Birmingham, England in 1866. He worked in iron and steel mills but boxing was his first love. His

---

[1] *Skaguay News* 12/31/1897.

[2] *Skaguay News* 11/19/1897, p. 4.

[3] *Tacoma Daily News* 04/08/1892, & Devere, William, pp. 92-95.

[4] *Creede Chronicle* 03/22/1892.

[5] *Illustrated Police News* 04/09/1892.

[6] Devere, p. 109-115.

[7] Ltr fr Frank A. Gibbons to Jeff R. Smith II 02/02/1887. Geri Murphy col.

[8] Hand-written Ltr fr Jeff R. Smith II to Mary Eva Smith 09/02/1889. Item 77, author's col.

[9] *RMN* 07/28/1893, p. 3. Newspapers and even Bascomb himself usually spelled his name "Bascom."

[10] *Aspen Times* 06/24/1893, p. 1.

[11] *RMN* 04/22/1895.

father, Bob Smith, was a celebrated fighter. Upon arrival in America, he located in Denver and remained there.[1] Four months after the Logan Park brawl, of which he was involved, Ed shot and killed Arthur Moody during a row.[2] Although the case outcome is unknown, Ed Smith was released and continued his boxing career.

Sullivan, Cornelius "Con Sullivan": Believed part of Doc Baggs gang (arrested with other members 1884).[3] Possible Soap Gang member in Creede (named in poem "Two Little Busted Shoes"), elected a Creede councilman, April 9, 1892.[4]

Taylor, John: Early Soap Gang member, apparently an active irregular. He may have been Soapy's mentor, the person called "Old Man" Taylor in early Soapy Smith biographies, but documentation is lacking. John Taylor and Jeff corresponded in 1886-87. Over time, Taylor found religion and broke with his criminal career in 1887.

Thornton, James "Duke of Halstead": A small-time crook, Probably from Halstead, Kansas, whose first known crime was stealing books from a store in 1886. He graduated into bar keeping for Ed Chase at the Palace Theater,[5] and the Mascot Theater on Blake Street, Denver.[6] In 1895 he opened an auction house in Denver with Soap Gang member Jackson.[7] In 1898 he worked for "Big Ed" Chase in the Inter-Ocean Club and hotel on Curtis Street.[8] He was the doorkeeper of Denver's Pavilion Club at the time of Jeff's death.[9] In December of 1898 he joined the Blonger gang where he was arrested for keeping a gambling room in the Blonger saloon at 1644 Larimer Street.[10] Thornton was shot dead in Chase's office of the Inter-Ocean in 1906 by Soap Gang member "Big Al" Hoffses.[11]

Triplett, Van B. "Old Man": Last name sometimes spelled "Tripplett." Soap Gang member in Denver and Skaguay. This long-time bunco man requires an expanded section. According to his newspaper obituary, he was born about 1841 in Virginia and was the originator of the gold brick scam. He began his criminal career young and prospered at it for forty years. He went to prison for swindling a Chinese man in Dayton, Ohio.[12] Sometime after his release in 1894, he joined the Soap Gang. Records show an 1876 arrest in Chicago for operating a bunco swindle.[13] He had a wife who was listed in Chicago's *Daily Inter Ocean* in 1893 as renting a furnished flat, waiting, it is supposed, for her husband's release from prison.

Famed con man George Devol wrote of Triplett,

> I had a partner at one time by the name of Tripp, and he was one of the smartest gamblers I ever worked with. He would play any and all games of

[1] *RMN* 07/15/1890, p. 3.
[2] *RMN* 11/17/1889, p. 6.
[3] *RMN* 04/19/1884, p. 8.
[4] *RMN* 04/10/1892, p. 2.
[5] *RMN* 06/04/1887.
[6] *Denver City Directory*, 1889.
[7] Hand-written Ltr fr George B. Fisher to Jeff R. Smith II, 11/08/1896. Item 12, author's col.
[8] DeArment, *Knights*, p. 177.
[9] *RMN* 07/20/1898, p. 10.
[10] *Denver Evening Post* 12/23/1898, p. 7.
[11] Parkhill, p. 67.
[12] *The Evening Times* 05/02/1901, p. 1.
[13] *Inter Ocean* 01/11/1876, p. 5.

chance, and would play them as high as any man in the country, and come as near winning all the time at most of them. He was a good, clever fellow.[1]

Devol recounted how he and "Tripp" as a partner would ride the Midwest railroads together, swindling travelers with three-card monte and stacked hands. Often Tripp would play the part of someone who was inexperienced with games of chance, such as a rancher or most often a cowboy. After playing this part in the swindle, Tripp would disappear only to reappear shortly "all dressed up so that no one would suspicion that he was ever a cow-boy."[2]

In Skaguay, Tripp impersonated a stampeder complete with pack (said to be filled with feathers, not the heavy contents of a gold seeker), working three-card monte at the Skaguay entrance to the White Pass trail. His job was to play his game, talk with returning stampeders, and discover who had gold. He would then direct or lead them himself to a "safe" assayer, saloon, or hotel in which the returnees would be relieved of some or all of their gold. Triplett operated the three-card monte game against John Stewart. Stewart's gold sack was grabbed by "Slim-Jim" Foster who handed it to Triplett, who in turn ran off while Foster and John Bowers held Stewart down.

After Jeff was killed, Triplett ran into the nearby hills. Alaska historian C. L. Andrews, who came to Skaguay six months after Jeff's death and who lived there for five years, reported hearing this account of Old Man Tripp's arrest:

> The story is told that Bowers came to Tripp, asleep in the forest on their second day out, shook him, and said, "Wake up! They're coming to hang us."
>
> "We should have been hung twenty years ago," was Tripp's reply. "I'm not going to stand it any longer. You're young and maybe can do it, but I can't, I'm going to get something to eat."
>
> They had eaten nothing but berries and roots. Tripp came down to Rice's restaurant and W. J. Rogers [a deputy] came to get him.
>
> "I've ordered a good dinner and I need it," Tripp said. "May I have it?"
>
> Rogers said yes. A crowd had gathered, angry and threatening.
>
> "They don't look good to me," Tripp said. "Will I be protected?"
>
> Rogers said there were two more guards.
>
> "Well, I'll chance it," Tripp said calmly.[3]

Afterward he was placed under guard in a third-floor room of the Burkhard Hotel.[4] Triplett was eventually tried, convicted of larceny, and sentenced to a year in prison.[5]

Vermillion, John Wilson "Texas Jack" and "Shoot-Your-Eye-Out Jack": Soap Gang member. Family members have identified him as John Wilson Vermillion, but some historians question the name.[6] According to Wyatt Earp, Vermillion was a carpenter by trade, but his skills included the use of a gun. He rode with Earp and "Doc" Holliday in 1882 on the large-scale manhunt for the killers of Wyatt's brother

[1] Devol, p. 164.

[2] Devol, p. 168, & pp. 164-68, 170-72, 183-85, 186-88, 217-18, 240-42.

[3] Andrews, *Alaska Sportsman*, p. 40.

[4] *Skaguay News* 07/15/1898.

[5] *Skaguay News* 12/23/1898

[6] Brand.

Morgan in Tombstone, Arizona.[1] At that time, he was known as "Texas Jack."[2] In May 1883, he joined Wyatt as a member of the "Dodge Peace Commission" during the Dodge City War.[3] By this time he had acquired a new moniker, that of "Shoot-Your-Eye-Out Jack." As yet no story accompanies this sobriquet. He joined the Soap Gang as a capper. Jeff mentions him as being present on April 2, 1889, in connection with an election fraud.[4] On August 18, 1889, he was arrested for "steering" in Jeff's mock auction house on Seventeenth Street. Arrested with Vermillion were Jeff, Bascomb, John Morris, and J. W. Allen.[5] He was with Bascomb and Jeff Smith in a brawl at Logan Park in August 1889, and he was with Jeff in a shootout at the Pocatello train depot on August 30, 1889. He is not mentioned as being with the gang again. Earp said Vermillion died in Chicago and was buried in Virginia.[6] An interview with Henry Edwards, however, indicates Vermillion died with his "boots on" in Utah.[7]

Walsh: Soap Gang member in Skaguay. Harry L. Suydam, in an article written for a magazine in 1901, Suydam, describes Walsh as

> a most brutal-looking man of almost herculean physique..., and he was known as Soapy's "right-bower." He was manipulating three English walnut half shells, under one of which was the alluring pea. Four men were apparently watching the pea. One of them had an axe on his shoulder, one carried a rifle, one had a fifty-pound sack strapped on his back and the other was leaning on a pack. All looked like the busy Argonauts of the trail. As a matter of fact, they were all accomplices, such as are known in mining camps as "boosters" or "cappers."[8]

Wilder, George W.: Soap Gang member in Denver and Skaguay. First recognized in 1890 as a self-proclaimed real estate speculator.[9] Arrested April 1893 as a "sure-thing" man with Frank Weldon, George Beck, Jeff Dunbar, A. B. Smith, John Bowers, James Jenks, and Handsome Casey.[10] Followed Jeff to Alaska. Arrested after Jeff was killed. Tried with Bowers, Foster, Jackson, and Triplett but acquitted.

Men of the bunco fraternity went to Jeff for opportunity, leadership, and protection. They wrote to him to share news of themselves and to ask him to send for them. Some Jeff regretted bringing into the Soap Gang. Some robbed him, and some became his enemy. But most kept contact with their boss for years after their last meeting. Loyalty was so strong in some cases among surviving old timers that decades after Jeff was killed, despite his widespread reputation as a ruthless bad man, they did not speak negatively of Jeff. They admired his shrewdness, polished

---

[1] Tefertiller, p. 233.
[2] Tefertiller, p. 233.
[3] DeArment, *Bat*, pp. 261-62.
[4] *RMN* 03/20/1890, p. 2.
[5] *RMN* 08/18/1889.
[6] *RMN* 08/18/1889.
[7] *Denver Post* 11/15/1914, p. 10. Item 163, author's col.
[8] Suydam, "Reign," p. 212.
[9] *RMN* 03/23/1890.
[10] *RMN* 04/25/1893, p. 3.

delivery of a swindle, organizational abilities, and standing as a political insider. They also admired him as one of them who could drink, shoot, gamble without regret, fight, and help the needy and desperate (even if he had helped to make them that way). With them he was square, and he was with them when they were In trouble. To them he had shown only good, and they were loyal to him for it.

Chapter 5
Soapy Smith Captures Denver and a Wife

Jeff, you have a lion by the tail. Swing it, don't let it swing you.
—Jefferson R. Smith II

The history of Jeff's first criminal empire in Denver shows how far a determined, intelligent criminal mind can go. Jeff had natural talent and skills refined by years of practice in cities and towns throughout the west. The particulars of his deals with city officials are impossible to know, but newspaper reports give clues to what took place behind closed doors. As Jeff became a fixture in the city, the *News* gave him the alias of "Soapy" and tried to end his rise, but Jeff would not be stopped. During his early years in Denver, Jeff continued to be in trouble, and it often seemed the law was close to shutting him down, but it always stopped short. Liking Denver and determining to settle there, he began to take root. And he married, a sure sign of settling in, though not of settling down.

Jeff's name was absent from the Denver newspapers for much of 1884 and for the first five months of 1885. He seems to have kept an extremely low profile as he established himself in the city. During this period, he might still have been traveling, and one trip might have led to a stay of many months. Eight years later, in 1893, the *Rocky Mountain News* published an uncharacteristically humorous story about Jeff, said to have been told by Jeff himself. The setting is among men aboard a train returning to Denver. Called upon for a story, Jeff told one that occurred on his return from the New Orleans World's Industrial and Cotton Centennial Exposition, which ran from December 16, 1884, to June 2, 1885.

SOAPY SMITH'S STORY
How His Eyes Were Blinded and How He Was Fooled.

The crowd of "sports" … found perennially partaking of the lavish hospitality of Col. Jefferson R. Smith, better known as "Soapy" Smith, the prince of bunco men, had drifted around to the prevalent bank hold-ups and railroad robberies as a topic of conversation. The party had been entertained with numerous blood-curdling tales of the James and Dalton gangs, interlarded with invitations from Jeff to "have something, boys." And a lull that succeeded one of the libations was broken by a suggestion that their host had not contributed to the fund of stories. Now, if there is one thing more than another that is characteristic of the Hon. Jefferson, it is his extreme modesty as to himself and his exploits. He blushingly announced that what he knew about robberies and desperadoes wouldn't hold a candle to the thrilling tales that had just been told, but he was finally induced to impose a severe strain upon his memory, and so began:

"It was several years ago—yes, Ed,[1] before I discovered the 'petrified man' at Creede. Don't interrupt me, or you'll make me forget. As I was saying, it was several years ago, during the world's fair at New Orleans. I had been down to take in the sights of the Mardi Gras festival. No, Ed, I said 'take in the sights.' I wasn't there on business, Shut up!

"Well, as I was about to remark before you inserted your insinuation, I was on my way back to Memphis after the festival was over. We had passed Little Rock and as I was feeling restless, I had been walking up and down the length of the train, from the smoker to the rear Pullman.

At the first station out of Little Rock I noticed a suspicious looking fellow board the train. At the next station another got on, and when the train station was reached and a third man mounted the car steps, my suspicions were aroused. You know I have quite a reputation as an amateur detective, and this conjunction of the planets incited my sleuthing propensities. I kept my eye on the trio and before long they got together in the smoker and began to hold a whispered conversation. I started to walk up the aisle past them to get a drink of water. Yes, sometimes, when I can't get anything else. Well, you know I am no sort of a hand to dress up and I looked rather rough in my slouch hat and high boots that day. I looked hard at them as I passed and I noticed that my glance had the effect of disturbing them considerably. I had on a big silver Mardi Gras badge, partially hidden by my coat, and I suppose they caught sight of that and the hump where my gun stuck out of my pocket and took me for a town marshal or a local officer of some kind.

"I went on up the aisle and was filling the cup at the water cooler when one of the trio got up and came forward. The car was nearly empty and I didn't know but he might attempt violence. But he held out his hand and said, 'How-d'ye do, friend.' I was surprised, but I shook hands with him, just to be polite, and was about to tell him he had the advantage of me, when he turned and walked back to his seat without a word.

"When I had recovered from the mild surprise that his behavior had occasioned I felt something crumpled up in the hand he had shaken, and upon looking I found it to be a crisp $100 note. 'Great Scott! What's this?' I thought. 'These fellows have been up to some mischief and think they can bribe me not to blow on them.' I happened to have a couple of thousand with me of course. If I'd been dead broke no one would have come near me.

"Did I get off at the next station and telegraph the police? No, you bet I didn't. I dropped into the nearest seat and spread my handkerchief over my face and the next thing I knew it was morning, and we were putting into Memphis.

---

[1] *Ed*: likely Big Ed Chase, Jeff's partner in many businesses, such as the Tivoli Club and enterprises, such as vote fixing.

"As I walked up the street the news boys were crying 'All about the big robbery,' and I bought a paper to see what it was. When I had read about ten lines I hired that boy to kick me ... round the city hall park, and then I went down to the Zoological gardens and let the monkeys make faces at me the rest of the day. Three men had broken into the court house of a county back in Mississippi and robbed the safe of the county treasurer of $12,000 in notes and coin! They had been followed to the nearest railroad, where they took the night train and that was the last seen of them. Twelve thousand dollars! And I was tickled over that measly little hundred. If I had only known—"

But here "Soapy" became entangled in his reflections and nobody thought it best to disturb him.[1]

The absence of Jeff's name from the newspapers ended in May 1885 when J. Brockman, a Denver resident, had Jeff arrested for swindling him. Jeff did not want to return the victim's money. The *Rocky Mountain News* reported the incident.

Says he was soaped by Smith.

An itinerant soap vendor, who sells prize packages of soap and who goes by the name of "Soapy" Smith, was arrested yesterday on complaint of a citizen who charges him with swindling. It appears that the citizen [J. Brockman] bought $30 worth of soap, under the impression, whether given him by Smith or not does not clearly appear, that he would realize $100 in prizes from the soap packages. All the money he did find in the packages appears to have been $1. He therefore says he was soaped by Smith and demands satisfaction.[2]

For the first time (on record), Jeff broke his rule against involving residents. Whether he did so deliberately or accidentally is not known. Also for the first time Jeff was identified in a *News* story as "Soapy" Smith.

The *Denver Tribune-Republican* also covered the arrest, writing of Jeff that

His occupation is that of a soap peddler, and he usually takes up his stand at the corner of Holladay [Market] and Seventeenth streets, where he attracts a large crowd of people by selling small packages of soap for $1 each, some of the packages containing bills ranging in value from $1 to $50, but the majority of the packages contain nothing but the small piece of soap.... Smith does business under a license issued to him by the city.[3]

The arresting officer, Henry W. Barr, could not prove Jeff had actually swindled Brockman, so he arrested Jeff for being in violation of the city lottery ordinance and had him held in jail pending receipt of $500 bond. The following day John P. Kinneavy, saloon entrepreneur and Jeff's friend, posted bail.[4] Records show that time and again Kinneavy would come to Jeff's aid. At the trial on the lottery charge, attorney Judge Miller represented Jeff and was able to get him off with a fine.[5]

---

[1] *RMN* 10/24/1893, p. 8.

[2] *RMN* 05/13/1885.

[3] *Denver Tribune-Republican* 05/13/1885.

[4] *RMN* 05/14/1885.

[5] *RMN* 05/14/1885, p. 2.

Smith claims that he does not pretend that everyone can be lucky and was very indignant when Judge Barnum fined him $25.00. He gave notice that he would appeal the case.[1]

Kinneavy was of Irish decent and is believed to have been raised in New York.[2] An early resident of Denver, he dabbled in its politics as a delegate in 1877.[3] During the yellow fever epidemic of the 1870s, he and his partner, Frank Parker, donated bar receipts from their saloon to aid victims.[4] Socially, Kinneavy was well liked by residents and peers. Of one Irish-American military organization, he was elected president.[5] In 1885, the *News* listed him as a wealthy land owner,[6] and by 1889, Kinneavy and co-partner T. W. O'Connor operated saloons at 1218 Sixteenth Street and another at 1321 Larimer, near city hall on Fourteenth. In 1892 he had a saloon at 1544 Larimer.

Certainly Brockman was not the only victim of Jeff's soap sale that day. The fine was $25, yet the victim lost $30. Jeff came away with $5 plus the money taken from others that day. No appeal of the case is recorded. On the day of the trial, the city council passed an ordinance against schemes like the soap racket, including

Any person who shall be engaged in any fraudulent scheme, device or trick upon the streets, through fares or public places or elsewhere in the city, or who by the aid, use or manipulation of any article or articles, thing or things what so ever in packages, boxes or otherwise arranged, whereby persons are induced, or sought to be induced, to purchase any such packages, articles or thing with a view to obtaining money, jewelry, or other property therein contained or therein connected in any manner. And it shall constitute no defense.[7]

The ordinance seemed designed to stop Jeff in particular and all bunco men in general. Some probably did seek more tolerant towns, but Jeff simply ignored the ordinance. Whether he felt it did not apply to him or that graft payments would shield him, the prize package soap sales continued. Nine days later, he was again in the news.

Slugging a Soap Man.

About 8 o'clock last evening a disgraceful fight occurred at the corner of Arapahoe and Sixteenth streets between an unknown person and the assistant for the soap peddler who is camped there during the day and evening. It seems that the unknown man had insulted the assistant and he proceeded to pound him up. After a number of blows were passed, most of which were struck by the assistant, Officer Bohanna appeared and marched them both off to jail.[8]

---

[1] *RMN* 05/17/1885.

[2] *RMN* 08/03/1879, p. 10.

[3] *Daily RMN* 09/07/1877, & 12/22/1877.

[4] Noel, *City*, p. 16.

[5] *RMN* 04/29/1880, p. 8.

[6] *RMN* 07/01/1885, p. 3.

[7] *RMN* 05/14/1885.

[8] *RMN* 05/22/1885.

Officer William Bohanna arrested both the assistant shill and the victim, but not Jeff. This is the first known recorded use of violence by the Soap Gang against their prey. Jeff was able to continue his street business for a solid month before the city council adopted a resolution on June 23, 1885, to rescind his peddler's license.[1]

So Jeff left Denver for an extended cooling off period. For forty-two days, from June 23 to August 1, 1885, there is no sign of him. Then his name appeared in an August 2, 1885, news account of a boxing match in Rawlins, Wyoming. Jeff was the timekeeper. Manager of one of the boxers was lawman and gambler Bat Masterson.[2] Jeff would be a timekeeper for other fights over the years. One occurred on November 18, 1887, eighteen miles from Denver, and another was in Boulder County, Colorado, in 1888. In this instance, one of the boxers was knocked down, and possibly when Jeff completed the ten count mark before the downed fighter again arose, the referee either did not hear Jeff's ten count indicating the fight was over or he chose to ignore the count and let the fight continue. Accusations of foul play were made but with no apparent repercussions.[3] Jeff again acted as timekeeper in a bout between "Denver Ed" Smith and Lawrence Farrell in 1894.[4]

While Jeff was away, bunco man Al Shoemaker tried to wear Jeff's mantle of master of the prize package racket. Like Jeff, he promised

> giving a man so much money for a certain package if the right one. Shoemaker as a successor to "Soapy" is a failure. "Soapy" is shrewd, good-hearted and generous. He likes to beat a sucker and spend his money with the boys. If he has a cent the half of it is the first man's that asks for it. Shoemaker is a cross between shrewdness and rascality. He is so thoroughly common that it is a surprise why any one should be roped in by him. Yet, Shoemaker will struggle. He might be able in his new role ... to gull the crowd for a while, and last night he attempted something out of his line—he attempted to play "Soapy's" sleight-of-hand trick and lost $50. Shoemaker shut up for the night. He will probably get some of his friends to stake him for $50 to-day and go into the business again, but his prestige is gone.[5]

Not much is known of Albert Shoemaker, or whether the *News* was correct in its assessment of his position in the gangs. In 1884 he was the leader of the ring of repeat voters and fraudulent registration.[6] Shoemaker disappeared from the limelight and did not reappear again until May 1892 when he was arrested for assault.[7]

The old adage that "a fool and his money are soon parted" was often observed in the 19th century, and newspaper reporters often poked fun at the ignorance of victims. Denver citizens found the stories of duped victims humorous reading, at times even agreeing with bunco men that victims deserved their losses. This attitude, however,

---

[1] *RMN* 06/23/1885, p. 8.

[2] *RMN* 08/02/1885.

[3] *RMN* 01/26/1888, p. 5.

[4] *RMN* 10/04/1894, p. 3.

[5] *RMN* 08/14/1885. "STREET STROLLERS."

[6] *RMN* 11/02/1884, p. 4.

[7] *RMN* 05/31/1892, p. 3.

was not enough to keep Jeff's bunco operations from public criticism and courtroom disfavor as the incidents of swindling increased. Jeff's solution was to erect a backstop of protection. He put the police, the courts, and the media on the payroll, management of which Jeff handled personally. Should cunning, skill, and planning not produce the illusion of lawfulness, that backstop kept trouble from breaking through to the Soap Gang and Jeff at its head.

Another dimension of Jeff's empire building required attention, the threat of violence and deadly force. If possible, rival bunco gangs would have Jeff evicted, jailed, or murdered to get him out of the way. Toughness was an effective way of keeping them at bay. Then, too, with an increase in operations, came an increase in the number of victims who, over their loss, might be inclined to put up a fight on the spot. Thus hard men of a fighting nature were allowed into the ranks of the Soap Gang. Strong-arming and outright robbery were normally frowned upon within the bunco fraternity. They raised consciousness to crime, and with sympathy nearly always in favor of victims, violence increased probability of arrest and prosecution even with bribes in place. Many were the quiet ways in which a victim could be rendered harmless, and they were usually worked with cunning and skill. However, periodically a victim could not be neutralized before, as the expression goes, he would "fly off the handle." Just as quick to react, however, were bunco men who were of a fighting sort. They felt their gain was rightfully theirs and tended to do whatever it took to keep it. Jeff was no exception. He was more than willing to put up a fight with his fists, cane, or pistol to keep money "worked" from a victim. This willingness imperiled each of Jeff's empires, hastened their demise, and eventually contributed to the sudden and violent end of his life.

In August 1885, the *News* reported a robbery in which the victim was drugged.

> John Lewis wandered into a Larimer Street dive last night and became intoxicated. While in that condition he was placed in a hack, taken outside the city limits and robbed of between $400 and $500. He was then dumped out on the prairie where he lay insensible till nearly morning, when he made his way to the city and reported his loss. He claims that he was drugged, and he probably was, as the gang who hangs around the notorious resort would not stop at murder if a $5 bill were in sight. This is the second occurrence of the kind that has happened at the same place within the past week.[1]

Drugging victims in saloons became popular for a period in Denver. It has not been established that Jeff knew anyone involved in these robberies or whether he was receiving tribute from those responsible. It can be guessed that he was and that probably he called a halt to them. They shocked the residents of Denver, who demanded something be done. A large percentage of these drug-induced robberies dropped off as quickly as they had begun, but they did not cease entirely.

Interest in arresting the guilty did not come from law enforcement but the ever-vigilant *Rocky Mountain News.* On the day of the story about the Lewis robbery, the *News* reported that about thirty bunco men were headed for Boulder and the fireman's

---

[1] *RMN* 08/25/1885.

tournament: "There are pickpockets and soap men and shell men, eight die men, top and bottom men, flim-flamers and the smiler with the shells, and all the rest of the boys."[1] Associating "the boys" with the robberies was an easy link for readers. Did the robbery of Lewis raise the profile of Soapy and the bunco brotherhood? The answer seems clear. Why else would "the brotherhood's" travel to Boulder be newsworthy?

The "eight die men" mentioned in the story ran a game called "Top and Bottom." It was a short con with gaffed, or altered, dice in which the victim bets that the top and bottom faces of three tossed dice either will or will not add up to twenty-one. It is based on the principal that players cannot see around corners. If they could see more than three sides of the cubes at once, they would notice not only that the tops do not come close to adding up to seven on opposite sides but also that some numbers are missing entirely while other numbers appear twice. The operator of "Top and Bottom" is a skilled sleight-of-hand artist who can switch sets of dice at any given moment.[2]

Jeff's name does not appear in Denver newspapers again until October 3, 1885, when he and another bunco man named Mike Rainey were arrested for assaulting John Koch, a probable victim. Koch failed to identify his attackers as Jeff and Rainey, so they were discharged.

With growth of Jeff's Soap Gang, sometimes stability and reliability trumped loyalty and friendship. In November 1885 Jeff was apparently faced with having to cut loose a confederate. His name is known only as Kit. In the first of two letters to Jeff, Kit complains at length over Jeff's poor treatment of him. The letter frequently becomes incoherent, betraying the writer's wounded and desperate state of mind.

> When ... I look back for 3 or 4 days and think how you have forgotten every tie of friendship that was between us, I am prepared for anything, and not surprised at nothing. Who has proven their friendship the most by acts, you and I, and who has forgotten the most, you or I. Loosing [sic] everything on earth, not only my money, but that which you know more than all, I prized. Sneered and laughed at by man and woman, one by one of our own party turned their back on me and then go part with my trinkets, thinking you were in trouble and give half to you and ... me with pants and cloths that a tramp would feel ashamed of. ... Then, when I told you I did not expect you to pay it [some bill of Kit's?] but to give me a few dollars, that I might get to work, I am told, if you haven't got it, you can't give it, and if I can do anything, go ahead.... ... And when I had tried to see Murphy to talk, but turned on by everyone and at last stay, to take my life when all this I went through and then ever clung to you and could not do or see you harmed....
>
> How have you, Jeff, repaid me? Let me tell you, when you see [me] damned, knowing that I dreaded anything public for reasons I told you and you only. What do you do? Try to shield me, as I have you? No, just the opposite. Having no crime to lay at my door, which, if you had, I would have been hung by you and yours. You talk of my little business matter a few years ago, then the woman, then someone that knows me ... then Fatty, who I

---

[1] *RMN* 08/25/1885.
[2] Scarne, p. 239.

never done anything but help, the same as the rest of you, talk about me ... with safe robbers, which all comes from you ... then you ask why I am not friendly. Who is the more than false one, you or I. ... And as for you, when everyone, even my lawyers, both say, you are in with it, I still fight for you.

Now, how would you like it if I should tell them, and others, as you have done, what I know about you and Fatty. Do you stop to think how deep you people are in? Do you think I don't know anything? Suppose when Fatty talks about me, and you also, I should go to someone and tell them that you were pretending to handle counterfeit money and that he went to get a directory with Murphy and you folks wrote a lot of letters. Now if I done everything [just listed], what would you do, or think of me? No, I have not even thought of such mean things and even in all my troubles, I have not made a confident [made someone a confidant], only of those that are interested in my case. You cannot find a detective, no officer, that you or Murphy knows in the city, that one word has ever been breathed to, by me or mine, but if any of them, or your friends think that it will be any help to them to know about those little things you and others have talked of, tell me and I will tell them all myself. No, Jeff, it is past. You can say nothing or bring up nothing. I care not how public that will.... I might have been ruined for life, as you will see when the time comes, and not while God lets me breath will I slip [and] tell [anything].

I am righted. I care not who suffers, for none cared for me. I would have come up, but a doctor from the lodge was here and you know my clothes are thin and he was afraid I might get cold for I have not got the swelling all out of my lower parts yet. I may come to the office tomorrow. I can say no more. I done all a human being can do to protect you.

Yours, Kit[1]

Jeff, it seems, had not come to the aid of Kit in a legal issue that involved "safe robbers." After obtaining two attorneys, Kit suddenly fled to Las Vegas, New Mexico. While claiming loyalty to Jeff, Kit grew deeply bitter until he could not refrain from making the veiled threat that he could expose Jeff, John "Fatty Gray" Morris, and Murphy (probably Tom Murphy) of counterfeiting and other crimes.

Jeff loaned Kit an unknown amount of money. By the end of November 1885, Kit was about to return to Denver for a court hearing, but not before writing to ask Jeff to leave Denver before his arrival.

Friend Jeff

I have just received a letter from my lawyers to be in Denver week after next. I shall sell [buy?] my ticket and you had better leave for a few weeks for I wish to harm you in no way or shape. I have never deceived you in any way and I think the time is not long when you will know it in your own mind if you do not admit it [already]. The money loaned me will be returned to you, every cent. You may not like my asking you to leave, but it is for your own sake and not mine. I have done my best to protect you, at my own loss, and shall

---

[1] Ltr fr "Kit," to Jeff R. Smith II, undated (believed Oct. or Nov., 1885). Geri Murphy col.

continue to do so, and it is your own gain to leave a little while. I write you for I may not be able to see you. Hoping this will find you doing well. I will close.

Yours, Kit[1]

It is not certain why Kit wanted Jeff to leave. Possibly Kit feared his testimony might implicate Jeff in criminal activities, and he wanted to protect Jeff. Perhaps Kit feared a meeting with Jeff. Kit's short letter contrasts sharply with the prior long one, both in length and tone. A communication from Jeff, particularly a stern one, could have produced this change. The outcome of this association, even the nature of the legal proceedings, is unknown, and Kit disappeared from record.

In the same month, an old friend wrote Jeff of his hope that Jeff would not only encourage him to come to Denver but also want to buy in with him as a partner.

Friend Jeff R. Smith

Thinking you would like to hear from an old friend I thought I would drop you a line informing you of my whereabouts.

I left New Orleans last March for California, where I remained long enough to work all the fairs, but I only got in 3 weeks graft at Santa Rosa, Petaluma, and Oakland, [−] Sacramento, Stockton, San Jose, and Salinas were queer. 5 weeks throwed away. Taylor was there but did not make any money. Tim Parker was there also, so was "Jew Ned," Sam Nathan and Big Burns, nobody made anything [−] absolutely nothing went in Stockton, and Sacramento. They even arrested them for playing poker at Sacramento. You never saw the like. The gang all disgusted. Tim Parker brought a young wife out from Boston ... and settled down in S. F. how is that for high?

I have a new fake, ... a great improvement on the Corona. ...[O]ne man can run it and the numbers can all be shown up, nothing to hide, when the Boosters win they can call out the number and show it to the suckers and the number that wins this time may lose the next and visa versa. Do you think I could get to open it up in Chase's this winter? It took better in Santa Rosa, Petaluma & Oakland ... than any other game in Sherman Tex. I ... took off more stuff [in] one night than all the rest of the games in the house at the J. T. Saloon in Sherman and the beauty of it is that nobody can get on to the fake, nobody has yet either in California or here. Write soon and tell me just what you think can be done or any other place in Colorado that I might go and work for a month or so. I got a partner now because it is too hard work for one man..., but if I can go to work in Colorado, I might buy him out and let you buy in. It will cost you $150.00 for half interest, which you can make in a week if there is anything at all doing, and I would rather have you for a partner than the one I got now because he is more of a gambler than a sure thing man and pays too much attention to gambling to suit me. Answer at your earliest convenience & oblige.

Your friend,   F. H. Anderson

Texarkana, Ark.[1]

---

[1] Ltr fr "Kit," to Jeff R. Smith II, 11/23/1885. Geri Murphy col.

Anderson's letter mentions several well-known confidence men. "Taylor" is possibly confidence man John Taylor, Soapy's probable mentor. "Big Burns" is surely "Big Ed" Burns, who became a noted member of the Soap Gang.

Anderson asks Jeff about being able to operate his swindle in "Chase's," a reference to the Palace Theater and Tivoli Beer Hall. Clearly illustrated are Jeff's connections to Ed Chase in 1885. Their alliance grew into joint gambling business ventures that lasted into the mid 1890s. In various capacities, the men seemed to have been partners. Stationary shows both names as proprietors, and their wives were friends.[2] One of Jeff's notebooks shows Ed Chase's name with the amount of $125. Other names appear in the same column, such as that of Ed Gaylord with the amount of $150, but it is not clear whether the money was being paid out or taken in.[3]

Edward "Big Ed" Chase, the legendary gambling czar of Denver, arrived in the mid 1860s. His name appears in Deadwood newspapers in 1878 in connection with a saloon there, but the extent of his involvement is not known.[4] In 1890, he was "elected" president of the Colorado Policy Association, a protection racket for policy shops in Denver.[5] Members paid for legal protection from prosecution. In the same format Chase later organized the Gambler's Protection Association to safeguard members from legal and illegal harassment. He was a city alderman from 1865 to 1868.[6] His strong political connections helped the gambling trade run "free and open" in Denver when Jeff first arrived. Chase seemed to prefer behind-the-scenes activity as opposed to serving in public office. "For half a century he made it his business to organize an underworld voting block whose support was traded for legal protection of his gambling establishments."[7] Chase was never ashamed of his methods. He believed the ends justified the means, admitting as much in a 1921 interview.

> I did many things to help out my friends among politicians in my long career. I had to do so to keep my friends and assure a proper degree of protection. Most ... candidates sought my help, but I made it a point to be pretty sure of the success of the man whose cause I championed. Possibly I did some things in the way of getting votes that the law did not sanction.[8]

Around 1877 Chase opened the Palace Theater and Tivoli Beer Hall, a combination theater, saloon, and gambling club in a two-story brick building.[9] Advertised as *Second to None*, it became Denver's premiere "leg-art" entertainment and gambling hot spot.

---

[1] Ltr fr F. H. Anderson to Jeff R. Smith II, 11/21/1885. Geri Murphy col.

[2] Ltr fr Hi Ki & Henry Edwards to Mary Smith, 10/15/1895. Item 43, author's col. A ltr in which Mrs. Chase "was pleased to hear from" Mary, sending "her kindest regards" and hoping she would return to Denver for a visit.

[3] Notebook, notes written in Jeff's hand, unknown date. Item #69, author's col.

[4] Deadwood.

[5] Parkhill, p. 80.

[6] *RMN* 02/22/1889.

[7] Noel, *City*, p. 39.

[8] Secrest, p. 89.

[9] Noel, *City*, p. 38.

Ed Chase's elegant (and notorious throughout the West) Palace Theater was at 1443–1457 Blake Street and entertained Denver's largest clientele. It had room for 200 players and 25 dealers and a bar with a 60-foot mirror. Midnight hors d'oeuvres included roast beef, pork, venison, antelope cutlets, breast of prairie chicken, wild turkey, quail, and salads. Not simply a gambling establishment, the Palace had a 750-seat auditorium featuring vaudevillian variety acts. The bill usually opened with songs sung by a bevy of young women seated in crescent formation, the master of ceremonies in the center, and two blackface comedians on the ends.

One by one the girls stepped to the footlights and offered ... song selections, interspersed with jokes from the comedians. Many of the young women were known as seriocomic songsters and early in the act each was dressed in skirts falling to about the knees. A man caught a cannonball shot from a cannon, the Palace performers concluded with a lively dance scene featuring the entire troupe, and the ladies' skirts went higher than the knee![1] ... Famous for everything from its racy stage shows to fancy buffets to peek-a-boo bosoms to gambling, booze, and murder, the Palace was known throughout the West.[2]

Young female entertainers were expected to mix with the customers whether inclined to prostitution or not. Box seats flanking the stage were heavily curtained to provide privacy for those who desired it.[3]

Ed Chase insisted that he was not a professional gambler, only a proprietor who leased gaming tables to gamblers. Under this arrangement, with the legal system the way it was, both parties were free of legal responsibility. By the time police responded to disturbances or accusations of cheating, the renter could not be found, and the owner could not be held liable for his tenant's wrong doing.[4] Nevertheless, like many of the other gambling establishments in the city, the Palace had its share of problems spill into newsprint.

Another murder at the Palace Theater, Denver. A.W. Munson shot and killed Thomas Miller last Sunday night. From the amount of blood that has spilled in that den, its floors must be a gorgeous gory red color.[5]

Choosing brides from among female employees of the Palace became a practice among gamblers there. In 1880, Chase himself chose his third wife, Frances Minerva, from among the Barbour Sisters, a feature Palace act. It was a successful union lasting until Chase's death more than forty years later. Chase's partner in the Palace, Ed Gaylord, impressed by Frances's ability to keep a gallivanting man like Ed Chase at home, later married the other Barbour sister, Addie. "Bat" Masterson,[6] who managed the theater and gaming hall from Chase and Gaylord around 1888, also

[1] Secrest, p. 130.
[2] Secrest, p. 137.
[3] Noel, *City*, p. 38.
[4] Noel, *City*, p. 38.
[5] *Georgetown Courier* 12/06/1888.
[6] Ortiz, p. 45.

found a wife on the Palace boards, a blond song-and-dance girl named Emma Walters.[1]

In his attraction to the lady performers of the Palace, Jeff was no exception. In November 1885, the *News* ran a story about how Jeff struck a man over the head with his pistol. The man had seized and kissed a woman with whom Jeff was talking, and Jeff had driven him off. His gun discharged, and it was feared he had shot the man. The *News* covered the excitement.

A NEGRO'S NERVE.
He Tackles a White Woman and Gets the Worst of it.

About 10 o'clock last night T. [sic] Smith, a gambler, was sitting in a back room attachment to John Kinneavy's saloon, corner of Sixteenth and Holladay streets, with a lady friend, when a colored man entered and without saying a word seized Smith's companion about the neck and kissed her. Smith naturally took umbrage at this and drawing a revolver struck the Negro over the head with it.... As the pistol, which was loaded, struck the Negro's head, one barrel went off and the neighborhood was aroused. Smith skipped out, as did also the Negro, whose name proved to be Arthur Jackson. Captain Swain was at once on the scene and caught Jackson as he was running across the street and took him to the city jail. Arrived here he washed the blood from his face and it was found that he was only slightly hurt. Smith subsequently gave himself up and he is being retained at police headquarters.

Colored men who know the man Jackson give him anything but a good name, saying that he has a weakness for attacking white women in the same manner as he last evening assaulted the woman who was with Soapy Smith.

The report of Smith's pistol caused a good deal of excitement for a few moments, but it soon died down when it was learned that no one was hurt.[2]

Probably the woman with Jeff was Mary Noonan, who would soon become his wife. This may have been the occasion of their first meeting. Versions of how Jeff met Mary vary, but all of them include Jeff's foiling unwanted advances on her.

The story told by Mary to her grandchildren and published in several biographies begins with Jeff attending a Palace Theater show. Jeff noticed Mary and wanted to introduce himself. Her name was Mary Eva Noonan, daughter of Irish immigrants and born in Louisville, Kentucky, in 1872, making her age thirteen when Jeff met her.[3] Rumors, not yet substantiated, have her a cousin to the outlaw Dalton brothers. The only positive clues are that her mother's maiden name is Mary Dalton[4] and that like the father of the outlaw brothers, she lived in Kentucky.[5] Eighteen days after Jeff hit

---

[1] DeArment, *Knights*, p. 168.

[2] *RMN* 11/04/1885, p. 5.

[3] b. 09/03/1872. d. 12/11/1947. Death certificate, author's col.

[4] Ltrs in family collections that the author has not actually seen. The author's father stated these Ltrs were given to another family member by Jeff R. Smith III and told to destroy them. The author was told by Joy Smith that they had not been destroyed.

[5] Shirley, p. 38.

Jackson on the head, Mary's name appears as a singer in the first of ten advertisements for the Palace Theater. They run from November 22, 1885, to January 6, 1886. Mary is listed by her stage name, Allie Nielson, which led early biographers to believe it was her real name. The advertisement for her reads, "First appearance here of the bewitching songstress."[1] A letter from 1887 indicates that for a short period, friends knew Mary as "Allie."[2]

In 1897, Mary told W. F. Hynes and Richard Davis how she and Jeff united,[3] and decades later, she related the same story to her grandchildren.[4] To Mary it was a fairy tale romance with Jeff her shining knight.[5] Mary said their first meeting was a dramatic event staged before the entire audience of the Palace Theater. Mary had just finished her performance and was leaving the stage when a man blocked her way. She tried to go around him, but he seized her. Jeff, who had been making his way toward her to introduce himself, bolted forward and with his cane deftly struck her assailant on the head. The man dropped where he stood but soon recovered and quickly fled. It is possible that Mary's version is true and that the woman with Jeff eighteen days prior was not Mary but a woman Jeff defended as well.

Following Jeff's rescue of Mary, an intense two-month romance ended in marriage. According to Smith genealogy, the wedding took place February 1, 1886. A photograph believed to have been taken at their wedding shows a young Mary and a mustached but beardless Jeff. The *News* reported the marriage and that the couple honeymooned at the elegant Charpiot's Hotel at 386 Larimer, between Seventeenth and Eighteenth streets.[6]

Jeff gave his personal affairs a very low profile, especially from his enemies and competition who would target his private life if they could. Additionally, he did not want his new wife to suffer embarrassment because of him. So Jeff kept his married life completely separate from his business affairs. Even neighbors did not know exactly who lived next door. One neighbor of the Smiths was Lafayette "Lafe" Pence, an attorney[7] and resident of Denver since 1885.[8] Later on, after Jeff had become somewhat notorious, in an 1894 interview, Pence said of his neighbor,

> I lived next to him for a couple of years and it took me a year to find out who he was. I used to notice him carrying home an armful of strawberries when I would have to be content with wishing for some, but I supposed he was some prosperous merchant or banker.[9]

To the very end, Jeff protected his family from his enemies and public exposure. At the time of his death, the majority of those who knew Jeff did not know he had a wife and children. In 1929 reporter W. F. Haynes remembered this protective trait:

[1] *RMN* 11/22/1885, p. 2.
[2] Ltr to Jefferson R. Smith II fr "Christine and Kirk" (last name unknown), 01/10/1887. Geri Murphy col.
[3] *RMN* 08/28/1929.
[4] Interview with John Randolph Smith, 07/02/1984.
[5] As told by Mary E. Smith to grandson John R. Smith.
[6] *RMN* 11/27/1885.
[7] *RMN* 05/03/1890.
[8] *The Register (Rock Valley*, IA) 03/23/1894, p. 3.
[9] *RMN* 03/30/1894.

"Jeff would sacrifice his life at any time to protect her [Mary's] good name; and any reflection on her conduct or character would meet his quick and furious vengeance."[1]

Before marrying, Jeff is believed to have lived in various hotels. After marrying, Jeff and Mary purchased a home at 341 Curtis Street,[2] a location some eight long blocks northeast of the city center. Decades later Mary told her grandson Randolph that Jeff kept her and the children away from the northern business district where he concentrated his activities.[3] Some historians inaccurately believed Mary knew little of her husband's activities. According to Jeff's grandson, John Randolph Smith, in the early days, Mary often helped Jeff cut out the paper squares Jeff used to wrap soap for his prize package soap sell. She also often traveled with Jeff on trips. No evidence indicates that Mary participated directly in any of Jeff's swindles and schemes, but she did become friends with the wives of some of her husband's friends and business associates, including the wife of Ed Chase.

A story Mary enjoyed sharing was the way she collected her husband's nightly income. While living in Denver, Jeff operated in the city almost everyday. After closing for the night, he often ventured into the Arcade Clubrooms or Murphy's Exchange and spent the night drinking and trying to "beat the tiger," the game of faro. When Jeff arrived home, often after Mary had retired, as he made his way down the hallway towards the bedroom, he would toss a roll of bills behind a picture that hung at an angle out from the wall. The next morning Mary would go through the house on a daily dusting routine. When she passed that picture, casually, and without interrupting the side-to-side motion of her duster, she would draw the frame from the wall, and into the apron pocket held open for it dropped the roll of bills. Rarely was there no money for her pocket.[4]

Other wealth came from property purchases. The county Assessor's report of 1886 shows that Jeff placed all their property, valued at $6,330, under Mary's name.[5] In September 1888 a "J. R. Smith" purchased lots 1-4 of block 28, "Downing ad" for $3,700 from G. H. Batchelder.[6] In 1889 the *News* listed Denver's wealthy land owners and land belonging to "M. E. Smith" [possibly Mary] is listed at $45,900.

Soon after the wedding, Mary became pregnant. It appears there was a medical difficulty, so for help with the birth, Jeff sent Mary to her mother's at 917 Locust Street, St. Louis, Missouri. A January 1, 1887, *News* story reported that Jeff made at least one trip to St. Louis to see his wife when she was close to giving birth.

> Mr. Jeff Smith, well-known in this city, returned yesterday from an Eastern trip, which included visits at Chicago, St. Louis and Philadelphia. At St. Louis Mr. Smith found his son, whom he had never met before and whose

---

[1] *RMN* 08/28/1929.

[2] *Denver City Directory*, 1886.

[3] Interview with John R. Smith, 01/1981.

[4] Interview with John R. Smith, 01/1981.

[5] *RMN* 10/29/1886, p. 3.

[6] *RMN* 09/06/1888, p. 5.

fighting weight is eleven pounds. Jeff says that during his absence of three weeks from this city he only saw sunshine two days.[1]

Jeff, however, did not see his son on that trip. He would not be born for another five weeks. The first child was a boy, christened Jefferson Randolph Smith III.[2] Friends of Mary sent Jeff a letter twenty-nine days before the birth, in January 1887, indicating how much Mary wanted to be at Jeff's side.

> I was over to Allies [sic] last night until after 11 o'clock. She seemed very uneasy, and had a severe headache. Otherwise she is very much the same as when.... [section missing] ... contented. She will never want for care as far as I am concerned. Allie said; if she new [sic] as much when you were here as she does now, she would have packed her trunk and went home with you. She never knew before how much she appreciated her home and husband as she does now, that she is here among her own folks [–] everyday seems a month until she is over her trouble and back with you once more, and it will be a long time before she will come here again.[3]

Jeff and Mary corresponded often, and Jeff would send gifts. A month after their son Jefferson was born, he wrote on March 7, 1887. Mary was still at her mother's.

> Dear Husband
>
> I received your letter and the little ring all o.k. It is very pretty but it is a great deal to [sic] large for the little darling. He got another one that very day, with his initials on it to [sic] and it first fit him. Mary Carroll gave it to him. She is just crazy over him.
>
> The reason I did not answer your letter sooner was because he was christened yesterday and we had a splendid time, was wishing you were here. He looked to [sic] sweet for anything. I got him one of those milk white cloaks I was showing you in the window when you were here, and a lovely dress. Well I might as well say a whole outfit. He just looked lovely. He is [an] awful good little dear, he hardly woke up to be christened, and when the priest poured the cold water on him he never cried. I guess he must take after you for being good for I know very well if they put cold water on me now I would scream and I don't think I ever heard mother say that I was such a good little baby.
>
> I think that fellow was awful good to give that little ring to you for little Jeff. I think Jeff will be able to walk and talk when that suits him.
>
> Dear Jeff, I guess I will have to close as the little fellow is waking up and he must get a little dinner.
>
> All the folks send love and were very sorry you were not here to see him christened. Kirk and Christine sends [sic] regards. Good-bye, answer soon.
>
> From your loving wife
>
> P.S. I kissed little Jeff just once for him [–] all the rest for myself.[4]

---

[1] *RMN* 01/01/1887, p. 4.

[2] b. 02/08/1887. d. 01/19/1952.

[3] Ltr fr "Christine and Kirk" to Jefferson R. Smith II, 01/10/1887. Geri Murphy col.

[4] Ltr to Jeff Smith fr Mary Smith, 03/07/1887, Jefferson R. "Little Randy" Smith col.

Another letter from Mary twelve days later asks Jeff to let her return to Denver. It appears concern for Mary's health and the age of the baby caused Jeff to want them in St. Louis.

> March 19th 1886 [the year was 1887, not 1886]
>
> Dear Husband
>
> I received your letter today and also the ticket for the ball. You ought of gone to the ball. It would cheer you up a little for I guess you are awful lonesome. They had a parade here but I did not get to see it. The day was too cold to take the baby out. You asked me if I was sick in your letter that I was going to a doctor. I did not feel very well but I am improving everyday and I feel much better now. You also said in your last letter be good to little Jeff for his Pa's sake. I don't understand you for sure and will be good to him for his own sake as well as anybody else. I felt awful about it but then I thought you might not have meant it the way I took it. Jeff I am ready to go out there anytime you say, or come after me. Little Jeff is getting bigger everyday and he is nice and heavy now and I don't think there is any danger of [for] him. I am nearly as fat as ever. You would not think I was sick at all. Well dear I guess I will close. Write soon. All the folks send love. Give all the folks out there my regards. Good bye from your loving wife. Also 20 kisses from little Jeff and big mama.[1]

In describing herself as "nearly as fat as ever," Mary was likely referring to the slow loss of weight from her pregnancy. She often signed her letters to Jeff, "From little Jeff and big mama." The latter term is probably one of endearment that arose with the progress of her pregnancy. Although christened Mary, Jeff addressed her and wrote to her as "Mollie." To her grandchildren, she was "Mammy." The name was apt because within the next several years, Jeff and Mary had two more children, Mary Eva, named after her mother,[2] and James Luther Smith.[3] They were born in St. Louis.

Jeff was exceptionally proud of his family. Mary later told of his strolls around the neighborhood with the children in their perambulator, how "he strutted down the street, like a peacock with chest thrust out."[4] Also an attentive father, Jeff shared life lessons with his eldest son. As a young child, Jefferson III had favorite memories of his father, one of which was how his father would sometimes say, "Jeff, you have a lion by the tail. Swing it, don't let it swing you."[5]

Two letters from Mary in March 1886 were addressed to Jeff at 1711 Larimer Street, Denver. Jeff had his mail delivered to a local cigar manufacturer merchant to keep his residence a secret.[6] While Mary was away, rather than living in their home,

---

[1] Ltr fr Mary Smith to Jeff R. Smith II, 03/19/1887. Jefferson R. "Little Randy" Smith col.

[2] Born July 4 between March 1887 & July 1889, when Ltrs in the Smith collections begin to mention her. Year died unknown. Ltrs refer to Mary Eva as Eva in order not to confuse her with her mother, Mary.

[3] Birth & death dates unknown.

[4] As told to author by his father, John R. Smith, who was told by Mary Eva Smith.

[5] As told to the author by his father, John R. Smith.

[6] Denver City Directory, 1889. p. 1066. (J. F. Chatard & Co.)

Jeff often resided in some of Denver's best hotels, including The Windsor[1] on Larimer and Eighteenth and the Batione[2] at 1720 Larimer, just east of Seventeenth Street across from the Chever Block where his office was located. He probably had at least three reasons for living downtown. The first was that he loved the atmosphere of the saloons and gambling clubs there. Second, he could afford the air of respectability and affluence the better hotels gave him. More important, staying in these hotels kept him close to his businesses and associates for purposes of oversight and direction.

As with any business, Jeff's profits rose and fell with economic conditions, politics at city hall, and whether or not the *Rocky Mountain News* was roasting Jeff in print. In March 1886, the *News* reported turbulent political weather.

The Thieves Must Go

Ten or twelve tin horn gamblers, holdup [men,] and all around thieves have received official notification from the police to leave the city, and several have already complied with the modest request, [−] others have asked and have been granted an extension of time in which to get their traps together. The police are determined to rid the town of suspicious characters. Besides those served with notices, there are a number of others on the list, and they will be notified within a day or two to make themselves scarce. There will be no favor shown to anybody who belongs to the non-producing class. Every man in town who has no visible means of support will receive a notification, if he hasn't sense enough to leave without one.[3]

Not certain is whether the police asked Jeff to leave, but between March and December, Jeff's name does not appear in Denver newspapers. Several bunco arrests occurred during this time, but Jeff's name is not mentioned. Letters to Jeff at the end of December 1886 indicate he was in Chicago.[4] A February 13, 1887, letter to Jeff shows he had been in St. Louis with his wife and children during Christmas.[5] He did not, however, stay away from Denver for long. Letters to Jeff began arriving in Denver in November 1886, addressed to 1711 Larimer Street. Jeff also began receiving letters from old friends and associates. It is probable he was trying to rebuild or enlarge his gang. John Taylor, perhaps Jeff's mentor and the "Old Man Taylor" of whom historians have written, sent Jeff a letter dated December 29, 1886, from the Brooklyn Hotel in San Francisco. (Spelling is as it appears in the Taylor letters that follow.)

Friend Jeff

I have just learned that there are parties hear from Washington with outfit to open a Bucket shop. They have the clock and a place to open and they have had Swartz, one of the poolroom proprietors trying to fix it for them but as soon as they open, I understand they will be pulled. I understand that the Chronical had a piece coppyed from ... the New York World ... of the 17th. I

---

[1] *RMN* 02/27/1886.

[2] *Denver City Directory*, 1887.

[3] *RMN* 03/13/1886.

[4] Ltr fr Eva Katherine & Emmie Lou Smith to Jeff R. Smith II, 12/26/1886. Jefferson R. "Little Randy" Smith col.

[5] Ltr fr John Morris to Jeff R. Smith II 02/13/1887. Jefferson R. "Little Randy" Smith col.

send you one cut [clipping] that one of the boys gave me today, so I don't know weather it would be policy [a "policy" operation?].... I understand the parties here are going to open and take chances. They say Bank[1] will open this week. They are dealing Koka Poka[2] all over town now. I don't know what to advise.... I don't want to see you lose any money so I thought I would let you know how everything [is]. ... I will now close, hoping these few lines may find you in good health and hoping to hear from you soon.

From your friend, John Taylor[3]

Three weeks later Taylor, still in San Francisco, wrote again on January 17, 1887.

Friend Jeff

I write these few lines to let you know that I am going away for a few weeks. I leave this afternoon for Los Angeles. I am going to try and work the lower country. They close[d] Bank on Friday. I heard Buckley had them stop on account of Lew Rickenbaugh [sic]. I hear that he tried to have Dublin kill[ed] in Arizona and they say that is the reason he had them stopped. Valentine has not showed up yet. The Bucket shop is running all right. You can write and if I stay any time in Los Angeles I can have it forwarded to me.

Yours Truly, John Taylor[4]

"Bank" is an old gambling term for the game of faro. It would appear that Buckley, possibly Christopher A. Buckley, known as "Boss Buckley" a San Francisco saloon proprietor and crime boss, was working with gambling king-pin Lewis Rickabaugh, in shutting out the competition.[5]

Jeff responded, and in eight days a letter from Taylor in Los Angeles, dated January 25, 1887, arrived in Denver.

Friend Jeff

I received your letter this morning and was glad to hear from you. I went to a sale yesterday and worked the shells and I turned a party for twenty dollars. There was another party there and they win $90 from a sucker and he caused a great fuss. ... There is three or four shell mobs here working besides the body backed [by "protection"]. It is desperate to think it will last very long as the papers are turning loss on them.[6] I have not received a letter from John Waller.... I will now close with my regards to all the boys. I hear from Tom Murphy [that he] was here in Los Angeles last year. I hope these few lines find you and your wife in good health.

From your friend, John Taylor[7]

---

[1] *Bank*: may be place where Policy bets are placed and/or a generic term for "open for business."

[2] *dealing Koka Poka*: this appears to be card game of some sort, but a search of several dictionaries under this spelling reveals nothing.

[3] Ltr fr John Taylor to Jeff R. Smith II, 12/29/1886. Jefferson R. "Little Randy" Smith col.

[4] Ltr fr John Taylor to Jeff R. Smith II 01/17/1887. Jefferson R. "Little Randy" Smith col.

[5] *Los Angeles Times* 01/12/1887 and 01/15/1887.

[6] *papers are turning loss on them*: possible interpretation: the papers are holding the losses complained about by the public against the police and whoever else is allowing "the games" to operate.

[7] Ltr fr John Taylor to Jeff R. Smith II 01/25/1887. Jefferson R. "Little Randy" Smith col.

Taylor spoke a little too soon about not receiving a letter from Waller. He received Jeff's letter, replied, and enclosed a letter to forward to Taylor. Waller had been traveling the country but had settled in Key West, Florida. Waller and his gang were reported doing well on the island, taking about $300 a night from short cons. In the letter, Waller invited Taylor to Key West, and if he did, Waller would set up a meeting with the marshal so that Taylor could operate.[1] The letter was never sent. In less than a month, religion changed the course of Taylor's life. He wrote on February 19, 1887, again from Los Angeles, to persuade Jeff to follow his lead before it was too late.

Dear friend Jeff

I received your letter yesterday and was glad to hear from you and glad to hear that you have a son. It ought to make you stop playing bank. You ought to know that there is nothing in it. You know what money you and I have lost at it, and you have seen what others have lost that play it, Jeff when you have so much money why don't you buy yourself a nice little home. If I was married and had the money it is the first thing I would do Jeff. ... I am sorry to hear of you having lost so much money. I hope you will stop playing before you get broke. I would like to hear of you getting even and then stop gambling all together. There is nothing in it. I am tired and sick of the life I have been living.

I have been very near giving up everything and becoming a Christian and living a Christian life. I have been tending religious meetings and I have received some wonderful blessings, and I don't know but I will give up everything. there is only [one] thing that troubles me and that is being in debt. If I had five hundred dollars so I could pay what I owe I would stop all faking. It would be my last. I may give up any day. If I do Jeff you will have to wait till I get up into Idaho and sell some of my property.[2]

Jeff, they had the Kansas City Kid arrested here, but they got him out on a habus Corpus and there was two or three officers waiting to arrest him, but he got away out of the courthouse.... They have Richie or Edwards arrested for a gold brick racket. He was two days undercover and had lots of chances to get away. The other parties got away. Bank is closed on account of the trouble.

They are having quite a time of it here. They had Texas Tom Ventriloquist arrested on a pigeon trick but he had an alibi. Tom is going to Denver so he can tell you all the news. It has rain[ed] here the last two weeks and I have not done anything. Jesup is also broke and in soak [drunk?]. I will now close hoping these few lines may find you and your wife and baby in good health.

From your friend, John Taylor[3]

---

[1] Ltr fr John Waller to John Taylor 01/23/1887, Geri Murphy col.

[2] It is probable that John Taylor owed Jeff money. No other information is known. Jeff was one to help out his friends financially if he could.

[3] Ltr fr John Taylor to Jeff R. Smith II, 02/19/1887. Jefferson R. "Little Randy" Smith col.

Taylor's letters paint a picture of busy bunco men operating policy shops, short-cons like the shell game, and the gold brick racket (selling a fake brick or bar of gold). "Richie" and "Edwards" could possibly be Guy Rich and Henry Edwards, alias Yank Fewclothes. The "pigeon trick" that got Texas Tom Ventriloquist arrested is a short-con racket, with many variations. A victim is convinced to give up a sum of "earnest" money to secure the rights to a share of a larger sum, for example, of a cashier's check found in a wallet.

Jeff heeded some of Taylor's advice. Two days later Jeff filed for ownership of 160 acres in Denver that he had been living on since January 28, 1887.[1] Jeff may also have had other parcels in Denver. In December he wrote to a real estate agent in Idaho about selling some Denver land. The agent's reply arrived in January 1887.

> My dear friend:
>
> I received your letter of December 31, 1886 in due time. This will be only a short business letter and to the point:
>
> A party wishes to know what you will take spot cash, for your block No. 35. on the upper end of town. Don't put on any fancy price if you want to sell it.
>
> If your price is satisfactory, you can get the cash for it. If you can sell it, I think the purchaser would improve it, so as to make your other property more valuable. Please answer at once, and oblige.
>
> Yours Truly, S. B. Dilley[2]

Nine days later Jeff bought the 160 acres in Denver. Possibly he sold land "on the upper end of town" in order to buy land for another home. Also possible is that this was part of a real-estate swindle to sell land Jeff did not own. One clue is that Taylor traveled to Bellevue, Idaho, where the agent in the sale was located. Not known is if S. B. Dilley was in on the swindle or its intended victim. Despite his professed wish to "stop all faking," Taylor himself may have written the letter, posing as Dilley. In Denver, Jeff was living at 1528 Glenarm.[3] Sanborn fire insurance maps show the Glenarm location as a house nine blocks from the corner of Seventeenth and Larimer streets.

From Bellevue a little more than a month later, Taylor wrote to Jeff a last.

> Friend Jeff
>
> I received your letter today and was glad to hear from you and to hear of you being in good health. As this [letter] leaves me at present I never felt better in my life. Jeff, I am sorry I cannot send you what I owe you in my letter but the party that wants to buy my block is in California and he is not expected back till the first of April. I tried to sell a lot today for two hundred and fifty dollars but the party could not pay in cash down. He is in business and he says he could not take the money out of his business.
>
> Jeff, all the money I have got is twenty-five dollars. I had forty dollars when I reached Bellevue and I paid twenty board[4] and I [indecipherable] fixed

---

[1] Land Filing 02/21/1887. Item 33, author's col.

[2] Ltr to Jeff R. Smith II fr S. B. Dilley, 01/12/1887. Geri Murphy col.

[3] *Denver City Directory*, 1887.

[4] *paid twenty board*: paid $20 for a place to eat.

one house and I have been working hard [indecipherable] papering and I have two rooms done to paper so it has taken the other twenty dollars.

Jeff, you would not have to ask me for what I owe you if I had it or could get it. It is the only thing that is worrying me.... It is the first time I ever was that much in debt. If I can send it to you by the first of the month I will do so.... Jeff, if it had not been for what I owe you I would of given up and become a Christian two weeks sooner than I did, but the day I gave up I told some ladies I would put it off for another year, but I went to a meeting in the afternoon and was converted. I am not sorry for the step I have taken.

I had my trip all planned out where I was going this spring. I was going to Spokane Falls, and from there into the [indecipherable] country. I thought ... I would get the wheel privilege at the races and it ought to be worth a thousand or so, so you see I gave up all my plans when I was converted.

Jeff, I was wishing you was here if you had not lost the money you did. I write for you to come here for you could of made lots of money building small houses and renting them out. You could build small houses for three to four dollars and rent them from $15 to twenty dollars a month. If I had a dozen houses, I could rent them. There is not a empty house in town that is fit to live in and this summer I don't think you would be able to get a room in town. There is not many strangers coming in yet. I look for a big boom in real estate this summer. I will now close with my regards to John Morris and all the boys and don't forget yourself.

From your friend, John Taylor[1]

In November 1887 a John Taylor was transferred to the penitentiary at Cannon City, Colorado, to serve a one-year prison sentence for forgery.[2]

It is unknown if Jeff heard from John Taylor again.

In February, John "Fatty Gray" Morris wrote to ask if he could rejoin his old Fort Worth associate. The letter referred to the easing of the gambling crackdown in Denver. Morris also mentions a new swindle called "Sucker Send" as opposed to "Straight Send."[3] This complex swindle, when successfully operated, required victims to go to a distant city to collect their winnings from a fictitious person. The advantage was that victims willingly left the area rather than the bunco men having to leave. No account is known of a victim returning to even the score.

Although gambling in Denver was still closed in February 1887, business must not have been all that bad as Jeff sent for Morris. Three months later, a telegram from Charles Anderson[4] in Deadwood to Morris and Jeff indicates Morris had indeed become a member of the Soap Gang.[5]

---

[1] Ltr fr John Taylor to Jeff R. Smith II, 03/28/1887. Jefferson R. "Little Randy" Smith col.

[2] *RMN* 11/16/1887, p. 5.

[3] See "Doc Watts," Chapter 4, for the full text of this Ltr.

[4] Charles Anderson may or may not be J. "Kid" Anderson. His name appears on the inside cover of Jeff's Notebook. It is circled and reads, "Charles Anderson [city listed but hole in paper makes indecipherable], 834 Folsom." Jeff's Notebook in author's col.

[5] Telegram fr Charles Anderson in Deadwood, SD, to "Fatty Gray" in Denver, 05/06/1887. Geri Murphy col.

Hard economic periods saw a rise in victim demand for the return of money taken by the Soap Gang. William Relue, one such victim, sent Jeff the following note:

Jan. 15th, 1887

Sir, if you will call at the Grand Central hotel, Room 7 and return to me that money you took from me on the 11th on the corner of Blake and 17th streets all will be well. If not I will see what can be done with you. If you comply with this [request] call between 2 and 3 p.m. this afternoon.

Yours respectfully, Wm. Relue[1]

Not known, but highly doubted, is whether Mr. Relue received any of his money back.

During these hard times, even victims were not beyond swindling. A newspaper clipping that Jeff saved tells this story:

Jeff Smith buncoed

Soapy Smith was buncoed out of $10.00 yesterday in the vicinity of Jeff's place[, which] still resounds with the horse-laughs given him. A Swede, name unknown, lost $40 in Jeff's place; and by a threat of complaining to the police induced "Soapy" to give him $200 for a check he had in his pocket. [Presumably, Jeff gave the Swede $160.] The fellow hastened out and ordered payment of the check stopped. Jeff was at the bank, however, before the Swede could get away and recovered $190.00 of the money.[2]

After all was said and done, however, Jeff was $30 ahead.

Once again Jeff decided to leave Denver until the current gambling reform subsided. He wrote to friends to ask if they knew of locations open to gambling. A.W. Kelso from Minneapolis wrote on March 22, 1887, about prospects there.

My dear Smith

Yours to hand this a.m. Since I came here a month or so ago, I have heard that last year during the season when there was [sic] thousands of strangers in the city and at lake resorts in the vicinity, that business was extraordinarily good, many plums having been pulled off.

Starting last season the city was [undecipherable] beyond question. Everybody being protected, but they all had to dive with a head [indecipherable]. This year there has been a number of new laws passed by the legislature. One, creating a board of police commissioner for the city. Some think that this board will not stand work [hold session?] this year. Others think they will. I am in a position that will enable me to find out as soon as any body. If anything can be done this year ... I am confidant you could make pretty plenty of sugar here.

I will keep my eye open to the main chance and if I should drop you a line or a telegram, you can bet that there is something worth coming after. Let this be confidential by all means.

Respt., A.W. Kelso[3]

---

[1] Ltr fr Wm. Relue to Jeff R. Smith II, 01/15/1887. Jefferson R. "Little Randy" Smith col.

[2] Newspaper clipping of unknown origin & date. Author's col.

[3] Ltr fr A. W. Kelso to Jeff R. Smith II, 03/22/1887. Geri Murphy col.

Frank Smith, Proprietor of the Turf Exchange in Pueblo, Colorado, also wrote back to caution Jeff about starting much in his city.

> May 8, 1887
> Friend "Soapy"
> Yours came this morning. I am intimately acquainted with the officials of the racetrack and fair grounds and have heard them "declare themselves," so that it would be no use to approach them on the "shell" question. I could "fix" things if any one could (and I should only be to [sic] happy to oblige you, if it were possible), but I know it would be useless to try it.
> As far as the town is concerned, I don't think there would be much money in it, outside of the race track. However, you or your friend might write to Bert Reynolds, proprietor of the Central Theater, (not using my name however, as he and I are not intimate) and get a table there and might fix the town to work the street daytimes, but I would not care to take any part of it: though should you come yourself I shall be pleased to assist you in any way in my power.
> I remain Very Truly, Frank L. M. Smith[1]

The letter indicates that Jeff still dabbled in the shell game.

It is not known where Jeff planned to go. The *Rocky Mountain News*, however, apparently found out (or thought it did) and in July 1887, published Jeff's itinerary.

> Soapy Smith, one of the local celebrities of Denver and one of the most pushing business men in the city, left last Tuesday evening in the rain for a month's sojourn in the East. While absent he will give away small samples of Denver's best soap and new crisp fifty dollar bills among his friends at Saratoga, Long Branch, Coney Island, Brighton Beach and other health and pleasure resorts. We are sorry to lose "Soapy" from among us, but will console ourselves by allowing the "Hifen" to unload its surplus amount of "soft soap" on the susceptible candidates. With Smith out of the way, the "Hifen" has no rivals in the state.[2]

How was Jeff's itinerary known? Possibly the *News* had cultivated a source within the Soap Gang. Equally possible, though, is that Jeff or a confederate purposely led a reporter to believe that Jeff was headed east when actually he went in another direction. No evidence shows he went east at this time. He may have gone as far east as St. Louis to see his family or in the opposite direction altogether. Jeff Smith could no longer afford to have his actions and his comings and goings generally known because whether true or untrue, his reputation linked him to any criminal event within his general vicinity. Another concern for Jeff was that publication of his travel plans would not only alert the law but also any rivaling bunco operations. Either entity, or both, could spell trouble. So he learned to be secretive or to misdirect the newspapers when he planned on traveling.

---

[1] Ltr fr Frank L. M. Smith to Jeff R. Smith II, 05/08/1887, Jefferson R. "Little Randy" Smith col.
[2] *RMN* 07/24/1887. *the "Hifen"*: Perhaps the name of a rival con man or gang. Standard sources for interpretation of slang and dialect do not list "Hifen."

One instance concerning Leadville shows the kind of attention his name generated. In May 1888, this story appeared in the *Leadville Herald Democrat*.

SOAPY SMITH IS COMING

One of the slickest and best known rascals in this whole western country is reported to be on his way to Leadville, where he will endeavor, and will probably succeed, in charming several hundred dollars from the unsuspecting miner, the cute Aleck ["smart Aleck"?] and the man who thinks he knows a good thing when he sees it. The gentleman referred to—Soapy Smith—is known to many people in Leadville, as he has been here frequently, and always with the same outfit, which consists of a small valise filled with small cakes of soap in little boxes, and a very pretty Mrs. Smith, who travels with him.

Soapy, as he is called from the nature of his business, is an artist in his line. He wears large diamonds, stops at the finest hotel and begins his work by taking his stand on the corner of a crowded street, where he opens the valise, collects a crowd by his witty talk and throws out his bait for the suckers.

After entertaining the crowd for a few minutes, he takes two or three soap boxes, puts a bill in one of them and tosses it into the satchel. The end of the bill slightly protrudes from the box. He offers anybody the choice of three boxes for $10.00.

Now appears the "sucker," who has seen the fifty-dollar bill go in the box. He knows where it is. He pays his $10, and, of course, gets left ["left out in the cold," that is, loses.].

The "smart" man now appears on the scene. He knows it is a swindle, but thinks he thinks [knows] Smith has over-reached himself. He pays $10, and gets the wrong box, too.

Smith has made as much as $200 a day at his business, and those who know him say that if he would let the faro bank alone, he could be a rich man in a short time.[1]

Jeff had a connection in Leadville. John G. Morgan, proprietor of the Board of Trade saloon there, wrote to Jeff with a request.

Leadville, Colorado November 9, 1886

Friend Jeff,

I wish you would look around in some of the pawn shops for a sand tell faro box 2L [—] may have a deck of blue water back cards in it. It has been soaked [sold to a pawn shop] since last Friday and the chances are that the fellow soaked it, soaked it for a square box [honest box] as he knows nothing about gambling, and the chances are the pawn broker too, is in for a square box as the deck in the box was so fine that it would take a good sport [a gambler in the know] to discover it. The box was made by Annie Ball and her name is on it. Now just go to the pawn broker and tell them to show you what

---

[1] *Leadville Herald Democrat* 05/02/1888.

boxes they have taken in since Friday and if you find any box just pay what was loaned on it and interest and no questions asked unless they tell you voluntarily. A young fellow that used to work for us I think stole it, and he left for Denver Thursday or Friday. Do not say anything to any one about it as a square sport [honest gambler] has no business with such things. With best wishes, I remain,

Yours Truly, Jno. [John] G. Morgan[1]

In the game of faro, a deck of cards is placed within a "dealing box" to prevent manipulation. A dealer draws cards from the box one at a time. Honest faro boxes are machined to exacting standards, and the dishonest ones are even more intricate in their workmanship. A "TELL-BOX" contains "An intricate and effective internal mechanism [that] enables the dealer not only to 'tell' the location of the cards, but to manipulate the cards in order to deal seconds...." A "SAND TELL-BOX" is "A faro dealer's box constructed to manipulate cards which have been slightly sanded on the backs."[2] A sanded, or rough, card will hold a smooth card, and when the box is triggered in such a way, it dispenses both cards. Then the dealer employs sleight-of-hand skill to manipulate the cards as needed.[3] Morgan wants his prize piece of "gaffed," or dishonest, equipment back, but he makes clear that Jeff should not ask any questions in the search because Morgan does not want it known his gaming establishment uses gaffed equipment.

From January through May 1888, Denver citizens read little of Jeff Smith in the city papers. But the absence of news was not for lack of Jeff's thriving bunco operations in downtown Denver. One cause of the apparent calm was Jeff's control of the police who patrolled his territory. Clark Secrest in his *Hell's Belles: Prostitution, Vice, and Crime in Early Denver* (2002) quotes from the doctoral dissertation of Anne Curtis Knapp, "Making an Orderly Society Criminal Justice in Denver, Colorado, 1858-1900" (1983). Knapp addresses how the police department was so corrupt and brutal

> that officers and supervisors seemingly spent the majority of their time ... deriving revenue from notorious houses, stealing money from arrestees, organizing votes for the Republican machine, collaborating with pawnbrokers ... involved in receiving stolen property, and accepting bribes from gamblers and tavern keepers in exchange for protection and favors.[4]

Jeff also courted newspaper editors and reporters to keep reports of criminal activities from publication. In one of Jeff's notebooks dated October 1, 1890, he lists $55 as being paid to the *Daily News.* Jeff had no known advertisements in newspapers, so the amount ($1,648 today) is surely far too much to pay for anything but a bribe.[5]

Then there were the victims, whom through one means or another, Jeff usually made sure remained quiet about their losses. If a victim did succeed in making a complaint, to begin with, the circumstances of civil procedure were on Jeff's side. An

[1] Ltr fr John W. Morgan to Jeff R. Smith II, 11/09/1886. Jefferson R. "Little Randy" Smith col.
[2] Maurer, p. 10.
[3] Maskelyne, pp. 194-199, "Sand Tell-Box" thoroughly discussed.
[4] Secrest, p. 160.
[5] Tom's Inflation Calculator. Memorandum notebook, 10/01/1890. Jefferson R. "Little Randy" Smith col.

out-of-town victim was not inclined to wait for a hearing. If he did, perhaps could be coaxed or tricked into leaving town before a hearing were held. A counter complaint against a victim was always a strong inducement to drop a complaint. Occasionally the name of "Soapy" would be seen in print, such as in the following instance:

> Some time ago Amos Daniels made complaint against Jeff Smith, better known as "Soapy" Smith, for defrauding him by a confidence game. The case was dismissed by justice Dormer yesterday on account of the non-appearance of Daniels, against whom the costs incurred were charged.[1]

However, such a slip was innocuous, leaving Jeff free to run his businesses in town and pursue the building of a calm, domestic existence on Glenarm Street.[2]

Having police cooperation produced two major benefits. On the last day of January 1888, Police Chief Henry C. Brady had his officers sweep the streets of confidence men and tinhorn gamblers. Fourteen men were arrested, all within proximity of Larimer and Sixteenth streets.[3] Seventeenth Street, where Jeff was based, was seemingly ignored. None of those arrested is known to have been a member of Jeff's Soap Gang. Not only were Jeff and his men exempted from the roundup, but their competition had been removed. Clark Secrest, Denver historian and author, describes the corrupt administration of chief Brady that made it possible for Jeff to operate unmolested:

> It is difficult to imagine a worse police chief than Denver's Henry C. Brady, before or since. His two-year term beginning in 1887 was marked by unprecedented laxity, corruption, and turmoil.[4]

The overcrowded, under-staffed Denver courts also worked to Jeff's advantage. Most businessmen and travelers could not afford to wait around for a hearing. More often than not, they accepted their losses and left the city. Occasionally, however, victims would become enraged over their loss and react violently. Jeff and his men were always alert for this possibility and kept "strong arms" at the ready. On Wednesday July 8, 1888, Jeff swindled two men who reacted with their fists. "A 'soap' man and two grangers [farmers] got into trouble yesterday morning, in which the grangers, as usual, got the worst of it."[5] Jeff always operated with steerers and boosters who were capable of physically handling unruly victims. In this instance, though, it appears Jeff alone battled the two grangers. Jeff no doubt learned early on about the inflammatory danger of bunco work. To protect himself, everywhere he went he carried concealed weapons. Once married, he also protected himself and his new family with life and accident insurance. One policy from the Pacific Mutual Life Insurance Company of San Francisco dates from November 29, 1888, to November 29, 1889.[6]

---

[1] *RMN* 06/15/1888.

[2] *Denver City Directory*, 1888.

[3] *RMN* 02/01/1888.

[4] Secrest, p. 162.

[5] *RMN* 07/05/1888.

[6] Life and Accident policy receipt, 04/02/1889. Item 26, author's col.

Three weeks later Jeff's soap sell racket was listed in the *News* along with a number of other swindles then operating in the city, under the headline, "The Street Fakir." Jeff is not mentioned by name, but his long-practiced prize package soap sell is described in some detail. Perhaps the calm Jeff had enjoyed by way of bribes was coming to a close. Titled "The Soap Game," the article addressed how

> the sucker who is abroad in the land has not tasted life until he has bucked the "soap" game. About one hundred packages containing soap are mixed up in a shallow box. The owner picks up one of the packages, and taking off the wrapper, then rewraps it, inserting at the same time a $20 bill: he drops the package in the box, and allows any of the by-standers the privilege of looking for it for $1. The man who is daring enough … picks up the identical package the bill is in and leaves the premises. He returns shortly, however, declaring he has been imposed upon—robbed, and when he asks redress the only answer he gets is "try your luck—$1 a chance."
>
> Denver is infested with all kinds of street fakirs, some of whom are on the streets from morning till night. Some make large amounts of money and others but very little, according to the ability of the man. These men have long since been hardened to the ways of the world. They are good judges of human nature, and know as soon as they set eyes upon a man whether he can be played upon, and to what extent....[1]

One victim Jeff "played" was of his own kind, a Portland, Oregon, bunco man named Jacob Kasenheim, known to peers as "Sleepy Jake." Kasenheim and two accomplices had developed a machine that made $5 gold pieces from "burmeze metal." To greedy dupes, they sold half interests in the money-making machines for upwards of $3,000. Successful in selling several of the machines in San Francisco before being caught, Kasenheim spent six months in prison. Upon release, he headed to Denver with about $2,000 and approached Jeff with an offer to join forces. William H. Morton described to the *Morning Oregonian* how Jeff swindled the swindler.

> "Soapy" knew of a possible customer—a mine-owner at Cripple Creek—who was returning on the next afternoon's train. As Jake could not write his name he never put his money in a bank as it was rather an embarrassing feat to check it out. According to the program, Jake took a seat near the door facing "Soapy" so as to observe his signals. "Soapy" entered from the rear end of the coach, and took a seat beside the supposed victim. "Soapy" did not attempt to "work" him, and after a few minutes general conversation "wigwagged" to Jake that it was no go. The buncoist got off at the next station, and as it was only a few miles back to Denver, and there was no incoming train, it was agreed to foot it back to town. After trudging along a few miles they were brought to a standstill by the command "Hands up!" and two masked men, with guns pointed at them stepped from behind a tree in the bend of the road. "Jake's" hands were elevated as high as he could reach. He was relieved of his $2,000. The highwaymen went through the

ceremony of going through "Soapy's" pockets, but it was only in order to throw dust to the eyes of "Sleepy Jake," for the supposed highwaymen were "Soapy" Smith's confederates.[1]

Perhaps the price of keeping the *News* quiet had risen too high, or perhaps the *News* felt that by keeping the story lidded, the cost to its crusading self-image was too high. Jeff and his prize package soap racket stand on the corner of Seventeenth and Market had become a fixture in the Denver business district. More days than not, he could be seen swindling the gullible of their currency and was becoming a symbol of organized crime in Denver, making of Jeff too inviting a target for the *News* to ignore.

In the latter 1880s, Jeff's roots in Denver were deep. He had married, maintained his wife and children in a nice home, and protected them from his way of life and its harms. He would do anything for his family—but give up criminal ways. He continued to gain influence at city hall and notoriety among bunco men across the country. In fact, among rogues Jeff had risen to the status of royalty. They applied in droves for membership in his Soap Gang, and if in good standing with the bunco brotherhood, they more than likely were allowed to try out for the big time. One of the newest applicants about to be hired was none other than Jeff's younger brother, Bascomb.

With success on a large scale, however, came an ominous shift. Hardened and dangerous men began to fill the ranks, rough and pitiless men like "Big Ed" Burns. Jeff would soon seek to widen his profits by opening a cigar store to front many schemes and by renting various locations for auction houses and other swindles. Jeff would also open his own saloon and gambling establishments. Both for good and bad, the future of Denver included Jeff Smith.

Chapter 6
Denver and the Tivoli Club

The slaughter pen
—The Tivoli Club as named by the *Rocky Mountain News*, October 1892

In 1880, Denver had 98 saloons. By 1889, the city directory listed 296,[2] and by 1890, 319.[3] Many of these were dives and fronts for gambling and criminal activity. They rarely closed, even on Sundays, which became a long-standing issue in city politics. Many saloons were hell holes of crime and violence, and the wayward visitor stood a better than even chance of leaving without his billfold, or worse—with contusions, broken bones, and perhaps a concussion. Decades passed as local lawmakers tried and failed to curb crime and violence in the saloons but not alienate the thousands who thronged to them. Not until Prohibition in the 1920s did Denver finally cap saloon crime.

The year 1889 held numerous transformations for Jeff. He entered the saloon business, greatly expanded his operations, and took in his younger brother Bascomb

---

[1] *RMN* 11/29/1888, p. 1. And *Morning Oregonian* 07/17/1898, p. 8.

[2] *Denver City Directory*, 1889.

[3] Noel, *City*, p. 116.

as a partner in business and crime. Prior to 1887, Bascomb was denied Soap Gang membership. Jeff felt his brother needed more schooling and experience before he could work successfully at his side. At age fourteen in 1883, Bascomb was already a trouble maker. In Belton, Texas, where he lived with his father, Bascomb tried to torch a hotel for not hiring him. The *Galveston Daily News* reported the story.

> An attempt was made yesterday evening to burn the Avenue hotel building by setting fire to a small store-room in the rear. It was discovered in time to prevent any damage. Bascom Smith, a youth, aged about fourteen years, who had made an unsuccessful application for work at the hotel, was suspected as the guilty party, and has been committed to jail in default of a $1500 bond.[1]

Jeff's sisters, Eva Katherine and Emmie Lou, writing from Belton on December 16, 1886, wrote to Jeff to keep him abreast of family affairs, including Bascomb's.

Dear Brother,

> I received your letter dated at Chicago yesterday and received the other one today, and the fifteen [dollars] for which you will please accept our heart filled thanks. I would rather you had sent presents for I know you have better taste. I don't know whether we can get something we need most. We had a very dull Christmas. Hope to have a better time New Years. Emmie L. says she is going to save her money to move away on. We are all well, yes Bascomb is a gambler. He makes some big winnings sometimes but it goes just like it comes. They say he is the shrewdest best monte dealer in town. I concluded that young mans [sic] ears are too large. Just look at them. I got a pretty long nose on now,[2] and the next thing you hear of I'll be away, away from Belton. I am mad at Papa. He makes fun of all my [undecipherable]. Em [Emmie L.] says come and see us. What would we give to see you. I received a letter from Cousin Bobo a few days since [—] he is a reporter for the Fort Worth Gazette. He always inquires about you. Well I will close hoping to see you another Christmas. With love to your wife.

We are your Affectionate Sisters

Eva K. and E. L. Smith[3]

Five months later Bascomb was still in Belton and gambling. In May 1887 the *Galveston Daily News* reported the following dangerous event.

---

[1] *Galveston Daily News* 09/21/1883.

[2] *ears are too large ... got a pretty long nose on now.* The ears seem to signify that Bascomb has grown large ones so that he can hear any and all praise of himself. Then Eva confesses wearing "a pretty long nose," suggesting nosiness (long-nosed, curious, prying, *OED*) or perhaps in the sense of making "a long nose: To put a derisive thumb to the nose" (Partridge, *Slang*). Another possibility is that the long nose alludes to when Moses learned from God that He is longsuffering (Exodus 34:6). Some sources claim *longsuffering* is a direct translation from the Hebrew for being long nosed, i.e., slow to breathe wrathful fire through the nose. Other sources claim this a mistranslation. It remains a somewhat popular idea and perhaps was so then. Eva could have taken the idea from church or religious writing. Seen in this letter by Eva is the inclination to employ, like her brother Jeff, literary devices—here, figurative language and, perhaps, biblical allusion.

[3] Ltr fr Eva K. & Emmie L. Smith to Jeff R. Smith II, 12/26/1886. Jefferson R. "Little Randy" Smith col.

C. B. Kirkland, a brakeman on the Missouri-Pacific railway, and Bascom Smith, a young sportsman of the town, had a difficulty this evening about sundown. Kirkland shot at Smith with a 38-caliber pistol, but missed his mark, and was arrested. He gave a $300 bond for his appearance in court to-morrow morning, when he will be examined.[1]

The date of Bascomb's arrival in Denver is probably some time after this shooting incident, but a letter to Jeff from Frank A. Gibbons, dated February 2, 1887, mentions Bascomb's placement in the gang three months prior.[2] It is possible Bascomb traveled between Belton and Denver for a time. His activities in Denver, however, are not officially heard of until 1889 when Jeff and Bascomb, under the business name of Bascomb, Smith and Company, opened a cigar store at 1531 Seventeenth Street, near the corner of Wazee Street, a block south of the train depot. Bascomb listed the business address as his residence.[3] The brothers sometimes roomed together at 3451 Larimer Street, known as "upper Larimer," in one of the many cottages there.[4] The store sold cigars, but it was just a front for criminal enterprise. The location was convenient for steering visitors from the train station to swindles in the back room at a small, green-covered poker table.[5] The establishment was located next to the saloon complex of George B. Fisher at 1535, 1537, and 1539 Seventeenth. Directly across the street was the Turre & Cuneo saloon at 1538 Seventeenth. A letter from Fisher to Jeff in 1896 shows the men were friends and that Fisher was well acquainted with members of the Soap Gang. It is probable, therefore, that victims were often brought to the Fisher saloon complex as prelude or finale to a swindle.[6]

Gambling for Jeff was a passion, and perhaps an addiction. His game of choice was faro. Obsessed with it, he worked hard to acquire money enough to "buck the tiger," the phrase by which the game was often known. After joining a game, he did not quit until either he or the bank was broke. A bystander reported Jeff's mode of play.

> That night I was in the Arcade when Smith came in. The place was ablaze with light and full of people, including the boys from the plains and mountains as well as Denver's own complement of gamblers. Games of chance were in progress everywhere. The ordinary plays were on, but everybody stopped when "Soapy" entered. He walked proudly through a lane of admirers as he found his way to the faro table. He was the center of attraction. No one else played. All had heard of his passion for faro, and many of us had seen him win a big pile with his sleight-of-hand during the day. We wanted to see whether he would be as successful when pitted against one of his kind at another game. He did not use chips..., but, empting his pockets of a large stack of twenty dollar gold pieces, proceeded to wager

---

[1] *Galveston Daily News* 05/18/1887.
[2] Ltr fr Frank A. Gibbons to Jeff R. Smith II, 2/02/1887. Geri Murphy col.
[3] *Denver City Directory*, 1889.
[4] *Denver City Directory*, 1889.
[5] Denver newspaper clipping of unknown origin & date. Author's col.
[6] Ltr fr George B. Fisher to Jeff R. Smith II, 11/08/1896. Item 12, author's col. This Ltr appears in full in Chapter 14. (See "Fisher" in Index for location.)

them as fast as his bets could be taken. At first he won everything, but afterward lost so heavily that it was generally reported ... he was dead broke. If such was the case he did not manifest any great concern, and at the close of the performance walked out of the hall as nonchalantly as he had entered.[1]

Faro is no longer played because, in an honest game, odds favor the house only slightly better than the player, 1¾% while upward from 6% in all other games. The odds made faro nearly the most popular gambling game of the 19th century. The problem for the player, though, lay in finding an honest game. Play involved the layout, a board with 13 playing-card spots, one for each numeral denomination and one for each face card. Another piece of equipment was the case, often referred to as a case-keeper. It was an abacus-looking device that kept track of the cards used in play so that players could tell at a glance what cards remained to be dealt. Another piece of equipment was a dealing box, a metal container for the deck of cards. It allowed the dealer to pull one card at a time from a thin slit on the side. Players wagered on the table layout which cards would exit the box as winner and loser. The first card out of the dealing box was the "banker card," or losing card, and the second out of the box was the "player's card," or winner card. Bets were won and lost on each "turn" from the dealing box, which continued until the deck was down to the three remaining cards. To "call the last turn," a player would bet on the order of the last two cards.

Dealing boxes came about as a way to prevent cheating. Made and sold by gambling supply houses, the boxes sealed a shuffled deck of cards from manipulation and allowed only one card at a time to be dispensed. A saying in the gambling trade, however, goes "Where there's a bill, there's a way"—a way to cheat. Special dealing boxes came to be manufactured that released two cards at a time rather than one. Called "gaffed," these boxes had a small button that could be pressed to release more than one card. This is the kind of box that John Morgan of Leadville wrote to Jeff about, the "sand tell box" of his that he hoped was in a Denver pawn shop. The two cards released went to a dispensed-card pile as if one card. Drawing the extra card during a game altered the cards to be wagered upon in "the last turn," and as the last two cards in a game usually entailed the highest betting, this previous manipulation shifted favorable odds from players to the house. Probably the majority of Denver gambling establishments owned gaffed dealing boxes. They were specially designed by gambling equipment companies such as Denver's George Mason and Company.

Jeff can be described as a gambler as well as a confidence man. When on a winning streak, Jeff often shared his winnings with friends and those in need. However when luck ran against him, Jeff sometimes became explosive and was a man to avoid. Gamblers made and lost fortunes playing faro, so problems with irate losers were bound to occur. Because of this inherent volatility and the temptation of players to cheat, such as by pulling back a bet or shifting it, faro was the only game that had as a part of its crew a heavily armed guard known as a "looker" or "look-out."[2]

---

[1] *Trail*, June 1920. p. 13.

[2] The author had a complete faro set up, with both a fair dealing box and a "gaffed" one. Many nights were spent playing, or "bucking the tiger," with friends. The *Dictionary of American Regional English*

Many who become hooked on gambling run into economic difficulties. One player of faro at Jeff's was forced into an agreement to quit playing.

> I, F.M. Pickerel do solemly [sic] swear that I will not play stake or be interested with anyone that does play at the game of Faro for the period of five years from the date here of dated September 2nd 1887 Signatured and sworn to begin this date of September 2nd, 1887
>
> F. M. Pickerel
>
> J.P.
>
> Henry N. Sales [Attorney and Justice of the Peace for Arapaho county][1]

The initials "J.P." signify a witness to the document and are possibly those of Soap Gang member Joe Palmer. The agreement does not specify a cause, but one can be imagined. Pickerel was engaged in a game of faro, perhaps a table operated by Jeff, in which he acquired losses, and Jeff, being in a generous mood, helped him out in return for a "promise not to play" agreement. Probably, though, generous altruism had little to do with the agreement. Rather, it was worth a loss to gain the abstinence, at least from Jeff's tables, of an addicted player who could not afford to play.

Jeff was not immune to excitement at the faro tables. A newspaper story tells how he once promised Mary he would refrain from playing faro for sixty days. At the end of that time, he handed over what he had saved by not gambling, $30,000. That night he played faro with $10,000 he had held back from Mary.[2]

As business and the economy were secure, Jeff approached gambling czar Ed Chase and succeeded in forming a partnership in a saloon and gambling hall, christened the Tivoli Club.[3] It opened sometime after February 12, 1888, when permission was granted by the city council to operate a saloon on the corner of Seventeenth and Market. The earliest mention of the Tivoli Club is published in the *NEWS*, on November 22, 1888 due to an anti-gambling raid by the city police. It was reported that the upstairs gaming portion of the house was under "proprietorship" of Jim Dunn, and that he had "roulette, faro and pokers games in full blast."[4]

The name Tivoli comes from the ancient Italian town of the same name. It resides northeast of Rome at the falls of the Anio river where it issues imposingly from the Sabine hills.[5] "Tivoli" was a popular name in the American west. Photographs from early Fort Worth show a saloon with that name when Jeff was there. Among likely reasons for choosing the name was the Tivoli Beer Hall, which was attached to Ed Chase's prestigious Palace Theatre on Blake Street. That Tivoli had since been sold and the name changed. The name was familiar to those who frequented the district

---

(*DARE*) lists "buck" as early as 1851 meant "To bet or lose (money) in gambling...." The *DARE* also lists "bucking the tiger" as first in print in 1859, meaning "To play [or gamble] against the faro bank."

[1] Agreement not to gamble document dated 09/02/1887. Jefferson R. "Little Randy" Smith col.

[2] *Seattle Post Intelligencer* 07/19/1898.

[3] Tivoli Club stationary showing names of both Ed Chase and Jeff Smith as partners. Jefferson R. "Little Randy" Smith col.

[4] *RMN* 11/22/1888, p. 1.

[5] Encyclopedia, 1892.

and was not something new to pique the curiosity of the press. Conceivably, Jeff sought the name as a tribute to the place in which he met his wife, Mary.

In partnering up with Chase, Jeff benefited from Chase's strong influence at city hall, which greatly helped protect Jeff's operations. A surviving piece of Tivoli Club stationary has the names of both Jeff and Ed as joint proprietors.[1] That the men remained friends well into the future is revealed in a letter to Jeff's wife in which Mrs. Chase "was pleased to hear from" Mary, sending "her kindest regards" and hoping she would return to Denver for a visit.[2] The women likely met when Mary sang at the Palace Theater and Mrs. Chase was there as one of the feature-act Barbour Sisters.

The new Tivoli at 1337 and 1339 Seventeenth Street occupied two stories, each with brick-walled quarters measuring 24 by 50 feet.[3] "Open day and night" and serving "wines, liquors, and cigars,"[4] the Tivoli Club advertised itself as a "headquarters for gentlemen, offering first class goods and First class attention."[5] The *News*, however, dubbed it "the slaughter pen."[6] Reports of swindles and violence, though no greater than in many other Denver establishments, such as the Palace Theatre and the Arcade, were numerous enough for the *News* to brand it with a bad name. Jeff was realistic about the threat of violence in Western saloons. He had been in enough of them to know that trouble was inevitable. While in Denver, Jeff purchased life and accident insurance policies, one of them for $5,000.[7]

As with most of Denver's saloons, gambling was located upstairs. It kept illegitimate activities from the prying eyes of the law man on the street, but it was also a matter of practicality. Being upstairs gave gamblers and swindlers time to clear out in the event of unwanted intrusions, such a police raid.[8] The 1890 Sanborn Fire insurance map of the street corner where the Tivoli resided gives a clue to why Jeff and Ed chose this location. It was one of the few buildings with numerous exits. The diagram shows a back door and stairway to various escape routes through several other buildings that exited around the corner onto Market Street.[9] Jeff and Ed likely had business friendships with their neighbors to insure access to their backdoors.

The Tivoli Club had two faro tables and two roulette tables. Seven dealers worked the faro tables while four men looked after the roulette wheels.[10] One of Jeff's business notebooks includes the word "wheel," a common name for roulette, but it could equally mean a policy wheel or any number of fortune wheel devices.[11] The

---

[1] Tivoli Club stationary, Jefferson R. "Little Randy" Smith col.

[2] Ltr fr Hi Ki & Henry Edwards to Mary Smith, 10/15/1895, item 43, author's col.

[3] Sanborn Fire Insurance map, Denver, 1893.

[4] Tivoli advertisement. Jefferson R. "Little Randy" Smith col.

[5] *Denver City Directory*, 1889, & stationary fr the Tivoli Club. Jefferson R. "Little Randy" col. The bill of sale indicates the Tivoli was located upstairs, 10/01/1891. Item 111, author's col.

[6] *RMN* 10/19/1892, p. 3.

[7] Life Insurance policy. The Pacific Mutual Life Insurance Company of San Francisco. 11/29/1888 to 11/29/1889. Policy #9510. Jefferson R. "Little Randy" Smith col.

[8] *RMN* 09/21/1891, p. 8.

[9] 1890 Sanborn Fire Insurance map, Denver, Colorado, sheet 58-b.

[10] *RMN* 05/08/1890, p. 7.

[11] Hand-written notebook ("memorandum") of Jeff R. Smith II, 1890-1891. Jefferson R. "Little Randy" Smith col.

1891 bill of sale lists "wheels" as well as safes, tables, chairs, and gas fixtures.[1] Also listed were several private card rooms for "friendly" games of poker.[2] A steam boiler in the corner kept the place warm. On the second floor off both sides off a hallway were rooms that may have been part of the Tivoli Club as well.

According to legend, few of the Tivoli Club's games were dealt fairly for out-of-towners, and on advice of attorney, Jeff placed a notice at the stairway that led to the gambling. "*Caveat Emptor*," it read, the famous Latin caution, "Let the Buyer Beware." Of course, few comprehended Latin, and if they did, none seemed to heed the warning.[3] Legend also has it that as part of a defense in court, Jeff argued that the Tivoli Club was an educational institution for the treatment and cure of gambling addiction, something on the order of the Keeley Institute for alcohol abuse.[4] The *News* even quoted Jeff's claim. "A man will be lured into a gambling hell and fascinated ... until he is forever lost." Then Jeff sprang the contrast: "After a man once comes to my place he is cured of gambling absolutely. He doesn't want any more of it."[5] It is hard to say if Jeff believed his claim, but perhaps he believed he could make people believe it. He is known to have used the argument again on an anti-gambling Skaguay newspaper editor, saying that when gambling addicts came up against him, he paralyzed them. "I take everything they've got" and they "never gamble again.... I tell you, I'm a reformer."[6]

Whatever trouble Jeff may have had over Denver's anti-gambling reform movements, it did not eat into his profits. In fact, for a time they and the operations that produced them climbed like 4th of July rockets. In a small, 39-page notebook with the word "memorandum" on the cover, Jeff recorded in his own hand the winnings, losses, and expenditures of the Tivoli Club for July 1890 through March 1891.[7] Dates of operation show all of Jeff's businesses open on Christmas 1890 as well as New Year's 1891. The notebook gives an inside, financial view of the economic successes and failures of the Club. Entries are mostly in order by date with one side tallying daily profits, listed as "winnings," and the other side tallying the losses, listed as "Looseys." Some months have so many indecipherable notes and money figures that a precise calculation is not possible. On a few pages Jeff broke down winnings and losses into comparisons between faro and the "wheel." That losses are recorded at all shows that gamblers in the Tivoli Club were not, or not always, victims, but rather, "patrons." Swindles and cons were likely conducted in the Club, but the faro and roulette games were honest (or honest enough) to ensure brisk return business among Denverites.

The following calculations are deciphered, insofar as possible, from Jeff's notebook for July through December 1890. Only summary winnings and losses are

---

[1] Bill of sale form with handwritten instructions & property contained inside the Tivoli Club, 10/01/1891. Item 111, author's col.

[2] *Denver Times* 10/07/1893.

[3] Collier & Westrate, pp. 138-139.

[4] *RMN* 09/08/1893, p. 3. & Collier & Westrate, pp. 144-45.

[5] *RMN* 09/08/1893, p. 3.

[6] *Denver Evening Post* 03/18/1898, p. 3.

[7] Hand-written notebook ("memorandum") of Jeff R. Smith II 1890-1891. Jefferson R. "Little Randy" Smith col.

presented. In the interest of furthering analysis, added to Jeff's listings are "Volume, Win/Loss" and "win/loss to volume." In most instances, including even summaries for January through March 1891, Jeff's handwritten notes are not decipherable, sometimes because they are so detailed and sometimes because the penciled calculations have faded with time.

> July 1890: Winnings: $1,783, Losses: $1,035, Volume: $2,818
> Win/Loss: +$748—win/loss to volume: +27%
>
> August 1890: Winnings: $1,440, Losses: $1,860, Volume: $3,300
> Win/Loss: -$420—win/loss to volume: -13%
>
> September 1890: Winnings: $4,657, Losses: $2,340, Volume: $6,997
> Win/Loss: +2,317—win/loss to volume: +33%
>
> October 1890: Winnings: $2,845, Losses: $1,723, Volume: $4,568
> Win/Loss: +1,123—win/loss to volume: +25%
>
> November 1890: Winnings: $1,420, Losses: $1,090, Volume: $2,510
> Win/Loss: +330—win/loss to volume: +13%
>
> December 1890: Winnings: $1,515, Losses: $2,255, Volume: $3,770
> Win/Loss: -740—win/loss to volume: -20%
>
> **Totals 1890**: Winnings: $13,660, Losses: $10,303, Volume: $23,358
> Win/Loss: +3,358—win/loss to volume: +14%

Jeff's notebook introduces the Silver Club in October 1890. The *News* reported its location to be "over the Tivoli."[1] Apparently the Tivoli's upstairs gambling hall was changed to the Silver Club while the downstairs saloon retained the original name. The intention seems to have been to create an exclusive environment in which to play faro and roulette. The News, however, did not like what it saw.

> It is chiefly a bunco place. It does not pretend to deal a "square" game even as the gamblers term it, except in exceptional instances. As THE NEWS reporter stepped in last night the dealer saw he was a stranger and promptly shoved the "carpentered" [gaffed] faro box into place.[2]

Here is evidence of one kind of game for "regulars" and another for "strangers," or visitors. Silver Club notation is so detailed and faded that winnings and losses for all months listed are not decipherable. Where evident, the figures are much lower than for the Tivoli Club, showing a lower volume of activity. The ratio of win to loss, however, is much higher. The following are two of five summaries to appear for the Silver Club:

> November: Winnings: $308, Losses: $95, Volume: $403
> Win/Loss: +213—win/loss to volume: +53%
>
> December: Winnings: $674, Losses: $80, Volume: $754
> Win/Loss: +594—win/loss to volume: +79%
>
> **Totals**: Winnings: $982, Losses: $175, Volume: $1,157
> Win/Loss: +982—win/loss to volume: +70%

---

[1] *RMN* 07/22/1893, p. 1.

[2] *RMN* 07/22/1893, p. 1. A "carpentered" faro box is a dealing box altered in a way that it can be manipulated by the dealer to give the house better odds. According to the 1893 Sanborn maps for 1893, 58-b, 1761 Market is on the northwest corner of Eighteenth and Market streets. Either the information is flawed or the Tivoli Club and the Silver Club moved to a new local in 1893.

In part, the reason for the relatively high losses at the Tivoli Club was faro. It was the game of choice throughout the West. As previously observed, the odds in faro are only slightly in favor of the house. On the pages in which Jeff separates the winnings and losses between the "wheel" and faro, the greater losses are at the faro tables.

Jeff did not always win when a victim played Tivoli Club games. On one occasion he came out decidedly for the worse although he took the victim's money. A *Denver Evening Post* story tells of Jeff's men having "lured a man upstairs to the gambling...."

> The word soon went out that the victim had money and "Soapy" went to deal faro, as was the rule when fine work was to be done. The victim was a miner who had spent several years in the mountains and was returning to his home in the East. He won a few bets, but began to lose. A well-known Denver man stepped in at this juncture and seeing what was going on, began to play also. But he "coppered" every bet the miner made. That is, whatever card the miner bet on, he bet against. The victim lost, but the citizen won. All kinds of inducements were offered to get the new player to stop, but he shook his head and listened to nothing that was said, declaring that the gambling house was public and his money was as good as any one else's. It would not do to kick up a row or the victim would "wise-up," quit playing, and in all probability complain to the police. The citizen was allowed to win $1,800. But the victim lost $2,500 and went back to the mines the next day on money borrowed from Smith to make another stake.[1]

Also in October 1890, "Big Hand" debuted in the notebook. Only one column appears under this heading, obviously winnings. "Big Hand" is believed to be the name Jeff gave the "friendly" poker games in which Soap Gang members played with visitors on an almost daily basis. Big Hand is listed in the notebook for 28 of the 31 days in October. The total three-month take for Big Hand is $4,087, today the equivalent of approximately $122,487.[2] The scheme required a team of 5 or 6, and their abilities and performance needed to be "spot on." The cost of this team was probably high, but then with profits running at 100%, Jeff could afford to pay well.

October: $1,843   November: $1,650   December 1890: $594
Totals: Winnings: $4,087, Losses: $0, Volume: $4,087
Win/Loss: +4,087 — win/loss to volume: +100%

The location of Big Hand games was no doubt off limits to all but those involved in the swindle. How the con might have been run was presented in the example of the Denver visitor who was "pinned" and "gripped" by Reverend Bowers and taken to the back room of the cigar store. Having the game in a closed location made it easy to set the scene right down to the chair in which the victim would sit.

An accomplished "deck mechanic" can control playing cards in a number of ways. The objective is to bring a victim along in a game until he is sufficiently comfortable and confident. Confederates in the game contribute by folding good hands or betting on low ones as if bluffing and then losing. After a stretch of winnings and good

---

[1] *Denver Evening Post* 07/31/1898.
[2] Tom's Inflation Calculator.

prospects, the victim is dealt a hand that seems unbeatable, causing him to wager big. Of course, the mechanic has dealt a member of the gang a higher hand.

A gaffed deck (containing marked or shaved cards) is one way for a deck mechanic to deliver the right cards to the right players. However, the surest method of delivering the final Big Hand of a game, or the coup de grâce, is to deal from a cold deck, that is, a deck stacked with cards in a pre-arranged order. Typically, the switch to a cold deck occurs after the shuffle and cut but before the deal. Of the ways the switch can be made, the simplest was for the dealer to slide his chair forward. In that movement, his hands drop below the table for just a fluid moment and switches one deck with the cold one in his lap. There were other ways of smuggling a cold deck into the game. One was through a runner who had come to deliver a message, or if in a private room of the Tivoli Club, a waiter with a drink tray (with the bottom concealed by a towel hanging from his arm). When the smuggler is within proximity of the dealer and the victim's attention is directed elsewhere by a confederate, the switch is made.

With the cold deck in play, the victim may receive, for example, a full house (3 of one kind and 2 of another) or 4 kings. Dealt such a good hand, the victim is likely to bet high, and is, in fact, encouraged to do so. When the betting is done and the cards laid out, the victim is stunned to see he has been beaten by, for example, a straight flush, 5 consecutive cards of the same suit.

Some places auctioned almost worthless watches and jewelry for many times their value, and newspapers called these places "mock auction houses." Jeff opened one of these places in February 1891 and listed the costs of opening in his notebook under "Auction House." The list including the following:

> Rent Feb. 27 ($70), fixtures ($35), coal ($2), help ($2), telegram ($3.75), Auctioneer ($25), Coal oil tray glass ($8), Gasoline Lamp & oil ($4), License ($100), Goods from E. ($250), Carpenter and doors ($30), Jack ($2)
> Total to open: $506.75

Unfortunately, "income" is not listed in the notebook, but an estimate is possible. If a $2.00 brass pocket watch is represented as a $30 gold watch and auctioned for $13, the margin of profit would be 550%! If the $250 in "Goods" that Jeff bought to be auctioned were to sell at a profit of 500%, $250 could be turned into $125,000. Even at 250%, the profit on one lot of cheap items could be as high as $60,000.

On February 19, 1891, the *News* reported complaints against auctioneer John Bowers. According to the notebook, Jeff's auction house opened on February 27, 1891, but the *News* report appeared eight days earlier. Bowers, then, was auctioneering for Jeff on the street before taking the business indoors.

Selling Snide Watches.

On complaint of William Nicols, a gentleman from the rural district, John H. [sic] Bowers, as auctioneer, at the corner of Seventeenth and Market streets, was arrested on the charge of obtaining money under false pretenses. Nicols claims that he bought a watch for $25 which the auctioneer represented as solid gold. Nicols took the watch and walked away as proud as a king, only to find a few hours later that all the gold had worn off his watch and that instead of being solid gold it was common dingy brass. He returned to the auctioneer who politely informed him that he could not buy the watch back as he was selling and not buying such articles. Bowers was placed under $300 bonds for his appearance at Justice Simmonds' court....[1]

A month later, on March 12, 1891, German visitor Joseph Fendrichs from Telluride, Colorado, was swindled in Jeff's auction house. He described to a *News* reporter how he had come up from the depot and put part of his money in a bank

> so that when I get to St. Joe I could take it out again by writing. When I walked back and a man say to me—"hello landsman, where are you going?" At the same time taking me by the coat and pushing me inside the shop.
>
> When he pull out my watch and say—"good movement but got some more here that are better." I said "all right, but I want my own watch." "Come here," he said, and took me in a back room. "Have you any money?" he asked. "Yes, some," I said. "How much" he wanted to know. "More than enough for the watches," I told him. "Let me see it," he said. "No, I will keep it; I don't want the watches!"
>
> All the time the other men were bidding on watches, and at last one said to me: "Their [They're] yours." "No," I said. "I never bid for them!" Then some one took my money from me and I left the place to come and see the police. We went back and one said: "Here, take $25 for the watch. But I wanted all my money and then he gave me $40 more and said that that was all I had given him for the two watches. He got from me $165.[2]

As auctioning watches for much more than they were worth was not a crime, the police or the courts could do little for victims. In the case of Fendrichs, however, he claimed money had been wrested from him. Whether he received more than the $65 returned to him, while unknown, is doubtful. Apparently he had no bill of sale.

Another tricky auctioning technique was to offer money back to someone for helping to rescue a fine watch that was selling for too little, plus $2 upon return of the watch that was purchased. J. E. Noon described to the police how he was taken in by the promise. As he was entering an auction house belonging to J. Kantrowitz's,

> they were auctioning the watch, one of the cappers having just bid $14 on the time-piece. Kantrowitz stepped around to him, told him it was a shame that the watch was going so cheap, and that if Noon would bid $15 he could have it; also that if he would come around later he could exchange the watch for the money and get $2 as a bonus. Noon bid, paid his money and left. He returned later to make the exchange suggested and get the $2 he had earned, but was fired out bodily.[3]

In August 1891 Jeff's auction house business was destroyed by fire. The *News* covered the disaster in an article titled "CLEANED OUT."

> A fire, caused by the explosion of a gasoline lamp, broke out in the auctioneer establishment of Jeff Smith, No. 1429-31 Seventeenth Street, at

---

[1] *RMN* 02/19/1891, p. 7.

[2] *RMN* 03/13/1891, p. 5.

[3] *RMN* 04/15/1892, p. 6.

12:30 this morning. The fire department was on hand promptly, but the entire stock, valued at about $900, and fixtures were lost, insurance $400.

The building owned by Florentine Spalti, was not injured to any great extent. It is not known whether this loss is covered by insurance or not.[1]

The profitability of the Tivoli Club, the Silver Club, and Big Hand operations can be stated with certainty for July through December 1890, which is as follows:

Tivoli Club, July-Dec: Winnings: $13,660, Losses: $10,303, Volume: $23,963
   Win/Loss: +$3,358—win/loss to volume: +14%

Silver Club, Nov- : Winnings: $982, Losses: $175, Volume: $1,157
   Win/Loss: +$807—win/loss to volume: +70%

Big Hand, Nov-Dec: Winnings: $4,087, Losses: $0, Volume: $4,087
   Win/Loss: +$4,087—win/loss to volume: +100%

Totals, July-Dec: Winnings: $18,729, Losses: $10,478, Volume: $29,207
   Win/Loss to volume: +28%

Totals in current dollars[2]: Win: $561,308, Loss: $314,026, Volume: $875,334
   Win/Loss to volume: +28%

For this six-month period of start-up enterprises, income was over half a million in today's dollars. No income is shown for the auction house. Potentially, its profit margin could have been larger than his other operations combined, even at half the estimate of a 500% return. As previously observed, a $250 investment in high end "cheap John" goods could be sold for $60,000, and this within a month! With auction house revenue added in, profit for a six-month period would be about 1.7 million in today's dollars.[3]

The notebook has more to reveal, this time about fictive and actual proprietors. It records Joe "Gambler Joe" Simmons three times. Two show amounts Joe owed, one for $20 and one for $300. The third is for $285 in a column under "Cash," dated November 1890. This may have been Simmons' pay for managing the club, an assumption based on Jeff's later having made Joe the manager in 1892 of his Orleans Club in Creede. However, according to the *News*, Henry Dutch was the manager of the Tivoli Club in February and October 1891.[4] This apparent discrepancy reveals a common practice among owners of tenderloin properties in downtown Denver.

Henry Dutch was the alias for William Deutsch. Under this name he owned several properties. In 1881 and 1882, he had managed Ed Chase's Palace Theatre's saloon and gaming annex, the Tivoli Beer Hall.[5] For ejecting a John Burns from the Theatre in March 1881, Deutsch was arrested for assault and battery.[6] In 1883 he was listed as the proprietor.[7] In 1887-1888 he was listed in the city directory as proprietor of the Alhambra Beer Hall at 1321 Seventeenth Street[8] and as its manager in 1889.[1] In

---

[1] *RMN* 08/08/1891, p. 2.

[2] Tom's Inflation Calculator.

[3] Tom's Inflation Calculator, $1 in 1890 = $29.97 in 2009.

[4] *RMN* 02/23/1891 and 10/27/1891, p. 3. The October listing states that Deutsch's is manager of a business at 1700 Market which is the exact corner of the Tivoli Club.

[5] *RMN* 03/06/1881, p. 8.

[6] *RMN* 03/12/1881, p. 8.

[7] *RMN* 03/06/1883.

[8] *Denver City Directory*, 1887 & 1888.

1886 a property on Seventeenth and Holladay streets (later named Market) was transferred to his name, where in February 1888 he received permission to open a saloon at that location. This property is believed to be Jeff and Ed Chase's Tivoli Club.

In city directories for 1890-91 and 1893-95, Deutsch is listed as proprietor of the Tivoli Club.[2] In June 1892 the *News* mentioned him as proprietor.[3] The city directory in 1897 lists the Tivoli Sample Room at the same location.[4] A business card lists his name for the "Tivoli Sample Room" located on the "corner 17th and Market streets."[5] A "sample room" was a step above a saloon in class, some of which served only wines. Deutsch's name also appears on a personalized glass whiskey flask, the label reading, "Fine Old Monogram whiskey, Bottled expressly for Wm. Deutsch, Tivoli Seventeenth and Market Street, Denver Colo."[6] Paperwork for the Tivoli Club indicates Jeff and Ed Chase sold it in October 1891,[7] but this was most likely a way to shield their names as proprietors during the anti-saloon reform movements of 1891. Undercover ownership was not a new idea in Denver. Ed Chase is known to have hidden his numerous gambling establishments and policy shops under the names of others who appeared as their owners on city records. As political weather changed, so did proprietors, at least on paper. Jeff and Ed reestablished their recorded ownership of the Tivoli in 1892. No matter the recorded "owner," when the Tivoli made headlines in the newspapers, it was listed as Jeff's place, and publicly he never denied it.

The first known account of a victim in the Tivoli Club appeared in a June 1889 edition of the *Denver Times*. The *News* printed Jeff's articulate defense against the charge, but the lead given the story expressed the paper's judgment.

STILL ANOTHER FAKE

The statements published ... last evening are refuted by trustworthy testimony, and designated false and malicious.... Mr. Smith, the proprietor, said: "when I read the account in the Times about my place I felt very much injured. That paper is worse than any highwayman in Denver. I am a married man making an honest effort to make a living for my family through a legitimate business. If the people responsible for that foul slander had come up to me and robbed me, it would be preferable than to stain my character. That man Hearie never lost a cent in my house. He never even sat down in my house that I know of. He used to come here to sell matches and other truck, and I always pitied the old man. The man got drunk and was robbed somewhere on Nineteenth street. He is working the old soldier racket as many other frauds do to gain sympathy. I was a soldier myself, in the twenty-

---

[1] *Denver City Directory*, 1889.

[2] *Denver City Directory*, 1890-1891, 1893-1895.

[3] *RMN* 06/19/1892.

[4] *Denver City Directory*, 1897.

[5] Tivoli Sample Room business card, Geri Murphy col.

[6] Whiskey bottle, Jerry Hazalet col.

[7] Tivoli sale paperwork, 10/01/1891. Item 111, author's col.

first artillery of Indiana and the One Hundred and forty-fifth infantry during the war. This would be the last house that an old soldier would be held up in."[1]

No records are known that indicate Jeff ever officially served in the US military.

Jeff read newspapers. They gave him political weather reports, listed prospective visitors, revealed opportunities for assisting politicians with their problems, and measured "Soapy Smith's" level of exposure to public view. At one time Jeff employed a clipping service to gather news articles about him from major newspapers around the state. Two of the last photographs taken of Jeff, one standing at the bar in his saloon in Skaguay and the other on horseback there, show him in possession of what appear to be newspapers. He was also interested in national affairs, including natural crises such as poverty, hunger, and epidemics and in man-made disasters. In these cases, he often responded by opening his pocketbook to make contributions and often encouraged his friends and others to do the same. The disastrous Johnstown, Pennsylvania, flood of May 31, 1889, was one of the worst natural disasters of its kind. After heavy rains, the 1852 dam 14 miles above the river valley town gave way and sent a 20-foot high, debris-filled wall of water roaring down the narrow valley. The catastrophe was of astonishing scale. In moments, Johnstown was completely destroyed, and over 2,000 people were dead, including over 100 entire families and nearly 400 children. The disaster was on the minds of everyone and in their conversations.[2] Jeff and friend John Kinneavy each gave fifty dollars out of their saloon businesses to aid the victims and their families, which in contemporary dollars amounts to $1,479.[3] The Denver Chamber of Commerce appointed a committee to solicit donations, and a list of those donating was published in the *News*. Of over 200 donations, 18 were for more than $50.[4] In September 1888 Jeff gave $10, or $296 today, to a subscription being taken for yellow fever victims in Jacksonville, Florida, no small amount for victims 1,475 miles away.[5]

In February 1888, John Kinneavy and partner Tim Connors[6] bought out gambler Clifton Bell's Jockey Club,[7] a saloon and gambling house on Sixteenth Street, opposite the Hotel Brunswick.[8] Kinneavy developed the Jockey into a high-toned establishment of good reputation. A *News* reporter visited one evening and described what he saw.

> The uptown gambling places are patronized by a slightly more prosperous class of people than those on Larimer street. At the Jockey Club on Sixteenth, between Lawrence and Larimer, there were seven tables in active operation at 10:30 p.m. Fifty-two men were playing or preparing to.... Nearly all were clerks and small business men. There are thirty employees.[9]

---

[1] *RMN* 06/20/1889.

[2] Johnstown Flood Museum.

[3] Tom's Inflation Calculator: $1 in 1889 = $29.57 in 2009.

[4] *RMN* 06/05/1889.

[5] *RMN* 09/20/1888, p. 8. Tom's Inflation Calculator.

[6] Tim Connors became a police officer, was involved in a shooting with Bat Masterson in 1897, and was indicted for election fraud. By 1905, he was Denver's police captain of detectives. (Secrest, p. 146)

[7] *RMN* 02/09/1888, p. 2.

[8] *RMN* 02/09/1888, p. 2. "Jockey" often spelled "Jocky."

[9] *RMN* 07/22/1893, p. 1.

Jeff had many associates in Denver. One was John Kinneavy, a well-regarded business owner with whom Jeff worked closely until Jeff left Denver in 1895. Another was Ed Chase, a well-protected, highly successful business owner and partner. Associates also included the proprietors of other saloons, like Johnny Murphy and his often bloody Murphy's Exchange. Jeff often marshaled them to support or to defeat one ordinance or another. Then there was the fluid Soap Gang of swindlers, card sharks, and strong-arm men, ranging from twelve to twenty-four. With the high and the low and rough, Jeff mixed well, including the religiously ordained.

Reverend Thomas Uzzell, the "Fighting Parson," had a special liking for Jeff, and for quite awhile Jeff's regard for the parson was mutual. In 1885, the parson assumed control of the religious and philanthropic activities of the People's Tabernacle. For many years it operated in a building and area near brothels and cribs on Blake Street near Twentieth.[1] For twenty-five years, the parson and his volunteer corps cared for the sick and the poor. The Tabernacle had a full-time doctor paid by the Congregationalist church, and it paid his patients' medical bills.[2] Under Uzzell, the church ran a free medical dispensary, distributed free clothing to the needy in winter, operated a free bathhouse, and regularly offered free classes in life skills, such as sewing. A night school tutored adults and children in basic academic skills, such as math and reading.[3] He did his best to assist all people in need, no matter their background or religion—or lack of it. Lyle Dorset in his *History of Denver* wrote of Tom Uzzell that he used his own money

> to open a "Friendly Shelter" in the heart of Denver's slums. There he fed, sheltered, and clothed as many as 400 men at one time who were disease-ridden, drunk, or down on their luck. He preached a little gospel to the indigents, but he never made conversion to Christianity, temperance, or middle-class morality a measure of worthiness or a requirement for help.
>
> Rather than conducting fund-raising drives for ... edifices, Uzzell solicited money to buy tents for the homeless and furniture and clothing for the needy.[4]

Uzzell worked out of the same Blake Street location from 1888 to 1901, when a new The People's Tabernacle Church and center was built at 20th and Welton streets.[5]

Carlyle Channing Davis was a partner with Colonel John Arkins in establishing the *Leadville Evening Chronicle* in 1878-79. Arkins sold out in 1880 and left town to buy into the *Rocky Mountain News* in Denver. Davis stayed and ran the *Chronicle* for many years. In 1916 he published an autobiography titled *Olden Times in Colorado*, and Parson Tom Uzzell figures prominently among its pages. The parson had come to Leadville in 1878 to build a Methodist church[6] and almost immediately established

---

[1] Denver Public Library, digital photograph information, call number C-166.

[2] *Denver Daily News* 07/12/1885.

[3] *Denver Daily News* 06/10/1886.

[4] Dorsett, p. 115.

[5] Denver Public Library, digital photograph call number C-166.

[6] Leadville.

himself as the "Fighting Parson." A "lot jumping" problem had existed, and when the parson went to check on a lot donated for the church, he discovered

> men unloading lumber upon it. Seeing that they were not disposed to listen to his wordy protest, Tom stripped off coat and vest, and made such a determined assault ... as to induce them to desist. Later, Tom said to me: "I made up my mind [that] if the Lord wanted me to recover that lot, He would give me strength to lick those fellows. And the result showed that He was on my side! ... It was strange that I didn't get hurt in that town [Leadville]. I used to go at all hours of the day and night, answering death-bed calls and visiting the sick, but never a word was ever said against me or my work.[1]

Carlyle Davis also told Uzzell's story about preaching a funeral five miles from town in winter for the co-owner of "a perfect den of vice" who had been shot to death. When the service ended, the huge crowd left in a hurry, and the man who brought the parson forgot him there. Among the last to leave were six prostitutes, and they offered him a ride. He accepted it, and they made him sit in the middle of them. He asked to be dropped off at the outskirts of town, but they refused, and the six most notorious women in town drove him home "right through the busiest streets in the town."[2]

Davis also retells Uzzell's story of the impression he made on Bishops Warren and MacCabe when they came to visit in 1879.

> I got a call, about dark one night, to go to a tough place and marry a couple. I asked my visitors if they would not like to accompany me. Both accepted the invitation, and as we were leaving the house, mother called to me,
>
> "Tom, you've forgotten your pistol!"
>
> Bishop Warren threw up his hands in holy terror. He didn't want to remain longer in a place where a preacher had to carry a gun.[3]

In interview given to the *News*, Uzzell reported that one of the Bishops said,

> "Good heavens, Mr. Uzzell. ... Do ministers carry pistols in Leadville?"
>
> "Oh, yes," he replied. "When I go out after dark I carry a revolver in one pocket, and a prayer book in the other."[4]

When Uzzell came to Leadville as its first minister,[5] he was afraid of being robbed by the numerous gamblers. Confidence man Charles "Doc" Baggs, however, convinced him that gamblers would not rob him but that riff-raff might. The parson found Doc's words true. In fact, he also discovered that when times were hard and the need great, gamblers were the most generous with cash donations.[6] And so the parson developed for the gamblers not just tolerance and respect but even liking. Uzzell performed the marriage ceremony for Baggs and his wife.[7]

---

[1] Davis, Carlyle, pp. 230-231.
[2] Davis, Carlyle, pp. 298--299.
[3] Davis, Carlyle, pp. 300.
[4] *RMN* 06/09/1886, p. 6.
[5] *RMN* 06/09/1886, p. 6.
[6] *RMN* 04/01/1890.
[7] *RMN* 12/27/1892, p. 4.

Jeff trusted and respected the parson. When Jeff gave money to the parson, he knew it would be used in the most effective and least judgmental manner. Isadore Leon, an acquaintance of Uzzell's, recalled in an interview the time she and the parson were walking in the business district of Denver when they came upon Jeff. The parson is said to have introduced him as "the greatest confidence man in America—and my friend."[1] Jeff throughout his life made contributions to men like Uzzell who helped not just those of one congregation or those who were religious but all people in need.

During the Christmas holiday, Jeff was said to be in his most charitable frame of mind.[2] Joseph Emerson Smith, an early Denver newspaper man, bears out this perception with a 1943 remembrance of Jeff.

> We newspaper men, if not downright fond of, were intrigued by him [Jeff]. We saw him on Christmas mornings presenting dressed turkeys to a long line of hundreds of the very poor at Seventeenth and Market, a wholesale commission house keeping open to supply the big birds.[3]

The story of Jeff's annual act of giving away turkeys to the poor at Christmas time was well-known to many in Denver. The *Denver Evening Post* made note that countless citizens missed the tradition when Jeff left.

> For years when the cold winds of winter were causing the people to seek shelter in some building as it blew the snow in great drifts, "Soapy's" conscience would hurt him. Every Christmas morning when happiness seemed only for the rich, he would buy a barrel of dressed turkeys and stand on the street corner. He would give one of the turkeys to every man who came along that had the appearance of being poor. When one barrel was gone he would get another and would put in the day in this occupation. He made many a home happy by doing this. Last year [1897] was the first time he missed giving something to all the poor people he met, and there is little doubt that his absence was noted more than that of any other one man who lived in Denver. Families who had not had a square meal in months got one on Christmas through the kindness of Smith. Yet the money [that paid for those chickens] was robbed from other people.[4]

Another report of Jeff's Christmas giving appeared in the *News* in 1892.

A huge dinner for Denver's poor

> Before the programs ... commenced, several members of the sporting fraternity, headed by the distinguished Jeff Smith, appeared at the back door and made inquiry for Parson Tom. The parson was at home to all callers.
>
> "We rather thought we would like to chip in on this play tonight, parson," said Jeff, "If you wouldn't object."

---

[1] Collier & Westrate, p. 149.

[2] Interview of John R. Smith about a conversation with Mary E. Smith regarding Jeff's Christmas charities. 12/12/1983.

[3] Smith, Emerson, *Colorado Magazine*, p. 16.

[4] *Denver Evening Post* 07/31/1898.

"Object," responded the parson, "not much; no one is barred out of this game," and into the parson's outstretched palm "Jeff" and his friends dropped $5's, $10's, and $20's until the pile counted up to $60, to be applied where it would do the most good.[1]

A sixty-dollar donation in 1892 would have amounted to $1,798 today.[2]

R. M. Eddy, thought to be a one-time Soap Gang member, spoke to a *Washington Post* reporter shortly after Jeff's death. Eddy said that Jeff

was one of the most kind-hearted men that ever lived. I will venture that there is scarcely a big city in the country where you couldn't find some man that could tell you of a good act that Jeff Smith had done him. In his palmy days in Denver and Creede, he gave away money recklessly to almost any applicant. When hard times came to Denver, ... with a well-known priest, he organized a score of free-lunch stands, and every sport in town was assessed at what Smith thought a reasonable figure. None of them demurred to giving up [a contribution], and nobody went hungry during that adverse period.[3]

A friendship between Jeff and the parson continued into the mid 1890s, and Jeff was last in touch with him from Alaska in 1897.[4] According to Uzzell, over eleven years, Jeff gave him $1,500 to $2,000, the equivalent of $44,355 to $59,140 today.[5] In an 1896 interview with the *News*, the parson said that when Jeff and his men would bring him money for his work, the parson felt compelled to accuse them of bribery, saying, "'Do you expect to shut my mouth with this?' And Soapy Smith has often said to me: 'No, Tom, we know you would shut up every last one of us if you could.'"[6]

The parson, a hero to many, persevered in serving the poor and destitute until his death in 1910. Though he helped more than most, thousands many times over, hard times still left many thousands unserved. Accepting this shortcoming, he decided on a simple epitaph for his tombstone, which is inscribed there: *He did his level best.*

So did Jeff. In 1884, roller skating was big as a popular pastime around the country. Trying to capitalize on the sport, Jeff wrote letters in search of a company that would give him a good deal on the purchase of several hundred pairs of skates. C. C. Lamos, Jeff's supplier of cheap John goods, wrote a handwritten response on company stationary.

Friend Smith

I got an order today from Waller, was a little surprised to see him in Texas. I have written to Balding [−] also to Wilkinson Hq [Headquarters], and other parties for them to send you their bottom cash prices on roller skates and guess they will attend to it at once.

---

[1] *RMN* 12/28/1892, p. 1.

[2] Tom's Inflation Calculator.

[3] *Washington Post* 07/24/1898, & *Denver Times* 07/25/1898, p. 2.

[4] Robertson & Harris, Appendix, Ltr fr Perry A. Clay to Jeff R. Smith, II, 04/13/1897: "Parson Uzzell showed me your telegram" (p. 229).

[5] Tom's Inflation Calculator, using 1889 as a median year.

[6] *RMN* 02/04/1896.

Am glad to hear you are still on earth, and catching on. I suppose Waller is worth from 25 to 30,000 by this time and we shall hear of him starting a Bank one of these days.

I should think Denver was a good place for business and it would be a fine town to stick to. Let me hear from you at any time, whether you want goods in our line or not.

Tom Lamos[1]

John T. Waller was one of the few known confidence men who retired comfortably wealthy. Around 1895 he moved to Dade City, Florida and invested his money in property and perhaps keeping a link to his past, he also invested in several traveling carnivals. He still held a sizable estate upon his death in 1915 at age 65.[2]

John Wilkinson of the Chicago-based John Wilkinson Company responded immediately with a typed letter on company stationary, quoting prices of from $1.85 to $2.60 per pair of skates when bought in lots of 200.[3] Whether or not Jeff ordered the skates is unknown, and so is what his plans for the skates might have been. He may have wanted them for cheap John sales or auctions. A romantic notion would be that he considered donating skates to poor children of the city through Parson Uzzell in time for Christmas. Not beyond possibility is that he considered doing both.

Jeff had motives for making conspicuous charitable contributions, including public relations and the pleasure of receiving plaudits from the public and his peers. Many of these acts, however, also occurred under cover of night and through the rear doors of charities, and were not generally known. Decades after Jeff's death, word of some of these other contributions surfaced such as from Alonzo B. Osgood, who had come to Denver in 1886 at age twenty-seven. In 1932, he shared his memory of Jeff.

Soapy was a good fellow, not half bad, not more than half bad anyhow. He would cheat you out of your shirt while you watched him, but he was the most liberal fellow I ever knew, and many a down-and-outer thanked the man for the cheerful giver he was.[4]

It was in Jeff's nature to help the unfortunate and not be stingy about it. Jeff's second nature, though, perhaps to the point of genius, was a compulsion to exploit for financial profit the frailties of human nature through charm and craft. This was his business profession, and he was ambitious in it.

Around the time Jeff opened the Tivoli in February 1888, he established a nearby office from which to conduct operations and expand his empire. Whereas most crime bosses kept themselves from view, Jeff had the audacity to open an office on the second floor of the three-story, upscale Chever Block building on the northeast corner of Seventeenth and Larimer streets. In 1941, the *News* quoted a person who had been in that office. He remembered "mahogany furniture, handsome rugs and well-selected

---

[1] Hand-written Ltr on company stationary fr Tom Lamos of Lamos & Company to Jeff R. Smith II, 10/20/1884. Jefferson R. "Little Randy" Smith col.

[2] *Dade City Banner* 06/04/1915.

[3] Typed Ltr on company stationary fr John Wilkinson of the John Wilkinson Company to Jeff R. Smith II, 10/23/1884. Jefferson R. "Little Randy" Smith col.

[4] *Denver Post* 08/26/1932.

paintings giving an air of opulence and dignity, despite the massive sideboard loaded with liquors, wines, cordials and crystal glassware."[1] In addition to directing operations from here, Jeff used the plush environment for "big store" swindles. He and Soap Gang members became rich mining men and bankers quite at home in the "severely dignified atmosphere" and where Jeff became the "financier handling millions for investment, or other character to fit the crime."[2]

William C. Black worked on the first floor of the Chever Block as a clerk with the Postal Telegraph Company. Black sent Jeff's telegrams, which he thought were going to Jeff's mother.[3] She, however, had died in 1877, so the telegrams were probably being sent to Jeff's wife in St. Louis. Perhaps helping to lead the clerk to a false conclusion was Mary's signature line on one return telegram the clerk delivered to Jeff: "from little Jeff and big mamma."[4]

The late 1880s had been a time of high and widening operations. Although Mary remained in St. Louis, probably for the sake of her health, circumstances in Denver were settled and secure enough that Jeff allowed his younger brother to join him, opening the Bascomb, Smith and Company cigar store. Profits from combined operations were soaring, Jeff had partnered with one of the most successful businessmen in Denver, Ed Chase, in the Tivoli Club, Jeff had started up the new Silver Club, and he moved into a posh, new office. This social ornament and plentiful funds would be enough to put anyone in a charitable mood, which Jeff exploited with characteristic skill. Success was coming fast and easily. Every bet was coming up a winner. The big wheel of fortune, though, is famous for variety, and it has yet to be successfully gaffed. As quickly and as often as winning numbers spin up, they spin misses again. Soon, what should have been a simple, profitable, even pleasant swindle turned into a riot that shook Jeff's empire and nearly caused its collapse.

Chapter 7

A Declaration of War

I did not mind so much being called a thief: I am use to it.
But no man can slur my family.

—Jefferson R. Smith II
Weekly Register Call, August 2, 1889

Jeff thoroughly believed himself a law unto himself. And why not? With policemen and politicians in his pay, no one had blocked his way, and so far, everything important had gone his way. The *Rocky Mountain News*, however, did not see things Jeff's way and refused to give him a pass. The *News* mounted direct attacks against him, and in time, as the paper hotly persisted, it became clear that both Jeff and the managing editor were willing to risk mortal combat than back down. After Jeff almost

---

[1] *RMN* 03/14/1941.
[2] Smith, Joseph, pp. 60-61.
[3] *Denver Catholic Register* 05/08/1941.
[4] *RMN* 03/16/1941.

killed the managing editor, the *News* declared all out war against him, but through it all, Jeff never hesitated in his aggressive climb.

Denver's social clubs often organized day excursions by train beyond the city limits. On Sunday, July 21, 1889, the destination of one such outing was Logan Park. The trip was heavily promoted, though by whom was not exactly clear. Advertised as "a dazzlingly beautiful spot for a day's picnic adventure,"[1] in reality, Logan Park was far from beautiful, far from home, and far from the law. For Jeff and the Soap Gang, it was a dazzling opportunity with a captive audience. Crowds dropped off in the morning would not be picked up until late afternoon. So, satiated with nature's beauty, people would enjoy diversion until the train arrived. Perhaps look over games of chance provided for their amusement.

That was the idea, to tempt willing members of the crowd to see if their eyes were quicker than the hand. Unfortunately for Jeff, his producers, and his performers, the day went wildly wrong, and the *News* had men there to report it. The next day's paper told a lured, violent story of unforgivable transgression against decency at Logan Park. And the man responsible for it all was "'Soapy' Smith." As on previous occasions of outcry, Jeff expected it to die down. But the *News* made sure it did not. The story's sensational and cynical slant was just the beginning of a sustained attack against Jeff, which in retrospect, appears to have been a calculated declaration of war against him.

LIKE RAGING FIENDS.

Scenes of the Most Fearful Brutality Mark the Bright Sabbath Day at Logan Park. Crazed Men Roll Fighting Upon the Ground, Frothing with Hate and Screaming Awful Blasphemy. Swindling Games and Unlimited Drink Lead to the Natural Result of a Mad Free Fight.

Logan Park was the scene of a wild, hilarious picnic for the "sure thing" men yesterday, and it was likewise a mournful funeral for the "suckers." The hot sun seemed to bring out both classes of useful citizens like ants from under a stone.

Never was there a more crying disgrace to any city than the scenes in Logan Park. It would have been ludicrous, if it had not been so shameful.

It was the opening day of the park for the year, and it is hoped that it was also the closing day. "Soapy" Smith was the master of ceremonies, and hauled the guests out, set them down in the midst of a vast sun scorched plain and told them to be good and make merry, until he came for them again, which was not until the sun had gone down. For many days before yesterday was blazoned the fact to the pleasure loving populace that on Sunday the twenty-first instant there would be a "grand opening" at Logan Park, where ice cream might be eaten, and red lemonade might be drunk, and the prehistoric ham sandwich might be swallowed to repletion. There was nothing said about the whole thing being a big trap set by the brotherhood of tin-horn gamblers, who slapped their pockets as they came home last night. It had been a field day.

---

[1] *RMN* 07/22/1889.

... A crowd of 300 to 400 pleasure seekers, with a *NEWS* reporter, set down fifteen miles from home, without even a sage brush in sight to excite thoughts of a park ... and the train just pulling out of sight....

... At the entrance to the grove of nine trees under the first leafy cottonwood was the man with that fossil racket of the "shells." ... Wearing a slouch hat that curved downward over his forehead in a point, he bent his head forward and peered from side to side into the faces of the group ... with that sneaking, furtive look that reminded one of no one so much as Uriah Heep.[1]

"Oo's a next man to put up?" he yelled. "Watch it now!" "Watch it!" "Ware is it?" "Five dollars wins ten!"

One of his "cappers" burst in through the crowd and carried off his $10 in a most bungling style of workmanship. But the geese didn't notice it. They were too anxious to be plucked. A young man, who was apparently loaded for sport, put up $5 and lost: put up $10 and lost: put up $20 and lost. He was growing wild with despair.

"Plays fair, gents! Don't tell if you knows ware it is! Everyman for hisself. Plays fair!" said Uriah with a chuckle. "Wunst more now," he said. "Twenty-five wins fifty!" he whined to the young man, who was looking gloomy as the grave. "Come on! Twenty-five wins fifty!" in a wheedling tone. The poor fish bit. His hand trembled so he could hardly lift the shell. His face worked convulsively.

"I've skinned ye again," shouted Uriah, "try again." The poor devil swallowed a sob and turned on his heel, but a crowd who had been looking on and sympathizing with the young man began to mutter.

"I'll smash ye in the nose," shouted Uriah to one who had been particularly emphatic in his remarks, "I'm a fighter, I am! Don't worry me! This yere's the way I make my livin'. What's it to you? How'm I goin' to dress my girl with silks ef I don' make money?" But he knew enough of human nature and its stormy outbreaks to pick up his plant and sneak over to another part of the ground. He made hundreds of dollars during the day....

Under every tree was a sharper with a "sure thing" racket of some older or newer design. The "tin-horns" and their "cappers" held the grounds. If some poor creature squealed when bitten and the crowd seem disposed to take up his grievance, every shark swam in that direction and the array was too formidable to make resistance possible.... The man with the purse full of $10 gold pieces, the soap racket man, the three-card monte man, the thimble-rigger and the shaker of dice occupied every point of vantage under the trees. There was nothing else to do. People must be fleeced or bored in a place like that. They chose the latter....

---

[1] *Uriah Heep*: a grasping, repugnant, self-proclaimed "umble" character in Charles Dickens' *David Copperfield* (1850).

In the midst of the so-called park, on one side of the dancing pavilion, beer flowed from a dozen bung-holes. There was no water; it was beer or nothing. It flowed in a steady stream down dozens of parched throats, and later in the day produced its usual riotous effect....

Many of the visitors, disgusted, attempted to leave the ground at 4 o'clock. The spiders who had drawn the flies into their net began to fear a stampede and [premature end to] the fitting close of a most successful day. Whether through collusion or not, the trains were not allowed to return until sunset.... Crowds left the park and wandered disconsolately up to the platform, upon the edges of which they sat for two hours, waiting for the train that never came.

A Bloody Fight.

But this simple swindling and beer drinking was not exciting enough for the crowd. As the evening came on, those who remained began to get worked up. The festivities were not sufficiently gory to meet their views so they started to remedy the evil. The result was that there was a small riot in which several men were cut up, a dozen or more covered with blood and one man, whose name is not known, seriously and perhaps fatally injured. The row was very sudden, no one knowing how it started or any of the particulars, which led up to it. Among the happy crowd of picnickers were several men who are continually aching for a fight and take every occasion to exhibit their fistic abilities before admirers of the art called manly. The first thing noticed was a scuffle between J. F. Davis and C. C. Bell, who were trying to spread one another over the field.... They came onto the grounds much the same as the ancient Spartans descended upon the coasts of Athens, prepared to take humanity as it came, regardless of the size or reputation of the men they were among. At any rate they tipped over an apple stand which an old man was running, in an instant three or four strangers sprang to his assistance..., and in less time than it takes to tell, fifteen or twenty people were mixed up, crowding and sprawling on the ground like so many snakes. They fought hard, and to hurt. The bartender Billy Allen became interested, and joined in the row, ostensibly, to quiet matters, but his appearance was like waving a red flag at an infuriated bull. Grasping a couple of beer glasses, he began to strike right and left, believing in the Irish tactics of hitting every head he saw....

When quiet was finally restored, the contestants were the sorriest specimens of human beings ever seen. Black eyes predominated, and bloody noses and red frescoed features were plenty. They all felt enraged and were anxious to again open hostilities.

Ed Smith, a brother of "Soapy" Smith, fell into an argument with someone at the little [train] station, which ended in a fight, in which beery members of the crowd took a hand, and of course Jeff was prompted to help his brother, which he did to the queen's taste.[1] A grand riot was

---

[1] *to the queen's taste*: perfectly, to perfection; exactly as would be desired. (*DARE*)

inaugurated and clubs, beer bottles and everything of a movable character could be seen swinging over the heads of struggling men....

Swinging a Hatchet.

There was bad blood in the crowd in the train when the union depot in Denver was reached; an unknown man started a row.... Someone picked a hatchet out of a soda box and struck Bell a stunning blow across the left cheek, laying open a gash about four inches long. Bell and Davis appeared at headquarters and informed Detective Howe of the fact.

Later in the evening Henry Clifton came into the police station in company with Jeff Smith and lodged a complaint against the latter for assault..., alleging that his life was in danger while Smith was at large. They wrangled in the office and officer Henry Smith arrested both. Jeff Smith for assault and Clifton as a witness in the case, which is so badly tangled up that no one seems to know anything about it, where it started exactly, or what was the direct cause. Several deputy sheriffs came on the scene and made ... arrests. Had it not been for their timely appearance the melee at the park might have resulted more seriously than it did.[1]

The tangle of events was by design. In the event of arrest, the routine among bunco men was to give varying and distorted accounts of what happened. The more confusion, the greater were chances of evading judicial consequences. C. C. Bell may be gambler Clifton Bell. The "Ed Smith" in the story was probably not Jeff's brother Bascomb but "Denver" Ed Smith, a local boxer Jeff used as a strong-arm. Jeff admitted being among the combatants, saying that he had to fight after being assaulted and knocked down. When asked why he joined the melee, Jeff said, "I had to stop the fuss."[2]

Although likely, it is unknown whether the event was sponsored and/or promoted by Jeff or if he and the Soap Gang just took advantage of the outing. No criminal complaints stemming from the affair could be found, nor any record that Jeff was in court over the Logan Park incident. He claimed he was not involved with the gaming and that he was there with his wife and children to watch a balloon ascension.

A week passed, but the Logan Park story and its connection to Jeff did not die down. "The proper role of a city's newspaper is to report the news," Colonel John Arkins, owner and managing editor of the *Rocky Mountain News*, might assert, and to take up the right and the good on behalf of its decent, law-abiding citizen readers. And if the news includes crazed behavior and blood letting, and if it identifies someone central to lawlessness, and if the campaign is hard fought long enough and gathers a following, and if it sells newspapers, lots of newspapers, well, so much the better for citizens and the paper that champions them.

John Arkins had worked his way up into newspapers. All up through the Midwest and South as far as New Orleans, Col. Arkins worked at the printer's trade after the close of the 'Civil' war. In 1873 he came to Colorado and for several

---

[1] *RMN* 07/22/1889.
[2] *RMN* 08/06/1889.

years worked as compositor and foreman in Denver offices. When the Leadville boom began he went into the new mountain mining camp and established the *Evening Chronicle*.[1] It was his first newspaper venture, and it made a great success and became a power in politics. In 1880 he sold the *Chronicle* and bought an interest in the *Rocky Mountain News*, the oldest paper in Denver. For over fourteen years he continued the management of the paper, making it a great success, not only financially, but as a newspaper of great and far-reaching influence. As an editorial writer he was practical, forceful, and fearless.[2]

For a man in Jeff's position, being caught in a negative light was a dangerous liability. Jeff depended on the favor of public persons of the Establishment, and the best publicity for Jeff Smith and his operations was none at all. So he did not respond, and the story did not die and news of him did not let up, but in fact became more critical and fierier. Jeff continued to wait. But waiting allowed new damage as the *News* began naming public officials with whom Jeff associated.

Soapy Smith was in conversation with some friends in the city hall when the subject of running him out of the city was brought up.

"Why," he said, "no one can compel me to leave this city, and so far as exposing me, that cannot be done, because I have the utterances of all the newspapers in my own hand, and they will not use my name. There is John Arkins, he will not permit my name to appear in the columns of his paper without my consent." [Mayor] Londoner laughed at his egotism and the manner in which he was branded a liar by the publication of an article in yesterday's *NEWS*.[3]

At last, Jeff paid a visit to *News* managing editor Colonel John Arkins. The object, as Jeff later testified in court, was to ask the editor to leave him alone:

I will state that I have always had the best opinion in the world of Mr. Arkins and thought he was a good friend of mine; I had nothing in the world against him.... ... I will state what happened to me and Mr. Arkins about a week before, in regard to Logan Park. I went into his office to talk with him; I walked into his office, and he says "how do you do;" I says "how do you do John;" I says "you have been giving me a good roasting;" I says "John, I am innocent of that; I am not doing anything at all; I don't like to get roasted when I [get] off a train;" I didn't ask him to make any retraction; I says "for God's sake, let me alone," and he said he would let me alone, and I went away with that understanding.[4]

---

[1] *Evening Chronicle*: launched January 29, 1879. (Davis, Carlyle, p. 126)

[2] *Chicago Daily Tribune* 08/18/1894, p. 7. Obituary for John Arkins: "... died at his home here [in Denver] today [8/17/1894 on his tombstone] of gastritis, aged 52 years. ... He leaves a widow and one son. ... Col. Arkins was a native of Pennsylvania, having been born in Fayette county Feb. 14, 1842. While called Colonel, and while looking every inch a soldier born to command, the title was only honorary. It was his pride that in the civil war he never got above the rank of corporal" ["Sgt" on his tombstone].

[3] *RMN* 07/29-30/1889.

[4] *RMN* 08/06/1889.

Jeff thought the problem solved, but he was greatly mistaken. Condemnation continued and widened to include his family, prompting a return visit to Colonel Arkins.

Jeff had sent his wife and two children to Idaho Springs, Colorado, on July 26, the day he met with Arkins. Three days later Jeff traveled there with William Scott Lee, the recent ex-mayor of Denver, and Deputy City treasurer James P. Hadley (who was known to forget to collect liquor fees in the saloons of Denver).[1] The purpose of Jeff's trip was to check on his wife and two children, who had been ill. When he arrived, Jeff had pointed out to him yet another *News* article that took particular pains to roast him. Jeff obtained a copy and found applied to him words like "prince" and "astute," but they were combined with words like "knaves" and "rascal."

SOAPY'S QUIET SNEAK.

The red and bleary-eyed sun looked down yesterday morning upon Mr. Jeff Smith with its wonted favor. The information may seem somewhat unimportant..., but be it known that Mr. Jeff Smith is a person of renown. In his dexterous toyings with the strong but muscle-bound arm of the law he has so successfully evaded due to his sneaking and contemptible crimes, he has obtained such a modicum of fame as is expressed in the epithet, "Soapy."

It was, therefore, upon Soapy Smith that the dissipated old luminary cast his beams such as they were. Soapy didn't kick. He is a philosopher. Any sort of beams, or anything else that he can get hold of for that matter, is good enough for Soapy. He is no calla lily. This little introductory is merely intended to lead up to the fact that the distinguished blackleg[2] mentioned was down at the depot superintending the sallying forth of his cohorts to prey upon whomsoever they might. Soapy, in the language of the fly-by-night fraternity, "has" Denver.

HE OWNS THE TOWN

A word of meaning is conveyed in that expression. He has it to do with it what he will in so far as all professional swindling and stealing is concerned. ... The city is absolutely under the control of this prince of knaves, and there is not a confidence man, a sneak thief, or any other kind of parasite upon the public who does not pursue his avocation under the license from the man who has become great through the power vested in him by those whose sworn duty it is to administer the laws without fear or favor.

This fellow had his plans mapped out. He doesn't go blundering about. As his satellites ... came up, he gave them their assignments. Some upon this train, some upon that. The exposure of his operations at Logan Park last Sunday in the NEWS had made it extremely desirable to keep away from there for a week or two. This was tough for Soapy, and he since daily rends the NEWS into tatters, being of practical mind, instead of his hair.

So Logan Park was barred.... Another point, which this astute rascal deduced from the Logan Park affair, was that it was rubbing it in too strongly

---

[1] *Denver Republican* 05/16/1891.

[2] *blackleg*: in this context, a cheat at cards or horseracing. A gambler who cheats. Collegiate dictionaries, informal usage.

to mass all his force at one place. That proceeding reaped much harvest, it is true, but it was killing the goose and cutting off the supply of omelets. The great army of chumps doesn't mind being defeated in detail, but it hates to be jumped upon bodily and torn and stripped and cast into cattle cars with contumely and derisive queries as to what it is going to do about it.

SCATTERING THE CROOKS

Therefore, it was that yesterday operations were conducted upon a different method. Instead of swooping down upon a single place and denuding the denizens thereof of their belongings, many places were gathered in. It isn't judicious to rob several hundred people on the same day. They set up a mighty roar which clangs through the corridors of the city hall and the county building in so disagreeably loud manner that the officials are filled with perturbation lest they have to do something about it. Such things are really unpleasant and Soapy felt within himself that last Sunday he had flopped into the bubbling dough in a way quite strange to his usual practice.

The predatory expeditions of the gang yesterday were really not entirely successful. First of all, there was a dearth of likely excursions to be worked, and secondly, they did not go to just the king of places admired by the sharks. The locomotive engineers went to Palmer Lake. ... Soapy's family is stopping at Idaho Springs. ...[1]

Week after week, attack articles on crime in the city from the *News* helped build a cry for reform in Denver. With his enterprises in the city pressured down, Jeff had indeed circulated operations into outlying towns, camps, and settlements. Even these movements were reported in the *News*, with Jeff identified as their director. Further, his every movement was painted in negative and cynical innuendo on the front page of the newspaper. This scrutiny and the constant personal attacks on his character (and the ruination of his business) made Jeff gnash his teeth and look for some indirect but effective way to end the war waged against him and his enterprises.

The *News* itself, though, brought things to a head when it wrote, "It is good to be Soapy's family just now, but maybe not so good after a while."[2] Jeff had kept his wife and children strictly removed from his business. They were not involved and were out of bounds. But not the *News*. To get at Jeff, its attacks aimed to embarrass and tarnish the honor of Jeff and everyone associated with him—associates, friends, political people, office holders, and his wife, the mother of his children. It was all bad, but the worst of it for Jeff was that Mary felt ostracized and that she had been driven from her hotel. Years later, Mary related to her children and grandchildren how she broke down and cried when she told Jeff how she was treated by other women at Idaho Springs. Jeff would have agreed with the proverbial expression that "Revenge is a dish best served cold." In this case, though, it seems he felt compelled to serve it hot.

In court, Jeff testified about what he encountered at Idaho Springs:

---

[1] *RMN* 07/29/1889, p. 1.
[2] *RMN* 07/29/1889, p. 1.

My wife got acquainted with several ladies in the neighborhood and at the hotel there, and when I arrived there I was pointed out as a thief and a vagabond. She spoke to a couple of ladies after THE NEWS reached there, and they turned their backs on her and wouldn't speak to her. I met a gentleman who says, "Did you see THE NEWS?" I said "No," and I went and got THE NEWS, and afterwards the proprietor of the hotel where my wife was stopping made some remark about such a character I was and that he didn't have any use for her in that house. Both of my children were sick, but she bundled up and came down here [to Denver] that afternoon.... I talked this matter over with this gentleman who was with me, and he says, "I believe I would go and see Arkins myself; he is a good fellow; I don't see why he should abuse you in that way." I talked with several men who said Arkins was responsible for it, and spoke about my going up there and having a talk and squaring myself with him. I said I would go and see him; I had this old cane when my foot was broken, and had it with me when I went into the [*Rocky Mountain News*] office and inquired for him....[1]

Jeff, Mary, and the children had returned to Denver from Idaho Springs around 6:00 p.m. that July 29, 1889, a Monday. Without delay, Jeff put his family on a St. Louis-bound train to stay with Mary's mother. Sometime after 7:30 Jeff enlisted Ned "Banjo" Parker to go with him to the *News* office for the purpose of visiting its editor. They stopped in Albert Nelson's saloon at 1637-1643 Curtis Street where Jeff asked the bartender if Arkins had been in that night. Hearing that he rarely came in, Jeff and Parker left the saloon[2] and went to the Patterson and Thomas Block, which housed the *News* office on Seventeenth Street near the corner of Curtis Street. Jeff asked G. S. Hoag in the office if Arkins were in and was told he would return in about half an hour. Jeff then asked by which door the colonel usually entered and exited and was told he normally used the front door. Jeff also spoke to a night engineer, asking him if Charlie Thomas[3] were upstairs. The engineer told Jeff to ask the elevator boy as he was not sure. "Never mind," the witness at trial said Jeff responded. "I want to see another party anyhow." Jeff then went back out to the street and waited for the colonel.

SOAPY THE ASSASSIN

Last night at ten minutes to 9 o'clock Jeff R. Smith attempted to murder Colonel John Arkins, president of the News Printing Company and manager of this paper. Never did ruffian commit a more utterly brutal deed.

Colonel Arkins had just left his office and was about to call a carriage. The streets were crowded with people and the electric lights shone brilliantly. Streetcars were passing, and ladies chatted as they walked along. It did not look like a favorable spot in which to commit a black crime.

---

[1] *RMN* 08/06/1889.

[2] *RMN* 08/06/1889.

[3] *Charlie Thomas*: Charles Spaulding Thomas, Denver city attorney 1875-1876; Senate 1888 & 1895; Governor of Colorado 1899-1901; elected Senate 1913 to fill vacancy caused by the death of Charles J. Hughes, Jr.; reelected in 1914 & served from January 15, 1913, to March 3, 1921. (Congress, Biographical Directory)

> In the shadow of a great doorway crouched the form of a being with murder in his heart. At his right hand and left were others come to see the murder done.[1]

In its reporting, the *News* was mistaken in a number of particulars and exaggerated others. Reported was that Jeff carried a heavy black cane, but the cane placed on exhibit during the trial was described as a light, wooden walking cane. The *News* account had the editor leaving, but Arkins testified that he was arriving at the office. The *News* reported "others" with Jeff, but witnesses stated that only Ned "Banjo" Parker accompanied Jeff that night.

Arkins stated that when he arrived, he saw Parker but not Jeff as his form was blocked by Parker's. When Arkins was about ten feet away, Jeff stepped out and said, "Oh, John!" Arkins glanced over his shoulder. Jeff threw up his left hand as though to shove him back, and with his cane in his right hand, according to witnesses, struck Arkins once over the head and knocked him to the sidewalk. While he was down, Jeff kicked him twice and struck him two or three more times with the cane. Witnesses claimed Jeff stooped over Arkins and felt his hip pocket, as if to discover a gun there, but no such claim was made at trial. Afterward, Jeff turned and walked rapidly to the corner and disappeared down Curtis Street. Parker, who was between Jeff and witnesses with a cane of his own raised to prevent interference, quickly walked off in the opposite direction.[2] Jeff testified about his actions.

> I had no intent of hitting Mr. Arkins until the moment he came. I spoke to Mr. Wyatt as he was getting out of his hack at the door. I says; "Johnny, how are you getting along?" "Oh," he says, "I am living yet," and just as I spoke up came the colonel and I struck him; I have no excuse for doing it; I says: "John, this is a fine way of treating me." And I struck him; I was half crazy, desperate; I have nothing and I did not know how I was going to get any money or anything, and I attributed all my troubles to this paper.

Once the attackers left, Arkins was helped to Dr. Dingle's drug store for medical attention. What happened next the *News* overstated and slanted all it could.

> In a few minutes thousands of people knew that the gang which infests the city had given a manifestation of its power by striving to murder the man who dared to stand boldly and tell the truth. Threats of summary vengeance were made by stern men and the threats grew into a fixed determination as hundreds of friends of the injured man came hurriedly from all parts of the city. The trembling fugitive in his hiding place heard the rumors and sought safety. Where did his thoughts naturally turn? To his friends, of course. And who are his friends? Let the record stand. It was to the police station that Soapy Smith fled for shelter after stopping at a saloon to brace his courage.

When the matter was reported to police headquarters, Lieutenant Phillips[3] had every officer on the beat notified.... Detectives were sent out in

---

[1] *RMN* 07/30/1889.

[2] *RMN* 07/30/1889.

[3] *Phillips*: probably W. J. Phillips, one of the first 13 police officers in Denver. Secrest, pp. 21, 44, 92.

every direction, and in a few minutes, Detective Scott located the would-be murderer in the Jocky [sic] Club saloon, and placed him under arrest.[1]

After the attack, Jeff made his way to his friend and bondsman John Kinneavy, proprietor of the Jockey Club. Jeff waited there until Detective Scott arrived. Then Scott, Jeff, and Kinneavy walked over to the courthouse where Kinneavy posted a $500 bond for Jeff, and the two men strolled out.[2]

On the next day, Tuesday, Jeff began to address damage control through public relations. He spoke to a reporter of the *Denver Times*:

> I would not care ... how much the *News* might roast me personally, although Colonel Arkins assured me after I had explained the matter to him, that he would not permit his paper to lie about me. Then to have that paper not only score me, but to drag my unoffending family into the thing was more than I could stand, and I assaulted him, that's all there is to it.[3]

A few days later, on August 2, 1889, Jeff called at the *Denver Republican* and made the following statement:

> "Arkins and I have been good friends for several years. I have done considerable work for him. When he wanted to go to the St. Louis convention and vote for Hill, he called me into his office. 'Jeff,' said he, 'I want you to do some work for me at the primaries.' All right, John,' I said; and I did the work. I carried the primaries for Arkins.
>
> "Now, I am no saint. I don't profess to be. But I am no worse than a hundred others, and John had no right, after all I had done for him to single me out for a thief, and proclaim that I was a blackleg. It was not grateful. My business is selling prize packages. No one is obliged to buy. When the Logan park matter came up John pitched into me. I had no more to do with Logan park than he did. I went to see John, and protested. 'John,' said I, 'this is no square deal. I had no more to do with Logan park than you did.' 'Jeff,' he replied, 'I would not say anything in my paper to injure you.' I took a cigar and walked out feeling first-rate.
>
> "Well, I sent my wife and babies to Idaho Springs. They are not very well and I wanted to give them the benefit of fresh air. To send them away I had to borrow money. Sunday I went up to see them. I think as much of my family as any man ever did. I went alone. I went for nothing else than to see my wife and little ones. I did not go to look for suckers or to work any game or anything else.
>
> "Did you see that outrageous article in the *News*? And that after what John had just promised me. It was a lie and it dragged my family in. I did not mind so much being called a thief: I am used to it. But no man can slur my family. There was no excuse for it. I would not and could not stand it. The reflection on my family was uncalled for totally, and most insulting. I was

---

[1] *RMN* 07/30/1889.

[2] *Denver Times* 07/30/1889.

[3] *Denver Times* 07/30/1889.

desperate when I read the article. What could I do? John had gone back on his word. I had no money. I had borrowed from everyone I could. To be picked out from a crowd I could tolerate, but to have my family assaulted was different.

"I went to the *News* office and called for John. I waited an hour for him. When he came I knocked him down. He yelled 'Murder! Police!' and I walked away. That's all there is to it.[1]

Jeff spoke to the *Times* again on the following Monday, August 5.

"The more I thought about it, I felt more hurt, and I could not refrain from hitting Colonel Arkins when I saw him. I was desperate. I had no money, my family was sick, and had been ostracized from Idaho Springs, I had no intention of killing Mr. Arkins, else I would not have gone around asking for him."[2]

In addition to public statements, Jeff tried to make personal peace with Arkins, sending a handsome easy chair to his office. Arkins immediately had it sent back.[3]

Granted were the district attorney's demands that the charge of assault be changed to attempted murder and that the bond be increased to $2,500. Again Kinneavy came forward with the bond.[4] Jeff was outraged by the charge. In court he proclaimed, "'If I was wanting to murder him I wouldn't tackle him with a stick.'"[5]

The *Denver Times*, not hostile to Jeff in settled times, saw how the tide was running heavily against "Soapy Smith" and pushed him forcefully away:

It was not necessary to ... do the formality of putting him behind bars, for his bondsman was at his heels, and was prepared to sign any bond that would release the prisoner. He was registered on the police record as a gambler by occupation. In a few minutes he walked forth in the cool night air, free to all intends and purposes, and as he believes, laughing up his sleeves at the work he had performed and the murderous design he had all but carried out.

Who dares to say that the *NEWS* has not been just in stating that Soapy Smith has the police power under his heel? Flushed with arrogance at the iron grip he holds upon those who should administer the law, he has said that his rule is supreme, and that to him who dares to thwart his plans, instant vengeance shall fall. This he has believed. When his murderous blows were falling, he was thinking of his safety from those who should punish. He said to himself, "They cannot, I am a law unto myself."

The *NEWS* has opposed this scoundrel. It has pointed out that he has supreme control over the lesser scoundrels. It has exposed his methods and drawn his plots into the light of day. It has urged that he could not daily pursue his career of robbery unless with the knowledge and consent of the

---

[1] *Weekly Register Call* 08/02/1889.

[2] *Denver Times* 08/05/1889.

[3] Ltr fr W. M. Arkins, a nephew of John Arkins, to Robert L. Perkin. (Perkin, p. 370)

[4] *Denver Times* 07/30/1889.

[5] *RMN* 08/06/1889.

authorities. The answer to this is a blow in the darkness of night, a murder in all but success. What are people going to do about it?[1]

Jeff's public relations defense worked a human angle. When Col. Arkins went back on his word to desist and then had gone on to slur his family, Jeff was, he asserted, provoked into thrashing him. This defense found understanding among some of the public. After all, Col. Arkins had gone too far before, and this was not the first time that very year that Arkins had been assaulted for his public pronouncements.

The first time occurred on the early morning of February 9, 1889, at Jones's barroom on Curtis Street, near the *News* building. While Arkins was in New York, the *New York Times* had quoted Arkins taking sides in a dispute between Kentucky Senator Joseph Blackburn and Judge A. W. Rucker of Colorado. Judge Rucker wrote to Colonel Arkins to ask if what he had said in the *Times* interview were true, and Arkins replied that, in general, it was. Rucker's reply was that "he would rawhide Arkins" for what he had said.

> Last night Senator-elect Wolcott and Chief of Police Brady called to see Arkins on important local matters. Arkins and Brady had not been on good terms, but both were personal friends of Wolcott, and he 'rounded them up,' as they say here. The conference at the *News* office lasted over two hours. After midnight they continued the conference on the streets, finally stepping into a saloon which is a favorite resort for local and State politicians.[2]

The three men were standing at the bar when Judge Rucker came in.

> The Judge walked up to Arkins, and without saying a word struck him a violent blow across the mouth with his open hand. The silk hat that graced the editor's head rolled on the bar, but the man stood as if petrified. Rucker stepped back after delivering the blow and said: "Take that, and if you are a man of courage you will resent it."[3]

Judge Rucker then reached for, or drew, a pistol (accounts vary), and Chief Brady immediately relieved the judge of his weapon and took him to jail for a stay of several hours. At a hearing the next morning, neither Arkins nor Rucker attended. Chief Brady presented the matter to the court, and a fine of $10 was assessed with an additional $6 for court costs. There seemed an end to that affair. It might not have been though. Just as in Jeff's case, Col. Arkins clearly did not know when to quit. The *Tribune* quoted what Arkin's said about Judge Rucker's weapon:

> "It was a fancy plated toy gun—one that children might play with, but not one that would be carried by a man who would shoot. He knew the chief would interfere, and it was a good place for a bluff. Before I had a chance to realize what was going on Rucker was a prisoner and was hustled out of the place."[4]

And *The Times* printed more of what Arkins said about the weapon:

[1] *Denver Times* 07/30/1889.
[2] *Chicago Daily Tribune* 02/09/1889, p. 2.
[3] *New York Times* 02/09/1889.
[4] *Chicago Daily Tribune* 02/09/1889, p. 2.

[A]nd looking around [I] saw Rucker flourishing a nickel-plated revolver. I want to say right here that a man who carries a nickel-plated revolver will not fire it on anybody, and you can publish that as coming from me.[1]

In Jeff's case, Arkins again had gone on and on, only worse than in Rucker's case, laying on sarcasm as thick as possible and then drawing in Jeff's family. Like Judge Rucker, Jeff came to call Arkins to account. And again like the judge, Jeff exploded.

So the power and reputation of the *News* through its editor were again brought into question. The paper and the editor had to defend themselves and prove they could not be backed down, so they escalated their war against Jeff, not just at home but beyond. Bulletins were sent across the country, containing the narrative of Jeff's criminal empire and of his attack against the editor of the *News*. The *Los Angeles Times* published the story under the heading, "A COWARD'S ACT."[2] Newspapers followed suit in San Francisco, Chicago, New Orleans, Boston, St. Paul, Omaha, Lincoln, Cheyenne, Leadville, Canyon City, Fort Collins, Las Vegas, and New York City as well as in many others.[3]

From the *Chicago Daily Tribune*:

> At 9 o'clock this evening Jeff T. [sic] Smith, alias "Soapy," attempted to murder Col. John Arkins, editor of the *Rocky Mountain News*. ... Smith called him by name, and on his turning struck him a blow on the left temple with a loaded cane, fracturing the skull. ...
>
> The *News* has been waging a vigorous war against Smith's gang, which has waxed powerful under the protection of the city authorities, and though many threats were made it has persisted in its course fearlessly. At the editorial rooms of the paper it is announced that the *News* will redouble its efforts to rid the city of the scoundrels that infest it.
>
> Col. Arkins' wounds are serious, but are not thought to be fatal.[4]

Quoted in the *News* from the *Cheyenne Leader*:

> The most notoriously corrupt and decrepit municipal organization in the West is that in Denver. The decent element ... seem to be entirely under the domination of a clique of ringsters who run things according to their own sweet will without regard to the good of the people. The natural consequence has been and is corruption in most of the municipal departments.[5]

Denver was indignant over the assault and at the wave of national criticism about the power Jeff Smith was said to possess over city officials. The *Denver Times* had little choice but to continue to side with the *News* in accusing and condemning Jeff:

---

[1] *New York Times* 02/09/1889.

[2] *Los Angeles Times* 07/30/1889.

[3] Newspaper clippings collected by Jeff R. Smith II. Author's col. Other cities were no doubt informed of the attack, but these are the only clippings the collection contains. Those containing dates are as follows: San Francisco: *Daily Evening Bulletin* 07/30/1889, p. 4. Chicago: *Daily Inter Ocean* 07/30/1889. New Orleans: *Daily Picayune* 07/30/1889, p. 2. Boston: *Boston Daily Advertiser* 07/31/1889, p. 5. St. Paul: *St. Paul Daily News* 07/30/1889, p. 2.

[4] *Chicago Daily Tribune* 07/30/1889, p. 2.

[5] *RMN* 08/05/1889.

This man Smith's demonstration of violence has warning in it. It shows the spirit of the vice so prevalent in this city. It demonstrates not only how evil it is but how desperate and presumptuous it has become. It tells how prompt, strong and determined a fight should be made against it. Smith should be promptly punished to the limit of the legal penalty. It cannot yet be determined perhaps whether or not his offense is a felony. If it be, he should have the longest term prescribed by statute in the penitentiary. If it be not, after he has received the slight punishment possible to be legally inflicted, he should be driven from the city.

Smith makes the common plea of his class. He says he is "no worse than a hundred others." By this, of course he means, "a hundred others" engaged in legitimate pursuits, but who sometimes do sharp things in business and pursue devious ways in politics. But he is worse than these hundreds of others. He makes all his money by practicing on the ignorance and cupidity of others. His pursuit is essentially vicious. It is a swindle upon individuals and demoralizing to the public. It is a common thing for gamblers and swindlers to plead occasional generous acts and amiable deeds as a palliation for their regular pursuits. Nothing but a change of calling can make those persons anything but enemies to society. And when they become violent it is time for the authorities to rise up and stamp them out.[1]

The next day, Wednesday, July 31, 1889, Jeff appeared before Justice Palmer. The courtroom was packed with friends and on-lookers while outside, people climbed onto windows and poles along the street to get a glimpse of the drama inside. Jeff's attorneys were successful in reducing the charge to assault to do bodily harm. The reduction dropped bond back to $500.[2] The *News* mixed into its reports of courtroom proceedings how one Jeff's "associates" criticized Jeff to his face, writing that even

gamblers and thugs, his associates, condemned his cowardly attack upon Colonel Arkins. One of them said to Soapy: "It is a dirty trick and a poor way to settle anything, to strike a man with a club without giving him a show."

No sooner had the bond been lowered than it was increased again when for the prosecution, the

Hon. T.M. Patterson appeared and was granted a hearing at once. He called the attention of justice Palmer to the fact that the complaint upon which Smith was arrested was assault with intent to murder while the bond upon which he was released Monday was given for the crime of assault to do great bodily injury. Mr. Patterson severely criticized the action of Judge Morris in admitting Smith to bail in $500 bond and for a less offense than that with which he was charged. He asked that the bond be fixed at $2,500 for Soapy's appearance on Monday. How serious an injury had been inflicted could then be determined to some extent.

---

[1] *Denver Times* 07/30/1889.
[2] *RMN* 07/31/1889.

"All right" said Soapy. "I will give a $10,000 or a $20,000 bond just as you like."

Mr. Caypless then appeared and the bond was fixed. John Kinneavy and Soapy signed it, Judge Palmer took his stub pen and wrote a bold signature at the foot of the sheet, and Soapy walked out.[1]

The trial was calendared for Monday, August 5, 1889, and the *News* worked very hard against Jeff until then in the arena of public opinion. In fact, for the issue of July 31, it published two stories that worked against Jeff and city hall, obviously developed prior to the attack on Col. Arkins. One story contained interviews of the mayor and police chief. It placed partial blame on them for allowing Jeff, with his bad reputation already four years old, to continue residing in the city. Mayor Wolfe Londoner was the first to be interviewed about driving Jeff and the Soap Gang from Denver.

"I have ordered these fellows to be sent out of town or watched. I gave explicit orders to that effect several weeks ago. If that is not done I am not to blame. This occurrence has been as much a matter of grief to me as to you. What more can I do?"

The reporter suggested that the reputation of this gang was enough to warrant more stringent precautions.

"Can you show me," replied the mayor with the air of a man who has you on the hip, "that Soapy Smith has been working his game in public? He will be stopped if he does."

"Has any attempt been made to get any evidence against him?"

"I told you I had given orders that he is to be watched. I don't know anything about his partners or associates. All that I know is "Soapy" himself. If there are others, orders have been given to watch them."

"Do you not consider a brutal attack of this kind a menace of the liberties of the citizens?"

"As to that, I think the way I should treat it would be to take a gun to those fellows. My life has been threatened I suppose fifty times since I have been in this chair. I keep a look out for them," and the mayor bristled and looked savage.

"Soapy Smith," he continued with an attempt to be jocular, "came to my store about four weeks ago and asked to be allowed to 'go to work.' I told him that that would never be allowed so long as I was mayor. He pleaded to be allowed, and I answered him, 'no.'

... Why," he said with a faint imitation smile, "it was only a week ago that he came down here to try to work us again for permission. He told Lieutenant Perry Owens that Colonel Arkins would come down himself to intercede for him." ...

"And his gang will continue to work unmolested?"

"I know nothing about his gang. I only know 'Soapy.' 'Soapy' introduced himself to me, as I told you. That is the way I came to know him." The mayor

---

[1] *RMN* 07/31/1889.

concluded with a grimace, as if he and "Soapy" might be on terms of hard, bitter enmity.

"You are not aware, then, that his flock wings its way to Logan and other parks every Sunday, and returns to find refuge here?"

"No, I don't know much about that. The police are watching them."

He went on, in response to a question: "Yes, I know something about the reputation of these people and can't say that there is no work being done by them, but they are watched and they are not doing it on the street. Still I don't see how we can rid the city of them. There is nothing against them that we can get hold of. 'Soapy' Smith, for instance, is a citizen. He has lived here many years." ...

"Are you aware that these men have staunch friends on the police force?"

"No sir!" with indignation on which the cream did not rise. "No, sir! We have none of that kind of men. We know our men." It was very dramatic and effective, and only called for an "Ah," in reply.

"How do you account for the prisoner's hospitable treatment last night?"

"Was he hospitably treated? Where is that bell?" and the mayor grasped wildly for the knob which was to summon a functionary from below. Tired of the farce, the reporter left.[1]

Then a similar visit was paid to Police Chief John F. Farley.[2] The goal of the interview was to shame the new chief into taking aggressive action against Jeff and his men, but the response was similar to the mayor's.

"I regret it very much," he began, in a deep lugubrious voice. "But what can we do? I have never been able to catch Smith in any open act. The patrolmen all have their orders to watch for him and the rest of them. They are to arrest them immediately, if detected. Those are the orders...."

"I thought I might catch him during the circus—kept a strict lookout, but we weren't successful."

"Are you not attacking the ranks and letting the heads go?"

"No; I don't think so. I don't agree that Soapy and men of his stamp are the leaders."

"You don't think by getting them out [that] their satellites will follow?"

"No; I don't think so. You mustn't expect too much, we can't do everything at once. I admit the town is still well stocked with crooks, but you must remember that when I took hold there were by actual calculation from 600 to 700 boosters and steerers attached to the gambling houses of the city. We are working them out gradually. We can't clean the whole thing out at once."

"You don't propose to strike at the head, then?"

---

[1] *RMN* 07/31/1889.

[2] When in 1889 he became Denver's new Chief, the *City Directory* listed him as manager of the Thiel Detective Agency.

"No! How can I? They are citizens, have a business," with a little trill on "business."

"What can I do? It is necessary that I should get plain, forcible evidence against them. If I don't and take him to court I only make a fool of myself, and if he gets off, there is only just so much more encouragement for his pals."

… "Soapy," he said by way of change, "seems to have a great many friends. That is shown by the way they run after him to give bail. He is very strong. We would have [to have] good evidence to do anything with him."[1]

The two officials played right into the hands of the *News*, which had its other story all but ready to embarrass them into action. The paper had already concluded that the two city officials must be in cahoots with Jeff, naming their association "the firm of Londoner, Farley & Smith."[2] Now the *News* would dare them to disprove it.

The day the interviews appeared, a companion story contained all the information about one of Jeff's men that the mayor and police chief said they desired for action to be taken. The Soap Gang member was John "Fatty Gray" Morris, and he was described "working" a victim. The article reported his name inaccurately as J. T. Gray, but the rest was painfully precise. His real name was John H. Morris, known to his peers as "Fatty Gray," an alias based on his being overweight and having a head of gray hair. Morris first met and probably worked for Jeff in Fort Worth in 1879-1880 and had come to Denver to work for him in 1887.[3] The *News* described him in 1889.

> He is a well-fed looking sort of chap, probably weighs 165 pounds, stands about 5 feet 7 inches, has cheeks round, well colored and healthy looking, wears his iron gray hair clipped short and sports a black mustache tinged with gray and a suspicion of dye. He is a smooth character and second only to "Soapy" himself in the success and scope of his work. Strange to say, too, he is quite well known to everybody except the police.[4]

His talents included the "diamond game," in which he swindled his victims by claiming he was broke and would sell his valuable diamonds at a cut rate price. Inferior stones

> are doctored up in such a way as to deceive even an expert. These pretty gems are worth between $20 and $25 a carat, good diamonds run from $80 to $100. Quite a nice margin…. "Fatty" gets his supply of brilliants from headquarters all nicely fixed up, well set and dazzling to the eye. He keeps a stock on hand. … When he gets his claws, soft and gentle claws, fixed upon a victim he makes known the fact that he is hard up and would like to float a loan. The lender suggests an appraiser. Why certainly; "Fatty" is just yearning for an appraiser to set a value on his property. It is a long felt want with him. Then comes in his fine work. He steers the lender against jewelers, who examine the gems and pronounce them to be worth so much.[5]

---

[1] *RMN* 07/31/1889.

[2] *RMN* 08/18/1889.

[3] Telegram fr Charles Anderson in Deadwood, SD, to "Fatty Gray" in Denver 05/06/1887. Geri Murphy col.

[4] *RMN* 07/31/1889.

[5] *RMN* 07/31/1889.

To learn all he could about Morris, the reporter pretended to be a land purchaser. He went to a real estate agent known to be in league with John Morris. Led to an office to wait for the agent to be free, the reporter was introduced to Morris, who happened to be waiting for the same man. During the wait, Morris started up a friendly conversation. When the agent arrived, he quickly saw that the reporter was not going to buy any properties, so the agent let Morris have a crack at him with his games.

Morris told the reporter about wanting to open a gambling house but lacked remaining funds to do so. He needed a loan and was willing to put up family diamond heirlooms as security. The reporter naturally brought up the question of appraisement. Few victims would lend money without knowing the value of the items at hand. Knowing this, the bunco man eagerly awaited the victim's request and was ready to recommend qualified jewelers for the job. A good appraisal equaled a larger loan.

Several jewelry houses appraised the value of the stones at $1,750, and the reporter offered $800. More appraisals were sought, each raising the value until the reporter presented a last loan offer of $900. Arrangements were then made for payment that afternoon. The newsman, however, walked away with no intention of lending Morris a dime. Instead, he went directly to his office to write his exposé.

The article, "Fatty Gray's Folly," published Morris's residential address, 2025 Arapahoe Street, to make it easier for the police to find and arrest him. "This individual," the article continued, "has a very neat little two-story brick house in which he abides at times and entertains therein sundry crooks and confidence....[1] The police chief had no choice but to arrest Morris the same day. Detectives Loar and Howe brought him in for safe keeping in hopes that some of his victims would come forward so charges could be drawn up.[2] Not arresting Gray would directly implicate the chief as being in league with the Soap Gang. No matter the deals Jeff may have had in place. It was mutually understood that should trouble come, all agreements were off.

A NEWS reporter called upon Chief Farley yesterday and asked him what action would be taken against "Fatty" Gray, whose methods of gulling the innocent were exposed in yesterday's paper.

"Well," answered that official, "I was not aware that 'Fatty' was practicing in the city.... I saw him to-day, and he admits to having been roped in by your reporter. He left me his address and states that he is prepared at anytime to face any charge that may be made against him by anyone, no matter who."

"Will you order him out of town?" asked the reporter.

"We have considerable to contend with. He says he is a citizen, and what steps can be taken to get rid of him? If he has been working his games here in the city, then he has stolen a march on me. You know he was at one time a companion of 'Soapy' Smith, but is not now. He is in business and defies anyone to prove anything against him. It does look as though he had tried to gull one of your reporters. If some of the men he has victimized will show themselves I will take all the necessary steps to deal with him in the

---

[1] *RMN* 07/31/1889.

[2] *RMN* 08/01/1889, p. 2.

proper manner." ... It is very improbable that any of them will do so as few people care to come forward and say they have been made fools of.

... The people Gray has been in the habit of defrauding cannot very well be produced, because they are strangers from all parts of the country, who, thinking they have the best of the bargain, leave the city as quickly as they came, and are unheard of afterward.[1]

The following day Morris was brought before a judge and quickly released due to lack of evidence. No victims of his swindle had come forward to give complaint.[2] Still, suspicion of corruption within city hall remained a topic of discussion all over the city.

The *News* had been very busy assembling the issue of July 31, but Jeff's side had not been idle. The *News* must have been astounded when that day, Ned "Banjo" Parker, Jeff's aide in the Arkins attack, strolled in to be interviewed.

Ned Parker, better known as "Banjo" Parker, called at THE NEWS office last night and disclaimed any connection with the assault upon Colonel Arkins. He says that he and Soapy Smith have not been good friends for some time, and have not been upon speaking terms until within the past three weeks. This, he claims, was owing to the fact that Soapy absolutely controlled the city, and that he was unable to do any "business" here until about three months ago, when he says he had to pay heavily for an "extra license." He says that on the night of the assault he was being shaved in the barbershop in the Patterson Block. Coming out, he proceeded up the street. Passing the prescription door of Dingle's drug store, he was called by Soapy Smith, who said to him, "They've been jumping on me again." He inquired what was meant, and was told of the article in THE NEWS, which he had not read. He bought a paper and was going down to the Windsor to read it, when Soapy called him again, saying: "Hold on a minute, I'm waiting to see Charley Thomas." After a few words, Parker says he started off again, when Soapy once more called to him, "Hold on, I am waiting to see a man, I don't want to see Charley Thomas at all. Wait a minute, and I'll go with you." Parker said he would go ahead, and had got a few feet away when he heard Soapy say, "Oh John," and a fall immediately afterwards. Turning around he saw Colonel Arkins staggering to his feet, saying, "Who struck me?" Parker says that he saw Soapy run around the corner of Curtis street, making a motion as though to draw a revolver. Thinking that if there was to be firing he would likely be struck, owning to his size, he turned back, passed THE NEWS office and went to the Windsor. This, he says, is all he knows about the matter, and is indignant at being ranked with Soapy Smith.[3]

A first conclusion might be that Parker was telling the truth. His account was plausible, accommodated the facts, and agreed with the *News* in condemning Jeff. However, the somewhat generally known practice among the bunco men was to deny

---

[1] *RMN* 08/01/1889.

[2] *RMN* 07/31/1889.

[3] *RMN* 08/01/1889.

working with or being on friendly terms with each other. Such posturing kept some of the brotherhood out of jail to work on freeing those who had been arrested. An additional advantage was that of creating "reasonable doubt." In this instance, Jeff thought best to have his man go to the newspaper office and tell a yarn.

The tactic failed. Parker was not believed, perhaps because his character was already known. The day after Parker's account was published, the following appeared:

> "Banjo" Parker who, it is stated, acted as a bodyguard to Smith in his dastardly attack on the manager of this paper, is a large overgrown specimen of humanity. He is a fat individual and has long pursued the soap and pen tricks as a means of livelihood. Six or seven years ago the writer met him up in Manitoba [Canada] where he was waxing fat on the credulity of the Canucks, but his little game was soon stopped as the police hauled him in and he was given twenty-four hours to leave the city. He is a dangerous vagrant. He has found other cities too hot for him, amongst them, so the writer is informed, Fort Worth, Texas. He should be shipped back east to his native state.[1]

Jeff's trial began on August 5, 1889. Procured were the services of three attorneys, Judge James Belford of Belford and Wikoff, Judge Barnum, and H.B. O'Reilly, Esquire.

Judge Belford, a popular Republican Denverite, in 1870 had been appointed an associate justice of the Colorado Supreme Court. Upon admission of Colorado as a State, he was elected as a Republican to Congress and re-elected to several terms. He moved to Denver in 1883 and opened a law firm.[2] Judge Belford was known as the "Red Rooster of the Rockies" because of his flaming red hair and "magnificently roseate beard."[3] In August 1891 he began writing for the *News* a series of controversial articles on modern spiritualism, evolution, materialism, miracles, ghosts, and the after-life.[4]

On the first day of the trial, the *News* was there early to watch.

> "Soapy," the assassin, was there early. He was restless and discomposed. He sat and walked nervously up and down or picked anxiously at his clothes or mustache. For the first time in his life this shameless bunco man was observed to be agitated and unnerved.[5]

Jeff testified that he was in the "auction business, selling prize packages." His attorney, Judge Belford, spoke on behalf of Jeff's unique trade.

> With regard to Mr. Soapy Smith's business, to be sure he wraps up a $50 bill in a soap package, puts it down in his bag, and the person that buys it probably don't get the $50; but if people don't want to lose they shouldn't

---

[1] *RMN* 08/02/1889.
[2] Congress, Biographical Directory.
[3] Perkin, pp. 363, 381.
[4] *RMN* 08/15/1891.
[5] *RMN* 08/06/1889.

buy a package of soap.[1] ... I have often backed three queens with a $50 bill and lost the pot, but I had no one to blame but myself.[2]

Then there was the cane. Jeff claimed he always carried the cane he used to hit Arkins due to a foot that kept falling asleep. He claimed he struck Arkins on the impulse of the moment and that it was not a planned attack. After the beating, Jeff told how he went to the saloon belonging to his friend John Kinneavy and then gave himself up. "I was ready to be tried on the charge!" he stated, adding what his attorney, Judge Belford, had proclaimed in court, that "The press was an outrage, and the enemy of the city!"[3]

Jeff's best defense came from Arkins himself. He told the court that he and Jeff had known one another for five or six years, that he had spoken with Jeff on several occasions, and that a week before the attack, Jeff had come to complain about being roasted in the *News* for the Logan Park incident. Arkins said Jeff had asked to be left alone, that he was not mixed up in the affair. Jeff had testified that Arkins promised to let up on him, and Arkins agreed that he had made the promise. The two had parted with good feeling towards one another with Arkins accepting a cigar from Jeff.[4]

A day later, on Tuesday, August 6, 1889, the trial was over. For Jeff, it could not have turned out better. The charge of attempted murder was reduced to assault with intent to do bodily harm. Jeff was ordered held for trial in district court on that charge, under bond of $1000,[5] and again with John Kinneavy present as bondsman, Jeff went free. Presumably the bond was forfeited, perhaps as a fine, because the trial was never held. It seems too serious a charge with far too much public attention for the matter just to have been forgotten. Far more likely is that Jeff found a way to have the case settled. It might have required forfeit of the $1,000 bond and paying more besides to certain persons, along with the promise of favors. But the case was apparently over, vanishing as if by some master sleight of hand. However, as would be shown over a year later, the case was not dead. It revived over a year later, but again it vanished and as mysteriously.

With the trial concluded, Jeff no doubt hoped the war with the *News* was over. It was not. However, clear now was that dislodging Jeff from Denver would be more difficult than originally thought. Jeff did not leave Denver for the last time until 1896. Col. Arkins, however, left the newspaper business exactly one year from the close of Jeff's trial and, in essence, acquittal. Perhaps the two assaults against Arkins in the previous year for his critical words as editor of the *News* had been enough.

Tomorrow the rumors regarding the sale of the *Rocky Mountain News* will come to an end. The *News* will change hands. Col. John Arkins, the President and manager of the company, will receive $390,000....[6]

---

[1] *puts it down in his bag*: use of a bag for mixing soap packages differs from other descriptions. This may be a switch bag, and possibly Jeff did use one during this period. A switch bag contains a hidden compartment. Money-laden bars of soap are switched with bars that contain no money.

[2] *RMN* 08/06/1889.

[3] *RMN* 08/05-06/1889.

[4] *Denver Times* 08/05/1889.

[5] *RMN* 08/06/1889.

[6] *Chicago Daily Tribune* 08/06/1890, p. 2.

1. Earliest known photograph of Jefferson Randolph Smith II, age 5 to 7. Circa 1865-67. Coweta County, Georgia. (Jefferson R. "Little Randy" Smith col.)

2. The Dr. Ira Ellis Smith house where Jefferson R. Smith II was born. Coweta County, Georgia. (Author's col.)

3. Smith family photo. (l to r) Eva K., age 2-4, Emily D., age 30-32, Jefferson R. Smith, Sr., age 36-38, and Jefferson R. Smith II, age 7-9. Circa 1867-69. Coweta County, Georgia. (Kyle Rosene col.)

4. Jeff R. Smith, age 9-12. Circa 1869-72. Coweta County, Georgia. (Kyle Rosene col.)

5. Jeff R. Smith (left), age 17-20, and unknown companion. Circa 1877-1880. Believed to be in Texas. (Howard Clifford col.)

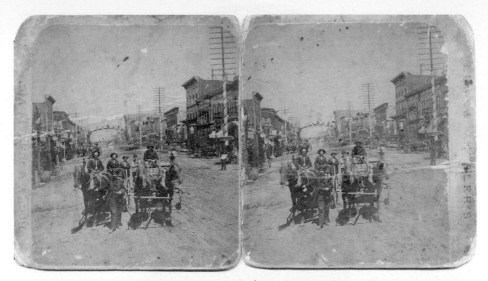

6A. Leadville, Colorado. Jefferson R. Smith II (3rd from left, back), age 19, sent this stereoview home to his family. He wrote on the back, "This is a crew of freighters we met in Leadville on the 21st of July 1880 in the morning on the day that Gen Grant arrived. You can see my photo by looking between the two wagons next to the man with the apron and his sleeves rolled up. (between the two men) J.R.S." According to other writing on the back, Jeff told his sister Eva that the former President (1869-77) was on horseback in the background. The *Leadville Weekly Herald* for July 24, 1880, reported the General's visit on page 1. Eva put a pin-hole through one of the stereoview photos to mark Grant's location. Astride his mount, Grant is said to be the blurry figure behind "the man with the apron," apparently crisscrossing the street decorated in his honor. (Kyle Rosene col.)

6B. Inset of 6A above, left side.

7. License for "Jeff Smith" to "hawk his prize soap." September 16, 1882. The $15.25 fee was high; in today's dollars it would be $417.55 (Tom's Inflation Calculator). (Jefferson R. "Little Randy" Smith col.)

8. Jefferson R. Smith II and Mary Eva Smith, photograph taken after their marriage. Circa 1886. Denver, Colorado. (Jefferson R. "Little Randy" Smith col.)

9. Men believed to be (l to r) John Morris and John Bowers. Circa 1889-1892. Denver, Colorado. (Kyle Rosene col.)

10. Bascomb Smith, his only known image. *Rocky Mountain News*, April 13, 1899. (Author's col.)

11. Jefferson R. Smith II. Circa 1890. Denver, Colorado. (Kyle Rosene col.)

12. Denver's "street of doom." Looking north down 17th Street from Larimer. In the three-story, brick Chever Block on the right, Jeff rented an office on the second floor and saloon space on the first. Beyond this building, just passed the large telephone pole, is the two-story building that housed the Tivoli Club. The façade of Union Station rises from the end of the street. Circa 1884. (Denver Public Library, Western History Collection, X-22053)

ONE OF SOAPY'S CUSTOMS.

13. Jeff giving out turkeys to Denver's poor. *Denver Evening Post* July 31, 1898. (Author's col.)

Jeff's reaction to the colonel's retirement in August 1890, if any, is not recorded.

Not all newspapers were against Jeff. After the trial, the *Denver Republican* in a commentary titled "This may be justice," the editor called Jeff's prosecution a great injustice. Described was how another Denver man had perpetrated a far worse crime and received less punishment. The other man had beaten his pregnant wife so badly that her child had died at birth. The courts could not decide if the baby had died as a result of the beating and so fined the husband twenty-five dollars. Pointed out was that for protecting his wife, Jeff was fined $1,000 ($29,570 today).[1] "It pays better," the editor observed, "to abuse a wife than it does to defend her."[2]

On August 2, 1889, the Denver police board succumbed to the demands of the *News* and passed an ordinance closing "all games of chance within the corporate limits of the city." Pressure on the city fathers was so great that they also saw fit to include closing down all gambling houses in the city. County Chief of Detectives DeLue announced that if he "found a gambling house open in Denver on Monday or after he would arrest everybody in it."[3] Denver witnessed an exodus of the city's gamblers to other less-regulated parts of the state. An article, "Across The Platte," describes how Jeff decreed a mass departure to the nearby city of Colfax to become "The Colorado Monte Carlo," where "a short ride across the viaduct will take the Denver sports out there." The article continued,

> Soapy, it is said on good authority, secured quarters on Golden Avenue, Colfax, on Friday and on the same evening moved the material part of his stock-in-trade over there. He is to be followed by others.

The "others" included Kinneavy and his Jockey Club and proprietors of the Missouri House, who "secured quarters near Colonel Smith's institution...."[4]

The main route west from Denver was Golden Avenue, named for the Rocky Mountain foothill town and supply center of Golden to which it led. At some point between 1863 and 1873, the road also came to be called Colfax Avenue.[5] Local historians deduce that landowners in the region were looking ahead to federal favor and assistance beyond territorial days, so to gain favor, the road was named after politician Schuyler Colfax.[6] In 1889 Eastern entrepreneurs were gathering up land for development as it seemed clear that Denver would soon press beyond its city limits.

"Colonel" Smith, as he called himself during this period, was applying leverage on Denver City fathers by actually or by feigning to join Eastern entrepreneurs in securing land west of the city. Denver property and business owners looked on this possibility

---

[1] Tom's Inflation Calculator.

[2] *Denver Republican* 08/07/1889.

[3] Unknown newspaper clipping, 08/01/1889. Clipped and saved by Jefferson R. Smith II. Jefferson R. "Little Randy" col.

[4] Denver newspaper clipping of unknown origin 08/01/1889. Author's col.

[5] Colfax Avenue officially named in 1896. (Colfax Avenue.com)

[6] Schuyler Colfax, in 1854 an Indiana Republican Congressman, served as Speaker of the House 1863-1869 and Vice President to Ulysses Grant from 1869-1873. Early Denver pioneer Daniel Witter married Colfax's half sister. He was a Federal tax collector for the region, a post that might have come to him through his marriage connection, and he owned considerable property along Golden Avenue. It is known that Colfax visited Denver and its western outskirts in 1865, 1868, and 1873. (Denver Post.com)

with worry. Threatening such a move surely put city hall in turmoil. Enormous numbers of contributions and sums of graft from the gambling fraternity would stop. Also ended would be the legitimate spending and circulation of ready money that the gambling trade brought to local businesses. That could dramatically diminish. A compromise must have been reached, for as suddenly as talk of moving began, it ceased.

The *News* watched and waited for Jeff or his men to go afoul of the law. Only twelve days after the trial ended, Jeff and some of his men were caught swindling at least six men from Colorado Springs at Jeff's "auction" house on Seventeenth Street. The *News* published the story on its front page under the heading,

SMITH AND HIS PALS.
An Exposure of the Means by Which a Great Soap Partnership Was Built Up.

Judge Belford was loudly called for to the police court yesterday morning, but failed to respond to his name. The legal Barberousa was wanted badly to defend "Soapy" Smith, late of the firm of Londoner, Farley & Smith, which dissolved with a crash the evening before.... Jeff R. Smith, Bascom Smith, (brother to Jeff R.), T. J. Gray, (familiarly "Fatty"), G. E. Roberts and John Vermillion [were] brought in the night before on the complaint of Henry Hedt, dewy "sucker" from Colorado Springs. ... "Sapo Viridis" Smith (sapo viridis being the botanical name for green soap) was green with rage at his quondam partners Farley and Londoner, and asked for a stay of proceedings until he could procure the attendance of his counsel Barbarous Belford. ...

The prosecuting attorney caused a storm of laughter in opening the case against the five bunco men by looking sternly at Sapo Viridis Smith, and inquiring gravely: "Where are your partners?" Some one pointed to Chief Farley in the skirts of the audience.... There was a roar like the bellow of a bull and it was with difficulty that the court room was restored to ... decorum.

A continuation to wait for Belford was seriously objected to so likely [was it] to impair the candor of the testimony given by the "suckers" who had been roped in at Soapy Smith's place on Seventeenth street the day before.... ...

Henry Hedt, the first witness called, was delightfully fresh and naïve. He was a cook in a restaurant in Colorado Springs and had come up to town to see life. He had bought three sticks of the firm's candy for 25 cents, then seven for 50 cents and finally fifteen for $1 with[out] drawing anything but a penholder. "Fatty" Gray had asked the auctioneer, Roberts, to wrap up a $50 bill in the candy packages for which Hedt was asked to put up $25. He put up $10. Sucker like, he still played on until he had squandered $17, when he complained to the police. He recognized Gray, John Vermillion, Bascom Smith and J. W. Allen as "cappers" for the layout who drew large sums of money incessantly while he was in the shop.

C. E. Shepard said he had spent $20 in the place, deriving ... a penholder and a knife. Pat Wilson encouraged by the luck of Vermillion, known as "Shoot Your Eye Out Jack," had invested $1.50 in candy, drawing blanks every time. J. W. Allen, a youthful "booster" for the establishment, had made a great deal of money out of a small investment.... ... Pat Wilson, John Hogel, Cart Olsen and M. J. Hickey, other innocents testified to having expended various sums for the candy which brought them in nothing.

Unfortunately, so defective are the ordinances, proprietors of this "skin" game are liable for nothing worse than vagrancy. The case will be resumed on Tuesday morning. The bond was placed at $1,000.[1]

Jeff's auction house had reinvented the prize package soap sell by exchanging soap for candy. A new Soap Gang member was John "Shoot-Your-Eye-Out Jack" Vermillion. An associate of Wyatt Earp in the early 1880s, he then was known as "Texas Jack."[2] For reasons yet unknown, his name had become "Shoot-Your-Eye-Out Jack" by the time he joined the Soap Gang.

After all its chest-beating against fake prize package sales and all its finger-wagging at defendants, the *News* expected the trial to produce convictions. Evidence and complainants were plentiful. What other outcome could occur but conviction and jail time or at the least, escort to the next train out of Denver and a warning never to return? The *News* was in the courtroom to witness the contrary outcome.

Sapolio Smith and his four retainers, "Fatty" Gray, Brother Bascom Smith, Auctioneer Roberts and Jack Vermillion ... appeared before Police Magistrate Barnes yesterday afternoon to transact the concluding business of their trial on a charge of vagrancy, begun last Saturday morning. ...

...Belford did not turn up. Sapolio Smith has asserted with a sob that when the "Red Rooster of the Rockies" got back he would be all right. Perhaps Belford did not enjoy the notoriety he was gaining as the much wanted attorney general for crookdom. At all events he found it wise to defer his return....

Attorney O'Reilly conducted the affairs of the quintet in a very breezy, cheerful manner.

"Soapy" remarked to a circle of friends before the case was opened that, seeing the magistrate had let off the Chinese gamblers at $1.50, he hoped to get through on $1.25, seeing that he was so much younger an offender. He didn't know there was anything wrong in it. No one had ever told him it wasn't allowed. Of course if he had been told it would have been different. But he hadn't, and he thought it was a trifle rough to be hauled up this way before any one had taken the trouble to call him into some dark corner and say, "Beware, Soapy, your business is off color. You will be called to time."[3] Going ahead, he said, imbued with an invigorating sense of his own moral rectitude and spiritually chastened passions, he considered it just infinitesimally tough and rough that the police should descend like wolves on a fold of lambs, as in the case of Marcos Bozzaris.[4]

---

[1] *RMN* 08/18/1889.

[2] Tefertiller, p. 233.

[3] *called to time*: "to come to time" is "to yield to authority, comply."(*DARE*) Hence, "called by authority to account"?

[4] *Marcos Bozzaris*: Hero of long-running Greek struggle for independence from Turkey. His long service ended when he was killed leading led a decisive night assault against the Turks. (Encyclopedia, 1892)

"Soapy" was withal cheerful and chipper, save for the aroma of injured innocence which floated around him and seemed to insure him a front-page advertisement on the calendar of martyrs. ...

The five [defendants] leaned languidly up against the magistrate's desk and declared themselves ready to withdraw their former plea of "not guilty," having "thought it over."

"But really," said Monsieur "Soapy," earnest leaning across the desk, "it was a straight game. Here, I brought some of the prizes up to show you," and he ... brought out a good haul of knives. ... "Look at them, judge," he said, "look at them," with an air of conviction, "the very best stock in the market, that's what we get."

"Very fine! Very fine!" grunted the magistrate glaring at the stack like a hardware merchant. "Very fine indeed!"

"We are ready to promise," added Soapy, "that we will never run the game again. We didn't know it was wrong, you know," he said with a sort of ephemeral wink. ...

"Well," said Magistrate Barnes, clearing his throat, "taking all things into consideration, I will fine you each $200 and stay of execution so long as you keep your promise."

"Soapy" was on the point of asking everyone out to have a drink on the strength of this pleasant permission, but stopped himself in time. ... [1]

It is improbable that Magistrate Barnes was unaware of Jeff's criminal enterprises. Just two days prior, Barnes had witnessed Jeff bail out one of his men in another swindle. With its usual tinge of contempt, the ever watchful *News* reported the event in its Tuesday, August 20, 1889, issue.

"Dan" Leery, commonly known amongst the confidence gang as "Mysterious Dan," came up before Magistrate Barnes yesterday on a charge of vagrancy. He was arrested Saturday night and bailed out by "Soapy" Smith. His standing with the police is sufficiently accounted for by that fact. The evidence was withdrawn against him yesterday morning, the "sucker" having "slept it over," and even the patrolman had forgotten what he had arrested him for.[2]

It would appear that the victim and the patrolman had been paid to drop the case.

In the issue of Wednesday, August 28, the *News* exposed how the Denver City Council had demanded a percentage of the tills of saloon owners. This amounted to a large increase over the fixed payments the saloon men had already been paying. The understanding had been that in return for the fixed payments, the city would keep police from interfering with their businesses and that closing time would be 2 a.m. If the increase were not met, Mayor Londoner, through Chief Farley, had ordered that the doors of all gambling establishments be closed at midnight or risk losing their licenses. The unprecedented source of the story was some of the saloon proprietors.[3]

---

[1] *RMN* 08/21/1889.
[2] *RMN* 08/20/1889.
[3] *RMN* 08/28/1889.

Jeff decided that peers who had "talked" to the *News* would be given an object lesson, and the police would give him a pass to do it. Fortified with the knowledge that no one could stop him, Jeff struck back.

Soapy Smith on the Warpath Without Fear of Arrest.

...Jeff R. Smith went into a faro layout a few nights ago and borrowed $25. Subsequently he returned and presented his watch, worth probably $15.10, and borrowed $50. Some time afterwards he sat down at one of the tables in the room and won something over $100. He was then asked to redeem the watch.

He pondered.

While he was so engaged it suddenly occurred to him that he had the town by the throat, and thereupon he arose from his seat and took the faro dealer by the throat likewise. Jeff carries a dirk about five inches long which opens out when a spring is touched. So he pulled the knife. He had the freedom of the city and why not? To be sure he was a distinguished personage, and as he placed the knife to the dealer's throat, he remarked in his suave, gentlemanly way:

"You ___ ___ ___ of ___, I'll swipe the gizzard out of you, you ___ ___ fool; give me my money, I'll redeem that ___ ___ watch when I see fit."

For some reason the dealer trembled and handed over the money, while the spectators wondered, did this man have a pull with the administration? It looked that way. While Jeff is a plain everyday, happy-go-lucky sort of fellow, and is devoid of canned up ostentation, he had the freedom of the town and proceeded to exercise it in a judicious manner. So he cut out the green cloth on the table, and hacked it up like a well trained butcher, after which he sauntered out of the room with the air of a man who had a decided corner on the town, the administration and the world. For several days the affair was talked of on the streets, and yet it has not come to the ears of the sleuth hounds of the city department. If it has, so much the worse for them, for "Soapy" disregarded the law, and the police have done the same. Were a bricklayer, a hodcarrier or a dry good clerk to strike a man in the face and bruise him slightly, he would be arrested and fined in the police court. Jeff Smith is a different person. He can threaten a man's life, the affair can be discussed in the club houses, and the chief of police will not so much as reprimand him.[1]

After this high-profile, public indictment of Jeff's behavior and the lack of response from authorities, perhaps Jeff's city hall friends persuaded him to take a vacation from Denver. Whatever the cause, a few days after Jeff lacerated the green cloth of the faro table and threatened its dealer, he was on a train. With him were a few members of the Soap Gang, believed to be his brother Bascomb, John Morris, and John Vermillion, and possibly "Auctioneer Roberts" as well as J. W. Allen. According to a letter to his wife, he was headed northwest to Spokane Falls, Washington.

---

[1] *RMN* 08/28/1889.

Despite withstanding attacks by the *News* and prevailing in the courts, Jeff may have often thought of the days when towns and cities of the West were wide open for exploitation without so much resistance, when for the purchase of a license either on paper or with a handshake, crowds could be worked until they were cleaned, officials were paid off, and it was time to move on. Denver had been that way for a time except that so many people came that moving on was not required. Crowds just kept coming. Then change set in. Jeff was up to it, but remembrance of the days of old across the frontier held an allure. Was there any frontier left? Perhaps. Perhaps in the Northwest, perhaps up Spokane Falls way in Eastern Washington. Word of the area was reaching Denver from Jeff's wide circle of friends, from miners, railroad workmen, and woodsmen coming from or going to the area, and from the Union Pacific Railroad, which in 1889 completed a line from Portland, Oregon, north by northeast to Spokane. Now it was possible to take a Pullman coach all the way from Denver up to see the place being called another Denver in the making.

It requires no very profound knowledge of Western geography, no very lengthy study of the State of Washington, to enable anyone to understand without difficulty some of the minor reasons why Spokane Falls should become a great and important city, the metropolis of a vast surrounding country. A glance at the map will show the mountain range that extends up through the Idaho Panhandle, and then along the British Columbia frontier, to the east and north of the city. These mountains are incalculably rich in ores of all kinds, and would amply suffice to make a Denver of Spokane Falls, even if she had no other natural resources to draw from.[1]

The route for Jeff likely would have been north from Denver to Cheyenne, Wyoming; west by northwest to Pocatello, Idaho; northwest to Pasco, Washington; and north by northeast to Spokane. A more direct route from the east through the Cascade Mountains would not be completed until 1892.[2]

An event earlier that month may have influenced Jeff's choice of destination. On August 4, 1889, Spokane Falls lost thirty-two blocks of the main business district in a horrific fire.[3] Conceivably, in this prime location Jeff saw special opportunity in the aftermath of the fire. Further, there were all the towns between Cheyenne and Spokane to look over.

On the other hand, it may have been as the *Denver Times* surmised, "that they were going to Ogden and other cities to 'work.'"[4] Then an explosive event occurred that caused Jeff to pick Spokane as a destination.

On Friday, August 30, 1889, Jeff's train made a scheduled stop at the Pocatello depot. During the wait, a man in railroad switchman clothes came up to the window of the railroad car where Jeff sat and fired at him five times, point blank. All but one bullet missed injuring him. It came so close that it mutilated half Jeff's mustache as it whizzed by. Jeff drew pistol and returned three shots, all striking their targets, two in

---

[1] Lomax, E.L., General Passenger Agent. (Union Pacific)
[2] *Online Encyclopedia.*
[3] History Link.org.
[4] *Denver Times* 09/01/1889.

one fleeing assailant and one in another. Next, railroad personnel "tried to mob" him, as Jeff put it, but "we stood them off," and Jeff and his party, with the aid of "a few good citizens," left Pocatello on a hasty, twenty-five-mile horseback ride north to Blackfoot. The newspaper there gave the shootout only two sentences:

Pocatello had a shooting scrape last week. Nobody killed however.[1]

Three days later, on stationary imprinted with the design and address of the St. Nicholas Hotel in Butte, Montana, Jeff made time to record in a letter to Mary the details of the event and assurances of his well being.

September 2, 1889
Dear wife,

I am all safe and with friends. I had a narrow escape but came out all right. Was sitting in the car at the depot at Pocatello and a man came up and shot at me without any warning through the car window. The smoke of the pistol blinded me for a moment, but I returned the fire and shot both my assailants, one through the thigh, and the other through the calf of the leg and the heel. Five shots were fired at me in all and how I was missed I can't tell. It looks like providence helped me out. I fired three shots, all of which took effect. The men shot were switchmen and were working for the railroad. The railroaders tried to mob me but we stood them off and got a few good citizens to help and escaped to Blackfoot. We returned the next day. I had my trial and was acquitted. Write to me at Spokan Falls,[2] Washington, Territory.

Bascomb is in Dillon, Montana. Kiss little Jeff & Eva for me. Give all my friends my best wishes and don't be afraid. Will let you know about other things in my next. I rode 25 miles on a horse in 45 minutes and I am very sore on my sitter. I also lost my mustache as one of the bullets cut half of it off (say nothing about that!) Write me who were my friends. I had to use the money in Pocatello or I would have been there yet. God bless you my dear wife,

Jeff

p.s. address plain Jeff R. Smith, Spokan Falls, Washington Terr. The man that shot at me was one of the men who got licked at Logan Park.[3]

The *Denver News* printed the following on the evening of August 30:

Arrested in Idaho.

The following dispatch was received at police headquarters last evening:

POCATELLO, Idaho., Aug. 30.—Police Headquarters, Denver, Colo.: Is Soapy Smith and gang wanted there? All arrested here. SIMPSON.

According to Jeff, though, in his letter to Mary, he and the men with him returned to Pocatello the next day, August 31, 1889. The police put them in jail while figuring out

---

[1] *The Idaho News* 08/31/1889.

[2] *Spokan Falls*: also *Spokane Falls*. Incorporated 1881 as "Spokan Falls," an "e" was added to the name in 1883, and "Falls" was dropped in 1891. The name comes from the first residents of the region, the "Spokanes," meaning "Children of the Sun." (Spokane, City of)

[3] Hand written Ltr to Mary Eva Smith fr Jeff R. Smith II, 09/02/1889. Item 77, author's col.

just what had happened and while waiting for a reply to a wire to Denver about whether Jeff was wanted there. Denver declined the offer to have Jeff returned.

Details of the shootout reached *The Denver Times* the day after the event, and the story appeared the next day. It was based on a dispatch from Pocatello.

JEFF SMITH SHOOTS A MAN

The Result of a Feud Between Rival Gangs "SOAPY" PROVES TO BE GAME From All Accounts the Shooting Was Justifiable—Pocatello Toughs Attempt to Drive Denver Experts Out of Idaho.

Jeff Smith, accompanied by "shoot-your-eye-out Jack," Fatty Gray and others, left Denver last Monday night [August 26], ostensibly for the mountains. It appears now, however, that they did not intend going on a pleasure trip, as they stated, but that they were going to Ogden and other cities to "work." It will be seen by the following dispatch that the party has not had smooth sailing since leaving Denver:

Special to The Times. POCATELLO, IDAHO, August 31.—On the arrival of yesterday's train from Ogden a shooting affray occurred, in which Samuel Belcher of Ogden was shot through the left leg and right ankle. Jeff Smith of Denver has been arrested as the party who did the shooting. From all facts that can be learned it seems that Smith was justified. A notorious gang at Pocatello, who have been "working" Ogden and other cities, attempted to kill Smith and his companions, but Smith was game and refused to quit the territory which the other gang claimed…. Three guns were drawn on Smith, but he, instead of running, pulled his own gun, shot Belcher and put the others to flight. He was immediately afterwards arrested and will be given a hearing to-day. Another statement as to the effect that the affair grew out of an old feud in which the gang headed by Smith was opposed to a gang being led by "the Rincon Kid."

It has been well known among "fly" people[1] that an attempt to kill Smith would be made as soon as he left Denver. The "Kid" and his gang are especially bitter against the smooth soap man and in frequent letters to people in Denver the "Kid" has expressed himself as determined to "do" any member of the Smith gang that he might meet.

A number of dispatches were received to-day by friends of Smith's in which "Soapy" declares that he was justified in shooting Belcher. However, one dispatch from another source states that Belcher was an innocent man—whom "Soapy" did not know and did not intend to shoot.

The following dispatch was received this afternoon by a citizen:

"I was honorably acquitted. Show this to my wife. Will write particulars."

Jeff Smith.[2]

Major discrepancies occur between Jeff's version and the Denver dispatch. Jeff wrote that two men attacked him while the dispatch reported three guns (three men?)

---

[1] *"fly" people*: Fly man. An expert thief. A professional criminal. (Partridge, *Underworld*)
[2] *Denver Times* 09/01/1889.

drawn against him. Jeff claimed Belcher was a beaten man at the Logan Park brawl, yet the dispatch wrote that Belcher was a member of a rival bunco gang attempting to rid his turf of encroachers. (Both reports could be true.) The dispatch reported that Jeff had been arrested immediately following the gunfight while Jeff wrote that he and his men escaped and returned the following day to sort out what had happened with authorities. The money he spent in Pocatello likely went to attorney and enhanced fees to ensure his freedom. The local paper did not publish statements from Jeff about the attack because probably Jeff was gone, immediately having resumed his journey.

The man Belcher is not listed in the 1889 Denver City Directory, but perhaps he and some of the others "who got licked" at Logan Park had been part of a Utah bunco gang that had come over to "work" the well-publicized event. Word was out that Jeff and some of his men were leaving Denver, on holiday. Belcher and the man or men with him could have been waiting for Jeff to come through Pocatello. On the other hand, they might have been from the environs of Denver and as disgruntled victims of Logan Park, were riding the same train, shadowing Jeff, gotten off in Pocatello, changed into railroad work clothes, and closed in on Jeff from outside to gun him down. Still another scenario is that Jeff and the men with him were "working" Utah towns and were being tracked by a rival local gang. If Jeff were going directly to Spokane from Denver, it would not have taken from Monday, August 26 (per the *Times* story), to Friday, August 30, to reach Pocatello. Moreover, the *Denver Times* reported Jeff had been on a train arriving in Pocatello *from* Ogden, which is south of the route from Denver to Spokane. However the true circumstances, clear is that a person or persons wanted Jeff dead.

Once exonerated on September 1, presumably Jeff and the others left. The *Idaho News* noted the departure: "The smell of gunpowder has been wafted away and the fightists are all gone."[1] Just where Jeff went next is not exactly clear. He could have gone north into Montana to Butte. That could be where he came by the stationary from the St. Nicholas Hotel in Butte, on which the next day, September 2, Jeff wrote Mary his four-page letter. For certain, Bascomb did go north toward Butte; Jeff wrote that Bascomb was in Dillon, south of Butte. Jeff also wrote that he could be written to in Spokane. He did not, however, travel northwest from Butte to Spokane, at least not by rail. The Great Northern would not have a railway through the Cascades until 1892.[2] Traveling the steep Cascades in 1889 would have been arduous.

Clear, though, is that Jeff intended on going to Spokane. In his letter to Mary, he asked her to address her letters "plain Jeff R. Smith, Spokan Falls, Washington Terr." This means of address was not uncommon, at least for Jeff. A number of letters in the Smith family collections are addressed in a similar manner. It was not wise to advertise a specific place of residence, even on an envelope in the US mails. That would be to invite another Pocatello! Jeff suspected someone in Denver, perhaps even a friend, had given out his itinerary and destination. Near the close of his September 2 letter to Mary appears this cryptic sentence "Write me who were my friends." It seems likely that in an off-hand way, Jeff is asking who might have been

---

[1] *Idaho News* 09/07/1889.
[2] *Online Encyclopedia.*

told of his whereabouts and/or route, who might have been inquiring after him, or who might have been inquiring about what had happened in Pocatello. After all, for the attack to be so direct, it must have been known that he was a passenger on that train.

Mary left the children with her mother and hurried to be with her husband, probably at Spokane Falls. While with him, she tried to fix his perforated mustache but without success.[1] Jeff may have resorted to shaving his face smooth and regrowing the beard and mustache that are known in all post 1889 photographs.

When Jeff returned to Denver, it may have been without a few members of his entourage. Vermillion is not heard of in the Denver newspapers again and is believed to have left the gang. John Morris also disappeared from headlines. It is thought he, too, may have dropped out. Four years later a "John Morris" was arrested for assault in Denver and fined $10, but it is not known if this is "Fatty Gray."[2]

Mid 1889 marks Jeff's first sequence of violent behavior and his first reported use of a knife and a gun. All within a month and a half, there had been fist-fighting, man caning, destruction of property with a knife, threatening a man with a knife, and a fierce shootout. The causes of these events are not hard to account for. The Logan Park affair that had gone so badly awry; the *Rocky Mountain News* declaration of war on Jeff and his businesses, including unrelenting public insult of Jeff and his circle; legal peril (and cost); and an explosive, sudden, and nearly successful plot against his life. Any of these events could have released the safety catch on Jeff's behavior. In matters large and small, violence seems to have become much closer at hand. A 1903 remembrance of Jeff during his Denver days illustrates the shift:

> Chief Roberts of the fire department,[3] who has just returned from a trip to the firemen's convention in the East, recalled this morning how "Soapy" Smith once brought a meeting of Red Men[4] to order.
>
> "We belonged to the same lodge," said Mr. Roberts, "and Soapy was the presiding officer one night ... at a meeting at which there was considerable turbulence over a disputed question. Soapy rapped on the desk with his gavel and shouted loudly for order. The members paid no attention to him."
>
> "Suddenly he whipped out a big navy 45 revolver and pounded on the desk with the butt."
>
> "If I can't rap you into order," he exclaimed, "I can shoot order into you." The meeting became so quiet that one could have heard a pin drop.[5]

---

[1] John R. Smith, as told to him by Mary Eva Smith.

[2] *RMN* 08/13/1893, p. 8.

[3] Fire Chief, 04/1894-04/1895 & 09/1897-04/30/1903.

[4] *Red Men*: Improved Order of Red Men. This fraternal order traces to pre-Revolutionary War societies such as the Sons of Liberty (responsible for the Boston Tea Party). After 1812, name changed to Society of Red Men, and after 1834, changed to Improved Order of Red Men. The Society remains extant. (*Cemeteries*) The Order is listed in the 1889 *Denver City Directory* under secret and benevolent societies. Two of these tribes met in the Chever block on the corner of Seventeenth and Larimer streets, where Jeff had his office. A ticket for a grand ball and installation of officers for the Improved Order of Red Men, dated 01/05/1895, is in the Jefferson Randolph "Little Randy" Smith col.

[5] *Denver Times* 09/05/1903.

Jeff was not only a member of the Improved Order of Red Men in Denver, but at one time was elected "chief." A newspaper article dated November 20, 1892 states that during one meeting of the organization

> Chief J. R. Smith of Comanche, No. 23, presented the tribe with a handsome and original war bonnet, which was taken from the head of a dead warrior at the battle of Wounded Knee, at Little Cheyenne. The bonnet is a fine piece of work, and the members of No. 23 feel proud to be the only tribe in the state whose chief can wear the original head dress of an Indian tribe.[1]

A "J. S." is listed in the *News*, as well as L. S. Palmer, as being members of Comanche, No. 23 on January 16, 1893. A ticket for a grand ball given by Comanche Tribe, No, 23, dated January 5, 1895 are some of the many treasured artifacts Jeff and Mary saved.[2]

Jeff had good reason to believe in one of his favorite proverbial sayings, that if "You have a lion by the tail, swing it, don't let it swing you." It was a sizeable lion Jeff had by the tail: city hall, more than one crusading newspaper, a legion of semi-independent Soap Gang members, other such competing organizations, victims of unknown volatility, and in general, the whole rapidly growing city of Denver. Huge, often snarling, and dangerous, it was difficult to manage and keep at bay, and sometimes required swinging. So it is not exactly a failing that Jeff apparently did not see the other lion that needed swinging, the one steadily creeping up on him, the lion of Jeff's own nature.

Despite so much adversity, though, things were going Jeff's way. As he observed in his September letter to Mary, "It looks like providence helped me out." And for about the next nine years, in general, providence would continue to help him out.

Chapter 8
Soapy Recaptures Denver

Gone To Church—Today is Sunday.
—Sign on the door of the Tivoli Club

As exhausting as it was, Jeff cherished being a boss in Denver. No circumstances could induce him to give it up, including threats of prison or death. He was, after all, a gambler, and successfully resuming control over his Denver operations was a big gamble. It meant working with crooked politicians and police officers, a treacherous breed whose loyalty was to themselves alone. Especially the politicians would turn on him if their interests were served or their self-preservation were at stake. Returning to Denver would also mean re-entering the war declared on him by the *News*. Further, reformers were mounting a new war by way of election blocks to shut down the entire gambling and saloon industry. A growing concern was the mounting wave of ambitious men like the Blonger brothers, men as determined as Jeff to hold the reigns of power if

---

[1] *RMN* 11/20/1892, p. 23.
[2] Geri Murphy col.

they could. At this time, it seemed that Denver wanted war on many fronts, and in returning to Denver, Jeff might be said to be ready to give it to them.

Jeff, though, had special powers, his wily ways. Even when he succumbed to frustration when his dignity was insulted, he knew to put a reasonable human face on an event, not to quibble over paying a fine, even a hefty one, and even to leave Denver for a time when the heat was high. Then in returning, he could feel his way into just how to do it, such as by instilling calm, working patiently to persuade, and re-establishing alliances. Crucial in this process was an ability to prime the money pumps that quenched thirsts and cooled brows, from elected officials to the judiciary to the police, including gamblers and swindlers and even the needy—and even those who ministered to the needy, right down to stray animals on the street.

Jeff left Denver on August 26, and in his September 2, 1889, letter to Mary, he wrote that he was going to Spokane Falls. No records of his activities there nor anywhere during his absence have yet been found. On October 17, 1889, forty-eight days after the Pocatello gunfight, Jeff was back in Denver and back in trouble. Oddly, given its previous coverage and efforts against Jeff, the *News* barely gave space on page six to report Jeff in court on the old charge of assaulting its managing editor.

> Jeff Smith has been held by the grand jury to answer for assault with intent to kill. He was present yesterday in the criminal division of the district court and gave a bond of $1,000, John Kinneavy becoming his bondsman.[1]

Another bond for $1,000? How did this ghost charge reappear? A good guess is that a certain power wanted Jeff out of the way. However, it seems other powers were glad to have Jeff back in Denver. His beneficial influences were being felt, the greatest evidence of which is the apparent reburying of the old charge, permanently this time.

Quickly resuming control of the city's underworld was surely satisfying, but Jeff was without Mary. She and his children were still with Mary's mother in St. Louis, presumably waiting for Jeff's signal to return. Jeff lived at 1631 Blake Street[2] while Edwards and his wife Hi-Ki lived in the Smith home on Curtis. At first this arrangement might have been temporary, but the Smiths were never again to live there. Edwards and his wife remained in the house until sometime after 1895 when Jeff sold it.[3]

Amazingly Jeff's name did not appear in the *News* for four months, and then only indirectly. His Tivoli Club was noted in the papers but without Jeff's name. Reform ordinances had forced all saloons in the city to close on Sundays. On one Sunday, February 17, 1890, Jeff hung a sign on the door of his club and the *News* noted it:

> Down Among the Dives.
>
> The door of the Tivoli saloon, which is always a favorite resort with a certain class, did not yield to the pressure which many brought to bear against it [*not* to observe the Sabbath]. On the panel was pasted a notice with the words: "Gone to church; to-day is Sunday."[4]

---

[1] *RMN* 10/17/1889, p. 6.

[2] *Denver City Directory,* 1890.

[3] Ltr fr Hi Ki & Yank Fewclothes (Henry Edwards & wife Hi Ki) to Mary E. Smith. 12/14/1895. Item 6, author's col.

[4] *RMN* 02/17/1890.

Major French, commander of Denver's Salvation Army, read about the sign and felt Jeff might be coming around to a religious way of thinking. Taking the initiative, the major led a march to the corner of Market and Seventeenth and presented Jeff with the opportunity to look good in a blue and red uniform. A reporter described the event:

> The army came to a halt just in front of his [Jeff's] place, and sent up "hallelujahs" enough to wake up…, and this song was sung as an inducement to Soapy to join the band, to the tune of "Climbing Up the Golden Stairs."
>
> "Soapy" would not bite even at this, but the little army received a few recruits from the crowd on the corner and marched happily to their hall on Lawrence street.[1]

Along with most of his peers, Jeff was a strong advocate for the Colorado Republican Party. His return to Denver was not just allowed by the Republican political establishment at city hall; it was welcomed. However, in what may have been revenge for wrongs Jeff perceived had been done to him by Mayor Londoner and Chief Farley, Jeff did not withhold all evidence of fraud in the registration and collection of votes in the mayoral election of April 2, 1889. Londoner, a Denver pioneer and businessman, was inclined to allow gambling and saloons, and he had enlisted Jeff's aid in securing his election. In addition to receiving expense money, Jeff no doubt also had assurances that his interests would be protected. However, after all that Jeff had gone through, he probably believed Londoner had not fulfilled his end of the bargain, so Jeff, in a round-about way, assisted the district attorney in court. The trial seeking ouster of Mayor Londoner because of gross election fraud began in mid March 1890.[2]

In the spring of 1889, Jeff, Ed Chase, "Bat" Masterson, John Morris, Ned Parker, John Kinneavy, city detective Sam "Sheeny Sam" Emrich and a host of others were involved in the criminal act of fraudulently registering hundreds of names to vote so that ballot boxes could be stuffed with hundreds of false and fictitious and votes.[3]

> Election day, April 2, 1889, turned into a carnival of abuses. Reportedly, because of their twenty-thousand-dollar slush fund, saloonkeepers were able to pay two dollars per vote. Bonuses for repeaters were generously awarded in the form of lottery tickets and free beer. Tramps and hoodlums from nearby towns were brought to Denver and marched to the polls by election-day special deputies.[4]

Fraudulent voting in Denver was an open secret for a long time, including Jeff's involvement. Appearing in 1910 was a book of remembrances about Denver in the 1880s and 1890s. As a young man interested in the law, Lindsey

> had read, in the newspapers, of how the Denver Republicans won the elections by fraud—by ballot-box stuffing and what not—and I had followed one "Soapy" Smith on the streets, from precinct to precinct, with his gang of election thieves, and had seen them vote not once but five times openly. I

---

[1] Denver newspaper clipping of unknown origin & date, cut out by Jeff R. Smith II. Author's col.
[2] *RMN* 03/19/1890.
[3] *RMN* 03/20/1890 & 03/15/1890, p. 6.
[4] Noel, *City*, p. 96.

had seen a young man, whom I knew, knocked down and arrested for "raising a disturbance" when he objected to "Soapy" Smith's proceeding; and the policeman who arrested him did it with a smile and a wink.[1]

Voting fraud might have continued as it had for years without general revolt had it not been for one abuse that was widespread. Many legitimate voters had been turned away, some even arrested, because their names had already been used by others to cast ballots. At first officials refused to investigate. The election was certified, over. But accusations continued and kinds of election abuses grew more numerous, until after eleven months, the Arapahoe County Court preferred charges and held trial in the matter. Jeff was subpoenaed to testify about what had happened in the Thirtieth precinct, site of some of the worst abuses. The *News* reported Jeff's testimony under questioning by District Attorney Lafe Pence. He said that if Jeff Smith

happens to be named to you gentlemen later as Soapy Smith, I trust that counsel and the court and jury will make allowance for it and not regard it as slang, because it has become a common and notorious name....[2]

Pence was denied the request, but the prohibition did not include the *News*.

Soapy had no intention of answering if he could avoid it. He was very good natured and was amused at the interrogatories of the attorney. Some things he would deny. On other points the answer would be that such things might have occurred but he had not seen them. On still others Jefferson Randolph Smith said his memory was at fault. As a rule, however, the witness endeavored to evade the questions or answer them equivocally. Mr. Pence did not allow this. As a result, many damaging confessions were obtained from Soapy.[3]

... His full name was Jefferson Randolph Smith, evidently having a youth of promise. His residence was 3451 Larimer.[4] Witness had been to the polls ... a little before 7 o'clock in the morning of April 2, 1889. ...

Witness had not furnished anyone with slips that day. "Soapy" declared that he had taken no one to the polls on that day. Most of the time he endeavored to answer all the questions evasively. He finally admitted that he had had a doorkeeper at his store [cigar store] that day. His store was just around the corner from the polling place. It was his custom to have a doorkeeper when he had work of a private character going on inside. The witness would not say that he had seen anyone given slips in his store. It might have been a fact that some men had been furnished with some. Witness had taken some of his friends to vote. His business was mostly around the polls that day. He tended door for awhile. The witness had not sent anyone to the polls that day. He had been in the saloon, close to the polling place, once or twice. Ed Chase was there about an hour. He might have been there two hours. The witness had taken some men to the saloon

---

[1] Lindsey, pp. 11-12.

[2] *RMN* 03/15/1890, p. 6.

[3] *RMN* 03/20/1890, p. 1.

[4] Noel, *City*, p. 188. Known as Upper Larimer Street, it was filled with cottages and corner stores.

to get a drink. There were men by the name of Erwin, Parker and Vermillion inside. The witness had seen [Chief] Dan Brady go into the saloon once as he came out. He had not seen Chief Brady there. The witness had not paid particular attention to what was going on. If any men had slips of paper while he was in there he had not seen them, at least he could not remember anything about it. There was an inner room to the saloon with still another one off that. Mr. Pence here drew a plan of the neighborhood. Soapy was then required to answer a good many searching questions. The witness denied having furnished slips during any part of the day to voters. He had taken a good many to the polls. They were always friends. The witness had furnished these men with straight Republican ballots that day. None of the men had changed clothing to his knowledge. He had himself not changed their clothing for them, nor any one else to his knowledge. In the inner room of his cigar store there was a table with ballots on it. If a cigar box was there with slips of paper with names written on them, Soapy had been so blind he had not seen it. The witness did not think there was anything under the table but the floor. There was money there on the table. Some two or three men had had slips of paper with names on them. They were in his store at the time. If there were any others he did not know it.

Ed. Chase had a book full of names. Some men had gone to the polls from the saloon. He had not seen any slips dealt out to voters. The witness was ignorant of anything going on within the saloon, not having been observing at the time. Before he left the stand Soapy drew a plan of his store for the jury's benefit, with the back and front rooms shown.[1]

Other testimony established that Deputy Sheriff Keller and Police Chief Farley had been on hand to suppress disturbances from quarrelsome voters. Also revealed was that only votes for Londoner were put in the ballot box. The others were discarded and replaced with ballots from those who were deceased, those no longer residing in Denver, and worst, those currently residing in the city but who had not yet voted.[2] Then when these arrived to vote, they were turned away for trying to vote twice.

Jeff was not cross examined by the defense, probably for fear he might expose more examples of fraud. Evidence already indicated that the election had been stolen in exchange for the promise that saloons would be left to operate relatively unmolested by the police, and of that there was plenty of evidence.

Despite the city ordinance prohibiting saloons within five-hundred feet of any church or school, parson Thomas Uzzell of the People's Tabernacle complained that his church was surrounded by a dozen saloons, whose patrons endangered his life many times. Yet, the parson added, the police were "Never around when trouble comes" although "they are always about when I give an oyster supper."[3]

---

[1] *RMN* 03/20/1890, p. 2.
[2] *RMN* 03/20/1890, p. 2.
[3] Noel, *City*, p. 97.

On election day, members of the gambling fraternity as well as tramps in Jeff's precinct had been sent to the Tivoli Club, the Silver Club, Bascomb's cigar store, and the Jockey Club. There they received a slip of paper containing the name of a registered voter. They would then go to the polling place where that name was listed and vote using the name on the slip of paper. It was found that over eight hundred fraudulent votes had been cast in this way.[1] The practice was noticed due to the back and forth travel of these voters. They were asked to vote just once, but some overzealous rogues repeated the process three and four times. These voters were known as *repeaters*.[2] Mike Maher, one of those so named, admitted in court that he alone had voted nearly one hundred times.[3]

Other voting precincts accused of allowing the same practice were controlled by Ed Chase and the Blonger brothers, Lou and Sam[4] of the Elite Saloon on Stout Street between Sixteenth and Seventeenth streets, and the Tourist Club.[5] None of these men was subpoenaed to testify.

Louis H. Blonger, born 1849, was a quick thinker and a fast-talker who got things done. In the Civil War, he joined the Union Army at age fifteen as a fifer. In the 1870s he went west with his older brother Sam. Sometimes with his brother, sometimes not, he became a supplier of drink, gambling, and entertainment in the boomtowns of Utah, Nevada, New Mexico, and Colorado. Legal power obtained through the backdoors of city halls enabled the Blongers to have competitors escorted out of town. Ed Burns, later member of the Soap Gang, was one to have this experience.[6] In the 1880s Lou Blonger gambled and hobnobbed with such Western legends as the Earps, Doc Holliday, Bat Masterson, Frank Thurmond, and Lottie Deno.

Samuel H. Blonger, born in 1839, was the tallest Blonger at 6-foot-3. He went west by wagon train in 1858 and hauled freight over the Sierra Nevadas. He is said to have scouted and fought Indians alongside Buffalo Bill Cody. Visiting home after the Civil War, he returned to the West with younger brother Lou. They teamed in dozens of towns, including Virginia City, Tuscarora, Salt Lake City, and Albuquerque. As a lawman in Colorado, he lost an eye in a gunfight; for the rest of his life he wore blue-tinted glasses. He followed the boom to Leadville in the late 1870s, lost a race to succeed Horace A. W. Tabor as mayor in 1879, and then went south with Lou to serve as city marshal of New Albuquerque. In the late 1880s he settled in Denver but continued to run mines at Cripple Creek until late in life. A prominent gambler and racing aficionado, he was probably an expert swindler as well.[7]

While serving as a deputy marshal in Albuquerque under his brother Sam, Lou helped prevent Wyatt Earp and Doc Holliday from being extradited to Arizona on

---

[1] *RMN* 04/06/1890.

[2] *RMN* 11/23/1891.

[3] *RMN* 03/31/1890.

[4] *RMN* 03/20/1890, p. 2. Samuel H. Blonger, b. 03/15/1839, d. 02/15/1914; Louis C. Blonger, b. 05/13/1849, d. 04/20/1924.

[5] *RMN* 05/08/1890, p. 7.

[6] *Albuquerque Morning Journal* 02/16/1882.

[7] Lou Blonger information: Blonger bros.com.

murder charges.[1] He settled in Denver in 1880 and ran saloons and policy shops on Larimer Street and later on Stout Street. Along with Sam, over the years, he owned valuable mining claims. Taking over from Jeff in 1896, until 1924, the Blongers made a career of influencing elections and political appointments and of running a protection racket that shielded Denver con men from prosecution. Convicted in 1923 of conspiracy to commit fraud, five months later, Lou died in prison.[2] Descendants of the Blonger brothers report that their relatives headed up gangs off and on during the mid 1880s but that during this time they were also often on the move.[3] In 1892 they operated a saloon and gaming hall at 1741 Larimer, referred to in the *News* as "Lou's Place." On April 7, 1892, their house was shut down because a "systematic bunco game was being carried on at this joint, and that the unwary were being roped in by the wholesale."[4] In October 1892 the Blongers, according to the *News*, operated a crooked faro game on Larimer in partnership with Jeff. The article also states that the gaming license was not paid to city hall but to Ed Chase and that no swindling house could operate in Denver without paying Chase a percentage of the profits.[5] Not known is if Jeff was in "partnership" with the Blongers or if he had to pay Chase to operate.

The *News* got behind the effort to oust Mayor Londoner, and though on April 5, 1889, the election was ruled invalid,[6] it would take two years and the Supreme court to force Londoner from office. Jeff no doubt worked on future elections with much improved methods of stuffing ballot boxes. In Jeff's scrapbook is a business card for the Matthews' Automatic Ballot Box Company in Denver. It advertised "Absolute Protection for the Purity and Secrecy of the Ballot Box."[7] A properly gaffed "honest" voting machine was probably among these improved methods.

The *News* also wanted the police chief's job vacated.

> John J. Farley is not expected to last much longer as chief due to his dealings with mayor Londoner and how he was involved with the vote scam, harboring gamblers and confidence men, and thieves, allowing houses of ill repute to run in respected residence portions of the city, failed to enforce the Sunday closing of saloons, let certain gambling houses run all night, refused to interfere with a water Co. laying pipes without permits.[8]

It must have been a great disappointment to the *News* when Farley was unanimously re-elected by the three commissioners of the fire and police board a year later.[9]

The *News* led a renewed reform movement to eradicate gamblers, thieves, and confidence men from the city, but it was business as usual for Jeff. Except for the inconvenience of attending court proceedings, the voting fraud trials produced no

---

[1] Blonger Bros.com.

[2] Van Cise, p. 347. Blonger Bros.com presents transcripts of obituaries, among them *RMN* 04/21/1924.

[3] Johnson, Craig, and Scott. 2005 communications with these descendants of the Blonger brothers, author's col.

[4] *RMN* 04/07/1892, p. 5.

[5] *RMN* 10/11/1892, p. 3.

[6] *RMN* 04/06/1890, p. 1.

[7] Business Card fr the Matthews' Automatic Ballot Box Company. Item 38, author's col.

[8] *RMN* 04/23/1890.

[9] *RMN* 05/08/1891.

convictions and did Jeff no lasting damage. This was also the case during the previous reform movement, mild inconvenience, and the many swindles of the Soap Gang continued. A little over a month after the trials, however, Jeff was exposed for a swindle gone sour in one of his establishments on Wazee and Sixteenth streets. The *Denver Republican* printed the victim's description of what took place.

I was coming up the street, said the Swede, when a stranger came up to me and said, "Hello there, partner; where are you from?"

I told him I had just arrived from Oakland, California, and was on my way to Kansas City. He said his name was Johnson and that he was also going to Kansas City. He proposed going to an office and getting scalper's tickets. I told him I had a ticket. He insisted on my going with him and I did so. Johnson said that he had just come in from Missouri and was going to start a restaurant in Denver. [W]e went to a place on Sixteenth street and there, the other man, Smith was met!

Anderson described how the friendly men fleeced him. Smith "gave a talk" on the value of metal" and offered for sale a silver bar. Anderson resisted "and hung back, fearing" robbery in some other way. He refused all other fortune-making offers, so "watches were shown in a case and tickets corresponding to them produced.

Johnson persuaded Anderson to draw a ticket and also reached for one himself. The former got card number 11 and Anderson a blank. Neither ticket was entitled to a timepiece. The tickets were again mixed and shuffled and the bait was sugared. Smith took from his pocket a roll of bills and apparently placed $250 and a watch as one tempting offer, saying that number 11 would rake the deck.[1]

The *Denver Republican* continued the account, but the *News* also covered the story from the point where Jeff stripped the money from Anderson's hand. Chief Farley's name was placed in the forefront in order to goad him into action.

FARLEY'S BAD BREAK.
He Says He Will Protect All Honest Men.

As soon as the rumor spread that "Soapy" Smith had snatched the money from Anderson, a NEWS reporter began a thorough investigation of the charge. ... The rottenness of the system is becoming more and more notorious.

In the confusion after the money was snatched, Jeff talked Anderson into signing a receipt for $150 but returned only $50. Jeff offered $20 more, then $30—refused. Anderson wanted his $100. By this time policeman Henry Minart had arrived, summoned by Bascomb, and when Anderson explained, Minart said "he would 'square the deal,'" but Jeff wanted Anderson taken to jail. Minart left with Anderson, and told Anderson "that he better skip town, and pointed him" toward the depot.

The Swede ... ran athwart Officer Ramsey. He thought that this officer should also know the condition of affairs and unburdened himself in a brief

---

[1] *Denver Republican* 05/03/1890. *rake the deck*: i.e., clear all from the deck, as of a ship. Rake everything in (no authority).

story of the transaction. Ramsey is a conscientious and efficient officer, and he recognized immediately that Anderson had been the victim of some put-up job. Accordingly he asked the poor fellow to go to headquarters and report the occurrence. Here the Swede was instructed to swear out a warrant for "Soapy," and the matter was then and there turned over to the sheriff, while Anderson was detained to act as witness. ...

A NEWS reporter interviewed Smith last night on the deal. He said:

"I will honestly give the facts in the case. This man Anderson came into my place. I do not presume to run a better shop than dozens of others around me. But I want a fair show, and ask that THE NEWS treat me squarely. Well, as I stated, this fellow came in and he became interested in the lottery racket, and he dropped his wad of $150. When he saw that he had lost he squealed and I compromised by returning him his money. He felt satisfied at this and gave me a receipt for that amount. After he left the place he must have gone directly to officer Minart, for he shortly afterward returned, accompanied by the policeman. Officer Minart asked him would he arrest me, and the fellow replied in the negative. But the policeman had not the authority to do so, as he did not witness the transaction and was not in possession of a warrant. The Swede then left the office and I presume he was steered up against Ramsay. The latter came off his beat and jumped upon me like a highway robber, arresting me without a warrant. I was locked up for four hours before the warrant was served, and then I had a hearing before Justice Morris and was bound over in $500. Attorney Pence [Lafayette] acted as my lawyer."

"Did you whack up[1] with Minart in this deal?"

"No, sir; most assuredly no. I don't know him more than any other officer on the force. The fact of my arrest and the charge of suspicion against me would lead me to believe that the police have a malice against me. Other places are permitted to run, and there are none of them any better than mine. I only ask a fair show and don't presume on working the baby act.[2] There are lots of suckers worked everyday and but little attention is paid to the matter. If Anderson lost $70 he did so after he left my place." ...

Chief Farley was asked had he heard anything regarding the squaring of the deal. He replied in the negative, but said that he would begin a vigorous investigation into the charge this morning.

"You can say," he concluded, "that we are determined to suppress bunco men, no matter who it strikes."[3]

The following day, May 4, 1890, The *NEWS* reported that Chief Farley had agreed to declare war on the thieves who were currently infesting the city. His first act

---

[1] *whack up*: A sharing out of stolen goods or illicitly obtained money, 1887. (Partridge, *Underworld*)

[2] *working the baby act*: "plead the Baby Act. To excuse oneself as too inexperienced." (Partridge, *Slang*) "Baby" B2 Special Combinations: "plead the baby act, to enter a plea that one is not legally responsible by reason of youth or inexperience." (*OED*)

[3] *RMN* 05/03/1890.

was to fire Officer Minart for his connection with the Soap Gang.[1] He then placed four policemen, officers Barr, Ramsey, Alexander, and Sullivan, on patrol of the area around Larimer between Sixteenth and Seventeenth streets. However, the chief also ordered that no one could be arrested without the officer explicitly stating the crime for which the person was charged. Arrests on "Suspicion" or for "safe keeping" were banned as a direct result of Jeff's apparently illegitimate arrest. The *NEWS* continued its report on policemen who befriended the Gang.

> Day after day detectives and policemen have been seen drinking and carousing with these fellows, and a gentleman who is in a position to know informed a NEWS reporter that he knew of a few of the officers who now sport $250 diamonds as a result of a little dicker with the gang. This he vouches for by referring to the record of the office and incidentally asking the reporter to notice the diamonds on the individual fences.[2]

In response to such embarrassment came city hall efforts to reform the police, but Jeff continued to operate pretty much as usual. With the policeman on the beat to detectives and captains as well as city hall officials themselves, Jeff practiced his congenial and persuasive ways. Since youth, he had built on a natural ability for leading all sorts of people where he want them to go, and he had not lost his touch. Diamonds suggest the rest. Jeff must have been thought to compensate handsomely, notwithstanding that his diamond supplier probably was Fatty Gray. Attractive bribes and graft that could be counted on as sources of regular income were hard to stop, perhaps impossible.

In the Anderson case, however, Jeff and a person identified as "Johnson" were bound over to district court on a charge of grand larceny, found guilty, and fined $300 each.[3] For some, apparently, this kind of "press" made Jeff a prize catch. Three weeks later, an ambitious young man tried to arrest Jeff. The *News* gave this account:

> James Dennis ... is a young man who aspires to the rank of detective on the city force. For the past few weeks he has loitered around the gambling houses and auction dives on Seventeenth St., and has been making frantic efforts to capture some noted thief, which would bring his name prominently before the public. Nothing has crowned his keen watch, and he appeared goaded on to desperation yesterday when he tackled Jeff Smith, or "Soapy" as the latter is called. Dennis had heard, he claimed, that Smith made some insulting remarks, but as he did not know "Soapy" he had a warrant sworn out for the arrest of John Doe. Going along Seventeenth St. yesterday, Dennis perceived Smith standing near the corner of Wazee, and going up to him he said: "I arrest you. I am an officer and have a warrant for you." "Well, come inside," replied Smith, "I can get bonds here." When the men went inside Smith asked Dennis to show his warrant, but the latter had none, and then

---

[1] Officer Minart was acquitted of all charges on 05/09/1890. (*RMN* 05/10/1890)

[2] *RMN* 05/04/1890. *diamonds on the individual fences*: diamonds worn by those having received this stolen property. *Fence*: purchaser or receiver of stolen property, 1698-1900, common world wide. (Partridge, *Underworld*)

[3] *RMN* 05/10/1890.

Smith requested his authority for making the arrest. Dennis could not display any, and presently the liveliest time ever seen on Seventeenth St. was enacted. Smith walked into the bogus detective, gave him the soundest laying out he had ever enjoyed, and then officer H. C. Smith came along and placed Dennis in custody on a charge of disorderly conduct and impersonating an officer.[1]

The notoriety that comes from "press" also caused Jeff to be accused of crimes he could not have committed. Report of one of these was published in May 1890.

Getting After Soapy.

Some person called at police headquarters yesterday to complain that he had been done up by a bunco man on the Twenty-third street viaduct and that he had lost $10. He gave a description of the thief who worked the old knife game and the police surmised that it must have been "Soapy" Smith. Smith had several witnesses to prove that he was not above Seventeenth street yesterday, but went to the police station and gave himself up when he heard that they were desirous of locating him. It appears now that any game turned in any part of the city is attributed to "Soapy." The manner in which the fellow is followed by the authorities does not reflect credit upon them. He admits that he is no angel, but the actual criminals who are now working the city should be attended to.[2]

Jeff's political career remained rather rough and flagrant. In the Democratic primaries of September 20, 1890, every ward, except the Ninth at Seventeenth and Wazee streets, was run without incident. The *News* reported the trouble there.

One of the exceptions mentioned was a high handed outrage perpetrated upon the judges of the primaries of the Ninth ward. At 7 o'clock, as the polls were closed, a crowd of toughs and bullies, with Soapy Smith in the lead, burst into the room where the election had been in progress, knocked down the judges and carried off the ballot box.[3] To heap insult upon injury two of the unoffending judges, who scarcely raised their hands to resist the invasion, were arrested and locked up at the city prison upon the charge of creating a disturbance. The third judge escaped a similar fate by running away.

The following is a plain statement of the case as presented by J. F. Healey, one of the judges of election:

" ... We opened the polls at 4 o'clock in the presence of a large crowd of 'Soapy' Smith's gang, in which were a number of the toughest characters of the city. Two tickets were voted upon—a fence and an unpledged ticket.[4] All passed off quietly until about fifteen minutes before 5 o'clock. From that time we had trouble. A man claiming to live at Thirty-eighth and Blake wanted to

---

[1] *RMN* 05/17/1890.

[2] *RMN* 05/08/1890, p. 7.

[3] *the judges*: city-appointed citizens to oversee polling site election procedures.

[4] *a fence and an unpledged ticket*: a known receiver of stolen goods and an independent candidate. The election judge seems to be saying that one of the candidates was a known criminal.

vote. I knew there was no house at that point and I refused to receive his ballot. I asked him who gave him the number. He said it was given by Andy Kelly. Somebody cried: "Get an ax and bust the door." Another shouted: "Wait till the polls close and we will smash the door and the heads of the judges too!"

"By this time a large crowd had assembled in front of the polling place and probably 200 votes had been cast. Somebody put a light on the outside of the window. I placed two candles in front of the ballot box one on each side, in order to show that we were doing the square thing. About a quarter of an hour before the polls closed a candidate for state honors visited the spot and insisted that we should allow a gang of toughs to enter the room previous to the time of commencing the count. He wanted the gang put inside as 'watchers.' I told him that it would first be necessary to get an order from Chairman Arbuckle of the county committee[;] then some responsible man would be admitted.

"At 7 o'clock we closed the polls and moved the table back in order to make room for the work. Just then the crowd cried 'they are going to stuff the ballot box,' and the next instant a rush was made, the door burst in and the crowd came at us. We fled for our lives, passing out at the back door with a great pack of human wolves in pursuit. Mr. Cain, who carried the ballot box, was knocked down and kicked in the head and face. The box was carried off by the crowd. Mallen escaped by swift running, but Cain and I were seized and taken to the city jail, where we were locked up for two hours before we were released through the efforts of C. P. Hoyt."

It was feared that the ballot box was finally placed in charge of Deputy Sheriff Stockton, who claimed the right to act as its protector. The prisoners were placed under bond of $400 each, to appear at 9 o'clock to-morrow morning. It is the opinion of Mr. Healy that the majority of the votes cast were in favor of the unpledged ticket. The Ninth ward will be contested.[1]

No record is known of legal action against Jeff or any other parties in the voting location attack that evening.

The last appearance of the Tivoli Club for 1890 concerns a shooting said to have occurred in October. On November 9, 1890 the *News* published a correction that "Gambler Joe" Simmons, the reported proprietor of the Tivoli, had wounded W. M. Shuck of Lyons, Colorado, with a glancing shot from his .45 Colt, and not Dick Hawkins as first reported (in October?). No other details were given.[2]

January 1891 foreshadowed rough times ahead for the Smith brothers. On January 15 Bascomb was fined $5 for being intoxicated, $5 for disturbing the peace, and $100 for carrying concealed weapons. Circumstances were not divulged, but it was reported that Judge Barnes gave Bascomb 24 hours to leave town for 6 months, or the fines would be implemented. Bascomb either kept a very low profile or took a

---

[1] *RMN* 09/21/1890, p. 2.

[2] *RMN* 11/09/1890, p. 7.

vacation from the main part of the city. His name is absent from the record until 1892 when he settled in Creede.

Sometime before January 23, 1891, a dealer named Smith (no relation) who worked one of Jeff's Tivoli Club gambling tables was fired. The reason is unknown, but Jeff later told a *News* reporter that "the man was such an unprincipled scoundrel that he was discharged."[1] This man Smith, "a medium-sized, rather good-looking, smooth face, with the exception of a mustache, black stiff hat and light over coat," strolled into the Arcade club rooms at about 8:30 p.m. on January 22, 1891, and placed a $100 wager at a faro table. The bet was a losing one, and the *News* covered what happened as the dealer collected the bet. Smith then drew his

> 45-calibre Colt's gun, cocked it and requested the dealer pass the money back. The bank dealer was not slow in complying with the request.
>
> The bravo[2] held the pistol in his hand, backed out of the room and walked leisurely down stairs and disappeared, although a crowd of about 150 men were in the room..., yet not a move was made to intercept the "tin horn."

Next Smith went into the Nickel Plate Club on Lawrence Street, arriving about 10:30. He went to a faro table, bet "$50 on the king and said: 'This all goes, see!'" The dealer said "All right," the $50 was lost, and the dealer said,

> "Well, you have lost your 'dough'....
>
> "The h___ I have! Give me that bet, and quick too," at the same time drawing the same big pistol as he displayed at the Arcade club rooms.
>
> The desperado backed out unmolested, in the same manner as he did making his other successful play. ... Detectives are looking for the would-be Jesse James, and it is quite possible that the "bad man from Market street" will languish in the city jail before morning.[3]

The robber made good his escape from the city. One year later, on March 8, 1892, the *News* reported that the robber was not named Smith but Dick Hawkins. On March 7, 1892, he executed the same scenario in Creede, and the *News* covered it.

BEATING THE WHEEL.

> Dick Hawkins and Two Pals Rob a Roulette Wheel in Creede. With Drawn Revolvers They Lay Claim to Twelve Hundred Dollars And Decamp. Now the Crowd Is Looking for the Bold Trio With Tight Neck Tie Ready.
>
> Special to The News. CREEDE, Colo., March 7.—The most sensational affair that has been witnessed at Creede occurred this afternoon at 3 o'clock. Dick Hawkins, a well-known Denver sport, and two "pals," robbed the Mint Exchange of $1,280. Dick Hawkins is the same individual who held up one of the faro banks for $200, the Arcade, in Denver, a year ago, and made good his escape. Hawkins began to deal faro this morning for Charlie [M.] Lorje [or Lorge], or "Sheney [sic] Charley," as he is called in Denver at the Arcade, where he has been running the principal roulette wheel.... ...

---

[1] *RMN* 01/23/1891.

[2] *bravo*: a daring villain, a reckless desperado. c. 1597-1876. (*OED*)

[3] *RMN* 01/23/1891.

Hawkins dealt all day and at the closest estimate the bank won nearly $1,000. At 3 o'clock Harry Smith and Jerry O'Brien, his two pals, came in and began playing. Instantly the trio drew their revolvers, took all the money and backed out the door. Captain Light, Captain [Jack] Kirwin[1] and Deputy [Mike] Delaney and a posse of men are in search of the robbers, and if found, quick retribution will be meted out to them.[2]

Two days later on March 10, 1892, *The Creede Candle* published more information on the robbery.

Dick Hawkins, one of the faro dealers at the Mint, ... on Monday night, with the aid of Harry Smith and Jerry O'Brien, covered the crowd with their guns, collared the bank roll of about $1,300 right out from the jaws of the tiger and made good their escape with the boodle. A posse was at once organized and many innocent young men who were supposed to resemble the absconding Dick because of a common lack of whiskers were held up and examined, but the looters were away, and the green on which they sported now knows them no more.[3]

If that were not enough bad luck for Lorje, the following day the train on which he was a passenger derailed, breaking his wrist and badly bruising his body.[4] It is not known whether Dick Hawkins and his confederates were ever apprehended.

In 1891, with saloon proprietors largely ignoring the Sunday closure law, those wanting it observed grew stronger. Not having faith that the present administration would enforce the law, reformers created the Law and Order League. Its goal was not only to close the saloons but also, eventually, to close every gambling house in the city. The News quoted them as saying about every gambling table in the city, "They are to be swept away into fathomless oblivion."[5]

The League was formed by some of Denver's best-known men of God and their flocks, including Reverends H. H. Beech, J. D. Rankin, E. A. Paddock of West Denver Congregational Church, A. A. Cameron of Calvary Baptist Church, A. S. Phelps of Immanuel Baptist Church, E. P. Thomas of Westminster Presbyterian Church, and Dr. Barns of Christ M. E. Church. The League demanded the state law against gambling be obeyed. Rev. Rankin reminded the city of the law's penalties and punishments, including penalties for property owners who knowingly rent space for the purpose of gambling and punishment of people who visit such establishments to gamble.

For keeping or renting a building for gambling purposes, or knowing that your property is so used, or that gambling instruments are kept there, and not cause complaint to be made, a penalty is attached of not less than $30 or more than $500, or imprisonment in the county jail of not less than ten or more than thirty days. And every day on which such places are kept open

---

[1] "Jack Kirwin was a tough deputy who infested South Denver during his halcyon days." (*RMN* 10/05/1892, p. 3)

[2] *RMN* 03/08/1892, p. 2.

[3] *Creede Candle* 03/10/1892.

[4] *RMN* 03/09/1892, p. 1.

[5] *RMN* 06/02/1891.

shall constitute a separate offense. For keeping a gambling resort or practicing gambling for a livelihood, the penalty is imprisonment for not less than three months, nor more than one year, and a fine of not less than $200, nor more than $500. For betting upon anything or playing any game for money, the fine is not less than $50 nor more than $150.

In spite of this, gambling is carried on openly in our city. There are twenty-five well-known gambling houses, employing 175 dealers and other helpers. It is carried on in many cigar stores and barber shops, and in almost every saloon in the city. There are also five grand lotteries with agents in all parts of the city.[1]

On February 22, 1891, the League went to District Attorney Stevens with a list of sixty-four saloons serving alcohol on Sundays, along with many of the gamblers' names who frequent these establishments. Among those listed were manager Henry Deutch of the Tivoli Club.[2] The organization with the assistance of the *News* continued to publish the offenders' names from latter February through mid April 1891.[3] The Tivoli Club is mentioned only once in the listings. The League demanded that the city enforce Chapter 25, Sections 153-160 of the general statutes of the state of Colorado for 1883. Section 156 of this chapter provides that

No person shall keep any description of building, or rent, or knowingly permit the same to be rented for the purpose of gambling upon the penalty of being fined not less than $80 or imprisonment for not less than ten days, or both. Any person who keeps a gambling device of any nature or is in the habit of gambling renders himself liable to imprisonment for not less than three months and a fine of not less than $200....[4]

Unknown is why the League did not also mention city ordinance Number 99, sections 6-8, enacted, October 1, 1884. Under certain conditions, these gave authority directly to the police chief and his officers, without complaint being filed or warrant, to seize any gambling equipment coming to their attention ("such as cards, tables checks [chips], balls, wheels") and deliver these to the "police court of the city of Denver, who shall order the same destroyed.[5]

District Attorney E. N. Stevens clearly stalled in trying to enforce this particular chapter. The city fathers knew they would lose out on great amounts of revenue by enforcing the ordinance. Even the *News*, a great supporter of reforms, nevertheless predicted that enforcement would only lead to more problems:

WILL RAISE CAIN

The large gambling fraternity in this city will be somewhat concerned as to the action of the league. In every Western town and city, gambling is rife, and the names of its devotees legion. ... Many cities in the West have made similar attempts, but it has always been found to be an impracticable test. In

---

[1] *RMN* 07/13/1891, p. 8.

[2] *RMN* 02/23/1891.

[3] *RMN* 02/23/1891, 03/09/1891, 03/12/1891, 04/11/1891, 04/14/1891.

[4] *RMN* 06/02/1891.

[5] *RMN* 10/17/1884, p. 7.

the mining towns it is an old maxim that the more numerous are the faro and poker tables the more prosperous is the town.

Should the league carry its point, there will be a mammoth exodus from the city and the hundreds of men who rely upon the green baize for a living, either as players or as table runners, will scatter among other cities where the merry clink of the glasses can be heard on the seventh day, and where the raking in and measuring out of the chips goes on unmolested. The first few raids ... would call for scenes of wild excitement, and add many a column to the never ending fight between those who view life and morals from different points. It would be no picnic for the league, but neither would it be altogether a Fourth of July celebration of hilarity for the knights of fortune.[1]

The Law and Order League hired ex-Deputy Sheriff William A. Glasson to seek evidence of saloon and gambling ordinance violations and report them to the District Attorney. Glasson and his agents found that although the campaign had previously some effect on saloon operations on Sundays, the saloon proprietors now began to defy the law openly. The *News* for February 23, 1891, quoted the report as saying that

everywhere the agents gained admittance they found the saloon doing a big business.... The saloon men, the agents claim, are becoming more brazen in their violation of the law. Side and back doors, which were formerly used to admit the thirsty, are now closed and the front doors swung wide open, when one desires to enter.[2]

Shortly after hiring Glasson, the League began to suspect Glasson's intentions and methods. After only a few months, the League dropped him from their payroll. Glasson claimed the League owed him over $1000, which the League adamantly denied. The "crusade against the gamblers," Glasson told the *News*,

was nothing more than a scheme to put money into the hands of the members [of the League], as they expected to get half the money from the fines, which they calculated would amount to $50,000. District Attorney Stevens took the proper course in refusing to put the county at an expense of $65,000 by prosecuting them [gamblers and others].[3]

Was Glasson paid by Jeff Smith, Ed Chase, and many others to make this statement to the *News*? It was a play out of the confidence man's handbook: *accuse the accuser*.

The District Attorney did refuse to prosecute gambling ordinance violations as doing so would surely deplete the city's treasury and destroy the city's economy, but the *News* and the League continued to publish the names of offenders.[4] Moreover, In June 1891, the News quoted this hard-hitting statement from Reverend Dr. Barns:

There are twenty-five well known gambling hells [sic] distinguished as "public." They are run by forty proprietors, and employ 175 dealers and helpers. The buildings in which the halls are located are owned by thirty

---

[1] *RMN* 06/02/1891.

[2] *RMN* 02/23/1891.

[3] *RMN* 06/26/1891.

[4] *RMN* 02/23/1891, 03/09/1891, 03/12/1891, 03/11/1891, 03/14/1891.

persons. Of these several are women, one a member of the last grand jury and one a member of the city council. Nearly every saloon in the city is a gambling house. Gambling is also carried on in many barber shops and cigar stores in different parts of the city. There are five grand lotteries in Denver, viz.: "Grand Mutual Contribution," "Colorado Policy Association," "Colorado State Lottery," "Denver Distribution Company," and "Denver City Gift Enterprise." They are owned and conducted by thirteen men. They employ writers in various parts of the city. In addition to these there is pool selling on the races, ball games and many other things. And all these are running in open violation of the most stringent laws.[1]

Saloons remained open but nervously on guard. They locked front doors and directed customers to rear and side doors. Saloons bold enough to have their front doors open had coverings over the bar and served drinks in other rooms.

The reform campaign made allies of the newly appointed fire and police board of three, who were eager to do their job. Saloon proprietors formed their own alliance, The Liquor Dealers' Association, and named Mart H. Watrous, proprietor of Murphy's Exchange, as president. With brewer Adolph Zang[2] and others at his side, Watrous met for several hours with Parson Uzzell and Judge M. A. Rogers in a vain attempt to offer amendments to a strict new ordinance, including one that would exempt from closure reputable establishments that catered to businessmen. The League could not be persuaded to compromise, and the proposed amendments were rejected.[3]

The Law and Order League gained permission to examine city licensing records and discovered that nearly three hundred saloons were operating without a license while others had paid their licenses only partially. Chief Farley was ordered to visit every city saloon and shut down all that had not paid in full. Some proprietors produced a "paid in full" receipt, yet their names did not appear on the city treasurer's record. So where was the money? The previous year, 1890, saw just under $50,000 in saloon license revenue, but for 1891, the books showed only $3,800.[4] This revelation, published in the *News*, along with saloon closures all over the city created a sensation. Upon reading the article, several hundred men gathered at city hall to ask what was going on. City Treasurer A. B. Place tried to explain the ninety percent decrease in revenue. He said it was "true that many saloon keepers" were

> operating without a license. The times ... have been hard on all classes of business, and in order not to shut off the revenues from ... saloons by closing them up I carried them along on part payment. This may not be exactly legal, but it is what I did, and I expected that as times improved the saloon men

---

[1] *RMN* 06/29/1891.
[2] *Adolph Zang* (1856-1916): son of Philip Zang, founder of oldest brewery in Colorado. In 1889 Zang Sr. sold the family breweries to a syndicate for $2.5 million but remained as figure head. Adolph Zang managed the breweries (*Portrait*) and had interests in banking and hotels. (Noel, *City*, p. 80)
[3] *RMN* 02/24/1891.
[4] *RMN* 04/14/1891.

would be able to pay up entirely. There is hardly a city in the country where the same practice does not prevail."[1]

The reformers celebrated when they were finally able to oust Mayor Londoner from office. He was given a bill for $1,592.10 to cover part of the cost of the 1889 election fraud investigation. Attorney Lafayette Pence for the City of Denver instructed deputies to take possession of Londoner's grocery store and placed a levy on its goods until a check for the amount named in the bill was produced.[2] More was to come. The Voorhees' bill, named for its creator, Colorado Senator Ralph Voorhees, called for the closing of all wine rooms where women were known to frequent.[3] The bill also called for all saloons to shut down business at midnight.[4] Two swindles involving "auction shops" were exposed in the *News* on the same day, indicating that although Jeff's Tivoli Club trade was affected by the reforms, he was still largely in business.

In mid March with only two swindles to report, the *News* observed that "Cases of bunco games have been rather scarce as of late." The first case involved a German tourist who had lost $165 in a watch-buying scam at McHenry & Charles M. Graff's on Seventeenth and Market streets. Chief Farley brought the victim into a meeting with Graff, who was induced to return the swindled funds. No charges were filed. It is known that the auction house of McHenry & Graff had been open since at least July 1890 and that John Bowers often worked as the auctioneer.[5]

A second headline read, "Seventeenth Street Sharks." William Oliver lost $42 "through the ... time-honored brace game."[6] Con man John Hayes was caught and arrested by Detective Holland. The victim was also detained as a witness.[7] Holding a victim until the hearing had become not uncommon as witnesses often disappeared.

The following day, Saturday, March 14, the *News* published an article asking the city fathers to "enforce the orders." It referred to city code section 161, which stated, that whenever officers know that "any person has ... any cards or other gambling devices," these persons be seized and taken "before some judge or justice of the peace," and that in enforcement of the law officers are even "directed to break open doors" to take possession of gambling devices and are "to convey all persons having possession of such ... before some judge or justice of the peace to be held or committed to answer any indictment which may be found against them"[8] With this kind of public demand for rule of law by force of wrecking-ball, added to the efforts of crusading leagues and newspapers and criminal investigations, matters were tense. And for some, the atmosphere provoked explosions.

---

[1] *RMN* 04/14/1891.

[2] *RMN* 03/14/1891.

[3] *RMN* 02/24/1891.

[4] *RMN* 03/06/1891.

[5] *RMN* 07/25/1890, p. 3.

[6] *brace game*: a game in which there is concerted cheating; brace box, in faro, a dealing box designed to facilitate cheating. U.S. slang c. 1875. (*OED*) Also generally, "A card game in which at least one player is cheated," like "Big Hand. (Partridge, *Underworld*)

[7] *RMN* 03/13/1891.

[8] *RMN* 03/14/1891.

At about 5:00 pm on Wednesday, April 8, 1891, Jeff was at the Turf Exchange saloon at 1728 Larimer Street. Standing at the bar, he, Jack Devine, Matt Keele, and Jack Flood were engaged in talk of the recent election for city aldermen. In the *News* the previous day, attorney Lafayette Pence had exposed more vote purchases by Republicans in the Seventh ward where hundreds of votes had been cast illegally.[1] Jeff was a member of the Seventh ward, and he supported Republican candidate John Begley for alderman and not Jack Devine's boss, John J. Noonan. Devine accused Jeff of working against Noonan, causing his defeat, and punctuated the remark by striking Jeff such a blow to the neck that it knocked him to the floor.

Devine was about to follow up when Jeff drew his revolver and began shooting. The first shot missed Devine, but the second struck his right shoulder as he fled out the door and down Larimer Street. Bystanders said another shot was fired at the fleeing man. Friends of Devine helped him to medical attention from two doctors who later stated his wound was not life threatening. The friends then hid Devine from Jeff as well as police seeking to arrest him. Back in the saloon Jeff surrendered to Officer Linton and went with him before Judge Ilangs, who set bail at $5,000. Word of Jeff's quick and accurate shooting made the Aspen papers[2] and the front page in Leadville.[3]

Jeff told a *News* reporter that the shooting was entirely in self-defense. Perhaps that was rightly so as Devine had a record of outbursts. At the time, he was free on bail for the murder of a drunken man at John Noonan's Ruby saloon, where Devine worked as a bartender. He struck and killed the man with a beer keg mallet to the head but later said the weapon was an iron-headed lemon-squeezer.[4] No record of charges against Jeff in the shooting were found. It is believed the cases against Devine and Jeff were intentionally shuffled around the courts until forgotten as both men were needed by corrupt politicians. In Devine's case it was only after the *News* had continued to urge an investigation of the case and the tenure of two Republican District Attorneys that tardy steps were taken.[5]

Nine days later, on April 9, 1891, the *News* reported that Judge Simmonds had fined Jeff $10 for assaulting a John W. Chambers.[6] No other details were published.

Jeff's shooting spree was not over. About three weeks later, in early May 1891, Jeff took pot shots at a man named Flynn who demanded his money back after trying to buck a "sure-thing" game.[7] No details or charges against Jeff were found. Given Jeff's past successes at finding his target, probably the aim was *not* to hit the man but urge him on his way. Still, this next use of force adds to an emerging pattern of violence. Jeff did not limit his violent attacks to victims and rivals but extended them to police officers as well. Mentioned only in passing within the pages of the *Denver*

---

[1] *RMN* 04/07/1891.

[2] *Aspen Times* 04/11/1891.

[3] *Leadville Daily & Evening Chronicle* 04/09/1891, p. 1

[4] *RMN* 04/09/1891, & 10/05/1892, p. 3.

[5] *RMN* 10/05/1892, p. 3.

[6] *RMN* 04/17/1891.

[7] Robertson & Harris, p. 92.

Evening Post Jeff had seriously stabbed officer Guyton for an unknown reason on an undisclosed date.[1]

On Monday July 13, 1891, William Oliver, who had been swindled back in March,[2] was apparently swindled again in a mock auction house. This time he got into a fist-fight with bunco man John Goodfellow. Both men were arrested for disturbing the peace.[3] The mock auction houses on Seventeenth Street had been relatively peaceful and out of the public eye for awhile, but the reform wave caught them up, too. This was not the only time a victim was enticed into Jeff's games a second time. In April 1893 a Rudolph Hann was led into the Tivoli Club and swindled of $130 in a rigged poker game. Hann went to the police and complained. With the aid of a policeman he was able to recover $35. Before night Hann was inveigled a second time into the club but supposedly escaped before losing any more money.[4] Here is evidence that Jeff's men were masters of human nature.

A businessmen's petition to ban the auction houses emerged, and when Fire and Police Board President Egbert Johnson was asked to sign, he promptly did so in large letters. He spoke to the *News* about a number of complaints that

> had been filed against the auction joints, but in no instance has the complainant been willing to prosecute a case before the police court. In the absence of formal prosecution the power of the police board[5] to revoke auction licenses is far from being satisfactory. The board is given authority to revoke auction licenses, but not until a complaint has been filed which is signed by ten reputable property owners residing in the same election precinct. The defendant must be given a hearing before the board, and if it is decided to revoke the license, the complaint shall be made before the city council. Should the council fail to set [a hearing] promptly the police board may settle the question at once by rescinding the license. Under this proceeding it would require about a month to close an auction room however discreditable it might be to the city.[6]

To counter the appearance of complacency, the fire and police board assigned several officers to some of the mock auction houses with orders to warn potential patrons that they were in danger of becoming victims of a bunco scam. The targets were the Seventeenth Street auction houses of Hooper, McHenry and Graff, and Smith and Palmer. Jeff Smith and Joe Palmer's house was in competition with the other two, but they worked with one another when it suited them. The *News* for July 26, 1891, describes how Jeff sealed Hooper's sale of a cheap John watch for $20.

---

[1] *Denver Evening Post* 01/11/1897, p. 6.

[2] *RMN* 03/13/1891, p. 5.

[3] *RMN* 07/14/1891, p. 3.

[4] *RMN* 04/04/1893.

[5] *police board*: In 1889 the State combined the Denver commissioners of fire, police, and excise into a board titled the Denver Fire and Police Board, the three members of which would be appointed by the Governor. This new board was in place but yet to become called by its official title. It will be in time.

[6] *RMN* 06/25/1891.

Yesterday a Bear Creek farmer was walking on Seventeenth street when his attention was attracted by the cries of an oily tongued salesman in Hooper's place. The man held a copper colored watch in his hand and exclaimed that he was about to give it away for $24. His distress at having the beautiful ornament thus torn from his possession was so graphically portrayed that the Bear Creek man was easily persuaded to invest $25 in the watch. He was made to believe that he would be given $5 for his bargain. No sooner had the money changed hands than somebody offered to give $60 for the watch, provided it was tested and found to be genuine gold. The stranger was hustled into "Soapy" Smith's establishment. "Soapy" was introduced as an expert jeweler. He looked at the watch, pronounced it gold and worth $60. Then he collected $4 for his "expert" testimony. As the dazed countryman wandered to the pavement he was taken in charge by a detective and conducted to police headquarters, where he made affidavit to the facts. The watch is in the possession of the police commissioners and entirely worthless. It is expected that the auction men will make a hard fight before the council but the police commissioners are determined that the full penalty of the law shall be meted out.[1]

Of the $25 the "countryman" paid for the watch, $5 was apparently returned as a sort of rebate. Of this amount, Jeff extracted $4 for his appraisal. The idea was that the man would then be on his way home with his $60 gold watch. Instead, however, he went to the police. The next day, Hooper went to police headquarters and refunded the farmer's $20. However, in two days' time the promise of shutting down the auction houses was forgotten. As the *News* reported on July 28, "Owing to the limited number of men on the police force, the commissioners decided not to place a patrolman regularly on duty in front of the auction joints to warn verdant strangers away."[2]

In July 1891 various proprietors of saloons and gaming halls met and formed an organization called the Liberal League. Its goal was to encourage a less stringent enforcement of laws against saloons and gambling. Although Jeff's name is not listed in the newspapers as being involved, he was most assuredly was. His good friend John Kinneavy was elected president and chaired its July 14, 1891, business meeting. Debated were details of a petition calling for an end to the Saturday midnight and Sunday closure law. The objective was to collect twenty thousand signatures for the petition from all the leading business firms of Denver as well as thousands of ordinary citizens.[3] Their argument was that all of Denver was suffering because of the loss of revenue generated by the mandatory closings. Saloon proprietors claimed great financial burden to themselves as well as the rest of the business community as scores of visitors and residents left the city on Saturday in order to be free to drink and gamble in outskirt resorts and towns on Saturday night and Sunday. A wholesale failure of saloons was threatened if the law remained in force.[4] By the end of July both

---

[1] *RMN* 07/26/1891, p. 7.
[2] *RMN* 07/28/1891, p. 8.
[3] *RMN* 07/15/1891, p. 3.
[4] *RMN* 07/14/1891.

factions, the Liberal League and the Law and Order League, had circulated petitions in favor of their causes. The Law and Order League claimed Sunday closings showed a drop in crime and a spike in economic prosperity whereas the Liberal League claimed the exact opposite. The Liberal League proposed to take legal action against Mayor Rogers, the fire and police board, and the chief of police for malfeasance. In a bold move they demanded that the city either remove the Sunday closing ordinance or proceed with enforcing the laws to the letter as fully defined by the state. This would mean the complete closure of all saloons and gambling houses, which would be immediately followed by a personal class action suit against the mayor, the police board, and the chief of police. No such lawsuit was filed throughout the 1890s.

Helping the right candidates to win in the coming November election was seen as the only hope for survival of the saloons and gambling houses within city limits. Although the 1891 Denver city elections included choices for judges to the supreme court, district court, and district attorney, the Liberal League focused on the race for Arapahoe County sheriff. The county courts favored the saloon proprietors and often reversed decisions against them, so every case involving the saloons was appealed to the county courts. With a sympathetic sheriff in office, the saloon proprietors and gambling houses had a chance of defying the fire and police board and the police court.[1] The Republican candidate for sheriff was William K. Burchinell, a Denver businessman whose sympathies were known to side with the saloon cause.

Burchinell was seasoned. A Civil War veteran and a Republican representative in the 1873-74 Pennsylvania legislature, he was appointed in 1874 by President Grant to head the US land office at Fairplay, Colorado. In 1878, President Hayes re-appointed him to the post, which was moved to Leadville. In 1883 he left that position, moved to Denver, and embarked on the mill business. He was elected Arapahoe County sheriff in 1892 and served until 1896.[2]

In October 1891, Denver Republican voter registration was plagued by accusations of fraud. Claimed was that at least two thousand illegally registered names had been placed on eligible voter lists.[3] It was reminiscent of the 1889 election fraud scandal. In the November 3, 1891 election, Denver Republican candidates captured every office they sought, including county sheriff, district court justices, and district attorney. Given this landslide, saloon proprietors at once began to defy police orders to close on the Sabbath. The *News* reported that on Sunday, November 22, 1891, over one hundred saloons and businesses were dispensing liquor to patrons. For the moment victory was in the hands of the saloons and gambling halls.

In September, ex-deputy sheriff William A. Glasson of the Law and Order League created a private investigative firm, the Glasson Detective Agency, and hired Joe Matthews to investigate an organization called the Trust and the man said to head it, "Big Ed" Chase. The Trust's single purpose was to protect and aid bunco men within the city.[4] Matthews kept after the bunco men under steady surveillance in an effort to

---

[1] *RMN* 08/26/1891, p. 3.

[2] *Burchinell:* Portrait.

[3] *RMN* 10/17/1891, p. 3.

[4] *RMN* 10/04/1891.

expose the Trust and its members, but he had no luck. Then in an egotistical move, he described for the *News* a fictional meeting he had had with Jeff at the Arcade, claiming that "Smith was finally thumped until he was condemned by the meat inspector" [Creative parlance that Jeff had been badly beaten]. Matthews manufactured this story, no doubt, for the benefit of those who had hired him, but he apparently did not know Jeff's reputation for retaliation. When the story was published, it was also reported that Jeff's standing had become at stake in places he normally socialized. "'Why,' said a well known sport, 'Jeff could not walk down Seventeenth Street from Larimer to Wynkoop without having the life guyed out of him.'"[1]

On Saturday evening, October 3, 1891, Jeff gathered up John Bowers, Felix Friend, and "Cap" William Sidney Light to accompany him on an unfriendly visit to the office of Glasson's Detective Agency, located in the Good Block building at Sixteenth and Larimer. At the stairway Jeff ordered two men to remain downstairs to prevent escape from above or interference from below while Jeff and another went upstairs. Newspaper reports do not detail who stayed downstairs and who went up with Jeff.

The *News* reported that "One of Glasson's men stated that a stranger came to the rooms and asked for Joe Matthews, and then returned with 'Soapy' and another man. They used bad language—so bad that it was insulting." Things were about to get a great deal worse. Glasson was not present, but detectives Gavitts and Joe Matthews were. Jeff and two others forced their way in, a fight broke out, and Jeff was knocked down by a blow to the face with a revolver and that later when he

> took an inventory of his physical effects he found that his nose was broken and he was talking through a space formerly occupied by two teeth. Then his war dance began, and the neighbors thought that an iron foundry had been started in the Good Block. Fifteen minutes later Smith was on the street. He requested a NEWS reporter to take the census of the population of the new graveyard he had just established in Mr. Glasson's rooms. He showed badges he had snatched from the bodies of his victims, and also claimed to have gotten valuable manuscripts from the detectives' private library.[2]

During the melee Matthews was able to escape, but agent Gavitt was not so lucky. He had been ill in bed in another room. He was pulled from a bed and beaten severely enough to require hospitalization. The furniture of the office was then attended to and drastically reduced in value. "The place resembled a spot that might have been kissed by a Kansas cyclone or one of Cleopatra's prize Egyptian storms," stated a reporter who witnessed the after effects of the attack. City Detective William E. Reno persuaded Jeff, Friend, and Light to give themselves up and accompanied them to the city jail.

Nothing is currently known of Soap Gang member Felix Friend, but "Cap" Light was Jeff's brother-in-law. He and Eva Katherine, Jeff's sister, had married in June 1887. "Cap," as he was called, short for "Captain," was a man to whom violence came

---

[1] *RMN* 10/04/1891. *the life guyed out of him*: i.e., "to be teased to death." *guy*, verb. To hiss: theatrical: fr c. 1870. May be fr Dutch *de guig aansteken*, to make fun. To make an object of ridicule: colloquial fr c. 1880. Also to poke fun. (Partridge, *Slang*)

[2] *RMN* 10/04/1891.

naturally, and as had come to be said about him, he was a "good sort of fellow—to get away from."[1] If they could, dead men who had come up against him might testify to that. Cap's record makes pretty clear why Jeff had Light accompany him to the Glasson office. Violence was on the agenda.

It is doubtful that Jeff lost two front teeth in the fight. Future descriptions of Jeff mention no missing front teeth. It is possible, however, that he let this part of the story float forward to gain public sympathy and support. In reality, Jeff and his men probably initiated the fight, giving the Glasson agents little time to react. Jeff probably profited from the files he confiscated, which contained personal and confidential information that spied-upon Denverites were certain to find humiliating and embarrassing. Possibly some of these were willing to pay handsomely or be inclined not to cause Jeff Smith enterprises trouble in order to keep damaging information from public scrutiny. All files pertaining to Jeff and his associates were no doubt immediately destroyed.

Arrest warrants were issued for Jeff, Light, and Friend, charging assault to do bodily injury and battery and for carrying concealed weapons.[2] After newspapers reported the warrants, no further information about the affair appeared. If any legal repercussions came to Jeff and his men, they were slight. The Glasson Detective Agency closed almost immediately and was not reported in the newspaper again.

Jeff was a boxing fan, but apparently in late 1891, he could not resist swindling Bob "Ruby Robert" Fitzsimmons (1863-1917), the great middleweight boxing champion. The earliest known public report of the incident was written five years after it occurred. The *RMN* discovered and exposed the story.

> There were any number of sporting men at the exhibition given by Bob Fitzsimmons at the Lyceum theater Saturday night, but only a few of them knew of an adventure that occurred to him on his visit to Denver five years ago, and the great pugilist did not refer to it during his short stay. He was shy of making the acquaintance of strangers however, and Otto Flotto, his Colorado manager, was careful to protect him from bunco men, for bunco men made a fool of Bob once, and he was not anxious to repeat his experience. It happened in this way:

> The lanky Australian was on his way East from the coast. He had made a good deal of money in California and when he reached Denver he was filled with that comfortable feeling that places one at peace with all the world. He was anxious to see the city and wandered away from his friends and down Seventeenth Street. He was enjoying himself immensely when two very affable gentlemen accosted him, calling him by name and reminded him that they had had the pleasure of meeting him in California. One was "Beef-steak Mike" and the other was a hand shaker named Brooks, but Fitz did not know it [the man's name]. Brooks was introduced as a nephew of Huntington,[3] a

[1] *RMN* 12/27/1893, p. 3.

[2] *RMN* 10/06/1891, p. 4.

[3] Huntington, Collis Potter: Built the Central Pacific as part of the first US transcontinental RR. Huntington helped lead and develop other major interstate lines such as the Southern Pacific and the Chesapeake and Ohio Railroad. www.netstate.com/states/peop/people/ct_cph.htm. Accessed 06/17/2006.

California millionaire. The fighter felt flattered and when the scion of the great Western family asked him to walk down to the depot and see his new private car Fitz consented.

At Market Street, the millionaire stopped. Something was on his mind.

"What's the matter?" asked Brooks apprehensively.

"I promised to see a friend here." Said Mike. "and it would be wrong for me to disappoint him, but I hate to leave you."

"Can't we go with you?" Brooks asked hesitatingly.

"It would be asking too much."

Fitz boomed on the two and they entered Soapy Smith's famous resort. There were a number of men engaged in playing cards and Mike's friend was among them. In a very short time Fitz was introduced in the game and lost $1,800, the story goes, all the ready cash he had, and then departed with his two new friends.

"Funny," he said, when they reached the street, "I couldn't win a blessed bit."

He didn't see young Mr. Huntington's private car, but half an hour later at Murphy's exchange on Larimer street he related his adventure and was told that he had been buncoed. "All right," he said, but he never "squealed," those who know say, and this is why Fitz did not cotton to strangers during his present visit to Denver.[1]

Nineteenth months later The *Denver Evening Post* published a much more detailed account that closely parallels the stories the author has heard from other family members. In this version Bowers posed as "colonel" Collis Potter Huntington himself. This was published a few weeks after Jeff's death.

When Fitz was here the first time, long before he had studied anatomy and discovered the solar plexus, he was picked up by the "Rev." Joe [John] Bowers, the same man that was with Smith when he was killed. This "pick up" consisted of an introduction that had been arranged for. Bowers was introduced as "Colonel Huntington, general manager of the Southern Pacific railroad, with headquarters in New York." "Colonel Huntington" said he was out here in his special car in a business trip and would in all probability leave for New York the following night. He invited Fitz and his wife to accompany him on the trip. Fitz wanted to get to New York and he welcomed the invitation gladly. He seemed to reach out for it and take it to his bosom.

"Colonel Huntington" suggested a walk as he did not like the curiosity seekers that followed Fitz to be gazing at him too. They got into a carriage and were driven several blocks as fast as the horses could go....

With the crowd behind, they left the carriage, walked for a time on Seventeenth Street, and met a friend of the colonel's, who joined them. When at last they came to a door not far from Seventeenth, the colonel knocked, and a voice invited them to enter.

---

[1] *RMN.* 12/28/1896. p. 8.

"Soapy" was on the inside but Fitz did not know him and he was introduced as Major Southern. The colonel and the major talked over "business" and a game of poker was proposed. Fitz had a little over $400 with him and was wearing a diamond in his cravat and a diamond in each of his cuff buttons.

The game dragged along for a time, not much money changing hands and to make it more interesting the $25 limit was taken off…. There were four men in it—"Major Southern," "Colonel Huntington," Fitzsimmons and the man they met on Seventeenth street. A jackpot was going around and had been sweetened until there was $50 in it. "Colonel Huntington" suggested that everyone sweeten [it] $10 just for fun, and with a "you-can't-bluff-me" air "Major Southern" said: "We'll make it $20 more." The other man, of course hurried in with his $20 which only left Fitz to be "bull-headed." He thought of the trip to New York in the "colonel's" special car and dropped in his $30. This made the pot worth $140—and "Soapy" was dealing.

"Colonel Huntington" was sitting next to the dealer, next Fitz, and then the man who was playing just to be "sociable." The "colonel" seemed disgusted and passed on the blind without looking at his cards. Fitz opened the pot and the sociable man stayed in. It was worth $140, but Fitz opened it low with an even $100. "Major Southern" looked at his hand and said: "Oh, I'll stay." He dropped in his hundred. "Colonel Huntington" picked up his cards with the remark that the pot was worth fighting for and he raised $100, making $250 he had put in.

When he said "fight" Fitz glanced at him, then skinned his cards down and his three tens were still there. He stood the raise. The sociable man said he did not know the game very well, but he guessed he would stay. "Major Southern" passed out. "Colonel Huntington" drew one card. Fitz drew two and the sociable man took one. Fitz caught a pair of sevens with his three tens and pulling all his money from his pocket, but $150. The sociable man raised the bet $150 and "Colonel Huntington" dropped out. Fitz only had a few dollars in change left and he was very much excited. He was about to speak for a showdown when the sociable man suggestively asked him what his diamonds were worth. Fitz replied $300, but he would let them go into the pot for $150 if it was agreeable. It was, of course, and into the pot went the cuff buttons. He was growing more excited every minute and somehow his cravat would not come undone. He grabbed the tie and jerked it from his neck, tearing it in two and threw the whole thing into the pot.

The sociable man had a king full on fours.

"Colonel Huntington" had a pressing engagement and hurried Fitz out of the room. He said he had some diamonds in his car that he would give the prize fighter while on the trip to New York.

The next night Fitz, accompanied by his wife, asked the depot policeman to show them "Colonel Huntington's" special car, as they were going East with that distinguished gentleman that night. After being assured that there was no special car in the city and had not been, it dawned upon Fitz that he had been against what is commonly known as the "big mit."[1] His wife had enough money to purchase the tickets for Chicago and they left that night, but not in a special car. Fitz tells this story when confidential.[2]

Information from within the Smith family is that Jeff had won some diamonds, now in the Smith family collections, from Fitzsimmons and that they possibly came from his cuff links. Fitzsimmons was a very flashy boxer of his time. The nickname "Ruby Robert" came from the rubies set in his teeth.[3] Jeff had the Fitzsimmons' diamonds set into a ring. One large diamond represented Mary, and two smaller ones on each side were for his son Jefferson and daughter Mary Eva.[4] Jimmy, the second son, was not yet born. Jeff gave this ring and the remainder of the diamonds to Mary. Years after Jeff's death, she had the diamonds removed and placed in rings that she gave to the grandchildren.[5] The ring and some of the diamonds are still in the family's possession.

On October 1, 1891, four days prior to Jeff's raid on the Glasson Detectives, Jeff sold the Tivoli Club and all its furnishings to Robert Gardner for $1000. Unknown is whether Jeff decided to get out of the saloon business temporarily or if it were just a sale "on paper" to remove his name from ownership. However, it is known that in time Jeff would once again be its proprietor. The sale, made out on a pre-printed form with the blanks filled in by hand, included everything deemed

> property in the Tivoli club rooms corner 17th and Market streets up stairs, consisting of safes, wheels, tables, chairs, gas fixtures and all other property contained in said room and now owned by me, the party of the first part.[6]

Jeff had shown himself to be a savvy, tough survivor. But even for Jeff, life in Denver in 1891 was challenging and often dangerous. As well as enduring the pains of assault on his character (including his family if close enough by) in the *News*, Jeff was on constant guard against the everyday hazards of fists and bullets. It was no place for a family, at least not yet as the struggle for control and calm was a constant. No wonder, then, that Jeff always looked beyond Denver for other opportunities, to points west in Utah or northwest in Spokane Falls. Then, too, opportunity might be at hand closer to home. To the south in Colorado were signs of a big new silver rush to a little camp called Creede, a name that was catching fire in Denver. Jeff's ability to survive

---

[1] big mit: This is the kind of swindle that ensnared Mr. Walker in the example with Rev. Bowers and is probably the game Jeff listed in his 1890 notebook as "Big Hand." A "mark" is brought into an elaborate scheme involving many actors, with the objective of relieving the mark of a large portion, or all, of his money. *Mit* or *mitt* is slang for *hand*. Suggested are the many hands involved in the scheme. "A big mitt," can also be "a municipal scheme undertaken with a view to private advantage of its promoters." (Mitt 3. slang, originally U.S., *OED*. Also Partridge, *Underworld*)

[2] *Denver Evening Post* 07/31/1898.

[3] Interview with David A. Jack, Fitzsimmons' great great nephew, by author, 07/11/2003.

[4] Story related to author by John R. Smith.

[5] Not until the late 1990s did Smith family members with rings speak of the diamonds for fear of retribution from victims. On the 100th anniversary of "Soapy's" death, members of the Smith family went to Skagway, Alaska. A relative who wishes to remain anonymous showed me the ring Mary had given to her father and permitted me to photograph it. Sadly the photograph roll was lost.

[6] Bill of sale form with handwritten notes, 10/01/1891. Item 111, author's col. Witnesses signing the contract were Natson E. Coleman and O. S. Barton.

and even thrive locally was proved, but could he expand beyond Denver and keep Denver, too—rise as some had high above the common fray?

So Jeff was inclined to look to Creede. What he saw decided him to advance on it, and in very short order, he made it his to rule as a little empire in what would be his shortest reign and perhaps most bizarre.

Chapter 9
Soapy Smith's Creede

It's day all day, in the day-time,
And there is no night in Creede.

—Jefferson R. Smith II
Creede 1892

Jeff reigned over the gambling and criminal population of Creede from the day he arrived until fire razed it. This period in Jeff's life ran like a carnival side show, complete with Jeff's most bizarre exploit, the famous petrified man. As soon as Jeff's Orleans Club was built, its bar and gambling began serving the throngs nearly twenty-four hours a day, all days of the week. Next came the violence for which boomtowns are known and the trouble that followed the Soap Gang everywhere it went.

Jeff's presence in Creede is well known, but the briefness of his presence there is not. As few as three months (February into April 1892) seem certain but no more than eight months seem possible (October 1891 into June 1892). But though brief, it was intense. As the boom grew, Jeff deftly stole a march on the most advantageous property in town, seized control of a large share of the gambling activities, bought (or won) at least two mines, became the dominant saloon man with his Orleans Club, and put the unmistakable stamp of himself on the town and its history from that day to this.

In latter 1891, the economic situation in Colorado had turned down, become bleak, and was worsening. Unemployment in Denver was reported at 3,373, an all-time high that was matched by a rising crime rate. For lack of funds, public maintenance ceased. As a sign of chaos, residents were fined for trying to repair street damage. Parson Uzzell was having trouble obtaining enough charitable donations for his aptly named Friendly Shelter. Under his church roof were 375 suffering citizens for whom he was struggling to care.[1] Normally he could count on Jeff and other gamblers for help, but they had their own money troubles. Fewer people had cash to gamble with. Additionally, Jeff and Uzzell's friendly relationship had suffered when the parson joined the anti-saloon and gambling reform movement.

The general situation in Denver had the bunco brotherhood seeking other locations in which to operate. Additionally, Jeff and his variety of sure-thing enterprises had become too well known to continue without constant trouble and increased exposure. Jeff had no thought of abandoning Denver. After all, the recent election results would ease pressures, but change would take time and so would a change in the economy. In the meantime, another strong revenue stream would be welcome.

---

[1] *RMN* 03/06/1891.

In January 1892, some gambling house and saloon proprietors once again threatened to desert Denver unless reform-sponsored restrictions subsided, but at this point, there was little that saloon-friendly city officials could do. Even some of the Republican city administrators who served under Mayor Londoner in 1889, referred to as "Londoner Boodlers,"[1] were preparing for criminal trials on charges of embezzlement, forgery, and fraud. To keep from being subpoenaed to testify against former allies, some of them may have asked Jeff to leave town.

Aggravating matters was a new ordinance, strongly backed by the *News*, requiring gaming houses to pay a hefty percentage to the city treasury, which was starved for funds. Conditions in general made an exodus from Denver eminent. But where and when to go for people like Jeff, used to having things their way, required planning, timing, quick action, and not just a little luck. Relocating to a camp already up and running for a time could be risky, not to mention dangerous. As it so happened, a new camp was about ready to expand. It had not blossomed yet but was about to.

Early in 1892, in the San Juan Mountains about 320 railroad miles southwest of Denver,[2] a tent city was spreading. In the 8,000-to-9,000-foot elevations, large silver deposits were located near Willow Creek, later to be named Creede. First discovery had occurred years before in 1889 when Nicholas C. Creede and his partner George L. Smith found silver in a high, narrow canyon. Over the course of that summer the partners established a mining camp, naming it Willow, and began developing a mine. Reportedly its name came from what Nicholas Creede exclaimed upon opening an extraordinarily rich vein of silver: "Holy Moses."

The remote site was above Wagon Wheel Gap, a steep, ten-mile, winding river canyon that channeled the headwaters of the Rio Grande. The question of how the rich ore would be transported brought the mine owners in the winter of 1890 to the Denver headquarters of the Denver & Rio Grande Railroad. Since 1883, rail service had ended where Wagon Wheel Gap began. There had been nowhere beyond for the railroad to go to, until now. After discussions with the railroad's president, David Moffat, the partners sold him the Holy Moses for $75,000. When news of the sale became known, prospectors and miners began traveling to the area. Mining sites throughout Southern Colorado were numerous, but none had been purchased outright by Colorado's richest man. When the Holy Moses went into production that year and a railroad bed was being laid up the Gap, Willow camp was renamed Creede.[3]

As growth continued through the summer of 1890 and more rich silver deposits were discovered, a rush began, and camps began forming on down the narrow gap between the silver-laden cliffs. String Town was next and then, from a gully between two great mountains, Jimtown spilled into an open valley. Then Creede became known as Upper Creede. More camps followed, extending further into the valley to a distance of two miles. All of these camps eventually became known as Creede.

---

[1] *Boodlers*: boodle, from the Dutch *boedel*: property, goods, chattels > illicit booty. A boodler is one who takes or gives boodle. And more: a ward politician who takes graft, a herder of illegal voting gangs, a fixer for criminals, a grafter who blackmails crooks and the innocent folks. (Partridge, *Underworld*)

[2] Davis, Richard, p. 67.

[3] Feitz, *A Quick History*, p. 26.

The Sherman Silver Purchase Act of 1890 made demand for silver not only strong but guaranteed. The US Treasury was required to buy, at market value, 4,500,000 ounces of silver each month. This demand and Creede's abundant supply of silver at one point caused a boom, with population during one period growing at three hundred a day. Which county the area fell into was uncertain, so Creede had no government, no organization, and no law. Money in the community suddenly began flowing as freely as mountain streams into the Rio Grande. At the height of the boom, ore from the mines produced $1,000,000 in silver each month. This kind of wide-open, rich environment, about $29,570,000 in current times,[1] was the perfect setting for a man of Jeff's talents.

Hundreds of carpenters tried but failed to keep up with demand for homes and buildings in the business district. In Upper Creede, space was at such a premium within the narrow canyon walls that a side of the stone mountain itself became the back wall of numerous structures. The din of saw and hammer persisted twenty-four hours a day, and all the lanterns from the saloons, hotels, and businesses reflecting off the canyon walls at night made it seem the sun still shone. Jeff, according to the *Denver Times*, coined the sentence "It's all day in the daytime and there is no night in Creede."[2] Cy Warman, editor of one of Creede's three newspapers, the *Chronicle*, employed the line in a poem.

Creede

Here's a land where all are equal—
    Of high or lowly birth—
A land where men make millions,
    Dug from the dreary earth.
Here the meek and mild-eyed burro
    On mineral mountains feed—
It's day all day, in the day-time,
    And there is no night in Creede.

The cliffs are solid silver,
    With wond'rous wealth untold;
And the beds of running rivers
    Are lined with glittering gold.
While the world is filled with sorrow,
    And hearts must break and bleed—
It's day all day, in the day-time,
    And there is no night in Creede.[3]

Author Richard Harding Davis commented from Denver on the mania for Creede.

> In Denver it faced you everywhere from bill-boards, flaunted at you from canvas awnings stretched across the streets, and stared at you from daily papers in type an inch long; the shop-windows ... advertised "Photographs of Creede," "The only correct map of Creede," "Specimen ore from the Holy Moses Mine, Creede," "Only direct route to Creede," "Scalp tickets to Creede," "Wanted, $500 to start drug-store in Creede," "You will need boots at Creede, and you can get them at_____'s." The Gentlemen in the Denver Club talk Creede; the people in the hotels dropped the word so frequently that you wondered if they were not all just going there.... It was a common language, starting-point, and interest. It was as momentous as the word Johnstown during the week after the flood.[4]

---

[1] Tom's Inflation Calculator.

[2] *Denver Times* 10/12/1895.

[3] Warman, p. 10.

[4] Davis, Richard, pp. 60-61.

By December 1891, a narrow gauge railroad ran to Creede,[1] and in time, two passenger trains arrived and departed each day, one of them a thirteen-hour Denver express. Freight trains came and went at all hours.[2]

Creede's business district began where Upper Creede's cliffs widened into the valley. Of those who lived and worked there, it was surmised that half the inhabitants were miners and semi-honest businessmen out to make a profit while the other half was made up of gamblers and confidence men.[3] Jeff understood this bifurcated sea extremely well. He had been moving and working in it all his adult life.

From Denver in early 1892, when Jeff first decided Creede was a good relocation bet, he sent a man there to reconnoiter a potential invasion of the Soap Gang. A few gambling house proprietor friends were also dispatched. Back came a hand-drawn map of the Creede area on Denver and Rio Grande Co. railroad stationary. It consists of a crude layout of the land, mines, and owners. At the top is written, "Last chance / every thing / takin and Develope / more or leasse."[4] The map seemed to show little possibility of obtaining real estate in Creede, but looks could be deceiving.

Jeff and his men arrived in Creede sometime after October 4, 1891[5] and before February 2, 1892.[6] On January 30, Jeff purchased a town lot from a W. J. Kurt for $100.[7] Five days earlier, on January 25, 80 acres of state land in Creede, leased to a V. B. Wason as "school land,"[8] was reported subleased illegally to squatters. Not known is where Jeff was when he purchased the lot, but 3 days later on February 2, 1892, Jeff was in Creede to file a non-payment action on a check for $750. J. M. Burkhart of Trinidad had written it to Jeff, perhaps had suffered buyer's remorse, or, more likely, saw himself the victim of a swindle, and on February 5 had stopped payment of his check. Jeff's document filing official protest of non-payment was written up and notarized by H. J. Alexander and given to the Miners Bank of Creede. Jeff had opened a checking account there.[9] The outcome of the attempt to collect is unknown. The document shows Jeff still had an account at Denver's First National Bank.

On Tuesday, February 9, 4 days later, Jeff acquired leases on lots 5 through 13 in block 24 on Cliff Street for a mere $22.50 a month. On the same day he also acquired lots 14 and 15 of block 24 for only $5 a month.[10] Names on the leases include Jeff, John Kinneavy, and L.S. Palmer, the latter possibly being Joe Palmer. The leases

---

[1] Davis, Richard, p. 67.

[2] Feitz, A Quick History, p. 35.

[3] Feitz, *A Quick History*, p. 9.

[4] Title of hand-drawn map, with misspellings, of Creede on "Denver and Rio Grande Railroad Co." stationary. Item 16, author's col.

[5] Jeff is known to have been in Denver at this time. (*RMN* 10/04/1891)

[6] Check made out in Creede to Jeff Smith, 02/02/1892. Item 19, author's col.

[7] Quit deed claim/purchase, 01/30/1892. Item 25, author's col.

[8] *school land*: "The 1875 Enabling Act for the Territory of Colorado authorizing the admission of Colorado as a state upon adoption of a state constitution, provided that two sections of every township would be 'granted for the support of common schools.' The Act provided that the lands be sold 'only at public sale' with 'the proceeds to constitute a permanent school fund' the 'interest of which to be expended in the support of common schools." (Macke)

[9] Protest of non-payment document made out in Creede, 02/02/1892. Item 19, author's col.

[10] Sub-lease documents, 02/09/1892. Item 22 & 23, author's col.

covered three-quarters of the west side of Cliff Street between Wall and Second streets, some of the most prime real estate in Creede. Additionally, saloons and gaming halls to be operated by Jeff and his friends came to be located on the east side of Creede Avenue, the main street in the camp and one block west of Cliff Street. Jeff also leased a lot just above the one on which he was living "to be used for a dwelling house."[1] Presumably this location would be for a family home. Mary and son Jefferson did visit Creede but never resided there.[2] Jeff's lease of this dwelling one week before the commercial property indicates his confidence of success.

Jeff obtained enough lots in Creede's business district for himself and some of his Denver friends. The problem was that some of these properties were on "school land." The state contested these leases and cancelled V. B. Wason's lease, intending itself to auction lots from the land to the highest bidder. The 102 "squatters" who had leased "school land" from Wason and who had already made improvements were ordered to vacate without reimbursement. They chose to stay and fight if necessary.

> The boast is openly made that the state may sell at auction and give title which may be good at some time, but that nothing less than Winchesters carried by militiamen can give possession.[3]

The state auction was scheduled for Friday, February 26, 1892. In the days prior to the sale, Creede was filled with investors wanting to capitalize on the misfortune of Creede's early settlers. Governor John L. Routt and other state officials arrived in the private car of Rio Grande and Denver Railroad Co. Treasurer J. W. Gilluly. He had brought two surgeons and medical supplies in the event of trouble as threats of violence were being made if the state proceeded as planned. The engine pulled "seventeen cars, with every available seat occupied and standing room at a premium...."[4] Numerous Denver real estate firms were among the new arrivals seeking to invest in the land sale. In the meantime, the governor remained locked in his sleeping car.

Two days before the auction, eight or nine hundred men met on behalf of the Wason leasers in a large tent at the center of the school land. The plan was to discourage, verbally—or physically if need be—outside bidding so that current lot holders could buy their properties from the state. At one point during the meeting, heard were gun shots and cries of "lot jumping" and "he is jumped." In meetings with state officials, representatives of the "squatters" argued that current leasers should be given a fair chance to purchase the land from the state, but state law prohibited such action.[5] Trouble looked probable.

The public sale on Friday morning, February 26, 1892, took place in a 40-foot circus tent. A stand was erected in front of the state auctioneer, occupied by E. H. Watson, chairman of the citizens' committee. He was ready to contest the sale of any squatters' lots. With him were 25 men of the committee all wearing red badges. Jeff

---

[1] Sub-lease document, 02/01/1892. Item 24, author's col.

[2] Statement by Jefferson R. Smith III in undated (circa 1936) newspaper clipping. Item 169, author's col.

[3] *RMN* 02/26/1892, p. 1

[4] *RMN* 02/26/1892, p. 1

[5] *RMN* 02/26/1892, p. 1.

had leased some of these lots, but his involvement with the citizens' committee, if any, is not known. However, the fact that men marched in wearing red badges fits Jeff's mode of operation. Some of Jeff's associates, however, were definitely involved. On March 2, the following Wednesday, while the auction proceedings were still ironing out differences, a committee was appointed consisting of S. T. Harvey, A. T. Jones, Clinton T. Brainard, John Kinneavy, E. C. Burton, John Lord, G. R. Miller, Louis Kerwin, and W. J. Allen. Kinneavy, of course, was one of Jeff's allies, and G. Miller could be George Miller and W. J. Allen could be J. W. Allen, both of the Soap Gang.[1]

Meanwhile, on the previous Friday, violence was expected, so the governor remained in the private car and received reports. State officials warned those present that if any problems hindered progress, the sale would be adjourned to Denver. No violence occurred, but plenty of "committee" member direction did. Its coaching strategy had a desired effect, and the bidding was without rancor. A *News* correspondent described how excitement was high and

> the crowd was enormous. When a lot was called upon which was a squatter's cabin, the improvements and the name of the claimant were read by the chairman of the committee of twenty-five and there were loud cries of "Let him have it!" "Throw out the man who bids over him!"
>
> The cries were hoarse with anger, but as one or two lots had been knocked down to squatters at the minimum price fixed by the state appraiser, good nature ... reasserted itself. There were calls of "They will do the square thing!" and "The speculators are all right!" The sale ran along for some time without particular incident, the lots bringing a price from $200 to $300.
>
> ... Lot 14, in block 28, was claimed by a woman. When the minimum price was called, cries of "Give it to the woman," went up.
>
> "Let her have it."
>
> "Do not bid over her."
>
> The first bid was made in the woman's behalf at $50. Martin Froody then raised the bid to $51, loud cries of "Put him out," were heard, and there was a rush in the direction of the auctioneer's stand where Martin stood. The confusion and noise was quieted with the utmost difficulty.
>
> Stretching his hand as high as possible, Martin with the gallantry which he averred every man from Denver should possess, announced that his bid was for the woman and Rev. Mr. Brodhead called lot 14, in block 28, for the "woman." At $51. Martin was loudly cheered and Denver friends pressed forward to take his hand.... ...
>
> A livery man with a leather coat and rubber boots mounted the platform of the belligerents and claimed a lot because upon it he had kept a few overworked mules. A woman in a plush sack took a position back of him and shouted that she had her children on the same lot and that there she made bread for them.

---

[1] *RMN* 03/03/1892, p. 2.

"Down with the livery stable; let the woman have it: she came here early, she makes bread," were the cries that lifted the tent. The cries in favor of the woman who made bread prevailed, and she received the lot.... ...

Women mounted the stand with babies in their arms and the kids took the real estate. For half an hour a woman in a fiery red dress held her position at the corner of the squatters' stand and cast her most seductive glances at the auctioneer. When the golden opportunity came she plead to be permitted to buy lot 12 in block 12, to carry on a small mercantile business. She gave her name as Louise C. Grebor and amid wild cheers took in the perpendicular patch of ground 25 feet by 125 at $105. ...

No sooner was it knocked down than she asked for the adjoining lot for her sister. Five hundred voices in the crowd asked as many questions.

"Where is your sister?" "What is the matter with one lot?" "You are overdoing it." "Come off!"

"Well," said Louise, "I have a business on one and she on the other and we straddle across."

Hats were thrown high in the canvas, shrieks of laughter split the air, the auctioneer leaned back and took an observation through the bottom of a beer bottle ... the crowd howled, "Let them straddle it."

"They need it," and accordingly Mrs. William Hoyt of New York straddled the second lot at the same figure. Louise went around back of the state auctioneer and from a black silk handkerchief, pulled a roll of bills, which was smilingly received by Registrar France and handed over to Bill Smith, who deposited them in his tin box....

During the excitement General Adams of Colorado Springs had his pocket picked and lost about $700. He had invested heavily in lots and was known to have money, by the toughs, who were lounging around for plunder. Money began to pile up upon the table of the land board, which was surrounded only by a rude railing.

Warden Bill Smith had charge of the cash box, and toward evening reports were sent in that a gang of thugs were organizing to make a rush for the box. There was a movement in the crowd and Bill Smith, who has the reputation of being one of the coolest men in the frontier, was somewhat worried.... For this reason and on account of the rush of business the sale was adjourned at 6:30 p.m., and a hasty exit was made from the side of the tent. Warden Smith took the precaution to stuff the rolls of bills into his outside pockets and to carry the box so that it might be taken, if anything....

... The names of those who planned the robbery are known, and they will be hunted down by the indignant settlers.[1]

Not known is if Jeff and the Soap Gang were involved. They could have been but probably were not. They had enough to manage (buildings to build, personnel to put in place, bunco sites to stake out) without a large robbery to plan, execute, and cover up

---

[1] *RMN* 02/28/1892, p. 1.

right from the start of their time in Creede. Jeff had every intention of sticking around as he successfully bid $1,800 ($53,226 today) for lot 20 on block 4.[1]

The following day, Monday, after the story was published, the *News* received and published Jeff's method of obtaining various lots at the auction.

SOAPY AT CREEDE.
He Is Said to have Played Con on the land Board.

Soapy Smith is stepping high to the music of a golden strained orchestra at Creede.... He no longer figures as the high roller in front of a faro layout, but is devoting his time to the acquisition of wealth. Press specials tell in pathetic strains the influence of a lovely woman at the camp, and recount how the gallant miners waived their privileges in competing for choice corners so that representatives of the fair sex might turn an honest penny in real estate speculation. Some of the best and most central sites have been snapped up in that way, but no one has connected Denver's noted con man as the instigator.

His old partners in Denver are having a great laugh over the deal by which, they say, Soapy outwitted the authorities, buncoed the state and school fund and pulled the wool over the keen eye of Governor John L. Routt to the tune of several thousand dollars. The women in loose flowing scarlet robes and glib tongues were acting as cappers for the far-sighted Soapy, and the title of the cream of Creede reality will soon be vested in Jeff T. [R.] Smith. So the story has reached the city, and those who have a personal acquaintance with the thimble rigger say it is true.[2]

Yes, apparently it was true. With the aid of some women from Denver, cheered on by the Creede Citizens' Committee, Jeff acquired some of the finest lots in Creede. Odds had been against his securing any valuable land at all, but a keen understanding of human nature and an adept hand at setting a scene and working a "play" had again ended as scripted. It was one of Jeff's most public cons and not his last.

Creede crime stories trickled out across Colorado. A *Silverton Standard* reporter wrote about his experiences and impressions upon first arriving in Creede by train.

"Change clothes for Creede," was the salutation which greeted our ears as the train left Wagon Wheel Gap. The passengers did not exactly change clothes, but many were seen to place their scarf-pins out of sight, run their watch-chains through the arm-hole of their vests and make other preparations for defense against the disciples of "Soapy" Smith whom they expected to meet at the depot. In a few minutes the train stopped at Jimtown and the passengers were not disappointed. The platform was lined with bunco steerers who worked most industriously and with apparent good results. In the near neighborhood wheels of fortune and the nut shell game attracted considerable attention and some money. ...

[1] *Creede Candle* 03/03/1892, p. 4. Tom's Inflation Calculator.
[2] *RMN* 02/29/1892, p. 6.

Not seeing any ore being shipped out during his short stay, the reporter expressed doubt about the future of the camp.

> As the resources from the mines would never support a town of 500 people, we had to look elsewhere..., and the sight of "Soapy" Smith and his 130 disciples only confirmed our opinion. ...
>
> As a show, Creede is a success, and if you avoid "Soapy" Smith, it is well worth the price of admission. ... [1]

A local newspaper, the *Creede Candle*, could not deny that crime was on the rise and feared trouble. A sign of it came during the early morning hours of March 9, 1892, nearly resulting in Creede's first murder. Jeff's Orleans Club was indirectly involved as the shotgun had come from the Club. A *News* journalist in Creede reported the event:

> Almost a murder occurred this morning in the miner's resort at 4 o'clock over a hard boiled egg. Dick Murphy, a little sporting Negro, who has worked in almost all the gambling houses in Denver and several in Creede, took a hard boiled egg from a Negro lunch man, Charles Murphy, well known to Denver, and refused to pay, whereupon the latter hammered the former's face into a jelly with the butt of a revolver. As soon as he escaped punishment he rushed ... across the street to Jeff Smith's place, where the barkeeper was sleeping, snatched a double barreled shotgun from behind the counter, rushed back across the street, and as Charles Murphy was coming out of the door drew up his gun and fired both barrels of buckshot.
>
> Murphy seeing by the electric light the raised gun dropped on his face and the contents of the gun lodged in the door, broke all the panes of glass in the right hand window and played havoc with the interior of the saloon. Had this occurred half an hour earlier at least half a dozen people would have been killed or wounded. [2]

The next issue of the *Candle* called for law and order.

> Creede's reputation for decency, law and order, ... is fast going glimmering, and only a semblance of peace remains. The spirit of fight is in the air, and everybody seems ready to settle any little dispute which may arise with guns or knife or fist. Four or five affrays of this kind are becoming the daily quota and the crack of the six shooter comes often. Fortunately no death has resulted from the lack of discipline, but unless something is done soon to curb the growing disposition to recklessness, a reign of terror is imminent. Every law-respecting citizen should do what he can to maintain order in the camp, and the incorporation of the town should be pushed as rapidly as possible, that police officers may be placed in authority. [3]

Law enforcement would come to Creede, but order and peace did not exactly follow.

Jeff and his associates began obtaining mining claims. How they came to own them, whether purchased, won through gambling, legitimate or otherwise, is not

---

[1] *Silverton Standard* 03/05/1892.
[2] *RMN* 03/09/1892, p. 1.
[3] *Creede Candle* 03/10/1892.

known. John Kinneavy held the Star mine, and Jeff invested in the Epsiladen mine[1] and later the Delaware quarry. The story of these mines, their successes or failures, and Jeff's association with them is not known.

Word soon spread that Jeff controlled Creede's gambling and criminal underworld and was staffing political offices there. The first camp election for mayor and council members occurred March 31, 1892, and except for Cy Warman as Aldermen, none of the names in the newly formed temporary council were old allies of Jeff.[2]

Creede rapidly grew. By mid March, 80 saloons and 60 gambling houses served the wide open camp.[3] Trouble was imminent, and Jeff did his best to hold it back. Some time in March he had "Cap" William Light, his brother-in-law, appointed deputy marshal. Although having an officer of the law on his side was a plus, favoritism was not Jeff's only consideration in choosing Light. Cap's law enforcement reputation was, to put a point on it, ominous. During the course of his career in Texas, he had shot and killed four men.[4] His fifth and last would be in Creede.

To govern Creede, Jeff sought the best. *The Reign of Soapy Smith* quotes a source who tells how Jeff contacted Herman Strauss of the Levi Strauss Company in Denver about becoming Creede's first mayor.

> Isadore Leon, still a Denver resident, recalls that, soon after the Creede boom started, he went there accompanied by Herman Strauss, dry-goods merchant and member of the famous philanthropic Strauss family, to investigate the commercial possibilities of the camp.... The proposition [from Jeff for Strauss become mayor] did not come to a head, but it is illustrative of the high type of business man which Smith sought for the municipal government. In a position to elect whom he pleased, he sought the best.[5]

In Denver, Strauss had a shop at 1625 Larimer Street, just a few doors from the Arcade Clubrooms and a short distance from Jeff's office in the Chever Block. Strauss probably knew Jeff or at least who he was. If extended, Strauss declined the invitation.

Creede saw a quick succession of lawmen. The first camp council meeting was held February 13, 1891, conducted by "Mayor" Atkinson. Elected as camp marshal was James Medows. But the names of these men do not appear in newspapers again. The absence possibly indicates several groups vying for political power in Creede. The March 10, 1892, edition of *The Creede Candle* identifies a Captain Jack Kirvin as acting city marshal, serving with a deputy's commission from the counties of Hinsdale, Rio Grande, and Saguache.[6] *The Candle* for March 8, 1892, lists Mike Delaney as a deputy marshal. In later years, Delaney became a Denver policeman and later still a Denver detective who aided the Blonger brothers in court. The future association matches a past one with Jeff. On April 1 Delaney is identified as city marshal, but *The Candle* for April 22 reported that the town board chose Peter Karg as city marshal.

---

[1] *RMN* 12/31/1893.

[2] *RMN* 04/01/1892, p. 2. Cy Warman is not known as an operative of Jeff's, but he was an admirer.

[3] *RMN* 03/14/1892, p. 2.

[4] *RMN* 12/27/1893, *p.* 3.

[5] Collier & Westrate, p. 85.

[6] *Creede Candle* 03/10/1892, p. 2.

Peter Card [Karg], the marshal chosen by the town board, is a straightforward young man and will make a good officer. He is connected with no clique and will have no strings on him to prevent him upholding the laws.[1]

Another camp election on April 9, 1892, identified a new mayor and councilmen. Cornelius "Con" Sullivan, one of Jeff's men, was elected as a councilman.[2]

Sometime between February 9 when Jeff acquired a prime business lot and February 18, 1892, Jeff opened the Orleans Club. *The Candle* does not list it by any name other than "Jeff's place."[3] This long, narrow, false-front saloon and gambling enterprise was in the heart of the business district on Main Street (also known as Creede Avenue). It is relatively easy to spot in photographs as it appears to have been the only place flying a large American flag from its corniced roof. The *News* for March 7, 1892, refers to Jeff's saloon, but not by name. "A little below" Kinneavy's place,

> where the large flag of stars and stripes is floated in his large place, was Jeff W. [R.] Smith, probably better known as "Soapy" Smith, of Denver, on account of his smooth and convincing manner, entertaining a party at his bar with stories of the marvelous richness of his mines.[4]

Jeff ran the Orleans Club, camp politics from behind the scenes, and extensive criminal activities. He also managed his Denver operations. Normal business activities kept him very busy, and added to these was a share of problems. The *Creede Chronicle* reported how an Orleans Club employee attempted to cheat Jeff out of a night's take at a faro table. A Memphis newspaper titled the *Commercial Appeal* filled in portions of the story in 1898 after Jeff's death. It all began when a miner just in from Chalk Creek visited a reporter named Taber at the *Chronicle* office and said he hoped his narrative of triumph would be published. It was "At dusk," Taber wrote,

> when he entered the Chronicle office, his trousers were stuffed like the trousers of a football player—stuffed with money. His face was flushed and his eyes dancing. He was a miner by profession, a gambler by instinct and a deep drinker. He told Taber frankly that he had expected a reporter would find him out at the hotel, but seeing the paper was shy on enterprise he had come in to give up the news of the Chalk Creek district. He hinted that seeing his name repeated in the paper would help him over at the new camp where he was mayor, magistrate, postmaster and notary public. "If that likeness could go on the first page," he said, sliding a photograph over to the reporter, "I'd be willing to pay for the cut." He offered to "open wine" for the gang, printers and all, if they would join him at the Albany for a midnight feed.
>
> In the twilight of the following day he called again. He was not nearly so frisky. The stuffing was gone from his trousers and the twinkle from his eye. Pulling a chair up to the reporter's desk, he began to pour out the story of his undoing. Hartigan [the editor], seeing a smile beginning to play about the

---

[1] *Creede Candle* 04/22/1892.

[2] *RMN* 04/10/1892, p. 2.

[3] Jeff R. Smith II acquired the lot for the Orleans Club on 02/09/1892; the *Creede Candle* mentioned "Jeff's Place" on 02/18/1892.

[4] *RMN* 03/07/1892, p. 2.

smooth face of the reporter, went over ... and Vaughn, the master mechanic (and general manager in the editor's absence) came in from the back room.

Half an hour later the man went out. "Say," he called back, from the door. "You don't need to mention names, but I'll stand by the paper if you give the outfit a good roast."

Taber had written the heading for the expose in the presence of the Chalk Creeker, and he [Taber] had cheered and applauded it. When he picked up the paper on the following morning he was delighted to see that it had not been changed or softened:

A DEEP LAID PLOT TO DO A MAN OUT OF MONEY.

Business Men to Form a Union to Protect Themselves Against the Sharks"

And there was the miner's "likeness" on the front page, top of the column, and right up against pure reading matter.

The miner had admitted in the interview that he had been in the habit of bucking the tiger [playing faro] at the Orleans Club, kept by one Sapolio Smythe, and that he had dropped several small wads there. Finally, one of his men up at the mines, who used to deal faro at El Paso, said he could beat Soapy's game, but it would take time and money.[1]

This El Paso man enlightened the miner of a fail proof system in which he had been beating the house at faro. He would go down to the Orleans Club and get a job dealing faro, the miner would come in and play at the man's table, and the two men would split a handsome take. First, though, as a sign of good faith and to seal their partnership, the Texan talked the miner into advancing him $500. The Texan then obtained employment at the Orleans Club as a faro dealer, and at a pre-arranged time, the miner would come in and play faro as usual, but at the Texan's table.

On the day the miner was to come in and play, Jeff saw his new dealer tampering with a dealing box. He said nothing at the time, but when the Texan came to work that night, Jeff assigned a different dealer. The miner came into the club, saw that the Texan was not dealing, but sat down at a faro table anyway and started to play. The miner lost from the start. He moved his pistol around to his front for the dealer to see. The dealer reached into his table drawer, withdrew a pistol of his own, and put it on the table. Setting the pistol down, the dealer said to the miner, "I call you." Jeff quickly got between the men and told them to put away their weapons. Jeff signaled for a new dealer, and the game proceeded. Jeff then called the El Paso employee to the bar.

"Here's a hundred for your week's work. Get a drink and a cigar and take the trail back to Texas."

"Why, what's up, Jeff?"

"Oh, nothing much, only if you're here when that sucker goes broke, he'll kill you. He thinks you've been robbin' 'im an' if you haven't you've been crooked with me, an' in that case the rules o' the house make it my duty to put your lights out m'self, see?"

---

[1] *Commercial Appeal* 09/04/1898, p. 20.

A few minutes later an unemployed Texas faro dealer with a cigar in his mouth was on the trail out of Creede. Later, after the miner related the incident to the *Creede Chronicle*, Jeff verified it.[1] Given Jeff's love of the flawless con, especially of those who would cheat him, highly possible is that the whole affair was set up by Jeff and a fellow Texan to make a fast $500.

Poems and stories contain hints and evidence of the personal and business lives of Jeff and his men in Creede. William Devere, "Tramp poet of the West," who visited Creede in 1892, recorded some very candid scenes. In Denver, he had been proprietor of the Palace Theater[2] and the Mascot Theater on Blake Street.[3] Soap Gang member James Thornton, the "Duke of Halstead" (Halstead, Kansas), was a bartender at the latter, so possibly Devere and Jeff were acquainted prior to 1892. Five years later, Devere published a book of poems in which several were in tribute to events in Creede. One of Devere's poetic verses addresses the Orleans Club, some of its inhabitants, and a few details about the crowded conditions in Creede at the time. It was originally published in the *Tacoma Daily News* on April 8, 1892.

"TWO LITTLE BUSTED SHOES."[4]

A Touch of Nature.

The Orleans Club at Jimtown,* Colorado, '92,
Was a joint where you could play all games from a split up to a blue.[5]
And the gang that hung around the club I'll say, 'twixt you and me,
Would hardly cut a figure at a Methodist Pink Tea.

There was "Big Ed Burns," and "Crazy Horse," "Jim Sanford," "Windy Dick,"
"Tom Kady,"[6] the shell juggler, "Joe Palmer," pretty slick,
"Joe Simmons, who could deal the bank and never lose a check,[7]
"Pete Burns," "Jim Bolen," and "Jeff Smith," all high cards in the deck. [1-8][8]

In the poem, the speaker, presumably Devere himself, comes into the Orleans Club to retrieve something in the traveling trunk he had stored there.

I happened in one morning to investigate my trunk;
I'd left it in the barroom, for I slept up in a bunk,
For sleeping berths were limited, and I could name a few
Who have stood up in the corner in Jimtown in '92. [25-28]

Some of Jeff's men that morning are in a "kidding, chaffing, guying" … "good natured" mood (11), and they gather round Devere at his trunk to "josh and kid" (31). The levity

---

[1] *Commercial Appeal* 09/04/1898, p. 20.

[2] Secrest, p. 139.

[3] *Denver City Directory*, 1889.

[4] *Tacoma Daily News* 04/08/1892, & Devere, pp. 92-95. Numbers in text refer to the poem's lines.

* The lower end of Creede Camp was called Jimtown. [Devere's note.]

[5] *from a split up to a blue*: From a low to a high wager. A "split" or Split Bet is a combination bet across two numbers as one might do on a roulette table. "Blue" refers to a blue-colored betting chip that was given a monetary value, usually higher in value than a white or red chip.

[6] *Tom Kady*: spelling often adopted for "Cady."

[7] *check*: casino and poker chips were called "checks" in the 19th century.

[8] Numbers in brackets and parentheses refer to "line numbers" in the poem.

ends when the trunk's lid is lifted and seen is what the speaker's wife had placed on top: "... two tiny little stockings and two little busted [open, empty] shoes" (38). These remembrances of the child and mother left behind at home go directly to the "great rough heart" (42) of the "gang that stood around" (41). From their silence, the speaker

> knew their thoughts in retrospect, flew o'er the western plain,
> To their patient wives and little ones they might not see again,
> And I knew the violet splendor of the hills whereon they roam,
> Was mingling with the unshed tears for little ones at home. [49-52]

The men are mesmerized and silent until the lid of the trunk is closed and locked again. Then one of them suggests they remove to the bar to "irrigate" (63) as if to regrow the carefree attitude that prevailed before the opening of the trunk.

> And "Big Ed Burns" proposed that we should have a toast or song,
> But after each had filled his glass with "Old Mcbrayer Booze,"
> We drank to wives and children and those little busted shoes.
> CREEDE CAMP, COLORADO, MARCH 8, 1892. [66-69]

Identified are some of the Denver Soap Gang members who followed Jeff to Creede and new men who joined him there: Crazy Horse, Jim Sanford, Windy Dick, Pete Burns, and Jim Bolen. The poem also tells a little about the way of things in Creede. For example, in terms of accommodation, because so many gang members are in the bar so early in the morning, apparently some of Jeff's men slept in the Orleans Club. The poem also opens a window on the humanity of these men on the frontier, far from home and family. In their silent demeanor, the poet finds a common strain in "each great rough heart" (42) that leads him to write, "they were not bad men, and I mean just what I say" (57), at least not bad clear through. Devere had "tramped" with such men, worked with at least one member of the Soap Gang (James Thornton, the "Duke of Halstead"), and was apparently liked by them. They "kid and guy" with him. Perhaps one reason they liked him was because he empathized with their loneliness, wildness, loyalty to one another, and even the regret they sometimes knew. Further, Devere could give authentic voice to their experiences and feelings. If renderings of the poet were sentimental, even deep purple with sentimentality, that was no reason not to like the man or his work.

As for torturing the lines and rhymes of his poetry and contorting its diction, on these counts Devere pled guilty. His Preface to the 1897 collection of his works reads, "I make no apology for the vernacular, the diction or the syntax...." He had no need to apologize. His aim, he wrote, was to "chronicle ... some vivified wild and wooly western stories, ... based upon events ... in the sub-strata of western life." [1] This regional poet made a lasting contribution to the preservation of the West of his day. Occasion will come again to look to him about the life and times of Jeff in Creede.

Sidney B. Remsen, an early Creede pioneer, witnessed Jeff playing faro in a tent. Remsen, who was forty in 1892, was interviewed by workers for the Civil Works Administration in 1934 about his experiences.

---

[1] Devere, p. 5.

In 1892, I came to the boom at Creede. This was the last [of] January and there were over 3,000 people in the camp, and by July there were 10,000. It was a tent-filled town with gambling houses. Soapy Smith was running the town, and he and his gang were getting rich. During February and March, many were killed by thugs in drunken quarrels over women and gambling. One night Soapy Smith entered a tent where faro and other games were running. Bets were not limited and the capital of the bank was $40,000. Soapy had watched the dealer for several nights while a band was playing and drunken men and women were betting their last dollars. There was scarcely standing room in the large tent. This dealer always had the cards stacked,[1] and Soapy understood how the cards run. Soapy bet $30,000 on the high card, and the dealer knew Soapy would win if he turned it, so he refused to turn it. Soapy's gun was at the dealer's ear and the card was turned — it was turn or die. Soapy won $30,000.[2]

No independent verification of this story of Jeff's winning such a large amount ($887,100 today) is known. However, stories of Jeff's gambling for high stakes ("going for broke") are numerous. Stories tell of nights Jeff left a gambling hall broke; this could have been a night he left one rich, very rich.

Miss Jo Campiglia of Denver related another interesting episode, this one probably in the Orleans Club. Her father at age eighty-five told her the story.

Business was so good that Soapy decided to take a trip to Denver to hire musicians for an added attraction to his new venture. My father, his brother, Tony, and another young violinist got the job as a trio, and went to Jeff's place and filled the hall with music while the gambling went on.

Then one very cold, snowy night one of the gamblers discovered a game was crooked and started shooting up the place. Somebody yelled: "Down on the floor, everybody!" My father hid behind a big, potbellied stove, Tony crawled under the bar, and the other musician crouched behind a beer barrel. The shooting went on for a long time … and continued far into the night up and down the streets of Creede.

… Smith paid the musicians in silver and gold currency and he paid them well. The tips they got from the lucky gamblers were extremely generous and they prospered right along with their boss. However, the shooting scrape frightened the young musicians and they quit their jobs and returned to Denver and they didn't work for Soapy Smith again.[3]

Miss Jo's story may tell about the night Joe Palmer shot it out with the "Louisiana Kid." *The Candle* reported the event occurred on Thursday, February 11, 1892.

There was a shooting affray in Jimtown last Thursday night. "Louisiana Kid," believing his rights had been trod upon in a social game of draw, laid [lay] in wait for manager Palmer of Jeff Smith's place and opened up his

---

[1] *Stacking*: Arranging a deck of cards in a preset order so that the dealer wins. "A stacked deck," idiom.
[2] Civil Works Administration interview with Sidney B. Remsen, 04/06/1934. State Historical Society of Colorado. Pam. 365 #1.
[3] Robertson & Harris, pp. 107-108.

artillery when Palmer came out of the house. Palmer did some shooting on his own account. The Kid was wounded, but got away, and was last seen hitting the pike for south. Palmer had both thumbs shot off and got a ball in the hip and a scratch on the head. For a while guns were kept hot in the camp but no serious results are reported.[1]

This is the first reported shooting directly involving the Orleans Club. *The Candle*'s brief account suggests only a somewhat significant event. The *News* correspondent in Creede, however, claimed the shootout occurred on the next night, Friday, February 12, and added quite a few more details, such as that the intended target was Jeff.

> The "Louisiana Kid" Goes Gunning for "Soapy" Smith.
>
> Special to the News. CREEDE, Colo., Feb. 13. — There was considerable excitement ... last evening caused by a gun play in which several parties were interested and several others mixed up. A young man known in the camp as "Louisiana Kid" went into "Soapy" Smith's place after losing some money on the games, made a big kick and received a blow over the head from a butt of a six-shooter for his trouble and was fired out of the place.
>
> Thinking he had been abused he laid in wait for Soapy's outfit and as soon as a couple of them showed up he opened up on them with his gun. They returned his fire and then the shooting became general. After the gun play was over it was found that Soapy's manager had both his thumbs shot off, a ball through his arm and a slight wound in the body. The "Louisiana Kid" received three balls, one in the head and the other two in the body. He then made good his escape and up to date nothing has been heard of him. Last seen of him he passed through Watrous and Bannigan's saloon and took up Wason's toll road toward Wagon Wheel Gap. Soapy's manager was taken away from the camp on the train to-day.
>
> The affair is trying to be hushed up by the tin-horns and the gambling fraternity of the camp. There is a report ... that if these affrays are not stopped that all of the gamblers will be run out.... The promiscuous shooting came very near causing the death of ... John Kepper, who is about to start a restaurant in the camp, was sitting in a building across the street and a ball came through the building and cut off both the rear legs of the chair he was sitting on, and caused him to suddenly find himself on the floor.... The report that a man was hung on the school land this evening caused nearly all the camp to rush down there, but it turned out to be merely a fake to draw the people down there by the saloonkeepers, and merely an effigy of a man.[2]

Joe Palmer's gun-fighting days were apparently over. Nonetheless he continued as a member of the Soap Gang. As the *Denver Republican* observed of Jeff,

> Kindhearted, generous Soapy Smith is known to many men. Many know him, too, as a man who would stand by his friends to the end. Many others

---

[1] *Creede Candle* 02/18/1892.
[2] *RMN* 02/14/1892, p. 2.

know him as a bitter enemy. When he thinks he is right, he stands by it, and when it is the other way, he stands by that, too.[1]

On Wednesday morning, March 2, 1892, less than a month after the first shootout in the Orleans Club, another occurred. This story did not make the pages of *The Creede Candle*, but it did not slip by the *News*.

Exciting Times in Creede

Special to The News. CREEDE, Colo., March 2.—There was a gun play in front of Jeff Smith's gambling house this morning at 1 o'clock. A tin-horn, who goes under the name of Charley Creek, had been taking in the town with a prospector named Jim Lanning. Lanning had been winning at faro, and when in Smith's place, Creek asked for $5. Cummings refused, and Creek, who is an opium fiend and who was drunk, drew a gun and fired at Lanning, who was walking away. The ball grazed the calf of the leg, inflicting a flesh wound. There were no arrests.[2]

Once Jeff was set up in Creede, more friends and associates relocated there. "Gambler Joe" Simmons took over Joe Palmer's job as manager of the Orleans Club, and according to the poem "Two Little Busted Shoes," he was very successful at dealing faro. Friend and bondsman John Kinneavy opened an "...elegantly furnished sample room where no gambling is allowed...."[3] Kinneavy's saloon was at the intersection of Cliff Street and Creede Avenue, at the base of the two huge cliffs that are unique to Creede. Thus Kinneavy's saloon was triangular. It was only about five doors from Jeff's Orleans Club and possibly located on one of the lots leased by Jeff. James Connors opened the Free Coinage Saloon.[4] "Reverend" John Bowers and Jeff's brother Bascomb also joined the party at Creede, intermittently. Acting as intermediaries, they shuttled from and to Jeff's Denver enterprises.

"Cap" Light likely appreciated Jeff's influence in securing him a commission as a Creede deputy marshal, but "Cap" surely came to regret accepting it. At 4:15 a.m. on Thursday March 31, 1892, "Reddy" McCann, a faro dealer from the Gunnison Exchange, was drinking heavily in the Branch Saloon and causing a ruckus. Earlier somebody had been shooting out windows and lights near the section of Main and Wall streets. McCann was believed to have been doing the shooting. It was Deputy Marshal Light's job to disarm the hip-pocket brigade, as the men who carried guns into Creede were called, so Light, under the influence of alcohol himself, entered The Branch Saloon accompanied by William Allen and approached McCann. The story appeared on page 1 of the April 1, 1892, edition of *The Creede Candle*:

Reddy McCann Shot and Instantly
Killed by Captain Light.

It is said that Light went into the place and was told by McCann that no — — — could take his gun away from him; that one word led to another until

[1] *Denver Republican* clipping cut out by Jefferson R. Smith II, 1892, month unknown. Jefferson R. "Little Randy" Smith col.

[2] *RMN* 03/03/1892, p. 2.

[3] *RMN* 03/07/1892, p. 2.

[4] *Creede Candle* 02/25/1892.

finally the deputy slapped McCann in the face; that following the slap came the guns and that Light was forced to shoot in self-defense.

Sheriff Delaney had previously taken two guns from McCann at different times, the latter time getting a sore hand as his part of the struggle.

McCann was a faro dealer at the Gunnison Exchange. He came to Jimtown from Salt Lake and had been in the camp about six weeks. ...

At the inquest, Mr. Schwartz, a friend of McCann, testified as follows: "At 4:15 a. m. Mr. McCann, deceased, went into Mr. Murphy's saloon and stepped up to the bar. In a few minutes Captain Light and William Allen entered the place and began to talk with Mr. McCann, and in my opinion both were under the influence of liquor at the time and they began joshing one another, and Captain Light slapped McCann in the face, knocking a cigar out of his mouth, and I saw them both reaching for their guns, and I dropped behind the counter and I do not know who fired the first shot. After the shooting was over I got up and found McCann laying [lying] on his back on the floor and the barkeeper and I walked up to him and he told us these two words, "I'm killed!" We sent for the doctor at once. We picked him up and laid him on the table, where he expired about fifteen minutes later. I was too excited to tell how many shots—about five or six I judge."

William Allen testified: "My residence is Jimtown, Colo., occupation, bartender. After I came off watch this morning at 4 a. m. Mr. Light and myself went over to Mr. Long's saloon to take a drink, and there met Mr. McCann. He and Mr. Light began to talk. I walked over to the stove and I heard a few words of tussing [cussing?]. Saw Mr. Light slap the cigar out of McCann's mouth and McCann drew a gun and commenced firing at Mr. Light. Then Mr. Light began firing at McCann. Then I saw McCann fall. Mr. Light turned and walked out."

To district attorney: "I did not go into the saloon alone. Mr. McCann was standing against the bar when we entered. Can not tell who spoke first, McCann or Light. They seemed like friends to me when they met. Did not think Light was angry when he slapped McCann. McCann drew ... first and he fired first. Can not tell who were present when the firing began, only Dave Allen, myself and Captain Light. Myron Long was attending bar at the time.

... [The coroner's jury retired to deliver and returned] in a few minutes the following verdict:

On the testimony hereby attached, we the jury, find that William McCann came to his death from a pistol shot at the hands of Captain Light, in self-defense.

Captain Light is reported as feeling sorry that the trouble arose, and it is said that he will resign his position. "I've had enough of this," he says, "and do not wish to be again placed in this position."

The Captain was for four years marshal of Beldon [Belton] and the same term in another Texas town. He is not a quarrelsome man, but will act when duty calls him.[1]

News of the fight reached as far away as Boston where it made the pages of the *Police Illustrated News*: "The first murder at Creede, Col., occurred March 31. Capt. Light shot and killed McCann, a gambler, in Long's saloon. Light has disappeared."[2]

It was Creede's first killing, but Light's fifth. Although the coroner's jury found he acted in self-defense, different versions of the fight surfaced, and a trial was called for. Light did not remain to find out if there would be a trial. His wife, Jeff's sister Eva, had a two-year-old boy and a daughter born sometime in 1892. Light and Allen quickly left Creede, Light to Denver and then to Temple and Allen to Pueblo to tend bar.

McCann's friends made their different accounting of the shooting known to the populace but were not invited to the inquest, and their version was not printed in the Creede newspapers. Their version, however, was published elsewhere. A few days later the *Leadville Daily and Evening Chronicle* published it as told by a visiting miner.

How They Kill People in Cold Blood at Creede.

"I did not see the shooting of 'Red' McCann by Light, a brother-in-law of 'Soapy Smith,'" said a miner who came in from Creede yesterday afternoon, "but learned all the particulars before leaving Creede. It appears that the Smith men up there travel in a gang, and are a perfect terror. It was shortly after 3 o'clock when five of them went into Dave Long's place, where McCann was standing. Light made some insulting remark to McCann, when the former knocked him down, and, drawing his gun put two shots into the defenseless man, killing him instantly. One of the gang then went outside and fired three or four shots two of which took effect in the casing of a window in Sponsillier's place just across the street. The gun was then placed in the dead man's pocket to make it appear as if the murder was in self defense. Light walked out, but was not arrested."

"Was a coroner's inquest held?"

"Yes, the coroner's inquest was held. No one was admitted but ... witnesses for the defense, and a verdict of self-defense was returned at once. To tell the truth, the jury was afraid to return any other verdict. There is a great deal of feeling over the matter up there, even among the business men, but they don't dare say anything. I was stopped several times by friends for expressing my opinion too freely about the matter. The whole truth is, the Smith element has the camp under a reign of terror. The murdered man was spoken of as a quiet, inoffensive fellow, never known to quarrel, and it is only a matter of time when a vigilance committee will be organized there to wipe the Smith element entirely out. Everybody seems afraid to say anything, but just now they are doing a heap of thinking."

"Does Bob Ford belong to the gang?"

---

[1] *Creede Candle* 04/01/1892.
[2] *The Illustrated Police News* 04/09/1892, p. 11.

"No. Soapy's men seem to have it in for Bob, but they are cowards and only shoot unarmed men. They know if they go for Bob they will find a man armed, and that he will shoot. I was told that one tough went looking for Bob with a shotgun a short time ago, but did not find him. I notice Light did not lose much time in getting away. No, he did not go on to Denver. I think he will go to Oklahoma, where he came from. My honest conviction is, the reign of terror will continue up there until the vigilantes run Smith and his gang out. I don't care to have my name mentioned in connection with what you publish, but I assure you what I have said is true. I have to go back there on business matters, and I have no desire to be picked out as a mark."[1]

An obituary for Light twenty months later in the *News* makes the story, in a way, even worse than the one above. This story had it that Light knew McCann's revolver was empty the night he shot him because Light had watched him empty it.

The shooting [of McCann] created considerable excitement, even in that abiding place of the unexpected.... In the town at that time the "variety" afforded the gamblers and miners all the recreation they wanted outside of the saloon. The painted fairies [showgirls] from all over the West flocked in and they made the place hum for a few months. A bartender named [William] Allen became enamored of one of these angels whose beauty had not been seriously marred by the excesses of the camp. He had as a rival Red McCann. The eventual quarrel followed and the girl agreed to take the man whose nerve showed up to the best advantage in a Creede shooting scrape. Captain Light was a friend of Allen's, and to him he confided the story. That night they started out to do their daily kalsomining,[2] and before entering a saloon they met McCann and a party of friends whose hilarity was such that they all began shooting off their guns in the air. The chambers were emptied and they all went into the saloon to liquor. McCann and Light exchanged words and the latter, always calm and composed, irritated McCann to such an extent that he pulled his empty gun on Captain Light. With that the deputy marshal nailed him, and before his gun quit smoking five cartridges had found a resting place in some vital part of McCann's anatomy. An inquest was held, but before the verdict was announced Light had left the camp.[3]

These two accounts indicate that the story told at the inquest was a cover-up for the murder of an unarmed man. Four months later on July 22, 1892, in Pueblo, Allen was arrested and transported back to Creede to face a murder charge. He was suspected of possibly firing his gun at McCann as well. He was standing at the roulette table with McCann between him and the bar. Light was near the door facing McCann. According

---

[1] *Leadville Daily & Evening Chronicle* 04/05/1892, p. 2.
[2] *kalsomining*: kalsomine or calcimine, trade name for a kind of whitewash containing lime. Here apparently used in figurative, informal sense of whitewashing, i.e., to gloss over or conceal faults or defects; give a favorable interpretation of or a falsely virtuous appearance to." (Webster's)
[3] *RMN* 12/27/1893, p. 3.

to some reports the shot which killed took effect in the victim's left side, the one toward the roulette table, could not have come from Light's gun.[1]

The friends of McCann in Creede had apparently been pushing for justice but four days later Allen was released owing to a want of witnesses.[2] The district attorney attempted to have Light extradited from Bell County, Texas, but the Hinsdale County authorities in Texas would not allow the transfer because Light was in their custody on assault charges.

Cap Light's life came to a sad and ironic end. After shooting and killing five men, he shot and killed his sixth on Christmas Eve 1893, himself by accident.[3]

———

In April 1892, Jeff may have seen signs of significant trouble brewing in Creede and prepared an exit. Eight days after the McCann shooting, Jeff reportedly sold the Orleans Club to a Sam Mayer.[4] It is believed, though, that the sale was in name only and that Jeff held control of the establishment. When on June 5, 1892, fire destroyed Creede, including the Orelans Club, Jeff returned to the fire-razed site, perhaps on June 6, to survey his losses. The *News* reported Jeff's saying that he proposed to erect a tent where the Orleans Club had stood and to reopen his business. He probably would not have made this statement had he no longer been owner.[5]

Robert Newton Ford, killer of the outlaw Jesse James, owned Ford's Exchange,[6] a saloon and gambling enterprise in Creede across from Kinneavy's. The *News* in early March 1892 printed its reporter's impressions of Ford's, how it

> fairly thronged. A platform with ropes around it and handbills gave one notice that a sparring match between local sluggers was to occur later in the evening. Meanwhile men and women were dallying with faro and craps and roulette, while different groups took their turn lining up at the bar....[7]

Cy Warman described his first impression Bob Ford in a letter to a friend:

> The first man I was introduced to when I stepped from the train, was Bob Ford, who in connection with the Governor of Missouri, removed Jesse James some ten years ago. He is a pale, sallow fellow with a haunted look, and he is always nervous when his back is to the door. Fitz, there is a great deal of wickedness in the world, and in a mining camp they make no attempt at hiding it.[8]

The first known mention of Ford in Creede came from a *News* reporter who had been dispatched to the camp to cover the daily news.

---

[1] *RMN* 07/24/1892, p. 2.

[2] *RMN* 07/23/1892, p. 2, & *RMN* 07/27/1892, p. 3.

[3] Light's life is fully traced in Chapter 4.

[4] *Creede Candle* 04/08/1892.

[5] *RMN* 06/06/1892, p. 1.

[6] Parkhill, p. 90.

[7] *RMN* 03/07/1892, p. 2.

[8] Ltr fr Cy Warman to Fitz-Mac, 03/17/1892, in *The Great Divide* 12/1893, p. 45. Item 126, author's col.

CREEDE, Colo., Feb. 11.—There is no let up in the boom. The number of people coming in seems larger than ever. Fifty carpenters came in on the train to-day to go to work on school land building.

A short one-round fight with two-ounce gloves came off to-night between Billy Woods of Colorado and George L. Lear, late of Leadville. Woods finished his antagonist in one short round and left him insensible when time was called. Bat Masterson was referee and Bob Ford kept the time.

The miners will hold another meeting next Saturday night at which time it is expected that a code of rules will be adopted for the protection of each other.[1]

Prize fighter Billy Woods was often employed as an enforcer during elections in Denver, and no doubt he found employment in Creede other than in the ring. According to the *News*, "He was ready to use his fists for the purpose of 'convincing' mistaken individuals who labor under the impression that they are entitled to cast a free ballot."[2]

Some historians have written that Smith and Ford were never on good terms because they competed for business and control of Creede's sporting element. In the same letter to a friend, Cy Warman mentioned the hatred he perceived the men held for one another.

I want to say that you did my friend Smith a great injustice when, in your day-dream you make him my slayer. He is my personal body guard. He is also a bitter enemy of Ford. Mark you, these men will meet some day—I say some *day* for it's never night in Creede—and whether he do kill Sapolio or Sapolio do kill him, or both do kill each other—especially the latter—the incident will render my positions all the more secure.[3]

Perception among the general population of Creede was that Smith and Ford were on bad terms. The miner from Creede interviewed in Leadville about the shooting of "Red" McCann was asked if Ford were a member of the Soap Gang. He said, "No. Soapy's men seem to have it in for Bob...."[4]

But not everyone found animosity between the two. In his book *The West From A Car-Window*, Richard Harding Davis wrote briefly of numerous "prominent citizens," including Bat Masterson, Bob Ford, and Soapy Smith. In these instances, Davis covered each citizen's line of business, yet he mentions nothing of Ford's Exchange or that Ford even had a saloon and gaming hall.[5] This may indicate that Ford's place was not in existence until as late as June 1, 1892. If so, the two were not business competitors.

Since back shooting Jesse James ten years earlier, in 1882, in the eyes of many, Ford was a coward, not a hero. Jesse's brother, Alexander James, predicted Ford's

---

[1] *RMN* 02/12/1892, p. 2.

[2] *RMN* 10/05/1892, p. 3.

[3] Ltr fr Cy Warman to Fitz-Mac 03/17/1892, published in *The Great Divide* 12/1893, p. 45. Item 126, author's col.

[4] *Leadville Daily & Evening Chronicle* 04/05/1892, p. 2.

[5] Davis, Richard, pp. 82 & 85.

life-long curse in 1882 when Alexander gave himself up to Missouri Governor Thomas T. Crittenden. He said, "but what must be the suffering of such a pitiful creature as Bob Ford? For paltry dollars he has, while on the verge of manhood, brought upon himself a blighting curse that will never leave him in all the years to come."[1]

No known evidence indicates that Jeff had anything against Ford, or if so, it was neutralized by friendship, that is, the friendship of a friend of Jeff's. Among the few reports of Ford's activities in Creede newspapers is one citing a friendship with Joe Palmer of the Soap Gang. On Easter Sunday evening, April 17, 1892, Ford and Palmer overindulged in Creede's finest liquors. As the evening wore on, the men grew wilder until Palmer, although partially thumbless since the barrage of bullets exchanged with the "Louisiana Kid," joined Ford in shooting up the town. It was said that the friends were not just "tying one on" for the fun of it. They had reason, and for Ford, a significant reason about which everyone knew. Two weeks prior, April 3, had been the tenth anniversary of the day Ford shot and killed Jesse James. For Palmer it was the collection of a debt. The Creede newspapers mentioned nothing of the cause, but the *News* correspondent got the scoop.

> John [Joe] Palmer and Bob Ford caused considerable excitement this evening in front of Benjamin's saloon. Palmer was trying to collect two hundred dollars owing him from Gus Ball. After being knocked down, Ball agreed to pay the amount, but as soon as he got up he skipped out and if captured by Palmer and Ford there will be trouble, as they are both under the influence of liquor and discharging their revolvers in the air. Ball owes a number of other debts in Creede.[2]

For three hours the shootists held target practice in the center of town, and no one dared interfere. While taking a walk John Spears became a moving target during the melee and the two shootists forced him to "jump into the dormitory of the Beebe House, and frighten the servant girls almost to death."[3] The long episode ended, when the pair ran out of ammunition and wound down into exhaustion. The *Chronicle* roasted Ford and Palmer for the incident and Ford swore vengeance.

Five days later, *The Candle* reported the shooting event and its consequences .

Ordered to Leave

> Sunday night was marked with more disorder than any previous one in the camp's history. Bob Ford and Joe Palmer got on a raid and shot Jimtown full of holes. Buildings were perforated, window panes broken, and the air badly cracked up with pistol balls. Not an officer was to be seen. One of them had a sudden attack of nausea and went home to bed. Another had forgotten his buttonhole bouquet and was ashamed to appear on the streets without it. So with one excuse and another, the hired supporters of the law kept out of the way and let the fun go on. It lasted from 9 to 12 o'clock, when the ammunition ran out and the jags got too big to carry, when it died out of its own volition.

---

[1] *St. Louis Republican* 10/06/1882.

[2] *RMN* 04/18/1892, p. 2.

[3] *Commercial Appeal* 09/04/1898, p. 20.

Unhappy citizens huddled and determined that both men should be expelled. "A delegation of six-footers waited upon the two" and informed them of the edict.

A few minutes later a hack drove up briskly to a door on Creede Avenue. Bob Ford and Joe Palmer came rushing out and piled into the hack, shut the door and pulled down the blinds. The order was given and the hack sped down the toll road to Wason.

A few minutes later an express wagon pulled up to the same door and sundry trunks, grips, and possessions of the two were piled therein, and it emptied its load at the depot. The out train that afternoon took the trunks and things on board and then stopped at Wason to pick up two male passengers, who seemed anxious and worried about something and who took a long, last look at the bluffs of Willow Canyon as the train pulled away for Denver.[1]

Jeff was a man who stuck by his friends. However, Jeff was not in Creede when Palmer was ordered to leave, having left about a week prior. Palmer was one of Jeff's men left behind to manage his interests in the camp. With the help of friends, both Palmer and Ford were allowed to return ten days after the incident, with the promise to behave themselves. It is probable that Jeff was involved at some level in persuading "Creede's leading citizens" to allow the men to return.

After the Palmer-Ford shooting spree, Creede wanted more officers on patrol. Apparently Frank Herald of the merchants' police was the only officer on duty[2] the night Ford and Palmer went on their binge. To protect his interests, Jeff no doubt did his best to see men appointed as police officers who would be brave enough to enforce the law and corrupt enough not to interfere with him. He mirrored this same balance in Skaguay, five years later. In a month's time, however, Creede residents complained about the new officers. As the *Creede Candle* put it, "Commissioning

bums and thugs to keep the peace has brought Creede into bad repute. Few officers, and they men of pluck, integrity and reliable conduct, is the need of the hour. Disarm the surplus officers and let us have peace.[3]

Businessmen from Denver, and other parts of the country, considered Creede as a new town for investment, and they wanted a reasonably peaceful environment. Jeff knew that to be successful as the head of Creede's underworld, residents needed a measure of protection, especially those who brought big money, investment, and jobs to town. Smith family stories tell how Jeff would parade important business men and worthy acquaintances around town and into many saloons to be introduced as "a friend of Jeff's." This seemingly casual tour was actually a formal communication to all confidence men that "this man" was not a target.[4]

Non-violent small businessmen of the criminal persuasion were allowed to operate but had to pay Jeff for the privilege and obey his rules. Anyone developing a profile as a swindler or posing a threat to Jeff's operations, especially those prone to

[1] *Creede Candle* 04/22/1892, p. 4.

[2] *Creede Sun* 06/09/1892.

[3] *Creede Candle* 06/17/1892.

[4] As told to author by his father, John R. Smith, who said his father, Jefferson R. Smith III, told it to him.

violent crime, was put on the next outbound train. Violent crime, such as strong-armed robbery, worked against Jeff's long-term success and was not tolerated.[1]

As a result of Jeff's rule, life in Creede had a peaceful veneer. In his first published book, Richard Harding Davis wrote about law and order in Creede:

> It is not at all a dangerous place, and the lawlessness is scattered and mild. There was only one street, and as no one cared to sit on the edge of a bunk in a cold room at night, the gambling houses were crowded ... every evening ... because there was nowhere else to go. The majority of the citizens used them as clubs, and walked from one to the other talking claims and corner lots, and dived down into their pockets for specimens of ore which they passed around for examination. Others went there to keep warm, and still others to sleep in the corner until they were put out. The play was never high. There was so much of it, though, that it looked very bad and wicked and rough, but it was quite harmless. There were no sudden oaths, nor parting of the crowd, and pistol-shots or gleaming knives—or, at least, but seldom.[2]

Not all of Jeff's protection from crime came free. Lot jumpers were a problem, and lot owners without "connections" could pay Jeff to protect their real estate. A hand-written contract for protection between George Patterson and Jeff reads as follows:

> This Agreement made and entered into this twenty seventh day of February A.D. 1892 by and between Geo J. Patterson of Creede Colorado party of the first part and Jeff Smith, Will Henry and C. H. Davis all of Creede, Colorado parties of the second part: Witnesseth That the said party of the first part for and in consideration of services to be performed herein-after mentioned and stipulated by the said second parties does covnaut [covenant] and agree to and with the second parties aforesaid that in case the lots belonging to the said first party and others lying west and south of the D and R. G. [Denver and Rio Grande] depot in South Creede shall be protected from lot jumpers to the best endeavors of the said second parties, then and in that event the party of the first part agrees to pay the said second parties one half of all proceeds arising from the sale of any or all of the aforesaid lots immediately upon the conclusion of such sale.
>
> The said first party further agrees to bear all expense of preparing said lots for sale and the proper holding of the same such as lumber for foundations and expenses of laying same.
>
> The said second parties agree to use due diligence in protecting the aforesaid lots from trespassers.
>
> Witnessed our hands and seals this 27th day of February A. D. 1892
>
> Geo J Patterson   Seal   Will Henry   Seal
> JeffR Smith   Seal   C.H.Davis   Seal[3]

---

[1] In the early to mid 20th century, mafia gangsters lived by this same philosophy. Al Capone was a big suppressor of local violent crime, except in cases, like Soapy Smith, where he utilized it himself.

[2] Davis, Richard p. 86.

[3] Protection contract, 02/27/1892. Item 31, author's col.

Another friend of Jeff's who came to Creede was "Bat" Masterson. He arrived sometime before February 11, 1892, at which time he had refereed a boxing match between Billy Woods and George Lear.[1] He needed little introduction in the camp as he had already made a name for himself in the Western states as a lawman, a gambler, and a prize fight aficionado. In the late 1880s Masterson dove into the saloon and gambling business but did not fare well as a proprietor. He possibly purchased the Palace Theater from Ed Chase but sold it in 1891.[2] When the Creede rush commenced, Watrous, Benniger & Company hired Masterson to manage the gambling section of the Denver Exchange, a combination saloon, restaurant, and gambling hall. Martin H. Watrous was a partner of John Murphy's in Murphy's Exchange in Denver.[3] The restaurant and saloon sections were said to be under the management of boxer Billy Woods,[4] but the February 25, 1892, edition of the *Candle* states that Woods "dedicated his new saloon Tuesday night with two sparring exhibitions."[5] It is not known if Woods had his own establishment or if the newspaper was referring to the Denver Exchange. Of the Exchange, a *News* reporter wrote that inside he observed "at least 500 keno, roulette and faro players of all kinds and conditions and ages."[6]

The Exchange was open around the clock, and according to a *St. Louis Globe-Democrat* reporter, it could not be told

> how much they rake off the gaming table every twenty-four hours. Every gambling device known to the west is carried on in their house, and every table is literally full night and day. Masterson walks around the house about sixteen hours out of twenty-four, and knows everything that is going on.[7]

Masterson also had discerning self-control that helped him keep order. Richard Harding Davis witnessed this ability when a man who was drunk slapped Masterson's face. Then

> the silence was so great that we could hear the electric light sputter in the next room; but Masterden [Masterson] only laughed, and told the man to come back and do it again when he was sober.[8]

Charlie Meyers, who worked for Masterson at the Exchange, described another incident in which Masterson had to quell an impending fight between Jeff and Jeff Argyle, known in Denver as "the Black Prince" for his wickedness and unwillingness to back down from a fight. In November 1891 Argyle had assaulted city Alderman McGilvray and the following day assaulted another man.[9] Collier and Westrate describe the 1892 confrontation between the two Jeffs.

---

[1] *RMN* 02/12/1892, p. 2.

[2] DeArment, *Knights*, p. 117.

[3] *RMN* 02/23/1891.

[4] DeArment, *Bat*, p. 332.

[5] *Creede Candle* 02/25/1892.

[6] *RMN* 03/07/1892, p. 2.

[7] *St. Louis Globe-Democrat* 03/05/1892.

[8] Davis, Richard, p. 85.

[9] *RMN* 11/24/1891, p. 8, & 11/25/ 1891, p. 4.

Jeff Argyle was dealing, and Tom Crippen was lookout. A row started, during which Soapy yanked out his gun and yelled, "Jeff Argyle, you're through as dealer in this game. You pull that card and you'll pull the next one in hell! I want a change of dealers."

There was no yellow in Argyle. He looked Soapy square in the eye and said, "If Bat Masterson tells me to pull, I'll pull it." I ran over to Bat, and he came to straighten things out just in time. Peg Leg Charlie Adams, who helped rob the Denver & Rio Grande Express, had piped up and said, "Soapy's right, and anybody who says he ain't is a damned liar." Nobody cared to dispute Peg Leg because he was wearing six-guns, had a derringer in his vest pocket and another in the palm of his hand.

About that time, Bat reached the scene. He was a friend of both Jeffs, so he sized the situation up for a second and then said, "Now, look here. You're both friends of mine, and I won't stand for this, be a couple of good boys and stop quarreling. You too, Peg Leg. What's the use of getting excited? You all know Jeff Argyle's a fair, square dealer or I wouldn't have him here. And we all know Jeff Smith's a square shooter. Two square guys have no call for any gun play with each other. Just remember that. Now, how about it?"

Bat usually had his men sized up right, and he proved it again this time. Soapy grinned and put up his gun. "Guess you're right, Bat," he said, and the game went on.[1]

The earliest known communication between Jeff and Masterson is a telegram dated April 15, 1887, sent by Masterson from Hot Springs, Arkansas. It concerns Dave Black, a young man in hiding for an unknown crime. "Tell Dave Black if you know his whereabouts," Masterson wrote, "not to leave [—] I can square him."[2] What came of the offer is unknown, but the Colorado State Reformatory at Buena Vista, which opened in 1891,[3] shows a David Black incarcerated there for a nonviolent crime.[4]

Masterson was well aware of Jeff's criminal activities, but other than the Denver election fraud of 1889, it is doubtful he was ever involved in criminal activity with Jeff. Possibly through Masterson, Jeff met famed gambler and lawman Wyatt Earp when he came to Denver. Masterson and Earp had known each other since their days in 1876 as Dodge City police officers. In her *Recollections*, Wyatt Earp's widow, Josephine, wrote of her husband's association with Jeff.

We remembered Soapy Smith from our visits to Denver and Creede, which Wyatt and I had visited at the urging of Bat Masterson. Soapy was not the kind of gambler Wyatt and Bat were. He played the sure things, rather than gambling in the true sense of the word. However, he fancied himself a true gambler and had once sat in a card game with Wyatt and Bat at Creede.[5]

---

[1] Collier & Westrate, pp. 99-100.
[2] Western Union Telegram fr Bat Masterson to Jeff R. Smith II, 04/15/1887. Geri Murphy col.
[3] The Buena Vista Correction Facility still operates today.
[4] Colorado State Reformatory Prison Records: 1887-1939. "Black, David (Alias), inmate number 9648, prison record volume number 21.
[5] Boyer, p. 161.

The men may have sat around the same card table in Creede. Masterson and Earp are thought to have dealt faro for Ed Chase in the Arcade,[1] so a good assumption would be that on occasion, the three men played cards together.

Also in her *Recollections*, Mrs. Earp directly quotes her husband as saying, "'Soapy knows all the tricks, … but he also knows what's good for him and doesn't try any of that nonsense on people like Bat and me, who are on to him.'"[2] Jeff probably would not have swindled Earp because Earp was Masterson's friend. Jeff and Masterson remained friends and continued to correspond for the remainder of Jeff's life. Topics generally involved Denver politics, gambling, and mutual friends. The last known letter to Jeff from Masterson, dated January 24, 1897, addressed Denver's gambling and political arenas, in which Masterson wrote, "Everything is running open here, but the play is very spotted."[3]

When a friend of Jeff's died, a proper send off was provided. The closer the friend, the more lavish the send off. Joe "Gambler Joe" Simmons and Jeff had worked together in Denver from Jeff's earliest times there and were best of friends. So when pneumonia, the scourge of the camps, fell upon Joe and he died of it on March 18, 1892, Jeff took it hard, openly displaying emotion. Both newspapers of Creede, a poet, and the Boston *Illustrated Police News* noted and published accounts of Jeff's mourning. Here is how the *Creede Chronicle* in its first issue presented the event on Tuesday, March 22, 1892.

"Can a feller buy a stack of blues in here, to-day?"

"Not to-day, pardner."

"What's the matter?"

"Well, Joe Simmons is being buried to-day and the house is closed until after the funeral."

"Who was Joe Simmons?"

"How long have you been in camp?"

"Came in on the afternoon train."

"Thought so. Well Joe Simmons was Jeff Smith's best friend. This is Jeff's house and not a card will be turned or a drink sold until Joe's remains have been carefully planted. You can slide up to the bar and gulp one to Joe's health beyond the range, but your money don't go."

The above conversation took place at the Orleans Club in this camp, Sunday afternoon. The inquiring party was a miner fresh from Leadville. The man who responded was the bar keeper at the Club.

After the drink, the mixologist waxed talkative. "I've known Jeff Smith," he said, "for a number of years, but I never saw him knocked such a twister as when he found out that Joe had to die. Down in Texas years ago both of 'em was kids together. They went to an old log schoolhouse and helped each other to annoy the teacher and get a little learning. Then they went to punchin' cows and worked for the same outfit, afterwards graduating into the

---

[1] DeArment, *Knights*, p. 173.
[2] Boyer, p. 161.
[3] Jones, Robert, p. 331.

Texas Rangers. They ran together, swore together, yes and I guess they skinned many a sucker together too, but they never gave a friend dirt.

Well Joe comes into camp when he hears the boom is on and went to dealin' for Jeff. He finally got sick—pneumonia—and Friday night a few moments before 12 o'clock, Jeff goes up to his room. Joe was dyin' and Jeff knowed it, but he tried to give him a stall that he was looking all right."

"Don't lie to me, Jeff," says Joe, "I know I'm dying. My last chip will be cashed in very soon and I want to say good-bye to you. You won't have no preachin' at my send-off, will you? No. Good. Just lay me out and wish me good health on the other side of the range. If there is another side and any health there. Good-bye, old pard, I'm off!"

"Them was the last words Joe spoke, and Jeff came down to the saloon and cried like a baby. He says to me, 'Chick [William], the whitest man on earth just died,' and I know what he meant.[1]

From the undertaker's at two o'clock, on Sunday March 20, in a heavy snowstorm, a long procession followed the wagon that carried Joe's casket. In the only covered "for hire conveyance" in Creede rode Jeff, John Kinneavy, Hugh J. Mohan, a Denver journalist, and the *Chronicle* reporter, Cy Warman, who reported the funeral in his newspaper. Fifty or more fellow mourners followed in a variety of wagons. Heading up the steep, snowy hill to Sunnyside Cemetery, Simmons' granddaughter, Beth Jackson, claimed that Joe's casket slid out of the wagon and had to be lifted back in.[2] Then half way up the hill, the horses could no longer pull their loads through the accumulated snow, so the mourners walked the rest of the way, carrying Joe's casket and a case of Pomeroy champagne. Once at the burial site, Jeff gave the eulogy.

The man whom we have just laid to rest was the best friend I ever had. You all knew him. Did any of you ever know him to do a thing that wasn't square with his friends? No. I thought not. Neither did I. The best we can do now is to wish him the best there is in the land beyond the range, or the hereafter, if there is any hereafter. Joe didn't think there was and I don't know anything about it. Friends, I ain't much of a speaker. But Joe was my friend and all he wanted was for us to gather at his grave and drink his health when he was gone. Let us do it.

Twelve bottles of Pomeroy were then opened and each of the assemblage took his glass in hand while Smith said: "Here's to the health of Joe Simmons in the hereafter, if there is a hereafter." The glasses were drained. Then all joined hands around the grave and sang "Auld Lang Syne."

Jeff followed a tradition held in high regard by gamblers, that the sporting element of a mining camp regard the last wishes of a dying friend as a duty to be faithfully performed. The editor of the *Creede Chronicle* came to admire the men of the gambling profession and published how he felt in the March 22, 1892, edition: "They

---

[1] *Creede Chronicle* 03/22/1892.
[2] Author's interview with Beth Jackson, 04/02/1991, author's col.

may be outside the pale of the world in many things, but they practice the broad principles of humanity. How many cultured centers of civilization do this?"[1]

With Jeff's eulogy, the *Illustrated Police News* included a large pen and ink drawing of Jeff leading associates in a toast.[2] The memorial service moved William Devere to compose a poem about the gravesite ceremony.

"JEFF AND JOE."
A True Incident of Creede Camp, Colorado.

Knowed Joe Simmons? Course I did.
Knowed him 'fore he up an' slid
'Cross the range that blustery day.
Did he slide? Well I should say!
Not the way you mean it, though,
Up the hill we toted Joe,
An' we laid him 'neath the rocks.
Death had called the turn, "Jack Box."
'Fore he cashed in Jeff Smith come,
Asked if nothin' could be done.
Jeff, yer see, thought well of Joe—
Knowed him thirty years or so,
Pal'd together down below.
Joe liked Jeff and Jeff liked Joe,
An' through all the changin' years,
Sheered each other's smiles and tears.

Worked together, tooth and nail,
Punchin' cattle up the trail;
Dealt the old thing; tackled bluff;
Each one blowed the other's stuff,
An' when one got in the hole,
T'other just dug up the roll.
So the gang all come to know
Joe liked Jeff an' Jeff liked Joe.

When the big excitement came
Every man that played a game,
Square or sure, that could succeed,
Packed his grip and went to Creede.
Gamblers, miners, suckers, marks,
Spieler, macers,[3] bunco sharks,
Men of money, men of greed—
Every one fetched up in Creede.

An' with all this human show
To the front came Jeff and Joe,
Opened up the "Orleans Club,"
Slept on tables, cooked their grub,
An' commenced to "cop the dough,"
Till old Death showed up for Joe.
Jeff dropped in to see the end
Of his staunch old pal an' friend,
For, yer see, he wished to know
The last wishes of poor Joe.

"Hallo, Joe, yer gainin' ground,"
Jeff remarked, a lookin' round,
But Joe answered; "Yes, the change
Just you answer, yeas or no,
If I ever throwed a friend,
Didn't I stay to the end
Through the toughest of the tough?
Did I ever take a bluff?
Did I, through my whole life long,
Ever do a friend a wrong?
Ever treat a poor cuss mean?
Haint I anteed my last bean?
Can you show me airy place
Where I weakened in the race?
Tell me, Jeff—my race is run.
And Jeff answered; "Nary one."

"Well," said Joe, "I'm glad of that;
It comes easy to stand pat.
When you know that you've done right,
Even Death itself looks bright.
So, old boy, don't preach or pray;
Keep the gospel sharks away—

---

[1] *Creede Chronicle* 03/22/1892.

[2] *Illustrated Police News* 04/09/1892.

[3] *macers*: swindlers who obtain goods fraudulently and sell it at half price. (Partridge, *Underworld*)

It's no use to call them late
Just to boost me through the gate.
Let the boys just gather 'round
From each bottle knock the neck,
Fill each glass with Pommery Sec;
Let each staunch friend drink this toast:
'Here's to old Joe Simmons' ghost!'
In the hereafter, if there be
Such a place for you and me,
Let the gang, all hand in hand,
A jolly, good an' jovial band,
Open out, an' all in line,
Sing together 'Auld Lang Syne.'"
Jeff said: "Joe, it shall be done."
And Joe answered: "Let her come!"

Maybe you don't think that we
Kept in all sincerity
Jeff's last promise to poor Joe!
Up the hill through blinding snow
Came the wagon with the box.
Up the mountain, 'round the rocks,
John Kineavy, Hugh Mohan
An' old boy Jeff led the van;
Up the mountain, through the snow,
Till they reached the grave of Joe.
There, with heads uncovered all,
Jeff Smith opened up the ball
An' asked if anybody there
Could say Joe Simmons wasn't square,
Or ever yet a wrong had done
To friend. All answered: "Nary one."

"Well," Jeff replied, "This is the end
Of old Joe Simmons, my best friend.
I promised him I'd do my best,
'An with the gang lay him to rest.
Now fill your glasses, fall in line,
An' sing 'The Days of Auld Lang Syne.'
They drank an' sang. The pure white snow
Fell softly on the grave of Joe.

An' as for Jeff—well, I may say,
No better man exists to-day.
Fell softly on the grave of Joe.
I don't mean good the way you do—
No, not religious—only true.
True to himself, true to his friend;
Don't quit or weaken to the end.
An' I can swear, if any can,
That Jeff will help his fellow man.
An' here I thank him—do you see?
For kindness he has shown me.
An' this I'll say, when all is o'er,
I only hope that you and me
May stand as good as he.

The Big Book says—that is I think
It says—that "whoso giveth drink
And food to even one of these,"[1]
The Savior he is sure to please.
An' sky-pilots say this is so,
But then, of course, I do not know
That either they or I can learn
A sinner how to call the turn.
But this I do know, every time,
(An' you can bet I'm dead in line,)
That whoso giveth up his pelf
For charity will please himself.
I've heard it said, time and agin,
That charity can cover sin.
But then, of course, I do not know
If this applies to Jeff an' Joe.
I know that I'm a wicked chap
Of course, an' I don't care a rap
About these Christians—do you see?—
That's catalogued as "Pharisee,"
Or who repent on the last day,
Then get their wings and soar away.
I'd rather (if I was allowed)
Fall in with the poor sinners' crowd.
I am not stuck on those that teach,
Or who don't practice what they preach.

---

[1] "whoso giveth ... even one of these": seems to be a variation on Matthew 18:6: "But whoso shall offend one of these little ones which believe in me, it were better for him that a millstone were hanged around his neck, and that he were drowned in the depth of the sea."

No man can tell me where I'll go | But when I'm called on to cash in
When I cash in my checks, and so | I hope I'll have an equal show
I know that I am prone to sin | With sinners just like Jeff an' Joe.

CREEDE CAMP, COLORADO, MARCH 27th, 1892[1]

In later years little was done to preserve the Creede cemetery, and today few of the names on the graves are identifiable, including Simmons'. But Devere's poem helps memory of the place to live on. A copy of the poem along with letters, news clippings, and business documents were found in Jeff's trunk following Jeff's death in Skaguay. Robert D. Jones published some or all of these documents along with brief commentary in the December 1907 and January 1908 issues of *Alaska-Yukon Magazine*. The poem reprinted in the second part with this introduction:

> The following was written by the "tramp poet" [William Devere] at a time when Soapy Smith happened to be in a prosperous and flourishing financial condition. He was so well pleased with the "poem" and the light in which it painted him that he made deVere [Devere] a present of a thousand dollars.[2]

No other evidence of such a payment is known to exist.

Joe Simmons died two days before the debut of the *Creede Chronicle*. The depiction of Joe's funeral service gave the newspaper the jump-start it needed and made it welcome in the Orleans Club and other sporting houses. Cy Warman, one of the founders and editor, later said, "It's a mistake to assume that gamblers do no good. Joe Simmons helped make the *Chronicle*."[3] Warman arrived in Creede three months following the camp's formation. He transported with him equipment to start a newspaper and a telegraph service. One day, after watching "Troublesome" Tom Cady maneuver the shell game, Warman entered a shanty saloon for a drink and later would write that it was here he was first approached by Jeff.

> In a little bushless spot by the roadside was a board shanty, upon the door of which was tacked a tin beer sign. Inside half a dozen workingmen—laborers or miners they might be—were sitting on wooden benches about the stove. They had been in animated conversation, but hushed it as they noted the entrance of a new comer. One small man with pale, lusterless hair and cold, gray eyes was recognizable as Tom, the shell man—"Troublesome Tom" they called him. I had seen a carpenter pause at Tom's three-legged stool that day, watch the game for a moment, then slowly slide his tool bag from his shoulder to the ground, put $5 on the table and pounce upon one of the

---

[1] Devere, pp. 109-115.

[2] Jones, Robert, p. 385. Part of the magazine's introduction (p. 329) to the documents is as follows: "The character of the man as he was is plainly shown in the correspondence which our correspondent unearthed in the dust-covered archives of the 'sheriff's library' in Skagway." The documents were said to have "been carefully preserved by Soapy" in "the scrap book of the notorious crook and gambler." On July 9, 1898, law enforcement may have set it aside for study, or someone may have taken the scrapbook from Jeff's trunk and hidden it. Since the 1907-1908 publication of the "correspondence," whereabouts of the scrapbook has remained unknown. Nor has anything come to light about the *Alaska-Yukon* "correspondent" Robert D. Jones.

[3] *San Francisco Call* 09/04/1898.

shells. He lost this five and two more, called the shell man a thief and demanded his money back.

"Yes," said the man, with his cold eyes fixed upon the top of the mountain. "I presume that's what you wanted with my money—to give it back."

Now the carpenter was pushed aside by a man who could guess. This man was able to win three times out of five.

Seeing that the game could be beaten, a merchant from Denver put down ten, tried again and lost. Crumbling a fifty-dollar bill in his left hand, the merchant watched the two half shells for a moment and then made a grab. "Turn it over, turn it over," he demanded excitedly, dropping the crumpled bill. Tom turned it over, but there was nothing in it—nothing for the merchant.

"Why didn't you turn it yo'se'f?" said the man with a Southern accent and a full black beard. "That fellow's a shark."

The merchant glanced at his questioner, flashed another bill and watched the shells. Suddenly he nailed one of them.

"Take yo' hooks off that shell." Said the dark man to Tom, "and let the gentleman turn it over."

"I don't see any money," said Troublesome Tom.

"There's my money," said the merchant, dropping the bill.

"You bet fifty?"

"I bet the bill," answered the merchant. Now the shell man moved his hand from the shell and allowed it to hover over the new note. The man turned the shell, slowly, but the pea was not there. Even as he turned it Tom's velvet fingers closed on the $100 bill.

Now this same man with the Georgia pronunciation came from behind the pine bar and spoke to me. He had no whiskers, but I could swear that this was the man that helped the merchant play off the hundred.

"You the artist that's going to start the daily paper?"

"Yes," I answered, and as my eyes wandered over the faces of the company my mind went back to Denver. "Goodbye," Col. Arkins of the News had said "When you come back you'll be wearing a wooden overcoat."[1] [S]omething in the air of this place ... recalled the colonel's prophecy.

"Going to make war on the gamblers?" asked Jeff.

"Not for gambling."

"What for then?"

"Sandbags,[2] six-shooters and masks" was the reply.

"Well, sir, if that's your gait, we can gallop in the same heat. My name is Jeff Smith, and when you're in trouble, say so, and I'll help you."

That is the way we became acquainted.[3]

---

[1] *wooden overcoat*: a coffin.

[2] *Sandbags*: used to stun or knock out victims before robbing them.

[3] *Commercial Appeal* 09/04/1898, p. 20. And *San Francisco Call* 09/04/1898.

According to Warman Jeff operated a small roadside board shanty saloon in the early weeks of Creede before opening the Orleans Club, or perhaps more than likely, Jeff operated several saloons in Creede as he did in Denver and would later in Skaguay.

Jeff had gained another ally in Creede, and the two men continued a friendly acquaintance for years. In Skaguay, 1897, Jeff received at least three jocular letters from Warman.[1] After leaving Creede, the newsman moved to Denver and became the railroad reporter for the *News*, giving travelers and business men the news on train time tables and other pertinent depot information.[2] Possibly because of Warman's friendship with Jeff, Warman's articles never mentioned gangs working the train depot.

Jeff did a great deal of good for those who might do him favors in return, particularly politicians and city officials. But he also did good by many who held no prospect of ever doing him a favor. Most of these were indigents and their families whom he did not know or those who ministered to them such as Parson Tom Uzzell. Part of this relationship to people took the form of "common courtesy." In a 1986 letter, Charles Elliott remembered how whenever conversation "turned to Soapy Smith, my grandmother would always say that as bad as he was, 'he was a gentleman.'" One story grandmother Elizabeth "Lizzie" Pfeiffer told about Jeff was the day she

> was going down along one of the sidewalks in Creede. They had board sidewalks in those days in places. She had two little daughters by the hand, ages would have been some where around four and six years old. The oldest was my mother, Lena, and the other sister was Violeta.
>
> As they approached one of the many saloons in Creede, there was a big crowd of men on the sidewalk and over flowing into the street. Soapy Smith had a box set up in front of the saloon and was running one of his famous shell games. It consisted of three half walnut shells and a pea. He would shuffle the shells around and take bets on where the pea was located.
>
> As my grandmother and the two little girls approached the game area, they started to go out into the street and around the crowd of men in front of the saloon. Soapy Smith saw them and stopped his game and told all of the men to get back off of the sidewalk so that the lady and two little girls could go through the game crowd.[3]

Jeff gave to social events in Creede, which were numerous. When an employee of his was married, Jeff contributed to the conviviality. Journalist Richard Harding Davis wrote about witnessing Creede's first wedding.

> The bride was the sister of Billy Woods's barkeeper, and "Stony" Sargeant, a faro dealer at "Soapy" Smith's [Orleans Club], was the groom. The Justice of the Peace, whose name I forget, performed the ceremony, and Edward De Vinne [William Devere], the Tramp Poet, offered a few appropriate and well-chosen remarks, after which Woods and Smith, who run rival gambling-

[1] *three ... Ltrs fr Warman*: 02/16/1897; 09/22/1897; 11/16/1897. (Robertson & Harris, pp. 221-223)
[2] Perkin, p. 391.
[3] Ltr to the author fr Charles Elliott of Monte Vista, Colorado, 07/13/1986.

houses, outdid each other in the extravagant practice of "opening wine." All of these are prominent citizens, and the event was memorable.[1]

The *News* reported that John Kinneavy presented the bride, a Miss Elizabeth Lelchering of Denver, with the deed to lot 9 in block 1. Mr. and Mrs. Bat Masterson stood with the couple as Jeff hosted the bridal party with a champagne supper.[2]

In boomtown Creede, Sunday was just another work day for the mines and saloons. With the lack of religious houses in the camp, some saloon-gambling houses allowed services in their places of business. The *Candle* reported the first such event:

Last Sunday was long on religious services. ... Rev. Joseph Gaston of Ouray preached in the Creede hotel that morning to a large congregation, and in the evening occupied the desk of the keno roller in the club room of Watrous, Bannigan & Co.'s saloon at Jimtown, making an impressive fifteen-minute talk to some 400 men, who stood with uncovered heads and paid close attention to his words. At the conclusion of his talk it was proposed to take up a collection, but this was refused. Then the call "First ball 41" was resumed and the cheerful sound of "keno!" came as an amen to the Lord's prayer.[3]

The *News* also described the mix of gambling and religion in an article on the gaming houses that were open on one particular Sunday.

Just below his place [Jeff's Orleans Club] one's ears are this Sabbath night fairly split with strains of music from the various dance halls on the other side of the street, until Mart Watrous' place is reached, which is filled with at least 500 keno, roulette and faro players of all kinds and conditions and ages. ...

Directly across from an unfinished building in which are neither doors or windows or plastering on this cold Sabbath night, float the sweet strains of music. ... Beside this building is the Texas Exchange, and opposite is Matt [Mart] Watrous' place. During the lulls between the singing and preaching you can hear "17 on the black," "single 0" and "keno" and occasionally a demi monde voice high above the noise of the crowd on the sidewalk.[4]

The *News* reported the return from Creede of Rev. E. A. Paddock, where he was building "a Congregational tabernacle on the school lands 25X60 feet in size. It will be of boards, with a tent roof, and will seat 200 people."[5] In the *News* he warned "all persons without plentiful supply of pocket money to remain away from Creede. 'The town,' said he, 'has an everlasting lot of people who haven't a cent to their name, and see nothing before them but starvation or counting the ties homeward.'"[6]

Looking back from 1914, Henry "Yank Fewclothes" Edwards said that

At the time Creede, Colo., was booming, Smith went there and characteristically declared himself the "big noise." He was instrumental in

---

[1] Davis, Richard p. 82.

[2] *RMN* 03/08/1892.

[3] *Creede Candle* 02/18/1892.

[4] *RMN* 03/07/1892, p. 2.

[5] *Creede Candle* 03/10/1892, p. 2.

[6] *RMN* 03/23/1892, p. 5. *counting ... homeward:* counting the railroad ties ahead as they walk homeward.

founding the first church there. The minister came to "Soapy" and asked him assistance in soliciting funds. The two collected $68, to the minister's dismay, but "Soapy" came to the rescue.

"Give the money to me," said "Soapy," "and I will show it to some of my friends and shame them into giving more. I will be back in a little while."

In an hour Smith returned and put $600 into the hands of the happy parson. He had gone to a gambling house and won $600 with the $68. The parson did not learn until years afterward where "Soapy" had "gathered" the money with which they built their church.[1]

Jeff might have helped Rev. Paddock with funds to build Creede's first church. The camp, however, had many churches. Congregationalists, Methodists, Unitarians, Baptists, and Catholics each had a church building.[2] Which was first cannot be certain.

Parson Tom Uzzell, however, had heard stories of Creede's ill repute and high-density population, and thought that another church might be a good idea, so he came to Creede to evaluate the situation. Uzzell arrived the first week of April 1892. He planned to stay only a few days and help in the building another church. Land, however, was not available anywhere close by, and Uzzell himself immediately ran into difficulty finding a suitable location to hold services. His first service was in a large tent that had been erected for a prizefight to be held that evening.[3] On Saturday, April 9, 1892, he held service in the Congregational Church, aptly named the People's Tabernacle.[4] Uzzell's service netted $75 in donations, and with these tucked in his wallet, he and his co-traveler, a Mr. Vincent, retired to their room in the Tortoni Hotel. The parson knew from experience that his funds needed guarding, so he placed his pants, with his wallet in a pocket, under his pillow, put out the light, and went to sleep.

Sometime that night he was awakened by sounds of retreat from his room. "There's a man in the room," the parson yelled, instinctively reaching for the gun he always carried. The men rose and gave chase, but the intruder was not found. Then Uzzell discovered that he had been robbed. Not only were the donations gone but so were his pants. News of the robbery spread through the camp. A search party formed, looked until well after daybreak, but did not find the thief. Later that day the pants were found in another room minus his wallet with the money inside.[5] The *Creede Candle* thought the thief should be hanged and said so rather cryptically.

> The culprit ought to be seen in the mountain air with only the blue sky above and the roaring cataract beneath. Parson Tom is one of the cleanest, brightest and most manly preachers in Colorado and the thief who stole his pants is the meanest man on record.[6]

[1] *Denver Post* 11/15/1914, p. 10. Item 163, author's col.

[2] *RMN* 03/14/1892, p. 2.

[3] Denver newspaper clipping of unknown origin, cut & saved by Jefferson R. Smith II, 02/20/1896. Jefferson R. "Little Randy" Smith col.

[4] *Creede Candle* 04/08/1892.

[5] Creede newspaper clipping of unknown origin, cut & saved by Jefferson R. Smith II, 04/12/1892. Jefferson R. "Little Randy" Smith col.

[6] *Creede Candle* 04/15/1892, p. 4

Several versions tell of how Jeff gave money to Uzzell. One states that when Jeff learned of the robbery he went to see Uzzell at his hotel. The *Denver Evening Post* described the encounter.

> The bunco man welcomed the parson and said he had heard that the reverend gentleman had been robbed during the night. "Soapy" sympathized with the loser of the $75 and the trousers and said: "Parson, I've just got a $20 note with me and I am going to play faro, and win out for you." He left the place, but returned in an hour and handed the parson $120, which he said he had won at bank [faro].
>
> Others told a different story. They said that "Soapy" had tried to win out for the parson, but lost $800 in doing it. Then he borrowed the $120 from two different men and gave it to Uzzell, at the same time telling him that he had won it at the gaming table.[1]

Jeff probably gave the parson enough money to replace the loss, perhaps more. Jeff had been generous with the parson in Denver. The source of the money, though, was likely neither from barrowing or gambling for that purpose but rather just out of pocket. With all of his Creede business ventures, Jeff had access to large amounts of money at any time. As for the robber, Jeff probably knew who he was, or if not, quickly found out and likely got the money back, or a good piece of it. Jeff was the "go-to" man for anyone wanting to do business in Creede, especially illegal business. Someone "operating" in Creede without Jeff's say so would quickly find himself out of business and most likely run out of Creede.

Jeff's past friendly association with Uzzell is a consideration. Jeff, of course, for the sake of charity, had often been the parson's occasional ally in Denver, and the two demonstrated a friendly familiarity. Cy Warman had even seen the men taking a meal together at Creede's Albany Hotel and wrote about it in a letter to a friend.

> The Albany is all right. It is the best place in the gulch; but, of course, you never know who is going to occupy the next seat. Last night, at dinner, the Rev. Tom Uzzell, the city editor and Soapy sat at one table[;] a murderer, a gambler, a hand-painted skirt dancer and a Catholic priest held another, while Miss Parsons, Billy Woods the prize-fighter, English Harry and I ate wild duck at a large table near the stove.[2]

However, in 1891 when Parson Uzzell aligned himself with the Denver Law and Order League, Jeff had to add his name to the long list of those who were unfriendly to his business interests. The League, after all, was among the principle causes that Jeff and others had come to Creede.[3] For reasons unknown, the parson gave up plans to start another church in Creede and returned to Denver. Was he made to feel unwelcome? A reasonable suspicion about the robbery is that Jeff had orchestrated it. Perhaps he wanted to rid Creede of the "do-gooder" who helped ruin Denver.

---

[1] *Denver Evening Post* undated clipping believed to be circa 1898-1899.
[2] Ltr fr Cy Warman to Fitz-Mac, 04/13/1892, in *The Great Divide* 11/1893, p. 47, col. 4. Item 126, author's col.
[3] *RMN* 03/02/1891.

The parson apparently got the money back. According to Uzzell in an 1896 interview, when Soapy learned of the robbery, he went around to the sporting men, collected "80 good silver dollars," and handed them to the parson before boarding a train back to Denver. Uzzell remarked, "The Lord taketh away and the Lord gave. Blessed be the name of the Lord!"[1] Among those hearing the parson, more than one might have thought: "The Lord is right, and his name in this case is Soapy Smith!"

The final scene of Uzzell's adventure to Creede occurred in Denver after he returned. According to the *Denver Evening Post,* Uzzell found his stolen pocketbook, empty, in his upper coat pocket. "How it got there is still a mystery that the parson does not try to solve. He carries the purse now."[2]

If he really wanted to, Jeff might have done more to help Parson Uzzell in Creede. Jeff had, however, something quite a bit bigger that he was working on. In the same April 15 issue of the *Candle* that reported the Uzzell robbery appeared the story of the unearthing of an amazing find: a petrified man.

Chapter 10

McGinty and a Dirty Little Coward

I don't begrudge having invested my $3,000 in this piece of stone because ... I am implicitly convinced that it is a genuine case of petrifaction and that not only myself and the medical world will be benefited ... but [also] the entire civilized world....

—Jefferson R. Smith II
Creede Herald, April 15, 1892

Back on March 3, 1892, to flesh out its first issue of 6 pages, the *Candle* carried the story of a find in California's San Joaquin Valley, a petrified man. The lime and cement carcass of 410 pounds was said to be that of a Mexican desperado who rode with Joaquin Murietta (1829 c.-1853), a California gold fields bandit.[3] Then a little over a month later, on April 9, the *Candle* reported how J. J. Dore had been digging about seven miles southeast of Creede, on a ridge east of the Rio Grande, when

> He came to a piece of stone shaped like a man's foot protruding from a bank of soil. There were evidences of a recent slide or falling away of the dirt which had brought the foot to view. His curiosity aroused, Dore used his pick and shovel and revealed enough of the body to convince him that he had found the body of a man turned to stone.
>
> He hastened back to town, got an assistant [George W. Lewis and a *Creede Herald* reporter,] ... engaged one of Hoover's transfer wagons ... and returned to the place. The four feet of soil over the body was removed and the promise of a perfect body fully verified. The curiosity was loaded into the wagon and brought to Jimtown where it was placed in [the] Hotel Vaughn....

---

[1] *Denver Evening Post* 02/20/1896, p. 4.
[2] *Denver Evening Post* undated clipping believed to be circa 1898-1899.
[3] *Creede Candle* 03/03/1892, p. 3.

In lifting out the body, the left arm and two of the toes were broken off.

It is probable that this is the most perfect and interesting petrifaction ever found. The man in life had been a well proportioned and perfect specimen of manhood. Every detail of flesh and muscle is shown in the stone just as it was in life. There is no sign of emaciation.... The muscles are as round and finely formed and the surface has the mark of the skin as well as a living man. It is a marvelous reality and eclipses the Cardiff Giant and Solid Muldoon[1] attempts to design a petrified body as much as the real form eclipses a rag baby.

What is the history of this man? ... There are proofs of a violent death. The throat has been cut by a knife, a great gash is down the right cheek, the forehead at the line of the hair had been struck with a heavy instrument [undecipherable] slash of a knife, and the arm and breast are badly mutilated.... These wounds were fresh when the body was interred and speak plainly of Indian butchery or fatal feud with fellow man.

That the man had been buried by white friends was evident from the posture and the hands crossed on breast.

It is believed that he was a member of Fremont's first expedition, which passed up this way in the winter of 1842 ... when all but the pathfinder and three men perished of privation or at the hands of Indians. They left a trail of dead behind them, and this brave fellow, who now is a sight for the curious, may have been one of that unfortunate band which penetrated the unknown West and made the oncoming of civilization possible.

No one can tell who or what he may have been. His grave was where no man would likely go and where perhaps no man had been until Dore wandered that way to explore the mineral resources of Creede.

The discoverer has been coining money from his find. It was laid in a box in a room of the tent hotel and there seen by hundreds, who paid 25 cents for

---

[1] *Cardiff Giant and Solid Muldoon*: Both were hoax petrifactions engineered by George C. Hull, a marked-cards hustler and New York tobacconist. *Cardiff Giant* was sculpted from stone, planted on the Cardiff, NY, farm of a confederate, and "happened upon" by well drillers on October 16, 1869. Acquiring the body as arranged, Hull successfully toured his ten-foot stone being and sold it to businessmen for $37,500. Later, P. T. Barnum offered $60,000 for the giant but was turned down. He had a replica created that drew large crowds. *Solid Muldoon*, the 2nd find, emerged near Pueblo, Colorado, on September 16, 1877. As related in the *NY Times*, this 7½-foot tall, 450-pound body possessed several startling features: "the great length of the arms and the ape-like appearance of the hands and feet. ... At the end of the backbone is a tail about two or three inches long, strongly suggestive of the truth of the Darwinian theory" (11/27/1877). *Solid Muldoon* was displayed in Pueblo for a time, toured, and finally sold to P. T. Barnum. Eventually revealed in the *Times* was how Hull in 1876 had tried for another *Giant*, run out of money, and gone to Barnum for financing. He supplied it and managed everything from there, including delivery to a former employee for planting in Colorado. The hoax was revealed in detail in a *Times* story on 01/27/1878. Several Internet sites in error have *Solid Muldoon* being displayed in Denver by "Soapy Smith." Muldoon seems to have been conflated with McGinty. In 1877, Jeff was 17 and probably working in Fort Worth. He may have been in Denver for a short time as early as 1879, but in 1877 Muldoon was already in New York with P. T. Barnum. (Waymarking.com & Museum of Hoaxes.com)

the privilege. Dore was offered and refused $5,000 cash for him, and will travel with it unless he can get his price.

Friday night some thief cut open the tent, entered and stole the broken left arm.... The left hand is tight to the heart and the loss is not important, but the thief will probably get a fat reward ... [for] return of the member.[1]

The *News* correspondent in Creede wrote that the petrified man, christened McGinty, was said to weigh nearly 400 pounds and was almost 6 feet tall. "The top of the head has the appearance of having been scalped.... The body is a bluish gray and is hard as a rock." The *Denver Times* said it was "prematurely bald ... of a darkish color."[2] A Mr. Baker offered Dore $6,000 for the body but was refused.[3] The following day the *News* correspondent claimed to have had small pieces of the carcass analyzed. With a report that the petrified man was nearly a third iron, the reporter called the find a fake.[4] People, though, apparently took no notice. They wanted to see McGinty.

As a news flash on the day of publication, the following was published in the "Around the Camp" section of the *Candle*:

Jeff Smith has purchased McGinty, the petrified man, and will travel with him. The price was $3,000. Jeff paid the money this morning and went down to get possession. Four others claimed ownership, and it required some lively discussion with fists and guns to get away with it.[5]

The *Creede Herald* jumped into the excitement with news that the petrified man had been stolen, recovered, and purchased by Jeff Smith.

PETRIFIED MAN.
"SPIRITED" AWAY THIS MORNING BY ARMED MEN.
Happy Finale—Compromised With the Owners—Jeff Smith Purchases the Remains and They Are Shipped to Pueblo. ...

On Monday evening last in the ... HERALD I had not only the pleasure but the satisfaction of publishing the discovery of the remains of A PETRIFIED MAN, and the corroboration of its identity, I am still further happy to state, was substantiated by the opinion of all the intelligent men of the camp of Creede.

But what was my astonishment this morning when I discovered the fact that the restaurant of Mr. Vaughan was surrounded in broad daylight by SEVEN ARMED MEN, who demanded possession of the petrified man.

I could hardly realize the truthfulness of the rumor, but individual investigation enabled me to learn that it was a fact. The helpless owner, as well as those who had been associated with him in the exhibiting this phenomenal freak of nature, were absolutely paralyzed. The box containing the form ... was spirited away. This morning they made representations to

---

[1] *Creede Candle* 04/15/1892, p. 3

[2] *Denver Times* 03/03/1896. Newspaper article clipped and saved by Jefferson R. Smith II. Jefferson R. "Little Randy" Smith col.

[3] *RMN* 04/11/1892, p. 1.

[4] *RMN* 04/12/1892, p. 2.

[5] *Creede Candle* 04/15/1892, p. 4.

Mr. Jefferson Smith that they had purchased THE STIFF from Mr. Dore for an almost inconsiderable sum and as it was supposed to be as valuable as the product of the Last Chance, Amethyst or any other mine in Creede, offered it to Mr. Jeff Smith for three thousand dollars.

This gentleman is of a speculative turn of mind, anticipating future results as cleverly as Mother Shipton[1] prognosticated them. Knowing the advantages the possession of such a relic of the past would be in his hands at the forthcoming [Chicago] World's Fair, he gave his note for that amount at once, which was honored this afternoon, and the discoverers of the PETRIFIED MAN, Mr. J.J. Dore and Geo. Lewis, went away happy. The important feature of this whole transaction lies in the fact that Mr. Smith was innocent of the manner in which the body had been secured and the exercise of implicit confidence he had in the gentlemen with whom he negotiated. They are not in town to-day, ... [and] on this afternoon's train the investor [Jeff] ... left ... with his property in his hands not a bit disgruntled.

To a HERALD reporter he said: "Mohan, I don't begrudge having invested my three thousand dollars in this piece of stone because from all the evidences I have secured I am implicitly convinced that it is a genuine case of petrifaction and that not only myself and the medical world will be benefited by my exhibition of it, but [also] the entire civilized world, because of its anatomical perfections. I myself, rough as I appear, may not seem to be a book worm, but when others are asleep, I am awake and I honestly believe THIS IS NOT A FAKE. The money I have invested is nothing to me because I know I will quadruple the same in one week's exhibition of the remains in the city of Pueblo alone. I bought the substance in good faith. I have seen the original owners and they have been paid the money required for his possession and I am only too glad to be the owner of it now. I take it away with me on the train to-day and with it my best wishes for the future of Creede, as I am deeply interested in many valuable mining properties here which, when I perfect my arrangements in Denver with reference to this, CREEDE'S WONDER, I will return to the camp with the money derived from my purchase and put ... holes in the ground enough to at least stake one hundred honest miners and give them a fair chance to earn a living. I am sorry I must go away so hastily, but my lite [my "guiding light"?] has always been that he who acts quickly, acts best; good bye. If you have no kind words to say of me in my departure, say nothing at all."

At that moment the whistle of the locomotive blew, announcing the departure of the lucky Jefferson Smith, whom he did not envy, but regretted

---

[1] *Mother Shipton*: Supposed English witch and prophet, 1488-1561. Her predictions of political fortune, London's great fire of 1666, and the world's end in 1881 were fabricated by others. She and her powers had an extraordinary hold on the popular imagination into the 20th century. (*Encyclopedia*, 1910)

after three months residence in Creede that he was not a part owner in as rich a mine as the successful Smith had invested his money in.*[1]

In the *Herald* Jeff said he planned on returning to Creede, but he does so only once, perhaps, over a month later and then in response to a monumental disaster.

Newspapers state that Jeff purchased McGinty, but the only surviving original document for the transaction is a lease for one month. At the end of this period, the body was to be returned to Dore. The lease is handwritten, apparently by J.J. Dore, on stationary from W. A. Thompson & Company, a saloon at the junction of Main and Cliff streets in Creede. It is signed by Dore and "J R Smith" and dated April 15, 1892.

The agreement made and entered into this the [15th[2]] day of April A.D. 1892 by and between J.J. Dore party of the first part and Jeff. Smith party of the 2nd part.

Witnessith that I, J.J. Dore party of the first part have this day leased to the said party of the second part — a supposed petrified Human body the same being found by me on the 9 day of April A.D. 1892, about 7 miles east of Creed[e] Colorado, for the purpose of exhibition to the public for the term of one month from date.

In consideration for which the said party of the second part agrees to and bind[s] himself [and] his Heirs or [?] to pay to the party of the first part, one-half of the net proceed after paying all nesessary [sic] expences [sic] and at the expiration of the time above mentioned to turn the body over [to] the party of the first part in as good condition as when received except in case of unavoidable accident, and to permit no one to disfigure or mutilate or in any way injure the said body.

Witness   J.J. Dore   J R Smith[3]

This agreement is an exercise in self-protection. It documents that Jeff *leased* "a supposed petrified human body" from its discoverer and puts Jeff at just about the furtherest possible remove from the petrified body while still giving him legal possession of it. This way if the body were ever proved a fake and charges brought against Jeff, evidence would show that he had been defrauded. That claim might summon hoots and laughter in a Denver courtroom, but the agreement was evidence for the claim and could bring an immediate dismissal—or no charges in the first place.

Why it was made public that Jeff *purchased* McGinty for $3,000 is not known, but the day's events help to explain. Excitement prevailed. The *Candle* reported "lively discussion with fists and guns," and the *Herald* reported the body spirited away, later guarded by seven armed men, and finally, taken from town by Jeff. Had Dore and Lewis tried to sell "the man" to others? Had others taken him by force? Did Jeff and

---

[1] *Creede Herald* 04/15/1892, p. 1. Item 114, author's col. *Sentence interpretation: "At that moment the whistle of the locomotive blew, announcing the departure of the lucky Jefferson Smith. Who did not envy and who did not regret that after only three months residence in Creede, he was not a part owner in as rich a mine as the successful Smith had invested his money in."

[2] *15th*: presumed as this small section became creased & apparently fell away.

[3] Handwritten lease for McGinty 04/15/1892. Item 112, author's col. On back of the lease is a note written by gambling kingpin Ed Chase: "Gaylord give Jeff Kinnivy's [sic] note of $1200—Edward Chase."

the Soap Gang have to retrieve McGinty? Were these events staged to sensationalize McGinty? The strange doings and speed of events make one or more or all of these possibilities probable. Other evidence suggests a high pressure conclusion to the transaction. The *Herald* reported the discoverers and owners of McGinty were no longer in town, giving the impression they were eager to be off to enjoy their fortune. More likely, however, is that they were told to leave town and not come back.

Was Dore actually the owner of the petrified man, or was he an actor in a scheme? Not at all unlikely, and in fact entirely possible, is that no money, or at least not much, changed hands because Jeff had owned the petrified man in the first place, had employed men to bury it, find it, bring it in, display it, and sell it (or lease it) to Jeff.

More evidence suggests that Jeff manufactured the petrified man. Judge Belford, Jeff's first chair lawyer in the Col. Arkins trial, is linked to the "Solid Muldoon" hoax. Belford knew the Pueblo man who had buried the creature near Pueblo in 1877 for P.T. Barnum and George Hull.[1] As a story to tell to pass time, Belford could have told Jeff of the failed affair. And no doubt Jeff knew the story of the Cardiff Giant and the many tens of thousands of dollars it had earned for its owners. That event was linked to the Muldoon story.[2] Those frauds had occurred in the late 1860s and 1870s. Now in 1892, prodded by the excitement out in Fresno, California, over an apparently petrified desperado found in a cave, the time might have seemed right for a reincarnation of a petrified man phenomenon. This time, though, it would not be the form of a man sculpted from stone or shaped in molds. It would be a real man. Such a product would not be hard to come by. Apparently at least one firm in Merced, California, was in the business of putting human bodies into a state of petrifaction.[3]

Subsequent evidence (to be revealed) shows McGinty to be the product of 19th century cadaver preservation practices. He no more came to reside in that hillside in 1842 than the other petrified men came to their resting spots years before. McGinty was put there in 1892. The planning, the execution, and the exploitation all bear the mark of a showman with the skills of a P.T. Barnum, or in other words, Jeff R. "Soapy" Smith. Although entirely characteristic of him, it is also the most bizarre and elaborate escapade Jeff had yet managed. The scripting even bears the profundity of flair so characteristic of Jeff. Even the struggle for ownership of the stony corpse, in which Jeff won out, could have been part of the script or added to it by creative playwright Jeff R. Smith. Needing to keep several paces from the center of attention, Jeff arranged for a third-party rival to purchase the find, showing how Jeff had nothing to do with its discovery or sale because he had to struggle to purchase it. People would not have believed the petrifaction genuine had Jeff hauled the entity into camp, claiming he had found it, not with Jeff's sleight-of-hand reputation. His having to struggle for possession in the end is the final degree of Jeff's separation from McGinty.

Dore's initial exhibition of McGinty in a tent adjoining the Vaughn Hotel was part of the plan of disassociation. The price of 25¢ for admission to view McGinty was a ruse.

---

[1] Cited as a reference by the man, W. A. Conant. *New York Times* 01/27/1878.
[2] See footnote above to "Cardiff Giant and Solid Muldoon" in *Creede Herald* story titled "Petrified Man" in this chapter.
[3] *Spokesman Review* 10/22/1896.

The real money came from those waiting in line, wiling away time by playing Jeff's games of chance conveniently set up to entertain the throngs. Rather than having to search out victims for his games, they came to him, or rather, to Dore's McGinty. Probably Dore was allowed to keep a portion of this admission money, perhaps even half, out of which he paid the Vaughn Hotel a fee for "use of the hall."

One account has McGinty moved to Jeff's Orleans Club and arranged under kerosene lamps with their flues painted black and placed in a draft so they would flicker. The account also has Jeff lecturing over the body to throngs of people.[1] While no evidence shows that Jeff ever delivered lectures on McGinty, given Jeff's personality and speaking skills before a crowd, it seems likely he would have been drawn to the opportunity to dazzle an audience with a fantastic story.

According to Clara Snow, a young child in Creede at the time, she and some friends tried to steal McGinty from where he was on display at the Theater Cominique. They were unsuccessful but not for lack of trying. She said they broke off part of an arm.[2] This remembrance may be fanciful because the *Candle* reported the arm as well as some toes had been broken off when McGinty was first unearthed. The *Creede Herald* also noted the arm's being broken off.[3] Additionally, the same April 15 *Creede Candle* story on McGinty closed with the report that on the evening of the previous Friday, April 8, "some thief cut open the tent, entered, and stole the broken left arm of the curiosity."[4] Given three sources, the breakage seems probable. Nevertheless, the arm must have been reattached in some permanent way because the surviving photograph of McGinty does not show an amputee. As for the toes, an ad Jeff placed in the *News* reads, "toe nails all complete, in a perfect state of preservation."[5]

News of a petrified man having been found in Creede spread all over the state. Cripple Creek, a gold camp in competition with Creede for status, attempted to out-do McGinty with a petrified female body. *The Creede Candle* poked fun and even gloated over the vain attempt to imitate their new celebrity citizen.

> Cripple Creek can't keep pace with Creede without faking. Creede had two murders in one day. Cripple Creek came in four laps behind, and then could only scrape up one. Creede found a genuine petrified man, and then Cripple Creek went right off and tried to make people believe they had found a petrified Indian girl. O, that camp's no good at all.[6]

After exhibiting McGinty for about a week, presumably by Dore, Jeff and his petrified man left town, as the *Creede Herald* reported on April 15, 1892. Not known is if he planned to return as he said, or if he was again misleading his competition and detractors. However, on December 30, 1893, Jeff filed "Notice of Intention to Hold Mining Claim" on a property named the Delaware.[7] This is property Jeff had either won

---

[1] Feitz, *Soapy*, p. 12.

[2] Interview with Clara Snow, by author, Del Norte, Colorado, 07/25/1985.

[3] *Creede Daily Herald* 04/01/1892.

[4] *Creede Candle* 04/15/1892, p. 3

[5] *RMN* 05/27/1892, p. 4.

[6] *Creede Candle* 04/1892.

[7] Notice of intent to hold the Delaware mining claim by Soapy, 12/30,1893. Item 109, author's col.

or purchased on February 19, 1892. The Notice formalizes intention to develop the Delaware either for ore or to sell it. No further record of the property is known.

In the *Creede Herald* interview of April 15, Jeff said he thought he could recoup his purchase price of $3,000 by exhibiting McGinty in Pueblo alone. Not known is if he and McGinty stopped in Pueblo, but in Denver Jeff did put McGinty on display at Murphy's Exchange.[1] Toward the end of March, however, there was a legal hurdle. The *News* carried the story, and so did the *Candle*, which stated, "George W. Lewis has sued Jeff Smith and J. J. Dore for possession of McGinty, the petrified man."[2] Exhibition had to be halted until May 22, 1892, when Jeff won full ownership rights. That afternoon, a Sunday, McGinty was taken to another saloon Jeff owned, the White Front. It resided across from Manhattan Beach, a private amusement park at Sloan's Lake four miles from downtown Denver.[3] Little is known of the White Front saloon. The only report of crime there comes from the *News*, October 10, 1892. A J. C. Stevenson of Washington, DC, complained "of a gang of bunco steerers at the White Front saloon.... He lost no money but was in imminent danger of bodily injury."[4]

Two days after Jeff won possession of McGinty, Lewis and a C. C. Ross were arrested for vagrancy. Ross was said to have made McGinty, but nothing came of this *News* story.[5] George Lewis, though, may have been in league with Jeff from the beginning as a third party to confuse legal standing. The court case could have been a maneuver to give Jeff complete ownership of McGinty. A George Lewis was reported to have joined the Charles "Doc" Baggs' gang in about 1875. In San Francisco 1882, he killed seventeen-year-old Ed Patterson. Later a George Lewis was employed by Jeff, but the only newspaper article addressing the connection does not say in what capacity.[6] The *News* cites a Lewis as having left Denver for the last time in 1886,[7] but he may have gone to Creede from somewhere in 1892 and returned to Denver to lodge his suit. Just over four months after his arrest for vagrancy, George Lewis was shot and killed by Eugene Borel in Ogden, Utah, February 26, 1893.[8]

McGinty made good money for Jeff, producing steady income from those wanting to view the wondrous stiff. Even more lucrative, however, were the games patrons played as they waited in line. Once crowds died down, McGinty became the draw for auction houses and other swindle joints. A week after sending McGinty to Manhattan Beach, Jeff took his petrified man back into the heart of the city, at 1643 Larimer Street, where the price of admission was a mere 10¢. In the background of the one known photograph of McGinty are display cases filled with what appear to be watches and other small items. This picture was probably taken in one of Jeff's mock auction houses. McGinty was later placed on view a few doors north of Champa Street. Handbills, similar to an ad in the *News* for May 27, 1892, advertised the attraction.

---

[1] *RMN* 04/17/1892, p. 8.
[2] *RMN* 04/27/1892, p. 4, & *Creede Candle* 04/29/1892, p. 4.
[3] *RMN* 05/22/1892, p. 6.
[4] *RMN* 10/10/1892, p. 2.
[5] *RMN* 05/24/1892, p. 3.
[6] *RMN* 03/02/1893, p. 5.
[7] *RMN* 03/02/1893, p. 5.
[8] *RMN* 03/02/1893, p. 5.

A petrifaction as natural as life, showing a fine specimen of manhood; every muscle, and even pores of the skin are plainly seen by the naked eye. Parts of the petrifaction have been analyzed by the most skeptical, and it has been pronounced genuine by all. $1,000 to any one proving to the contrary. Skeptics, Doctors, and all scientific men are especially invited. On exhibition at 914 Seventeenth St. Admission 10 cents.[1]

Thereafter for years, McGinty was a conspicuous resident of Denver, especially to visitors. The yearly Knights Templar Conclave was important to the economy of Denver, so important that Chief Sam Howe ordered his police detectives to arrest all bunco steerers and sure-thing men found working the streets. Eighteen were arrested on August 8, 1892.[2] Known is that Jeff used his petrified man as a magnet for the street hustlers of the Soap Gang, but so far as is known, McGinty himself was never in trouble. During the Knights Templar Conclave even four years later, in August 1896, thousands were said to have visited the petrified man. Along with fame, though, also came challenges to authenticity, but Jeff always spoke up for McGinty.

Some pronounced it spurious and some genuine. To the scoffers Mr. Smith proudly displayed a chemist's certificate.... That man runs two ounces in gold to the ton," said he.[3]

During the four years Jeff owned McGinty (1892-96), Jeff sold half interests in the petrified man over and over. Henry Edwards said that "until his [Jeff's] death he was selling interest in the thing."[4] Edwards might have been given to overstatement, but Jeff did sell interests in the petrified man often. His methods for doing so and then legally regaining possession are unknown. Possibly contracts included a clause that gave Jeff the edge in regaining full ownership. Beyond the suit he won in March 1892, so far as is known, no others against Jeff involving the petrified man occurred.

In October 1896 in Hillyard, Washington, a suburb of Spokane, Jeff sold McGinty a last time. The buyer was a Great Northern Railroad mechanic. The *Spokesman Review* covered the story, beginning with how "Soapy Smith, as he is commonly known, is one of the slickest confidence men on the coast. He is known in every city of the west ... and has a great number of friends among the police officers." Then the *Review* quoted from the *Denver Times* about how the mayor of Hillyard had written to the mayor of Denver bout the "stone man" and

the social standing of one Jefferson Randolph Smith. ...Smith is in Spokane, and a few days ago he met a man named Ennis.... It appears Ennis had money, and Smith had none. Now Smith has money and Ennis has none.... Up to date the petrified man is still in the possession of the Pacific Express Company. ... The famous corpse has many a time been the salvation of Smith. It has been sold a hundred times, but each time there is a long string on it, and Smith always gets it back.... Just how Smith will again become the possessor of the stone man is not known: But it is safe to say that ... it will

[1] Fr photograph of original handbill in Denver Public Library, Denver, Colorado.
[2] *RMN* 08/09/1892, p. 7.
[3] *Denver Times* 03/03/1896.
[4] *Denver Post* 11/15/1914, p. 10. Item 163, author's col.

again repose in a box, to be shipped to some distant city, and again sold at a neat figure. The man is supposed to have come from the petrified man factory of Merced, California.[1]

McGinty remained in Washington state, and nothing is known of any efforts to retrieve him. Jeff probably thought about it, though, during money-making ventures in Skaguay.

This author believes that McGinty is still on public display. Since the mid 1950s, he has been greeting the curious at Ye Olde Curiosity Shop in Seattle, Washington. Known there as "Sylvester," he stands in a glass case among the many "curiosities." A brochure describes him as a man 45 years of age, 5'-11" tall and weighing 121.3 pounds. Comparison of photographs of McGinty and Sylvester shows them to be strikingly similar. For example, the arms and legs of both McGinty and Sylvester are in the exact same positions in relation to the rest of the body.

In 2001, The *Mummy Road Show* TV series on the National Geographic Channel devoted an episode to Sylvester the petrified man. The goal was to determine whether Sylvester was a petrified mummy or a man-made concoction. He turned out to be both. X-rays revealed Sylvester to have been a living human being and that upon death had been preserved. Then in 2005, the TV show revisited Sylvester and submitted him to new technology. CT and MRI scans revealed internal organs so remarkably preserved that an embalmer must have preserved the body very "shortly after death."[2] Chemical examination revealed high levels of arsenic, the chemical used in 19th century embalming and also to halt the natural process of decomposition which destroys human bodies. *The Mummy Road Show* wondered, "Who put Sylvester into the arsenic one day in the late 19th century is unknown but the motive was to preserve him for fairground display, to make a buck. Maybe a showman did it, maybe a business man who sold bodies to sideshows."[3]

In life, Sylvester's real name and history are unknown, but circumstantial evidence indicates he was a criminal by trade. The x-rays show he had been shot in the head with a shotgun but lived to tell the story. The pellets remain in his skull, and skin tissue had healed over the wounds. Sylvester's death was probably caused by a bullet that entered the middle body and traveled upwards to the collar area.

Like McGinty, Sylvester has his own legend. Jeff Smith's petrified man appeared in 1892 out of a hillside near Creede. Sylvester appeared in 1895, half exposed from shifting sands near Arizona's Gila Bend Desert. Dry desert conditions were said to have petrified the corpse.[4] Are Sylvester and McGinty one and the same? It seems to this author highly likely that they are. One piece of conflicting evidence is that most newspaper accounts describe McGinty as "darkish in color"[5] while the one known surviving photograph shows him as bright white. This difference, though, could be due

---

[1] *Spokesman Review* 10/22/1896.

[2] *Seattle Times* 11/20/2005.

[3] Mummy.

[4] Ye Olde Curiosity Shop.

[5] *Denver Times* 03/03/1896.

to the over-exposure effect of flash powder. The darkish color, however, is also a positive piece of evidence. Seattle's Sylvester is exactly such a color.

Height and posture, though, provide the greatest similarity between the two. Study of hundreds of photographs of petrified or mummified corpses and comparison of them to one another shows no similarities—except between McGinty and Sylvester. Add to this resemblance that McGinty passed for the last time from Jeff's ownership in 1896, that Sylvester's story begins in 1895, and that McGinty was last known as going to the same state where Sylvester now resides, and the odds grow in favor of the two being one. With the persistence of research efforts and time, a paper trail consisting of such things as bills of sale, storage receipts, and diary entries may reveal with certainty that McGinty went on to a new identify and career as Sylvester. If so, Soapy would likely be pleased to know that his over one-hundred-year-old sideshow is still on the job.

One possibility regarding the previous identity of McGinty is the "Louisiana Kid." Reported wounded in the head and body after shooting it out with Joe Palmer and the Soap Gang on February 11, 1892, the "Kid" was never heard from or seen again, at least not as he had been known. Scans of Sylvester show wounds similar to those of the "Louisiana Kid." *The Mummy Road Show* examiners of Sylvester state that Sylvester was manufactured into a petrified state "very quickly after death." If the "Kid" had died of his wounds and been gathered up by the Soap Gang, as a cadaver of convenience for petrifaction, then two extreme possibilities come to mind. This author can imagine a petrifaction firm informing Jeff that "We can make you a genuine looking petrified man. Just deliver us a body." Even if such a firm were as far off as California, rail service could have delivered it in two days if on ice, and the "Kid" might have already been frozen, having died of his wounds while taking flight. It was, after all, winter at a high elevation when he fled into the night, severely wounded.

While Jeff was in Denver, on June 5, 1892, a disaster of the worst kind struck Creede: fire. It had previously broken out on April 14 in John Kinneavy's triangle-shaped saloon before it had opened for business. Quickly discovered, it was easily extinguished.[1] Fifty-two days later, a new blaze began in Kinneavy's, but this time it broke free, roared into the business district, and grew into an inferno well beyond the camp's ability to contain. It consumed the entire business district, right down to the ground, including Jeff's Orleans Club. Amazingly no lives were lost, but the loss of property was enormous. The *Denver Republican* reported the ensuring trouble:

> Following the fire, a wild debauch was entered into by the sots and fast women of the camp. Free liquors were had for the stealing, and many cases of wines, bottles of whiskey, boxes of cigars, and such goods were seized and hundreds were drunk before the flames had half burned down. Prompt work by the respectable element of the camp prevented this lawlessness from getting too far. Dozens of men were commissioned special officers by the mayor and these ... arrested robbers, and took away the liquors.... Good order was soon restored and maintained for the rest of the day.[2]

---

[1] *Creede Herald* 04/15/1892.
[2] *Denver Republican* 06/05/1892.

Jeff told the *News* that he lost two buildings in the fire, totaling $8,000 in value, neither being insured. He was reported to have already bought a tent one hundred feet in length and that he would return to Creede to erect it where his buildings had stood. Jeff estimated the total loss at $300,000 but was optimistic about Creede's future:

> The business portion of the town will be moved to a safer place further down the stream. I have been in every important mining camp of the world, but have seen none equal to Creede. I verily believe that within twelve months there will be 10,000 miners at work in the district. Every man that has a prospect hole stands a fair chance of making a fortune."[1]

Beyond this optimistic view and Jeff's stated intention to return to Creede, no records show that he did, although he might have. The business district would be rebuilt, a miniature of its former self, and Creede live on, but without Jeff and his associates. However, as late as December 30, 1893, Jeff still had property and mine interests in Creede that were looked after by a M. F. Stilwell who was under contract to do so.[2]

On May 29, 1892, Bob Ford opened a dance hall in Creede.[3] It was razed 7 days later by the big fire. He purchased a large tent and reopened a makeshift saloon. On June 8, 3 days after the fire, Ford, the killer of Jesse James, was shot dead. He had entered his tent saloon, followed by a man with a shotgun. The man was Edward Capehart O'Kelley, ex-policeman of Pueblo and ex-marshal of Bachelor City, near Creede. Ford was facing away when O'Kelley said, "Hello, Bob." As Ford turned, O'Kelley sent Ford to his death with a double barrel shotgun blast to the throat.

O'Kelley and Ford had had several altercations in Pueblo. These were probably the reason for the killing.[4] Some accounts claim that Jeff may have talked O'Kelley into murdering Ford. Jeff could have been in Creede at the time. He was reported saying that he would return to look after his properties and the loss of the Orleans Club, but no evidence of Jeff's being in Creede after the big fire has been found. The men were not on friendly terms, but, Jeff had used his influence on Ford's behalf because Ford was a friend of Jeff's man Joe Palmer. Moreover, no legitimate reason is known for Jeff to want Ford dead. Ford was a troublemaker, but he was no competition or identified threat to Jeff's dominance or commerce.

However, according to a story handed down through the Smith family, members of the Soap Gang often teased Ford. A little after he went to bed, from the street would begin the faint singing of a song Ford had come to hate.

... Jesse had a wife,	But that dirty little coward,
A lady all her life,	That shot Mr. Howard,[5]
Three children, they were brave.	Has laid Jesse James in his grave.[6]

---

[1] *RMN* 06/06/1892, p. 1.

[2] Contract to look after properties 12/31/1893. Item 109, author's col.

[3] *Creede Candle* 06/03/1892, p. 4.

[4] Ries, p. 72.

[5] *Mr. Howard*: the alias James was living under.

[6] As told to author by his father, John R. Smith. Full lyrics to this song are available online (Nelson-Burns).

Boomtown Creede was a high point in Jeff's career. With acuteness and subtlety, bravado and style, power and restraint, Jeff exercised leadership and all his various skills. The financial profit accruing to Jeff and his associates and friends must have been enormous. Thousands of men thronged Creede in those early boomtown winter months, and most of them had money to spend. To Jeff as well as others in his sphere, he must have seemed on the way to achieving his potential as a significant player, another Big Ed Chase—in time, perhaps bigger. But especially for a gambler, even one said to be lucky, that ever-spinning wheel of fortune cannot always favor the player. And Jeff Smith was not just a serious gambler at the faro table. He was a passionate and daring gambler in all things. When rebellion against Jeff and the Soap Gang appeared in Creede and the *Candle* became crammed with new ordinances, Jeff packed up McGinty, put his Orleans Club and other properties in capable hands, and moved on. As timing in the arrival to a new boom-camp was crucial, so was the point at which to leave. Not heeding the danger signs could be deadly as persons other than Jeff would learn in Skaguay six years later.

Chapter 11
A Denver Killing and the Panic of 1893

A man will be lured into a gambling hell and fascinated so that he will go again and again, until he is forever lost. After a man once comes to my place he is cured of gambling absolutely. He doesn't want any more of it.

—Jefferson R. Smith II
Rocky Mountain News, 9/8/1893

No sooner had Jeff returned to Denver and the Tivoli Club than political friends old and new rushed him back into politics. Known as one who could deliver strict control of the saloons and the streets as well as gently work the halls of power, Jeff was called upon to employ his abilities. But no amount of control and work could keep the seeds of national economic trouble from sprouting into the Panic of 1893. The stress of these busy, frustrating, and occasionally desperate times helped summon the most violent behavior yet in both Jeff and Bascomb, several times nearly costing them their lives. Additionally, as Jeff witnessed the dramatic increase of suffering among Denver's populace, he engaged in his greatest recorded period of charity work and personal giving.

At the April 1892 local Republican convention, Jeff was elected alternate delegate from the fourth district, precinct five.[1] Jeff may have been willing to become publicly involved in politics because things were so bad. The national economy was disintegrating and Denver was in trouble. Jeff and the Soap Gang had an increasingly hard time separating victims from their hard-earned, ever-more scarce dollars.

Toward the end of July 1892, Jeff and John Bowers were arrested. Bowers had made the usual acquaintance of an out-of-towner named John Cully. Posing as a prospector, Bowers said he would like to show Cully some ore specimens. Entering a

---

[1] *RMN* 04/24/1892, p. 3.

room above the Tivoli Club, the pair found the usual "big hand" swindle, staged and waiting. Invited to sit in, Cully flatly refused, and a fight erupted. By the time police arrived, the melee had progressed downstairs and outside. Cully was found cornered between a telegraph pole and a wagon, defending himself with an umbrella. Jeff, according to the *Denver Republican*, held a cigar cutter and Bowers a cane. Jeff denied connection with the fight, but a bystander told a different story. Jeff grew agitated, accused the bystander of lying, and reaching over the shoulder of one of the officers, struck the witness between the eyes with his fist. Jeff, Bowers, and Cully were arrested, the Tivoli Club was closed for the night, and Jeff was charged with assault.[1]

Not known is how the fracas was resolved, but it probably followed a familiar pattern. Jeff's friend John Kinneavy went to the Denver jail to post bail. At the hearing the defense argued that the trouble was just the result of a misunderstanding. That is, if charges for the arrest ever made it to a hearing. Jeff's influence among both the police and city officials was well in hand at this time. The city license for the Tivoli Club, under the name of William Deutsch, had come due, and it was renewed without objection.[2] As for Cully, he likely paid a fine, finished his Denver business, and did not set foot on Seventeenth Street again except to go to his train at Union Station.

During the first week of September, the Arapahoe County Republican party held its 1892 convention in Denver. As a delegate, Jeff controlled the district G voting block. Additionally, to secure the nomination for the "right" person, he and Ed Chase were said to be responsible for distributing payoffs, or "boodle," during the convention.

> Jeff Smith is the individual who is known as "Soapy" Smith. This appellation was well earned by his former lucrative occupation of selling small cakes of soap from the street corners and pretending to place $50, $10 and $5 in certain of the packages.... Since giving up this plebian style of gaining a dishonest livelihood, Smith has run sure-thing gambling houses in Denver and Creede and made a great deal of money from the unsophisticated by operating the shell game and three-card monte through his employees in mining camps, at resorts and at out of town picnics. He has squandered the money, it is true, but that has only served to make his rapaciousness the greater. Earl B. Coe, the Republican nominee for congress, owes his nomination to "Soapy" Smith in great part. Ed Chase and Smith distributed a large amount of tramway and Coe boodle among the delegates to the Republican county convention, and he is ready and preparing for the same kind of work on election day.[3]

The convention caucus floor swirled with boisterous dissent as men shouted vile language at one another. Several times, violent outbreaks caused the chairman to summon the police, who entered the crowd with batons. Several delegates drew revolvers, but no shots were fired. However, in the ensuing fights, tables and chairs were smashed to splinters.[4] The dissention was over which Republican candidate to

---

[1] *Denver Republican* 07/27/1892.

[2] *RMN* 07/31/1892, p. 8.

[3] *RMN* 10/05/1892, p. 3.

[4] *RMN* 09/06/1892, pp. 1-2, 6.

back for Congress. "The Ring," as head Republican Denver officials were called, was able to thrust the unknown Coe into the lead position. The Ring saw this collections attorney and real estate scalper, who had no political experience, as the perfect choice. He was entirely willing to be told by the Ring what to do. Appointed chairman at the Republican county committee, Coe had authority to fill the positions that formed what was known as "the Combine." This group essentially controlled the county executive committee whose goal was to control the coming election.

Each Combine member had his own agenda, and Jeff was an employee or associate of most them, as will be seen, in the election of 1892. The Combine included very powerful and ambitious Denverites, including the following: **Nathaniel P. Hill** hoped to head an anti-silver delegation and to go into the cabinet under President Benjamin Harrison. **David H. Moffat** hoped to control the legislature conjointly with William Evans in getting laws enacted to force out their competition. **William Gray Evans** of the Denver City Tramway Company worked with Moffat to eliminate competition for street railways and paving contracts worth millions of tax-payer dollars. **Joe H. Smith** expected to become chairman of the fire and police board and run the politics of the city. **A. M. Stevenson** expected to be chairman of the board of public works. **Bill Hamill** desired to perpetrate himself as railroad commissioner. **Dave Kelly** expected a fat contract to furnish onyx for the new capitol building. **Bill Griffith** desired to make himself even on his losses on the *Denver Sun* and to float a bunco land scheme in Arizona with Coe in the event of the latter's election to Congress.

With the right people in elected office, **Jeff, Ed Chase, Jack Devine, Mike Ryan, and Billy Woods** could look ahead to staying out of the penitentiary whatever they might do. Ryan was a good example of what could be done. He was supposed to have been serving time in Cañon City prison for drugging and robbing a farmer of $5500, but he was released on a "supersedeas" bond[1] issued with the help of Justice J. C. Heim—who was running for governor. Other than the unique ability of Ryan to steer election fraud, no other reason has been discovered for his release.

During the course of primary electioneering, gamblers who had backed William Burchinell for sheriff changed alliances. The shift put Burchinell in search of revenge. On the evening of September 5 the bitter sheriff ordered the closing of every gambling house, pool hall, and policy shop in the city. Police were not notified of the order, so confusion and debate ensued over whether the order was actual. The *News* interviewed Burchinell, who said he planned to keep the gambling dens closed for about a week or so until he could weed out the undesirable class. It would appear his plan was to put those who did not side with him out of business. The *News* interviewed several of the gambling house proprietors, including Jeff, who said,

> "The sheriff is sore because a certain clique of gamblers who have always been on his side switched. It was directly due to the primary results."
> "Will you close your gambling tables?"
> "Perhaps."

---

[1] *Supersedeas bond*: "writ of supersedeas," legal idiom. "A writ commanding the stay of legal proceedings which ought otherwise to have proceeded...." (*OED*)

Smith [also] has an establishment in Jefferson county, opposite Manhattan Beach and now smiles serenely when he thinks of it—the only place in sight for the fervid pursuer of fickle fortune.[1]

A majority of the Republican county committee revolted against the Combine and elected George Cook chairman in place of Coe. The *News* reported the revolt and thought "that was that" until the following day. The Combine flatly refused to accede. Republican delegates wanting to see Cook were forced to undergo questioning by Combine rogues. Jeff was more than willing to see people pushed around for the good of the Combine. A shooting in mid October, however, preoccupied Jeff for a time.

Two checks in the author's collection, made out for a total of $1,700,[2] indicate that dupes were still being taken for large amounts of money but that it was becoming harder and more dangerous to collect it. Clearly Jeff believed his line of work had become hazardous enough that when offered a life and accident insurance policy with his subscription to the *Denver Times*, he bought it. The policy came from the Travelers Insurance Company of Hartford, Connecticut.[3] Naturally, Jeff wanted to be sure his family could care for itself financially in the event he suffered an accident. On the policy, Jeff listed his occupation as auctioneer. Given his true profession and its hazards, however, should Jeff's heirs have tried to collect on the policy, benefits might have been denied. Among the events that would void the policy were accidents or death that involved intoxication, dueling or fighting, violating the law, and exposure to unnecessary danger. Two months later, Jeff almost involuntarily tested the bounds of his policy. It was the evening of October 11, 1892, when Jeff used his gun and a gambler named Cliff Sparks died on a barroom floor.

Cliff Sparks, a gambler, was killed in Murphy's Exchange at 11:50 last night. He was shot through the body by either Jim Jordan, another gambler, or by Jeff Smith, known more familiarly as "Soapy."

The tragedy was the culmination of a row between Jordan and Tom Cady. Cady is a shell game fakir, working for Smith. Sparks fell and died in a few minutes. The abdominal aorta was severed by the bullet which passed through him. Smith and Cady escaped from the rear of the building. Jordan was arrested by Officer Hunt, who met him as he was going out of the side front entrance of the saloon. Jordan had a hot revolver of heavy caliber in his hand.... All he would say was that it was an accident.

Earlier in the night Jeff Argyle, proprietor of the Missouri gambling house, and Tom Cady had trouble in the exchange gambling room, next door above the scene of the homicide. They had a quarrel over poker chips. Cady sprang to his feet and struck Argyle in the face, knocking him off his chair. Argyle rose and pulled his revolver. Special Officer Gardiner seized Argyle's arm as the latter fired. The bullet, through this move, struck Cady's chair. Both men

---

[1] *RMN* 09/05/1892, p. 5.
[2] Bank drafts fr J. Webber, (1) $1500, 07/03/1892, & (2) $200, 12/22/1892. Jefferson R. "Little Randy" Smith col.
[3] Life insurance policy, 08/19/1892, item 17, author's col.

were arrested and Cady was subsequently released. Cady went directly to Murphy's Exchange again and was joined by Jeff Smith and Cort Thomson.

"Troublesome Tom" Cady had the altercation with "The Black Prince" Jeff Argyle in the upstairs gambling room of Dale & Company above Murphy's Exchange, and both had been arrested. However, the *Denver Republican* states that the row between Cady and Argyle started in the Missouri Club, in which Argyle was actually the manager, not the proprietor as stated in the *News*. Argyle, a noted killer, a year before had gunned down a bricklayer playing at one of his Missouri Club faro tables.[1] Upon learning of Cady's arrest, Jeff posted bail for his friend at the jail, and together they went to Murphy's Exchange. In the first-floor saloon were Clifton Sparks, James B. "Gambler" Jordan (aka Henry Gilmore), and Corteze "Cort" Thomson, a friend of Jordan's and not known to be on good terms with Jeff or Cady. As Jeff and Tom

> entered the bar-room of the saloon Jordan met them. They drank together and the affair earlier in the night came up. Jordan said to Cady that he was sorry for it. "Yes, you are, you ___ ___ ___ ___" responded Cady as he instantly struck Jordan in the face.[2]

The *News* published what it could learn of the details.

> Jordan drew his pistol. Smith drew his. Mart Watrous grabbed Jordan and carried him toward the front of the bar-room near the lattice work partition.
>
> In a statement, Watrous said he grabbed Jordan and threw him down in an attempt to keep him from drawing his gun. As he did, Jordan said, "Let me go, or we'll be killed."[3] ...
>
> Murphy pushed Cady, Smith, and Thompson back toward the rear of the room. The two principal combatants were fully thirty feet apart. Cady started for Jordan again and Murphy struck him. Cady said to Smith: "Shoot him," meaning Murphy.
>
> Sparks, who had been standing back from the bar, midway between the front and the rear, stepped forward to protest against the shooting and Murphy jumped back out of range and Jordan and Smith shot at almost the same instant. The bullet from Smith's pistol crashed through a plate glass ... partition leading to the front, an elevation of seven and a half feet from the floor. Jordan's bullet was not found up to 2 o'clock this morning. Which hit Sparks has not yet been determined. Jordan intended to kill Cady, and Smith meant to kill Murphy, without doubt.
>
> When the patrol wagon arrived the doors of the place were closed and an eager crowd surged outside in the pouring rain, vainly endeavoring to see through the drawn curtains.
>
> Inside was confusion. Policeman Hunt ... held Jordan by the collar with one hand, while in the other he held the smoking revolver taken from his

---

[1] Parkhill, p. 92.

[2] *RMN* 10/12/1892, p. 1.

[3] *RMN* 10/20/1892, p. 6.

prisoner. ... At the other end of the bar lay the innocent victim of the evening's quarrels, breathing his last. The bullet, fired either by Jordan, his friend, or Jeff Smith, his enemy, had entered just over the left hip, passed clear through the body, severing the abdominal aorta, and came out an inch above the right hip bone.

The cutting of the artery caused death before Surgeon Wheeler had time to examine the wound. A dozen men stood about ... gaping at the dead body and the hole in the partition made by the other bullet. Murphy was applying ice to a huge contusion under his left eye, caused by the blow from Cady's cane in his attempt to arrest the latter and Jeff Smith. ...

Mart Watrous, the proprietor..., saw the quarrel leading up to the shooting and had just released Jordan when the gun, or guns, went off. ... "I was standing in front of the bar," he said, "and Cady and Jeff Smith had just finished drinking. Jordan was standing near them at the time and as Cady turned around, he said to him: 'Tom, I'm sorry you got into trouble.'"

"'You're a liar, you ___ ___ ___,' said Cady, and he hit Jordan in the face. Jordan reeled back, and drew his gun as he did so. I jumped and caught him and ran him against the bar in the corner near the folding door. I saw a gun in Jeff Smith's hand. I let go of Jordan, and as I did so I heard a shot go and saw Sparks fall.

"There may have been two shots—I think there were, judging from the course the bullet must have taken that went through the glass—but I only heard one report."

"As soon as Cady had been bailed out after his trouble with Argyle, he returned to my place, accompanied by Jeff Smith. Jordan, Sparks and the others were there, and Smith proposed the drinks. In the conversation that followed, the latter accused Watrous and myself of acting unfairly in not trying to get bail for Cady as well as Argyle.

"In the heated discussion that followed, Cady called Jordan a ___ ___ ___, and struck him. The men were separated, Thompson and Mart hauling Jordan back to the front of the room, while I pushed Cady the other way.

"As I made for Cady he cried to Smith, "Shoot, Jeff; shoot the ___ ___ ___, I called to Sparks, who was behind me, to stop the row, and he stepped forward. At that instant I heard two shots in close succession and saw Sparks stagger. As he reeled toward the bar Cady ran at him and felled him with a blow on the head. ... "Just then I heard Smith cry, 'Tom, let's get out of this,' and he and Cady started for the rear room. I followed ... and knocked Cady down, and turned toward Smith. As I did so Cady picked up the cane I had dropped and dealt me a blow under the eye. Both ... ran out the back door and disappeared. ... "Sparks was facing Cady and Smith when he was shot, and I can't tell which shot him."

Thompson's statement corroborates that of Murphy in all its details. He helped pull Jordan back and held the latter until he had drawn his revolver and threatened to shoot him, when he let go. He heard two shots and saw Smith shoot, but couldn't say which it was that shot Sparks.

Smith gave himself up at 1:30 o'clock this morning. He had a heavy revolver, with all the chambers loaded, and Thompson and Murphy were arrested and jailed as witnesses.

The police restrained people from entering the saloon, but outside, within ten minutes, there were fully 300 men.

Sparks has been a gambler in Colorado and Denver for fourteen years. He was 40 years of age and unmarried. He was dressed finely and wore good jewelry. His father is a physician in St. Joseph.[1]

The next day's *News* reported more information from the coroner's jury. The story began with how the Jeff Argyle and Tom Cady trouble

had little to do with the shooting of Sparks. Jordan drew his revolver to avenge an old fancied wrong. He drew to kill either Smith or Cady. He cared but little which. He was nervous and saw his enemies, each with a weapon. Before he could raise to gain aim, his finger pressed the trigger and the ball flew in a wrong course. The weapon fired at him was used with equal haste. Neither party desired to take any chance, and their bullets went wild. A witness well known and whose word cannot be doubted stated that Jordan's revolver belched forth its leaden ball when he was holding it on level with his wrist. The same witness is quite sure of the course of this death messenger. Jordan's bullet, he says, killed Sparks.

The cause of the ill feeling between Smith, Cady and Jordan is said to have originated in Chicago several years ago. The three men were together in a deal of some kind, the profit of which was several thousand dollars. Cady and Smith had control of the money and a settlement satisfactory to Jordan has never been reached.

The coroner's inquest was commenced at 2 o'clock and lasted until nearly 8. ... The testimony of Johnny Murphy was the most important. Testimony that would have been much more valuable could not be obtained and the coroner reported this fact to the district attorney.

An excited group in the front room of the morgue awaited the verdic' of the jury, which was as follows:

"The deceased came to his death in Murphy's exchange, 1717 Larimer street, Denver, Arapahoe county, Colorado, about 11:50 p.m. October 11, 1892, by a gunshot wound caused by a pistol ball fired from a revolver in the hands of James Jordan. We further find that said shooting was felonious, and that Thomas Keady or Cady was accessory to the same."...

William Vance, one of the coroner's employees, was the first witness. He said: "I received word by telephone that a man was dead at Murphy's exchange. I entered the bar room and on the floor, two-thirds of the way down the bar, a man lay with his feet towards the back part of the building and his head almost against the partition, and an overcoat over his head. I hunted for a revolver, but found none. In undressing him I found the bullet

---

[1] *RMN* 10/12/1892, pp. 1-2.

had gone through the overcoat on the left side, through all of the clothes and through the man, again through his underclothes and coat, and lodged in the right overcoat pocket."

John W. Murphy was kept on the stand much longer than the other witnesses to the affray. His testimony went more in details. After narrating circumstances down to the time blows were exchanged, witness continued:

"I told Jeff to be quiet. Just at this time a shot was fired. I then let go of Cady and rushed towards Smith. As I did so Sparks staggered and fell, Cady striking him at the same time. I caught hold of Cady again and he struck me crying, 'Jeff, get him. He has a knife,' meaning me. He then picked up my cane and struck me twice, at the same time the police entered and Smith and Cady went out the back door. I went where Sparks was lying, and Sparks said to me in a low tone, 'John, what do you think of it?' I replied, 'Cliff, it is off at Sheepshead. You are gone.'[1] He did not reply to this. He had spoken his last word. There were two shots fired, possibly three. I think Cady fired one shot. I think that the shot that killed Sparks was fired by Cady. I did not see Jordan fire, as Watrous had him in the corner. Sparks was standing facing the back end of the bar. Cady and Sparks were standing together not four feet apart. Sparks' left side was towards Cady. Smith was in front of him when the shot was fired. I do not know whether he shot or not. Cady had a small derringer, with a caliber not less than 44." ...

The omission of Smith's name from the verdict created some surprise, even chagrin among many interested. Cady having [been] held as an accessory was largely due to Murphy's testimony. He was arrested by Lieutenant Clay and Detective Currier early in the day at his residence on Curtis street. He with Jordan and Smith were transferred to the county jail on a warrant for murder sworn out in Justice La Bert's court by officer Hunt. Deputy Sheriff DeLue served the papers, and took them in a hack to their new quarters. No effort was made to procure a bond. The preliminary hearing will probably take place to-day. Judge Furman has been retained by Jordan and Mr. Barton by Smith and Cady. The verdict of the coroner's jury does not necessarily release Smith.

The history of the men engaged in the shooting is interesting. The deceased is an old-time Western gambler and has been in Denver on and off for seventeen years. For years he was a member of the notorious "Doc" Baggs gang, composed of expert confidence men. At the time of his death an indictment for robbery hung over his head. He was married in Chicago eleven years ago to a young lady from Council Bluffs. His domestic life has always

---

[1] *"Cliff, it is off at Sheepshead. You are gone."* Murphy appears to have chosen to tell Cliff Sparks that he was mortally wounded by way of allusion to *sheepshead*, or *schafskopf*, a card game. Probably of German origin, it is traced out of Wisconsin (1886). Players lay down cards in succession. "It is off" may refer to what is called a "smear," or an uncommon set of cards that have been played. Who wins is not known until all players have laid down their cards. A possible interpretation, then, is that "the others in this game have made their plays, including a smear, and you can't win against it." Sparks had been "smeared," and it was not in his cards to win. (*DARE, sheepshead,* 5)

been happy and last night his widow left with his remains for his old home in St. Joseph, Mo.

The rumor that Sparks had been robbed after death of a valuable watch and a diamond pin was found to be untrue. Deceased did not have a watch on his person at the time of his death. His diamonds were transferred by the coroner to Mrs. Sparks.

The records of Jeff Smith and Cady are too well known to rehearse.[1]

Yarns over time have come to tell of a man claiming to be a friend of Sparks' coming onto the scene and weeping over his dead friend, placing his head down to the dead man's chest as if to listen for any sign of a heart beat, and with no one the wiser, removing Sparks' diamond stick pin with his teeth. The story started because Sparks had no watch on his person at the time of his death. It was determined that he had entered the saloon not wearing a watch. The diamonds on Sparks that were said to have been stolen were in fact removed by the coroner and given to Mrs. Sparks, a common procedure at the time.

The *News* published how things stood.

Groups of well-known gamblers yesterday discussed the shooting in all the downtown saloons and the general impression prevails that the scene enacted in Murphy's exchange on Tuesday night will prove but a prelude to a bitter warfare between a well known gang of men who live by their wits and dollars gained by fleecing. The ill-feeling has been smoldering of late and needed but slight provocation to fan it into a blaze of crime.[2]

No one could agree on who precisely had shot Sparks. Cady and Jordan were held without bond. Jeff was arraigned before Judge Burns and charged with the murder. With Judge Belford at his side, Jeff pled not guilty. Belford filed a motion to separate Jeff's trial from that of Cady and Jordan. The motion was granted. On October 13, 1892, two days after the shooting, Jeff was released by Justice Le Bert on bond of $10,000, which was signed by Ed Chase.[3] Accusations stated that Jeff was released six days before his preliminary hearing due to his strong political ties in the county Republican party.[4] The *News* questioned the ethics of the court in releasing Jeff for any amount of money.

Whether Jeff Smith is in any way responsible for the murder of Cliff Sparks or not has little to do with the case. A man charged with murder is usually held without bail until the preliminary hearing. This rule is seldom deviated from. The testimony in the corner's inquest was necessarily incomplete. It was held hurriedly but twelve hours after the murder and some of the most important and unprejudiced witnesses were not subpoenaed. The coroner did not have time to learn who were present at the time of the shooting. Two of the principal witnesses, Cort Thomson and John Murphy, testified that the shot

---

[1] *RMN* 10/13/1892, p. 5.
[2] RMN 10/13/1892, p. 5.
[3] *Boulder Daily Camera* 10/14/1892, p. 1.
[4] *RMN* 10/19/1892, p. 8.

that killed Sparks came from where Smith and Cady were standing and it has not surely been determined which of these two men had the pistol.

Another point that has caused general comment is that warrants charging the men under arrest with murder were sworn out before the inquest was terminated. In every case where law reigns untrammeled by political chicanery the warrants are not sworn out until after the inquest, and then the coroner performs this duty....[1]

Jeff had to spend two days in jail, and in addition, his Tivoli Club was ordered closed.[2] Murphy's Exchange was allowed to continue operating although it was the location of the shooting and held a worse reputation. The *Denver Republican* in noting this fact, figured favoritism in its October 14 issue, questioned the reasoning.

The Fire and Police board just yesterday had discussed the killing of Sparks and the best plan to pursue in preventing such crimes in the future. For some unaccountable reason they have proceeded to close the gambling house of "Soapy" Smith and Dale & Co.[3] They give as the reason that "these places have been the scene of many disorderly occurrences." Exactly what evidence they have that Dale & Co. have kept a place that was disorderly does not appear. On the contrary the facts are that it is one of the most orderly houses of its kind in Denver. It is one of the places that has not been troublesome to the police. No gambling house in Denver has so clean a record and none has been run with so little police interference.

The prime cause of the murder Tuesday night was a quarrel entered into by Jeff Argyle of the notorious Missouri club [−] where a year or more ago, "The Black Prince" shot a bricklayer and [at] "Troublesome Tom Cady," the manipulator of the walnut shells. That the trouble which ended fatally began in the Missouri club no one who knows the facts questions for a moment. The scene of action was transferred to Murphy's Exchange, where shooting was indulged in and Cady arrested.

Was it for this then that the Missouri club was allowed to remain open, that Murphy's Exchange is open, and that the gambling house of Dale & Co. is closed?

In Argyle's place the "Black Prince" shot a player at his faro table and within two years, in Murphy's Exchange, there have been three shooting scrapes that ended fatally. Yet these slaughter houses are allowed to remain open, and the unsuspecting gamblers or plain man is invited to enter and get himself shot or carved up.... On the other hand, a place where never yet has occurred a fatal affair, is hit upon by the Police board and ordered closed. Thus the ruling spirits are satisfied and the long suffering public is in as great danger as ever.[4]

---

[1] *RMN* 10/14/1892, p. 2.

[2] *Denver Republican* 10/14/1892.

[3] *"Soapy" Smith and Dale & Co.*: Jeff had sold the Tivoli Club in October 1891 to Robert Gardner. At some point it appears he became partners in "Dale & Co." in owning the Tivoli Club again.

[4] *Denver Republican* 10/14/1892, p. 3.

The *Denver Republican* could have no idea it had moved too quickly in the publication of its opinion. Two days later, a Soap Gang steerer nearly killed a woman in a private room of the Tivoli Club. According to the *News*, "Jeff Dunbar, one of Soapy's steerers, and a general all around athlete in the art of heeling,"[1] was fleecing a Miss Flossie Leigh of her money. On October 15, 1892, less than a week after the Sparks killing, Dunbar asked Flossie to meet him at the Tivoli Club. The purpose of the meeting was never determined, but it seems likely to have involved a "sure thing" transaction. A detail to emerge was that when it came time for Flossie to produce money, she refused.

> He became abusive and the woman got up to leave, when Dunbar pulled out his gun and struck her violently over the top of the head with it. As she staggered to the floor he struck her a second blow on the forehead, and she sank bleeding and senseless to the floor.

> Dunbar immediately fled out the side door and the men in the saloon, attracted by the noise of the assault, ran in and found the woman senseless on the floor, her scalp torn and bleeding from the blows. A doctor was summoned and the wounds dressed as hastily as possible. Miss Leigh was placed in a hack and driven to her home. Her skull is thought to be fractured near the base and it is not certain that she will live.

> A warrant for the arrest of Dunbar was sworn out ... and is now in the hands of the constable for service whenever he can find Dunbar.

> This is the first attempt in Soapy's new blood-letting establishment.[2] It is just possible that the next woman who ventures into the death trap will be instantly killed.[3]

Dunbar appears never to have answered for his assault.

Cady and Jordan were held without bond for the murder of Sparks. Cady was also charged with being an accessory.[4] On November 20 Jordan was released on $7,500 sureties signed by Mart Watrous and Sam Blonger.[5] Ten days later they did the same for Cady.[6] One year and fifteen days from the date of Sparks murder, the trials against Jeff, Jordan, and Cady began. Jeff, represented by Judge James Belford in a separate trial, pled not guilty. Cady was found not guilty on October 28, 1893, as no evidence existed that he had fired a shot.[7] This left the fault with either Jeff or Jordan.

In Jeff's case, it apparently took about two months to convince Judge Burns to drop the murder charge. Newspapers had interest in the complex death, but in tracking it for over a year, media sometimes seemed to lose track and events have to be inferred from their lack of mention. Jordan's case was the last to go to trial. The

---

[1] *art of heeling*: (1) "heeler": a working dog that urges animals onwards by nipping at their heels (4.b. *OED*). (2) "to heel": to lariat an animal by the hind leg. (*Scribner's Magazine* 1887, *DARE*) Hence the art of herding, roping, tripping up.

[2] *Soapy's new blood-letting establishment*: a reference to the new partnership with Dale and Co.

[3] *RMN* 10/16/1892, p. 3.

[4] *Boulder Daily Camera* 10/14/1892, p. 1.

[5] *RMN* 11/20/1892, p. 15.

[6] *RMN* 11/30/1892, p. 2.

[7] *RMN* 10/28/1893, p. 3.

previous coroner's verdict had charged Jordan with felonious murder. At trial, his defense was lack of intention as his pistol had discharged prematurely. Finally, the charge of murder against Jordan was dropped as well. The question of who shot Cliff Sparks was left unanswered.

After Jeff's death in 1898, Denver barber William H. Morton, who often cut Jeff's hair, described the method he thought Jeff used in the Sparks killing.

> Smith was a dangerous man and a shooter. He was a smooth fighter, though, and he shot only when he saw that the crime could not be traced to him. His enemies claimed that his usual way was to corner his man, get four or five of his associates around and then have all of them shoot together. All used the same kind of revolvers, and the man who fired the fatal shot could never be found. The killed party was never hit by more than one bullet. A man named Sparks was killed in this way in Denver. Four shots were fired by Smith and his three associates. Three bullets struck three different corners and one struck Sparks. Smith was tried for the crime and escaped punishment. Five or six murders in all were attributed to Smith.[1]

In a 1914 interview with the *Denver Post,* Henry "Yank Fewclothes" Edwards spoke about the gunfight that night. "'Soapy' was charged with the crime. It couldn't be proved against him and he was freed, althou[gh] several witnesses declared on the stand that they had seen Smith fire."[2] Good friend to Jeff that he was, Yank would or could not say outright that Jeff had gunned down Sparks. In one of Jeff's notebooks appears a column of names and money amounts. Watrous' name is at the top of the list with "$200" beside it (about $6,000 today).[3] As the notebook is undated, not known is if the money were being paid out or taken in. Whether Jeff paid Watrous to obscure what he had witnessed cannot be known, only suspected. Who shot Sparks cannot be certain, but a point of note is that if Jeff did not hit Sparks, then it would be the only known shooting incident in which he used his gun to no effect. One comment can be made with certainty, that Murphy's Exchange was a dangerous place. On the back of an historical photograph of the site appears the following handwritten note: "Larimer Street from 17th — Old 'Murphy's Exchange' whose history is written in blood."[4]

Cort Thomson, arrested early on as a witness in the Sparks shooting, testified that he saw Jeff draw his gun and that either Smith or Cady had killed Sparks.[5] This testimony surely created a grudge between Jeff and Thomson, including Thomson's devoted wife, famed Denver bordello madam Mattie Silks. Six years later in 1898 that grudge against Jeff, which became mutual, bore bitter fruit. Mattie, whom Jeff had frightened out of Skaguay, made devastating public accusations against Jeff and the Soap Gang that were read up and down the West coast and in Washington, DC.

---

[1] *Morning Oregonian* 07/17/1898, p. 8.
[2] *Denver Post* 11/15/1914, p. 10. Item 163, author's col.
[3] Notebook, handwritten notes by Jefferson R. Smith II, unk date. Item #69, author's col. Tom's Inflation Calculator.
[4] Denver Public Library photograph, circa latter 1890s, call number X-25715.
[5] *RMN* 10/20/1892, p. 6.

Accounts vary about when and where Mattie Silks was born; some say 1846 in Kansas, others 1848 in Indiana. Accounts agree, however, that in 1865 at about age nineteen, Mattie owned and operated a bordello in Springfield, Illinois. After about ten years as a madam of working girls among cowboys and miners, she came to Denver in 1876, a few years ahead of Jeff. By 1887, Mattie owned and operated three "houses" in Denver, all of which thrived due to her proactive, generous relationship with city hall and the Denver police. She met Cort Thomson sometime in 1877. He was a handsome athlete who often won local running competitions. At gambling, though, for which he had a mania, he rarely won. Mattie successfully vied for his attention by lavishing him with as much money as he could gamble. When in 1884 the first wife of Cort Thomson died, Mattie married him.[1]

It was not an easy marriage as Cort could be "poison mean."

"Cort Thomson was an unusually handsome fellow, slightly under medium height," says Colonel W. S. Billy Thompson, of Denver, former bartender at the Exchange; "he was what you'd call a 'swell' dresser—the best of everything, trim and neat, and not much jewelry.

"Because of the similarity of our names he always called me 'Cousin Bill.' When he was sober you couldn't want to meet a pleasanter fellow, but when he wasn't, it was time to look a little bit out. He could be poison mean.

"One night when Cort had a few too many George Watrous, the head bartender, tried to give him the bum's rush. Cort reached for his hip. I knew he carried two pistols in his hip pockets, so I grabbed him from behind and said to George, 'Get behind the bar and let me handle this. Cort will do what I say, because we're cousins. Aren't we, Cort?'

"Cort said, 'Sure, Cousin Bill,' I took him outside and called a hack and sent him home."[2]

Talk about town was that Jeff Smith was a protected favorite of his city hall friends. It is not hard to figure why. Five days after the slaying of Cliff Sparks, on October 16, 1892, the *News* published a front-page political cartoon showing the city fathers around a table, planning the next election strategy.[3] The cartoon caption reads, "Districting of Arapahoe County by the Republican Leaders—"Planting" hobos for Registration and Voting." Jeff is studying a map of the county as others point to areas where "help" would be needed. Like a field officer, Jeff was relied upon to supply that help through lieutenants. And Jeff's price if successful, protection. Among the coterie of cronies are **Jack Devine** (quick-tempered, political hanger-on whom Jeff shot in an 1891 fight), **Mike Ryan** (saloon keeper, election fraud expert, and all-around bad man), **William H. Griffith** (president and manager of the *Denver Times*), **"Big Ed" Chase** (Jeff's business partner, policy shop king, and specialist in forming underworld voting blocks), an unidentified man (behind "Big Ed"), **William Gray Evans** (head of the Denver Tramway Company, a monopoly[4]), **Dave Kelly** (Denver business man and

[1] Rutter, pp. 134-143.

[2] Parkhill, p. 236

[3] *RMN* 10/16/1892.

[4] Dorsett, p. 75.

contractor), **A. M. Stevenson** (attorney and fixer for the Denver City Tramway Company[1]), **Bill Hamill** (the Denver mine king), and **Joe H. Smith** (County Clerk and Recorder). These men often appear in political cartoons of the period, and prominent among many of them is a bearded figure always identified as "Soapy Smith."

In the cartoon, the group is meeting in "Boodle[2] Hall." A prominent picture on the wall is of the Denver Tramway Co, with "God Bless Our Home" appearing in its upper left. The smoke coming from its stack forms a balloon for the motto "We want the earth." The environment is completely unsavory, reeking of crooked politics backed by brutal power. Above the door are four aces atop crossed pistols, a bowler-hatted strong man stands just outside the door, and to the right is a shelf of liquor, glasses, box of cigars, a lantern (for under cover of darkness work?), a set of dice cups, and hanging in a bunch to be taken down quickly for immediate use are a night stick, sap (or black jack), and a pistol. On the table are four shot glasses, a bottle of "Old Rye," a box of cigars and open box of spilled matches, an apparatus with a "patent False Bottom," and another sap and brass knuckles. Holding the voting district map in place are a pistol and dagger stabbed through the map into the table.

On October 18, 1892, the Combine decided that their associates should disgorge some of their plunder. The major gambling houses were ordered to "donate" $500 each to the Republican campaign fund, under the threat of having their businesses closed down. Several were known to have paid, including Jeff Argyle, who demanded a stipulation that the charge of assault to murder standing against him, when he shot at Cady, should not be pressed. Jeff had the Tivoli, the White Front, and an interest in the Blonger gambling house at 1744 Larimer Street, but he was not assessed. No doubt his services were valued contributions.[3]

Jeff left little doubt that he considered himself above the law. When police interfered in his business, he sought to stop them. If stopping them failed, he punished them. Shortly after the Dunbar episode, on Tuesday, October 18, 1892, the *News* reported how a John Tarpey was about to be robbed in the Tivoli Club when a detective rescued him. Jeff retaliated.

SOAPY SMITH'S DEFIANCE.
He Puts Up a Cruel Job on Denver's Detective Department.

---

[1] *A. M. Stevenson*: Judge Ben Lindsey in his book *The Beast* (1910) tells of meeting Stevenson when Lindsey and partner Gardener first started practicing law and took the case of an injured child against the Tramway Co. After two trials, their cases resulted in hung juries twice. One night Stevenson came to call, saying, "Hello, boys. ... How's she going? Making a record for yourselves up in court, eh? ... Wearing yourselves out, eh? Working night and day? Ain't you getting about tired of it?" The reply was they had gotten 11 to 1 each time and would win yet. "Uh-huh," Big Steve continued. "You will, eh? ... Now I'm a friend of you boys, ain't I? Well, my advice to you is you'd better settle that case. Get something for your work. Don't be a pair of fools. Settle it." Big Steve was asked why, and the reply: "'Jury'll hang. Every time. I'm here to tell you so. Better settle it." (Lindsey, pp. 22-23)

[2] *Boodle Hall*: where boodlers plan graft payments to key politicians & officials, plot illegal voting gang activity, determine how to fix juries, lay out blackmail schemes.... (Partridge, *Underworld*)

[3] *RMN* 10/18/1892, p. 1.

Soapy Smith is getting bolder and bolder every day in his open contempt of the law. His importance as one of the chief heelers[1] in Tramway Boodle hall has swelled him like a toad, and he flaunts his crimes and his defiance in the face of the authorities—apparently with impunity. Soapy goes regularly on every day with his bunco game, and his dive at the Tivoli saloon registers unqualified voters by the dozen, finds time to stand preliminary hearing on the charge of murder and, just for a nightcap, as it were, slugs somebody—or his henchmen do it for him—or drugs and robs them. Soapy's excuse is that he is compelled to do it to keep in line with the dark methods of Boodle hall.

John Tarpey is a man well advanced in years, who has marched in Uncle Sam's infantry for just twenty-seven years. He received an honorable discharge from Fort Logan the other day and a permit to the old Soldier's home at Leavenworth. Tarpey had about $200 on his person when he was enticed into Smith's slaughter pen Monday afternoon. He met some pleasant gentlemen there who smiled and smiled, and yet were villain still.[2] They were Soapy's heelers.[3] And Soapy pays them to smile. They were spending his [Tarpey's] money for him, and early in the evening had him in that condition where he was ripe for their sandbags. Just about this time somebody happened to drop into the place and saw what the gang was up to. This somebody notified Chief of Detectives Howe, and he detailed Detective [William] Ustick. Tarpey was rescued, but with only $125 in his pocket, and placed in jail to recover from the effects the vile liquors with which Soapy's heelers had plied him.

This action on the part of the detectives made Soapy sore. He immediately bowled up on a good brand of whisky, which he was compelled to buy at some other establishment than his own, and then started out. He called up detective headquarters by telephone from half a dozen places, and each time made complaint that somebody's house had been entered and robbed, giving a different name and a different address each time. Imagine the result. All the men in the department were out sleuthing burglaries that never occurred, putting in their spare moments swearing at the capricious fate that had sent them on such wild goose chases. Yesterday morning they learned that Soapy had planned and executed the hoax and was around publishing it from the housetops.

The police board is beginning to think now that Soapy is really in earnest in his defiance of law. What are they going to do about it?[4]

---

[1] *one of the chief heelers*: "heeler": one who follows at the heels of a political leader or "boss"; an unscrupulous or disreputable follower of a professional politician. (5. *OED, NY Herald* 1877)

[2] *smiled and smiled, and, yet were villain still*: allusion to Hamlet's saying, "one may smile, and smile, and be a villain; / At least I am sure it may be so in Denmark." William Shakespeare's *Hamlet*, 1.5.108-109.

[3] *Soapy's heelers*: (1) "heeler": a working dog that urges animals onwards by nipping at their heels (4.b. *OED*). (2) "to heel": to lariat an animal by the hind leg. (*DARE, Scribner's Magazine* 1887) Hence those who herd, rope, trip up.

[4] *RMN* 10/19/1892, p. 3.

The following day Tarpey was released from his safe-keepers only to find that he had purchased a fake train ticket while at the Tivoli Club and was obliged to stay another night in Denver.[1] It is unlikely he went out drinking again. At the following fire and police board meeting Jeff's misdemeanor offenses were mentioned and deplored, but the board did not act, except to demote the detective who had rescued the old soldier.

> ...Soapy's antics with the detective department, an account of which appeared in yesterday's News, was duly brought to the attention of the board yesterday and the members discussed ways and means, and President Johnson mentally execrated him for making monkeys out of the officers. Further than this the board did not go—the members didn't believe they had any power to pull him up for his misdemeanors. This practically gives Soapy and others of his ilk a license to play pitch and toss with the whole department. Soapy and his friends of Boodle hall will not be slow to take advantage of this license. ...
>
> William Ustick was transferred from the detective to the police department....[2]

Despite many legal issues, Jeff's economic situation was good. On October 19, 1892, the *News* published that Jeff was a silent partner of men who had purchased a hotel not far from Blake and Nineteenth streets.[3] A week later Jeff's name was in the *News* regarding a victim's $500 bank draft that Ed Chase had cashed for him.

CONFIDENCED AT CREEDE.
An Old Man's Story Implicating Highly Moral Republicans.

> The Union National bank wishes to know whether it should pay H. F. Harder or Ed. Chase a ... draft for $500, and to that end brought an action ... heard on Saturday by Judge Rising and in which a decision will probably be handed down to-morrow morning. ... While the question presented to the court is purely one of law, aside from the issue of fact as to whether Chase was an innocent purchaser for value, the details as to how Chase came into possession of the paper in dispute make interesting reading.
>
> Defendant Harder is an elderly man, the great mistake of whose life was in showing up at the new mining camp [of Creede] one day last spring with a roll of greenbacks. Not only this, but early in the game he bit many times and oft the seductive fluid which intoxicates. He had more friends than anybody. His chance acquaintances insisted on his drinking round after round with them, and the result was that Harder was soon paralyzed, according to his own statement. He does not know who the men were that induced him to do it, but he started in to beat the "bottom and top" [top and bottom] skin dice game. Of course he was unsuccessful, and in a dazed condition found that all his stuff, including this $500 draft, was gone. It had been signed in blank. The next trace of the valuable paper was at the Union National bank in Denver,

---

[1] *RMN* 10/20/1892, p. 6.

[2] *RMN* 10/20/1892, p. 2.

[3] *RMN* 10/19/1892, p. 3.

where it had been cashed by Ed Chase, to whom it had been assigned by Soapy Smith. ...Chase poses as the "innocent purchaser," and demands the entire pound of flesh.[1] The inside facts as to the transaction could be learned no doubt fully from Soapy, but while he glibly gives directions at [Republican] headquarters in the Cheesman Block as to the conduct of the campaign, on the subject of the Harder draft he is as dumb as an oyster.[2]

The case was decided in Harder's favor, and Chase was ordered to repay the bank.[3]

As so often before, Republican voter registration for the election was expected to be fraudulent, and the *News* was keeping careful watch. It noticed and asked why only four vagrancy arrests had been made as compared to the previous year's twenty-two. Assumed was that the fire and police board was intentionally ignoring the "vags" and hobos until after the election so they could be registered.

> The saloons and dives in the lower part of town, along Blake and Market streets, are crowded with a mob of hobos, all with a plentiful supply of beer money. On election day Jack Devine and Soapy Smith will get in their work by discovering them in their dark hiding places.[4]

Combine leaders knew Jeff could produce victory. According to the *News*, Jeff was paid $25 a day for services and provided with cash to buy drinks for an army of repeat voters.[5] Jeff was needed, yet a thorn he felt was the fire and police board order that kept the Tivoli Club closed. Feeling confident, Jeff made a demand.

> He Tells the Gang That His Gambling Hell Must Run.

> After the murder of Cliff Sparks the police board closed Soapy Smith's gambling house at Seventeenth and Market streets. ... Yesterday Stevenson, Cook, Griffith, Evans and Hamill promised Smith and Ed Chase that the place would be reopened next week.

> This information is official and accurate. It comes direct from the inner council chamber of boodle hall. Smith and Chase several days ago notified their fellow members of the executive council that if the rooms were not allowed to run they would not only stop working for the gang ticket, but would make public what they know of the inner workings of the machine. The bosses ... begged Smith and Chase to keep quiet. They pointed out that it would ruin the chances of the ticket if Soapy's place were allowed to open before election. ... Smith and Chase were obdurate.... Promises that the rooms would be permitted to open after election were spurned. ... Stevenson, Griffith, Hamill et al., then gave way and passed their solemn promise that the place would be reopened next week.

---

[1] *demands the entire pound of flesh*: allusion to the merchant Shylock's insistence on what is due him, "a pound of flesh most near the heart." William Shakespeare's *The Merchant of Venice*.

[2] *RMN* 10/24/1892, p. 2.

[3] *RMN* 11/15/1892, p. 4.

[4] *RMN* 10/28/1892, p. 8.

[5] *RMN* 11/01/1892. Tom's inflation calculator shows $25 in 1892 currently equivalent to about $639.

A vote for the Harrison ticket is a vote for Soapy Smith, Ed Chase, Stevenson, Jack Devine and the combine.[1]

Chase's name appearing in connection with the Tivoli suggests that Chase continued to have an interest in the gambling house. Not clear is if the Tivoli remained closed between October 13 and early November. Jeff Dunbar buffaloed Flossie Leigh in the Tivoli on October 16, and Tarpey was swindled there on October 17, 1892. Possibly the Tivoli had been allowed to reopen but then closed again after October 17.

Concern for public safety during the election led the fire and police board on October 30 to order Jeff Argyle and Tom Cady to stay out of the city's saloons. Argyle, however, was allowed to roam the Missouri House, of which he was manager. This order did not sit well with the Combine as both men were needed to gather voters.[2] When voter registration began, the *News* began listing names said to be fraudulent.

Passions this election season ran high on whether the monetary system would be based on gold alone (supporters were called gold bugs) or a bi-metal system of silver and gold at a ratio of 16 to 1. Republicans gold alone, and Democrats and Populists supported gold and silver. C. McFarland, a silver supporter, walked into the Cheesman Block on Saturday, November 5, 1892, looking for Dave Kelly to secure a small sum owed him. In the middle of the corridors he bravely but foolishly held up a silver dollar and cried, "That's the sort of man I am. That is what I am going to vote for." Immediately surrounded by supporters and members of the Combine, he was jumped.

> Bill [Bascomb] Smith, a brother of Soapy's, jumped at him [McFarland] and struck him in the face. Others joined in and he was kicked and pulled over to the stairs, down which he was thrown. Last night he bore cuts over his eyes and behind his right ear as proof of the treatment he received.
>
> ... It was in this delectable resort of bummers and heelers[3] that an ex-sheriff of Larimer county had his pockets picked on Friday.[4]

On the day before the election, the *News* published a statement made by Jeff, which if true would show just how above the law he felt he was.

No Law for Soapy.

> Jeff Smith, usually called "Soapy," made the statement publicly yesterday that he would be —— —if any law could keep him from casting as many crooked votes as he —— —pleased, and he didn't give a —who knew that was his position.
>
> "I will cast as many fraudulent votes as I want to." Said he, "and there is no —— —law can prevent me."[5]

On election day morning, the polling office for District F, precinct 6, located at 1328 Eighteenth Street, was visited by Jeff, Devine, Chase, Leonard DeLue, Mike Ryan, Tom Keyes, and boxer Billy Woods. They ejected the poll watcher and appointed a man named Jarecki in his place. Five fraudulent voters at a time were

---

[1] *RMN* 10/29/1892, p. 5.

[2] *RMN* 10/30/1892, p. 15.

[3] *bummers and heelers*: bums & political followers.

[4] *RMN* 11/06/1892, p. 9.

[5] *RMN* 11/08/1892, p. 5.

marched in to cast ballots. Repeat voters wore yellow tags. It is believed they were paid per vote, and the tags helped keep count.[1] Lafe Pence, a candidate for Congress, arrived to keep an eye on Jeff and Chase. Pence also wanted to talk to Jeff about something, but Jeff was not interested. To show the degree of his disinterest, prompted by Lafe's tenacity the day before, Jeff jumped into his buggy and sped off.[2]

Any politician could recognize the advantage of having Jeff work for his side, or of *not* having Jeff work *against* him. Such a one was Lafayette Pence. "Lafe," as he was known, had been the prosecuting attorney for Arapahoe County during the 1889 election fraud case. Jeff must have been impressed with his work because in 1890 he hired him for a criminal case.[3] Now Lafe was a Populist Party candidate for Congress, and he wanted Jeff not to work against him. The Populist party platform, however, called for political and social reforms that vastly differed from Jeff's views on how the political machine should be run. If Jeff did do anything regarding Pence's campaign, it would be to help him lose. So Jeff refused Lafe's persistent entreaties to discuss the coming election. But Pence would not give up.

In August 1894, the *Denver Mercury*, a Republican mouthpiece, looked back to the day before the 1892 election to illustrate Pence tenacity. He was in his horse-drawn buggy when he saw Jeff in his coming the other way.

> To try and follow Jeff was useless, and there was only one thing to do—get by his side and stay there. This Lafe did. He deliberately jumped from his own buggy and at once clambered in the back end of Jeff's carriage and announced his intention of staying there.
>
> "Get out, Pence," said Jeff. "I've got business on hand."
>
> "So have I," responded Lafe.
>
> "But you are not my kind of people.... I'm against you. Get out."
>
> "See here, Jeff," responded Lafe, "I'm dead on to you. You are going to come after me with some of those slick tricks of yours and I'm afraid of you."
>
> "Slick tricks nothing. Get out!" demanded Jeff.
>
> "I won't do it!" said Lafe. "You can't lose me. I'll stay in this buggy…!"
>
> "I'll fix you!" said Jeff between his teeth, and suiting the action to the word he whipped his horse into a run, turned corners so quick that the buggy ran on one wheel, but still Lafe clung to the back end like a major.
>
> Finally Jeff stopped when he saw it was no use and turning to Lafe said: "Lafe, you are a daisy, ain't you?"
>
> "That's what I am," answered Lafe.
>
> "A dead wise fowl," said Jeff.
>
> "Correct!" responded Lafe.
>
> "Suppose I get out and walk?" inquired Jeff.
>
> "I'll follow you," replied Lafe.
>
> "See here, Lafe," insisted Jeff, "you are a game fish, but you're on the wrong side. I've got to help beat you."

---

[1] *RMN* 10/24/1892, p. 4.

[2] *RMN* 11/09/1892.

[3] *RMN* 05/03/1890.

"Jeff," said Lafe, looking seriously, "I'm going to go to Congress, and if I lose sight of you to-day I'm a goner. Now you can adopt any measure you please, I'm with you. I'll never let you lose me this day if I die trying to keep up."

Do what he would Jeff could not shake him off, and after the polls closed and Lafe had swept the field in spite of all that could be done, Jeff said to him: "Lafe, you are the gamest bird I ever saw, and if you didn't deserve that election I don't know of any Populist who did."

Col. Smith, in spite of himself, looks pale since Lafe's return, and if he gets another nomination this year [1894] Jeff swears he will either disguise himself by shaving ... or go and hide out where Lafe can't find him.[1]

Pence was indeed game, and he had a long and mostly successful life, but he was unsuccessful in his 1894 reelection attempt.[2] Jeff, who now referred to himself as "Colonel Jefferson Randolph Smith," grew somewhat friendly with Pence, and the two corresponded on political issues. One letter of response from Pence to Jeff in June 1894 indicates that Jeff asked Pence if he might be interested in running for governor of Colorado. Pence, however thankful for Jeff's kind words, declined the offer.[3]

No matter the hard times in political circles, if business had been good for the gamblers and confidence gangs at Christmas time, to feed and clothe the poor, they were apt to donate a percentage of their profits to the church of their choice. Well known throughout Denver's underworld was how no one in Denver helped the poor more than Parson Uzzell. Jeff had gone to the rear door of the Tabernacle on December 27, handed the parson $50 in assorted bills, and told him to put the money to use where it would do the most good.[4] Three days later the *News* published a story of another nighttime visit, this time to the parson's home.

HEARTS ARE TRUMPS.

As Parson Tom Uzzell was sitting in his home on Mary Street in North Denver last night, toasting his toes before a cheerful fire, he ... was indulging in that unpurchasable luxury—a reverie. He was thinking of all the poor souls in the bottoms, members of his flock, who had been enabled to pass a cheerful Christmas by reason of the generosity of the Denver people. ...

It was while these dreams were chasing each other at a Nancy Hanks[5] gait through Parson Tom's thinking works that the door bell rang. The pull

---

[1] *Denver Mercury* 08/25/1894.

[2] Lafayette "Lafe" Pence (1857-1923). Attorney. Moved to Rico, Dolores County, Colo., in 1881 and practiced law until 1884; member of the State house of representatives in 1885; settled in Denver in 1885 and continued the practice of law; prosecuting attorney for Arapahoe County in 1887 and 1888; elected as a Populist to the 53rd Congress (March 4, 1893-March 3, 1895); unsuccessful candidate for reelection in 1894 to the 54th Congress. (Congress)

[3] Ltr to Jefferson R. Smith II fr Lafe Pence, June 3, 1894. Jefferson R "Little Randy" Smith col. (See "Pence" in Index for location of this Ltr.)

[4] *RMN* 12/28/1892, p. 1.

[5] *Nancy Hanks*: famous trotting horse named for mother of Abraham Lincoln. "[S]he never once broke stride, and she stood as a superlative example of the standardbred (of that time [1892]) at its best." (Harnesslink.com)

given that bell indicated that somebody had hold of the cord who meant business. The preacher of the slums was jerked out of dreamland without any ceremony. He swore—swore just like the deacon in the "One Horse Shay"—and he wondered what in the "Sam-nation sixty" was up.[1]

When he went to the door three big, two fisted men told him they wanted to see him, and they wanted to see him bad. They were taken into the parlor. He thought to himself: "Well, gentlemen, you seem to have the best of me." The visitors did not say much. They sized up the parson, and he in turn looked them over thoroughly. While each was doing his own thinking, one of the strangers reached for his hip pocket.... Out ... came a roll of paper a yard long, with names and figures on it—here, there and everywhere.

"Count up those figures," was the command of the parson's visitors, and Tom began to count.

"I make it $429.50," he said, after adding up the long columns." ...

"This," they said, "was the contribution of the employees of a few of the club houses of the city, and was given him to help in taking care of the poor of Denver during the winter."

And then, while Tom's eyes were glistening and he was thinking how best to express his gratitude, his brusque but warm hearted callers bade him good night without leaving their names. They, however, left the "roll of honor" for him. The names on it are those of members of the sporting fraternity.[2]

The story did not make Jeff happy. The list did not include his name nor those of his closest gambling associates. So Jeff acted. On Christmas Eve Uzzell was busy preparing a dinner for children when a message came that a number of men wanted to see him in the ante-room. He told what happened next to the *Denver Evening Post.*

I sent back word that I was very busy and asked them to wait a few minutes. They sent back word that they could not wait and so I went to see what was wanted.

In the ante room I found twenty men, all strangers to me, all but one, Soapy Smith, who stepped forward and said: "I want to introduce to you Parson Byers." I shook hands with the man and when he took [back] his hand I found a $10 bill in my hand.

All the others now came forward and shook hands, each leaving with me a bill like the first.

"What does this mean, gentlemen?" I asked.

"It means that our money is just as free as anybody else's," said Soapy, and then all hands wished me good night and left.

---

[1] *swore just like the deacon in the "One Horse Shay"... "Sam-nation sixty":* "The Deacon's Masterpiece: or The Wonderful 'One-Hoss-Shay,'" a 120-line poem by Oliver Wendell Homes, published *Atlantic Monthly* 1858. "Shay," Americanism of *chaise*, light, open two-wheeled carriage. "swore just like the dean," "'I dew vum,'" *I do vow*, as close to a curse as a deacon, or parson, comes. "wondered what in the 'Sam-nation sixty' was up." Meaning unknown but may be related to "What the Sam Hill," a long-time euphemism (Welsh) for "What the hell."

[2] *RMN* 12/31/1892.

It seems that what were called the legitimate houses had ignored Soapy and his tinhorns and they took this method of asserting themselves.[1]

In the telling of the story a second time in 1898, Uzzell seems to have inflated the amount given by the first "legitimate" gamblers to $1,000. Perhaps Uzzell hoped that the current gambling houses, not to be outdone, would donate as much.

With the giving season past, it was back to the business of taking. In the first month of 1893, John Bowers assaulted Deputy Sheriff Hanson, William Jackson drew a pistol in the Arcade, and Frank Brown committed petty larceny.[2] Bowers, not in the public eye since assaulting John Cully in July 1892, was fined $10 and costs.[3] Bowers was arrested again at the end of April with other "sure thing" men in a friendly poker game swindle about which the victim complained and the *News* duly reported.

Detectives Ordered to Round Up the Entire Fraternity.

H. Slade of Salt Lake complained to the police yesterday afternoon that he had been buncoed out of $150 in a gambling house at Seventeenth and Market streets. The game was friendly poker, but there were odds of 2 to 1. Several complaints of late have come into the police station against the class of gamblers known as "sure thing" men, so Chief Veatch, after hearing Slade's story, ordered Chief Howe to land in jail all the sharps found on the streets. As a result, Detective Carberry, Connors and Carrier soon had George Wilder, Frank Weldon, George Beck, Jeff Dunbar, A. B. Smith, John Bowers, James Jenks and Handsome Casey all behind the bars.[4]

W. K. (probably W. H.) Jackson while gambling in the Arcade attempted to "back his play," as stated in the *News*, with a gun and was arrested by Officer Palmer.[5] Known as "Professor" Jackson, he was now a key member of the Soap Gang. Bowers, Jackson, and Brown followed Jeff to Alaska.

Jeff was so well known by this time that he hired a clipping service to help him track how he was portrayed in the press. Jeff saved these clippings and clipped articles he found that named him in current events, namely the Colorado elections of 1893 and 1894 in which the words "fraud" and "Soapy Smith" became synonymous. Clippings came from such Colorado newspapers as *The Silverton Miner, The Ft. Morgan Herald, The Burlington Banner, The Boulder Camera,* and *The Lamar Sparks.*[6] A clipping from the latter reads as follows: "It is understood that Soapy Smith of Denver positively refuses to be the Republican candidate for governor this year. He will, however, do all in his power to redeem Colorado."[7] It seems unlikely that Denver Republicans would have considered Jeff a viable gubernatorial candidate. He was more useful behind the scenes.

---

[1] *Denver Evening Post* 12/25/1898, p. 14.

[2] *RMN* 01/28/1893.

[3] *RMN* 01/11/1893, p. 2. *cost:* court costs.

[4] *RMN* 04/25/1893, p. 3.

[5] *RMN* 01/26/1893, p. 3.

[6] Newspaper clippings cut out by a clipping service for Jeff R. Smith II. Author's col.

[7] *Larmar Sparks* 07/19/1894.

A front-page cartoon in the *Denver Sun* portrays how an active political underground of criminals, already rewarded with appointments of various sorts for past electioneering services, sought to have Republican George Graham appointed as police commissioner.[1] A large crowd of formally attired men fill a hall before a nearly naked giant figure seated on Colorado Senator "E. O. Wolcott's Throne." The throned figure wears a dunce's cap upon which is written "Wolcott's Man Friday." In this person's outstretched hand are three rolled up scrolls upon which are written "Appointment." At the time it was not clear who controlled appointments, the governor or state officials, but clearly the senator was seen as having influence. Denver fire and police board appointments would eventually lead to legal battles between the governor, members of Denver city government, and their powerful criminal allies. The next spring, in 1894, when the governor called up the national guard to enforce his appointments, Denver city fathers called upon Jeff Smith, among others, to assemble forces at city hall to withstand what became a siege. This cartoon features the beginning of the disagreement leading to that face off in the center of Denver.

Before the throne a letter lies open, addressed "U. S. Senate, Washington DC" and dated "June 17th 1893." It begins, "Dear George." The addressee may be the "Man Friday," that is, an assistant, though a powerful one, to the senator. It continues, "Don't forget our friends." It concludes with "Yours, Ed." Standing beside his letter, before the figure, and half facing the crowd of "friends" is Big Ed Chase, chief political strategist and owner of gambling and collector from gambling establishments across Denver. In his hand is a parchment that reads "place"—signifying a coveted *place* of power in city or state government. Across his back appears the label "Gangster." Immediately to his left is his partner, whose name appears in large dark letters on his right arm: "Soapy Smith." Jeff holds a parchment with his "place" named on it: "Cesspool Cleaner." As the cleaner of such an area, implied is that he knows it well.

Other men named in the cartoon, from left to right, include the following: ***Crocker*** (partially out of the picture along with the parchment he holds). This is William Crocker, a police officer and one-time guard at the county jail who stood trial at various times for false imprisonment, assault with intent to kill, assault and battery, blackmail of prostitutes, and complicity with criminals.[2] ***Clark*** (parchment held reads "Patrolman"). Culver E. Clark was a police officer who later stood trial for false imprisonment, "assault to kill," assault and battery, blackmailing prostitutes, and "complicity with criminals."[3] ***Soapy Smith. Ed Chase. DeLue*** (holds no parchment but appears to be offered one by Ed Chase). Leonard DeLue had a long career in Denver with feet planted on each side of the law. As a deputy under Sheriff Burchinell, he often appeared in newspapers stories about arrests. He also frequently turned up as recruiter of criminals, polling site disrupter, and strike breaker. A Denver city publication for 1913 lists him as police commissioner,[4] a position no doubt secured, or at least sanctioned, by Lou Blonger, and after law enforcement, he remained

---

[1] *Denver Sun* 01/22/1893.

[2] Secrest, pp. 199-200.

[3] *RMN* 10/15/1890.

[4] *Police Commissioner.* Denver, City of (1913), pp. 2, 18.

connected with Blonger while operating the DeLue Detective Agency until about 1923.[1] ***Sheeny Sam*** (holds two parchments, one reading "Chief [of] Police," the other unclear). This is Samuel Emrich, a Denver city detective and participant in the fixed election of 1889. He was also involved with DeLue and others in swinging the election of 1893. On June 14, 1904, he was "sentenced to sixteen years imprisonment for the murder of William Malone, a saloon keeper, in a quarrel in the latter's saloon."[2] ***Jerecki*** (holds two parchments, one reading "Gangster," the other "Gas Smeller). "Jerecki" may be the "Jarecki" identified as the Combine-installed election watcher when Jeff and others marched into the Eighteenth Street election site. ***Arnett*** (holds one parchment reading "Gangster"). This is probably William H. Arnett, a deputy sheriff along with DeLue under Sheriff Burchinell. It seems Arnett stepped across the line of the law less often than DeLue but often enough to be considered a loyalist to city hall in 1893. He went on to a long career with the federal department of justice.[3] ***Mortimer Carr, Alias Morgan*** (holds one parchment reading "Gangster"). To date, no further information about him is known. ***Ike Stein*** (holds one parchment reading "Chief of Fire Dep"). To date, no further information about him is known. ***George H. Graham***, an Auction and Commission Merchant with A. H. Weber,[4] is not figured in the cartoon although he is its subject. The caption appearing under the whole cartoon reads, "Will Governor Waite," who was yet to take office, "contribute to this by appointing George H. Graham upon the fire and police board?"

City officials warned gambling houses that they must support appointment of Graham to the fire and police board and a prescribed 1893 election ticket, or they could expect to be shut down. The political climate in Colorado was rapidly heating up.

The collapsing economy sparked radical political campaigns nationwide. In June 1893, a full-scale depression, historically known as the Panic of 1893, was tearing down the US economy. Silver producers found their mines and smelters unprofitable and began closing them. Whole industries began crumbling, including 194 railroad corporations; of 500 banks to close nationally, 12 were in Denver, 6 on the same day, July 18, 1893, and 3 more the following day. Depositors not retrieving their funds beforehand lost their money as federal insurance protection was then unknown. The nation's unemployed, about 2,500,000, began drifting into the cities in search of jobs and food. In Denver, hundreds of men roamed the streets, begging for work, food, and shelter. Denver newspapers reported a steady rise in holdups by hungry men and in suicides by the desperate who had given up hope. Faced with these conditions, on July 27, 1893, the city set up a refugee camp at the foot of Sixteenth Street at River Front Park.[5] The national guard furnished tents for 400 men; another 200 slept in grandstands. Parson Uzzell helped screen applicants. The city fed between 500 and 1,000 people each day for over two weeks. Many residents feared Denver would not

---

[1] Van Cise, pp. 14-15. Leonard DeLue is named Leon Dean in Van Cise. Also see BlongerBros.com. Search "DeLue."

[2] BlongerBros.com. Search "Sheeney [sic, Sheeny] Sam."

[3] BlongerBros.com. Search "Arnett."

[4] *Denver City Directory*, 1887.

[5] Arp, p. 33.

recover from the economic collapse. To help the troubled city, railroads offered reduced fares out of town and later issued free tickets. The economic crisis was ultimately blamed on the federal government for changing to a gold standard rather than staying with silver and gold. This belief influenced many votes in the previous election and would again those to come.

Jeff's saloon, gambling, and bunco businesses suffered a lack of quality gamblers and victims. As a sign of hard times, in March 1893, it appears Jeff spread employment of the Soap Gang into saloons owned by associates and friends. Jeff himself presided over the gambling rooms at the Ingersoll Club at 1653 Larimer near Seventeenth.[1] Joe Palmer was a saloon keeper on Seventeenth near Champa, where he was arrested in May for larceny involving a stranger from Yuma, Arizona.[2]

On a boxing bout wager, Jeff ran into some luck. On March 4, 1893, he placed big money on "Denver Ed" Smith against Joe "Kangaroo" Goddard. "Denver Ed" was not favored, and his against-the-odds victory was a surprise. The *News* noted Jeff's win, though not the amount, and named him "the luckiest man in town. Mr. Jefferson Smith, 'Soapy,' is always a winner. If this keeps up he will soon be a mascot."[3]

While Jeff was always occupied with making money, he seems never to have lost sight of the struggle of the masses. Frequently Jeff found time and capital to aid those in need. When on February 17, 1893, police clerk Sam T. Inman committed suicide over financial problems, Jeff took out his wallet to help the man's family.

> Jeff Smith performed yesterday another of those acts of generosity and charity for which he is noted. When he heard that Sam Inman had left his family in very poor circumstances he at once put his name down for a large amount on a piece of paper and got a number of his friends to do likewise. The fund has reached $362.00.[4]

The amount does not seem like much today, but an inflation calculator for 1893 shows it to be about $10,850 today.[5]

Jeff's giving, however, had a practical side. The gift was surely also a contribution towards improved relations with the fire and police board. Inman, an ex-deputy sheriff and ex-lieutenant of police, was a clerk of the police court, but his position was to be eliminated. He was also a gambler going through a losing streak. The game of faro was his favorite, which is possibly how Jeff came to know him. He was survived by a wife, son, and daughter. In a note to his daughter he wrote that he had not a dollar to his name and on the previous day had lost $175 gambling at the Nickel Plate Club, the Chicken Coop, and the Jockey Club.[6]

In May 1893, one of Jeff's men inaccurately judged a victim and lost ten dollars. The *News* covered the story.

---

[1] *RMN* 03/21/1893, p. 4.

[2] *RMN* 05/03/1893, p. 3, & 05/11/1893, p. 3.

[3] *RMN* 03/04/1893, pp. 1-2. *mascot*: in the sense of being "a lucky charm to betting men."

[4] Denver newspaper clipping of unknown origin, cut & saved by Jefferson R. Smith II, 02/19/1893. Jefferson R. "Little Randy" Smith col.

[5] Tom's Inflation Calculator.

[6] *RMN* 02/18/1893, p. 3.

SOAPY SMITH BUNCOED.
An Innocent Swede Does Up the Wily Thimble Rigger.

Soapy Smith was buncoed out of ten great big silver dollars yesterday morning by a country Swede named Nels Larson. Larson and his wife on their way from the coast to Boston stopped over a few hours and Larson, who had heard of the growler [the tiger, faro] attempted to buck it in the Tivoli Club. He … lost $40 in cash and $270 besides, for which he presented a draft on [a] Boston [bank] for $470. Soapy Smith was out at the time and one of his men cashed the check and gave Larson only $200 in change. The Swede went to his wife, and when she heard of his loss she made him telegraph to have payment on the draft stopped. Jeff Smith heard of this and he had a lively chase to catch Larson to get his money back. Larson and his wife had, meantime, applied to the police for aid. Just before the train pulled out all interested parties came together, and Smith was compelled to accept $190 back for the check for which he had given $200.

"First time I ever got caught," said Jeff to Detectives Cook and Peterson, who accompanied Larson.[1]

Three weeks later, a police sweep led to a number of Jeff's men being arrested for vagrancy, including John Bowers, George Wilder, and George Baker. Given his feeling on the subject, Jeff probably assisted the defense in arguing that the men were "citizens, not vags." Proposed was that the Denver vagrancy ordinance was unconstitutional. The judge agreed and dismissed the case against the men.[2]

For several days, the *News* scapegoated the gambling halls with articles about men with little money who had gambled it away in crooked games. As a result, homeless men angry, and a few considered taking back some of that ill-gotten cash by force. Beginning July 26, 1893, for two nights it was feared that bands of hungry men might mob gambling halls. The first night was without attack but made fearful enough by wandering crowds of men. Before the second night, Sheriff Burchinell took no chances and swore in about fifty deputies. They were heavily armed and assigned to gambling halls alongside well-armed gamblers. That night, had any men from among the larger crowds that assembled near Larimer rushed any of the establishments, the bloodshed would have been horrific.[3] Jeff, who was prepared to fight, expressed his concerns and hopes to a *News* reporter.

Jeff on Guard.

Hon. Sapolio Smith on Thursday evening, when it was broadly intimated that a raid on the gambling houses was intended, was on the battlements. Laying his armament aside for a moment, he delivered himself of the following characteristic remarks: "There mustn't be any more of these mobs in Denver. It's a bad business. Now, take to-night fer instance. There's this restless, excitable crowd ready to hand, and I know of four or five miscreants who are circulating about trying to stir up an assault on a couple of business

---

[1] *RMN* 05/06/1893, p. 3.
[2] *RMN* 05/21/1893, p. 14.
[3] *RMN* 07/28/1893, p. 3.

houses [that are] supposed to have considerable cash on hand. They'd better not try it, for we've got men enough interested in preserving this city to make ignominious failure a certainty for them. We business men can't afford to have this city destroyed—as soon as the clouds roll by, and that'll be blessed soon, she's going to be a bird!"[1]

Reported in the same issue was an incident involving Bascomb as a deputy.

Arrested for Assault to Kill.

John Cooney was arrested at a late hour last night for an assault to kill at Nineteenth and Larimer. His head was badly beaten. It is claimed by his friends that he is an innocent party, and that he was assaulted by two deputy sheriffs—Bascom Smith and Ingersoll. The stories of the different parties are conflicting. Two shots were fired in the melee.[2]

The police managed to keep the crowds moving so they quickly tired, and by 10 p.m. they had completely dispersed. The next day, Saturday, railroad cars loaded with unemployed men were rolling eastward. Some known or suspected troublemakers were forcibly placed on the first train cars. Slowly the fear of mob violence dissipated.

For the first five months of 1893, Bascomb had no serious trouble with the law. But toward the end of June, he killed a man. While at Creede in 1892, Bascomb made an enemy of one Harry "Shotgun" Smith, said to be a booster for Bob Ford's Exchange. The trouble began with a fistfight in a Creede saloon. Dick Hawkins, a friend of Harry's, attempted to shoot Bascomb, but before steadying his aim, one of the Soap Gang floored Dick with the swing of a cane.[3] Hawkins had come up against the Soap Gang before and lost. In 1890 he dealt faro at the Tivoli Club. After Joe Simmons loosed a shot in his direction to settle an altercation, Hawkins was fired. He then gave up Denver but not before robbing the Arcade and Nickel Plate. Hawkins showed up in Creede and with his pal "Shotgun" Harry, robbed the Mint Exchange.[4] Hawkins thought it best to remain scarce, but "Shotgun" Harry Smith returned to Denver to work for the Blongers, grafting and dealing faro at 1744 Larimer.[5]

On June 23, 1893, Harry Smith went on a drinking binge and made the deadly mistake of visiting the Tivoli Club and provoking a fight with Bascomb there. The *Mercury* published what happened.

THE KILLING OF SMITH
He simply Went Looking For Something, and Found it.

The killing of Harry Smith at 17th and Market streets, last Friday night ... was no more than dozens of men expected. When sober he was a good hearted fellow, but when in his cups [he] was a perfect madman. Whisky sets many a man crazy and Harry Smith was simply one of that many.

---

[1] *RMN* 07/29/1893, p. 2. "clouds roll ... be a bird!" Interpretation: As soon as these storm clouds roll by, which will be soon, Denver will be like a bird, flying high again."

[2] *RMN* 07/28/1893, p. 3.

[3] *Denver Republican* 04/14/ (illegible date).

[4] *RMN* 03/08/1892, p. 2.

[5] *RMN* 06/24/1893.

The story is briefly told. He had a spite at Bascomb Smith, a young man who attends exclusively to his own affairs, and on the night in question he [Harry Smith] "loaded up" and proceeded to settle. Bascomb kept out of his way. He even ran from him; and when he could run no farther, he mixed up with his opponent, drew bead first, and that is why he is alive instead of dead. Had he been the sixteenth part of a second late, he would have been dead instead of the other fellow. As it was, he was fortunate, because he shot first and saved his life, although he was compelled to take the life of his enemy.

Men who go roaming around the streets looking for something generally find it. Harry Smith is not the first one to qualify this assertion. Many have gone before him and many will follow after. And when one pauses to consider, how idiotic does it look to see a man with a gun strapped to him, looking for some one whom he can kill! ...

A man who has brains will rely on those brains to carry him through. A man who has little brains is compelled to rely on a club, a gun or a knife.

For the dead man ... there should be nothing but pity. For the man who killed him in self defense there should be nothing but forgiveness because he simply defended himself, and self preservation is the first law of nature.

Did the editor of the MERCURY get behind that ice chest while the firing that killed Harry Smith was going on? Well yes, he got right behind it, good and hard! The editor of the MERCURY has a very healthy stomach, but he can't digest hot lead.[1]

The *News* reported that the fight took place at 9:30 inside the Tivoli but ended on the sidewalk just outside. It also wrote how that afternoon Harry had purchased a gun from the Solomon pawnshop for $10. About 8:30, he entered Goldsmith and Wacker's saloon at 1718 Larimer, already drunk. He spotted Bascomb and Jimmy Blaine at a table in the rear, went up to Bascomb, and said, "I can whip you in any kind of fight." He then pulled his gun, struck Bascomb on the head, and told him to "draw and shoot." But Bascomb was not armed. Before Harry started shooting, the bartender and Blaine forcibly removed him to the street. Meanwhile, Bascomb went to his room, retrieved his "big 45-caliber," and went to the Tivoli Club. A half hour later, Harry came in, asked Jeff the whereabouts of Bascomb, and was told that he was not there. Jeff proposed a drink but then noticed Harry had a pistol in his right trouser pocket. So rather than a drink, Jeff induced Harry to leave. He did, but twenty minutes later he returned to find Bascomb standing at the entrance. Harry was verbally abusive while Bascomb tried to reason with him. Frustrated, Harry yelled, "You —. I can meet you at your own game," and again drew his revolver. This time Bascomb was ready and had his gun out a moment in advance. Grasping one another, they wrestled into the entrance of the Tivoli. Bascomb fired a shot that blasted Harry's left wrist and made Harry drop his revolver. Bascomb fired three more shots in rapid succession, two of which "lodged into the right breast just above Harry's heart, piercing his lungs and exiting through the shoulder." A bullet that missed hit Fritz Beck, a spectator, taking off

---

[1] *Mercury* 07/01/1893.

a piece of his right ear. Harry fell on his back, his head striking hard on the flagging. Bascomb jumped over Harry and ran up Market Street and into a Chinese laundry. He was followed by Officer Barr, who upon reaching the laundry met Bascomb walking out to surrender, saying, "I shot the man to save my own life."

Harry Smith and Bascomb went by patrol wagon to city hall, where the police surgeon dressed Harry's wounds. Growing delirious, Harry started asking for Jeff, but at times he cried out, "If Bascomb was here now, I would fight him. Bring him in." Jeff came, "spoke to him kindly and the dying man seemed relieved. At times he imagined that he had killed Bascomb and then he would cry out, 'I got him. I got him.'" Harry was taken to St. Luke's hospital where he died at 11:30 p.m.[1]

The *Aspen Weekly Times*, quoting an unknown source, published the following.

Denver, June 23.—Great excitement was caused among the gambling fraternity tonight by the murder of one of their number. About 10 o'clock Bascom Smith, a brother of the famous Jeff Smith, engaged in a fight at Seventeenth and Market streets with Harry Smith, who, however, is no relative of the first named Smiths. The fight ended in Harry Smith being shot three times and wounded so badly that he died at midnight. Both men had guns, but Harry Smith was wounded in the gun hand at the start and was not able to use his revolver. ... Harry Smith ... is quite well known throughout the state. While in Creede he and a companion ... robbed a faro bank at the point of a shotgun. Since then he has been known as "Shotgun" Smith. Since his arrival in Denver he has several times put a hundred dollar bill on the faro layout and after losing has produced a gun, taken his money and departed. Bascom Smith, the killer, is under arrest.[2]

Bascomb was charged with murder, but the charge was dropped on grounds of self-defense.[3] Luckily for Bascomb several credible witnesses were in the Tivoli Club that evening, including *Mercury* editor Nathan Baker. In November 1898 the *Denver Evening Post* remembered the killing. In a series of editorials titled "Unpunished Denver Murders," Bascomb's shooting of Harry Smith made number 10 on the list.[4]

On July 4, 1893, Jeff refereed a boxing match at Denver's Broadway Park. The *News* labeled the Reddy Gallagher-"Denver Ed" Smith match "an unscientific exhibition," that is, a fake. The fighters did show a degree of bravery by enduring a paying crowd of three thousand that was sorely disappointed. At one point the fighters circled, striking out but too far apart to do anything but fan one another. During the third of the four scheduled rounds, "the crowd began to hiss and cry fake." When all the dancing with but a few "playful taps" was over and Jeff did not even render a decision, the crowd left with blood in its eye. What "the game" was is not clear. No attempt was made even to pretend the match was a real contest. Perhaps with the

---

[1] *RMN* 06/24/1893. And 06/25/1893, p. 4.

[2] *Aspen Times* 06/24/1893, p. 1.

[3] *RMN* 06/29/1893, p. 7.

[4] *Denver Evening Post* 11/26/1898.

admission money in hand, Jeff and the boxers were indifferent. During the fight, Jeff even leaned against the ropes, chatting with police Sergeant Norcott.[1]

About 1:15 the next morning, July 5, 1893, a report of continuous shooting was telephoned to police headquarters.

> It was a startling report that a man with black whiskers, a soft hat, a big revolver and a public-spirited jag, who looked like [undecipherable] insurgent, had turned himself and his armament loose on the residents there.
>
> An officer who went to investigate discovered that the author of the scare was Señor Colonel Jefferson Randolph Smith, amusing himself by shooting 45-caliber bullets through the windows of the Glenarm bar. The colonel swore he thought the cartridges were blanks, and went laughing on his way. [2]

Apparently Jeff was not arrested for the offense. Probably drunk, he had disturbed the peace, endangered public safety, and destroyed private property, and yet was seemingly allowed to go on his way. Did he privately recompense the owners of the Glenarm? Probably—unless Jeff thought he owed them the damage.

This light, even humorous, treatment in the press examples the effectiveness of Jeff's efforts to befriend newspapermen. By showing members of the fourth estate a good time at the Tivoli Club, Jeff could not only minimize bad press but also garner its support. Jeff surely feted Nathan Baker of the *Mercury* for his coverage of the shooting death of Harry Smith. During its short existence, the *Mercury* backed Jeff's political aspirations and criminal business. No matter how much he tried, though, Jeff could not strike a friendly connection with the editors of the *News* or the *Denver Times*.

Near July's end, the latter newspaper published several finger-pointing articles at bunco men for a recent rash of swindles on lower Seventeenth Street. Jeff rebutted the articles with a letter that was published the day he penned it, July 28, 1893.

> Ed Times
>
> In several of the last issues of the Times I see that the bunco men are holding high carnival on lower 17th St. I beg to inform you that there are no bunco men on 17th St. and that if you will send out a man to investigate you will find I am telling the truth. The gentleman that writes the articles about the conductor worrying his passengers [about the danger of being buncoed on the streets of Denver] is either a malicious liar or a fool of the rankest type. I have talked to the proprietors of the Times on different occasions and think they mean to do justice to all, but will state once for all that you are misinformed beyond a question of a doubt. Soapy Smith who is supposed to run a bunco business has not been open for two weeks, and I would suggest that you employ a reporter that is more truthful or not so prejudiced. I will sign myself
>
> Rspt. Jeff R. Smith
> alias "Soapy"[3]

---

[1] *RMN* 07/05/1893, p. 3.

[2] Denver newspaper clipping of unknown origin, 07/04 or 05/1893. Jefferson R. "Little Randy" Smith col.

[3] *Denver Times* 07/28/1893. The original handwritten Ltr to the *Times* is written on stationary fr the Iron Mask Hotel, Gilman, Colorado. The published form possesses no place, date, & addressee. Except for some differences in punctuation, the Ltr was published as written. Item 108, author's col.

When once in a while an officer was thought to be aiding Jeff in a swindle, the *News* felt obligated to publish the accusations.

Police Board Hears the wail of an Innocent Texan.

Officer George Saunders was on trial before the fire and police board yesterday for alleged complicity with Jeff Smith. The complainant was J. Ayers, a locomotive fireman from Wichita Falls, Tex. The board acquitted Saunders, but ordered that Jeff Smith must return to Ayers the ... money lost in his gambling room. The evidence for the defense was that Ayers came into the Tivoli with a couple of men.... He didn't know how to play and let them buck the tiger with his money until he lost five $50 drafts on [a] New York [bank] and $52 in cash. The men were strangers that Ayers met. His verdancy on this showing is beautiful.

Ayers' story is that while looking at minerals in a window of the Brown hotel he was picked up by a pleasant gentleman interested in that subject who gradually led him to the Tivoli. After he dropped his wad he says Smith gave him one of the $50 drafts and advised him to go East. Instead he went down to Chief Detective Hopkins, who turned him over to Lieutenant Clay, who detailed Officer Saunders to go with him to the Tivoli. He recovered $57 more and says Saunders then advised him to hie away eastward. He sought further relief from members of the Brotherhood of Locomotive Firemen. They stopped payment of the $50 drafts and had Saunders hauled up. The board announces that it is unable to find anything to implicate the officer, but will compel the return of the rest of the money.[1]

A week later Jeff and Ayers appeared before the fire and police board. Details of the meeting were eagerly published in the *News* the following day.

Jeff Smith and the young fireman, Ayers, who dropped $302 in the Tivoli, were callers on the police board yesterday. Ayers has received all his $50 drafts but one and on it he got $30 cash. He demands that he receive the draft and be allowed to keep the $30 besides for loss of time and expenses. Smith has tendered him the $20 balance, but he declines to take it.[2]

It seems likely that there the matter stalemated.

Nineteen days later Jeff was in the newspapers again for swindling two Californians of $250 at Jeff's Silver Club.

Californians Fall into the Clutches of Card Sharpers.

Colonel Sapolio Smith relieved two genial gentlemen of the trouble of carrying $250 to Chicago and expending it amid the gayeties of the "Midway plazory" yesterday. The original amount was $300, but the colonel returned $50 in his generosity of soul, and the guests continued their way to the magic White city.[3] The colonel says he is a great reformer. "A man," says he, "will be lured into a gambling hell and fascinated so that he will go again and

---

[1] *RMN* 08/12/1893, p. 8.

[2] *RMN* 08/20/1893, p. 4.

[3] m*agic White city*: the 1893 Chicago World Columbian Exposition exhibit buildings were painted white.

again, until he is forever lost. After a man once comes to my place he is cured of gambling absolutely. He doesn't want any more of it."

It was this wise: The two men are from Pasadena, Cala. They are M. Martin and Edwin White. They wore their pants in their boots, had their upper lips shaved and their chin-whiskers swayed and waved in the breeze as they alighted from the West. A very agreeable gentleman met them, learned that they were en route to the Columbian exposition and took them up into the northeast corner of the second floor of Seventeenth and Market streets [the Silver Club?] to get some pretty illustrated guide books to the fair. They went upstairs, were given the books and agreeably entertained. One of them sat down with their friend at a game of stud poker. The friend won and won and laughed like a schoolboy over his luck. He was going to the world's fair, too, in the afternoon. He pushed half his big pile of chips to his California friend, and then they both won.

Then the Californian caught three kings and an ace in the hole. Next to him was a man with three queens who was playing desperately and had great beads of perspiration ... on his brow. The Californian knew the other had three queens because he had caught a glimpse of them. The man had plenty of money and the Californian pushed in $300 beside his chips. Just at this juncture a quiet self-contained, but coarse looking man at the end of the table put up his money and called. He had three aces and two jacks.

The Californians went to the police station. An officer was sent to see Colonel Sapolio with them. The colonel took the visitors aside, gave them $50 and a nice, quiet little talk about how sorry he was that his doorkeeper had allowed card-sharpers to get into his place when he sought to entertain only gentlemen and the visitors went back to the depot.[1]

In the same issue of the *News*, the fire and police board was considering a complaint by Alexander May against Gillam and Powell of the Denver Mutual Contribution Company. It operated a policy wheel on the northeast corner of Seventeenth and Market streets, the same intersection on which the Tivoli Club was located, making it practically certain that Jeff controlled of it. May claimed he paid $2 for a ticket with the numbers 34-43-69. May's numbers came up, and he was to win $230, but the house refused to pay. The house discharged a Thomas Reed, writer of policy tickets there. Claimed was that the ticket was sold after the wheel had turned and Reed and May knew the winning numbers. May went to the fire and police board to have the place closed down, and Reed testified that the game was thoroughly crooked: numbers on the wheel were often removed, and winning numbers were frequently changed. How the board responded to this evidence is not known.

Jeff constantly had trouble managing his two lives: the one as crime boss and the other as civic-minded business and family man. Some newspapers waged constant war against Jeff's predominant self, the leader of successful confidence men. Highly skilled in the confidence arts himself, Jeff loved using his god-given talents and

---

[1] *RMN* 09/08/1893, p. 3.

shrewdness to set up first-rate swindles and seeing them played so well that victims never knew they had been taken. However, he cherished community acceptance and applause. Jeff had a gift for organization and leadership, and as has been written by more than one historian, had he channeled his abilities towards honest endeavors, he could easily have climbed high. Perhaps, though, that climb would not have been so easy. For Jeff, there had always been two ladders, one for each side of himself, both equally appealing. So he climbed them both, the legal and illegal, shifting from one to the other, higher and higher, until inherent instability caused them to diverge. The wonder is that he climbed them to such heights.

Jeff loved to discuss city, state, and national politics. He also had a talent for writing that he liked to exercise. As eventful and hectic as his life was, he made time to write short stories and poems on politics and social issues of the day. A few of these found their way into the pages of several Denver newspapers, including the *Mercury*.

A TWILIGHT TALE
(By Jefferson R. Smith)

Scene.—A western miner in the east becomes weary from a walk over the dusty roads, and sitting on a stile near a New England farmer's residence, buries his face in his hands as he thinks of the wife and babe he left in his mountain home, and who are still looking with tear dimmed eyes for that aid which will never come.

FARMER:

Where are you going, stranger?
You look quite weary, most dead;
It's easy enough for one to see
You've no place to lay your head.
Come, come, speak up. Speak up my boy,
And tell me where you're from;
If there's any good that I can do
I'll do though you're a "bum."
"Bum?"[1] well, I'll retract that word
In these hard times of peace,
When all of us are struggling so
To keep up life's hard lease,
And so if you'll excuse me, friend,
For talking cold and hard,
From this time on I promise you
I'll call you simply "pard."
And now speak up and tell me,
Have you no home, my friend?
If so, your face so honest looks
That aid I'll surely lend."

MINER:

"Well, friend, then I will tell you

Since you speak so frank and kind,
I have in the far off silver state
Those whom I left behind.
There's Maggie, she's my wife,
    you know,
Long years we've worked together;
I at the mine, she at our home
With heart as light as feather.
Nor is this all," said the miner
As he brushed away a tear;
"Have you ever had a blue-eyed babe
Who to your heart was dear?
An angel dropped from heaven?
A cherub baby boy?
Well, I had one in the Rockies
Who filled my soul with joy.
Was I a man out there, you ask?
Did my heart bleed for the poor?
Go ask the weary pilgrim
Who passed my cottage door.
You know we're all God's people,
And we've all read that word

---

[1] The statement refers to use of the word "bum" by the *News* to describe poor & homeless men in the city.

That "He who giveth to the poor
But lendeth to the lord."[1]
You see I worked hard in the mines
And never lost a day;
I always made good wages
For the mine was on the pay,
But they had some legislation
Up at Washington one day,
That robbed us of our labor to
Help gold-bugs,[2] so they say.
So, as wife and babe were starving,
Had naught on earth to eat,
I'm hunting work so I can send
Them home some bread and meat.
But I find more idle men here
Than in the silver state,
And people tell me it comes from
A gold-bug interest rate;
That the people voted wrong last fall
For president, they say,
And that Cleveland's czar-like methods
Have brought this gloomy day.
I read about his babe last night
In silks and satins fine,
And my thought went back

to my mountain home,
And I sadly thought of mine.
That thought kept me awake last night;
Say, friend, I never slept,"
Said that great big-hearted miner,
And he bowed his head and wept.
FARMER:
"Here, friend take this five dollar note;
There's a mortgage on my land.
And this was interest money.
But I have got the sand
To help a suff'ring mortal,
And boldly make a stand
Against this gold bug monarchy.[3]
Here, stranger, here's my hand —"

What! dead? and on life's highway,
In an honest search for bread?
Oh, Cleveland, punisher of babes,
God's curses on thy head!
May an angel following thy trail
With a blood red flaming sword
Teach thee; "Who giveth to the poor
But lendeth to the lord."[4]

The dramatic format and the unforced meter of the lines allow the reader to enter the difficult worlds of the Farmer and the Miner, to sympathize with their hard times,

---

[1] *He who giveth to the poor / But lendeth to the lord. Holy Bible.* Proverbs, combination of 28:27 & 19:17. 28:27: "He that giveth unto the poor shall not lack; but he that hideth his eyes shall have many a curse." 19:17: "He that hath pity upon the poor lendeth unto the Lord; and that which he hath given will He pay him again." In employing this combination, Jeff is in interesting company. The sentence is very close to one employed by famous Puritan preacher and theologian Jonathan Edwards (1703-1758). Edwards sentence is "He that giveth to the poor lendeth to the Lord." The sermon is titled "The Duty of Charity to the Poor" (now also known as "Christian Charity"). The sermon was first published in Scotland in 1788 in a collection titled *Practical Sermons*. It probably did not appear again until the 1860s when collections of Edwards' sermons began to be published, but not widely. The combined verses from Proverbs may have become proverbial in Jeff's time, and Parson Uzzell might have employed it. (Edwards)

[2] *gold-bugs*: political nickname for advocates of a single gold standard (*OED* 10a(b)) as opposed to those who supported bi-metalism (gold & silver as a standard at a ratio of 16 parts silver to 1 part gold). This had been the standard since the U.S. Coinage Act of 1792 (*Gilded Age*, p. 191).

[3] *gold bug monarchy*: In 1893, President Grover Cleveland insisted on repeal of the Sherman Silver Purchase Act (enacted in 1890) and pressed for gold alone as the currency standard for the country. The monarchy is Cleveland and his administration (*Gilded Age*, p. 191).

[4] *Mercury* 09/30/1893. Jefferson R. "Little Randy" Smith col.

find uplift in the Farmer's charity, feel the irony of one with little giving it all to aid the afflicted, and experience regret over how help for the farmer had come too late.

The poem supports no political party, neither gold-standard Republicans, whom Jeff supported in elections, nor Populists, who were for bi-metalism but who would shut people like Jeff down. Rather, the poem points to the suffering of the masses victimized by the Panic of 1893. It also seems to give voice to the experience of its author during Southern Reconstruction and to all classes who had been marginalized and dispossessed by economic and social upheaval. The Farmer's curse upon President Cleveland is more than political show. For the expiring Miner, and thousands like him whose livelihood is dying or already dead, something akin to an angry blow has be been delivered to the cause of so much strife and suffering. And in the call for an avenging angel is the satisfaction of having delivered an inspired *coup de foudre*, or sudden thunderbolt, from the moral high ground. Hitting back at those perceived to have caused such widespread trouble and anguish, the poem in publication must have given Jeff considerable satisfaction, including that which authors feel when their work is thought worthy enough by others to be given flight among readers.

The day after the poem appeared, October 1, 1893, Jeff wrote to Mary. The brief letter shows the strain of this intense period, but whatever the causes of his tightening emotions, financial problems were not among them. Many in the nation were suffering economically, and dupes on lower Seventeenth Street may have thinned dramatically, but the letter makes plain that Jeff was in no danger of financial collapse.

> My dear own Mollie
> On the 10th of October or a few days before, I want you to be ready to go with me to Chicago. We will stay there 4 or 5 days and have a time of our own. We will leave the babys [sic] with mother and paint the town red. I have been almost crazy since you left. But I am still alive.
> Love to all, Jeff[1]

Jeff and Mary did leave the children with their grandmother in St. Louis and take a train to Chicago. Years later Mary told her grandchildren about that exciting trip to the World Columbian Exposition, commonly called the Chicago World's Fair. It commemorated the 400th anniversary of the arrival of Christopher Columbus in the Western World. The Exposition site on the shores of Lake Michigan devoted 55 acres to exhibit buildings on such topics as transportation, electricity, and the arts. Concessions covered another 50 acres. Total acres amounted to over 600, development of which cost as astounding $22 million (about 700 million today)[2].

At the time, the Exposition was the most popular destination in the nation. "There is in the life of any great city a moment when it becomes fully conscious of its place in history. For Chicago that moment was 1893."[3] The psychologist William James wrote, only half humorously, to his novelist brother Henry that "EVERYONE says one ought

---

[1] Ltr fr Jeff R. Smith II to Mary E. Smith. 10/01/1893. The stationary bears the letterhead of the Iron Mask Hotel in Gilman, Colorado, covering "Gilman" with "Denver." Item 1, author's col.

[2] Tom's Inflation Calculator.

[3] Miller.

to sell all one has and mortgage one's soul to go there; it is esteemed such a revelation of beauty."[1] Thomas Edison declared, "No man who makes his living by his intellect can afford to miss the Fair."[2] The Exposition consumed three times more electrical power than the host city of Chicago. In the midway, the most popular feature was the Ferris Wheel, this Exposition's Eiffel Tower. The very first of its kind, standing 264 feet high, George Ferris's Wheel carried 36 cars, each with space for 60 persons whose one revolution ride took 25 minutes. Beginning in May 1893, the Exposition's 184 days received 27 million visitors who had opportunity to see such legends as Buffalo Bill Cody, Inventor Thomas Edison, escape artist Harry Houdini, boxer "Gentleman" Jim Corbett, and musician Scott Joplin.[3] Not known is if Jeff "worked" the crowds, but with that many "customers," he might not have passed up the chance.

Since 1889, Jeff had not seen fit to have his family at his side. He had tried that once, and the *News* had made Mary suffer for it. Jeff's letters to his family express love and how he missed his family. Fairly regularly, he would travel to St. Louis to visit or have them journey to him. Not known is if Mary ever again came to Denver, but she and the children did visit Jeff in Creede. Plans to build a home and resettle there were abandoned when it became clear that Creede had reached its climax. Jeff settled for keeping his family secure and stable in St. Louis and considered resettling there. He worked at ingratiating himself with the St. Louis underworld, as a St. Louis news story tells,[4] and he received letters from St. Louis politicians and legislators.[5]

For possible relocation in Chicago, it can be safely assumed Jeff investigated the criminal underworld power structure. Chicago Mayor Carter Henry Harrison had maintained close ties with longtime Chicago crime boss Michael Cassius McDonald. "King Mike," as he was known, was the main man Jeff would have had to see if he wanted a place in the mostly Irish underworld gambling domain. Jeff was probably well aware of the mayor's support of wide-open gambling, prostitution, and liquor, the very things Denver officials often sought to shut down. Naturally, Mayor Harrison was enthusiastically supported by Chicago's criminal bosses. Allowed to operate were "saloons and gambling houses, protected bunco steerers and confidence men and brace games of all kinds without hindrance." As the mayor once declared, "You can't make people moral by ordinances and it is no use trying. This is a free town."[6] As a business location, surely Chicago would have been a city to Jeff's liking.

On October 7, 1893, the *Denver Times* published Jeff's travel plans not only to Chicago but also elsewhere. That Jeff's trip would also be for business is suggested.

Col. Sapolio Smith Leaves for the Windy City.

Col. Jefferson (Sapolio) Smith, lord-high ruler of 17th st., leaves [Denver] for the East [Chicago] tonight to be gone several weeks. While absent he will

---

[1] James.

[2] Hirschl.

[3] Miller.

[4] Fr Jeff Smith's scrapbook: "'Soapy' was only arrested once in St. Louis, although he lived here off and on for years. Detectives McGrath and Tracy took him in." (Jones, Robert, p. 333)

[5] Ltrs dated 1896 & 1898 fr Jeff Smith's scrapbook: the second Ltr fr Cronin, on letterhead "HOUSE OF DELEGATES," concludes, "With regards from all the boys." (Jones, Robert, pp. 332, 336)

[6] Franch, p. 113.

leave his work in charge of his able lieutenants. He will visit Midway Plaisance[1] and Carter Harrison,[2] and show the Midway inhabitants and the windy city's mayor how he does business in the Queen City of the Plains.

After he has done Chicago to a turn Col. Smith will journey to Washington, where he will labor with the law-makers for a few days, and from there he will proceed to Atlanta, Ga., returning via St. Louis. Col. Smith says he is deeply grieved at being left off the Speak-Easy ticket, having been defeated for the office of sheriff by William Arnett, and instead of remaining in the city will relieve his troubled mind by dining on the Georgia 'possum, pawpaw[3] and persimmon.

He says he has been invited to address the Georgia Democrats on the free coinage [of silver] issue, and in order to get his subject well in hand has been studying with a distinguished editor for the past few weeks.

Col. Smith says he is not fully decided what political ticket he will support locally, since bolting the Speak-Easy nominees, but will return before election day, so as to have his ward ___ [install?] the men of his choice, and it is ___ [surely?] able to suppse [sic] that Sapolio will ___ [support?] the winning ticket, for in ad- ___ [dition?] to being an artist in his peculiar ___ [sort of ?] business, there are no flies on him ___ [when ?] he gets down to political work. As Jeff ___ [proposes?] so goes his ward.... ... For four long weeks will the ___ [Colonel be?] missed from his 17th st haunt.[4]

No corroboration shows Jeff attempted to run for sheriff of Arapahoe County nor that he visited Washington, DC, with political motives nor that he ventured to Atlanta.

Jeff was probably preparing for his trip when a newspaper article again described bunco gangs infesting lower Seventeenth Street. Complaints of their exploits had become incessant, bringing the *Denver Times* to call it "The Bunco Parade."

The bunco men are working 17th street quite swiftly these days and passengers who walk up that street arriving on the trains are watched for and the unwary are usually trapped. Hardly a day passes but someone is roped in and robbed of what money he may have.[5]

The article describes one swindle involving the giving away of free World's Fair (World Columbian Exposition) books. Victims were met walking up Seventeenth Street from the train depot and informed of the giveaway occurring at the Tivoli Club.

One of the passengers walked up 17th street and was met by one of the fellows who obtained recognition and began by talking of a World's Fair book

---

[1] The recreational area of the Chicago Columbian Exposition of 1893.

[2] *Carter Harrison*: 5-term mayor of Chicago. On October 28, 1894, two days before the close of the World's Columbian Exposition, he said in a speech, "I intend to live for half a century still, and at the end of that time New York will say, 'Let us go to the metropolis of America [Chicago].'" That evening he was shot to death in his home by a deluded person. (Hirsch!)

[3] *pawpaw*: "papaw." Of the custard-apple family, growing in the central & south U.S., having oblong, yellowish, edible fruit with many seeds.

[4] *Denver Times* clipping cut out by Jeff. He wrote at the top in pencil, "Sat. 10/07/93." A bottom left portion of the clipping is torn away; words "supplied" are signified by "[?]." Item 127, author's col.

[5] *Denver Times* 10/07/1893. Clipping cut out by Jeff R. Smith II. Jefferson R. "Little Randy" Smith col.

which some old fellow rooming at the Tivoli was giving away. The stranger had not heard of it. The bunco man said that he was going out on the same train with the other fellow and asked him to go over with him to the Tivoli, as he wanted to get one of the books for his wife. So they went to the place and the bartender was asked where the man was who had the books desired, and he replied that he was upstairs in his room.

The familiar "Big Hand" scenerio followed: a walk upstairs, three or four men playing cards where the old man with the "books" should be, word that he was out but would return, and an invite to pass the time until the old man's return in a friendly game of poker. The bunco steerer then

asked for a dollar's worth of chips and requested his victim to take some, too. The stranger in [by] this time had "tumbled" to the situation and made a rush for the door, fearing that he would be robbed outright and made his escape, going right back to the depot.

Last week another instance happened of the same nature, only the fellow was taken for $40.... He had been in the city making purchases and ... was induced to enter the Tivoli and came out having lost a check for quite an amount and about $80 in cash. He had reached the depot intending to go home, when he related what had happened to him and he was advised to go to the city hall and enter complaint, which he did. ...Smith was sent for. In the meantime, steps had been taken by the chief to have the check headed off. The ... interview with Smith resulted in all of the checks and money being returned but about $40, which Smith said he would not give up unless compelled to do so as the result of a law suit and the matter was dropped. The young fellow from Boulder felt very foolish over his experience, and when asked how it happened that he allowed himself to be taken in replied that it was done so slick that he did not know what was happening ... until it was too late. He said that ... when he saw what kind of crowd he had gotten into he was afraid of [for] his life and remained in the game hoping that something would happen to allow him to get out.

To one familiar with the workings of the street these fellows can be seen any day working ... in pairs and singles at the hours of the train arrivals. They do not get very close to the depot, as the officers there have been waging a vigorous warfare against them for months. ... Hardly a day passes that complaints are not being lodged with the officers at the depot, and the only thing that they can do is recommend the victims to apply for relief at police headquarters."[1]

Never had Jeff and the Tivoli Club been implicated in so many crimes in so short a time. Returning from his trip, Jeff learned that a petition signed by twenty-six merchants in the vicinity of Union Depot had been presented to the fire and police board. Requested were stricter measures against confidence men and bunco steerers along Seventeenth. Two days later, on Monday, October 30, 1893, Jeff appeared

---

[1] *Denver Times* 10/07/1893. Clipping cut out by Jeff R. Smith II. Jefferson R. "Little Randy" Smith col.

before the board. Claiming the petition was not unanimous and that he could secure a counter petition, he was allowed to circulate one, but in the meantime, he was ordered to stop all street activity with which he was associated.[1] The following day Jeff's petition was complete. It was not exactly a counter petition as it pertained to one site, not a general vicinity, but its twenty-three signatures showed impressive support. Dated October 31, 1893, it was addressed "To the Honorable Fire and Police Board of the City of Denver, Colo."

> We, the undersigned, business men of Seventeenth St. [now operating in the City of?] Denver, would respectfully state that we have known Jeff R. Smith for a number of years and we state that we know Mr. Smith to be an honorable gentleman, a man of his word, and of the most strict business integrity, and we desire to see him continue business at his old stand at the corner of Seventeenth and Market streets.

Respectfully.

D. May May Shoe & Clothing Co.	
James B. Belford	
Charles M. Graff	
Denver Collateral Bank.	1400 17th
Geo Stevenson	1412 17th
Thos Morrison	1420 17th
The Schivenfeld Mercantile Co.	Cor 17th & Blake
A. Badenhof _ Vice Presdt	
Union Hotel . G. N. Beard . Prop.	
C. W. Bowman	1520 17th
Geo B. Fisher	Cor 17th & Wazee
W.J. Rosenthal	1526 17th
F. Goodman Wholesale Tobacco}	1507 & 1509 17th
Weil Bros Wholesale Liquor dealers}	1631 Blake
Royer & Shynock Hardware}	1750 Larimer
Inter Ocean Hotel .	
Nathan L. Baker Editor Mercury}	
August Endhink	1414 17th
St George Hotel	1529 17th
Davis Turner, Prop.	
Ramon Solis — Solis Cigar Co.	
F. Spalti — owner Block	17th & Blake
S. Wachtee & Co.	1717 Larimer
Sam Mayer	1638 Larimer
Wm Deutch owner Block	17th & Market
Andy Keeley — McPhee & McGinnity	18 & Wazee
Thos. F. Begley	1417 Larimer[2]

---

[1] *RMN* 10/29/1893, p. 5, & *RMN* 10/31/1893, p. 7.
[2] Handwritten petition, 10/31/1893. Item 110, author's col.

The fire and police board, knowing Jeff very well, questioned the validity of the signatures on the document. A clipping cut from an unidentified source reveals Jeff's hopes in his attempts to manipulate the board.

> In the suave, affable manner, which so highly distinguishes the proprietor of the Tivoli Club, he told the board that he was only too anxious to accede to its wishes and would instruct his corps of assiduous assistants to discontinue their attentions to those gentlemen of simple habits who so eagerly desired to witness the operations of Mr. Smith's club-rooms. He impressed on the board, however, the fact that his lieutenants never tried to affect Denver citizens with their persuasive eloquence, but confined their efforts to visitors whose dress and actions betrayed their rustic occupations.
>
> The colonel naively questioned [discussed?] the genuineness of the signatures to the petition, and the board adjourned the hearing of the case until he could prove the truth of his assertion.[1]

Jeff wisely did not say that he himself had collected the signatures on the petition. Very possibly some, if not all, were indeed forged. The record does not show their validity having been determined. Jeff's defense before the board must have surprised or even shocked more than one of the board members. To present a petition from Jeff's immediate business community, declaring Jeff a man of his word, and then for him to claim Denver citizens were never swindled, only rustic visitors (who were, after all, customers of much of that community) took one hundred percent brass. Given Jeff's ability to deliver a spiel with a wink and a smile, however, might have earned him a less stern rebuke from the board. However it was delivered, though, its nature and effect seem clear. Accounts of swindling related to Jeff drops from publication until May 1894. Jeff's bunco scams probably continued but were scaled back, perhaps a little less aggressive, and a great deal more fine tuned.

Since Jeff's Chicago visit, he had endured a string of bad luck. He was down in the dumps as two articles in the *Denver Times* make evident.

> There are all kinds of hard luck, and every person who gets in a bad way seems to think his fortune is a little worse than anything he has ever heard of. A party of story tellers were telling their experiences to one another, there being no policeman present in an uptown barroom the other night, when in stepped Col. Jefferson Smith, who as a story teller, has no equal.
>
> The Colonel has been in pretty hard straits lately, his troubles having been aired through the press, but since the election he feels more contented..., and after taking a drink at the bar and listening to the story tellers a few moments he invited the boys to take a round on him and then started in to relate his story of hard luck.
>
> "Now, you boys may think you know what hard luck is, but you don't know a thing about it," began the colonel, by way of introduction.

---

[1] Newspaper clipping of unknown origin & date (probably late October or November 1893), cut by Jeff R. Smith II. Author's col.

"I have had some pretty tough times myself, but this fellow that I am going to tell you about was in about the hardest luck of any poor devil on earth.

"I knew him in Dallas, when he was flying high and had money to throw at the birds, but luck turned against him until he went broke and finally quit the town. I didn't see the poor fellow again until one evening about three months afterward, when a party of us were playing a game of poker at a little wayside saloon in Southern Kansas. The party had just met by accident and we were using corn for markers, not having any chips.

"We were playing along quietly when in comes this friend of mine, looking about as seedy as any poor devil you ever saw. He had been bumming around the country until his clothes were getting pretty shabby; he needed a shave and was a hard looking 'mark' in general.

"I did not recognize the man when he appeared, neither did he know me, but after watching the game for a few minutes he stepped out and was gone about a half hour, when he came back and rather nervously pulled his chair up to the table and asked for a hand in the game. I noticed his nervousness but paid no attention to it until it came around his time to ante.

"Instead of putting up his money he ran his hand into his pocket, pulled out a handful of corn and poured it onto the table.

"'Hold on stranger,' I said to him politely, 'we're not playing reds tonight.' And the stranger fainted in his chair.

"When he came to his senses he told me that he thought he had a snap[1] when he saw us using corn for chips, and had gone out to a big corn crib and picked up the first ear of corn in his reach. He would have been all right, only he got a red ear.

"But to show you what hard luck he was in, we went back the next day and searched that whole corn crib over and found that he had gotten hold of the only red ear of corn in the crib."

The boys all admitted the fellow was in hard luck and drank to his good health and success in the future.[2]

As if to prove that the tables could turn, Jeff soon had a run of bad luck.

HAS A SURE HOODOO.
TOILS AND TRIBULATIONS OF A CHEVALIER OF FORTUNE.
On Every Hand He Is Haunted By Pitfalls and Death Traps ... An Unparalleled Chapter of Injury, Sickness, Poisoning and Fractures Precipitated Upon Hon. Jefferson R. Smith.

The Honorable Jefferson Randolph Smith has been distinctly in a state of mind for two weeks past.... Day after day he has stuck close to the Tivoli bar, rarely venturing half a block away, and all the time his face has worn the sad expression of a man who has found himself on a dead card—not in it.[3]

---

[1] *a snap*: an easy job, of stealing. fr c. 1885. (Partridge, *Slang*)

[2] *Denver Times*, 11/15/1893.

[3] *on a dead card—not in it*: uncertain. Having to bet on a losing card—not in the game?

"I don't as a rule believe in a fellow squealing," he began. "If the game runs against you, double up and wait is my style. But there are some runs of luck that outdo human nature. I had one of them a month ago, I hit a run of hard luck that leaves anything I ever struck before out of sight. I won't attempt to deny I'm rattled; it's fazed me, simply fazed me. It began on my Chicago trip. You see I wanted to see that fair; I don't expect to be around time for the next one. Then I owed $2800 in town and wanted to pay it. Instinct told me the Windy city was the place to get the stuff.

"At first everything went my way. I picked up a cold thousand on the train going out and felt right in line when I struck the town itself. Inside two days I had the long green right down in my jeans—$3000, $2800 for my friends and the rest for me. I saw the show, too; that hadn't cost me a cent. I gave a little dinner also at my hotel—no, not the Palmer, the Auditorium, second floor, front, private. Turkish bath, music room, parlors, and opera house, you know—that cost a nice little roll, but I didn't worry about that; it didn't [hurt?] my little thirty hundred at all. Then I came home. That's when my troubles began.

"It was avidity that did it," he resumed. "I didn't run across any creditors around town and I got to thinking I'd have a little more dough for me. I went up to Bob Austin's place[1] and hit the wheel. In two hours, I was minus the little thirty hundred and had got desperate. I didn't care for myself by that time; it was my debts that worried me. I'd got to get that $2,600 back, and I dropped $500 more of my own trying it.

"Then I made up my mind to quit and I went down the street in a dead funk. It wasn't so much the losing that hurt me; it was the thought of having made a sucker of myself—got my figure and then pressed up for more. Well, then, as I said before, I discovered that my hard luck had only just begun. I dallied round in the early morning and got the neuralgia in my eye. That made me so blind that in going up the street I couldn't see a coal hole, and down I went like McGinty.[2]

"That sent me to bed. If a man wants to think he's a Methuselah, just let him get a pair of eyes on him that won't read and then get laid up on his back. He'll live a year a day and not half try.[3]

"While I was at my very worst and thought it surely must be time to call the turn,[4] along comes Tom Clark with a capias[5] and tells me the grand jury has indicted me for murder. Wasn't that rough, though? I never said a word— I just ambled over to the court on the day set to go and felt pretty sure I was

---

[1] Probably Gavin & Austin's at 1617 Larimer Street as described in the *RMN* 07/22/1893, p. 1.

[2] *down I went like McGinty*: "Down Went McGinty," wildly popular song by Joseph Flynn, 1889, about a hard-luck Irishman who kept falling off a wall, down a coal hole, down to the bottom of the sea. (Lee, p. 392)

[3] *live a year a day and not half try*: make a day seem like a year.

[4] *call the turn*: end the game, of life? figurative. Betting on the order of the last cards in the pack. c. 1864, 1889. II 8.d. Cards. (*OED*)

[5] *capias*: arrest warrant.

going to hang—nothing would have surprised me but what did happen. They decided not to try me; laid me over to another occasion. I braced up a little and was just walking out of court when I saw something that made my heart jump—it was a nickel on the floor; I was sure my long run was changed. That was where I got fooled. I was pretty stiff yet, and in bobbing down for the coin I broke my silk suspenders.

"If there's a more wearying feeling on earth than results from an accident of that nature I don't know it. I fixed the feeling though, with a pin I found on the floor. Then I went to jump on a cable car and that d__d pin hooked into my flesh and tore away about three inches of me, I felt sore, but that wasn't the worst of it—blood poisoning set in, and I've earned a doctor bill of $40 fixing it up!

"Now I haven't but just got over this when along comes Big Jack of the Inter-Ocean and takes a shot at me, and I find I haven't any gun! Jack swears he means to kill me on sight. The hardest luck of all is he don't do it. I've been down to his hotel and over to the Central and pretty much everywhere, but he is no place to be found. I'm beginning to feel like the Wandering Jew! ... I believe a year's monking would do me good," and the Hon. Jefferson R. limped away.[1]

On December 19, Jeff filed a $5,000 damage suit against Charles G. Chever and William B. Palmer at whose property at 1705 Larimer the offending coal-delivery hole was to be found.[2] (Outcome of the suit is unknown.) The "capias for murder" is not identified but probably concerned the Clifton Sparks shooting of October 1892. The Big Jack referred to as taking a shot at Jeff is probably the Jack Devine whom Jeff had shot and wounded in an altercation over the outcome of the 1891 election.

Jeff often extended a helping hand to others, especially friends and peers. Sometimes, though, he regretted doing so. One such occasion began a few days after Jeff appeared before the fire and police board. John Wright, an ex-city detective, came to Jeff for help, which he rendered. About a week later, Jeff felt compelled to undo what he had done when an ill-clothed, emaciated woman with two children in like condition also came to Jeff for help. A reporter for the *News* wrote up the entire story.

AN ACT OF JUSTICE.
Jeff Smith Was First Charitable and Then Just.

Retributive justice in the person of Jefferson R. Smith dropped the bandage from her eyes yesterday and took a good square look at things, with a result highly commendatory, both to the erstwhile blind goddess and her wide awake representative pro tempore.

... Justice and Jeff went together at the sight of a deserted and forlorn wife and her helpless babes and together rubbed their palms in stern satisfaction as they heard the prison door clang behind the unworthy cause of

---

[1] *RMN* 11/08/1893, p. 8.
[2] *RMN* 12/20/1893, p. 8.

all this misery and woe. Verily, it was a sight to warm the heart of the philanthropist who has not grown too angelic to take delight in just retribution.

On the first day of the present month Stella Sheedy, a well-known character, was arrested by Detectives Carberry and Currier, charged with robbing a laboring man named John McNamara. John Wright, ex-city detective, ex-convict and crook, was taken as her accomplice. The woman has her habitat in the block at 1425 Larimer street, a noted resort frequently raided by the police. Wright is her paramour and is said to assist her in her schemes.

At the trial before Justice Pickens, the woman's methods were fully aired. The case of McNamara was an example. Wright allured him into Stella's room and there the pair proceeded to rob him of all he had. But in this instance they bit off more than they could masticate. The victim showed fight and raised such a noise that the police were called in. They found Wright with two swollen eyes and in a generally dilapidated condition. When McNamara took an inventory, he found that he was $14 short.

The couple were arrested and the woman got thirty days in the county jail.[1] Wright escaped conviction, although it was shown that he was an ex-convict and general tough character, and that he had a wife and children in this city whom he had deserted for this dissolute woman. He set to work immediately to effect his paramour's release from a restraint especially unpleasant to him, as it deprived him of the means of "earning" a livelihood.

He had an acquaintance with Jeff Smith, and he went to him for aid. Unacquainted with the man's domestic history, the genial and accommodating Jeff agreed to go on the appeal bond [for $300], and a supersedes from the county court was secured.[2]

An hour later Detective Carberry, who had made the first arrest, met the woman on her old stamping ground…. She appeared highly elated and told the officer how "Johnny had got me out." … But the very instrument used for its subversion was destined to work the final triumph of right.

Yesterday morning as the colonel, the title by which the rejuvenated Jeff is known, stood in the door of his establishment at the corner of Seventeenth and Market streets, his attention was called to a most forlorn looking object coming up the street. It was a woman with a babe in her arms and a little girl toddling along by her side. All were in rags and as a particularly energetic gust of wind swept up the street it showed how thinly all were clad.

Jeff accosted the woman and was surprised to learn that she was looking for him. He revealed his identity and heard a story that metamorphosed the man in an instant. She was the wife of John Wright…. Her husband had deserted her for another woman and she was left in absolute want, to provide for herself and babies. Wright had refused to contribute a cent toward their maintenance, while he had spent all his ill-

---

[1] *RMN* 11/04/1893, p. 2.
[2] *RMN* 11/05/1893, p. 8.

gotten gains on his dissolute companion. His wife had worked at everything she could get to do, as the worn and calloused hands she showed to Jeff bore eloquent testimony, but she and her little ones were now on the verge of starvation and about to perish from the cold and she had sought him for assistance.

The answer she received was so immediate and hearty as to almost bewilder her. First he gave her a sum of money which would keep her from want for some time to come. Then he rushed off to undo ... writ of supersedes by paying all the costs and then withdrawing from the appeal bond. In company with Deputy Sheriff Ingersoll he went to the Sheedy woman's room on Larimer street to re-arrest her. Upon forcing an entrance..., they were not surprised to find her and her pal about to fleece a very unsophisticated individual from the rural districts. He was extricated from their toils and sent on his way rejoicing, while mistress Sheedy, very much against her will, was relegated to a more appropriate abode in the county jail, where she will languish out the term of her sentence, with no more writs of supersedes to look forward to.[1]

Jeff was mindful of how aiding the poor, needy, and desperate of Denver helped his reputation. These acts, though, usually showed little, if any, calculation. They were too often spontaneous, anonymous, or mixed in with the sponsorship of others to be clearly open to the charge of being self-serving. Those who really knew Jeff and how ingrained in him was the belief that he had the right to take suckers for all they had, looked at his charitable acts with suspicion or wonder, if not disbelief. How could a consummate, life-long confidence man with a determined and sometimes ruthless gang also be a generous benefactor?

While some did not believe Jeff's acts of generosity, Jeff apparently did. He performed them regularly and with conviction as part of his business persona, one he regarded as having such public standing and character that he thought it appropriate to seek elected office. In the pages of the city's newspapers, for a time, he hinted at his election prospects numerous times, and he may have run, or prepared to run, for county sheriff in 1893. In November, he sought support for a run for city alderman. In mid November, the *Denver Times* quoted him as saying, "He says there is no question as to his being elected Alderman from the Third ward at the election next spring."[2] When hearing of Jeff's political aspirations, the Combine, the higher Ring, and people in general must have shaken their heads and thought, "Not possible." Jeff's name, despite being seen on occasion in favorable and charitable lights, was synonymous with Denver's crooked politics and constant crime, not to mention its connection with violence that ended with men being wounded or dead. Additionally, at the time, Jeff was still under indictment for the murder of Clifton Sparks.

One man of influential public standing who stood by Jeff for many years apparently did so in part because of his charitable works. This man was in a better position than most to know Jeff and all of his doings. He was Jeff's lawyer in the Col.

---

[1] *RMN* 11/11/1893, p. 3.
[2] *Denver Times* 11/15/1893.

Arkins attempted murder trial and in the Cliff Sparks murder trial: Judge James B. Belford. In an October 16, 1896, letter penned in Denver to Jeff in Spokane, Judge Belford paid Jeff a superlative compliment along with a gently stated reservation. It appears at the close of a friendly letter about politics and his ill health and poor financial state:

> I do not know that I will ever see you again on this earth, but I do know that one who has to my own knowledge so generously and so munificently helped the poor, relieved the distressed and encouraged the weak, will not be among the damned, whatever his short comings may be.[1]

For the rest of his life, Jeff pursued dreams of becoming an important *public* political figure, and while in Denver, he was willing to risk his life to keep Denver aligned with his political loyalties. Jeff had opportunity to prove this commitment when Colorado's new governor called up the state militia, sent it into Denver, and gave it orders to fire upon city hall if those inside, Jeff Smith among them, would not vacate.

Chapter 12
King Gambler and The City Hall War

Regarding "Soapy Smith, *"He is one of the greatest characters in the west.... ... You never knew anyone to have such power.*
—Colorado Congressman Lafe Pence
Washington, DC, March 20, 1894[2]

By 1891, the general population of Colorado had lost confidence in Republicans and Democrats. To address the worsening problems of the common people, fusing with Democrats in some places, a third party emerged: the People's Party. Interest in Populism, as it was called, surged among farmers, miners, and rural working people, and they flocked to Populist candidates who addressed their concerns.

Enter Davis Hanson Waite. Raised in New York state and having studied law in his lawyer father's office, at age 25 in 1850, he made his way west. Waite worked on newspapers, as proprietor of mercantile ventures, as Republican representative in the Wisconsin and then the Kansas legislatures, as rancher, and as school teacher in Missouri. Returning to New York during the Civil War, he studied for and passed the bar, and he also owned and operated a newspaper. Arriving in Leadville, in 1879, he practiced law and looked for silver, moved to Ashcroft in 1880, and finally settled in Aspen in 1881. There he practiced law, served as a "Police Judge" (Justice of the Peace), was the first Pitkin County Superintendent of Schools, edited *The Aspen Times* and *Chronicle*,[3] and became owner and publisher of *The Aspen Times* in 1883.[1]

---

[1] *Jones*, Robert, pp 336-337.
[2] *The Register* 03/23/1894, p. 3.
[3] In the *Aspen Times*, the following advertisement appears fr July 16, 1881, to March 24, 1883: "DAVIS H. WAITE, Attorney-At-Law and Police Judge, Aspen, Colorado. Will be prompt in collections and remittances; do all kinds of conveyencing with neatness and dispatch; will obtain Government Patents and give special attention to Mining Cases in the District and United States Courts."

With the economic downturn in 1891 and while secretary of the Knights of Labor, Waite launched the labor-oriented *Aspen Union Era,* became a co-founder of the Colorado Populist Party in February 1892, and in July became the Populist candidate for governor.[2] While campaigning, he advocated various Populist themes (an end to corruption, a reasonable work week, curbs on monopolies), but the flag he hoisted highest in speeches before large crowds was the one for the free coinage of silver. Waite drew Silver Democrats and some Republicans, and despite the Republican party machine, a Populist victory, coming mainly from Colorado's rural districts, could not be checked. Elected were a majority of populists to the Colorado State House, a near majority in the Senate (by one vote), two Populist Colorado Congressmen to Washington (John C. Bell and Lafe Pence), and as the eighth governor of Colorado since statehood in 1876, the sixty-eight-year-old Populist Davis H. Waite.[3]

Waite's agenda as governor included strengthening Populist political power. After recreating a demand for silver to put miners back to work, other Populist planks included government control or even operation of transportation and communication monopolies, an eight-hour work day,[4] and women's suffrage. The gift of suffrage, Waite thought, would bring thankful women to Populism along with their opposition to gambling and vice, and drink. Thus would be weakened that rival of Populism, the Prohibition Party. Waite had many plans for enhancing the Populist Party, and backing them was the iron will of a committed redeemer.

While in Aspen, Waite was "noted for his opposition to drunkenness, gambling and other forms of vice, and as justice of the peace he was especially severe upon those guilty of such offenses."[5] He brought this severity into Colorado politics. "Governor Waite was," wrote Clyde King in *The History of the Government of Denver,*

> an honest and irate believer in the suppression of all gambling and vice and hence used all his power for the enforcement of the state laws pertaining thereto; Denver had always been rather tolerant of such vices, though not always more so than other large cities, and laws and ordinances pertaining thereto were just sufficiently enforced to prevent an outbreak of adverse public opinion. Preceding governors were in sympathy with the policy of the leaders in Denver..., and hence there was no friction...; but all was different with Governor Waite. He was impulsive, sure of the eternal righteousness of his convictions, and could brook no control.[6]

This orientation made Waite an enemy of not only Ed Chase and Jeff R. Smith as heads of the gambling and saloon men but also of Denver's mercantile community, of its banking establishment, and of its many city officials. To them, gaming, the saloons, their entertainments, other lesser upstanding attractions, and a variety of side

---

[1] *owner and publisher of The Aspen Weekly Times*: On May 19, 1883, his name first appears on the masthead as follows: "D. H. Waite & Co., Publishers."

[2] *National Cyclopaedia of American Biography, The*. Vol. VI. NY: James T White & Co., 1896.

[3] Ubbelohde, p. 221.

[4] Ubbelohde, p. 221.

[5] *The Cedar Rapids Evening Gazette* 04/13/1894, p. 7, col. 5.

[6] King, p. 211.

businesses, such as auction houses, were a general and often personal boon. People came to Denver for these things as well as business, and along with the general prosperity of Denver as a major destination city, officials who allowed the attractions to flourish received a regular income from it (also known as graft).

Waite's impulsive, hard-charging approach to change often took the form of firings for "incompetency, neglect," and, his favorite, "malfeasance" (or "evil doing" in public office). So numerous did these events become, many accomplished with increasing physical force, that they led at last to armed confrontation between the state militia and the regular and deputized men of the Denver police and sheriff's departments, called The City Hall War. And throughout this two-year period, the person whose name most often appeared in print as opposing Governor Waite's reforms? "'Soapy' Smith."

Jeff did not lead opposition against the governor, but reports often reveal him in the vicinity of conflicts. If Jeff were sighted and reported on, writers usually reminded readers that Jeff Smith was also known as "Soapy" Smith, the notorious crook.[1] When being out of sight counted most, Jeff was far from the action, but the governor and Populist allies had often spotted him among the opposition or connected with crime in news stories, and some with newspapers, including Waite and a son-in-law publisher, made "'Soapy' Smith" a convenient figurehead of lawlessness and all things unsavory.

Not all newspapers, however, disparaged Jeff. One supporter was Nathan Baker, owner and publisher of the *Denver Mercury*. From the excellent send up he gives Jeff in early March 1894, it seems Jeff was considering a run for city council.

THE THIRD WARD

Since Col. J. R. Smith has moved his residence to the Third Ward, the property holding element of that section ... always on the look-out for good city legislative timber, have been discussing him as the next member of Denver's council.

The citizens of the third ward could go a great deal farther and fare much worse. Col. Smith is in the prime of manhood, is shrewd in legislative matters, always goes to the front on important questions that will benefit Denver, and above all things else, his friends know that he can be relied upon with the most implicit faith.

During the recent [economic] panic..., when men were clamoring in front of the banks for their money and when the snapping of a twig would have precipitated a riot, he proved himself a pacificator of no small moment, and during the days that followed when hungry men were roaming the streets and wealthy property holders were nervous and unable to decide upon a course to pursue, he not only took large sums of money from his pocket to assist Rev. Thomas Uzzell in feeding them, but in many ways quieted those who were talking of pillaging the town.

The MERCURY has no means of knowing how Col. Smith feels over this action on the part of the people in mentioning his name for the council, but if

---

[1] Newspaper clippings during the years 1893-1894 obtained by Jeff R. Smith II through a clipping service he hired. The clippings and the bill for the service, author's col.

they keep it up and he is nominated, out of the two thousand and five hundred votes in that ward it will poll not less than two thousand.[1]

One week later, perhaps motivated in part by political ambition, Jeff showed his willingness "to go to the front" to protect his way of life, that of his friends, and his political beliefs. Later on, Baker in his paper would again reward him for doing so.

Denver was well known, though no more than Chicago, for its saloons with their risqué tableaus and saloon girls, houses of prostitution, "sure thing" cons, other frauds, and, though illegal, plentiful games of chance. Also well known was that "corruption, disorganization, and poor leadership" persisted in the police department. For these and political reasons, in 1889, the state exerted control by establishing a board of three commissioners, one each for fire, police, and excise (taxation).[2] The idea was for the commissioners to act separately, but the board always acted as a unit. Salaries for these positions were not high, but they were significant, especially during hard times: $3,000 for the chairman (who was the fire commissioner), $2,500 for the other two commissioners, and $1,800 for a secretary.[3] The governor made appointments for two-year terms, with "advice and consent of the senate," and the governor had "power of suspension or removal at any time for cause, to be stated in writing, but not for political reasons."[4] The board was important and powerful. It determined policy and made rules, but it could not fix saloon license fees lower than "$600 per annum nor allow them to be open on Sunday or after midnight...." The board could grant, refuse, or revoke licenses. So board members were of significant interest to the saloon men, and they were extremely important to city government. "[L]icences granted to retail liquor dealers alone brought into the city treasury" well over $100,000 a year.[5]

Waite tapped into the problem of corruption in his 1892 campaign when he publicly questioned why so many criminals were being prematurely transferred from Cañon City Penitentiary to the Denver County Jail and then quickly paroled. Why, he asked, are "criminals" being "protected" instead of "punished"?[6] It seemed painfully obvious that criminal interests were influencing state, county, and municipal justice, and Waite understood this influence to extend to the Denver fire and police board. So as part of his platform he promised that his first task would be to rid the capital city's government of corruption. He did not waste any time in shaking and shaping things up.

In early February 1893, Waite embarked upon his mission. He appointed a new fire and police board: "C. B. Stone, chairman, D. J. Martin and J. H. Phelps."[7] On February 15, he fired the Colorado State Medical Board treasurer for malfeasance. This treatment was controversial because the doctor had long served, never charged with dishonesty, and was not now. The firing was over his not following state rules for

---

[1] *Denver Mercury* 03/10/1894.

[2] Secrest, p. 163.

[3] King, p. 184. Tom's Inflation Calculator: $1 in 1894 = $29.97 in modern dollars, so $89,910 for the chair, $74,925 for the other commissioners, and $53,946 for the secretary.

[4] People v. Martin, pp. 568-9.

[5] King, p. 185.

[6] RMN 10/16/1892.

[7] *Aspen Times* 02/04/1893, p. 1.

the collection and disbursement of funds.[1] This was the first case of the governor's precipitous removals, in this case for something that could have been easily corrected.

Otherwise, the transition of government proceeded smoothly. On Friday, March 10, 1893, for example, was a showy public ceremony at city hall as the new fire and police board replaced the old. Fire and police units paraded before a reviewing stand, with the governor represented by his wife.[2] By early May, however, the governor was investigating charges of corruption against two of his appointees. On the Monday evening of May 8, "Members of the board called on the governor...," *The Aspen Times* reported. "That the meeting was anything but pleasant there is plenty of evidence."[3] What happened two days later made plain the subject of the meeting.

AFTER THE POLICY MEN
The Shops Will All Be Closed in Denver At Once.

Denver, May 10.—The office of the Colorado Policy association, No. 1833 Fifteenth street, conducted by Edward Chase, was raided at 1 o'clock this afternoon under instructions from the fire and police board and Chief Veatch. Joseph Waterman, an employee, was arrested, as well as Mr. Chase. ... Both were immediately taken to police headquarters, but were promptly released on $1000 bail furnished by Jeff R. Smith.[4]

Ed Chase, Jeff Smith, and in-court "friends" had produced this show of arrest many times before,[5] and it created the desired effect, a period of calm. Twenty days later by the end of May, when asked, Waite replied, "No; I haven't done anything more about an investigation of the fire and police board."[6] Then by Saturday, June 17, 1893, the governor fired Commissioners C. B. Stone and George H. Phelps. They had served a little more than three months. The cause, according to *The Aspen Times*, was "'incompetency and neglect' in connection with the charges of holding up [supporting] the gambling fraternity" by not prosecuting a "Mr. Coryell for his work in collecting money for the gamblers for alleged police protection. ... Trouble Anticipated."[7]

---

[1] *Aspen Times* 02/18/1893, p. 1.

[2] *Aspen Times* 03/11/1893, p. 1.

[3] *Aspen Times* 05/13/1893, p. 1.

[4] *Aspen Times* 05/13/1893, p. 2.

[5] ... *many times before*: In a book of remembrances about his early days in Denver as a lawyer, Judge Ben Lindsey describes a meeting with Ed Chase. Lindsey was offered the job of district attorney by way of a fixed election; Lindsey's lawyer partner would be counsel for Chase's gamblers. At a meeting, Lindsey was told, "Mr. Chase ... doesn't expect to run [gambling] wide open all the time. Whenever the District Attorney has to make a demonstration, *he's* [Chase is] willing to pay up [with an occasional prosecution, conviction, and fine]. ... They don't want you to do anything crooked.... All they want is fair play. You know gambling can't be stopped as long as men want to gamble. You can handle the thing in a practical way. ... You needn't be afraid of offending your friends." After Chase had left the meeting, Lindsey was told "we could make $25,000 a year... without the slightest danger of becoming 'involved'—and at the same time gain all the credit from the community of enforcing the law and prosecuting the gamblers. ... The game had been played in this way, in Denver, before." Lindsey evaded the situation. (Lindsey, pp. 62-63)

[6] *Aspen Times* 05/27/1893, p. 2.

[7] *Aspen Times* 06/24/1893, p. 3.

Trouble came. On Monday, June 19, the governor named Judges Jackson Orr and A. J. Rogers to serve the unexpired terms of the fired commissioners. They would join remaining member D. J. Martin. Orr had been a captain in the Union Army, a lawyer in Iowa who served in the State house and then two terms as a Republican Representative in Washington. Moving to Silverton, Colorado, in 1874, he had been three years a county judge (1875-78) before coming to Denver to sell real estate and practice law. Along the way he had shifted from Republican to Populist. Andrew Jackson Rogers had been a New Jersey lawyer and two-term Democratic Representative in Washington. After an unsuccessful bid for reelection, in 1867 he became a lawyer for New York City during the infamously corrupt Tammany Hall period, including the reign of Boss Tweed. When serious reform came in 1892, Rogers moved to Denver.[1] Here, in the highly critical words of Charles Hartzell, a Republican state senator from Arapahoe County and a serious anti-populist, Rogers "was quickly seized with an acute attack of Populism."[2] So quick was the bond between Waite and Rogers that critical pundits nicknamed Rogers "Jersey Lightning" and "Ajax."[3] Rogers' appointment, however, had to be withdrawn because "it was discovered that," according to Hartzell,

> an appointee on this board must have resided in Colorado one year prior to his appointment. Nothing could be done except to wait; and so they waited, and promptly when the time arrived Ajax was installed....[4]

When Rogers was withdrawn, quickly tapped for as police commissioner was George W. Trimble—affluent[5] former Leadville banker, unscathed veteran of numerous law suits, entrepreneur, and co-founding director of the successful Denver National Bank.[6]

On Saturday, June 24, District Court Judge Graham administered the oath of office,[7] but when the new commissioners came to work on Monday, the old ones, Stone and Phelps, were still there. The new men "demanded possession...," but the former commissioners "refused to surrender." Mayor Van Horn ordered Chief Veatch to report to the new members in his office, but Veatch refused, was fired, and replaced by a lieutenant. Veatch joined Stone and Phelps in refusing to be discharged.[8]

---

[1] *Orr and Rogers*: Congress, Biographical Directory.

[2] Hartzell, p. 28.

[3] Ajax: This Greek hero of the Trojan War is described in *Bullfinch's Mythology* as "gigantic in size and of great courage, but dull of intellect."

[4] Hartzell, p. 29.

[5] "The Little Johnny mine" in the Leadville area "raised to affluence a dozen other lucky co-owners-- ... Geo. W. Trimble...." (Davis, Carlyle, p. 312)

[6] *George W. Trimble*: Real estate investor in Ohio (1872), mining entrepreneur, co-founder of Miners' Exchange Bank of Leadville (1878), merged with Bank of Leadville (Oct 1878), H. A. W. Tabor, president. "This bank ... came to a disastrous end on July 25, 1883, in debt nearly $450,000 (Stone, p. 402). Trimble became receiver to settle debts & received $24,000 for his work. He survived various law suits over land and bank claims (Brice v. Somers 1872, Jones v. Bank of Leadville 1888, Tabor v. Bank of Leadville 1906). Co-founding "director" of the Denver National Bank of Denver, Dec 4, 1884 (Stone, p. 401).

[7] *Aspen Times* 06/24/1893, p. 3.

[8] *Aspen Times* 07/01/1893, p. 3.

So on Tuesday, just before noon, the old commissioners were removed by force. the mayor enlisted a police officer, building inspector, plumbing inspector, and nine others from around city hall and "took forcible possession of room 1.... No blood was shed in the transaction."[1]

Perhaps it is unfortunate that blood was not shed. Had it been, the courts might have become involved much sooner, clarified authority, and spelled out how removal of public officers should be accomplished. Instead, because the raid was successful, a signal was sent, that even in city hall superior numbers and the threat of force could settle a dispute. This was round one in the bout between the new Populist governor and the men who ran Denver, and it went to Waite. So would round two when Trimble was summarily removed in favor of Rogers, but not round three when it came to "the midnight sneak" into the Cañon City Penitentiary, nor round four when Waite sought to remove more commissioners by military force. That round, called The City Hall War, was a dangerous stand off. At the time, the outcome seemed an even score, but as the rounds wore on, it could be seen that the governor had been badly hurt.

By Friday, June 30, ex-Commissioners Stone and Phelps filed complaints in district court against Orr and Trimble for "usurping," or taking without right, their offices. It was a "quo warranto" proceeding, meaning that, to be determined was "by what right," if any, did Orr and Trimble "depose" Stone and Phelps?[2] In the meantime, the new fire and police board—Martin, Orr, and Trimble—went about overseeing procedure, granting and renewing licenses, holding hearings on infractions, and making appointments. On July 17, they named a new chief of police, A. W. Kellogg, of the firm of Kellogg, Warren & Co., mining engineers and brokers.[3]

The fire and police board, perhaps particularly because of the fierce anti-gambling governor was looking over its shoulder, cast about for a plan to keep a lid on trouble in downtown Denver and settled on posting special policemen in saloons and public houses "for the purpose," as they later explained,

> of preserving the public peace; preventing riots and disturbance; preventing minors, intoxicated persons, or others under disability, from frequenting such house; to apprehend persons guilty of any disturbance or breach of the peace, and for the purpose of giving information as to the presence and whereabouts of suspicious characters; to ascertain the names of persons frequenting such houses and carrying them on, and the places where gambling was carried on..., with a view to restricting and controlling the said evil and vice, in order to [achieve] its eventual suppression.[4]

In the meantime, the governor busied himself with silver issues and preparing to persuade the legislature that a special session was needed. At a convention of delegates from silver-producing states held in Denver on July 11, the governor made a speech that was heard all the way to New York City:

---

[1] *Aspen Times* 07/01/1893, p. 1.
[2] *Aspen Times* 07/01/1893, p. 1.
[3] *Aspen Times* 07/22/1893, p. 2.
[4] People v. Martin, p. 568.

The Colorado Silver Convention to-day was both big and sensational. Coliseum Hall, the largest in the city, contained fully 2,000 people.... The sensational feature of the day was the speech of the Populist Gov. Waite. ... In conclusion he said: "The war has begun; it is the same war which must always be waged against oppression and tyranny to preserve the liberties of men.

"Our weapons are argument and the ballot—'A free ballot, and a fair count.' And if the money power ... attempt to sustain its usurpation by 'the strong hand' we will meet that issue when it is forced upon us, for it is better that blood should flow to the horses' bridles rather than our national liberties should be destroyed."[1]

The violent imagery and apparent call for armed insurrection brought a chorus of criticism[2] despite his not, apparently, meaning to issue such a call. His intent, rather, judging by the Biblical allusion, apparently was to say that those on the side of the God of the book of Revelations have a powerful ally. Revelations 14:19-20:

And the angel thrust his sickle into the earth, and gathered the vine of the earth, and cast it into the great winepress of the wrath of god. And the winepress was trodden without the city, *and blood came out of the winepress, even unto the horse bridles*, by the space of a thousand and six hundred furlongs.[3]

Biblical allusion or not, the imagery drew steady criticism and caused the governor to be christened "Bloody Bridles." But Waite also had enthusiastic supporters. *The New York Times* reported on them at the next Silver Convention in Chicago that August:

A number of enthusiastic delegates had been shouting "Waite" for two days, and when the Chief Executive of the Centennial State mounted the platform their cup of joy was overflowing. Cheer after cheer was given by delegates, who stood up and waved their hats wildly, and the ovation terminated with "Three cheers for Gov. Waite."

The Governor spoke at great length. His speech was marked by many indulgences in tirade and abuse, each of which was heartily applauded by the convention. Toward the end of his remarks he said:

"The proposal by false friends of silver and their allies in Wall Street to adopt the present price of bullion silver as compared with gold as a new money ratio, would simply crystallize all wrongs and injuries the money power has inflicted upon the people.... This, as a compromise, beats the one the devil proposed to Jesus Christ on the mountain." ...

"If the money power shall attempt to sustain its usurpation of our rights by strong hands, as in other lands, we will meet that issue if it is forced upon us. For it is better, infinitely better, rather than our liberties should be destroyed by the tyranny that is oppressing mankind all over the world, that we should wade through seas of blood—ya, blood to the horses' bridles."

---

[1] *New York Times* 07/11/1893, & fr the speech quoted in full in *Aspen Times* 07/29/1893, p 2.
[2] *Aspen Times* 07/29/1893, p. 2.
[3] Holy Bible. Revelations 14:19-20. Emphasis added. A furlong: 1/8 of a mile, X 1600 = 20 miles.

As these last words were spoken the convention burst into applause which lasted several minutes. The delegates and spectators cheered, clapped their hands, and waved their hats. It was a great triumph for the Colorado man.[1]

The governor changed the emphasis of his allusion from God's power to God's wrath. In fact, God was pretty much left behind in deference to blood, "seas of blood." If blood it took to motivate the base and build political momentum, blood Waite would provide.

Applauded so vigorously, Governor Waite may have felt he was heading to the moon. His Biblical imagery had stirred the people, and in a next speech, he had enhanced it and was admired even more. With the people and the right and the inspired word of God on his side, what could he not achieve? A time would come, though—and soon—when he would feel forced to demonstrate the power he had so easily claimed. As history now shows, the governor was not going to the moon after all, but coming back, and at a high rate of speed.

In August, the governor met resistance to his proposed call for a special legislative session. At some point this month, his new-found advisor and friend A. J. Rogers met the one-year requirement for appointment, and the governor removed Trimble in favor of Rogers. There was no hearing, no controversy, not even any notice, just the fact of the removal. Feeling offended and wronged, and no stranger to judicial proceedings, Trimble quickly filed suit in district court and won. The decision, however, was immediately appealed to the Colorado Supreme Court, which also had before it the state-appealed district court cases of Stone and Phelps against Orr and Trimble (now removed from office). The cases were joined under the title Trimble v. People. Chief Justice Hayt wrote a lengthy decision that reversed the lower court, and "Trimble v. People" would often be quoted in future cases of removal. With regard to the Denver fire and police board, however, the topic was far from settled law.[2]

To pump life into his special session, the governor called a miner's convention in Salida. There, "the people" would help determine topics for the legislature to address. Scheduled for early December,[3] the convention would be prepared by advance men, who were to have all in readiness when the governor arrived. Then suddenly a matter of malfeasance arose with a member of the Colorado Penitentiary Board, Fred Reynolds, and the warden of the prison at Cañon City, Frank McLister.

Over the weekend of December 3 and 4, a son-in-law of the governor, ex-Deputy Warden Bruce, delivered news of the offense. He had just been fired by Warden McLister, and when Waite heard the son-in-law's report, before going to Salida, the governor fired a commissioner on the penitentiary board and the warden, appointed Solomon J. Toy the new warden, and authorized Toy and Bruce to take charge of the prison. They took "the night train from Denver" to Cañon City, arriving "about one o'clock," and while the warden slept at his home, the pair gained entrance at the prison by posing as sheriffs. Once inside, Bruce and Toy found "a few sympathizers"

---

[1] *New York Times* 08/03/1893.

[2] Trimble v. People.

[3] *Aspen Times* 11/25/1893.

and "disarmed all sleeping guards...." When McLister arrived at the prison the next morning, he was "refused admittance" and "notified that he had been superseded."

Immediately resorting to the courts, McLister found that "the Governor had no power to remove the warden except upon the request of, and charges preferred by, the Board of Penitentiary Commissioners," and these unanimously supported McLister including his firing of Bruce. McLister regained control of his prison the same day. As for the fired commissioner, the charge of malfeasance was based on prison money being kept in the bank owned by the commissioner and no interest being paid on it. That commissioner just ignored the firing, and so did the other two commissioners. The governor appointed an entirely new penitentiary board, but it was ignored by the Cañon City Penitentiary, and the old board went on with its business as if no dispute existed. In time the governor applied to the Colorado Supreme Court for a ruling, but it declined official action as it lacked jurisdiction.

The Aspen Times did its best to set Populist fire to the incident. This paper, previously owned by the governor, was now owned by another son-in-law of his, B. Clark Wheeler, "a mining man, a state senator and a personage of considerable influence in the Populist party."[1] Reported was how ex-Deputy Warden Bruce promised "some very sensational matter in connection with the prison management," but none ever appeared. The governor's Attorney General Engley was reported as saying, "It was an assassination of law and order and the interested parties are criminally liable." He was not speaking of the nighttime doings of Bruce and Toy but of the warden and the commissioner. Warden McLister was reported as having "fortified himself" in the prison, but the paper allowed him to be quoted in his own defense: "If I have been guilty of any act which calls for my discharge, then I am ready to step out. All I want is for matters to be conducted in a regular manner."[2] And so, in this affair, the governor again signaled that he was given to over-reaching and to sudden acts to seize control. The Denver fire and police board, the Denver saloon and gambling men, and the Denver Republican establishment and their lawyers all took notice.

In the meantime that December, the governor arrived in Salida and went to the hall he had rented at his own expense for the convention. But it was empty. According to Hartzell, "the Governor raved and fumed" and sent out his people with orders to fill that hall. "By dint of much effort, eighteen men were finally rounded up, who agreed to listen to the oracle, and, after having properly nerved themselves, his excellency was sent for."[3] What was presented over the course of a four-hour harangue was a rehearsal of the thirty-two items of business the governor was to present to the special session of the Colorado Legislature. Among the proposals was an 8-hour workday for all labor, a law against the "sweating system" (sweat shops), a law against usury, and number one was a plan that "struck the hearers dumb with amazement": Colorado silver would be sent to Mexico where it would be minted into Mexican dollars and returned to Colorado to be used as "full legal tender for all debts, both public and private." Ballots among the 18 were immediately taken, and 10 voted for the package

---

[1] Cedar Rapids Evening Gazette 04/13/1894, p. 7.
[2] Aspen Times 12/04/1893, p. 2.
[3] Hartzell, p. 20.

of charges, a majority of 2.[1] Waite finished drafting the "Business to be Transacted" by the special session on December 25, and it was published the next day along with the governor's call for a special session to begin on January 10, 1894. Waite promoted his session by appearing before the Business Men's Club and the Farmer's Alliance, receiving withering criticism from the former and praise from the latter.[2]

The first meeting of the session was opened at noon by the governor, who again was heard in New York City. The *Times* headline ran as follows:

> The Members Having Listened to the Governor's Tale of Woe, Want to Go Home—Probably Will Adjourn To-day—Absolutely Refused to Have the [governor's] Message [to the legislature] Printed—No "Blood to the Bridles" in It, but Plenty of Wailing.[3]

Populists kept the session from being adjourned, and the governor did all he could to promote his foreign coinage plan. The legislature, though, refused to take the proposal seriously, dubbing the proposed Mexican silver coins "fandango dollars."[4] Hartzell reports that the governor then "apparently lost all interest in the session, and turned: his attention to "appointees whose conduct ... was not giving him entire satisfaction."[5] These principally were two of his new appointees to the Denver fire and police board.

On Wednesday, January 17, the governor ordered Commissioners Martin and Orr to "appear before him" that Friday to answer charges against them.[6] These included "knowingly sending special policemen to the gambling houses of Denver for" the protection of those houses and for "failing" to arrest "persons whom they knew to be in open violation of the law...."[7] The accused argued that their intent in posting the special policemen was far from what the governor charged, but rather, as has been listed, to preserve peace, to prevent disturbance, to collect information, and to make way toward eventual suppression of gambling.[8] In his 1911 *History of the Government of Denver*, King reports that

> The governor ... reminded them that the law not only required such dens to be suppressed, but authorized the officers of the law to break into them and seize all their "machinery of vice." Admonishing the commissioners to enforce the law abolishing gambling, the governor allowed them to return to their positions.[9]

For the next six weeks the governor and his man Rogers sought to guide Orr and Martin in their fire and police board duties. Included were recommendations "to remove certain members of the police force and of the fire department ... [although they] long had been faithfully serving in their ... positions..." and to replace them with

---

[1] Hartzell, pp. 20-22.
[2] *Aspen Times* 12/30/1893, p. 2.
[3] *New York Times* 01/11/1894.
[4] *fandango dollars. Gilded Age Dictionary*, p. 519.
[5] Hartzell, p. 26.
[6] People v. Martin, p. 570.
[7] People v. Martin, p. 566.
[8] People v. Martin, pp. 567-8.
[9] King, p. 213.

Populist appointees.[1] Rogers argued for these firings as well as for other directions of the governor, but Martin and Orr stood against him, all of which Rogers reported to the governor. The struggles continued to an impasse, and in the quiet that followed, the besieged commissioners and the many policemen and firemen loyal to them imagined a plot being hatched for their removal. On Wednesday, March 7, the governor made his move, firing Martin and Orr for malfeasance and neglect, and on the next day, he named their replacements: Dennis Mullins as fire commissioner and Samuel D. Barnes as police commissioner.

The reaction was broad and immediate. Martin and Orr refused to vacate their offices, the governor encouraged his new appointees to take the offices by force, and by late afternoon, Wells, Taylor & Taylor, counsel for Martin and Orr,

> secured from Judge Graham a temporary writ of injunction restraining governor Waite from calling out the militia [as it was rumored he threatened to do], restraining Mayor Van Horne from arming a posse of men to assist in forcing Commissioners Orr and Martin out of their offices, and restraining the governor's new appointees from taking their seats.

That evening, sheriff's officers served writs of stay to all concerned parties, and when the governor received his, a newspaper reported that he was

> wild with rage. He arranged, it is said, to pounce down on the headquarters tonight and forcibly take possession. "These men have got to go," he said.[2]

Commissioners Martin and Orr remembered the removal of Stone and Phelps and of Trimble by Rogers. They remembered how Rogers was at Trimble's desk even before Trimble was informed of his removal. And they remembered the dark-of-night penitentiary plot of Bruce and Toy. So Commissioners Martin and Orr put Police Chief Kellogg and Sheriff Burchinell in charge of marshaling "a large force of deputies" to "assist in preventing the new commissioners from taking forcible possession." The mayor said he would give the new board an office somewhere and called for "the entire police force ... to surrender.... ... All who came over would be" retained. As for Rogers, took up "waiting in harmony with the governor and the new commissioners."[3]

The conflict had been enlarged. Now it was not just about gambling in Denver but about "home rule" in Denver and opposing radical gubernatorial rule. It was about power and self-determination, and whether they would be surrendered or defended and preserved. And so became aligned almost at once such people as the railroad and tramway man William Gilpin; other utility people (gas, garbage, sewage, electricity...) who did not like being targeted by Waite for monopoly practices; members of the banking community whose colleague George W. Trimble had been so rudely dismissed; A. M. Stevenson, one of the most effective political and judicial inside fixit men in Denver; D. H. Moffat, president of the First National Bank of Denver, one-time president of the Denver and Rio Grande Railroad, investor in vast Denver Real Estate, owner of vast mining interests, and principle investor in the Denver, Northwestern, and Pacific Railroad. (Moffat co-signed a $5,000 bond as surety for

---

[1] People v. Martin, p. 568.

[2] *Galveston Daily News* 03/09/1894, p. 8.

[3] *Galveston Daily News* 03/09/1894, p. 8.

Martin and Orr on the Graham injunction).[1] And, of course, for Jeff R. Smith and Big Ed Chase, the root issues were gambling and saloon activities. Feeling exceedingly confident in the company of other such powerful men, Jeff and Chase were ready to act. The power elite casts a large and hospitable shadow, one not only inviting but also highly unwise to evade.

By the weekend, word had spread about the injunction and what had been said in court to prompt Judge Graham to issue it, specifically,

> that the governor threatened to call out the militia and that the mayor was swearing in a large force of special police to oust the petitioner from his seat by violence. ... "Do you say, Mr. Taylor, [Judge Graham asked] that the governor is resorting to these high-handed measures without trying means that are lawful and peaceable?"
>
> "We have every reason to believe it true, your honor.... We can prove that officers ... have been interrogated as to whether they would march under orders or would prefer to disobey and be cashiered [fired]."
>
> "Do you allege ... the petitioner ... unjustly removed?" inquired the court.
>
> "No, your honor. We consider that to be immaterial. We leave that matter in abeyance, and simply ask that the petitioner be protected from the violent and high-handed measures that are threatened. If the threats were to be carried out, bloodshed would follow, and the fire and police forces, on which the city relies for protection, would be demoralized. It would be a public calamity, and so it is for the public welfare that we seek this writ."[2]

On Monday and Tuesday, March 12 and 13, the governor tried to ride out the standoff by going about business as usual, but the effrontery of those occupying city hall against his executive orders was galling. Returning from a trip and finding the situation unchanged, the governor wanted to act. His counsel pointed out how "the matter was then in the courts for settlement" but the governor replied, "Oh, damn the Courts!"[3] *The Aspen Times* reported events in the atmosphere of the gathering storm:

WAR CLOUD IN DENVER
Governor Waite Has Ordered Out the Colorado National Guard
HE HAS ASSERTED HIS DIGNITY

> The Injunction of District Court Judge Graham Will Be Defied—Martin and Orr Must Step Down and Out and the New Police Commissioners, Barnes and Mullins, Will Be Inducted Into Office—The Governor's Orders Not Subject to Review By District Judges.
>
> At 10 o'clock Wednesday night Governor Waite, commander in chief of the national guard..., issued the following order, says the Denver News:

(Special Order No. 242)

> Brigadier General E. J. Brooks, Colonel A.W. Hogle, commanding First Battallion, C.N.G. [Colorado National Guard]

---

[1] *Denver Times* 03/11-14/1894, reprinted *Aspen Times* 03/17/1894, p. 3.

[2] *Denver Times* 03/11-14/1894, reprinted *Aspen Times* 03/17/1894, p. 3.

[3] Hartzell, p. 34.

You will immediately upon receipt of this order, order the troops of your command to assemble at the armory at 1 p.m. on Thursday, March 15. You will report to Brigadier General T. J. Tarsney, who will assume command.

DAVIS H. WAITE

Governor and Commander-in-Chief.

When the governor returned from Colorado Springs Wednesday evening he went into private conference with Adjutant General Tarsney and ex-Mayor Platt Rogers, who is chief council for the new police board. At the conclusion of this conference the orders were issued and there is little room for doubt that the governor proposes to use the national guard to place Commissioners Barnes and Mullins in possession of their offices and declare martial law until that end is accomplished. Judge Graham in refusing to modify his injunction laid down the proposition that the governor's power ends with his appointments and that he has no power to induct his appointees. The governor seems to intend to demonstrate that Judge Graham was in error. ...

Platt Rogers, attorney for the new board, stated...: "We will bring matters to a head [by entering into contempt of court]. ... "

"What will you do to get into contempt?"

"I do not care to say just what will be done. No, it will not be necessary to wade in blood up to the bridles. No blood will be shed."[1]

News on the evening of March 14 that the militia was marching on Denver triggered a call to arms. Policemen, firemen, politicians, and sheriff's deputies were ordered to report for duty, and for the rest of the night, they came to the castle-like city hall at the northwest corner of Larimer and Fourteenth streets. The call was also heard beyond the rank-in-file of city employees. Generally accepted was that Waite's appointees were ready to ban, permanently, all gambling in the city. This and that the new commissioners would be installed by force provoked the ire of the wagering community. Upwards of two hundred gamblers, bunco men, and "hard cases" came forward to be commissioned as deputy sheriffs and special police.[2] To all of the assembling combatants, the governor threatened their world order, their loyalties, and, in such dire economic times, their livelihoods. They were prepared to fight.

Before sunrise on March 15, 1894, Denver was awake. Newspapers confirmed that the governor had ordered the militia to Denver and proposed to use it if the old commissioners would not vacate their offices.[3] About 9 o'clock, crowds began gathering at city hall. People left or did not go to work but instead joined others streaming toward the city government center to see what would happen.

While Police Chief John Stone was organizing his forces,

First Lieutenant Clay and Deputy Sheriff DeLue were collecting arms and ammunition in two express wagons. With dispatch, they made the rounds of the gun stores and pawnshops, gathering shot guns and rifles wherever they

---

[1] *Aspen Times* 03/17/1894, p. 1

[2] *Castle Rock Journal* 03/21/1894.

[3] *Decatur Daily Republican* 03/16/1894. Note: this Georgia paper presented an uncommonly detailed, chronological account of events on March 15, 1894, in Denver and is often relied upon in this chapter.

could be bought or borrowed.[1] ... At 10 o'clock, two wagonloads of breech-loading shotguns and ammunition were delivered.... The department was now equipped with a shotgun and two 45-caliber Colt's revolvers for each man.... A quantity of dynamite cartridges was also stored in police vaults ready for an emergency.[2]

A cartoon depicting the event appeared on the front page of the *National Populist* newspaper. In it, Jeff carries two kegs of dynamite at the head of a "Committee of Safety," marching to city hall. Following him was a parade of gamblers, bankers, brokers, politicians, and hobos carrying signs. One reads, "Governors have no power which gamblers need respect."[3] The *Denver Republican* reported that "Jeff Smith arrived at the head of the guerrilla contingent, and men wearing red badges bearing the words, 'Special Police,' began to grow numerous in the corridor."[4]

By 11 a.m., the streets were "blockaded with a seething mass" of spectators. Police Chief Stone appeared at one point to make a public statement:

> We will hold the city hall against all attacks from the outside, if it takes dynamite to do it.... We have 110 men on duty, and they will be here as long as they are needed. They are all loyal men, and have been too long in the service to permit anyone to intimidate them. We are prepared for any emergency, and we will risk everything to protect the property which the citizens and tax-payers have entrusted to our care. No interference with the fire department will be permitted. The city hall will not be surrendered while the courts are dealing with the city. If the governor wants blood to the bridles we will give it to him; but he can't have the city hall.[5]

By noon, some distance away at Twenty-sixth and Curtis streets, the armory was surrounded by as many spectators as city hall, and arriving militiamen had difficulty gaining entrance. But at 2 o'clock, when apparently no accommodation with city hall had been reached, Adjutant-General Tarsney and Brigadier General Brooks as his second, issued the command to advance. Company E proceeded, and behind it fell in the bicycle signal corps. Company B came next, and behind it, Company K. "The most notable thing in the military procession as it moved through the streets was a big battering ram, mounted on an express wagon. It created a good deal of laughter, notwithstanding the serious nature of the whole affair."[6]

As General Brooks and four aides-de-camp led the way up Fourteenth Street, members of the chamber of commerce stepped forward to appeal for calm. General Brooks told them that he must obey the governor's orders. At this time,

> an aide, upon being pressed by the crowd, drew his sword and raised it with a flourish. This threat angered the crowd; they jeered him, hissed him, and

---

[1] *Denver Republican* 03/16/1894, p. 1.
[2] *Decatur Daily Republican* 03/16/1894, p. 3.
[3] *National Populist* 03/24/1894, p. 1.
[4] *Denver Republican* 03/16/1894, p. 2.
[5] *Decatur Daily Republican* 03/16/1894, p. 3.
[6] *Decatur Daily Republican* 03/16/1894, p. 3.

groaned, while someone in the crowd cried: "Coward." One man threatened to take the aide from his horse and settle him.[1]

When the first regiment and Chaffee light artillery arrived at city hall, it set an offensive line on Fourteenth Street. Large armaments consisted of 2 6-inch, 12-pound Napoleon cannons, 2 Gatling guns, and the battering ram. The cannons were aimed at the second story of city hall.[2] Anxious curiosity turned to fear, which spread quickly through the city. State and city officials scrambled with court officials in an attempt to order the governor to withdraw the troops, but the reply was that he would not.

One plan that emerged was to have the governor arrested, but Judge Graham refused to sign the warrant. The governor's camp feared attempted assassination.[3] Several threatening letters had been received that day.[4] Guards were posted inside and around Waite's residence.

Within city hall, policemen, deputy sheriffs, gamblers, and assorted underworld figures thronged hallways, offices, and windows, waiting and ready for whatever action the militia would take. The *Denver Republican* described the defensive force:

> The solid stone building was now an arsenal and manned from the basement to the tower above the roof by armed men.
>
> In the basement were about 150 policemen, deputy sheriffs and special policemen. Every entrance was barricaded ... by armed men. On the floor above 42 uniformed policemen faced the front door in close array, the front rank men to the number of 30 having rifles or shotguns. Flanking these were about 50 deputy sheriffs and specials [special police] carrying clubs and revolvers.
>
> On the second floor the Fire and Police board rooms, corridors and stairways were guarded by armed men. ... In the room to the east of the building on the third floor was the bomb brigade with their store of giant powder, dynamite, fuses and caps. The explosives were all ready to be hurled through the windows, and men accustomed to the handling of such missiles stood ready to use them.
>
> A floor higher [were] knots of sharpshooters—men who have made records with the rifle and revolver—waited silently to pick off the gunners and militia officers at the first overt act. ... But this was not all. Even the tower above the roof had its quota of riflemen ready to open fire at the first hostile movement of the state troops.[5]

After a tense period of waiting,

> A delegation arrived with a message from the governor, stating that if the city hall was not vacated within thirty minutes orders would be sent to the troops to bombard the building with cannon balls. This created much excitement among the mob and much activity among the besieged garrison.

---

[1] *Decatur Daily Republican* 03/16/1894, p. 3.

[2] *Denver Republican* 03/16/1894, p. 1.

[3] *Denver Republican* 03/16/1894, p. 1.

[4] McCook, p. 135.

[5] *Denver Republican* 03/16/1894, p. 2.

Jeff Smith and five others climbed upstairs into the third story and took up places at two windows. They took ready-to-fling stacks of giant powder and dynamite torpedoes [to throw] into the street as soon as the militia menaced the civic citadel.[1]

Various other sources report that Jeff, wearing two .45 caliber revolvers,[2] stood with a contingent of his men, at the ready with a

large quantity of dynamite. The men had all been sworn to defend the building against the attack of the militia and the most desperate and disreputable characters in the city had been employed to explode the dynamite without regard to the consequences.... The explosives were fitted with fuses and detonating caps, and were to be hurled into the midst of the state troops if they approached the hall too closely.[3]

The *Denver Times* reported how at one point Jeff leaned out, apparently with dynamite in hand, and called down to soldiers near the city hall perimeter.

Say, you guys had better make a sneak. I've got enough of the stuff to send us all to hell, and as I am nearer to heaven than any of you, I'll not be the first to die.[4]

The standoff between the heavily armed, determined forces was intense. One shot could have caused both sides to open fire. Members of Denver's "most influential citizens" sent messages to the militia, to the governor, and to the police, arguing that to prevent massive bloodshed, they must stand down and pursue peaceful resolution. But to no avail. "The governor declared he would order the militia to fire upon the city hall regardless of the crowds of spectators, and the police board within as stolidly maintained" that it would "resist attack." Chief of Police Stone "said he would die before he would surrender."[5]

Among the militia was equal determination:

Captain Barrlett, chief of the [national guard] sharpshooters, had a dozen picked men under his command. He appeared pre-eminently ready for business in fatigue uniform, leggings, black slouch [hat] pulled over his eyes and with saber unsheathed. "I've got a dozen men who can shoot," he explained. "I can depend on them to pick the heads out of those windows."

He stationed them at intervals along the edge of the crowd.

The chief interest of the crowd centered on the brass Napoleons. There were 40 rounds of solid shot in the caissons, besides shells and plenty of ammunition. Being old muzzle loaders, firing would be slow work and the Winchesters in the city hall could pick off the gunners as they loaded and swabbed, and the carriers as they ran to the rear for powder and shot.

---

[1] *Denver Republican* 03/16/1894, p. 2.
[2] *RMN* 04/01/1894, p. 4.
[3] *Denver Republican* 03/16/1894, p. 1.
[4] *Denver Times* 08/01/1898, p. 2.
[5] *Decatur Daily Republican* 03/16/1894.

"But," said a grim looking lieutenant, "we can tumble that building on their heads with a dozen shots."[1]

Through infiltration, the city hall defenders had the element of a flanking surprise. *The World* reported that in the streets,

> There was every reason to believe that in this mass of people were several hundred deputy sheriffs, drawn from the lower part of the city, and it was stated without reserve that the moment one of the guns was fired, the gunners would be seized and torn to pieces.[2]

The *Denver Republican* agreed that members of the sheriff's department milled around near the militia.

> All through the crowd were men with deputy sheriff's badges and armed who had been sent there. It was claimed to keep the troops back. They had instructions to pay particular attention to the gunners in the artillery if they attempted to load the guns.[3]

Supporting this view is Ben Lindsey, a young law student, who wrote of the events that day in a remembrance:

> My brother was a militiaman, and I kept pace with him as his regiment marched from the Armouries to attack the City Hall. There were riflemen on the towers and in the windows of that building; and on the roofs of the houses for blocks around were sharpshooters and armed gamblers and the defiant agents of the powers who were behind the Police Board in their fight.[4]

The long day wore on. At one point, someone outside the hall lit a firecracker, and it was feared general firing would begin. Miraculously, it did not.[5] *The World* reported that later in the afternoon, a meeting of citizens seeking the arrest of Governor Waite assembled at the offices of former Judge Caldwell Yeaman, now corporate lawyer of Yeaman and Gove,[6] to consider

> the advisability of proceeding against the governor on the question of his sanity. Under the law he can be taken into custody on the affidavit of a sufficient number of reputable citizens that he is a dangerous lunatic, or that they have every reason to believe him such. He can be detained until such a time as he had had a proper trial on the question of his lunacy.[7]

No such plan, though, was put in motion.

Rogers and Ward, attorneys retained by the governor, telegraphed notice that if by 5 p.m. he did not assure them he would drop his warlike attitude and call off the attack, they would wash their hands of the whole matter. Late that afternoon, "a committee of citizens from the chamber of commerce" called upon the governor at his guarded residence. "When asked to come out, his face was pale, and at the request of

---

[1] *Denver Republican* 03/16/1894, p. 1.

[2] *The World* 03/17/1894.

[3] *Denver Republican* 03/16/1894, p. 1.

[4] Lindsey, p. 18.

[5] *Denver Republican* 03/16/1894, p. 2.

[6] Fifield, p. 62.

[7] *The World* 03/17/1894.

Mrs. Waite he remained standing in the door."[1] They again asked Waite to submit the ousting of city officials to the Supreme court, pleading that if any outbreak of fighting occurred, the loss of life and property would be great.[2] "The result was a failure to get him to consent to anything. 'I shall order the militia to fire,' he reiterated. "The people may assassinate me if they will, but I propose to have my way."[3]

Just after this meeting, the governor played his last card. Brigadier General McCook of the regular US Army recorded it in the annual report of 1894 to the secretary of war. The general received a letter from the governor "at about 5.20 p.m.," requesting the assistance of US Soldiers. General McCook, who was in Denver and seeing that "property of the United States ... was now in serious jeopardy," telegraphed orders to the commanding officer at Fort Logan to send at once "five companies ... with 100 rounds of ammunition per man and rations for twenty-four hours. Special train will leave at once for your post." The general then informed the governor that troops were on the way and recommended that he return the national guard to its Armory. Waite, however, replied that he did not want to. At 6 o'clock the general also called Chief Stone to say "he had ordered troops from Fort Logan to protect the chief and aid him in preserving order."[4]

At 7:30, General McCook met with the governor, who said he wanted the general "to assist him in taking possession of the city hall." The general said he could not and explained what he could and could not do. Under federal law, US "troops could be used only for the protection of Government property and for the preservation of peace, provided a crisis was imminent." The governor persisted, again asking for combat support and for the general to hold his "troops in reserve for the National Guard to fall back upon in case they were repulsed." The general "replied that the United States troops could not be used for such a purpose." There the meeting ended.[5]

McCook also reported that five companies of the Seventh Infantry arrived at 8:30 p.m. and that as soon as their arrival became known, "The crowds of people about the city hall dispersed, and in a few moments later the National Guard returned to their armory, and peace and quiet were restored to the city."[6]

At 8:45, released by the governor, the militia returned to barracks at the armory. The City Hall War was not over, but its military campaign had ended. One death had occurred, but not among combatants. A spectator had fallen "from his perch on a storm-door entrance to the hall, striking head first upon the pavement...."[7] Sometime about 9:30, General McCook wrote that he was visited by "committees from the Board of Trade and the Chamber of Commerce and many other citizens...." They had come "to express their thanks for the prompt action taken in bringing the troops to Denver."[8] As for the city hall defenders, their victory celebration sounded long into the night.

---

[1] *Decatur Daily Republican* 03/16/1894.

[2] *Denver Republican* 03/16/1894, p. 1.

[3] *Decatur Daily Republican* 03/16/1894, p. 3.

[4] *Decatur Daily Republican* 03/16/1894, p. 3.

[5] McCook, p. 134-35.

[6] McCook, p. 135.

[7] *Decatur Daily Republican* 03/16/1894, p. 3.

[8] McCook, p. 136.

However, with victory came defeat in the court of public opinion. Reported throughout Colorado and well beyond was how criminals, at least in part, participated in governing the centennial state's capital city. As the *Denver Times* observed,

> The alliance of the gamblers and the bunco men with the old fire and police board is not a pleasant thing to contemplate. It has come to a pretty pass if the interests of the city and the lives and property of citizens cannot be protected without the assistance of such men.[1]

And the *New York Times* published this associated press dispatch:

> The public were in consternation to-day at learning that all yesterday afternoon great stores of giant powder and dynamite cartridges had been carried up into the tower of the City Hall, where a gang of desperate fellows, led by "Soapy" Smith, the famous gambler and bunco man, stood ready and willing to throw the deadly stuff into the militia below, regardless of the fact that men and women in dense masses surrounded the small and determined company of young soldiers.

Counter balancing this negative was another report in the *Times* that "A number of prominent men" had assembled "to consider the advisability of proceeding against the Governor on the question of his sanity."[2] Other papers in other cities also picked up on the thread of this story, such as *The Evening Times* in Cumberland, Maryland:

> When prominent citizens like D. H. Moffat, W. S. Cheesman, Donald Fletcher, J. J. McNamara, J. S. Appell and others meet and seriously consider in a secret night meeting the propriety of having the governor held for lunacy as a means of safety to the public, the gravity of the situation must be great.[3]

On this same theme of competency, the *News* in Frederick, Maryland, picked up Denver District Attorney Steele's angry response to the conflict:

> "If anybody is killed in the controversy between Governor Waite and the old police board, the person who does the killing and the one who incites the act will be tried for murder." ... This means that Governor Waite will be tried for murder if anybody is killed in the dispute now on. At least twenty people have called on the district attorney and urged him to have the governor tried as to his sanity. It is said that Dr. Eskeridge, Pfeifer and H. E. Lemon are willing to swear he is insane.[4]

As for Jeff, his press in Denver was considerably better.

SMITH A BRAVE MAN.

His Deeds at Denver Put Him on a Par With More Pretentious Heroes.

The following extract from the Denver Mercury will be read with gratification by the many friends of Col. Smith in this city:

---

[1] *Denver Times* 03/16/1894.
[2] *New York Times* 03/17/1894.
[3] *Evening Times* 03/17/1894, p. 3.
[4] *News* 03/17/1894, p. 1.

"It was only last week that the Mercury in speaking of the much abused club room men of Denver, said that they always come to the front in the interest of the property holders.

Now the proof.

When old Dave Waite; that personification of bull-headed executive idiocy; ordered out the state troops to slaughter law abiding citizens and create panic in Denver, Col. Jefferson R. Smith went to the front with picked men, stood at the city hall and in the name of law, order and good government, announced he was ready to defend with his life, if necessary, the property of the people.

Col. Jeff Smith is called the king gambler, "Soapy," a "sure thing" and God only knows what, by a gang of parasites who are no good on earth; but gambler as he is, he exhibited more manhood in standing by the courts and peace officers than nineteenth twentieth's of those moral pulpit-pounding ministers who are always howling against the saloons and club rooms.

People who believe in giving justice to whom justice is due, will now please admit that Col. Jefferson R. Smith has established the undisputed right to be called one of Denver's most reliable citizens. And that's what he is.

It might be well enough in this connection to state that while this fracas was going on Thursday last, Dean Hart was hid in his wine cellar, and he had that plug hat,[1] with a rosette on it, drawn down clear over his ears!"[2]

The City Hall War received national attention, and people wanted to know more. On March 19 when the Colorado Washington delegation was asked about it, Jeff's old neighbor and former lawyer Congressman Lafe Pence was willing to speak up:

"SOAPY" SMITH.

Who the Leader of the Denver Opponents to Governor Waite Is.

Washington, March 20.—Governor Waite of Colorado and his recent actions form a common topic of current gossip. No one is better able to talk of Colorado matters than that brilliant young representative, Lafe Pence. He told a good story of "Soapy" Smith, whose recent exploits in Denver at the head of the mob is much talked of. "He is one of the greatest characters in the west," said Mr. Pence. "He is probably not over 30 years of age, and by no means impressive in his build. He is, however, the king of the lawless element in Denver. If Smith and four men were in the city hall tower and five dynamite bombs were thrown into the militia, the world would naturally say that Smith and the other four men each threw one. But I am willing to bet that if the bombs had been thrown and Smith had been indicted, each of his four companions would have sworn that Smith begged them not to throw a single bomb, and that in the scuffle one of the men threw two, which would account

---

[1] *plug hat*: a round, hard felt hat with a narrow brim.
[2] Newspaper clipping of unknown origin regarding story in *The Denver Mercury*, March (unknown date) 1894. Jefferson R. "Little Randy" Smith col.

for the five. You never knew anyone to have such power. He never lets one of his followers go hungry if he has a dollar in his pocket, and they know it.[1]

Perhaps because of this story, Jeff sent the Congressman a telegram, which was subsequently published.

> Hon. Lafe Pence, House of Representatives
>
> All quiet here, but more trouble is expected. Be assured the interest of the community will not be neglected. Col. Jeff. Randolph Smith[2]

More trouble was expected, but not all of it in Denver. On the morning of the city hall confrontation, in the Cripple Creek mining area to the southwest, El Paso County Sheriff M. J. Bowers (no relation to John Bowers) sent six deputies to arrest leaders of miners who were illegally striking. Instead, the deputies were arrested by pro-miner deputy sheriffs in the area. The effect in the county seat of Colorado Springs was that

> Every able-bodied man in sight had been deputized and armed, and a military formation was being effected as rapidly as possible. The sheriff was going in after his men with all the force he could muster.[3]

Governor Waite knew of the trouble that evening and in fact had been monitoring the growing unrest for sometime. Anticipating that he might want to send the national guard to the area, he had pressed General McCook to help him "take city hall." With the matter of the insubordination there in hand, he would then be free to send the state's military elsewhere. Stalemated in Denver the night of March 15, however, he did the only thing he could to prepare for eventualities: call up the national guard throughout the state. The entire force consisted of two regiments, one headquartered in Denver and the other to the south in Pueblo, with a total muster force of about twelve hundred men.[4]

Early on the morning of March 16, the governor emerged from his residence and invited the men who had been guarding him to come in for breakfast. Afterward, he ordered them back to the armory and went to his office to meet with General McCook.[5] The governor argued further over the use of US troops, and when the general reasserted that they could not be used for other than as stated the previous night, the governor said he wanted them out of Denver. The general refused. He had taken an extraordinary step in ordering troops to Denver, and the next order would have to come from Washington. It soon arrived: the troops should remain for as long as the general saw fit. The telegram to the Colorado Congressional delegation from nineteen Denver civic leaders, including D. H. Moffat and Sheriff Burchinell, probably made the decision an easy one. In part, they wrote, "If [the troops are] removed, we anticipate a renewal of the tumult of yesterday, and probably a bloody riot as the governor has ordered all the organized militia of the State to Denver."[6]

---

[1] *Register* 03/23/1894, p. 3.

[2] *Boulder Daily Camera* 03/21/1894.

[3] Rastall, p. 13.

[4] *Decatur Daily Republican* 03/16/1894, p. 3.

[5] *Daily Kennebeck Journal* 03/17/1894, p. 2.

[6] McCook, p. 136.

Mobilizing all of the state's guard probably was not for the purpose of forcing removal of the two civic commissioners, but the governor was not inclined to give Denver the satisfaction of an explanation. The reason for putting all of the guard on alert, however, was soon apparent. Throughout the day in Colorado Springs, according to B. M. Rastall in his examination of the mining strike, rumors were rife: men reported killed or wounded, miners in arms everywhere and guarding roads into the mining district. Not knowing fact from fiction but unnerved by the commotion, Sheriff Bowers late in the day of March 16 telegraphed the governor:

> To Davis H. Waite, Governor of Colorado: Five hundred armed men are at Altman. Two deputies were shot tonight by the mob. I cannot control them with my posse. Send troops at once. M. J. Bowers, Sheriff.[1]

The governor replied early the next morning:

> Denver, March 17, 3 a.m. Sheriff El Paso county, Cripple Creek: You ought first to summon posse comitatus[2] of your county. If they cannot maintain order then call upon me as governor for aid. Calling the troops must be last resort. I will order troops held in readiness immediately. Wire me here.[3]

Men were reported killed, but in fact, no one was. In fact, no one was shot or even hurt. The report of the five hundred armed men was likely true, however, and the number was growing. That report alone would have been enough to prompt the governor to do what he did: issue orders for the immediate removal to Cripple Creek of Company A of Colorado Springs, Company C of Pueblo, and Companies B, E, and K of Denver, including "the Chaffee Light Artillery, about three hundred men in all, to proceed with all possible dispatch to ... preserve the peace." Adjutant-General Tarsney and General Brooks left immediately. It might have been to preserve peace that the governor dispatched the guard, but as things played out, it is as likely that Waite saw a political opportunity to form a large Populist enclave of miners in Republican El Paso County.[4]

When Jeff telegraphed Congressman Pence that "more trouble is expected," Jeff meant Denver, not the conflict to the south. Denver was still full of military activity. Its citizens on Saturday, March 17, were still jumpy, and none more so than those on guard at city hall, as the following news report examples:

> Great excitement prevailed on Larimer street at 11 o'clock by the appearance of the light artillery in marching order, [and] the staff officers on horseback followed by two gatlings.
>
> At the city hall the policemen grasped their rifles and rushed to the windows and doors to prevent an attack, but the artillery ... was only going to the railroad yards to load for Cripple Creek.[5]

---

[1] *Aspen Times* 03/24/1894, p. 3.
[2] *posse comitatus*: a body of men summoned by a sheriff to enforce the law of a county.
[3] *Evening Times* (Cumberland, MD) 03/17/1894, p. 3.
[4] "The interest of Governor Waite in the miners was undoubtedly a political one...." (Rastall, pp. 41-42)
[5] *Evening Times* 0317/1894, p. 3.

A city full of soldiers was unsettling, and a strident Populist press added to the uncertainty, especially to those within city hall and their supporters beyond. Here is a sampling from the governor's son-in-law's paper, *The Aspen Times*:

> Some efforts have been made to avert the impending crisis but the governor as commander-in-chief of the state troops, is firm in his stand that justice must be done, or by the eternal, blood will flow and the responsibility will rest upon the corrupt gang at the city hall who have set themselves up against the governor's rights, have defied the law and are willing to commit murder. The grand old governor will endear himself to many here and to the people over the state generally if he will ... wipe up the earth with this corrupt and villainous gang of political spoil hunters, men who recognize no law except the law of brute force.[1]

That Saturday, the governor formally asked the Supreme court "to determine ... what persons were entitled to the offices of fire and excise commissioners." Announcement of this news produced a general relaxation of tension. The following Sunday, March 18, General McCook even ordered US troops back to Fort Logan. But it was a false calm. While the high court was required by the constitution to give an opinion when requested by the governor, "it does not require, nor does the constitution permit, this court to render judgment in connection with such opinion."[2] It should not have been a surprise, then, and probably was not to Wells, Taylor & Taylor, counsel for the plaintiff commissioners, when on Saturday, March 24, "The supreme court sent the fire and police board case back to the district court..., so the matter is left where it was ... when the governor called out the militia to seat his appointees. ... "

> The unanimous opinion of the court was adverse to the governor in all things, except that the court recognized his right to remove and appoint members of the board. It was declared that his power ended there and he could not induct his appointees into office, and his employment of the militia for this purpose was greatly in error and unauthorized by law.[3]

The press gave the governor no deference and published such statements in the unanimous opinion as "By no rule can the power of the governor be construed to be such as to call out the militia to induct an appointee into office. This, the court holds, is a dangerous exercise of arbitrary power that tends towards anarchy and despotism."[4] When the press caught up with the governor after the opinion was released and was asked to comment on it, he said, "I have absolutely nothing to say upon this subject."[5] That statement meant to many that the governor was in one of his planning modes, and "Considerable uneasiness was caused by rumors that the governor had threatened to take the matter into his own hands in defiance of the supreme court."[6]

---

[1] *Aspen Times* 03/17/1894, p1.
[2] People v. Martin, p. 570.
[3] *Fresno Morning Republican* 03/25/1894, p. 1.
[4] *Atlanta Constitution* 03/25/1894, p. 19.
[5] *Sunday Leader* 03/25/1894, p. 1.
[6] *Hamilton Daily Democrat*, Ohio, March 26, 1894, P. 1.

When the Martin and Orr case went to the Supreme court on March 17, the following Monday, Judge Graham went on vacation. Still in force was his injunction, which forbade any action to remove Martin and Orr from their posts. Additionally, Wells, Taylor & Taylor had filed for a writ of contempt with Judge Graham against not only Governor Waite but also Mayor Van Horn, Commissioner Rogers, and newly appointed Commissioners Barnes and Mullins for "having violated the injunction."[1] After all, the governor had summoned the militia, and the mayor and newly appointed board had tried to reorganize the police force and deputized men to assist in the conflict. But Judge Graham had not acted on that application, and with his being away, Judge James Glynn from the Thirteenth District Court (in the small, high plains town of Sterling) was summoned to conduct a hearing on the application for contempt of the injunction. He began the hearing on the morning of March 19, and when on Friday, March 24, the Supreme Court sent the removal of commissioners question back to the Second District Court, it came to Judge Glynn. He was quick to act.

The following Monday, March 26, Judge Glynn dismissed the charge of contempt, quashed the injunction, "censured Martin and Orr for arming men and placing dynamite in the City Hall," and "asserted that Mullins and Barnes were de facto and de jure[2] entitled to the office and that Martin and Orr had no color of title to the offices."[3] Populist newspapers the next day, Tuesday, March 27, were exuberant, leading the story with headlines like "WAITE IS VICTORIOUS" and "Wipes Up the Earth With the Old Denver fire and police board."[4] The Mayor and new board acted swiftly. They ordered Police Chief Stone replaced by John J. Farely, fired two lieutenants of police who refused to come over to the new board, fired all police officers who had shown disloyalty to the new board, and ordered the old board from city hall. Six patrolmen guarded the rooms, however, so the new board, remaining in the mayor's office, appointed an entirely new police force. Late that day, Wells, Taylor & Taylor asked the Supreme court to reinstate Judge Graham's injunction, but the court declined any action until the next morning when it would "hear arguments on the application."[5] On duty that night were "two police departments for the city of Denver."[6]

The Supreme court heard arguments all of the next day from both the State and Wells, Taylor and Taylor. At about 4:15 p.m., the three justices took a brief recess and returned to announce that the Supreme court did not have jurisdiction to rule on the case. In other words, due process had not yet been completed in district court. Following this bombshell came another: Shortly after the Supreme court's ruling, Judge Allen, a regular member of the Second District Court,

> issued another injunction restraining Commissioners Barnes and Mullins from interfering with Orr and Martin in their possession of the fire and police board. The immediate effect was to nearly precipitate a riot at the city hall.

---

[1] *Daily Gazette* (Janesville, WI) 03/19/1894, p. 2.
[2] *de facto and de jure*: (1) *de facto*: "in fact." Often used in place of "actual" to show authority even though legal requirements have not been met. (2) *de jure*: lawful, as distinguished fr de facto (actual).
[3] *Daily Gazette & Bulletin* 03/27/1894, p. 1.
[4] *Aspen Times* 03/27/1894, p. 3.
[5] *Aspen Times* 03/27/1894, p. 3.
[6] *Daily Times* 03/27/1894, p. 1.

Wells, Taylor & Taylor had been ready with papers

> alleging great danger of violence and disturbance and praying an injunction until the pending quo warranto[1] proceedings instituted by District Attorney Steele shall have been heard.

The injunction was issued at 7 o'clock in his chambers, with Walter Cheesman (owner of the Union Water Company) and D. H. Moffat putting up the bond. Papers to be served upon the new board members were given to Deputy Sheriff Tom Clark, who arrived at city hall about 9:20 that evening.[2]

Earlier, at about 6 o'clock, Mayor Van Horn and the new commissioners were in the mayor's office, working on their re-organization. The appointment of Farley as police chief had been rescinded and given to Henry M. Behymer.[3] He, however, could not be found, so police lieutenant Oswald was put in charge of going down to meet with the old police force in the basement and giving them their new orders. "Long before 9 o'clock the corridors of the building filled with spectators." Jeff and Ed Chase had heard of the trouble and came to city hall to see if help were needed.[4] Word of a new injunction had circulated, and excitement was high. Judging help from their quarter was not needed at that time, they retreated but would check back later on. At 9 o'clock, Oswald went to the basement with a Lieutenant Mahoney. These new officers "circulated among the men of the incoming and outgoing runs and asked them to join forces with the new board." Lieutenant Clay of the old board

> shouted that an injunction had been issued and the papers were on the way for service. The men cheered, cried that they would stand together, and crowded around Clay and Oswald.

Acting Police Chief Oswald said he did not think there should be any hard feelings, and Clay agreed but said he would bet "any man in the crowd ... that an injunction had been issued." Oswald said he would take that bet at "$100 to $5." Now "Not only the policemen, but the whole crowd from upstairs had thronged into the basement ... and there was a great uproar." Oswald said he did not believe there was an injunction and that all men wanting to "come over to the new board could come upstairs to the office of the park commissioner" and be sworn in. But "The men set up a series of hoots and howls, followed by shouts that they would stand by the old board."

At 9:20 Deputy Clark with the injunction arrived, but "big Lieutenant Mahoney" with some of his "new" policemen made his way to the outward-swinging door and with them and Clark on the outside, Mahoney ordered the door shut. Chief Stone forced his way to the door and hit it with "a ferocious rap. The door opened half an inch. Mahoney said: 'Keep that door locked, Dan,' and bang shut it went instantly...." Stone and Mahoney then had "words," ending with, if Mahoney "talked too much," Stone would have him put out of the building, and Mahoney replied, as he walked away, that he would like to see him try it. Then the door opened, new board police and observers

---

[1] *quo warranto*: Latin, literally, "by what warrant," i.e., by what authority is an action taken.

[2] *Aspen Times* 03/31/1894, p. 1.

[3] Farley ... Behymer: "Yielding to pressure from Gov. Waite, the new board has selected H. M. Behymer, a populist, for chief of police, instead of ex-Chief Farley." *(Daily Gazette* 03/29/1894, p. 1)

[4] *Aspen Times* 03/31/1894, p. 1, & as follows.

retired, Deputy Sheriff Clark entered with the injunction, and the old board police congratulated one another.

Soapy Smith, Ed Chase and other prominent citizens, who had been present earlier in the evening, returned soon after and triumphantly strode not only on the sidewalk but into the basement of the city hall itself, where they consulted with the authorities concerning the maintenance of order and the proper suppression of the persons outside who dared to remain on earth.[1]

Attention then turned to "serving" members of the new board with the injunction. They were thought to be in "the park room," but it was dark and the door locked. Deputy Sheriff Clark and others went around to "the windows on Fourteenth" Street and were hoisted through, but found no one. The door to the mayor's private office was tried but found locked. The men then went to the mayor's hallway office door, which was also locked. They persuaded the colored janitor, Henry Reed, to be hoisted over the transom and to unlock the door from the inside. Next, they opened the inner office door with a piece of wire and there found "Messrs. Mullins and Behymer" and another man "in the dark." Tom Clark then made "service" of the injunction at about 10:30. Mullins "said he was following the advice of counsel in avoiding" being served. "The crowd had quietly gone home by this time and the danger of trouble was over.[2]

Perhaps the danger of physical violence was over for the night, but trouble continued. On Friday, March 30, on his own motion, Judge Glynn

quashed the injunction issued by Judge Allen against Barnes and Mullins…, making a conflict of authority, as Glynn and Allen are co-ordinate judges. This was followed by a counter move from the old board [via Wells, Taylor & Taylor] obtaining a writ of prohibition from the Supreme court restraining Glynn from acting in the matter at all.[3]

This action revalidated Judge Allen's injunction against the new board. Not at all flagging in the injunction battle, new board lawyers applied to the Supreme court the next day, Saturday, March 31, "for a writ of prohibition directed against Judge Allen." The high court responded by issuing writs for Judge Glynn and Judge Allen to turn over their records on the case. This development caused the old board to suspect

that the new board would attempt to seize the rooms by force. A garrison of ten men was established in the office and thirty rifles were hastily moved upstairs. All available men were hastily placed under arms in the basement.[4]

The two applications to the Supreme court, however, had turned the legal tumblers that opened the legal door to the high court. Associate Justice Elliot (in the decision to come on April 16) wrote,

during the three weeks following [March 7] there were legal proceedings in the courts…; but not until Saturday, March 31st, was any application made to this court by which the controversy could be settled and determined; on the

---

[1] *Aspen Times* 03/31/1894, p. 1. Events are presented in a neutral journalistic fashion until this last six-word clause. Presumably the story had been picked up fr another paper or a press service.

[2] *Aspen Times* 03/31/1894, p. 1.

[3] *Reno Weekly Gazette And Stockman* 04/05/1894, p. 5.

[4] *Aspen Times* 04/07/1894, p. 2.

Monday following [April 2], this court indicated its willingness to take original jurisdiction.[1]

The Populist press was concerned. Reported was that evidence from both sides would be presented, including how Martin and Orr would testify that in "conferences with the governor ... he is alleged to have insisted that the department should be made a political machine."[2] The old board defense accepted that the governor had the "power of suspension or removal ... at any time, for cause to be stated in writing, but not for political reasons."[3] These last four words were the point of leverage, that the governor sought to remove Martin and Orr "for political reasons only" because they were not "of the same political faith ... and had refused to fire persons not of the governor's party and to fill their positions with those who were.[4] Well known was the governor's attempts in this regard. The new board had just seen the governor's desire to appoint Populists. He had insisted that the new board's appointment of Chief Farley be rescinded and given to Henry M. Behymer, an undertaker for many years, a deputy sheriff for a few years, and a "loan agent." What qualified him, apparently, was his enthusiastic Populism.[5] The new board complied, but the appointment of Behymer was decried so roundly, even among Populists, that he served as police chief but a single day before being replaced by Hamilton Armstrong, a foreman for a printing company but a person of acknowledged leadership ability.[6] Nervousness and frustration showed up in print, such as *The Aspen Times*:

> Down in this neck o' the woods the people would like to see Governor Waite call out force enough to forever quiet the most corrupt political combination that has cursed any city in the West. The Denver "Soapy" Smiths would not be missed if the state militia were to wipe up the earth with them.[7]

The days proceeded into April, and still by Friday the thirteenth, the high court announced no finding. The two boards kept operating in their separate offices in city hall, the fire department had separate leaderships but the same force, and the two police forces under the two chiefs found ways to work together. And there was Sheriff Burchinell's force of deputy sheriffs to flesh out thin spots or places where contention might temporarily arise. That Friday the thirteenth was an unlucky one for Populists in the controversy, though word of it did not appear in any Populist paper:

> It appears that the truculent and terrible Gov. Waite of Colorado is indebted for his bloody-thirsty [sic] propensities to the sanguinary inspiration

---

[1] State v. Martin, p. 570.

[2] *Aspen Times* 04/07/1894, p. 1.

[3] State v. Martin, p. 569.

[4] State v. Martin, p. 568.

[5] *Behymer, Henry M.*: background: 1880 census, undertaker (1887 Denver City Directory), undertaker (1890 Directory), deputy sheriff, loan agent (1892 Directory).

[6] *Armstrong, Hamilton*: Denver City Directories 1887, 1890. He served as Denver Police Chief from April 17, 1894, to January 10, 1921 (Secrest, fn 78, P. 51). Governor Waite was not finished with Behymer, though; he had the board appoint him Denver's Chief of Detectives. His performance and that of the Populists he appointed came to be such a joke (taken up by Charles Hartzell, pp. 51-52), that after five weeks, Chief Armstrong removed him (Secrest, p. 170).

[7] *Aspen Times* 04/07/1894, p. 2.

of the still more truculent and terrible Mrs. Waite. During the business men's conference over the situation in Denver, ... Mrs. Waite pushed herself into the chamber of and interrupted the speakers as she cried out with clenched hands "that the fight must go on until the last national guardsman in the state lay dead on the pavement."[1]

Other commentary from the press tended to this same critical tenor, of the governor and sometimes his wife as well.

If the press at large across the East and Midwest had Governor Waite and his wife to criticize, *The Aspen Times* had Jeff. During this time, Jacob Coxey's Army of out-of-work men, commonly called "commonwealers," was crossing Colorado on their way to Washington to demand attention to their economic plight. The following notice about them appeared in the *Times'* regular Saturday issue of April 14:

Should the commonwealers come to Denver Governor Waite will urge the city to treat them kindly, feed them and send them on their way without unnecessary delay. The governor says he will not call the militia out unless Soapy Smith and Sheriff Burchinell are unable to preserve the peace and ask for assistance.[2]

The *Times* might not have been engaging in idle sarcasm. It might have had inside information, for in just a few days, Jeff would receive appointment as a deputy sheriff.

On Monday, April 16, the supreme court handed down a decision in favor of the governor. He had statutory power under the laws of Colorado to appoint members of the fire and police board and to suspend or remove them "at any time for cause, to be stated in writing, but not for political reasons." Further, the court asserted that "It is a presumption of law that every public officer does his duty" and observed that "Charges of improper motives [for removal] are easily made, are often untrue, and are always hard to prove." Authority must reside somewhere, and it resided with the governor. For his decisions in this case to be challenged and submitted to judicial procedure "would involve much delay—perhaps a trial by jury with right of appeal—and thus the wheels of municipal government would be blocked" in ways not tolerable in "a great city." So it must be "upon the conscience of the executive" to "restrain and control his official conduct" insofar as his actions be taken "not for political reasons."[3]

And so the decision concluded with a "Judgment of ouster" to take effect on or before noon the following day. Martin and Orr were not charged with any offense. Although they had held their offices unlawfully for forty-one days after being dismissed, the decision stated that they were not to be fined.[4]

In the governor's office, *The Aspen Times* reported "unadulterated joy on the part of the friends of the governor." "Populists" came calling at his office "all day to congratulate him on the victory." The governor was quoted as saying, "I am happy indeed that the court has proven equal to its responsibilities."[5]

---

[1] *Register* 04/13/1894, p. 2.
[2] *Aspen Times* 04/14/1894, p. 4.
[3] State v. Martin, pp. 576-78.
[4] State v. Martin, p. 579.
[5] *Aspen Times* 04/21/1894, p. 1.

On the next day, April 17, the transition in city hall took place without incident. Sheriff Burchinell, however, not being sure how things would go down, undertook one of the more improbable actions of the City Hall War period: the official appointment of Jeff as an Arapaho County deputy sheriff. It occurred on the day of the transition, probably in the morning. Given the recent past history of discord and with police forces in disarray, the sheriff wanted to be ready. It seems likely that many such appointments were made that day, and Jeff, having proved able to lead men to city hall on March 15 and able to calm subsequent disturbances there, could be a valuable man to have ready to serve. And so the following document was prepared and signed:

To Whom it may Concern:

Know all Men by these Presents, That posing especial confidence and trust in the integrity and ability of Jeff R. Smith I, WM. K. BURCHINELL, Sheriff of said County of Arapahoe, in pursuance of, and by authority vested in me by law, have appointed, and do hereby confirm him, the said Jeff R. Smith to be a Deputy Sheriff in and for said County Without Compensation from County And all of his official acts legally performed while acting as such Deputy Sheriff are entitled to full faith and credence.   Witness my hand and seal this 17th day of April 1894

[signed] Wm K Burchinell   Sheriff of Arapahoe County[1]

When word got out that Jeff was a lawman, Burchinell denied it. He also denied that Jeff carried any legal weight during the siege at city hall.

I will say that I did not put a single deputy sheriff in the city hall…. If Soapy is running around making arrests then he is doing so illegally and is liable to arrest for impersonating an officer. For all I know he is a special policeman [but not a deputy sheriff].[2]

Eventually, the sheriff admitted giving Jeff a deputy sheriff's commission but that it had since been revoked.[3] A commonplace practice among political figures was to deny involvement with Jeff. It was nothing personal. Most of them worked with him and liked him, but denial was sometimes a necessary part of that friendship.

Sheriff Burchinell was doing what a veteran of conflict should do, be prepared. Another measure he took was to place an order for fifty Winchester rifles, model 1886, 40-82 caliber. Engraved with "Arapahoe County," they were shipped in July.[4]

During the period of conflict and uncertainty, on Thursday, March 17, a friend of Jeff's died. Mourning the loss and moved by death, Jeff again picked up his pen.

Billy Larimer
By Jefferson R. Smith

(note-when Billy Larimer, a well known member of the liberal class, died in his room at Seventeenth and Market streets, Thursday night last week, he made the unique request that his friends who were in the room with him, play the banjo while his spirit

---

[1] Deputy Sheriff appointment form: Portions written in are underlined. Author's col.

[2] Newspaper clipping of unknown origin & date cut by Jeff R. Smith II. Author's col.

[3] *Denver Republican* newspaper clipping of unknown month & year (probably June, 1894), saved by Jeff R. Smith II. Author's col.

[4] Arapahoe.

was leaving its earthly body. His request was granted, and while "Old Black Joe" was being played and sung he passed away with a smile on his lips.)

Jim Bush[1] was playing the banjo
At eleven o'clock at night;
While Billy he was lying low—
Grim death he had to fight.
But nothing could be done for him,
Of life he'd had his lease.
Doctor Dulin and the nurses said
Death soon would bring him peace;
For all of us poor sinners
Someday have to "cash-in,"
Be we religious rascals
Or delve in open sin.
The boy to whom my pen alludes
Was Billy Larimer,
He was a prince, I tell you,
And true as he could be;
He never to a friend said no,
Nor a stranger turned away,
And all will wish to see him right
With the angels judgment day.

He asked to have the banjo played
As his life passed slowly out,
And the music seemed to please him
For he turned and looked about.
And then he softly breathed his last
While we with sorrow blest
Knelt down and offered prayer that he
Might have eternal rest.
The K.P.? [Knights of Pythias] Yes,
    they buried him—
A grand and loyal band—
And I hope that he will meet them
In that bright and happy land.
Bill, to no church did he belong,
But I'll take my chance with him
'Long side of pious hypocrites
Who sing a pious hymn.
And when I'm called to pass away,
Just let the banjo play and play.[2]

————————

After the transition from the old board to the new, *The Aspen Times* was prolific in forecasting the future:

> The most important matter remaining to be developed is the policy of the new board towards the gambling houses. The members of the board decline to state what course they will pursue, but a populist who stands so close to them that his utterances have almost the force of an ex cathedra dictum says that every gambling house in town will be closed.
>
> "The program which is mapped out," said he, "is to shut every one of them and keep them shut. The governor and board are committed ... and there will be no half measures. Lower Seventeenth street will also be cleaned of the bunco men who have infested it. All these people have been helping to hold up the old board with money and physical force. Jeff Smith will be arrested every day so long as he attempts to continue his present occupation. The district attorney may turn them all loose or refuse to prosecute if he likes, but the board will keep right on arresting."[3]

---

[1] *Jim Bush*: manager of The Midway saloon at 1703 Larimer Street, Denver, Colorado.
[2] *Denver Mercury* 03/31/1894.
[3] *Aspen Times* 04/21/1894, p. 1.

The Populist *Aspen Times* had an especially sarcastic warning for Jeff. It was buried on page 4, but it stood out as a single news note, as if a personal message to Jeff and his friends.

> Governor Waite is waging a relentless war upon the gamblers in Denver. Soapy Smith and others of his stamp will not be prominent as he was under gang rule. The virtuous "Soapy"—well it's too bad [for "Soapy" that] Governor Waite can't appreciate talent like his.[1]

Future events suggest that Jeff received this message and others like it and that in time he helped author, or at least favored, an outrageous symbolic reply.

Competing Denver fire and police boards, duplicate police and fire forces, standoffs with the military at city hall, and appointment of Soapy Smith as a deputy sheriff were over and would not return. But in many ways the war with Governor Waite was not over, and the worst for a number of people was just ahead.

Chapter 13

Gambling Goes Underground—
"Confidence" Games Across the Bridge

Declare yourselves! Be men, not slaves!
Stand up—don't weaken! Fight for your rights....

—Jefferson R. Smith II
Denver Mercury 08/26/1893 & 06/02/1894

Rules under the old board required saloons and gaming halls to close at midnight and on Sundays. The week the new board took office, it told proprietors to prepare within a few days to close their doors.[2] The following Monday gambling establishments were ordered permanently closed by noon the next day, Tuesday, April 24, 1894. The *News* covered the gloomy affair on the day the order was issued.

LAIR OF THE TIGER.
AFTER TO-DAY IT MAY BE HARD TO LOCATE.
Big Gamblers Say They Will Close Up And Wait for Business Men to Squeal,
But Little Fellows with Skin Games Expect to Grow Fat—The Colfax Monte
Carlo Will Not Materialize ... —Other Suburbs May Harbor the Beast.

Yesterday was a doleful one for the sports. They stood disconsolately about in front of the closed gambling resorts sadly discussing the situation. None of them had any idea of securing any other kind of employment. They will live on hope for a few days, and, doubtless, in twos and threes migrate to some more sportive settlement.

The big houses, like Gavin & Austin, the Arcade, the Jockey Club and Samson & Scott's, will not make any attempt to start again to-day.... The morning will be spent in packing up the wheels and other paraphernalia of a

---

[1] *Aspen Times* 04/21/1894, p. 4.
[2] *RMN* 04/18/1894. And *Denver Republican* 04/20/1894.

gambling hall. Some of the smaller places will die hard and run till noon. The last public drawing of the policy wheel will be at noon....

The policy men have no intention of giving up their business, and it is stated that they can easily evade the law. The wheels will be transported to one of the suburbs, where the regular drawings will take place and half an hour afterwards printed slips bearing the list of successful numbers will be found in a dozen or more cigar stores....[1]

The Aspen Weekly Times continued the account on the day of closure.

Denver's Gambling Fraternity Preparing to Get Out of Town.

DENVER, April 24.—"Gone a Hunting," was the inscription on a sign which hung on the door of a Market street policy shop this morning. The sign was put up as a joke, but nevertheless it was a truthful explanation of what the policy men and gamblers of the city were doing.

They had all decided to obey the order of the new police board, which went into effect at noon, and ... were scattered over the suburbs hunting for localities to set up their establishments anew.

Larimer street which has been the mecca of Denver gamblers, seemed to contain more idlers than usual today. ... Blonger's, Argyle's and other places on Larimer and Market, including Jeff Smith's Tivoli, were closed tight and so were the three policy shops on Larimer and Fifteenth streets respectively. ...

It was the general impression that if Colfax allowed the dispossessed gamblers to reopen in that town it would soon have the entire Denver fraternity established within its limits. The business men of the town according to conversations had this morning by a Times reporter, were almost unanimously in favor of receiving the gambling men.

A petition to sanction gambling in the town was circulated yesterday and nearly 100 business men signed it. The town board is divided on the question. ... Mayor King is undecided. The friends of the gaming men, however, hope to have the board give the desired permission.

Colonel Jeff Smith and several other gamblers have hired places in Colfax with the understanding that the bargain will be off if the trustees object.[2]

According to the *Rocky Mountain News*,

The outlook is that Colfax will not be invaded to any material extent just at present. Probably two or three small houses may be started there, but the idea of establishing a gilded Monte Carlo has been abandoned. Colonel J. Randolph Smith has circulated a petition in the little town and has secured sixty-five signatures. The petition is addressed to the mayor and trustees and asks them to sanction public gambling. Mayor King has not quite made up his

---

[1] *RMN* 04/23/1894.
[2] *Aspen Times* 04/28/1894, p. 3.

mind about the question and he holds the balance of power, as the board of trustees is evenly divided. ... Mayor King will wait until the gamblers appear.

"It is no use hunting the tiger before it appears," he says. "I will let you know what I think of the gambling houses later." The business men along Golden avenue are very anxious to have the gamblers with them. They are in favor of them to a man.[1]

Jeff became known as the "green cloth diplomatist," and the gamblers watched his every move with more than usual interest. On April 24 Jeff was in Colfax, standing in front of a saloon when he was introduced to local Trustee David Peabody. An impromptu debate broke out that attracted a crowd of nearly a hundred spectators. The *News* published some of the exchange.

"Ah! 'Soapy' Smith, is it?" said Peabody.

Smith nodded.

"Are you coming over here to soft-soap the people of Colfax?" asked Mr. Peabody.

"No, not at all," was the response.

The argument upon gambling then began. "If there was a string of prayers from here to the moon," said Peabody, "I would not be in favor of allowing the gambling houses to keep open in Colfax."

"I have a pretty tough name," said Jeff, "but I am willing to put my record alongside yours for assisting charity. I have given several thousand dollars to churches. I was intended for a preacher myself."

"But you fell from grace!" interposed Peabody.

"No, no, not at all," replied Smith: "I thought I could do more good in the business I'm in than as a preacher."[2]

Gambling in Colfax did remain open. Jeff opened a gaming house as did Charles Pierson of the Arcade and a few select others.[3]

Within days of the closure in Denver, gambling was back but hidden now in basements and attics, with hidden entrances resembling those of "speakeasy" clubs of the 1920s. Sympathetic judges aided with verdicts that favored gamblers.

Gamblers Must Be Caught Actually in a Game.

Judge Frost yesterday discharged A.W. Gilman, accused of running a private gambling room in the Hallack & Howard block, Seventeenth and Arapahoe streets. Sergeant McPhee and other officers testified that they had to break in the door. There was gambling apparatus in the room, a number of men were sitting around and the box under the "kitty" hole in the table contained over 100 chips. They could not swear that gambling had been going on because they did not actually see it. The defense was that there had been no gambling since Monday at noon, when the order went into effect.

---

[1] *RMN* 04/23/1894.

[2] *RMN* 04/24/1894, p. 3.

[3] *RMN* 09/06/1894, p. 1.

The finding of the court emphasizes the difficulty which will be met by the police force in attempting to suppress gambling under the conditions which will surround it. Actual evidence showing that gambling was in progress will be hard to get, because the rooms will be kept locked and look-outs will warn those within of the approach of the police in time to allow the game to stop and the players to pick up magazines or newspapers.[1]

Jeff and Ed Chase had no intention of permanently leaving Denver. The new police chief, Hamilton Armstrong, beholden to the new fire and police board that had appointed him, made an effort to shut down gambling. The first to be hit was Ed Chase, and the *News* covered the event in detail.

JIG OF THE GIGS UP.
POLICE BEGIN A WAR ON ALL POLICY SHOPS

Ed Chase, King of the Policy Men, and Half a Dozen of His Writers Are Unceremoniously Pulled—His Place at 1333 Fifteenth Street Searched and the Freshly Oiled Wheel Found in the Dusty Attic—....

The police are after the policy players. Yesterday the first blow was struck by the arrest of Ed Chase and half a dozen of his writers. Since the organization of the new fire and police board, the proprietors of the local policy associations have been saying little, but have continued....

The game of policy is to the poor man the most seductive of all forms of gambling, for he sees in it the possibility of making a big winning from a small investment. He may win once in a thousand plays, and if he does he gets back an amount equal to that he lost on previous guesses. The policy fiend thinks by day and dreams by night of "gigs" and "saddles" and "horses" and "spiders,"[2] and any number impressed on his mind in an unusual way is invariably played for all it is worth. ...

Ed Chase, who has amassed a fortune at the business, is the recognized power behind the wheels which revolve in Colorado. ... For a long time he has been allowed to work among a class of people who can ill afford to invest even a trifle in such a snap game. Hundreds of dollars are paid in at each policy shop by these unfortunates who are controlled by the gambling mania.

At a central place the numbers are drawn from a small brass wheel at 12 o'clock noon and 5 o'clock in the afternoon of each day of the week. In the parlance of the legitimate gamblers the game is a "sure thing." The percentage against the policy fiend is enormous, but as he is usually unable to figure it out he plays on in ignorance. In order to lure on the superstitious a dream book has been published, so that if an inveterate gambler dreams of

---

[1] *RMN 04/26/1894.*

[2] *gigs, saddles, horses, spiders*: "Policy bets were placed on groups of numbers from 1 through 78.... Borrowing from horse-racing terminology, a two-number betting combination was called a 'saddle,' a three-number combination a 'gig,' and a four-number combination a 'horse.' Gigs were the most popular play, but bets could be made in combinations of up to 25 numbers." Presumably, a "spider" would possess an eight-number combination. (Yronwode)

something unusual he consults the book.[1] If his teeth fall out while he is asleep he plays the 7-11-44 gig. For a ten-cent investment he stands a show to win $11.80. If he dreams that he is falling over a precipice the book tells him that his lucky gig is 3-17-27.

When Sergeant Tarbox visited Ed Chase's main office yesterday at 5 o'clock he found a dozen men inside, and on each face was written the expectant look of the policy fiend. A drawing was interrupted by the unwelcome presence of the police.

"You are under arrest," was the greeting Ed Chase got when he was arrested a few minutes later.

"What for?" was his query.

"For running a gambling house and carrying on a policy business," replied the sergeant.

"But we do not run a gambling house and the policy numbers are drawn from a hat," retorted Chase.

Upon his refusal to show the officers through the building at 1333 Fifteenth street, the officers decided to forego any formality. They found no wheel on the first floor, and the same ill-luck attended them in their visit to the second story; but away up near the roof in a dark room in the rear of the building they found a brass wheel. Every other article in the room was covered with dust. The wheel was innocent of such neglect and the bearings had been freshly oiled. The prospective "gigs" and "saddles" and "spiders" and "horses" were still in the cylinder.[2] The fortune maker was confiscated and taken to city headquarters along with Chase, whose fortune it had helped to make. Gus Brohm, a partner of Chase's, was also arrested....[3]

Men were removed from the Denver police and fire departments because of their allegiance to the old board. Many others were fired or let go simply to make room for appointees deemed desirable by the new board. Senator Charles Hartzell listed how the fire chief, who had served since about 1878, and Police Chief Farley, who had a good national reputation, were removed to make way for Populists, such as Populist State Senator Hamilton Armstrong. And so,

> from the top to the bottom, these departments were quickly filled by those whose sole recommendation was loyalty to the Populist party.... The Governor himself, and even his estimable wife, showed the greatest enthusiasm in directing the employment of the faithful, and many who had just arrived from outside places were quickly placed on duty.

Police Commissioner Rogers complained, though, of the "inability to give employment to twenty-one hundred Populists in two hundred places...." Further, there had

> been a succession of almost daily changes—generally at the dictation of the Governor—until the new appointees refuse to buy uniforms, well knowing that

---

[1] *the book*: One such book was *Aunt Sally's Policy Dream Book*, Wehman Bros., 1889. (Yronwode)

[2] *still in the cylinder*: figurative. No numbers had yet been generated by that cylinder, or wheel.

[3] *RMN* 05/08/1894.

they are liable to be dropped any day, and many of them parade the streets of Denver, with no official sign other than an immense club.[1]

In early May, 125 men, "largely ex-police and ex-firemen, left Denver in command of ex-Chief of Police Veatch." The force was headed for Cripple Creek to serve as deputy sheriffs in the labor trouble there. "They were armed to the teeth, and prepared for immediate action."[2] The news of unrest among miners, mine owners, and law enforcement had also caused "a large influx of a rough element into the district..., and tramps, and criminals, and roughs of all descriptions flocked in from all directions."[3] The hostility between miners and El Paso County deputy sheriffs was developing

> into a more sinister mood generally. Small bands of [striking mining] men raided throughout the district, stealing provisions and arms and ammunition, getting into drunken rows, and sometimes maltreating non-union men.[4]

The disgruntled Denver exiles headed by Captain J. C. Veatch "were joined at Colorado Springs by about 50 more" men. There they found themselves again against Governor Waite, who made no secret of backing the striking miners. Some 37 of the 40 mines of the Cripple Creek district were shut down by the striking miners. Their number at the armed camp at Bull Hill and their stronghold at Altman was between 500 and 600 while eventually Sheriff Bowers would command, not a posse, but a regiment of deputies numbering "about 1200."[5] The national guard had already come and gone once, and the governor would soon send it again.

In the aftermath of the City Hall War in Denver, many ex-city employees as well as gamblers and crooks abandoned Denver. But not Jeff. He stayed and fought to keep his position. On May 11, 1894, 3 days after Chase's arrest and 20 days after Chief Armstrong's original threats of a crackdown, the *Denver Republican* reported Jeff's arrest for "disturbance." The charge involved three bunco cases. Clark Secrest reports the case in his book on "Crime in Early Denver":

> L. B. Casebier, a visiting school teacher from Kansas, and two other tourists ... complained to Armstrong of being befriended and then robbed in a Denver vice and gambling den. Casebier, who was knocked unconscious during the assault, alleged that ... [Jeff] was in on the caper.... Casebier indignantly announced, "I shall never speak to another stranger while I am in this city unless he is properly introduced to me." Armstrong ... boisterously announced "a general war on suspected poker clubs," which was a hollow threat and the gamblers knew it."[6]

Sometimes office holders had no choice but to assist Jeff. One example occurred on April 20, 1894. John Bowers and two others were arrested for vagrancy. Jeff went to city coroner H. H. Martin, who had a number of outstanding debts among the sporting crowd, and as partial payment, asked him for a favor. When Bowers

[1] Hartzell, pp. 39-40.
[2] Rastall, p. 17.
[3] Rastall, p. 15.
[4] Rastall, p. 16
[5] Rastall, p. 23, & Stone, vol. I, p. 841.
[6] Secrest pp. 164-165, & *Denver Republican* 05/11/1894.

appeared in court on the vagrancy charge, his attorney argued that bunco steerers should not be charged with vagrancy because they are well paid for their services. Coroner Martin, though, was the hole card. He testified that Bowers was his employee in the collections department. Charges against Bowers were dropped.[1]

On the same day, an elderly woman visited the *Mercury* newspaper office. She was a washwoman barely making enough to care of her child and crippled husband. She had heard about some trouble Jeff had recently had with the law and felt the need to help him. "You see," she explained,

> I never knew anything about Jeff Smith only what my husband had said [about] his being the king of the gamblers, and that naturally made me afraid of him. Well, you remember that night when Parson Uzzell was giving out loaves of bread to all the hungry people? I went to the [People's] Tabernacle one night, but I got there too late. Every loaf of bread was gone, and not a penny in the house. I don't know what I was doing only standing alone when a gentleman came close up to me and ... pushed a piece of paper in my hand, and before I could even talk, he said: Take that, lady, it will get you all the bread you want.
>
> I turned to say thank you, sir, but he was gone.... I am only a woman, but I have got a vote and so has my husband, and anybody who does an act like that for us shows that they have hearts that are in the right place, and I think that they are better than the people who abuse them.[2]

Jeff loved being seen as a benefactor. He enjoyed the elevated standing—a big reward just for helping someone in need. Jeff also longed to be a hero and a title to go with it. A military rank would help fill the bill, but he was not interested in serving in the US armed forces. Although never in the military, he once told a newspaper reporter he had served during the Civil War.[3] In 1893, he even adopted the title of "colonel." Jeff had enjoyed power and authority during the day-long City Hall War as the leader of a company of special policemen and later as a deputy sheriff. Drawn to military style leadership, Jeff saw another opportunity for it only two weeks after the City Hall War, when Jacob Coxey's Army made its march on Washington, DC.

During the economic panic of 1893, conditions for the working man plummeted. Banks failed, so did commerce, and men lost their jobs. The surplus workforce, in turn, drove wages down. Conditions were deplorable and ever worsening. In his survey of causes for the "The Cripple Creek Strike of 1893[-1894]," Rastall reported how

> millions of laborers were idle. It was estimated that in the city of Pittsburg alone 100,000 men were out of employment. In every city men were eager to seize an opportunity to work for their board alone, and rumors were current of men offering themselves as slaves for life for a promise of mere subsistence.[4]

---

[1] *RMN* 04/27/1894.

[2] *Denver Mercury* 04/28/1894.

[3] *RMN* 06/20/1889. "I was a soldier myself, in the twenty-first artillery of Indiana and the One Hundred and forty-fifth infantry during the war."

[4] Rastall, p. 3.

A little over 100 miles northwest of Pittsburg and about 200 miles northeast of Cincinnati in the town of Massillon lived Jacob Sechler Coxey. Once a laborer in steel mills, through hard work and family support, he became a quarry owner and employer. This true son of toil was seized with Populist zeal in 1891, and by December 1893 he was originating a famous movement. Coxey had developed a plan for employing "millions of unemployed men driven to enforced idleness by the closing of mines and factories, and the introduction of labor-saving machinery."[1] In 1891, he sent his plan to Congress. It had been introduced as a national roads bill, but it went nowhere. In 1892, he formed the J. S. Coxey Good Roads Association to promote a roads program to relieve unemployment and build up the country. This time he would build support through a petition drive and forward it again to Congress. Coxey was engaged in this work when he attended the 1893 Bimetallic Convention at the Columbian Exposition in Chicago. There Coxey met Carl S. Browne. According to Lucy Barber in *Marching on Washington*, Browne impressed Coxey with his passion and organizing experience, and saw that Browne "might help the Good Roads Association. Coxey sought out Browne and convinced the westerner [from California] to visit him in Massillon."[2]

Browne arrived, and between December 7 and January 31, 1894, they drafted two bills for Congress, one for national roads and the other to finance them, published them in a bulletin, and began circulating petitions. Would signatures by the tens of thousands be enough to gain traction in Congress? He and Browne, who had experience organizing political events, went round and round in their thinking.

Enter Jeff Smith. In August 1893, he submitted an opinion letter on the labor crisis to *The Denver Mercury*. It appeared on the 26th, and in September *The Mercury* also printed his story of the silver miner who starved to death. Probably through Associated Press services, the letter reached the *Washington Star* in the District of Columbia, there to be labeled a piece of Western impudence.[3] But the letter also made its way around the country and in December 1893 appeared in the Ohio *Cincinnati Enquirer*. It struck strident tones from first to last.

March On![4]

Let The Workingmen Go Straight To The National Capitol

Editor Mercury: Why not tell the laboring men to go to Washington? The gold bugs should not be allowed to corrupt Congress as they did in 1873.[1] Let

---

[1] Coxey, p. 45.

[2] Barber, p. 17.

[3] Unknown Denver newspaper (Denver Mercury?) 06/02/1894. Clipping cut by Jeff R. Smith II. Jefferson R. "Little Randy" Smith col.

[4] *March On!*: This title and the words "sons of toil" appear in a popular labor song that emerged sometime prior to 1885. "Often old songs were given new words to suit the industrial era, such as 'Marching to Liberty,' sung to the tune of the 'Marseillaise' [anthem of the French Revolution, 1792]. Known as the 'Workers' Marseillaise,' it was especially popular at rallies and demonstrations" (Avrich, p. 137). The spirit of the letter's appeal is distinctly labor oriented as well. However, though Jeff may have been in sympathy with the millions of unemployed, he was never in league with the International Working People of America (IWPA) or the Knights of Labor. In fact, "Only those associated with idleness (bankers, speculators), corruption (lawyers, liquor dealers, gamblers), or social parasitism (all of the above) were categorically excluded from membership in the Order. (Fink, p. 9)

those who are out of work march on to Washington, fill the streets of the great city with honest sons of toil and tell the government of the United States that they must have relief. Let them say to Grover Cleveland, the stuffed prophet of Buzzard Bay,[2] that they have the same right to live as he; that their families are suffering for bread, and that the end of his play to the powers of Wall Street must cease. Let them march to Washington by every road. Let them stand face to face with the President and John Sherman, and tell them and the Representatives of the people that they demand to be recognized.

Make up half a million or more men and all go. If they want to jail them, then let them go to the officers like men and be fed from the greatest public crib. Don't pillage and burn, but just go there and get free grub and clothes.

Let the laboring men do this. They have made all the money in the country, they have made the government, and as the government owes them a living let them go to Washington and get it.

March on to Washington at once!

Let the gold bugs see your suffering. Fill the public squares and demand a surrender for the right, for humanity!

Declare yourselves! Be men, not slaves! Stand up—don't weaken! Fight for your rights, and stamp the Rothschild's and stuffed prophet out of sight!

Hurray for free silver and an honest government!

Jefferson R. Smith[3]

Did the December issue of *The Cincinnati Enquirer* with Jeff's letter reach the Coxey household? Did it influence the plan to rescue labor and save the nation? Perhaps. But whether directly or indirectly, or by historical synchronicity, Jeff's call and the Coxey/Browne plan both envisioned a massive march on Washington. Coxey explained twenty years later that he and Browne had "very little faith that Congress would do more than pigeon-hole" their rescue bills, and so "the idea was conceived of presenting the demand to Congress in the form of *a petition with boots on*, and accordingly, on Feb. 28, 1894, Bulletin No. 3 was issued, giving plan of organization...." This Bulletin, picked up broadly by the press, announced an embarkation date, Easter, March 25, their "line of march, design of badges, rules, notice of meetings to be held en route," and the May 1 "date of arrival at the Capitol."[4]

On March 19, Senator "William Peffer, a Populist from Kansas who knew Coxey, introduced the two bills...."[5] The demonstration, then, ending with Coxey's speech on the capitol steps, would be a living petition of citizens on behalf of the legislation. This manner of lobbying by the people, however, was brand new, alien. Given the labor unrest since the deadly Chicago Haymarket Riot of 1885, "Labor" easily aroused fear.

---

[1] *Congress in ... 1873*: With so little silver in circulation as currency, it had become undervalued, so investors had been trading it abroad for gold, thus further decreasing silver circulation. So Congress in 1873 authorized the Treasury to stop minting the silver dollar (*Gilded Age*, p. 191).

[2] *Grover Cleveland ... Buzzard Bay*: Buzzard's Bay, Massachusetts—Cleveland's summer retreat.

[3] *Denver Mercury* 08/26/1893 & 06/02/1894.

[4] Coxey, p. 46, emphasis added.

[5] Barber, p. 18.

As planned, on March 25, 1894, the march began. It was led by African American Jasper Johnson, who carried the "Stars and Stripes." Then came Carl Browne on horseback followed by Coxey in a carriage with his wife and "recently born son with the odd and political name of Legal Tender." Next came the Army of the Commonweal,[1] composed of about 100 men and a 6-piece band. "In town after town…, the Commonwealers, trying to march in the disciplined ranks of solders, repeated their performance…."[2] A contingent of curious reporters followed along. Eventually, more than 40 joined the army on its 700-mile march to Washington.[3] The objective was to bring attention to the plight of America's unemployed and to advocate for the Roads bills. The goal was for 100,000 unemployed "sons of toil" to join the army along the way. The actual numbers varied, growing and waning between 300 and 600 at any one time. "In addition, sixteen … divisions," Coxey wrote,

> were en route to Washington City from California, Colorado, Washington, Wisconsin, Illinois, Iowa, Oklahoma, Indiana, Pennsylvania, Massachusetts, New Jersey, and other states. The barriers they encountered, hardships they endured and incidents of the marches have become matters of history.[4]

In Denver, Jeff set out to gather 1,000 men to make a "division" for Coxey's Army. On April 27, 1894, Jeff negotiated with the railroads for free passage of men wanting to join Coxey's movement. The same was being successfully negotiated with the Florence and Cripple Creek Railroad for 300 mining men by a man representing himself as "General" J. S. Sanders.[5] The railroads in Denver, though, wanted nothing to do with the scheme—unless, of course, each man paid in full for his ticket.[6] It is possible that Jeff considered not only leading these men to Coxey but also joining the march and assuming a leadership role alongside Coxey himself. After all, Jeff had the prerequisites, among them, extensive knowledge of these types of men and leadership experience with their roughest sort. Then, too, he held the title of "colonel."

After negotiations with the railroads, Jeff telegraphed Lafayette Pence in the House of Representatives about his plans.[7] Jeff wrote him as well; however, the letter's contents are unknown. Pence replied on June 3, 1894.

> House Of Representatives U.S.
> Jeff R. Smith, Esq.,
> 1703 Larimer St.,
> Denver, Colorado
> Friend Jeff:
>   I am in receipt of yours of the 28th inst. I am not surprised that the railroads refused to haul men east, as that seems their policy everywhere.

---

[1] *Commonweal*: commonwealth or "general welfare."

[2] Barber, p. 23.

[3] Barber, p. 20.

[4] Coxey, pp. 46-47. These "matters of history" are numerous and harsh, including starvation, commandeering trains, shootouts with law enforcement, and arrests. None of these other "divisions" succeeded in joining Coxey's march.

[5] Rastall, p. 4.

[6] Newspaper clipping of unknown origin saved by Jeff R. Smith II. 04/27/1894. Author's col.

[7] *Atchison Daily Globe* 04/26/1894.

We all regret the trouble you are having in the state over the strikes at Cripple Creek and especially over the late floods. I sincerely hope the damage has not been so great as reported. Your letter bears out the reports we have received as to the scarcity of money in the west. It is about the same in the east. The latest news is to the effect that the crops are failing and if that should happen, the desperate outlook for the people this fall will be worse than ever before. I am grateful to you for your kind words about myself, but I have no idea whatever of standing as candidate for governor and have so written to all the friends who have mentioned the matter to me. The fact of the matter is, it looks to me like a losing game for a man to hold any office and I am not at all clear in my mind as to the course I will take this fall. I don't know when we will get away from here but probably not before the first of August. The assistant door-keeper joins in best regards to yourself. He is a very popular officer and our silver men only regret that we did not elect him door-keeper last fall. Mr. Coleman who is with me sends best wishes.

Very sincerely yours,
Lafe Pence[1]

Jeff was the personal acquaintance of a number of state and federal government officials, including such members of Congress as Colorado's Senator Edward Wolcott, Representatives James Belford and John Shafroth, and Texas Representative Joseph Bailey.[2] The assistant doorkeeper of the House of Representatives referred to in Pence's letter is Jeff's cousin, Edwin "Bobo" Smith, who had served in that position fourteen months earlier.[3] Nothing is currently known of "Mr. Coleman."

On April 30, 1894, Jacob Coxey's "Industrial Army" arrived in Washington with roughly 500 men, a fraction of the 100,000 Coxey hoped for. Public support had dissipated after stories of trouble were reported. One of these lasting several days concerned the Butte Miners' Union in Montana. A sizeable number of its men wanted to join Coxey's Army and asked the Northern Pacific to transport them. Refused, they seized a train and began east. When federal marshals intercepted them, two miners were killed, but still in possession of the train, the men continued east for two more days before being stopped.[4] The miners from Cripple Creek received a train ride to Cañon City and from there, transport on the Denver and Rio Grande to Pueblo. Not being offered further transport, they hijacked a Missouri Pacific train and started for Chicago. A purposely wrecked train on the tracks did not stop them; they just cleared the way and continued. A second wreck forced them to abandon that train, but they "took" another and made it half way across Kansas before US marshals stopped,

---

[1] Ltr to Jeff R. Smith II fr Lafe Pence, 06/03/1894. Jefferson R. "Little Randy" Smith col.

[2] Ltr to "Dear Brother Jeff" fr Edwin B. Smith, 03/27/1898. "I saw Senator Wolcott and he asked to be remembered to you. Congressman Bell of Colorado and Congressman Shafroth also ask me about you every time I see them. Bailey of Texas wants to know when you are coming back here." Item 3, author's col.

[3] Ltr to Captain George Waterbury fr Edwin B. Smith, 08/21/1893. Edwin signs Ltr "Assistant Bookkeeper, House of Representatives." Item 41, author's col.

[4] Barber, p. 21.

arrested, and dispersed them.[1] Barber reports that the *New York Times* caught the "prevailing attitudes of reports" on the march with its headline about the Montana men's death: "'Blood Flows from Coxeyism.'" To back the point was news of stolen trains, wrecks to stop them, and violent arrests. Barber, however, found that "Coxey and Browne's march caused few such violent incidents."[2] But in the public's view, violent insurrection was at hand.

Many thousands viewed the army's march down Pennsylvania Avenue. One estimate put the number as high as 30,000. The "racial and class composition was equally divided between blacks and whites and seemed to consist overwhelmingly of workingmen."[3] After the seven-mile parade to the southern edge of the Capitol grounds, tension grew as Coxey and Browne continued. Then Browne made a run for the capitol. Police tackled him and clubbed him into submission. Browne's break was a planned distraction, and Coxey quietly made his way to the steps and mounted five of them. There he began to read a prepared statement. Police stopped him, however, and led him away.[4] Coxey was released but then arrested the next day. He was charged with having violated an 1882 US Statute against displaying banners and walking on the grass of the Capitol grounds. It did not matter that Coxey had not walked on the grass but carefully kept to pathways through the thousands of spectators who stood on the grass, nor that his banner consisted of a lapel pen measuring "'3 inches by 2 inches wide.'"[5] Coxey, Browne, and Christopher Columbus Jones, an old man in rumpled clothes and a silk hat who represented Pittsburg labor, were tried by jury.

On May 2, among those attending the arraignment of Coxey, Browne, and Jones were seven congressmen and senators. Also attending was Adjutant-General Thomas Tarsney, commander of the state militia during the day-long City Hall War. He had come to offer his services as a lawyer. Whether Governor Waite sent Tarsney or he asked for leave to come is not known. When the trial began the next day, several congressmen assisted the lawyer defending Coxey and another defending Browne and Jones. Among these were Representative Lafayette Pence and Representative Thomas Hudson of Kansas, both Populists. They worked with the defense of Coxey through to his being found guilty and sentenced. On May 22, Judge Miller "asked the usual question whether the defendants had anything to say about why sentence should not be passed." When it came Coxey's turn, he said, "I do not appeal for mercy, because I have committed no crime, ... but I do ask for justice." Judge Miller sentenced the 3 to jail for 20 days and fined Coxey and Browne 5 dollars each. The criminals were taken directly to jail in a van called "The Black Maria." With them was a dozen white and negro workhouse prisoners. Coxey, Browne, and Jones were in handcuffs; their companions were not.[6]

---

[1] Rastall, p. 4.

[2] Barber, p. 20.

[3] Barber, p. 34.

[4] Barber, p. 35.

[5] Barber, p. 36.

[6] *New York Times* 05/03/1894 ("Coxey Placed Under Arrest") 05/04/1894 ("Coxey Defender A Senator) 05/22/1894 ("Coxey in the "Black Maria'"). Congressional persons appearing in court to help with the

The army without its leaders fell into disarray. Many left for other locales. Some begged on Washington streets and door to door and were often arrested. On June 11, Coxey and the other two were released. Jones returned to Pittsburg and Coxey with his family to Massillon, there to prepare an unsuccessful run for Congress. Only Browne remained. He promoted parades, street-corner protests, and bizarre demonstrations, such as dressing as Lady Liberty on July 4. The press termed him "an insane and desperate performer."[1] By early August, remnants of the army in various locales were set upon by Maryland and Virginia police and military forces. In his book *The Coxey Plan* (1914), Coxey reported a raid on one camp "in the night, by fifty heavily armed policemen...." Those rounded up were "confined in the Maryland workhouse for ... not having any work to do...."[2] Barber reports that "By August 14, the last 165 men were either riding trains or walking out of Washington," thus ending the first march of US citizens on the nation's capital.[3]

How might the future of "Colonel" Jefferson R. Smith have been altered had he succeeded in transporting a thousand men east? Would his leadership have enhanced the effectiveness of the "March"? Only one thing can be concluded for sure, that the history played out on the national stage would have been different. Jeff knew how to rally men and gain followers, how to get their trust and loyalty, and how to put on a show. Conflicts and trouble would have been resolved quite differently, perhaps with orchestrated violence. Jeff's past and future make that conjecture pretty much certain.

Jeff may have fooled some into believing he was a hero, but he could not fool those he victimized on nearly a daily basis. Many victims of Jeff's skinning houses and street swindles never knew who he was as they were from out of town, but those who complained and the public at large came to see him as a criminal and nothing more. Approaching mid May 1894, Jeff was once again in the *News* as a criminal.

> Another and more flagrant case occurred last night. Sol Correll, a young man suffering from both consumption and asthma, came to police headquarters and complained that as he was passing the Midway saloon at Seventeenth and Larimer streets..., Jeff Smith came out and suddenly struck him in the face, knocking him down. Correll said that three weeks ago he was buncoed out of $40 at the Royal bar on Larimer Street and supposes that Smith connected him with the arrest of Noonan & Dillon [two men charged in the case]. Special Officer Bowie soon arrested Smith, who was taken to the city hall, where he gave bonds for his appearance in court to-day.

> Correll had the temerity to go out on the street and had not proceeded 100 yards from the city hall when he was arrested by deputy sheriffs and taken to the county jail on a charge of disturbance—probably because he

---

defense by speaking out or conferring with counsel include Sen. William Allen of NE (Populist), Sen. Lucien Baker of KS (R), Rep. Haldor Boen of MN (P), Rep. Lafe Pence of CO (P), Rep. Omer Kem of NE (P), Rep. Thomas Hudson of KS (P), Rep. John Van Voorhis of NY (R). Adjnt-Gen. Tarsney's name does not appear in the *Times* trial accounts after May 2. *Black Maria: "'The van that conveys prisoners to gaol'" (1869] but prob. current since 1840 (Partridge, *Underworld*).

[1] Barber, Chapter 1.
[2] Coxey, p. 51.
[3] Barber, p. 39.

was first robbed and then knocked down. Later he was released on a bond secured by the police authorities and sought his doctor. He is on his way to Akron, where he hopes to find health.[1]

The Midway saloon at 1703 Larimer, located in the Chever Block, was managed by J. S. Bush. According to the *News*[2] it was owned by Jeff. A Midway business card saved by Jeff remains in the family collection.[3]

Jeff may have used his influence with the sheriff's department to effect this arrest. That the city police department rescued Correll, as it were, is a likely sign of lingering bad feeling stemming from the fire and police board struggle of months before. Another sign of continuing conflict was reported in the *News* the following day.

> Bascomb Smith, a brother of Jeff Smith, recklessly discharged his pistol at Thirteenth and Market last night, and when Officer Shuck attempted to arrest him he resisted with tooth and nail, finally flashing a deputy sheriff's badge. The policeman was never phased, however, and Smith was gathered in.[4]

Eight days later, two German families who spoke only German had a stopover in Denver on their way to Alamosa. They were encouraged to find Mr. Hooper of the Denver & Rio Grande Railroad as he spoke fluent German and would help them with needs. The *Colorado Evening Sun* of May 19, 1894, told the story.

FIN DE SIECLE SMITH[5]

> Those who are best acquainted with Colonel J. Randolph Smith are also well aware of the kind of business in which he takes especial delight, but this morning the colonel closed up a little deal which may result disastrously for the genial king of Seventeenth street. This morning as the colonel descended the stairway of his luxurious atelier[6] above the Tivoli and ambled gently up the street meditating on the peculiarities of the hayseed, the colonel met a messenger who informed him that Colonel Hooper of the Denver & Rio Grande would like to see him in his private office.
>
> Visions of an annual pass or perhaps of a chance to exchange experiences with the passenger agent of the Denver & Rio Grande floated before the colonel's eyes and he steered himself toward the Equitable Building.

The article details how two German families disembarked the Rock Island train, "glanced round with a perplexed air," and attracted "the attention of Colonel Smith's

---

[1] *RMN* 05/11/1894.

[2] *RMN* 06/29/1894, p. 8.

[3] Business card for the Midway saloon, Geri Murphy col.

[4] *RMN* 05/12/1894.

[5] *FIN DE SIECLE SMITH*: *fin de siecle* (French) = "end of the century." Formerly meant to suggest the progressive ideas, customs, and freedoms to come in new century to come. The sense of the headline could mean "The much too free and liberal Smith." It also could allude to the end of the age of Soapy Smith. Gambling and buncoing was being pressed out of Denver, and these events in Colfax were signs of the end of Jeff's days in Denver. After the turn of the century, the phrase came to signify decadence, i.e., a decline in morals, art, literature, etc. Deterioration, decay.

[6] atelier: artist's studio or workshop.

city man, who inquired if he could assist them." They said yes, and the man, who "could speak German like a native," said he would take them to Herr Hooper's office,

> but somehow he became mixed on the topography of the city, and no doubt wanting to give them an idea of the city took them across the Sixteenth street viaduct. At the other end of the long bridge their new friend invited them into a palatial thirst parlor, where, he said, Colonel Hooper generally passed the noon hour. However, Mr. Hooper was not in at that moment, and in order to beguile the time, pretzels, wienerwurst and Annheuser-Busch were ordered, and also a pack of cards and some chips.

While waiting for Mr. Hooper, the German families lost about $219, approximately half of what they had. So kind was Mr. Smith's agent, however, rivaling the kindness of "even the colonel himself," that he refunded $19 of the money. He also gave them a check for the rest of their cash. They could cash it in Alamosa when they arrived. Then, as Mr. Hooper still had not arrived, they left the hospitable German-speaking man and found T. C. Henry, head of the Alamosa colony they were to join. They

> related to him the pleasant little entertainment which Mr. Hooper had provided for them and also the kindness of his agent in offering to take care of their money. Mr. Henry jumped to the conclusion that this was some of Mr. Smith's work and he immediately went to Colonel Hooper and told him the particulars.
>
> The Denver & Rio Grande Railroad always endeavors to encourage enterprise, but Mr. Hooper when he heard of this transaction thought it a little too fin de siecle and that was the reason Colonel Smith was invited to visit Mr. Hooper as stated above.
>
> When Colonel Smith arrives a proposition will be made directly to him to either return the money or suffer the consequences.[1]

The outcome of the meeting between Mr. Hooper and Jeff was never published.

Nineteen days later, on June 7, 1894, Jeff was again in the lime-light. For two days the *News* published accounts of his attack on City Detective Griffiths.

> If there is any vigor in the law Soapy Smith will be sent to the penitentiary. He is a professional swindler and has attempted murder before. There is not a more desperate nor dangerous person than he in Colorado who is allowed to run at large.
>
> His assault of Wednesday upon a police officer who was seeking in his saloon for one of the protected thugs who live by robbery, and who but a few hours before had stolen a victim's money, was in keeping with his usual methods of assault. Sneaking up behind the officer he dealt him a murderous blow with a revolver, the officer having no reason to suspect his deadly purpose. He [Jeff] continued to strike his stunned and fallen victim until others interfered to stop him. This man Smith is a power in county politics. He is the right hand man of the sheriff for desperate and inhuman deeds. He may commit any crime and the influences that have protected him in the past will

[1] *Colorado Evening Sun* 05/19/1894.

save him in the future so far as the county authorities can effect it. He brooks no criticism or exposure. Any one who attempts it is liable to be murdered.

Is there not vigor enough in the laws and virtue enough in its administrators to bring this cowardly and unconvicted criminal to justice? Why denounce miners at Cripple Creek while this menace to life and property runs at large.[1]

Griffiths had entered the Midway saloon looking for and finding Soap Gangster George Wilder, accused of buncoing a man named Ed Baker. Wilder submitted to arrest peacefully and asked the detective to wait a few moments so that he could get his bondsmen to avoid going to jail. Jeff and Chief of County Detectives DeLue entered the saloon, and Jeff shook hands with Griffiths.

"After I had shaken hands with Smith," said Griffiths, "and was speaking to Wilder, Smith drew his gun and struck me from behind. He hit me on top of the head, stunning me and struck me again as I was falling. He then stuck the gun in front of me and backed me out the door."

DeLue, said Griffiths, did not show the least inclination to help him or to stop the row. ... The other side say that Griffiths started a wordy war with Smith, who acted in self-defense, but the officials at headquarters say that Griffiths is not of a quarrelsome nature and does his work quietly.

Jeff was arrested and charged with assault to murder, resisting an officer and interfering with an officer while on duty. He was held on $3,000 bond.[2] Two days later the charge was reduced to simple assault and Jeff was fined $10 and court costs.[3]

Wilder's case was still on the books on June 13 when he and Jeff met with Wilder's victim, Ed Baker, in an attempt to convince him not to testify against Wilder.

A talk about the matter followed and Smith called Baker a fool for attempting to prosecute his case against Wilder. He then invited Baker to take a drink and the latter declined. More talk followed and Jeff appealed to a hackman at the corner, asking his opinion in the question at issue. The hackman said the business was none of him and declined to talk. "Soapy" said he could get a civil answer out of any man he talked to and incidentally told Baker that if he did not leave the city at once he would do him up. Quite a crowd gathered and in the excitement Smith drew a gun. Officer Connors arrested him without trouble, and he was released at the station on $200 bonds.[4]

Wilder did not show up in court for his case. He was found at the Tivoli Club and locked up in the city jail on June 14 for "safe keeping and vagrancy." At 11 p.m. that evening Jeff, accompanied by Senator J. H. Balsinger and Orren Allen, arrived at the jail with a $1,000 bond for Wilder's release. Clerk Hickey refused the bond on the grounds that Wilder was being held for "safe keeping." Debate of the matter with the

---

[1] *RMN* 06/08/1894.
[2] *RMN* 06/07/1894, p. 8.
[3] *RMN* 06/09/1894, p. 5.
[4] *RMN* 06/13/1894, p. 8.

clerk became heated, and an angered Jeff struck the desk with his fist to emphasize his argument. The clerk threatened to arrest Jeff and started around the door to get his prisoner, just as Chief Armstrong entered the room and managed to calm the men.

"There's no use talking, Mr. Smith," said Armstrong. "I won't let Wilder out of jail. I'll have him in court tomorrow morning if it takes the whole police force to do it." Balsinger called the clerk a vile name and Armstrong caught him by the arm.

"You can't run me in," yelled Balsinger, the whole police force can't do it."

"Well, you'll come back and apologize to this man tomorrow morning, or I will run you in," answered the chief. Hickey reached for the alarm bell button and Smith caught his wrist and held him. Loud language was used by both sides and the officers in the building flocked into the room.

Threw Up His Hands.

Smith raised both his hands and kept them elevated until the affair was over. He is a quick man with a gun, but knew that if he had made a motion to get his weapon he would have been shot down. A few minutes later Armstrong released Wilder from jail, Senator Balsinger becoming responsible for his appearance today.[1]

Appearing directly under this story is another concerning Jeff and Cripple Creek miner T. F. Coxgriff, who had

> applied for protection at headquarters yesterday. He said that Soapy Smith had threatened to run him out of town and he asked permission to carry a gun as he had lived in mining camps for fifteen years and had never yet been chased out of the community in which he lived. Smith claims that Coxgriff was hanging about his place and became a chronic nuisance.[2]

Wilder went to court the next day as promised. He made no defense and bond was set at $300. Resolution of the case was never reported, but so far as is known, the last comment in the *News* about it held true: "Ed Baker left for Oregon last night and it is likely that the case will never be heard again."[3]

Then after Wilder's appearance in court that day, which Jeff attended, in Overland Park, for an unknown reason, Jeff arrested a man. The police doubted his authority, but Jeff exhibited a deputy sheriff badge that had been given to him by Sheriff Burchinell.[4] The outcome is not recorded, but the "fall out" was. On June 19, 1894, the *News* charged that the sheriff had

> appointed a very large number of the lawless element as deputy sheriffs. Professional gamblers, tin horns, [and] confidence men of every degree are said to bear the badge of the office, and to flash it when themselves or one of their pals gets into trouble to protect him.

[1] *RMN* 06/15/1894, p. 8.
[2] *RMN* 06/15/1894, p. 8.
[3] *RMN* 06/16/1894, p. 8.
[4] *Boulder Daily Camera* 06/18/1894.

One of the rights that follow being commissioned a deputy is to carry a gun, and everyone of this element with a commission does carry one. When Soapy Smith and men of his ilk who are deputies flourish revolvers and strike down police officers who don't walk along according to their lines of duty, is it not time that the extent of this outrage upon law and order should be discovered and proper steps taken to rectify the outrage?[1]

The *Denver Republican* usually supported Jeff but this time did not:

The sheriff says he gave Jeff Smith a commission for some special work several months ago, but has since revoked it. The Colonel still retains his commission and badge.

It is strange, in the face of the sheriff's statement, that nearly every bunco steerer arrested by the police has in his possession, a revolver and deputy sheriff's badge. Bascomb Smith, who was arrested last week, was thus equipped, although Mr. Burchinell denies having ever given him a deputy sheriff's commission.[2]

No doubt Jeff enjoyed the power and prestige of the deputy sheriff commission and badge. Further, though, flashing it at the right moment kept swindled victims from going to the real police. Apparently Jeff had a supply of badges that he dispensed to his men. With badges having become controversial, though, it would have been prudent to retire them, and for a time they were.

Police headquarters at city hall that summer experienced a stream of visitors who came to complain of being duped out of cash and items of value. Police Chief Hamilton Armstrong, recently appointed by the new board and Governor Waite, was under pressure to crack down on criminals. If he did not make inroads against them, suspicion would grow that he was in league with the bunco men. So Armstrong declared war. He ordered the arrest of all bunco men found working their games on the streets.[3] He was largely unsuccessful, however, in curtailing criminal activity, and the stream of complaints remained as steady as before.

Typical among these complaints was that of Cyrus B. Hawley of Marion, Kansas. In a saloon he met two friendly men who invited him join them in a drink. One, though, led to another. But it only took two. After the second, he remembered nothing until awakening in a closet. Staggering out and regaining his senses, he found his pocketbook gone. At police headquarters, Cyrus said he believed he had been drugged. Officers agreed, saying events followed methods used by Jeff's gang.[4]

The Soap Gang was unyielding, persistent, and creative. Dr. C. W. Lyman of Boston was one who learned of the swindlers' abilities. In late June of 1894, he had come to Denver for a physicians' convention. The good doctor was flattered to find his photograph and story in the local newspapers. People were impressed. So was the Soap Gang. The *Denver Republican* told his story.

---

[1] *RMN* 06/19/1894, p. 4.

[2] *Denver Republican*, unknown month and date (probably June, 1894) saved by Jeff R. Smith II. Author's col.

[3] *RMN*, undated clipping saved by Jeff R. Smith II. Author's col.

[4] *Denver Republican*, undated clipping saved by Jeff R. Smith II. Author's col.

In his after-dinner geniality Dr. Lyman felt in a mood to discard for the nonce something of his Beacon Hill reserve, so when the most clerical-looking steerer on Seventeenth street sauntered up to him and remarked that it had been "a regular dog day." The doctor beamed through his glasses and said: "Aw—yes, indeed: quite so, quite so."

"Nights much cooler than in Boston, though." Went on the man who lives by his wits—and that settled it.

For fifteen minutes the Boston physician and the Seventeenth street clergyman talked about Ibsen,[1] the last [Boston] fire, the Concord School of Philosophy and other pleasing topics. Then the supposed clergyman proposed a street car ride, to which Dr. Lyman assented.

In telling Chief of Detectives Behymer about it yesterday morning, Dr. Lyman said they rode in a cable car over a long bridge, much longer than the one between Boston and Cambridge, and stopped in the center of a small dirty town in which dogs and children abounded.

"That's Colfax," chuckled the chief....

After leaving the car the doctor's companion proposed soda water. They could not find a drug store, and so entered a saloon. There the regulation antediluvian programme[2] was carried out. The clergyman met "the colonel" and introduced him to his friend the doctor. The clergyman had not met "the colonel" before in years, and so they must go into a nice quiet room off the bar and compare notes. Of course the doctor would go along? He did.

By a remarkable coincidence three men were playing poker in the room, and still more remarkable, they were acquaintances of "the colonel."

"Poker, I declare!" exclaimed the colonel, "Just like college days!" It was like "college days" to the clergyman too, and not to be outdone in a boast about wild oats, the doctor uttered a low remark to the same effect. ...

After that it was easy sailing for the two bunco steerers. They and Dr. Lyman took a hand in the game "just for old times' sake." When the "sucker hand was dealt out Dr. Lyman held three kings and two aces, bet $58 cash and a $1,000 check on the Manufacturers' bank of Boston, and lost the pot to the colonel, who showed down four deuces.

"Most remarkable cards," remarked the clergyman and he said it was time to go, to which the colonel assented. The doctor's wishes in the matter of departing were not consulted, but he left with the other two, who saw him safely to his car and left him.

The doctor spent the night "diagnosing" what had happened and concluded he had been duped. Next morning he went to the police and "told the whole story to Chief Behymer," who had the doctor telegraph his Boston bank with instructions not to honor the check. Then every bank in Denver was called and given the same instructions.

---

[1] *Ibsen*: Henrik Ibsen (1828-1906), Norwegian playwright, by the 1890s called the father of modern drama.

[2] *antedeluvian program*: a routine older than the flood of Biblical times.

Then Marshal France of Colfax was sent for. The chief of detectives wanted the Colfax official to pull the house[1] in which the Boston physician was buncoed, but for some unaccountable reason the marshal seemed loath to do it. He said that if the house was pulled Dr. Lyman must first be arrested. This so alarmed the man from the Hub[2] that he begged the Colfax marshal not to arrest anybody, it was all right. The doctor went his ways and was not heard of again until 6 o'clock last evening.

Then he came back to police headquarters with alarm depicted on his face and his whiskers much disordered. The bunco man was after him again. In the corridor of the American house, the Seventeenth street clergyman met the doctor and in very unclerical language told him that his check was no good. If he did not pay the $1,000 at once he would be arrested.

The doctor demurred, pleaded and coaxed to be let off. "All right; seeing that you are a stranger here—and a green one at that—I'll let you off at $500," said the bunco man. Dr. Lyman promised to consider the offer and then posted for the central station.

The chief of detectives emphatically told the much-badgered and swindled homoeopathist[3] to pay nothing and particularly pay no attention to bunco steerers.[4]

Although the genial reverend is not named he is certainly "Reverend" John Bowers. His job was made much easier by the city newspapers. They published everything he needed to know about his prey. Bowers could introduce himself as from the doctor's hometown and discuss topics likely to interest the man, thus instilling confidence. Bowers took the doctor across the bridge to Colfax and the same saloon used in several other swindles, such as of the German families. Jeff, whom the *Denver Republican* identified as "the colonel," was waiting to participate in the gentle heist. The story makes obvious that Marshal France was on Jeff's payroll. The outcome of the affair never made it into print, but it is doubtful Jeff or Bowers suffered at the hands of Marshal France.

This period of transition set in motion by Governor Waite is characterized by an air of recklessness and confrontation. The saloon men, gamblers, and bunco community were under pressure but not in the least ready to surrender. How the power struggle would end and what the landscape would look like later on was still very much uncertain. It might be said that the day of the City Hall War was the climax of the struggle and that the drama was drawing toward its final scenes. Although coming after the climax, however, those scenes would not be lacking in drama, audacity, and pathos.

---

[1] *pull the house*: "pull in," or bring in to a police station, persons in that house, i.e., saloon. Colloquialism?

[2] *the Hub*: Occupying a position analogous to the hub of a wheel; a central point of revolution, activity, life, interest, etc. Applied to Boston, U.S., & playfully to other places. (*OED*)

[3] homoeopathist: one who practices homeopathy, treatment of diseases by the administration (usually in very small doses) of drugs which would produce in a healthy person symptoms closely resembling those of the disease treated. (*OED*)

[4] *Denver Republican* 06/20/1894.

In the Cripple Creek mining district, the 500-to-700 determined force of striking miners and the 1200-man deputy army of Sheriff Bowers were approaching the point of pitched battle. On June 8 formations of deputies were advancing on the miner-fortified Bull Hill. The miners had no artillery, but they did have a huge bow-gun that could deliver "beer bottles filled with dynamite."[1] The hill was also mined with dynamite, and the miners were well supplied with small arms. Tarsney ordered Brooks to catch up with Sheriff Bowers and demand that he turn back the deputies. Brooks overtook the Sheriff and commanded him to turn back. Bowers argued that he had authority to proceed, but Brooks replied that he "would be compelled to fire upon the deputies unless they ceased their march immediately."[2] Bowers reluctantly ordered a retreat. He also signed a paper to that effect, and Brooks had to show it to other deputies elsewhere advancing. Though the deputies argued with Brooks, he succeeded in turning them back.

On the next day, Saturday, June 9, with the deputies refusing to disband, a summit meeting between the sides was held at Altman, the miner's stronghold. Included were Tarsney, Brooks, Bowers, representatives of the El Paso County Government, the miners, and the mine owners. A seven-point agreement was reached. The seventh point was that "Persons for whom the sheriff has or may have warrants [are] to be arrested and turned over to the sheriff at Colorado Springs."[3] Many arrests immediately followed.

And so in latter June 1894, General Tarsney, as he had done for Jacob Coxey in May, again exchanged his military uniform for a lawyer's suit of clothes. He had been in Colorado Springs for several days, working on a defense team for arrested miners, and on Friday, June 22, 1894, he had retired to his room in the Alamo Hotel at the city center. Shortly after midnight the porter brought word to Tarsney that he had a telephone call at the hotel desk. Tarsney hurried down to the lobby and had just stepped up to the telephone when a masked man with a pistol in hand came up to him and said, "We want you." Another masked man stood behind the first near the door. Tarsney asked what was wanted and was told to come along. Tarsney said he didn't want to and tried to retreat, but the masked man sprang forward and "struck General Tarsney a vicious blow with the weapon," staggering him.[4] Then told he was to be killed, Tarsney begged for time to write a note to his family, but the reply was that "there was no time to waste."[5]

Another masked man appeared at the door to cover the porter and desk man while the second came forward to assist the first in dragging Tarsney outside. Beside two hacks (coaches for hire) with unmasked drivers stood four more masked men. Tarsney was forced inside one of the hacks, followed by some of the men, and others entered the other hack. One masked man climbed up with each of the drivers, and they were off "at a mad gallop" east two blocks on Cucharras Street and left on Weber

---

[1] *bow-gun ... dynamite*: Rastall, p. 31.

[2] *fire upon the deputies*: Rastall, p. 32.

[3] Rastall, p. 34.

[4] *Davenport Daily Leader* 06/24/1894, p. 1.

[5] *Cedar Rapids Weekly Gazette* 06/28/1894, p. 5.

straight north out of town toward Austin Bluffs. About fifteen minutes later, three police officers rode at a gallop "in the direction" the kidnappers had gone. But they "had a poor trail to follow. It was pitch dark and they only knew that the masked party had headed north."[1]

Thomas J. Tarsney was a battle-hardened man. At nineteen in 1861, he and two of his brothers enlisted in the Fourth Michigan Volunteers. He left service four years later at the rank of colonel's orderly sergeant. Tarsney had been wounded only once though he fought in dozens of skirmishes and battles, including Antietam, Chancellorville, and Gettysburg. While 2 of his brothers became lawyers and went on to Congress (one from Michigan, Timothy E. 1885-1888, and one from Missouri, John C., 1889-1896), Thomas went west to railroad as a fireman and then an engineer, at last settling in Pueblo, Colorado, where he and his wife Lucy ran Clifton House, a place for railroad people.[2] Finally following the path of his brothers, he studied law and in 1886 was admitted to the bar in Colorado.[3] In 1893, Governor Waite made Tarsney his adjutant general, the commander of the Colorado National Guard. Tarsney probably was appointed for his strong Populist standing, not his military training, all of it "on the job." Still, he had four hard, long years of military life at war, service within an officer's command, administrative experience as a lawyer, and maturity. He was fifty-one when appointed and still could ride out on his own alone, meet up with officers and Indian police, and negotiate a successful end to Indian troubles.[4] But nothing, not even the horrors of the Civil War Battle of the Wilderness in which he was wounded, could prepare him for what was to follow.

Between 3 and 5 miles north, near the bluffs, and off the road away, the coaches pulled up, and Tarsney was dragged out and brought to a circle of about 15 masked men. Sherman Crumley, driver and owner of one of coaches, said, "Several times on the way out I heard them threaten Tarsney's life."[5] Supplemented by abundant cursing, the threats against Tarsney's life continued. A leader among the masked men suggested that every man who wanted to could tell

> the general all they proposed to do with him, why they proposed to do it, and their opinions of him. He was accused of waging war against the mine owners and deputies, he was accused of handling the state troops in the interests of the strikers; he was accused of issuing an order to the troops to fire upon the deputies from the twelve pounders; and finally, he was accused of indirectly being the cause of the death of the [two] deputies who were killed during the Bull Hill campaign. For this they threatened to kill him. Every humiliating threat and form of profanity was hurled against him.[6]

---

[1] *Davenport Daily Leader* 06/24/1894, p. 1.
[2] *History of the Arkansas Valley, Colorado* (1881).
[3] Colorado State Archives.
[4] *Aspen Times* 05/20/1893, "That Navajo Scare," p. 4.
[5] *Davenport Daily Leader* 06/24/1894, p. 1.
[6] *Cedar Rapids Weekly Gazette* 06/28/1894, p. 5. Note: This telling of events are reported to have come fr Tarsney himself, given in interview in his Denver home. The following summary is taken this article.

When the men had had their say, Tarsney was invited to speak for himself. He said that not he but General Brooks had been in command at Bull Hill and that his orders came from Governor Waite. This said, after a brief conference with the men, the leader announced that the general would receive a hundred lashes. Tarsney then asked to be shot as he would not survive such punishment. After another brief pause, the leader told one of the men "to get his implements and do his work." Shortly, the man "returned with a pail of coal tar, a brush and a rag and a feather pillow. The general was then disrobed and the tar and feathers administered.

Blackened and feathered, the general was allowed to put his clothes back on. He then was guided to a road and told to head down it. Said the leader,

"Roswell lies in that direction [west]. Keep straight ahead. Don't ever set foot in Colorado Springs or Cripple Creek again or your life will pay the forfeit." ... So suddenly had life been given the tortured man, so great was the strain through which he had passed, so severe were his physical sufferings, that he scarcely realized the situation.[1]

According to Crumley, driver of the hack, and another person later on, Tarsney then thanked the spokesman and others among the masked men, again and again, "for sparing his life," and shook their hands.[2]

The general began to walk. He was followed for a time by someone on horseback, but whoever it was soon turned off, and Tarsney was alone in the pitch dark and pre-dawn cold at the 6,000-foot elevation. As he followed the road, the tar drying and cracking as he walked, his movements became more and more painful, but he traveled mile after mile. Several times he saw farm houses but said he dared not approach them. Being "hatless, in soiled clothing and his face covered with tar and feathers," he thought he would be too frightening to behold, perhaps even attacked in self-defense. Finally, though, near dawn, in pain and exhausted, he went to a farmhouse for help.

He had come to the house of Andrew Malloy, "a ranchman, who had been a deputy at Cripple Creek" during the conflict.[3] Nevertheless, he was given aid and comfort, a breakfast, and the ministrations of Mrs. Malloy, who may have done more harm than good. She tried to remove the tar "from his face, neck, and hair" with coal oil. It removed most of the tar, but her work caused abrasions, inflammation, and some blistering. As would later be learned, the coal oil may have increased damage to his eyes caused by the tar. Still, the kindness of taking him in and attempting to relieve his suffering were gratefully accepted and appreciated, so stark in contrast were they to the treatment he had suffered some 5 hours previous. He learned he had walked northwest about 14 miles and that it was about 11 miles further to Palmer Lake, the closest locale along the railroad. Malloy drove Tarsney there, where he telegraphed the governor, and a special train was dispatched to retrieve the tortured national guard commander.[4]

[1] *Cedar Rapids Weekly Gazette* 06/28/1894, p. 5

[2] *Davenport Daily Leader* 06/24/1894, p. 1, & Hawarden Independent (IA) 08/10/1894, p. 3.

[3] *Littleton Independent* 06/29/1894.

[4] *Cedar Rapids Weekly Gazette* 06/28/1894, p. 5

Arriving in Denver about 3:15 p.m., he was driven home and attended by National Guard Surgeon Kling and Tarsney's orderly, Victor Goeth. They succeeded in removing the rest of the tar. Later, after rest and dinner, "to a party of sympathizing friends [he] related the story of his trouble."[1] Often during the telling of his "humiliating experience his feelings overcame him."[2]

Who was responsible? The answer must be "Many." Plausibly frustrated, angry, sullen ex-deputies had undertaken the deed spontaneously. Their every advance against the miners had been frustrated either by the miners, their own superiors (Sheriff Bowers or "Col. Veatch" as he was being called), or the national guard. When advancing on Bull Hill, General Brooks had chased them down as if bad children and given them a humiliating dressing down.

> "Get back to camp, every one of you," he began. "I am in command here and you have broken faith with me already. So you must face right around and return to where you came from. I have here an order from Sheriff Bowers which tells you to go back."
>
> The fire-eating deputies looked at one another and then began a tumultuous consultation. No one man appeared to be in command, and from all sides came a volley of orders, advices and expostulations. To words of expostulation General Brooks gave the simple answer that they must obey. The national guard was now abreast of the county officers and halted close to their lines. The deputies did not hesitate any longer, but upon an order from some one wheeled around on their tracks and began the journey back....
>
> Many of the deputies showed great resentment at being ordered back to camp and tore off their badges in anger. Quite a number left camp that night to return to Colorado Springs....

As the deputies passed by some of the militiamen, they "hissed" the deputies. General Brooks immediately silenced his men with threat of the guard house, but this correction did not cool the anger of the humiliated and frustrated deputies.[3] On the night of the outrage, reported seen "was a meeting of twenty-five deputy sheriffs at Antlers Park at 10 o'clock, and it is believed the plot against General Tarsney was hatched there."[4]

On June 25 or 26 four to six men, supposedly members of Jeff's gang, arrived in Colorado Springs apparently to operate some street games. They were arrested and brought before Chief Dana who warned them to leave town. No other information on this group of men is known.[5]

How involved was the community of Colorado Springs, a threatened Republican, anti-Populist stronghold, and the many owners of mines, including David Moffat of Denver who owned most of the forty mines in the region? They wanted their mines reopened, the miners' union crushed, and if need be, Governor Waite's national guard

---

[1] Colorado Springs Gazette 06/24/1894, p. 2.

[2] *Cedar Rapids Weekly Gazette* 06/28/1894, p. 5

[3] *New Castle News* 06/16/1894, p. 2.

[4] *Cedar Rapids Weekly Gazette* 06/28/1894, p. 5

[5] *RMN* 06/29/1894.

outnumbered and backed down? Principally the mine owners but also local business owners and county government put up the money for Sheriff Bowers to underwrite the costs of a deputy army that grew to 1200 men.[1] Only a little more money and not much persuasion could have purchased a band of men angry enough to perform a late-night mission of revenge. Here is plausibility. Though General Brooks had been the primary actor, the adjutant general had been conspicuous throughout the days of confrontation, and here he was back, defending the transgressing miners in court.

But also involved were Denver interests. Among them was Lou Blonger, keeping a low profile at the time as a participant in "policy," operator of various criminal schemes, and "fixer." He now had an office on Seventeenth Street and several saloon and gaming dens. Lou owned a share of the Forest Queen gold mine, one of thirty-seven mines affected by the strike. A claim in 1891, it hit big in 1892. Mine revenue helped Lou and his brother Sam strengthen themselves in Denver, and now like the other mine owners, that revenue had been blocked. And for Lou as well as Jeff Smith, Ed Chase, and many others in their circle, there had been all the trouble in Denver with city hall and now the pressure to close down gambling, the buncoing arts, and the rest of it. According to the *News* the Smiths and Blongers joined forces, referring to them as the "Smith-Blonger bunco-steering brigade."[2] Tarsney had been at the head of the city hall trouble, too, with his cursed militia. Then there was County Detective Leonard DeLue. The Blongers as well as Jeff and all the so-called Boodle Hall men were connected to DeLue. After ex-chief Veatch had fielded a 105-man force of ex-policemen and firemen and been brought to a standoff by some three hundred miners,

> Orders were sent to Denver for an additional force of guards and County Detective DeLue began to recruit men for service. It was expected that 125 men would leave for Cripple Creek Saturday morning.[3]

So about a quarter of the deputy army, amplified by men from Leadville, Pueblo, and Colorado Springs, were Denver men who either had ties to or experience with the Denver Combine. Any one of these, and likely many, could have been in regular contact with Denver people, and perhaps Denver bosses. Further, most of them had a grudge against Governor Waite and his point man, Tarsney.

The Cedar Rapids Weekly Gazette published a June 23 dispatch from Denver that explored for a cause of Tarsney's being made a target:

> General Tarsney was the personal representative of the governor during the police board troubles when the militia were opposite the city hall. His undaunted bearing at the time antagonized the police and their sympathizers, and it was freely stated that if shooting commenced he would be the first man to fall.

---

[1] Owners Send a Large Force of Deputies to Fight if Necessary. The owners of mines at Cripple Creek have determined to resume work on their properties now that the railroads have been built into the camp. To do this they knew that it would be necessary to send in non-union miners and enough deputies to protect them. (*Fairplay Flume* 05/31/1894)

[2] *RMN* 07/05/1894, p. 5.

[3] *Castle Rock Journal* 05/30/1894, p.2; *Colorado Transcript* 05/30/1894, p. 2; *Fairplay Flume* 05/31/1894, p. 2.

In the earlier stages of the Cripple Creek trouble he was legal advisor for some of the miners and since the settlement of the strike has resumed his services in that capacity. While the militia were in the field at Cripple Creek he was again the direct representative of the governor through whom orders were transmitted to General Brooks. In this service he found himself opposed once more to many of the men aligned against him at the city hall. The A. P. A. was bitter in its threats against General Tarsney.

The A. P. A.—the American Protective Association—in 1894 was a secretive order with about a million members.[1] It was born of anger over wide-spread unemployment, resentment of immigrants in general, and immigrant Catholics in particular. And a noticeable A. P. A. contingent was part of Veatch's force. The *Colorado Springs Gazette*:

> There is no doubt but the A. P. A. movement cuts quite a figure in the fight, and it is not an unusual thing to hear one of the deputies express his sentiments that American miners will work in the Cripple Creek mines before they are through. Over Commander Veatch's headquarters floats the American flag, and every once in a while some pent-up spirit breaks fourth with the shout, "America for Americans!"[2]

Finally, although perhaps "all of the above" may have found scapegoat satisfaction in Tarsney's cruel treatment, another and most probable cause was a desire to embarrass, frustrate, and warn off the militant, labor-loving, anti-capitalistic, trouble-making Populist Governor, Davis H. Waite. Tarsney had received the terrible dressing down and application of tar and feathers, but symbolically it was delivered to Waite, and Waite knew it. Upon Tarsney's first arriving home, before his interview at length, the general said, "They told me that their first intention had been to give me 100 lashes and then hang me, but they compromised on the tar and feathers."[3] There is but a single clear conclusion to the question, "Why wasn't Tarsney just tormented and lynched?" It was a common enough practice throughout the west and south in 1894.[4] And that is because Tarsney's abductors were told not to. The general, it would seem, was valued more as a living, humiliated and defiled representative of the governor whom the governor would be forced to look at and work with thereafter.

Toward the end of July, 1894, the leader of the men who performed the outrage against Tarsney was tracked down to the home of his parents in Missouri. He was "Joseph K. Wilson of Denver..., 28 years of age, [and] one of the ... deputies commissioned ... during the Cripple Creek strike war and in command of a squad of mounted men."[5] Tarsney and Denver Detective George Peterson arrested Wilson and brought him back to Denver. Then while being transported to Colorado Springs, Wilson confessed, naming Sheriff Bowers, Deputy Sheriff Mullins, hack owners

---

[1] A. P. A.: Gilded Age Dictionary.

[2] *Colorado Springs Gazette* 05/29/1894.

[3] *New York Times* 06/24/1894.

[4] *lynching ... a common enough practice*: Between 1882 and 1968, there were 4,742 *known* lynching in America. (McMurty, p. 28.)

[5] *Aspen Times* 08/04/1894, p. 3.

Sherman and Walter Crumley, several national guard soldiers, other men, and even the wife of one of them, who supplied the feathers by donating a pillow.[1]

The broadly watched-for trial, anticipated to begin in latter August, never began. On Monday, August 20, 1894, promptly at 2 p.m., Justice McCoach and sixteen men charged with assaulting General Tarsney were assembled for a hearing to determine if evidence merited a trial. Sheriff Bowers and Under Sheriff Mullins were not among this group. The proceeding was being held in Colorado City, south of Pueblo and about ninety miles from Colorado Springs. All was in readiness to begin except no prosecutor appeared. Finally, the judge himself left court to look for him, and returned at 2:45 with District Attorney Cockran, who immediately asked the court to dismiss charges against all the men. He said the grand jury "had refused to return true bills on the evidence...." Cockran said that Tarsney's lawyer, a Mr. Stidger, had promised new evidence to bring into trial by the time of the hearing. Cockran had been waiting for the man, but after an hour beyond when the lawyer said he would appear and still with no word from him, nothing could be done but dismiss the cases. "Thus have ended the cases against the men arrested by order of the Governor...," concluded a news dispatch, and "They [Governor Waite, General Tarsney, et al.] have made themselves ridiculous, and are being laughed at out of court."[2]

The grand jury had not believed all of Joseph Wilson's confession nor the confessions of some others who had been arrested. Their stories, unsubstantiated and conflicting, did not add up, and so there could be no "true bill." Whether or not conflicting stories were employed by self-initiative or direction is not known, but it was a familiar practice among criminals in Denver. Suspected was that the man had received direction from higher up.

Waite apparently thought so. On June 26, he had offered a reward of up to $1,000 "for the arrest and conviction of the persons who committed or aided and abetted in the said outrage..., payable at the rate of $200 for each person ... until the full sum of $1,000 and not more shall be paid."[3] Failing to secure any evidence, the reward was increased to $2,000 and the amount upped to $250 "for the arrest and conviction of each and every person (not exceeding eight in number) who furnished money for ne purpose of bringing about the outrage" against General Tarsney, "or who furnished money for the purpose of aiding any of the participants ... to leave the State." The person to contact was Attorney Frank Owers of Leadville. The reward notice appeared in newspapers from Denver to Pueblo in early September. It appeared four times in the *Colorado Springs Gazette.*[4] In 1894, $2,000 and $250 were sizeable amounts ($59.940 and $7,493 today[5]) but apparently not enough to uncover those who triggered the outrage and kept their identities so well hidden.

Even before the charges were dismissed against those who had been arrested and the reward money increased, Waite was hitting back through his former

---

[1] *Aspen Times* 08/07/1894, p. 3.
[2] *The Weekly Gazette* (Colorado Springs) 08/23/1894, p. 8.
[3] *Aspen Times* 06/30/1894, p. 2.
[4] *Colorado Springs Gazette* 09/05-06-10-11/1894, p. 3 X 3, p. 7 X 1.
[5] Tom's Inflation Calculator.

newspaper at those he suspected. Without evidence, no one could be accused outright, least of all a big mine owner and railroad man and banker like David Moffat and all the other moneyed Republicans in the Denver Ring, no one, that is, except Soapy Smith, who was already branded as infamous. On July 21, *The Times* went after Jeff in three different stories:

> Soapy Smith is a good republican—give this boss bunco's band another whack, and the redemption business will go merrily on. [p. 2] ... Let us see; Dynamite Soapy Smith is a shining light in this "law and order" party that is going to "redeem" the state this fall. [p. 4] ... Denver Soapy Smith should be carefully protected, but Cripple Creek laborers should be shot down and the state would suffer no ills in consequence. [p. 4][1]

August 8, 1894: "Such a governor is unpopular with the "Soapy" Smiths of the country and stands in the way of whisky-dive politicians" (p. 2). Same August 8 issue:

> Now, what has Governor Waite done to "injure the credit of the state?" The people who are asked to believe this would like to have republican newspapers explain. Is it because he smashed the Soapy Smith gang of political blacklegs in Denver?[2] Is it because [listed are land deals and labor's rights].... Is it because he refused to permit the murderous gang, that brutally assaulted General Tarsney, to drench Cripple Creek with the blood of miners? [p. 4][3]

August 11, 1894:

> It is the "gang" that inaugurated this republican business and if anybody thinks for a moment that the Soapy Smith contingent has any idea of relinquishing their chances for a "pull" at the spoils, his verdancy is of a rich emerald hue. ...
>
> Joseph R. Wilson, the man arrested in Missouri for being implicated in the tarring and feathering of General Tarsney, has made a full confession. It is said that one or two others have also confessed to a participation in the outrage. As the confessions criminate officials and prominent men in Colorado Springs it is now conceded that the affair was concocted by General Tarsney's political enemies. It illustrates the methods of the republican redemption league, the moving spirits of which are such men as Soapy Smith, Burchinell and the rest of the gang at Denver and Colorado Springs.[4]

On August 13, 1894, at a Populist meeting in Denver, Police Chief Henry Behymer spoke on behalf of the governor about how Jeff was getting out of politics.

> I was talking to Mr. Smith yesterday.... To Colonel Randolph Smith. Colonel Jefferson Randolph Smith. Some people call him Soapy Smith. I asked him what he was doing in politics this fall. He replied, "Nothing." "Why, colonel,

---

[1] *Aspen Times* 07/21/1894, pp. 2 & 4.
[2] *blacklegs*: blackleg. Brit. derogatory a person who continues working when fellow workers are on strike.
[3] *Aspen Times* 08/04/1894, pp. 2 & 4.
[4] *Aspen Times* 08/11/1894, p. 4.

how is that?" said I. "You have always been active in politics." "Yes, Behymer," said he, "but to tell you the truth, the Republican party is getting too corrupt. I can't train with them any longer."[1]

As the Colorado campaign for governor heated up and Thomas Paterson, editor of the *Rocky Mountain News*, endorsed Republican Albert McIntyre, Waite and his Populist son-in-law hit back in their paper by keeping its spotlight on Soapy Smith: "That does settle it! Thomas [Paterson] has unmasked and he and Soapy Smith will be found side by side working for the "redemption" of Colorado."[2]

Jeff and the Soap Gang now favored settling with victims rather than appear in court. This approach angered police and those fighting to convict or evict Jeff and his associates. In July the police had an excellent case against John Bowers, "Big Al" Hoffses, and James Thorton for swindling $108, but Jeff convinced the victim not to prosecute. Details are unknown as the case never came to court, but according to the *News*, it involved a large roll of paper money with only a few genuine bills on top.[3]

Three days later Dr. W. P. Robinson of Utah met members of the gang in Denver and was invited to Colfax for a little recreation. Robinson was led to poker game with Bowers, Hoffses, Thornton and "John" [W. H.?] Casey in which he lost $280 by lending cash for a fraudulent check. Robinson went to Police Chief Armstrong and gave descriptions of the men. Recognizing the descriptions Armstrong sent Officers Remley and Wright on a hunt for the bunco men. The two officers met with Jeff who

> coolly informed Remley that the money would be returned if there would be no prosecution. Later Chief Armstrong saw Smith and the latter agreed to turn the men over to the police this morning. If he does not do so Chief Armstrong says he will make Denver an equator town for the king of the bunco men.[4]

Six days later Jeff "turned over" Bowers to the police, who was soon after released on bonds. While at city hall with his prisoner, Jeff placated Armstrong, saying, "Well, chief, ... you have brought me to a stand still. Hereafter I will do the square thing."[5] It should be no surprise that the men were tried and discharged[6]. Four years later, Jeff had the exact same opportunity to thwart prosecution but turned it down. It was a rare and disastrous mistake.

Less than a month later Jeff and Bowers confronted a medicine street hawker on Larimer Street. Jeff struck the vendor over the head with his cane. The reason for Jeff's anger was that the hawker, to lure in a crowd, was exposing the secrets of the shell game operation and other tricks used by Jeff and his men.[7]

---

[1] *RMN* 08/13/1894, p. 8.

[2] *Aspen Times* 09/15/1894, p. 4.

[3] *RMN* 07/08/1894.

[4] *RMN* 07/11/1894.

[5] *RMN* 07/17/1894, p. 2.

[6] *RMN* 07/31/1894, p. 6.

[7] *RMN* 08/09/1894, p. 3. And 08/10/1894, p. 5. And *Greeley Tribune* 08/16/1894.

The year 1894 had contained about as much turmoil and brinksmanship as any year could. And for Jeff Smith, more, much more, was to come. The year was just half over, and Jeff was approaching a breaking point.

Chapter 14

The Aftermath of 1894

I beg to state that I am no gambler.
A gambler takes chances with his money, I don't.

—Jefferson R. Smith II
Rocky Mountain News, December 2, 1894

The Governor Waite-guided city fathers of Denver were fed up. On September 5, 1894, after a full summer of crime, they ordered all houses of ill repute and gambling establishments, especially the Tivoli Club, closed down.[1] Crime and gambling, however, were not coequals, and not everyone was against gambling. If anti-gambling factions were to be pushed back, associated action was needed. The following day of the shutdown the *News* published a rumor that Governor Waite had made a deal with the gaming house proprietors to reopen gambling in Denver if they would give their backing to him rather than the Republican candidate.[2] Whether or not gambling would return to the city was news, and newspapers had an ear to the ground about it. So it was that when the leading dozen gamblers of the city met in a room over Hebard and Higgins' saloon on Market Street, on a Saturday afternoon, September 15, 1894, it was news. The meeting, including Jeff, Ed Chase, and John Hughes, was called for the purpose of forming the Gamblers' Protective Association, and several newspapers carried the story.[3] Its two bedrock purposes were to reopen Denver's gambling houses and support efforts to defeat Governor Waite in the next election.

Within a week another meeting was held and the name of the organization was changed to the Knights of the Green Cloth. The *News* reported that Jeff informed the membership that "he believed that the people were beginning to see that faro was in reality a highly moral and intellectual game. 'They see,' said 'Soapy,' 'that there is not enough money in circulation, and before I get through I expect to convince them that it is not the demonetization of silver which has cursed Colorado. I find people putting their money into savings banks. Now, this is dead wrong. The faro bank is the only safe bank. It is run by honorable, high-minded men, who would scorn to do evil."[4]

Though Jeff's Tivoli Club was "closed," his other criminal activities prospered, fixed poker games being the swindle of choice. In an 11-day period Jeff's men were arrested in 4 separate incidents involving crooked poker in a room at the St. Charles Hotel on Market Street. On September 27, 1894, Bascomb, Jackson, and Hoffses

---

[1] *Denver Daily News* 09/06/1894.

[2] *RMN* 09/06/1894, p. 1.

[3] *RMN 09/21/1894, p. 2. 09/25/1894, Leader* 09/22/1894, & *Denver Republican* 10/13/1894.

[4] *RMN* 09/25/1894, p. 3.

14. Jeff in front-page cartoon (3rd from left at the table) helping plan a crooked election. *Rocky Mountain News* October 16, 1892. (Author's col.)

15. Junction of Cliff Street (left) and Creede Avenue (right), Creede, Colorado. The triangular building (center) is John Kinneavy's sample room (saloon). On June 5, 1892, the fire that destroyed the business district started here. Jeff's Orleans Club is a short distance down Creede Avenue from Kinneavy's, on the left. A large US flag is raised above it. Circa spring 1892. (Denver Public Library, Western History Collection, X-7905)

16. Orleans Club on Creede Avenue. Men in formal business attire pose upon substantial foundation works for support wagons heavy with supplies and ore. Jeff's Orleans Club with the American flag on top is on the right. Circa spring 1892. (Courtesy Creede Historical Society)

17. McGinty the petrified man (below left) rests in a box in Denver. (The photo is turned to facilitate comparison.) The cases behind McGinty appear to contain watches, indicating McGinty may have resided in one of Jeff's auction houses to attract customers. Circa 1892-1895. (Jefferson R. "Little Randy" Smith col.)

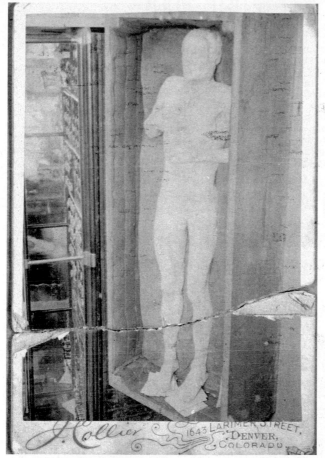

18. Sylvester (above right). The author believes this is McGinty, now known as "Sylvester." He is still "on the job" as an attraction at Ye Olde Curiosity Shop, Pier 54, Seattle, Washington. (Darryl Beckmann photog.)

19. Petrified Man advertisement for McGinty in Denver. Circa 1892-1895. (Denver Public Library, Western History Collection, F-23860)

20. Jeff pouring out sentiments at the burial ceremony for Joe Simmons. Sunnyside Cemetery, Creede, Colorado. *Illustrated Police News*, April 9, 1892. (Author's col., item 70)

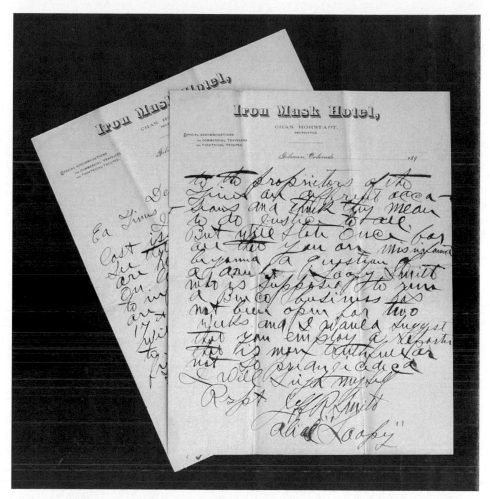

21. Letter to the editor of the *Denver Times*. Jeff wrote to inform the paper that it was "misinformed," that there are "no bunco men working 17th Street," and to "suggest" that the paper "employ a reporter that is more truthful and not so prejudiced." (Author's col., item 108)

22A. Front-page cartoon of Jeff with two kegs of dynamite, leading a parade of "Gamblers, Thugs, Murderers and Rogues." This criticism was part of the fall out from Jeff's participation in the City Hall War. *National Populist*, March 24, 1894. (Author's col., item 96) 22B. (below) Inset of 22A.

Denver City Hall War, March 15, 1894. 23. (above) A large crowd assembled to observe the standoff between Governor Waite's Colorado National Guard and the Old Fire and Police Board's forces, members of which hang out of city hall windows and stand atop its roof. 24. (below) National Guardsmen in formation, awaiting orders. Two cannon are behind them, and behind these, supplies and caissons. (Denver Public Library, Western History Collection, X-22120 and X-22118 respectively)

To Whom it may Concern:

Know all Men by these Presents, That reposing especial confidence and trust in the integrity

and ability of _Jeff R Smith_ I, WM. K. BURCHINELL,

Sheriff of said County of Arapahoe, in pursuance of, and by authority vested in me by law, have

appointed, and do hereby confirm him, the said _Jeff R Smith_

to be a Deputy Sheriff in and for said County

Without Compensation

from County

And all of his official acts legally performed while acting as such Deputy Sheriff are entitled to full

faith and credence.

Witness my hand and seal this _17th_ day of

April 189_4_

Wm K Burchinell

SEAL

Sheriff of Arapahoe County.

25. Deputy Sheriff commission signed by Sheriff Burchinell, for Jeff R. Smith, April 17, 1894, Denver, Colorado. (Author's col., item 29)

26. A shell and pea operator along one of the Alaskan trails to the Klondike. Circa 1897-1898. (Author's col.)

were arrested after a poker game with a greenhorn. Jeff furnished the bonds.[1] Eight days later Bowers and Jackson in a card game took $240 from a Freeman Libby.[2] Three days later on October 8, George Wilder, Hoffses, George Van Orten, and John Kerr were arrested for cheating at poker.[3] Newspapers gave one "long-con" game, extensive coverage.

Alexander Blair was a sheep farmer whose range was near Rawlins, Wyoming. Returning from Kansas City where he had sold several carloads of wethers[4] for a good price, he stopped over in Denver on Sunday, September 30, 1894. On Monday he met an old friend named Jackson whom he had known years prior in Wyoming. Jackson showed Blair around the city, and they talked old times. It is probable that Jackson was W. H. Jackson of the Soap Gang and that he passed on crucial personal information about Blair to another member of the gang, believed to be John Bowers. On Tuesday Blair shopped about town for sheep shears. At the door of a hardware store on Arapahoe Street, someone stopped and addressed him by name. Although not recognizing the man's face, Blair was pleased with his manner.

The man introduced himself as "Taylor," a partner in a company interested in purchasing mines in Northern Wyoming and Arizona. Upon stating that he knew both states well, Blair was offered payment for services as a guide to the mines. Blair expressed interest, and Taylor took him to meet the other two partners, one of whom was Jeff. A deal was made whereby Blair would guide the party at $5 per day and expenses. The trio invited Blair to join them in a private room at the St. Charles hotel. Refreshments were brought in, and a friendly game of poker was suggested. When the game was over, Blair was a little behind, owing the pleasant Mr. Smith the small sum of $29. Blair wrote out a draft for this amount on the First National Bank of Rawlins. In a later interview Blair stated,

> I lost $29, ... and as I didn't have the change one of the men told me to write a check. I am a very poor writer and it's about all I can do to write my own name. One of the men filled out the check and it was for $29. I signed it....[5]

Jeff informed Blair that if he would visit Jeff's office everyday for any consulting that might be needed, beginning immediately until they were ready to leave for Wyoming, Jeff would pay him $5 a day. Blair agreed. On the fourth day, October 4, Jeff regretfully informed Blair that the partners had decided not to invest in the Wyoming-Arizona mines, so his services would no longer be needed. Paid for his services as agreed and with nothing to hold him in Denver any longer, Blair left for home. Jeff and the other partners accompanied Blair to Union Station and bid him a friendly farewell.

Once home, Blair was shocked to discover that his bank had cashed the check he had signed, not for $29 but for $1,029. Blair realized at once that his check had been

---

[1] *RMN* 09/28/1894, p. 8.

[2] *RMN* 10/05/1894, p. 5.

[3] *RMN* 10/09/1894, p. 8.

[4] *wethers*: castrated rams.

[5] *Denver Sun* 10/13/1894.

altered and that his paid stay in Denver for four days was to give a Denver bank time to clear the check with Blair's Rawlins bank.

Blair immediately returned to Denver and in Justice Howze's court swore out a complaint that resulted in an arrest warrant for Jeff Smith on the charge of forgery. An informant alerted Jeff of the warrant, and before he could be apprehended, Jeff walked into the office of the clerk of the court and said; "Well, I hear I am in trouble. Make out a bond." The papers were prepared, signed, and Jeff walked out a free man.[1]

At a hearing on October 18 before Justice Woodson, for reasons unknown, Blair did not appear. The *Denver Post* reported Jeff's statement to the court:

> He said that the complaining witness was an old-time poker-shark, who owns 10,000 sheep in Wyoming, and the only trouble with him was that he was beat at his own game.
>
> "Somebody told Blair," said Jeff, "that I was a richer man than Dave Moffat, and he afterwards tried to obtain $500 from me. When he comes to Denver again I will have him arrested on the charge of blackmail and perjury."
>
> The court after absorbing the eloquence of Jeff's appeal dismissed the charges, and the happy southerner joined his faithful subjects. Rev. Bowers and Jackson were waiting at a safe distance…, and Jeff informed them that the docket was once more cleared of its black marks against the Smith family.[2]

After the Blair case Justice Woodson openly declared that he would no longer take bunco cases in his courtroom. He stated that the blame for failing to convict thieves was too often laid upon the justices and that he was tired of being unfairly blamed.[3]

The "black mark" against the family may have been cleared that day in the Denver courtroom, but another more personal blot on the family name was being closely guarded from discovery. About this time Jeff learned that his sixty-four-year-old father had been committed for alcoholism to the Texas State Lunatic Asylum in Austin.

> 10/11/94—
> Robt. Gardner[4]
> 402 Gains Ave., Hot Springs, Ark
> Dear Sir:
>   Your letter of the 7th received. No change in Mr. Smith's condition since last writing, I do not think he will recover. His general health is quite feeble. In case of death do you desire that he be buried here.
>   Respectfully,   F. S. White, Supt.[5]

Jeff had left home early in his life in part because he did not get along with his father. Still, when such debilitation entered the picture along with the stress he knew it

---

[1] *RMN* 10/13/1894, & *Denver Republican* 10/13/1894.

[2] *Denver Post* 10/18/1894.

[3] *RMN* 10/20/1894, p. 4.

[4] *Robt. Gardner*: husband of Emmie Lou, Jeff's sister. (Ancestry.com, 1900 US Census)

[5] Ltr fr F.S. White to Robert Gardner, 10/11/1894. Geri Murphy col. Note: The Ltr was typed on stationary from the asylum, but at some point someone, probably a family member, tore the heading, "Texas State Lunatic Asylum," from the letter, obviously to keep others from learning the location.

brought into his sisters' lives, the trouble was yet another weight he carried during this turbulent period. A storm was coming into Jeff's and Bascomb's lives, and this news of their father's being committed and his enfeebled state surely contributed to it.

I. R. Noe fell into the clutches of the Soap Gang and lost his watch. His description of the bunco man led police to J. G. Bell at Mattie Silks' bordello on Market Street. Bell returned the watch to avoid arrest. When officers arrived at Noe's room on Sixteenth Street to return his watch, they came upon John Bowers and W. H. Casey in the hallway near Noe's door. Surmised was that they were waiting for Noe to come out, either to rob him of more valuables or to punish him for going to the police.[1]

Bowers and Casey were arrested and taken to the police station. There, the pair proposed a bargain: if freed, they would leave Denver. Chief Armstrong agreed to the offer and gave them twelve hours to depart. He also gave them a firm warning: should they ever return, he would lock them up, and lock them up again as fast as they could make bail. Armstrong announced to the newspapers that as fast as he could locate the rest of the hooligans, he would offer them the same choice as Bowers and Casey.[2]

Guessing that Bowers and Casey would not heed his warning, Armstrong ordered his officers to keep a vigilant eye for the pair, and a few days later, Casey was arrested for vagrancy and given sixty days imprisonment. Jeff obtained a writ of supersedes, and despite wondering whether the writ was genuine, police at headquarters freed Casey. On the same afternoon Bowers was arrested on the same charge. Jeff posted bail, and Bowers was released. In the late afternoon W. K. Jackson, J. Anderson, and Jeff's brother, Bascomb, were also arrested. Jeff asked the police chief for the cause of the trouble, and "Armstrong informed him that a new order of things was being inaugurated and that the bunco men must keep off the streets." The *News* referred to the men arrested as the "Big Five."[3] For release of Bowers, Anderson, and Jackson until their court date, Jeff signed surety bonds. Constable Tibbitts of Judge Cater's court signed Bascomb's bond.

Although the police crackdown put a severe crimp in the gang's activities, it did not stop them. On October 26, 1894, a Louis West was befriended by a preacher who enticed him into a poker game in which West lost $60.[4] Jeff, Bowers and another unnamed member of the gang were arrested and later discharged when West could or would not identify the trio.[5]

The election of 1894 was a vastly important event to the City of Denver and the State. The Colorado Populist Party once again nominated Governor Waite, but against opposition, including that of General Tarsney.[6] True, the Waite administration had the bad fortune of being in office when the financial panic of 1893 struck, which had put

---

[1] *Denver Republican* unknown date but believed to be early October, 1894. Article cut out and saved by Jeff R. Smith II. Jefferson R. "Little Randy" Smith col.
[2] *Denver Republican* unknown date but believed to be early October, 1894. Article cut out and saved by Jeff R. Smith II. Jefferson R. "Little Randy" Smith col.
[3] *RMN* 10/18/1894, p. 8.
[4] *RMN* 10/27/1894, p. 1.
[5] *Denver Evening Post* 10/29/1894, p.2. And *RMN* 10/30/1894, p. 3.
[6] *Daily Chronicle (Marshall, MN)* 11/16/1894, p. 1.

45,000 Coloradoans out work,[1] and the economic downturn had endured. Waite tried to cope with the problems on behalf of the working class, and any administration would have had to be lucky to establish a good record to run on in such hard times. Good efforts might have been enough, but Waite's had often been bizarre, such as his "fandango dollars" proposal, and dangerous, such as risking a military battle in the middle of Denver. Even on small issues, such as with the well-liked and respected, honest treasurer of the medical board whom Waite had fired on procedural grounds, Waite took the extremist course. He did not back his appointees, such as all the commissioners on the fire and police board, and not even the long-suffering General Tarsney. The general thought he should manage the compensation of the militia under him, not the inspector general, but Waite eventually assigned the job to the inspector general. Tarsney threatened resignation over the decision,[2] showing disillusionment with the man for whom he had endured so much.

Waite's opposition, McIntyre, hit him hard. "...Populists had disgraced Colorado in the eyes of the nation, frightened off capital, and fostered a spirit of anarchy" were his arguments. The Populists and the Democrats publicized that "a vote for the Republican ticket would be a vote for the saloon." Women were asked if they wanted to be found voting the same ticket as 'Soapy' Smith, the gamblers, saloon keepers and prostitutes of Market street."[3] Come the November election, Waite received 75,000 votes to McIntyre's 93,500.[4] Subsequently, Waite blamed fickled women, to whom he had given the vote, as well as the "15,000 gamblers and lewd women" of Denver for his defeat. Waite was wrong in at least two respects. The number is probably grossly inflated. The population of Denver in 1895 was estimated at 90,000.[5] That would make 1 in every 6 Denver residents a gambler or lewd woman. Second, Waite's opposition in Denver, though also beyond, was far greater than he stated, including E. B. Field of the telephone monopoly, Walter Cheesman of the Union Water Company, Daniel Sullivan of the Gas and Electric company, Bill Evans of the Tramway company, and, of course, David Moffat. Waite had seriously threatened the stability of the city and their business interests, and they got him out of the way. If Soapy Smith rounded up a few voters to help in the cause, including itinerants and women who were lewd, that was all to the better for the business at hand. Walter Cheesman probably summed up the attitude of the wheeler-dealers best in stating that "of course, you understand, politics with us is a matter of business."[6] With that Jeff Smith would have entirely agreed.

A new administration was approaching on the incoming tide of time, and all the gambling and saloon men needed to do is wait. Governor-elect McIntyre had been quoted as saying that "he is not a crank on the subject of gambling and will not interfere with private clubs.... He does not proposed to interfere with private rights," and he offered this attitude as a "feeler" to what he called the "better class" of

---

[1] Abbot, p. 144.
[2] *New York Times* 08/01/1894.
[3] *Boulder Daily Camera* 10/04/1894, p. 1.
[4] Abbot, p. 144.
[5] Leonard, *Denver*, p. 110.
[6] *Abbot, pp. 256-57.*

professional gamblers. *The Aspen Times* could not resist, of course, taking a swing: "It is quite probable," the paper wrote, "that later some concessions will be made [by Governor McIntyre] to that good, loyal redeemer, Soapy Smith."[1]

Some, however, were so eager for a return to pre-closure days that in latter November they circulated a petition and sent it to the fire and police board and out-going Governor Waite. It asked for reconsideration of the policy closing gambling clubs because the effects were proving extremely harmful. Buildings were tenantless, the influx of money to the city was severely diminished, and "trade and all kinds of business" were negatively affected. Suggested was that Chief Armstrong settle on a "class of responsible men" as would conduct gambling "halls with decency and propriety and under such regulations and surveillance as the police department may prescribe." Signers included two banks, Appel Clothing, George Trich Hardware, and forty-three prominent businesses.[2] Subsequently, though, when learned that Jeff might have initiated the petition, many signers asked that their names be removed. Jeff, however, in a letter to the *News*, presented an adamant denial of participation in the petition drive. It might have been better, though had he not written the letter on sheriff's detective department letterhead stationary.[3]

> To the News: Wishing to set myself right with the public, I beg to state that I am no gambler. A gambler takes chances with his money, I don't. I had nothing to do with the businessmen's petition, and under no circumstances would I sign such a document. Hoping that the clergy will kindly leave me out of that "class," I remain with best wishes for all good men.
> Jeff Smith[4]

Nine days later, the *Denver Evening Post* published a detailed interview with Jeff.

JEFF SMITH TALKS.
The History of the Now Famous Gambling Petition.

Jeff Smith spurred by the criticism of the ministers of the city over his association with the business men's petition, unburdened himself in the following interview:

"I had nothing to do with obtaining the names that were attached to the petition. Lew [Lou] Blonger and Mark Watrous are the gentlemen to whom all the honor of the much agitated petition belong. They labored hard and incessantly and were rewarded with the satisfaction that it has killed gambling forever in Denver. For never again will the click of the merry ivories be heard within the city precincts.

"The existence of the petition was not known to over five gamblers until it had been presented to the fire and police board, and not one in ten of the gamblers favored the petition or do they to-day. There is no course left for the incoming governor to do but keep the gambling houses closed, for public

---

[1] *Aspen Times* 12/15/1894, p. 4.

[2] *New York Times* 11/27/1894.

[3] Undated (circa December 1, 1894) original draft of letter handwritten by Jefferson R. Smith II on stationary of the office of the sheriff's detective department. Jefferson R. "Little Randy" Smith col.

[4] *RMN* 12/02/1894.

opinion would be so powerful that the mere talk of it might cause a public calamity.

"While I myself am in favor of the opening of the gambling houses, I want it distinctly understood that I am no gambler, never was or never will be.

"It pains me deeply to read the names of the firms who have signed the obnoxious petition under a misapprehension. For it stamps the men who obtained the names as the cleverest 'sure thing' men in our mighty nation.

Do these firms desire the public to believe that they were ignorant of what they were signing. I know different, for I have investigated the matter myself and found that the very ones who, in their anxiousness to escape public condemnation, have denied all knowledge of their wrongful acts by letters of apology, were the ones who assisted Messrs. Blonger and Watrous.

"Petitions have killed gambling forever here and now let them work out their own salvation."[1]

Was Jeff part of the petition drive? Probably he knew about it, but it seems likely he did not participate in securing signatures. He knew that his reputation could be a black mark against it. Besides, at the moment, he did not want further association with professional gambling. A former gambler could perhaps secure public office, something Jeff still had interest in (as events would show), but to ask the electorate to vote for a current gambler was not a gamble a savvy gambler like Jeff would take.

Late in 1894, Jeff moved the Tivoli Club in secret to 1729 Market Street.[2] Detective DeLue learned of the location and ordered Detective Schinttman along with officers Dougal and Waitman to keep close watch on the site. At noon on December 12, 1894, John Bowers was observed leading a victim into the place. Five minutes later the officers broke in with revolvers drawn and arrested Bowers, Hoffses, Casey, Jackson, John Van Orton, and intended victim Charles Williams. At the Rock Island Railroad ticket office, Williams had met Bowers, who had asked where he was headed. Williams replied Topeka, and Bowers said he was going there himself and was pleased to meet a traveling companion. Bowers then led Williams to Jeff's place and bought a stack of chips for $1 but had not yet induced Williams to play when the officers arrived. They took the men and several stacks of chips, one table, and $1 in money to the police station.[3] Newspapers give no hint of the outcome of the arrest. The early entrance of the police prevented a victim, let along evidence of gambling.

Next in December John Bowers was arrested for "Bunco steering," but Jeff was able to have him released.[4] Jeff still had influence, but Denver was becoming a different town, one in which it was difficult to rest easy. He was losing control of activities he used to dominate. Though his deftness in the conning arts had not diminished, the times apparently wore on him and could put him into a wistful mood. Its evidence appears in a poem that found its way into the *Denver Mercury*.

---

[1] *Denver Evening Post* 12/11/1894.

[2] *Denver City Directory*, 1895.

[3] *RMN* 12/07/1894, p. 3.

[4] Defendant's Recognizance form. A bond of $300 to appear in court on 12/18/1894. Jefferson R. "Little Randy" Smith col.

Boyhood Days
By Jefferson R. Smith

I rose this morning feeling fine,
And thought how quick I'd passed the time,
It seemed to me but yesterday
A happy schoolboy I did play.
No trouble, or care, or worry, or fret;
I wish I was a schoolboy yet.
When a boy I had no debts to pay
I cared not if it stormed all day:
I had no bother about silver or gold;
I never thought that I'd grow old;
I knew nothing of Wilson's Tariff bill,[1]
I never heard of Hawaii Lil.[2]
There was no such pest as Grover C;[3]
And the country was in prosperity.

My great ambition was to be
A soldier great, and the whole world
      to see;
Or a statesman, like our Webster-Clay;
And live an idol' the same as they.
But ambition changed; yes, very soon;
And my only thought was to gold
      doubloon
And I have looked for many a day
To find a man who ain't built that way.
The farmers, merchants, bankers, all
Will be the same till the judgment call.
Oh it's nothing but bother, worry, or fret
I wish I was a schoolboy yet.[4]

The poem explores the lost riches of carefree boyhood when admirable prospects lay ahead. The scramble for money found in every man, though, and other realities changed his ambition, and his compensation, "nothing but" effort, anxiety, and a worn-down state. Better by far were those boyhood days, free of burden. The poem also points to the wish for military and political greatness. This ambition had not been left behind. Never having served as a military officer, though, Jeff had to give himself the title of colonel. Who knew, though? Perhaps he would have opportunity to earn it yet.

The year was ending with some not totally unexpected developments. Governor Waite after the election had asked General Tarsney to resign his post as adjutant general, but he had refused to vacate. So far, the governor had not called upon the militia to remove him by force. Tarsney said he would retire when the governor did, as requested by a majority of 20,000 votes cast in the previous election.[5] Tarsney's count was off, but not by much; Waite's loss was not by 20,000 but by 18,500. As for the ringleader of the masked men who tormented and tarred and feathered the general, Wilson, he "Has Fled The Country," read the headline.

> Wilson is the man whom Gen. Tarsney traced to Missouri and brought back to Colorado for trial. Pending his trial Wilson was locked up in the El Paso county jail. About a month ago he was liberated on a bail bond and is now missing. He is thought to be in Mexico.[6]

As for Jeff, the Denver City Hall War had brought him greatness and disaster. He proved to friends and peers that he was a leader of men, ready to lay down his life for

---

[1] *Wilson's Tariff bill*: The Wilson-Gorman Tariff Act of 08/27/1894 included the first graduated income tax law. The Supreme Court declared it unconstitutional the following year.

[2] *Hawaii Lil*: The Hawaii revolution of 01/17/1894 deposed Queen Liliuokalani.

[3] *Grover C*: President Grover Cleveland.

[4] *Mercury* clipping of unknown month & year (after Aug 1894), saved by Jeff R. Smith II. Author's col.

[5] *Daily Chronicle* (Marshall, MN) 11/16/1894.

[6] *Daily Gazette* (Janesville, WI) 12/07/1894.

a cause. That high point, though, had been the beginning of the end of gang rule as it had been in the city's government. New powers were emerging, including expanding public utility companies. With these edging into the main stream and Jeff was feeling his fit with Denver becoming uncomfortably tight, he again had been studying a potential greener pasture, a locale where he was unknown, a place so distant that his past would not be likely to catch up with him, a least for a long while. The site that had caught his attention lay vast and inviting to the south, way south of the boundaries of his homeland, Mexico. So the end of the year for Jeff was devoted to journeying south and deep into old Mexico, some say in an attempt to take over the country.

Chapter 15

The Mexican Adventure
And Burning Every Bridge

Come at once; bring everything you can.
—President Don Jose' de la Cruz Porfirio Diaz of Mexico

Jeff was an American version of "The Man Who Would be King." In this famous 1889 short story by Rudyard Kipling, an adventurer in a far-off land ascends to the position of a god by means of innate shrewdness, and he tends to pursue good. Realities, however, drag him back to earth in mortally harsh ways. Jeff would play out this semi-tragic scenario several times, and at least twice he would strike back blindly at powers that denied him his rightful place in the scheme of things. The first of these fate-shaping conflicts would soon occur.

In latter December 1894, Jeff received a letter from old his friend William Daily, addressed in care of the Arcade Saloon. The handwritten letter is on stationary from New Hutchins House, Houston, Texas, and dated December 17, 1894.

> Well old Pards
> Its about time I was droping a line. I was at the Cotton Pallace at Waco. It was a Bloomer, no one made a dollar. Bob Gardner has a house open there. ... I will start tonight for the city of old Mexico whare I can get licens to play Three card monte for one dollar a day. I will join Big Smyley at Montira [Monterrey], Mexico.
> Very Resp.   Your Friend, Wm Daily[1]

Appearing to Jeff between the lines was a message of opportunity. Actually, it was one of added opportunity and means. True, south of the border lay new territory to harvest in the traditional way, with short cons and auctions, but something more was there, something vast and grand in terms of an opportunity to be seized. And if ever there were a man to seize an opportunity like this one, it was Jeff R. Smith II.

---

[1] Ltr to Jeff R. Smith II fr William Daily, 12/17/1894. Jefferson R. "Little Randy" Smith col. "Spelling" is all as it appears in the Ltr.

So Jeff, Bowers, and Jackson prepared to travel down into old Mexico to assess possibilities. Deciding to keep their destination secret for the time being, they planted one of their false-lead stories in the *Denver Republican*.

Soapy Will Travel.

Denver is more or less threatened with the loss of three of her most prominent citizens. Colonel J. Randolph Smith, "Rev." Joseph [John] Bowers and "Doctor" W. H. Jackson have declared their intention to go to Japan. Yesterday they displayed railroad and steamship tickets to Yokohama, reading via the Atchison, Topeka & Santa Fe railroad and San Francisco. They say they will leave today for their Oriental destination. They announce that their object is a visit of pleasure and sight seeing....[1]

Two days later Jeff received a cryptic telegram from Monterey, Mexico. "Take a sleeper at Laredo remain in car until 7 am. L. H. Smylie."[2] And so as the year ended with the men traveling not west but south.

Bascomb is believed to have been left behind to assist with Denver operations, but he was soon in trouble. On January 5, 1895, Bascomb was arrested for malicious mischief. He had smashed furniture in a house on Market Street during a quarrel and slashed the arm of Georgie Roe, a probable prostitute, with a knife. Jackson is known to have returned to Denver on or before January 30, 1895, as he was arrested for vagrancy on that day.[3] What came of these arrests is not recorded.

Mexico in 1894 was under the dictatorship of President Don Jose' de la Cruz Porfirio Diaz, and ever-present revolutionaries looked for chances to overthrow him. In November 1893 the *News* began publishing accounts of Northern Mexican revolutionaries when in a surprise attack, the rebels captured the custom's house at Las Paloman.[4] When several cities then fell to the rebels, their successes caught the Mexican President off guard. The Diaz regime raised an army of thirteen thousand to fight the rebels, but it was poorly equipped and lacked telegraph communication. In consequence, cities continued to fall, and rebel forces grew. In the US it was generally thought that the Diaz government could fall if the fighting became general. At the least, the rebels kept the Mexican President from exercising total control of the country. As Jeff read of these developments, he began to see an opportunity for both men to profit: a second army, private and well-funded, of mercenaries fighting for the President of Mexico, organized, outfitted, and led by Jeff Smith. His would be an army of soldiers of fortune and a Mexican version of the French Foreign Legion.

Jeff sent an outline of his idea to the Mexican dictator and received an invitation to the national palace in Mexico City. Possibly impersonating a United States military colonel, Jeff embarked for the capital to discuss his grand plan for solving the rebel problem. Apparently the meeting went well. Returning to Denver from Mexico about January 20, Jeff began to prepare for a military expedition into Mexico and left again

---

[1] *Boulder Daily Camera* 12/27/1894, p. 1, & *Summit County Journal* 12/29/1893, p. 5.
[2] Telegram fr L.H. Smylie to Jeff R. Smith II, 12/29/1894. Geri Murphy col.
[3] *Denver Post* 01/30/1895.
[4] *RMN* 11/12/1893, p. 1.

on the 29th. He must have felt confident because this time he left information about his doings behind. The *News* had details and published them on February 1, 1895.

"SOAPY" FLIES SO HIGH

Offers His Services To The Mexican Government. He Is Now Said to Be at the Capitol of Our Sister Republic Ready to Lend His Services in Case of War—"Rev." Joe [John] Bowers, Tom Keady [Cady] and Other Friends Are With Him—All Are Heavily Armed.

"Colonel" Jefferson Randolph Smith and his hand man, Parson Bowers, are now in Mexico. They left Tuesday and according to their "say so," took fifty Winchester rifles with them.

Since the "colonel" returned from his Southern trip a couple of weeks ago, he has been in close communication, he claimed, with President Diaz of Mexico whom, it is said, went against the "colonel's" game to the tune of several thousand dollars.

He concluded that the "colonel" was just the man he wanted for war purposes, so he sent the wily "Soapy" back to Denver for recruits. An advertisement was inserted in a paper in this city stating that 500 men were wanted for Mexico. The advertisement attracted ... a large crowd, but no one seemed to know who the agent was, and everything was done on the quiet.

On Tuesday morning Smith and Bowers were at the Union depot, and exhibited a telegram said to be from President Diaz, which read: "Come at once; bring everything you can." ..."Soapy" and "Rev." Bowers both had tickets for Mexico, and boarded the south-bound train.

This morning another of the contingent also bought a ticket for Mexico. He was Tom Keady [Cady], the manipulator of the three shells. He also exhibited a telegram, but it was not from President Diaz, and it read:

"Dead easy game. Come at once. Signed Smith."

Keady [Cady] did not know what the message had reference to, unless it was the war that is expected to break out, but he was going down more for a visit than anything else.

When the trio get together down there they will furnish the natives with a game and if they don't beat them out at it there will be sent up a wail that is only familiar to these men.[1]

The *News* saw the trip as little more than Jeff's looking for fresh pastures for swindling, but a distance of about 1600 miles seems rather far to go for run-of-the-mill swindles, especially since being apprehended in Mexico by rebels could mean indefinite detainment or death. Rather, the preponderance of belief is that the private army Jeff was recruiting was no daydream and not part of a swindle, but rather, a serious undertaking. These pursuits, of course, do not rule out that Jeff had other plans for making money illegitimately. Larger prizes, though, were to be had, among them mercenary pay, power over a region and perhaps more, and especially a military rank and personal and military fame and glory. In later years members of the Smith

---

[1] *Denver Post* 02/02/1895, p. 6.

family often spoke of their belief that Jeff considered the situation an opportunity to seize control of Mexico.[1] This goal may have become enlarged through the lens of often-discussed family lore, but myth is said to have roots in reality.

Probably several members of the Soap Gang who accompanied Jeff to Mexico City in January assumed the roles of ex-US officers and American dignitaries. At the meeting with Diaz, Jeff asked for and received an advance sum of money, possibly equivalent to several thousand dollars in start-up money to finance an all volunteer army. The Mexican President expected in return assistance in putting down the resistance. The exact amount Jeff obtained is unknown.

Few details of what took place while Jeff was in Mexico are known. It is certain that Jeff roomed at the Iturbide Hotel[2] and that some of his men performed the familiar swindles on the peasantry. The only known remnants of his visit are a few letters that mention the trip and two items taken from the office of the Mexican President, perhaps even his desk: a sheet of official presidential stationary and an envelope. Did Jeff want them for forging stationary upon which to forge letters? Possibly. Or did he want them simply to prove to friends that he had indeed met with the Mexican leader.[3]

Jeff and others with him traveled between Denver and the Mexican capital for almost two months. While absent from Denver, certain members of the Soap Gang looked after Jeff's interests, and the swindle games continued as usual.

One reason Jeff went to Mexico may have been to evade prosecution in several court cases. One of these involved Thomas Moody, a livestock dealer from Omaha. In late October or early November 1894, Moody came into Jeff's place on Market Street and sat down with the wrong group of poker players. Moody's playing met with varying success for a time, and then he drew four queens. His assumption, of course, was that he had the hand of a lifetime, a sure thing, but he did not have enough cash to call the pot. He offered a check made out to Bascomb, and it was accepted as a bet on his hand. Then came the shock of discovering that another player held four aces. The check was turned over to a Mr. Meyer who in turn sent it to South Omaha for collection. Once back in Omaha, Moody asked his bank not to honor the check.[4] Jeff sued for non-payment, and a friend in Omaha, Thomas Dennison, kept Jeff abreast of the situation in handwritten letters on stationary from The Denver hotel at 1321 Douglas Street. (Dennison's letters include his grammar and creative spelling.)

November 9, 1894

Friend Jeff

I just seen the lawer and he tells me that the bank has gaven up the fight and will bring the money in to court and then the fight will be between Moody and Myers so that looks like the bank was not weling to stand aney more of the expense and truble of fighting a loosing fight so it will come up

---

[1] Stories of taking over Mexico were often told by numerous Smith family members, including Randolph J. Smith and Joseph J. Smith.

[2] *RMN* 05/04/1895, p. 2.

[3] One sheet of personalized stationary and one personalized envelope with the over under initials of "P" & "D." Jefferson R. "Little Randy" Smith col.

[4] *RMN* 12/14/1894, p. 2.

at the next terem of the court well [undecipherable] went the best they could for us here and I gess the same in Denver.

Regards to the boys   Thomas Dennison[1]

A month passed before Jeff discovered Dennison's assumptions were wrong.

December 14, 1894

Friend Jeff

The check case came up today in the county court and was desided a gainst us on the ground that we did not show that the man that presented the check to B Smith was Thomas Moody. So we will appeal to the district court and I will let you know what more evidence we will need. Three [undecipherable] tellers in the bank hear swore that it was the same signature. I all so want to show that B Smith has no intrest in that poker game all so that Thomas Moody is the one that was in Denver on that day and if he ever gambled in Montrose. I will send you a letter teling you what I want and you tend to it. My advise would be to have Moody arrested for pergery. I wish Harris would make his statement more plainer to what Moody told him. Can't you get someone to sware that Moody told them that all he wanted was half back because he had a partner and could not go home without the money.

Thomas Dennison[2]

The affair did not appear in Denver newspapers for over a month. Then Moody made an unexpected return to Denver, and the *News* published his story on December 15, 1894, the same day Dennison penned another letter to Jeff.

Friend Jeff

Inclosed you will find clipping from morning paper which [undecipherable] reporter has written how they swore three bank cashiers that swore positively that the name on the check was written by the same man that wrote the name of Thomas Moody on his deposition.... ... I would rather spend the hole business twice [on lawyers and expenses than] to see that dirty son of a Bitch Moody get one cent of it. Why don't you write over to Tom Hebler at Montrose and find out who is Moody's partner and find out if he ever gambled and what his reputation is to been honest.... ... this next time I will let you know just what we want and you get it Tom Parkhurst & Hopper live stock [undecipherable]

Thomas Dennison[3]

In response to Moody's complaint, Jeff and John Bowers were arrested on December 18 for bunco steering and paid a $300 bond.[4] At trial, Moody claimed to have been drugged in a saloon and that he did not remember anything from 2 to 5 p.m. that day, including making out a check. Its amount is not known but presumed in excess of $1,000. Experts examined the signature on the check and said they found

---

[1] Ltr fr Thomas Dennison to Jefferson R. Smith II, 11/09/1894. Geri Murphy col. Spelling is as appears.

[2] Ltr fr Thomas Dennison to Jefferson R. Smith II, 12/14/1894. Geri Murphy col. Spelling is as appears.

[3] Ltr fr Thomas Dennison to Jefferson R. Smith II, 12/15/1894. Geri Murphy col. Spelling is as appears.

[4] Bond paperwork, 12/18/1894. Jefferson R. "Little Randy" Smith col.

considerable differences between it and others on documents Moody had signed.[1] Jeff's attorneys claimed that three tellers at the Omaha bank said the signature on the check was Moody's.[2] The hope was that Moody would tire of the expensive case and settle out of court for half the amount. Attempts were made to discredit Moody as a gambler in Montrose, Nebraska. Even Moody's business partner was spied on in an effort to determine his gambling habits. The presiding judge finally decided the case in favor of Moody and Jeff collected nothing.

W. H. Jackson and Alton E. Hoffses appeared to be in charge while Jeff and John Bowers were in Mexico. Also during Jeff's absence, L. E. McNulty, another victim from Omaha, lost $200 in Denver on February 4, 1895, in a dice game when a crookster snatched it from the table and ran. The Gang then scattered except for a bogus police officer who threatened to arrest McNulty for gambling. McNulty, however, did not scare off. He went to police headquarters,[3] but none of the bunco men could be identified.

Apparently Jackson and Hoffses had broken into Jeff's supply of sheriff's badges. In early February 1895, Robert Russell of Chicago had come to the end of his stay in Denver and was walking along Seventeenth Street in search of a discount ticket home. There he met Silas King, a member of the Soap Gang, who said he knew a man who handled discount tickets and would sell one to Illinois for only ten dollars. Russell could not pass up such a great bargain and agreed to follow King to Sam Walker's saloon at Nineteenth and Curtis. Once inside, King asked for Bill Clark, the man with the tickets. Told he was out but would return soon, the men decided to wait. Drinks were ordered, a dice game initiated, and soon Russell was minus $130. Then a man appeared, flashed a deputy sheriff's badge, and arrested Russell for gambling. While being escorted to jail, Russell pleaded ignorance of the law, being a visitor to the city, and the sympathetic "officer" offered to release Russell if he would leave Denver immediately. Russell agreed. But once away from the officer, Russell grew suspicious and found his way to police headquarters. Soon Silas King and L. Woodward were under arrest on charges of buncoing and impersonating an officer.[4]

Having had enough of phantom officers of the law, the police had an officer named Smith dress as a tourist and go to Seventeenth Street down by Union Station. He was approached by Jackson who introduced himself as a mining specialist from Mexico. Jackson, looked very much the part, dressed as he was in Mexican attire and sporting a wide sombrero. Jackson invited Smith to a cigar, and both men entered King's Cigar Store. Jackson attempted to purchase two cigars with a twenty-dollar gold piece, but King was unable to make change. Jackson said he would go to another store for change and be right back, leaving Smith with King. Jackson's real reason for leaving was to call in Soap Gang associates James Thornton, James Thompson, and Alton Hoffses to make their play on the compliant mark.

[1] Denver newspaper clipping of unknown origin & date, saved by Jeff R. Smith II, titled "*Four Aces did the Queens.*" Author's col.

[2] Ltr to Jeff R. Smith II fr Thomas Dennison, 12/14/1894. Geri Murphy col.

[3] *Denver Post* 02/04/1895.

[4] *Denver Post* 02/07/1895, p. 2.

Jackson soon returned, and after paying for the cigars, he invited Smith to see some "feather work" he had brought up from Mexico. Smith agreed, and the men went to Connor's saloon where Jackson inquired after a "Professor" Thompson, who naturally was out but would soon to return. Jackson invited Smith to indulge in a few drinks. After a short while "Professor" Thompson arrived, and the three retired to the Pioneer Block. They entered room 22 where the "Professor" was staying and surprised several men who were using the room to pass the time in a friendly game of poker.

As gambling was now positively illegal in Denver, the poker players required Jackson and "Professor" Thompson to vouch for Smith. After the routine enticement to the game, Smith identified himself as a police officer, arrested everyone, and escorted them to jail. Landlord Ed Chase posted their bonds.[1] The outcome of the arrest is unknown, but apparently neither Jackson nor Hoffses received jail time. Eight days later when Bowers returned, they were swindling again.

In the same day's newspaper reporting Officer Smith's dramatic arrest, the *Denver Post* obtained copies of police files listing forty-three policy shops running wide open within city limits. Governor Waite's fire and police board had been completely replaced by Governor McIntyre, who on January 29, 1895, appointed an ex-city treasurer, an insurance salesman, and ex-police chief. Pressure perhaps was lightening on "Policy," but buncoing was a different story. On February 27, 1895, the *Denver Post* noted the return of a well-known con man.

"REV." BOWERS HOME

Two Cases of Bunco Reported Soon After His Arrival. He Is Not Accused of
Doing the Jobs, but It Is a Strange Coincidence—One of the Victims Was
Induced to Enter a Poker Game and the Other Wanted to Purchase a
Cheap Railroad Ticket—Old Schemes as Good as New Ones.

"Rev." Joe [John] Bowers registered at Ed Chase's hotel, in the Pioneer building, from the City of Mexico at 10 o'clock this morning. Clerk Jackson assigned the "reverend" gentleman to room 22 on the top floor.

The sign "H. Anderson, mineral expert," now appears upon the door. The "preacher's arrival spread with lighting rapidity throughout the city. Among the prominent callers were W. H. Jackson, Al Hoelfas [Hoffses], Kid Mitchell and a host of other less celebrated gentlemen. All joined the wandering "preacher" and drank to his good health.

The ceremony was interrupted to welcome John H. Baker, a Union Pacific engineer from Pocatello, Idaho. A little game of stud was engaged in and Baker left $55 for their future enjoyment. He demanded his money and was given $10 and told to get out. Afterward he called at police headquarters and Detective Schlottman [known as "Sledge-hammer Jack,"[2]] obtained his $55. The bunco men claim that they lost $10 by the operation.

---

[1] *Denver Post* 02/19/1895.

[2] *Sledge-hammer Jack*: "Schlottman, on the police force in 1894 & 1895, was known around town as 'Sledge-Hammer Jack'" (Secrest, p. 136). Fr the *Denver Republican* 05/14/1900: "To keep the police out, most of the gambling houses built great doors, believed to be proof against any assault of the

A. H. Schnider of Lake City, Col., was another caller who wanted to purchase a return ticket to his home for $3. He got no ticket and now mourns the loss of $12.

The County court this morning returned executions for $14.50 against W. H. Jackson and Al Hoelfas [Hoffses] on cases they appealed from the police court. Landlord Chase paid the amounts.

Bowers referring to his visit in Mexico, reported business excellent. Colonel Jefferson Runnymead Smith[1] will arrive in a few days, said the "preacher." He has been entertaining the citizens of Mexico, by selling them his soap, with $10 bills around each package.[2]

The day Bowers returned from Mexico, Joseph Gottlieb, owner of a pawnshop at 1607 Larimer, filed a complaint against Bascomb. Charged was that he had entered the shop, picked up a valise, and tried leaving with it. Gottlieb protested, barred the way, and received a blow to the eye. Bascomb was arrested for robbery and assault and battery.[3]

Meanwhile in Mexico, President Diaz suddenly cancelled Colonel Jefferson Smith's army-building contract. When, where, and how the President communicated this news to Jeff is not known. It is thought, however, based on later accounts, that Jeff was in Mexico City, in which case, he may have received the dismissal in person, though probably not from Diaz himself. Dictators do not need to deliver their unpleasant messages in person. Had he done so, with opportunity to turn on his charm and needing to reach for some eloquent flimflam, Jeff might have stood a chance. Probably, though, assistants or military men or both probably delivered the summary message or may have summoned Jeff to receive it. If word came in written form, it has not survived.

The most probable scenario is that sometime in latter February or early March, President Diaz received reliable information that the Colonel Smith who represented himself as a soldier was an imposter and that he was instead a notorious gambler and confidence man. Possibly the President was sent word by the *News*, although any number of Jeff's enemies could have done the same. With hopes of military greatness in Mexico shattered, Jeff, as stories tell, also had to endure the Mexican dictator's warning him never to put boots on Mexican soil again. Doing so would mean

---

police. The chief had made a 16-pound hammer with a long handle. Equipped with this Schlottman was sent and any door that failed to open at his order was splintered with the sledge."

[1] *Jefferson Runnymeade Smith*: A tangential but somewhat interesting note: Runnymede is forever associated with King John and June 19, 1215, the date he signed the Magna Carta (Great Charter) and the beginning of England's constitutional monarchy. Runnymede is the site of the signing, which is either an island by that name on the Themes river in Surrey or marshy land on the south side of the Themes below London. What has Runnymede to do with Jeff R. Smith? The writer seems to have tried to cast the story as a satire, but it often slips into unartful sarcasm. "Runnymede" means a meadow that is runny with water, or "a marshy meadow." Was the writer seeking to attach "swampy" to Jeff? For allusional meaning, the name requires no easy stretch of thought.

[2] *Denver Post* 02/27/1895.

[3] *RMN* 02/28/1895, p. 5.

imprisonment, even execution.[1] Jeff had no friends in Mexico's capital to help him work the system. Beginning at the top of the dictatorship and being discovered by the dictator himself, Jeff could do nothing but take the stern rebuke and move on. In addition to the private blow to his pride, he must have been in for another when it came to explaining to confederates who had followed him that the adventure was off.

Ignoring the warning, however, Jeff made several more trips to Mexico but apparently only so far as Monterey—about 500 miles northeast of Mexico City. The last solid reference to Jeff's being in Mexico appears on a postcard, one side of which advertises one John Haley who was apparently "well connected" there. On the card Haley writes to Jeff,

> What about the concession you wanted me to get you? Please tell Julio Levies if he wants anything in Monterey to write me stating what he is willing to pay. The faro game here is doing well. Do you intend to return to Monterey if so when?
>
> Truly yours   John Haley

The advertisement on Haley's card gives insight to the type of work he prefers:

Nota Bene[2]

> I will manage, compromise, or fight to a finish Law Suits in any part of Mexico. ... Will assist in getting Concessions from the City, State and Federal Governments, and make a specialty of
>
> EXTRADITING FUGITIVES
>
> from the United States. I will have nothing to do with Divorce Suits, Shadowing, reporting the conduct of Employés, nor hunting husbands and wives that are "lost, strayed or stolen."
>
> I have some of the best legal advisers in the Republic. State your case, and if I take it I will give you my references.   Truly yours,   JOHN HALEY
>
> Monterey, Mexico.[3]

On March 1, 1895, Jeff arrived in Denver was immediately interviewed by the *Post* about his two-month stay in Mexico.

> He Returns From a Pleasant Trip to Mexico.
>
> Colonel Jefferson Runnymeade Smith arrived in Denver yesterday from the City of Mexico, where he has been the honorary guest of President Diaz for the past two months.
>
> The colonel entertained his many friends with glowing and interesting accounts of his experience at the Mexican capital, and with many tears of regret for the dear friends he left behind, he referred to his numerous trips into the interior with his "grip" filled with neat packages of soap and a trio of indispensable shells.

---

[1] Collier & Westrate, p. 195.

[2] *Nota Bene*: Latin, literally, "Note Well."

[3] Ltr fr John Haley to Jeff R. Smith II, 09/12/1895. Item# 4, author's col.

Jeff denies that he left Denver to avoid taking part in the old police board row, and treats with contempt the report that he intended to join the revolution in Nicaragua.

The colonel remarked that he returned home simply to meet his old friends and, if possible, to increase the list of his acquaintances. [1]

Eight days later, Jeff announced his candidacy for Alderman in the Ninth Ward. Besides the desire for power and prestige, Jeff's most probable motivation for seeking public office was to work for the continued relaxation of restrictions on gambling. Whatever the reasons, Jeff was serious about running. He closed up one of his swindle offices to remove the chance of an investigation working against him. The *Denver Evening Post* covered the spectacle.

WILL ENTER POLITICS

Colonel Jeff Smith Will Let the Countryman Alone. The Firm of Smith, Bowers & Jackson Has Been Dissolved and Jeff Will Endeavor to Get the Nomination For Alderman in the Ninth Ward—What Mr. Smith Thinks of Politics and Banking.

The Hon. Jefferson Runnymeade Smith, late of the City of Mexico, but now a permanent resident of Denver, has decided to retire from active banking business and enter the field of politics.

No more that alluring sign, Smith, Bowers, Jackson & Co., banking and mining brokers, will appear upon the handsome plate glass window to tempt the unsophisticated tourist to deposit his loose cash in the vaults of the three Napoleons of finance. ...

"I am going to be an alderman," said the bashful Jefferson to an interested gathering of friends in City Clerk Vick Roy's office this morning.

A number of the city fathers were present when the statement was made and all became intensely interested, for Jefferson is always interesting, even when in earnest.

"Yes," continued Jefferson, "I will be your opponent, Phillips, in the ninth ward for the nomination for alderman, and a right merry fight I'll give you, too.

"The banking firm is dissolved and Rev. Bowers will manage my campaign.

"If I am defeated for the nomination by the Tramway or water company influence ... I will run independently and I will come pretty near getting there."

Phillips for a moment was too overcome with surprise to utter either his approval or disgust. [2]

The article may have been pure sarcasm, but Jeff's plans were no joke. He may have had intended to stay clear of the wrong side of the law but probably only long enough for the public to forget past transgressions and elect him. Once in office, Jeff would perhaps graduate to large scale swindles or to just plain lucrative and effortless graft.

---

[1] *Denver Post* 03/02/1895.
[2] *Denver Post* 03/09/1895.

The criminal organization of the Blonger brothers, Lou and Sam, was expanding. Would they care to see Jeff in public office, especially after Jeff in print had blamed Lou for the awkward businessman's petition against the ban on gambling? Possibly, if that letter were just for show. Then there were the newspaper editors of the city, most of whom would be against Jeff's holding public office. Even with Jeff's ability to get out the vote, his being elected would not be easy. The stiff headwind could even be felt to increase when just two days after Jeff announced his candidacy, *The Denver Post* informed the public that attending a hearing on charges of robbery and assault and battery of Joseph Gottlieb would be Bascomb Smith, "'Colonel' Jeff's Brother."[1]

City elections would take place on Tuesday, April 2, 1895. On the Saturday before, occurred a much publicized but very weak raid on only a single gambling club. Arrested were owner John Hebard and 18 players. When the patrol wagon arrived at police headquarters, Jeff and Ed Chase were already preparing bail for the men. At headquarters Police Chief George Goulding released 15 of the 18 players as he was informed that only 3 men were actually gambling and the remaining men only seeking shelter. The *Denver Evening Post* called the chief's raid "simply a big bluff" to influence the election. This would seem to be the case as on Monday all the cases involving gambling were postponed until Wednesday, the day after the election.

According to the *Post*, fourteen gambling halls were currently running in the city, and these were split into two competing groups known as the "big eight" and "little six." Hebard, as one of the "little six" felt his place was intentionally chosen rather than hitting one of the larger "clubs" as part of a "war of extermination." The *Post* reported that as a member of the "big eight," Ed Chase was preparing to open for business the day after the election with guaranteed protection from closure.[2]

The election on Tuesday was won by the Republican candidates, but the *News* called it won by fraud. Hired were 133 special policemen to watch over the polls, but these were cogs in the well-oiled Denver Combine politics. These "policemen for a day" made sure that "repeaters" and fraudulent voters were allowed to cast their votes unmolested. The *News* claimed that as a reward, all gamblers who aided in this election would be allowed free reign in the operation of their gaming houses.[3]

Jeff was one of the most prolific leaders of fraudulent voters. Unfortunately for Jeff, he apparently revealed evidence of his work to someone who was a *News* informant, which was published the following day.

> Colonel Jefferson Smith grew confidential. He took the News informant into the place where the boodle was being distributed and as he knew the gentleman, unfolded the whole plan.
>
> Throwing back an overcoat that lay upon a trunk in the robber's den, the colonel showed a bunch of slips upon each of which was written a name.
>
> "There," said Soapy, "that is all I have left of about $800. All the rest have been used in the Third and Fourth wards."

---

[1] *Denver Evening Post* 03/11/1895.
[2] *Denver Evening Post* 04/01/1895, p. 2.
[3] *RMN* 04/03/1895.

There were about fifty remaining, and the other 750, names of dead, and those who are no longer legal voters, had been fraudulently cast for the corporation ticket at $2 apiece.[1]

Despite published accounts of atrocious election fraud, no indictments followed. When asked about this lack, the fire and police board and district attorney claimed that no complaints of fraud had been received.[2] Also noted was that since election day, gambling houses had reopened and saloons stayed open on Sundays, all without interference by the police. As for Jeff's desire to be nominated for alderman in the ninth ward, it was never realized. It is doubtful he was considered a serious candidate given his candor regarding his line of business.

The explosions began just after Saturday midnight, on Sunday morning, April 21, 1895. Perhaps it was as the *Post* stated, "a desperate effort to get even for all of their injured feelings for the past year...."[3] Much had happened to feel injured about: failure to secure men a train ride to Coxey's Army, shut down of Denver gambling, constant arrest of his men, humiliation in Mexico, debilitation and decline of the elder Jefferson Smith, lack of domestic calm and companionship with his wife and children, pressures of the election campaign (both as a fixer and a candidate), rising Blonger Brothers influence, erosion of his position in the Combine.... Whatever the cause or causes, the effect was explosive. Here was no beating of a Colonel Arkins that could be defended on moral grounds but savage beatings of personal, political, and professional friends in high places. The sixteen years of Jeff's building himself up in Denver were beaten down that morning by none other than Jeff himself, with the enthusiastic help of his brother, Bascomb. What made him do it? Over the three years left to him, Jeff probably often wondered.

On Monday, April 22, Newspaper headlines blazed: *STRUCK THE CHIEF* (the *News*). *SMITH'S WAR PAINT: JEFF AND BASCOM[B] AND THEIR RAMPAGE SATURDAY* (*Denver Times*). *HIT AT EVERY HEAD: The Smith Brothers run Amuck Through the City* (*Post*). Each paper chronicled what happened, but the stories differed in important ways. Each agreed, though, that events had begun late Saturday evening. The Smith brothers were drinking about town when they learned that Police Chief George Goulding and others were at Jennie Rogers' brothel.[4] Then came one of those impulsive thoughts that requires a lamentable description: "It seemed like a good idea at the time." And the idea this time was to pay a visit on Chief Goulding at Jennie Rogers'.

According to the *News*, based on "stories whispered ... at the police station," the chief and two saloonkeepers were in one of Jennie's rooms. One was not identified; the other was Tom Sewall, proprietor of the Side Line Saloon. Arriving at Jennie's, Jeff and Bascomb asked to see the chief but were told they could not. The Smiths then "became enraged," went to a room where they thought Goulding would be, and hit it

---

[1] *RMN* 04/03/1895.

[2] *RMN* 04/04/1895. And 04/06/1895, p. 4.

[3] *Denver Evening Post* 04/23/1895.

[4] *Jennie Rogers*: Her real name is probably Leah J. Tehme. She was a highly successful Denver brothel madam and competitor of Madam Mattie Silks. (Secrest, pp. 235-239.)

several times "with the butt of a revolver." The door "cautiously opened and the Smiths forced their way in." Not stated is who opened the door, but it was not Sewall or the chief because they "jumped to their feet and started to eject the intruders."

> Just what happened then is hard to explain, but in a very short space of time the chief was on the floor in one corner of the room and Sewall was staggering to a chair, the blood flowing from a number of severe wounds on the top of his head where one of the Smiths had hit him with a gun. The actions of the third man in the room are not explained by the inmates, but it is believed that he escaped through a window.

> The racket inside the house, added to the screams of the women, drew a big crowd to the sidewalk. Among them were two patrolmen, one of them being officer Alexander, it is said. Just as the officers decided upon entering the house the chief and two Smiths appeared and walked away as though nothing had happened to disturb the peace of the neighborhood. The officers, seeing their chief with the two men, saluted and awaited orders, but none were [sic] issued, the party continuing rapidly down Market street.[1]

The *Post* had quite a few more details about the fight.

> Tom was knocked to the carpeted floor by a stunning blow straight from Jefferson's shoulder. He struggled to his feet and ... Jeff's devoted brother delivered a second punch that for a moment dazed Tom and sent him toppling.... The noise of the scrap aroused the house, and frightened females in scanty attire were soon running frantic through the building.

> Their appeals to the three combatants did not tend to shorten hostilities for with the Smith family's second blow Tom braced himself against the satin embossed wall and reached for his gun.

> This belligerent effort called for immediate action on the part of Jefferson and little brother Bascom, and in an instant their guns flashed in the air and descended with considerable force on Tom's cranium. A second blow from Jefferson's 45 sent Tom sprawling to the floor with blood spurting from a deep gash over his left eye and two long scalp wounds.

> The appearance of the life-giving fluid sent a thrill of horror through the congregated females, who viewed the encounter from a safe distance on the stairway, and two of them were soon in the throes of hysterics.

> The victim of the assault lay bleeding on the floor and Jenny Rogers, the mistress of the notorious bagnio, rushed to his side and put an end to the murderous assault. She ordered the Smith family to leave her house, which they did without further ceremony.[2]

Chief Goulding must have had a good relationship with the *Post* and the *Times* because in their accounts he does not appear on the scene until later or become involved until a disturbance is heard. Then,

---

[1] *RMN* 04/22/1895.
[2] *Denver Post* 04/23/1895.

The chief, in pursuit of his duty, went into this house, and, as he was standing in the hall making inquiries of Miss Rogers, he heard noises produced by a scuffle in one of the parlors, and in the next moment Tom Sewall appeared, followed by Jeff Smith and Bascom Smith, who had their guns drawn. The chief at once stopped the fight, and as Tom Sewall would not agree to prosecute the warlike brothers assaulting him the chief had to allow the belligerent brothers to depart, Jeff Smith promising to go home at once. ... Jeff Smith made an attempt to strike at the chief, who was in 2005 Market street performing duties for which he draws a salary from the people.[1]

Some, such as the *Aspen Times*, had it that the Smith brothers' "first victim was Chief of Police Goulding, whom they pounded into submission."[2] To the contrary, Goulding was unharmed. At least he wore no reported marks or abrasions. The *News* continued the story with the chief escorting Jeff and Bascomb away from Jenny Rogers' house and then parted from them. As for "Sewall, whose head was badly damaged," a friend took him to Police Surgeon Mack at city hall. Fire Captain George Duggan was there, and Sewall asked if the Smiths had been arrested. Told they had not, Sewall asked why. The captain said he did not know as the chief had not yet been in. Sewall suspected Goulding had come in with the Smiths and insisted on looking

into the chief's private office. This privilege was granted and a search was even made under the chief's big desk, but no Smiths were found. Sewall hinted ... that he had been injured by "Soapy" Smith, and that the chief was mixed up in the affair. He said, sarcastically, that he wanted to bail Smith out, and afterward told the officials that in case any inquiry was made they should say that the wounds [his] were caused by a cable car accident.[3] ... Quietly, however, it is said, he told Captain Duggan that he would kill Smith on sight and his actions seemed to warrant the threat.

While this was going on..., however, the two Smiths were not idle. ... After Goulding and Connors left the Smiths the latter went into Blonger's place on Larimer near Seventeenth.[4]

In the *Denver Times* story, the chief and Detective Connors had gone "down upon Market street to see if the new police regulations for the government of the resorts [brothels] were being properly observed." So they are together before arriving at Jennie Rogers'. Further, this account has the chief taking information to Rogers about one Donna Dare who had just started working there. But in the *Post*, the chief and Connors arrive at Rogers' "resort a short time after the assault." The point of drawing attention to the discrepancies is that they suggest it was Connors who was in the room with the chief and Sewall when the Smiths pushed in and that Connors is the one who left the room through the window. In a follow up article by the *News*, the chief said,

"On Saturday night I went out as is my custom, in company with an officer—I never go alone—to visit various downtown places and see for

---

[1] *Denver Times* 04/22/1895.
[2] *Aspen Times* 04/27/1895, p. 2.
[3] The previous day Sewall was reported as having been run-over by a cable car. (*RMN* 04/21/1895, p. 4)
[4] *RMN* 04/22/1895.

myself how they are running. After visiting Wisch's and some other places, I said to Detective Connors, who was with me, I'll go over to Jennie Rogers', as I want to see her on some business."[1]

In sum, it appears probable that Chief Goulding and his model detective were closeted in Jennie Rogers and that what Jeff and Bascomb had heard about the chief's being there on other than the "people's business" is true. They may have gone there just to razz the chief and that it was a razzing that went bad—very bad.

The *News* has them going directly to the Blonger Saloon, but the *Post* has them visiting the "Casa Bianca" saloon first. Goulding in the *News* later on, though, said he arrested the Smiths in the "Casablanca saloon"[2] and was taking them to jail "when Sewall and friends overtook" them in a carriage and said he would not prosecute them. So the chief and Connors let Jeff and Bascomb go, and to the Blonger saloon they went, shadowed by Officer Kimmel.

According to R. K. DeArment in *Knights of the Green Cloth*, Lou and Sam Blonger opened "their modest [saloon] establishment in Denver in 1880," and Lou "contributed a percentage of his saloon profits to the crime lord [Jeff and/or Ed Chase] with never a murmur of protest."[3] Not known is if the Blonger saloon of 1895 is the one opened in 1880, but for certain Jeff and Bascomb went into a Blonger saloon at "1644 Larimer street." From this point on, the accounts in all three papers on April 22, 1895, vary only slightly. In the Blonger saloon, the brothers "were looking for trouble, and became quite noisy" (*News*). "They attempted to pick a fight with some gamblers..." (*Times*).

> Officer Kimmel went into the place and told the Smiths that the noise must stop at once or there would be two arrests. This settled the Smiths to some extent, and they retired from the place, muttering maudlin apologies to the officer. [*News*] ... Next they went into the big Arcade saloon.... [*Times*]

Officer Kimmel's ordering them from the Blonger saloon may have saved their lives. Collier and Westrate claim that "Shortly afterward it was revealed that Lou Blonger, gripping a double-barreled shotgun, had been crouching beneath the cigar counter, prepared to fire the moment Soapy opened the card-room door."[4] Had Jeff and Bascomb not left and instead succeeded in making trouble or in trying to see Lou Blonger, Jeff's life may have ended in 1895 instead of 1898.

The brothers' night of fun was not over. They crossed the street and entered the Arcade Clubrooms for a few more drinks. Jeff began a heated discussion with "Sheeny Charley" M. Lorje (or Lorge), the barkeeper.[5] Jeff accused him of being a cheap stud dealer and then physically assailed him. No match for both Smiths, "Sheeny" stopped defending himself after being knocked to the floor by Jeff's pistol-whipping, which opened a deep, jagged gash on the left side of his skull.

---

[1] *RMN* 04/23/1895.
[2] *Casa Bianca saloon* and *Casablanca saloon*: the Casablanca is likely the Casa Bianca; this latter name turns up several more times.
[3] DeArment, *Knights*, p. 381.
[4] Collier & Westrate, pp. 207-208.
[5] The *RMN* misspelled his last name as "Lord."

Jeff was just starting the fight with Lorje when Arcade proprietor John J. ("Square-Shooter") Hughes, who was reading a newspaper in the dining room, heard the commotion and came into the room. In 1887 Hughes had partnered with "Big Ed" Chase in ownership of the Arcade.[1] Chase sold his interest in the club to Hughes, who was now sole proprietor. Hughes saw Jeff hit Lorje in the head with the butt of his pistol and attempted to stop him from doing the man further harm. Jeff apparently resented the interference and turned his rage on Hughes, calling him nothing but a cheap waiter and "hasher." Hughes ordered Jeff out of the Arcade. Enraged, both Jeff and Bascomb attacked Hughes. Easily overpowering him, they clubbed the unarmed Hughes repeatedly across the face and head with their revolvers until friends of both Hughes and the Smiths separated them.

Officer Kimmel, who had heard the commotion, came into the Arcade to ask what was going on. The barkeeper said nothing was seriously wrong, and Officer Kimmel left. Then Jeff and Bascomb calmly walked out and down Larimer towards Sixteenth. The barkeep later explained that he was afraid to say anything to the officer while the Smiths were there as he was certain the brothers would "kill the whole works,"[2] that is, "attack anyone in sight." John Hughes' condition was critical. His skull was fractured, and he had deep, serrated gashes across his forehead, face, and between the eyes. The brothers had done a thorough job, just short of murder.

At the corner of Sixteenth and Larimer, Chief Goulding and Detective Connors arrested Jeff and Bascomb without incident. As the four men made their way to police headquarters, Officer Kimmel caught up with them and said that none of the assaulted men would make complaint against either man. Upon being released, Jeff and Bascomb promised to go home.

Just before daybreak, Chief Goulding slipped into police headquarters to see if reporters had been around to ask about his doings that night and was told that the *Rocky Mountain News* had indeed been there. In its first report of the story, the *News* had Goulding leaving town out of shame, but this was not correct. The chief had hidden in his office. When reporters from the *News* finally caught up with Goulding, he claimed that he was not even present at the fight. Rather, when it commenced, he had only just arrived to deliver a message to Jennie Rogers. His explanation only made matters worse when it proved to be a half truth. He produced the message he was "delivering," but it turned out to be a response to a telegram Jennie Rogers had sent about one of her working girls. Now not only was the chief known to call on such places but he also became known as "Jennie's messenger boy."[3]

Three days after the affair in the brothel, Goulding denied ever seeing Jeff and Bascomb until after their attacks at other locations, not at the brothel. The *News* stated that it was not part of Goulding's duty to "hold court in his own mind, decide whether he can or cannot make a case and hold or release the prisoners accordingly." In an interview with the *News*, Goulding said of Jeff,

---

[1] DeArment, *Knights*, p. 173.

[2] *RMN* 04/22/1895, *Denver Times* 04/22/1895, & *Denver Post* 04/22/1895. Denver newspaper clippings saved by Jeff R. Smith II, Jefferson R. "Little Randy" Smith col.

[3] *Road* 04/27/1895. clipping saved by Jeff R. Smith II. Jefferson R. "Little Randy" Smith col.

I do not believe that Soapy has been doing any business lately, and he will not be allowed to do so. I propose to run all confidence men, thugs and vagrants out of town. There is no man who would be more pleased than I if Smith had to leave the city. If he should ever try to hit me with a gun he had better hit hard the first time.[1]

The following day, Hughes recovered enough to swear out complaints against Jeff and Bascomb for attempted murder. The next day, Officer Kimmel arrested the brothers on Market Street. They were released on $500 bonds. Arraignment came on May 15, 1895, the charge, assault to kill. Bonds were fixed at $1000 each. This time no John Kinneavy posted bond, nor Ed Chase. Hughes was an associate and friend, and hard to understand was why he should be attacked, beaten, and nearly killed. Another bridge had been burned that night, and there was no immediate way back.

Bonds were set at $1,000 for Jeff and $1,000 for Bascomb, and they were furnished by attorney G. M. Allen.[2] Trial was set for July 1, 1895.[3] Jeff hired attorney James B. Belford for his defense.[4]

The Road, a Denver magazine, defended Jeff's actions at Jennie Rogers' brothel.

The citizens of Denver ought to extend Jeff Smith a vote of thanks for jumping the chief. We hope every time he is caught lolling around a house of prostitution guzzling wine that some body will kick him on the end of the spine hard enough to drive it through his skull. Soapy isn't half as bad as the Republican political whelps who use him.... We don't pretend to be Colonel Jeff's official organ nor do we endorse his life work but this we will say: that he is a mighty insignificant case of confidence man compared with the gang who have been using him.

Give Jeff a chance ... and ... he will shine with respectability along side of some of our millionaires who pose as honest men. Jeff has a good wife and four little children[5] he loves as well as any father can, and he is not a bad man at heart—far from it. He is honest *in his way* and does not rob his fellow man under the cloak of religion or the guise of eminent respectability. He is generous—far more so than many bankers we can mention. Use Jeff right and he will do fairly right, but hunted, deceived, buncoed and used as a butt for all the Republican perfidus[6] political jobs—what can you expect of him?[7]

The Road often sided with Jeff. A damaged clipping from it cut by Jeff and placed in his scrapbook expresses the editor's thoughts about Jeff.

---

[1] *RMN* 04/23/1895, p. 5.

[2] Denver newspaper clipping of unknown origin saved by Jeff R. Smith II, 05/16/1895. Jefferson R. "Little Randy" Smith col.

[3] *Denver Evening Post* 06/01/1895.

[4] Relied upon for this sequence of events: *RMN* 04/22/1895, *Denver Times* 04/22/1895, *Denver Post* 04/22/1895, *The Road* 04/27/1895.

[5] *four little children*: Mary and Jeff had 3 children and possibly 2 at this time.

[6] *perfidus*: Latin, disloyal. *Perfidious* is likely the word (idiom), meaning deliberately faithless, basely treacherous; fr *perfidy*: deceitfulness, faithlessness, treacherous.... Hence "all the Republican political jobs calling for lying and treachery."

[7] *The Road* 04/27/1895.

Colonel Jefferson Randolph Smith is a philosopher and a gentleman. We mean it.

He should be made chairman of the reception committee appointed by the Chamber of Commerce, to meet Eastern capitalists. We want to say right here, and we mean every word of it, the Colonel represents interests ten times more legitimate than the bunco mining deals and corner lot fakes, headed by what some are pleased to term, "our very best citizens." ...

We doff our hats to Jeff. His business takes nerve and sagacity and doesn't injure the country in the long run half as much as the jackrabbit lot schemes for..., Jeff "blows" his "stuff" in Denver, while the Leets and Moffats,[1] when they make a raise, lock their stuff up and help no one.[2]

The year continued badly for Jeff. He must have known his empire in Denver was ending. Added to the change in underworld politics and control was the bad news six months earlier that Jefferson Sr. had been institutionalized. Three days after the Hughes assault, on April 23, 1895, the Superintendent of the asylum wrote to Mr. Gardener (husband of Jeff's sister Emmie) in Temple, Texas. The news was not good.

Dear Bob:-

Replying to your card of the 22nd., in regard to J. R. Smith, regret to say that he has not improved any mentally since I came, and the out-look for his recovery is very gloomy; his physical condition is good, sleeps well, eats plenty, and I am doing all I can for his comfort. Any time you would like to hear from him, drop me a line and I will take pleasure in replying to your letter.

Your friend,   C. T. Simpson, Supt.[3]

According to Geri Murphy, one of Jeff's great-grandchildren, Jeff Sr. did not appear to have died in the asylum. When he was released is not known, but he died in the city of Austin where the asylum was located.[4]

Jeff was irate over his diminishing position in Denver, but amazingly, and despite the rampage, he found that he still had clout. On April 30, just ten days after the Hughes attack, Bascomb had been arrested and found to be a walking arsenal. His guns were confiscated, but Jeff was able to have him released on bonds.[5] That he was not kept in jail as a danger to society shows how much Jeff could still accomplish with the police.

Several reports had it that Jeff had been showing a deputy sheriff's badge but no mention is made of whether he did so in a swindle or just to show it off. Sheriff Burchinell sent Jeff a letter regarding the matter, and the *News* received word of it.

---

[1] *Leets and Moffats*: David H. Moffat, longtime capitalist centered in Denver; John E. Leet, highly successful Denver real estate entrepreneur and city activist. (Hall, pp. 496-98) (Hall, Frank. *History of the State of Colorado*. Vol. IV. Chicago, Blakely Printing Co., 1895.)

[2] *The Road* 1894 newspaper clipping that Jeff tore out of the paper and upon which he wrote in pencil, "1894 Road 17th," Item 106, author's col.

[3] Ltr fr C. T. Simpson to Robert Gardener, 04/23/1895. Geri Murphy col.

[4] Interview with Geri Murphy who had communications with the institution still in existence. Records do not show that Jefferson R. Smith Sr. died in the asylum. April 2006.

[5] *Denver Evening Post* 04/20/1895, p. 4.

BURCHINELL IS POLITE.

Protest to Soapy Smith About Displaying a Deputy's Badge.

Sheriff Burchinell has addressed a letter to "Soapy" Smith, informing him that reports of Smith's displaying a deputy's star had reached him, and that he had instructed his deputies to arrest Smith upon a recurrence of this conduct. Sheriff Burchinell chafes at the suggestion that Smith is a deputy sheriff, and says he has no right to carry weapons as such.[1]

Four days later, on Wednesday May 15, 1895, the day of his arraignment, Jeff went drinking with gunman Joe Palmer. Obviously he was upset over the legal proceedings. By mid-afternoon they were, in the words of the *Times*, "as jolly as a pair of pirates."[2] Notified of the inebriated men, the police were on the lookout for them. It was mid afternoon when officer Kovsky located Jeff leaning wearily against a pillar of the First National Bank. Upon being searched and found to be carrying a large revolver, he was arrested for carrying a concealed weapon. At headquarters he was released with a warning to go straight home. Instead he procured another pistol, and using a belt and holster, Jeff strapped the gun on his waist in full view of the community. He then linked up again with his drinking buddy, Palmer.

Around six that evening, Jeff and Palmer were parading Larimer Street. They stopped in front of the Arcade to voice opinions on recent events. Officer Kimmel approached the men and tried to talk them into going home, but they resisted. Sergeant Lew S. Tuttle arrived, and the two policemen were placing the pair under arrest when Jeff grew quarrelsome. He argued that his gun was not concealed and that city gun laws allowed him to have it. With brazen deliberateness, Jeff drew his pistol from its holster and began cocking the hammer and slowly releasing it back down. Then he began pointing the revolver towards the crowd of on lookers that had gathered. Palmer grew panicky and said, "If yer goin' to shoot'er up, Jeff, I'm widge," and made a dive for his own pistol. Officer Kimmel grabbed Palmer's arm just in time to stop him and probable bloodshed. Jeff and Palmer were arrested. Both men were held until shortly before midnight and released on bonds of $1,000 each.[3]

Differing from the *Times* account of events, the *News* reported that Jeff had two revolvers at the first confrontation before he strapped on still another gun, and that before being arrested, without resistance, Jeff and Palmer had gone into the Arcade. The *News* did not mention any hammer-cocking, pistol-pointing or Palmer's attempt to assist. The *News* quoted Chief Goulding's saying, "I will not release either prisoner unless he gives $5,000 bonds...." And the *News* reported that he later changed his mind and at 12:40 a.m. released Smith and Palmer on bonds of $1,000 each.[4]

The following morning before Judge Webber, Jeff was fined $3 and costs for being drunk and $50 and costs for carrying concealed weapons. Jeff appealed the weapons charge. Palmer was fined $3 and costs for drunkenness. Palmer had passed

---

[1] *RMN* 05/11/1895, p. 8.
[2] *Denver Times* 05/16/1895.
[3] *Denver Times* 05/16/1895.
[4] *RMN* 05/16/1895, p. 8.

his gun to a friend when he was arrested, so the charge of carrying a concealed weapon was not pushed in his case as none was on his person when arrested.[1]

Whether on his own inclination or at the suggestion of friends, Jeff quickly left Denver, jumping bond. He went to St. Louis to see Mary and their children at her mother's. His attorney was not pleased that he had left. In an unfamiliar formal style, on May 26, 1895, he wrote to Jeff in St. Louis, pleading for his quick return.

> Dear Sir.
>
> The cases in which you are interested have been continued until next Saturday, June 1st. At that time you are required to be present and plead the charge, being a felony, no plea can be put in your absence. The cases cannot be tried before the 24th of June but you must be here to plead to the [indecipherable] on next Saturday. I was shocked that you had jumped your bail and left the country for good, and Col. Dennison wanted to have your bond forfeited. This I protested and the court gave me until next Saturday to have you here. My advice is to be here without fail.
>
> Truly yours   James B. Belford[2]

To say that Jeff was having a bad year would be an understatement. It started out well enough but soon went into a steep decline. Colonel Smith, veteran of the City Hall War of 1894, had become a military advisor of Mexico. He had cast his net into foreign territory with the dream of catching command of an army of his own, only to come home disappointed over how his past had blocked his dreams. He threw his hat into the political ring for alderman of Denver but again past crimes kept him from realizing this goal. Just when elections turned in favor of the gamblers, with much help from Jeff's fraudulent voters, and gambling restrictions in Denver were easing, an underworld power shift and big political tug-of-war handicapped Jeff's methods of operation. Struggling against an advancing end to his dominance, he appears to have snapped, savagely assaulting several men. Jeff's Denver days were nearing an end, and soon he would be a wanted fugitive.

Chapter 16
Colonel Jefferson Smith, Insurgent Mercenary

They mistook me for a pawnbroker, who was in town for a no good purpose, instead of the peaceable and law-abiding citizen that I am.

—Jefferson R. Smith II
Denver Times, July 1, 1895

In 1895, Jeff remained a man who would be king. However, he remained a man who had lost his kingdom and could not find another. In towns and cities from west to east and back again, either bad luck or his own reputation, which had preceded him, barred his way, and sometimes brutal resistance prevented his stopping for long.

---

[1] *Denver Evening Post* 05/16/1895, p. 2.
[2] Ltr to Jeff R. Smith II fr James B. Belford, 05/26/1895. Geri Murphy col.

Nothing, though, stopped Jeff's search for the right place in which to settle and bend to his will. In his search, he became no ordinary traveler but a wanderer, a will-o-the-wisp—apparently here or there, receding when approached, and vanishing. His presence would be reported one place but then reported in another at the same time, only to have been in the first place after all. Or not.

In February 1895 Cuba revolted against Spain in a bid to become an independent nation. A partial cause of the rebellion was the depression of 1893, which severely affected the Cuban sugar industry. Repressive measures taken by the Spanish aroused the sympathy of Americans, and in particular one who was prone to action.

Cuba's Freedom is Assured

Captain General De Campos of the Cuban Government forces will soon have a foreman to fight who may prove harder to crush than even the redoubtable and many lived Jose Marti.[1] The new enemy to Spanish domination in the war-torn island is none other than Colonel Jefferson Randolph Smith of Seventeenth street Denver.

If the United States government does not interfere, the colonel proposes within the coming month to land a force of Mexican guerrillas in Cuba, all armed with Martini-Henri rifles of the most modern pattern, and march at their head to the succor of Jose Marti and his insurgents....

Whether it is love of bleeding liberty, or love of loot, or ambition to become a great military leader that has inspired the versatile "Soapy" to turn from mercantile pursuits to the warpath, is not known. Certain it is, however, that he is about to become a soldier of fortune.

Very quietly, and with more or less secrecy, Colonel Smith took his departure from this city last Sunday evening on a Burlington train. With commendable caution, too, he revealed his mission to but a few persons....

After Jeff left , though, the ultimate destination of his journey "leaked out": Cuba.

He is first to go to St. Louis, where a trusted American agent of the insurrection will meet him. This man, who like Colonel Smith, is a diplomat and soldier of fortune, will have letters of introduction to the Denver ally of Jose Marti, and likewise a big "wad"... amounting to $6,000.[2]

Jeff was to purchase the rifles in St. Louis and ship them to New Orleans and then to Tampico, Mexico, with Jeff disguised as a merchant. During his trip, an army consisting of mostly Mexicans was to be raised in and around the cities of Mexico and Chihuahua. Once the army numbered several thousand, with Jeff at the head, it was to be transported to Cuba.[3]

Seven days later President Cleveland called on US citizens to avoid giving aid to the insurgents, and Jeff gave up his plans for Cuba and another military dream.[4] It is not known if Jeff really planned to see the adventure through or whether it was all just

---

[1] *Jose Marti* (1853-1895): Cuban-born, anti-colonialist writer and revolutionary. He died in one of the first skirmishes against Spain in the revolution he helped to foster.

[2] *Denver Republican* 06/05/1895.

[3] *Denver Republican* 06/05/1895.

[4] *Denver Times* 07/01/1895.

a complex ruse for a chance at the $6,000 that had been raised for "the cause." It is equally possible that the story was his attempt to lay down a false trail for the Denver prosecuting attorney to follow in case he sought Jeff's extradition. On July 2, 1895, Jeff and Bascomb's bondsman, Gaines Allen, surrendered the bonds, and Mart Watrous and R. L. Barra offered to replace Allen as bondsmen, which was accepted.[1]

According to Jeff, he went to St. Louis when David R. Francis, ex-governor of Missouri, sent for him. Francis was running for senator and wanted Jeff's help in the election.[2] Perhaps Jeff saw the chance for election spoils in the form of a new territory to run if he could get Francis elected. Moreover, should things go well, Jeff could be with his wife and children again. But things did not go well, not at all. Jeff clipped the newspaper story telling what happened.

> Detectives McGrath and Tom Tracy ... have been suspended. They took advantage of the chief's absence from the city Wednesday and went on a hilarious tear.
>
> After visiting several downtown resorts, the detectives entered a hack and went out to the saloon out on Chestnut Street. There they met "Soapy" Smith. Tracy thought Smith wanted to insult him, and McGrath proceeded to knock an apology out of him. "Soapy" Smith is the man who stood off the Colorado militia with a Winchester during the trouble between Gov. Waite and the police two years ago, but Detective McGrath, reinforced by a jag, proved too much for "Soapy," and he and Tracy hammered the Denver man till he was nearly unconscious and drove him out into the darkness. Then the detectives resumed their pilgrimage in the bad lands.
>
> Chief Desmond was asked about the detectives' suspension this morning. At first he denied it.... Finally he admitted that he had suspended them, and said he would appear against them both for neglect of duty.[3]

According to one St. Louis newspaper, two other detectives also took part in Jeff's beating, making it four against one, and Jeff received a broken nose.[4] The *Denver Evening Post* claimed the two detectives were drunk.

> The bartender pointed "Soapy" out to them and said he was a bad man from the west. The detectives wanted to gain some notoriety, and approached Smith, saying: "You are 'Soapy' Smith, a gun-fighter from Denver, ain't you?"
>
> "Soapy" acknowledged ... their identification, but said he was no fighter. Some words passed, when one of the detectives pulled his revolver from his pocket and struck Smith over the head. The other detective drew his gun, and before "Soapy" could defend himself he was badly beaten. The detectives sent him to police headquarters on the charge of vagrancy, which charge they trumped up against him to save themselves. "Soapy" was so badly hurt that the police surgeon was obliged to dress his wounds.

[1] *Denver Evening Post* 07/02/1895, p. 2.
[2] *Denver Times*, 07/01/1895.
[3] Unknown St. Louis newspaper clipping, saved by Jefferson R. Smith II, 1895 (most likely June) Jefferson R. "Little Randy" Smith col.
[4] Jones, Robert, p. 333. Unknown and undated St. Louis newspaper clipping.

While this was being done Chief Harrigan came into the office and inquired how Smith got hurt. The detectives said he had resisted arrest and they were obliged to "trim him up." By some means the chief found out the true state of affairs and asked "Soapy" to bring charges against the detectives for their cruel treatment.

"I thought of that," said "Soapy," "but I investigated and found that both men have families depending upon them for support and I decided not to do it."

The chief insisted, saying that he did not want such men on his force and some one had to make the charges.

"Well, I'll never make them, and if I am subpoenaed I'll testify that I started the fight," said "Soapy." He left town the next day and the detectives are still on the force.[1]

Why did the detectives attack Jeff? A whispered word from a local crime boss to the police, honest or otherwise, might have been the trigger. That the local newspaper printed Jeff's alias of "Soapy" is a good indication that his reputation preceded him or was intentionally surfaced by his rivals. No matter the blame, it was enough to keep Jeff from setting up operations in St. Louis.

Back in Denver the Soap Gang still seemed to have things under control. Joe Palmer opened a saloon at the corner of Eighteenth and Lawrence streets, believed to be the Missouri House,[2] which was not much more than a front for rigged poker games.[3] Jeff continued to receive pleas from his attorney, Judge Belford, to return to Denver and face trial. In a June 22, 1895, letter, Bascomb urged him to return as well.

Dear Jeff

I was up to see Allen, the man that went on our bonds and he says you must be here for trial and says you should be here next Friday so you could [undecipherable] look around for your self so to keep them from having a fit. Write me and tell them what you are going to do. They don't seem to think you are going to come back so let me know what you are going to do. I had a prop[4] made to mail. You know old John the bartender in the Arcade told me if we would leave town that it won't be all right. I wrote you a letter before this today.

Yours as ever   Bascom[5]

Five days later Bascomb sent Jeff a telegram addressed to 917 Locust Street, St. Louis: "'Come at once Bowers got back this morning. Answer. E. Bascom Smith'"[6]

---

[1] *Denver Evening Post*, undated clipping, circa 1898-1899.

[2] *RMN* 11/15/1896, p. 11, & *RMN*, 12/27/1896, p. 5.

[3] *Denver Evening Post* 06/18/1895 & 07/01/1895, p. 2.

[4] *prop*: a stick pin or tie pin or stud, diamond or otherwise. (Partridge, *Underworld*) Perhaps this was a gift Bascomb enclosed to his brother.

[5] Handwritten ltr fr Bascomb Smith to Jefferson R. Smith II, 06/22/1895 on stationary fr the DeCunto, Barra & Company saloon, located at 1933-35-37 Larimer Street. Geri Murphy col.

[6] Telegram to Jefferson R. Smith II fr Bascomb Smith, 06/27/1895. Jefferson R. "Little Randy" Smith col. Perhaps Bascomb put an "E" before his name thinking it would shield his identity and Jeff's

Jeff arrived in Denver on July 1, 1895, the day his trial was to begin. But defense attorney Belford had secured a week's delay. The injuries his client sustained in a St. Louis assault prevented him from testifying in his own defense in the case of assault with which he was charged. The irony escaped no one's attention. As Jeff left the court, he consented to an interview with the *Denver Times*.

Colonel Smith's Wounds.

"You can see for yourself," said he as he withdrew into the quiet of the bailiff's office, "that my wounds are calculated to impose somewhat of suffering on one who is advancing in age, and who possesses not the sprightly energy and youthful activity of earlier years. These injuries, as you must know were inflicted by the uncultured, unsophisticated and vulgar minions of the law in East St. Louis, who ignorantly mistook me for a pawnbroker, who was in town for no good purpose, instead of the peaceable and law-abiding citizen that I am. Be it said to the credit of the superiors of these men, however, that as soon as my true character was represented to them, they incontinently dismissed the presumptuous fellows in question from their positions, in addition to levying large and burdensome fines against them. To all of which your enterprising and popular paper has heretofore given publicity.

"In justice to myself," continued Colonel Smith, with some degree of ... sadness in his voice, "I would like to say that this trip of mine to St. Louis was not made for the purpose of avoiding any engagements, such as the present one ... contracted previous to my departure from Denver. Not at all.

"Certain ill-tempered and witless newspaper reporters here represented that such was the case and that as an effective means of ridding myself of any temporary embarrassment these engagements might occasion me, I had gone to the Cuban Islands to lend myself to the cause of the insurgent armies. This was a wholly false and unjust statement of my object in leaving Denver. For while I am free to admit that my whole heart and sympathies go out to the down trodden and oppressed people of those isles, nevertheless I do not consider that my poor abilities would suffice to materially advance their noble struggle for liberty and for escape from painful and disgraceful thralldom. ...

"No, sir! I left Denver and went to St. Louis on other business. Knowledge of my somewhat successful endeavors (you will pardon the seeming egotism of the remark I am sure)—knowledge of my somewhat successful endeavors on behalf of political aspirants in the West had in some manner come to the ears of my old friend Dave Francis, ex-governor of Missouri, you know, and he being desirous of promoting by what honorable means he could [achieve] a laudable ambition to sit in the seat of an United States senator, he sent for me. Thinking, no doubt, that I might be of some slight service to him in furthering this ambition.

---

whereabouts. Such a thin disguise, though, perhaps indicates that the "E" is merely the telegrapher's mistake.

"The Democracy of the state is somewhat divided on the matter of free silver coinage, and Governor Francis is desirous of coming into popular favor—and into the senate at the same time—by espousing the cause of Mr. Grover Cleveland. If the calling of a state convention for the purpose of taking action on this money question could be 'staved off.' Vulgarly speaking, there was hope that the administration would be able to capture the Democracy in regular convention and declare for Mr. Francis for senator.

"My part was to stiffen the back of Maffott, chairman of the state committee, and to—" [Jeff stopped speaking.]

Colonel Smith became somewhat too weak at this point to continue, and begged to be allowed to continue the interview at some other time. Which was reluctantly agreed to.[1]

The week passed, and Jeff did not show up for trial. Once again he fled the city, probably upon learning that his chances of keeping out of prison were slim. Jeff may have returned to Denver with the intention of getting Bascomb out of the city, the two of them leaving the state together. It is a mystery why Bascomb did not go with Jeff when he had the opportunity. A letter from W. R. Phelps in Victor, Colorado, addressed to "Col Jeff. Smith, care of Lou Blonger, Larimer street," indicates that Jeff, although listing his residence as 1421 S. Fifteenth Street,[2] was no longer in Denver and that Blonger was steadily rising in power. The letter eventually reaching Jeff from Victor, Colorado on July 16, 1895, bore no cheer.

Friend Jeff

Geo. Jordan who put up that money for you has just spoken to me. The money was not his and he is in the hole anyhow. He went to Judge McIntosh for the cash, and of course the judge did not have it. Jordan holds a receipt for the money, and is going to compel the judge to refund it. Under the circumstances this will place me in the box, for I cannot permit judge McIntosh, nor any friend to suffer through my actions, and of course you know he would not have done anything in the matter, but for me. Now Jeff, I am not able to pay him this money, having my brother, a little boy, to care for.... Please do not compel me to answer it, for it will compel me to lose property which I am paying for in monthly payments. I hope you will dig up the amount & remit it to Jordan at once & not place your friends in this disagreeable position. Let me hear from you at once.

Yours as ever,   W. R. Phelps[3]

Jeff headed back to St. Louis. There he placed his properties, reported to be valued near $10,000 (about $312,400 today) in his wife's name.[4]

---

[1] *Denver Times* 07/01/1895.

[2] Denver City Directory 1895, p. 973.

[3] Ltr fr W. R. Phelps to Jefferson R. Smith II, 07/16/1895. Geri Murphy col.

[4] Tom's Inflation Calculator. Unknown Denver newspaper clipping saved by Jefferson R. Smith II. The content suggests the date to be late January or early February; "1896" is written at the top. Jefferson R. "Little Randy" Smith col.

Bascomb, as much trouble as he was already in, just could not stay away from it. On Monday night, July 22, 1895, he committed another near deadly attack.

> Bascomb Smith Visits the Casa Bianca Saloon and Takes Part in A Row Between the Inmates—One Of Them Seizes His Gun and a Struggle for Life Ensues—One of The Combatants Sent to the Hospital, While Another with His Nose Broken Escapes the Surgeon.

> The Casa Bianca saloon [at 1933 Larimer Street] is perforated with two bullet holes, or rather the wood work of the mirror is. The balls were intended for Louis Petit, and he escaped death only by a miracle. Bascomb Smith, brother of Jeff Smith, used the weapon, an ugly 45 gun. He is locked up in the city jail. Petit has a pair of badly burned hands and Alfred Delplank is in the hospital ward at the jail with one side of his head bruised and cut, while another Frenchman, the name unknown, who escaped during the excitement, is wandering around somewhere in the city with a part of his nose missing.

The brawl began shortly after 11 o'clock between Delplank and another man, two Frenchmen. Bascomb, finding himself in the vicinity, was "about to interfere" when Petite told him not to interfere. According to the story patrons told, that statement caused Bascomb to draw, "and a moment later his gun flashed in the air and was pointed directly Petit's stomach." Grasping the pistol just as it fired, Petit received flash burns to his hands but succeeded in causing the bullet to pass under his arm. "With a mighty effort," Bascomb turned the gun upward towards Petit's head, but again the Frenchman "caught the weapon with both hands" and turned it again before it fired. Then "giving a vigorous push" to his assailant, Petit fled the Casa Blanca with Bascomb right behind him.

> Officer Gilmore, who had been attracted by the shooting, grappled with Smith on the sidewalk and struggled with him until Patrolman Palmer arrived and managed to wrest the weapon from Smith's hands. The latter and Delplank were taken to police headquarters where Delplank's wounds were dressed. The other Frenchman with the lost nose escaped and so did Petit.

Petit was found and "promised to appear as a witness" while the other man had yet to be found. When Delplank was "attacked by a number of" men, Bascomb said that only then had he interfered. "He would not say that he had fired the shots.[1]

The following morning Bascomb was fined $25 and costs for carrying concealed weapons and $10 and costs for disturbance of the peace. Being free on bond pending trial for assaulting Hughes, Bascomb was considered a flight risk and so was arrested that same day, with bond raised to $5,000.[2] Joe Palmer notified Jeff of the situation.

> Friend Jeff,

> Yours of the 2nd at hand. Was glad to hear from you. I have telegraphed to St. Louis trying to find you. Bas is in [jail]. His bond is $5,000 and I cannot get … a bond for him. Ther is no friends here. Every body is laying off and mocking one another. Will send you a clipping out of this mornings News.

---

[1] *RMN* 07/23/1895, p. 6.
[2] *Denver Evening Post*, 07/23/1895.

Hoping to hear from you soon. Let me know what to do for Bas. Can get a bond on your say so, that is if you will telegraph you will be responsible.

Joe Palmer.[1]

Jeff could not find a bondsman for Bascomb. Judge Belford tried to juggle the court system so that Jeff could return without fear of arrest in order to be a witness in Bascomb's defense. But Belford was not successful, so Jeff stayed clear of Denver. For a short time he roomed in Colorado Springs, awaiting word from his attorney.[2]

In the latter part of July, Jeff was in Texas where a letter dated July 23, 1895, was addressed to him.[3] On August 3 "Jeff Smith and wife" are listed as guests at the Washington hotel in Galveston, Texas.[4] On August 5 in a letter to Jeff, addressed to San Antonio, Henry Edwards wrote that gambling was completely shut down in Denver and that no bunco men were working the city.[5] This was not wholly true according to the *Denver Evening Post.* The paper set its editorial sights on "Big Ed" Chase and felt that police Chief Goulding should be doing likewise.

Chase was the silent man behind Jeff Smith, and Jeff, as his successors are [now] obliged to, contributed 40 per cent of his earnings.

Any who refuse to pay the rake-off are refused police protection by Chase and before they have time to get their second wind are under arrest and in police court on a fine of $100 or $200 for vagrancy.[6]

Jeff was willing to return to Denver to help his brother but was sternly cautioned to stay clear of the city or face prison. However, Jeff's attorneys, Judge Belford joined by Thomas Ward, succeeded in delaying the forfeiture of Jeff's $1,000 bond. During this time it seems Jeff still hoped to regain his position in Denver. Then on August 3, 1895, attorney Ward sent a typed letter to Jeff in San Antonio, regarding his services.

My Dear Sir: -

Your letter of the 31st, came to hand this morning. As I told you in my conversation with you and wrote you in my letter, I am so situated that I cannot undertake your case without the payment of the fee, to-wit, $250, and that should be paid by the 5th of August. You will probably get this letter Tuesday and ... I do not feel that I can go ahead without the money. I will, however, wait until the 6th before I withdraw from the case in order to let you telegraph me if you have the money and that the same is placed in some one's hands here so that I can get it. I can say very frankly to you I cannot get the case continued unless I have the money, and if I should have the money I am certain I can.

I have not seen Judge Belford at the time of writing this letter. He told me, however, the other day that unless the money came, he would withdraw

---

[1] Ltr fr Joe Palmer to Jefferson R. Smith II, 08/06/1895, Geri Murphy col. Ltr exactly as written.

[2] Ltr fr Jefferson R. Smith II to Henry Edwards, July 23, 1895. Ltr is mentioned in another ltr fr Henry Edwards to Jefferson R. Smith II, 08/16/1895. Geri Murphy col.

[3] Ltr fr James B. Belford to Jefferson R. Smith II, 07/23/1895. Jefferson R. "Little Randy" Smith col.

[4] *Galveston Daily News* 08/03/1895, p. 4.

[5] Ltr fr Henry Edwards to Jefferson R. Smith II, 08/05/1895, Jefferson R. "Little Randy" Smith col.

[6] *Denver Evening Post* 07/25/1895.

also. I do this in order to enable you to make arrangements here to get your attorney to represent you in the trial of the case on the 14th or 15th.

I hope that you can make the riffle[1] and so I desire you to send me a telegram whether you get the money or not. In case you get the money, have some bank in San Antonio make arrangements with the American National Bank here so that I can reach it at once.

Yours truly,	Thomas Ward [2]

All the emphasis on "money" might have meant that a bribe was needed. On the other hand, Jeff's payment of legal fees could have been seriously delinquent. However it was, Ward and Belford must have received an acceptable reply from their client as they continued working for him. That money then was a problem for Jeff seems to have been known among those dealing with him. Four days later, Mart Watrous, half bond holder with Frank Barrow for $2,000, also wrote to Jeff in San Antonio. He conveyed how Belford and Ward had expressed confidence in being able to secure a continuance but that Jeff had to be in open court on August 14. Watrous also wrote that he had spoken to Hughes but that "he expressed himself as indifferent." Then Watrous practically pleaded with Jeff to show for his court date.

I sincerely hope, Jeff, that you will be here on the 14th, (which I am sure that you will) for the reason that if you shouldn't I know that the district attorneys' office will immediately ask for a forfeiture of the bond, and I know that you would not want to place me in that position. The general supposition here is that you will not be here but I think differently and have offered to bet on the point.

The general opinion is here that the case won't amount to anything.

Gambling is entirely closed here and it looks to me as if it would remain closed. There are other matters of news that I could tell you but as you will be here soon you can learn them yourself.

Please drop me a line in answer to this and let me know when you start.

Yours truly,	Mart H. Watrous[3]

But Jeff did not return for his court date, instead crossing from Texas back into Mexico. He wrote Watrous and Belford from Mexico City, and Watrous, writing to the Iturbide Hotel in Mexico City, responded with good news about court scheduling.

Friend Jeff: -

Your letters received; also saw your letter to Judge Belford. Mr. Belford and Mr. Ward were over to the district court this morning looking up the records of your case. The criminal division of the district court did not convene on the 14th, therefore they have had no session of the court as yet..., and Judge Belford claims that on that account there can be no special session of the criminal division until the regular session in September, and he will ask for a continuance of your case next Tuesday upon those grounds.

---

[1] *make the riffle*: shuffle this deck of cards, or, prepare to deal with this situation.

[2] Ltr fr Thomas Ward Jr., to Jefferson R. Smith II, 08/03/1895. Jefferson R. "Little Randy" Smith col.

[3] Ltr fr Mart H. Watrous to Jefferson R. Smith II, 08/07/1895. The ltr is typed on stationary fr The Colorado & Arizona Mining Company of Denver. Jefferson R. "Little Randy" Smith col.

Watrous worked in how as yet no forfeiture of the bond had occurred and would not "providing Belford is sustained in the position that he takes." Jeff was advised not to return "until you hear from us" by telegraph and to write "every few days" so his whereabouts would be continually known.

> You need not experience any anxiety of either Mr. Ward or Judge Belford withdrawing from your case as they will both be there at the finish, and Judge Belford told me to say to you in the letter that if you had any chance to make some money there not to spend your time running up here until such a time as they wanted you; but when you come, to bring some money with you.
>
> You must not get down in the mouth, Jeff, as everything will come out all right in the end. All I ask is for you to drop me a postal every few days to keep me posted as to your whereabouts, and come when we telegraph for you; and you can rest assured that we will do the best that we can....
>
> All your friends join me in best wishes.
>
> Yours truly,   Mart H. Watrous [signed]
>
> P.S. Please address your letters to me to 918 16th St.[1]

Watrous was putting the best face he could on the situation, and Jeff's attorneys may have been willing to "be there" with Jeff "at the finish," but they needed money and were again saying so, with Belford claiming that he was going broke.[2]

On August 16, 1895, on Brown Palace Hotel stationary, Henry Edwards also wrote to "Col. Jeff R. Smith" Jeff at the Iturbide Hotel. The envelope was postmarked August 18 in Denver and August 21 in Mexico City.

> Friend Jeff:
>
> Your card of 11th, inst. Just received. I also received a line from you at Colorado Springs on the 23rd of July and another from San Antonio on Aug. 5th, in which you stated that you would be here in a few days, as you would leave there the next day. Had you sent me your address I certainly would have written you. John Kinneavy gave me your card to him, and asked me to attend to it. I saw Judge Belford this morning and Tom Ward and the Judge went over to the west side court to see about it. Court was called on the 12th, but as no judge put in an appearance, court was set for the 20th. Judge Belford said he would be there on that date, and have your case postponed till September. He said he would write to you today, giving you all the points in the case. Gambling has been closed here for two weeks. Harvey Day and Whitford have opened over at Colfax. Banningan is fixing up a pool room in the place formerly used by Higgins & Hebard where they were in Colfax. The con men are not working. Bill Daily came here last Monday. I met Ellen Dalton yesterday. Denver is very quiet. Hoping this will find you well and prospering.
>
> With kind regards I remain   Yank.[1]

---

[1] Ltr fr Mart H. Watrous to Jefferson R. Smith II, 08/16/1895. Typed on stationary for the Mescal Milling Company of Denver of which Watrous was the Treasurer. Jefferson R. "Little Randy" Smith col.

[2] Ltrs fr attorneys to Jefferson R. Smith II, 07/23/1895, 08/07/1895, 08/16/1895, and 08/20/1895. Geri Murphy col.

Jeff may have yearned to return to the Denver of old, but Edwards' letter gave little sign that the city would ever again be as open as it was. Jeff continued to keep his distance from Denver. So, apparently, did John Bowers. His sister, Annie Bowers, wrote Police Chief Goulding in August 1895 to ask the whereabouts of "J. L. Bowers." Her inquiry made the pages of the *Denver Evening Post* but without indication of from where she was writing. The last time she had heard from him, she wrote, "'was when he was proprietor of the Tivoli saloon at the corner of Seventeenth and Market streets.'"[2] Was Bowers exaggerating to his sister about being the Tivoli's one-time proprietor or co-partner? It can be assumed that she knew nothing of her brother's life of transgression.

If any truth is in the story, in late August Jeff traveled to Gillette, known as the "Monte Carlo of Colorado," and aligned with promoter Joe Wolfe. Since July 1895, he had been organizing and advertising the first bullfight to take place on US soil. Wolfe chose Gillette because trains to and from boomtown Cripple Creek made a stop there. At a cost of close to $10,000, Wolfe built an arena in the center of the town's horserace track, which could be seen from every passing train. As the story goes, Wolfe allowed Jeff to manage all saloon and gambling concessions outside the entrance to the arena, which was set to open on August 24, 1895. Presumably Wolfe would receive a share of the profits.

The bullfights were expected to draw about 50,000 spectators over the course of three days. Ten bulls and several matadors were coming up from Mexico for a first class demonstration. The first series of mishaps occurred at the US/Mexico border. Apparently Wolfe did not know that the US policy allowed no Mexican bulls into the country. As replacements, in haste he purchased ten Hereford bulls in the US.

The Colorado Humane Society sought legal means to have the event banned, and sensing a controversy, newspapers took up the debate over whether bull fighting should be allowed in the US. Newly elected governor Albert McIntyre sided with the Humane Society but refrained from taking official action.

Next, city and county governments squared off. On the first day of the fights, county sheriffs were ordered to arrest Wolfe. The city of Gillette, eager to see the bullfights proceed, had its police officers place Wolfe under protective custody to prevent his removal. However, for Wolfe, a more serious problem was at hand. Surprisingly, even with all the free publicity, only about 3000 tickets were sold, a fraction of the predicted sales. One reason for the relatively low attendance was the pre-sale of counterfeit tickets. Additionally, it is possible that many would-be patrons had drunk up or gambled away their ticket money in Jeff's makeshift saloons and gaming tents. Jeff may also have been involved in selling forged tickets.

The bullfighting itself was a failure. The cause was largely due to the bulls Wolfe had purchased. He may not have realized that the nature of the average Hereford bull tends toward shyness. Thus the contest between the placid bovines and the experienced matadors became a wholesale slaughter. One bull had to be shot dead to end its suffering, which did not please the crowd.

---

[1] Ltr fr Henry Edwards to Jefferson R. Smith II, 08/16/1895. Geri Murphy col.
[2] *Denver Evening Post* 08/14/1895, p. 4.

Then before the third day, El Paso County deputy sheriffs shut down the event and succeeded in arresting Wolfe. In addition to losing $8,000 of his $10,000 investment, he paid $82.50 in fines. Upon release, Wolfe left the state and never returned.[1] If indeed Jeff had been there, he alone profited from the adventure.

Possibly Jeff had not been part of the affair. Letters, all postmarked Mexico and saved by Jeff, indicate he may have been in Mexico before, during, and after the bullfights (August 24-26), and as late as August 29, 1895.[2] Then again, he may have received these letters upon a return to Mexico after the Gillette adventure.

Perry Clay had been a captain in the Denver police department under Chief John Stone. After the Colorado Supreme Court decided the issues of the City Hall War in April 1894, Clay, Stone and fifty-six other officers under the old fire and police board "voluntarily retired." Clay and Stone then became co-editors of a newspaper titled *The Patriot*, which addressed Republican interests. Judge Lindsey in his retrospective exposé of Denver corruption, titled *The Beast* (1910), wrote that "Perry Clay's *Review*..., long supported by the advertisements of saloons, dives and brothels, is now disguised as a temperance advocate; and in this disguise, delivered free, from door to door..., it carries the arguments of the corporations to the homes of 'the church element.'"[3] Not surprising, then, is it to find a very friendly letter to Jeff from Clay. He was responding to an August 1895 letter from Jeff in Mexico. Clay mentions the Gillette bullfights but not as a witness. Had he been one, there might have been confirmation of Jeff's being present or not.

Friend Smith:

Your agreeable and welcome letter was [undecipherable] in on me like an irrelevant dream. Had you addressed me from "The Paradise of the Peril"[4] I would not have been surprised that to know of you, again in the land of dreamy eyed Caribbean, on [one?] home of the bull fighter. Speaking of bull fighting, we are now having it here in Colo. – at Gillett, in the Cripple Creek district. They are now enjoying the national sport of Spain of whom the great Ferdinand & Isabella were patrons, and the excitement of which has thrilled the great and good earth for many hundreds of years. The people you mention are not doing well, gambling in Denver. There's some going on, but it is very quiet! Several have started in Colfax again, and may do well unless sons of bitches graft them to death. Of con men, you know that the past two years has developed and produced an unexampled crop of the lowest most disreputable, knocking sons of bastards that the world ever knew. We are doing very well with our paper, much to the annoyance of some of your friends and ours. We expect to live and be flourishing when they are in hell. If

---

[1] Sprague, pp. 177-187.

[2] Ltr fr Henry Oliver to Jefferson R. Smith II, 08/29/1895. Jefferson R. "Little Randy" Smith col.

[3] Mardos, & Lindsey, p. 183. Clay became Arapahoe under sheriff in 1896 and served until 1898, at which time he purchased a half interest in the *Denver Examiner*. For his loyal service to Republicans, in the words of Judge Lindsey, Clay has since been politically rewarded with the clerkship of the district Court. The last record of his service thus far seen shows him still serving as a "Clerk of district Court" in a Colorado Court of Appeals action in 1913. (*Pacific Reporter*, vol. 133, p. 420)

[4] *"The Paradise of the Peril"*: Clay may be referring to Cuba.

I was sure this would reach you, I would write fully. Stomas[1] sends his regards to you, while I ask you to believe me, ever your friend and well wishes.

> Perry A. Clay[2]

Clay's letter sketches a bleak picture of Denver's gambling atmosphere as well as hinting at the power changes occurring there.

Four days later, on August 29, 1895, H. Oliver, confidence man and supplier of buncoing props, writes to "Col Jeff R. Smith" on National hotel, Minneapolis, stationary. He is responding to a letter from Jeff in Mexico City at the Hotel del Jardin.

> Friend Jeff.
>
> I was surprised to have your letter forwarded to me today. I suppose you want some more of that Homestake Stock, you said U.S. Bonds [—] did you mean the Homestake Stock or not [—] let me know at once so I can get you more.[3] I will have to go to Chicago to get it. I have been here for 4 weeks and this is even worse than St. Louis outside of having a chance to play faro. I tell you gambling is a thing of the past, for a few years anyway and there must be some other way invented of getting the coin. I intend going to Atlanta, Ga. To run club rooms thru the Cotton Expo.... Now Jeff I want you to give me a chance to make some money as I certainly am capable of making it or of helping you in any scheme you may have on. I wish you would correspond with me regularly and I will keep you advised of anything you wish. My wife is going to move from our present flat in Chicago and send your letters to 338 State st., "Social Saloon" as they will reach me from there. ... If you want any other kind of flash bonds or paper[4] give me the description and I will try and get it for you.
>
> Yours very truly   H. Oliver[5]

Letters to Jeff indicate that gambling all over was suffering from reform movements.

Bascomb now faced two charges of assault with intent to kill. His bondsmen, having grown weary of their legal responsibility, surrendered Bascomb to the court. He was jailed on August 17, 1895 and remained incarcerated until his trial on August 20.[6] The Hughes trials of the brothers were postponed as was the forfeiture of Jeff's bond. He promised a return to Denver by September 1 for a trial date of September 12.[7] Jeff received a "Liar's License," a joke certificate dated August 26, made out to "Jeff Randolph" humorously signed by "U. R. A. Mother."[8] Possibly it came from bondholder

---

[1] Stomas: this is D. P. Stomas, someone whom both Jeff and Clay knew in Denver. Jeff lent him $250 while in Spokane, Oct 1896. (Item 27, author's col)

[2] Ltr fr Perry A. Clay to Jefferson R. Smith II, 08/25/1895. Geri Murphy col.

[3] *Homstake Stock ... get you more:* Oliver apparently deals in counterfeit stocks and bonds.

[4] *flash bonds or paper:* flash, adj 3, 2: Counterfeit, not genuine, sham. (*OED*) Jeff may have obtained a supply of such documents, which turn up with his arrest later on in New Orleans.

[5] Ltr fr H. Oliver to Jefferson R. Smith II, 08/29/1895. Jefferson R. "Little Randy" Smith col.

[6] *RMN* 08/18/1895, p. 4.

[7] *RMN* 08/20/1895, p. 8; *RMN* 08/21/1895, p. 8; & *Denver Evening Post*, 08/21/1895, p. 8.

[8] Liar's License, 08/26/1895. Geri Murphy col.

Watrous, who typed a last letter of hope to Jeff on August 27, 1895. It was addressed to Jeff R. Smith, Esq., La. Calle de la Independecia, Mexico, Care Hotel Del Jardin.

> Friend Jeff: -
>
> Your letter of the 21st at hand. It is an old saying that "it's darkest just before dawn" and I sincerely hope that this may prove true in your case. I am confident that it will be only a question of a short time, with your capabilities and rustling qualities, before you will get hold of some money; and a man certainly deserves it who will go into that country after it.
>
> I saw Judge Belford yesterday, and he said that when it was necessary for you to be here that he would let me know; so if you will keep me posted as to your whereabouts from time to time [I] will telegraph you.
>
> Gambling is still entirely closed here, and I am afraid it will be sometime before they [people on the inside] succeed in getting things shaped up [put into shape so that gambling can resume?]. ...
>
> I saw "Yank" to-day and showed him your letter. He said that he had received a letter from you a few days ago, and that he would write you to-day and send you papers.
>
> Your friends all join me in best wishes.
>
> Yours truly,   Mart H. Watrous[1]

On September 11, 1895, someone named "Joe" in Monterey, using stationary from the Hotel Hidalgo, wrote to Jeff at the Jardin Hotel in Mexico City.

> Friend Jeff,
>
> Come here on first train or as soon as you can. As there is a chance to do some big business. You must not delay, as you know delays are dangerous. Bring a good man with you.
>
> Yours,   Joe[2]

It is not known if Jeff went to Monterey. If he did, he should not have as he was expected to appear in a Denver court the next day.

On September 12, 1895, Jeff again did not appear in court. The district attorney asked for forfeit of his bonds, and the request was granted. Jeff's bondsmen, Mart Watrous and Frank Barrow, were out $2,000. Jeff was now a fugitive.

At trial on September 16,[3] Bascomb was found guilty of assault to commit great bodily harm. The *News* eagerly reported details of the trial.

HIS LAST ROUNDUP.
Bascom Smith Convicted of Assaulting
John J. Hughes with Intent to Kill on the West Side.

Bascom Smith, brother of Jeff Smith, was tried yesterday upon indictments charging him with assault to kill and assault to do great bodily injury. The complaining witness in each case is John J. Hughes, of the Arcade saloon.

---

[1] Typed ltr fr Mart H. Watrous to Jefferson R. Smith II, 08/27/1895. On stationary of the Mescal Milling Company. Jefferson R. "Little Randy" Smith col.

[2] Ltr fr Joe [?], to Jefferson R. Smith II, 09/11/1895, Geri Murphy col.

[3] *Denver Evening Post* 09/12/1895, p. 2.

The testimony of the witnesses recalled to mind the memorable night of April 20, last, when the desperate Smith brothers, each armed with two revolvers, paraded the down town streets, searching for their enemies and intending to settle with blood the many imagined grievances that suggested themselves to their beer-fuddled brains. The chief actor in this performance was not present in court yesterday. Jeff Smith's bond has been forfeited and Jeff is now far away from Denver.

Dr. H. H. Martin informed the jury regarding the injuries sustained by Hughes. Other witnesses examined by the prosecution were Bartender Cooley, Officer Kimmel, Harry Lyon, Ball, a colored porter, and a man named Jackson. The substance of the evidence was that the Smiths were drunk on the night of the trouble and that each was in a vicious mood.

Bascom Smith was the only witness for the defense, although his attorney, John Deweese, made use of the testimony of witnesses for the state. It was claimed by the defense that there was cause for the assault and that Hughes was struck in the general scrimmage that followed the first blows....

Shortly after 5 o'clock the jury retired and at 5:30 o'clock a verdict of guilty of assault to commit great bodily harm was returned.[1]

On September 20, 1895, Bascomb was sentenced to a year in the county jail.[2] A few days later the *News* marked the small victory against the controlling Republican gang.

The Hon. Bascom Smith has been sent to the county jail for a year. If he will lay his delicate ear to the cold and cruel wall next Thursday he will hear the gang convention chanting in mournful numbers the sad strains of that hymn, "We Shall Meet but We Shall Miss Him."[3] The removal of Bascom from active participation in the campaign this fall is a serious blow to the party in which he has been so long recognized as a power.[4]

Within a month's time Jeff returned to the US, stopping in Dallas where he was arrested for vagrancy. A telegram issued to Denver police chief Goulding was shown to a *Denver Times* reporter who wrote a news story.

JEFF SMITH IS A VAG
That Is How the Famous "Soapy" Is Booked in Dallas, Texas.
FALL OF THE KING OF BUNCO STEERERS.
The Man With a Past an Inmate Of a "Lone Star State" Prison Cell.

Dallas, Texas, Oct. 12. Quackery Soapy Smith inmate vagrancy enclosure. Arnold, Sheriff. This is a copy of a telegram which was received by Chief of Police Goulding this morning. It is in cipher and to be translated it signifies:

That Jefferson Randolph Smith, alias Soapy Smith; once king of Colorado bunco steerers and past aide-de-camp to President Diaz of Mexico;

---

[1] *RMN*, 09/17/1895, p. 7.
[2] *RMN*, 09/21/1895, p. 2, & *Denver Evening Post*, 09/21/1895, p. 7.
[3] song titled "The Vacant Chair (We Shall Meet But We Shall Miss Him)." Popular song since 1862.
[4] *RMN*, 09/22/1895, p. 12.

once captain general of Cuban armies in America and past custodian of the only original ossified man, has fallen so low in the estimation of the authorities of the highly moral town of Dallas as to be arrested and charged with being a common vagrant. This is all very pathetic but the translation of the telegram does not altogether lack humor, for Chief Goulding is asked if he wants the only Soapy. Goulding hastened to reply that he did not want him and he hoped that he would continue to be an ornament to Dallas. At first it was decided that Soapy might be used as an attraction in the Mountain and Plain festival, but now he can only be admired at a distance.

There is, however, a criminal charge against Smith in connection with the brutal assault made upon John J. Hughes several months ago, but Bascomb Smith, the main actor in this affair, is now in jail and repentant, and the county authorities hardly believe that it is worth while to spend money to bring Jeff Smith back. He is such a pleasant figure at a distance of say, 600 miles. When Smith left town he deserted his bondsmen.... The day for the trial arrived, the defendant did not appear and the bond was declared forfeited. ...

Soapy Smith is a name familiar to nearly every man in Colorado. He is probably the last of his race—a relic of by-gone days, when desperate men armed with a brace of huge pistols, were allowed to trample on the laws of county and state.

Soapy Smith appreciated the fact several years ago that Denver had become too civilized for him, and, after various escapades in Mexico and attempts to ... aid Cuban patriots, he settled down in Texas.

There was a time Smith would say ... to be a Texan was equivalent to having four aces in every jackpot—but ... Texas has become civilized like Colorado, Oklahoma and other western territories and states. Bad men are no longer wanted, and they are treated with little ceremony. Soapy Smith was no doubt drawn to Dallas to witness the great fistic carnival,[1] and now he will have to receive returns from the great fight behind bars.

"It was day all day in daytime, and there was no night in Creede," was coined by Smith and put into verse by Cy Warman.[2]

"It's night all night in the night time, and there is no day in Dallas," is his latest refrain.[3]

It is not surprising that Goulding did not want Jeff returned. He was a reminder to the city in general and to the chief in particular that Jeff had opened closed doors in Jennie Rogers' brothel and found Chief Goulding there.

---

[1] *fistic carnival*: the proposed heavyweight title fight between James J. Corbett and Robert Fitzsimmons, scheduled for October 31, 1895, in Dallas. Populist Governor Culberson called a special session of legislature and succeeded in passing a law that made prizefighting a felony. The fight was cancelled.

[2] The 2-line refrain fr Warman's 2-stanza, 1892 poem reads, "It's day all day, in the day-time, / And there is no night in Creede."

[3] *Denver Times* 10/12/1895, & *RMN*, 10/13/1895, p. 4.

Jeff did not remain long in the Dallas jail. Once released, he visited his father and sisters, who were still residing in the state. He told them of Bascomb's imprisonment and had them write the Colorado governor to ask for Bascomb's release. Jeff also visited Galveston and Houston, most likely searching for a new home location. As late as mid October 1895, Henry Edwards was forwarding Jeff's Denver mail to Texas.[1]

Soon after Bascomb's conviction, the Denver confidence men again flourished. According to the *News* of October 17, 1895, the two main bunco gangs were now directed by Ed Chase and Lou Blonger. With Jeff out of the city, the Chase and Blonger factions began vying for overall control. Members of the Soap Gang still resided in Denver, and while some remained loyal to Jeff as they managed his few remaining interests and property within the city, others began working under different bosses, apparently switching sides. More than likely, though, they were just trying not to be squeezed out altogether. James Thornton appeared to be with the Blonger Gang but later also worked with W. H. Jackson when he worked for Chase.[2] Jackson eventually reunited with Jeff and others in Alaska.[3] Thornton stayed in Denver where in December 1898 he was arrested for running a gambling house owned by the Blongers at 1644 Larimer Street.[4] Chase eventually ceded his throne to the Blongers.

In late October Jeff ventured to Spokane, Washington. From there he wired Henry Edwards to pack up McGinty, the petrified man, and ship him to the Spokane suburb of Hillyard by Pacific Express (cash due on delivery). Jeff had sold a half-interest in McGinty for $250 to one R. B. Ennis. The two men rented an empty storeroom on Riverside Avenue and posted a large sign informing the public that the celebrated petrified man was to be exhibited. Jeff left Spokane without paying the delivery charge, and Ennis did not have the $31 to take possession, so McGinty remained in storage at the Pacific Express Company.[5] Ennis waited for Jeff to return, and when he did not, Ennis contacted local authorities. The *Spokesman-Review* covered his plight.

> Mayor McMurray [of Denver] has received a letter from the mayor of Hillyard, Wash., inquiring as to the social standing of one Jefferson Randolph Smith, also as to said Smith's code of morals, and to what extent the gentleman's word is as good as a gold bond.
>
> The mayor ... referred the inquiries to the police authorities.
>
> It seems that Denver's "illustrated" citizen,[6] J. Sapolio Smith, has once more disposed of a half interest in his far-famed petrified man. According to the letter, Smith is in Spokane, and a few days ago he met a man named Ennis..., a machinist in the employ of the Great Northern [Railroad] shops. Ennis, it appears, had money, and Smith had none. Now Smith has money and Ennis has none. ... [Smith] wired to his "dodger," Yankee Hank, to send it by the Pacific Express C. O. D. [And now there is] a bill of $31 on it.... Up to

---

[1] Ltr fr Mary E. Smith to Hi Ki and Henry Edwards, 10/15/1895, item 43, author's col.

[2] *RMN*, 02/09/1897, p. 2.

[3] *RMN*, 10/17/1895, p. 4, & *RMN*, 10/18/1895, p. 2.

[4] *Denver Evening Post* 12/23/1898, p. 7.

[5] *Spokesman-Review* 10/22/1895.

[6] *illustrated citizen*: "illustrious" citizen?

date the petrified man is still in the possession of the Pacific Express Company. Ennis is out $250 and Smith is out of town.

The famous corpse has many a time been the salvation of Jeff Smith. It has been sold a hundred times, but each time there is a long string on it, and Smith always gets it back. The corpse first made its name in Colorado history at the time of the Creede boom. Smith and his pals procured it in New Mexico and sneaked it into Creede and buried it in a lonely spot on Bachelor mountain. One day amidst great excitement a prospector discovered it. It was dug up and ... became a nine days wonder. When the first novelty wore away, Jeff put up a job to have some of the "gang" steal the corpse and a mock battle in which a thousand pistol shots played a prominent part told the story of how Jeff Smith rescued the body of the petrified man from the ghouls. In the heyday of its fame and prosperity the corpse came to Denver and was exhibited on Seventeenth street, and it attracted large crowds and made much money for "Sapolio."

Just how Smith will again become the possessor of the stone man is not known, but it is safe to say that ere many moons it will again repose in a box, to be shipped to some distant city, and again sold at a neat figure.

The man is supposed to have come from the "petrified man factory" of a Merced, Cal., man, who a few years ago indulged in the profitable business of making petrified men to order. One petrified man is quite a curiosity, but the manufacturer was so industrious that the market was soon overstocked, and there are but few who are able to make their stone man bring such excellent figures as J. Sapolio Smith.[1]

On November 3, 12 days later, Edwards wrote from Denver's Ingersol Club:

Friend Jeff:

Yours of Oct. 30th at hand, and was pleased to hear from you. Have just returned from a visit to Ba's [Bascomb's]. His case came up at west side court yesterday, but was postponed until next Saturday, the 9th inst. He does not wish to be tried for this case till his present term has been served. Has employed Messrs. Hilton & Walker as counsel, and they think they will be able to have it put off, if they are not successful in having this case quashed altogether. He is looking well, and weighs 159 lbs., but is very anxious to regain his liberty. Received a letter from Bowers, who promised to send him fifty dollars, but the money had not come. He must have money in order to have the lawyers work for him. I hope you will use good horse sense and judgment, and not get into the same box he is in. Things are in a worse shape than when you were here. It is no use trying to live here, unless you have money as people are talking about what is due them, and say they must have it. Hard times is the cry. There does not seem to be any money in this election. Plenty of double crossing going on. Baker says that some people

---

[1] *Spokesman-Review* 10/22/1895. As presented in a previous chapter, the author believes McGinty now comfortably and somewhat famously resides at the Ye Olde Curiosity Shop in Seattle, Washington.

will not be able to square their accounts, and will stay closed. He told me that he had written you. Watrous said he would write you, and hopes you will make some money before you come back. With kind regards and best wishes, as ever

Yank.[1]

The following day Watrous did write to "Jeff R. Smith, Esq., Dallas, Texas":

Friend Jeff:

Yours of October 30th at hand. Every thing quiet here and there are being no inquiries made about you, although my impression is that they expect you to return soon after the election or when it is convenient for you to do so. In fact they do not seem to be at all anxious in regard to the matter; therefore, I would advise you to try and get hold of a little money to fetch with you when you come. As you know, that's what makes the mare go. I understand that the grand jury found an indictment against Bascom for assault with intent to murder. I think his trial comes up very soon.

To-morrow is election and it looks as if the Republican ticket will be elected.

Gambling is open here at the present time but it is hard to say whether it will remain so long. Money is very scarce and business very quiet.

I think some of going to Cripple Creek this month, but a letter addressed here will always reach me. With best wishes, I remain.

Yours truly   Mart H. Watrous.[2]

Watrous does not mention the $2,000 bond that he and Frank Barrow had forfeited for $1,000 each. Presumed is that, somehow, Jeff repaid the men for their loss.

In mid November Jeff made a daring return to Denver. Among reasons for coming, one was to secure a loan. On November 18, 1895, he borrowed $1,725 from the First National Bank of Denver,[3] equivalent to $51,200[4] today. With his siblings in need, he likely used some of it to help them. Jeff also owed attorneys and perhaps forfeited bond money to Watrous and Barrow. Jeff might have had a silent co-signer or an undisclosed asset, but he also must have had a solid record with the bank. It knew of his recent trials and that he might never return to Denver.

The day Jeff took out the loan, Bascomb wrote to him. Jeff had not risked arrest by visiting his brother in Jail, so probably Bascomb did not know Jeff was in Denver.

Dear Bro Jeff,

I thought I would write to you. I have written several times but never got any answer. I just received a letter from Emmie and Eva. It is too bad Bob, Emmie's husband, has lost his mind and is in jail at Belton and our sisters are in a very bad fix. If I was out or ever get out, I could help them to get along some way. For Christ's sake, if you can go there, or can do anything for them, do it, for they are in a bad fix. If I had any money I would send it to

[1] Jones, Robert, p. 380

[2] Jones, Robert, p. 380.

[3] Andrews, "Real," p. 38. Shows a copy of a check found in a trunk in Skagway, Alaska.

[4] http://www.halfill.com/inflation.html accesses 03/17/2008.

them if it was the last I had, but I have not got any money, not one cent and am in a very bad fix myself. But I may get out some time and if I do I will go to hard labor rather see my own blood suffer for anything. I have learned a very dear lesson, but I think it will be a good thing for me. I saw Mr. [Perry A.] Clay and he said he got a telegram from you. He said he would do anything he could to get me out but you know how that is. That may [be] the last of it. The Grand Jury found another bill against me. I will go out to plead not guilty to assault and intent to kill. I don't know how I will come out. Everything goes wrong and it would not surprise me if I get in the pen before they get through with me. Old Dennison was fired out of office a day or two ago. He won't have the pleasure of prosecuting me anyway. I said to Clay that I heard you was coming back. He said he would be glad to see you again. The Grand Jury found a bill against Sam Blonger for obtaining stolen goods. It was about a check I got him to get the money... when you had the joint over Solmon's Pawn shop. The check was for six hundred dollars. Suppose you remember it. Bowers and Jackson won it, so they want me for a witness. What would you do if you was around. I don't know of any more to write so I will close.

From your Bro Bascom Smith   County jail[1]

Bascomb apparently did not know Jeff had already been to see their sisters in Texas.

The check to which Bascomb refers concerns Sam Blonger, John Bowers, and W. H. Jackson and their swindling S. H. Wolcott of Catskill, New Mexico, out of a check for $600. On January 31, 1894, the con occurred over Solmon's pawn shop in one of Jeff's gambling rooms. According to the *Denver Evening Post*, Wolcott was steered there by Bowers. That day, Bascomb, on behalf of Jeff, visited the Blonger saloon at 1644 Larimer and asked Sam to cash the check. Blonger declined but directed Bascomb to Edward Quentin at the State National bank. He had been in the habit of cashing these kinds of checks for a fee of $20.

Bascomb's dilemma was that if he turned state's evidence, he might help himself but break loyalty with his friends. In his letter Bascomb asked Jeff what he would do in the same situation, but Jeff's answer, if he made one, is unknown. At the time of the swindle, Lou and Sam Blonger had a working relationship with the Smith brothers, but that may have soured after the attack on Hughes. At trial, bank employee Quentin testified that Blonger had guaranteed the check, but as Blonger had no other connection to the check, he was found not guilty of wrong doing nearly two years after the fact, on January 7, 1896.[2]

During the two-to-three weeks preceding the Blonger trial, District Attorney Greeley Whitford and his officers visited Bascomb in the county jail at least a half-dozen times, urging him to turn state's evidence against Sam Blonger. According to Bascomb, Whitford enticed him into trading state's evidence against Blonger for immediate release from his one-year prison sentence, dismissal of cases against him, and appointment to a position on the city police force.

---

[1] Ltr fr Bascomb Smith to Jefferson R. Smith II, 11/18/1895. Geri Murphy col. The author has replaced errors for readability.
[2] *Denver Evening Post* 01/08/1896.

The day preceding the Blonger trial, Bascomb was due in court on the second charge of assault. The district attorney's office asked for a continuance because two prosecution witnesses were out of town. Bascomb's attorney, Judge Hilton, objected and read to the court a prepared statement of charges against Whitford, as Bascomb expected that a Nolle Prosequi[1] would be entered and that he would be acquitted of all charges. The District Attorney did not deny encouraging Bascomb to testify against Blonger but denied a deal. However, later in private with the court judge, Whitford all but admitted a deal, saying that with Bascomb's cooperation, "a radical change" would take place at once. Bascomb's trial continuance was granted until January 27, 1896.[2] Some deal making may have taken place as no record of a trial outcome could be found and no additional prison time was added to Bascomb's sentence. Not known is what Jeff did with the bank loan or what he did in Denver during this time.

Jeff might have attempted to purchase a Galveston gambling house. A bunco friend wrote to Jeff in Houston in December 1895 about working there.

> Friend, Jeff.
>
> I heard you are still in Houston. Have just came over from Paris [Texas] but done no good. Are you going to get that Galveston House? I see that the big chief of Dallas got quite a little personal in the Denver Mercury. Jeff if you get a house anywhere outside of Houston and can use me I will come.
>
> Yours Truly   Fred Brownsill
> c/o Cabinet Saloon, Fort Worth[3]

Clearly Fred Brownsill had some sort of trouble that he wanted to avoid in Houston. Jeff was about to acquire the same desire. In December 1895,

> A little Affair in Houston, Texas, Caused Jeff to Bid His Country Good-Bye for a While—His Hand Seen in the Death of a Houston Gambler—Had Put Up a Great Scheme to Break Up a Green Baize Monopoly.
>
> Irrepressible Colonel Jefferson Randolph Smith, some time of Denver, late of Houston, Texas, and now attached to the army of President Diaz of the Mexican republic, has become disgusted with the United States, according to a report that reached this city yesterday, and is a self-made exile in a foreign land. "Soapy" [was] mixed up in a shooting scrape in J. O. Dalton's gambling house..., and for the present he feels more at ease among the dons and duennas than among the plain citizens of this country.
>
> This is so because if he remained within requisition reach of the Lone Star state authorities he might be made defendant in a conspiracy-to-murder trial. On the 5th of December the colonel and W. R. Riddle, familiarly known as "Dick" Riddle, went into J. O. Dalton's saloon and gambling house in Houston with the avowed purpose, so it is said, of the killing of Dalton. That gambler stood in the way of a plan "Soapy" had devised to control the gambling business in the Texas town he had chosen for his home. Riddle

---

[1] *Nolle Prosequi* (no-lay pro-say-kwee): n. Latin for "we shall no longer prosecute." 1. A procedure by which the Attorney General may terminate criminal proceedings. (*QED*)

[2] *Denver Evening Post* 01/08/1896, & *RMN*, 01/09/1896.

[3] Ltr fr Fred Brownsill to Jefferson R. Smith II, 12/03/1895. Geri Murphy col.

acted the part of hired villain in the tragedy that ensued, but being slow with a gun he met the fate that was intended for J. O. Dalton. His first bullet missed "Soapy" Smith's rival and in the exchange Dalton killed him.

After the shooting the story of "Soapy's part in the job was brought to light and that former distinguished citizen of Denver moved out hastily. It was reported here yesterday that he is now wearing the military uniform of President Diaz. The same information came in a letter to C. D. [Charles] Pearson of the Arcade saloon, so it is said. ...

The story of the Preliminaries to the killing of Riddle is interesting. Here and there ... can be seen ... Colonel Smith's characteristic enterprise and Richelieuan[1] diplomacy. Several months ago "Soapy" left Denver, forced out by rival bunco men and political activity. He sampled a number of southern cities and finally pitched his tent in Houston. There he found a "good thing," but it happened to be another fellow's. J. O. Dalton ... held a monopoly of the "green baize" business in the town, and grass was short for outsiders.

"Soapy" Smith was only a few days in Houston before he realized that gambling there was a close corporation industry, with Dalton in charge. Being a man of resource, he [Jeff] was not discouraged by this fact, and it was not long before he found a following ready to back him in any kind of effort to shake Dalton's supremacy. A look over the situation convinced the new combine that the Dalton gang could not be got rid of by ordinary methods, so extraordinary ones were resorted to.

One of "Soapy's" men was to get up a quarrel with the Denver gambler's rival, and if Dalton caught a fatal bullet in the fight—why, then, there would be a dead boss gambler and room for a bright man in his place.

"Dick" Riddle, a dead shot and game sport, volunteered to polish off the man who was non persona grata to Col. Smith. It was all to be done on the level—no murder about it—but Dalton to be given an even break for his life. The programme was carried out in the following order:

Accompanied by Col. Smith, Riddle, revolver in hand, walked into Dalton's gambling house on the evening of December 5. They descried J. O. Dalton superintending a faro table, and when within easy range of him "Soapy" stepped aside, shouting to Dalton: "Look out there, John; you'll get winged!" ...

Dalton looked up, saw the pistol in Riddle's hand, and ducking, he reached for his own weapon. Riddle pulled the first trigger, his bullet going wide, and a second or two later Dalton fired. His aim was true. The bullet hit Colonel Smith's partner inside the right shoulder at the juncture of the breast and neck, deflecting downward, passing through the lung tissue, and lodged

---

[1] *Richelieuan*: after the ways of Cardinal Richelieu (1585-1642), "the greatest French statesman of the 17th century." ... "'I venture on nothing without first thinking it out; but once decided, I go straight to my point, overthrow or cut down whatever stands in my way, and finally cover it all up with my cardinal's red robe.' Such are the words put into Richelieu's mouth; and whether he said them or not, they represent fairly enough his deliberation, resolution, and cold severity." (*Encyclopedia Britannica*, 1892.)

in the abdominal cavity. "It's all off," remarked "Soapy," and he [and apparently Riddle] walked out of Dalton's house, satisfied that there was no gambling throne for him in Houston.

At 11:50 o'clock next day "Dick" Riddle died of his wounds. Dalton surrendered himself to the police, was charged with murder and released on $500 bonds by Recorder Hill. On December 7 an inquest held on the remains of Riddle resulted in a verdict declaring his death to be a case of justifiable homicide and exonerating J. O. Dalton from all blame in connection with it.

Some one had "leaked" the story of the plot entered into to oust the boss gambler from power by killing him. Presumably Col. Smith suspected some such thing for he disappeared from Houston on the night of the shooting.

Before leaving, it is said that he wrote the letter to C. O. [Charles] Pearson setting forth..., "My native land, good-night," to the United States, and intended to take service under the banner of Mexican President Diaz. A man from Houston, who visited police headquarters yesterday, said that the information contained in the letter to Mr. Pearson was common gossip among Jeff Smith's associates in the Texas town.

In contrast to this unidentified clipping, apparently from a Denver paper, is the *Galveston Daily News*. It published vastly different witness accounts at the hearing.

The first witness was Max Bowman. He said it was yesterday between 1 and 2 o'clock p.m. he was standing over [in] the saloon and heard some parties coming up the stairs and looked; it was Dick Riddle and some other; Dalton said to him: "Hello Dick, old fellow," Dick said, "You — of a —, you don't like me, and I'll kill you," and he struck Dalton; it was in Dalton's place of business; Riddle had a pistol in his hand; it was a deadly weapon; he struck Dalton; I never saw Dalton carry a pistol in my life; Dalton is a much smaller man than Riddle; I don't know much after I heard the shots fired; I then left.

Ed Carpenter said: "I live in Corsicana, but am now in town for awhile. Between 1 and 2 o'clock in the afternoon yesterday I was in that place. I heard a noise and Dalton came in hurriedly, and Riddle was behind him, and said to Dalton, 'You — of —, you don't like me, do you.' Riddle had his gun out and I saw them come together; I heard the shot and saw Dalton turn and get his gun. He went behind the table; I didn't know why at that time he went behind the table; I didn't see but one shot fired: Riddle looked mad; after the first shot I retired: Riddle had a little one-barrel pistol in his hand; it happened over a saloon in this city yesterday."

S. C. Anderson: "I am stopping in town at 526 Louisiana street; may be here sometime; yesterday between 1 and 2 p.m. Dalton was in his place and I heard a noise and looked and saw a man struggling with him; the other fellow said, 'You don't like me, you — of —.' They were stooping over and one shot was fired, and the other fellow (Riddle) fell at the first shot, and Dalton shot again: I know that the other fellow fired the first shot; it happened in Houston; the room is about 8 x 12 feet: Mr. Riddle fired the first shot; it was upstairs; there was no other way of exit or ingress."

Charles Davis said: "I was in the club room over the saloon yesterday; — don't know the time; I heard some men come up stairs and looked and one said to Dalton, 'You don't like me, you — of —,' and struck at Dalton with a pistol in his hand and knocked him up against the stove; Dalton and he ... were struggling; I heard shots, several of them; don't know who shot them; Smith came down stairs leading Riddle, and at the post Riddle sank down and some one said to him, 'Dick, are you hurt?' 'No, I am only killed,' he answered."

Mr. Williford said; "I was in the place and heard a noise up stairs and saw a Negro porter run down and I started up to see what was the trouble and heard some one say, 'you — of —,' and heard the shooting, but didn't go further up; I had no business there then; I saw three men going up stairs arm-in-arm; two of them were McDade and Riddle; I heard them make no remarks going up; I didn't know the other man; I heard six or seven shots fired; I am certain of that."

Jerry Lucas, colored, said: "I am porter in the Mint saloon, and I saw yesterday three gentlemen coming up stairs abreast, and I was coming down stairs and was about half way when I heard the shots, and then made the rest of the way down in quick time."

Said Mr. Bowman, recalled: "Yes, there were six or seven shots fired; I saw Riddle sitting in the door and two men take him up and carry him up the street; one of these was Jeff Smith."

Here the attorney for the defense stated that the defendant would admit that Riddle was dead, and that Dalton did the shooting that caused his death.

Officer Cliff Ellison: "I know Dick Riddle and also the defendant...; I talked with Riddle and he was going to run Dalton out of the town; it was twenty-five minutes before the shooting; Riddle is dead; I saw the wounds; there were two—one in the right shoulder and the other in the right groin...."[1]

Despite their absence from witness accounts, words of warning from Jeff to Dalton probably uttered. They were to disassociate himself from Riddle. Had Riddle been successful, what Jeff said no doubt would have been used in his own defense. Jeff, though, apparently warned Dalton of the impending danger too soon, and Dalton was quicker and more accurate than Riddle anticipated. The unknown newspaper clipping recycled the old news of Jeff's association with President Diaz. That was for color as the affair of the private army in Mexico had been terminated in 1894.

If Jeff went to Mexico, he did not stay long. About December 20, 1895, in New Orleans, he took a suite of rooms on Royal Street and paid for them in advance. On December 28, the *Daily Picayune* reported Jeff, Edward Keeley, William White, alias "Holland," and Charles Meary, alias "Major," had swindled J. R. (or R. P.) Landry of out of $34 in a poker game. Landry complained to the police who arrested the four and sent them before Judge Aucoin for violating the city's ordinance against gambling. The

---

[1] *Galveston Daily News* 12/06/1895, p. 3.

charge labeled the group "dangerous and suspicious characters." Jeff was listed as "J. Randolph, alias Smith." The *Picayune* story was unusually detailed:

> On Keeley was found $180 in confederate money, $37 in United States currency and a gold watch and chain. White had a check for $7000 on the German National Bank of Denver, Colo., signed by Jackson Shorts. On Meary was found one deposit check No. 12,427, dated June 12, 1894, signed by J. Otis Stevens & Co., for $1000, and $30 in currency. Besides a gold watch and chain and $5 found on Randolph, there were found several blank checks on every bank in the city.[1]

The judge gave them a choice of a $25 fine each or 30 days in jail. The fines were paid.[2] The *Denver Republican* reported that Jeff was not able to pay his fine and was in jail.[3] A week later Jeff wrote to the *News* from St. Louis to deny that he was in jail.[4]

Jeff had gone to St. Louis to be with his wife and children, and while there he received a letter from attorney Belford.

> My dear sir,
>
> Your letter read. If you will keep sober and avoid saloons, my advice is for you to come here and at once. You must disconnect yourself from Bascomb.
>
> Truly yours,   James B. Belford[5]

Bascomb's second trial on the charge of assault to kill for the near shooting of Louis Petit back in July 1895 was about to take place, and if Belford was to be successful in helping Jeff return to Denver, he would have to distance himself from his brother, something he did not wish to do. In letters to Bascomb and his sisters, Jeff mapped out a publicity campaign for getting Bascomb out of jail.

As planned, Bascomb wrote to the editors of all the Denver newspapers and asked them to print a response from Jeff in which he claimed to be tired of being a fugitive from justice and roaming the country that came with it. He wanted to return to Denver and stand trial but that he needed a bond to keep him from being jailed upon arrival.[6] At the same time, Bascomb filed a petition for pardon with Governor McIntyre, promising to reform and leave Denver forever. The Smith sisters, Eva and Emmie, also wrote to the governor from Temple, Texas, on January 15, 1896.

> To Governor McIntyre:
>
> Dear Sir—We write you in regard to Bascom Smith, who is now in jail in Denver, and, if you would only pardon him, [it] could and would be of great help to his sisters. We have been very unfortunate, indeed. Away from all

---

[1] *Daily Picayune* 12/28/1895, p. 3.

[2] *Daily Picayune* 12/28/1895, p. 3, & an unknown New Orleans, La, newspaper clipping saved by Jefferson R. Smith II, 12/28/1895, Jefferson R. "Little Randy" Smith col.

[3] *Denver Republican* 01/20/1896.

[4] *RMN*, 01/25/1896, p. 2.

[5] Ltr fr James B. Belford to Jefferson R. Smith II, 01/13/1896. Jefferson R. "Little Randy" Smith col.

[6] Unknown Denver newspaper clipping saved by Jefferson R. Smith II. "1896" is written at the top. Believed to be late January, early February. Jefferson R. "Little Randy" Smith col.

relatives, bereft of husband and father, and brother in jail. Now, if you will only pardon him you will have long gratitude and prayers of

Eva K. Light

Emma L. Gardner.

P. S. —We are in destitute circumstances, and don't know what to do.[1]

The plan was probably to time Jeff's arrival in Denver with the release of Bascomb so the brothers could flee the state together. Jeff must have known that if he left as planned, he probably could never again return without risking arrest. Amazingly, however, well into 1897 Jeff was still registered as a citizen of Denver, residing at 1421 S. Fifteenth Street.[2] Perhaps until the end, Jeff harbored hopes of returning

About 2 p.m. on January 30, 1896, a Union Pacific train eased to a stop about two miles north of Denver at Fortieth Street. A little freight would be unloaded and such few passengers who resided thereabout would disembark. Ten-to-twelve "fierce looking men, and a woman" were seated together, and one left their number. He stepped from the train, walked quickly to a waiting closed carriage, and had no sooner entered than it jolted off. The others in the group remained on the train for the short ride into Union Station, observed by Special Union Pacific agent Scott. Ordinarily he might have continued surveillance of this rough-looking crew, but instead he left the train immediately to use the telephone. His call was to the police to report that the fugitive Jeff Smith was somewhere in Denver. Jeff had learned he had no chance of his securing a bond to protect him from arrest in Denver, so he took an enormous risk and came back as unobtrusively as possible.[3]

After notifying the sheriff and district attorney, Police Chief Farrington dispatched eleven detectives and as many policemen to comb the streets for bunco men who might give up a lead on Jeff's location. The search was not successful although Jeff remained in Denver all day. At 3 p.m. officer Kimmel met Jeff entering the Brown Palace Hotel, one of Denver's best. "'Won't you come in and have a drink,'" Jeff reportedly said to Kimmel. The officer declined, and Jeff had gone on his way. Kimmel later claimed that he was unaware Jeff had returned and that his superiors were searching for him.[4]

No one admitted to having seen Jeff after that. Unable to locate him, the police came to question whether Jeff had been in the city at all. He quickly learned that the police knew of his presence and were looking for him, and with a bold exception, kept to unfrequented ways. Later that night, Jeff and his entourage boarded a train for Cripple Creek.[5] The *News* reported that Cripple Creek authorities "declared that Jeff Smith could not live in that city." The paper also made a prediction: "If they intend to keep the threat, lively times may follow."[6]

---

[1] *Denver Evening Post*, 01/29/1896; *RMN*, 01/30/1896, p. 8; & *Denver Republican*, 01/30/1896.

[2] Denver City Directory 1897, p. 1000.

[3] *RMN*, 01/25/1896, p. 2. As late as 01/25/1896 Jeff was still in St. Louis.

[4] Unknown Denver newspaper clipping saved by Jefferson R. Smith II. "1896" is written at the top. Believed to be late January, early February. Jefferson R. "Little Randy" Smith col.

[5] *RMN*, 01/30/1896, p. 6, & *Denver Republican*, 01/30/1896.

[6] *RMN* 01/30/1896.

Why Jeff came to Denver for part of one day is unknown. Why were ten men and a woman traveling with him? Stories circulated that they were going into business at Cripple Creek. Others felt they were on their way to the "fistic carnival" soon to occur at the Mexican border near El Paso.[1] Still others thought they were on their way to Southern California to establish a gambling empire.[2] Could Jeff have been attempting to arrange Bascomb's freedom? Amid the flurry of rumor, Jeff shocked the city when, on February 3, 1896, he appeared in a Denver courtroom.

The Famous Jefferson Returns to Stand Trial.

Colonel Jefferson R. Smith created a sensation by appearing in the West Side court this morning and tendering bonds for his appearance at trial for assault to kill. Colonel Smith was dressed in a fashionably cut suit, and still wore the whiskers, which have given him such a distinguished appearance. He was accompanied by Patrick Burns, an Elyria saloon keeper, who went on his bond.

Smith is charged with an assault to kill John J. Hughes, of the Arcade. He and his brother Bascom accumulated a couple of jags several months ago and then pounded up Hughes with six-shooters. Bascom Smith is now serving twelve months in the county jail for the offense.

It is said that Jeff Smith has been in the city since last week and that he took his time to deliver himself up to the West Side court. He is well provided with money, having a prodigious roll and $20 packages of silver dollars. He was a visitor to the First National bank this morning.[3]

In the same issue of the *Denver Evening Post* on another page, the police were quoted as stating that the Jeff's reappearance was nothing but a hoax, a trick to cover some other play.[4] Not recorded is what happened in court or with authorities about charges against Jeff. An agreement of some kind must have been reached, however, because Jeff was not arrested and allowed back in Denver several more times. Apparently, though, the agreement did not include Jeff's permanent return to the city.

Understandably, historians believe that Jeff went to Cripple Creek to attempt a takeover of its underworld. There were signs of his being there, and not alone. "Big Ed" Burns, probably one of the "ten fierce men" traveling with Jeff, was arrested in Cripple Creek for vagrancy. However, Jeff's interest was not in the established mining center but in Victor, a booming mining community to the southeast. Discovering that Jeff was in town and to ascertain whether

---

[1] *fistic carnival* : "the boxing carnival to take place in El Paso" included bouts on Feb 11, 12, & 13, ending on the 14th with Peter Maher vs. Robert Fitzsimmons. Jeff might have planned on attending. Bat Masterson was there in charge of 100 men managing the fighters' train, but a dozen Texas Rangers were also there to prevent the fight from occurring on Texas soil. Mexican soldiers were also present, across the border. Maher had eye trouble that postponed the bout until Feb 21. Just over the border in Mexico that afternoon, Fitzsimmons knocked out the Irishman in the 1st round. (*New Era*, 01/01/1896, p. 6; *Lincoln Evening News* 02/10/1896, p. 2, & *Oakland Tribune* EXTRA 02/21/1896, p. 1)

[2] *Denver Republican* 01/30/1896.

[3] *Denver Evening Post*, 02/03/1896, p. 1.

[4] *Denver Evening Post* 02/03/1896, p. 5.

colonel Smith was to referee tonight's fight, the reporter lied his way [in]to the hotel Victor ... and requested ... an interview. Mr. Smith stated that he had nothing for publication, but that the fight would be on the square, in fact that "if there was no fight there would be no decision." The gentleman said that he was in Victor on money business, and that eastern parties were interested with him. In speaking of the outlook, the colonel said that he thought the whole district was coming to the front ... [and] that no better place for the investor of money could be found. "Soapy" called himself non-partisan, and those who attend the mill[1] tonight will see a fight and to the finish.[2]

This information comes from a damaged newspaper clipping that Jeff saved. Nothing is known about the "money business," how long he was in Victor, or the boxing match.

Jeff was back in Denver on February 19, 1896, to visit The First National Bank of Denver. He borrowed $1,750 — $25 more than in November 1895. Records show that seven month's later, Jeff paid back the amount in full.[3] On the day Jeff took out the loan, he was leaning against a building's stone pillar on the corner of Larimer and Sixteenth streets when Parson Uzzell walked by. The parson gasped and extended his hand in friendship. The following day's *Evening Post* reported their conversation.

"I never drink — no more." Said Soapy.

"The Lord be praised," said the parson.

"Where you hail from?" asked Soapy.

"The vineyard of the Lord!" said the parson.

"Your breath don't show it." Remarked the pseudo gambler. "Dear parson, you must excuse me, I'm in a fearful hurry — mining business. I'll call on you at the tabernacle in the very near future. Goodbye. May the Lord bless you. Amen." And Soapy hurried up the street.[4]

Uzzell continued the story by telling the reporter how in 1892 in Creede, Jeff had helped him after he was robbed. Unknown is if Jeff called on the parson during that week in Denver. Before leaving for St. Louis, Jeff did visit the offices of *The Road*.

Our esteemed friend, Col. Sapolio Smyth [sic] called on us one day this week to inform us that he still considered Denver his home and proposed to remain here. He says all the stories published about his making gunplay in Texas, shipwrecked on the coast of Cuba, etc., are lies. Said he:

"I have been living quietly in St Louis trying to restore to health a sick member of my family. I wish the public would please remember I have a good wife and five children[5] and that I would willingly turn my hand to anything to earn an honest living. But will anybody give me a chance? That is the question. I consider bunco steering more honorable than the life led by the average politician and I think it infinitely more honorable than wrecking savings banks and stealing the taxpayers' money by putting it in the hands of

---

[1] *mill* : "—4. A fight, esp. with the fists: fr ca. 1819, 1860, 1890." (Partridge, *Slang*)

[2] Damaged undated newspaper clipping found in Soapy's scrapbook. Item 132, author's col.

[3] IOU for $1750, 02/19/1896 marked "Paid," 09/15/1896, item 28, author's col.

[4] *Denver Evening Post*, 02/20/1896, p. 4.

[5] There were only three children. Was Jeff exaggerating or was the newspaper wrong in its reporting?

such men as have disgraced this state [by] wrecking national banks. I would like to open a cigar store or a chop house[1] but if I did, every political heeler in the town with a pull would be on my neck. I don't know what to do, but something I must and will, for I don't propose to let my family go hungry."

There is something pathetic about the plea Soapy makes for an existence and there is more truth than poetry in all he says. That he has robbed people right and left ... he himself does not deny, but the most of his plunder went to the coffers of big church-going thieves whose "pull" at the court house and city hall protected him. One good thing can be said of Jeff— he never robbed the poor. He always laid for big game and usually landed it. In his game of robbery, it took tact, skill, courage and nerve. The people who are robbing the city, county and state through vicious legislation are never arrested and their robbery requires nothing but cash to buy votes. It is a distinction without a difference—unless it can be in favor of Jeff.[2]

Jeff came again to Denver in March, and the *Denver Times* recorded that when he left, McGinty, the petrified man, went with him. McGinty had been on display in a Larimer shop but was removed and crated for travel. The paper reported Jeff said he planned to tour the petrified man through Southern states.[3] Another account, already discussed, claimed McGinty had been sold five months before.

No city allowed Jeff to linger for long. While a fugitive, Jeff ran an ineffective defense from beyond the jurisdiction of the courts, and though he seemed to be making progress in it, in his absence, underworld power shifted to others. Now he seemed to have nowhere to go. In his wandering, searching for an opening, the next big mineral rush, Jeff ran afoul of the law and of every kingpin bunco boss in every city in which he tried to set up. They all knew him or knew of him and had successfully stifled his attempts to move into their territory. There was only one direction he had not explored: the far Northwest, and beyond that, "The Last Frontier."

Chapter 17
Swindling the Great Northwest

Gold here in big quantities, all country talking up here.

Jefferson R. Smith II
Letter to Mary, May 10, 1896

Appearing in American newspapers for years had been dispatches about gold strikes far to the north, in Canada and a place called Alaska. Few knew much about these far flung expanses, but Jeff had been keeping an eye on that vast far corner. As one whose name was known from the Midwest to Louisiana and throughout the West, Jeff did not stand a chance of keeping a low profile against the tall reputation, and not just in underworld and law circles. In Chicago in 1896, a Dr. M. A. Holmes gave a talk

---

[1] *chop house*: chop-house, "A restaurant, especially one of poor quality." (*OED*, 1690, *DARE*, 1806-1940)
[2] *The Road*, 02/29/1896
[3] *Denver Times*, 03/03/1896.

titled "Soapy, a Famous Gambler."[1] So Jeff had an eye out for any place of promise where he stood a chance of not being shadowed by his reputation. Spokane was such a place for a time, a smaller Denver, central to mineral riches in the region, but the speed of communications and the ease of travel, even way out in Western Washington, made him not anonymous but known, and known well, all too quickly.

But if a big gold rush occurred in the North, not the Northwest, but a thousand miles or more to the north, in the District of Alaska or the Yukon District of the Canadian Northwest Territories,[2] there again could be a place, if arrival were early enough, in which he could not just prosper but make it big for a long while.

On March 19, 1896, in Gillette, Jeff was arrested and held on unspecified charges. He claimed he was there on behalf of a friend, looking for a contractor who was building a home close by.[3] According to a letter from a Robert J. Byrne, Jeff was still in town on Sunday March 29 when Jeff lent him twenty dollars. Byrne returned the loan by post from Denver the following Tuesday along with words of thanks.[4]

Some of Bascomb's trouble with women over the years had found its way into print. In April 1892, for assaulting Bascomb, Eva Brown, "a fairy," was arrested.[5] The next report, appearing March 6, 1895, was grief stained. Additionally, it helped keep Denver's door barred to Jeff.

> Jessie Smith, mistress of Bascom Smith, brother of the notorious "Soapy," committed suicide this morning by taking morphine. She had a few minutes before received a note from the county jail from Smith, who is a prisoner there, in which he had upbraided her for some supposed neglect.[6]

She was Jessie Wise, "who for many years past has led a life of shame on Market street." Known as "Smith" to many as she had been with Bascomb, according to one newspaper, for 6 years, Jessie was his 25-year-old mistress. "She had a few minutes before received a note from the county jail from Smith, in which he had upbraided her for some supposed neglect."[7] Visiting Bascomb almost daily, she brought "delicacies" to ease his prison life. On March 4 she did not have the money to purchase the food he liked and so did not come to the jail that day. Angered, Bascomb penned a letter, which was found next to her body at 2114 Market Street. Bascomb wrote,

> Dear Jessie—What is the matter with you? Why did you not come over today? Be sure and come to-morrow, for I want you to go somewhere for me, so don't fail to come. I don't know why you don't come, and I guess I will have

---

[1] *Daily Inter Ocean*, unknown month and day, 1896, clipping saved by Jefferson R. Smith II, author's col.

[2] *District of Alaska ... Northwest Territories*: Alaska was a "District" fr 1884 to 1912 at which time it was designated a "Territory." Fr the Northwest Territories (1880), Canada carved out Yukon District in 1897.

[3] *RMN*, 03/20/1896, p. 7.

[4] Ltr fr Robert J. Byrne to Jefferson R. Smith II, 03/31/1896. Jones, 12/1907, p. 336.

[5] *RMN*, 04/23/1892, p. 5. *"a fairy"*: "A debauched ... woman, especially when drunk" (Partridge, *Slang*). May also refer to an opium smoker. The little lamp used in smoking is called "the fairy" (Partridge, *Underworld*).

[6] *Aspen Times* 03/07/1896, p. 1.

[7] A Belle Wise was charged with keeping a lewd house, *RMN*, 10/15/1886, p. 2. "Jessie Wise raised merry cain in a hack for three hours. Then she abandoned the vehicle and kept up the circus in the street until arrested by Officer McDermont for drunkenness and disturbance." (*RMN*, 08/20/1891, p. 3.)

to have you brought over day after to-morrow and put in jail. I can see that you don't keep straight. Don't fail to come to-morrow, for I expect to get out Saturday, and I want you to go and do something for me. I have got a lot to tell you, so come by 2 o'clock if you can. Yours,   Dear Bass.[1]

The county jailer permitted Bascomb to visit the morgue where the remains of his mistress lay. "The meeting between the impassioned lover and the silent figure before him was most affecting. Unnerved by the tragedy, Smith wept like a little child."[2]

In his note to Jessie, Bascomb wrote that he expected to be freed on Saturday. Perhaps he was expecting the pardon for which he had applied.[3] He was not released, however. Another high-level appeal to free Bascomb may have occurred. Two newspaper accounts have Jeff calling on Colorado Governor McIntyre to plead Bascomb's case. Jeff reportedly said, "This is pretty tough, for a row with a cheap gambler, whose only injury was a black eye. Any other man than my brother would very probably have gotten off with a fine or nominal punishment."[4] These reports appear on April 6 and 7, 1896, so the event may have occurred sometime between April 1 and 5. The story is somewhat in question, though, because Jeff is believed to have been in Seattle on April 1, booking passage for an April 6 or 7 sailing to Alaska. The close timing, however, does not rule out Jeff's having met with the governor.

Nor was this the last attempt to help Bascomb out of prison. The *Denver Evening Post* reported on April 17, 1896, that a Mrs. Julia Killam and a number of other women advocated for Bascomb's release. Nothing is known of the lady or the other women. Conceivably, Bascomb or Jeff could have persuaded or induced them to undertake the effort. Even the district attorney came to agree that Bascomb should be pardoned, but the governor took no action.[5]

During the uncertain period of early 1896, Jeff traveled to the west coast. An undocumented story tells of his arrest in San Francisco on an unknown charge.[6] At the tail end of March Jeff is thought to have been in Seattle where he is believed to have booked passage to Alaska on April 1, 1896, aboard the *General Canby*.[7] This vessel was owned by Homer Pennock, after whom the town Homer in Cook Inlet is named. Della Murray Banks and her husband went to Cook Inlet in April aboard the *Excelsior* as members of the Pennock gold mining party. In 1945, Banks wrote of her experiences that spring of 1896, and she describes the *General Canby*,

> a tugboat Pennock had bought in Tacoma.... He had had it remodeled to carry both passengers and freight, although little could be said for the accommodations. [When "she arrived early in May,] She brought supplies, some men from Denver, and an Englishman....[8]

One of the men from Denver most certainly was Jeff Smith.

[1] *Aspen Weekly Times* 03/07/1896, p. 1; *Denver Evening Post* 03/06/1896, p. 2; & *RMN*, 03/07/1896, p. 2.
[2] *Aspen Weekly Times* 03/07/1896, p. 1; *Denver Evening Post* 03/06/1896, p. 2; & *RMN*, 03/07/1896, p. 2.
[3] *Denver Evening Post*, 02/24/1896, p. 2.
[4] *Denver Evening Post*, 04/06/1896, p. 2, & *RMN*, 04/07/1896, p. 7.
[5] *Denver Evening Post*, 04/17/1896.
[6] Robertson & Harris, p. 154.
[7] *Seattle Times* 03/31/1896.
[8] Banks, p. 39.

The *General Canby* docked in Juneau in mid April. That would put Jeff's sailing date about a week before, on April 8 or 9. Jeff stayed a few days in the relatively settled and growing mining capital of southeast Alaska. Here gold had been discovered near tide water in 1880 by Joe Juneau and Richard Harris, who traced it several miles up into Silver Bow Basin above Juneau. By 1896, placer and hard rock mining had become a mainstay and was steadily expanding. The largest mines were the Mexican, Ready Bouillon, Alaska Juneau, and Treadwell across the channel on Douglas Island.[1] Jeff took to the streets to attract miners, their families, and merchants with his prize package soap sell. Even this far north, though, there was sufficient law to stop his trade with an arrest and prosecution. Both made the pages of Juneau's *Alaska Searchlight.*

John Rudolph was brought before Commissioner Mellen on the 24th charged with gambling. His mode of procedure was what is termed by the "profesh" as "flim-flaming the guys"—or he would pretend to wrap up ten and twenty dollar bills with a cake of soap and sell it for five or ten dollars as the case might be. Juneau has a number of "guys" who are eager to bite at the scheme, and had it not been that an officer took the "flim-flamer" there is no doubt he would have reaped a rich harvest. And yet they say there are no suckers in Alaska.[2]

Jeff tore the page from the small newspaper and mailed it to Mary in St. Louis. At the top, he wrote in pencil, "The money I wrapped up was borrowed. I have nothing. Fined $25.00 cost and stopped from work." This is Jeff's last recorded use of the prize soap racket although it seems unlikely he would have given it up entirely. Jeff used the name "John Rudolph" to keep from being recognized. The soap racket and many other cons required shills and steerers. Jeff mentions no others with him, but it can be assumed that a few Soap Gang members were traveling with him. The clipping Jeff sent contained two passages about miners going to Cook Inlet and into the interior of Alaska where gold had been found and a rush was believed imminent.

When it came time for the *General Canby* to continue its journey north, someone in Juneau recognized Jeff and sent word to the *Rocky Mountain News*[3] that he had been seen boarding the steamer with prospecting miners, destination Cook Inlet, where the city of Anchorage would be built.

Russian trappers and explorers in 1849 had reported gold being found on the Kenai Peninsula, South of Cook Inlet. Other relatively big finds occurred in 1861, 1870, and 1872.[4] From 1880 to 1895, 18 significant finds are recorded, 3 in Canada (Cassiar Bar, 1884; Stewart River, 1885; Miller Creek, 1891) and 15 in Alaska in places with names like Rampart (1882), Fortymile (1886), Yaktaga (1893), and Girdwood (1895).[5] Gold seekers in Alaska during this period entered through Cook

---

[1] Davis, Trevor, p. 28.

[2] *Alaska Searchlight* 04/1896, p. 15. Item 15, author's col. Jefferson R. Smith III kept "John" but changed "Rudolph" back to "Randolph" in naming the author's father John Randolph Smith.

[3] *RMN* 05/06/1896, p.7.

[4] DeRoux, p. 34.

[5] Littlefield.

Inlet. No diminutive slip or portage, this Inlet is about 50 miles across at the mouth, 150 miles long, and then branches into two arms, each of about 25 miles.

Venturing into the little-known areas of Alaska was dangerous. To be encountered were bogs, freezing temperatures, storms, deeply crevassed glaciers, and abundant but also aggressive wildlife—bear, moose. Just getting there on coastal waterways was dangerous. Ships had captains who were unfamiliar with frequent violent storms and heaving seas, fluctuations of tides of from 25 to 30 feet (even 40 in a tidal bore), reefs, and rocky outlays, many of which were uncharted. Jeff indirectly affirmed these conditions in a short letter to Mary.

> May 10, 1896
>> Cooks Inlett near Coal Bay, 600 miles from Juneau on board the Gen.
>> Canby 2500 miles north of San Francisco.
> Dear Mollie
>> Am well, will be to my destination tomorrow if nothing goes wrong. Have had a hell of a trip. You can write to Resurection Creek, Cooks Inlett, Alaska. Have no time to write now as we hail a steamer bound for San Francisco to mail this. Have heard no word from you since I left Denver.
>> Yours Jeff   Love to all[1]

Jeff had spent the last ten days aboard the *General Canby*, and it could well have been "a hell of a trip" as crossing the Gulf of Alaska can be notoriously rough. The only way he could get a letter to his wife was to include it with mail handed off to a south-bound steamer or packet ship like the *Dora*, either in a port or, less likely, while underway in usually heavy seas.

Jeff made one more entry on this letter to Mary. Turning the letter sideways, he scrawled, "Gold here in big quantities [−] all country talking up here-" Indeed, in the relatively immediate vicinity had been 3 large strikes in 1894-95 (Prince William Sound, Girdwood, and Nelchina). Gold had already been discovered in 1890 in Hope (up Resurrection Creek 2 miles) and Sunrise, up the coast about 12 miles and then up Six-Mile Creek about 2 miles, and those areas had not yet been fully prospected. Further up the Resurrection Creek valley, extending some 24 miles to interior creeks, showed promise. Finds here would not match the immensity of George Carmack's that summer, 400 miles (as the crow flies) to the east in Canada, but they were all substantial.[2] In such an immense country, with 18 substantial and some large finds since 1880, it naturally followed that the country would be talking up gold.

---

[1] Ltr fr Jefferson R. Smith II to Mary E. Smith, 05/10/1896, item 11, author's col. Presented as written. *near Coal Bay*: Coal bay lay "on the northern shore of Kachemak bay inside the Homer spit." *Resurrection Creek* is a tributary to Turnagain Arm, Cook Inlet. Jeff was likely given this location as a place where mail could be sent; "the camp" so named at that time lay about 2 miles from tide water up the creek valley between mountains rising to about 1500 feet. Early on, prospectors call the location Hope City (*Geographic*). *600 miles from Juneau*: a modern map shows the distance to be on the order of 825 miles; the distance north from San Francisco, depending on the route, is about 2500 miles.

[2] *400 miles (as the crow flies)*: the closest established route to Carmack's site of discovery was 1,600 miles from Jeff's location, back to Skagway in Southeast Alaska, over the Chilkoot trail, and 600 miles down lakes and the Yukon River to the Klondike River and then into the adjacent interior creeks.

Other ships arriving at the location that would become Homer and having to wait for the late breakup of the Inlet ice were the steamers *Utopia* and *Lakme*, containing together, as Mrs. Banks tells us, "four hundred men headed for the Turnagain Arm district. They camped on the spit...."[1] During this wait at some point, Mrs. Banks met Jeff. He "was a dark-haired, medium-sized, mild-mannered man," she wrote of him forty-nine years later, "and I was quite surprised after my introduction to him to learn that he was the notorious Denver confidence man."[2]

Jeff also wrote to Bascomb while apparently camped on the spit, as a couple of details from his letter match Mrs. Banks' remembrance. This letter made the press:

> Dear Bas. —Well I am 600 or 700 miles more on my way. Over 400 men are camped here on ice waiting for a thaw. You can write here but I may never get the letter. Have done no business yet. I expect to look for gold with the balance of the guys. Regards to all the people in the jail. I don't suppose the governor has done anything for you. Take it easy; the world was not made in a day.
>
> Your brother.   Jeff.[3]

Jeff seems to have reached the head of Cook Inlet the following day. A letter to a friend from there, apparently dated May 11, came to publication over a month later.

Col. Sapolio Smith Heard From.

> A citizen of Greeley received a postal card Saturday from the notorious "Soapy Smith." The card was written from "Cook's Inlet, Six Mile Creek-Alaska,"[4] and dated May 1 [11?]. An attaché of the Tribune made the following extract: "This place is 2,500 miles north of San Francisco, 1,500 miles from a railroad or telegraph office and 600 miles to the nearest post office. There are about 2,000 men in camp looking for placer claims and we think we have it. Only one woman in camp. I expect to be in Denver next fall in time to aid my brother redeemers.[5]   Your friend,"
>
> "Jeff Smith."[6]

Mrs. Banks met that "one woman" to whom Jeff referred. "She was red-headed, and attractive in a bold way. She and her husband were running a restaurant at Hope."[7]

Jeff had left on the *Utopia* when Mrs. Banks came up on Homer Pennock's *General Canby*, returning on a supply trip. She describes conditions that Jeff had seen and experienced two to three weeks before. The setting must have convinced Jeff that

---

[1] Banks, p. 38.

[2] Banks, pp. 38-39.

[3] *Denver Evening Post* 06/10/1896, p. 6.

[4] *Six Mile Creek-Alaska*: from tidewater to camp lay about 2 miles up the creek in a narrow valley below mountains rising to 3,000+ feet. Named Sunrise in 1899 (*Geographic*).

[5] *redeemers*: employed in a political sense, not religious, to signify one who engages in redemption, "3.a. The action of freeing, delivering, or restoring in some way" (*OED*). The religious connotation is likely intended to carry sarcasm for moral views against gambling and other behaviors branded as vices by certain Populists.

[6] *Greeley Tribune* 06/18/1896, p. 8.

[7] Banks, p. 41. Paragraphs later in the narrative, Mrs. Banks wrote, "As for the red-head, her husband shot and killed her in Dawson a few years later."

the region was not right, at least not yet, for his kind of operation. Mrs. Banks wrote how the twenty-five-mile long, narrow Turnagain Arm

> can be entered only at high tide, for at low tide it is nothing but mud flats. A bar at the entrance causes the water to pile up and go in a large bore, sweeping everything before it. Woe betide the small craft caught on the mud flats by the ebb tide, since the incoming flood tide will swamp her.

On her first day there, Mrs. Banks visited the camp and came back to the ship for the night. Too excited to sleep, she went up to the deck and

> was standing at the rail when the mate yelled suddenly, "Hold on there!" Came a creak and a groan, and the world seemed to slither out from under me. The Canby keeled over on her side in a mud ravine, and hung there tilted at a forty-five degree angle.
>
> Just the tide going out, that was all! ... Luckily, I happened to be on the upper side of the ship, else I'd have landed in the mud and perhaps underneath the hull! The whole surface of the Arm is intersected by these ravines, some shallow and some twenty-five or thirty feet deep.
>
> We had tied up to the bank, fastening a cable to a tree. The weight of the Canby was too much, and had uprooted the tree. By four-thirty [a.m.] I was back "up town," having been hauled ashore by the mate over an improvised gangplank.[1]

No, here was not yet the right place or time for Jeff. He did not expect to find another Denver, where naive and willing customers disembarked their conveyance and flowed up to the feet of Jeff's associates. But better had to be done than this. So it seems likely Jeff was ready to return almost at once.

The first available ship into the area, arriving ahead of the returning *General Canby*, was the steamship *Utopia*. It had dropped anchor at the head of Cook Inlet, disembarked its chartered cargo and hundred passengers bound for the Susitna River region, likely looped to the Sunrise-Hope beach sites to take on passengers, and returned south. Jeff boarded and paid passage to Seattle, but had he known what lay ahead, he might have waited for another ship.

First, the *Utopia* was missing its master. He was Captain Dynamite Johnny A. O'Brien, an explosive Irishman from Cork who had gone to sea at 15, become a captain at 25, fought pirates, and who at the slightest infraction, battled insubordinates with his will and sometimes his fists. The nickname "Dynamite" seems to have grown out of his quickness to detonate when faced with dereliction of duty or disrespect for his station aboard ship. Once in Nagasaki "he had disposed of two larger opponents in less than thirty seconds." They had not liked O'Brien's tossing overboard their "two bottles of vile-looking liquor."[2]

Switching from the Puget Sound-China run in the early 1880s, Captain Johnny, as he was often called, skippered steamships along the far North American coast. By 1896, he knew the waters from Seattle up through the "Inside Passage" to Canadian

[1] Banks, pp. 40-41.
[2] Dalby, pp. 90-91.

ports and on to Ketchikan, Petersburg, Sitka, Juneau, and Dyea (near future Skaguay at the head of Lynn Canal), Prince William Sound and Cook Inlet, the Aleutians and Dutch Harbor, the Bering Sea and St. Michael to the east and Nome to the west.[1] But all his thirty years at sea and his hail health at age forty-five could not keep him upright when his appendix burst.

What happened next varies in different versions, but the one told in Milton A. Dalby's *The Sea Saga of Dynamite Johnny O'Brien* (1933) carries the clearest ring of veracity. To prepare for this biography, Dalby met regularly with O'Brien in his eightieth year in the months before his death in August 1931. Dalby also had access to the captain's diary as well as other records.[2] The biography is unsentimental and often realistically hard-hitting in its clear-cut accounts of brutal first mates, murderous cooks, loves, murders, numerous fights, and men perishing in storm-whipped seas. The following sequence is based primarily on Dalby's biography of O'Brien.

When the *Utopia* reached lower Cook Inlet, it encountered a heavy outflow of ice and so "came to anchorage in Seldovia Bay, with two other vessels, until the ice cleared...." It was here that O'Brien suddenly collapsed in terrific pain. Dalby recounts how since no doctor had been aboard, a hurried survey

> of the anchored ships revealed a fortune-seeking miner who had once been a surgeon. He shook his head dolefully over O'Brien after a hasty examination.
>
> "About a thousand to one shot to pull through," he told the *Utopia's* hovering officers. O'Brien was partially conscious and heard the remark. "I'd operate if I had any tools but I haven't any," the ex-doctor went on.
>
> O'Brien painfully roused himself. "Doc, I heard you say I had a long chance to pull through. I'm a sport and God knows I don't want to die in this damn place. Go ahead; all you need is a knife and a pair of scissors."

These tools were "honed to razor sharpness and roughly sterilized." Since the ship was "rolling somewhat," men carried the captain ashore in the bitter cold to "a rough hut," slipping "repeatedly on the icy ground." Here he was "placed on three planks laid over two packing boxes" for the operation. O'Brien said he did not know what anesthetic was used but that "it was at least partially effective." He said he was conscious at times during the operation "but felt no marked pain."[3]

"O'Brien lay in a bunk in the hut for several days," recuperating. In the meantime, ice had cleared sufficiently to allow ships up the Inlet, and the *Utopia's* 100 restless miners wanted to join them. So somewhat behind the other vessels, the *Utopia* also made the 200-mile voyage to the head of Cook Inlet but without its ailing captain. He was left in a better accommodation than the hut, "the galley of some ill-fated ship," as Mrs. Banks described it, but she and her husband had transformed it into their home.

---

[1] Dalby, p. 176.

[2] Dalby often refers to interviews with and diary accounts of Captain O'Brien, e.g., interview, p. 43, and diary, p. 50. Also included are numerous photographs and a shipmaster's ticket, 1890, p. 210.

[3] Dalby, pp. 176-77.

> The Captain of the utopia was ill, apparently from appendicitis. We had
> been moved hastily from the derelict galley ... so as to give over our quarters
> to the sick man, they being the quietest and the cleanest spot.[1]

When Jeff returned to Coal Bay at the Homer Spit on the *Utopia*, the captain was
returned to his cabin to continue his recuperation.

At some point, Jeff learned that "The vessel's coal supply ran very low, the
bunkers were scraped almost bare," apparently a Seattle provisioning error. Coal was
to be had, just not the $300 ($9,372 today) for a sufficient supply of it.[2] So, from his
bunk aboard ship, O'Brien ordered coal dug "from the bottom of the bay" where "a
straggling coal formation was uncovered" when the tide was out. Over the next two
days, ten tons were taken into the *Utopia's* coal bunker. Bitter cold made the wet,
back-breaking work even worse, and on the third day, the crew refused to dig any
more. Such was the state of things when

> A knock came on O'Brien's door and a bearded man entered. He smiled.
> "When do you sail, skipper?" he asked.
>
> "No coal, mister, and no money to buy any with, dammit...."
>
> Out came a bulky wad of crumpled bills. "How much do you need?"
> O'Brien told him, and three hundred dollars were quickly peeled off.
>
> Coal was purchased, and during the three days ... before the *Utopia* was
> ready to sail the bearded stranger spent much time in O'Brien's cabin. His
> name? "Just Smith, skipper!" He ... tended O'Brien as carefully as a nurse
> might. He kept the cabin clean and brought O'Brien such food delicacies as
> could be found. If O'Brien wondered a little about the two heavy-framed
> revolvers which nestled under either armpit he said nothing, for they were
> none of his business.
>
> The *Utopia* sailed and O'Brien slipped into uneasy sleep with the
> welcome pounding of her engines in his ears. But when he awoke—it was
> some eight hours later, the cabin clock disclosed—all was quiet and the ship
> seemed anchored. He called feebly but none heard him, and Smith was not
> about. He gripped a stout water glass and hurled it through a cabin window
> and out onto the deck. The mate came running in response to the crash.
>
> O'Brien demanded the cause of the ship's halting and was told that the
> purchased coal was of wretched quality, and that the engineers refused to
> burn any more of it. "So we've decided to anchor here under the lee of Cape
> Elizabeth[3] and wait for a supply of good coal," the mate explained. "The crew
> agrees with the engineers," he added.
>
> O'Brien exploded..., and then had to grip his side in mad pain. "Why in
> the devil wasn't I told about this? Who do you think is master of this ship?"
>
> "We didn't think you were in any condition to handle the ship, captain."
>
> "Call Smith, the bearded passenger, at once," O'Brien demanded.

---

[1] Banks, pp. 10 & 38.

[2] Tom's Inflation Calculator.

[3] *Cape Elizabeth*: this island lies at the eastern mouth of Cook Inlet (*Geographic*).

"Dynamite Johnny explained to Smith the situation and asked if he might borrow his guns—the damn crew was mutinous and needed a little convincing that the "old man" knew what was best for 'em!

An unusual fifteen minutes followed on deck. O'Brien was aided to a deck chair by Smith and, with a revolver in each hand, called the crew to file by him and swear that they would help get the ship into Juneau where an ample supply of good coal would be obtained. He stormed at the engineers particularly and shook the weapons at them threateningly.

"If that coal was good enough to steam on for six or seven hours it's good enough to get into Juneau with," he shouted. "By the Rock of Cashel[1] I want steam up in this old tub and I want it in a hurry! Understand me?"

And apparently he was understood for the *Utopia* crossed the Gulf of Alaska without trouble and refueled in Juneau. When the vessel reached Seattle it was a pale O'Brien who went ashore on the arm of his friend Smith. He had weighed nearly 160 pounds when the *Utopia* had sailed...; he was reduced to 120 when he came ashore. He spent the next month in a hospital.

Dalby reported from O'Brien that members of the Soap Gang

frequently traveled on O'Brien's ships although their identity was not always known. O'Brien found Smith kind-hearted and generous; indeed such was his reputation in Skagway outside of purely business hours! He returned ... [to Skagway] with O'Brien on the *Utopia* [in 1897] and, at O'Brien's urgent plea, kept a tight grip on his gang of cut-throats and gamblers during the trip north.[2]

On June 2, 1896, after an absence of two months, the steamer *Utopia* docked in Seattle.[3] Upon disembarking, Jeff registered at the Butler hotel on Second and James streets, listing his residence as Denver.[4] For the next two months Jeff traveled between Seattle and Spokane Falls.

That August from Spokane, Jeff attempted to defraud J. Hugh Bauerlein of a mining claim. Jeff sent Bauerlein of the Denver Stock & Mine Exchange an unsigned check for $2,500. Hoped for, probably, was that the claim papers and unsigned check would be returned for signature. Bauerlein responded on his letterhead stationary:

Newlin's Gulch Gold Camp, Aug 13, 1896

Mr. Jeff R. Smith
        Spokane, Washington
My dear sir,
Your registered letter with enclosed check for $2500 (not signed) received. I herewith return the same to you for your signature.
A big strike has just been made in the adjoining property owned by the "Covade" company.

---

1 *Rock of Cashel*: ancient Irish fortress symbolizing "foreign brutality, spiritual strength, and Irish courage" (Cashel).
2 Dalby, pp. 178-79.
3 *Seattle Times* 06/02/1896.
4 *Seattle Times* 06/03/1896.

I am pleased to learn that you have been so successful. I am sure you will be well pleased with the investment you are making with me.

Yours truly   J. Hugh Bauerlein

You can return it to me signed, to room 4 "Denver Stock & Mine Exchange" care of "Covade Mountain Gold Mining, Tunnel & Milling Company."[1]

The printed check was on the "First National Bank, Denver Col." It seems doubtful that Jeff had funds there. The check might have been one in his possession from when he had an account there, or it could have been acquired from the "flash bonds and paper" supplied by H. Oliver.[2] How or if Jeff pursued the matter is unknown.

Who from the Soap Gang was with Jeff during this period is not known. Bowers and "Red" Gibson were not with him. They had been arrested in Colorado Springs on August 7, 1896, for vagrancy, fined $50 plus costs, and given two hours to leave town. The police made them leave their trade tools, including false whiskers, saps, and revolvers.[3] Bowers' name is not mentioned again in Denver until March 1897 when his wife Isabel divorced him for lack of support while he in his own defense questioned the paternity of their second child.[4] At some point Bowers joined Jeff, perhaps about this time. Arrested in Denver for vagrancy, Gibson and Soap Gang member J. C. Leary were *asked* to leave the city. Both men eventually joined Jeff in Skaguay.[5]

In July 1896, Mary penned a two-page letter to her husband on Denver Ingersoll Club stationary.[6] She crossed out Denver, Colo." and wrote "St. Louis Mo." July 189<u>6</u>.

Dear Husband,

I would have written to you sooner but Jeff swallowed a fish hook and I did not want to worry you until I found out if it would be necessary for him to go under an operation, but he is getting along all right and doesn't seem to suffer. If he passed it, it must have been away from home for I watched him very closely. Jeff, I have never got a cent out of the rent but $11.85 cents and I had to send that right out to Brown & Bro. to pay insurance on that extra $15.00 they took out. I will send you all the statements from agent and Brown & Bro. when I hear from you again for I do not want to lose them and you might have left where you are before they would get there. I wish you would let me know how our insurance runs or if it is yet due. Inclosed you will find last notice from Brown & Bro.

It is dreadful hot here, sufficating [sic] lots of rain and then intense heat. I nearly went crazy the day Jeffy swallowed that hook but I know now he will be all right.

---

[1] Ltr fr J. Hugh Bauerlein to Jefferson R. Smith II, 08/13/1896, item 9a, author's col.

[2] Bank check made out to J. Hugh Bauerlein for "<u>Twenty five hundred</u> Dollars," "not signed," dated 08/06/1896, item 9b, author's col.

[3] *Denver Evening Post* 08/07/1896, & *RMN* 08/08/1896, p. 8.

[4] *Denver Evening Post* 03/24/1897, p. 8, & *RMN* 03/25/1897, p. 3.

[5] *RMN*, 09/29/1897, p. 8.

[6] Ingersoll Club in Denver: The *News* in 1893 claimed that Jeff presided over gambling there. (*RMN* 03/21/1893, p. 4)

Well Jeff I will close hoping to hear from you at once. Jeff & Eva & Jim
send love and kisses and the same from your
true Mollie
P.S. Eva nearly went crazy over your picture and the dollar you sent her, and
poor Jim cried all day. M[1]

Mary signed her name "Mollie," as she occasionally did. Jeff surely asked himself how
an eleven-year-old boy came to swallow a fish hook.

The letter was posted August 11, 1896, to "Jeff R. Smith, Spokane, Wash., C/of
Grand Hotel," and was postmarked received on August 14. This was three days before
George Carmack made the biggest gold discovery in the history of Canada's Klondike
region. News of the discovery, however, did not reach the outside world until the next
summer. Freeze up on the Yukon was fast approaching, and no one would be entering
the interior area or going "outside" until the following year. After making his big find on
Rabbit Creek, which Carmack renamed Bonanza Creek, he traveled about 65 miles
down the Yukon River to register four claims with the Northwest Mounted Police at the
camp called Fortymile. Up the Fortymile River, gold had been discovered in 1886, and
since 1893, this camp, where the river met the Yukon, had been active. On the way
there and when he arrived, Carmack told every person he met about the discovery,
and, as told by Alaska Historian R. N. DeArmond in *The True Story of the Discovery of
Gold At Bonanza Creek* (1997), "By November a total of 338 claims in the Bonanza
Creek area had been filed with the Police Inspector." The only "rushes" or "stampedes"
in 1896 to the golden creeks south of the Klondike River were from between Fortymile
and Bonanza Creek.

Eleven months would pass before the world began learning of the region's
enormous riches. Miners, made wealthy after their spring/summer "clean up" of the ore
they had mined all winter, carried the word when they came out in July 1897. Coming
1601 miles down the Yukon on the flat-bottomed *Alice* and *Portus B. Weare*, at St.
Michael they boarded the steamers *Excelsior* or *Portland*. When the *Excelsior* docked
in San Francisco on July 14, 1897, excitement spread quickly when each passenger
disembarked with a reported average of from $30,000 to $90,000 in gold. The same
occurred on July 17 when the *Portland* docked in Seattle. There, however, as
DeArmond writes, a

Seattle reporter wrote that the ship carried "a ton of gold," and that headline
went out across the country. The actual amount was closer to two tons. ... If
there is an exact date for the start of the great Klondike Rush, July 17 is it.[2]

In 1896 and the first half of 1897, the big rush Jeff was looking for was yet to
appear. From the Northwest, though, he was watching for it. Jeff often stayed in
Spokane Falls, which according to the *Spokesman Review* was a bunco haven.

The fame of Spokane is spreading and as a result during the last week a
dozen or more noted confidence men have struck town and in a quiet manner
have commenced to ply their vocation. They are all said to be "slick"

[1] Ltr fr Mary E. Smith to Jefferson R. Smith II, July (day unknown), 1896, item 13, author's col.
[2] DeArmond, *Bonanza Creek*, pp. 40-43. *Gilded Age*, "Klondike Gold Rush." *Geographic*, "Fortymile."

individuals and while as yet have made no effort to capture any large game have been quietly laying their wires so to do. As yet they have confined their attention to working outside saloons, but with the big crowd that will be here this week to attend the races these gentry will no doubt try to do some bigger business. The police have them spotted and if they attempt to try any "funny business" they will at once be arrested.[1]

Jeff's Spokane establishment of choice was the Owl Saloon. An envelope postmarked August 1896 and addressed to "Col. J. R. Smith, Spokane Falls, Washington, Terr.," from the district attorney of Denver, Greeley W. Whitford, has a penciled note written on the face of the envelope, "In Owl Saloon."[2] On November 18, 1896, Bat Masterson wrote regarding money that was collected in the Owl Saloon for a mutual friend.[3] A letter from Jeff, dated February 1897, lists the Owl as a return address.[4]

A letter of response from George Mason indicates that Jeff was running games of chance in Spokane.

GEO. MASON & CO.
Playing Cards and Ivory Goods, 1413 Eighteenth Street.
Denver, Colo. Aug. 10, 1896
Friend Jeff:

Yours at hand and will say am glad to hear from you and you are still on earth. We have a new small Tivola. We made a few weeks ago a New Orleans Belt with 50 spaces [—] there is [sic] 2 prizes and 3 blanks. It is a good deal larger, that is, the basket, than the old style and makes a better showing. We made it for one of you x lieutenants Power and the gang and think they are doing well with it, as they were running at Fisks Gardens and done well. Since then I see in paper they were arrested at Colo Spring and fined 50.00 and a few hours to get out of town. Since then I have heard nothing from them or seen them. There is nothing going on here at all and it seems worse than ever. We will soon make some drop cases, that is as soon as we can get at them [i.e., get to making them]. Ed Chase sent over a note for that machin[e] saying it belonged to him and he paid what charges was on it. The machine we put the celluloid on and fixed up. But your jewelry spindle is still here. Jeff wishing you success we remain yours
Resp.   GEO. MASON & CO.[5]

---

[1] *Spokesman Review* 06/23/1896.

[2] Envelope addressed fr Greeley W. Whitford to "Col J. R. Smith," 08/04/1896, item 166, author's col.

[3] Jones, Robert, pp. 330-331.

[4] Ltr fr Jefferson R. Smith II to Mary E. Smith, 02/15/1897, item 63, author's col.

[5] Jones, Robert, p. 333. Notes: *Tivola*: probably *tavola*, the Italian word for "table, plank, board." New Orleans Belt ... 3 blanks...: an imprint on the table for some sort of gambling game containing a belt of 50+ spaces, presumably for bets. *the basket*: may refer to a "bird-cage" dice rolling basket device such as used in "chuck-a-luck." *x lieutenants Power*: nothing is yet known of this apparent ex-lieutenant of Jeff's. *Fisk's Gardens*: a pleasure resort south of Denver, owned by A. C. (Archie Campbell) Fisk, entrepreneur and Denver business leader. (Bright, "Englewood"; *Cyclopaedia of American Biography*)

Jeff was known to purchase gaming equipment from this company, which was located near the Tivoli Club. Once established in Skaguay, Jeff paid Mason $1000 for a roulette table. As shipping was costly, the table and legs were built in Skaguay.[1]

Another document showing Jeff in Spokane includes a promissory note for $250 from D. P. Stomas.[2] Made out on a printed form with "Wash." supplied, it is made for $250, dated "Oct. 13th 189<u>6</u>" and due "<u>5 days</u> after date without grace...." At the bottom appears "Due <u>Oct 18</u>[th] 189<u>6</u> At <u>Spokane</u> [signed] <u>DP Stomas</u>." Not indicated is what the money was for.

James H. Cronin had owned a saloon in St. Louis since at least 1888, and by 1895, he was the owner of two saloons and was a Delegate from the 1st Ward in the city government.[3] He wrote to Jeff in Spokane on the ornate letterhead stationary of the St. Louis House of Delegates and would use it again 1898. As Cronin's salutation and the content of the letter make clear, he was a friend of Jeff's and an "associate."

> Legislative Department
> HOUSE OF DELEGATES
> St. Louis, October 28, 1896.
> Friend Jeff:
> Yours of the 24th received this a.m. and was glad to learn of your return to civilization and that you are enjoying good health and I hope that you have made a barrel of money. Now in regard to the election in Missouri my candid opinion is that Bryan[4] will carry it by at least 50,000 and it might go as high as 75,000.... As to the general result I think it is safe to say that Bryan will be our next president. The enthusiasm manifested in Illinois and Indiana, which are no longer doubtful states and will surely go for Bryan leads me to make this prediction.
> Many thanks for the beautiful pictures. Will send you by express two pair of knucks today. With best wishes believe me
> Your friend,   James H. Cronin[5]

While Jeff was in Spokane, Bascomb completed his prison sentence and was released on September 20, 1896. He promised to "go straight" but fell back into old habits. Twelve days later he was arrested for carrying a concealed pistol. The *Denver Evening Post* described the events leading to his arrest.

> Bascomb's thirst continued all of yesterday and far into the night. Whisky induced a desire for war and Smith carried his artillery with the bravado of a Leadville militiaman. At midnight Bascomb became involved in an argument with Miss Dora Harris, who was a sweet faced babe in gay "Paree" just 45 years ago. Bascomb and Dora flirted and quarreled. When the reformed

---

[1] Notation fr Harriet Pullen about Jefferson R. Smith II paying $1000 to ship the roulette table up to Skagway, made on her copy (Jones, Robert, p. 333). The author's father, John R. Smith, purchased the roulette table from the Pullen museum in 1973.

[2] Document fr D. P. Stomas to Jefferson R. Smith II, 10/13/1896. Item 27, author's col.

[3] St. Louis City Directories, 1888 through 1895.

[4] William Jennings Bryan, Democratic Candidate for president in the 1896 national election.

[5] Jones, Robert, p. 332.

county jail graduate missed a roll of $25 he threatened to inaugurate an extended slumber in Riverside [cemetery] for the giddy French girl. She retaliated by having Bascomb jugged for carrying concealed weapons. Now la petite Dora languishes in a prison cell pending her trial on a charge of larceny from the person....[1]

Jeff wrote to friends in Denver, trying to establish contact with his brother. It must be presumed Jeff had learned of the problems that had come of Bascomb's behavior. One reply came to Jeff at The Grand Hotel in Spokane, arriving November 12, 1896. It was from George B. Fisher, who penned in flowing script a letter of three pages on his own letterhead stationary: "Established 1879 / Geo. B. Fischer / Jobber and Dealer in / Old Whiskies, Imported and Domestic Wines. / Fine Cigars A Specialty. / 1535 to 1539 Seventeenth St. Cor. Wazee." The letter betrays a friendship of long standing.

November 8, 1896

My Dear Jeff.

You must pardon my delay. Election day I was sick in bed, so did not vote, came near having pneumonia. However it passed off without assistance. Tomorrow an auction shop is to open across the street, also a place on Wazee near 17th. The firm of Lester, Jackson & Thornton [−] my neighbor "Kastner" says these firms represent McKinlys [President William McKinley's] advance agents of prosperity, so business is expected to boom this month. I hear of Bascom but I do not see him. He usually comes in the store nights when I am away. Should I see him will have a talk with him.

My dear Jeff, I regret much the result of the national election. The laborer has disfranchised himself, the producer has declared against the perpetuation of independence, the masses has [sic] expressed themselves as incompetent to legislate for themselves, while the east has slaped [sic] the youth, energy and progression, square in the face. A rebuke that intelligence can rally from and forgive, but never forget. The Nov thinking, has insulted the philosopher, the parent and grand parent, has anathemized [anathematized] and coerced there [their] offshoots of nature, because they simply desired to perpetuate home government, happiness and prosperity. In the next four years President McKinly [sic] will be critised [sic] by every nation in the world. The Swiss government will be studied from coast to coast, [the] United States for 4 years will be a political study room. Initiative and Referendum will be recognized as the only political panacea to bring peace and prosperity — to a liberty loving people. We are all quite well now. Henry & Yank[2] join in good wishes, I received a picture of Mr. Ewing's child, it is beautiful,

I am as usual   Geo. B. Fisher[3]

---

[1] *Denver Evening Post* 10/02/1896.

[2] *Henry & Yank*: this first "Henry" may be a person other than "Yank" as it is unclear why Yank's other first name should be preceded by "Henry &."

[3] Ltr fr George B. Fisher to Jeff R. Smith II, 11/08/1896, item 12, author's col.

Jackson and Thornton, the men opening the auction shop, are surely Soap Gang members W. H. Jackson and James "Duke of Halstead" Thornton. Yank is most assuredly Henry "Yank Fewclothes" Edwards.

Bascomb remained in Denver and thereafter in the West, never again to work with Jeff. He continued to find trouble as revealed in a November 18, 1896, letter to Jeff from friend William "Bat" Masterson. He begins gently with salutations, commiseration over hard times, and works up to news of deep concern over Bascomb's doings:

> Friend Jeff:
>
> Your letter received and very glad to hear from you. It would have pleased me much better had you stated that you were prospering. Well, Jeff, I am hanging on the raged [ragged] edge myself. The election went against me so far as the governor is concerned, but the ticket I supported elected the entire Arapahoe county delegation to the legislature and it looks now as though we may be able to get the city charter so amended as to abolish the fire and police board and let the right to control our city affairs revert back to the mayor. If this can be done it will be passed by the legislature in time for our April election and things may be as they used to be.[1]
>
> I have not seen Bascom since he was released after completing the year's sentence. I hear of him, however, and always in some kind of trouble. He has been arrested twice of late for disturbance and discharging firearms down in the neighborhood of 20th and Market streets, and you know the kind of people who frequent that locality. If I were you I would advise him to leave here, as it is only a question of time until he will get a "settler" and every time the papers speak of him they generally say the brother of "Soapy" Smith, who was last heard of skinning suckers in Alaska. So you see you are not getting any the best of it.
>
> I think Bruce will get out all right in time, but it will cost coin. He got into it by getting drunk with Jeff Argyle, "another good thing" as you know.
>
> Bruce received a $100.00 already from Spokane collected in the Owl. You tell Brownie and St. Clair that, will you? Bruce is a poor writer and may not have acknowledged receipt of the money.
>
> Well, Jeff, I wish you good luck,
> Remember me to all friends you see.
> As ever yours,   W. B. Masterson[2]

The "Bruce" referred to by Masterson may be a little-known, possible Soap Gang member Jimmy Bruce, also known as "The Great Gobble Fish."[3] The letter clearly shows the strong bond within the bunco brotherhood. Its members were willing to send

---

[1] *things may be as they used to be*: the board was not abolished, and the governor continued to appoint its members until 1903. In that year, as decided by the Colorado Supreme Court, determination of commissioners came under the jurisdiction of the city, not the state. (King, p. 238)

[2] Jones, Robert, p. 330-331.

[3] *The Great Gobble Fish*: How Jimmy Bruce came by his moniker at present is unknown.

money over long distances to friends and partners in "the business." It also shows that Jeff as well as Bruce and Masterson had friends and associates in the Spokane area.

Masterson was not exaggerating Bascomb's troubles. The *Denver Evening Post* lists five charges against him, including vagrancy, drunkenness, disturbing the peace, carrying concealed weapons, and discharging firearms.[1] He was fined a total of $153 and had his "elegant, silver-plated, highly engraved revolver confiscated."[2] On November 5, 1896, he was in court for stealing a woman's expensive diamond-encrusted jewelry.[3] According to the *Post*, Bascomb still had some friends in the current administration and received an order to leave town rather than face fines still owed from his October melee.[4] Bascomb left for an unidentified destination.

In early 1897 Jeff wrote to Masterson in Denver from Los Angeles. The content of Jeff's letter is unknown, but Masterson's reply survived.

> Friend Jeff:
>
> Your letter from Los Angeles received. Glad to hear from you.
>
> I suppose you were in the new camp of Randsburg. I believe you are a little like myself—"let the new camps run for other people." I do not intend to ever again go to a new camp: at least until it has demonstrated that there is something in it besides wind.
>
> Everything is running open here, but the play is spotted. It has got to be a piking game all over town. A decent change ... will attract a crowd of sufficient size to obstruct a view of the table.
>
> "Plunk" has got the police department "buffaloed." ... The mayor will not permit his being railroaded in the police court, and the newspapers have tendered him all the space he wants in which to air his grievances. I enclose you the chief's left lead and "Plunk's right hand cross counter. "Plunk" invites more of the game and threatens to bawl the police department out in the papers. .... I hope the war goes on. I have promised to do the press work for "Plunk" and incidentally furnish a few facts.
>
> I am against the department for the reason that it is in with the gambling trust headed by Ed Chase and they would get me killed if they could. You might furnish me a little ammunition for a future use if it should be needed. Your name will never appear directly or indirectly under any circumstances. ... Hope you are well and prospering.
>
> Yours   W. B. Masterson.[5]

The person referred to as "Plunk" is Frank Salter, a one-time member of the Soap Gang and one whom Masterson saw as having influence in Denver politics. In November 1893 Salter had been arrested on charges of highway robbery for relieving a Miss Dollie Emerson of some diamonds. A week after being released on bail, Salter visited Joe Howard of the Central Theater. Howard had caused the arrest of Salter,

---

[1] *Denver Evening Post*, 10/31/1896, p. 2.

[2] *RMN*, 11/03/1896, p. 8, & *Denver Evening Post*, 11/02/1896, p. 10.

[3] *Denver Evening Post* 11/05/1896, p. 8.

[4] *Denver Evening Post* 11/11/1896.

[5] Jones, Robert, p. 331

and Salter showed his appreciation by "plunking" Howard on the head with a loaded cane. Salter was arrested and charged with assault to murder. He still had pull with the police court, however, and was released on a $500 bond.[1] Masterson asked Jeff for any scandalous information he might have about the police department, but Jeff's reply, if one was made, is not known. Surely Jeff had a few stories to tell.

Masterson probably did help Salter with the press in two ways. Also found in Jeff's Skaguay scrapbook was a *Denver Times* clipping headlined "'Plunk' Has A Word" and "He Pitches Into the Police Department in Characteristic Language." What the *Times* meant by "characteristic" is not clear as other writing by Plunk has not come to hand. But if Masterson did help with the writing, he likely applied brakes to a florid and abrasive style. It is a longish "letter to the editor," longer than most, so it could be that in addition to helping out with the writing, Masterson used some "pull" to have the whole of it printed. Its slant is a self-interested defense and set of accusations, none pertinent to Jeff at this time but of sufficient interest for him to save the clipping.[2]

In January, Jeff wrote to Cy Warman, and is believed to have been in Spokane when a reply from "1239 B. D. E., Wash. D.C." reached him on February 2, 1897.

> My dear "Soapy,"
>
> I have your note of Jan. 22, and here is my address at the top of this page. I see your cousin of the Post often, and the other evening his charming sister wrote me up at a little entertainment where I read some of my western rhymes, she is a very nice little girl. I may drift—in fact I hope to drift—to Los. A. [Los Angeles] myself before another winter.
>
> My regards to dear old Creede, one of the whitest of them all—and good hunting to you
>
> Truly Yours   Cy Warman[3]

Hunting apparently had been good. For $1.00 Jeff bought from one Martin Murphy his 1/8 interest in a gold mine located about 150 miles north of Spokane. The bill of sale, appearing to be Martin Murphy's hand, evidences having been written under duress or in something akin to distraction, hurriedness, or inebriation. Words are repeated. The word *heirs* is misspelled and rewritten, again incorrectly. Punctuation and capital letters appear (or do not appear) in odd places, and the description is not clear, requiring a closing reference to where the claim is recorded. Dictation of the contents could account for confusion and so many anomalies. The document is on stationary from the Grand Hotel, apparently Jeff's principal residence in Spokane, and is presented as written. Martin began by filling in the date line (underlined) this way:

> To all Persons Concerned.   Spokane, Wash., Jnury 24th 1897
> This agreement entered into between Martin Murphy party of the first part and Jeff R Smith party of the second part, For and in consideration of the sum of $1.00 One Dollar, I Martin Murphy do sell transfer assign and sell to Jeff R Smith his hrirs hriress assigns and administrators forever. My One

---

[1] *RMN*, 11/30/1893, p. 3, & 12/05/1893, p. 5.
[2] Jones, Robert, pp. 332-32.
[3] Ltr fr Cy Warman to Jefferson R. Smith II, 01/24/1897, item 107, author's col.

eighth interest also the One eighth interest of Phil ORourke's in the Bunker and Sullivan Claims in the Slocan District more fully described in Dowion and B.B. Records Recorded in the town of Kaslo.　　　Principal Martin Murphy
　　　Witness Jas. E Walker[1]

Was this a legitimate purchase, extortion, settlement of a gambling debt, or the remnant of a swindle? One dollar in 1897 is worth about $31.24 today,[2] but it still seems a small amount for the sale of an interest in a gold mine and suggests other considerations.

Jeff was doing well in Spokane, but he was watching for signs of a better location, which probably would occur in the North as occasioned by a big gold rush. Gold, however, as the saying goes, is where you find it, and going up with the prospectors, as Jeff had in 1896, was not the best way of finding the best place to be at the right time. To be proactive, however, Jeff had written to Cousin Edwin in Washington, DC, to ask him to use his influence to secure permits to operate at Fort St. Michael in Alaska. This site at the head of the Yukon River looked early on to be a prime location for a major settlement. Edwin replied in a letter dated November 18, 1897.

　　　Dear Jeff:
　　　　　Your letters were gladly received. Always anxious to know how you are doing. You say you want me to send your permits. The letter to Col. Randall is all the permit the war department will give. That letter which I have already forwarded you grants you every concession you are after. I hope you will not get in any trouble with the minimums of the law.
　　　　Your brother　　Ed. B. Smith[3]

While watching the North, Jeff looked south, way south. He wrote to Charlie E. Pratt and T. Jeff Davis in Guatemala to ask about opportunities. Both men replied to convey the horrible state of affairs there. Davis added, "'If you have got any enemies you want to fix, send them down here.'"[4] In February Jeff wrote to Mary on stationary from the Russ House hotel in San Francisco. Not known is if Jeff had recently visited that city or obtained the stationary from someone who had, a common practice. His letter to Mary Dated Februay 15, 1897, reads, in a large pen hand,

　　　Dear Wife
　　　　　This far on my journey to the North God bless you
　　　　　　　Jeff
　　　　　　　Owl Saloon
　　　　　　　Spokane[5]

The short missive shows how fixed Jeff's sights were becoming on Alaska.

Within two months, he went to St. Louis to see Mary. On May 2, 1897, a "Charlie," possibly Charlie E. Pratt, wrote to Jeff from The Spokane hotel in Spokane for assistance in a detailed plan to swindle his cheap partner:

---

[1] Mine claim transfer between Jefferson R. Smith II & Martin Murphy, 01/24/1897, item 7, author's col.

[2] Tom's Inflation Calculator.

[3] Ltr fr Edwin B. Smith to Jefferson R. Smith II, 11/18/1897. Jefferson R. "Little Randy" Smith col.

[4] Ltr fr T. Jeff Davis to Jefferson R. Smith II, 02/08/1897, Jones, Robert, p. 335.

[5] Ltr fr Jefferson R. Smith II to Mary E. Smith, 02/15/1897, item 63, author's col.

Friend Jeff:

I was sorry that I did not get in to see you in Denver as I passed through. Cripple Creek is N.G. except about one house. We, "The Old Man and I," went to Denver, Salt Lake and the Carson fight.[1] Only opened up at the latter place. Must have quit at least twenty thousand to the good. Went back to Salt Lake, from there to Butte. Neither place any good—that is, Butte is all right, but the anti-gambling law goes into effect July 1st. We heard so much about this place [Spokane] that we concluded to run over. Well, I have never seen anything like it. Since I have been here in this hotel, they have been playing poker, and one man they say is over twenty thousand dollars winner in [the] last week—5 to 10 thousand a sitting is nothing for them to lose, and it is the same at dice, faro bank, etc. The old man is trying to get a place to open. He is the tightest wad I ever saw. He could have gotten nicest house in town here for only a difference of 25 a month, but by his squabbling some other parties got ahead of him. We have another small place in view, and may have to take it now. Soon as we do I want you to come, and if I wire..., I want you to come without delay. Bring some man if you can who is not a "profesh," but a business man—and make a good flash or change in. The old man will turn for money if there is a change in. He dealt a hundred and two hundred for Al Smith and those New Yorkers and I dealt lucky enough to beat them. In fact, I have won over $100,000 for him in the past two years, and as I said before he is the stingiest, greediest old bloke that ever lived, actually begrudges that he has to eat (as it costs something). I got a letter from the old folks—below Greenville—asking me to send them fifty as the high water, etc., had raised hell with them. I was short 15 of it and tried to make a borrow of the old man of the 15—and I got it—NOT. So I had to soak my super.[2] Now, what I want you to do is this: Bring someone as above stated and change in about 5,000 to make a change in, and limit, and cop out a few thousand each for the 3 of us. I will do the work for one-third if you have to get some[one] to furnish the money. If you are in shape to handle the proposition alone, why of course I want it cut in two parts. ... I can give you from $500 to $1,000 a deal[,] the best of it—if you will make a flash like I said 5 or ten M.[3] Do not keep this letter unless you have to—and when you can, tear it up. The old man is coming up, so I will close.

   Yours, etc.,   Charlie

P. S. -From the reports the country up above here is great. In fact, it is those boys that ... come down here that make the high rolling plays. Have seen them downtown stacking up 20s all over.... Nearly all gold used out here.[4]

---

[1] Carson fight: refers to heavyweight championship boxing match between James J. Corbett and Robert Fitzsimmons on March 17, 1897, in Carson City, Nevada. Fitzsimmons became champion that night.

[2] *soak my super*: cheat or not pay my landlord.

[3] *flash ... ten M*: make a show of $5,000 or $10,000. M = $1,000.

[4] Ltr fr "Charlie," to Jefferson R. Smith II, 05/02/1897, Jones, Robert, p. 333.

At the time this letter was sent, Jeff was still in St. Louis, but the letter mentions his being in Denver, too. Jeff is known to have answered from St. Louis as Charlie sent a reply by telegram.

THE WESTERN UNION TELEGRAPH COMPANY
Received at 412 & 414 Pine Street, St. Louis, Mo.
[From] 667 Ch. Enfl Ch. 2:53 p.m. 15 Paid.   Spokane, Wn., May 26 [1897]
Jeff R. Smith, Hotel Rozier, St. Louis:
Didn't answer because thought you were coming right on everything good shape so don't delay.
Chas.[1]

How or if this scheme to con "the old tight wad" was put into action is not recorded.

Before returning to Spokane, where Jeff probably had a few enemies, he used a news-oriented form of messaging in a newspaper to announce to friends that he was headed back. A clipping he cut out and saved tells the story.

THE SEAL CAME BACK

"Jeff," the pet seal belonging to "Doc" Brown, after exploring the waters of Lake Coeur d' Alene, has concluded he likes those of the Spokane River, in the vicinity of Spokane, better, and has returned. Perhaps it was because of his fondness for the "Doc." Whatever the cause, he is back.

Several weeks ago "Jeff" was sent to the Lake, where he could have abundant room in which to disport himself. ... A large bathing pool was fenced in for him in the bay at the ranch owned by George Forster. There "Jeff" seemed contented for a time. It was a lonely spot, however, and "Jeff" craved company.

He broke out of the pool and went to Coeur d' Alene city, where he was seen Friday. He was reported from there, and "Doc" Brown sent a box of fish up to him. Before they had arrived, "Jeff" had started for Spokane.

Yesterday he was seen in the water above Washington Street Bridge. He seemed glad to see familiar faces, wagged his tail and tried to stand on his head, as an evidence of his joy. "Doc" Brown will secure permission from the owners and have a home built for him on the island, where he may spend the winter.[2]

Coeur d' Alene, the lake and the city, are about thirty miles east of Spokane. It would appear that Jeff had traveled to Coeur d' Alene but had met with little success and wished to return to Spokane. Perhaps it was anticipated that a rival gang would not welcome his return, so, perhaps with the assistance of a reporter, he sent the coded message to let friends know he was coming. "Doc" Brown, a friend and Spokane associate of Jeff's, tried to convince Jeff to stay put, but Jeff was already on his way. Later on, Brown sought permission from the rival boss for Jeff to stay in Spokane during the winter when visiting from Alaska.

---

[1] Telegram fr "Charles," to Jefferson R. Smith II, 05/26/1897, Jones, Robert, p. 333.
[2] Unknown, undated Spokane newspaper clipping saved by Jefferson R Smith II, author's col.

The Spokesman-Review for Monday, July 12, 1897, published a story about a gold brick bunco man, "One of the most notorious and dangerous criminals of the United States..., none other than 'Rebel George,' alias W. H. Knowlton and a hundred others aliases." A probing reporter interviewing the man in jail, portrayed him as evasive and unstable. Toward the end of the interview, asked if he knew Jeff, the man, now thoroughly painted as a rascally criminal, replied, "No, I don't know 'Soapy' Smith. I know of him, but never met him." Jeff thought more damage had been done to his reputation. He clipped the story and sent it to Mary in St. Louis, writing at the top, "Same old story what next. I can't do no good."[1]

Three days later, on July 15, 1897, the *SS Excelsior* docked in San Francisco with more than a ton of gold. Word of the treasure ship brought huge crowds, and word steadily spread across the country. But on the evening of July 16 when Seattle learned that the far richer *SS Portland* was bound for its port, the city was electrified. Pierre Berton reports how *The Seattle Post-Intelligencer* "chartered a tug, loaded it with reporters, and sent it ... to intercept the *Portland* as she entered the sound." The reporters got stories from excited passengers and sped back to Seattle aboard the tug. *P-I* extras had been on the streets for awhile when the *Portland* "nosed into Schwabaker's Dock at six" a.m. and was met by five thousand people. Since word had begun to spread the evening before, Jeff would have had time to arrive by night train from Spokane and be among the waterfront throng. The *P-I* wrote that a ton of gold was aboard. But there was not. The more conservative *Seattle Daily Times* announced a half ton, but that amount was also incorrect. The true tally was two tons. The sixty-eight passengers disembarking that Saturday morning, July 17, 1898, had among them "at least" 4,000 pounds of gold valued at $900,000, or in today's dollars, about $28 million.[2] The great gold rush Jeff had been waiting for was on.

Chapter 18

Skaguay, the Klondike Gold Rush, Seattle, St. Louis, Washington City, and New York City

This is my last opportunity to make a big haul. Alaska is the last West.
I know the character of the people I shall meet there and I know
that I am bound to succeed with them.

—Jefferson R. Smith II, 1897
The Trail, published January 1920

Jeff was about to identify what he had been searching for, the perfect base camp for the rule of one man. Skaguay would prove a paradise for the Soap Gang rogues. All the new town needed was a little organization, and that was one of Jeff's specialties. According to his wife and Cousin Edwin, Jeff planned on making a killing in

---

[1] Clipping fr *Spokesman Review* 07/12/1897, item 129, author's col.
[2] Berton, pp. 98-99. The value per troy ounce (12 ounces per pound) in 1898 was $18.98 (Green). The value of $1 in 1898 is about $31.24 today. (Tom's Inflation Calculator)

Alaska and then going into a "straight" business and being a solid family man. For Jeff, the problem would be in knowing when to quit.

In the port of Seattle, everything changed overnight after the July 17, 1897, "9 O'CLOCK EDITION" of *The Seattle Post-Intelligencer* hit the streets and flashed by wire across the country. The headline and story ran two columns wide:

GOLD! GOLD! GOLD! GOLD!
Sixty-Eight rich Men on the Steamer Portland.
STACKS OF YELLOW METAL!
Some Have $5,000. Many Have More, and
a Few Bring Out $100,000 Each.[1]

Tens of thousands of people worldwide suddenly prepared to go north to the gold fields. The location of those fields was not at all clear. Maps of the area were incomplete and few, and the event occurred so quickly that *The Seattle Daily Times* "wasn't sure whether to typeset Clondyke, Klondyke, or Klondike, and used the three spellings at random."[2] Known, however, was that American routes meant a sea voyage from San Francisco, Portland, or Seattle. After a brief, intense competition for supremacy, Seattle won out as the major point of embarkation. The chamber of commerce underwrote an advertising campaign, and "Entire industries sprang up to meet the miners' needs...," including such essentials as housing, information, and supplies.[3] Immense crowds preparing for travel jammed the streets, shutting down streetcar services. Skilled and unskilled workers, clerks, newspaper reporters, doctors, barbers, policemen, the poor, and the wealthy walked out on their jobs and families to book passage on one of the few ships heading to Alaska. Even Seattle's mayor, W. D. Wood resigned his office, formed the Seattle and Yukon Trading Company, and prepared to head north.[4]

Within ten days an estimated fifteen hundred people had left on chartered steamers to Alaska, with many more in line behind them for any ship that could float. That first summer 10,000 Seattle residents left town for the gold fields. Many more would have gone, but transportation was insufficient. Attempting to meet demand, ship owners put worn out and even dangerously damaged vessels into service.[5] C. B. Richardson, a gold seeker, recorded the crowded conditions aboard ship on the hazardous journey that was common to so many.

> Fort Wrangell,[6] Jan. 30.—We arrived here at 11 p.m. The coast is lined with rocks and hidden reefs, and the sea being very rough the boat [could not] put into port until morning. Our captain lost a boat a few weeks ago, but passengers and crew were saved. ...[E]very old tub that could be made to

---

[1] *Seattle Post-Intelligencer* 07/17/1897, p. 1.

[2] Boswell, p. 107.

[3] Boswell, p. 109.

[4] Berton, p. 102.

[5] *Salt Lake Semi Weekly Tribune* 02/15/1898, p. 10.

[6] *Fort Wrangell*: shortened to "Wrangell" in 1902. "Named by Russians after Admiral Baron Ferdinand Petrovich von Wrangell. Erroneously spelled Wrangle and Wrangel" (*Geographic*). In this book, the name is spelled "Wrangell" despite how it appears in source materials.

float has been pressed into service for the Alaska trade. "The City of Seattle," our boat, is said to be the best and fastest in the service. On her last trip she lost two passengers, one being killed by a lantern falling from the mast, and the other was washed overboard. We had three dogs washed off the deck last night. They followed us for a short distance before sinking. All along the coast you pass thousands of little, uninhabited islands and Indian villages, and the scenery is truly grand. ... The worst part of the trip is at Queen Charlotte's sound. Here the "City of Mexico" went down a few weeks ago, and the sea is always rough. We were all in the dining-room when the boat entered the sound, and as the wind was blowing a gale, in a few minutes nine-tenths of the passengers were making a wild rush to get out. The dishes were rolling over the floor, and nearly everyone was sea-sick. We have 600 persons on board and lifeboats for but 280, and this is on one of the best boats. The crowd is composed of men from all over the world; a few from England and the great cities; a large number of hardy Western men; a few women with little babies; and then we have a large number of gamblers, three-card men, the Soapy Smith contingent, and sure-thing bunco players, etc., and a few painted fairies. A large percentage of the men have mortgaged their homes or exerted every resource to get money to come, and say they will strike it rich or never return. Few have the means to get back. They are a determined, desperate lot, and will explore the great unknown country if grit means anything. There are about 100 dogs on the deck that make the night hideous with their continual howling....[1]

With regard to the man killed by a falling lantern, a story is told about Jeff Smith's mixing into the affair and saving the captain some trouble. In so far as can be determined, the story is first told by Alaska historian C. L. Andrews, who made something of a small study of Jeff Smith. Andrews came to Skaguay to live in 1898 shortly after Jeff was killed, and while living there until 1903, he came to know many of the people who had dealings with Jeff outside the Soap Gang.[2] Though without specific attribution, another reason for relating the event, beyond Andrews' reputation and credentials, is that Jeff's hand seems such a good fit to the glove of this story.

The *City of Seattle* was headed north in the usual state of ships on the Seattle-Skaguay-Dyea run, jam-packed with sea sick people complaining about tasteless food and filthy, stinking conditions. Andrews tells how "Hunter was captain and E. T. Pope was purser" and "The ship was loaded with adventurers setting out to become miners...." They had heard of the all-powerful "miner's meetings" and were given to trying them aboard ship as the journey progressed.

The spirit of adventure was particularly high in two young men who, as Andrews writes, were "of careless and irresponsible disposition." They climbed the foremast,

---

[1] *Salt Lake Semi Weekly Tribune* 02/15/1898, p. 10.
[2] *C. L. Andrews* is Clarence Leroy Andrews (1862-1948). He spent 51 years studying, writing about, and filming Alaska and its people. His *The Story of Alaska* (1931) went through many printings over 20 years. Andrews does not site the source of the story of Jeff on the *City of Seattle*, but he does mention people in it whom Andrews seems to have known.

and "One of them grabbed the halyards that controlled ... the range light..., which weighed some ten pounds..., laid hold of the loosened line, and used it as a swing." The ship had reached Queen Charlotte Sound, and the ship had begun to roll "in the usual long swell running in from the ocean." One of the young men began "having a hilarious time swinging with the roll of the ship out over the water from one side to the other." The youth could have met with a number of fatal mishaps (hitting the mast, falling to the deck, being flung into the sea), but the ten-pound light came loose, struck his head, and killed him.

The event raised the ire of the already discontent passengers, and some of them felt the need for a miner's meeting. A committee was appointed "to look up the victim's family and arrange a suit for fifty thousand dollars' damages against the shipping company." It was during these proceedings, which had grown "pretty hot," that Jeff appeared. He said that he knew the dead man and asked if anyone else did. No one did. Jeff then spoke to a man he knew, standing next to the body, and asked him to look in the dead man's pocket.

> "He's got that medal of mine that I showed you yesterday. Look for it, Bill. All right, then, I'll look. I'm not afraid. He's been sleeping in my room. He has no ticket. Now, here in this pocket he has a sealed package with Jefferson R. Smith written on it. It isn't important. I knew he took it."

> Soapy produced the medal and the package from the dead man's pockets, then turned to the crowd again.

> "Now, you scum, if you want to stand up for a man who's a stowaway, a cheat and a bum, I'm off with you."

> That stopped the miners' meeting. Soapy had turned the trick by his methods and ability to handle a crowd.[1]

What object might Jeff have had in playing the crowd as he did? At least two advantages are clear cut. First, making an appreciative friend of the ship's Captain Hunter would be a valuable business connection. It could produce toleration of the "large number of gamblers, three-card men, the Soapy Smith contingent, and sure-thing bunco players" (seen by C. B. Richardson) who plied their trade among the hundreds of captive passengers. Second, Jeff may have found pleasure in facing down an angry crowd, plying his sort of persuasions, and getting his way. Within just a couple of weeks, he would do the same thing with angry men in Skaguay and again get his way, once more pretty much with his voice alone.

The Seattle Post-Intelligencer proclaimed that "'so far as Seattle is concerned the depression is at an end. A period of prosperity, far greater than anything known in the past, is immediately at hand.'"[2] Merchants, saloon proprietors, gamblers, prostitutes, and confidence men saw a golden opportunity to profit from the stampeders and headed northwest by the thousands from all over the country. Profit from gold seekers headed to the Klondike was to be found at three points. First, the exit ports to Alaska, with Seattle quickly becoming chief among them. Second, the two drop off ports for

---

[1] Andrews, "Real," pp. 7 & 36.
[2] *Seattle Post-Intelligencer*, 07/21/1897.

Klondikers in Alaska, Dyea and Skaguay. Third, the goldfield camps and nearby towns. Jeff abandoned plans for a "hotel" in St. Michael and opted for Skaguay.

To set up operations there, Jeff needed financing, so he shared his plans to profit from the stampede with potential investors. One of those to respond was Felix B. Mulgrew. Having come into some money, he was willing to place $3500 of it with Jeff. But within a couple of months, Mulgrew needed some, and preferably all, of it back. He was way down on his luck, but that just seemed to spur new wheeler-dealer plans. He wrote from San Francisco on November 29, 1897.

> Jeff R. Smith, Esq.:
>
> Dear Sir—"A friend in need is a friend indeed." I'm busted—up a stump, and about as desperate as you were when we first met. That Spokane trip cost me about $4,000, all in all, including [the] $3,500 I advanced you. When I got back and paid some debts, helped along some poor people, I soon found myself down to cases, or within a few hundred of being so. It was a case of "dig up" again, so I started for the Klondike. A party here agreed to pay my wife and children $50 a month for a year, in consideration of a half-interest in what I located. Well, I didn't get there. Our river boat broke down and we were frozen in at the mouth of the Yukon. I had to borrow money to get back to Frisco.
>
> I don't know which way to turn. As I had about $7,000 only a few months ago, those who knew me naturally think I ought to have money now. I ... must raise at least $200.... ... If I had $200 to $300 I would get on my feet and pull out. I have a chance to book 100 people for Dawson at $300 each, including 1,000 lbs. of provisions.... That would give me $30,000. I can get a 150-ton boat, to carry 100 passengers, delivered at St. Michael, for $20,000. Such a boat would give 100 tons freight capacity, aside from the 50 tons allotment to passengers, and at 5 cents per lb. I can take in $10,000 from freight. Thus I would take in about $40,000, while $30,000 would pay for the boat, grub, etc. That would clear the boat and give about $10,000 in cash, and to that could be added what the boat would earn next year on the river. I would let her freeze up somewhere near Dawson and use her for a hotel.... I have two or three capitalists on the string for this plan.... I'm dead broke now, and I want you to be my friend if it breaks a leg – or breaks somebody else.
>
> My wife often speaks of "Dr." Smith and always says: "Jeff will pay you when he prospers." I feel sure you will..., but a little now is an absolute need.
>
> In Seattle recently I heard you had been in town and was flush. I met Mr. Thompson, who told me you had gone to Nashville. I wired you there, to the track. I am sending this letter to Mr. Thompson to forward, as he probably knows your address. For the gods' sake do not disappoint me. My wife sends best wishes for your happiness.
>
> Yours truly,   F. B. Mulgrew[1]

---

[1] Jones, Robert, pp. 385. Jones has Mulgrew's initials as "H.B." They are, however, "F.B." Karen Hendricks, a great-great granddaughter of Felix B. Mulgrew, confirmed the spelling on 02/15/2008.

Often responsive to requests for financial help, Jeff probably sent Mulgrew at least some of what he asked for. Jeff's good payback record to creditors, including banks and individuals, suggests Mulgrew got his investment back, although when is not certain. With the profits Jeff would make in Skaguay, he easily have could done so.

Captain William "Billy" Moore knew that one day a transportation route to and from the Western Canadian Northwest interior would be in demand, and since locating what would be named the White Pass in June 1887 with Skookim Jim, George Carmack's brother-in-law, Moore was obsessed with the pass, the trail to it, and the valley below with its deep-water port. It was an opportunity for development he felt compelled to seize.[1] Beginning in October 1887, Moore and his sons developed the valley land, complied with American laws in establishing a townsite, called Mooresville, and in claiming a plot of 160 acres. "They registered both in Washington [DC] and Ottawa [Canada]."[2] As funds allowed, the Moores "erected a dwelling and a small wharf, constructed a wagon road ... four miles up the valley, and made the pack trail to the summit."[3] In 1896, months before George Carmack's big gold discovery, early railroad speculators for the future White Pass & Yukon Railway gave Moore financial support to secure a right of way through his site.[4] Mooresville was one mile short of 1000 miles from Seattle, and one mile short of 100 miles from the city of Juneau.

Steamship companies quickly identified the closest drop off points to the gold fields. The route lay north through the Inside Passage of islands of British Columbia and Southeast Alaska to the head of Lynn Canal. Here were two locations about six miles apart. One had deep water relatively close to shore and a trail leading to a summit gap named the White Pass.[5] The other location, divided from deep water by two miles of muddy tidal shallows, led to the Chilkoot Pass.[6] Both terminated at Lake Bennett, the head of a 600-mile navigable route across lakes and down the Yukon River to the Klondike. Both trails had advantages and disadvantages. At 30 miles to Lake Bennett, the Chilkoot was shorter but 614 feet higher with a staggeringly steep climb at the end. The 40-mile White Pass was not as steep but took longer. Because of the goods that needed transporting, amounting to a ton that the Canadian Mounties began requiring in early 1898,[7] packing on both trails was so hellish that thousands turned back. An old timer who had been over both trails was asked which was best. "He thought quite a while, then he shook his head and said: 'There ain't no choice. One's hell. The other's damnation.'"[8] A San Francisco paper offered a sense of the trail scene.

---

[1] Minter, pp. 25-29.

[2] Dickey Diary, 10/12/1898: in entry regarding his attending a "'Citizens' Meeting' where it was decided to raise funds to fight Mr. Moore's claim to the town site." Learned details of claim there.

[3] *Morning Oregonian* 04/27/1898, p.8, & Minter, p. 39.

[4] Minter, pp. 51-52.

[5] *White Pass*: elev. 2886', Ogilvie named in 1887 for Canada's Interior Minister Thomas White (*Geographic*).

[6] *Chilkoot Pass*: elev. 3500', named after the Alaska Native Chilkoot who inhabited the region (*Geographic*).

[7] Berton, p.154.

[8] McKeown, p. 101.

Ten thousand, fifteen thousand, twenty thousand men forever pressing onward, treading on the next man's heels, strangers to each other, and yet all moved by a common impulse; tugging, pushing, sweating, making themselves beasts of burden; strangely incurious as to the concerns of all but self; silent, preoccupied, their eyes fixed on a single goal, a bleak, inhospitable region of eternal silence; their only lode stone, gold. Such is the character of the innumerable host moving over the Alaskan passes into the Yukon basin. If one falls by the wayside, the others pass him by. The sense of social community and obligation seems to be forgotten. It is every man for himself, and every man's life is in his own hands and no other's.[1]

All of this was yet to come. In the beginning, back on Monday, July 26, 1897, just nine days after the steamship *Portland* arrived in Seattle with its "Stacks of Yellow Metal," the *Queen* anchored in deep water near Mooresville and asked Captain Moore for permission to unload passengers and supplies onto his land. The *Queen's* Captain Carroll did not know whether his passengers were entering the United States or Canada as the area was claimed by both countries.[2] Moore consented, believing that his years of patience and hard work were finally going to pay off and that he would soon be a wealthy man. Moore quickly found that he was mistaken. The stampeders were in too much haste to care about his property rights. They pushed him aside and took possession of his land, and thus the new camp was conceived in lawlessness.

Moore watched helplessly as they swept in from the sea.... The horde was ruthless, unthinking, and in a hurry. Down went his trees, leaving a field of jagged stumps in a sea of mud. In went their stakes, as plot after plot of choice land was wrenched from his acres. Up went their tents as frantic men sought shelter from the relentless wind and rain. The miners had arrived, and they were tearing Moore's dream to bits.[3]

Onboard the *Queen*, 29-year-old John Douglas Stewart from Nanaimo, British Columbia, had disembarked at Dyea with 35 other miners headed for the Chilkoot trail.[4] Stewart's return through Skaguay would be directly related to Jeff's demise.

The tent city on Moore's land was renamed "Skaguay," after *Skaqua* or *Shgagwéi* as then known by the Tlingit, meaning "windy place with white caps on the water."[5] With arrival of an official government post office, the spelling changed to "Skagway," but early businessmen and residents resisted the change well into the 1900s.

As *The Skaguay News* would later put it, "During that first harsh winter of 1897 the frantic stampeders acted on greedy impulse and abandoned all humanity and reason as they charged at a crawl up the White Pass and Chilkoot trails." The Chilkoot trail was too steep for horses, but for the four years the White Pass trail handled foot traffic, from 1895 to 1899, an estimated 3,000 horses died on the trail, thus giving the

---

[1] *San Francisco Examiner* 04/10/1898.
[2] Pennington, p. 241.
[3] Minter, p. 72.
[4] Pennington, pp. 241-242, & *Seattle Times*, 07/24/1897. Stewart's name is listed as "John C. Stewart," which is believed to be the reporter's mistake.
[5] *Daily Alaskan* 04/22/1913, & *Skagway Alaskan*, summer edition, 2008, p. 16.

White Pass an additional name, "Dead Horse Trail."[1] Gold seekers who did not make it over the passes before winter were forced to retreat to Dyea and Skaguay to wait out the winter. Many stampeders who made it over the passes found they were not properly provisioned to last the winter in the desolate Klondike. Starvation was feared, but while it came close to some, it did not become reality. The Canadian government found a way to deliver food and supplies. In early February 1898, the Northwest Mounted Police (NWMP) took matters into its own hands and published the requirement that all prospectors must possess a minimum of 1,150 pounds of food and other necessities amounting to 2,000 pounds. Lacking these minimums meant being turned back.[2]

The date of Jeff's arrival in Skaguay is not certain. Jerry Daily, one of Jeff's partners, told "Bat" Masterson that their first visit to Skaguay was for 23 days. Jeff left Skaguay for an "outside" visit on September 14, 1897, so the date of his arrival in Skaguay may be pegged as Sunday, August 22, 1897, 27 days after the first ship of miners arrived.[3] The *Utopia* left Seattle on August 14 with a "J. R. Smith" among its passengers. The ship was scheduled to leave on Friday, August 13, but superstitious passengers and a flexible Captain O'Brien opted to wait a day. When reporters asked about the delayed departure, they were told that it was taking longer than anticipated to load cargo.[4] As travel to Skaguay from Seattle then could take about a week, it is more than likely that the "J. R. Smith" is Jeff aboard the *Utopia*. Moreover, after he came south in 1896 with Captain O'Brien, the captain's biography has Jeff returning "from Seattle with O'Brien on the *Utopia*" along with some of "his gang of cut-throats and gamblers...."[5]

Jeff, Daily, and two other unnamed members of Jeff's "crew" disembarked in Skaguay and worked 19 of the 23 days they were there. In that time, according to Daily, they made $30,000 and divided it 4 ways before Jeff returned to Seattle.[6]

Newcomer Hal Hoffman described Skaguay in August 1897,

> Skaguay is, at this date, a city of eleven frame or log houses, a saw-mill, five stores, four saloons, a crap game, a faro layout, blacksmith shop, five restaurants, which are feeding people all the time, a tailor shop, on which is hung the sign "bloomers fitted for shotguns;" a real estate office, two practicing physicians, another professional pathfinder whose specialty is shown by the sign painted on a board nailed to a tree, "teeth extracted;" some 300 tents, and a population of about 2000 men and seventeen women. Four of the women are accompanying their husbands into the Klondike. The others are unchaperoned.[7]

---

[1] *Skagway News*, Summer edition, 1992.
[2] Berton, p. 154, & Rennick, p. 27.
[3] *Denver Evening Post* 11/15/1897, p. 7.
[4] *Seattle Post-Intelligencer* 08/14/1897.
[5] Dalby, p. 179.
[6] *Denver Evening Post* 11/15/1897, p. 7.
[7] Harris, pp. 466-467.

The first physical evidence of Jeff's presence in Skaguay is a letter to Mary dated August 28, 1897. Enclosed were receipts for $1,500 to Mary,[1] the equivalent of about $47,000 today.[2]

Scagway[3]   Aug 28, 1897

Dear wife

I got Mrs. Scovell, the wife of elder Sylvester Scovell,[4] the correspondent of the N.Y. World, to send you $500 as I did not know if [I] could send it myself or not.[5] Since then I have had luck in a trade and send $1000 more, making $1500 on this boat the Queen. It will be shipped by express to you from Seattle, Wash. This makes $1600 all told. Take up that mortgage and cash yourself up. That is, keep the money yourself. And don't go saying anything in St. Louis as you will never get a cent out of anything in St. Louis.[6] Write to Juneau. Be sure and send $1000 to 1,300 at least to Brown & Bro Denver to pay mortgage.

Yours till death,   Jeff[7]

Upon arriving in Skaguay, Jeff had to pay for food and shelter for himself and for the men who accompanied him.[8] In order to send $1,500 to Mary, Jeff likely profited several times that amount. The policy for bunco gangs, including Jeff's, dictated that the men be paid first. Next came the costs of lodging, food, and supplies. Anything after that was Jeff's for gambling and personal endeavors. It is very doubtful that Jeff sent all his spare money to Mary. After all, to take care of "running the show" including everyone's needs, Jeff needed to take care of his own, which included his pastimes. So it can be safely assumed that he made a considerable amount of profit in the six days between his arrival and the day he sent Mary the money.

As with other mineral rushes, the majority of merchants came to Skaguay to make a profit and move on to the next boomtown. Those remaining probably did not originally plan to. All of the merchants, though, depended in part on the trade of residents, and of course, they themselves were residents, short-term or not, and did not want to be victimized nor have others like them made victims. Aside from the aggravation of loss, that would inhibit trade and eat into everyone's profits.

---

[1] Receipt for $1000 and for $500 fr Jefferson R. Smith II to Mary E. Smith, 08/28/1897, respectively, items 20 & 21, author's col.

[2] Tom's Inflation Calculator.

[3] Scagway: The name has been spelled variously since 1882 when it was recorded as *Schkaguè*. In 1891 it was recorded *Shkagway*. Other numerous spellings have been *Skagwa* and *Skaguay*. This latter spelling was predominate until a post office was established in November 1897, but the change was slow in coming. A military post early on was titled Skaguay, and A. C. Harris's widely distributed *The Klondike Gold Fields* (1897) spelled the name Skaguay. (*Geographic Dictionary of Alaska*, 1906).

[4] *Scovell*: spelled *Scovel*. Mrs. Scovel's first name is Frances; she hailed from St. Louis.

[5] *New York World* 02/17/1898, p. 1. Sylvester Scovel was in Havana on 02/15/1898, covering the arrival of the battleship *Maine* for the *New York World* and witnessed the explosion that sank the ship.

[6] never get a cent out of anything in St. Louis: possibly meant is something like "Don't mention this income from your husband as you will never profit anything there in doing so."

[7] Ltr fr Jefferson R. Smith II to Mary E. Smith, 08/28/1897, item 59, author's col. Spelling & punctuation have been regularized somewhat for readability.

[8] *Denver Evening Post* 11/15/1897, p. 7.

Understanding the need to leave residents alone, Jeff made the same promise to Skaguay merchants he had made in Denver, Creede, and other camps. He and the Soap Gang would keep exclusively to transients. Many merchants secretly supported the buncoing enterprises because of the money the gang freely spent in their local stores rather than leaving town and being spent elsewhere. If Jeff's operations kept sizeable amounts of money in town to be spent there, so much the better. Moreover, they were relieved of guilt as they themselves were not performing criminal acts. All they had to do was ignore what was going on. What they did not know could not hurt them. Or so at first they thought. Shea and Patten in their *The "Soapy" Smith Tragedy* (1907) address the change that occurred among merchants and business men who yielded "to the hypnotic influence of this arch-rascal." Made "hungry for the lavish patronage of the gang of rogues," in general, the town

> condoned, aided and abetted. There was a reign of terror in Skagway. Honest men were intimidated. The people were cowed. It was the policy of the gang to prey upon transient travelers and leave such residents as did not oppose them unmolested. The better element became calloused and submissive.[1]

Jeff probably openly prophesied to the businessmen that one way or another the stampeders' money would end up in someone's hands. Why let it go to Canadian merchants when they could just as easily have it. Besides, if his victims could be so easily duped, then they could not possibly be intelligent enough to survive in the wild. Such men could easily become taxing burdens and blights on a community. Jeff was more than willing to put these "new-comers" on a ship for home before such problems could arise. Jeff convinced many that he was doing his victims and the residents of Skaguay a much-needed favor. The businessmen, however, were reaping huge benefits from Jeff and his Soap Gang's activities. In more than just small ways, the businessmen of the town were partners in those activities.

In Jeff's funeral sermon, Rev. Sinclair pointed to this partnership by noting how

> in new and only partially organized towns, the same discrimination between the pure and honorable, and those who are more or less associated with wrong-doing is not so sharply drawn. Many who would not be seen in [the] South or East associating with gamblers, prostitutes or "grafters," will walk with such on the streets, cultivate their custom in business, or even tolerate their influence in civic affairs. Amid such circumstances it requires some extra moral courage, and extra firm faith in ... moral principles ... to choose principle at a loss of profit, and purity of mind and body at a loss of popularity and pleasure. This is made even more difficult by the feeling among many that their present residence is only temporary, that they are really exiles from home merely to make a "stake," and that necessarily many of the maxims and customs of the home land are suspended here.[2]

---

[1] Shea, p. 4.
[2] Skaguay News 07/15/1898. Reprint of Rev. John A. Sinclair's Funeral Sermon.

The camp community had attempted to establish law. On August 12, 1897, a group of "residents" with the help of a miner named Dave McKinney held meetings to set up a self-appointed city council. At this time the Committee of 101, a vigilante society, was organized. Little is known of the early activities of this group, but it is mentioned in the December 31, 1897, edition of *The Skaguay News*.

> The town is without a legal city government simply because the Congress of the United States in its wisdom, has seen fit to enact no laws which would give Alaska any measure of local self-government, and the laws which have been applied to the territory are wholly inadequate to meet any emergency. There has been a nominal supervision exercised over the town by the Committee of 101, a body of men elected by the people during the first great influx into this place. It was sort of a committee of safety, or vigilance committee, but this has fallen into a state of innocuous desuetude, for the very good reason that there has been nothing for it to do.[1]

Certainly Captain Moore would disagree. The stampeders decided to plot the town differently than he had. He could only watch as his land was cut into 3600 lots and sold without his consent or a share of the proceeds.[2]

Several early residents argued that the situation in Skaguay was not a battle between good and evil. Captain Baughman of the steamer *Humboldt* saw the conflict as between two rival groups operating at the same time,

> neither bent on occupations designed to attract the most solid citizens in any community. Nor did either faction parade the shield of virtue until a miscalculation by Smith's crowd on what the public would put up with gave the others an opportunity to step in as upholders of the law, and at the same time put their rivals to rout for good. Smith and his tribe were more clever in making money through shady unproductive enterprise. They were hard to compete against. Better to crush them.[3]

Skaguay pioneer George Dedman echoed this perception:

> There was considerable jealousy and bad blood between the real estate swindlers and the confidence gang under Soapy Smith. It was a case of the pot calling the kettle black."[4]

The feud continued to simmer, and the citizens "were afraid to criticize either side for fear of getting in bad."[5] Denver had the same problem as reported in an 1889 issue of the *Rocky Mountain News*,

> The News has frequently asserted that there was no hope of reform from either one of the factions, which are known respectively as "the gang" and the "gang smashers." As between the two there is no choice—both are equally corrupt, equally venal. "The gang" is supposed to be the fellows who are now

---

[1] *Skaguay News* 12/31/1897, p. 2.

[2] Minter, pp. 74-76.

[3] Ryan, pp. 5 & 19.

[4] *Denver Post* unknown date (post 1898), author's col.

[5] *Oregon Journal* clipping, unknown date, & *Denver Post*, unknown date (post 1898). Author's col.

in power, and want to remain there; the "gang smashers" are the fellows who have fallen out with "the gang" and want to get in office.[1]

Frank H. Reid worked as a bartender at the Klondike saloon, in which Jeff is believed to have held an interest. In 1900, the *Rocky Mountain News* quoted Dr. J. S. McCue, who was in Skaguay at the time, saying that Reid "had formerly been a friend and worker of Smith's."[2] Reid soon found opportunity to employ a skill he had learned in a Michigan college, that of surveyor.[3] Perhaps with foresight, while bartending at the Klondike, Reid "acquired a set of survey instruments from a down-and-out engineer," and at an early citizens' committee of stampeders in the fall of 1897, he made his abilities known and was appointed surveyor. Not long after, Reid managed to nominate himself City Engineer.[4] On August 18, 1897, Reid, William C. Fonda, and W. Thibaudeau surveyed the town site.[5] By December 31 Reid was advertised as the official surveyor with complete records for all lots in town. Skaguay built itself around these plans, including a proposed narrow gage railroad bordering the eastern edge, even though they were not officially adopted until March 8, 1898. Unfortunately for Capt. Moore, the new plans left his cabin directly in the middle of the intersection of Main and McKinney Avenue. In October 1897, the new city council ordered the cabin moved. Moore fought the order, but the city forced its removal to another location.

Moore was not the only one. In an interview in 1900, City Assessor Harry Suydam described how the process worked in 1897.

> During part of this winter I spent several nights a week attending ... "miners' meetings," some of which were held to compel men who had built along the trail to move their cabins and conform to our new street system, which had been adopted by the majority of citizens. These pioneers who were blocking our fast-growing town streets with their buildings, fought hard to be left alone; but it was a physical impossibility to build any town with zig-zag trails, or alleys, running through our cross section of streets.

> Our methods were apt to be summary in those days. We would march in a body to the objectionable building, and, though we were often opposed by rifles, shotguns and axes, the offenders would invariably weaken after a stiff fight, and then their property would be demolished. If no resistance was offered, both buildings and their contents would be moved in a careful manner.[6]

In one month's time since the arrival of the first ship on July 26, 1897, Skaguay progressed from a beachhead of transients to a confused and seething boomtown of 5,000 to 6,000 residents and stampeders with 1000 new ones passing through each

---

[1] *RMN*, 09/21/1889, p. 2.
[2] *RMN* 01/28/1900.
[3] Mayberry, pp. 18-19.
[4] Minter, p. 74.
[5] Spude, p. 40.
[6] Suydam, *The Reign*, pp. 213-214.

week. At the height of the rush to the Klondike, between August 1897 to August 1898, the population of Skaguay fluctuated between 10,000 and 20,000 residents.[1]

That first winter, stampeders in Skaguay bought land on which to build crude cabins for shelter until they could leave for the Klondike. The moment they left to begin transporting supplies up the trail, lot jumpers squatted on the land and sold it to the first stranger who would buy it. When the rightful owners returned, they found their property had been sold, and if gone for long, perhaps resold half a dozen times. Then the current occupant would staunchly resist removal.[2] US Commissioner John U. Smith had been appointed Recorder of Town Lots, and his poor administration of recording contributed immeasurably to the problem.[3] But it was not just incompetence that led to problems. This Smith, "John U." (and no relation to Jeff) was a Portland, Oregon, lawyer who was appointed in July 1896 as US Commissioner of Alaska. He was a man who, as Governor Brady said, had "a hunger and thirst for fees"[4] and who went after them both legally and illegally. He had been on the job less than four months before the US president and secretary of the interior had received from Governor Brady "Formal charges ... against John U. Smith" for "usurpation of unwarranted authority, of taking extortionate fees for his services, and other grave irregularities."[5] With regard to lots in Skaguay, the *Morning Oregonian* in February 1898 reported from the *Alaska Mining Record* that

> "Through his 'bureau of information,' which is conducted through his many grafters, he advertises townsite locations, creates a stampede of the people, who begin locating lots in every direction, and a few weeks later John U. himself establishes an office ... and announces that he is ready to record lots at $5 apiece. In addition to this, he will tell you that it is necessary to have your lot surveyed—which is all rot—and this will cost you another $5 or $10.
>
> "Smith first had his office at Skagway. After all the available land in that section was located, he immediately began doing business in Dyea. He was next heard from at Sheep Camp. Soon ... he went to Haines Mission, put up a tent and soon began doing a flourishing business. ..."[6]

Next he tried to do business up the trail at Lake Lindemann beyond the Chilkoot and White Pass summits, but that was in US and Canadian disputed territory, as the boundary had not yet been established, and the Canadians ordered him to desist.

Confusion exists about who was behind the Bureau of Information. Jeff Smith had a Skaguay establishment by this name (which will be addressed). It could be, though, that about land sales, the two Smiths had reached some sort of understanding, and perhaps not for the last time. Another connection between the men might have been Frank Reid, a trained surveyor who for a time worked as a bartender in the Klondike saloon, in which Jeff is thought to have been a part owner. Did Reid pay both Smiths a

---

[1] *Skagway News*, Summer edition, 1992.
[2] Suydam, *The Reign*, p. 214.
[3] Minter, p. 74.
[4] Hunt, *Distant*, p. 56.
[5] *New York Times* 11/23/1897.
[6] *Morning Oregonian* 02/14/1898, p. 5.

fee from the "fee for lot" surveying work that came his way? To John U. Smith, perhaps, but to Jeff, probably no. When Reid became a surveyor, he seems to have aligned himself with Jeff's competition, the secret city vigilance organization, later naming itself the Committee of 101.

To decide disputes over lots was "an executive committee of five, who sat twice a week to hear and adjust grievances...." Harry Suydam, the Assessor, was one of these, "and whenever our decisions were disputed..., we were empowered to call on two hundred enrolled citizens to execute our sentence." Suydam reports that more than once the committee was "threatened with shooting, and twice I was held up, and once beaten for my pains...."[1] Lack of clarity and lax authority often resulted in wearing down the resolve of original property owners, causing them to give up.

Saloon proprietors from the start were very successful in Skaguay. The District of Alaska required alcohol sales permits to be purchased from the governor as well as the US Internal Revenue Service,[2] but few heeded the law. The first issue of *The Skaguay News*, on October 15, 1897, reported 11 saloons in town.[3] At the height of the gold rush, running without interference, Skaguay had 5 breweries and 70 of Alaska's 142 saloons. Organized crime was also running with little interference. Stampeder Alexander MacDonald in a 1905 book about his experiences wrote, "I have stumbled upon some tough corners of the globe during my wanderings beyond the outposts of civilization, but I think the most outrageously lawless quarter I have ever struck was Skaguay."[4] Major Samuel B. Steel, Superintendent of the Yukon Northwest Mounted Police, wrote that Skaguay

> was about the roughest place in the world. The population increased every day; gambling hells, dance halls and variety theatres were in full swing. ... At night the crash of bands, shouts of "Murder!" cries for help mingled with the cracked voices of the singers in the variety halls. ... One Sunday morning..., bullets came through the thin boards [of our cabin], but the circumstance was such a common event that we did not even rise from our beds."[5]

William Hunt in *Distant Justice: Policing the Alaska Frontier* (1987) believed that "Steele exaggerated" for the purpose of distinguishing Skaguay from Dawson and enhancing "the Mounties' reputation."[6] The apparent calmness of the statement does seem to make the event seem common. But it should be noted that the Mounties in Skaguay had no authority to act as peace officers, so what else could be done during the apparent fight outside except to continue to "lie low" in their beds. Stray bullets penetrating walls at this time, while not common, was no exaggeration.

Skaguay News man E. J. Stroller White reports such an event in one of his more sober columns about those times. One "night a man was killed in the Klondike Saloon and the stranger who did the shooting fled to the street, pursued by a crowd of

---

[1] Suydam, *The Reign*, p. 214.
[2] Alaska Public Safety.
[3] *Skaguay News 10/15/1897*.
[4] MacDonald, p. 3.
[5] Steele, pp. 295-298.
[6] Hunt, *Distant*, p. 55.

enraged friends of the deceased." White had been sleeping underneath the printing press in The *News* building when five shots were fired after the man "just as he passed the printing office." Two of these hit the sidewalk, but three flew into the building. The next morning White secured "several sheets of boiler iron with which to surround" his sleeping area.[1]

Skaguay was the Promised Land for Jeff. His arrival added man-made villainy to the hazards already imposed by nature. The Skaguay Valley in which nestled the town bottlenecked in the steep mountains, and through it victims were forced to file. The bunco men literally had gold seekers going and coming from the tidal camp. Conversely, this natural funnel would later hinder escape for the Soap Gang.

As the newly appointed deputy US marshal of the district, James Mark Rowan was stationed at neighboring Dyea along with a detachment of soldiers. When Skaguay outgrew Dyea, Rowan moved his office there. On February 25, 1897, 100 soldiers of the 14th Infantry arrived in Skaguay to establish a post. In addition to being available to supply stampeders with relief should it be needed and control in case of large-scale civil unrest, the US Army was there to keep peace with Canada. Under the command of Colonel Thomas M. Anderson, post headquarters were later moved to Dyea as a better strategic location.[2] Federal law, then as now, stated that the military could not be called out to Skaguay unless the need for martial law was imminent.

When a legal matter needed resolving, it was lodged with the US Commissioner in Dyea, a four-mile boat voyage from Skaguay. Once made, the complainant had to guarantee attendance at a hearing. The guarantee was required because too many litigants continued their journey to the gold fields instead of attending hearings and trials. To those seeking justice in the courts and a mining claim over 600 miles away, it was a matter of priorities. This slow legal system worked to the great benefit of Jeff and his Soap Gang, as few victims were willing to wait out the slow turning of the wheels of justice. Jeff knew what he was doing, as he had done it all before in Denver and Creede. For him Skaguay was a gold rush within a gold rush.

Jeff hated the Alaska winter[3] and would have preferred to spend it down in the states. With business so good, though, he would endure the wind, rain, snow, and cold. Something else, though, made Jeff leave Skaguay while his operations were so successful, Mary. Receiving word that she was ill, on September 14, 1897, Jeff boarded the *SS Queen*[4] and docked in Seattle eight days later. *The Seattle Daily Times* interviewed passengers returning from the Klondike, and Jeff was one of them. In his interview he claimed to have earned $18,000 to $20,000 during his short stay in Skaguay,[5] amounts equivalent today to between about $562,320 and $624,800.[6]

US Attorney Bennett and US Marshal James McCain Shoup were also on board the *Queen*. They claimed that the residents of Skaguay had forced Jeff out of Alaska.[7]

---

[1] DeArmond, p. 61.
[2] Sorley.
[3] Statement made by Mary Eva Smith to her grandson Randolph J. Smith (circa 1927).
[4] Ship roster information provided by Howard Clifford.
[5] *Seattle Daily Times* 09/23/1897.
[6] Tom's Inflation Calculator.
[7] *Denver Evening Post* 09/23/1897.

In November 1897 "Bat" Masterson returned from Washington state and spoke to the *Denver Evening Post* about Jeff's departure from Alaska.

> I saw very few people from Denver. I heard of but did not see Soapy Smith. The report that he was driven out of Skaguay was erroneous. I met his partner Jerry Daily, at Spokane. He said they were in Skaguay twenty-three days and 'worked' nineteen days while there. During the nineteen days they captured $30,000, which was divided into four parts, over $7,000 each, but Soapy got the most of it ultimately. He received a telegram that his wife was sick in St. Louis and went to that city to be with her. They did not have time to bother with him at Skaguay, for everybody was too busy looking out for themselves.[1]

Jeff must have discovered that Mary was better, probably by telegraph, because nine days later he was still in Seattle, lodging in the business district called Pioneer Place, known today as Pioneer Square. Gold rush Seattle had become notorious for wide-open gambling and prostitution. Like the old clunker ships that were given new life and sent to Alaska, old buildings and warehouses were remodeled into saloons and gambling dens. By day, Seattle bustled with activities associated with outfitting and transportation. By night, according to one newspaper headline, it became "a hot town" that catered to the needs of a largely transient population.[2] One of the amusement houses in which Jeff spent his nights was the Horse Shoe Grill Room and saloon located at 914 Front Street.[3] This place was to Seattle what the Arcade was to Denver, making it a popular destination among Seattle's leading gamblers and underworld figures. On October 1, 1897, a sizable affray erupted between two groups of men, one of whom was Jeff. Denver's *Rocky Mountain News* reported what was known of the confrontation.

ROUGH AND TUMBLE FIGHT

> Jeff Smith and Jimmy Dugan Badly Beaten Up in a Saloon Row.
> Special to The News. SEATTLE, Wash., Oct. 1. —Jeff Smith, Jimmy Dugan and Elmer Maybury, formerly a Denver sport, engaged in a fight to-night in the Horse's Shoe saloon, during which Maybury was stabbed once in the arm and his clothes cut several times. Ed. Gaffney, a local athlete, who took Maybury's part, narrowly escaped a deadly thrust from Dugan's knife. Smith and Dugan were badly beaten up. An old grudge on the part of Smith toward Maybury was the cause of the row. The saloon floor was covered with blood. A plate glass mirror was broken and guns were in sight all around.[4]

No record of arrests or other details could be found. As no known grudge existed between Jeff and Maybury, the fight might have been over "turf," in which a local gang did not appreciate Jeff's presence. What is certain is that Jeff now had enemies in Seattle. He continued on his way to St. Louis.

---

[1] *Denver Evening Post* 11/15/1897, p. 7.
[2] *Seattle Daily Times* 10/07/1897.
[3] Seattle City Directory 1895-96. A 2" by 2" advertisement, p. 402. And Seattle City Directory 1898, p. 498. Today the site is 614 Howard Building next to the Pioneer building at Pioneer Square Park.
[4] *RMN* 10/02/1897.

Mary's illness must have had no lingering effects as no further recorded word of it is known. After time with his wife and children, in November 1897, Jeff traveled to Washington, DC, on business and pleasure, and got together with his double first cousin, Edwin Bobo Smith. They had not seen one another since they were boys in Round Rock, Texas, twenty years before. Edwin recorded the day of their meeting.

> One day in the latter part of 1897, a telephone message came from the Willard Hotel that a gentleman who declined to give his name wanted to see me. It seemed a bit mysterious, but I went and there was Jeff; but in the bearded stranger, it was hard to recognize my ancient alter ego. There was an emotional moment and then he plunged into the object of his visit: "I am here ... because of some important business and to see you. The thing I have set my mind on is going to Alaska; the states are about played out, overcrowded, and Alaska is the last frontier. Up in the Klondike there is more gold than ever California or Australia produced and the early birds are going to get the big rewards. What I'll thank you to do for me is to get a permit from the war department to operate a hotel up there; the miners must have meals somewhere and a place to lodge, for it is a pretty tough country and a long way from civilization. They will need amusement, too, and my hotel will provide music, dancing, and if they want, poker, faro, roulette and so forth. ... But we don't have to go into such details with Uncle Sam do we?" He was reassured on this point and elated when told he could hope for a government concession in forty-eight hours. Well, his request was granted and meanwhile he was taken in tow to see the nation's capitol.[1]

In 1897 Ed was a reporter for the *Washington Post*. This position and his prior service in the US Congress gave him numerous influential contacts, and he used them to try to help Jeff make a respectable name for himself. In a 1920 interview for *The Trail* magazine, Edwin said that Jeff wanted a concession for a hotel site on the government reservation at St. Michael, Alaska.

> His intention seems to have been to seek an honorable fortune in the frozen north and then to return to Washington and establish himself in the respectable life of a hotel proprietor. His cousin made a vain effort to keep him out of Alaska, but he expressed the greatest confidence in the success of his schemes in that distant region and was intent upon going.... "This ... is my last opportunity to make a big haul. Alaska is the last West. I know the character of people I shall meet there and I know that I am bound to succeed with them."[2]

In another writing, Ed interviewed Jeff for his newspaper.

> Mr. Jefferson R. Smith of the state of Washington, who has been in Alaska for the past 3 years,[3] was entertaining a party at Chamberlain's last

---

[1] Smith, Edwin, & ltr fr Jefferson R. Smith III, 06/15/1941.

[2] *Trail*, p. 9.

[3] *past 3 years*: Jeff, of course, had resided in Alaska for fewer than three months. Perhaps the thought was to enhance Jeff's authority on the state of affairs in Alaska.

evening with descriptions of the gold country, and the life of the hardy adventurers who have gone onto that region.

Any man in good health, said Mr. Smith, can stand the climate, and most people get fat and robust while staying up there. I have slept for weeks in wet clothing and never knew what it was to be sick. But of course a man wouldn't go up there purely for the climate, and it must be confessed that the long winter nights are very monotonous.

The rush of the people next spring will be something unprecedented in the annals of the world. I believe at least 200,0000 fortune hunters will make for the Klondike just as soon as the weather will admit.[1] I notice that agents sent out by Victoria merchants are trying to make it appear that the British Columbia town is a better place for out fitting than Seattle. This ought not to pass unchallenged. Seattle is ... the best place to get equipped, as the merchants there are in every way better provided with all the necessities needed by the miner, nor will a single cent of tariff tax be imposed on outfits brought in from the United States, although that falsehood was also circulated in the interest of Victoria.

I think there is gold in Alaska beyond imagination of man to depict, and I have been over the greater part of it, and in the British possessions as well, [−] of course, not all the people that are going after gold will succeed; only a small percent, in fact will acquire a big amount, but the few who do make a strike will take out enough to satisfy them. As soon as a considerable population gets in there, no doubt there will be a move to obtain for the territory a regular territorial form of government. This will be bitterly fought by the big steamship and trading companies and mining syndicates. They have no taxes to pay now, and they are well content to have the present status maintained.

I was at Skagway when there were 6,000 people there, and never saw a more orderly crowd. A move was made to get up a law and order society, something after the fashion of the California vigilantes, but the thing was so utterly uncalled for that its promoters were forced to abandon the project. There was no stealing, no homicide, not even simple fights, and I consider this a remarkable thing when you take in[to] consideration the mixed character of these sojourners made up of adventurers from every part of the country.[2]

To portray Skaguay as an inviting destination and perhaps to cover some of his own deeds there, Jeff was obviously exaggerating and sometimes outright lying.

Ed led Jeff around town and introduced him to numerous Washington dignitaries, including Senators George Graham Vest of Missouri, William Morris Stewart of

---

[1] *200,000 fortune hunters*: the number may seem an overstate, but Pierre Berton in his *Klondike* (1972-2001) records the following: "...it has been reckoned that in the winter of 1897-98 one million people laid plans to leave home and family to seek their fortune in the Klondike and that, at the very least, one hundred thousand actually set out" (Berton, p. 116).

[2] *Washington Post* 11/11/1897.

Nevada, George Laird Shoup of Idaho, Edward Oliver Wolcott of Colorado, Congressman John Calhoun Bell of Colorado, well-known Washington journalist Marse Henry Watterson, and ex-Texas Representative Colonel Ochiltree. Jeff was making an impression in the nation's capital. Richard Harding Davis, editor of *Harper's Weekly*, was in town and had read the *Post* interview. Davis had known Jeff in Denver and Creede, and in 1892 had published *The West From A Car Window* in which Jeff figures several times. Davis contacted Ed and set up a dinner engagement. William F. Hynes, a Denver justice of the peace and political figure, joined the assemblage at the Raleigh hotel. During the meal Jeff was his usual highly entertaining self, full of humorous anecdotes. At the conclusion of the evening the men lounged in the lobby before exchanging good-byes. In parting Ed, drew his cousin aside and thinking he was out of hearing range, said, "'Jeff, give up the whisky or the gun!'" Davis heard the statement and at outside the hotel, he declared, "Well, boys, I believe it is true that after all there is something good in the worst of us, and perhaps something bad in the best of us." Ed quickly added, "And God only knows what's in the rest of us!"[1]

To the *News* in 1929, Hynes spoke his mind about meeting Jeff:

> To a stranger he would pass on the street for anything but what he really was. He appeared rather like a fairly prosperous businessman. He was popular even with the officer who sometimes sought him for consultation. He was always armed; usually he carried a pet white-handled pistol.[2]

In a 1937 revision of his manuscript about Jeff, Ed mined deeper into his recollection of Jeff's Washington visit:

> Meanwhile he was taken in tow to see the nation's capitol; first of all to the Senate chamber where he especially wished to meet Senator Edward Wolcott, of his own state, whose brilliant oratory put him on a pedestal. There was a bond between them, growing out of gaming; both were plungers and many an all night session had been spent together in "fighting the tiger" in Denver's sporting lairs. There was a hearty greeting and a luncheon at which Wolcott inquired of Jeff the cause of his visit. When told, he said: Jeff are you going up there to mine gold or skin suckers?
>
> The other grinned: A little of both, Senator. And if anything real good turns up, shall I put you in on it?
>
> By all means put me in and notify me by wire what money I am to put up; I'll take your word for everything.
>
> At the Chamberlin's famous club where nightly gathered the bon vivants, Jeff met distinguished companions, getting introductions through Wolcott to such notables as Marse Henry Watterson, former Texas Representative Col. Tom Ochiltree, Senator William Stewart of Nevada, Senator M. C. Butler of South Carolina, and many authors, actors, and artists. To say he enchanted them is simple truth; the tales he spun fascinated his audience. Ochiltree,

---

[1] *Denver News* 08/28/1931.
[2] *RMN* 08/28/1929.

often styled the modern Munchausen,[1] gaped at one who easily outclassed him. He would combine romance with reality beyond any of the raconteurs of the day. When all but the habitués had left and the talk still revolved about the spectacular stranger, Senator Wolcott said:

"In this man, Jeff Smith, the elements are strangely mixed. He has sins to answer for, of course, but there is much to his credit side of the ledger. With a friend, his word is as good as a bond. If he has been spoliator, he has never failed to divide his depredations with the needy. No beggar ever appealed to him in vain, and wherever humans are hungry, he is the first to give out rations. The poor out our way look on him as Jim Fiske[2] used to be regarded in New York. They said ... he never went back on the poor; It's the same way with Jeff. All the little children in his block run to meet him. I have told him that he should have located in New York where squeamishness is not prevalent, and where he would have been one of Dick Croker's[3] most trusted lieutenants. Denver is too much of a 'pent-up Utopia' for his special kind of talent; the biggest city in the world is not too large for him."

When the time came for him [Jeff] to leave Washington, a dozen of his new acquaintances urged him to remain longer; John Chamberlin, formerly famous in New York sporting circles, proffered him free lodging and board indefinitely; Alfred Henry Lewis[4] offered a percentage of a new novel Jeff had inspired. My own entreaties were added, but to no avail; irrevocably his thoughts were fixed on the new El Dorado.[5]

While being enjoyed and respected in Washington, Jeff remembered his family. On Sunday, November 14, 1897, from the Raleigh Hotel on its stationary, he wrote to his ten-year-old son, Jefferson. Perhaps some topic of conversation that evening had struck a chord with Jeff that brought him to write.

Dear son Jeff-

I wrote to mama from Fayetteville, N. C., and I guess the letter is to hand by this time. I want you to look out for your hand, hurry up, and learn your books, as you won't have the chance all the time as you have now. You know that a man that don't know how to read and write and count is no good, and if he drinks whiskey and beer he is sure to be a bum. Don't be crazy to play all the.... [text missing][6]

The rest of the letter is lost. An interesting part of the letter involves a father telling his son to "look out for your hand." A family story called "The Curse of Wagon Wheel Gap" tells how a victim of Jeff's games near Creede put a hex on the Smith family. Forever,

---

[1] *Munchausen*: Karl Friedrich Hieronymus Freiherr von Münchhausen (1720-1797): 18th C teller of tall tales.

[2] *Jim Fiske*: 19th C New York confidence man.

[3] *Dick Croker*: 19th C New York crime boss.

[4] *Alfred Henry Lewis* (1857-1914): journalist and author of 18 books. (*New York Times* 12/24/1914)

[5] Unpublished manuscript by Edwin Bobo Smith, 06/15/1941. He never finished it, dying five months later on 11/01/1941. Geri Murphy col.

[6] Ltr fr Jefferson R. Smith II to Jefferson R. Smith III, 11/14/1897, Geri Murphy col.

the hand of all first-born males would be impaired. Fear of this curse was renewed in the Smith family when the first grandson was born with a deformed left hand.

Jeff was getting around. After being with his family in St. Louis and before going to Washington, Jeff went to North Carolina, as mentioned in the letter to his son. A reason for the trip is not known nor has the letter to Mary from there survived. From Washington, Jeff went to New York City for thirteen days.[1] On November 30, the *Rocky Mountain News* reported Jeff "in New York organizing a Klondyke expedition to start from the East in February."[2] Then on December 7, the *News* reported that

> O. L. Smith has returned from New York, where he met a number of Denver men who are pushing Klondyke schemes of various kinds. Among the boomers encountered by Mr. Smith were "Doc" Darnell, Jim Duggan and "Soapy" Smith. The Denver talent is making a success of arousing interest ... and Duggan prophesies that the company of which he is one of the principals will transport 1,000 Eastern gold-hunters to the great placers of the North.[3]

Nothing more is known of these men or this activity. It could have been a rumor, an honest enterprise, or a swindle. That it was the latter would be the safest bet.

William Devere, author of the poems "Two Little Busted Shoes" and "Jeff and Joe," was in New York at the time. In an 1899 interview, Devere spoke of Jeff's visit.

> About eight months before he was killed Smith came to New York to visit several of his friends, among them myself and Frank Keeney..., who is now manager of the Metropole hotel. Smith stayed in that hotel for two weeks and in that time he made a friend of every guest and hanger-on at the hotel. He had a wonderful faculty of making friends, and he never wronged a friend. When news of his death came, every man in the Hotel Metropole was ready to assert that Jefferson Randolph Smith was one of the cleverest gentlemen he had ever known. ... Soapy Smith ... was another man with a bad name who was a good fellow. ... He was a born leader of men.[4]

Nearly a half year later, in a letter dated "Mar, 27, −98" on *Washington Post* stationary, Cousin Edwin wrote to Jeff to convey remembrances from Congressmen who still reminisced over his visit to the capitol.

> Dear Brother Jeff:
>
> Glad to get your letter. I am so busy you must excuse me for not writing sooner. I saw Senator Wolcott and he asked to be remembered to you. Ex-Congressman Bell of Colorado and Congressman Shafroth[5] also ask me about you every time I see them. Baily of Texas wants to know when you are coming back here. He will be the next speaker if the House goes Democratic. I wish you would write and give me all the news. I want to print [it] in the Post.
>
> Your brother Ed[6]

---

[1] *Morning Telegraph* 11/27/1897.

[2] *RMN* 11/30/1897, p. 8.

[3] *RMN*, 12/07/1897, p. 10.

[4] Waterloo Daily Courier 12/21/1899.

[5] John Franklin Shafroth became governor of Colorado fr 1908 to 1912.

[6] Ltr fr Ed Smith to Jefferson R. Smith II, 03/27/1898, item 3, author's col.

Those connections along with Edwins' faithful efforts secured Jeff something he very much wanted: permission to build at an American gateway to the Klondike. In October 1897, to help control the disorder created by the gold rush, the US government opened Fort St. Michael on St. Michael Island, District of Alaska. It was in a new place of abundant opportunity without competition, and at 2,000 miles from Seattle, surely it was far enough away that his name would not be there to greet him. Situated near the mouth of the Yukon River, it would be the transfer point from ocean-going vessels to flat-bottomed boats that would ply the Yukon River to and from Dawson City, the boomtown nearest the gold-laden creeks. The authorization appeared on a single typed page.

65828 A. G. O.

War Department,
Adjutant General's Office,
Washington, January 28, 1898.

J. R. Smith Esq.,
Care E. B. Smith, Washington Post,
Washington, D.C.

Sir: –

I have the honor to inform you that a suitable location for the business purpose of your company, as far as grounds, etc., [per the] available permit, on the military reservation of Fort St. Michael, Alaska, has been approved by the Secretary of War, and the papers forwarded to the Commanding Officer at that point, with instructions that, upon presentation of this letter, he shall without delay proceed to stake out the grounds, etc., necessary for your business, under the enclosed regulations, and permit you to enter upon and use them, pending the completion of the formal permit by the signature of the Secretary of War and seal of the Department.

Very respectfully,

Sm'l Breck [signed]
Adjutant General.[1]

With the order came an eight-page booklet entitled *Regulations Governing The Use and Occupancy of Lands Within the Limits of the Military Reservation of Fort St. Michael, Alaska.*[2] The permission and the rules for using it arrived about the second week of February. Now Jeff had a decision to make. He could build a hotel at what surely would be a major American entrance to the Klondike. Through it would pass, coming and going, vast amounts of money and gold, and many were the ways he knew how to take a share of it. But first, much needed to be done. To build the hotel, he would have to raise many thousands of dollars, arrange for supplies and builders, probably leave right away by steamship around the Aleutian island range, a voyage of about 2000 miles, stand the cost of bringing up his men.... Or should he stay where he had already staked a successful claim to a temporarily captive migrant population of

---

[1] Land use Permit fr war department, 01/28/1898, posted this date but bearing no date of receipt, item 45, author's col.

[2] Booklet, 1898, item 36, author's col.

thousands, knowing that tens of thousands more would be arriving in the spring? Skaguay was certain to be a huge success that spring whereas.... Round and round went the planning and comparisons of outcomes. And then the battleship *Maine* blew up in Havana harbor and hearts began a patriotic beat. When news of the explosion reached Skaguay about February 22, Jeff might have immediately conceived of forming an army company of men around the event. He knew if he chose to lead the way, men would follow. A double murder had occurred, and Jeff successfully talked down angry townsmen and probably prevented the lynching of the shooter. And business (gambling, sure-thing operations, land speculation...) was booming. Busy with it all and collecting a share from dozens of operators and activities in Skaguay, more than ever before, it seems likely Jeff one day put the letter of permission in his trunk and tended to the business at hand.

Chapter 19
Striking It Rich in Skaguay

In the boom town at the entrance to White pass, "Soapy" is a power and a prominent citizen. The sporting fraternity owe allegiance to his cause and when the place is incorporated will further his ambition to be Chief of Police.
— *San Francisco Examiner*, February 25, 1898

Although Jeff was reported in New York at the end of November, at a Thanksgiving masquerade ball, *The Skaguay News* listed a "J. Smith" attending as a Tin Goblin. Also listed was William Saportas, a new Skaguay "associate" of Jeff's, attired as a Northwest Mounted Police officer.[1] As Jeff had done in Creede, he worked at developing relationships with merchants, civic leaders, and newspapers. Jeff was not shy about approaching those he thought he could work with. In Seattle he told Willis Loomis, an ex-Denver police officer, "I'm going to be the boss of Skaguay. I know exactly how to do it, and if you come along I'll make you chief of police." Loomis declined.[2] Not known is the extent of Jeff's influence in Dyea. Evidence, though, shows that he had felt things out there. On the back of an envelope received in late January 1898, Jeff scribbled, "Wells Dyea Saloon ok."[3] In long form, this note to himself might read, "Wells of the Dyea Saloon is ok to work in with our kinds of cons." Adding to speculation that Jeff had influence in Dyea is a notice that appeared in an 1898 issue of a Florida newspaper, the *Gulf Coast Breeze*, stating that those who operate in Dyea, Sheep Camp and along to the base of Chilkoot are under the leadership of Tom Cady, a notorious Colorado camp confidence man."[4] Cady was an

---

[1] *Skaguay News* 12/04/1897, p. 4.
[2] Berton, p. 103.
[3] No Wells or Dyea Saloon is on record with the Klondike Gold Rush National Historical Park, but listed is a Dyea Beer Hall. Envelope addressed to Jeff R. Smith jr. c/o Horse Shoe Saloon, Seattle, WA. Postmarks show Washington, DC, 01/17/1898 & Seattle 01/23/1898, item 66, author's col.
[4] *Gulf Coast Breeze* 06/10/1898.

instrumental member of the Soap Gang in Colorado, and if he were truly in charge of Dyea's underworld, then he was doing so as an associate of Jeff.

From Skaguay pioneer Harriet Pullen, it was learned that Jeff paid the George Mason Company in Denver, a wholesaler of gambling equipment and supplies, $1000 for a roulette wheel and equipment, including shipment to Skaguay.[1] To keep down enormous shipping costs, the wooden table and legs were manufactured in Skaguay. Chances are it was one of the first wheels of its kind in the camp. Two letters to Jeff from Mary in March 1886 were addressed to Jeff at 1711 Larimer Street, Denver, which was next door to George Mason and Company. Knowing Mason personally, Jeff probably also purchased other gambling gear, honest and crooked, from the firm. Where the wheel was placed is not known, but period photographs show it was not in Jeff Smith's Parlor. There would not have been room for it there.

Rev. Robert M. Dickey wrote in his diary for "8 Oct Sailed up the Lynn Canal & anchored off Skagway in afternoon." In 1895 at age 27, he had been recruited from Ireland by Rev. James Robertson, Superintendent of Canadian Presbyterian Western Missions. Two years later, Dickey was in the second of a three-year curriculum at Winnipeg's Manitoba College when Robertson recruited him for the Klondike. Not even yet ordained, Dickey was reluctant, but Robertson convinced him he was the man to go. On September 5, 1897, Dickey was bade farewell as the "'first Missionary to the Klondike'" and ordained at Victoria, British Columbia, on September 16. On October 2, he embarked for Skaguay aboard the Canadian SS Quadra.[2]

Found among the papers of Rev. Dickey is the clipping of a news story titled "First Divine Service." "In Skaguay" is added in Dickey's hand. Penned at the bottom appears "From the Globe 10 Nov 1897 / Report of special correspondent." This article is helpful in detailing what happened next and in putting certain matters into perspective concerning Jeff.

> The Quadra had the honor of bringing to Skagway their first clergyman, Rev. R. M. Dickey, sent by the Presbyterian Church of Canada. He intended going through to Dawson at once, but that being so difficult and finding here a population of 1,500 without the ministrations of religion, decided to stay for the winter at all events. He went on shore on Saturday [October 9, 1897] and posted up notices about the town that Divine service would be held in a hall above the new hotel at 3 o'clock on Sunday. At that hour 70 persons had assembled. There were twelve women, wives and daughters of traders. Some Indians and a noted pugilist and gambler were among the motley congregation. Mr. Dickey stood in front with a Bible in his hand and conducted the service. ... His rich, sympathetic voice stirred their memories and scenes of childhood, bringing back the old mother and the home. ... After the service a photograph of the scene was taken, then a committee meeting was held, and they offered to build Mr. Dickey a church and have it ready in

---

[1] Table was in possession of Harriet Pullen until 1973 when the author's father purchased it. In a Dec 1907 issue of Alaska-Yukon Magazine, Mrs. Pullen circled a published ltr fr George Mason to Jeff and wrote, "Soapy paid [$]1000. for a roulette table bought at this place. Mrs. Pullen has the table."

[2] Dickey Diary for all dates shown.

three weeks. The well-known gambler occupied a front seat and followed the service attentively, afterwards giving the verdict that Mr. Dickey was the right sort of stuff. Of that there is no doubt, Mr. Dickey making an excellent impression. His pluck in volunteering to go to the Yukon at this season indicates the right man for the work.[1]

Rev. Dickey recorded that the service for seventy was held in Burkhard Hall and that they sang "the old familiar hymns & tears were in many eyes. At close, asked" was if services and a Sunday school were wanted regularly, "& every hand went up." Then "those interested" were asked to wait to arrange time & place. "70 waited & unanimously decided to build a church. Building committee appointed. Ladies appointed to raise funds." They met that day and "divided the town into districts for collection."[2] Not recorded by Rev. Dickey is how the "well-known gambler" occupied a front seat" and afterward affirmed the minister was "the right man for the work." Seeming certain is that this gambler, this "well-known gambler," was Jeff R. Smith.

Rev. Dickey worked, from 1940 when he retired from the Presbyterian Church until his death in 1950, on a fictionalized account of his experiences in Skaguay, on the Trail, and in the Klondike. In that account, titled *Gold Fever* (1997), Dickey included most of the clipping from *The Globe*. He left in the "noted pugilist" but did not include the "well-known gambler"—nor where he sat (up close) and especially not that the gambler affirmed him. In his book, Rev. Dickey, in fact, paints "Soapy" Smith as the primary antagonist during Dickey's six months in Skaguay. So it would not do to have "Soapy" affirming him, especially not in matters concerning the building of the Union Church, and especially not where it came to the contribution of money to the church. Here's why:

In Philip Godsell's *They Got their Man* (1939), related is the often-repeated story about how

> When a transient apostle appeared penniless in Skaguay, despairing of his hope of erecting a church and mitigating the evils of the place ... it was Soapy who came to the rescue ... handed over $200 that lay on the gambling table before him. Visiting every civil and honky-tonk and gambling joint in town, Soapy handed the amazed preacher that night an additional $500 with the promise of more to come.[3]

On June 20, 1944, Rev. Dickey saw fit to write to the widow of Rev. John Sinclair, the Canadian who had replaced Dickey in Skaguay in April 1898. Dickey wrote that he need not tell Mrs. Sinclair how Godsell's story

> is an absolute falsehood. Your dear husband and I were the only ministers of any denomination in Skaguay. The story is a malicious slander and an insult to the church. I wrote to Godsell and told him it was absolutely false.[4]

---

[1] *The Globe* 11/10/1897, a clipping fr among Rev. Dickey's papers and photographs of the Klondike Gold Rush period.

[2] Dickey Diary for 10/10/1898.

[3] Mills, p. 23.

[4] Mills, p. 24, the footnote for which reads, "'John A Sinclair Papers.' Letter of June 20, 1944, fr R.M Dickey to Mrs. John A. Sinclair. In possession of Jas. M. Sinclair, Winnipeg" (Mills, p. 85).

At the time Jeff was alive, Skaguay had but one church, and for it, Rev. Dickey never solicited funds. Reports indicate this work was done by "the ladies," who canvassed the town, and by members of the congregation. The sequence of the fund raising was covered in *Skaguay News* articles that Rev. Dickey included in a chapter in his book about the building of the Union Church, which was dedicated on December 12, 1897.[1] The articles were clipped by Dickey and paper clipped to his diary.

The story of a preacher in Skaguay soliciting money in saloons for a church appeared in various publications, usually without attribution. Martin Itjen in his "Early Days of '98" tourbook (1934) is an exception. Itjen wrote that "A minister went" into a saloon "one day in June, 1898,[2] soliciting aid to build a church. The gamblers and patrons donated freely, some $5.00, $10.00, and $15.00 each and some donated labor." This description is clearly transported from *The Skaguay News* report of the regular Sunday church service of October 24. Stated was that the pastor said that "although the response had been liberal, yet they were" still short $120. Then

> One man after another stood up ... and gave five, ten, twenty and in one case sixty dollars. Even the children came forward with their dimes and received the hearty applause of the people. Altogether over $200.00 were subscribed in the meeting, and that amount has since been added to.[3]

Rev. Dickey in his diary for October 24 recorded how "At close [of service] told them we still wanted 120. Amid great enthusiasm over $200 subscribed." And the entry for October 25: "Collected nearly all the money promised yesterday."[4]

But in the saloon in Martin Itjen's published version,

> The minister also approached Soapy, who was playing faro, saying, "Mr. Smith we have planned to build a church here in Skagway, but we need money, would you help this cause?"
>
> Soapy pushed a bunch of bills that he had on the table towards the minister, saying, "take that." "Thanks," said the minister, "set down your name." Soapy replied, "never mind, just put down cash and get out." The bystanders estimated the amount to be about $200. Charlie Walker ... was the eye witness to this affair who is a florist in Skagway at this time.[5]

So this was Itjen's documentation. However, the newspaper report and Rev. Dickey's handwritten diary are better. Nothing in Dickey's life contains even a hint of soliciting in this way, or any way, and even Jeff would likely have been offended at how these stories portrayed him, as a flamboyant braggart in the first story and an abrupt lout in the second. In telling the story of Rev. John A. Sinclair, James A. Sinclair in *Mission: Klondike* (1978), working from his father's papers, diary, and correspondence, probably put the matter much nearer the truth of the situation. To the

> missionary, Jefferson Smith was an enigma. Obviously here was a mountebank with the manners of a southern gentleman. Dickey was struck

[1] Dickey, *Gold*, pp. 28-34.

[2] *June 1898*: this was six months after Skaguay's Union Church had been built.

[3] *Skaguay News* 10/29/1898.

[4] Dickey Diary, dates indicated.

[5] Itjen, p. 24. The amount of $200 being given by "Soapy" is repeated on p. 27.

with amazement and horror at all that Smith represented; yet citizens, who from a moral standpoint should have been his bitterest opponents, were charmed by the man's magnetic personality.[1]

No published subscription list to the church is known, unlike at least two others to appear in Skaguay with Jeff's name on them (the Rowan widow's fund and the hospital). While it seems unlikely Jeff would have given $200 (about $6,248 in today's dollars[2]) and more in total than was even needed, he might have given something. Rev. Dickey might not even have known about it unless he were told, and he probably would have been. If Jeff were "the well-known" gambler at the first church meeting, "in the front row," and stayed for the decision to build the church, he likely made a contribution along with the others, and it seems likely Rev. Dickey knew about it. The contribution was not the problem. It was the story of how it was made, portraying Rev. Dickey as having gone to saloons and among gamblers to ask for money.

Immediately after the December 1897 dedication of the Union Church, in addition to regular services and Sunday school, other needed activities were identified. Rev. Dickey listed them in his *Gold Fever*. Needed were

> (1) A day school. There are thirty-five children in the community and more coming. We must provide for their education. (2) A reading room, writing room, and library. (3) A hospital. We have sick people in a dozen shacks and tents. (4) Clubs for men, women, and young people.[3]

Work on these needs began, but the church had yet to identify a fifth important project.

On December 4, 1897, Skaguay held its first election, and the seven newly elected members of the town council passed ordinance #1. It addressed the need to round up stray dogs of every description that had overrun Skaguay and that were starving and freezing to death.[4] They had been bought or stolen in Seattle, the most suitable of which for the climate and packing were Malamutes and Huskies. These sold for $300 and $400 each. According to a Seattle newspaper, the scarcity of dogs for packing created demand for even "little dogs not much larger than pugs."[5] However, "For all the good they were to prove to their owners," wrote Henry Woods,

> they might just as well have been shot. Indeed, it would have been a merciful act that would have saved them from the abuse, the stupid cruelty, and the dire suffering they were doomed to experience at the hands of their owners and from the rigors of a climate for which they were utterly unfit.[6]

Not clear is when the Union Church undertook to form a humane society for horses and dogs, but its start was probably at the Sunday service of October 24. Dickey in his diary for October 21 records meeting "Captain Lauridson. Good old Xn [Christian] Says not being able to do the people any good he did something for the horses. So he used to go out over the trails & bring home & doctor the horses left to

---

[1] Sinclair, p. 44.
[2] Tom's Inflation Calculator.
[3] Dickey, *Gold*, p. 39.
[4] *Skagway News*, Summer edition, 1995.
[5] *Seattle Daily Times* 11/11/1897.
[6] Morgan, Edward, p. 32.

die."[1] In *Gold Fever*, Dickey lay out how some packers, "only some mind you," were so abusive that they overloaded, underfed, improperly sheltered, and, in short, worked their pack animals until they died or were so weak and injured that their owners would abandon them on the trail. "Often they didn't even have the mercy to shoot them. So Captain Larry, as Lauridson is called, began "gathering food scraps and hauling them by dog team out to starving animals...." Sympathetic friends began to help, and Dickey announced an appeal for help at a Sunday service, "and the response was generous." Horses began being doctored as well as fed and led back to Skaguay for rehabilitation. Subsequently, "a fifth project" was suggested

> for this Union Church..., a humane society—an organization that will defend and protect the animals.... Our humane society can organize a scrap collection so that every house, shack, and tent will be visited regularly. We can organize haying parties ... to clear the snow and cut the long grass underneath. Those who can't help in these ways can contribute money for hay and oats and dog food. How many will join the humane society?"
> I think every hand went up. Enthusiasm was in the air.[2]

According to early biographies of Jeff, he was partial to animals and in Skaguay started his own adopted-a-dog program that campaigned to have most every household in town adopt at least one of the poor mutts, which surely otherwise would die. In the winter of 1897-98, hundreds of dead pack animals lay under cover of snow beyond sight of people in town, but in Skaguay, as Robertson and Harris in their biography of Jeff write, "Small mounds of snow literally dotted the town, beneath each" of which lay "a dead dog." Jeff, in his usual excessively generous charitable manner, is said to have adopted six of the poor critters. No records of this activity is known to exist, only undocumented, word-of-mouth accounts of this humane deed.[3]

Jeff was personally involved in at least three saloons and their activities, and throughout Skaguay in general, all gambling was under his control. Joe Briggs of Durango, Colorado, had traveled to Skaguay in January 1898, and in an interview upon his return, he said, "'Soapy' Smith of Denver fame, has three joints in Skaguay and it is safe to say they are strictly on the bunco order."[4] Harry Suydam also stated in an article that Jeff had control of three gambling halls in Skaguay.[5]

At the time of Jeff's death, John Clancy "was interested with Jeff Smith in a private enterprise."[6] Perhaps, then, one of the first saloons Jeff became involved with was in partnership with Frank W. and John E. Clancy, brothers already in the saloon trade in Seattle[7] and Dyea.[8] Their establishment stood at the corner of Runnalls and Shoup streets (7th and State today). *The Skaguay News* for December 31, 1897,

---

[1] Dickey Diary for 10/21/1897.
[2] Dickey, *Gold*, p. 31 & 47-48.
[3] Robertson & Harris, p. 193; Collier & Westrate, pp. 244-45; Bronson, p. 103; Satterfield, p. 69.
[4] *Daily Journal* 03/03/1898, p. 4.
[5] Suydam, p. 215.
[6] *Skaguay News* 07/15/1898, p. 3.
[7] Alaska Searchlight 12/17/1894.
[8] *Dyea Press* 03/12/1898.

contains a large, two-column, half-page advertisement and a write-up under the heading "Clancy's Place."

> Of all the places of resort in Skaguay that known by the above name is one of the best known and most popular. Located in the business center of the city, it is always to be found by the newcomer, and all old-time residents know Clancy's.
>
> All visitors to this place are treated with uniform courtesy. There is music and dancing every evening. Clubrooms are maintained in connection, and a first-class cafe is soon to be added. The management leave no stone unturned to make their visitor enjoy themselves.[1]

Rev. Dickey was out on Thursday night, November 11, 1897. He

> Visited bowling alley, shooting good game. Also Clancy's Saloon. Weary looking girls exerting their last strength to lead men astray. Gamblers stealing hard earned money from men who ought to have more sense."[2]

A business card found among Jeff's belongings after his death reads, "Clancy & Company, Music Hall and Clubrooms, First-Class Restaurant in Connection." The eatery opened sometime in January 1898.[3] The back of the card lists mileage from Skaguay to 24 locations, beginning with "Summit of White Pass—18" and ending with "Circle City—888." Dawson City was listed at an even 600 miles.[4]

Frank was listed as the general manager,[5] and Jeff was no doubt the "& Company," a silent partner in order to shield the business from his reputation.[6] It is likely that Jeff managed the gambling, including the $1000 roulette wheel Jeff had shipped from Denver. In six months Jeff helped Frank win a seat on the city council.[7]

Another saloon in which Jeff is believed to have had a controlling interest was the Klondike. Located in a tent near the northeast corner of Broadway and McKinney (5th Avenue),[8] it was advertised under the proprietorship of Ira Coslet and Ward.[9] By the end of December they moved the saloon to a two-story structure at the corner of Broadway and Holly (6th Avenue today) and added "Music Hall" to the name. A December 31, 1897, *Skaguay News* advertisement billed the Klondike as "the largest and best equipped place in Skaguay," with "Scotch and Irish Whiskies, fine wines and all the leading brands of cigars." It had clubrooms for gambling and furnished rooms upstairs for lodging. A dance hall and theater were connected with free entertainment every night.[10]

---

[1] *Skaguay News* 12/31/1897, write-up, p. 10; advertisement, p. 12.

[2] Dickey Diary, entry for 11/11/1897.

[3] *Skaguay News* 12/31/1897, p. 12. Clancy advertisement reads in part, "Will have after January 1st a first-class Short Order Cafe in connection. Open Night and Day."

[4] Clancy and Company business card, circa 1897, item 32, author's col.

[5] *Skaguay News* 02/11/1898, p. 1.

[6] *Daily Alaskan* 02/28/1898.

[7] *Skaguay News* 06/17/1898.

[8] Spude, p. 7.

[9] *Skaguay News* 11/05/1897. "Ira Coslet and Ward" were J. G. Cosslett and Edward Ward.

[10] *Skaguay News* 12/31/1897.

Frank Reid is believed to have been a bartender at the Klondike when it was only a tent, and that this is where Jeff and Reid first met. On July 8, 1898, Jeff fired the rifle shot that eventually killed Reid. The long-standing story has been that Reid also killed Jeff in the same short gun fight, but this story, as will be revealed, is in serious doubt.

Roy Daniel White knew Jeff in Denver and Skaguay. In an interview recorded in 1968, White said the following about Jeff and Reid:

> Oh, yes, he was a partner of Soapy's, but then he wanted to run Skagway. That's what they got into the quarrel with. ... He was a clever son-of-a-gun all right. He wanted to put himself in a little ... but Soapy wouldn't stand for it. He was Soapy's partner—then he split. He was gonna take the town on his side. Soapy didn't want that and that's why they shot it out. I wasn't in Skagway [when Soapy was killed]. I was in Candle.

White's reason for the shootout between Jeff and Reid does not seem possible as a main cause, but it might have had something to do with why Reid's gun came so quickly into play. White did not think highly of Reid, stating that "He was crookeder than Soapy ever was."[1]

On Monday, January 31, 1898, at approximately 2 a.m., Andy McGrath was at the upstairs bar in the People's Theater on Holly Street. One account of what happened had it that bartender John Fay cheated McGrath out of change. Another account had McGrath drinking with a theater girl whom he accused of stealing over $100 from him. McGrath complained to proprietor Jake Rice,[2] and a quarrel ensued, which attracted Fay. Rice and Fay then jumped McGrath, knocked him down, and threw him out. McGrath left the theater, vowing to return. *The Seattle Daily Times* wrote that McGrath was heard saying as he left, "I will come back and settle for this."[3] However, others claimed he "left, promising ... to get a gun and square accounts."[4]

Expecting trouble, Fay armed himself with a pistol and waited in the lower saloon. McGrath went across the street where he found Deputy US Marshal James Mark Rowan sitting in an all night lunchroom.[5] McGrath asked for the loan of the deputy's revolver. Rowan said no to the loan but volunteered to go to the theater with McGrath to settle the dispute. Another account appears in Rev. Dickey's diary for January 31:

> Heard of shooting affray last night. Row in theatre. Lamont [McGrath] badly beaten [−] went for gun. Marshal Rowan out taking fresh air—said he wd go with him & see what was matter. Entering door—men inside fired [−] killed both & another man wounded. Rowan's wife gave birth to child few hours before.[6]

Fay was hiding behind a faro table, and when the men entered, without warning, Fay shot them. McGrath fell and died within minutes. Rowan, severely wounded, staggered to Dr. Moore's office, but he soon expired. Both men had been shot in the

---

[1] White, Roy Daniel.
[2] *Daily Alaskan* 02/28/1898.
[3] *Seattle Daily Times* 02/06/1898, p.1.
[4] Suydam, p. 215.
[5] *Daily Alaskan* 02/01/1898, & Suydam, pp. 215-216.
[6] Dickey Diary, p. 32.

groin. Harry Lamont, former proprietor of the Nugget Saloon, and Billy "Bonanza King" Jones, the city fireman,[1] were outside the theater. Startled by Fay's gunfire, Jones drew his pistol and accidentally fired it, hitting Harry Lamont in the legs.[2] The *Daily Alaskan* reported the formation of a vigilante mob eager to deal out justice.

> The indignation of the law-abiding citizens of this city had reached the high-pressure mark by mid-day, and they decided to call a public mass meeting and inquire into the cause of the double tragedy and devise ways and means of bringing offenders to justice. At 3 o'clock [January 31], promptly, many of our best citizens and businessmen had assembled in the church. Determination was depicted upon every countenance, and it was evident there was no foolishness or false pretense with them. Major Strong was elected chairman of the meeting, and [attorney] Sam L. Lovell secretary. On the motion it was decided that a committee of twelve men be appointed to devise ways and means to meet the conditions and investigate the shooting affair and arrange for the punishment of the murderer.... There is liable to be some interesting developments this afternoon.[3]

The Committee of 101 was resurrected. General consensus among those who have recorded the events of this period is that this group was made up of ordinary residents seeking justice, but some pioneer residents of Skaguay later claimed that two gangs were bidding for control of the town and that this organization was trying to take advantage of a bad situation for its own ends.

Immediately after killing the two men, John Fay hurried to Jeff for protection. Fay was in hiding when the new church bell tolled that afternoon, calling all concerned to determine what was to be done about the double homicide. Major Strong led the vigilante meeting, or tried to. Arguments swayed between seeing Fay fairly tried and seeing him hanged. Jeff addressed the group to call for calm, rationality, and preservation of law and order, but he also threatened to shoot anyone who tried to carry out a lynching.[4] Tom M. Ward,[5] a local merchant, said he knew the whereabouts of Fay and that he had agreed to give himself up if guaranteed protection and a fair trial. Rev. Dickey, now living in a lean-to behind the church, was likely a witness. His diary entry for the next day confirms details: "Citizens meeting about murder. Ward stated Fay had confessed & wd give himself up if promised protection. Ten—mostly gamblers [—] appointed guard [—] Major Strong to appoint 12 men to try him."[6]

Jeff wanted law and order as much as most residents did, but for different reasons. A system of checks and balances included "due process" of law, thus checking impulsive vigilante ways with the slowly turning wheels of justice. Jeff's

---

[1] Suydam, p. 216.
[2] *Daily Alaskan* 02/01/1898 and 02/05/1898.
[3] *Daily Alaskan* 02/01 & 05/1898.
[4] *Seattle Daily News* 02/07/1898.
[5] *Ward*: may have been the same Tom Ward who later joined the vigilantes in the hunt for the Soap Gang after Jeff's death.
[6] Dickey Diary for 02/01/1898.

businesses actually ran smoother and safer under a well-regulated legal system than under miners' justice, which was often swift and violent.

The meeting reconvened at 3 p.m. the following day, again with Major Strong presiding. Twelve men were appointed to bring in a verdict but then were unwilling to do so for fear of legal retaliation later on. They recommended another committee be formed to look into the matter and that a judge be appointed for sentencing. Major Strong was disappointed with the nonverdict and even more disappointed when he was nominated to be judge. He begged to be excused from the honor, but the crowd insisted.[1] Jeff may again have addressed the group, and emotion began to rule as it seemed Jeff's argument for a legally constituted trial was gaining support and that Fay would escape justice. Rev. Dickey did address the group, as his diary tells:

> [Feb] 2 Citizens meeting–Committee reported that Fay sd [should] be held for trial. Feeling high. Made a pacific speech to crowd for which criticized next day in Alaskan. Urged [people] not [to] wreck vengeance on Fay but get after the gang and its leaders. One hundred citizens to be appointed from wh[ich] 12 to be chosen to try Fay next mg [meeting] at 9 [p.m.].[2]

Apparently elected from a next meeting that evening were ten new jurors to investigate and arrange punishment for John Fay. *The Seattle Daily Times* listed them as "Captain Josias Martin Tanner,[3] Mr. Willis, H. C. Grady, C. B. Beeson, Mr. Shea, Ira Coslet,[4] Mr. Beebe, Col. Fisher, A. T. Brown, and Peter Annence."[5]

Then word spread that upon learning of her husband's death, Mrs. Beryl Rowan had died of shock and grief along with her infant son, James Mark Rowan II.[6] The story prompted another mob scene in the streets, demanding that Fay be handed over for immediate execution. The news, however, proved to be untrue. Story of the deaths of mother and child had even reached *The Seattle Daily Times*,[7] but the newspaper updated its story: "Mrs. Rowan is yet alive, though in a precarious state of health, and the baby seems to be doing well."[8] *The Skaguay News* struck back at the "accustomed untruthfulness" of the *Times* and other "Puget Sound newspapers" for stating

> that Fay ... was saved from hanging by the intimidation of an irresponsible class of people resident in the town. This is a base libel on the great majority of Skaguay people, who are of the law abiding and law-maintained class."[9]

The statement could have been written by Jeff himself. In fact, it might have been.

During jury selection, someone announced, "Men, there is a government boat steaming up the bay, and this mob will soon get its desserts," meaning that authorities

[1] *Denver Times* 01/06/1901.
[2] Dickey Diary for 02/01-02/1898.
[3] Tanner descendants state the correct spelling is Josias. Susan Tanner Schimling to author, 04/15/2007.
[4] *Ira Coslet*: J. G. Cosslett is believed an associate of Jeff.
[5] *Seattle Daily Times* 02/06/1898.
[6] *Morning Oregonian* 02/08/1898, p. 6; *Milwaukee Sentinel* 02/08/1898, p. 7; & *Denver Times* 01/06/1901.
[7] *Seattle Daily Times* 02/06/1898, p. 1.
[8] *Seattle Daily Times* 02/11/1898, p. 2. Beryl Rowan and son James Mark Rowan II moved to Seattle; James eventually attended a Catholic boarding school. Author's interview with family descendant Renee Rowan, 07/23/2008.
[9] *Skaguay News* Supplement, 02/18/1898.

would charge the mob with illegal actions. Then someone else shouted, "Let's get Fay and do the job before they cheat us out of him." Major Strong replied that no boat was coming and asked that he be given until nine the following morning to decide a sentence. A bloc of the vigilantes did not want to wait. They elected a judge from their own crowd to convict and sentence the murderer without further ado.[1]

Jeff did not wait for further developments. He went to US Commissioner John U. Smith and demanded his help in protecting Fay. Agreeing to take immediate action, the commissioner was taken to Fay's hiding place, and on the spot, he deputized Jeff's men, who were guarding and protecting Fay, and ordered them to escort the prisoner to a ship that would take him to Sitka. There Fay would be held for trial.[2] News of Fay's being shipped out was not discovered until Thursday, February 3, and then only slowly. Again, Rev. Dickey's diary catches this piece of the event: "Enquiries [−] where is trial−no one knows. Soon find Fay gone. John U Smith had sworn in guards as deputy marshals & had taken him away. Indignation."[3] *The Seattle Daily Times* put the news in print on February 7, 1898: "Ed Fay Not Hanged."

> Ed Fay, the murderer of Rowan and McGrath at Skaguay, was not hanged; his friends, headed by Soapy Smith, the gambler, organized and threatened to use their guns if Fay was hanged. Fay was therefore sent to Juneau.[4]

Not known is if Fay were a member or supporter of the Soap Gang, or if Jeff even knew him personally. His defense of Fay may have been entirely business. Allowing the vigilantes to have their way would set a precedent. Then Jeff could expect swift and harsh retaliation from armed, emotional mobs who rarely sided with Jeff's kind. No matter his reasons, however, the actions he took to stop the lynching of Fay was what any officer of the law or legal court would have been expected to do. Jeff often had occasion to represent himself with this fact in defense of himself. That, however, did not count for anything among a certain element of men in Skaguay. Among them from then on, Jeff was seen as having helped a double murderer escape justice.

A somber event occurred the next day, Friday, February 4, 1898: Rev. Dickey's burial service of Marshal Rowan. Three others were also buried by Dickey that day, apparently of natural causes. Pneumonia and spinal meningitis were abroad in the camp, killing many. Dickey buried two more, "John Sutherland & Hazel Atkinson," the next day. The mood of the town, grim in the midst of so much disorder and death, likely spurred another meeting of (what Rev. Dickey calls in his diary) the "Citizens Protective Association. He recorded their "Behavior fair, but smoking & spitting a lot."[5]

On February 11, 1898, *The Seattle Daily Times* published an article titled "Toughs rule the roost." Interviewed had been officers of the *City of Topeka* who confirmed

> reports of lawlessness at Dyea and Skaguay. Both of these towns are in the hands of a gang of scoundrels and gamblers who should be made to

---

[1] Suydam, p. 217.
[2] *Seattle Daily Times* 02/11/1898, p. 2, & *Denver Times* 01/06/1901.
[3] Dickey Diary 02/03/1898.
[4] *Seattle Daily Times* 02/07/1898.
[5] Dickey Diary 02/05/1898.

decorate the lower end of an elevated rope. Hold-ups and serious violations of the law are of almost hourly occurrence and scenes are daily enacted that would put to blush even the tough element of older communities.

The respectable portions of the very cosmopolitan population of these two towns are so decidedly in the minority that they are forced to bow in diplomatic submission to the gang of which a fellow who [undecipherable] in the name of "Soapy Smith" is said to be the recognized leader.[1]

Petitions circulated in Skaguay asked the governor and federal government for assistance. Requested was that the army be brought in to protect the citizens of Skaguay and stampeders along the trails.[2] Jeff used the opportunity to upstage the emerging vigilantes and gain sympathy among residents. To assure the town of his interest in its welfare, Jeff headed up a subscription for the deputy marshal's widow. It was published in *The Skaguay News* under the title of "The Rowan Fund."

The amounts subscribed for the benefit of Mrs. J. E. [M.] Rowan, wife of the late deputy marshal, killed by Ed Fay, and the persons subscribing are published below. The list is still open to receive subscriptions, and may be found at the First Bank of Skaguay, where subscriptions will be received for a week longer. The general expenses, amounting to $119, have already been paid. Following are the names of the persons contributing:

Jeff R. Smith	$ 50
W. J. McIntosh & Co.	50
Jake Rice [proprietor of Jake's Place and The People's Theater]	50
Hoff & Gem Saloon	50
Clancy [John and/or Frank Clancy]	50
Chas. B. Sperry [vigilante, later headed Citizen's Committee]	20
A. P. Stoel	10
J. H. Brooks [Joe Brooks, famed packer]	10
Sam Howard	25
A. Mona [Proprietor of The Yukon Sample Rooms]	10
D & D Saloon	10
Hotel Mondamin	25
Jos. Burkhard & Co [Burkhard Hotel]	20
F. F. Clark [Manager of the Burkhard Hotel]	5
D. Duff	5
Payton, Reynolds & Cohen	30
Skaguay Real-Estate & Improvement Co.	10
M. Quinlan	2
Green & Roberts	15
Miller & Spires	15
Total	$414[3]

[1] *Seattle Daily Times* 02/11/1898, p. 2.

[2] *Seattle Daily Times* 02/11/1898, p. 2.

[3] *Skaguay News* 02/18/1898, p. 3.

Jeff's name comes first because he headed the drive, and his friends and associates gave many of the larger amounts. Others include key businessmen and important citizens. The subscription made *The Seattle Daily Times* but not in a positive light.

> To square themselves with the community the gamblers have started a subscription of $1000 for Mrs. Rowan. "Soapy" Smith is out with a list. He secured $700 in less than an hour, and will have no difficulty in getting the other $300. The talk he put up in getting subscriptions was rather humorous under the circumstances. "Marshal Rowan protected us when he was alive," he said, "and it is only right that we should help his widow now that he is dead."[1]

Amounts were overstated. Funds collected were taken to the First Bank of Skaguay on Holly Street where residents could continue giving to the Rowan fund. When collections ceased on March 3, the total was $424. After expenses Mrs. Rowan was presented with the balance, $305.[2] Though far less than $1000 dollars, the amount was not inconsiderable, worth over 31 times as much today.[3]

Jeff at this time was on a good-citizen-of-Skaguay campaign. On the same day the Rowan subscription was published, an article appeared about a large meeting that had taken place the night before. The topic was fire protection for the town.

> Skaguay's unparalleled growth demands that steps be taken to insure fire protection as far as possible. The means now being taken should have the earnest support of every citizen.

Jeff was the main speaker among six men who spoke on the issue.[4] Knowing firsthand from Creede what a major fire could mean to a town and its (and his) businesses, Jeff was instrumental in setting up Skaguay's first fire brigade.

At the same time, on the other side of the citizenship coin, to the criminal element, Jeff was without doubt the boss of Skaguay. He was the go-to man for good-paying work and for protection, and for them, his rules were law. To his rivals, he was the uncrowned king of Skaguay and feared. However, all in all, to many of the residents and merchants, Jeff was no longer just a gambler but also an effective champion of law, order, rationality, and the common good.

Ten days later, on the last day of February, further evidence of good-citizen Jeff appeared. The *Daily Alaskan* published another subscription list, this time of those who had contributed to the community hospital site and building that had been purchased from Packer Joe Brooks. "Jeff R. Smith" was fourth from the top with a $25 donation. Previously, when the Union Church adopted the idea, as reported in Sinclair's *Mission: Klondike*, "a board of three trustees was named with Reverend R. M. Dickey as chairman."[5] A committee was formed to canvass Skaguay for contributions, and one night as canvassing lists were being reviewed, Dickey's *Gold*

---

[1] *Seattle Times* 02/11/1898, p. 2.
[2] *Skaguay News* 03/04/1898, p. 3.
[3] Tom's Inflation Calculator: $1 in 1898 = $31.24 X $424 = $13,246; $305 = $9,528 today.
[4] *Skaguay News* 02/18/1898.
[5] *Daily Alaskan* 02/28/1898, & Sinclair, p. 53.

Fever narrator, Quebec, tells of coming "to one entry that read, "Jefferson Smith $25." The person who collected that donation said,

> "...I was passing Jeff's place, and he came to the sidewalk and said, 'I understand you're collecting money to build a hospital. That's something any of us may need sometime—I'd like to help.' And he handed me $25."

After a debate about not accepting tainted money, Rev. Dickey (named "Dominie" in *Gold Fever*) said, "If Soapy wants to contribute to a good cause, we have no right to prevent him." When asked what was thought "of the stories being circulated about Soapy's benevolences," Dickey replied, "I believe some of them are true....'[1]

Examination of Skaguay's newspapers suggests that Jeff's bunco activities were not extensive, but this was not the case. Jeff well knew the importance of controlling the media and of keeping effects unlinked in the public mind from a common cause. As he had done elsewhere, Jeff compensated those who agreed not to print all the crime that occurred in town. Additionally, even those who disagreed with Jeff were apt to soften the news for reasons of civic pride. Jeff was able to manipulate the Skaguay newspapers, but he could do little with those in "the states," where his activities, although often exaggerated, were described with relish. Seattle and San Francisco headlines told of horrid conditions in Skaguay, and this representation spread to newspapers as far away as New York. Presented was that Jeff ruled a criminal underworld at the southern gateway to the Klondike. Skaguay merchants feared that all the negative reports would discourage newcomers. One of the worst reports came from officers of the *Noyo* when the ship arrived in Seattle from Skaguay on February 25. Interviewed, these officers said,

> that the conditions of lawlessness and disease there are beyond description.
>
> "Soapy" Smith of Denver and his gang are in full control and law-abiding people do not say a word against him.
>
> Hold ups, robberies and shooting affrays are a part of the daily routine. Eight frozen bodies were picked up on the Skaguay trail Feb. 15. Two hundred are sick at Skaguay with a disease resembling cerebral spinal meningitis. Twelve died in one day.[2]

The *Daily Alaskan* published counter editorials stating that the reports were not only false but outright lies made up by the city of Juneau to hurt Skaguay's reputation. The main editorial came from doctor Arthur H. Bryant, who added,

> Tonight I understand there is to be an indignation meeting of the citizens. Let all attend and let the world know exactly where and to whom these reports can be traced and when the source is found any intelligent person will see at once that he is in the presence of a cold-blooded and infamous liar.[3]

On the day the *Noyo* account was published, the *San Francisco Examiner* featured a drawing of Jeff with an article about his criminal affairs. Above the drawing reads, "This gambler aspires to be an Alaskan chief of police. Rules the sporting

---

[1] Dickey, *Gold*, p. 72.
[2] *Seattle Post-Intelligencer* 02/25/1898.
[3] *The Daily Alaskan* 02/28/1898.

fraternity at the gateway of the gold fields and thinks he would be the best man to preserve peace in the district." The caption under the drawing reads, "Soapy Smith, the uncrowned king of the town of Skaguay." The story itself exposed his methods.

"Soapy" Smith, one time known as Jeff, gambler, politician, "sure-thing" man, has added to his other titles that of "shah of Skaguay." He also longs to be called "Chief." In the boom town at the entrance to White pass, "Soapy" is a power and a prominent citizen. The sporting fraternity owe allegiance to his cause and when the place is incorporated will further his ambition to be Chief of Police. ... The story of the career of the would-be policeman teems with tales of adventure. He is known all along the pacific coast as a most desperate gambler.

The article correctly exposed Jeff's past in Denver, including a detailed exposé of the prize soap sell racket. But even in this damning article, the reporter apparently felt compelled to include that Jeff also had a good side.

He made fortune after fortune and spent it all in riotous living and in good deeds, for it must be said of "Soapy" that no hungry man ever asked aid of him and was refused.[1]

Jeff's infamous past had caught up with him. Too soon every Skaguay resident would know his full identity. An obviously powerful friend in San Francisco, known only as "John," wrote to Jeff about the article and to warn him about a "squealer" thought to be in Skaguay. This interesting and colorful but long and somewhat repetitive letter has been shortened; otherwise, with a few assists, it appears as written.

Esmond House, 43 Sixth Street
San Francisco, Cal., Feby. 25 1898
Jeff Smith, Esqr.
Chief Police, Skaguay, Alaska:
Friend Jeff:—Today's San Francisco Examiner gives you quite a good send off with a large picture of you. It seems by this able sheet you will be the next or first chief and if so I am glad of it, so you can regulate some of the wolfs that's in our line of calling. They must have some man of judgment to regulate them or they will break up any place they go. There is one in particular, who is strickly out for himself and I here he is in your town (Skaguay); he will undermine you or any one else in order to gain his own point. I tell you Jeff he Dutch or John Rennels[2] would put you and everyone else in jail to have the graft himself. If he had his way in this city while with me he would have had many of the gang drove out or put in the workhouse. You will always find him sneaking around talking to officers and telling other people['s] bisness to them. Jeff he ... is beyond a doubt one of the most dangerous men in the country and avoid[s] any principle. The only friend or God he knows or acknowledges is the mazuma[3] and to reach that he will stop at nothing, he has not a charatable or Honorable hair in his head. When I had

---

[1] *San Francisco Examiner* 02/25/1898.
[2] *I ... Rennels*: I tell you, Jeff, he, this Dutch, as he is called, whose name is John Rennels, would put....
[3] *mazuma*: money, cash, US slang, fr Yiddish (*OED*).

to drop him from the pay roll he got drunk like any cheap guy on 5¢ beer—large glasses, and combined with old McCormick to write me and the police department up through a pettifogging attorney here [—] he with McCormick in their letter given to the Daily Call newspaper claimed that I had the Chief of Police right and was given him the chief money. Now I and everyone else knows this to be true that Rennels and McCormick are the guilty ones—.... Such people ought to be in the sewer. You can rest assured he is your enemy. He has roasted you to me more than once and told me what smart capers he cut while in Denver, Col.

There was nothing bad enough he did not say about you he can give you plenty of taffy[1] while there is money in it but he is full of deceit, if you touch his pocket you can find out where his Dutch heart is if he has any. There is only one thing to do with him to keep him on the walk [—] drive him out of town for you or anyone else can not do a thing he will not tell officials to get into favor. I learned that deceitful rascals faults at my own expense. Why Golden Gaggers and others would have driven him from here a pauper only for me, and he repaid me well for my favors shown him by writing up the police dept & saying I was giving them percentages. ... They put some of the gang on the tramp, but I am living well & eating the same & no trouble on my mind, for I am O K and treated all as I would wish to be treated myself. ...McCormick, Atkins & others ... are dead letters here as well as many other places. Their pedigree is ahead of them in many citys. Any information or anything I can do for you here I will do cheerfully in the way of ordering anything you might want. Hoping I may have the pleasure of hearing of you been elected Chief & with best wishes I remain

Your Friend and well wisher. JOHN.

[P.S.] This is no heresay. The cop, the attorney who wrote the article and Billy Atkins who was there listening to Dutch getting McC to do it all tell me Dutch is to blame for all.[2]

It is unknown if Jeff identified a man named Dutch in Skaguay. John wrote how it is important for "men of judgment" to "regulate some of the wolfs that's in our line of calling." If not, "they will break up any place they go." Words of wisdom Jeff well understood. As long as a bunco boss could keep his men content, the less reason for them to get out of hand and cause trouble for one and all.

Thirteen days after the San Francisco article appeared, another exposed more about the bunco men and the shell games along the White Pass trail.[3] These articles and others like them took aim at the character of Skaguay. Never before had this much bad publicity been written about any of the camps in which Jeff had operated. Skaguay's merchants surely began to question continued alignment with Jeff, fearing that their own fortune-making schemes might come to a premature end.

---

[1] *taffy:* crude flattery, soft soap, US slang (*OED*).
[2] Jones, Robert, p. 334.
[3] *San Francisco Chronicle* 03/10/1898.

Joseph T. Cornforth wrote a letter dated March 5, 1898, that was published in the *Denver Evening Post*. It speculated on trouble to come.

Mr. Jeff Smith is in Skaguay playing his old-time games with the shells and ball, three-card Monte, etc. He has 30 men in his outfit. They stick together like rats when there is a quarrel and work the town to the queen's taste,[1] skinning every stranger at the first opportunity.

As Skaguay grows and there is a settled state of feeling, the best people of the town are becoming very much worked up about him and talk is now strong of calling a public meeting and inviting him to light out for other parts.[2]

Since the death of Deputy US Marshal Rowan, rivals for Jeff's control had held several meetings and revived the Committee of 101. Some residents considered gambling to be the cause of Skaguay's unruliness and crime, and calls to ban it were made, with one of its strongest supporters being O. W. Dunbar, proprietor of the newly created *Morning Alaskan* newspaper. Soon after the anti-gambling stance was published, Dunbar reported that he was visited by "a neatly-dressed man of medium height." After determining Dunbar was the proprietor and owner, the man said, "I'd like to have a talk with you," and Dunbar recorded what the man said next.

"You see, I'm somewhat of a newspaper man myself, and my brother is one of the best newspaper men in Colorado. In fact, there's not much about the business I don't know, from the duties of battery boy to the writings of the editorials. And I want to tell you right here that 'you're off' on that gambling proposition, especially about 'Soapy' Smith. I'm sure you're wrong there, because I'm 'Soapy' himself.

"You see, there are gamblers and gamblers. Now, these crap game men only make tin-horn gamblers, for this reason: When a man runs up against one of them he loses his money slowly, but surely. He wins a little occasionally, and becomes fascinated with the game. Then he winds up by becoming a gambler himself. But when they 'run up' against me 'it's off with them.' They're just paralyzed. I take everything they've got in short order, and they just throw up their hands and swear they'll never gamble again—and they don't. I tell you, I'm a reformer, and 'you're off' on the proposition.

"Besides," "Soapy" continued, "if these fellows are allowed to go through to Dyea and on to Dawson with all their money it will operate to the serious disadvantage of Skaguay and as a good citizen you should stand in and encourage 'reformers' of my stamp."

Dunbar said that "after wishing the editor a pleasant good morning," he departed.[3] It is doubtful Jeff's favorite argument on behalf of himself as a reformer swayed Dunbar's opinion much. Perhaps Jeff could see that, because according to Dunbar's daughter Claire, Jeff also offered an inducement. The daughter had come with her father to Skaguay to work side by side with him in producing the paper and claimed to

---

[1] *to the queen's taste*: to perfection. An expression (*OED*).
[2] *Denver Evening Post* 03/18/1898, p. 3.
[3] *Denver Evening Post* 03/18/1898, p. 3.

be a witness to the conversation. Decades later she wrote of it, of what else Jeff said, and what happened thereafter.

> In the course of the conversation that followed, Soapy offered Oscar Dunbar $50 an issue to keep his name out of the *Alaskan*. "That shouldn't be hard to do for that price, should it?" he inquired.
>
> "It shouldn't be," was the reply....
>
> An hour later a messenger appeared ... and produced two bottles of Mumm's Extra Dry and a box of Soapy's best cigars, which he handed to the editor with "Mr. Smith's compliments." Claire's father, in answer, picked up the latest edition of the Alaskan, still wet, and handed it to the boy, saying, "To Mr. Smith with the compliments of Mr. Dunbar." The paper contained another editorial ... describing how soapy had tried to quiet the editor.[1]

On Monday evening March 7, 1898, between 6 and 7 miles from town on the White Pass trail near Porcupine Hill, Peter Clancy Bean, a twenty-five-year-old miner from Williams, California, was murdered. Powder burns were on his face and a .38 caliber slug in his left breast. Near his body was his empty pocketbook. However, the *Daily Alaskan* reported $300 in gold was found in his belt as well as $33.72 in cash in his pockets.[2] It was believed his killer, or killers, were frightened away before searching the corpse.[3] His killer was never discovered, but it is unlikely that this was the work of the Soap Gang.

In 1909, Will Irwin serialized *The Confessions of a Con Man* in the *Saturday Evening Post* and then in 1913 *The Confessions* appeared as a book. This long-time "grafter," as he called himself, worked for Jeff in Skaguay and had this clear-sighted perspective on the work of the Soap Gang.

> Alaska people have talked like a dime novel about the Soapy Smith gang in Skaguay. Only lately, a paper said that our "coffee and doughnut men"[4] used to rob and kill people, and drop their bodies in the bay. That is rank foolishness. Grafters don't work that way. Soapy wouldn't have protected any man who did. The straight money from three-card monte and the shells came so easy that we would have been crazy to take such risks, even if we had been thugs and murderers. A man who knows anything about graft realizes the rattle-headedness of such talk. And I know better than any one else, because I was on the inside.[5]

Conning, doping, even strong-arming if necessary figured into the modus operandi of the Soap Gang, but not outright homicide.

Nevertheless, the day following Bean's murder, the Committee of 101 posted $10^{1}/_{4}$" X $7^{3}/_{8}$" handbills around the camp, warning the bunco men that they were no longer welcome in Skaguay.

---

[1] Henderson, p. 59.

[2] *Daily Alaskan* 03/09/1898.

[3] *Seattle Daily Times* 03/12/1898, & *Morning Oregonian* 03/16/1898.

[4] *coffee and doughnut men*: no listing for this expression found. The sense may be that these are not hard-drinking, violent criminals but men of a gentler sort.

[5] Irwin, p. 172.

WARNING!

A word to the wise should be sufficient! All Confidence, Bunco and Sure-thing Men, And all other objectionable characters are notified to leave Skaguay and White Pass Road Immediately. And to remain away. Failure to comply with this warning will be followed by prompt action.

101.

Skaguay, Alaska, Mch. 8, 1898[1]

After publishing the warning in the local newspaper and posting it around town and along the trails, the Committee expected bunco men to make themselves scarce. It was reported in Seattle that approximately forty gamblers and confidence men had fled Skaguay to Juneau on small steamers.[2] By the time the news reached Portland, included was that all gambling in Skaguay had been closed down.[3] Most bunco men might have heeded such a warning, but not Jeff. He had no intention of abdicating his throne. In fact, he counterattacked almost at once. Not to oppose the 101 would give the organization momentum. To renew support of residents, he called an informal town meeting of those interested in "law and order" and broadcast it in the newspaper.

Announcement.

The business interests of Skaguay propose to put a stop to the lawless acts of many newcomers. We hereby summon all good citizens to a meeting at which these matters will be discussed. Come one, Come all! Immediate action will be taken for relief. Let this be a warning to those chechawcos [sic] who are disgracing our city! The meeting will be held at Sylvester Hall at 8 p.m. sharp. (signed) Jefferson R. Smith, chairman.[4]

At the meeting Jeff named himself and those behind him the law-abiding element, and to rival the 101, he formed the Law and Order Society, which boasted 317 members. On Saturday, March 12, 1898, Skaguay awoke to an Answer to the Committee, published in a newspaper and plastered about town on 8" X 5¼" handbills, some of them tacked to the doors of some members of the Committee.[5]

ANSWER TO WARNING

The body of men styling themselves 101 are hereby notified that any overt act committed by them will be promptly met by the Law abiding Citizens of Skaguay and each member and HIS PROPERTY will be held responsible for any unlawful act on their part and the law and order society consisting of 317 citizens will see that Justice is dealt out to its full extent as no Blackmailers or Vigilantes will be tolerated.

The Committee.[6]

Then came a series of shootings and robberies that shook the town. On Sunday, March 13, 1898, Sam Roberts was shot at point-blank range and killed just outside his

---

[1] 101 Handbill, 03/08/1898, Alaska State Museum, Juneau, Alaska.

[2] *Seattle Daily Times*, 03/12/1898.

[3] *Morning Oregonian* 03/16/1898.

[4] *Dyea Trail* 03/11/1898.

[5] DeRoux, p. 9.

[6] *Dyea Press*, 03/12/1898 and an original 317 handbill at the Alaska State Museum, Juneau, Alaska.

cabin.[1] Inside, Roberts' partner heard the shot and ran out to see the murderers running away. It is rumored that Roberts may have been one of Jeff's associates and that he was murdered in retaliation for something he had done.[2] *The Seattle Daily Times* claimed Roberts was a member of the Soap Gang who had been operating a gambling game and was shot as he was returning to his cabin with his previous night's winnings. Two days later, on March 15, Alexander McLain, a businessman, was sandbagged and robbed in front of his home.[3] Additionally, another man, unidentified, had apparently been robbed, knocked unconscious, and thrown from a wharf into the bay, where he drowned. Of this murder, only these few facts, published in *The Seattle Daily Times*, are known.[4]

Armed, violent robbery did not match Jeff's way and seem unlikely to have been perpetrated by the Soap Gang. Such crime, especially if occurring serially, invited not just legal interference but worse, vigilante justice, which could lead to even worse, martial law—any of which worked against the bunco man's interests. One theory is that these were the crimes of hopeless men who had turned desperate. Another is that a number of strong-arm thugs and violent criminals had converged on Skaguay about this time, so many that Jeff could not immediately control them all. Despite Jeff's "law-and-order" campaign, these crimes were blamed on Jeff and the gamblers.

One method said to be used by the Soap Gang was that of grabbing a victim's wallet or poke and running off with it. When an intended target brought forth his wallet in one of Jeff's establishments, a member of the gang would jump up, grab the wallet, and dash out the door. Others would then rise in orchestrated attempts to stop the thief, only to block the door after the ruffian had escaped. This play was not first among methods of extracting cash from victims, but last, after other enticements had failed. The Soap Gang included some very dangerous characters who were violence prone, but Jeff allowed them to uncoil only when required, never as a practice. As for holdups and murder, to repeat Irwin's con man's professional view from within the Soap Gang, "we would have been crazy to take such risks, even if we had been thugs and murderers."[5] It could be, too, that the number of murders were played up for various reasons (propaganda against Jeff, against Skaguay, to boost newspaper circulation). Historian Clarence L. Andrews wrote that

> It is doubtful whether many murders were perpetrated in Skagway during Soapy's time. I came to Skagway about six months after his death. I knew the U.S. Marshal and the Commissioner who tried the cases in connection with Smith's gang. I knew most of the men who lived in Skagway, and for five years I listened to their conversations. I have searched the records and

---

[1] Not to be confused with Sam Roberts, the proprietor of The Office saloon on Broadway. who participated in the July 4 parade four months later.
[2] *Dyea Trail* 03/11/1898, & *Seattle Daily Times* 03/17/1898.
[3] *Morning Oregonian* 03/16/1898.
[4] *Seattle Daily Times* 03/12/1898.
[5] Irwin, p. 172.

newspaper files, and have found little verification of a large number of killings considering the number of men who were passing through.[1]

The spate of robberies and murders, however, was alarming and caused the Committee of 101 to request the aid of Colonel Anderson of the US Army stationed at Dyea. Soldiers arrived in Skaguay to quell any violent reaction to these crimes, but there was none. US Commissioner Smith and Deputy US Marshal McInnis had temporarily closed gambling on Wednesday, March 9, 1898.[2] Colonel Anderson could not legally impose martial law unless officially called or otherwise clearly apparent to protect property and lives. With no threat visible, the army returned to Dyea.[3] Officials under Jeff's control successfully convinced the commander that peace was being preserved and that gambling was restricted to "legitimate" gambling only. Within days the gaming houses were once again wide open.[4] A line said to have come from one of Jeff's letters, whether true or not, fits the moment perfectly, "We have got them licked and mean to rule absolutely."[5]

Looking at the handbills side by side, neutral Skaguay residents might find it hard to decide who the "good" guys were. One warned criminals and "objectionable characters" to leave while the other from "Law abiding Citizens of Skaguay" warned the former against illegal acts. The group that replied to the Warning from the "101" claimed a membership over three times larger, "317 citizens." But that particular number must have been recognized by some, if not most, as the street address of Jeff Smith's Parlor. Some humor was likely intended but also a symbolic warning, that Jeff was behind a large, organized, and determined force.

Jeff professed himself a public benefactor of the foolish and unprepared. He claimed to be the means of weeding out the unfit who were sure to perish in the frozen North or become a burden to their community. The greatest kindness one could do for such people, he claimed, was to force them to leave Skaguay on the first boat home, after they had spent or lost all their money, of course. Merchants were easily persuaded that it was better for people lose their money in Skaguay where it would be put back into circulation in local businesses rather than be lost in Canada. Jeff knew how to appeal for support among the powerful merchant class of Skaguay.

But with opposition from this semi-secret group calling itself the 101, Jeff felt he needed a sizeable armed force to back his rule of Skaguay. He had visited with powerful men in the nation's capital and had impressed them, and he had already been granted a request by the department of war for authority in Fort St. Michael. So he felt that he was in a position to ask for more authority with a reasonable expectation it would be granted. Jeff had become the American version of *The Man Who Would be King*. All he needed was an army unit to secure his crown.

---

[1] Andrews, "Real," p. 38.

[2] *Pagosa Springs News* 03/25/1898, p. 2.

[3] *San Francisco Examiner*, 04/10/1898.

[4] *Morning Oregonian* 03/17/1898, p. 6.

[5] Collier & Westrate, p. 233.

Chapter 20
The Uncrowned King of Skaguay

We made a beeline for Soapy Smith's saloon.
We knew it was the first thing they'd ask us about back home.

—One of three young Klondikers

Skaguay's criminal element looked to the guiding, experienced hand of Soapy Smith. With the backing of a wide variety of bunco men, rouges, and ruffians, Jeff quickly held control of Skaguay's underworld. With these men Jeff opened and operated some of the most bizarre businesses he had ever conceived, including a Merchants Exchange, the Real-Estate & Information Company, a cut-rate ticket office, and a telegraph office. Jeff's enterprises grew quickly and were among the most successful in the camp. Perhaps one of his boldest and proudest accomplishments was a saloon bearing his name across the top front, Jeff Smith's Parlor. With the coming of the Spanish-American War,[1] his saloon became headquarters for the Skaguay Military Company, which he formed and commanded as its "elected" captain.

Because of Alaska's distance and harsh conditions, most of the Denver gang did not join Jeff in Skaguay. Those who did include John Bowers, George Wilder, Ed Burns, W. H. Jackson, Charlie Adams, and Frank Brown. Some newcomers were W. F. Foster, alias "Slim-Jim," brothers John and Frank Clancy, Van B. Triplett, alias "Old-Man Trip," William F. "Billy" Saportas, A. L. White, alias "Sheeny Kid," William Tener, H. L. Bronson, alias "Red," J. Degrauder, alias "Doc," and Charles Butler.

In November 1898, a James Finnegan who claimed to know Jeff "quite intimately" talked to the *Denver Evening Post* about Skaguay Soap Gang activities.

> He had 100 to 150 slick rascals in his gang, who lined the wharves at Skaguay and as soon as passengers would alight from the incoming steamers they would line up, leaving a narrow passageway through which to elbow your way. With ill-concealed eagerness they would ask for news, especially about the war with Spain, and would pay 50 cents for fresh newspapers from the states. Talking earnestly and ... exclaiming at every victory of Uncle Sam's boys, they would lead the victim down to a saloon ... known as "Smith's place." Here three-card Monte, shell games and roulette were in progress continually. A fellow evidently fresh from the Klondike (a member of the gang) would be dropping nuggets and winning others back and setting up drinks for the crowd.

> Your new friend would ask you to try your luck after he had paid for your drink. If you refused, two evidently tipsy prospectors drinking at the bar would start a fight under your very nose. In the melee you would get slugged and

---

[1] *the Spanish-American War.* 04/19-08/23/1898, about 10 weeks' duration. The US battleship *Maine* blew up in Havana harbor 02/15/1898. Over 200,000 "volunteers and National Guard troops ... rushed to the colors." *Gilded Age.*

robbed. If you wouldn't try your luck and drop a ten or twenty, they would save you the trouble and rob you anyway.

They had other schemes. One day I was watching an incoming steamer and saw a prosperous-looking man of middle age descend the gangplank. A sickly looking fellow hobbled up and began talking earnestly to him. ... The invalid tells him that Alaska's climate is killing him; that he must return to the United States. He has two lots and a comfortable cabin that he will sell for $100. They go up to the house he says he has to sell and as soon as the new arrival steps in the door, a masked man draws a bead on him with his shotgun and orders him to throw up his hands. They relieve him of his money, his watch and chain and other valuables and lock the door upon him. When he finally escapes the robbers are out of sight.[1]

Jeff would not have orchestrated outright robberies, but he surely knew they occurred and may have demanded a percentage of them after the fact. Jeff was the man in front and on top, the one who made it possible for others to run games and operate their schemes. With Jeff's ok, they could operate and then pay him a percentage of their profit. Without Jeff's ok and if they did not want to pay a share, the only choice was not to operate. Will Irwin's unnamed con man confessor worked three-card monte in Skaguay for Jeff and had a clear perspective of Jeff's position.

When we reached Skaguay we found a job for Soapy at once. ... Soapy's job was to act as protector for the whole gang, bribing officials who would take money, and intimidating those who wouldn't. For that he charged a sixth of our profits, after the nut [expense] was taken out. Many kicked at the price. A gang of shell-workers struck out ... toward Dawson and worked independently.[2]

With so many people working for and with Jeff, it might be wondered how he kept track of what was going on or whether an opposition group was forming. It was just because of large numbers, though, that Jeff had a psychological edge. In Skaguay, his "associates" were so numerous that few were sure who worked for Jeff. The ordinary citizen hesitated to voice opposition for fear of addressing one of Jeff's men.

Jeff and the Soap Gang's methods were almost identical to those employed in Denver and Creede, including reliance on topography. Rather than a train station from which streamed fresh victims, there was the beach and later the wharves. A function of *Daily Alaskan* reporter William Saportas was to greet, interview, and gain the confidence of select passengers debarking the ships, a practice not uncommon at the wharves in San Francisco and Seattle. Unlike reporters in those cities, though, Saportas sought personal information about how well funded a gold seeker might be and how long he would be in town, details to be passed along to "associates" up the street. He would also answer questions and steer newcomers to one of Jeff's establishments, depending on which swindle seemed appropriate to the prey. Saportas and his brother, E. W., also operated a packing and information business, a

---

[1] *Denver Evening Post* 11/27/1898, p. 12.
[2] Irwin, pp. 168-69.

legitimate business that was also perfect for gaining information about those in town preparing to advance up the trail.

William F. Saportas probably arrived in Skaguay a few weeks earlier than Jeff did in latter August 1897. It appears his brother E. W. Saportas and he might have been on their way to Dawson in the stampede that year. Packer Calvin H. Barkdull, writing in 1952 in his late 70s, told how Saportas had come to his office to arrange for packing his outfit to Bennett. Saportas paid half the cost in advance and was to pay the rest upon delivery in Bennett. But, according to Barkdull,

> He did not show up in Bennett to receive the goods. When I returned to Skagway he told me he had lost his money in a gambling game at Soapy's place, and that Soapy had then offered him a job at three hundred dollars a month on the staff of the Skagway newspaper. I was to sell his outfit in Bennett, take out the freight charges due and give him the rest, which I did.[1]

A conflicting story, however, also involves Saportas and the selling of an outfit at Bennett. It involves Sylvester Scovel, the man whose wife wired Mrs. Smith money on August 28, 1897. In this year Scovel was "America's most celebrated newspaper correspondent." In covering events in Cuba from 1895 to early 1897 for Joseph Pulitzer's *New York World*, he had interviewed rebel leaders, been captured by the Spanish, helped American forces, and seasoned his reporting with bravado and flair. When the Cuban isle overheated, the *World* sent Scovel to other locations, including Europe. When the great Klondike gold strike occurred, Scovel came to cover the event and brought along his new St. Louis socialite wife, Frances. Another correspondent, E. Hazard Wells for the Scripps newspaper chain, met Scovel in Skaguay on August 12, 1897, and remarked that except for Scovel, "there are no other bona fide newspapermen in the vicinity. Several miners have told me that they are to send news to various papers...."[2] Perhaps Saportas was one of these and had met Jeff through the Scovels, or perhaps the Scovels met Saportas through Jeff. By August 20, Tappan Adney, reporting for *Harper's Weekly* and the *London Chronicle*, had arrived. He reported "A large painted cloth sign" that indicated "the location of the correspondents of enterprising newspapers, and the half-dozen newspaper men here gave us a hearty welcome."[3] Adney, however, recorded no names.

Scovel's implausible idea was to make the trip to Dawson an extended honeymoon and another exciting adventure to report. He would spend the winter there, reporting. Then in Bennett he learned that mail deliveries in and out of Dawson would likely number only three that winter. So he hit upon the sensational idea of dog sledding copies of the *New York World* into Dawson along with supplies and selling them at fantastic prices. Return dogsled runs would carry his dispatches "outside." The plan, though, would need to be cleared with his paper.

So leaving his wife in a tent in Bennett, he returned over the Chilkoot to Dyea and sailed to Seattle to wire the idea to his paper. His superiors turned him down flat. He was to come to New York at once or find other employment. Scovel boarded an east-

---

[1] Barkdull, p. 10.

[2] Wells, p. 32.

[3] Adney, pp. xix, 41-42.

bound train and telegrammed a young man in Skaguay whom he had met on the way through: William Saportas. Perhaps Saportas had been a correspondent for an outside paper and Scovel met him as a fellow journalist. Not even one paper was in Skaguay at this time. The first issue of *The Skaguay News* appeared on October 15, 1897, and the first issue of the *Daily Alaskan* on February 1, 1898. Scovel's telegram, believed to have been sent September 22, 1897, would have gone to Seattle and then taken another seven days minimum to reach Skaguay. It asked Saportas to go to Bennett, find Scovel's wife, sell their outfit, escort his wife back to Skaguay, and deposit her on a ship to Seattle. Funds would come from sale of the outfit. "As an incentive to Saportas, Scovel promised to 'have the *World* send you full credentials as a special correspondent' in Alaska."[1]

Saportas did all that was asked of him and more. He not only found the distraught wife, who had not seen her famous husband for a month, and brought her to Skaguay; he also accompanied her aboard ship to Seattle. Not known is if Saportas received a correspondent's credential from the *World*, but he could claim to have one on the strength of Scovel's telegram. It could have been with this promise in hand that Saportas introduced himself to Barkdull when Saportas asked him to sell an outfit at Bennett. Writing fifty-five years after the event and remembering Saportas as Jeff's man, Barkdull could have filled in what he did not know with what seemed logical.

However it was, Saportas seems to have been one of Jeff's men early on. Jeff left Skaguay from latter September to late November or early December 1897. He might have forged a connection with Saportas before leaving but certainly later on. At 26 going on 27,[2] Saportas had reporting skills and that credential from Pulitzer's *World*, and he had management skills. In November 1897, an advertisement for Holly House, in which Jeff is thought to have had an interest, named "W. F. Saportas, Proprietor."[3] This restaurant and lodging business was on Holly Street between Runnals (State today) and Main streets. Later ads advertised "first class accommodations with the best quality goods and cigars."[4] Jim Pitcher, Klondiker and packer, reported that his

> headquarters were at the Holly House, a small hotel with a bar, a dining room and as I recall several sleeping rooms. I was never in one of the sleeping rooms, for all rooms had been engaged even before the furniture was put in. It was necessary to be a brother-in-law of the manager to get possession of one. ... I lived in a cabin with about eight other fellows near this hotel.[5]

Pitcher also recorded that "Captain Wood of the North West Mounted Police had his headquarters at the Holly House" during the three months" Pitcher was in Skaguay.[6] Pitcher's identifying Holly House as "headquarters" is explained by another Saportas skill, packing. A *Skaguay News* note included how "W. F. Saportas ... is now engaged

---

[1] Campbell, p. 154.
[2] 26 ... 27: CA Death Index, b. 29 Jan 1871, NY City; d. 12 June 1942, Los Angeles (Ancestry.com.)
[3] *Skaguay News* 11/19/1897, p. 4.
[4] *Skaguay News* 12/31/1897.
[5] Pitcher, p. 18.
[6] Pitcher, p. 19.

in transporting eighty tons of freight for the Canadian government to the lakes."[1] By December's end the brother of Saportas, E. W. Saportas, was listed in *The News* as General Manager of the Packing, Guide & Information Company of Alaska.

> Freight contracts entered into from Tidewater to River Navigation and onward. Guides furnished for Mountain Passes and River Rapids. Information relating to Climate, Outfits, and Best Methods of Travel.[2]

E. W. was killed in the *Clara Nevada* disaster. In a wild storm on the night of February 5, 1898, with apparently a fire on board, she was driven onto Eldred Rock, splitting the ship open. Of the approximate 100 aboard (39 crew and some 61 passengers), all were lost. So fierce was the event and aftermath, only one body was ever recovered.[3]

William Saportas at some point in February or March 1898, probably at the behest of Jeff, became a reporter for the *Daily Alaskan*. When Oscar W. Dunbar returned to Astoria, Oregon, on a visit to his wife, J. Allen Hornsby,[4] a medical doctor, active in city meetings but apparently at loose ends in town, became editor of the *Alaskan* in Dunbar's absence. Where Jeff failed to secure favor with Dunbar, he seems to have succeeded with Hornsby. So Jeff had two friends on the inside of that paper. Later accused of receiving graft from Jeff in return for withholding news about him, Hornsby was fired and forced from town, and so was Saportas.

W. E. "Slim-Jim" Foster's assignment, like Saportas's, was to funnel a fresh victims towards Jeff's establishments. Working from another page of the Denver con man's playbook, Foster and the other steerers often gained the confidence of their quarry by warning them of crooks who lurked in the new camp, adding, "Why not go over to the Merchants Exchange? They're an honest outfit that will see your gear over the pass without over charging. I can vouch for them."

Van B. "Old-Man" Triplett was an aging, professional bunco man. His earliest known criminal record dates from Chicago in 1876 where he was arrested in a swindle gone awry.[5] In Skaguay, he "steered" newcomers, but he also worked the shell game and three-card Monte racket along the White Pass trail, posing as a stampeder. He played his short con swindles and conversed with returning stampeders to find out who among them carried sufficient cash or gold to make them worth the Soap Gang's time in Skaguay. He also "worked" those who were ready to begin the trail from Skaguay. If found to possess ready money, they were warned of impending bad weather or of sickness on the trail and urged to remain in Skaguay until it was safe, thus giving the gang another chance at their money.

Harry Suydam, an early resident of Skaguay, saw first hand how the shell men operated along the trails. In a 1901 article, he told of watching

> a most brutal-looking man of almost herculean physique. His name was Walsh, and he was known as Soapy's "right-bower." He was manipulating

---

[1] *Skaguay News* 12/31/1897, p. 4.

[2] *Skaguay News* 12/31/1897, p. 2.

[3] Gibbs, pp. 71-73. *Skaguay News* 02/18/1898, p. 4, postulates that the ship caught fire and blew up.

[4] Hornsby: the name most often appears in print as "J. Allen Hornsby." The middle name is sometimes spelled "Allan." The "Allen" spelling is adopted throughout.

[5] *Inter Ocean* 01/11/1876, p. 5.

three English walnut half shells, under one of which was the alluring pea. Four men were apparently watching the pea. One of them had an axe on his shoulder, one carried a rifle, one had a fifty-pound sack strapped on his back and the other was leaning on a pack. All looked like the busy Argonauts of the trail. As a matter of fact, they were all accomplices, such as are known in mining camps as "boosters" or "cappers."

A stranger happened along, and at once the dealer talked a little louder; the cappers became more active. Just as the new arrival came up, one placed a $20 gold piece on the box, picked up the shell that covered the pea, and promptly pocketed one of the dealer's double eagles.[1] The stranger was interested to see such an easy game, and began to look over the cappers' shoulders. Then, quite accidentally, one capper backed out to allow the stranger to get nearer the dealer, and when he pressed forward, excited at the game, the fellow got his shoulder behind him and crowded him to the front.

The new comer hesitated after being asked to lift the shell just for fun, but encouraged by the cappers, he consented, and sure enough the pea was uncovered. Then all the cappers laughed at him merrily, and the dealer threw the bait to give him another chance. He immediately saw the shell that covered the pea, for the dealer carelessly let the shell rest on it. Then down into the gold sack the innocent dived, while every man in the crowd craned his neck to see the size of the sack, and almost before the man could raise the shell the dealer had pocketed his $20. He protested, but all the cappers only laughed heartily, while the dealer good-naturedly arranged the shells to give him a chance to get his money back.

Suydam reported seeing a man lose $600 in just minutes before realizing "he was 'bucking a sure-thing game.'" If a player resisted, he stood little chance because "these men were always expecting trouble, and were ready for it." One of Jeff's shell-and-pea men would not even bother "lifting a shell for less than $20...." Suydam believed it "not uncommon for the boss to make $2,000 in one day on this game."[2]

The Skaguay News and Suydam told of one victim who successfully stood up for himself. A packer had stopped at one of these set ups and lost a great deal. When turning from the seven gamblers who had conspired to take the victim's money, ready to go on, the packer was "jeered by the cappers and dealer." That was too much.

He ... turned and knocked one of them down, another gambler engaged him and met the same fate. A third was about to go down under the doughty fist of the victim, when the gambler pulled a revolver and flourished it at the man. Thus challenged, the victim himself drew a small gun and stepping back a few steps, opened up on the crowd of gamblers, and did not stop firing until he had emptied his weapon three times. At the same time, the seven

---

[1] *double eagles*: the name for the largest denomination US metal currency until the California gold rush was the $10 "Gold Eagle." In 1849 Congress authorized the $20 gold piece, and its nickname doubled. *Gold.*

[2] Suydam, "Reign," p. 212.

gamblers were firing as fast as they could at the man, who had stood out boldly and was a good target. Fifty or more men packing on the trail, witnessed the battle very unwillingly, for the bullets were flying in all directions and made it very dangerous in the vicinity. As it was, an innocent packer sitting on his sled up the trail was the only man hit by a bullet, with the exception of one of the gamblers who was said to be hit in the hand.[1]

As Suydam concluded his version, "The casualties, as usual, were disinterested parties, three onlookers being slightly wounded by spent bullets, and one horse was shot dead while packing along the trail."[2]

Harry Suydam helped Frank Reid survey Skaguay and shared a tent with corrupt US Commissioner John U. Smith. Later Suydam was city assessor and shared quarters with Deputy US Marshal Sylvester S. Taylor. Of him Suydam wrote, "Many dark deeds I was cognizant of, but was powerless to remedy."[3] When Taylor replaced the murdered James Rowan, Jeff immediately befriended Taylor and put him on the payroll. From 1891 to 1896, Taylor had been constable and deputy sheriff in Nanpa, Idaho, and during a portion of that time, he was a deputy US marshal. From May 1896 to January 30, 1898, he had been city marshal of Nanpa.[4]

Doctor Howard Atwood Kelly also witnessed the shell games along the Skaguay and Dyea trails and described them in his journal, circa March 25, 1898.

> The most prominent feature of the landscape is the activity of the shell-game men and their cappers. How any one can be deceived by these crooks is a mystery, but many are. They look evil, and are evil. Great numbers lose heavily and a good many have had to give up their journey and turn back, all funds being lost. ... Shell-game tables extend from Dyea to Sheep Camp and one comes across them every hundred yards or so. The U. S. soldiers here do not look like soldiers. They are slovenly. Too often they are seen watching the shell-games and never once have I seen them do anything in the nature of police work. They are inefficient and not respectable. No one has any respect for them. ... I never saw a shell-game after leaving Sheep Camp. The terrain up above was too tough for these tender creatures![5]

In addition to free-wheeling games of chance, Jeff owned merchant services, for example, the Merchants Exchange. Here, according to legend, new arrivals were told that the supplies they had purchased in "the states" were the wrong kind. But the "cheechako"[6] was not worry; the wrong supplies would be taken in partial exchange for appropriate supplies. Then after a short interval, the "wrong supplies" were reshelved to be sold to another stampeder whose outfit included the "wrong supplies."

---

[1] Pennington, pp. 88-89.

[2] Suydam, "Reign," p. 214.

[3] Suydam, "Reign," p. 213.

[4] Criminal case 1028-US v. Sylvester S. Taylor. Record Group 21 – US District Courts. Box 16 – 01/01/05(2). National Archives and Records Administration, Pacific Alaska Region, Anchorage, Alaska.

[5] Davis, Mary, pp. 43-44.

[6] *cheechako*: Chinook jargon for "newcomer," *chee* new; *chako* to come. A newly arrived immigrant in the mining districts of northwestern North America; a tenderfoot, greenhorn.

Jeff discovered in Seattle that everyone, including himself, wanted information about Alaska and the Klondike. Here was another opportunity. In Skaguay Jeff opened an information bureau. Harry Suydam as City Assessor noted that Jeff had

> two cabins in close proximity to the wharves, on which were posted large signs, which read, "General Information Bureau." Inside of these cabins was always a well dressed-man behind the counter, who could entertain a visitor about the condition of the different trails, charges for packing, etc., until his confederate came in. The conversation would lead to cards, and, quite incidentally, he would produce a pack, and begin throwing three of them.[1]

In addition to playing a friendly game of cards if opportunity arose, instead of giving out information, the real objective was to collect it. Desired information included the background of newcomers, their immediate plans, whether they traveled alone, how much cash they had on hand, and whether they were armed.

John M. McCawley worked as a newsboy when he came with his father to Skaguay. In a recorded interview, he recalled how bunco men, including John Bowers, tried to swindle his father in the Information Bureau office. Their interaction began on the beach when a young fellow "dressed as a westerner with a cowboy hat," stepped up and observed how the "old man" had a large number of items.

> "If you're going up, I'll help you pack you're bundles up." Now this is a bunco man see, and when we got them up above the tide line, he was through, and my dad knew that a man who would do a turn for you like that, well you should ask him to have a drink whether he would or not, so my father asked this man to have a drink, and we went across to a saloon near the tide line, and I went in with 'em. A little boy from the farm with all ears and had never seen anything before.
>
> So they had their drink, and while they were having their drink, another man stepped up and sort of butted in. Now he was a second bunco man, but we didn't know it. The first man was through, but the second man had said that he had bought a team of horses to take his outfit into the Klondike. And he said that his outfit was small and that he could take my father's outfit along with his just for help of my dad along the way. After they had their drink, he says, "Let's go up and see the horses." Now there were no horses, but we didn't know it. So while on the way up to see the horses, there was a little building across the way that says Information Bureau. And he says, "Let's ... get a map," and we went across to get the map. And the man that was running the place, he says, "I'm just out of maps, they're in the post office. You wait while I go down and get them." And he went ... out..., and his purpose we figured out was to notify the head bunco man that they had a live one in the Information Bureau. So my father still thought the man with the

---

[1] Suydam, p. 215. Suydam ends the paragraph in such a way that the bunco men many times killed their victims. The author chose to leave this part out as bunco men were known to use their intelligence to make their money, not murder. It does not make sense to go through all the work of renting a cabin, setting up a three-card Monte game, just to kill the victim at the conclusion. Why not just wait in hiding on the trail for victims to forcefully rob and kill.

horses was ok. And now in comes the bunco man, and he says, sort of like he's half drunk..., "Give us a map." The man with my father says, "The man that's running the place is just out to get the maps. Wait here, he'll be right back." So then he started his bunco game playing. He says, "You know, they had a game in Dawson, I suppose you're going to the Klondike?" And my father said, "Yes." "Well," he says, "you ought to be careful when you get in there because they're the worst set of thieving rascals you ever ran into. ... They had a game called three-card Monte." And he said, "I bought one of the games before I left, and I'm going to learn to play it while I'm out. By the way I never treated my ole' man very good." He saw that my father was an old man, and he wanted to make a story for him. So, he says, "I'm gonna pay the mortgage off of the farm and just set the ole' man up in fine shape." He says, "I'd like to learn to play this game," and he says, "Let's practice." And he took out the three-card Monte, it was wrapped up in a hanker-chief. As soon as my father saw that, he knew this fellow was a bunco man. He'd seen that before, but he still thought the fellow with the horses was ok. And so he wanted my father to gamble on the cards.... He says, "Now you don't need to bet any money. They're using gold coins. They're twenty dollar gold pieces, see?" And his pockets was full of 'em. And he says, "Every time you turn the right card, I'll give you twenty dollars." My dad knew that trick. He tried to jog on [nudge] the other fellow not to have anything to do with it, but the other fellow kept on playing, and he kept gettin' twenty dollars. And I was sittin' back there wondering as a boy why my dad didn't get some of those twenties? When this fellow wouldn't take the nudgings..., my father dropped on to the fact this other man with the horses was a bunco man too. So he told them, "Well, fellas, you've got the wrong man. I knew that game before either one of you fellas was born." So then their head bunco man, he says, "Oh well, he's an old man, an old broke son-of-a-gun," a little stronger words than that, and he says, "We couldn't get nothing from him anyway." My dad said that was a ploy [for] a greenhorn man to pull his money out and the con men would conk him over the head and be gone, but my father said to him, "I'd rather be an old broke son-of-a-gun than I would to be a thieving rascal like you are." So they walked off and left us. And [we] went on ... to a normal life in Skaguay, and we would hear stories about men losing their money, and they would say they lost it up at Soapy's place, and then it got so that everybody in Skaguay knew all the gang, and there were about twenty-five men in the gang.

When asked if one of the men was Soapy, McCawley said no, that it was Bowers.

Later as a newsboy, John McCawley witnessed the pre-swindle meetings of victims and the Soap Gang giving testament to the size and power of the gang.

We kids selling newspapers on the street, we got to know all the men, and we would see them with some captured fellas.... They'd walk them up the street and take them to Soapy's place. We'd start to follow to see what was going to happen. There would always be side men, and they would say, "You kids get on back, get out of the way, get away from here." We were afraid to follow them up. They would take them up to Soapy Smith's. He had a long building…. They had a barroom next to the street where they served the liquor. Next to that was a gambling room where they had five tables. Roulette and faro and different kinds of games. I wouldn't remember now just what they all were.[1]

The Skaguay Real-Estate & Investment Company on McKinney Street (5th Avenue today) next door to the post office was another operation believed to have been under Jeff's control. J. Allen Hornsby, Arthur H. Bryant, and John G. Price operated the office. Their advertisement read,

Real estate bought and sold, houses to rent, business chances, investments made for non residents, special attention paid to the care of property placed in our hands. Mining properties bought and sold & examined. Headquarters for quick cash sales. References, all the prominent men in the city.[2]

Skaguay property often illegally changed hands. As in Creede, Jeff made the most of property protection rackets. Hornsby was on Jeff's payroll, and Price is believed to have been Skaguay's first attorney. Assumed is that Jeff used his services from the very start. Of special note is the line "investments made for non residents." The wording suggests that residents should stay clear of this firm, it being an unwritten but often professed practice that the Soap Gang worked principally on out-of-towners.

The cut-rate ticket office operated much as it had in Denver. Tickets on outbound steamships were offered at a discount, but the tickets, which never materialized, were just a ploy to get victims inside the establishment where they could be tempted by various swindles while waiting for the non-existent ticket to be obtained.

One of the more brazen scams Jeff worked on stampeders was the Telegraph Office. Travel between Skaguay and Seattle took about a week, and after that long at sea, the weary traveler was eager to be in touch with loved ones and associates at home. Seeing an opportunity, Jeff opened a telegraph service that would send a message anywhere in the US for only $5. More could be made than just this fee, however. Upon entering the "office," a victim learned the key operator had stepped out for a moment but would soon return. Encouraged to wait, he would be surrounded by newfound "friends" who chatted with him and offered the usual pastime games of chance. When the key operator appeared, if the victim still had the $5 fee, he could send his message. If believed to still have funds enough, he would be followed and after a short time informed that a reply telegram had arrived and awaited him back at the office—for an additional $5. Then the friendly games of chance might be employed again to obtain even more, if not all, of the victim's money.

In 1897-1898 no telegraph line ran to Skaguay, but the line from the Telegraph Office that disappeared into Lynn Canal made it appear there was. A line did not reach Skaguay from Juneau until 1901.[3]

---

[1] McCawley interview.
[2] *Skaguay News* 02/11/1898, & *Daily Alaskan*, 02/28/1898.
[3] *Collier's Weekly* clipping, 11/09/1901.

Jeff's services operations took advantage of the ignorance and gullibility of most stampeders. How many were victimized cannot be calculated, only estimated to be in the thousands. As Will Irwin's confessional con man reported of Skaguay arrivals, "They all had money; and most of them were reckless with it."[1] Most who "lost" their funds were quick to fault nature rather than look dim-witted. Author Richard O'Connor touched upon this point in *High Jinks on the Klondike*. "Hundreds of stampeders who returned home from Skaguay in dejection attributed their defeat to the rigors of the journey when actually they had been laid low by whisky, women and dice."[2]

Depending on the situation and the demeanor of the victim, Jeff sometimes returned money to a defrauded prey. Being caught broke and trapped in Skaguay often helped their case. Jeff would give them enough for passage homeward and a few words of advice, perhaps something like, "Learn from your mistakes, but never let on to others that you made any. It would be embarrassing to admit that you were a failure up here." Jeff might laugh in the face of a victim who had tried to cheat him at his own game, but to the naïve who blundered into a loss, he might try to send him along with enough spine to hold him upright and get him home.

Jeff also helped men whom he had not had a hand in defrauding. Stephen Stephens, a newspaper boy of fourteen in 1898 Skaguay, remembered how

> It was the same way with down-and-outers who came back over the trail. He would bawl them out for being hungry and for not coming to him sooner. He would then see the stranger out of trouble. He would do all these things, and yet he would not scruple an instant to rob a prospector of his gold and send him away a pauper. It all depended on how the stranger came to him.[3]

Dr. W. T. Barrett wrote of his having observed Jeff look after some of his men when they were afflicted by disease.

> I met Soapy Smith many times during our ten days stay in and near Skagway through D. Moore, a resident physician who was attending dozens of cerebrospinal meningitis cases, many of whom were associated with Soapy in gouging the public. Soapy often accompanied us on our daily rounds and seemed rather a delightful fellow to meet, one that would pass in any ordinary community as a successful business man—mild mannered and much interested in the humanities. His record, however, as an outlaw leader was well known to both American and Canadian authorities.[4]

Jeff looked after his men, and he was generous toward many of his victims. He was also indifferent to the plight his schemes brought to most victims. Jeff's character was an inscrutable spectrum of opposites and consistent contradictions.

Skaguay was so free-wheeling a bustling enterprise, it is somewhat surprising that Jeff would have time and interest to devote to trying to control neighboring Dyea. If he tried, it does not appear he had much success at it. Jeff's partner John Clancy had a "Clancy and Company" ad in the Dyea newspaper, listing a location at River Street

---

[1] Irwin, p. 168.
[2] O'Connor, p. 32.
[3] *Literary Digest*, p. 49.
[4] Barrett, p. 55.

and Wilson,[1] but Jeff apparently was not able to control the newspapers there. The *Dyea Press* freely warned of Soap Gang activity. "Dyea has everything that every other town in Alaska has, except 'Soapy' Smith."[2] Located in the same issue was this warning: "Don't play the shell & pea games in Wrangle and Skaguay or you will have to walk home."[3] Not being able to influence public and merchant opinion through the community's media, Jeff stood little chance of establishing the kind of control in Dyea that he enjoyed in Skaguay.

In the late winter and early spring of 1898, Jeff and John Clancy partnered in obtaining a small, false-fronted, single-story wood-frame building at 317 Holly Street on the north side, between Broadway and State streets. The 18-foot by about 40-foot building had been constructed for the First Bank of Skaguay, which occupied the structure from October 1897 until February or March 1898 when the bank moved to larger quarters. The front had to be altered to accommodate a bar, and Jeff added electricity and a sign on the outside. Nighttime interior photographs show illuminated light bulbs hanging from the ceiling. Electric lighting was rare, expensive, and something to show off, not obscure behind shades. A final touch outside was a large trim piece set atop the front. Painted across it in large letters was the name of the place, "Jeff Smith's Parlor." The *Daily Alaskan* gave the saloon a warm write-up:

> Jeff R. Smith's new saloon parlors were opened on Saturday afternoon and were visited during the day by Jeff's many friends and well-wishers. The pretty back parlour is as cosy as a lady's boudoir—Jeff's friends predict for him a large measure of success.[4]

The Parlor was probably open by March 9, 1898, the date sworn complaints were filed against Jeff and eight other men for gambling there.[5] Three days later Jeff used the 317 address number as the Committee member count in answer to the Committee of 101. Records are unclear about who actually owned the Parlor and the date of purchase. However, there is no question that Jeff was in charge of it.

"Jeff's Place" as some called it, was advertised as the "Most Elegantly Furnished Resort in Alaska" with "Choice Wines and Liquors [−] Havana Cigars" with "Special Attention Paid to Service."[6] Three interior photographs show signs of elegance. Though small, the Parlor had a large bar with a white, ornate front and a dark mahogany top, backed by mirrors and long-necked decanters on a shelf. Paper of fancy design covered trimmed walls, the ceiling had a rectangular painted or papered design, and the floor had circular tiling. A small table resided along the east sidewall window. On the west wall behind the bar hung political and patriotic pictures. One image that was constant in three photographs was the American flag with a superimposed picture of President McKinley. Two photographs show the Cuban

[1] *Dyea Press* 03/12/1898.

[2] *Dyea Press* 05/14/1898.

[3] *Dyea Press* 05/14/1898.

[4] Sinclair, p. 127. Printed as written.

[5] US Commissioner's Records, pp. 143-151.

[6] *Skaguay News*, 06/17/1898, p. 3.

revolutionary flag while another shows it facing an American flag, suggesting solidarity with Cuba against Spain in the Spanish-American War.

A small enclosed area in the back with a framed opening may have remained from when the building was a bank. A safe could have resided around the corner in this small enclosure. The space could have been used as Jeff's Office, a club room, or both. One photograph shows a man sitting in a chair inside the opening. Evidence indicates that some gambling took place in the Parlor but none of "big hand" swindles or of gambling devices. An advertisement for the parlor states, "No Cards, No Games." That, however, could have been a policy taken up later on. Speculation has it that Jeff eventually kept gambling from his place because it did not fit the image of the public-spirited citizen Jeff wanted to promote. In control of plenty of gambling throughout Skaguay, he did not need it in the little building from which he sought to shine as a law-abiding businessman and that became the headquarters of Smith's Military Company. His name hung preeminently in large letters across the top front of the building, and criminal trouble would have attached to his name. Skaguay had a city hall, but it was inside Jeff Smith's Parlor that most civic matters were determined. Mont Hawthorne told of having visited "Soapy Smith's gambling place," a location he wanted to see before heading up the White Pass trail. Hawthorne was not precise with dates, but the narrative of his solitary journey from Astoria to Dawson is clear and detailed, and from some events and a date dropped along the way, his visit to Jeff Smith's Parlor may be estimated to be early March. Mont had seen Jeff about town.

> He never went around talking and bragging and shoving folks. He moved quiet and soft like.... Folks around town claimed he was in the women business just as much as he was in gambling. But if that was so, then he sure run his affairs like they do a department store, because down there at his main gambling place he didn't have a bunch of dance hall girls hanging around taking a man's mind off his business. That place was for gambling, and folks done it there, too. ... It was terrible crowded, we just walked around and looked and let the rest of them take the chances. It was just an ordinary dive, with a bar and card games, and the rest of the usual skin games. The place sure wasn't very fancy, just made of up and down boards. It must have been about forty foot by thirty foot.[1]

Actually, the building was smaller than that. A modern measure of the reconstructed façade is only eighteen feet. The building might have been about forty feet long.

Next door was a small restaurant "in connection" with the Parlor. It was remembered by Royal Pullen, son of Skaguay pioneer Harriet Pullen. He was ten years old in 1898 when he worked as a newsboy for *The Seattle Post-Intelligencer*. In a tape-recorded interview with members of the Smith family, he described what he remembered of Jeff and one of his saloons, possibly Jeff Smith's Parlor.

> It didn't have anything very plush. ... There were red curtains in the saloon, but not in the restaurant. There were just tables with oils cloth on them. ... He had a little restaurant in there, and then the gambling hall and

---

[1] McKeown, pp. 112-13.

saloon was right next to it, and that's where he entertained us newsboys. He had little tables. ... I guess there must have been 25 or 30 of us news kids, and an oyster dinner was really something. He had a backroom that was his office, where they carried on. I was never allowed back in there. ... We were 10- and 11-year-old kids. They don't allow you around. They'd say, "Sonny, go on, this is no place for you." ... He was a good guy as far as we were concerned. He liked us kids, and we liked Soapy. He wasn't mean. There wasn't anything about Soapy that was mean. He always would pay us. The boy who got to him first with the news from the states got a silver dollar because it took the papers anywhere from a week to two weeks to get there. Those old gamblers and panhandlers were really nice. I had a lot of friends amongst them, I really did. I might as well tell you that I had a lot of friends among the prostitutes too. Some of those were really fine women. They were really good friends.[1]

Skaguay could be rough and tumble, but newspapers across the nation exaggerated the wickedness of its frontier environment Jeff's Place. Three young arrivals to the camp had heard of the notorious "Soapy" Smith's and purposely sought it out, hoping for a glimpse of the bad man.

We made a beeline for Soapy Smith's saloon. We knew it was the first thing they'd ask us about back home. "Did you go to Soapy's place? Did you see him?" Well, we never saw him but we were in the headquarters.... And it was a big disappointment, let me tell you. It looked just like any ordinary saloon. We didn't see anybody that even looked crooked in the place. We called for our drinks and paid. Then, just as we were about to throw the liquor down, a volley of shots let loose that raised us off our heels. Wasn't anything. Just one of the men in there that had shot off his revolver to scare us greenhorns. He called us "cheechakos." That's the name they had up there for the new arrivals. Well, they all had the laugh on us. They saw they scared us bug-eyed. We beat it and went back to the boat. We were just boys, the three of us. We never in our lives had been "shot at" before. But we were no different from the rest. The Klondike was full of boys like us. Greenhorns.[2]

In a recorded interview with Smith family members, Roy White, who met Jeff in Denver and worked for him in Skaguay, gave another glimpse inside Jeff's Place.

Charlie Anderson stopped over there. Charlie was quite a heavy drinker ... and he got to drinking there. Charlie had $600 and Soapy sold him 6 claims. Now Soapy didn't know those claims were worth a penny. You see, the way he got the claims is this: a miner would come in and they'd get broke [and] for a few meals and a drink or two, they'd sell ... some claims. They were ... legal, all registered. ... Soapy sold 6 claims to Charlie for his $600. We went on down to Candle.... He ... wanted to see those claims ... up by Candle, about 8 miles out. So we got a feller to go over there with him where the

[1] Pullen, Royal, recorded interview.
[2] Winslow, pp. 113-14.

claims were, and by golly right from the grass roots it was rich. He took about a million dollars out of those 6 claims. Soapy sold him a fortune.

Jeff hired White to deal cards and tried to interest him in working the prize package soap racket on Skaguay crowds. White had lost some fingers railroading, and that loss was apparently one reason Jeff took to him, as White eventually makes clear.

He took quite a liking to me.... I had bought a horse taxi for $150 first, and I had that on the corner. Everybody got to like'n me. I'd drive 'em, some of them would get in, just let me drive 'em around, just because I was right on the [undecipherable]. Soapy, he got to like'n me. ...

He says, "You're into small money; you should be in a bigger load of dough. You got talent." ... I says, "I'm doing all right." [Jeff says,] "How much you make'n?" I says, "Not too much, 7, 8, 9 dollars a day." "That's chicken feed," he says. "You should be make'n more money, you're smarter than that. I'll show you something I'm not going to use anymore. I'm in a bigger [business?] now." He says, "I'm not going to use it anymore, but it's a good one. Start you off with a good bankroll." ...

He'd do almost anything for you, but if he didn't like you, ... he was quite an enemy. But anybody who was down, it was a known fact that Soapy would always feed them, give 'em a little money to get out of town, get a job. He was very liberal that way, open hearted.

He had hands as soft as a girl's..., very limber, very good, too, fast with his hands. He could do anything with cards, dice too. He was dynamite with dice,.... .... He could do anything with cards like nobody's business. There were gamblers who didn't want to play him, but when they seen me with no fingers on, they figured I couldn't cheat 'em even if I wanted..., so that's the reason I got hired for deal'n.[1]

On February 15, 1898, while anchored in Havana Harbor, the US battleship *Maine* suddenly exploded, killing 258 of its crew. Spain was blamed although reliable reports indicated that the interior explosion could not have been the work of Spain. The US declared war on April 25, but because Spain had declared war on the US the previous day, the US Congress backdated its declaration to April 21, 1898. But Jeff did not need a declaration of war to swing into action. Reaching Skaguay a week later, word of the *Maine's* sinking stirred patriotic zeal in the hearts of Skaguay's residents, and as expressed sometime later by *Skaguay News* reporter Elmer J. Stroller, "in no heaving breast in Skagway did patriotism seethe, bubble, ferment and boil more intensely than in that of Jefferson Randolph Smith...."[2]

Within seven days of the Committee of 101's distribution of handbills, Jeff had created his own Alaska army unit with himself as captain, "elected by its members in true democratic fashion."[3] Jeff foresaw the public relations power of this effort, and it was affirmed: people applauded it. And now he had another power if needed, the

---

[1] White, Roy interview.
[2] DeArmond, "Stroller," p. 16.
[3] DeArmond, "Stroller, p. 17.

Skaguay Military Company under his command. Should "disturbances" occur, such as vigilantes might cause, Captain Smith could call up what amounted to his own private army. The 101, with no stomach to oppose an organized unit of "Patriots," shrank behind doors and bided time.

Chapter 21

The Skaguay Military Company

*Spain will send her battleships to seize our ports,
and they will try to capture our ships. But, be damned to them ...
we'll stake our lives against their plots.*
—Captain Jefferson R. Smith, Commanding
Skaguay Military Company meeting, circa April 1, 1898

Never believe I'm dead until you see me in the morgue.
—Jefferson R. Smith II
said to his wife Mary

The causes of the Skaguay Military Company are several. First was the plight of Cuba in general. Since 1895, Spain had suppressed the Cuban people most brutally, killing not only freedom fighters in battles and skirmishes but also over 100,000 noncombatants. The American people were at first incensed that a European power was operating militarily so close to American shores, but with news of the carnage, which newspapers were eager to report, people were shocked and angered. Then with the blowing up of the US battleship *Maine* in Havana Harbor, the drum beat to war began. In Skaguay, Jeff heard that sound, measured the sentiment, which he himself probably shared, and envisioned a volunteer Skaguay military force. It is no wonder that he was able to organize a military company so swiftly. He had been rehearsing the act since 1894 when he proposed such a force to President Diaz of Mexico, and he had had it in mind subsequently when troubles in Cuba began to flair.

Two other significant causes begin with the secretive vigilante Committee of 101 and its "Warning." Jeff claimed a committee of 317 in a bold "Announcement" by way of reply, but at the time, that number was hyperbole—breath-catching, but overstatement to be sure. So to put flesh to the number, Jeff saw a means of recruiting a sizeable body of men and of sealing his own stature as its leader. Finally, there was the Warren bill. It authorized funds for such units as Jeff's volunteer company. On "March 8, 1898, Secretary of War Russell A. Alger allocated $250,000 for organizational expenses, $197,000 for transportation and horses, $31,392 for equipment, and $15,000 for subsistence."[1] Only 11 days span this allocation and the approximate date of Jeff's creation of a volunteer military company. However, the speed at which news could cross the country was ever increasing through organized cooperation among newspapers via telephone and telegraph. News from coast to

---

[1] Singer.

coast could be in print within a day, and news from Seattle could easily have reached Jeff in time to lend impetus to his plans.

Jeff went about forming the Skaguay Military Company by working people into a state of wanting and needing it. He called for and led patriotic assemblies to address war fears and the need for readiness. Wasting no time, he followed up by executing a plan to recruit, organize, have recognized, and administer an all-volunteer military force created, in theory, for use by the President of the United States. Minutes of the formation, a necessary part of applying for recognition, are as follows:

At a meeting of the citizens of the United States of America residing at the city of Skaguay, a territory of Alaska, held at the Bauer Hall,[1] for the purpose of organizing a military company in the territory of Alaska for the purpose of offering its services to the Government of the United States as volunteers in the event of a war with Spain: Said meeting was called to order on the 18th day of March, 1898, at said hall by J. [John] Callahan,[2] who then and there stated to the meeting its object and purpose. Mr. Callahan was then unanimously elected Chairman of the meeting, and J. M. Donaldson, unanimously elected Secretary of the meeting.

It was then moved and seconded and carried that all citizens of the United States being desirous of membership in said company to be organized at Skagway for the purpose enumerated at the opening of the meeting, that each person takes oath of allegiance to support the Government of the United States, etc. and in the event of war with Spain to enlist their services for a period of two years after which oath so taken their names to be subsequently subscribed thereunder. Thereafter the oath hereto annexed was then read to each individual member who desired to become a member of said military organization and when taken he thereafter subscribes his name thereto.

UNITED STATES OF AMERICA,)

)   ) ss.

District of Alaska.   )

We the undersigned citizens of the United States of America being first duly sworn deposes and says that he is a citizen of the United States and will support the Constitution thereof, and if called upon as a member of that military organization known as the "Skaguay Military Company", organized for the purpose of responding to any call or demand made by the President of the United States in the event of a war with Spain for the period of two years, and if so called will enlist and become enrolled in accordance with any rule or regulation of the United States now adopted under the military regulations.

George Arnold, William D. Barr, James Beedle, Dave Blake, Fred Bluff, F. Boker, Charles Boston, J.L. Bowers, S.P. Bowser, Ben H. Brewer, Al Britting, Ed Burns, T.H. Callahan, John W. Campbell, Martin J. Casey, Frank Cleveland, James Collins, A. Comey, Bob Delford, Jack Dolan, William

---

[1] Probably H. A. Bauer, Holly Street store owner. Empire Theater program, item 117, author's col.
[2] *Seattle Times* 07/24/1897.

Dugan, C.P. Duke, John Dureivan, John Eldridge, John M. Every, Dick Flemming, Joseph Gamack, James Gilbert, J.D. Harrigan, Pete Headly, C.E. Hill, James Holt, Al H. Isaacs, D.I. Kennedy, Lewis Kulb, Joseph Land, Andrew Lang, H.D. Laras, B.L. Leroy, D.M. Levine, Harry Linnell, Frank Luthers, James McCan [?], James McCarty, Ed McGowan, William McGuiness, J.T. Miller, Arthur Morgan, Jerry Mugivan, Thomas Murry, F. Nold, William O'Kieff, James O'Neil, Tim Parker, James Pitcher, George Pitcher, Cal Powen, George Powers, Thomas Reenan, Phil B. Robertson, G.E. Rudaugh, J. Shannon, C. Shepard, B. Smith, D.S. Spencer, Robert Stockton, Ed Stranger, E. Sulival, Mike J. Taysee, R.L. Tiegald, George Troll, L. Twedall [?], G. Vigh, H.L. Vinton, Ned Williams, John W. Wilson, T. YaGaron [?], Wm. W. Yeakens, Jack Young.[1]

That the meeting aforesaid after the names hereto subscribed and the oaths therein taken adopted the following resolution: Be it hereby resolved that we proceed at this time to elect by ballot the following officers for said company, to-wit: A Captain, First Lieutenant, Second Lieutenant, First Sergeant, Second Sergeant, Third Sergeant, First Corporal, Second Corporal.

That in accordance with said resolution so adopted, the following officers were then and there unanimously elected for said company:

Captain, Jeff R. Smith,

First Lieutenant, John Foley,	Second Lieutenant, J. M. Donaldson,
First Sergeant, J. T. Miller,	Second Sergeant, R. B. McAndrew,
Third Sergeant, James Clancy,	First Corporal, D. H. Wilder,

Second Corporal, John W. Campbell.

It was then moved and seconded that a copy of those resolutions, together with the minutes of the meeting so held, and the oath subscribed by the members of this meeting be sent by mail to the President of the United States of America, at Washington, D. C. and a copy of same be forwarded to Hon. John G. Brady, the Governor of the territory of Alaska.

It was then moved and seconded that said meeting be adjourned subject to the call of the Captain of said company.

Dated this 19 day of march, 1898.

[signed]   J. M. Donaldson   J Callahan
                  Sec   Chairman[2]

Company members number 85, including 3 officers and 5 noncommissioned officers. Of the 79 enlisted men, 2 were apparently promoted: First Sergeant J.T. Miller and Second Corporal John W. Campbell. Names on the roster from the Soap Gang

---

[1] These 79 names, here appearing in a single paragraph in alphabetical order by last name, in the original typed document appear in two unalphabetized columns. The order may have been taken from a "sign-up" sheet. The document is creased and faded, so the spelling of some names cannot be certain, but most are.

[2] Documents of the Skaguay Military Company, 03/19/1898, item 34, author's col. The day and month are written in as are the names (as signatures) and positions of secretary and chairman.

include John Bowers, John Miller, and Ed Burns.[1] Recruiting a company of men ready to be soldiers for their country in so short a time took considerable skill, but then to ride the wave of patriotism to the top by being elected captain of the company was a master stroke. In Denver and during the Mexican and Cuban adventures, Jeff was just a self-proclaimed colonel. Now he had been "elected" captain.

Jeff left open the invitation to join his army company, and more came forward. The fever to "join up" spread to Dyea where more than 400 called on Colonel Anderson, commander there. He, however, could not respond without specific orders. Anderson had reported that 4 companies were no longer needed in the Lynn Canal region. In response, 2 of the 4 companies along with Anderson were ordered to return to Vancouver, Washington, the following May.[2] No doubt some of those patriots who were turned away signed up with Captain Jeff's Company.

Without delay, Jeff had eight copies of the minutes, enrollment, and letters of enclosure, dated March 19, 1898, typed up by Dr. Lewis Garrison, paying $10.50 for the job.[3] One copy each was mailed to President McKinley and Governor Brady, offering the services of the Skaguay Military Company. Only a few weeks prior, Jeff had been recognized by the war department when given authority to locate at Fort St. Michael. Now he sought recognition from the President of the United States.

Skaguay, Alaska, March 19, 1899.

To Hon. William McKinley
President of the United States,
Washington, D.C.,
Sir:— I take pleasure in enclosing for your perusal the minutes and enrollment of the Skaguay Military Company, organized for the purpose of responding to any call you may make for volunteers in the event of war with Spain.

It is the desire of the company to commence drilling at once, having secured the services of an ex-army officer for that purpose and we wish to know if we may be furnished with the necessary arms, accouterments, etc., for that purpose. This organization, we hope, will become a permanent one and one which will not be far behind any other organization of this kind in responding to the demand in time of trouble. I am

Very respectfully,
Your obedient servant
Jeff R. Smith [signed]
Capt.[4]

---

[1] *Ed Burns*: that this is Jeff's man of many years is confirmed by an 04/01/1898 ltr fr L. E. Hanks in Seattle. He wrote to Jeff to ask Burns to give Jeff a reference on Hanks' behalf. The letter reads, "My Dear Mr. Smith: After you consult with Mr. Ed Byrnes [Burns] please inform me by return mail if you have any place for an average broad spieler and fair T. B [Top & Bottom] man. If so please write me at once here by return of mail, please give my regards to Hughy Higgins, Ed Byrnes and other friends. Very Respectfully, L. E. Hank." (Jones, Robert, p. 383) "Top & Bottom": see index.

[2] *Skagway, News*, Summer Edition 1992, & *Morning Oregonian* 05/20/1898, p. 2.

[3] Bill for eight copies fr Dr. Lewis Garrison to Jeff Smith, 03/19/1898, item 57, author's col.

[4] Document fr Jeff Smith to President William McKinley, 03/19/1898, author's col.

Jeff directed that marching and drilling of his company begin right away, and it seems likely he often reviewed it personally. One can imagine his enjoyment of this role and of the satisfaction he felt in knowing that members of the 101 witnessed the quasi military show of force and were powerless to do anything about his command of it. The Captain of the Skaguay Military Company continued this development of the Company for months. According to the June 1, 1898, edition of the *Sitka Alaskan Report*, men of the Company continued to drill "every night."[1]

A most likely entirely fictional story concerns how Jeff used the recruitment process to rob volunteers who signed up for the Military Company. The story first appeared in a Vancouver newspaper and was republished in the *San Francisco Call*, June 3, 1898, in which Jeff promised

> The men who enlisted $5 a day and rations. Many joined and Smith and his gang fixed up a building as headquarters where recruits could enlist. They were told they would have to be medically examined and were requested to take off their clothing and step into an adjoining room. There they found a doctor who pretended to test their lungs, and then left them stark naked. The would-be soldiers waited in vain for his return and then passed out, only to find their clothing, cash, guns, etc., gone. Smith and his gang left for the mountains and the Skaguay citizens had to be appealed to before the men could leave the building.

In November 1898 the *Denver Evening Post* published a more detailed story as part of a long article about Jeff as told by James Finnegan of Aspen.

> About the smoothest thing Smith ever did was to start his recruiting office for the Untied States army. He secured office quarters of three rooms the first being the office, the second the doctor's room and the third, opening out on to the alley.... The men disrobed here, placing their clothes on chairs.
>
> "The doctor" would darken the center room and then begin to test your eyes by suddenly removing a black box from two large lamps shining like the most powerful electric lights by the agency of highly polished reflectors. The room would [be] absolutely dark and the effect was to almost stun you. ...
>
> When the applicant went back to get his clothes he found he had been robbed. Some experienced even the loss of their shoes.
>
> A friend of mine had $1.00 in his clothes in addition to a bunch of keys and a piece of tobacco. When he returned he found his coat, trousers, tobacco, money and even his keys gone. He kicked to the "doctor."
>
> "Well," said the "doctor," "there's the door and you know what a place Skagway is. Why didn't you lock it?"[2]

Finnegan claimed to be intimate with Jeff, but too much of his account of Skaguay makes this author wonder if he had ever been there. He described Jeff's saloon as being near the wharves and filled with gaming equipment whereas Jeff Smith's Parlor was seven blocks inland and held no gaming equipment of any size.

---

[1] *Sitka Alaskan Report* 06/01/1898.
[2] *Denver Evening Post* 11/27/1898, p. 12.

No other known reports of men complaining that they had been robbed in this way are known. In fact, not even any reports of "physicals" are known. Jeff wanted the Company to be a force in which its members, the town, and not least of all himself could take pride. Such a force could hardly be sustained if its men were robbed as a first experience. Even Collier and Westrate, who document nothing and present many details and stories about Jeff and the Soap Gang that could not be true, reject that Jeff was behind the robberies. They counter the story, however, with what appears to be another fabrication: "This dastardly work was reported to Soapy, who wrathfully ordered the perpetrators rounded up and hauled before him." The perpetrators "attempted to laugh off their performance as a practical joke," but "Soapy" was not amused and "compelled them to disgorge their ill-gotten booty on the spot and return it to the rightful owners, after which they were forced to apologize to their victims."[1] That the Company remained active for nearly four months strongly suggests that the men were not abused, at least not as told in the story of its recruits being robbed.

Jeff was popular once again in Skaguay, and he sought to extend his enhanced reputation, setting his sights back on Seattle. In February 1898 *The Seattle Daily Times* had called Jeff a crook who controlled Skaguay. Now Jeff sent a rebuttal, which the *Times* published.

HON. JEFF. R. SMITH, ESQ.
Writes From Skaguay Correcting False Impressions. Makes a Polite Request Which The Times Most Cordially Grants—States That He Is On The Side of Law and Order and Was Never Convicted of Crime.

"Soapy Smith" of Skaguay sends The Times the following courteous letter, which is cheerfully published:

Skaguay, Alaska, March 22, 1898.

Editor The Times—Dear Sir: I have noticed at different times various pieces similar to the one enclosed in regard to myself. I beg leave to state that I have no gang, and that I have not been ordered out of Skaguay, or any other place, and that I expect to live here as long as I see fit to. I have taken the side of law and order here time and time again, and all reports like the one enclosed are base falsehoods. I helped a lot of citizens stop a murderous mob from hanging a man that no one knew whether guilty or not, and thereby caused the dislike of some of the members of the murderous outfit. I acknowledge I have been in the saloon and gambling business for a number of years, and when all games and saloons were placed under strict police surveillance. And I have never had any trouble in my place of business; was never convicted of any crime in my life, and don't think that I am being treated right. I don't think you want to hurt me or my business by publishing such stories, as I am sure I [have] never done you or anyone an injury without cause. I am still here in business, and expect to remain. Respectfully yours,

JEFF R. SMITH.

Called "SOAPY."[2]

[1] Collier & Westrate, p. 268.
[2] *Seattle Daily Times* 03/30/1898. Original clipping fr Soapy's scrapbook, item 143, author's col.

So Seattle was addressed. Next came San Francisco. Its papers delighted in stories about Jeff, the more sinister the better, and one of his severest critics was the *San Francisco Examiner*. The opportunity to alter that criticism came when that paper sent Edward F. Cahill to investigate and report on conditions in Dyea and Skaguay. Learning he was on the way, Jeff prepared a VIP tour. When Cahill went home, charmed by Jeff, he gave Skaguay and its notorious citizen a clean bill of health. His article was titled "What I Saw Of Real Life & Death at Skaguay And Dyea" and began, "When hell freezes over it will be like Skaguay. ... That is what I was told. What I found was different. I found a community in which there is order without law...."

Cahill's accounts of Skaguay's and Dyea's trails, merchants, and residents were so positive they glowed. Additionally, Cahill discredited stories of rampant lawlessness and disease. It seems highly probable that Jeff altered Cahill's view of the "sure thing man" because in depicting him and his helpers on the trail, the newsman repeated Jeff's long-held business philosophy. Cahill ventured onto the trail, probably with helpful direction at the least, and at the most, he was guided there by Jeff himself. In realistic detail, Cahill described how in the icy climate the con man

> is found blowing his nimble fingers and running his little shell game seated on the snow by the slippery trail, while his cappers stand around habited like "farmers" to beguile the unwary Klondiker, sweating like a beast of burden, to drag his heavy sled up the hill. The sure-thing man's code of morality is the most extraordinary and perhaps unexpected thing about him. He resents with bitter anger and scorn the name of thief or vagrant, and, in fact, he will not rob you except by rule. If you do not cross his lines you are perfectly safe, and he holds that if you are fool enough to go up against his game he has a perfect right to take every advantage that his skill permits. In fact, he insists loudly that he is a law-abiding citizen and when heedless people in Skaguay talked about a vigilance committee the confidence man, exulting in his numbers and his might, stood up in line to keep peace with an ugly gun, and the peace was kept. ... I met one of the tribe of an evening at a road-builder's camp at the head of the White Pass. He shall be nameless here because outside of his calling he seemed a decent sort of fellow and rather shame-faced about his "business," as he called it, although he made no secret of his methods.... It is not all profit in the shell game, which, old-fashioned as it is, was yet the favorite and most lucrative means of polite swindling. The retinue of cappers and steerers is expensive and they are paid about twice as much as, let us say, a locomotive engineer or other skilled mechanic.
>
> "No, it isn't all profit by any means," he explained. "I have to clear $100 before I make a white quarter for myself. I have to pay the men wages, their board, and their whisky. After I clear the $100 it begins to mount up pretty quick." He admitted that he had taken in something like $250 on that day.
>
> "You are operating among the packers?" was asked.
>
> "No, I don't do business with packers. They have not much money, and I don't want their little $15 or so. What I'm after is the men that's going into

Dawson. It makes me sorry sometimes to have to separate them from their little wad, but—well, it's them or me."

"You are not doing any work in Skaguay now?" one asked.

"Naw," in a tone of contempt. "There's nothin' in Skaguay—nothin' but stranglers."

"Stranglers?"

"Yes, vigilantes."

Cahill then focused on Jeff Smith.

It is possible that … some injustice has been done to Mr. Smith which should be corrected, if only out of regard for the distinguished family to which he belongs, for the sun never sets on the Smiths. "Soapy" Smith is not a dangerous man, and not a desperado. He will fight to very good purpose if he must, but he is not in the least quarrelsome. Cool in the presence of danger, absolutely fearless, honorable in the discharge of those obligations which he recognizes, generous with his money, and ever ready with a helping hand for a man or woman in distress, he bitterly resents the imputation that he is a thief or vagrant. It is true that if you go up against his game you will certainly lose your money, but it is a process of painless extraction. I may as well acknowledge an imperfect sympathy for those who let themselves be swindled in the persuasion that they have themselves a sure thing. … You may lend "Soapy" Smith $100 or more at any time and be certain to get your money back with interest sooner or later, all without a scratch of the pen. …

Not the least amusing trait of "Soapy" Smith's character is the eager interest which he takes in the preservation of law and order. The interest is, of course, not purely unselfish, for he realizes that crimes of violence create a sort of public opinion likely to be unhealthy for his own peaceful, if peculiar, industry. He feels that there are times when fine distinctions get confused, and therefore he is always foremost for law and order coupled with life, liberty and the pursuit of a sure thing.[1]

Jeff showed the highly positive article to a limited few. Although it put Jeff and Skaguay in a favorable light, residents might not take kindly to an unbeatable gambler who had a hand in civic matters and who had a military company under his command.

At some point during the visit, Cahill attended a Skaguay Military Company meeting, and Jeff, perhaps stimulated by the reporter's presence, made a speech that led to a memorable performance by one and all. Standing on a chair among cheers and "warlike yells," Jeff addressed the need to preserve

the safety of the American coasts and stressed the necessity of guarding them to the death against supposedly projected plans of the Spanish fleet to raid cities and shipping.

"Spain will send her battleships to seize our ports," he cried, "and they will try to capture our ships. But, be damned to them and we'll stake our lives against their plots. … Do you realize our country's danger?"

---

[1] *San Francisco Examiner* 04/10/1898.

As these statements are attributed to Jeff by Collier and Westrate, they may be fact or fancy. However, the less unreliable Cahill in his poem "Skagway Guns!" portrays something of what Jeff said about a potential invasion of US soil by Spanish forces—"They'll never land!"—and what happened next.

> Whereat he loosened from his belt and laid upon the bar
> The weapon which for several men had set the gates ajar;
> An' Soapy Smith, the card sharp, drew an ivory-handled beaut',
> An' put it on the counter, an' the crowd all followed suit;
> The muzzle of the daisy that took off the Marshal's ear
> Laid right beside the weapon which had punctured Rhino Pierre;
> An' near by was the gentle, inoffensive little thing,
> That had wafted Bunco Charlie to the place where angles sing;
> Then Soapy Smith, the card sharp, standin' near 'em on a chair,
> Observed, "When Spain gets to the coast she'll find a welcome there!
> We'll box these guns and ship 'em by the first boat on the run
> To President McKinley, who abides at Washington!
> An' in the hist'ry books we'll read the Nation's proudest boast,
> How Skagway men sent Skagway guns to save the Eastern coast;
> It bein' the one town where men made sacrifice sublime,
> Because their country could not build the coast defense in time.[1]

The day before the poem appeared in the *Examiner*, through his secretary, the President responded to Jeff. The letter probably reached Skaguay by April 16.

> Executive Mansion
> Washington
> April 9, 1898
>> The President directs me to acknowledge the receipt of your communication of the 19th ultimo,[2] enclosing the minutes and enrollment of the Skaguay Military Company, organized for the purpose of responding to a call for volunteers in the event that they should be needed, and to inform you that it has been referred for the consideration of the Secretary of War.
>> Very Truly yours,
>> John Addison Porter [signed]
>> Secretary to the President
> Capt. Jeff R. Smith,
> Skaguay, Alaska.[3]

It is believed that Jeff framed and hung this letter in Jeff Smith's Parlor as public witness to the fact that the Skaguay Military Company, "Capt. Jeff R. Smith" commanding, was officially recognized by the President of the United States.

Another letter is said to have followed from Secretary of War Russell Alger. It commended the initiative of Captain Smith and the patriotism of the Company's

---

[1] *San Francisco Examiner* 04/10/1898.

[2] *ultimo*: Latin, "of last month," i.e., March.

[3] Ltr to Jeff Smith fr John Addison Porter, the secretary of the president, 04/09/1898, author's col.

officers and men but declined their service due to the high cost of transport from Alaska. Although the letter's contents are reported, neither it nor a copy is known to exist.[1] E. J. Stroller White, of *The Skaguay News*, thought Jeff preferred to keep "mum about the war department" politely declining "services of Smith's Alaska guards...."[2]

Possibly Jeff was sincere in his quest to marshal aid for the country. True, his search for a military title had been a long one, so he had a personal interest in being officially recognized. But signs show that the Skaguay Military Company was much more than a scam or padded with Soap Gang members, only a few of whom had signed up. Possibly, though, the names of more gang members had been left off the roster to keep the company clear of controversy. Further, perhaps Jeff felt it would be making hostages of fate for too many names of the gang to be listed in one document. In fact, to this day no complete list of those who worked with and for Jeff exists.

A sincere sign of Jeff's commitment to military service appears in his own hand. On April 19, Congress recognized Cuban independence, demanded Spanish withdrawal from Cuba, and authorized the President to use force to attain these ends.[3] War was declared as of April 21. In a letter to Mary dated April 26, in anticipation of the declaration, Jeff wrote, "I will have to go to the front if called on."[4]

Earlier in April, Jeff had written to Mary to send money and share his travel plans. Postmarks show his letter took nearly a month to reach St. Louis.

> Dear Mollie   Skaguay Apr. 4th 1898
>
> I send 100 more today by express making $400 all told. Tell Kirk, there is nothing here for him or anyone in Skaguay now. There may be this fall. I am going to Dawson as every tin horn that went there have got rich. I hate the trip, 800 miles in a little canoe and sleep out at night. It is hell but I am going to tackle it. Will write you who goes with me and when I start. About June 1st you better sell in Denver or go at once and fix it up as it is due in May. Love to all   Your husband Jeff. Skaguay[5]

Nothing shows that Jeff went to Dawson. Perhaps he thought better of trying to go as supposedly Mounties knew who he was and were prepared to turn him back. Telling friends to stay away for the time being suggests either slackening good times in Skaguay or that opportunities were exhausted, or both. Surprising, too, is that Jeff still owned property in Denver. Perhaps he had held on to it in the hope that he might one day return as he had done in 1892 when he left Creede.

The day before Jeff wrote to Mary, two miles above Sheep Camp at a tent city about eighteen miles from Dyea, disaster struck. It was Palm Sunday, April 3, 1898, at 2 a.m. when from the mountain 2,500 feet above, a heavy snow pack gave way, came roaring down, and buried everything before it to a depth of thirty feet.[6] Men

---

[1] The National Archives reported in 1963 that "The Adjutant General's Office acknowledged Captain Smith's letter on April 9, 1898, but the records do not include a copy of the reply." Ltr fr the National Archives and Records Service, item 168, author's col.

[2] DeArmond, p. 20.

[3] *Gilded Age*.

[4] Ltr to Mary Smith fr Jeff R. Smith II, 04/26/1898, item 64, author's col.

[5] Ltr fr Jeff R. Smith II to Mary Smith, 04/04/1898, item 44, author's col.

[6] *Skaguay News* 03/27/1898.

immediately began digging for people encased within the heavy, wet snow. Across ten acres the buried were heard calling for help, praying, and cursing. Within twenty minutes, about a thousand responders were digging mightily, but only a few people were rescued, and four of these soon died.[1] Most victims suffocated. Over the next four days of digging, three new avalanches buried even more people. Eventually, the loss of life was put at seventy. An exact number was never determined.[2]

Stories are told of Jeff's having taken advantage of the dead in the slide. Ella Lung Martinsen, in retelling of her father's time as a Klondiker, quotes a Skaguay merchant as saying, "When news of the avalanche reached Skagway, he [Jeff] immediately sent up some of his gang posing as rescue workers ... to rob the dead!"[3] The version picked up by historian Pierre Berton is that Jeff "had himself appointed coroner" and that "Near the site of the tragedy he" had a morgue set up for the purpose of identifying bodies. The need to search for identification was perfect cover for stripping "each frozen cadaver ... of rings, jewelry, cash, and other valuables."[4] Good reason exists, however, to believe this account is more "'Soapy' Smith fiction."

The *Dyea Trail* made mention of robbing corpses.

> A number of bodies had been taken from the slide, and it is alleged on good authority that some of them were looted of money and valuables. But every suspicion of this kind ceased with the appointment of the Citizens' Committee, which was composed of the most prominent and respected men of Dyea and Sheep Camp. This Committee examined each body carefully, made a minute memoranda of all personal effects and made the best disposition of the same that was possible under the circumstances....[5]

The paper does not mention "Soapy" Smith in connection with the Sheep Camp disaster. With the rivalry between Dyea and Skaguay openly discussed in their respective newspapers and with the *Trail* often mentioning the Soap Gang, one would think that if Jeff had set himself up as a coroner at or near the disaster site, his presence would have made the *Dyea Trail*. Like the story of the recruits who had been robbed, this one also seems to have germinated from a single seed. In this case, though, the seed was indeed a J. Smith, but a different J. Smith.

> From the scene of the snowslide comes a story which goes to show that ... Commissioner John U. Smith was not deprived of either nerve or ubiquity.... He was early on the spot, and at once proceeded to assume full control and direction of everything.... In the pursuance of his official authority ... he took charge of the outfits of victims as fast as they were disinterred, with a view of administering the estates, and was down to his knees in snow and up to his ears in business when the surviving partners of the unfortunates ... persuaded him that they were entirely fit and able to do the

---

[1] Berton, pp. 257-58.
[2] *Skagway News* 03/27/1998, p. 5.
[3] Martinsen p. 379.
[4] Berton, p. 259.
[5] *The Dyea Trail* 04/09/1898, p. 1.

work themselves. Then a "miners' meeting" was called, and the committee appointed by it relieved Mr. Smith of his remaining self-imposed duties.[1]

This report in *Morning Oregonian* tells of an impertinent interloper of self-appointment named Smith seeking to work his will over the dead and their effects. Not hard to imagine is how easily the report about one Smith, first name John, could be pinned to another Smith, first name Jeff. Some myths grow from talkative sorts of people with fanciful or enhancing imaginings. Others grow from fact, in this case, the work of a somewhat locally notorious Smith being assigned to an even more notorious Smith.

False reports seem to follow notoriety. From Wrangell, Alaska, came report that

irrepressible Soapy Smith and his "regimental" grafters will be passengers on the next steamer from that port. "Soapy" ... decided that he would do Tacoma during the mobilization of the National Guard at that place. An advance guard of six of the Smith brigade arrived last night on the *North Pacific*.[2]

Then another false report was created by an imposter named Harry Green. He had been a member of the Skaguay Soap Gang, but when he left that spring, in a conversation with a reporter aboard ship, he pretended to be Jeff. Discovering the deception, Jeff sent a threatening letter to the offender. Green replied on April 12, 1898, the day he checked into the Hotel Northern, signing the register "Jeff Smith."[3]

Mr. Smith:

Your letter of the 28th just received by chance. I happened to drop in to Seattle today.

When I left Skaguay on the 21st Mar, I left on the boat Ning-Chaw, and there was no one on that boat but a lot of your friends, such fellows as Luther Woods, Johnnie Miller, Bill Toregdy, and Big Down, a lot of Arizona and Texas friends of yours and mine. This talk that was made to the reporter was made all through a josh, they named on the boat to the reporter. Luther Woods' name was supposed to be Jerry Daily, my name was supposed to be Jeff Smith's brother. Big Down [was] supposed to be Harry Green, Roberts' partner. They asked for Harry Green on the boat running from Victoria to Seattle. They referred the reporter to Big Down that was supposed to be Harry Green, the man that come back from fish creek, with a lot of gold nuggets, a wealthy man. Now you can see the crowd on that boat was doing it more for a josh on the reporter than anything else. You have never known me to be a knocker[4] on no body living. I don't like to have the name of being a knocker. I am not making any apology to anybody if I would of done it. You know I don't like a reporter or policeman any how. The reporter in Victoria had it that Soapy Smith's gang got run out of Skaguay and we were supposed to be the gang.... In regards to making it pretty warm for me when I return [to Skaguay], I never intended to go back when I left..., and if I ever happen to get back, I'll not hide from nobody. I have not done it yet, and I

---

[1] *Morning Oregonian* 04/14/1898, p. 8.
[2] *San Francisco Examiner* 04/27/1898.
[3] Hotel Northern ledger, 04/12/1898.
[4] *knocker.* "One who speaks ill of another." Americanism. (Partridge, *Underworld*)

never will. There is as good a blood in me as there is in anybody there. You will find me at Seattle or Spokane any time. I am sorry I have to write this kind of a letter because I have a lot of friends amongst you fellows, such as Agerman Daily and all others that I know. I don't want them to think for one moment that I was to fault for any josh like that. No more news.

    Remain yours,   Harry Green.[1]

Green used Jeff's name again in Tacoma, on May 1, 1898, when the newspaper there mistakenly reported "Soapy" Smith arrested there.

    TACOMA, May 2.— Eight tough gamblers from Seattle came over to the campground of the First regiment of Washington volunteers yesterday, and attempted to open up a nutshell and other flimflam games. The commanding officer was advised of their presence, and at once sent a detail to drive them off the premises. Two of the gamblers drew revolvers, but they were overpowered before they had time to use them and placed in the guard house ... until civil officers could be summoned.

    The prisoners were taken to the county jail, where four of them gave bail in the sum of $500. The other four are still in jail. It is understood that "Soapy" Smith, of Skagway, was at the head of the gang.[2]

The real Jeff in Skaguay was furious. Not known is if he ever made it "warm" for Green for stealing his name and damaging it. With opportunity, doubtless he would have.

A month into spring, Jeff grew concerned over not hearing from home. Moreover, the gathering war clouds were seen even from distant Skaguay. Writing on April 26, 1898, he could not yet have known that war had been declared just days before.

    Dear Mollie

    No word from you. What is wrong? I am captain of the 1st Co. of Alaska and will go to the war if there is any. I suppose it is on now. I expected to go to Dawson City. But now I will have to go to the front if called on. Write here.

    Love to all. Your husband,   Jeff —[3]

Jeff asked why he had not heard from Mary. The answer was that with the declaration of war, the mails had slowed even more than before. Jeff also confirmed his commitment to the Skaguay Military Company and that if called, he would "go to the front." Later, with war having come, news shows Jeff at his post with his men.

ALASKA REGIMENT
A Thousand Loyal Men Who Wish To Offer Their Services

    Alaska wants to send a regiment to fight the Spaniards. ... A telegram will be brought down on the next steamer from the authorities of Sitka, addressed to Gov. Brady of Alaska, who is now in Washington city. This

---

[1] Ltr to Jeff Smith fr Harry Green, *Alaska-Yukon Magazine*, 12/1907, p. 334. Small corrections to spelling and punctuation have been made to promote readability.

[2] *Morning Oregonian* 05/03/1898, p. 3.

[3] Ltr to Mary Smith fr Jeff R. Smith II, 04/26/1898, item 64, author's col.

telegram will ask that he tender the services of one thousand loyal Alaskans to President McKinley.

According to advices just received from the north, Dyea and Sheep camp will place 300 men in the field at the first call. As many more will come from Skagway, where "Soapy" Smith has a well organized company of volunteers. Four hundred men could easily be enrolled at Juneau and Douglas Island. The remainder of Alaska's thousand would come from Sitka and Wrangell. There is not much chance that President McKinley will need his Alaskan troops but they are ready. ... It is said ex- ... Commissioner John U. Smith, of Skagway, is anxious to go to war. He was an officer in the Oregon National Guard. He may come down on the next boat.[1]

In the meantime, bad publicity continued to track Jeff, some of it untrue. For example, the *Rocky Mountain News* reported his arrest in Tacoma on May 1, 1898.[2] Whoever the person might have been, it was not Jeff. He was in Skaguay, preparing for a May 1 parade, the very first in Skaguay and perhaps in all Alaska. In that pageant Jeff would lead the officers and men of the Skaguay Military Company. Before parade day, badges were made for the Company. Jeff sent one to Mary in St. Louis and one to a newspaper, which wrote a story looking back on Jeff, the badges, and parade.

Soapy Smith's Badges.

Captain of Skagway Company equips his men for parade.

"Soapy" Smith, the best known gambler in all Alaska, is nothing if not patriotic. At Skagway he has formed a military company composed of some of the best men of that camp as well as a number of patriotic gamblers. "Soapy" now registers as Capt. Jefferson R. Smith. Skagway had a monster war ratification celebration a few weeks ago in which Smith's company took a prominent part.

Just before the parade started, a Skagway printer suggested to "Soapy" that his men should all wear badges. Smith said he didn't see how he could have forgotten that important detail and asked what 200 badges would cost. The printer replied that the job must be done in style and that the badges should be red, white and blue. He said he would print two hundred on slips of paper for $18. "Soapy" put up the money and soon the badges were turned out.

One of them was received here yesterday. It reads: "Freedom for Cuba. Remember the Maine! Compliments Skagway Military Company, Jeff R. Smith, Capt." Red and blue ink was used on white paper and Smith said he would not have done without those badges for $100.[3]

The Skaguay News covered the spectacle and the *Denver Evening Post* picked up the story.

---

[1] Undated, unknown newspaper clipping, fr Jeff R. Smith's scrapbook. Item 144, author's col.

[2] *RMN* 05/03/1898.

[3] Unknown, undated newspaper (most likely Seattle, 05/1898) clipping cut out by Soapy for his scrapbook. Item 139, author's col.

Never in the history of Skaguay has such a public demonstration—such a general outpouring of the people been witnessed as last Sunday evening. The occasion of the gathering was in answer to a dodger,[1] generally circulated to the effect that at 8 o'clock Sunday evening a public meeting would be held on Fifth avenue, in front of the city hall, for the purpose of ratifying the action of the United States in declaring war against Spain.

Early in the day preparations ... began. Business houses, offices and private residences were gaily decorated with flags and bunting and it is safe to assert that had the stock of goods not been exhausted..., that from the business place or residence of every American citizen in the city would have been unfurled the stars and stripes. By 7 o'clock ... upwards of six hundred men and many ladies could be seen on the streets wearing red, white and blue badges which read: "Freedom for Cuba! Remember the Maine! Compliments of Skaguay Military Company. Jeff R. Smith, captain." At 7:30 o'clock a procession nearly two blocks in length formed on Broadway, led by a carriage containing Dr. Hornsby and Moore, Walter Church and Deputy United States Marshal John Cudihee, and headed by the Skaguay Cornet band. Standard Bearer Tanner of Denver, Colo., proudly bore a large silk flag on which is inscribed the words, "First Regiment of Alaska Militia."

Beside him marched Captain Jeff R. Smith of the Skaguay guards.

Following were members of the United States Army, the Skaguay guards and citizens in all upwards of four hundred men, to say nothing of a number of women, who [being] patriotically inclined, donned male garb, and joined in the procession. Along [the way] were seen many banners and transparencies on which were inscribed such mottoes as "Death to Weyler," "Down with Spain," "Freedom for Cuba," etc. To the soul inspiring strains of "Marching Through Georgia," the procession headed up Broadway to Seventh avenue thence west to Main street and to the post office, where the nation's flag was saluted, and with bared heads, the gallant members of the procession and upwards of two thousand sidewalk escorts listened to the melody of that old tune so dear to the heart of every American, "The Star Spangled Banner." From the post office the march was continued to the United States customs house on State street, when heads were again bared and that time-honored American melody, "Yankee Doodle," floated out on the evening breezes.

From the customs house the procession headed for the city hall, where Captain Smith gave the order to "break ranks." And a general round-up took place on Fifth Avenue before the city hall, but the avenue was crowded the entire distance between State and Broadway. By previous arrangement Dr. J. A. Hornsby had been selected as chairman of the "spread eagle" portion of the exercises, and for ten minutes he entertained the large crowd with the kind of patriotic speech that causes a man to want to take the next steamer for the scene of action. Dr. Hornsby retired by introducing the well known attorney, Walter Church, who, in his usually happy, eloquent and pleasant

---

[1] *a dodger: a small handbill or circular. (OED, meaning 3, 1884, 1888)*

manner, delivered an address aptly appropriate and pointed. He was followed by Attorney I. N. Wilcoxen, a battle-scarred veteran of the last war. Mr. Wilcoxen is still able and willing to battle for the stars and stripes, and before his able address was concluded all his hearers were ready to enlist in the good cause. F. T. Kellar followed in a speech rampant in vim, vigor, humor and patriotism. He is only a "boy" but the war spirit is strong within him.

Jeff R. Smith, captain of the Skaguay Guards, made the closing address.

While Jeff's eloquence is not of that style which is said to make arches of Irish oak resound, yet he has a manner which causes his hearers to vociferously applaud. He closed his address by asserting that he had actually captured Weyler, and had him then and there in custody.[1]

The *Seattle Post-Intelligencer* quoted Jeff's closing remarks.

"There is one man, who in this terrible strife, has transcended the bounds of fair war. He has murdered the helpless and weak, debauched women and starved little children. Mr. Chairman, this man we have with us today. I have him here, and now we will proceed to hang and burn Butcher Weyler."[2]

The *Denver Evening Post* continued.

At that moment "Weyler" was run up on a pre-arranged wire and properly hooted at by the crowd. A big bonfire was at once started, and Weyler was burned in effigy amid the deafening yells of upward of two thousand enthusiastic Americans.

This ended the greatest public demonstration ever held in Skaguay. From start to finish it was a success in every detail and although the participants hailed from every corner of the Union there was not heard during the event a single rough, coarse or offensive word from the lips of any man. The best people in the city were present, and everybody went home feeling that the evening had been profitably and patriotically spent."[3]

Perhaps the most interesting description of the parade comes from *Skaguay News* reporter Elmer J. ("Stroller") White. Decades later he wrote a series of remembrances in newspaper columns, and this one was titled "Smith's Alaska Guards." White described an interruption that occurred in front of the Princess Hotel, which was operated by madam "Babe" Davenport. At the parade approached, she ran into the street followed by five or six of her "employees," all of whom wore uniforms "barely visible to the naked eye." Babe grabbed the bridle of Jeff's horse, stopping him, and demanded that he immediately organize a "Ladies Auxiliary" of the Skaguay Military Company so they could join in the parade. Jeff "shooed" the ladies back, saying, "Your turn will come later," and proceeded. No part of the town was slighted, and after about an hour and a half of marching, the parade stopped in front of Jeff Smith's Parlor, White reported, where Jeff gave a stirring speech that ended with

---

[1] *Denver Evening Post* 05/24/1898, p. 10.
[2] *Seattle Post-Intelligencer* 05/09/1898.
[3] *Denver Evening Post* 05/24/1898, p. 10.

"I am sure that you will ... follow me...." And with that he turned smartly on his heel and marched into the saloon. ... And follow him they did, and it just happened that seven extra bartenders were there, aproned and waiting....[1]

"Stroller" White, as the life-long newsman called himself, did not include the burning in effigy of Weyler, and news stories did not include the stop at the Palace Hotel. The success of the events that day established an apparent momentum. Various newspaper accounts estimate that after May 1, 1898, the ranks in the Skaguay Military Company swelled to between 300 and 400 volunteers.[2]

John Bowers is known not to have been in Skaguay for the parade. He may have left Skaguay during the initial Committee of 101 handbill warnings in March. By mid April he was sighted by Denver authorities and when questioned, said he was visiting friends. Police Chief Farley gave him twenty-four hours to leave, but two weeks later he was still in Denver. When asked by an *Evening Post* reporter about his stay, he replied, "'I don't do nothin' now but speil the boards,' which means that he works the three card Monte racket."[3] On May 4, 1898, Bowers was arrested in Colorado Springs as part of a swindle gone sour and was jailed when he could not pay the $50 fine.[4] Jeff wrote John W. Murphy care of the Horse Shoe Saloon in Seattle, looking for Bowers. Murphy responded on May 9, 1898.

Friend Jeff:

I understand Bowers has gone back to Skagway. I wrote him to Victoria and Vancouver, but have rec'd no answer. I was in good shape here to get on my feet but old Bull had me pinched on a deal that Bowers and I was in, and because I didn't turn the proceeds over to him, he had Durff swear his life against me, &c., which caused me some trouble. Bull has lost many friends and is not in it. I will have things all right in a few days. Jeff, it makes no difference what people say for or against you. I am always your friend and I hope you are doing well. I will make some money here but it won't be through the Bull click. Write me soon as you get this. I have two letters for Bowers. One from Skagway and I think it is from you. As soon as I know where Bowers is I will forward them on to him.

Write by return mail. Ever your friend.   JNO. W. MURPHY.
                                            Care "Horse Shoe Saloon."[5]

Possibly this Murphy is the former operator of Murphy's Exchange in Denver.

News of Jeff's military company spread. Here is one notice to appear in May 1898 in *The Seattle Post-Intelligencer.*

According to advices brought down on the Al-Ki, ships are being taken at Wrangell and Juneau to form volunteer companies to act with Jeff Smith's Skaguay Company.[1]

---

[1] DeArmond, pp. 18-20.

[2] *Seattle Post-Intelligencer* 05/09/1898, p. 3, & an unknown, undated newspaper clipping. Jefferson R. "Little Randy" Smith col.

[3] *Denver Evening Post* 04/23/1898, p. 8.

[4] *Denver Evening Post* 05/04/1898, p. 2.

[5] Ltr to Jeff R. Smith II fr John W. Murphy. (Jones, Robert, p. 383)

Such notices, neutral-to-good ones instead of bad, must have pleased Jeff. People he did not even know were writing to him and praising his efforts. In June 1898 one such person sent Jeff a gift for his patriotic endeavors.

> Yesterday afternoon Jeff Smith received through the mail a box containing a white piquet ascot cravat, with a hand-worked American & Cuban flag above the scarf pin. On the back of the cravat were written the words: "From Miss A. A. Stevens, Seattle, to Capt. Jeff Smith." Jeff has no acquaintance with the young lady, and can not understand the matter.[2]

At the end of April 1898, a rumor of Jeff's death circulated in the states and reached Mary in St. Louis before it was dispelled. James H. Cronin of St. Louis, saloon owner and Delegate to the city government, was able to calm Mary's fears with letters he had received from Jeff dated after his reported death. Cronin wrote to Jeff, on the ornate House of Delegates stationary, on May 2, 1898.

> Friend Jeff,
>
> Yours of the 19th April, received this morning, and was glad to hear from you, it was reported here that you were killed up there, and your wife was here to see me this morning. She was very uneasy. I showed her the letter I received from you which made her feel better.   You stated in your letter that you were Captain of the Alaska Guards. I don't think you will be bothered very much as war is nearly over, so the papers state.   Jeff if you make more money than you can handle why ship it in to me, I will take good care of it.
>
> Answer this as soon as you receive it as we would like to know how you are.   I wrote a letter to you about two weeks ago, I guess you have received it by this time.   I remain as ever
>
>   Yours most sincerely   Jas. H. Cronin
>
>   per. WJD[3]

Jeff had once told Mary, "Never believe I'm dead until you see me in the morgue."[4] This statement did nothing to ease her apprehension when having to wait weeks for communication from him. The mails as usual were taking a long while. Cronin's letter was postmarked in St. Louis on the day it was dated, May 2, and was postmarked Skagway[5] on May 16—two weeks later.

Cronin was correct in stating the war would soon end. On May 1, 1898, while Jeff was parading his militia around Skaguay, American Commodore George Dewey was annihilating the Spanish fleet at the battle of Manila Bay in the Philippines, the turning point in the war. News of the victory may have eased tensions in the states, but up in Skaguay Jeff did not stop fueling patriotic fervor, and citizens still followed him.

---

[1] *Seattle Post-Intelligencer* 05/09/1898.

[2] *Skaguay News* 06/17/1898. Jeff was wearing this ascot the night he was killed. It now resides on display, spattered with Jeff's blood, at the Skagway City Museum.

[3] Ltr to Jeff Smith II fr James H. Cronin, 05/02/1898, item 49, author's col. "per WJD," the initials of the person to write the letter; apparently Cronin dictated it.

[4] Mary Eva Smith to grandson, John Randolph Smith.

[5] *Skagway*: about this time the spelling was changing from Skaguay to Skagway; so Cronin's address lines (envelope and in letter) spell the name, and so reads the Skagway postmark.

From Los Angeles in March 1898, John J. Shay wrote to Jeff about a batch of bunco men heading towards Skaguay.

> I received a letter from Daily (Old Bill), he is in Tacoma. You will no doubt see him up your way. Jeff, with all his faults, the old man loves the very ground you walk on. "Treat him kindly." Kid Collins left for Seattle last night. Thence to Skagway. There is none of the gang here now but Link Howard, and I think Davis, alias Poker Davis, will be in Alaska ere long. Billy Cardwell (Senator Whit's clerk), says [to me] "Who are you writing to, Jeff...?" I said yes. "Well then," said he..., "give him my kind regards, for he is a good fellow." By the way, Jeff, Frank Cole blowed the mineral and got not a quarter from same, and is on the hog train. He is trying hard for someone to stake him for Alaska, and owing to his being a good rustler, you might have the pleasure of seeing him in the near future, and ... [let's not forget] to mention Mr. Coy Kendall, who worked for me so long, and then went to work for Cole, is now on his way to Alaska and will no doubt call on you, and Jeff, I wish to state he is a perfect and good man, honest as the day, and no better man lives, and kindly do what you can for him, use your influence in getting him something to do, tending bar or anything else, for he is most worthy. Please give my regards to Kempter (Dutch) and to all the boys, and not forgetting yourself. I remain,
> Very truly yours,   JOHN J. SHAY.[1]

Jeff replied to Shay, who again responded with news about mutual friends.

Los Angeles June 28, 1898

Dear old friend Jeff:

> First of all I want to thank you many thousand times for the number of papers you have sent me. Not alone myself, who takes an interest in reading the valuable and clean little sheet that it is, but many businessmen and miners as well. They seem to take a great interest in reading same and express their great surprise in learning the enterprise of the people of Skagway. Am sure the paper being here does your town no harm. Henderson just came back, and states that Capt. Jack Lamey had left for ... North Spokane, but a letter to Republic, Wash., would reach him. Jack made no money with Henderson on his staff. Ed is a good man. "<u>No</u> better," but out of his line of business & C. H. Davis is out at some springs. And not a grafter in town. Burk has gone back to the city. Will enclose old Bill's [Bill Banks] letter. Kid Collins was here short time ago— stayed but a few days and left again. Was sorry to see him leave, a good fellow he is. Cole was in yesterday, the first time in many weeks. He is broke and has been for a long-long time. He would make a good booster, and more than willing to join the band. However, he should go mining again. King Warren is in San Francisco. I had a letter last week from him. He tells me he is going to Alaska. Jeff, as always I am glad indeed to know of your doing well, and as I told the boys here, ... you had more brains than them all put together. You stood your ground in

---

[1] *Ltr* to Jeff Smith II fr John Shay, 03/10/1898. (Jones, Robert, pp. 380-381). Slightly edited for readability.

Skagway and now have the people's confidence and respect. Success to you is my earnest wish. My business still continues to be good. Am perfectly satisfied and happy, and hope this will find you the same, and any of my friends who might be there. I wish best wishes. I remain forever your friend
John Shay[1]

Stateside members of the bunco brotherhood were gravitating north. How many actually arrived in Skaguay and went to work under Jeff probably will never be known as the key to the success of Jeff's operations was secrecy. Jeff gained the support of the local newsmen by managing good press from the outside as well as from prominent citizenship roles in Skaguay, such as organizing a militia for the Spanish American War effort. Merchants and saloon men were flourishing, and so was the new deputy marshal (thanks to Jeff's teaching him how to be obtuse). From "operators" working the trails and out of several saloons and businesses night and day, running three-card Monte, the shell game, rigged "big hand" poker games, and occasional "snatch and run" robberies, a river of money flowed into the little back room in Jeff Smith's Parlor and into Jeff's hands. John Shay was right. Many residents did respect Jeff. As for those who opposed and hated him, they feared him, too. How was a man who headed a military company, supported by the community at large, to be taken down? So Captain Smith drilled the Skaguay Military Company on a regular basis, held court in Jeff's Place, also known as "the real city hall" of Skaguay, and the leaders of the Committee of 101 met in secret and watched for Jeff to make a mistake.

Chapter 22

Conspired to Murder
And the Fourth of July

In justice to our beloved country I would implore your speedy investigation as there is an organized band of cut-throats in control.

—Commissioner Lewis Levy
to the US Attorney General, June 6, 1898

It was Soapy's greatest hour.

—Rev. John A. Sinclair
written of Jeff's participation in Skaguay's Fourth of July Parade

Although deplored, murder was never much of a surprise in frontier towns. The robbery and death of a Skaguay prostitute in May 1898 was no different. In this case, however, the event was brought to the attention of a large "outside" audience, including the US Government, because of a Denver madam named Mattie Silks. She told *The Seattle Daily Times* that Jeff's men had carried out the murder with the knowledge of the deputy US marshal. Jeff countered the story with a suit against the *Times*, but the bell, as the saying goes, could not be unrung. The story helped generalize the belief that Soapy Smith headed ruthless criminals and controlled

---

[1] Ltr to Jeff R. Smith II fr John J. Shay, 06/28/1898, item 65, author's col. Slightly edited for readability.

Skaguay. On the day before the murder, the White Pass & Yukon Railway Company came to town. Well aware of Jeff's control, the Company was not about to let him get in the way of its railroad. The balance of power in Skaguay was about to shift.

Late on Saturday, May 28, 1898, Ella D. Wilson, a prostitute, was murdered in her Holly Street cabin. The shocking details were published up and down the west coast.

SMOTHERED TO DEATH.

Mysterious Murder of a Mulatto Woman in Skagway.

Skagway, May 29, via Port Townsend. June 3.—A mysterious murder occurred here last night. Ella D. Wilson, a mulatto woman, was smothered to death in her house on one of the busiest streets of the town by some unknown person. The murder was not disclosed until this afternoon. The woman was found lying in her bed. Around her neck a pillow-case had been drawn tightly, with the ends thrust in her mouth for a gag. Her wrists and ankles were tied together with sheets. Over her head and face a pillow was pressed down, and death had evidently resulted from smothering. Robbery is supposed to have been the motive for the crime, as the woman's trunk had been rifled. She was thought to have had about $2000.... There is no clue to the murderer. The murdered woman had lived in the principal towns on the Pacific coast.[1]

Charles Augustus Sehlbrede, a former state legislator and lawyer from Roseburg, Oregon, was the new US Commissioner for Dyea and Skagway, replacing John U. Smith. He had assumed his duties on or about May 5. On May 21, 1898, a Saturday, Sehlbrede probably thought he was home to stay for the evening with his wife and two girls when word of the death came.[2] Sehlbrede wrote in the official inquest record how report of the death indicated "that a murder had been committed," so he "immediately went to Skaguay" and appointed a "coroner's jury to inquire into the cause of death."

The inquest record is peculiar insofar as it is incomplete in the extreme. Recorded is the woman's name, that she lived "in a house on Holly Street, that "Dr. J. Allen Hornsby performed the post mortem examination," and that

> The witnesses and jury were instructed to be present at the office of the U.S. Marshal on Tue. morning at 10 o'clock, May 31st 1898. The following jurors were present: E. J. White, W. F. Saportas, Albert Fleming, W. M. Leslie, H. A. Smith, and J. D. Barry.[3]

There the record ends, with no statement of finding, no sworn statement by the jury, no date, and no "C.A. Sehlbrede" signature, which appears at the end of dozens of other hand-written official records. The *Daily Alaskan*, however, reported a finding in its May 31 issue, "unintentional murder."[4] Seeming likely is that the inquest record was left in such a state of incompleteness because, simply, it had been forgotten, left undone in the turmoil of so many events following hard upon the other.

---

[1] *Morning Oregonian* 06/04/1898, p.2.
[2] Pioneer web site, & Morning Oregonian 04/29/1898, "Sailing of the Elder," passenger list and notice of posting that supersedes Smith.
[3] Inquest Record 1898-1935.
[4] *Daily Alaskan* 05/31/1898.

That the murder was unintentional is likely true. A sequence of events leading to Wilson's death might have gone like this: on the afternoon or early evening of Saturday, May 28, 1898, one or perhaps two assailants subdued, gagged, and bound the victim. The location of the little house on Holly is not known, but if it were within the two blocks between State and Alaska streets, there would have been significant foot traffic, and even gagged, Ella Wilson could have been heard crying out through the thin boards. A pillow applied to the face and sufficient pressure to the pillow would have muffled that sound. This force could have extinguished her life.

Two names of men on the jury are known associates of Jeff, W. F. Saportas and Dr. J. Allen Hornsby. Beyond being on Jeff's payroll to keep Soap Gang trouble from appearing in the pages of the *Alaskan*, this pair would have been inclined to help out in other ways, such as promoting a non-inflammatory finding by the coroner's jury. Member E. J. White is none other than *The Skaguay News* reporter who became known as Stroller White, Klondike Newsman. He definitely is *not* thought to be an associate of Jeff. Deputy US Marshal Sylvester Taylor is all but named in Sehlbrede's inquest entry, which indicates that jurors met in his office in the Occidental Hotel Building on the morning of May 31, 1898. Taylor was also Jeff's man, body and soul. The report of "unintentional murder," however, was to be far from the end this story. Early the following month a report came down upon the town from the outside in the manner of an avalanche.

Mattie Silks, the highly successful Denver bordello madam, and Corteze "Cort" Thomson, her gambler husband, were surely still bitter towards Jeff over the 1892 shooting of Cliff Sparks in Denver. Thomson had been arrested as a suspect, and the pair had blamed Jeff for his arrest and the legal trouble that followed. Thomson was indeed a combatant in the shootout, but he was not the killer. Most likely it was Jim Jordan or Jeff who sent Sparks to his grave. This ill feeling might have something to do with the story she gave a *Seattle Daily Times* reporter who was at the docks to meet passengers returning from the North.

Details about Mattie Silks in the North in 1898 vary widely among writers.[1] Based on dates that are certain as well as various realities, here is this writer's interpretation of events involving her in 1898. At the peak of the Klondike gold fever, Silks, her husband, and some of her "girls" came from Denver to Seattle sometime in May 1898. Returning from a non-income-producing sojourn in England, Mattie and Cort found Denver in a depressed state, which affected Mattie's business income. Her problems were nothing, though, that Klondike gold could not fix. In Seattle she learned of the need to hike the 40-mile White Pass trail or the 30-mile Chilkoot with its stratospheric climb at the end. Now 40 years (and probably more) and growing heavier, with Cort in poor health, with "girls" not of the outdoors type, and with extensive outfitting that

---

[1] *The Wildest of the West* (1951) by Forbes Parkhill gives Mattie Silks comprehensive treatment, and writers draw details about Silks from Parkhill more than from anyone else. His book lacks detailed documentation, but the pedigree of sources identified in the Acknowledgments (e.g., Charles Nolan, long-time confidant of Silks, and Philip S. Van Cise, Denver district attorney who put Lou Blonger in prison) lends the book credibility. Many details, though, are wrong. For example, Parkhill has the Silks' taking the train to Whitehorse and a steamboat from there to Dawson. Rails did not reach the summit until February 1899 and did not connect to Whitehorse until July 1900 (Satterfield, p. 155).

would be required, Dawson by the overland route was not attractive. But what about Skaguay as a destination, only a boat ride away? She knew that Jeff, who ruled there, had no liking for her or Cort, but she also knew Jeff was a business man. Perhaps a mutually attractive professional arrangement could sooth hard feelings.

No record shows husband Cort or any "girls" going to Skaguay, but Mattie's presence was recorded, dramatically. Proposed is that this savvy business woman came alone to discover if she could operate there, and if so, at what price. What she found was the niche for her kind of business already filled and thriving. The Red Onion at Holly and State streets with its 10 10X10' upstairs rooms was booming,[1] so were the little houses along the well-established, block-long red-light district on Shoup Street (7th Avenue today) between Broadway and State streets, and so were the saloons like Clancy's, teaming with dance hall girls willing to please.[2] Still, *Madame* Silks, as she preferred to be called, knew how to wedge in, and she probably earnestly pressed Jeff about operating in Skaguay. Mattie knew better than just to arrive and set up. Her business could not work that way, depending as it did on the protection of power brokers like Jeff. So a cost of operation may have been discussed, and then on Sunday evening, May 29, 1898, having retired to her room in the Occidental Hotel on Broadway, she was thinking on the matter or perhaps waiting for word from Jeff. Then she heard words she did not expect to hear, words coming through the wall that frightened her so much that she immediately boarded the southern-bound SS *Farallon*. When a *Times* reporter encountered her on the Seattle dock and asked what news she might have to report, Madame Silks told a startling story.

CONSPIRED TO MURDER

A Terrible Tale of Crime Comes From Skagway.

What A Mrs. Silks Says

Marshal Taylor, "Soapy" Smith and Two Toughs Said to Be Running the Town and Murdering at Will—Awful Condition of Affairs.

If the story told by Mrs. Mattie Silks, a passenger who arrived in Seattle from Skagway on the steamer Farallon this morning, be true it is time something was done by the United States Government to straighten out the lawless condition of affairs at Skagway. According to Mrs. Silks' story Deputy United States Marshal Taylor of Skagway is a consort of murderers, a sharer with them in crime, and "Soapy" Smith has taken to murdering people for their money. Briefly told, Mrs. Silks' story is as follows:

On the afternoon of May 28th Ella Wilson, a mulatto prostitute, was strangled to death and robbed in her house on one of the principal streets of Skagway. A large trunk in her room, which was supposed to contain her money, was found broken open. It was the only thing in her room that was molested.

Deputy United States Marshal Taylor took charge of the body and began an "investigation" to discover the perpetrator of the deed. Mrs. Silks says that she occupied a room in the Occidental Hotel in Skagway, and adjoining her

---

[1] *Red Onion Saloon* website.
[2] Spude, pp. 138-45.

room was the office of the Deputy United States Marshal. The only partition separating the rooms was one of thin boards. The night after the murder, she says she heard Marshal Taylor, "Soapy" Smith, one Bill Tanner [Tener] and one Bowers—the latter two being well-known crooks—talking in Taylor's office while they were dividing up $3800. She says she gathered from their conversation that the money was what had been taken from Ella Wilson and that the murder had been committed by Tanner [Tener] and Bowers, at the instigation and with the consent of Taylor and "Soapy" Smith.

But that was not all. Mrs. Silks says that while she sat in her room she heard this outfit plan to strangle her to death in the same way in which Ella Wilson had been served. After hearing this plan Mrs. Silks came to the conclusion that Skagway had become too hot to hold her and she immediately took her departure on the first boat.

One of the passengers who came down on the Farallon said this morning to a reporter for The Times: "The condition of affairs at Skagway is a disgrace to civilized government. The United States officials make no pretense at enforcing the law. They are making money hand over fist, and any sort of crime can be committed as long as the officials of the United States get their share of the loot. The only law that is respected is the rifle or the revolver, and unless something is done pretty soon Skagway will be absolutely unsafe for any man to venture into who values his life."[1]

By the time Silks' story reached Skaguay, Ella Wilson was buried, the investigation had led nowhere, and her small estate (½ interest in a house and lot, 2 trunks, bedding, tent, stove, stove wood, wearing apparel) was being appraised for sale.[2] No one in Skaguay publicly admitted to believing Silks' story, and "outside" papers were being condemned for the slanders told about Skaguay. A very short statement about the story Silks told appeared after Jeff was dead, reading, "Little as we believed it at the time, it now looks as though the story told by Mattie Silks was true."[3] The thing about that story, though, is that not only was it likely true; it is quite likely also untrue, or at least in part.

Among the many in Western camps and towns, from Fort Worth to Leadville to Creede and even Denver, who knew that "walls have ears" was Jeff Smith. He had lived in rooms up and down the west where it was possible to hear the slightest sound through the thin boards of an adjoining room—a step, a voice, even a whisper. Further, Jeff made it his business to know who of any import to him was in town and where that person was. That kind of intelligence and a heightened state of awareness were parts of his business model. Given this background, a distinct possibility, or indeed, probability, is that Jeff knew exactly where Mattie Silks was staying while in Skaguay, that she was known to be in her room next door when Jeff, Marshal Taylor,

---

[1] *Seattle Times* 06/04/1898, p. 2.

[2] Probate Book A 1898-1903. All of this was accomplished on May 31, 1898. By June 23, her goods were valued at $130 against claims for "administration etc. of about $170" and were ordered sold.

[3] *Skaguay News* 07/15/1898, p. 3.

Bowers, and Tener met in the Marshal's office in the Occidental Hotel, and that every word heard by Mattie Silks that night was spoken for her hearing.

Another interpretation of the incredible discussion that Mattie Silks overheard does not seem possible. It is no insult to Ella Wilson to doubt that she was robbed of $2,000 as reported in the *Oregonian* or of the $3,800 that Silks said she heard being divided up? These amounts are equivalent to about $62,480 or $118,712 in today's dollars.[1] Skaguay was reported to have had "more than a hundred prostitutes" at this time,[2] and as Anne Butler demonstrates in her *Daughters of Joy, Sisters of Misery*, in general throughout the west and in frontier towns, "The occupational circumstances" of prostitutes, especially those on their own,

> rested on such a shallow economic base that the general inflation and uneven cash flow ... only added further instability.... Mired in personal and professional disorder, prostitutes seemed unable to use their pitiful wages as a means to extricate themselves from prostitution...."[3]

Michael Rutter in *Upstairs Girls: Prostitution in the American West* (2005) writes that "in the heyday of a boomtown, a woman might make between $40 and $175 a week...,[4] much above what other kinds of work open to women paid but far short of producing thousands in a few months. There were exceptions, such as Klondike Kate Rockwell and Mattie Silks, who amassed tens of thousands, but Ella Wilson was not one of these exceptions. If not for the notoriety of her death, her name would be obscured among the many women in that unlawful but tolerated and dangerous profession who had been murdered.

So if Jeff knew that he and the others could be heard by Mattie next door and were tossing around such high numbers and talking as though Jeff had directed men to rob and murder Ella Wilson and that Mattie Silks would be next, and that the marshal knew what had happened and what was proposed, only one conclusion is possible. Jeff wanted to scare the woman out of town. If so, then the plan worked so well that it took immediate effect. But more was to come, which Jeff probably should have foreseen: the possibility that this woman, who already carried a grudge against him, would likely use the event to hurt him. When a reporter came up to her on the dock in Seattle to ask what news she might have for publication, she was only too eager to tell what she had heard.

Finally, why should Jeff want to scare Mattie Silks out of town? Having been a success at her game for decades, she probably felt confident enough to pressure Jeff into letting her set up in Skaguay. What kind of pressure? Perhaps the implication, or even overt threat, that she possessed an encyclopedic knowledge of the "Denver 'Soapy Smith'" that could prove embarrassing to the Captain of the Skaguay Military Company. She also might have had a chat with Marshal Taylor without Jeff present and without knowing that Taylor was Jeff's man. However it was, it would have been memorable at some point about June 11, 1898, to be within the vicinity of Holly and

---

[1] Tom's Inflation Calculator.

[2] Morgan, Lael, p. 271.

[3] Butler, p. 51.

[4] Rutter, p. 7.

State streets after a newsboy had earned his dollar from Jeff for delivering a June 4, 1898, copy of *The Seattle Daily Times*. Jeff's audible reaction to the Mattie Silks' backfire on Jeff within that paper probably was heard through many a wall near Jeff Smith's Parlor.

By June 24, for publishing the Silks' story, Jeff and Marshal Taylor had filed a libel suit against *The Seattle Daily Times*. Each asked for $25,000 in damages.[1] Jeff also sued the *San Francisco Examiner* for $25,000 for defamation of character, hiring attorney Walter Church to serve papers to the newspapers.[2] The suit was filed on July 2 in Seattle.[3] The *Seattle Times* retaliated in its July 4, 1898, issue.

SOAPY SMITH IS ANGRY

He Wants $25,000 From The Times for Defamation

HIS REPUTATION "INJURED"

But He Will Have to Prove That He Had a Character Capable of Being Defamed. He Really Takes Himself Seriously.

"Soapy" Smith is aggrieved. "Soapy," as everybody knows, lives at Skagway, and among the initiated is regarded as a man who does just about what he pleases up there without let or hindrance. This time the cause of "Soapy's" grief is a publication, which appeared in The Times on June 4, 1898, under the head of "Conspired to Murder." "Soapy" says this article had damaged his "reputation" to the tune of $25,000, and he proposes to invoke the majesty of the law to collect the aforesaid amount. "Soapy's" attorneys today served papers on The Times, demanding that amount. Tacked onto "Soapy's suit is one by a gentleman named Taylor, who says he is a Deputy United States marshal at Skagway and who claims that he too has been damaged $25,000 worth. Taylor, however cuts little ice. "Soapy" is the "main guy."

The article over which these Alaska magnates have allowed their wrath to rise until they could no longer hold it in, will be recalled by the readers of The Times. Briefly stated, it was a story ascribed to Mrs. Mattie Silks, who formerly lived at Skagway. Mrs. Silks occupied a room in the Occidental Hotel at Skagway, adjoining the office of Deputy Marshal Taylor. There was a colored woman murdered and robbed at Skagway during the last week in May, and Mrs. Silks claimed she overheard Taylor, "Soapy" and two other men dividing the money which had been taken from the colored woman and plotting at the same time to kill her (Mrs. Silks). Mrs. Silks decided to go afar from Skagway and stand not on the order of her going, which she promptly did. The Times published her story.

It is this article that made "Soapy" so sad that it will take $25,000 to brighten him up again. Of course "Soapy" knows that before any court will give him damages for a smirched reputation, he will have to prove that he had a reputation that was capable of being smirched that much. "Soapy" is a

---

[1] *Skaguay News* 07/11/1898.
[2] *Denver Times* 07/03/1898.
[3] *Daily Alaskan* 07/11/1898.

wise man, however, and probably took this into consideration before he began his "suit." As for Taylor—well, as said before, Taylor cuts little ice. "Soapy" is the "main guy."[1]

The Silks' story had hurt Jeff, Marshal Taylor, and town merchants, who continually feared that a bad reputation would cause travelers to and from the Klondike to avoid Skaguay. Lewis Levy, one of the commissioners for parks in Tacoma, Washington, had gone to Alaska on business, probably private. He had returned on the *Farallon* with Silks, and reading her story in the *Times* prompted him to tell his own story. Putting it into letters, the first he wrote was on June 6, 1898, to S. A. Perkins, a powerful City of Tacoma entrepreneur who had partnered in founding the Athletic Club, owned two city newspapers, and sat on the Republican National Committee.[2] "Some of the experiences I have had," Levy wrote to Perkins,

> are beyond description. I have seen American citizens deliberately plundered before the marshal's eyes in dens kept for that purpose.... I had to pay the marshal $20 after he had recovered stolen property, before he would make a return to the court commissioner, as he threatened to turn it back to the thieves unless I did so.

No doubt Perkins shared Levy's story among his Washington state and Washington, DC, friends and colleagues. Levy also wrote to the US attorney general on June 9, 1898, stating "that it would be very dangerous for a government agent to go there, if his business was known."[3]

Above the grim story of the death of Ella Wilson in the *Morning Oregonian* had appeared a short news story:

> Port Townsend, June 3. – The steamer Farallon, which arrived here tonight from Alaska brings news that in addition to the indictment of eight customs officers, the grand jury at Sitka has brought in two true bills against John U. Smith, ex-United States commissioner at Skagway, on charges of extortion and accepting bribes. Smith has been arrested.

The gears of justice were slow, but they turned. It took from November 1897 to June 1898, but John U. Smith had been removed and then arrested. Jeff, Marshal Taylor, and the merchants of Skaguay had good reason to be unhappy. Stories like those of Silks and Levy oiled judicial wheels and sent perceptions of lawlessness in Skaguay throughout the country. As a result, the tempers of some were shortened, causing them to consider speedier sorts of justice, such as provided by a bullet or a rope.

As for Mattie Silks, Cort, and "the girls," they did not stay in Seattle, and they did not return to Denver. Rather, they went to Dawson mostly likely by way of the all-water route: 3,000 miles from Seattle through the Aleutians to St. Michael and 1700 miles by steamer up the Yukon to Dawson.[4] None of the entourage is recorded among the Mountie logs of people embarking down the Yukon from Bennett. Forbes Parkhill in *Wildest of the West* (1951) claims Mattie hiked the Chilkoot, but given the scenario

---

[1] *Seattle Times* 07/04/1898.

[2] Hunt, *Tacoma*, pp. 59, 164, 202, & Tribune.

[3] Hunt, *Distant*, p. 61.

[4] Berton, p. 190.

SUITS - - $28.00
PANTS - - 7.00
AND UPWARDS

FIRST CLASS FIT
AND WORKMANSHIP

JOHN McDONALD

606 SECOND STREET . . .   May. 10 # 96   Merchant Tailor

~~Seattle, Wash.~~ Alaska 189__

Cooks Inlett Nor Cool Bay
600 miles from Juneau
an Board "Gen Canby"
2500 miles North S. Francisco   Dear Mollie
Am well, will be to
my destination tomorrow
if nothing goes wrong
Have had a hell of a trip.
You can write to
Resurection Creek
Cooks Inlett Alaska
Have no time to
write more as we hail
a Steamer bound for San
Francisco to mail this
Have had no word from
you Since I left Juneau
yours Jeff — Love to all —

Gold here in big quantities all country talking up here —

27. Letter from Jeff to his wife Mary, written aboard the steamer *General Canby* in "Cooks Inlett" (Cook Inlet), Alaska, May 10, 1896. On the side of the letter Jeff penned, "Gold here in big quantities [—] all country talking up here." (Author's col., item 11)

28. Jeff with hands in his pockets before the doorway to Jeff Smith's Parlor, 317 Holly Street, Skaguay, Alaska. John Bowers (r) looks to Jeff, smiling. Perhaps Jeff said something amusing; the two men to Jeff's left also appear to smile. Circa May-June 1898. (Ralph MacKay col., 1970-58-464, Archives, University of Alaska Fairbanks)

29. Jeff Smith's Parlor. Banners indicate circa July 1898, Skaguay, Alaska. (Cynthia Brackett Driscoll, Brackett Family col.)

Warning !

A word to the wise should be sufficient !

All Confidence,

Bunco and

Sure-thing Men,

And all other objectionable characters
Are notified to leave Skaguay and
White Pass Road Immediately.
And to remain away.
Failure to comply with this warning
will be followed by prompt action

101.

Skaguay, Alaska, Mch. 8, 1898.

30. (above) Handbill from the Committee of 101. (Alaska State Museum, Juneau, III-O-86a)
31. (below) Handbill from the 317. (Alaska State Museum, Juneau, III-O-86b)

ANSWER
TO WARNING

The body of men styling themselves 101 are
hereby notified that any overt act committed by them
will be promptly met by the Law abiding Citizens of
Skaguay and each member and HIS PROPERTY
will be held responsible for any unlawful act on their
part and the law and order society consisting of 317
citizens will see that Justice is dealt out to its full
extent as no Blackmailers or Vigilantes will be tolerated.

The Committee.

32. Inside Jeff Smith's Parlor. Of the 12 men in this "Flashlight Photo" (as noted bottom r), 4 are known and identified by number: (l to r) Nate Pollock (1), Van Triplett (looking away, 4), Jeff R. Smith (5), John Bowers (high collar, 8). Under the ledge of the bar hang two towels for patron use. Jeff wears his stickpin in his tie and carries a newspaper in his coat pocket. Circa May-July 1898, Skaguay, Alaska. (Theodore E. Peiser photog., Library of Congress, 13094-262-8544)

33. Inside Jeff Smith's Parlor. Of these 6 men, the first 4 (l to r) are known: Nate Pollock, John Bowers (probably), John Clancy, Jeff Smith. Flags on the left wall include (l to r) the American flag with a photo of President McKinley superimposed, the revolutionary Cuban flag, and the American flag. Circa May-July 1898, Skaguay, Alaska. (Alaska State Library, Wickersham col., Theodore E. Peiser photog., ASL-P277-001-009)

34. Inside Jeff Smith's Parlor. Three of these 7 men are known: (l to r) John Clancy (1), John Bowers (3), and Jeff Smith. Jeff wears a pin in the shape of a marching soldier with rifle shouldered. Circa May-July 1898, Skaguay, Alaska. (Denver Public Library, Western History Collection, Theodore E. Peiser photog., Z-8905)

35. Jeff R. Smith on his horse, Holly Street, Skaguay, Alaska, awaiting the July 4, 1898, parade to begin. Jeff Smith's Parlor is partially visible far left. The alley where John Stewart was relieved of his gold is to the right of the Parlor. Jeff appears to be wearing the white ascot draped with US and Cuban flags sent to him by an admirer. The poster on the building in the middle advertises the Fourth of July. (Courtesy Royal British Columbia Archives Collections, James A. Sinclair col., John A. Sinclair photog., ZZ-95358)

36. Fitzhugh Lee, the captured eagle given to Jeff, resides in a cage aboard a wagon made into a patriotic float for Skaguay's July 4, 1898, parade. The small boy dressed as Uncle Sam is John Clancy's son. Jeff Smith's Parlor and Jeff's horse can be seen to the far right. (Courtesy Royal British Columbia Archives Collections, James M. Sinclair col., John A. Sinclair photog., ZZ-95358)

37A. Patriotic bunting on Jeff Smith's Parlor indicates this photograph was taken on May 1, 1898, probably just before the parade of the Skaguay Military Company. A large crowd of citizens (children, women, men in formal dress) appears fresh and staged for a group photograph to commemorate the occasion. Nearly every face looks to the camera. Jeff is at attention on his mount, his posture erect and right arm straight down. Behind Jeff, a man standing among men holds a large sign reading, "The Skaguay Military Company." This eastern side of Holly Street (6th Avenue today), between Broadway and State streets, was a business section. A little sign on the right of Jeff Smith's Parlor reads, "Merchant's Lunch," and down the street (r to l) from Jeff Smith's Parlor are various businesses: H. Bauer General Merchandize, H. B. Litt Ready Made Suits and Cloaks, Louvre Café, Barber Shop, Theatre Royal, New York-Alaska Trading & Mining, N. H. Wilson Druggist. (See inset below.) (Alaska State Library, William R. Norton col., ASL-P226-117)

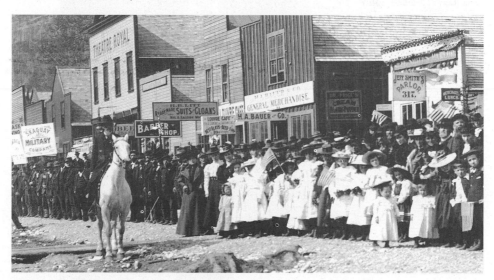

37B. Inset of 37A above.

38. Jeff on his horse, riding along Broadway toward Holly Street, Skaguay, Alaska. This photograph was taken by Rev. Sinclair on July 7, 1898, at about 9 a.m. (Sinclair, p. 131). Others would later claim it was taken on July 4, 1898. (Alaska State Library, William R. Norton col., John A. Sinclair photog., ASL-P266-067)

39. John Douglas Stewart (right) with his sack of gold. Skaguay, Alaska July 14, 1898. (Alaska State Library, William R. Norton col., ASL-P266-090)

documented by her story in *The Seattle Daily Times* and everything that would be required of the trip (journey back up past Skaguay through Dyea, "packing" for 7-to-10 people, boat building...), that does not seem possible whereas just booking passage from Seattle for everyone does.

Once Mattie and company were in Dawson, Parkhill is specific. She "rented a good-sized frame building on Second Street for $350 a month" from the "proprietor of the Sour Dough Saloon," named Jenkins. Moreover, Parkhill quotes Silks as saying,

> "The protection money I paid in Denver was penny-ante stuff alongside what the redcoats of the Mounted police demanded," she later told her Denver friend, Charley Nolan. "I had to pay them fifty dollars a day for every day I operated at Dawson City, but I'm not kicking. It was worth it."[1]

At the end of three months, with winter approaching and her husband ill, Mattie packed everyone up and left on the *Susie*. That would have been September 16, 1898, or shortly before. On this date the last outbound riverboat of the season, the *John Cudahy*, left Dawson.[2] When asked by Charley Nolan back in Denver how she made out in Dawson, Silks said that after all expenses, which included, "passage both ways, the protection money, and Cort's gambling debts, I have a net profit of $38,000 for my ninety days at Dawson City...."[3] It could be that Mattie at some point came to think that by scaring her out of Skaguay, Jeff had done her a favor.

––––––––––

Rev. John A. Sinclair, arriving in Skaguay on May 20, 1898, was Rev. Dickey's Canadian Presbyterian replacement at the Union Church.[4] A faithful diarist, Sinclair recorded his Skaguay experiences between May 20 and August 1898. His son, James M. Sinclair, expanded his father's diary into a biography titled *Mission Klondike* (1978).

Rev. Sinclair took a comfortable room with board for $1 a day at the Golden North Hotel, "a temperance hostelry" run by Thomas Whitten and his wife.[5] Finding discord at the Union Church, Sinclair wanted to confer with his predecessor. Dickey was at Bennett, conducting services, building a boat, and waiting with thousands of others for the ice to go out so the water journey to Dawson could begin. Sinclair made the "knees shaking" and "heart pounding" climb to Bennett in a day.[6] At Log Cabin, he found "Greasy and slatternly women, begrimed and ragged children and rough, shifty-eyed men ... in a sea of mud and filth."[7] In Bennett at the first place they stopped for food, there was none because the cook had gone to bed. "At that moment, a seductive looking woman strolled into the bar, her walk and carriage leaving no doubt in one's mind as to her profession." Sinclair had reached one of the rough edges of the frontier.

Over three days, Sinclair made copious notes of Dickey's stories of "frustrations and achievements" in Skaguay and sketches of those from whom he "could expect

––––––––––

[1] Parkhill, p. 268.
[2] Adney, p. 455.
[3] Parkhill, pp. 269-70.
[4] Sinclair, p. 84.
[5] Sinclair, p. 86.
[6] Sinclair, p. 91.
[7] Sinclair, p. 93.

stanch support" and those from whom he "could expect no consideration."[1] Then it was back to the relative comfort of the Golden North but also numerous difficulties. Young parishioner store clerks were gambling and losing their employers' money, and especially troublesome was the Episcopal clergyman who had taken physical possession of the Union Church. He was selling an "Electro-Magnet for the Cure of the Liver" and was seeing "female 'patients'" late at night *at the church*. Then there was the law of Skaguay. Golden North proprietor Whitten told Sinclair,

> There are so many in business here ... who are involved with Jeff Smith and are coining money from the sporting element, that they willingly tolerate Smith's influence in civic affairs. His word is the law!

Rev. Sinclair's reply, no doubt via Rev. Dickey:

> For want of properly constituted authority, revive your Committee of 101. Do it quietly. Document all the evidence of skullduggery. Meet with Governor Brady. Meet with Judge Sehlbrede. But work discreetly.[2]

That apparently happened as an almost immediate mobilization on July 8 shows.

One of the more bizarre stories told about Jeff in Skaguay involves North West Mounted Policeman Captain Zachary Taylor Wood and two subordinates.[3] In early June 1898, they were ordered to transport $150,000 in customs fees (other versions of the story say $224,000 in bullion from the Klondike) across District-of-Alaska soil to the Canadian *Tartar*, which would be waiting in Skaguay's deep-water port. The route chosen was the Chilkoot trail and through Dyea because, as the story goes, taking the White Pass meant chancing a robbery attempt by "Soapy" Smith and his gang. At Dyea harbor, the Mounties loaded the heavy cargo into a skiff, rowed to the tugboat *Lady of the Lake*, and made for the wharf where the *Tartar* was tied up. Covering the gold transport was the story that Captain Wood was going to a new duty assignment.

As related by G. S. Howard in *The Quarterly: Royal Canadian Mounted Police* (1983), Wood said a rowboat full of men "suddenly bore down astern of the tug as it chugged towards Skagway." In response, Wood ordered his men to shoulder arms and shouted a warning. When the tug tied up at the crowded wharf, between the Mounties and the *Tartar* stood Jeff with men whom Wood recognized as Soap Gang members. Jeff reportedly approached Wood, followed by most of his gang, offered welcome, and invited the captain to stay a few days in Skaguay before embarking on his long voyage. In the context of the story, this welcome was a brazen pretext to keep the men in town so they could be robbed. The story tells how Wood refused Jeff's invitation, saw to the loading of the heavy bags onto the *Tartar*, and sailed at 1 p.m.[4]

Jeff probably did meet the Mounties as told in the story's different versions.[5] However, he did not go with his gang but, more likely, with members of the Skaguay

---

[1] Sinclair, p. 95.

[2] Sinclair, pp. 98-106.

[3] *Zachary Taylor Wood*: grandson of Zachary Taylor (1784-1850), 12th President of the United States.

[4] Howard, and Hunt, *Distant*, pp. 55-56.

[5] In the version Rev. Dickey tells in his narrative, Wood "threatened to sink the other boat if it came any nearer." Further, on the wharf, Jeff and his men were between the Mounties and the *Tartar*. The three unloaded "their charge, and marched along, wheeling the cargo toward the" ship. When they "reached

Military Company, not to rob the foreign visitors but to welcome them. This would be in keeping with Jeff's way of thinking, one officer to another as an international gesture of goodwill. Thus, as a show of respect, he might have sent members of his Company in a boat (albeit in a lowly rowboat), not to board the *Lady of the Lake* but to welcome it. In the universally negative tellings of the story, though, the skiff "suddenly bore down" on the tug as if the steam-powered vessel could not have easily outmaneuver and outrun a rowboat containing a number of men. Colonel Steele, who gave Wood the assignment and to whom Wood reported, gave the story a page in his *Forty Years in Canada* (1915). In Steele's telling, the event occurred on June 9, and Wood "had to threaten to fire on the men in the row boat full of men, who appeared determined to run them down and were only kept at a distance by the threat of shooting."[1] In another version, this one by Philip H. Godsell, "From out of the shadows loomed" the rowboat...." This time the tug is a "Police boat," and the rowboat, "Loaded with ruffians, ... bore swiftly down" on the tug "until it became obvious they intended to ram the Police boat."[2]

These distortions are accompanied by another, that Captain Wood knew members of the Soap Gang "by sight." Not even the Skaguay Committee of 101 claimed that. Moreover, all of the versions have Wood immediately leaving Skaguay as if having run a gauntlet and needing to put danger behind him. Not so, reported *The Skaguay News*.

> Captain Wood..., who was stationed here during the fall, winter and spring...,[3] and who left nearly a month ago for Lake Bennett, was crossing palms [shaking hands] with his many friends here.... Capt. Wood was on his way to Victoria, and left on the *Tartar* for a hurried ... trip in connection with the Canadian customs. Were it not ... that he is a true son of Britain, he would be a welcome adjunct to the country over which waves the stars and stripes.[4]

Rather than being jostled in a threatening manner, the wharf crowd, including Jeff, probably was giving Wood a friendly greeting.

Jeff would not have led holdup men in a public place in the middle of a June day against well-armed policemen of a foreign land. That would have caused an international incident and made its leader the object of a manhunt. Jeff, of course,

---

the waiting bandits," they "began to jostle the Mounties...." At that point, "A squad of" Royal Navy "reservists, fully armed," came off the *Tartar* and "rushed down the wharf. The thugs, seeing that serious opposition was at hand, quickly dispersed." This version concludes much as the other: "According to the generally accepted version of the event, Soapy remained and welcomed the major as if they were best friends and invited him to stay a few days in Skaguay. The major just as courteously declined with profuse, if cool, thanks." Rev. Dickey was not in Skagway when this meeting occurred, he having left for Dawson on April 1, 1898 (Dickey Diary). He was retelling the "story that reached us in Dawson..." (Dickey, *Gold*, p. 129).

[1] Steele, *Forty*, p. 313.
[2] Godsell, p. 75.
[3] Wood had resided at Holly House and probably is the one to award Saportas a big packing job the previous December. (Pitcher, p. 19, & *Skaguay News* 12/31/1897, p. 4.)
[4] *Skaguay News* 06/17/1898, p. 1.

probably did intend to rob the Canadians if he could, but by indirect means under cover of civility and ceremony such as might be accomplished over an extended stay. Perhaps the Mounties did react stiffly to Jeff and his men, and took away the perception that a robbery could have occurred then and there. After all, they were in charge of a very large amount of cash and gold. But more than likely, the crowd posed no menace; the *News* notice of welcome counters that. Rather, the Soap Gang's standard approach was to leverage human shortcomings by presenting a "sure thing." Within the hearts of all men, even Mounties, were weaknesses that just had to be fished for patiently and artfully when a "pile" was at hand—in this case a huge pile of gold and cash. And if opportunity to cause it to disappear availed, of course the Soap Gang would not hesitate.

At that time Jeff could have used a portion of that gold. He, Frank Clancy, and William Saportas were attempting to bring to Skaguay a huge attraction: the title fight rematch between James "Gentleman Jim" Corbett and "Ruby" Robert Fitzsimmons.[1] According to the *Denver Evening Post,* quoting from a copy of *The Skaguay News*, Jeff had asked the citizens and the railroad to put up a purse of $50,000 to entice the fighters to the city. It would be an excellent investment.

> Smith showed the citizens, on paper, how the town would make a profit of $1,000,000.... He said there would be at least 50,000 strangers in attendance, and each one would be compelled to leave ... $20, which would make $1,000,000 left in Skaguay. ... [F]rom the tenor of the article it is inferred that the citizens do not take much stock in the scheme. Fitzsimmons and Corbett have not yet been consulted..., but if "Soapy" gets hold of them they will undoubtedly consent to the fight taking place in Skaguay."[2]

Jeff and Skaguay surely would have benefited from the extravaganza. Jeff may have worried that Fitzsimmons would recognize him as one of the Denver men who years before had "taken" his diamonds, but if so, it did not slow Jeff's sales pitch. Jeff might have been able to convince the fighters to come to Skaguay where, unlike most of the rest of the country, their fight would not be against the law, but he was not able to convince the Railway and most Skaguay merchants to put up a guaranteed purse of $50,000. So the plan was added to the list of Jeff's promising but missed opportunities. Jeff, however, had another plan in motion to promote Skaguay. Gold.

In the same issue telling of Jeff's attempt to secure the Fitzsimons-Corbett fight, *The Skaguay News* reported "considerable excitement" in town

> over recent rich quartz finds in this immediate locality. On Wednesday of this week Jeff Smith, who has located a claim within less than two miles of the city, had about twenty pounds of ore in small pieces brought in, from any piece of which can be seen protruding in from one to a dozen places, solid chunks of gold, worth from two to 40 cents per "protrude." Mr. Smith says the vein from which this ore was taken is two feet in depth and of unknown width

---

[1] *Skaguay News* 06/17/1898.
[2] *Denver Evening Post* 06/29/1898, p. 2, & *RMN* 07/03/1898.

and length. There is no doubt but that if the class of ore exhibited exists in quantity of any magnitude, the vein is one of the richest in Alaska.[1]

That this find is a variation on McGinty seems almost certain. Nothing indicates such a claim near town. It would be no surprise to learn, however, that Jeff had sold and resold the claim numerous times.

Arriving in force on Friday, May 27, 1898, was the White Pass & Yukon Railway Company, Superintendent Frank Herbert Whiting at its head.[2] Coming from Denver, it seems likely that the engineer and foreman would have heard of "Soapy" Smith, but if not, he soon would.

Formed in 1896 and backed by investors in England, the Company began planning a railroad into the Yukon. In June 1897, a month before news of the Klondike Gold strike reached the "outside," Company men conferred with Captain Moore about surveying his land.[3] They advanced him funds to help construct his wharf to establish rights to use it and to construct and operate a railroad on his land. By July 1897, the rail company was attempting to improve the White Pass trail and prepare it for tracks. Arriving in Skaguay a year later to begin construction, the Company met opposition from every major group: merchants, saloon men, property owners, city government, other transportation companies operating along the White Pass, and Jeff Smith. The Company sought legal jurisdictional powers that included authority to collect royalties, distribute the mail, recruit and direct a police force, and generally administer affairs in this region of the District of Alaska. Though not legally granted, the Company claimed to have these powers. The battle for control of Skaguay had begun.

Originally, the tracks were to be run from Moore's Wharf along the east bluff. Land owners along this path expected to make many times the value of their property by selling it to the railroad. To circumvent high expectations, the rail company proposed to the city council that the tracks run down the middle of Broadway, the main street. No one held deeded rights to any part of Broadway, only to properties facing it. Business owners opposed both routes because travelers would be, potentially, prevented from visiting town.[4] Stampeders could just step off a boat and onto a train with their freight and not set foot in town. For those returning from the interior, the case could be the same, and without an ounce of that Klondike gold left in Skaguay. Claims were made that the railroad was bribing the council, and talks slowed even further.

Transportation issues were something new for Jeff. Previously, railroads brought victims to him and removed them after being relieved of some or all of their valuables. In Skaguay, the geography had required a change from railroads to ships, but the effect was the same. Geography and climate, moreover, had been advantageous, bottling up Stampeders until winter snows retreated from mountain passes and ice

---

[1] *Skaguay News*, 06/17/1898.

[2] Minter, p. 179.

[3] Minter, p. 66.

[4] The tracks were moved from Broadway to the route along the east bluff, and even at the time of this writing, the author has spoken with travelers who did not know Skagway was much of a town and did not bother to visit it. Having purchased rail tickets ahead of time, they stepped off the boat, walked up to wharf, and stepped onto a train, which then rolls toward the White Pass, out of sight of the town.

from lakes and rivers. Now, however, geography and progress were creating a nearly seamless link from the sea to the interior and threatened to remove a stop in Skaguay.

This issue also concerned merchants, and the city council called delay after delay as it searched for middle ground. Each delay, though, cost the Railway time and money. Supplies piled up, idle men were needed payment and housing to be kept ready to work, and the future date of revenue flowing back to the Company, counted on in its plan, became less and less certain. The Railway wanted to reach Bennett before winter, but progress from tidewater had not even begun. Beyond the barrier of the city council were other barriers. High, sheer, rock walls from which a rail bed had to be blasted and carved. Property rights of those living on or owning and profiting from property on the trail, including Jeff, who had an interest in the Bracket Road.[1] Three governments—the US, Canada, and England—which had yet to come to the negotiating table, not to mention the state of Washington, the province of British Columbia, and the District of Alaska. All this hindered the right of way the Company felt it had secured even before stampeders had arrived. Certainly it did not feel a need to deal with the likes of "Soapy" Smith.

After three weeks of debate, at last the city council granted "right of way" down the center of Broadway. Early on the morning of June 15, 1898, 500 men were laying track. By nightfall one mile of the thoroughfare had been graded, tied, and railed.[2]

Just after the first mile of track was completed, the council was asked to approve the hiring of a night watchman for the town. Jeff spearheaded the quest.

> At a called meeting of the city council held Tuesday evening, H. C. Bowman was employed to act as night patrol or watchman at the stipulated salary of $100 per month. The person to whom is due the credit of making possible the employment and payment of a man who will devote his time in protecting both life and property in the city is Jeff R. Smith, who, through his individual efforts, succeeded in raising from the liberal and loyal business men of the city, the money to not only employ one watchman, but he raised within a few dollars of the amount necessary to employ two, as he succeeded in securing a guarantee of $160 per month for this purpose. As soon as the $40 per month is guaranteed, a second watchman will be employed.[3]

What were Jeff's motives in leading this effort, beyond being featured in a role he enjoyed, that of public benefactor? Involved may have been a profit motive of perhaps $100 a month (about $3,124 today).[4] Was nighttime crime up? In short, yes, particularly the threat of fire. The *News* called it "INCENDIARYISM."

> Two attempts were made late Saturday night or early Sunday morning, to kindle fires under buildings in the most densely crowded portions of the city. One was under the store of Keelar, the money king, while the other was in some buildings in the rear of the Grotto saloon, run by J. H. Foster. Fortunately both fires were discovered before much headway had been

---

[1] *RMN* 04/13/1899.
[2] *Skaguay News* 06/17/1898, p. 2.
[3] *Skaguay News* 06/17/1898, p. 2.
[4] Tom's Inflation Calculator.

gained, and were extinguished…. If the dastard who is attempting to burn the town is apprehended…, he will have occasion to wish he had died of cholera infantum.[1]

The stories of Jeff's night watchmen and of "Incendiaryism" appear on the same page. The proximity of these events suggests a fire protection racket. Dramatizing the need for watchmen was not one but two fires set by some pyromaniac or "barn burner" with scores to settle, either of which could have leveled the town should a blaze arise during one of Skaguay's frequent winds. Best would be to have someone on the lookout for the work of such a person and of course for the occasional accidental fire. Not doing so could mean having the town expunged in a conflagration. On this matter, Jeff was probably regarded as an authority because of what had happened in Creede in 1892. Would $200 a month be too high a price to protect against losing everything?

As for Jeff, from the men he hired as watchmen, it would not be thought overbearing to ask them to contribute half their salary for the privilege of holding the position. Splitting the job between two watchmen would, presumably, make for only 15 nights each to "watch" the town. At the time, in Portland, a man could have a bunk in which to sleep and 3 meals a day for $.35, for $10.50 a month. The same could be had in Skaguay for $1.30 a day, or $39 a month.[2] On $50 a month, a watchman could have the necessities and $11 left over, and time to pursue other employment were it wanted. One can hear Jeff explaining all this to the watchmen, including how unlikely it would be that they would have to worry about looking for fires intentionally set.

George Brackett had improved a rough section of the White Pass trail, and for a small fee stampeders could use it. A story from the early startup of this section, called the Brackett Wagon Road, has roughnecks pushing Brackett aside and taking control of his enterprise and has Brackett going for help to Jeff, who immediately put the road back into Brackett's hands. After Jeff was killed, his brother, Bascomb, claimed that Jeff owned an interest in the Brackett Wagon Road.[3] No documentation supports the claim, but it is possible. Trading "protection" for a share, as in Creede, was among Jeff's enterprising ways. If such a sequence occurred, it is possible that those who hijacked Brackett's right-of-way were members of the Soap Gang and just playing their part in a protection racket swindle that netted Jeff an owner's interest in the road.

Jeff's associates did not see the railroad workers as residents and sought their money. Michael J. Heney, the Whitehorse and Yukon Railway Company construction manager, allowed no liquor in the railroad camps, so a Skaguay saloon proprietor sent a man to set up a tent saloon just outside their Rocky Point camp. Commonly believed, but without provenance, is that the proprietor was one of Jeff's associates. Heney ordered the man to remove the tent, but he refused, saying he "guessed it had as good a right to be there as Heney's" tent. Heney felt otherwise. After summoning camp foreman Hugh Foy, Heney pointed to a big boulder above the saloon tent and

[1] *Skaguay News* 06/17/1898, p. 2. This news item appears just above notice of "A Night Watchman Employed" and Jeff Smith's spearheading the effort among businessmen. *died of cholera infantum*: died of cholera as an infant.

[2] *Morning Oregonian 02/12/1898, p. 8.*

[3] *RMN* 04/13/1899.

within hearing distance of the occupant, told Foy to remove the rock by 5 the next morning, and "not a minute later." Believing the order a bluff, the man went to bed.

With the dynamite placed well before 5, at 4:55 Foy sent word to the man of the impending blast. He refused even to get up, so Foy went himself and told the man, "In one minute I will give the order to touch off the fuse and that rock will arrive here or hereabouts" in about 60 seconds. The man told Foy to go to hell. Foy yelled, "Fire!" and left to take cover. The man joined him shortly, in his underwear, and together they witnessed the blast and total destruction of the tent and its contents. Without recourse, the man headed down the trail in his underwear, cursing railroad men.[1]

On Saturday, June 25, 1898, Jeff assaulted F. R. Staples, a miner. He went to Dyea, filed charges with Commissioner Sehlbrede, and he issued a warrant for Jeff's arrest on a charge of assault and battery. Deputy US Marshal Taylor arrested Jeff, who pleaded not guilty. He then asked for and was granted a three-day continuation. On the day the continuation expired, in court Staples refused to prosecute and paid costs of $1.95.[2] Not known is what Jeff did to persuade Staples to drop the case.

The following day, a new McGinty was found, this one very much alive.

GENERAL FITZHUGH.
A Great American Eagle Captured and Brought to Skaguay—
Now on Exhibition at Jeff Smith's.

General Fitz-Hugh Lee came to Skaguay yesterday, and was the object of much attention.... The general is not the man upon whom are centered the eyes of the world for his gallant service to his country in Cuba,[3] but an immense American eagle, as full of fight as a cocoanut is of meat, and with an armament that would put the Vesuvius to shame. His beak is a variable [veritable] "iron virgin" for ferocity, his talons are an inch and a half long and sharp as a dagger. He is as large as a large gobbler, measuring 9 feet from tip to tip.

The great bird was caught ... about thirty miles down the canal by Frank Howard and three companions ... on a prospecting tour. He was found wedged in between two rock walls.... When they saw him, he showed fight instantly, and they were obliged to lasso him first, then throw a heavy blanket over him. Yesterday the boys arrived in Skaguay with the bird in a big dry goods box, heavily grated, and with a large rope fastening his legs together. Even then he ... was open to any engagement to fight.

The boys took him to Capt. Jeff Smith as a present, a big wire screen cage has been built for him ... behind the saloon, where he now is monarch of all ... within his reach. Yesterday a full grown hen was put in the cage, and with one stroke he tore her head off, and scattered her limbs and feathers all about him. He had half eaten her before her heart had ceased to quiver.

---

[1] Graves, pp. 61-63.
[2] United States Vs. Jefferson Smith, Section 537, case 273, 06/25-06/28/1898.
[3] Fitzhugh Lee was the American Consul General based in Havana, Cuba.

Jeff Smith will put General Fitz-Hugh in the parade of the fourth, and will then box him carefully and send him as a greeting to ... regiments in Cuba.[1]

With the approach of the July Fourth holiday, Skaguay was full of excitement. The Commercial Club, consisting of business owners, took early control of planning the celebration and appointed a committee to arrange "for the proper observance and celebration of the Glorious Fourth." Skaguay would have a parade, of course, and the committee decided it would consist of three divisions and three marshals, with Commercial Club President C. W. Everest as grand marshal.[2] Jeff's name does not appear as a planner or as being in the parade, but by July 1 his name appears in the plans as marshal of an added forth division. The *News* published the program.

[1] Grand Marshal, C.W. Everest and aids J.F. Burkhard and A.P. Tony [2] Band [3] Marshal First Division—S.L. Lovell and aids [4] Veterans [5] Children's' Float with Goddess of Liberty [6] News boys [7] Chilkat Indians [8] Grotesque characters [9] Bicyclists [10] Marshal Second Division—C.N. Hanson and aids J.G. Price and Sam Roberts [11] Knights of Pythias [12] Ladies Cavalcade [13] City Brewing Float [14] Gentleman's Cavalcade [15] Skaguay Brewing Float [16] Floats and displays of Skaguay business and industries [17] Marshal Third Division—F.W. Whiting and aids Messrs. Heney and Wilson [18] Railroad employees [19] Mechanic's Floats [20] Marshal Fourth Division—Jeff R. Smith and aids Wm. Tener and J.H. Brooks [21] Skaguay Guards and "Fitizhugh Lee" [22] Man of War Float [23] Brooks Pack Train.

The parade will form on Broadway at 1:30 p.m., and after parading the prin- [unreadable line] ... front of the city hall where speeches will be delivered by the orators of the day, Messrs. R. W. Jennings, Walter Church, Judge Sehlbrede and Dr. Campbell.

After the speaking, the athletic sports will take place on and contiguous to the Seattle and Skaguay dock, as follows:

1. 100 yard Foot Race, open to all. 2. 50 yard Sack Race, open to all. 3. 100 yard Fat Men's race—contestants must weigh 200 pounds or over. 4. 75 yard Ladies' Race, open to all. 5. Bicycle Race. 6. Tug of War—8 men. 7. Climbing Greased Pole, open to all. 8. Horse Race, ¼ mile, at low tide. 9. Indian Canoe Race, at low tide.

Prizes were donated by local businesses, including clothing, accessories, cigars, stationary, and a keg of beer. Frank Clancy donated a bottle of wine.[3]

Listed as marshal of the fourth division and dead last in the big parade no doubt sat ill with Jeff. He surely reasoned that given his success with the May 1 parade, no one knew better how to lead a patriotic celebration than he. The committee had planned the parade, but Jeff would make it a huge success. He extended "a courteous invitation" to Samuel H. Graves, president of the White Pass and Yukon Railway, to

---

[1] Unknown Skaguay newspaper clipping, 07/01/1898, item 145, author's col.
[2] *Skaguay News Supplement* 06/17/1898, p. 1.
[3] *Skaguay News* 07/01/1898, p. 2. Skagway today models its parade after the original of 1898.

join him as one of his aids. Graves had arrived in Skaguay just days before, on July 2. Still learning the political landscape and having heard rumors about Captain Jeff R. Smith, Graves declined.[1] Others, like Harriet Pullen, also declined invitations, but Jeff changed her mind with a personal appeal. She wrote about it in a small book about Jeff's reign in Skaguay.

> A few days prior to July 4th, '98 "Soapy," whom I had not met previously, called at my home..., and informing me that he was to be marshal of the Fourth of July parade, requested that I ride in said parade. At first I declined, but "Soapy," who had a masterful way about him, and could be very earnest when he so desired, pointed out to me that if all the prominent people of the town declined to participate as I had done, the parade surely would be a failure, and that it was my duty as a citizen to take part. I therefore consented and on the day in question was in line with many others. It was during the parade that I had my second interview with "Soapy" [−] when galloping up and down the line on his white charger, he stopped and thanked me for taking part, then wheeled and headed for another part of the parade.[2]

Monday July 4, 1898 was the most festive day yet seen in Skaguay, and most likely in all of Alaska up to that time. First thing in the morning the city was shaken by thundering echoes as shotguns were fired and dynamite placed under anvils was detonated.[3] Red, white, and blue bunting brightened city buildings. American flags and patriotic banners fluttered everywhere in town. According to some accounts, Jeff and his associates handed out candy, peanuts, and firecrackers to the children.[4]

Once the parade got under way, Jeff managed to make it to the front and stole the historical position as the apparent grand marshal. He rode his dapple-gray horse followed by Fitzhugh Lee in a large wood and wire cage on a wagon decorated with six American flags and traditional tri-colored bunting. John Clancy's six-year-old son, Frank, rode on the wagon behind the driver, dressed as Uncle Sam.[5] Rev. Sinclair reported that "At scheduled intervals the Guards would exercise a neat maneuver and fire a volley into the air as" Jeff would lift his hat "and acknowledge the plaudits of the crowd. It was Soapy's greatest hour."[6]

Of the post parade activities, Rev. Sinclair wrote in his diary, "Soapy was much in evidence. He was seated on the platform along with Governor Brady, Dr. Campbell and Messrs. Church, Humbert and Everest."[7] As official plans did not include Jeff as a speaker, he might have considered some stratagem by which he would be called upon to say a few words. No record, shows, though, that Jeff addressed the crowd. *The Skaguay News* reported how the Fourth "was a great day for amateur photographers,

---

[1] Graves, p. 18.

[2] Pullen, Harriet, p. 10.

[3] DeArmond, p. 53.

[4] Collier & Westrate, p. 273.

[5] *Alaska Sportsman Magazine*, "I Was Just A Kid", 10/1955.

[6] Sinclair, p. 130.

[7] Sinclair, p. 131. "Dr. Cambell" is Rev. Dr. Cambell. "Church," might have been the Mr. Church, one of the original organizers of the 101. "Humbert" is unknown. "Everest" is C. W. Everest, the original grand marshal picked for the first division of the parade.

as every man, horse, mule and float was 'snapped' at on every corner...."[1] These picture-takers probably photographed the decorated speakers' platform as well. Rev. Sinclair is reported to have taken up a good picture-taking position,[2] but photographs of this venue have yet to surface in the present. One day they may.

Following the afternoon games and competitions, a grand ball was scheduled at Clancy and Company's Music Hall on Seventh Avenue—admission, free. "Everybody will be at the grand ball Monday night," wrote *The Skaguay News.* "The largest and best dancing floor in the city. The best band in Alaska has been secured for the occasion."[3] As Jeff was surely "and Company," he likely helped plan the event.

Rev. Sinclair had quickly learned who Jeff was and "refused an introduction to him."[4] However, Sinclair was deeply interested in Jeff. As an amateur photographer and filled with the sense that special history was occurring around him, Sinclair took some of the most famous photographs of the con man ever captured.[5] One of these was taken on July 7, 1898. Appearing in indirect quotation of Rev. Sinclair's diary is a description of how one of the most well-known of these photographs was taken.

> A brisk wind ushered in the morning of July 7th, so much so that the Reverend J. A. Sinclair sought the shelter of a derelict shed that fronted onto Broadway. Here he set up his camera and tripod, determined to get an action picture of Jeff Smith riding by on his spirited gelding. He knew that every morning at 9:00 Smith passed this way en route to his saloon on Holly St.

Rev. Sinclair got his photo. The account continues with how the minister little realized "when he clicked the shutter that he again would be photographing the same subject within thirty-six hours...," except then he would be in a "mortician's back room," dead.[6]

In a report to the secretary of the interior, Governor Brady wrote that during his visit to Skaguay over July 4, he saw only two or three drunks and no rowdies. "Everything is orderly now, but there is a character there now by the sobriquet 'Soapy Smith' and he seems to have the gambling element completely under his control." Brady also expressed the fear that Jeff "might find it convenient to have the [railroad] men strike just after a payday and rush them into the town to help his business."[7]

---

[1] Skaguay News 07/08/1898, p. 2.

[2] Sinclair, p. 130. "Union Church's resident minister, with camera in hand, was standing at a vantage point to take a snapshot of the Governor."

[3] *Skaguay News* 07/01/1898.

[4] Sinclair, p. 139.

[5] *most famous photographs of the con man*: these appear in *Mission Klondike* (1978), the biography of Rev. Sinclair, which makes clear, often in Rev. Sinclair's own words, that he himself took the photographs. Several of these photographs appear in the 1907 booklet *The "Soapy" Smith Tragedy*, and their ownership is claimed by William Howard Case and Herbert Horace Draper. Their names are etched in the prints of the photographs. Case and Draper, as they were long known in Skagway (1898-1907*), likely purchased or traded for prints of Rev. Sinclair's photographs. *(in Skagway: Case, 1898-1920; Draper, 1901-13) Waugaman, pp. 31-34.

[6] Sinclair, p. 131. Regarding the photograph of Jeff astride his horse, until 1979, popularly believed was that this photograph had been taken three days earlier as Jeff rode in the July 4 parade.

[7] Brady to secretary of the interior, 07/07/1898. Interior department, Alaska territorial papers. Record Group 60. Federal Records Center, Seattle, Washington.

With Governor Brady was his seven-year-old son, Hugh. He later wrote that his father tried to strike a deal with Jeff. If Jeff would give up Skaguay, the governor would make him a deputy marshal at Sitka. Jeff is said to have respectfully declined.[1]

Jeff had been king of Skaguay. Those opposing him did so in secret. Then came the railway and a shift in the balance of power. Samuel Graves, the railway's president, was on site and later wrote a book about his experiences, *On The "White Pass" Pay-Roll* (1908). He recorded what he found in Skaguay in July 1898, no law except that of a criminal monarch with a military company acknowledged by the President of the United States. "The criminal element," Graves wrote,

> had the advantage of being thoroughly organized and armed, and skillfully led by a man named "Soapy" Smith, who was the uncrowned King of Skaguay. He was not a constitutional monarch, but his word was all the law there was. [Thus,] the criminal element ... had things all their own way, until the railroad builders began to oppose them on behalf of decency and order, and to form a nucleus round which the law-abiding element could rally."[2]

Independence Day showed that Jeff was popular with many of the merchants and residents, and perhaps even more powerful than the railroad men thought. They must have known that Jeff would not voluntarily abdicate his throne or resign from his military unit and move aside so that the railroad people could run things. A peaceful, non-violent surrender of Jeff's power would not take place. All they could do was wait along with the secret Committee of 101 for the right opportunity. Four days after the big July 4 celebration, the moment Jeff's enemies had been waiting for arrived.

Chapter 23
The Robbery

By God, trouble is what I'm looking for!

—Jefferson R. Smith II
July 8, 1898

Captain Henry Munn, an Artic explorer, who slept fitfully in Skaguay for six nights, reported "shooting on the streets every night."[3] Colonel Sam Steele, Superintendent of the North West Mounted Police, observed that "Skaguay at this period was about the roughest place in the world. ... At night the crash of bands, shouts of 'Murder!' [and] cries for help mingled with the cracked voices of the singers...."[4]

Merchants feared that reports, exaggerated or not, of Skaguay's criminal dangers would cause stampeders to choose other routes to and from the interior. Indeed, although other routes took up to three weeks longer than through Southeast Alaska, increasing numbers of Klondikers were already shipping their gold and were themselves returning from Dawson down the Yukon River to St. Michael on Norton

---

[1] *Lynn Canal News* 07/10/1980.
[2] Graves, p. 16.
[3] Munn, p. 75.
[4] Steele, pp. 295-296.

Sound and south by ship through the Bering Sea into the Pacific. Many, however, still returned via the Dalton overland trail or up the Yukon to Bennett and down the Chilkoot or White Pass trails to the deep-water port at Skaguay.

John Douglas Stewart was one of these. A miner in his early fifties, in 1897 he left his family in Nanaimo on Vancouver Island, British Columbia, for the Klondike. According to his daughter, Hazel Stewart Clark, in a 1958 article, he returned after "many months" of enduring "Claim jumpers, crude dwellings, monotonous food" and had "done well enough to improve his home, indulge his family somewhat and do a little traveling." Soon, however, in 1898, "he conceived the idea of going back to try again," this time with his cousin "for wages" in the Atlin area, which is in the extreme northwest corner of British Columbia, about 120 miles east of Skaguay over the White Pass and across and down lakes. This time Stewart did considerably better.[1]

In July 1898 he was making his way home when he met packer Calvin H. Barkdull at Bennett and said he wanted to go to Skaguay. Barkdull had "idle" pack animals,

> so I told him I would take him and his war bag to Skaguay for twenty dollars if he would pay for his own meals and lodging on the trail. He thanked me and gave me twenty dollars, and I gave him a good, sure-footed horse.... ... We arrived in Skagway about four p.m. July 7.... Stewart thanked me..., threw his war bag over his shoulder and went down town.[2]

Finding no immediate sailing available, for July 7 and 8, Stewart took room 55 in the Hotel Mondamin.[3] When Jeff Smith's Parlor opened for business in March 1898, Jeff took up residence in the Mondamin, room 61.[4]

Stewart had a canvas poke containing 158[14]/[17] ounces of gold that, according to court records, was worth $2,600.[5] *The Skaguay News* reported his gold worth $2,670 and $87 in cash in his pocket.[6] Stewart placed the gold in the safe at Kaufman's store.[7] In the morning Stewart would be robbed of all his gold and $76 in cash.

Accounts conflict on how Stewart was robbed but agree that they began on the morning of July 8, 1898. At approximately 10:00 a.m., Stewart met John Bowers and "Slim-Jim" Foster. Bowers represented himself as a buyer of gold for a large assaying company. Bowers and Foster feigned ignorance of the Klondike and pressed Stewart for information. Gaining the confidence of Stewart, they persuaded him to walk with them and, according to Stewart, led him into Jeff Smith's Parlor for a drink. Bowers asked if Stewart wanted to see "the bird eat," the bird being Fitzhugh Lee, but nothing more appears in Stewart's testimony about the eagle or the Parlor except that the

---

[1] Clark, pp. 40-41.

[2] Barkdull, p. 11.

[3] Hotel Mondamin register for July 1898.

[4] Evidence for residence there includes the following: Envelope addressed to Jeff in Skagway on which someone wrote "61," 03/27/1898, item 53, author's col. Envelope addressed to Capt. Jeff. R. Smith at box 61 06/16/1898, item 52, author's col. Hotel Mondamin register, 07/1898.

[5] Criminal case 1015-US v. W. E. Foster, Van B. Triplett, John Bowers. Record Group 21 – US District Courts. Box 16 – 01/01/05(2). National Archives and Records Administration, Pacific Alaska Region, Anchorage, Alaska.

[6] *Skaguay News* 07/08/1898, & 07/15/1898.

[7] *Tacoma Times* 12/27/1898.

three-card monte game and the robbery occurred in the saloon.[1] Stewart might have meant within the saloon area because witnesses say the events occurred in an alley beside the Parlor.

The most credible account of the robbery comes from three witnesses, first, a man and woman who heard everything that occurred through an open window in an adjoining building. Their story coincides with Stewart's except about where the events took place. According to them, Bowers and Foster led Stewart down the alley between Jeff Smith's Parlor and another building next to the Hotel Mondamin. Stewart was talking about the Klondike when "Old-Man" Triplett happened along and joined in the conversation. Triplett started talking about money he had lost in a gambling game and told how he had paid a gambler $5 to show him how the 3-card gambling trick was done and then offered to show the trick to the 3 men. Triplett pulled out 3 cards and began a game of three-card monte on a convenient box top. Foster said he knew how the trick was done and asked Stewart for $5 to bet against Triplett. At first Stewart demurred, but with a little coaxing, he pulled out his roll of cash amounting to $87. He planned to pull out $5 when Foster grabbed the whole roll and put it down, and with the turn of a card Triplett won all the money.[2] The remaining story of the robbery from the two witnesses match what Stewart stated on the witness stand.

> "I told Foster I should hold him for the money, and the old man, Van Triplett, said we acted as if we could not trust him, and gave some of the money back, and then said he would give us a chance to win it [all back], so Foster turned the right card and [Triplett] started to give him the money, but said, 'Supposing you had bet that in earnest, did you have the money to put up?' Foster said, 'No,' and turning to me said, 'You have the money,' and I said no, I did not have any money; that he took it all, but he said, 'You have some dust,' and wanted me to get it just to show the old man that we had the money in case the bet had been a real one. Bowers and I went to Kaufman's store to get the money and Van Triplett and Foster remained behind. We came back with the dust and I unrolled it and showed them the sack, and the old man said he did not know if that was gold, and Bowers said, 'Open it and show it to him, as he don't know gold dust when he sees it,' but I did not open it, and [was] just about to roll it up again, when Foster grabbed it and handing it to the old man, said, "Git!" and I started to grab the old man when they held me and said if I made a noise it would not be well for me. I pulled away from them and started after the old man, but could not see him and then went across the street and asked a party where there was an officer: that I had been robbed of $3,000 by some men over there."[3]

The third main witness, Abe L. Ritter, claimed to have seen Stewart scuffling in the alley with three men whom he knew to be members of the Soap Gang.

Stewart's daughter, Hazel Stewart Clark, told a different version based on what she said her father had told her. "It was in a hotel in Skagway, the day before his boat

---

[1] *Tacoma Times* 12/27/1898.
[2] *Daily Alaskan* 07/09/1898.
[3] *Tacoma Times* 12/27/1898.

was to sail, that he met two strangers" who convinced Stewart to put his gold in the hotel safe due to all the robberies. "This he did." The next morning, Stewart tried to claim his gold, "only to be told that there was nothing of his" in the safe. Then he was told that, "in fact, no one there had ever seen him before."[1] However the events occurred, one thing was certain. Stewart had lost everything.[2]

Next, according to the daughter, Stewart went to the deputy marshal, but he offered no help. At trial, Stewart was able to pick out the two men who had victimized him. Then the defense proceeded to assemble witnesses who testified to Stewart's lack of character and swore that he was a professional gambler who lived in Skaguay and had never been in the mining business.[3]

The daughter wrote that John Stewart's real story as she related it was never told in her father's lifetime (he died in 1930) because of a contract he had signed with a reporter for a San Francisco newspaper that gave the newspaper exclusive rights. The newspaper never published the story, and Stewart, faithful to his word, never spoke of it, except to his daughter.[4]

Stewart found Deputy Marshal Taylor, but he was of no help. Taylor told Stewart that if he would keep quiet for a time, he would see what could be done, and with that Taylor turned away and walked up the street with a carpenter to oversee work Taylor was having done on his new house.[5]

Stewart ran into the packer with whom he had come to Dyea, Calvin Barkdull, and told him what had happened. Barkdull could vouch that Stewart had had a sack of gold but could not say how much was in it. Barkdull went to his boss, Charles H. DeWitt, and relayed the story, to which DeWitt exclaimed, "My God! This won't do! If word gets down the river that the first man coming out by way of Skaguay was robbed, no one else will come this way."[6]

Commissioner Sehlbrede over in Dyea was apprised of the situation by telephone, and he promised to come over to Skaguay as soon as he could get a boat. "He telephoned back, asking that every precaution be taken to allay any agitation, so that he could be free to act when he came."[7]

As the day proceeded, Stewart and others told his story of robbery to anyone who would listen, and reactions were resentful and angry. Resident Harriet Pullen wrote,

> Quickly the feeling spread that at last the two forces were coming to conflict and that one or the other must prevail, and there was a great air of expectancy, the business men laying low and refusing to take sides, in order that they could take the side of the victors, no matter how the battle turned out.[8]

---

[1] Clark, p. 41.
[2] *Dyea Trail* 07/09/1898, p. 1.
[3] Clark, p. 41.
[4] Clark, p. 40.
[5] *Daily Alaskan* 07/09/1898.
[6] Barkdull, p. 45.
[7] *Daily Alaskan* 07/09/1898.
[8] Pullen, Harriet, p. 12.

Because of the time it took for the commissioner to arrive from Dyea, it was almost six p.m. before warrants could be placed in the deputy marshal's hands, and even then, the warrants were for two "John Doe's" and a Richard Roe, a person who remains unknown. Taylor surely knew whom the warrants were for, but he did nothing to perform the basics of his job. "To protect and serve" to Taylor meant Jeff, the Soap Gang, and himself. Throughout the day talk on the street had focused on the robbery. At the time of the incident, few knew who the guilty parties were, but the blame was being placed at Jeff's door. Rumors of impending violence spread, and numerous citizens opted to stay out of harm's way by staying indoors.

When Jeff learned of unrest over a robbery and rumors of his involvement, he took to the streets, mingled with the crowds, worked to placate concern. Probably he was dressed in his usual attire and for certain wore the silk ascot with the crossing US and Cuban flags sent to him by the admiring young woman in Seattle.[1] Claiming that no one had been robbed, Jeff's position was that Stewart had lost his gold in a square game. Between 2 and 6 p.m., according to the *Daily Alaskan*, "at least a dozen men went to Soapy Smith and tried to get him to disavow the robbery and give up the men." Jeff, however, maintained his position and "declined to do anything about the matter," finally stating in exasperation "that if Stewart had not 'hollered,' he [Smith] would feel like going out and getting him a piece of the money"[2] back. Jeff succeeded in convincing some that Stewart had not been robbed. According to *The Skaguay News*, in contrast with the *Alaskan*, Jeff told several businessmen he would make amends.

> During the early part of the excitement, Smith partially promised several men, including the writer, that ... [if there were] no "roar" made in the papers, the gold would be returned by 4 o'clock that evening, and that his influence would be used to prevent his men from in any way interfering with returning Klondikers in the future.[3]

During this period of turmoil, the vigilantes of the 101 regrouped. Members were split between two organizations, the Merchants' Committee and the Citizens' Committee.[4] Leaders of the Merchants' Committee approached the White Pass & Yukon Railway Company for help in ridding Skaguay of Jeff and his gang. Sensing serious trouble, the railroad dispensed firearms to some workers in the event of armed conflict. Seventeen officials of the Railway, including President Samuel Graves, attended a meeting of the Merchants' Committee, which elected Graves its chairman and determined to meet again that night at eleven. Graves sent two of his men, Heney and Hawkins, "up the Pass to prepare our camps for" what he termed the "hard fighting" that seemed "inevitable."[5] The Citizens' Committee called for a mass meeting of the town to be held that evening.

Inside the Parlor, Jeff was drinking. As witnessed by many in Colorado, when Jeff drank, he was dangerous. Venturing outside with some of his cohorts, Jeff walked to

---

[1] The ascot, complete with blood stains, is on display at the Skagway City Museum.
[2] *Daily Alaskan* Extra 07/11/1898, p.2.
[3] *Skaguay News* 07/15/1898, p. 1.
[4] After Jeff was killed, the Citizens' Committee absorbed the Merchants' Committee.
[5] Graves, p. 20.

the corner of Holly and Broadway and through a crowd of about twenty men. They were discussing the robbery, and someone said as Jeff passed that he was "such a coward that he had to have a gang of men with him." Jeff turned and faced the crowd "with an oath" and threatened "to litter the street with corpses. No one defied him...."[1]

Then there was Frank Reid. Louis K. Pratt, an attorney formerly of Denver, reported seeing an altercation between Jeff and Reid earlier that day, writing, "Jeff was armed and Reid was not, and was compelled to submit to abuse."[2]

Jeff had said the gold would be returned by four, but the hour passed with no word from Jeff. When told by a *Skaguay News* reporter that unless the gold was returned there would be trouble, Jeff is said to have replied, "By God, trouble is what I am looking for."[3]

As soon as Commissioner Sehlbrede arrived in Skaguay, he sent for Jeff to come to the marshal's office. Jeff arrived at six o'clock. There in the presence of the marshal and a *Daily Alaskan* reporter, Sehlbrede demanded that the gold and the men responsible be turned in. Jeff, however, stuck to his argument, saying that

> the boys who had the money won it in a fair game and they should keep it. He also said he had a hundred men who would stand behind him and see that they were protected. The judge finally told him he [Smith] could not afford to stand up for a gang of thieves; but he [Smith] almost screamed—"Well, Judge, declare me in with the thieves. I'll stay with them," and with that he passionately beat the table with his fist and left the room.[4]

Still seeking a peaceful resolution, an hour later Sehlbrede sent for Jeff again, and he came. This time Jeff offered to give up one of the men on the condition that Jeff could pick the prisoner's guards. Sehlbrede declined the offer. Presumably at this point, Jeff left the meeting, for Sehlbrede next got around to asking the men present in the room whether if he issued warrants, they would arrest Smith and his whole gang.[5] The reply was unanimous and emphatic: Jeff and every one of his men would be brought in. Sehlbrede added that "he wanted the men ... alive if possible, but dead if necessary."[6] His statement all but guaranteed bloodshed, and the town went wild at the news. Many feared violence while others were thirsting for it.

Violent rebellion against Jeff and the Soap Gang was eminent. Timely arrival in a new camp was crucial to taking control of it. Also crucial was a timely exit, especially in Jeff's trade. He had plenty of practice at making timely and successful exits from other towns, usually not much the worse for wear. Unfortunately for Jeff, however, when it came to clutch situations, he was bold and ready to fight for what he believed was his. Still, after making his stand, if required, he had often made timely escapes, such as when Col. Arkins received his punishment, when a bullet had found Cliff Sparks in

---

[1] *Daily Alaskan* Extra 07/11/1898.

[2] *Denver Times* 07/20/1898.

[3] Sinclair, p. 133, & *Skaguay News* 07/15/1898, p. 1. In *The News*, the line appears this way: "By ——, trouble is what I am looking or." [sic]

[4] *Daily Alaskan* 07/11/1898.

[5] *men present in the room:* the *Daily Alaskan* does not say who these men are.

[6] *Daily Alaskan* Extra 07/11/1898, p. 2.

Murphy's Exchange, and when Dick" Riddle had received a fatal bullet in J. O. Dalton's Houston saloon. In fact, Jeff may have had plans to exit Skaguay on an instant's notice should he fail to face down the escalating uproar. On July 8, from one Capt. S. E. Bright, Jeff had purchased the schooner *Janus*.[1]

Frederick Arthur Callerman was living in Skaguay. His brother, a machinist with the Railway, came to Frederick's room in the early evening of July 8 to announce that a posse was being assembled to arrest Soapy and his gang. Frederick declined to join, telling his brother that things were working up to a killing and he wanted no part of it. Frederick's brother replied that they were not to kill Soapy, just take him in.[2]

Citizens' Committee member J. T. Hayne, foreman of *The Skaguay News*, called for a meeting at Sylvester's Hall at 9 p.m. The *News* reported that with

> an ominous look worn by several hundred men..., a meeting was started in Sylvester's hall, but the space being inadequate to accommodate the crowd, an adjournment was taken to the Juneau dock....[3]

This dock, or wharf, was owned by the Skaguay Wharf Improvement Company. More commonly known as the Juneau Wharf, it was slightly south of the southern end of State Street. Skaguay had four wharfs at this time. First was Captain Moore's, which was against the bluff; second was the Alaska Southern's; and fourth, closest to the Skaguay River, was the Seattle Skaguay Wharf. The wharf to which the meeting adjourned was third in this array.[4]

At the meeting on the wharf, Thomas Whitten of the Golden North Hotel was elected chairman. Whitten appointed four men "to guard the approach to the dock in order that no objectionable characters might be admitted to disturb the deliberations of the meeting."[5] They were Captain Josias M. Tanner, Frank H. Reid, Jesse Murphy, and John Landers. They were an unarmed except for Reid, who had a .38 revolver somewhere on his person.[6]

Captain Josias Martin "Si" Tanner, age 48, acquired the title of captain while running steamers and barges to and from Skaguay.[7] Jesse Murphy was an Irishman from Portland, Oregon, who worked for the White Pass and Yukon Railway.[8] A J. Murphy is listed as a passenger on the *Queen* on its first 1897 run to Skaguay, and a Jesse A. Murphy is listed aboard the *Willamette* sailing for Skaguay from Seattle about a month later.[9] Nothing is known about John Landers.

Frank H. Reid, age 54, born in Peoria, Illinois, had been a schoolteacher in Oregon in 1877. In 1877, Reid served with Mart Brown's volunteer militia that crossed

[1] Probate paper on sale of ship. Skagway City Museum.
[2] Ltrs to the author fr Barbara Tacorda, daughter of Frederick Callerman, dated 02 and 03/1987.
[3] *Skaguay News* 07/15/1898, p. 1.
[4] "Map of Skaguay Alaska, U. S. A., March 8, 1898" (Spude, 46). The Juneau Wharf was also known as "the Third Wharf" (*Skagway News* headline 07/15/1898).
[5] *Skaguay News* 07/15/1898, p. 1.
[6] *Daily Alaskan* 07/11/1898.
[7] *Skagway News* (The Skaguay Alaskan) Summer tourist edition, 1995. Interview with Donald M. Tanner, grandson of Captain Josias Martin Tanner.
[8] *Morning Oregonian* 07/19/1898, p. 8, & Graves, p. 24.
[9] *Seattle Times* July 24, 1897, & *Seattle Post-Intelligencer* 08/29/1897, p. 3.

the Cascade range into the Eastern Oregon Blue mountains in the Piute Indian War.[1] On November 7, 1879, Reid shot and killed a neighbor, James Simons, during an argument near Sweet Home, Oregon. In a statement just before death, Simons told his side of the story. He had been walking to town with a load of wood in one arm and a stick in his other hand when Reid appeared carrying a cocked shotgun. Not on friendly terms, the two provoked one another. Simons said he did not talk to Reid's kind, and Reid replied that he would *make* Simons talk to him. Reid leaned his shotgun against a fence, and Simons dropped his armload of wood, keeping the stick in hand as the men continued arguing. When the distance between them grew close, Reid grabbed the shotgun and shot Simons. Reid fled but within a month returned to stand trial. Pleading self-defense, he was acquitted.[2]

As has been stated, Reid had bartended at the Klondike tent saloon in which Jeff is believed to have had an interest. With the equipment left at the Klondike by a needy stampeder, Reid went to work for the city council as a surveyor. If Reid had ever been "in" with Jeff, the council work caused him to realign with the Committee of 101.

Alaska historian C. L. Andrews, a post-Jeff Smith resident of Skaguay who had been Reid's student in Oregon, wrote that Frank Reid "was a quiet and determined" man.[3] But Andrews had not seen Reid since. Remembrances of him by Skaguay residents reflect a personality much rougher than that of a school teacher and civil engineer. Cecelia Selmer Price, a long-time historian of Skaguay, held the impression that "Reid was a crooked bartender at best."[4] Mabel Reed, who lived in Skaguay with her parents in 1897-98, knew Frank Reid and wrote in her *Skagway Memories* (1988) that he "had been known to have a very colorful vocabulary; he did a lot of swearing and using [of] foul language."[5] Royal Pullen, a Skaguay newsboy, was asked by members of the Smith family, "What kind of man was Reid?" He replied that he

> knew him as well as a youngster would know him. I never thought much of him. He was a tough individual. He was after the almighty dollar like anybody else..., and of course as I grew up I realized he wasn't too nice a character.[6]

So the some 200 outraged men who were meeting further down the Juneau Wharf assigned these 4 men to block anyone who might not be of the right frame of mind. Such a one would be Jeff Smith, who was moving toward them at a fast clip down State Street with a Winchester rifle. This was exactly the kind of set up that Jeff's enemies had been hoping for. All day Jeff had had opportunity to make amends or even leave Skaguay, but instead he chose not just to stand and fight but to face down a fevered mob alone. Three days before, one of Jeff's men had felt a change in people on the streets. He found Jeff and told him that he and another man "were overdue in Seattle." Jeff's reply: "You ain't got no nerve."[7] That surely was something

---

[1] Andrews, *Story*, p 307, fn 6, & Mayberry, pp. 18-19 & 42.
[2] Linn County records, 1880, State of Oregon v. Frank Reid.
[3] Andrews, *Story*, p. 196.
[4] Pullen, Royal, interview. Mrs. Price attended.
[5] Reed, p. 20.
[6] Pullen, Royal, recorded interview.
[7] Irwin, p. 171.

Jeff had plenty of, that and an all-or-nothing approach to things. Perhaps, though, Jeff did not realize just how enflamed his opposition had become. Moreover, fueled with alcohol and frustrated as he was at not being able to lay the Stewart robbery to rest, instead of talking down the mob, or even less likely, buffaloing it, had Jeff made it to the meeting, he might have fired it even hotter. Perhaps it was fate or just ill fortune that Jeff would first encounter a man who was infused with the mob's spirit. In response to a question about the tension between Frank Reid and Jeff, the latter's grandson, Joseph Smith, said, "Did you ever play king of the mountain? Those two were playing king of the mountain."[1]

A contest of wills may have been in the mix, but also more, a fate that lurks about certain men. Writing of that July 8 day in Skaguay, the *Morning Oregonian* ten days later caught its pulse, writing how "Iron nerve and nimble wit sustain" such men as Jeff

> through emergencies where less determined or resourceful spirits would succumb.... But soon or late, the day comes when the very devil is in the run of the cards, and nerves somehow seem unsteady.

Had that day come for Jeff, and further, as the *Oregonian* concluded, when "Luck, long a steady reliance, at last forsakes its protégé"?[2] In this case, a *yes* or *no* answer does not seem possible—just *maybe*.

Chapter 24
Shootout on the Juneau Wharf
My God, don't Shoot!

—Jefferson R. Smith II
July 8, 1898

When Jeff left his Parlor and as he quick-stepped along State Street to the Juneau Wharf, he probably thought he could bluff his way out of trouble. Jeff's fate, however, had already been sealed. Tension among the bunco men, the real estate grifters, and the vigilantes had been growing for some time. Now the breaking point was at hand. The confrontation would be explosive and deadly, and would unleash a mob of vigilante followers against the Soap Gang. The Citizens' Committee would emerge in control of the town. However, that control would depend on a bloody secret.

On the evening of July 8, 1898, most accounts put Jeff inside his Parlor saloon, drinking with friends and planning his next move. However, Dr. J. S. McCue later said he had been with Jeff "at a hotel just fifteen minutes before he went out to the wharf."[3] William "Bill" Saportas as a reporter for the *Daily Alaskan* was one of Jeff's men who could attend vigilante meetings and report their activity to Jeff. Sometime around 9 p.m., Saportas came to Jeff and slipped him a note that read, "'the crowd is angry, if you want to do anything do it quick.' ... [signed] 'S.'"[4] Jeff stuffed the note in his pocket

---

[1] Smith, Joseph interview, 07/02/1977.

[2] *Morning Oregonian* 07/18/1898, p. 4.

[3] *RMN* 01/28/1900. This might have been the Hotel Mondamin, just around the corner from Jeff's Place.

[4] Wickersham, p. 23.

and decided to face down the vigilantes by confronting them at their meeting place. Said to be well under the influence of alcohol, Jeff grabbed a Winchester model 1892 .44-40 rifle and possibly his Colt model 1889 New Army .41 caliber double action revolver.[1] With 6 or 7 of his men following at a distance, he walked west on Holly to State Street and turned south toward the Juneau Wharf 6 blocks away.

This wharf, between 15-to-20-feet wide, came straight in over the mud and gravel beach at a height of 10 to 6 feet.[2] At the wharf entrance, John Landers was talking with another man. About 60 feet down the wharf against the west railing, Josias Tanner and Jesse Murphy stood near one another. Frank Reid stood further on, alone, a short distance from Tanner and Murphy. The men were to identify Soap Gang members and prevent them from coming to the meeting then in progress "at a point half way to" Sperry's "ware house...."[3]

Three of the four men on guard were reportedly unarmed. Clarence L. Andrews, writing in a 1947 article, identified himself as a Skaguay resident who knew Commissioner Sehlbrede and Tanner as a deputy US marshal and who listened to the stories of the men of Skaguay for five years. Andrews wrote that Reid's weapon "was a .38 Smith & Wesson,"[4] and the newspapers reported that it was a .38. Years later Matthew M. Sundeen, age 33 in 1898, wrote that,

> Reid carted an old Smith and Wesson six-shooter, an ancient gun he had used in the rip-roaring days of the west and which he considered the best gun in Skagway. He said it never failed him but its failure finally cost his life.[5]

Sometime between 9 and 9:30 p.m.,[6] Jeff approached the wharf entrance. He held his rifle almost casually over his right shoulder, the muzzle pointing upwards and to the rear. At the entrance, Jeff stopped, and the men who followed came up to him. They remained there as Jeff proceeded alone up the center of the wharf. It is said he advanced without hesitation, cursing. Approaching Landers and the other man, Jeff ordered them off the wharf. They obeyed, jumping over the side to the beach about six feet below. Andrews wrote that these men, named Brownell and Singfeld, went under the wharf.[7] Jeff continued, passing Tanner and Jesse Murphy without addressing them, nor did they offer resistance, and kept right on toward Frank Reid, who called out, "Halt, you can't go down there." Tanner later said he did not recognize Jeff until he heard him speak.[8] Witnesses claimed Reid and Jeff argued for a few seconds, swearing at one another,[9] but none agreed on what was said.

---

[1] *Winchester.* serial # 66224, manufactured in 1894, in the Smith family collection. *.41 ... revolver.* this weapon was not reported as being on Jeff's person at the time of his death.

[2] Pullen, Royal, recorded interview.

[3] *Skaguay News* 07/08/1898, p. 1.

[4] Andrews, "Real," p. 38 & 40.

[5] *Fairbanks Daily News Miner* 06/23/1941, p.5.

[6] *Skaguay News* 07/08 & 15/1898 states fight occurred at 9:30 p.m. while the *Daily Alaskan* 07/11/1898 states the fight occurred at 9:00 p.m.

[7] Andrews, "Real," p. 39.

[8] US v. (1) Turner Jackson and George Wilder.

[9] *Daily Alaskan* 07/09/1898.

Generally believed is that at this point Reid still had his revolver tucked away and that Jeff still had the Winchester shouldered, but about what happened in the few seconds before gunfire erupted, accounts differ greatly. Reid may have shown Jeff that he was armed. Some claimed Reid drew his weapon first while others claim Reid did not draw until Jeff attempted to shoot him.

Jeff suddenly swung his rifle off his shoulder and struck at Reid.[1] Whether intending to shoot at that moment or to club Reid aside is uncertain. Reid raised his left arm to block the fast-approaching barrel. It struck and cut his arm, but he managed to grab the barrel and yank it away from the general direction of his head and press it downward.[2] The *Daily Alaskan* wrote that Reid grabbed the rifle barrel without being cut but that during the scuffle Jeff pulled it free and hit Reid's arm as he swung the rifle at Reid again.[3] Now the men were face-to-face, inches apart. Had Jeff meant to shoot Reid, he would have taken a position at least a few feet from Reid, far enough to aim his rifle. Therefore, one view is that Jeff intended to stun Reid, if need be, with a blow to the head. Using a pistol or rifle as a club was not uncommon in the frontier west.

When Reid grabbed the rifle barrel with his left hand and pressed it down, with his right he drew his revolver (if not already drawn) and pointed it at Jeff. At that moment Jeff is said to have shouted, "My God, don't shoot!" Reid, however, pulled the trigger. The result was a heart-stopping click. The hammer had fallen on a faulty cartridge. Reid tried to shoot again as Jeff jerked his rifle from Reid's desperate grasp.[4]

Both men fired in near perfect unison. It sounded to some as if one shot had been fired. "One witness said it looked as if the guns were spitting fire at the same time."[5] Then a number of shots followed, ranging between five and nine according to different testimonies. As reports tell of a total of five entry wounds in the two men, the minimum number of shots fired had to be five. The exchange occurred very rapidly. Reid received a bullet to one leg. Reid fired two more rounds, one grazing Jeff's left arm and the other striking his left thigh above the knee and exiting the other side. Chambering his Winchester, Jeff sent a bullet into Reid's lower abdomen and groin.[6] With his upper body buckling forward from the impact, Reid fell face down upon the planking, severely wounded. The fight between the men was over.

Uncertain at this time is whether Jeff was standing or also had fallen. The stock of his rifle was broken when received by the widow, which indicates that either it was broken in Jeff's fall or later, possibly in some purposeful act of vandalism or rage.

Seconds after the shooting ended, Jeff's men bolted toward their wounded leader, weapons drawn. Murphy rushed over to Jeff and grabbed his Winchester. Judge Wickersham believed Murphy picked up the rifle from the ground where Jeff had dropped it.[7] Matthew Sundeen was on the scene talking with the guards moments

---

[1] *Daily Alaskan* 07/09/1898.
[2] *Daily Alaskan* 07/09/1898.
[3] *Daily Alaskan* 07/09/1898.
[4] *Daily Alaskan* 07/09/1898.
[5] Andrews, "Real," p. 39.
[6] *Daily Alaskan* 07/09/1898.
[7] Wickersham, p. 22.

after the fight,[1] and others, like John F. Greene and a Mr. Schwartz, claimed that Murphy wrestled the rifle from Jeff's hands.[2] At this point, as stated by eyewitnesses, including Murphy himself,[3] Murphy turned the rifle on Jeff. The author believes this is the moment when Jeff said, "My God, don't shoot!" But Murphy pulled the trigger and sent a bullet through Jeff's heart, killing him instantly.

Murphy then, faced with the charging gang members, raised the rifle toward them and took aim. Coming up on the scene, W. H. Jackson with revolver in hand, pointed it at Tanner,[4] who testified that Jackson was "possibly twenty or thirty feet" away.[5] At that time Tanner was unarmed and could do nothing but watch, surely expecting to be fired upon, but Jackson did not fire. In his testimony later, Jackson did not know Tanner and that he had pointed his gun at "somebody that stood on the corner of the wharf."[6] Murphy was aiming Jeff's rifle at the gang as members of the vigilante meeting came running to see what had happened. Someone yelled out, "They have killed Soapy; and if you don't clear out quick they will kill you too."[7] Not wanting to engage in a gun battle in which they were vastly outnumbered, the gang slowed up, stopped, backed away, wheeled, and fled.

This is the author's long-considered view of how the shootout on the Juneau Wharf occurred. It is *not* how the official version was presented then nor how it has been presented for over a hundred years. That version, simply, is that in the exchange of gunfire, Frank Reid fired the heart-piercing bullet that killed Jeff Smith. How and why Reid could not have killed Jeff, based on strong authority, is simply explained.

After the gang had fled, Andrews relates how Tanner rushed over to Reid and asked for his pistol, which lay under him. Reid replied that he was badly hurt, but he managed to roll off his gun. Andrews wrote, "Tanner took it. Except for two empty shells and one unexploded cartridge it was empty."[8] Apparently Reid's pistol that day had but three cartridges in it, only two of which had been fired at Jeff. As would come to light the next day, however, Jeff's body had received three bullet wounds.

The following morning the *Daily Alaskan* led with a headline that was probably in its largest font: "Arch Desperado Dead." The headlines of *The News* read, "Soapy Smith's Last Bluff Called By Frank Reid." Details presented by both papers differed greatly, and this was just the beginning of differing and ever-changing stories of what happened that July 8, 1898, in Skaguay. Many years later Jeff's son clipped a story that reflected past tellings of that story and that heralded numerous variations to come.

Many garbled and highly purpled are the versions of this incident given by various historians. So many accounts have been told and so many

---

[1] *Fairbanks Daily News Miner* 06/23/1941, p. 5.
[2] *Morning Oregonian* 07/19/1898, p. 8. And *The Sun* (New York) 10/25/1908, p. 9.
[3] *Morning Oregonian* 07/19/1898, p. 8.
[4] US v. (1) Turner Jackson and George Wilder.
[5] Federal Reporter, p. 485.
[6] Federal Reporter, p. 482.
[7] *Daily Alaskan* 07/11/1898.
[8] Andrews, "Real," p. 40.

refutations of the story have been made to tourists in Skagway that there is no one now who is sure of anything about that day, except for the outcome.[1]

It is not possible to tell in what order the gunshot wounds were received, but it can be shown that Reid and Smith dealt out and received relatively minor wounds before each received one serious enough to end their fight with one another. Reid received a bullet to one of his legs, believed to be the left, but the fight-ending shot for him was the one down through the abdomen into the groin. It sent him face forward onto the wharf, seriously and painfully injured. Nevertheless, Skaguay newspapers and most vigilante accounts report Reid then fired one or more further shots at Jeff and that it was one of these that delivered his instantaneous death. However, when shown the information that is known about Reid's groin wound, Major R. O. "Slim" Ackerman, the gun editor for *Real West* magazine, wrote,

> It is unlikely that anyone could do all of that additional shooting after taking a .44-40 in the groin.... The .44-40 is a heavy bullet. For an early one, it had good shocking power at such close range. Reid would have been doubled up pretty badly. As an army officer and as a Federal agent, I've seen enough men shot to vouch for that....[2]

The Skaguay News reported that Jeff had been struck by three bullets, one of which entered the anterior (front) surface of the left leg, a third of the way between the knee and hip. The wound extended horizontally through the limb. That was one bullet. A second bullet grazed the left arm near the elbow but did not penetrate the skin. It is clearly seen in one of the post mortem photos. That was a second bullet. Then there is a third bullet, the one that ended Jeff's life. It entered three inches to the left of the left nipple, going "clean through the body, making its exit under the left shoulder blade and piercing the center of the heart during its course. Death was therefore instantaneous."[3]

However, the *Daily Alaskan* reported that the deadly bullet entered Jeff's chest on the right side, passed straight through, and exited the left side of the body under the armpit.[4] Photographs of the autopsy do show the bullet wound under the left armpit, but it cannot be told whether it is an entrance or exit wound.

On the dock Reid was semi-conscious when crowds from the meeting reached him. He is reported to have asked, "Did I get him?" and was told he had. Several men went for a stretcher and returned with a makeshift one, and shortly a dozen men carried Reid toward his house. When doctors Moore, Cornelius, and Bryant met them and took a quick look at Reid, they ordered him taken to the hospital, but they quickly changed their minds and ordered that a room be found at once. Mr. Brogan of the Occidental Hotel "told the doctors to take the house." Reid was carried to an upstairs room where his wounds were tended.[5] In great pain, Reid was administered morphine and at his request his leg was massaged.[6] He was next moved to Dr. Moore's office

---

[1] Unknown and undated newspaper clipping, author's col.
[2] Ltr to the author fr Major R. O. Ackerman, 06/10/1986.
[3] *Skaguay News* 07/15/1898.
[4] *Daily Alaskan* 07/09/1898.
[5] *Daily Alaskan* 07/09/1898.
[6] *Daily Alaskan* 07/11/1898.

where he could be properly examined. About five the next morning, Dr. Whiting, the railroad surgeon who had been sent for, operated on Reid. He found that the bullet had entered two inches above the groin on the right side and exited one inch to the right of the tip of the spinal column. Later reported was that "The pelvis or hip bone was shattered and he [Whiting] took out a dozen pieces of splintered bone."[1] Before probing began, Reid asked for a cigar, which he received, "And this he calmly smoked while the shattered fragments of his anatomy were being removed."[2]

The following day, Reid was taken to Bishop Rowe Hospital, and as the days passed, hope grew that Reid would recover.

> Considering the terrible nature of his wound he is progressing most favorably and will, it now can be said, undoubtedly recover. He heard with pleasure the finding of the jury justifying the shooting, but it was with no feelings of relief as he had no misgivings of his own upon the subject. "I could not have done differently..., and therefore have no regret to bother me."[3]

On the night of his death, Jeff had lain where he fell for sometime, blood from his wounds drenching the wooden planks beneath. In time, the stain became a an "attraction." So was it pointed out to George Pringle in 1901 by a tour guide:

> "You'll have to see the spot where Soapy died." The Skaguay man who said this was rather proud of the celebrity which the bandit had brought to the place. ... I judged by my friend's tone that he expected me to be deeply impressed with this particular sight. So down to the sea we went and out on the wharf. As we walked down he outlined the story of Smith's career in the camp. On the pier he showed me a dark stain, covering about a square foot, made by the life-blood of the man who for half-a-year forced Skaguay to pay him a tribute in hard cash.[4]

The *Daily Alaskan* reported that "After Reid had been attended to, Judge Sehlbrede went down to the wharf to view Smith's body." Bobby Sheldon, a newspaper boy in 1898, remembered Jeff's body on the wharf:

> He was sprawled out with his Stetson lying there, but nobody dared put his feet together or place his hands over his heart. They didn't dare show sympathy for fear somebody would pull out a gun.[5]

Commissioner Sehlbrede assigned five men to guard the body and later "ordered them to remove it to the undertaking establishment...."[6] This was Ed R. Peoples undertaking parlor at Broadway and Johnson Street (8th Avenue today).[7]

---

[1] *Daily Alaskan* Extra 07/11/1898, p. 2.

[2] *Skaguay News* 07/15/1898.

[3] *Daily Alaskan* Extra 07/11/1898, p. 1.

[4] Pringle, pp. 241-42. George Pringle was in Skaguay for a day before heading to Dawson for the Canadian Presbyterian Church (Mills, p. 76).

[5] Sheldon, interview, 1973.

[6] *Daily Alaskan* Extra 07/11/1898, p. 2.

[7] Address advertised in undated (pre-05/02/1898) Empire Theater program. Item 117, author's col. "Johnson Street" is 8th Avenue today.

Royal Pullen in an interview with the Smith family told a different story about the removal of Jeff's body from the wharf. He said that the woman who had been living with Jeff paid four men a hundred dollars each to remove the body.

> You see, nobody would touch Soapy after he was shot. ... They were just scared to touch him. This woman came down ... and she offered one hundred dollars a piece if they'd carry him off, and they did. They took him down to the morgue. Cost her four hundred bucks according to the story.... That was the story that went around. I don't know how much they got.

When asked by members of the Smith family who the woman was, Pullen responded,

> I don't know, I didn't know her. I knew her at the time, sure. She was just one of the red light district women he was living with. Each of these men had their own woman up there.[1]

The end of the story is not disputed, that Jeff died in an instant on the Juneau Wharf that night and that Frank Reid was so badly wounded in the groin area that he suffered greatly for twelve days before he too died. But who killed Jeff Smith is not settled. Witnesses cannot be relied upon because they have proven to be too numerous and too various. As Clarence Andrews, Skaguay resident from 1898 to 1903, wrote in 1947, "If all the men who claimed to have seen the shooting of Soapy Smith were laid end to end, the line would extend to the equator and back again."[2] To examine some of these witness accounts, however, and to examine the evidence and authorities who have commented on it are profitable and interesting exercises. In a history that has taken as its guiding star honesty about the nature of the man at the center of a myth, at stake is something far more valuable than gold—the truth.

Chapter 25

Witnesses and Accounts of the Gunfight

"Nonsense," I said, "He's only bluffing."

—Samuel H. Graves
President of the White Pass & Yukon Route[3]

Without doubt, the gunfight on the Juneau Wharf had witnesses. That there were more than just a few witnesses is doubtful. Over the years, however, many witnesses have come forward. Most have repeated the official story while others have added to the event, some with descriptions so preposterous that it is hard to believe the storyteller had ever been to Alaska let alone been a witness. So many varying accounts make all of them suspect. Whatever pieces of truth may be in them seem hopeless mixed with exaggerations, half-truths, and lies.

Perhaps one of the most famous residents to claim to have seen the gunfight was Skaguay pioneer Harriet Pullen and her youngest son, Royal. Fearing trouble might be at hand that evening, she had taken her youngest son, Royal, and gone looking for her

---

[1] Pullen, Royal, recorded interview.
[2] Andrews, "Real," p. 38.
[3] Graves, p. 23.

twelve-year-old, Dan. In her version, she was approaching the wharf when "Soapy" passed her, "carrying his Winchester and remarking to himself, 'I'll fix them.'" In her version, she wrote how Jeff was

> Almost immediately ... challenged by Reid, who called "Halt!" Soapy apparently had not noticed Reid up to this time, as he immediately halted and cried out, "My God, don't shoot!" Reid, however, immediately aimed his Colt and pulled the trigger. The gun, however, misfired, and just as he was about to fire again Soapy raised his Winchester and the two guns roared almost simultaneously.

Then occurred "a mad stampede ... all over town," Reid was carried away,

> and before I could realize what had happened my son Royal and I were practically alone with the dead outlaw. One or two men approached but passed on, one man in particular kicking him as he passed. Then it was that my small son, not half as scared as I was, pulled me by the hand up to where the dead bandit lay and looking him in the face exclaimed, "Why Mamma, that is the man that bought all us kids candy, and now he's dead!"[1]

Robert "Bobby" Sheldon was 90 years old in 1973 when the author and his father, John Randolph Smith, met with him. Sheldon said he witnessed the argument between Smith and Reid and saw Smith point his rifle at Reid, saw Reid grab the barrel with his left hand, and saw Reid reach for his own revolver with his right. This witness also said Smith was the first to fire and that Reid fired 3 shots before both men collapsed on the dock. However, 4 years later when interviewed by Klondike Gold Rush National Historical Park officials, Sheldon changed his story considerably.

> I was about fifty yards away. Mrs. Bert McKenzie, the wife of the engineer on the passenger train, was right near me when she heard the shot. She put her hand on my shoulder and said, "We better be getting out of here and maybe go into the Sylvester building. We don't know what direction those bullets are going to be going." But ... no other bullets came our way and we didn't go into the building. But finally after it was all quieted down and Soapy was dead.... [tape ends][2]

Railway President Samuel Graves also claimed to have been a witness. He and Frank Herbert Whiting, a Railway superintendent, had been to see that "1500 tons of rails and sleepers" were being unloaded from a ship at the Alaska Southern Wharf, which ran between the Juneau and Moore wharves. Returning, they

> noticed the crowd assembling on the other wharf for the mass meeting, but neither of us paid any attention to it till we had left our wharf and were in the street leading to the wharf the crowd was on.
>
> We were about 50 yards from the two men holding the entrance, and the crowd was about 75 or 80 yards farther on down the wharf when suddenly Whiting said, "By the lord, here comes 'Soapy'—now look out!" "Nonsense," I said, "He's only bluffing." While I was speaking, he passed near enough to

---

[1] Pullen, Harriet, pp. 12-13.
[2] Sheldon, interview, 1977.

touch me. He was ostentatiously armed with a couple of big revolvers and a belt of cartridges across his arm, as he shouted at the crowd to "chase themselves home to bed."

I stood laughing till I saw he was followed about 25 yards behind by a bodyguard of 14 of his picked men who were grimly silent and displayed no arms, though they were notoriously always armed to the teeth. These men followed "Soapy" past me and shut out my view, so I moved to the sidewalk and saw Soapy go up to Reid and make a bluff to hit him over the head with the barrel of his rifle. Reid put up one hand and protected his head by catching the barrel. "Soapy," failing to shake off Reid's hold, jerked back the rifle suddenly, which brought the muzzle against Reid's stomach. Reid still held Soapy's rifle with one hand as before, but he put the other slowly in his coat pocket, and without taking it out again commenced to shoot his revolver. "Soapy" at the same instant began to pump shots from his Winchester into Reid's stomach.

It would be impossible to say which fired first, the shots were absolutely simultaneous. Each fired four shots, though one of Reid's first shots had gone clean through Soapy's heart. It was not murder so much as a sort of spontaneous killing. Neither man had any intention of killing…, but they must have seen death in each other's eyes at the last moment and both fired together. They fell together in a confused heap on the planking of the wharf, "Soapy" of course stone dead, and Reid dying. It all happened in an instant.[1]

Graves tells the reader that he has been quoting from reports he had written to his company. Then Graves links a Railway employ, Jesse Murphy, to Jeff's shooting. Graves in his report even puts Jeff's rifle into the employee's hands.

Meanwhile, his bodyguard were within 25 yards of the two prostrate men and of the remaining entrance keeper, a little Irishman named Murphy who worked for us. When his guards saw "Soapy" fall, they gave a ferocious yell and drew their "guns" (as they call their heavy revolvers), and sprang forward for vengeance on the unarmed crowd, and it looked as if what I had mistaken for a comedy was going to become a shambles. But the little Irishman was the right man in the right place and rose to the emergency, as our White Pass men have a way of doing. "Begob, Sorr," he said to me an hour later, "I had nawthing but a pencil whin I saw thim tigers making jumps for me." But he had his quick wits, and like a flash he had snatched "Soapy's" Winchester from the dead man's hands, and the leader "Tiger" saw Murphy's eye gazing at him along the sights. Involuntarily, the "Tiger" checked his rush and was passed by another of the Guards. That instant Murphy shifted his sights and covered the new leader, and the same thing happened. By the time he had in turn covered a third leader, the "tigers" behind realized that the three or four first of them were sure to be shot and they were not in such a hurry somehow. Then the men in front realized that they were not being supported

---

and looked round to see why—the rush was over, and in another moment the whole fourteen "Tigers" broke and fled.

At that instant the crowd on the wharf, that had stood paralyzed with terror, became a blood thirsty pack of wolves and with a yell they started in pursuit, unarmed. It was lucky that I had moved aside on to the sidewalk. The "Tigers" swept past me and in another moment the crowd, jumping over the dead "Soapy" and the dying Reid in their mad rush, tore by me yelling "Get your guns, citizens."[1]

The evidence, insofar as it is possible to ascertain, strongly suggests that Graves omitted some important seconds of time, probably no more than ten. The omission probably occurred after Murphy took the rifle from Jeff's hands and before he aimed it at Jeff's men, who were approaching on the run from the wharf entrance. Murphy saw the fire fight between Reid and Smith and saw Reid face down, apparently gravely wounded. The wound to the upper leg probably caused Smith to fall but not lose consciousness, and Smith's men were coming on the run, weapons drawn, according to Graves. So Murphy pulled the rifle from Jeff's hands or picked it up, fired into Jeff's torso, and turned the rifle on the approaching gang members. Given this scenario, seen by Jeff's men and by Tanner, Murphy's co-guard, what Tanner said next (as Andrews implies was told to him by Tanner) had tremendous impact: "They've got Soapy and they'll get you next."[2] Jeff's men had just seen Murphy shoot Jeff point blank, saw 200 men on down the wharf about 150-to-200 feet, poised to rush forward, and saw Murphy with the same rifle aimed directly at them. Of course they ran. Chased by the mob on the pier, which as Graves writes, had become "a blood thirsty pack,"[3] Jeff's men ran for their lives.

Also given new meaning by this scenario is a sentence in Graves' report that seems misplaced in the chronology of events. In the report, Graves applies a curious evaluative statement to the instantaneous shooting between Smith and Reid, how it was not murder but a "spontaneous killing." What makes it curious is how it obviously was not spontaneous but incremental. The two men had had "words" earlier, had more words on the wharf, and scuffled. Then by most reports, Reid fired first on Smith, but the weapon misfired, a point Graves leaves out of his report. Instead, he tends to slant the fairness of the exchange against Reid by indicating Reid fired without drawing his weapon from within his pocket. How could Graves' possibly have seen that from, as he writes, "50 yards from the two men"[4]? The men did come to the point of shooting it out in short order, but not "spontaneously." So why did Graves choose the words "spontaneous killing"? Was he seeking to help Reid? Probably not. Having arrived in Skaguay only seven days before, Graves likely did not know Reid. Graves writes that he had written and submitted the report on July 9, the day after the event, but no word appears about Reid's tenuous condition. Further, Graves in his book, written ten years later, does not mention Reid again, the man upon whose tombstone is inscribed "He

[1] Graves, pp. 24-26.
[2] Andrews, "Real," p. 40.
[3] Graves, 26.
[4] Graves, p. 23.

gave his life for the Honor of Skagway." No, Graves neither knew Reid nor did he "honor" him.

But Graves did know Murphy, or at least learned who he was shortly after the shooting. Murphy was an employee of the Railway of which Graves was president. He also bestows "honors" on "the little Irishman" by writing that he "was the right man in the right place and rose to the emergency, as our White Pass men have a way of doing."[1] Other considerations are to be measured, but Graves' connection to Murphy could have influenced Graves' decision to leave those important few seconds out of his report, the time in which an excited Murphy in fear of the armed and conscious Smith and of his approaching armed men, took Smith's rifle, put a bullet through Smith's heart, and turned the rifle on Smith's men. To describe such a sequence of events, Graves' evaluation seems right: "It was not murder so much as a sort of spontaneous killing."[2] Graves in his report, though, did not apply the words to Murphy but to Reid and Smith. Spontaneous as Murphy's shooting of Smith might have been, it was the intentional killing of a wounded, unarmed man. Presented with those facts, it seems likely that a fair-minded grand jury would likely have return a true bill of murder.

————

On Saturday, July 9, Commissioner Sehlbrede ordered an inquest at Peoples' undertaking rooms into the cause of Jeff's death. A limited post mortem surgical examination (as an *autopsy* is defined) was performed by Dr. C. W. Cornelius[3] of Skaguay and Dr. Fenton B. Whiting, chief surgeon for the White Pass and Yukon Railway hospital.[4] A coroner's jury of five "leading citizens," according to *The Skaguay News*, attended the post mortem and then worked through the day, calling witnesses and sifting evidence, with only one adjournment, "for luncheon," "...until nearly half past four...." Then the jury findings were announced, that death was instantaneous "by reason of a pistol wound piercing the heart" and that Frank H. Reid fired it in self-defense.[5]

Rev. John Sinclair also attended the inquest and witnessed sections of the autopsy. In his diary for Saturday, July 9, 1898, he wrote that he went to the inquest for awhile, "taking my camera along to get a picture. But Mr. O'Donnell,[6] solicitor for the deceased, had had U. S. Commissioner Sehlbrede order that no photos be taken." When the adjournment for lunch came, however, O'Donnell came to Sinclair and asked him to "conduct a funeral service for Smith next Monday, promising to pay me well for it." Rev. Sinclair "complied" but refused payment.

> When he insisted, I told him I would much prefer some relic such as Soapy's small derringer pistol which he always carried with him in a holster concealed

---

[1] Graves, p. 25.
[2] Graves, p. 24.
[3] Dr. Cornelius advertised in a program for the Empire Theater as a Physician and Surgeon with an office on the corner of Main and Holly streets. Item 117, undated (pre-05/02/1898), author's col.
[4] Minter, p. 178.
[5] *Skaguay News* 07/09/1898 & 07/15/1898, p. 1. Not 5 but 6 jurors took part—their names listed elsewhere.
[6] *O'Donnell:* advertised in *Daily Alaskan*, "O'Donnell & Weldon. / Attys-at-Law. / Occidental Hotel Building."

under the waistband of his trousers. O'Donnell at once agreed he would secure the derringer for me. I am happy to have it as there is no doubt it will be an interesting souvenir and much sought after.

O'Donnell later "came quietly" to Sinclair and said that because he "was a clergyman," he could take photographs for his "own private use. "So," wrote Sinclair, "I have negatives of the corpse, one very lifelike with eyes open, one showing the breast exposed and surgeons conducting the post mortem and the third showing the bullet wounds.[1]

This author strongly suspects Sinclair was tricked into accepting a false relic when he was given the derringer. Sinclair's son wrote that Jeff's widow gave the derringer to Sinclair; however, Mary fought hard to collect and obtain everything belonging to her husband. She was never known to give anyone anything that had belonged to her husband except to her children and grandchildren. Further, Mary's stories never included having given Rev. Sinclair a weapon having belonged to her husband. The derringer is a Colt's model 1872 (Thuer model), .41-rimfire caliber and was not listed with Jeff's personal effects. What is most suspicious about it is that it is a rimfire model, which in 1898 was long outdated. Center-fire ammunition came out in 1873. As a man of the modern age, Jeff could easily afford a newer, reliable weapon for protection. His two known weapons are the rifle he died with and a double action revolver, both modern, well made weapons. That Jeff would carry an antique for self-protection is not believable. It should also be noted that the chance of purchasing rimfire ammunition for that particular derringer in 1898 Skaguay would have been slim to none.

Jeff died without a will, so on July 16, 1898, John E. Clancy was appointed administrator of Jeff's estate, estimated not exceeding $250 in value.[2] By July 22, Charles Hansen, L. Guthrie, and H. E. Battin (one of the leaders of the Citizens' Committee) were appointed as "three disinterested persons" to undertake appraisal of the estate, which was accomplished by August 6. Listed were the following:

Money ($88.60) An undivided one-half interest in one lot on the NE Corner of Hobart and Broadway streets.... ($35.00) 1 Watch (Given to Mrs. Smith) 1 Colts Revolver ($7.50) 1 Winchester rifle (Broken, $2.50) Fixtures and stock in saloon known as Jeff Smith's Parlor on Holly Street... ($277.50) Liabilities of saloon ($636.15) J. R. Smith's one-half interest in same (_____) Trunk and Contents ($15.00) Recapitulation: Personal Property: $148.60 Real Estate: None Total: $148.60[3]

That so little was appraised and appraised so unclearly make it a good guess that much of what Jeff had owned in Skaguay was stolen. Conveniently, fees accruing to Jeff's estate by July 21 for administrating Jeff's death amounted to the exact amount of cash found on Jeff's person. Charges included

---

[1] Sinclair, pp. 135-136.
[2] Probate Book A 1898-1903, pp. 51-52
[3] Probate Book A 1898-1903, pp. 53-54.

Coroner and Summoning Jury ($15) Jury ($6) Stenographer at Inquest ($10) Autopsy ($15) Probate Court Fees ($15) [Subtotal] $61. Amount turned over to R. P. Weldon, Atty. for Administration ($27.60) [Grand Total] $88.60.[1]

The cost of the funeral ($100) and the total "expenses of administration" and the inquest came to a total of $191.00. As the official recapitulation listed the value of Jeff's estate at only $148.60, on August 10, 1898, Commissioner Sehlbrede ordered the sale of Jeff's personal property to satisfy the debt.[2]

On September 21, 1898, Clancy asked Commissioner Sehlbrede to discharge him from his duties as administrator. The request appears in Probate records as a written statement, a kind of report, to the court, which is entered as a "Final account." It appears to be written in Sehlbrede's hand and probably based on a conversation with Clancy. It contains legalize ("Comes now, "above entitled," "prays," "Honorable court") that saloon owner Clancy would not have used, and no attorney's name associated with the document. That Sehlbrede himself composed the "Final Account" and wrote it directly into the official Probate Book is suggested by small errors, such as repeated or omitted words. The commissioner was likely willing to undertake the matter "on the spot" because Clancy, as the document indicates, "will be compelled to leave the District of Alaska in a few days."

A few points of interest appear in this "Final account." It states that the administrator "took charge of all the property of the said deceased that the administrator could get knowledge of." This language suggests other property about which it was thought "knowledge of" could not be gained. The document states that the sum of $148.60 was applied to the "liabilities of the said estate, accruing since the death of the said deceased, amount to the sum of $190.00"[3] and that the balance had been paid out of the administrator's own money. It states

> That the widow of said deceased has made a trip to Skaguay Alaska, for the purpose of investigating the management of said estate, and full opportunities have been allowed her by the administrator for so doing, and ... has even proposed to allow the said widow or anyone else interested to take the entire property left by the said deceased if the person so taking the same would [a]gree to settle the bills as aforesaid; but so far as the administrator knows—everyone interested is satisfied with his management of said estate.[4]

Not known is if Mary was apprised of this offer or if she knew what remained of Jeff's possessions or what price might have been quoted to her. Eventually several personal items were given to her and her son before she left town, including his watch, the broken rifle Jeff used against Reid, and some of the contents of the trunk, such as personal letters, the Fort St. Michael authorization document and brochure, and various receipts. Most of the trunk contents were appropriated by person or persons unknown. These might have included Clancy and "Si" Tanner. Letters to Jeff continued

---

[1] Official copy of estate fees, 07/21/1898, item 42, author's col.

[2] *Probate Book "A,"* p. 54.

[3] $190.00: the amount previously listed was $191—apparently a discrepancy. (*Probate Book* "A," p. 224)

[4] *Probate Book* "A," p. 224.

to arrive in Skaguay after his death, including one from Mexico.[1] The postmaster saved some of these and gave them to Mary. Apparently Clancy saw fit to keep some of Jeff's personal property. In a 1955 article, Clancy's son Frank wrote that his father had been the executor of Jeff's estate, which he incorrectly wrote was valued at $500 and included "some personal property," a "pearl handled pen-knife," and a Colt .45.[2]

Thus concluded the legal affairs of Jefferson R. Smith in Skaguay, hurriedly, with errors and a lack of clarity, and this depreciating statement: "...said estate has been shown to be of such trifling importance, the funds so meager, also the administrator instead of receiving any compensation for handling the said matter is out his own money in the matter of said expenses...." This "sweeping up," as it were, obscures Jeff's possible holdings and the extent to which Clancy was allowed to benefit from Jeff's death, such as by assuming control of Jeff Smith's Parlor. This treatment of Clancy suggests special consideration for his cooperation after Jeff's death. (This shadowy matter will be explored subsequently.)

Is it possible that Jeff with all his sources of income in Skaguay could have died with money and property worth but $148.60 (or about $4,642 today)?[3] Indeed, times occurred when Jeff was low on funds, if not broke, but in Skaguay in the summer weeks before his death, income from the "enterprises" under his control was at its height. When Jeff first arrived in Skaguay, he was reported to have made $30,000 in less than a month's time. He was known to have sent his wife at least $500 at a time in the beginning and is thought to have sent her money on a regular basis. One newspaper reported that Jeff had about $100,000 invested in St. Louis real estate.[4] Jeff's income in Skaguay surely rose as his dominance increased. Legal documents also show that Jeff had ownership of a schooner named *Janus.* Jeff purchased the ship from Capt. S. E. Bright on July 8, 1898. After Jeff's death Bright claimed Jeff had not paid him for the boat although he had given Jeff a bill of sale. The *Janus* was returned to Bright on July 23, 1898.[5] *The Seattle Post-Intelligencer* estimated that in a 20-to-25-year period Jeff had made $1,5000,000 in grafting but that he had spent it all.[6] Mary claimed that he was worth in the neighborhood of $40,000,000, that Skaguay was his last venture, after which he planned on retiring.[7] Mary told her grandchildren that she thought he had been giving wealthy business friends in Seattle and San Francisco cash, gold, and land deeds to hold for him. Suspected is that after his death, these *friends* just kept these assets for themselves. Specifically Mary told her children and grandchildren that Jeff had been dealing with John D. Spreckels of San Francisco, son of Claus Spreckels, the Sugar magnet, and that it was he who

[1] Letters ... Mexico: Envelope (author's col., item 51) addressed to Captain Jeff R. Smith. Partially obscured Mexican postmark shows June 1898. Another in Mexico shows July 1. Then Seattle July 9 and finally Skaguay, Friday July 15. The postmaster added in pencil, "Deceased."
[2] Clancy, p. 25.
[3] Tom's Inflation Calculator.
[4] *Seattle Post-Intelligencer* 07/22/1898.
[5] Probate paperwork returning *Janus* to S. E. Bright, 07/23/1898. Skagway City Museum.
[6] *Seattle Post-Intelligencer* 07/19/1898.
[7] Mary E. Smith to her children and grandchildren as they grew up.

kept the bulk of Jeff's Alaska earnings.[1] No letters or documents have yet been uncovered to substantiate a connection between the men. A possible link between Jeff and John Spreckels was the latter's ownership of the *San Francisco Call*. Jeff always made it his business to try to establish a friendly acquaintanceship with the large newspapers in order to protect himself and his environment, in this case Skaguay, from bad press, so having a monetary interest in a large paper would have interested him.

The large number of people falsely claiming to have witnessed the gunfight along with their varied accounts has only added to the trouble of trying to research the already cloudy truth of what actually occurred on the Juneau Wharf on the evening of July 8, 1898. The theft of Jeff's personal and business documents has also subtracted from the information that may have helped solve remaining mysteries. Thankfully, enough information about Jeff's death has survived to give us a true glimpse into the nature of his death, or rather, as the evidence tends to show, Jeff's murder.

Chapter 26

Reports and Cover Ups,
Theories and Last Rites

The way of the transgressor is hard, to quit.
—Jefferson R. Smith II
as quoted by Rev. John A. Sinclair[2]

Theories about Jeff's death made their way in print and in person to Mary during her trip to Skaguay and for a long time afterward. She arrived in Skaguay aboard the *Rosalie* on the morning of August 3, 1898, and she stayed about a month. At first, friends of Jeff still living in Skaguay did not approach the widow, fearing reprisal from the Citizens' Committee. Before she left, however, several of Jeff's friends came to her to share what they thought and knew. She heard the story that Jesse Murphy had actually killed Jeff, how Jeff's partner and now estate administrator John Clancy had been exonerated, how Murphy had been hushed up and official information falsified. Unfortunately, no record of these visits exists, but evidence tends to bear them out.

Over the next few decades, old friends, loyal associates, and ex-members of the Soap Gang visited Mary and the children in St. Louis. The visitors, some of whom Mary had known personally, came to pay their respects and talk about old times with Jeff. When the first wife of Jefferson Randolph Smith III died, Mary offered assistance in raising her grandchildren. John Randolph Smith, the author's father, went to stay with his grandmother for a series of visits, as did the other grandchildren. John related times when the visitors came to call. They would sit for hours with Mary and her son, Jefferson, drinking and exchanging stories. John admitted recalling only portions of what he saw and heard as a young boy, but some memories remained vivid. One of these occurred in 1927 when he was ten. One old friend of Jeff and Mary's stood out

---

[1] Mary E. Smith to her children and grandchildren as they grew up.
[2] *Skaguay News* 07/15/1898, p. 2, reprint of funeral sermon delivered 07/11/1898.

because of his clothing. He was well dressed but attired in the fashion of a past era. Visitors also included those who had a command of magic, an art for which John had a fascination. He remembered these men as being among the best "magicians" in the business. On the visit of one of these, the consumption of alcohol was heavy, and John was a tag-a-long with his father to see the visitor to his train. On the way to the station, the man vomited in the family car. The old bunco man pulled a handkerchief from his pocket and wiped his face, and as he did, John saw a handful of small dice spill to the floor of their car. Then when he and his father had returned home, John was given the chore of cleaning up the vomit. It was one of the few times he did not mind this kind of task as he wanted those dice to add to his magic collection, six of them as it turned out.

Plenty of witnesses to the gunfight on the Juneau Wharf loved to tell their story, but missing are accounts from the seven or so Soap Gang members who followed Jeff to the wharf that night. Some, if not all, must have seen the entire gunfight from a short distance away. They ran towards Jeff to aid him before deciding to turn and run. These men, some sentenced to jail, must have talked to people about the shootout, but no record of what they saw is known to exist.

From 1898 to well into the 1900s the Smith family received hints that someone other than Reid had killed Jeff. According to John Randolph Smith, some of Jeff's friends felt the gunfight was started intentionally in order to kill Jeff before he could order an all out attack on the Citizens' Committee meeting on the Juneau Wharf.[1] Rev. Sinclair stated this fear at the time: "Had Soapy been left one breath with which to rally his men, probably a score of citizens would have been injured."[2]

So who did kill Jeff? Much circumstantial evidence and one authoritative document points to Jesse Murphy. According to "Si" Tanner, who was practically on top of the event, Murphy, not Reid, sent Jeff to his grave. The night Jeff died, Commissioner Sehlbrede appointed Tanner to replace Sylvester Taylor. Three days after the shootout, Tanner sent a message about it to Colonel Steele of the North West Mounted Police. Tanner's original message is not known to exist, but fortunately Steele's report of it does. On July 11, 1898, in his monthly report, Steele wrote,

> According to the information I received from the Deputy Marshal, a man named Murphy is credited with the killing of Smith and not Frank Reid as reported in the newspaper.[3]

In the following month's report, Steele confirmed the facts as related to him by Tanner.

> On the 11th instant, I informed you of a shooting affray which occurred in Skaguay. "Soapy Smith" attempted to murder a Mr. Reed [sic] who was organizing a party to recover money for a returning Klondiker named J. D. Stewart who had been robbed of same by some of Smith's gang. In the struggle, etc., "Soapy Smith" was shot and killed from his own gun by a man

---

[1] Smith, John Randolph interview 07/07/1987.
[2] *Skaguay News* 07/22/1898, p. 4.
[3] RCMP files, 07/31/1898.

named "Murphy." Mr. Reed [sic] (who received two bullets from Smith's gun) died a few days afterwards.[1]

After the fight Jesse Murphy immediately insisted it was he who had killed Smith. A letter to Dr. H. R Littlefield from Dr. Cornelius, published eleven days after the gunfight, clearly indicates that someone in power, most likely US Commissioner Sehlbrede, took his claim seriously enough to order another autopsy examination.

> The shooting, Dr. Cornelius says, is the best thing that ever happened to Skagway next to the new railroad. Dr. Cornelius performed the autopsy on Smith's body for the coroner's jury. A man named Murphy claimed after the first autopsy that it was his bullet that killed the gambler, and it was necessary to perform a second [autopsy] to determine that Reed's [sic] bullet did the work.[2]

If a second autopsy took place, it was likely performed the same day as the first, July 9. No word of a second post mortem appeared in Skaguay newspapers, and but one official record of inquest was required. It lists the following six jury members in addition to US Commissioner Sehlbrede as "Exofficio Coroner": Godfrey Chealender, Frank F. Clark, Alfred E. Cleveland, William O. Henn, Anton Laumeister, and C. L. Niece. Witnesses who were sworn and testified included D. C. Bronell, O. F. Laird, J. M. Murphy, "Mr. Peoples" (the undertaker), J. F. Smith, J. M. Tanner. Also listed were doctors S. W. Cornelius and F. B. Whiting.[3]

It will be remembered that *The Skaguay News* reported how the jury "worked through the day ... until nearly half past four...."[4] Why did it take all day to determine a cause of death and how it came about if what had happened were as simple as Jeff's having been shot through the heart in a gunfight with Frank Reid? But it was not as simple as that because witness Jesse M. Murphy told a different story that was simple and straightforward. When Smith and Reid fired upon one another and both were wounded, Murphy ran over, snatched Smith's rifle, and fired a point blank shot into Smith's chest. So did the jury not believe Murphy? Was there actually confusion over who had had killed Jeff and what weapon had ended his life? Did Sehlbrede require a second post mortem to determine, if possible, the kind of bullet that had pierced Jeff's heart? These questions specifically will probably never be answered—unless one day a diary or letter from one of the principals surfaces, stating what went on.

In the meantime, though, evidence shows beyond a reasonable doubt that Reid did not kill Jeff. Tanner said Reid's pistol contained three shells, two expended and one not, while Jeff's body had three bullet wounds, one in the leg, one that grazed his forearm, and one that pierced his heart. Murphy and Tanner were the two men closest to Jeff when he was shot dead, and by Murphy's own word and Tanner's (as recorded by Steele), Murphy killed Jeff.

After the coroner's jury finding on July 9, no verbal or written accounts from Murphy are known to exist. Did he give in on his own, or was he helped, such as by

---

[1] RCMP files, 07/31/1898.

[2] *Morning Oregonian* 07/19/1898, p. 8.

[3] Inquest Record, pp. 5-6.

[4] *Skaguay News* 07/09/1898 & 07/15/1898, p. 1.

being told that if the results showed that he caused the homicide, he might be arrested on a charge of murder? After all, Murphy deliberately shot the unarmed, wounded man. Although it is doubtful Murphy would have been convicted, he surely was uncomfortable with thoughts of incarceration and legal entanglement. The *Daily Alaskan* barely mentioned that Jeff's death was the subject of a coroner's jury, only that the jury justified Reid's shooting of Jeff Smith.[1] Murphy's name was not mentioned in print, and he was never heard from again.

In a 1941 interview, Matthew M. Sundeen described what witnesses told him about the shooting on the Juneau Wharf. He had been in a nearby hardware store when the shooting took place and rushed up just after it had happened. There he learned from men directly involved that a carpenter named Murphy had killed Jeff.

> He [Jeff] encountered Reid, who told him to "stop where he was or he would shoot," according to Sundeen.
>
> "Soapy kept coming and Reid aimed his gun and pulled the trigger. Soapy would have been dead right then if the gun had worked."
>
> According to Sundeen, Reid pulled the trigger three times, but the gun only clicked. Soapy shot him through the groin. On his hands and knees…, Reid still tried to shoot, Sundeen said.

Murphy Gets the Credit

> Then a carpenter named Murphy came up from behind Smith, grabbed the rifle barrel, spun Smith around several times, as they fought for the gun, the old timer related. Murphy, he said, finally jerked the gun away, and as he did so, Smith fell. The gun was jammed, but Murphy instantly cleared it and shot Smith through the heart, killing him instantly.
>
> The reason Reid got the credit, according to Sundeen, is that "while Reid was dying in the hospital he kept asking, 'Did I get him?' To make him feel better they told him he shot Smith through the heart."
>
> If Murphy was the man, perhaps the pioneers thought it would cause less trouble if Reid was given the credit.[2]

Sundeen's version has Reid attempting to shoot first but due to a faulty weapon, never firing a shot. This story vastly differs from those of all others. Reid's weapon did misfire but also probably fired. Perhaps the intervening fifty-one years skewed Sundeen's remembrance of what witnesses told him. However, clear enough is what they said about Murphy, which corroborates what Tanner told Steele—that Murphy killed Smith.

If differing versions were not complicated enough, still another was told to the *Morning Oregonian*, which published it eleven days after the shooting.

> "Smith," said Mr. Schwartz, "attempted to break up the citizens' meeting and was grabbed by Reed [sic] and a carpenter named Murphy, also a Portland man. He turned his rifle and shot Reed. He then attempted to shoot Murphy, and a scuffle for the possession of the gun ensued. Reed, who had fallen, got on his knees, pulled a revolver and fired two shots. One of the

---

[1] *Daily Alaskan* 07/11/1898, p. 2.
[2] *Fairbanks Daily News Miner* 06/23/1941, p. 5.

bullets passed through Smith's heart. Reed and Murphy are now the popular idols of the town, and nothing is too good for them. ..."[1]

Here is a possible scenario but obviously incorrect in at least one particular. Murphy was being afforded no hero's treatment, at least not publicly.

John F. Greene, a Skaguay store proprietor who attended the vigilante meeting on the Juneau Wharf, stated that Soapy

> tried to hit him [Reid] over the head with the butt. Frank grappled with him, and Soapy shot him through the groin. Then Jim [Jesse] Murphy ran up to help Frank, who was still fighting. Together the two men twisted the muzzle of that rifle around until it was against Soapy's chest, then one of them—people say it was Murphy, but I like to think it was Frank—pulled the trigger....[2]

Another person to weigh in with knowledge of the shooting was Will Clayson, an early resident of Skaguay during the gold rush. In 1936 he proclaimed, "It is popularly believed Reid killed Smith, but those claiming to know assert Murphy fired the fatal shots."[3] Just who those people were who claimed to know, Clayson did not say.

In 1959 appeared a book by Richard C. Anzer about his adventures in the Klondike Gold Rush. Just days after the July 8 shootout, he arrived in Skaguay to join his father, John A. Anzer. The father, who had been in town at the time of the shooting, told his son that Jeff had been killed with his own rifle.[4]

Why was Murphy hushed up? What was the motive for giving Reid credit over Murphy? This author believes that, simply, those who had just taken charge of Skaguay, namely, the leaders of the Citizens' Committee, wanted to keep intact what had just been won. After Jeff was killed, Citizens' Committee members went on a vigilante rampage, and more violence and death was feared. When news of the shootout reached Captain R. T. Yeatman, commander of the US Army companies in Dyea, he offered military assistance. Commissioner Sehlbrede declined it. Captain Yeatman quoted Sehlbrede in a letter to the adjutant general on July 8, 1898: "We have control of matters here. We do not need you. If we do, we will let you know."[5]

During the ensuing hours and then days, Captain Yeatman kept in constant telephone contact with Commissioner Sehlbrede and let it be known that martial law could be declared in Skaguay unless civil control were clearly in evidence. Had Yeatman discovered that the killing of the previous night had been of an unarmed, wounded man and that no arrest had been made, he most likely would have imposed martial law. Further, Murphy would have had to be arrested and kept incarcerated unless a sizeable bond were posted. And if so, those who posted it could come under suspicion of protecting Murphy, perhaps even of having hired him to kill Jeff. Another problem with involvement of the military was that it might insist on the appointment of

---

[1] *Morning Oregonian* 07/19/1898, p. 8.

[2] *The Sun* 10/25/1908, p. 9.

[3] *Nome Daily Nugget* 11/19/1936.

[4] Anzer, pp. 12-14. Richard claimed to have been a shill for Jeff in 1894 in Pittsburgh and Chicago. The claim could be true. Jeff and Mary were known to have visited Chicago in October of 1893, and subsequently Jeff was often on the "railroads" to points south, east, north, and west.

[5] Hunt, *Distant*, p. 64.

new people to leadership positions. After all, the man who did the killing was a member of the Citizens' Committee, even specifically assigned to be among those who guarded the entrance to the Juneau Wharf.

No. In the face of these possibilities, one leading to the next, and the next, it would be best to endorse the story that the severely wounded Reid had killed Smith in a shootout. That would be far easier to manage than the troublesome story that Jesse Murphy wanted to tell, about how he had snatched the rifle of the prone, wounded Smith, and how as Smith pleaded for him not to shoot, Murphy fired anyway, point blank to the heart.

The Citizens' Committee dreaded the possibility of martial law. Speaking to a crowd in front of city hall, Tanner disclosed that fear when he reminded listeners that Captain Yeatman had come from Dyea with soldiers and had left only when Tanner, as acting marshal, and leading business men had assured him that "order would be maintained and that the men arrested would be protected and have a fair trial."

> Captain Yeatman, of the U.S. squad, said before leaving Monday, that, in the event of an unlawful move on the part of the people here, he will return with his men and take charge of the city....[1]

Skaguay newspapers never disclosed Murphy's side of the shooting. Only through word of mouth and in other publications did word spread that he had killed Jeff, not Reid.

Some accounts tell of still another man shooting at Jeff. These may be tied to the Murphy account but have become hazy with retelling over time. One such report comes from Mabel Pearce Reed. She was five years old at the time of the shootout but claims to remember that night well. She had come with her parents to Skaguay in 1897. On the day of the fight, the father was in the Klondike and his family in Skaguay. Mabel described what she remembered of that night in her self-published *Memories of Skagway: 1897-1901* (1988).

> A lady friend of Mama's was living in the hotel down in town, she invited us to stay with her. She felt it was dangerous for us to be alone while all the unrest was going on. I don't think Mama was worried, she didn't want to miss out on all the excitement. She tucked Papa's forty-four in her waistband and we walked to the hotel. Even though it was late, maybe ten o'clock at night, I remember leaning out the upstairs window and watching a crowd of men milling around and then moving toward the wharf.
>
> Papa was "inside" on July 8, 1898, when Smith was shot, but talked to a man who was with Frank Reid on the wharf. This man Harvey (I don't know his last name) ... said the men were out on the wharf having a meeting about running Smith out of town. Four men were posted at the foot of the wharf to keep Soapy or any of his men from going down to the meeting.
>
> Frank Reid was one of the four men on the wharf at the water line. There was a chain across the pier and when Smith came up ... Reid said, "Jeff, if you cross that chain I'll have to shoot you."... Smith had a rifle hanging over

[1] *Skaguay News* 07/11/1898.

his arm pointing down, when he stepped over the chain Frank Reid and Harvey both fired at him. Reid's gun misfired but Harvey hit him. Smith shot Reid as he (Smith) was falling and Reid fired again this time killing Smith.[1]

When Mabel's father returned to Skaguay, the man named Harvey told him what had happened and never to repeat the story, as he was ashamed of his participation.

In 1918, her father broke his promise and told his daughter, Mabel, what Harvey had said. Her father then made her promise never to repeat the conversation. She kept her promise until 1988 when she revealed it her in her book. In 1989, several months before Mabel died, the author interviewed her. Mabel steadfastly claimed that she had accurately retold what her father had told her about the shooting.

She also related a story of how Jeff helped a woman.

> It became known in Skagway that ... Mrs. Reynolds, needed a sewing machine so she could earn some money. Her husband had been "inside" a long time and she was ... low of funds. Soapy Smith heard of her plight and bought a machine for her. She didn't know him and was surprised by his gift.[2]

Frank Reid is included among the memories Mabel included in her book.

> Reid had been known to have a very colorful vocabulary, he did a lot of swearing and using foul language, so Mama was surprised when he asked for the ladies quartet from the church to sing for him as he lay dying. Mama sang alto in the quartet and said they sang every afternoon until his death.[3]

A key piece to the ambush theory is the exoneration of John Clancy, Jeff's partner in Jeff Smith's Parlor. Without doubt, brothers John and Frank Clancy were involved in Jeff's criminal activities. From their earliest times in Skaguay, Jeff and the Clancys ran saloons together. It is not possible for Jeff to have partners not involved, one way or another, in his line of work. John appears in two photographs with Jeff in his parlor. In one he is behind the bar, and in the other he stands beside Jeff, surrounded by Soap Gang members. In a letter dated June 13, 1898, from Seattle, Jim Wilson, possibly "Diamond Jim" Wilson (the highly successful Dawson businessman and gambler and later proprietor of the Anvil Saloon in Nome[4]) wrote to introduce a Soap Gang prospect. Addressed to "Frank Clancy or Jeff Smith," the letter reads,

> Dear Friends   This will introduce to you Morris Behan a brother of Hugh Behan He is all right and any thing you can do for Him will be appreciated by your friend as ever.   Jim Wilson[5]

Reference letters of this kind were common on the upper level of the bunco brotherhood.

After Jeff was killed, the Citizens' Committee went on a manhunt for members and friends of the Soap Gang. Numerous innocent men were falsely accused and roughed up. The vigilantes made an effort to apologize publicly to some who were

---

[1] Reed, p. 20.
[2] Reed, p. 19.
[3] Reed, p. 20.
[4] O'Connor, pp. 234-35.
[5] Ltr addressed to Frank Clancy and Jeff Smith fr Jim Wilson, 06/13/1898, item #8, author's col.

found to be wrongly accused, for example, "The citizens committee requests the News to assure Mr. Wm. Fielding that his detention was wholly the result of misinformation." Enough such victims of misinformation were around that a general statement of apology appeared in the same July 15, 1898, issue of *The Skaguay News*:

> It is most unfortunate and greatly to be deplored that reflections have been cast on the character at some of our most reliable and esteemed citizens by groundless imputations. It is deeply regretted, not only by the men themselves, but by the committee and the whole people as well. The committee was perfectly honest in its acts, but the best of men will sometimes err in judgment. To err is human, to forgive, divine.[1]

Businessmen and Skaguay residents who had no criminal association with Jeff and the gang feared they would be accused by competitors and enemies of being Smith associates. A number of merchants had good reason to be afraid. They feared for their businesses and even their lives, yet the Citizen's Committee spared both John and Frank Clancy any harshness whatsoever. No records indicate that they were even questioned as other innocently accused residents had been. Rather, on the morning after Jeff's death, Commissioner Sehlbrede appointed John Clancy "administrator" of Jeff's estate.[2] Charles B. Sperry, head of the Citizens' Committee, was appointed surety on the bond that guarantees an administrator's lawful and diligent performance.[3] Additionally, in the pages of *The Skaguay News*, John Clancy received a complimentary statement exonerating him of any wrongdoing whatsoever.

> It is but justice to state that against Mr. John Clancy, who was interested with Jeff Smith in a private enterprise, not a hint of suspicion has been breathed. He was in no way connected with the shady part of Smith's business, and no one more deeply deplores the sad condition of Frank Reid than does Mr. Clancy.[4]

This extraordinary treatment makes highly probable that John Clancy made some kind of deal with the Citizens' Committee. But was it made before or after Jeff's death? One theory is that the Committee approached Clancy before Jeff's death with a proposal. Clancy would receive full exoneration and be allowed full ownership of Jeff Smith's Parlor for supplying information about the Stewart robbery, the missing gold, the names of the guilty men, and the names of as many members of the gang as he knew. Having every gang member and perhaps some business competitors forced to leave Skaguay would be to Clancy's advantage. Should Clancy's help become known, anyone loyal to Jeff might be inclined to kill Clancy or expose him. Could John have helped set Jeff up to save his own neck and profit from Jeff's fall? Well, Frank Clancy obtained title to Jeff Smith's Parlor and quickly changed the name to the Mirror Saloon and then to Clancy's Café, a "Gentleman's Resort." Additionally, there is the sterling, public exoneration of John Clancy. Outcomes tend to support a yes answer to the question of whether the Clancys, particularly John, helped the Committee of 101.

[1] *Skaguay News* 07/15/1898, p.3. *To err ... divine*: Fr "Essay on Criticism" (1711) by Alexander Pope.
[2] *Probate Book "A,"* pp. 51-55, 223-225.
[3] Probate, pp. 51-52.
[4] *Skaguay News* 07/15/1898, p. 3.

Another theory holds that when Jeff and his men left the parlor on the evening of July 8, going right on Holly towards State Street and thence to the Juneau Wharf, Clancy slipped out, went left on Holly, right on Broadway, and thence to the wharf to warn the vigilantes that Jeff and his men were coming. Clancy would have had to run all the way, of course, because Jeff was moving at a good clip. No witness reported Clancy making this sprint.

One report, though, put Clancy on an evening walk with his wife and six-year-old son down by the Juneau Wharf shortly after nine p.m. Of course, "evening" at that time of year in Skaguay was (and is) broad daylight. As they walked, John Clancy saw Jeff coming their way. This report appears in a 1955 article by Clancy's son Frank.

> He [Smith] was armed with a Winchester and a colt .45 revolver. He was headed for the wharf.... Father tried to dissuade him from his mission, but it was no go. Soapy took out the .45 and pressed it against Father saying, "Johnny, you better leave me alone."
>
> Father replied, "If you want to get killed, go ahead." Mother was crying, so Father took us home. If I remember correctly we lived at Ninth and Main.[1]

A theorist may propose that Clancy's apparent demeanor at that meeting was one of relative indifference to what Jeff was doing, a show, of sorts, to distance himself from Jeff. Clancy, however, had to have known the feverish state the town was in, so what was he doing on a walk with his family while others hid within doors? Was he putting on a show, strolling with his family nine blocks from home on what was without doubt the most tense and dangerous evening in Skaguay's history?

After Jeff's death, Clancy claimed he knew nothing of his partner's unlawful activities, but something that night triggered a deep-seated fear in Clancy. According to Mary McCarty, John Clancy's granddaughter, like Old Man Tripp, John Bowers, Slim Jim Foster, George Wilder, and others from among the Soap Gang, John Clancy hid out in the hills that night.[2] Of course, this part of the story was not generally known at the time. In the spirit of theorizing, this possible event could mean that Clancy thought his association with Jeff and the Soap Gang was all too clear. It also could mean that Clancy had inside knowledge to trade for immunity and added booty. The outcome for Clancy would indicate that he made the trade.

Jeff's brother Bascomb learned of the events surrounding his brother's death and openly questioned the handling of his estate to the widow. While Mary was still in Skaguay trying to collect the estate, Bascomb wrote to her from Port Townsend, Washington, about what monies he felt she might be entitled to,

> Mrs. Smith,
>
> Dear Friend, yours to hand and glad to hear from you. I know they will say that Jeff had nothing when you went up but I think the Saloon must be a part his [—] only way it looks like he would have paid for something and the 2,100 that they claim that they found in his trunk must belong to him for they claimed that the man lost 3,200 so I think you can get that. Did you get Jeff's

---

[1] Clancy, p. 18.
[2] Interview with Mary McCarty, John Clancy's grand-daughter, by the author, 10/13/1987.

personal effects? I suppose they stole everything. I will be here for a week, so write to me here as I will get it. Let me hear all the news.

Yours as Ever   Bascom Smith,

Care of Tom Sanders Saloon[1]

In an interview with the *Rocky Mountain News* a year after his brother's death, Bascomb told some of what he learned from Mary and friends of Jeff.

Soapy Smith Shot in the Back and Robbed

Thieves fall out and we may find out some time what became of Jeff's property. There are men in Skaguay now who claim to have killed my brother. I have been told that Reid did not kill him, but that another man in the crowd fired a bullet into his back while he was struggling with Reid.

This is part of the statement of Bascomb Smith, the only brother of the late Jefferson R. Smith, who arrived in the city yesterday, after an absence of three years.

Bascomb resembles the famous gun fighting "Soapy" as closely as though he were a twin brother. The eyes, features and general bearing are the same and the voice has the same ring. It is the intention of Bascomb to make Denver his home for the future, providing he can find paying employment. He came from Vancouver, B. C., where he has lived most of the time during the past two years.

"Soapy" was killed and his followers scattered to the four winds on July 8, last. He has been the King of Skaguay and partner of John Clancy, keeper of the principal saloon In town. When war broke out, he organized the Skaguay Guards and offered to take them to Cuba. The Secretary of War, Russell Alger wrote him a letter stating that the guards could not be put into service, but thanked him for his efforts in behalf of his country.

"There are very few honest people up in that country," Said Bascomb last night. "I was told that my brother had $80 in cash in his clothes when he died, also that he owned several lots in Skaguay, a half-interest in Clancy's saloon which was taking in probably $200 a day and an interest in the White Pass Trail.

The widow never got anything out of the estate. The money was gone and there was no trace of the lots, as they had never been recorded. Even a letter of thanks from the secretary of war could not be found and nearly everything in Jeff's room had been stolen."[2]

A theory that the White Pass and Yukon Railway had a guilty hand in Jeff's killing was slowly revealed. It was no surprise that Murphy's name, an employee of the railway, was not mentioned in the newspapers as claiming to have killed Jeff. The railroad perhaps had the most to lose if Jeff remained in power, and the most to gain if he were removed. The railroad controlled the most important facts regarding the gunfight as the lead doctor working on Jeff's body during the autopsy was employed

---

[1] Ltr to Mary Smith fr Bascomb Smith, 08/08/1898, item 48, author's col.

[2] *RMN* 04/13/1899.

by the railroad. They could control and manipulate the cause of death, the number and location of bullet wounds, where they came from, and who fired them. The autopsy report was the official and final word on the subject, and few could dispute it.

The president of the White Pass and Yukon Railway gave some damaging evidence when he published his work diary in 1908. It exposed just how involved the railroad men were with the vigilantes.

> In times of peace, prepare for war. There's 200 cartridges, anyway said the purchasing agent, coming into the engineers' mess tent, where we were at breakfast this morning, laying them down with four Winchester repeating rifles (one for each of us) on the breakfast table.
>
> It seems that the citizens have determined to call Soapy to an account and have notified him that the stolen gold dust must be restored within 24 hours, and that Soapy is not inclined to comply, saying the money was lost in a square game. The citizens have called a mass meeting to consider what steps are to be taken, and it means a fight, and they look to us to lead them.
>
> After breakfast Heney, Hawkins, Hislop and myself received urgent invitations to attend a small and select meeting of prominent citizens, hastily summoned because of the feeling that nothing definite was likely to result from mass meetings. Seventeen of us attended this meeting (euphemistically called the 'Merchant's Committee,' but in point of fact a vigilance committee pure and simple), but no action was taken beyond electing a chairman and adjourning to 11 P.M. when it was quite understood ... that 'active measures' were to be adopted. Being manifestly the least qualified for such a position, you will easily understand that I was unanimously chosen for chairman, despite my protests. However, I have fortunately our three H's (Heney, Hawkins and Hislop) to advise me, and it would be hard to duplicate such a trio. The first thing we decided upon was to send Heney and Hawkins up to the Pass to prepare our camps for the hard fighting which seems inevitable, leaving Hislop and myself in Skaguay to deal with the local situation and attend the meeting tonight....
>
> Having attended to these matters and our daily grist of construction affairs, I found an Italian bootblack and made a contract with him to black my boots for twenty-five cents, which seems high unless you saw the boots. But he hardly got himself into action when I felt a light touch on my shoulder and saw Hislop apparently deprecating the performance.
>
> It is hardly wise just now he said.... I thought he meant that it was a poor investment in view of the fact that the boots would soon be bad as ever. But he explained that the public feeling was very excited and ran high, and that while it did not necessarily follow course that a man was honest because he had dirty boots, on the other hand there was an irresistible presumption that if his boots shone, he must earn his living by questionable methods.[1]

---

[1] Graves, pp. 20-21.

If the report in the October 10, 1898, *Denver Evening Post* is correct, a wax impression of Jeff's face was displayed in Denver.

> An enterprising showman in Denver is advertising a wax impression of the face of Soapy Smith, the late, who was killed in the boots he wore at Skaguay, Alaska. Great paper signs on the windows of the place where the exhibition is given announce in flaring headlines "Jefferson Randolph Smith, the hero of many encounters." The show is being given on the ground which Smith himself traversed almost daily previous to getting into his fatal trouble.[1]

Not known if this was a death mask molded in Skaguay or one made while he lived in Denver, or if it was a fake. If a mask existed, no record is known of what might have become of it.

Jeff's corpse awaited what would come next. The body resided where the autopsy had occurred, at E. J. Peoples' Undertaker's Parlor at Broadway and Shoup (7th Avenue), which served as the city morgue. Rev. Sinclair received word from other ministers in town that they would not help serve Jeff's last rites. "But I knew I was right," Sinclair wrote in his diary, to be "determined to give the remains a decent burial even if I should afterwards be invited to leave town because of my action." Rev. Sinclair than took precautions against that possibility. He wrote out his sermon in advance so that what he said could not be reinvented later, and he "persuaded" a Mr. Butler, one of the well-known members of the vigilante committee, to attend the service "as a safeguard against misunderstanding and mob violence." And so on July 11 at approximately 3 p.m., in a brief ceremony, Sinclair wrote how,

> in the dreary morgue, in the presence of a few who were not afraid, in the presence of no mourners, with the exception of his late mistress whose presence I felt was no tribute but rather, an insult to his living family in the East; in the presence of an ever-loving God, I closed the chapter of this poor desperado's career.

Eight people accompanied Jeff's remains to the cemetery. A driver and the undertaker conveyed the coffin in an express wagon. Before it in "a hack ... rode Mr. Butler, three lawyers who had done business with Soapy, a late partner of the deceased and myself." Rev. Sinclair wrote feelingly about the loneliness of the procession, contrasting it with all those who "rode or walked in" parades with Jeff, "marking the declaration of war with Spain...," and all those who had been proud to wear his July 4th badges..., but of whom now "not one had the courage to do his remains justice."[2]

The driver of the wagon is unknown. The undertaker is E. R. Peoples. In addition to ads in the newspapers as an Undertaker and Embalmer at Broadway and Shoup (7th Avenue), he had a shop at Broadway and Johnson (8th Avenue) that sold Upholstered Goods and Furniture, Shades, and Carpets.[3] One of the lawyers was probably Mr. O'Donnell, whom Commissioner Sehlbrede had appointed to look after

---

[1] *Denver Evening Post* 10/10/1898, p. 3.
[2] Sinclair, pp. 138-139.
[3] Peoples' business ads in order listed: *Daily Alaskan* 07/22/1898; *Skaguay News* 01/06/1899, & 12/09/1898.

Jeff's affairs, and he may have brought along his partner, Mr. Weldon.[1] The third lawyer is probably Walter Church, he who had helped Jeff file suit against The *Seattle Daily News* for liable. More of Mr. Butler than that he was a "prominent member of the vigilante committee" is not known. The "late partner of the deceased" was John Clancy. The woman who attended the "brief service" in the morgue, whom Rev. Sinclair identified as Jeff's "late mistress," did not go the cemetery.

Mention of a woman said to be Jeff's mistress exists in four writings published after Jeff's death. One concerns the woman whom Royal Pullen said was his mistress and who paid four men $100 each to carry Jeff's corpse from the wharf to the morgue.[2] A second concerns a woman who was leaving Skaguay on the day after Jeff was killed. The *Daily Alaskan* wrote, "The woman who lived with Soapy endeavored to leave town on the City of Seattle. She was brought back and examined and her trunks were searched."[3] That event occurred at some point before Stewart's gold had been found. The third is Rev. Sinclair's mention of the service "in the dreary morgue ... in the presence of no mourners, with the exception of his late mistress...."[4]

The fourth and last mention of a mistress in Skaguay appeared in a *San Francisco Examiner* article republished in the *Denver Evening Post*. Referred to is

> a woman with whom he [Jeff] took up in Skaguay. Whenever he made a winning at faro she always reminded him of his marital obligations so far as they applied to the maintenance of his family. One night he was wildly squandering about $2,500, which he had just won when this unusual woman entered ... and quietly requested ... a thousand dollars.
>
> "There's the 'dough,'" said Smith, pointing to the pile of gold and bills, which he had placed upon the bar to "lie as long as it lasted."
>
> Without a word she abstracted from the heap the sum she had asked for, while "Soapy" watched her with drunken gravity and his guests in the revel eyed the process with poorly concealed disapproval.
>
> "Come home when you've blown the rest of it," was her parting admonition.
>
> That thousand dollars was not spent for wearing apparel to adorn the person of the woman who took it. She sent it to the wife whose place she had taken. The people at the Skaguay express office said it was not her first visit to them on a similar errand.[5]

Except for again rehearsing the theme of the mistress with the "heart of gold," the story's lack of ornamentation and gravity suggests some grounding in reality.

Rev. Sinclair may have been hoping his funeral sermon for Jeff Smith's brief ceremony would reach a larger audience, for it reflected not just on Jeff but as much on certain citizens of Skaguay without whom Jeff could not have flourished. So Sinclair

---

[1] "O'Donnel & Weldon" ad: "Attys-at-Law. / Occidental Hotel Building." *Daily Alaskan* 07/13 & 22/1898, p.1.
[2] Pullen, Royal interview.
[3] *Daily Alaskan* 07/11/1898.
[4] Sinclair, p. 138.
[5] *Denver Evening Post* 08/08/1898, p. 4, & the *Washington Post* 08/14/1898.

must have been pleased when asked to allow publication of his sermon. Of the eleven paragraphs of two thousand words, published in *The Skaguay News* of July 15, 1898, the following sections demonstrate its charitable content and public purposes.

"Good understanding [of God's laws] getteth favor; but the way of transgressors is hard." PROV. 13:15.

The principle contained in our text ... has often been disputed by men who have taken inadequate views of life. ... Poor Smith thought he made this proverb truer to the facts of life, I am told, by revising it to read, "The way of the transgressor is hard TO QUIT." But in his disobedience of the laws of God and men, he found ... real and awful realities. ...

It is an old maxim, "Speak only good of the dead," and it is fitting for fellow mortals, taught by Christ of our own weaknesses, to be temperate in judgment. To those ready to condemn summarily a poor fallen woman, Jesus said: "Let him that is without sin among you cast the first stone;" but in the very sentence in which He forgave her, He mentioned what was wrong in her past, saying: "Neither do I condemn thee; go and sin no more."[1]

We lament that in the career of one who has lived among us there is so little that we can look back upon today as unmistakably good or heroic. Deeds were done which may have been charity or which may have been policy. Not knowing the heart, we cannot judge, but can hope for the best. ... His remains lie there today cold and still in solitary death, no worthy mourner near his bier, no tears of sorrow shed by his fellow citizens, no loss—but the opposite—felt by the most patriotic, deserted where he fell by the companions with whom he chose to be numbered, and whom, he fancied, he was protecting and leading. In an awful sense he lies "Unwept, unhonored, and unsung."[2] ...

In the sense of relief which all unmistakably feel over the destruction of an organization which has long lain like a leaden incubus upon the freedom of our citizenship, paralyzing the temporal, moral and spiritual development of the city, it is hard for us to feel sufficiently that sympathy which we should for a misguided and fallen fellow mortal. But ... when we look within, and thus see our own elements of weakness, and look about and see the atmosphere in which he lived, we should feel some pity for one in whom these same seeds of evil bore their ghastly fruit. His dead body is symbol of our own mortality, of our own helplessness in High Heaven's hands, and fatal career the symbol of our own lesser follies. Therefore as fellow mortals, ourselves prone to err, we have assembled to give decent and Christian burial to these poor remains, leaving judgment to God, and mourning the awful cloud of sorrow and dark memory which has fallen upon his wife and family in the east.

But today our minds must revert rather to the living, than the dead. And here again we see how "the way of transgressors is hard." Men, who, like

---

[1] *"Let him ... stone. Neither do I ... go and sin no more."*: John 8:7 & 11.
[2] *"Unwept ... unsung".* fr "The Lay of the Last Minstrel" (1805), Sir Walter Scott.

their unfortunate leader, foolishly fancied that without secrecy, without shame, without fear, they could prey upon the unsuspecting, could cleverly outplay the uninitiated gambler, could violently bluff the wronged into silence and submission, today find ... themselves marched by armed citizens before the judgment bar of their fellows, who can scarce restrain a revenge [that is] natural after so long an oppression. Oh, friends, when I heard the earnest "amen" from all parts of that jail full of frightened prisoners last night at the close of my prayer with them for God to protect the innocent, to prepare the guilty for just retribution, and to comfort and care for their dear ones at home I felt as never before how hard was the way of transgressors and how natural it was for the helpless to cry to the Lord in the day of trouble. ... May it be that the hardness of the transgressors' way may soften the transgressors' hearts.

Still another class of men are finding the way of transgressors hard. I have reference to many who followed the world-wide policy of "keeping in with these men for the sake of business." The old maxim, "better have a man a friend than an enemy," has its limitations when applied to conduct. It can never lead us to countenance wrong-doing without numbering us among the transgressors.

It is true that especially, in new and only partially organized towns, the same discrimination between the pure and honorable, and those who are more or less associated with wrong-doing is not so sharply drawn. Many who would not be seen in [the] South or East associating with gamblers, prostitutes or "grafters," will walk with such on the streets, cultivate their custom in business, or even tolerate their influence in civic affairs. ... This is made even more difficult by the feeling among many that their present residence is only temporary, that they are really exiles from home merely to make a "stake," and that necessarily many of the maxims and customs of the home land are suspended here. Looking at things from the point of view of the present merely, the way of the transgressor appears easy and profitable, and the way of the upright hard. Many, for such reasons as these, have long given countenance to the transgressors....

But we see men who associated with Smith's pals in the recent past, now flourishing Winchesters and clamoring for their punishment. This inconsistency is another added to the list of their transgressions, and will breed a contempt which will make their future way hard if they remain in Skaguay.

Permit me in this connection to point my hearers to a few lessons and duties which the tragic events of the past few days have thrown into clear relief. First of all, ... the work of reform will not be complete when every member of the "Smith gang" has been punished or deported. They were not the only baneful incubus smothering the morals and prosperity in this town of promise. The work of your vigilance committee will not be complete until all who are not engaged in fair and honorable business are made to feel that Skaguay has no place for them. All "grafters" should get a hint to leave; all whose business is to get the hard earnings of others without giving an adequate and honorable return should be promptly asked to close up; all who want to make gold out of their own and others' shame, should be firmly dealt with, and should get no recognition and no condonement from any who honor the virtue of their own wives, sisters, and daughters. ... In sounding this call to duty I would not be understood as encouraging anything like heartlessness or persecution. When Jeff Smith was alive, I refused an introduction to him. But today if he were alive and suffering, I would be at his bedside for the same reason as I conduct these sad obsequies. ... Let us ... show them ["wrong-doers"] an example of fairness and mercy which they forget to render others. Let us "trust in God and keep our powder dry," as the pious Cromwell[1] said when acting as his nation's liberator. Let us learn from poor Smith's mistaken career and awful end, what a curse even great and cultivated talents may become to the possessor and to others, if devoted to unconsecrated ends in life. Let us learn from the unhappy fate of his associates, and from the fears of those who lent countenance to his wrong-doing, that ... the way of transgressors [is] hard.

In any crisis we may have to face in the future, when tempted to either dally with wrong and wink at evil, or on the other hand to mete out intolerant or disproportionate retribution to the fallen, let us remember "Vengeance is mine, I will repay," saith the Lord,[2] and that "Good understanding getteth favor, but the way of transgressors is hard."

Rev. Sinclair found the cemetery harsh and forbidding. In his diary he wrote how it "had refused to conceal" Jeff's "chief lieutenants as they endeavored to hide from armed citizens" who had captured them there the previous night. And now, so it also

seemed loath to receive his mortal remains into her stony bosom. But rather, after hours of laborious digging and quarrying, the plot spared a meager foot of covering for his coffin.

Sinclair could not shake the pitiless cemetery. It was a forlorn "city of the dead," a "rough, unkempt, stone-marked field," and as uncaring were sounds thereabouts: "the monotonous roar of the mountain stream, broken only by the complaining creak and rattle of passing freight wagons on their way in search of gold...."[3]

---

[1] Cromwell, Oliver (1599-1658): English Puritan, head of England after execution of Charles I (1653-58), able administrator and general, brutal suppressor of Irish Catholics.

[2] *"Vengeance ... saith the Lord*. Romans 12:19.

[3] Sinclair, p. 139.

Chapter 27
Rounding Up the Soap Gang

Take back your gold.

—Soap Gang Prisoner Singing Solo
Between 2 and 3 a.m., Monday, July 11, 1898

When Jeff was killed, Soap Gang members fled for their lives, and the Citizens' Committee mobilized a massive manhunt, vowing to cleanse the city of Jeff's associates. The natural features of Skaguay that had slowed and bottled up the passage of Klondikers and made them subjects within Jeff's kingdom now denied the gang's escape. Special marshals guarded the wharves. Armed railroad men blocked the White Pass in several locations. Special marshals and vigilantes combed the town and surrounding hills. Dyea's Deputy US Marshal Snook was on the lookout for suspects in Dyea and on the Chilkoot Trail. The North West Mounted Police were on the lookout for gang members at the borders, ready for any conflict. The White Pass summit was equipped with an air-cooled Maxim machine gun while at the Chilkoot sat a Norden .303 caliber water-cooled machine gun, both capable of firing 500 rounds a minute.[1] Gang members could only run, hide, and hope a getaway route would somehow open.

The Citizens' Committee, led by Chairman Sperry, met with Commissioner Sehlbrede to ask that Deputy Marshal Taylor be removed because of his affiliation with the gang and replaced with Si Tanner until US Marshal James M. Shoup could come from Sitka to appoint a new marshal. The commissioner agreed to the appointment of Tanner, who selected twenty-five deputies to serve under him. Sehlbrede ordered Tanner to close all saloons and their gambling operations until the threat of violence was over. They remained closed until July 15, 1898, the morning after the last of the gang was sent to Sitka to stand trial.[2]

The Citizens' Committee organized the manhunt into two main search parties. The first group had the duty of rounding up accused gang members while the second focused on finding John Stewart's gold. S. H. Graves, president of the Railway, was closely involved and described roundup activities in a report to his company. He ran to his Railway "office tent and telephoned" camps three and five, told what had happened, and instructed two of his lead men, Heney and Hawkins, to have guards hold anyone without a signed pass and to be ready to come to Skaguay should they receive a call for help. "We put armed guards on all the wharves," Graves continued,

> with orders to shoot on sight if anyone tried to escape in a boat. Thus escape by land or water was cut off.... Some tried to get away in boats and were

---

[1] Gun and information on display at the RCMP Museum, Regina, Saskatchewan, Canada.

[2] *Morning Oregonian* 08/27/1898, p. 9. "By July 14...," 14 "of the more notorious members of the gang" were "herded aboard the steamer Athenian in handcuffs" for transport "to Sitka for trial." (Minter, p. 215)

caught by our guards. Some tried the Pass, and Heney and Hawkins got them, and the rest we got by an organized search of the town…, except a few who took to the mountains where we shall starve them out. But we got more than we could find jail room for, so we selected thirty-one of the leaders, and let the rest go with a warning to get out of town, and keep out. Now our job is to save the men we have in jail from the infuriated mob, which is clamoring for their blood.[1]

Royal Pullen described the hunt for gang members to Jeff's grandchildren.

They shot all night. You could hear the shooting and see the flashes in the hills when they were shooting. They weren't shooting at anything, they were just shooting. The gang was hiding in the hills. One guy hid under our house, until dark, and then he tore out. Mother wouldn't tell on him. We didn't want the guy to get shot. He stayed under there until it got dark and then he beat it.[2]

At Lake Bennett, newly appointed Deputy Marshals Boswell, Joy, and Barney arrived to supply information and descriptions of the gang to Mounties. Every house suspected of harboring gang members was searched. About 8 p.m. on July 9, Citizens' Committee member Pierre Humbert found Deputy US Marshal Taylor sitting in his cabin with a baby on his knee. He was ordered to stay inside his home and told that if he left it he would be "hanged or killed by the mob." Later, Taylor offered to return $600 of Stewart's gold to Governor Brady if allowed to leave Skaguay a free man. His request was denied. Once Stewart's gold was found, approximately $600 was missing. Taylor was likely given this amount as payment for not performing his duty in the case.[3]

Jeff had Taylor under his pay, so it was no surprise when it was discovered that two thirds of the city council of six was also under Jeff's control. At a special meeting, tendered were the resignations of J. H. Foster, Frank E. Burns, and W. F. Lokowitz. Council member J. Allen Hornsby was not there because he was being fired from his position as editor of the *Daily Alaskan* for complicity with Jeff Smith and was being "asked" to leave town. As Counsel member Spencer could not attend the meeting, the single remaining "member, Chairman Sperry," had by himself "to make, second, put before the house and vote on a motion to adjourn." Even "The new school board" that day reported it was "now 'shy' a member."[4] The Citizens' Committee soon replaced the four counsel members with men of its own and then had control of the city.

Both Skaguay newspapers later admitted keeping news of Stewart's robbery out of their pages, claiming they did so to keep peace until Commissioner Sehlbrede could repair the problem.[5] The *Daily Alaskan*, however, had more to explain after "discovering" that its editor had been on Jeff's payroll.

[1] Graves, pp. 26-27.
[2] Pullen, Royal interview.
[3] Whiting, p. 2. & US v. Sylvester S. Taylor. Whiting wrote that Taylor was found "with a baby on each knee, for protection and also, sympathy."
[4] *Skaguay News* 07/15/1898, p. 3.
[5] *Daily Alaskan* 07/09/1898.

> The mission of the Daily Alaskan is to give the news and all the news, fairly and impartially. That the issue of Friday evening contained no reference to the stealing of the gold dust, the first cause in the momentous events that have followed, it was a great disappointment to the proprietor as [well as to] the Daily Alaskan's many readers. The former editor, J. Allen Hornsby, who was solely responsible for this disappointment, has been discharged in consequence, and we have confidence that the gentleman selected to succeed him will materially aid in our endeavor to make this journal thoroughly newsy and reliable.[1]

In a *Denver Post* interview, Skaguay pioneer businessman George Dedman said that Jeff was paying $500 a week to the owners of both newspapers to keep detrimental news about himself and Skaguay from being published.[2]

The Skaguay News reported 25 men arrested, one put under home detention, and one kept under surveillance.[3] Unknown is how many more were allowed to extricate themselves from the environs of Skaguay. Andrews reported in 1947 how

> It was not generally known how many were included in Smith's gang. Dr. Whiting and Keelar, the "Money King," later compiled a list of the roughnecks who were supposed to have belonged, and both those men were in a position to judge fairly well. There were 192 names on their list, all of them suggestive of the underworld and many of them unprintable. The sobriquets range from "Soapy" Smith and the "Lamb" to "Moon Face Kid," "Slim Jim," "Blackjack Doctor," "The Queen," "B. S. Jack...."[4]

Waiting for an opportunity to escape town, some of the gang hid out in the Astoria Hotel. There, on Saturday evening, July 9, around 10:30, Tanner found Jackson, who the night before had pointed a weapon at Tanner on the Juneau Wharf. Jackson lay on a cot, his head covered by a blanket. Tanner later told how he struck a match, and upon "removing the blanket, he recognized Jackson, and told him he was the man he had been looking for...." Jackson replied, "You are mistaken."[5] Tanner thought not, dragged Jackson from his bed, and took him to city hall, behind which was the jail.[6]

Bowers, Foster, Wilder, and Triplett slipped out of town past the slaughterhouse and up the waterworks trail into the hills on the eastside of town. The *Daily Alaskan* told the story of what happened there.

> The first night they slept near the lake and remained in hiding all the next day. Saturday night, almost famished with hunger, they hit the trail again and came down to the slaughterhouse with the hope of escaping by boat or of getting back to friendly cabins. It seemed too risky to attempt to pass the lines of armed patrolmen, however, and shortly after 2 o'clock they started back up the trail. Tripp, who is an old man, was tired out and refused to go

---

[1] *Daily Alaskan* 07/11/1898.
[2] *Denver Post* unknown date (post 1898). There is no additional verification of this claim.
[3] *Skaguay News* 07/15/1898.
[4] Andrews, "Real," p. 38.
[5] *Federal Reporter*, p. 481.
[6] *Daily Alaskan* 07/11/1898.

back. His companions expostulated with him for an hour, but he stuck to his declaration that he "would rather be hung on a full stomach than die of starvation in the ____ ____ mountains." So he was at length permitted to return.[1]

At 5 a.m. on Sunday, July 10, 1898, a Citizens' Committee guard spotted Triplett near Herman and Shoup (Spring Street and 7th Avenue today).[2] He was headed for some breakfast. When found at the Pack Train restaurant, Triplett was feasting on beefsteak and mushrooms. He asked to be allowed to finish his meal before being taken in, and his request was granted. The jail being full, Triplett was taken to an upper floor of the Burkhard Hotel where a guard was placed over him.[3] Triplett told his captors that he was the man who had snatched Stewart's gold sack, took it to Jeff Smith's Parlor, and handed it over to the bartender, probably Harry Bronson,[4] who gave it to Jeff. Triplett claimed he did not know what happened to the gold after that. When news of the robbery spread, Triplett said he told Jeff that "the people were making such a stink about the job it would be wise to give the stuff up," but Jeff made no reply.[5] Triplett said he "stayed low," hiding in the Astoria Hotel, and did not go with Jeff and the others to the wharf.

Rev. Sinclair recorded how all day Sunday, July 10, 1898, the hunt for gang members continued, especially its principal members.

> All day the street past the jail, where all the other members of the gang were confined, was black with excited citizens, many armed with Winchesters. Every now and then a rush would take place around someone bringing in a message from the trail, or a posse of armed men marching in another suspect or another known "bunco" man.[6]

Triplett gave his captors the last known location of Bowers, Foster, and Wilder. An armed posse of 30 men scoured the hillside all day Sunday and into the early evening, looking for the men, but did not find them. In the early evening Tom Ward and 8 others were searching the hills near the cemetery. John Patten and James Little had a hunch that Bowers, Foster, and Wilder might be in the area, so they hid near a little bridge just north of the cemetery and waited for Ward and his men to leave, which they did around 8 p.m. About 8:30 the 3 fugitives stepped into the open about 50 yards to the east of Patten and Little and began walking straight towards Patten's hiding spot. When they were about 15 feet from him, he stood up, aimed his Winchester rifle at the men, and demanded their surrender. They did so without resistance. Bowers, Foster, and Wilder were marched into town about midnight where under cover of darkness they were taken to the city hall jail.[7]

---

[1] *Daily Alaskan* 07/11/1898.

[2] *Daily Alaskan* 07/11/1898.

[3] *Skaguay News* 07/15/1898, & *Daily Alaskan* 07/11/1898.

[4] *Harry Bronson*: he was later charged by the Committee of Safety with accessory to robbery and receiving stolen property (*Daily Alaskan* 07/15/1898, p. 1).

[5] *Daily Alaskan* 07/11/1898.

[6] Sinclair, p. 136.

[7] *Skaguay News* 07/15/1898.

The *Skaguay News* incorrectly states that a few minutes later they were marched over to the Burkhard Hotel. They were not moved until a few hours later, about 3 a.m. Rev. Sinclair wrote in his diary about his and Rev. Wooden's being given permission earlier to visit the prisoners and of the surprises they encountered there.

We went and were surprised at the welcome we received when these poor unfortunates knew our mission. I spoke, first assuring them that we came knowing how much they all realized the seriousness of their position and to offer them that consolation and hope that God alone can give.

Rev. Sinclair told the men they could appeal to God for protection "if innocent, and for his mercy and strength ... should they be guilty.... ... Dr. Wooden spoke feelingly" along the same line. The prisoners were afraid before, the words of these well-spoken, reverend men encouraging them to accept their trials and fate with God's help, but now they were abject. And Rev. Sinclair kept at them.

I then prayed to our Heavenly Father who knows all hearts and all past records, to look in mercy on His unfortunate children, to protect and vindicate the innocent, to prepare the guilty for punishment, and to protect, comfort and sustain their dear ones in the homeland. To my surprise, every prisoner was on his knees and from all parts of that room came fervent "Amens" at the close. Rising, I could see many a one brush away a tear. Several came to shake our hands before we got to the door.

When we were ready to leave the cell, we found that the guards would not let us out without a signed order from Tanner, the Marshal, and he had disappeared! Here we were, the preachers, locked up with the Soapy gang and my congregation waiting at the church and wondering what had become of me. But unique situations are the rule in Skaguay, so Wooden and I made the best of our times by visiting with our fellow prisoners.[1]

The men Sinclair saw and spoke with included Frank Brown alias Blue Jay, Thomas Rauschman alias Jap Tommy, A. L. White alias Sheeny Kid, and Bert Madison, all captured at Dyea. William Fielding was captured at Sheep Camp. Those arrested in Skaguay were Nate Pollock, W. F. Saportas, Charles Bromley, William Tener, John Clear, H. L. Bronson alias Red, B. O'Brien, T. Jackson, John Hawkins, C. L. Hussey, M. J. Talpy, J. A. Swain, Henry Smith, J. Leary, F. J. Dugronder, R. Kingsley, James H. Neiman, and Charles Butler.[2] It is absurd that the jail guards would not immediately release Sinclair and Wooden. Was Tanner intentionally detaining them as punishment for giving comfort to the prisoners? Eventually Tanner was located and the clergymen were released.

Since the night of the gunfight US Army Captain Yeatman had been regularly telephoning Commissioner Sehlbrede to ask if order had been restored. Sehlbrede assured Yeatman that he had everything under control, but with the capture of Old Man Tripp and then Bowers, Foster, and Wilder, a crowd had assembled, kept growing, and at last reached the critical mass of a mob that wanted to seize the

[1] Sinclair, pp. 136-37.
[2] *Skaguay News* 07/15/1898, p. 1.

prisoners. About 11:30 "Sehlbrede hurried to the scene and begged the people to maintain ... good order...."[1] That appeal somewhat calmed the turmoil, but it renewed and continued growing until by 2 a.m., Monday, July 11, Sehlbrede called Captain Yeatman and asked him to bring his soldiers.[2] Sehlbrede then ordered Tanner to transfer Bowers, Foster, and Wilder to the same third-floor Burkhard Hotel area occupied by Van Triplett.[3] Some of the men helping to guard the prisoners were F. F. Clark, Dr. J. A. Cleveland, Tom Word, W. J. Rogers, and Captain Sperry, chairman of the Citizens' Committee. Once together, the inmates began to sing. One soloist sang, "Take Back Your Gold," a sad love song composed in 1897.[4] Word continued to spread that the four men responsible for the robbery had been captured and were being held at the Burkhard. Soon several hundred men were noisily demanding that they be allowed to interrogate the prisoners about the whereabouts of the sack of gold and then to deal with them "as the crowd saw fit."[5]

Suspected was that Jeff had a silent partner and treasurer. This possibly prominent person might have Stewart's gold.[6] Tanner and H. E. Battin kept trying to calm the mob, and at one point Battin attempted to deflect hostility.

> You all know that Soapy Smith has silent partners. The Committee is trying to get at these partners. They are the men to hang if you must take the law in your own hands, which I don't think you will. Men who elevated themselves on a pedestal of seeming morality and robbed the public. Those are the men your Committee is trying to locate.[7]

Railway Chief Surgeon Dr. Fenton Whiting was in the crowd with Railway Chief Contractor Mike Heney, and they both hoped to see the prisoners strung up. In a letter to a friend in 1929 that Whiting never expected would be read by the public at large, he described the chain of events and his shocking participation in them.

> It was 3 A.M., and we had been quite busy all night, rounding up the gang. We finally got wind that these men were up there, and soon many hundreds of men had gathered out in front, all bent upon one "solemn thought"—to get hold of these rats, and string them up. Old Si Tanner, the Marshal stood in the hall way to upstairs, pleading with crocodile tears in his eyes, for "peace and harmony," and to "let the law take its course." ... Yes, old Si was bringing into play every inch of his unnatural eloquence.... Heney and myself were out there in the bunch, casually talking over the hectic situation, and the Sun was just about to announce another day up over Mt Dewey.... I thought I would go on upstairs, and make a survey of the situation before we made our grand rush for the "goal"—the three up there whom we so badly wanted.[8]

---

[1] *Daily Alaskan* 07/11/1898, p. 1.

[2] *Morning Oregonian* 08/27/1898, p. 9.

[3] Ltr fr Fenton Whiting, 07/27/1929, Alaska Historical Library. MS4, Box 13 #3.

[4] Pritzkow.

[5] *Skaguay News* 07/15/1898, p. 1.

[6] *Skaguay News* 07/15/1898.

[7] *Daily Alaskan* 07/11/1898.

[8] Whiting, p. 2.

Here is the confession of one man among many feeling the blood lust that transforms a crowd into a mob. This medical doctor just before on the same type-written page had extolled the wisdom of "Old Hipocrates." Now he was detailing his desire to lynch the prisoners and, next, how he went about reconnoitering a way for the mob to extract them from their guards. Whiting supplied a transition of sorts from Hipocrates. He shared the measure of himself as he remembered it over thirty years later: "I was young then, and full of everything, from gold ol' Rye, to good ol' real PEP, and didn't give a 'tinkers"[1] for "nothing' or nobody." Such an assessment of self in any setting has to be among the most unsettling ever written by a man of medicine.

Whiting did manage to get into the upstairs of the hotel for a look-see. Si Tanner let him "pass without a word, knowing me as he did for some time as a personal friend." On the third floor he saw the three guards "with their beautiful Winchesters, looking me square in the mug. ... Huddled" behind them were the "three arch criminals, crouching down on their knees, frightened nine-tenths to death already, and expecting to be yanked out by the coat collar, and informally strung-up." Whiting knew 2 of the 3 guards and "felt pretty sure" that they would not shoot him in a struggle for the prisoners.

Whiting then returned downstairs to Heney to report. After hearing the situation, Heney said,

> "Well, Doc, let's go on up and take the chance, it will be a nice diversion from this tiresome monotony of hanging round here all day." We both laughed like Hell, and shook hands, and got ready for instant action. But, just then, the unexpected happened as it always does.

A guard poked his head out the window and "announced to the impatient throng ... that a prisoner had escaped out the window...."

> The guards had paid so much attention to the throng's impending approach that they had entirely ignored the trembling prisoners huddled behind them, and one of them, Slim Jim, had actually jumped out the third story window down to a shed below and from there to the ground.

Whiting wrote that he then ran as fast as he

> could out around to the alley, where, much to my surprise, I really did run in, face to face, with the notorious and desperate "Slim Jim" standing up there against the wall, casting furtive glances in every direction, planning the best avenue of escape. I didn't kill him, because he didn't have a gun on him, but covered him with a most beautiful six inch Colts, which I had only previously bought in Seattle, and was anxious to see just how good it would work. He wilted at the sight of it, as I poked it under his homely mug, and grabbed him by the coat collar, and literally dragged him out into the open. Luckily, there was no one there but him and me, but way off at the end of this alley, stood a man who looked like a cowboy with a lasso in his hand—a nice new [undecipherable] inch rope, all coiled, and ready for action, like the proverbial

---

[1] *tinker's damn*: tinker: 1a, craftsman who mends pots; 1d, tinker's curse, cuss, or damn—not to care, or be worth a curse or damn," with ref to reputed addiction of tinkers to profane swearing (*OED*).

"rattler." He glanced at us and immediately took in the situation, and at my gesture, came forward on the run, swinging the "lasso" over his head as if in a round-up. But it was a case of "love's labor lost,"[1] for, in the meantime, the citizens had phoned across to Dyea, where the Federal troops were stationed, and they had arrived..., unbeknowns [sic] to ... us. The troops were in the lead, unfortunately, and the mob of hundreds of irate citizens had actually forced them over in our direction..., and as I plowed along half dragging Slim with my left hand, and holding "Old Reliable" in my right, I actually stumbled over and knocked down Capt. Yeatman, in charge, and trampled him down in the dust much to his disgust, of course. He was about as big as a hickory nut, and got up, brushing off his natty uniform, madder than hell!! I tried to look pleasant to him, this in the apparent face of martial law.... His face was quite flushed-up, to put it mildly, and just what he told me in sonorous tones would not sound well at a Methodist camp meeting.[2]

If the portrait Whiting paints is accurate, which seems likely, Yeatman and his sixteen soldiers probably saved Foster's life and prevented hundreds of armed and angry men from overwhelming the half dozen men seeking to protect the other suspects. *The News* reported that even "Several of our best citizens, heavy property owners and honest men, were anxious to pull on a rope Sunday night."[3] Yeatman ordered two soldiers to take charge of Foster, much to the "disgust" of Whiting and the cowboy who had "the rope still coiled in his ready hands." The soldiers took Foster back up with the others. Whiting reported that he and Heney then retired to the Board of Trade saloon where they "'lifted several'" drinks "and brooded over just what 'might have been' had not the damned federal troops arrived at that unfortunate time." And over that "might have been," Heney told Whiting, "That was tough luck, Doc."[4]

In the same letter to his friend, Dr. Whiting told of meeting Jeff Smith.

He came up to me on the street, and announced himself as "Jeff Smith—they often call me Soapy up here," he remarked, with a bland smile. "Anyway," he resumed, "come on over to my place and make yourself at home," handing me a cigar from his vest pocket at the same time, and stating that "Any --- -- - ---- [son of a bitch] who bothers you over there won't do it to anybody else again." We strolled on over to Jeff Smith's Parlors [sic] as the sign read, and entered. Inside there was an interesting picture, one which would make a "movey" blush with shame when it came to toughness.[5] We sauntered on up to the bar, and Soapy commanded with a very graceful gesture to the "Bar-keep" to bring out his best. He did so, pronto, and we libated in the usual

---

[1] *"love's labor lost"*: William Shakespeare's 9th play is titled *Love's Labor's Lost* (1588-95).

[2] Whiting, pp. 3-4.

[3] *Skaguay News* 07/15/1898, p. 3.

[4] Whiting, p. 4.

[5] *interesting picture ... a "movey" blush ... toughness*: this interesting, somewhat enigmatic sentence may refer to a raw, perhaps pornographic picture hanging in the Parlor. "Movey" may be "movie." The movies in 1929, of course, at the time of Whiting's writing, were highly popular and not yet subject to serious censorship, which was enacted in 1933 and began to take effect in 1934.

manner of those soulful times. As we faced about, and smoked our cigars, there before us stood an array of faces which had graced many a rogue's gallery—gunmen and killers from Creede, Cripple Creek, and Denver ... out West for their own good health and peace of mind, but also for their leader's bank account and prosperity. We stood there at the bar and smoked casually and talked over current events of the day. He reminded me of a typical Southern planter of the pre-slavery days—handsome, wonderful manners, and a fluent speaker, with an ebony Van Dyke beard and a cowboy hat....

Whiting noted that "'Soapy' ... didn't dare to job me, due to my association with the White Pass & Yukon Railway, but wanted our moral support." So it was that the "gang stood there" and "soon caught the idea" that Jeff was befriending Whiting

and marked time. This was an unusual affair—a social one, and they resumed their usual pastime, that of fumbling with the cards at the tables, and mixing in an occasional drink....[1]

Another version of Foster's escape was published in *The Skaguay News*. Once on the ground, he made a mad dash "before a hundred men, nearly all of them armed, were following him and shooting at him at every jump." Foster was apprehended near Bond (4th Avenue) and State streets, "and for a few minutes it looked as if the rising sun would shine on 'Slim's' body dangling from a limb." Tanner appeared, though, "recovered his man and quietly marched him back to the guarded room" in the hotel.[2]

Still another version of the escape was told by the *Daily Alaskan*. In this one, it was not Foster but Bowers, who upon hearing the threats of the crowd, "made a dash through the second story back window." Then "There was a rush for the rear of the hotel premises. A score more shots were rapidly fired." Reaching Broadway, "he was again in custody and pleading for his life," for

Then the demand to lynch him was renewed with some force, and Bowers pitifully pleaded for mercy or at least a little time. Leading citizens surrounded him, however, and coolly held back the more excited of the crowd.

Just in the nick of time up came Capt. Yeatman with seventeen or eighteen of the regulars from Dyea.[3]

Had Skaguay had another paper, even another version might have been told.

A common theme among the versions, however, is the mob mentality that called for bringing the four men to immediate and violent justice. Probably it was well that soldiers had come, or the accused, characterized by *The News* as "past grand masters in crime," might have had their last look at the sun that early Monday morning in July. Even so, the soldiers had not been called by the Citizens' Committee or Tanner, but by Sehlbrede, and as they wanted to preserve control, the soldiers

were politely asked by the citizens committee to withdraw..., after being thanked for their consideration in Skaguay's behalf, and assured that their act

---

[1] Whiting, p. 4.

[2] *Skaguay News* 07/15/1898, p. 1.

[3] *Daily Alaskan* 07/11/1898, p. 1.

in coming was appreciated, although for the good name of the town, it was deemed best that they return, which they did at about noon Monday.[1]

Before leaving, Captain Yeatman told Sehlbrede that "in the event of an unlawful move on the part of the people," he would "return with his men and take charge of the city...." In that event, because Alaska was a "prohibition district, all the saloons would not only be closed, but all the property pertaining to saloons" would be destroyed.[2] The Citizens' Committee surely feared that martial law would not only end their reign but also cause travelers to avoid the town, especially one without a single saloon.

Not lost on the leading citizens of Skaguay was that names conveyed perceptions for good or ill. When Captain Yeatman threatened martial law because violence appeared imminent, including lynching, the Citizens' Committee, on the morning of July 11, 1898, appointed the Committee of Safety, which, of course, suggested keeping the city as well as the prisoners safe. This committee would decide who among the detainees should be charged with crimes and sent to Sitka for trial, who should be strongly offered the opportunity to leave Skaguay (or in other words, be deported), and who, if any, should be released with an apology. This committee consisted of 11 members, with Commissioner Sehlbrede as chair. The other members included H. E. Battin, E. J. Brannick, F. E. Burns, Sam Freeman, S. H. Graves, Pierre Humbert, E. O. Sylvester, J. M. Tanner, F. H. Whiting, and Thomas Whitten.[3]

Railway President Graves' report of "July 13th" to his company shines light on the Committee's treatment of prisoners. The prisoners had "disclosed nothing of any value," had begun "to talk about 'their rights,'" and could cause

> trouble because of course we have no shadow of law to warrant their imprisonment, and still less for taking the money found on them and using it to pay for the stolen gold dust and for a fund to pay the expenses of legal prosecutions against those that we have got legal evidence against, and to pay the cost of "deporting" the others. This being so, before the mob got too tame, I took one of the prisoners who referred to his "rights," by the shoulder and led him to the window of our room from which he could look down on the mob, and said to him, "You are quite right, we have no authority for holding you a moment against your will. If you say the word, I will turn you loose into that mob this minute. What do you say?" This was more than he had bargained for, so he began to hedge, as I expected. Then I said, "If you don't want us to turn you loose this minute, you must sign this paper...."

The prisoner was handed "a written request to the Committee" for him to be held and protected "until he could be handed over" to legal authority, "and in consideration" for this service, "authority was given us to apply all money" taken from the prisoner.

> He rather "jibbed" at signing this, and wanted to consult the other prisoners, but I said, "No, sign or step outside. ... So he signed. Then we put

[1] *Skaguay News* 07/15/1898, p. 1.

[2] *Skaguay News* 07/15/1898, p. 3.

[3] *Skaguay News* 07/15/1898, p. 2. F. H. Whiting was a supervisor with the Railway and no relation to Dr. F. B. Whiting.

him in another room, and sent for all the other prisoners, one by one, and repeated the same proceedings until all had signed....[1]

Some Committee of Safety members, no doubt influenced by the Citizens' Committee at large, used their powers to eliminate certain business competitors for their own personal gain. It was all too easy to find enough witnesses (seventy-three were reported to have appeared[2]) to accuse a competitor of being in league with Jeff and cause his deportation. No solid record reports how many were forced from Skaguay. One resident reported "a dozen or more were gotten rid of" in this manner.[3] Several of Skaguay's businessmen who were deported complained loudly once they reached the safety of the states. They claimed innocence and that they had been exiled so that members of the Citizens' Committee could seize their businesses and property. One of these is believed to have been Thomas Rauschman, known as "Jap Tommy." Elmer J. "Stroller" White wrote that Rauschman had nothing to do with Jeff's activities, but rather, he did own the Comique Concert Hall, and the Committee wanted possession of it because of its stage and large seating capacity for their meetings.[4] Another of those accused and questioned was C. F. Moody, president of the First Bank of Skaguay. Moody was believed to be one of Jeff's "silent partners." In Seattle Moody had plenty to say about the accusation.

> C. F. Moody, president of the First Bank of Skaguay, arrived in Seattle Wednesday on the steamer Oregon. Shortly after his arrival he took occasion to make a strong and emphatic denial of the widely circulated story that he was run out of Skaguay by the citizens for the reason that he was accused of concealing in the vault of the bank the dust and nuggets stolen from a Yukoner by one of "Soapy" Smith's gang.
>
> Mr. Moody avers that he is the victim of a conspiracy and that an attempt is being made by his enemies to ruin his reputation and drive him out of business. He declares, however, that he will continue to be a resident of Skaguay and run his bank just as long as there is such a town. To a Post-Intelligencer reporter, at the Hotel Seattle, yesterday, Mr. Moody said:
>
> "All talk detrimental to my reputation was started by my enemies. The report that I was ordered to leave town by the committee of citizens was a lie.... It was believed that "Soapy" Smith deposited the stolen sack of gold in our bank, owing to the fact that he called at the office on the night the robbery occurred. I appeared before the committee of citizens, told my story and the gold, it will be remembered, was afterward found back of Smith's saloon.[5]

A total of fifteen men were known to be deported. The account of the first ten to leave appeared this way in *The Skaguay News*:

> J. Allen Hornsby, W. F. Saportas, Nate Pollock, C. S. Hussey, Bradley O'Brien, Chas Bromberg, J. Swain, J. Leary, Frank Brown and Henry Smith.

[1] Graves, pp. 28-30.
[2] *Skaguay News* 07/15/1898, p. 2, fr "Report of the Committee."
[3] *Morning Oregonian* 08/27/1898, p. 9.
[4] DeArmond, p. 40.
[5] *Seattle Post-Intelligencer* 08/05/1898, p. 6.

They were accordingly marched to the wharf where after being lined up, the command "hats off" was given and the gang was photographed, after which they were placed aboard the big steamer [*Tartar*] which soon after quietly pulled out....[1]

"The committee kept up its work unceasingly, and by Wednesday night, a second crowd, consisting of five men and one women, had been selected for deportation. They were shipped on the steamer" *Tartar*. Included were William Tener, Billy O'Donnell, Jim Hawkins, Bert Markinson, Mike Torpy, and his wife "Vie," who was held on the charge of "keeping a disorderly house."[2] The men left on the *Tartar* without trouble, but not Mrs. Torpy. Refusing to board ship, she was detained under guard.[3] "Vie" is probably "Violet Tarpy," a pick-pocketing California gang member who made her living "by luring marks into hotel rooms where cash could be appropriated in any number of ways, theft, robbery, blackmail."[4] In Denver she was arrested with other members of the Blonger bunco gang and bailed out by Lou Blonger. Apparently she felt she was better off staying in Skaguay. Mike returned, passing through Skaguay again on August 4, 1898, and *The Skaguay News* took note,

> Mike Tarpey [sic], one of the recent Tartar's passengers for below, passed through here yesterday on the Topeka for Sitka, to which place he goes for the purpose of visiting his wife, "Vie," who is a member of Skaguay's delegation at present detained in Sitka's "Skookum House." "Vie" is held on the charge of conducting a "bad shop," and her husband's visit is for the purpose of securing her release. We do not know that anyone here objects to her release, provided she keeps herself "skace" in the future.[5]

The following December "Vie," her last name spelled "Torpey," was running a brothel near the corner of Skaguay's State and Sixth streets for which she was indicted and ordered to appear before a Juneau grand jury.[6]

Generally believed was that most of the Skaguay deportees were wanted men and would be nabbed by law enforcement in Seattle. According to the *Daily Alaskan* for July 25, 1898, Seattle Police Chief Reid "gave instructions that the deportees were to be picked up for safekeeping. It is proposed that Seattle not be made a dumping ground for the criminal element of Skaguay." However, no evidence indicates that any of the deportees was taken into custody. The same issue of the *Alaskan* reprinted news from a Seattle newspaper about William Saportas and J. Allen Hornsby.

> W. F. Saportas will return [to Skaguay] on the next steamer. He says he came out to look after some business matters. He thinks that Soapy Smith wanted to commit suicide when he went down to the wharf. He thinks that the

---

[1] *Skaguay News* 07/15/1898, p. 2. A famous Case & Draper photograph of men apparently on Moore's wharf are thought to be the men described. But there are 9, not 10, and all but 2 are wearing hats. If the photograph described in the *News* exists, it is not known.

[2] *Daily Alaskan* 07/15/1898.

[3] *Skaguay News* 07/15/1898.

[4] *RMN* 11/11/1895.

[5] *Skaguay News* Supplement 08/05/1898, item 138, author's col. *"skace"*: archaic form of *scarce* (*OED*).

[6] US v. Mrs. M. J. Torpey.

matter might have ended very differently had not Soapy ran up against the nervy Reid. He agrees with the prevailing opinion in the north that Skaguay will be a much better town now that Smith is dead.

This orientation was blatantly self-serving from the person whom most of Skaguay knew to have been in the employ of Jeff. Moreover, widely known was that when Jeff's clothing was searched, a note was found that read, "'the crowd is angry, if you want to do anything do it quick.' ... [signed] 'S.'" Further, the handwriting was identified as belonging to "one 'Billie' Saportas."[1]

As for Hornsby, he

> was very indignant at the treatment he received at the hands of the vigilance committee, and expects to receive an invitation to return by the next boat. He said: "I was sent out of Skaguay in a most arbitrary manner. The United States Commissioner said there were no charges against me, but that he had no power to combat the citizens' committee that had put me on the boat at the point of loaded Winchesters. Everyone was very much excited, and although I was very badly treated I am not 'squealing.' The only thing they seemed to have against me was that I did not publish an account of the robbery [of Stewart] in the Friday evening edition. I could have explained the omission satisfactorily, but was not given the chance. Several of my enemies are at the bottom of the trouble, but it will turn out all right."[2]

It is not known if Hornsby returned to Skaguay, but the US Census for 1900 shows a John Allen Hornsby as a miner and previously a physician living in Eagle City, a District of Alaska mining community. Born in 1859 in St. Louis, records show him as a physician in a hospital in that city in 1880 and still a medical doctor there in 1890. By 1910 he was superintendent of a hospital in Chicago and then in 1920 a physician in a Washington, DC, hospital. He appears to have died in 1939, age 80.[3]

As for Saportas, he resorted to what some have done in romance when in trouble and gone off to join the French Foreign Legion. William, though, who was not that romantic, did not go so far. At the Presidio in San Francisco on October 4, 1898, at the age of 26 years, 8½ months, he joined the US Army. He was made a clerk, served his enlistment, enlisted again and continued enlisting. He received good-to-excellent reviews, rose to sergeant, sergeant major, and into the officer ranks to captain. Saportas received postings all over the country, and apparently in his travels, he met again the wife of the formerly famous *World* Sylvester Scovel, whom he had rescued from Bennett and who had become Scovel's widow. He married her in Hawaii in 1917 and is presumed to have remained so until his death June 1942.[4]

---

[1] Wickersham, p. 23.

[2] *Daily Alaskan* 07/25/1898.

[3] John "Allan" & "Allen" Hornsby, 1860 US census, 1889-1890 St. Louis Directories, 1900, 1910, & 1920 US Census, & *Dictionary of North American Authors*, all accessed through Ancestry.com.

[4] Campbell, p. 159. & Records fr US Army Enlistments, 1910 & 1920 US Census, 1925 Kansas Census, & CA Death Index, all accessed through Ancestry.com.

Deputy US Marshal Taylor did not fare well after Jeff's death. On Tuesday, July 12, 1898, US Marshal Shoup learned of the shootout on the Juneau Wharf. The following day he wrote to the attorney general.

> About twenty lawless characters are in the hands of the committee, and it is supposed that a number will be lynched. U.S. Deputy Marshal S. S. Taylor is accused of being in collusion with the robbers and is also in custody. There being no other marshal there, I leave today for Skagway.[1]

Shoup arrived on Thursday, July 14, and within hours fired Taylor from his position and appointed Tanner in his place. The *Daily Alaskan* reported "ex-Deputy Marshal Taylor" was charged with attempted extortion from a stampeder, but as the complainant left Skaguay for the interior, that charge was set aside, leaving only the charge of "willful neglect of duty, laid by Mr. Stewart." Taylor was brought before the Committee of Safety July 15, 1898, to answer to the charge. "He waived examination" and was ordered held pending posting of $5,000 bond until trial could be held at Sitka. Deputy US Marshal Tanner took Taylor into custody.[2]

At noon on the previous day, Stewart's gold was found by A. L. Remick. A Committee of Safety report, published in both papers, stated that it was found "in a trunk in an outbuilding in the rear of Smith's saloon." The Committee may have been mistaken about the "outbuilding" as none was known to exist there, only the little back room in the Parlor. In the same edition of *The News*, a paragraph about the gold stated it "was found yesterday about noon in 'Soapy's' trunk in the back room of his saloon." The sack contained 125¼ ounces, worth approximately $2,100. Missing was approximately $600, according to Stewart. Also found in the trunk were business documents belonging to Jeff Smith as well as letters written to and from him.[3]

To be wondered is why it would take six days to find a large sack of gold in a trunk in the small back office of Jeff Smith's Parlor. After all, Jeff had been a focus of the Stewart robbery, and with Jeff dead, one would think his effects would have been searched right away. It seems probable they were but that the gold had not been there then. So where was it until A. L. Remick found it? Probably in someone's possession who finally thought it best to let it be found among the dead man's things and thereby put an end to the question. The mob mentality had become fixed on finding Stewart's gold, and if its rising anger were not dampened, spontaneous hangings could result.

On July 14 Commissioner Sehlbrede and the Committee of Safety held secret preliminary trial hearings in the warehouse on the Seattle Wharf. Brought before the Committee were nine members of the Soap Gang, who were in custody. Triplett, Foster, Bowers, and Harry Bronson were charged with larceny. Wilder, Jackson, and John Clear were charged with felony assault with a dangerous weapon. Al White was charged with larceny and being armed with a dangerous weapon. Charles Butler was charged with inciting to riot. Bronson and Butler were "permitted to leave town" due to a lack of evidence. Trial for the remaining men was to begin the following day. Bond

---

[1] Hunt, *Distant*, p. 63.

[2] *Skaguay News* 07/15/1898, p. 3, & *Daily Alaskan* 07/15/1898, p. 1.

[3] *Skaguay News* 07/15/1898, p. 2, & *Daily Alaskan* 07/15/1898, p. 1. Report of the Committee is the same in both papers except that the weight in *The News* is 125⅓ ozs. while in the *Alaskan* it is 125¼ ozs.

for Bowers, Foster, and Triplett was set at $25,000 each, and for Jackson, Wilder, and Clear, the sum was $5,000 each. None of the men could raise bond, so all remained incarcerated. John Clear demanded an immediate trial and was given until 1 p.m. to find an attorney. Walter Church, the only attorney present, declined to take his case.[1] Clear's fate is unknown. Ironically, Church had represented Jeff and ex-Deputy US Marshal Taylor in their libel case against *The Seattle Daily Times* earlier that month.

Marshal Shoup wrote to the attorney general for the District of Alaska, "Everything was turned over to me as soon as I arrived and none of the citizens offered any resistance or obstruction." But Reid's condition was worsening, and Shoup feared "An attempt would immediately follow his death to lynch some of the prisoners by overcoming the guards...." In consequence, Shoup wrote, "I chartered a boat and brought all the prisoners to Sitka."[2] A photograph taken on the steamer *Athenian*[3] show Bowers, Jackson, Triplett, and Foster handcuffed to one another for the voyage.

The *Daily Alaskan* announced on July 15 that tranquility had returned to Skaguay. Tanner ordered the citizens' vigilante force relegated and asked that all guns lent for the crisis be immediately returned, including all effects taken from those arrested.[4]

Twelve days after being shot, on Wednesday, July 20, 1898, bed ridden since the gunfight, Reid died of his wounds. The Union Church funeral was the largest Skaguay had witnessed. A photograph shows a closed coffin in the church, draped with a military-type flag. Below the casket were heaps of flowers, and a wreath lay across a top-most corner. A large wreath and smaller cuttings from trees made a backdrop. An honor guard of two men "at rest" with rifles stand at each end of the casket.[5]

The *Daily Alaskan* covered the event in detail.

> The body of Mr. Reid lay in state at the church from ten until one.... Many ... paused by the bier for a last look at the placid features, and many remained in order to secure seats for the services. Thus long before one o'clock, ... all of the seats ... were occupied and the crowd outside unable to enter the church was very large. It filled the whole street.

Episcopal Rev. Dr. Wood performed services inside. Then "a platform was arranged at the approach of the church, on which Rev. Dr. Sinclair" gave an "eloquent tribute to the memory of Skaguay's hero.[6] The *Alaskan* reprinted Rev. Sinclair's "tribute" and then described the "long procession of vehicles crowded with people" as well as

> some on horseback, others on foot, that followed the remains of Mr. Reid to the cemetery, and formed a pageant imposing and impressive. Then came the soldier's funeral, and prayers by the chaplain, the salute from the rifles of

---

[1] *Skaguay News* 07/15/1898.
[2] Shoup to Attorney General, 07/22/1898. National Archives, Washington, D.C., Record Group 60.
[3] Minter, p. 225.
[4] *Daily Alaskan* 07/15/1898.
[5] Becker, p. 37.
[6] *Daily Alaskan* 07/22/1898, p. 1.

40. The start of the shootout on the Juneau Wharf. Frank Reid (left) grabs Jeff's rifle and pulls the trigger of his own pistol, only to have it misfire. Standing to the rear are Jesse Murphy and J. M. Tanner. (Art by John Bruce)

41. The final seconds of the shootout on the Juneau Wharf as Jesse Murphy prepares to shoot the wounded, unarmed Jeff in the chest with his own rifle. Frank Reid lies gravely wounded on the right. Josias Tanner and a group of Jeff's "associates" do not appear in the artist's rendering. Tanner stood off to the right, and Jeff's men were down the wharf at its entrance. (Art by John Bruce.)

42. Early postcard of Skaguay, Alaska. The Juneau Wharf where the shootout took place is left of the center with the triangular end. (Author's col.)

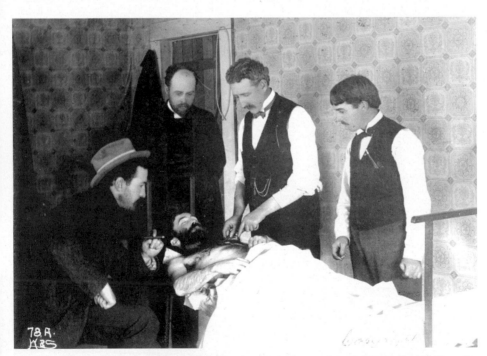

43. The corpse of Jeff R. Smith undergoing the start of an autopsy. (l to r) Dr. Whiting sits, smoking a cigar and Rev. John Sinclair watches as Dr. Cornelius cuts into Jeff's chest. An unknown man looks on. Photograph taken with Rev. Sinclair's camera (Sinclair, p. 136). (University of Washington Libraries, Special Collections, negative no: Hegg 17A)

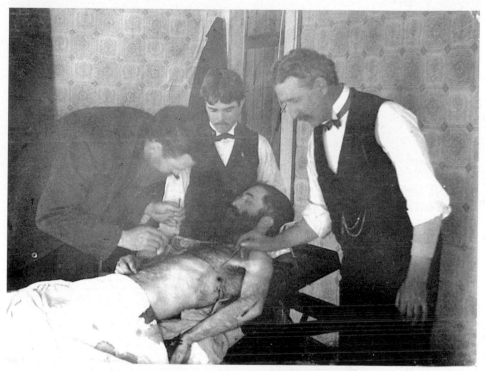

44. A graphic autopsy photograph of Jeff's corpse. (l to r) Dr. Whiting uses a tool in his left hand to lift skin from the chest cavity; with another tool in his right hand, Whiting points to something, perhaps an entry wound or damage to the heart. An unknown man looks on while Dr. Cornelius points with a tool to another wound. The crease from a bullet clearly appears along Jeff's left arm. The blood-soaked sheets probably betray previous probing of the bullet wound Jeff had received to his leg. (John A. Sinclair photog., author's col.)

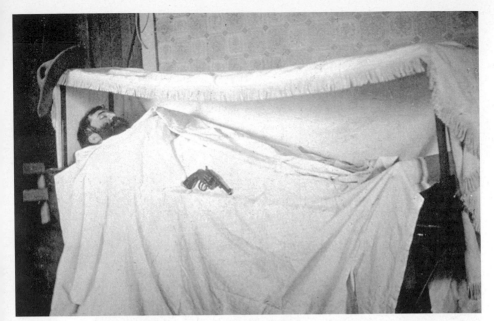

45. Jeff R. Smith II resides in the morgue in the same room and on the same table on which the autopsy was performed. Placed at his side is his large caliber, double action revolver. Jeff's hat hangs above his head. (H. C. Barley photog, Cynthia Brackett Driscoll, Brackett Family col.)

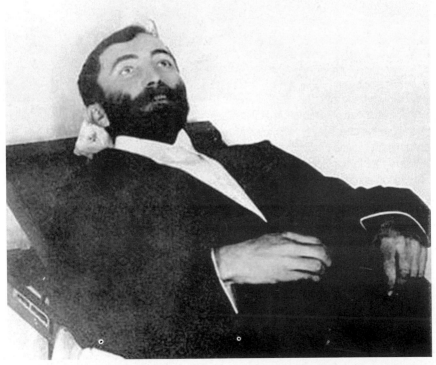

46. Jeff's open-eyed corpse propped up on an examination table. Rev. Sinclair wrote in his diary that he had "negatives of the corpse, one very lifelike with eyes open..." (Sinclair, p. 136). (Alaska State Library, William J. Kerr col., John A. Sinclair photog., ASL-P453-062)

The notorious "Soapy" Smiths grave.
In a gun fight with Frank Reid - both mortally wounded

47. Jefferson R. Smith's grave, Skaguay, Alaska. Rev. Dickey wrote at the bottom of this photograph, "The notorious 'Soapy' Smiths grave. In a gun fight with Frank Reid – both mortally wounded." (John A. Sinclair photog., Dickey Family col.)

48. Vigilantes gathered outside city hall, Skaguay, Alaska. Circa July 9, 1898. (University of Washington Libraries, Special Collections, John A. Sinclair photog., Negative no: UW 3783)

49. Nine Soap Gang members before being deported. They are believed to be at the entrance to Moore's Wharf, Skaguay, Alaska. The *Skaguay News* reported the names of ten men to be photographed before they were shipped out, as follows: "J. Allen Hornsby, W. F. Saportas, Nate Pollock, C. S. Hussey, Bradley O'Brien, Chas Bromberg, J. Swain, J. Leary, Frank Brown and Henry Smith" (07/15/1898, p. 2.). Only two of these names can be positively matched to men in this photograph: Pollock, fourth from the left, and Saportas, sixth. (Alaska State Library, Case and Draper col., Case & Draper photog., ASL-P39-0843)

50. Shipped to Juneau for trial were (l to r) W. Foster, John Bowers, W. Jackson, and Van Triplett. A photographer caught them together in handcuffs aboard ship. (Author's col.)

51. Envelope addressed to Capt. Jeff Smith from an unknown person in Mexico. Bearing a June 1898 postmark, the letter arrived in Skagway too late to be delivered. Across the top, someone in the Skaguay post office wrote, "Deceased." (Author's col., item 51)

52. "Soapy Smith's Skull." This is the label placed on the painted natural formation in the cliff near Moore's Wharf. The painting appeared in 1926 as a boost to tourism; an article alluding to the "Ironic Monument" appeared in 1927 (*Literary Digest*). The monument to a bad man still welcomes guests to Skaguay. (Author's col.)

53. Personal belongings.   (l) Jeff's silver-plated match safe (item 121).   (top) Six of Jeff's faro cards (item 159).   (c middle) Clancy and Company business card (item 32).   (c bottom) Henry Edwards business card. On back Jeff wrote "Yank is a great fellow. Jeff" (item 47).   (r) Gold-plated stick-pin engraved with Jeff's initials, "JRS" (item 120). (Items from author's col.)

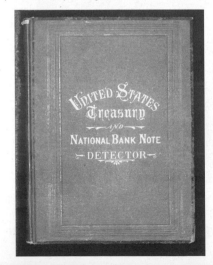

54. (l) *United States Treasury National Bank Note Detector* (1877). The book aided in detecting counterfeit bills. For purposes of comparison, it contains "proof impressions from the original government engraving plates" for US bank notes ranging from the one dollar bill to the one thousand dollar bill. Ink stamps inside show Jeff purchased this book from George Mason and Company of Denver. (Item 115, author's col.)

the comrades, and the bugle call of "lights out, and rest"; and all the earthly honor possible had been paid.[1]

At the gravesite, the choir, which had sung before in the Union Church, sang "Nearer My God to Thee" and was joined by "hundreds of citizens. Rev. Wood pronounced the benediction, a military chaplain offered a prayer, a commander made a short address, flowers were distributed, and the chaplain made "closing remarks." Finally, an honor guard fired a "salute to the dead…, and a bugle sounded 'taps.'"[2] That same day the first locomotive in Alaska and the first for the White Pass and Yukon Railway rumbled down Broadway on new tracks laid down its middle.[3]

Four days before his death, Reid made a will dated July 16, 1898. It directed, first, that his "body be decently buried" and that when his executor, Leslie Butler, had "sufficient funds in hand, [he] pay all funeral expenses and the expenses of my last sickness." And "Second, I give and bequeath unto my brother, D. U. S. Reid, now in Eugene, State of Oregon, the sum of One (1) Dollar." Third, his executor was directed to manage his "rights, title and interest" in a one-sixth interest in and to a 39-acre tract of land "fronting on Skaguay Bay" and to "sell and dispose of [it] in trust for the presiding Pastor or Board of church Directors of the Presbyterian Church Society. And fourth, he directed that his "personal estate … be sold" and that the proceeds "given to the president of the Women's Relief Corps of the Town of Skaguay" for its "use and benefit." The 27 items left by Reid, including the real estate, were valued at $487.40, and Commissioner Sehlbrede ordered them sold for cash on August 3, 1898.[4] Disbursements do not appear in the Skaguay Probate record, but presumably they were distributed as requested. Reid's possessions were listed in detail, down to one pair of shoes and a clothes brush. However, his pistol is not mentioned. Apparently Tanner, who picked it up the night of the shootout on the wharf, still had it.

By September funds were being collected for a stone monument to replace the wooden marker over Reid's grave.[5] The work was completed on January 27, 1899, at a cost of $450. The monument reads,   Frank H. Reid
Died
July 20, 1898
Aged
54 years
He gave his life for the honor of Skagway

John Stewart may have been a robbery victim, but in Skaguay he was not appreciated as explained in the July 15, 1898, issue of the *Skaguay News*.

It was more for the good name of Skaguay, rather than sympathy for Stewart, that our people rejoiced at the recovery of the sack of stolen gold. Ordinarily intelligent business men manifest very imperfect sympathy for a

[1] Fr the Rev. John A. Sinclair diary. James M. Sinclair, *Mission: Klondike*, Mitchell Press Limited, Vancouver, Canada, 1978.
[2] *Daily Alaskan*, 07/22/1898, p. 2.
[3] *Alaska Geographic*, p. 29.
[4] *Probate Book A*, pp. 135-38.
[5] *Skaguay News* 09/23/1898.

man who goes against sure thing games, or [men] who go mooning around looking at eagles in the rear of saloons with sacks of gold in their hands. Such men need guardians, but their softness and verdancy[1] in no way palliates or excuses the men who take advantage of innocence and rob them. Neither the penitentiaries nor asylums for feeble-mindedness are as full as the conditions of the country would justify.[2]

By November that contempt towards Stewart turned to something akin to hatred.

J. D. Stewart, the man who is alleged to have been robbed of his sack of gold while gazing at the proud bird of freedom in Soapy Smith's back yard on the 8th of July last, came to Skaguay two weeks ago and will be on hand to testify before the U.S. District court against the alleged robbers when court convenes at Juneau the latter part of the month. It is to be hoped that after the robbers are fairly started on their way to San Quentin, Stewart will submit to a surgical operation and have some oatmeal mush or other equally soft substance injected into his brain cavity.[3]

Two months later Stewart made a gesture of thanks. He contributed some of the gold returned to him to "plate" a US deputy marshal's badge for Tanner.[4]

Bowers, Triplett, and the others were sent to Sitka to await trial, which was held in Juneau before a federal grand jury on November 9, 1898. The defendants originally retained Seattle defense attorney Edgar Caypless,[5] known to the *Rocky Mountain News* as "par excellent" and one of the "loudest talkers in the business."[6] Caypless was a one-time resident of Denver and had defended Jeff and members of the Soap Gang at least once since 1888.[7] It was he who defended Jeff in the assault trial of John Arkins in 1889.[8] However, by the start of the trial in Juneau, the gang had hired attorney W. T. "Billy" Hume[9] and W. E. Crews, who argued that the "indictment did not state facts sufficient to constitute a crime," and further, that the court had "no jurisdiction."[10] Ironically, at the same time the Soap Gang members were appearing at their trials, the same court was just getting around to the trial of John Fay for the January 1898 murders of Deputy US Marshal James Rowan and Andrew McGrath. The wheels of justice in the District of Alaska were again turning, but also again so very slowly and not always, truly.

The defense argued that Stewart had lost his money in a square game and that no force had been used against him. The prosecution countered with the two witnesses who claimed to have heard the entire incident. It was their corroboration of

---

[1] *verdancy*: archaic, greenness. *verdant* = green.

[2] *Skaguay News* 07/15/1898, p. 2.

[3] *Skaguay News* 11/11/1898.

[4] *Skaguay News* 02/03/1899. This badge and other relics are on permanent display at the Alaska State Museum in Juneau.

[5] *Denver Times* 08/20/1898, p. 5.

[6] *RMN* 12/15/1889, p. 2. Alaskan newspapers misspelled his name as "Caypiese."

[7] *Denver Times* 08/20/1898, & *RMN* 08/30/1888, p. 9.

[8] *RMN* 07/31/1889.

[9] *Skaguay News* 12/09/1898.

[10] US v. (2) W. E. Foster and John Bowers.

Stewart's claim of having been robbed that produced arrest warrants. The defense wanted this testimony quashed as the witnesses, while they may have *heard* the incident, did not *see* it. However, the prosecution produced a new witness, Abe L. Ritter, who said he saw Stewart scuffling in the alley with the three men whom he knew to be members of the gang. Frank E. Burns, Citizens' Committee secretary, also testified as did Mr. Kaufman, the man whose store was said to have housed Stewart's gold. The defense asked for and received several continuances based on a writ of errors and a subpoena of defense witnesses, many of whom could not be located. The court ultimately rejected all points of "error," and the trial proceeded to a conclusion.

In the last month of 1898, the cases against three of the four men involved in robbing Stewart were concluded. Bowers and Foster were charged with larceny, or theft, and assault and battery while Triplett was charged with larceny only. They were all found guilty, sentenced, and taken aboard the steamer *Cottage City* for transport to Sitka to serve their sentences.[1] Bowers was sentenced to a year for larceny and six months for assault and battery.[2] He served his full time and was released in March 1900.[3] Foster was sentenced to a year and fined $1,000 for larceny, and six months for assault and battery.[4] After "Slim Jim" Foster had served one year, President McKinley commuted his sentence due to his having contracted consumption.[5] Van B. "Old Man" Triplett was sentenced to a year for larceny and served his full time.[6] After his release, he returned to Chicago, dying there in poverty on May 1, 1901, at age 60.[7]

George Wilder and W. H. Jackson[8] were indicted for the murder of Frank Reid. Wilder was acquitted, and so was Jackson. Wilder went free, but not Jackson. He was still indicted for the assault and battery of John Stewart and for the assault of Tanner on the night of the gunfight on the wharf when Jackson aimed his revolver at Tanner. Jackson's trial was continued on December 17, and on January 6, 1899, he was found guilty and given a maximum sentence: 10 years "hard labor" at McNeil Island penitentiary, Washington.[9] On January 10, his attorneys filed a writ that identified 18 errors, including allowing Frank Burns, a member of the Citizens' Committee, to be a Grand Jury member as well as a witness for the prosecution. The court of appeals denied all 18 errors but adjusted one part of the sentence. The court stated that the term "hard labor" was not a legal option to add to Jackson's sentence and could not be enforced.[10] In March 1903, the *Sitka Cablegram* announced that President Theodore

---

[1] *Skaguay News*, 12/23/1898.
[2] *Skaguay News* 12/23/1898.
[3] *Morning Oregonian* 12/18/1899, p. 3.
[4] *Skaguay News*, 12/23/1898.
[5] *Morning Oregonian*, 12/18/1899, p. 3. *consumption*: dated term for "tuberculosis."
[6] *Skaguay News* 12/23/1898, & *Morning Oregonian* 12/18/1899, p. 3.
[7] *The Evening Times* 05/02/1901, p. 1.
[8] *W. H. Jackson*: named Turner Jackson in the indictment.
[9] US v. (1) Turner Jackson and George Wilder.
[10] Federal Reporter, pp. 488-490.

Roosevelt pardoned Jackson.[1] However, a letter from the warden of McNeil Island states that Jackson was released on September 30, 1905, by writ of habeas corpus.[2]

Ex-Deputy US Marshal Taylor's case was special. Marshal Shoup said that when he appointed the man, he came "with exceptionally strong recommendations, having served in a similar capacity in Idaho…, where his reputation as an officer was unassailable."[3] When Rev. Dickey was in Skaguay (October 8, 1897 to April 1, 1898[4]), he associated with Taylor, had dinner with him "and his friendly wife in their snug home." In the fictional account of his time in Skaguay, Dickey characterized Taylor as "Strange and puzzling…," "clever," acting "With great courage," a man of feeling who "completely broke down" in telling of a little girl who had died some ten years before.

> And yet some people in Skaguay suspected that he was in fraternity with Soapy Smith and his league of cutthroats. We never believed that. And yet…. … Our conclusion was that he was a big-hearted man who fully determined to do right but who had in some way come under the power of Soapy and that he writhed under it. … There was something there, but whatever power Soapy had over him we never knew. It may be that he found himself powerless to enforce the law strictly and decided to follow a mediating path with the law breakers to amend their effect as best he could. Having submitted to appeasement once, perhaps he was in Soapy's power….[5]

The town also liked Marshal Taylor, or so it seemed from the press. For example, on July 1, there was this notice:

> Marshal S. S. Taylor will in a few days begin the erection of a five hundred dollar dwelling on his lot on Fifth avenue near the river. When completed it will be the finest and most pretentious residence in the city.[6]

Even in *The News* of July 8, the Marshal was offered sympathy from his many friends:

> United States Deputy Marshal S. S. Taylor received the sad news Tuesday [July 5] of the death of his father, Dr. S. S. Taylor, at Palo Pinta, Texas, ten days before. Dr. Taylor was eighty years of age…. Marshal Taylor's many friends here sympathize with him in his trouble.[7]

On Wednesday, July 13, after relieving Taylor of his star and ordering him held for prosecution, Marshal Shoup said, "I became convinced that he had not performed his duty as an officer."[8] The *Alaskan* reported that Taylor "is said to be prostrated over the situation in which he finds himself."[9] On July 15, the front-page of the *Alaskan*

---

[1] *Sitka Cablegram*, 03/08/1903.
[2] Ltr fr Warden O. P. Halligan to US District Court clerk, 11/16/1911, & US v. (1) Turner Jackson and George Wilder.
[3] *Skaguay New* 07/15/1898, p. 3.
[4] Dickey Diary.
[5] Dickey, *Gold Fever*, pp. 84-85.
[6] *Skaguay News* Supplement 07/01/1898, p. 2.
[7] *Skaguay News* 07/08/1898, p. 2.
[8] Hunt, *Distant*, p. 64.
[9] *Daily Alaskan* 07/13/1898, p. 1.

announced "a charge against Taylor of willful neglect of duty.... ... He waived examination and was held ... for trial.... The marshal took him into custody."[1]

At trial in Juneau, Taylor's defense was that because he had only "John Doe" warrants, he could not know who the robbers were. Certainly Taylor knew who they were, but his and Jeff's practice had been to delay action until a "situation" could be pacified. Jeff had worked this approach so many times that he was an artist at it and probably was too confident and insistent on it. Perhaps his "nerve" and loyalty to past practice blinded him to the Citizens' Committee of vigilantes and its readiness to whip up an immediate storm over the matter. Taylor was able to use the suddenness of events to his advantage. He testified that he had been in pursuit of the robbers for only three and a half hours before members of the Citizens' Committee ordered him to stay inside his cabin or risk being lynched. He took the warning seriously and did not venture out until US Marshal Shoup formally arrested him on July 14, 1898.

But this was only one piece of Taylor's defense. Others included "heartfelt references to his wife and four children" and reference to "his sterling past as constable, deputy sheriff, and U.S. deputy marshal in Idaho." Finally on December 10, 1898, Taylor was acquitted of negligence.[2] Evidence of his wrongdoing as a lawman was ample, but none of it was evidenced in court. An example was the report to the US secretary of the interior from Governor Brady that he, Brady, had received a report of Taylor's willingness to return $600 "of Stewart's money if the vigilantes would let him go."[3] Then there was the damning evidence of Lewis Levy, the Tacoma man who had written to friends in Washington, DC, about how he had seen

> American citizens deliberately plundered before the marshal's eyes in dens kept for that purpose.... I had to pay the marshal $20 after he had recovered stolen property, before he would make a return to the court commissioner [of my property], as he threatened to turn it back to the thieves, unless I did so.[4]

Jeff had the lawman well ensnared, and not just with the threat of ruining his reputation. Jeff was also providing Taylor with the means to build his fine new house by the Skaguay river. When Stewart, mussed up and distraught over the theft of all of his gold, came to Marshal Taylor for help, the marshal told him to keep quiet about it, and he would see what could be done, "but in a few minutes the marshal started up Broadway with a carpenter to oversee some work he was doing..." on Taylor's house. Stewart was another man who was going to help pay for it.

Though acquitted of negligence, Taylor's career as a lawman was over. His name was now manacled to the legendary "Soapy Smith," and no key could unlock it. Taylor took his wife Maud and four young children back to Idaho, and with the help a person named Pleasant Taylor, perhaps a cousin, who was a Showman and "Movey Projectionist," Sylvester became a "Manager of Show." That profession must have worked out for him because in 1910, living with Maude and two more children in the

[1] *Daily Alaskan* 07/15/1898, p. 1.

[2] Hunt, *Distant*, p. 65.

[3] Hunt, *Distant*, p. 64.

[4] Hunt, *Distant*, p. 61.

family, Sylvester's occupation was that of "Showman, Vaudeville and Movey Projectionist." He died comparatively young, though, in 1916 at age 49.[1]

The attempts of the main members of the Soap Gang to escape Skaguay were in vain. The harsh elements and concerted manhunt had blocked their escape. Their only chance was to risk being hanged by vigilantes and trying their luck with the judicial system. Temporary Marshal Tanner's temporary deputy marshals, Captain Yeatman's soldiers, and fate kept them from being hanged. All but Wilder did not fair as well with the court. As for the Soap Gang, it shattered on the evening of July 8, 1898. What it had been, however, would not be forgotten, especially not its leader.

The *Rocky Mountain News* could see the permanent mark that Jeff Smith had carved into history. In an article announcing his death, the paper wrote that

> He was a character the like of which will probably never be seen again in the history of the country. He left a few friends who will regret his death, but the majority of people who knew him were relieved when they heard that he had been killed. The evil which he did will live a long time after him, and his bunco record will be a monument which will last all ages.[2]

The paper was right about the monument but not exactly about its content. To be sure, a record of crimes spanned decades, but there was more, so much more to the spell of the man giving rise to the monument of myth. With the obsidian shine chipped away, however, one finds an inner sheen off human traits: charisma, empathy, manners, generosity, hardness, audacity, pride, daring, nerve, human magnetism, an insatiable hunger to be on the grift, and an indomitable will to succeed. It could go on, this list of traits about the man within the myth.

Chapter 28

Post Soapy

He never threw down a pal.

—Henry "Yank Fewclothes" Edwards
Interview in November 1914

The days and weeks after Jeff's death were filled with confusing facts leading some people to believe that Jeff was not dead. With a choice between rumor of Jeff's death and life, the preference was for life. For example, the following appeared in the *Morning Oregonian* two days after Jeff's death.

CONTEMPLATING AN ENTERPRISE HERE.

"Soapy" Smith, who attained considerable notoriety during his residence at Skagway, is said to have arrived in Portland, and to be contemplating opening up a place of business in his peculiar line. He is reported to have engaged quarters adjoining the Cyclorama building on Third street, and the scheme he purposes launching will no doubt be a paying one—for Smith.[3]

---

[1] 1880, 1900, 1910 US Census, Taylor/Holloway Family Tree, accessed through Ancestry.com.
[2] *RMN*, undated clipping, circa 1898.
[3] *Morning Oregonian* 07/10/1898, p. 5.

For the family, when certainty over the news reached St. Louis, bewilderment and great sadness followed, which turned to anger upon learning that Jeff had been apparently murdered and then robbed. For entrepreneurs, this was a period of attempting to profit from Jeff's death. For others, it marked the end of a violent era.

Enterprising men such as C. F. Niece of Skaguay tried to cash in on Jeff's death by taking "several hundred papers" to Dawson that contained

> an account of the "Soapy" episode, but, while he made expenses on the trip, he did not reap a very rich harvest. A few copies of the NEWS extras of July 9th had reached Dawson in advance of him, and these Mr. Niece found pinned up on the walls of every saloon and hotel in the goldopolis.[1]

A majority of the newspapers in the US and Canada published news of Jeff's death. C. D. Ven and Herbert Sacage, two enterprising men, read about the fallen bad man in Victoria, British Columbia. They immediately prepared to obtain, by any means necessary, the corpse of the infamous Soapy Smith. Along with a Dr. Richard Croft, the men planned to tour the cadaver through California, Colorado, Idaho and Montana. The paying public would have the opportunity to cast their eyes upon the actual corpse of the "bad man of the north."[2] Nothing more was heard of this plan.

Some were glad to hear of Jeff's demise, among them Harry Suydam, Skaguay's ex-City Assessor. He recalled hearing of the demise.

> I was at Circle City when a Skaguay newspaper brought the news.... Though we were almost one thousand miles from the scene of the tragedy, the news came like an electric shock. The single copy of the newspaper was carried off to a big gambling hall, and everybody in town was packed into the place listening eagerly while the story was read aloud. A deep sigh of relief went up when the audience learned that "Soapy" had "cashed in."[3]

Many of Jeff's friends learned of his death from newspaper reports. The news was published in Denver on July 16, but the date was misreported, and friends claimed the news could not be true. Some had received letters from Jeff dated after that date.

> A report received in this city last night to the effect that Soapy Smith had been killed in Skaguay on June 19, was not credited today. His friends are endeavoring today to ascertain if there is any truth in the statement. The report came from Seattle and was credited to a party of men returning from Alaska. They said Colonel Smith was shot and killed on June 19 by a former US engineer. No other information is had.
>
> Smith's friends in Denver do not believe the story, because of mail recently received from him. Chief Farley of the police department received a poster several days ago advertising a Forth of July celebration in Skaguay to which Colonel Smith had signed his name with a legal pencil. The poster is supposed to have been mailed after June 19.[4]

---

[1] *Skaguay News* Supplement, 08/05/1898, item 138, author's col.
[2] *Denver Times* 07/22/1898.
[3] Suydam, "Reign," p. 220.
[4] *Denver Times* 07/16/1898, & *Denver Evening Post* 07/16/1898, p. 2.

Denver enemies of Jeff, however, felt no sorrow when his demise was confirmed.

> There is not a man on the Denver police force who did not breath a sigh of relief when he read that "Soapy" was dead. It was bound to come, and all realized that, but the question bothering the police officials was how long "Soapy" was to go about killing other men.[1]

Nearly two weeks after Jeff's death, Mary read of it in a St. Louis newspaper. In later years she told her grandchildren how false reports had been received "a dozen times" before, so upon reading the real one, it was not believed.[2]

> Mrs. Jefferson Randolph Smith, according to St. Louis papers, laughed when she heard the story, for Soapy had told her never to believe him dead until she had seen his dead body. Mrs. Smith lives in St. Louis at 917 Locust St.
>
> "I will not believe my husband is dead until I see with my own eyes his dead body. He has warned me often not to believe reports of his death without positive information, and I do not believe he is dead now and will not believe it until I have proof of the most positive sort. During the years we have been married Mr. Smith has been reported dead a dozen times, yet after each report he either turned up or wrote me that he was alive and well. Only two weeks ago, I read in the newspapers that he had been killed in a snow slide in the Klondike, and my husband was alive and prosperous. Only a few days ago I got a letter from him in which he stated that he had tired of Skaguay, and intended leaving at once for Dawson, where he said, a better game was awaiting him. I believe that now my husband is in Dawson ... not shot and killed in Skagway."[3]

But not hearing from her husband worried Mary, and she soon decided to make the long trip to Skagway and find out for herself if Jeff were truly dead. With her son, Jefferson Randolph Smith III, and Bascomb as escorts, Mary traveled by rail to Seattle. For reasons unknown, Bascomb remained in Port Townsend, about fifty miles northwest of Seattle, while Mary and young Jefferson boarded the steamer *Rosalie* for Skagway.[4] A reporter for *The Seattle Post-Intelligencer* published what he observed.

> A little, pale-faced woman, with dull heavy features and drooping eyes, dressed in deep mourning and wearing a crepe bonnet with a rusty veil that hung far down below her back, sat in a corner of the social saloon of the steamer Rosalie last night. All about her was strewn baggage, old valises, boxes, bundles and packages wrapped in newspaper. On the seat beside her a small boy lay at full length, his feet hanging down over the arm of the bench and his head lying in her lap.[5]

Mary and Jefferson arrived in Skagway on August 3, 1898. The *Skaguay News* wrote of her visit.

---

[1] *RMN* undated clipping (circa 1898).
[2] John R. Smith to author, 1985.
[3] *Seattle Post-Intelligencer* 07/22/1898.
[4] *Morning Oregonian* 08/07/1898, p. 11.
[5] *Seattle Post-Intelligencer* 07/28/1898.

Mrs. Smith, widow of the late Jeff R. Smith accompanied by her eleven year old son, Jefferson Jr., arrived Wednesday morning on the steamer Rosalie. In the afternoon, they drove to the cemetery to visit the grave of her husband, at which place her sorrow and grief is described as having been most acute and touching. She is a quiet and reserved little woman who evidently feels her position very keenly. Young Jeff is a bright, active little lad who is very solicitous in the care of his mother. They will remain here several days. The remains of the late husband and father will not be disturbed, but will be left where they are.[1]

The *Daily Alaskan* also covered the Smiths in Skagway.

Mrs. Jeff Smith Here

Mrs. Jefferson Randolph Smith arrived on the Rosalie with her eldest of three children, a bright boy of eleven. She is a woman small of stature, a brunette of very pleasing appearance and charming manners and was attired in deep mourning. She went out to the cemetery this afternoon to visit her husband's grave. What she will do as to the removal of the body she has not yet decided.

The same issue had two advertisements for photographs of her husband.

Soapy Smith and all his pals, Stewart and his sack of gold, and many other interesting pictures at Case and Drapers.

PEISER has the best pictures of Soapy Smith. For sale at the Pullman Gallery Ninth and Main St. Price 50.

The same issue also published appointment of the executor of Frank Reid's estate, Leslie Butler with the assistance of attorneys Price and Fuller.[2]

While in Skagway Mary was given a sealskin coat. In a 1977 *Skaguay News* interview, one of Jeff's grandsons, Joseph Jefferson Smith, was quoted as saying that John "Clancy probably gave it to her, to settle the account." Joseph's wife, Thelma, added, "She came home with a sealskin coat. She wore it forever. It wouldn't wear out, so somebody had a guilty conscience when they gave her the sealskin coat."[3]

Mary was in Skagway when in Otero County, Colorado, a man claiming to be her son was arrested. The *Denver Evening Post* wrote that insanity was suspected. "He is perhaps some aspirant for military honors who hopes to get into the army through the son-of-a-distinguished-father entrance."[4]

According to the newspaper Mary planned to stay in Skagway only a few days, but that was soon lengthened to twenty days. According to her grandson John R. Smith, Mary said that at first she was not well received. Few would openly talk to her for fear of being implicated as an associate or friend of the Soap Gang. Slowly, first in secret, friends and supporters of Jeff began to confide to Mary what they knew of the events that led up to his death, including information about Jeff's property.[5]

---

[1] *Skaguay News Supplement*, 08/05/1898, item 138, author's col.
[2] *The Daily Alaskan* 08/03/1898.
[3] *Skagway News* 07/02/1977.
[4] *Denver Evening Post* 08/08/1898, p. 5.
[5] John R. Smith interview with author, 07/01/1985.

Friends and family feared Mary would find an unforgiving and unfriendly attitude from the residents. Mary's letters from Skagway, though, reported things were working out and that she was "fine."[1] She gathered what the Citizens' Committee would let her have and on Tuesday, August 23, 1898, she sailed for home. Captain O'Brien, still grateful to Jeff for his help in 1896, paid Mary's passage to Seattle.[2]

> Mrs. Jeff R. Smith and son returned to the Sound on the steamer Rosalie Tuesday from which place they will go to their home in St. Louis. Mrs. Smith came back here to look after any property her husband might have had, but found that he left nothing. It is said Soapy carried a heavy life insurance in favor of his wife, but there was a question about whether it would be paid without litigation.[3]

Mary left at least one admirer in the North, George H. Light, a miner returning to Dawson whom she had met on the *Rosalie*. Light wrote at least seven times, but she replied, apparently, only once, on September 22, 1898. It took until June, 1899, for the letter to arrive in Dawson. Light's reply is rendered as he penned it.

> Dear Friend Mrs Smith your Litter of Sept 22 Reseve[d] to day June 18 [—] Was [good?] to Here From you but Sorry to think that i Have got but one Letter from you[.] i have Roat 6 Letter[s] to you. i just came up from Egal [Eagle] City[.] i Was down this [way] awl Winter and i Rote [to you] from this [place.] i Send you the price list [of things] from [here] and good[s.] i Wanted you [to] come to Egal City but i think Dawson is the best Place for you if you bring any good[s] With you[.] Mrs Smith[,] i am Wating for you every day[.] i Have a Home For you So When you get to Dawson you Have a Home to go to and Some one to take good car of you and See that you [not] Want Wants For any thing as Long as you Stay in Dawson[.] Mrs. Smith[,] i was Sorry to Here that you Was Sik after going Home From the White Pass. i Have been ... awl over the Country gitting Claim[s]. i Have Ennofe Claim[s] to give you Haft of them and Have Ennoufe Left[.] Mrs. Smith[,] ... I [would] incourge you more on this Letter but ... i Havent Seen you for along time And you mite change your Mind Since i Saw you Last on the White Pass[,] but i Hoop Not For i Would Like to See you once More And if you don't Like Dawson i Will See that you git back to St Louis Mo, but i think that When you git to Dawson City that [you] Will Like the Plase and Wait till We have Ennofe money and come out togather for i [will] see that you Shell git the best of Car[e] While you are Here With me.
>
> Mrs. Smith[,] i Will Have to bid you good day for this is No Night[.] Here it is awl day Lite Here. give My best Regard to the Little one and tell Jeffei that i got Some gold Nugette[s] Here for Him
>
> And Some for you to[,] Mrs Smith[,] When i See you good by yours truly
> Geo Light

---

[1] Ltr to Mary Smith fr Jack P. (possibly Jack Pugh), 08/04/1898, item 14, author's col.
[2] Newspaper interview of John O'Brien, unknown publisher and date, author's collection, & Itjen, p. 79.
[3] *Skaguay News* 08/26/1898.

[p.s.] if you Should come to Dawson When i am away[,] Call at the Liadeau Co Store [and] you Will find Where i am.[1]

Mrs. Smith never visited Dawson City.

While in Skagway, Jefferson made friends with children about his age as well as several adults who had been friends or admirers of his father. He kept in touch with some of them for years. In 1902, Jeff wrote to one of his friends, looking for another with whom he had lost contact. George W. Meller replied on November 5, 1902.

Mr. Jefferson Smith, Jr.

Dear Friend Jeff

Your most welcome letter was received yesterday and I am glad to hear that you are all well and in good health. ... We had a big fire here last night. The big saw mill of the town burned to the ground but no other damage was done although the wind was blowing awful hard.... Say Jeff you asked me in your letter about your friend but there is no freight wagons running between here and White Pass. It is all done by rail road. ...I don't hardly know where to look for your friend, and you were asking about your father's grave. I was up to see it about two weeks ago and things look very good. The grave is in good condition. I was speaking to a man that knew your father and he spoke awful well of him and he said your father owned the biggest part of this town at one time and he said the biggest business men of the town today are the men your father was keeping up when he met with his misfortune. Well Jeff I wish you could have been with us on our trip from the Philippines to here. We had a fine old time. We were on the water for over fifty days. We stopped in Nagasaki, Japan, for five days and in Honolulu 5 days and laid over in San Francisco ten days, so you can imagine the time we had when we were turned loose in the good old U.S. after being imprisoned way back in the hills for almost two years. Well Jeff I guess I better close for this time. Hoping to hear from you soon again, with best regards to you all, I'll remain your old friend.

George W. Meller, Co M. 8th USA Skagway, Alaska[2]

In time, Mary remarried. Her husband's name was John P. Little, a policeman no less. A letter from Jeff R. Smith III shows she visited Denver in 1906 for at least two weeks.[3] She moved to Milwaukee, Wisconsin, where she outlived her second husband. She loved her beer and whiskey mix, which she told her grandson John was "for her rheumatism." Mary passed away on December 11, 1947, age 75.

Some refused to believe Jeff was dead. A claim that Jeff had been sighted was made in San Diego eight months after his death, but the matter was put straight by one Arch Bodine of Denver.

All this about "Soapy" Smith being alive, as wired to the newspapers from San Diego, and that he is in San Diego, is moonshine, said Arch

---

[1] Ltr to Mary Smith fr Geo. Light, 06/?/1899, item 2, author's col.

[2] Ltr fr George Meller to Jeff Smith III, 11/05/1902, item 103, author's col. Slight edits made for readability.

[3] Ltr to Mary Smith fr Jeff R. Smith III, 03/01/1906, item 72, author's col.

Bodine, who has a restaurant at 1327 Fifteenth Street. Bodine was in Skagway last October [sic] when "Soapy" was killed, and did not leave for several months afterwards. I was near him when he was shot, and I helped to put him in the wagon. After he was carried from the wharf to the morgue, he lay there for two days under a sheet, and hundreds of people saw him. There are lots of men in the west who look like "Soapy," but just paste it in your hat that Smith is as dead as a doornail. They didn't take any chances on his coming back to life in Skagway.[1]

Except for some lesser details, Bodine had the main one right.

Bascomb returned to Denver in 1899,[2] but the Blonger brothers controlled the underworld, and since Bascomb had turned state's evidence against Sam, it is not surprising that he was not welcome there. He traveled to Seattle where he slipped into the lowest crevasse of human existence, that of opium addict. *The Skaguay News* saw the story in a Seattle paper and reprinted it.

A brother of the late Soapy Smith is in the city hall charged with smoking opium. He was caught with six other white men in a six by ten room in the attic of 516 Washington Street. He gives his full name as John Smith. - *Seattle Post Intelligencer*

The above is probably correct as Soapy frequently mentioned a brother with whom he did not associate on account of the brother's dissolute habits. Soapy was ashamed of him.[3]

It is probable that "John Smith" was Bascomb. Both Jeff and Bascomb commonly used aliases when arrested. However, very doubtful is it that Jeff was ashamed of Bascomb. Jeff, who had witnessed ill-advised behavior among the human race for much of his life, including some of his own, would not have been likely to be ashamed of it in his own family. But would he have severed ties for the sake of being successful in his own sphere? Probably the answer to that question would have been yes.

In October 1899 Bascomb was arrested for vagrancy.[4] The charge could mean Bascomb was "down and out," or it could mean he was caught running a scam. Then for years Bascomb dropped from sight. In 1908 rumors circulated that he had been killed in Seattle, so Jeff Smith III wrote to the chief of police in an attempt to find him. A typed reply on department of police stationary arrived in May.

Jeff Smith,

St Louis, MO.

Dear Sir:-

Our delay in answering your letter in re to Bascom Smith was that we were trying to get him definitely located, he left here in 1902 and went to Denver Colo since then we have not heard from him, the Smith that was reported as having been shot by a woman named Nellie was Charlie Smith,

[1] *Denver Republican* 03/16/1899.
[2] *RMN* 04/13/1899.
[3] *Skaguay News* 02/03/1899.
[4] *Morning Oregonian* 10/29/1899, p. 10.

Bascomb was not killed and as far as we can learn is alive, if you should write to the Chief of police at Denver he may give you the desired information in regards to him.

Respectfully,
[signed] Irving Ward, Acting Chief of Police.[1]

It would appear that the acting chief or one of his men knew Bascomb.

Jefferson contacted the Denver police as suggested, but Bascomb was not to be found. Jefferson wrote to his aunt Emmie Lou in hopes that Bascomb would eventually contact her, but he never did. In a 1912 letter to Jefferson, Emmie Lou conceded that "It don't look like we will ever get any trace of Bascom."[2] One of the various old family genealogical trees made by descendants over the years contains a penciled-in date that Bascomb died in 1920 at age 51.[3]

Jefferson wrote Edwin B. Smith in 1905 about his father. Ed replied, "Your father and I were sincere friends and I honor his memory."[4] The two continued to communicate until Edwin's death in 1941.

As the years passed, Skaguay residents from 1898 slowly began voicing their feelings about conditions at that time. Jeff was not without enemies, but a number of people expressed a fondness for him. Dr. J. S. McCue knew Jeff in Denver and later in Skaguay. "I want to say this for Smith," he wrote,

> that he was a better man than nine-tenths of the residents of Skaguay, and the trouble which led to his death was more the fault of others than his own. ... If Smith had been killed two weeks before, no one in Skaguay would have had a bigger funeral than he.... He was town marshal, and while he was there in Skaguay, he kept the town clear of murderers, hold-ups, and other criminals. He knew that if it got the name of being a hard town it would hurt his business, and people with money would not come there. ... Soapy ... kept many a poor man from starving to death. He was always a good friend of mine, and I would trust him ... before I would some of them in that town.[5]

Denver Soap Gang member Henry Edwards had this theory about Jeff's death:

> A bunch of con men opposed to Smith were trying to horn in and get the pull with the big bugs. Stopping to exchange a few words with a vigilance committee, contrary to his usual custom of 'firing first and talking afterwards,' caused his death."[6]

Sixteen days after Jeff was killed, an obvious admirer spoke to a reporter:

> Washington Post: "I shall be greatly interested in hearing the facts as to the killing of Jeff, alias 'Soapy' Smith, at Skaguay." Said Mr. R. M. Eddy of Juneau, Alaska, at the Riggs.

[1] Ltr to Jeff Smith III fr Chief Irving Ward, 05/15/1908, item 73, author's col.
[2] Ltr to Jeff R. Smith III fr Emmie Lou Gardner, 10/16/1912, item 76, author's col.
[3] Recorded in Muscogee County, Georgia, is the death of a "Bascom Smith, 12 Jul 1919, Certificate 9756-A." (Ancestry.com) The years are close.
[4] Ltr to Jeff Smith III fr Edwin B. Smith, 02/16/1905, item 55, author's col.
[5] RMN 01/28/1900.
[6] The Denver Post 11/15/1914, item 163, author's col.

"Skaguay has been on its good behavior of late, and though Smith was classed with an element of somewhat adventurous men, he was not at all inclined to stir up trouble, and by his pleasant address never wanted for friends. Besides, he was one of the most kind-hearted men that ever lived. I will venture that there is scarcely a big city in the country where you couldn't find some man that could tell you of a good act that Jeff Smith had done him. In his palmy days in Denver and Creede, he gave away money recklessly to almost any applicant. When hard times came to Denver in association with a well-known priest, he organized a score of free-lunch stands, and every sport in town was assessed at what Smith thought a reasonable figure. None of them demurred to giving up, and nobody went hungry during that adverse period.

"With the sports with whom he associated Smith was easily chief. He was clear-headed and willing to fight if necessary to maintain his supremacy. In a big mass-meeting held in Skaguay early this year he was chosen Captain of a military company to fight the Spaniards, and the company offered its services to President McKinley. If they had been accepted, not a man would have welched on going to the front.[1]

Once beyond the Skaguay vigilantes, former, semi-undercover gang member William Saportas spoke of Jeff: "He is the most gracious, kindhearted man I've met. To know him is to like him."[2]

Belinda Mulrooney was twenty-five when she crossed the Chilkoot at the head of her own packing outfit. When twenty-six she erected the largest building in Dawson, the Fair View Hotel. And she was thirty-nine when in a Seattle hotel room rented for the purpose, the 135-pound Belinda trapped (with the help of two men) a 6-foot-tall man who had attacked her sister's reputation. For that "there was nothing left for me to do but whip him, which I did, thoroughly." Advised by her friend and admirer Judge Wickersham to appear in court on the resulting charge of assault, she paid a $150 fine.[3] All of this and much more is true about this exceptional woman. At age fifty-six in 1928 and again at age ninety in 1962, her remembrance of an association with Soapy Smith may be true or partially true. One aspect of it, however, seems surely true, that Belinda wanted to remember the event with "Soapy" Smith in it.

In the spring of 1898, her Fair View Hotel in Dawson was nearing completion. So the expensive structure would attract a rich clientele and start paying off its mounting debt, she was in a rush to appoint it in dazzling fashion. Supplies had been ordered and shipped to Skaguay, but with the rush to Dawson at its height, packing services would be hard to secure. "The only way to get the shipment," she wrote,

> was to go out and bring it in myself over the White Pass. I ordered it all, cut glass chandeliers and silverware, china and linen and brass bedsteads, I signed a contract with a fellow named Joe Brooks, a thick-set Vancouver

[1] *Washington Post* 07/24/1898, & *Denver Times* 07/25/1898, p. 2.
[2] Berton, p. 334.
[3] Mayer & DeArmond, pp. 312-13.

drayman who had some mules and a pack train, and paid him $4,000 down and [agreed to pay him] the balance at Lake Bennett to pack my stuff in.

With arrangements for shipment to Bennett complete, Belinda went to the lake to arrange for scows to transport the goods to Dawson. However,

> Brooks took my freight out a mile along the trail and dumped it there for a better offer to haul whisky. There was a clause in the contract that if he didn't deliver, the pack train was mine. He just laughed at me and said, "What are you going to do about it?" He was fond of drink and had so much money he didn't know what to do with it.
>
> I went back to Skagway and I was boiling mad. Soapy Smith was clean and he was intelligent looking. I thought he was the most perfect gentleman there. He looked like a minister and had this soft southern drawl. Soapy was my hero, and I went to him for advice. I told him what had happened and how I owed $8,000 and had to get this gear to Dawson.
>
> "I'll see what I can do for you, Belinda," he said.
>
> He picked up a good tough bunch of men and we lit out with his crew and took possession of the pack train, unloaded the whisky and packed my freight. Brooks had a pinto he rode all the time and I took that for myself. That's what Soapy did for me and I liked him.[1]

A Denver merchant, Joseph T. Cornforth, who visited Skaguay in the spring of 1898 wrote to a friend about meeting up with "None other than our well-known, suave townsman, Soapy Smith" before having been in town two hours. Cornforth discovered that Jeff had "accounts at the merchants' stores for provisions and fuel for the needy people here" and that they "amount to several hundreds dollars a week." Additionally, the visitor learned that Jeff paid "for the funerals of friendless persons, and I can assure you that that is no small item. What are you going to make out of a character like that?"[2] Of course, Cornforth was among many who recognized and applauded so much giving and puzzled over so much conning. In general, in announcing the demise of Jeff R. Smith, alias "Soapy," *giving* received the emphasis, as in the *Denver Times*.

> Soapy Smith had his faults but there are many men in Denver who were at one time hungry and looking for a dime, who will remember that his heart and purse were always open to the poor. Perhaps the good lord will remember all those little kindnesses as well as will the beneficiaries.[3]

The same was true in the *Leadville Herald Democrat*: "When the recording angel makes up his ledger with Jefferson (Soapy) Smith, there will be innumerable works of charity to be recorded in his favor."[4]

---

[1] Mayer, *Klondike* (1989), pp. 156-157, fr *Sunday Sun*, p. 28. In Mayer & DeArmond (2000), the historians find it "unlikely that Belinda had any contact with Soapy Smith." She may have hired a man whom "Belinda calls 'Broad'" who "may have been associated with Smith previously. We have been unable to determine whether Broad was his real name or a pseudonym." (Mayer & DeArmond, fn 12, p. 359)

[2] O'Connor, p. 60.

[3] *Denver Times* 07/21/1898.

[4] *Leadville-Herald Democrat* 07/17/1898.

Among two remembrances of Jeff appearing in the *Arizona Republican* in latter July 1898 was a story about Jeff's *giving back* to a young man who had lost his way. He was a collector of funds for a big dry goods outfit, Daniel and Frazier. After the young man had lost "all of his own money," he began

> dipping into a sack which Smith knew contained the firm's collections. When the collector had lost $100 of his employers' cash, Smith quit playing. Wrapping a $100 bill within a $5 bill, unobserved by the youth, he offered it to him for $10 [for the $5 and whatever the bill might be that was wrapped within it], then for $8, $5, $4, and $3. Bystanders wanted to buy the wad at the last named figure, but Smith would sell only to the collector. That young man had been disappointed so much within the preceding hour or two that he wouldn't invest in golden eagles at a dollar apiece. Smith finally put the money in the collector's vest pocket and lectured him upon the folly and danger of gambling with other people's money.[1]

Knowing Jeff better than most was Denver Soap Gang member and family friend Henry Edwards. In a 1914 interview, he spoke candidly about his friendship with Jeff.

> I never talk much about Jeff Smith. He was the warmest hearted man I ever knew and writers ... always get things mixed and paint up the bad side of his career. He never threw down a pal. I never talk about him except to warn young persons from gambling. Never gamble, if you would respect yourself. It makes you treacherous and spoils friendships. If you will let vice alone and put your energies in other directions you cannot fail.
>
> He died with many good deeds to his credit, as well as the other kind, but it is always the bad things he did which people remember. He loved his wife Mollie ... and his family. He was never cruel and used to give back money lots of times when he had worked on somebody who really needed it badly. There wasn't a stingy bone in his body....
>
> Smith's personal bravery was never questioned. He feared neither police departments nor things of the mining frontier. For twenty years he was the prize bunco steerer of the West and his bunco games were masterpieces of their kind....
>
> Smith had a bright sense of humor. Although a desperado, his deeds of kindness would have done credit to any man. A man in want was never turned down by Jeff.... He often risked being thrown in jail to help a pal out of trouble.
>
> Smith was not strong physically or of commanding appearance but he was always a leading personality in a mining camp and many a man breathed easier when the word came that 'Soapy' Smith died here with his boots on and a cigar in his mouth.[2]

---

[1] *Arizona Republican* 07/20/1898, p. 5, & other remembrances, 07/22/1898, p. 4.
[2] *Denver Post* 11/15/1914.

List of Images

(between pages 160 and 161)

1. Earliest known photograph of Jefferson Randolph Smith II, age 5-7, circa 1865-67.
2. The Dr. Ira Ellis Smith house where Jefferson R. Smith II was born, Nov. 2, 1860.
3. Smith family photo: Eva, Emily, Jefferson Sr., Jefferson Jr., circa 1867-69.
4. Jeff R. Smith, age 9-12, circa 1869-72.
5. Jeff R. Smith age 17-20, and unknown companion, circa 1877-80.
6. Leadville, Colorado. Jeff R. Smith, age 19, with "crew of freighters" the day General Grant came to down, July 21, 1880.
7. License for "Jeff Smith" to "hawk his prize soap," Sept. 16, 1882.
8. Jefferson R. Smith II and Mary Eva Smith after their marriage, circa 1886.
9. Men believed to be John Morris and John Bowers, circa 1889-92.
10. Bascomb Smith, his only known image, April 13, 1899.
11. Jefferson R. Smith II, age 29 or 30, circa 1890.
12. Denver's "street of doom," view north down 17th Street from Larimer," circa 1884.
13. Jeff giving out turkeys to Denver's poor, drawing, July 31, 1898.

(between pages 352 and 353)

14. Jeff in front-page cartoon helping plan a crooked election, Oct. 16, 1892.
15. Junction of Cliff Street and Creede Avenue, Creede, Colorado. Kinneavy's sample room and Jeff's Orleans Club, circa spring, 1892.
16. Orleans Club on Creede Avenue, circa spring 1892.
17. McGinty the petrified man in Denver, circa 1892-1895.
18. Sylvester, at Ye Olde Curiosity Shop, Pier 54, in Seattle.
19. Petrified Man advertisement for McGinty in Denver, circa 1892-1895.
20. Jeff pouring out sentiments at burial service for Joe Simmons, drawing published April 9, 1892.
21. Letter to the editor of the *Denver Times*, by Jeff writing to correct misinformation about "bunco men working 17th Street," July 28, 1893.
22. Front-page cartoon of Jeff with two kegs of dynamite, leading a parade of "Gamblers, Thugs, Murderers and Rogues," March 24, 1894.
23. Denver City Hall War: A large crowd assembled at city hall, March 15, 1894.
24. Denver City Hall War: Colorado National Guardsmen in formation, two cannon, supplies and caissons, March 24, 1894.
25. Deputy Sheriff commission for Jeff R. Smith, April 17, 1894.
26. A shell and pea operator along one of the Alaskan trails to the Klondike, circa 1897-98.

(between pages 512 and 513)

27. Letter from Jeff to his wife Mary, written aboard the steamer *General Canby* in "Cooks Inlett," Alaska, May 10, 1896. "Gold here in big quantities [—] all country talking up here."
28. Jeff standing before Jeff Smith's Parlor, 317 Holly Street, Skaguay. With him are John Bowers (r) and five other men, circa, May-June 1898.

Works Referenced

Abbreviations: **col** = collection, **Ed/ed** = edition/editor, **JRS** = Jefferson R. Smith II, **na** = no author, **nd** = no date, **np** = no place or no publisher, **nr** = number, **p/pp** = page/pages, **Rev** = Revised, **RtoR** = reel-to-reel, **U** = University, **unk** = unknown, **UP** = University Press, **vol** = volume.

<u>Books, Dictionaries, Directories, Films, Interviews, Magazines, Music, Records, Web Sites*</u>
    *All web sites accessed July 2009 unless otherwise noted.

Abbott, Carl, Stephen J. Leonard, & David McComb. *Colorado: A History of the Centennial State*. 3rd ed. Niwot: UP of Colorado, 1994.

Adney, Tappan. Introduction, Ken Coates. *The Klondike Stampede*. NY: Harper, 1899. Vancouver, BC: UBC Press, 2003.

Alaska Geographic: Skagway, A Legacy of Gold. "White Pass and Yukon Route Railroad" vol. 19, nr. 1 (1992): pp. 28-37.

Alaska Public Safety, Alcoholic Beverage Control. "History of Alcohol Control in Alaska." http://www.dps.state.ak.us/abc/history.aspx.

Ancestry.com.

Anderson, William U., *A History of Coweta County from 1825 to 1880*. Newnan, Georgia: Newnan-Coweta Historical Society, 1977.

Andrews, Clarence L. *The Story of Alaska*. Caldwell, ID: Caxton Printers, 1938-1953.

---. "The Real Soapy Smith." *The Alaska Sportsman* (Nov 1947): pp. 6-7, 36-40.

"Bass, The Story of Sam." Na. *City of Round Rock* website: www.roundrocktexas.gov/home/index.asp?page=953.

"Belton, Texas." Na. *The Online Handbook of Texas*. Texas State Historical Assoc. (TSHA): www.tshaonline.org.

Anzer, Richard C. ("Dixie"). *Klondike Gold Rush*. NY: Pageant Press, 1959.

Arapahoe County, sheriff's dept., history: www.co.arapahoe.co.us/Departments/SH/History/cityhallwar.asp.

Arp, Louisa Ward. *Denver in Slices*. Denver: Sage Books, 1959.

Autopsy defined. *Death: The Last Taboo*. www.deathonline.net/what_happens/autopsy/index.cfm.

Avrich, Paul. *The Haymarket Tragedy*. Princeton UP, 1984.

Banks, Della Murray. "Homer's Gold Seekers: A Game of Bluff." *The Alaska Sportsman* (Oct 1945): pp. 10-11, 36-43.

Barber, Lucy G. Ch. 1. "Without Precedent: Coxey's Army Invades Washington, 1894." *Marching on Washington: The Forging of an American Political Tradition*. Berkeley: UC Press, 2004.

Barkdull, Calvin H. "I Saw Soapy Killed." *The Alaska Sportsman* (June 1952): pp. 8-11, 45-50.

Barrett, Dr. W. T. *Personal Experience of Trial Life*. Victoria, BC: St. Ann Archives, nd.

Becker, Ethel Anderson. *Klondike '98: E. A. Hegg's Gold Rush Album*. Rev. ed. Portland, OR: Binfords & Mort, 1949-1972.

Beckmann, Darryl. *Lecture notes from The Life and Times of Alexander the Man Who Knows: A Personal Scrapbook*. Rolling Bay, WA: Rolling Bay Press, 1994.

Berton, Pierre. *Klondike: The Last Great Gold Rush, 1896-1899*. Rev. ed. Anchor Canada, 1972.

Blonger Bros.com: www.blongerbros.com. Search site at bottom of page.

Boswell, Sharon A. and Lorraine McConaghy. *Raise Hell and Sell Newspapers: Alden J. Blethen & The Seattle Times*. Pullman, WA: Washington State UP, 1996.

Boyer, Glen G. *I Married Wyatt Earp: The Recollections of Josephine Sarah Marcus Earp*. Tucson: U AZ Press, 1979.

Brand, Peter. Tombstone Vendetta. Extracted from *Who was Texas Jack Vermillion?* www.tombstonevendetta.com/vermillion.htm.

Bright, William. *Colorado Place Names*. 3rd ed. Boulder: Johnson Books, 2004.

Bronson, William. T*he Last Grand Adventure: The Story of the Klondike Gold Rush & the Opening of Alaska*. NY: McGraw-Hill, 1977.

Buffum, George T. *Smith of Bear City and Other Frontier Sketches*. NY: Grafton Press, 1906.

Butler, Anne M. Daughters of Joy, Sisters of Misery: Prostitutes in the American West 1865-90. Chicago: U of IL Press, 1987.

Campbell, Joseph. *The Year That Defined American Journalism: 1897 and the Clash of Paradigms*. NY: CRC Press, 2006.

Cashel, Rock of: www.destination360.com/europe/ireland/rock-of-cashel.php.

Cemetories and Cemetery Symbols. "Improved Order of Red Men." cemeteries.wordpress.com/category/red-men.

Clancy, Frank J. "I was Just a Kid." *The Alaska Sportsman* (Oct 1955): pp. 16-18, 25.

Clark, Hazel Stewart. "A Man of Honor." *The Alaska Sportsman* (Mar 1958): pp. 40-41.

Colfax Avenue.com: www.colfaxavenue.com/history.php.

Collier, William Ross, & Edwin Victor Westrate. *The Reign of Soapy Smith, Monarch of Misrule*. Garden City, NY: Sun Dial Press, 1937.

Colorado Department Of Corrections: exdoc.state.co.us/index.html.

Colorado State Archives: www.colorado.gov/dpa/doit/archives/index.html. Search bottom of page.

Colorado Corrections Records: 1887-1939: www.colorado.gov/dpa/doit/archives/pen/prison.html.

Congress, Biographical Directory. 1774-Present: bioguide.congress.gov/biosearch/biosearch.asp.

Coweta County, History Of. No ed. Newnan, GA: Newnan-Coweta Historical Society, 1988.

Coxey, Jacob S. *The Coxey Plan: A Cure for Hard Times*. Massillon, OH: Jacob S. Coxey, 1914.

Dalby, Milton A. *The Sea Saga of Dynamite Johnny O'Brien*. Seattle: Lowman & Hanford, 1933. This book has been quoted beyond standard "fair use" in tracing Jeff R. Smith's time in Cook Inlet, 1896. Due diligence was exercised but not successful in discovering a copyright holder for permission. The copyright of 1933 was not renewed with the Library of Congress.

DARE. Dictionary of American Regional English. Vols. 1-4, through Sk. Cambridge, MA: Belknap Press, 1985-2002.

Davis, Carlyle Channing. *Olden Times in Colorado*. Los Angeles: Phillips Publishing, 1916.

Davis, Mary Lee. *Sourdough Gold: The Log of a Yukon Adventure*. Boston: W. A. Wilde, 1933.

Davis, Richard Harding. *The West From a Car Window*. NY: Harper & Brothers, 1892.

Davis, Trevor. *Looking Back on Juneau: The First Hundred Years*. Juneau: Miner Publishing, 1979.

Deadwood, A collection of newspaper clippings: www.deadwoodpoker.blogspot.com.

DeArment, Robert K. *Bat Masterson: The Man and the Legend*. Norman: U OK Press, 1979.

---. *Knights of the Green Cloth: The Saga of the Frontier Gamblers*. Norman: U OK Press, 1982.

DeArmond, R. N. Afterword. *The True Story of the Discovery of Gold At Bonanza Creek: A Tlingit Legend recorded by Dr. Frederica de Laguna*. Wood Engravings by Dale B. DeArmond. Juneau: LapCat Publications, 1997.

---. *"Stroller" White: Klondike Newsman*. Skagway: Lynn Canal Publishing, 1989.

Denver City Directories, 1883-1896. Denver Public Library, Western History Collection.

Denver Post.com. Ed Quillen. "The mystery of Colfax." *The Denver Post* (05/16/2006): www.denverpost.com/archives/index.html. Archived (search at URL by date and title).

Denver Public Library. Western History & Genealogy: history.denverllbrary.org/images/index.html.

Denver, City of. Denver: Published by City Government, 1913.

DeRoux, Kenneth. *All That Glitters: A Centennial Exhibition on the Alaska-Yukon Gold Rushes.* Catalog for exhibition, Alaska State Museum, Juneau, May 10-Sep 22, 1996. Juneau: Alaska State Museums, 1996.

Devere, William, "Tramp Poet of the West." "Jeff And Joe: A True Incident of Creede Camp, Colorado." *Jim Marshall's New Pianner and Other Western Stories.* NY: M. Witmark, 1897.

Devol, George. *Forty Years a Gambler on the Mississippi.* Cincinnati: Devol & Haines, 1887. Reprint in facsimile, Bedford, MA: Applewood Books, 1996.

Dickey, R. M. *Gold Fever: A Narrative of the Great Klondike Gold Rush, 1897-1899.* Ed. Art Petersen. Juneau: Klondike Research, 1997.

---. Diary. Unpublished. Covers period 08/31/1897 to 10/16/1899. Yukon Archives, Whitehorse, Canada (accession number 94/93).

Dorsett, Lyle W. *The Queen City: A History of Denver.* Boulder: Pruett Publishing, 1977.

Edwards, Jonathan. "Christian Charity." Sermon. www.biblebb.com/files/edwards/charity.htm.

Emory Presidents. emoryhistory.emory.edu/people/presidents/LMSmith.htm.

Explore North: Explore Circumpolar North. explorenorth.com/library/communities/alaska/blStMichael.htm.

Federal Reporter, The. Cases Argued and Determined in the Circuit Courts of Appeals and Circuit and District Courts of the United States. St. Paul: West Publishing, 1900.

Feitz, Leland. *A Quick History of Creede: Colorado Boom Town.* Colorado Springs: Little London Press, 1969.

---. *Soapy Smith's Creede: the Silver Camp In 1892.* Colorado Springs: Little London Press, 1973.

"McCook, Report of Brig. Gen." *Report of the Secretary of War to Two Houses of Congress.* Vol. I. Washington: Government Printing Office, 1894. Pp. 132-36.

Fifield, James C. *The American Bar: Contemporary Lawyers of the United States and Canada.* Minneapolis: James C. Fifield, 1918.

Fink, Leon. *Workingmen's Democracy: The Knights of Labor and American Politics.* U IL Press, 1985.

Force of Evil. Film. Dir. & Writer Abraham Polonsky, with John Garfield, Thomas Gomez, Marie Windsor, Barbara Woodell. MGM, 1948.

Franch, John. *Robber Baron: The Life of Charles Tyson Yerkes.* Chicago: U IL Press, 2006.

Gallagher, "Reddy" Stephan. International Boxing Research: www.ibroresearch.com/Boxing Records/Gallagher_Reddy/IBRO -- Stephan Reddy Gallagher.htm.

Geographic Dictionary of Alaska. 2nd ed. By Marcus Backer. Washington: Government Printing Office, 1906.

Gibbs, Jim. *Alaska Maritime.* Atglen, PA, Schiffer Publishing, 1997.

Gilded Age *Dictionary. Historical Dictionary of the Gilded Age.* Eds. Leonard Schulp & James G. Ryan. Np: M. E. Sharpe, 2003.

Godsell, Philip H. "Skagway Terror." *Fury: Exciting Adventures for Men* (Oct 1957): 34-37, 73-78.

Gold, Only: www.onlygold.com/coins/double_eagle_fs.asp.

Graves, Samuel H. *On the White Pass Payroll.* Chicago: Lakeside Press, 1908.

Great Divide. "Letters between Cy Warman & Fitz-Mac." Reprinted in *The Great Divide* (11/1893): pp. 44-47.

Green, Timothy. *Historical Gold Price Table*: www.google.com/search?hl=en&q=gold+value+per+troy+ounce+in+1898&btnG=Google+Search&aq=f&oq= in pdf format.

Harnesslink.com "Nancy Hanks." "Superlative example of the standardbred Pedigree of the Week with Frank Marrion (02/07/2008): www.harnesslink.com/www/Article.cgi?ID=60637.

Harris, A. C. *Alaska and The Klondike Gold Fields.* Chicago: Monroe Book Company, 1897.

Hartzell, Charles. *A Short and Truthful History of Colorado During the Turbulent Reign of "Davis The First."* Denver: C. J. Kelly, Printer & Binder, 1894.

Henderson, Grace G. "Soapy Smith's Least Favorite Cheechakos." *The True West Frontier Times* (Mar 1975): pp. 29, 50, 58-62. Writer indicates direct quotation from Claire Dunbar Roberts appearing in the *Spokesman-Review*, 07/01/1934, 09/23/1951, & 03/15/1953.

Hirschl, Jessie Heckman. "The Great White City. *American Heritage* vol. 11, nr. 6 (Oct 1960): www.americanheritage.com. (Search title.)

History Link.org. *The Free Online Encyclopedia of Washington State History.* "Great Spokane Fire." www.historylink.org/essays/output.cfm?file_id=7696.

History of the Arkansas Valley, Colorado. Chicago: O. L. Baskin, 1881.

Howard, G. S. "Badman of Skagway Meets Insp. Wood." *The Quarterly: Royal Canadian Mounted Police* vol. 48, nr. 8 (Fall 1983): pp. 21-47.

Hunt, Herbert. *Tacoma: Its History and Its Builders.* Vol. II. Chicago: S.J. Clarke Publishing, 1916.

Hunt, Inez & Wanetta W. Draper. *To Colorado's Restless Ghosts.* Denver: Sage Books, 1960.

Hunt, William R. *Distant Justice: Policing the Alaskan Frontier.* Norman: U of OK Press, 1987.

---. *North of 53: The Wild Days of the Alaska-Yukon Mining Frontier: 1870-1914.* NY: Macmillan, 1974.

Inquest Record 1898-1935. Historic Records of the Office of the Magistrate, City of Skagway. Vol. 55. Microfilm Roll 17C. Alaska State Archives, Juneau, AK.

Irwin, Will. *The Confessions of a Con Man as Told to Will Irwin.* NY: B. W. Huebsch, 1913.

Itjen, Martin. *The Story of the Tour on the Skagway, Alaska Street Car.* Np.: np., 1934.

James, William. A letter to Henry James, Sept. 22, 1893. "Familiar Letters of William James – II." Edited by his son, Henry James. *The Atlantic Monthly* (Aug 1920): *The Atlantic* online: www.theatlantic.com/issues/96may/nitrous/jamii.htm.

Johnston, Alva. *The Legendary Mizners.* NY: Farrar, Straus and Young, 1942.

Johnstown Flood Museum: www.jaha.org/FloodMuseum/history.html.

Jones, Mary G. and Lily Reynolds. *Coweta County Chronicles for One Hundred Years.* Atlanta: Stein Printing, 1928. Reissued: Greenville, SC: Southern Historical Press, 1997.

Jones, Robert D. "Correspondence of a Crook." *Alaska-Yukon Magazine* (December 1907): pp. 329-337, & (January 1908): pp. 378-387.

King, Clyde Lyndon. *The History of the Government of Denver with Special Reference to Its Relations with Public Service Corporations.* Doctoral thesis, U of Pennsylvania, 1911.

Leadville. Colorado: *A Guide to the Highest State.* www.americanguides.org/colorado/cities/coleadville.htm.

Lee, J. J. & Marion R. Casey, eds. *Making the Irish American: History and Heritage of the Irish in the United States.* NY: Glucksman & NYU Press, 2006.

Leonard, Stephan J., & Thomas J. Noel. *Denver: Mining Camp to Metropolis.* UP of CO, 1990.

Lillard, John F. B. *American Past-Time of Poker.* NY: Harper, Gibbings & Co., 1896.

Lindsey, Judge Ben B. *The Beast.* NY: Doubleday & Page, 1910.

Literary Digest Magazine, The. "Soapy Smith's Skull: An Ironic Monument to a Two-Gun Tyrant" (Sep 3, 1927): pp. 48-52.

Littlepage, Dean. *Gold Fever in the North: The Alaska-Yukon Gold Rush Era.* Catalog for exhibition, Anchorage Museum of History and Art, May 8-Nov 9, 1997. Anchorage: Alaska State Museums, 1997.

MacDonald, Alexander. *In Search of El Dorado: A Wanderer's Experience.* London: Unwin, 1905.

Macke, Daniel. "A New Trust for Colorado's School Land...." Center for Wildlife Law. U of NM's School of Law's Institute of Public Law: wildlifelaw.unm.edu/pubs/trust.html?PHPSESSID= wKAL7KyBDvTrKTA1eBLx21.

Mardos Memorial Library of Online Books and Maps. Portrait and Biographical Record of Denver and Vicinity, Colorado. www.memoriallibrary.com/CO/1898DenverPB. (Scroll to "Name Index.")

Martinsen, Ella Lung as told by her father Edward B. Lung. *Black Sand and Gold: True Alaska-Yukon Gold-Rush Story.* Portland, OR: Binford & Mort, 1956, 1967.

Maskelyne, John Nevil. *Sharps and Flats, a Complete Revelation of the Secrets of Cheating at Games of Chance and Skill.* NY: Longmans, Green, & Co., 1894.

Maurer, David W. "The Argot of the Faro Bank." *American Speech* vol. XVIII (Feb 1943): pp. 3-11.

Mayberry, Genevieve. "The Hero of Skagway." *The Alaska Sportsman* (Aug 1941): pp. 18-19, 41-43.

Mayer, Melanie J. & Robert N. DeArmond. *Staking Her Claim: The Life of Belinda Mulrooney, Klondike and Alaska Entrepreneur.* Athens: Swallow Press & Ohio U Press, 2000.

Mayer, Melanie J. *Klondike Women: True Tales of the 1897-98 Klondike Gold Rush.* Athens: Swallow Press & Ohio U Press, 1989.

McCawley, John M. Interviewed by Randolph J. Smith, 09/22/1963. RtoR tape. Author's col.

McKeown, Martha Ferguson. *The Trail Led North: Mont Hawthorne's Story.* NY: Macmillan, 1948.

McMath, Robert C., Jr. *American Populism: A Social History 1877-1898* NY: Hill & Wang, The Noonday Press, 1993.

McMurty, Larry. "Hometown America's Black Book." *The New York Review of Books* vol. 47, nr. 20 (Dec 21, 2000): pp. 28 & 30.

Miller, Donald L. "The White City." *American Heritage* vol. 44, nr. 4 (Jul/Aug 1993): www.americanheritage.com. (Search title of topic.)

---. *City of the Century: The Epic of Chicago and the Making of America.* NY: Simon & Schuster, 1996.

Mills, Thora McIlroy. *The Church and the Klondike Gold Rush: The Contribution of the Presbyterian Church to the Yukon During the Gold Rush, 1897-1910.* Toronto: United church of Canada, Victoria University, 1977.

Minter, Roy. *White Pass: Gateway to the Klondike.* Fairbanks: U of Alaska Press, 1987.

Morgan, Edward E. P. & Henry Fitzwilliam Woods. *God's Loaded Dice: Alaska, 1897-1930.* Np.: Caxton Printers, 1948.

Morgan, Lael. *Good Time Girls of the Alaska-Yukon Gold Rush.* Seattle: Epicenter Press, 1998.

Mumey, Nolie. Creede: *The History of a Colorado Silver Mining Town.* Denver: Artcraft Company, 1949.

Munn, Henry Toke. *Prairie Trails and Artic Byways.* London: Hurst, 1932.

Museum of Hoaxes, "Cardiff Giant": www.museumofhoaxes.com/hoax/Hoaxipedia/Cardiff_Giant.

Nelson-Burns, Leslie. Lyrics to song about Jesse James: www.contemplator.com/america/jessej.html.

Noel, Thomas J. "Good Shepherd (1981)." *Colorado Catholicism*. The Archdiocese of Denver, 1989: www.archden.org/noel/07013.htm.

---. *The City and the Saloon: Denver, 1858-1916*. Lincoln: U Nebraska Press, 1982.

O'Connor, Richard. *High Jinks on the Klondike*. NY: Bobbs-Merrill, 1954.

OED. *Oxford English Dictionary, The Compact*. 2nd ed. Oxford, Clarendon Press, 1994.

Online Encyclopedia. encyclopedia.jrank.org/SOU_STE/SPOKANE.html. "Spokane," WA.

Ortiz, Lenny. *Denver Behind Bars: The History of the Denver Sheriff Department and Denver's Jail System, 1858-1956*. Boulder: UP of Colorado, 2002.

Pacific Reporter, The. Vol. 133. Various court decisions. St. Paul: West Publishing, 1913.

Parkhill, Forbes. *The Wildest of the West*. NY: Henry Holt, 1951.

Partridge, Eric. *A Dictionary of Slang and Unconventional English*. 7th ed. NY: Macmillan, 1970.

---. *A Dictionary of The Underworld: British & American*. NY: Bonanza Books, 1949-1961.

Pennington, Gerald L. *Klondike Stampeders Register: A Chronology of the Klondike Gold Rush 1897-1898*. San Diego: Windsor Associates, 1997.

People v. Martin and Orr. *Colorado Reports: Cases Adjudged in the Supreme Court of Colorado at the September Term, 1893, January and April Terms, 1894*. NY: Banks & Brothers, Law Publishers, 1894. Pp. 565-579.

Perkin, Robert L. *The First Hundred Years: An Informal History of Denver and the Rocky Mountain News*. Garden City, NY: Doubleday, 1959.

Pioneer History to about 1900, Churches of Christ & Christian Churches in the Pacific Northwest. ncbible.org/nwh/OrCoast.html.

Pitcher, Jim. *Sourdough Jim Pitcher: The Autobiography of a Pioneer Alaskan*. Anchorage: Alaska Northwest Publishing, 1955-1985.

Pringle, George C. F. *Tillicums of the Trail*. Toronto: McClelland & Stewart, 1922.

Probate Book A 1898-1903. Historic Records of the Office of the Magistrate, City of Skagway. Vol. 27. Microfilm Roll 8C, & original vol. Alaska State Archives, Juneau, AK.

Pullen, Harriet S. *Soapy Smith: Bandit of Skagway; How He Lived; How He Died*. Skagway: Skagway Tourist Agency, nd.

Pullen, Royal. Interviewed by John R. Smith, Joseph J. Smith, Thelma A. Smith, Justin & Ester Smith. Anaheim, CA, circa 1966. RtoR tape. Author's col.

R.C.M.P. files. Record Group 18, vol. 154, files 445 & 447 of 1898, 07/31/1898.

Rastall, B. M. "Cripple Creek Strike of 1893." *Colorado College Studies* (June 1904): pp. 1-48.

Red Onion Saloon. "History." www.redonion1898.com/history.html.

Reed, Mabel Pearce. *Skagway Memories: 1897-1901*. Self published, 1988.

Reedstrom, Ernest L. *Scrapbook of the American West*. Caldwell, ID: Caxton Printers, 1991.

Rennick, Penny, ed. *Dawson City*. Vol. 15, nr. 22. Anchorage: AK Geographic Society, 1988.

Ries, Judith. *Ed O'Kelley: The Man Who Murdered Jesse James' Murderer*. Marble Hill, MI: Stewart Printing & Publishing, 1994.

Robertson, Frank C. & Beth Kay Harris. *Soapy Smith: King of the Frontier Con Men*. NY: Hastings House, 1961.

Round Rock, USA. Na. Kiwanis Club of Round Rock, 1972.

Rutter, Michael. *Upstairs Girls: Prostitution in the American West*. Helena, MT: Far Country Press, 2005.

Ryan, Gerald. "Little Known Facts About the Life and Death of Skagway's Soapy Smith." *Alaska Life* (Apr 1942): pp. 4-5, 19, 22.

Satterfield, Archie. *Chilkoot Pass*. Rev. ed. Portland, OR: Alaska Northwest Books, 2004.

Scarne, John. *Scarne on Dice*. 8th ed. Chatsworth, CA: Wilshire Book Co., 1992.

Seattle Times web site. "CT tells mummy's secret: Preservation no accident." *Seattle Times* (11/20/2005): seattletimes.nwsource.com/html/localnews/2002634994 mummy20m.html.

Secrest, Clark. *Hell's Belles: Prostitution, Vice, and Crime In Early Denver*. Boulder: UP CO, 2002.

Shea & Patten. *The "Soapy" Smith Tragedy*. Skagway: The Daily Alaskan Print, 1907.

Sheldon, Bobby. Interview conducted by Howard Clifford and John R. Smith, 1973.

---. Interview conducted by historians and reporters during dedication of Klondike Gold rush National Historical Park, June 1977.

Sinclair, James M. *Mission: Klondike*. Canada: Mitchell Press, 1978.

Singer, Donald L. "Soapy Smith: Uncrowned King of Skagway." Paper. Fornightly Club of Redlands, CA. Presented Smiley Public Library, Redlands, CA, 01/02/2003: www.redlandsfortnightly.org/papers/singer03.htm.

Smith, Edwin Bobo. "Boyhood Days of Jefferson Randolph Smith II and Edwin Bobo Smith." Unpublished manuscript in author's col., 1937.

Smith, John Randolph. Grandson of JRS. Interviewed by author 07/07/1987.

Smith, Joseph Emerson. "Personal Recollections of Early Denver." *The Colorado Magazine* vol. 20, nr. 1 (March 1943): pp. 56-71.

Smith, Joseph. Grandson of JRS. Interviewed by Jeff Brady, 07/02/1977.

Sorley, Lewis Stone. *History of the Fourteenth United States Infantry From January 1890 to December 1908*. Privately Printed, 1909.

Spanish American War, Historical Dictionary of the. Westport, CT: Greenwood Press, 1996.

Spokane, City History: www.spokanecity.org/services/about/spokane/history/default.aspx?Tab=History.

Sprague, Marshall. *Money Mountain: The Story of Cripple Creek Gold*. NY: Little, Brown, 1953.

Spude, Robert L. S. *Skagway, District of Alaska, 1884-1912: Building the Gateway to the Klondike*. "Occasional Paper No. 36. Fairbanks: U of Alaska, 1983.

St. Louis City Directories. Gould's. 1888-1895. Ancestry.com.

Steele, Samuel B. *Forty Years in Canada: Reminiscences of the Great North-West with Some Account of His Service in South Africa*. London, Jenkin's Press, 1915. Toronto: McGraw-Hill, 1972.

Stone, Wilbur Fisk, ed. *History of Colorado*. Vol. 1. Chicago: S. J. Clark Publishing, 1918.

Sullivan, Edward Dean. *The Fabulous Wilson Mizner*. NY: Henkle, 1935.

Suydam, Harry L. "Scowing the Yukon." *Recreation* vol. X (Jan-Jun 1899): pp. 9-13.

---. "The Reign of 'Soapy' Smith." *Frank Leslie's Popular Monthly* vol. 51, nr. 3 (Jan 1, 1901): pp. 211-221.

Tefertiller, Casey. *Wyatt Earp: The Life Behind the Legend*. NY: John Wiley & Sons, 1997.

Tom's Inflation Calculator: www.halfhill.com/inflation.html.

Trail, The, vol. 13, nr. 1 (June 6, 1920): pp. 10-13. Letters from people who wrote in about the article "'Characters' of the Early Days: 'Soapy' Smith, The Gambler." By Barkalow Barnacle. *The Trail* vol. 12, nr. 8 (Jan 1920): pp. 5-11.

Tribune Almanac, January 1898. A Political Register. Ed. Henry E. Rhoades. NY: The Tribune Assoc, 1898.

Trimble v. The People. *Colorado Reports: Cases Adjudged in the Supreme Court of Colorado at the September Term, 1893, January and April Terms, 1894*. NY: Banks & Brothers, Law Publishers, 1894. Pp. 187-198.

Ubbelohde, Carl, Maxine Benson, & Duane A. Smith. *A Colorado History: Revised Centennial Edition*. Boulder, CO: Pruett Publishing, 1976.

Union Pacific. *Oregon, Washington and Alaska: Sights and Scenes for the Tourist.* Omaha: Union Pacific System, 1890. No page numbers; Spokane section. Booklet of approx. 50 pp.

US Commissioner's Records, Vol. 1, RG 506, Ser. #57, "Journal. U.S. Commissioners Court for Dyea, Alaska, Civil & Criminal Activities" (OS569), pp. 143-151. Alaska State Archives, Juneau, AK.

US v. (1) Turner Jackson and George Wilder, criminal case 1014. (2) W. E. Foster and John Bowers, criminal case 1024. (3) US v. Sylvester S. Taylor, criminal case 1028. Record Group 21 – US District Courts. Box 16 – 01/01/05(2). National Archives and Records Administration, Pacific Alaska Region, Anchorage, AK.

US v. Mrs. M. J. Torpey. NA-RG 21, Sitka Criminal Files, 1884 – 1900, Box 16, file 1022.

US v. Sylvester S. Taylor. Criminal case 1028. Record Group 21 – US District Courts. box 16 – 01/01/05(2). National Archives and Records Administration, Pacific Alaska Region, anchorage, Alaska.

Van Cise, Philip S. *Fighting the Underworld.* 2nd ed. Cambridge, MA: Riverside Press, 1936.

Warman, Cy. *Mountain Melodies.* Denver: Cy Warman, nd. (circa 1892).

Waugaman, Candy. "Capturing Alaska's Image: Pre-Statehood Alaskan Photographers." *Alaska History* vol. 17 (Spring/Fall 2002): pp. 25-53.

Waymarking.com. "The Solid Muldoon." www.waymarking.com/waymarks/WM38RN.

Wells, E. Hazard. Ed. Randall M. Dodd. *Magnificence and Misery: A Firsthand Account of the 1897 Klondike Gold Rush.* Garden City: Doubleday, 1984.

White, Forest. "The Panic of 1893 in Colorado." Unpublished Masters Thesis, U CO, 1932.

White, Roy Daniel. Interviewed by John Randolph Smith and by Justin and Ester Smith at 125 North Daisy, Long Beach, CA, 02/10/1968. RtoR tape. Author's col.

Whiting, Fenton B. Ltr from Whiting to someone named "Georgie." 07/27/1929, 10 pp. single-spaced, typed. Alaska Historical Library, MS4, Box 13 #3.

Whittington, Mike. "Sam Bass and Round Rock." *Texas Ranger Dispatch Magazine*: www.texasranger.org/dispatch/19/Sam_Bass/bass.htm.

Wickersham, James. *Judge Wickersham's "Old Yukon:" Tails – Trails – Trials.* Washington DC: Washington Law Book Co., 1938.

Winchester Model 1892, Dates of Manufacture for: www.savage99.com/winchester1892_dates.htm.

Winslow, Kathryn. *Big Pan Out.* NY: Norton, 1951.

Ye Olde Curiosity Shop web site: "Sylvester the Mummy Bobble Head." Product information. Ye Olde Curiosity Shop: www.yeoldecuriosityshop.com/catalog/product_info.php?products_id=161.

You Can't Cheat an Honest Man. Film. Dir. George Marshall, written by W. C. Fields as Charles Bogle. With W. C. Fields & Edgar Bergen. Universal, 1939.

Yronwode, Catherine. "Aunt Sally's Policy Players Dream Book." *Hoodoo in Theory and Practice.* www.luckymojo.com/auntsallys.html.

Yukon Genealogy. Gold Rush Data Base, Yukon Government. www.yukongenealogy.com.

Brochures:

Male Academy Museum, Newnan, Georgia. Brochure, circa 1995.

Collections, Private:

Geri Murphy.   Jeff Smith, California.
Kyle Rosene.   Jefferson R. "Little Randy" Smith, California.

Encyclopedias:

Cyclopaedia of American Biography. Vol. VII. N.p.: James T. White, 1892.
Encyclopaedia Britannica, The: A Dictionary of Arts, Sciences, and General Literature. 9th ed. Chicago: R. S. Peale Co., 1892.
Encyclopaedia Britannica, The. 11th ed. NY: Encyclopaedia Britannica Co., 1910.

Newspapers (includes date or dates consulted):

Clippings: Numerous clippings among the Smith family collections, many cut by Jeff R. Smith II ("Soapy"), show no newspaper name or date and are cited in footnotes as information allows.

Adair County News, The (Columbia, KY), 1910.
Alaska Searchlight (Juneau, AK), 1896.
Albuquerque Morning Journal, 1882.
Arizona Republican, Phoenix, 1898.
Boulder Daily Camera, 1892.
Castle Rock Journal (CO), 1894.
Cedar Rapids Weekly Gazette, 1894.
Chicago Daily Tribune, 1894-1899.
Colorado Evening Sun, 1894.
Colorado Springs Gazette, 1894
Colorado Transcript, 1894.
Commercial Appeal (Memphis, TN), 1898.
Creede Candle, 1892.
Creede Chronicle, 1892.
Creede Daily Herald, 1892.
Creede Sun, 1892.
Daily Alaskan (Skaguay), 1898.
Daily Arkansas Gazette (Little Rock), 1873-79.
Daily Chronicle, The (Marshall, MN), 1894.
Daily Evening Bulletin (San Francisco), 1884.
Daily Gazette and Bulletin, The (Williamsport, PA), 1894.
Daily Gazette, The (Janesville, WI), 1894.
Daily Inter Ocean (Chicago), 1881.
Daily Journal (Telluride, CO), 1898.
Daily Kennebeck Journal, The (ME), 1894.
Daily Picayune (New Orleans), 1889.
Daily Register Call (Central City, CO), 1879-1880.
Daily Rocky Mountain News, 1873-1879.
Daily Standard (Portland, OR), 1882.
Daily Times, The (Portsmouth, OH), 1894.
Davenport Daily Leader (IA), 1894.
Denver Catholic Register, 1941.
Denver Daily News, 1885-1894.
Denver Evening Post, 1893-1898.

Denver Mercury, 1893-1894.
Denver News, 1931.
Denver Post, The, 1895-1929.
Denver Republican, 1890-1899.
Denver Sun, 1893.
Denver Times, 1893-1903.
Denver Tribune-Republican, 1885.
Durango Wage Earner, 1907.
Dyea Press, 1898.
Dyea Trail, 1898.
Evening Times (Cumberland, MD), 1894.
Evening Times, The (Washington, DC), 1901.
Fairbanks Daily News Miner, 1941.
Fairplay Flume (CO), 1894.
Fort Worth Daily Democrat, 1879-1880.
Galveston Daily News, 1880.
Georgetown Courier, 1888.
Georgia Weekly Telegraph & Messenger (Macon), 1881.
Globe, The (Toronto-based but considered a "National Newspaper), 1897.
Greeley Tribune (Greeley, CO), 1896.
Gulf Coast Breeze (Crawfordville, FL), 1898.
Hawarden Independent (IA),1894.
Hazel Green Herald, The (Hazel Green, KY), 1910.
Idaho News The, 1889.
Illustrated Police News, The, 1892.
Inter Ocean (Chicago), 1878.
Lamar Sparks, The (CO), 1894.
Leader, The (location unk), 1894. JRS clipping.
Leadville Daily and Evening Chronicle, 1879-1892.
Leadville Weekly Herald, 1880.
Leadville-Herald Democrat, 1888-1898.
Lincoln Evening News (NE), 1896.
Littleton Independent (CO), 1894.

Los Angeles Times, 1887-1929.
Lynn Canal News, 1980.
Milwaukee Sentinel, 1898.
Morning Alaskan, The, 1898.
Morning Oregonian (Portland), 1898.
Morning Telegraph, The (NY, NY), 1897.
National Populist (Denver), 1894.
New Castle News, The (PA), 1894.
New Era, The (Humeston, IA), 1896.
New York Times, 1876-1899.
News (Frederick, MD), 1894.
Nome Daily Nugget, 1936.
Oakland Tribune (CA), 1896.
Oregon Journal, post 1898.
Pagosa Springs News (CO), 1898.
Register, The (Rock Valley, IA), 1894.
Reno Weekly Gazette And Stockman, The, 1894.
RMN. Rocky Mountain News, 1883-1941.
Road, The (CO), 1895-1896.
Salt Lake Semi Weekly Tribune, 1898.
San Francisco Call, 1884-1898.
San Francisco Chronicle, 1898.
San Francisco Examiner, 1898.
Seattle Daily News, The, 1898.
Seattle Daily Times, 1896-1898.

Seattle Post-Intelligencer, The, 1897-98.
Seattle Times, The 2005.
Silverton Standard (CO), 1892.
Sitka Alaska Report, 1898.
Sitka Cablegram, 1903.
Skaguay News, The 1897-1899.
Skagway News, The, 1977-1998.
Spokesman-Review (Spokane), 1896.
St. Louis Globe-Democrat, 1882.
St. Louis Republican, 1882.
Summit County Journal (CO), 1893.
Sun, The (New York), 1908.
Sunday Leader, The (Euclaire, WI) 03/25/1894.
Tacoma Daily News, 1892.
Tacoma Times, 1898.
Times. Aspen Weekly Times, The, 1881-1900.
Washington Post (DC), 1897-1898.
Waterloo Daily Courier (IA), 1899.
Weekly Gazette, The (Colorado Springs), 1894.
Weekly Register Call (CO) 1889.
World, The (Denver), 1894.
Yankton Press and Union and Dakotaion, 1874.

Magazines:

Alaska Life, 1942.
Alaska Sportsman, The. 1941-1958.
Alaska-Yukon Magazine, 1907-1908.
American Speech, 1943.
Collier's Weekly, 1901
Colorado Magazine, The, 1943.
Frank Leslie's Popular Monthly, 1901.
Great Divide, The, 1893.

Illustrated Police News, 1892.
R. C. M. P. Quarterly, no date.
Recreation, 1899.
Trail, The, 1920.
True West Magazine, 1995.
Washington Post, 1898.
Weekend Magazine, 1962.
Wild West Magazine, 2006.

Registers, Hotel

Hotel Mondamin, Skagway. In possession of Eagles fraternity, Erie #13, Skagway, Alaska.

Songs

"Take Back Your Gold." Music: Monroe H. Rosenfeld. Words: Louis W. Pritzkow. Joseph W. Stern & Co., NY, 1897. Ozark Folksongs: Religious Songs and Other Items. Vol. IV. Reprint of 1946-50 ed. Columbia, MO: U of Missouri Press, 1980.
"The Vacant Chair (We Shall Meet, But We Shall Miss Him)." Music: George F. Root. Words: Henry S. Washburn. Savannah: John C. Schreiner, 1862.

US Census: 1880 & 1890

Index

Abbreviations: **Dvr** = Denver; **ed.** = editor; **fn** = footnote; **f & p board** = fire and police board commissioner, Denver; **L&OL** = Law and Order League, Denver; **SF** = San Francisco; **Sy** = Skaguay; **SMC**: Skaguay Military Company; **USA**: United States Army; **WP&YR** = White Pass and Yukon Railway

Rincon Kid, rival gang head   168
Ring Con Kid, aka Tom Quinn   87
Rio Grande River   235
Rising, judge, Dvr   262
Ritter, Abe L., Sy   526-27, 579
River Front Park, Dvr 270
River Street, Dyea, AK   481
Road, The 14, 376, 406
Roberts, fire chief   170
Roberts, G.E. "Auctioneer," Dvr 88, 162-63, 165
Roberts, Green &, Dvr   461
Roberts, Sam, murdered, Sy   468-69, 521
Roberts' partner, Sam Roberts, Harry Green
     468-69, 497
Robertson, Frank C. & Beth Kay Harris   455
Robertson, Phil B., SMC   488
Robinson, W.P.,dr., victim, Colfax
Rocky Mountain News (*RMN*)   6, 10, 43, 51,
     57, 60-65, 70, 72, 74, 76, 83-86, 88, 93, 95-
     99, 104-106, 109, 115, 117, 119-21, 125-40,
     143-56, 158-66, 169-74, 177-78, 180-83, 185-
     93, 197, 199, 203, 205-06, 208, 213-14, 217-
     20, 223, 231-32, 237-38, 241, 246-53, 255,
     257, 259, 262-64, 266, 268, 271-72, 274-78,
     282, 289, 311, 323, 325, 328, 335-39, 347,
     351-52, 355, 357, 361-62, 364, 367, 370-71,
     373, 375-78, 392-93, 395, 401, 403-04, 434,
     438-39, 443, 448, 555, 578
Rocky Point camp tent saloon smashed   519-
20
Roe, Richard, Sy   528
Rogers and Ward, Waite's attorneys   309
Rogers, Andrew Johnson "Ajax," f & p board
     297, 300, 302-03, 316, 327
Rogers, Jennie, madam, Dvr   371-74
Rogers, M.A., judge, Dvr   187
Rogers, Platt, ex-mayor, f & p board counsel
     305
Rogers, W.J., special deputy, Sy   548, 567
Roosevelt, Theodore, president 580
Rosalie, SS   586
Rosenthal, W. J., Dvr 285
Ross, C.C.242
Ross, detective, SF   40
Round Rock, TX   26-28, 30, 32, 34
Routt, John L., governor, CO   202-03, 205
Rowan, James Mark II   457, 459
Rowan, James Mark, marshal   442, 457, 460,
     462, 466, 477, 578
Rowan, Mrs. Beryl, widow's fund   454, 457,
     459, 461-62
Royal bar, Dvr 335
Royer & Shynock Hardware   285

Rozier, Hotel, St. Louis   427
Ruby saloon, Dvr   189
Rucker, A.W., judge, Arkins insulted   151-52
Rudaugh, G.E., SMC 488
Rudolph, John, alias Soapy Smith, Juneau 410
Runnals Avenue (see *State Street*), Sy   474
Runnymeade, sarcastic name for Soapy Smith
     367 (fn), 368-69
Russ House hotel, SF 425
Russell, Robert, victim, Dvr 365
Rutter, Michael 510
Ryan, Mike, politico, Dvr   249, 259, 264
Sacage, Herbert583
Sacramento, CA   101
Salem, OR   39
Sales, Henry N., attorney, judge 124
Salida, CO300-01
Salinas, CA   101
Salt Lake City, UT   38, 66-68, 84, 176, 426
Salter, Frank "Plunk," gang   423-24
Salvation Army, Dvr 173
Samson & Scott's, club   323
San Antonio, TX386-88
San Diego, CA 587-88
San Francisco Call 41, 490, 546
San Francisco Examiner   492, 511, 558
San Francisco   40-41, 60, 82, 85, 109-10, 118-
     19, 152, 242, 361, 409, 411-12, 418, 425,
     428-29, 432-33, 450, 463-65, 472, 492, 504,
     527, 545, 574, 587
San Joaquin Valley, CA   235
San Jose, CA   101
San Juan mountains, CO   57, 199
San Quentin prison, CA   578
sand tell faro box   116-17, 123
Sanders saloon, Tom, Port Townsend, WA 555
Sanders, J.S., Coxey general   332
Sanford, Jim, gang   210-11
Santa Rosa, CA101
Sapolio Smith (Soapy Smith)   51, 70, 163,
     209, 219, 272, 277-78, 282-83, 395-96, 406,
     412
Sapolio Soap   45, 51
Saportas, E.W. 88-89, 473, 475
Saportas, William F. "Billy" 89, 450, 471-75,
     506-07, 516, 532, 566, 572-74, 590
Saratoga, NY   115
Savannah, GA   19, 24-25
Schaftner, Joy Smith 9
Schivenfeld Mercantile Co. 285
Schlottman, police detective   366 (& fn)
Schwartz, Mr., Creede   215
Schwartz, Mr., Sy   535, 549

Erratum: Wrangell, Fort, AK
Add pp. **429-30, 497, 499, 502**